perfacile

patior)
fruor)
fungar } Abl. part stem + urus + tenses of sum
vescor) Pass Pariph.
utor .

act pariph.

Pass Pariph.

pres. stem + nd + usa um o
tenses of sum

ad
ante
con
dē
in
inter
prae
pro
sub
super
p not
(circum)
ob

PLATE I   STATUE OF CAESAR IN ROME

That Julius Caesar was a famous man;
With what his valour did enrich his wit,
His wit set down to make his valour live:
Death makes no conquest of this conqueror;
For now he lives in fame, though not in life. — RICHARD III.

C. IULII CAESARIS

COMMENTARII RERUM GESTARUM

CAESAR'S COMMENTARIES

THE GALLIC WAR, BOOKS I–IV, WITH SELECTIONS FROM BOOKS V–VII AND FROM THE CIVIL WAR

WITH AN INTRODUCTION, NOTES, A COMPANION TO CAESAR AND A VOCABULARY

BY

FRANCIS W. KELSEY
UNIVERSITY OF MICHIGAN

ALLYN AND BACON

Boston　　　New York　　　Chicago

DAAA

PREFACE

Tʜɪs edition aims to interest the High School pupil in Caesar, to assist him by notes adapted to his stage of progress, and to facilitate his accomplishment of the second year of Latin work with appreciation of and respect for the subject, and with a firm foundation for further study.

America's entrance into the world conflict has aroused universal interest in warfare. Viewed in the light of the great struggle, Caesar's Commentaries take on a new interest. Modern armies have clashed on the battlefields of the Gallic War; modern camps are laid out in a way to suggest the manner of the Romans. The strategy of Joffre and of Hindenburg finds its prototype in that of Caesar, and modern armor, especially in types of helmet and breastplate, strikingly resembles that of ancient times. In countless ways — even to Caesar's statement, "Of all these the bravest are the Belgians" — the World War reproduces on a larger scale the campaigns of Caesar.

Such points as these it has seemed worth while to attempt to bring out in the Introduction, the Notes, and the Companion to Caesar. In the Syntax a statement of a rule is accompanied by specific illustrations from Caesar; the exercises in Latin Composition are designed to strengthen the pupil's grasp of the Grammar. The Maps and Plans cannot fail to add definiteness to the study, and the pictures will aid the student to visualize the scenes and objects described or referred to in the text.

In preparing the book my obligations have been greatest to the well-known works of Dr. H. Meusel and Mr. T. Rice Holmes; on the side of the illustrations, to the *Manuel* of Joseph Déchelette. Mr. George R. Swain allowed the use of his unique series of photographs, and Mr. G. F. Hill, of the British Museum, furnished a number of casts of Roman coins.

Many teachers have helped me with suggestions, of which I wish here to make acknowledgment; I am especially indebted to Miss Frances E. Sabin of the University of Wisconsin. Messrs. Allen and Phillips, of the Phillips Academy in Andover, have kindly permitted the use of their *Latin Composition*, and Dr. Gilbert H. Taylor rendered assistance in reading a part of the proof.

FRANCIS W. KELSEY.

Ann Arbor, Michigan.
January 15, 1918.

CONTENTS

PLATES [1]

The colored plates, and the plates illustrating the bridge across the Rhine, are from the designs of H. Rheinhard.

MAPS

The maps are based upon those in the Atlases accompanying the works of Napoleon III and Stoffel (p. xxxvii), with modifications from many sources, particularly, G. Veith's *Geschichte der Feldzüge Caesars* and, for Pharsalus, J. Kromayer's *Antike Schlachtfelder in Griechenland*.

[1] A full List of the Illustrations, with references, will be found on pages 665-674.

INTRODUCTION

i. Warfare Ancient and Modern

Since the Roman period the art of war has undergone great changes. These have resulted from the invention of gunpowder and other explosives, from the use of field glasses, from the utilization of electricity, steam, and gasoline to provide means of communication and transportation, and finally, from

Figure 1. — Wolf-holes before Alesia.

Constructed by Caesar in 52 B.C., and discovered by excavation.
At the left of the wolf-holes are rows of hedge entanglements.
In front of the rampart are double trenches, and above we see the palisade and towers.

the mechanical perfecting of every kind of weapon. Nevertheless the most recent military operations have exemplified the use of means and methods of warfare devised by the ancients and skillfully employed by Caesar in the campaigns of which he has left a record in the Commentaries.

As a part of his defensive works when he was besieging Alesia Caesar made many wolf-holes. These are round holes with sloping sides, in the center of which a strong pointed stake is firmly implanted. A glance at the illustration (Fig. 1) will show how slow and difficult an advance would be, particularly at night, over ground thus prepared ; for the soldier picking his way, no matter how carefully, would run the risk of slipping and impaling himself upon the projecting point.

Figure 2. — Wolf-holes near Ypres, in Belgium.

These wolf-holes were constructed by the German army in 1914.

On the further side, near the left, the posts carrying the barb-wire entanglement are visible. (Courtesy of the Press Illustrating Company.)

Precisely such wolf-holes have been used in the Great War, as, for example, along the German line near Ypres, in Belgium (Fig. 2). In front the line is protected by barb-wire entanglements. Corresponding with these are the hedge entanglements used by Caesar (shown in Figure 1, behind the wolf-holes), which were made by firmly planting in rows, and closely interlocking, branches of trees with the projecting ends stripped of bark and sharpened to a point

The Romans were the first nation to make trench-digging an essential part of warfare, but they limited it to the fortification of camps and to siege operations Since the Roman trenches were not used as passageways, they were generally left V-shaped, as those seen in Figure 1 ; but occasionally trenches were made with perpendicular sides, as the long trench, or moat, 20 feet wide, before Alesia (Map 17). In modern warfare trenching has become still more important, and now under many conditions soldiers are taught to " dig themselves in." But the process of digging is still the same, as may be seen from the comparison of a Roman trenching tool (Fig. 3) with the type of spade supplied as a part of the equipment of a soldier in the United States Army (Fig. 4).

When digging within range of the enemy's missiles the Roman soldiers protected themselves by movable shields, **plutei** (Plate IX, 4–5), and sappers' huts, **vineae** (Plate IX, 9). In trenching close to the Russian lines near Warsaw in 1914 the Germans used standing steel shields which were moved forward for the protection of the trenchers. A curious parallel to the ancient sapper's hut is the armored " one-man tank," designed for exceptionally hazardous service in front of the lines (Fig. 5).

Figure 3. — Roman trenching tool.

Discovered in the remains of the Roman Camp at Saalburg, near Homburg, Germany.

The wooden handle has rotted away.

The packs, **sarcinae**, of Caesar's legionaries were fully as heavy as those of modern infantry, perhaps heavier. They were carried on a forked stick over the left shoulder (Fig. 6), while the soldier of to-day has his pack strapped on his back (Fig. 7). The day's march of a small body of United States Infantry over fair roads will average approximately the same as that of Caesar's legionaries, about fifteen Roman miles. On forced marches recently European armies, moving on excellent roads and utilizing medical science to conserve the soldier's strength, have equaled, if they have not surpassed, Caesar's forced marches in the Gallic War.

In fighting there has been a surprising return to the methods of Caesar's time.

Caesar's legionaries held their weapons until they were within close range of the enemy, twelve to twenty yards; then they hurled their pikes. To-day in trench fighting the place of the pike is taken by the hand grenade, thrown often at even closer range; and soldiers are trained in the throwing of gre-

nades just as the legionary was in hurling the pike (Fig. 8).
"Rifle fire in this warfare plays small part," wrote Owen John-
son from the front in 1915; "cartridges are all very well for
machine guns, but for men, hand grenades and the cold steel."
Soon after the first soldiers from the United States arrived in

France, in 1917, it was found that by reason
of skill acquired in playing baseball, they
surpassed the European soldiers in throwing
grenades, in point of range as well as accuracy.

The "iron" of the Roman pike (Fig. 49,
p. 61) finds a parallel in a late type of French
bayonet (Fig. 9). The length is nearly the
same. The pike iron has a four-grooved point,
barbed; the bayonet is grooved on the four
sides, so that it makes a wound very similar
in character. But even the spear has not
gone out of use; in the Great War long lances
have been used by divisions of cavalry on
both sides.

More remarkable still is the return of recent
warfare to the use of the helmet as a protection for the head, and of a metallic shield to
protect the grenadier when exposing himself
by throwing grenades (Fig. 8). In shape,
however, the French helmet (Fig. 10) has as
much in common with a certain type of ancient
Gallic helmet (Fig. 11) as it has with the helmet of the Roman legionary (Fig. 12).

Figure 4.— Mod-
ern trenching
tool.

This is the trench-
ing tool supplied to
soldiers of the United
States army.

Modern armor seems to have reached its fullest development
in the equipment of the Italian barb-wire cutter. His helmet
(Fig. 13) is supplemented by a metallic veil, and his body is
protected by a cuirass, his legs by greaves. This specialized
armor, well designed for the purpose, is less flexible than the
defensive equipment of the Roman legionary (Fig. 33, p. 19).

The modern helmet has been found serviceable in protecting

the head against shrapnel; hence we may well believe that the ancient helmet greatly reduced the casualties from the leaden bullets thrown by means of slings (Fig. 14), as well as those from blows.

The Gaul, as is noted elsewhere (p. 638), in fighting used a spear or dart, shield and sword, but his spear (Figs. 40 and 43) was not so effective as the Roman pike, and his sword was of an altogether different type (Fig. 39). Oddly enough, recent fighting in France has revived the use of wickerwork shields somewhat like those of ancient Gaul (Fig. 48, p. 60). As a protection against liquid fire French soldiers before Verdun in 1916 " carried big oblong shields of interwoven

Figure 5.—" One-man tank."
Designed for the protection of wire-cutters under fire.

osier, covered with clay, against which the flaming liquid fell harmless," though the men, protected by masks, found " the smell terrible, almost suffocating."

In the night attack of Caesar's men upon the Helvetian corral, in 58 B.C., some of the defenders hurled darts from behind the wheels of the carts (I. 26); in 1916 a provision train of motor trucks, conveying supplies to General Pershing's force in Mexico, was attacked in a ravine, whereupon " the truck men and their soldier guard took a position behind the steel wheels of the cars," and routed the Mexicans by the accuracy of their fire.

Though the contending armies are vastly greater than those of Caesar's time, the Great War affords striking illustrations of the principles of military formation, tactics, and strategy[1] which he knew and applied.

---

[1] Under " Tactics " military men include the disposing of forces on land or sea in order of battle, and all manœuvres in the presence of the enemy;

In the battle with the Helvetians, and also in that with the Germans described in Book I, the more open formation of the smaller Roman force, whose soldiers were trained to fight with initiative, gave it a distinct advantage over the mass formation, called by Caesar *phalanx*, to which it was opposed. The mass formation of the modern German army is altogether different from that of ancient times; but again and again, in the Great War, German ranks, advancing with men almost touching elbows, have suffered much more heavily than British forces trained to attack in extended order and advancing against equally intensive fire.

Figure 6. — Roman legionary in marching order.

His pack is suspended on a forked stick over the left shoulder.

When Caesar first came into contact with the Germans, he was so impressed with their arrangement of cavalry that he made special mention of it, and afterwards he employed German horsemen as mercenaries. Each horseman, he tells us (I. 48), was accompanied by a foot-soldier; these foot-soldiers were swift runners, and

"Strategy" refers to the larger operations of war; it includes the laying out and conducting of campaigns as well as the execution of single movements designed to outwit and thwart the enemy.

exceedingly brave.   In our illustration, which pictures a charge of the Scots Greys in northern France in the autumn of 1914 (Fig. 15), nimble footmen are seen charging with the cavalry.

The transportation of troops by train and auto truck has simplified the concentration of reserves to hold a threatened point; yet no modern general has surpassed Caesar in insight and quickness of decision in moving troops in time of battle in order to forestall or checkmate the movements of the enemy. This was well illustrated in the Battle of Pharsalus, where his quick shift in forming a fourth line to support his greatly outnumbered cavalry (C. III. 89, and Map 20) gained an initial victory and contributed in no slight degree to the sweeping success of the day.

Figure 7. — United States sailor standing with heavy marching-order equipment.

The marching-order equipment of the United States soldiers is the same, whether in land or naval service.

A typical stratagem of Caesar was that by which he accomplished the crossing of the Elaver (now Allier) in 52 B.C. (VII. 35). Vercingetorix, on the opposite side of the river, had broken down all the bridges. Caesar encamped in a wooded spot near a place where the piles of a bridge had escaped destruction. The next morning he concealed two legions in the forest and ordered the rest of his forces to march up the river, spreading them out so that the marching column seemed as long as usual. Thereupon Vercingetorix also marched upstream, on the opposite side.   When he was far enough away, Caesar brought the two legions out of concealment, quickly rebuilt the bridge, recalled the troops that had marched up the river, and transferred his entire army across before Vercingetorix could interfere.

A similar stratagem was successfully employed in 1915.   The German and Austrian commanders wished to cross the Vistula in Poland at a point northwest of Ivangorod.   They moved their forces upstream in such a way as to lead the Russians to believe that they intended to force a crossing at some distance northeast of the city. At the point previously determined upon, material for pontoon bridges was brought to the bank of the river loaded on wagons which were covered over with straw, so that they were reported by the Russian aviators merely as loads of straw; since the Russian commander had no information to the contrary, slight attention was paid to them. The ruse made it possible for the pontooners to start building the bridges before their presence or purpose was suspected. When the Russians finally brought their artillery to bear at the threatened point, it was too late to check the work; the Teutonic forces completed four bridges over the river and marched across.

In the naval battles described in the Commentaries Caesar did not command his fleet in person, though in one instance he and his army witnessed

Copyright by Underwood and Underwood, New York.

Figure 8. — French soldier hurling a hand grenade.

He is standing in a trench. His head is protected by a steel helmet. With the left forearm he holds a shield.

the engagement from the land (III. 14). The tactics employed
have analogies in modern warfare.

On the Mediterranean Sea from a very early period there
were two types of ships, those propelled by the wind, that is

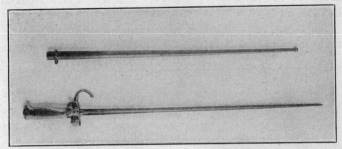

Figure 9. — French bayonet, with scabbard.

The bayonet can either be fastened at the end of a gun and used for thrusting, or de-
tached and handled as a long dagger.

by a force outside the ship, and those propelled by a force inside the ship, by oarsmen. Since the Mediterranean is relatively narrow and almost tideless, since also ships driven by
oars could be manœuvred more easily and with much greater
steadiness of movement, the oar ship was developed into a war

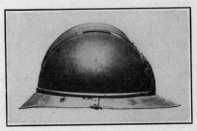

Figure 10. — French helmet, type of 1915, front and side views.

This helmet was worn by Richard N. Hall, a graduate of the Ann Arbor high school
and of Dartmouth college, who served in a volunteer ambulance corps in France and was
killed by a shell on Christmas eve, 1915, when driving his ambulance in the Vosges
mountains.

vessel and was highly specialized to this end (Fig. 146, p. 427), while low-decked sailing vessels were used for freight and ordinary passenger service. It was a freight ship on which St. Paul and his military escort sailed for Italy, suffering shipwreck at Malta; the battleships, or galleys, of Caesar's time (p. 636) had ordinarily three banks of oars.

The boisterous waves and high tides of the North Atlantic made impracticable, except under extremely favorable condi-

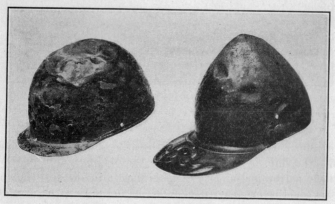

Figure 11. — Early Gallic helmets, of bronze.

Now in the British Museum. The neck-protector of the helmet at the right is ornamented in relief.

tions, the use either of galleys, which had to be built low in order to enable the oarsmen to dip their oars, or of the type of sailing vessel employed on the almost land-locked Mediterranean. Hence before Caesar's time the Venetans in northwestern Gaul (modern Brittany) had developed a strongly built high-decked sailing vessel, which, though small when compared with sea-going ships to-day, was able nevertheless to withstand the buffeting of ocean waves and to outride the gales. From Caesar's description (III. 13) it is evident that the Venetan ship was not like the type of vessel used later by the Vikings, but in essential features resembled the famous *Half-Moon* with which

Henry Hudson in 1609 crossed the Atlantic, discovering the river which bears his name.

Caesar found that he could not complete the conquest of northwestern Gaul without destroying the Venetan fleet. In the naval battle, of which we have a vivid account in Book III of the Gallic War, the two types of vessel were brought into hostile contact; the light and fast Roman galley, adapted for ramming and boarding, and carrying legionaries as its fighting men, was pitted against the Venetan sailer, which was so strong that it could not be rammed and so high that boarding was extremely difficult. Only quick ingenuity (III. 14), and sheer luck in the dying down of the wind at a crucial moment, gave to Caesar's men a complete victory.

Figure 12. — Helmet of a Roman legionary.

When not worn the helmet could be suspended by a cord passed through the ring at the top. The crest was fastened in the same ring before the soldier went into action.

Altogether different were the tactics of the sea-fight off Massilia, described in the second book of the Civil War (pp. 425–431). Just as on land at Pharsalus, and on both land and sea in the Great War, we find substantially the same military equipment on both sides, so in the sea-fight between Brutus and the fleets loyal to Pompey the type of battleship on both sides was the same, and victory rested with the side which had superior skill and fighting power.

Long after the nations of western Europe had developed to a high degree of effectiveness the wooden warship propelled by sails and armed with cannon, the galley continued to be used by the pirates of the Barbary States in northern Africa; "the vessels employed by the Barbary Corsairs were essentially rowing-boats,"[1] though after the sixteenth century they increasingly used ships like those of the European powers. Mu-

---

[1] *African Shores of the Mediterranean*, by C. F. and L. Grant (New York, 1912), p. 280. This work gives a graphic description of life on the modern galleys, and the lot of the galley-slaves, chained to the rowing-benches. The

tual jealousies of the European states allowed the Barbary corsairs to flourish until the nineteenth century. For a time the United States paid blackmail to the masters of the Tripoli pirates in order to safeguard American sailing vessels from their swift galleys and frigates, and our country did not free itself from the menace until 1815.

Like the galley, the modern battleship, with steam power replacing man power as propelling force, developed the tactic of ramming. This tactic had its best known exemplification in time of peace, in the accidental ramming and sinking of the battleship *Victoria* by her sister ship, the *Camperdown*, at the British manœuvres in the Mediterranean in 1893, in consequence of a mistake in orders. In recent years there has been a notable increase in the size and range of cannon mounted upon battleships, accompanied by a corresponding increase in the effectiveness of torpedoes; decisive engagements are now ordinarily fought at long range. Nevertheless in 1917 the British torpedo destroyer *Broke* rammed a German destroyer, and the marines, as in the olden time, finally fought hand to hand, the British gaining the victory.

ii. Caesar's Commentaries and the Great War

In September, 1914, the German armies, retiring from the drive toward Paris, established a line of trenches across the northeastern part of France. One portion of this line passed north of the city of Soissons, whose name is derived from that of the Gallic people called Suessiones; thence it ran eastward, not far from the river Aisne, which is so called from the river's ancient name, Axona. East of the village of Berry-au-Bac the German line of works crossed the Aisne to the south and passed east of Reims, which takes its name from the ancient people called Remi, and occupies the site of the Gallic city of Durocortorum, or Bigfort.

---

subject is more fully treated in *The Barbary Corsairs*, by S. Lane-Poole (New York, 1902); and G. W. Allen, *Our Navy and the Barbary Corsairs* (Boston, 1905).

This part of France in antiquity was reckoned as belonging to Belgium; for the southern boundary of Belgium, or Belgic Gaul, was along the rivers called by Caesar Matrona and Sequana, which have given us the modern names Marne and Seine. In this region, as also in eastern France and in the countries east of the Adriatic Sea, we find many points of contact not only between ancient and modern names but also between the events recorded in Caesar's Commentaries and those of the most recent history.

Figure 13. — Italian barb-wire cutter.

His wire-clippers are on the end of a long pole. He stands in front of the entrance of a well-screened refuge. (Medem Photo Service.)

The marshes along the Miette brook, near Berry-au-Bac, in 57 B.C., prevented a frontal attack by the Belgians upon Caesar's legions drawn up to receive them (Map 5). Across the same marshes when dry, in September, 1914, the Germans ran intrenchments, which during the winter filled with water; this caused inconvenience, to be sure, but safeguarded that part of the German line from attack by either infantry or cavalry.

When the Belgians tried to ford the Aisne, in the face of Caesar's archers and slingers, the stream was choked with dead (II. 10); dead and wounded again clogged the Aisne in 1914, when French and English troops near Berry-au-Bac built pontoon bridges within range of a murderous artillery fire.

Caesar commends the bravery of the Belgians who attempted to cross the Aisne over the bodies of the fallen (II. 10). Of all the peoples of Gaul, he elsewhere declared (I. 1), "the Belgians are the bravest." In 1914, the bravery of the modern Belgians was lauded by friend and foe alike, when at Liège and other points, against overwhelming odds, they tried to stem the tide of German invasion.

Thessaly, unlike the rest of Greece, has broad and fertile plains, well adapted to the raising of wheat. In 48 B.C., when Caesar was obliged to withdraw from Dyrrachium (now Durazzo), he led his half-starved troops into Thessaly and encamped in the midst of ripening grain-fields (C. III. 81); thither Pompey came to find him (Map 19), and the battle of Pharsalus followed. In June, 1917, one reason assigned for hastening the abdication of Constantine, King of Greece, was that the allied forces wished to make sure that the ripening harvests of Thessaly should be subject to their control; and immediately thereafter French and British troops occupied Pharsala (the ancient Pharsalus), as well as Larissa, on the site of the Larisa to which Pompey fled after the great battle. So it happened that the grain-fields of Thessaly were a factor in determining the site of the decisive battle between Caesar and Pompey, and, almost two thousand years later, in hastening the downfall of a Greek ruler.

The occurrence of similar events of war in the same localities may be ascribed in part to the influence of geographical features upon military operations, in part to continuing antagonism between adjacent populations of different stock. Broadly speaking, the military operations of the Germans in the western campaigns of the Great War have in no small degree been determined by the same physical conditions which first brought Caesar into hostile contact with Helvetians and Germans, and afterwards facilitated his conquest of northern Gaul.

To the Helvetians, bent upon migrating to western Gaul, the Jura mountains (Map GALLIA[1]) presented an almost im-

---

[1] A general map of Gaul has been placed at the end of this volume.

passable barrier, on the west side, while a northerly route
would have exposed them to attack by Ariovistus. In consequence they were obliged to follow the exceedingly difficult
route through the Mill-race gorge of the Rhone, Pas de l'Écluse
(Map 2), and at once aroused Caesar's apprehension; for the
Rhone was the boundary of the Roman Province.

Between the Jura mountains and the Vosges (ancient Vosegus) there is a broad opening in the mountain barrier along
the east frontier of modern France. Through this gateway
Ariovistus and his German hordes were pressing into Gaul,

Figure 14. — Roman slingshot, of lead, shown in two views.

Inscribed FERI POMP[EIVM], 'Strike Pompey,' referring to Pompeius Strabo, against
whose army it was hurled when he was besieging Asculum, in the southeastern part of
Italy, during the Social War, in 91–90 B.C.

having already seized upon the fertile plain now known as
Alsace, between the Rhine and the Vosges mountains. The
issue of the Helvetian campaign imposed upon Caesar the
obligation to protect his Gallic allies against Ariovistus; and
his first step was to seize the natural stronghold of Vesontio,
now Besançon (I. 38), which he made a military base. In
the last century France, fearing a German invasion by the same
route, transformed Besançon into a fortress of the first class.

The victory over Ariovistus enabled Caesar to fix the upper
Rhine as the boundary between the German territory and central Gaul. Secure against danger of attack from this side, he
was free to carry his conquest northward into Belgium. In
contrast with the highlands of central Gaul, and the mountainous country in the south, the greater part of ancient Belgium, corresponding with modern Holland, Belgium, and the
northernmost corner of France, was low and fairly level. It

was therefore an easy matter for Caesar, after the battles at the Aisne and the Sambre (Book II), to overrun the country, before western Gaul, or the mountain strongholds of the Arvernians in the south, had been conquered. The accessibility of ancient Belgium hastened its conquest by Caesar.

When Caesar invaded Belgium he had not the excuse of a previous attack by Belgians. He had heard that they were arming, and forthwith marched into Belgic territory. In 1914, German armies marched across Belgian territory, and held it in subjection, not because there was the slightest prospect that Germany would be attacked by Belgians, but in order to secure a quick and easy route through that neutral country into France; for along the line of direct contact between French and German territory the routes were more difficult, and other points of vantage besides Besançon had been strongly fortified on the French side.

To Caesar the Rhine seemed the natural boundary of Gaul on the east. By the defeat of Ariovistus, and later by the destruction of the Usipetes and Tencteri (IV. 1–15), he checked German invasions. All Gaul became Romanized. For a part of its course the Rhine formed the boundary of the Roman Empire; "to maintain the frontiers of the Rhine and the Danube," said the historian Freeman, "was, from the first century to the fifth, the great object of Rome's policy and warfare."

After the fall of the Western Empire Gaul was overrun by the German Franks, the "spearmen," whose name survives in that of the country France.

After the defeat of Napoleon at the battle of Leipzig, in 1813, the Allies offered to leave to him "the natural boundaries of France: the Rhine, Alps, Pyrenees, and Ocean." Bitter indeed since then have been the strifes over the lands lying west of the Rhine, arising from acceptance or rejection of the stream as a political boundary; the "Watch on the Rhine" in preference to all other patriotic songs became the German national hymn. No element in the historical content of

Caesar's Commentaries is more significant than this, that they disclose to us the age-long struggle between peoples of Celtic and Germanic origin aligned along the Rhine, a struggle which has reached its awful culmination in our own time.

Besides issues and events of larger significance, Caesar's Commentaries make mention of military practices, and instances of bravery, to which the Great War has furnished abundant parallels.

Figure 15. — Charge of Scots Greys at St. Quentin, in 1914.
Highlanders, holding to the stirrups, are keeping up with the horsemen.   (Courtesy of Collier's Weekly.)

In his conquest of Gaul, Caesar exacted many hostages. Hostages have also been seized by the Germans in conquered cities. On September 12, 1914, at Reims, then in German hands, the names of eighty persons were posted, with the following printed proclamation (translation from the French):

"In order adequately to assure the safety of our troops and quietness on the part of the population of Reims, the persons named have been seized as hostages by the commander of the German army. These hostages will be shot if there is the least disturbance. On the

other hand, if the city remains absolutely quiet and free from disturbance, these hostages and inhabitants will be placed under the
protection of the army."

Regarding the fate of the hostages held by Caesar we have
no information.   Hostages taken by the Germans, as the records
show, were in some cases shot, in others carried off to prison
camps.

Among the most inspiring passages of the Commentaries
are those in which Caesar makes note of the bravery of his
men.   Thus in describing the first expedition to Britain he
tells us how the soldiers of the tenth legion, following their
eagle-bearer, plunged into deep water, advanced against a storm
of missiles from the shore, and drove the British back, effect-
ing a landing (IV. 25).

Less spectacular, but not less brave, was the advance of the
Italian infantry across the Isonzo in the assault upon Goritz
in August of 1916.   "With water up to their necks," writes
Lord Northcliffe, who witnessed the movement, " carrying their
rifles high above their heads and ecstatically singing patriotic
songs, they forded the broad stream and carried the eastern
bank.   The enemy's shrapnel, which, falling among them,
churned the water into foam, failed utterly to check or even
retard their charge.   Those who fell wounded in the water
insisted upon being helped to gain the eastern bank, saying,
'Then they won't send us back.'"

Few modern officers have shown themselves more courageous
and resourceful than the heroic Baculus, who was almost done
to death in the battle at the Sambre (II. 25), but was restored
to health and twice thereafter saved the day by his quick
resolve and indomitable will (III. 5; VI. 38).   No instance of
individual bravery stands out so conspicuously, however, as
that of the centurion Scaeva, who fought at his post, at the
gate of a redoubt, though one eye was put out and he was
wounded in shoulder and thigh; in his shield, after the battle,
120 holes were counted where it had been struck by arrows

(pp. 434–435). In June, 1916, E. A. Bigorne, machine gun oper-
ator on the front in France, remained in an advanced position
after every other man in his trench had been killed, when it
was obvious that an assault of the enemy was preparing. He
gathered the ammunition of his fallen comrades, and when the
assault came he still held his post, using his machine gun so
effectively that he repulsed charge after charge against his
trench, accounting for 800 Germans in killed, wounded, and
fleeing, before he was relieved.

Caesar publicly commended Scaeva, and made him a present
of money amounting to more than $8000; Bigorne received
the decoration of the Legion of Honor, said to be the highest
award ever given to a private soldier in France.

iii. The Civilization of the Gauls

Excavations and discoveries in France in recent decades have
thrown new light upon the civilization of the Gauls in Caesar's
time. To give an account of these within narrow limits is
impossible. It may suffice to say that remains of city walls
have been found on the site of Bibracte and other Gallic cities,
so constructed as completely to verify Caesar's description of
a Gallic wall in Book VII (chap. 23); that burial places and
unearthed town sites in France, western Switzerland, Belgium,
and England have yielded an incalculable number of objects of
common life, now available for study in museums; and that
with the help of such objects it is permitted to picture to
ourselves the varied and picturesque life of ancient Gaul and
Britain in a way unknown to previous centuries.

Disregarding the highest estimates, we may reckon the population of Transalpine Gaul in Caesar's time as twelve or thirteen
millions; there were perhaps a fourth as many inhabitants as
are found in the same area to-day. There were in Gaul not a
few cities, some of which, as Avaricum with its 40,000 souls,
would be reckoned as important towns in modern times.

The growth of towns implies advancement in both commerce
and industry. In Caesar's time there was already developed

Caesar Born July 12 100 B.C. in Rome.

in Gaul a system of roads, with bridges across the rivers; and there is reason to believe that in many cases the line of a Gallic road was followed later by a Roman road, which in turn is now represented by a highway or railway.

Raw materials for industry and commerce were furnished by farming, by stock raising, and by mining (III. 21, and VII. 22). The Gauls were particularly fond of horses (IV. 2), the quality of which improved under their care. It was therefore no accident which led the Romans to import Gallic horses, and which gave to the Gauls such a lead in the invention of vehicles that the Romans borrowed from them the names of two kinds of cart, *carrus* (I. 3) and *carpentum*. From the Celtic, through the Latin and French, come our words " car " and " chariot "; and through the Anglo-Saxon, our word " cart."

The horse is a constantly recurring figure on Gallic coins (Figs. 17, 18, etc.). The fine quality of the horses still raised on Gallic soil is indicated by the fact that in 1910 there were imported into the United States from France and Belgium more than 4500 horses, nearly four times as many as were imported in that year from all other European countries.

The implications of Caesar's language about importations into Gaul, in Book I (chap. 1), Book II (chap. 15), and Book VI (chap. 24) are borne out by other evidence. The most convincing proof of the influence of both Greek and Italian traders, and of the commercial progress of the country, is to be found in the extensive and varied coinage of the Gallic states[1] in Caesar's time. The Gauls minted their own metal, though they had not the skill to produce coins of so fine workmanship as those of the Greeks and Romans. Their coinage was still in the imitative stage, reproducing, often crudely, designs of foreign coins which circulated among them.

Not a few Gallic coins were copied from a variety of widely

---

[1] In the United States the word **cīvitās** in passages relating to Gaul should not be translated " tribe," for the reason that in this country the word " tribe " is so closely associated with the American aborigines that to many it suggests a condition of savagery.

current Macedonian coins known as *staters*. An example is Figure 16, which is thought to have been struck by the Ambarri (I. 11). The head and the two-horse chariot are unmistakable copies of the obverse and reverse designs of a stater; and the unintelligible letters on the reverse, underneath the chariot, are the work of a Gallic coin-maker who did not know Greek, and imitated, without understanding them, the letters of the Greek name ΦΙΛΙΠΠΟΥ, "of Philip," which is found on the Macedonian coin.

Figure 16. — Gallic coin, perhaps of the Ambarri.

Gold. The Macedonian coins, from which this is copied, are of fine workmanship.

The head is that of a youth. The two-horse chariot on Greek coins was associated with games.

Just as clearly of Roman origin is the type of the two-headed Janus, found on a coin of the Mediomatrici (Fig. 17). On the reverse the Gallic designer has made a fanciful use of the chariot design, which appears on Roman coins as well as Greek; the charioteer has been resolved into the graceful curves which we see above the horse, while the chariot seems to be represented by a rosette underneath the horse, symbolizing a chariot wheel. The Gallic craftsman wished to make the horse prominent.

Figure 17. — Coin of the Mediomatrici.

Gold. Obverse, two-headed Janus. Reverse, design derived from a chariot type.

It is not surprising that in Caesar's time the Greek alphabet was in common use in Gaul (VI. 14), employed, for example, in making up the census lists of the Helvetians (I. 29); for Massilia, established originally as a Greek colony and trading post, was already an old city, having commercial relations with many Gallic states (p. 611).

Nevertheless we occasionally find Roman letters on Gallic coins, as in Figure 18, which reproduces a coin struck a short

time before the downfall of Gallic power, in 52 B.C. The face on the obverse is intended to be a portrait of the Gallic leader Vercingetorix, but is highly conventional. Much more true to life is a later portrait of Vercingetorix on a Roman coin whose designer must have seen him when a captive in Rome (Fig. 145). In military matters Vercingetorix confessedly imitated the Romans (VII. 29).

Figure 18. — Arvernian coin.

Gold, alloyed with silver.

Obverse, head of Vercingetorix, spelled VERCINGETORIXS, with helmet.

Reverse, below the horse, two-handled wine jar; above, scroll-shaped ornament.

Various objects of metal, pottery, and other permanent materials, of which a few examples are shown in the illustrations to the notes of this book, strengthen the conviction that while the northern parts of Gaul were more backward, the higher classes in the central and southern portions of the country in Caesar's time had adopted a more refined mode of life (I. 1); thus the terrified women of Gergovia threw down silverware to the Roman soldiers scaling the wall (VII. 47). The common people were housed in round thatched huts, but people of means had houses of stone.

Figure 19. — Relief, on a marble altar.

Discovered at Nîmes. The war trumpet ends in a fanciful head with wide open mouth, pointed ears, and a crest. The bronze-covered shield is skillfully imitated in the marble.

The altar was a votive offering, erected by a Roman soldier, of Oriental birth, at Nemausus, now Nîmes.

Notwithstanding their use of writing for ordinary purposes, including "documents public and private" (VI. 14), the Gauls did not develop a literature. This may be due in part to the insistence of the Druids that their body of doctrine, poetic and mystical though it was, should be transmitted only by memory (VI. 14). As the Druids were the intellectual leaders of the people, their practice in this respect must have discouraged literary effort.

This all-powerful priesthood, regarding which Caesar in Book VI gives the earliest authentic information, in their teachings united a theory of the universe with the doctrine of transmigration of souls. The power of the Druids in temporal affairs came from this fact, that while acting as arbiters and judges in disputes of every kind, they were enabled to enforce their decisions through the terrible penalty of excommunication (VI. 13).

Figure 20. — Coin of the Treverans or Leuci.

Bronze. Obverse, head copied from a coin of Augustus.

Reverse, bull, and inscription GERMAN[VS] INDVTILLI L[IBERTVS], 'Germanus, freedman of Indutillus.'

Outside the limited field of coins and minor objects the Gauls made almost no progress in art before the Roman Conquest. That they were ready for development in the fuller appreciation of art, if not also in expression, is evident from monuments of Gallic origin dating from the earlier years of the Roman occupation, in which an awakening of the artistic impulse is manifest. An example is the relief in Figure 19, showing a Gallic oval shield with metal covering and a war-trumpet with the head of a monster. Wind instruments with heads of animals or monsters, not of Gallic origin, may be seen in collections of musical instruments today.

Figure 21. — Coin of Tasciovanus, British ruler.

Gold. Obverse, tablet inscribed TASCIO, for TASCIOVANUS, between ornaments.

Reverse, horseman galloping to the right; on some of the coins he seems to be holding a trumpet. The significance of the letters SEGO is not clear.

Gallic and British coins struck after the Conquest indicate to us the adoption of Roman fashions within a few decades after Caesar's death, not only in Gaul but even in Britain. On the coin reproduced in Figure 20 we find a prominent man of the Treverans (or of the Leuci), designated in the Roman style as "Germanus, freedman of Indutillus."

Figure 22. — Coin of Tasciovanus.

Silver. Obverse, winged horse,
Pegasus, walking toward the left;
letters TAS, irregularly placed, an
abbreviation for TASCIOVANUS.
Reverse, winged Griffin,
springing toward the right.

Figure 23. — Coin of
Cunobelinus.

Bronze. Inscription, CUNOBELINI,
TASCIOVANI F[ILII], 'of Cunobelinus,
son of Tasciovanus.'
On the reverse is a centaur with a
mantle, blowing a trumpet.

Inscribed with Roman letters also are gold coins of the British Virica (Fig. 140), as well as gold and silver coins of Tasciovanus (Figs. 21, 22). Tasciovanus was a contemporary of the Emperor Augustus. He was the father of Cunobelinus, the hero of Shakespeare's drama Cymbeline, as a bronze coin of Cunobelinus shows (Fig. 23).

Figure 24. — Coin of Lug-
dunum.

Bronze. Reverse: prow of a
galley with beak; above, an obelisk, and a globe emitting rays.
Inscription, COPIA; the official
name of the colony was COLONIA
COPIA AUGUSTA LUGDUNUM.
On the obverse of this coin
the heads of Julius Caesar and
Augustus are shown.

Both the Griffin and the Pegasus of the silver coin (Fig. 22), and the Centaur of the bronze (Fig. 23), were designs taken from the Graeco-Roman mythology, and current in the Classical Art of the period. They may have been brought to Britain by skilled crafts-men directly from southern cities, or have been introduced by way of Gaul; in either case they confirm the infer-ence, suggested by the Roman letters on the coins, that Roman influence was strong in Britain in the interval between Caesar's expedi-tions and the Roman Conquest of the island (p. 611).

Complete Romanization of at least a part of central Gaul is indicated by a coin struck soon after 31 B.C. at Lugdunum, modern Lyons, which was one of the first Roman colonies established in Gaul outside the Province (Fig. 24).

iv. CAESAR AND THE HISTORICAL WRITERS

The historians have written more about Julius Caesar than about any other Roman. There are, nevertheless, wide differences of opinion in regard to his motives and character.

In the eyes of some Caesar was a monster of wickedness, a despot guilty of subverting the liberties of his country. Others have viewed him as a statesman and patriot of exalted aims. To others still his career has seemed to mark the culmination of the inevitable trend of the Roman state toward absolutism, and they have interpreted it as the opportune appearance of a will and personality powerful enough to dominate, and fuse into lasting union, the inharmonious elements of a political life rapidly drifting into anarchy. Men's views of Caesar have generally been colored by their attitude toward the type of government which he established.

The extant Greek and Latin writings in which Caesar has a prominent place are now accessible in excellent translations; nearly all are included in the *Loeb Classical Library*.[1] Accessible in English also, with few exceptions, are the most important modern works in foreign languages dealing with Caesar and his times.

The earliest characterization of Caesar which we have, in Sallust's *Catiline* (chaps. 53, 54), forms part of a comparison between him and Cato. A biography of Caesar in Greek, together with biographies of Pompey, Crassus, Brutus, Cato, and Cicero, was included by Plutarch in his *Lives*, published near the end of the first century A.D. (translation by B. Perrin, 10 vols., *Loeb Classical Library*, 1913–). Plutarch records

---

[1] The volumes of the *Loeb Classical Library*, established by James Loeb of New York, have the original text and the English translation on opposite pages (publishers, G. P. Putnam's Sons, New York).

also a number of Caesar's sayings, with the incidents which called them forth, in his *Moralia* (*Plutarch's Essays and Miscellanies*, translation revised by W. W. Goodwin, 5 vols., Boston, 1906; Vol. 1, pp. 246–248). In 120 A.D. Suetonius published a biography of Julius Caesar as the first of his *Lives of the Caesars* (translation by J. C. Rolfe, 2 vols., *Loeb Classical Library*, 1914).

The closing period of the Roman Republic was treated with much detail by two late Greek historians, whose works in great part still survive. About the middle of the second century A.D. Appian wrote the *Civil Wars* (translation of Appian's works by Horace White, 4 vols., *Loeb Classical Library*, 1912–13); and in the earlier part of the third century Dio Cassius composed his *Roman History* (translation by H. B. Foster, revised by E. Cary, 9 vols., *Loeb Classical Library*, 1914–). The ancient literary sources are well summarized and evaluated in the *Annals of Caesar, A Critical Biography with a Survey of the Sources*, by E. G. Sihler, which follows the life of Caesar year by year (New York, 1911).

To the ancient material relating to Caesar belong the coins struck by his order, and a number of portraits. The most important coins are interpreted by H. A. Grueber in *Coins of the Roman Republic in the British Museum* (with 123 plates; 3 vols., London, 1910). The portraits of Caesar are discussed at length, but without adequate critical preparation, in *Portraitures of Julius Caesar*, by F. J. Scott (New York, 1903). The bust of Pompey in Copenhagen, three portraits of Cicero, and three of Caesar, are presented in *Greek and Roman Portraits*, by A. Hekler (New York, 1912; plates 155–161). Several gems with the portrait of Caesar are published by A. Furtwaengler, *Die Antiken Gemmen* (3 vols., Berlin, 1899, plates 45, 46).

Among the modern biographies the first place must be given to *Julius Caesar and the Foundation of the Roman Imperial System*, by W. Warde Fowler (New York, 1892). Less satisfactory is *Caesar, a Sketch*, by J. A. Froude (New York, 1883).

Interesting sidelights on Caesar's career are found in *Cicero and his Friends, A Study of Roman Society in the Time of Caesar,* by G. Boissier, translated from the French (New York, 1898); *The Life of Cicero,* by Anthony Trollope (2 vols., London and New York, 1880); *Cicero and the Fall of the Roman Republic,* by J. L. Strachan-Davidson (New York, 1896); and *Social Life in Rome in the Age of Cicero,* by W. Warde Fowler (New York, 1909).

Still of interest for the student of Caesar, though in most respects superseded by later works, are *Lectures on the History of Rome,* by B. G. Niebuhr (3 vols., 3d edition, London, 1853); *History of the Later Roman Commonwealth,* by Thomas Arnold (2 vols., London, 1845); and *The Decline of the Roman Republic,* by George Long (5 vols., London, 1874).

Of special importance are the interpretations of Caesar's career in the fifth volume of *The History of Rome,* by Theodor Mommsen (5 vols., New York, 1895); in the first portion of *The Romans under the Empire,* by C. Merivale (reprinted in 8 volumes, New York, 1890); *The Roman Triumvirates,* by C. Merivale, a volume of the series *Epochs of Ancient History;* the third volume of the richly illustrated *History of Rome,* by V. Duruy (6 vols., London, 1883–86); the second volume of G. Ferrero's highly imaginative but suggestive *Greatness and Decline of Rome* (5 vols., New York, 1907–09); and the third volume of *The Roman Republic,* by W. E. Heitland (3 vols., Cambridge, 1909).

It would be interesting if to the diverse modern estimates of Caesar's character and life-work we could add a statement by himself regarding his aims and achievements. In default of the written word, however, we have not a few suggestions in the imagery of the coins issued by his authority, the types of which were suggested, or at least approved, by him. Thus we are warranted in believing that he wished men to recall the story of his lineage (Fig. 153) and the origin of the name Caesar (Fig. 164), as well as his victories in Gaul (Fig. 159), Spain (Fig. 161), the East, and Africa.

A suggestion of Caesar's attitude toward his task, or at least
the attitude he assumed, may be conveyed by a gold coin struck
in 49 B.C., after Pompey had fled across the Adriatic (Fig. 25).
Here we find, on the reverse, a design symbolizing his victories
in Gaul; the design of the obverse shows the head of Pietas,
the deified personification of loyalty to duty, particularly duty
to the gods.   Pietas in this connection has no relation to the

Figure 25. — Coin of Caesar struck in 49 B.C.

  Gold, aureus. Obverse, head of Pietas, wearing a wreath of oak-leaves ; the hair behind the head is gathered into a knot ornamented with jewels. The goddess is further
adorned with an earring in the shape of a cross, and a necklace. The significance of the
figure LII (52) is uncertain.
  Reverse, symbols of victories in Gaul ; cf. Fig. 159, p. 595.

office of Supreme Pontiff (Fig. 157).   It suggests that Caesar,
like the Trojan Aeneas in the Virgilian epic (Aen. I. 378), was
the instrument of heaven in the accomplishment of a mission.
  Illuminating studies relative to Caesar and the transformation of the Roman Republic into the Roman Empire, are *Roman
Imperialism*, by J. R. Seeley, in his *Roman Imperialism and
Other Lectures and Essays* (Boston, 1889) ; *Seven Roman States-
men of the Later Republic*, by C. Oman, with four studies devoted
to Crassus, Cato, Pompey, and Caesar (New York, 1902) ; *Caesar
and Alexander*, in *Lectures on Modern History*, to which are
added two essays dealing with ancient history, by Friedrich
Schlegel (London, 1849) ; by suggestion rather than by direct
bearing, the essay entitled *The Roman Empire and the British
Empire in India*, by James Bryce, in his *Studies in History
and Jurisprudence* (Oxford and New York, 1901).

Indispensable for the study of Caesar's Commentaries on the historical side are *Caesar's Conquest of Gaul* by T. Rice Holmes (2d edition, Oxford, 1911), and his *Ancient Britain and the Invasions of Julius Caesar* (Oxford, 1907). Very useful are the *History of Julius Caesar,* by Napoleon III, with the Atlas, on which have been founded most of the maps illustrating Caesar's campaigns in Gaul (2 vols., New York, 1866); two works by C. Stoffel, *Guerre de César et d'Arioviste et premières opérations de César en l'an 702* (Paris, 1890), and *Histoire de Jules César, Guerre civile* (2 vols., with Atlas, Paris, 1887); and *Histoire de la Gaule,* by C. Jullian (4 vols., Paris, 1908-13).

Both the historical and the literary significance of Caesar's Commentaries is estimated in *The Commentaries of Caesar* by Anthony Trollope, in *Ancient Classics for English Readers* (Philadelphia, 1871); in the *History of Roman Literature* by C. L. Cruttwell (London, 1878), *History of Latin Literature* by C. A. Simcox (2 vols., New York, 1883), and *Literary History of Rome* [3] by J. W. Duff (London, 1914). The title of the Commentaries is treated by F. W. Kelsey in *The title of Caesar's work on the Gallic and Civil Wars* (*Transactions of the American Philological Association,* vol. 36, 1905, pp. 211-238).

v. Caesar in Literature and Myth

Of deep human interest, and touching Caesar at many points, are the *Letters* of Marcus Cicero; among them are included a few letters written by Caesar and others intimately associated with him (edition, with full notes, by R. Y. Tyrrell and L. C. Purser, 7 vols., in part 3d edit., Dublin and London, 1901—; translation of the *Letters to Atticus* by E. O. Winstedt in the *Loeb Classical Library,* 2 vols., 1913.)

About a century after Caesar's death Lucan, reacting against the absolutism of Nero, composed the *Pharsalia,* an epic poem in ten books having for its subject the struggle between Caesar and Pompey, commencing with the crossing of the Rubicon. The poet's sympathies were with Pompey and Cato; but, even so, from the very force of his personality Caesar is the domi-

nating character.   (Text with notes by C. E. Haskins, London,
1887 : translation by Edward Ridley, New York, 1896.)

In modern times the singular power of Shakespeare's *Julius
Caesar* has apparently deterred other dramatists from attempting the theme.   The scene of the tragedy, *The False One*, by
Beaumont and Fletcher (first published in 1647), is laid at Alexandria after the battle of Pharsalus ; the young King Ptolemy,
Achillas, and Septimius (C. III. 104), who is " the False One,"
all appear, as well as Cleopatra, Labienus, and Caesar, who de-
claims over the head of Pompey, presented to him by Achillas.

Recently John Masefield, in *The Tragedy of Pompey the Great*
(New York, 1911), has skillfully developed an interpretation of
Pompey's actions altogether different from the view that will
present itself to most readers of Caesar's *Civil War*.   Bernard
Shaw's *Caesar and Cleopatra* is an amusing caricature.

Fewer historical novels concern themselves with the closing
days of the Roman Republic than with the first century of the
Empire.   The best of them all is *A Friend of Caesar*, by W. S.
Davis (New York, 1900).   The hero of *The Wonderful Ad-
ventures of Phra the Phœnician,* by E. L. Arnold, son of Edwin
Arnold (New York, 1890), in the first of his several eventful
lives weds the daughter of a British ruler and joins with the
natives in trying to prevent the landing of Caesar's forces.

To the domain of the essay, containing much suggestive gen-
eralization and psychological analysis, belong the sections and
passages relating to Julius Caesar in *The Tragedy of the Cae-
sars, A Study of the Characters of the Caesars of the Julian and
Claudian Houses*, by S. Baring-Gould (3d edit., London, 1895) ;
Roman Days, by V. Rydberg (2d edit., New York, 1887) ; *Im-
perial Purple*, by Edgar Saltus (Chicago, 1892) ; *Ave Roma
Immortalis*, by F. M. Crawford, New York, 1902) ; as well as the
older works, *Causes of the Grandeur and Decadence of the
Romans*, by Montesquieu (new translation by J. Baker, New
York, 1894 ; chap. 11, with the translator's note) ; and *The
Caesars*, by Thomas de Quincey (in vol. 6 of his *Collected
Writings*, edited by D. Masson, Edinburgh, 1890).

Wonderful portents accompanying the death of Caesar are described by Virgil in the first book of the *Georgics*, while the transformation of his soul into a comet is set forth by Ovid at the end of the *Metamorphoses;* thus within approximately a half century after his death the miraculous had gathered about his memory and had found literary expression.

Other marvelous stories about Caesar were current in the Roman Empire, and were reflected in later writings. The *Gesta Romanorum*, a collection of edifying tales made about the end of the thirteenth century, tells us how, as Caesar started to cross the Rubicon, a huge ghost stood in his way, and how Caesar met the challenge (Latin text edited by H. Oesterley, Berlin, 1872; trans. by C. Swan, 2 vols., London, 1824, vol. 1, p. 99).

The most persistent tale related to the safe-guarding of Caesar's ashes. In the earlier part of the first century A.D. a massive granite obelisk was brought to Rome from Egypt and erected in a circus near where St. Peter's church was afterwards built; on the top a large ball, or sphere, of bronze was placed (Fig. 26). The obelisk remained standing to modern times; until 1586, when the ball was taken

Figure 26. — Bronze ball supposed to contain the ashes of Julius Caesar.

After the murder of Julius Caesar his body was taken to the Forum, and there burned.

In the Middle Ages his ashes were supposed to be preserved in the large round ball on the top of the obelisk which, till 1586, stood at the side of St. Peter's church in Rome, and now stands in the Piazza in front of St. Peter's. (Illustration from an engraving made in 1569.)

down and found to be solid, many believed that it contained the ashes of Julius Caesar, placed there in order that, in the quaint language of a medieval guide-book, " as in his lifetime the whole world lay subdued before him, even so in his death the

same may lie beneath him forever" (*Mirabilia Urbis Romae.*
Latin text, H. Jordan, *Topographie der Stadt Rom*, vol. 2,
p. 625; translation by F. M. Nichols, London, 1889, pp. 71–72).

One version of the Swan Legend, most commonly associated
with Lohengrin, tells us how a sister of Julius Caesar eloped
with a Belgian prince, and in her northern home had a beautiful
white swan. Her husband joined forces with Ariovistus and
fell at the battle of Vesontio. Now in Caesar's army was a
hero, Salvius Brabon, who was descended from the Trojan
Hector. Hunting near the Rhine he saw a snow-white swan,
"playfully pulling at the rope which bound a small skiff to the
shore. Salvius leaped into the boat and cast it loose from its
mooring. Then the bird swam before him as a guide, and he
rowed after it." The swan conducted him to the sister
of Caesar, who made herself known to him; he brought Caesar
to her castle, and the conqueror embraced his sister with joy.
Salvius asked Caesar for the widowed sister's hand; Caesar
consented, and Salvius Brabon became the first Duke of
Brabant (S. Baring-Gould, *Curious Myths of the Middle Ages*,
second series, Philadelphia, 1868, pp. 332–335).

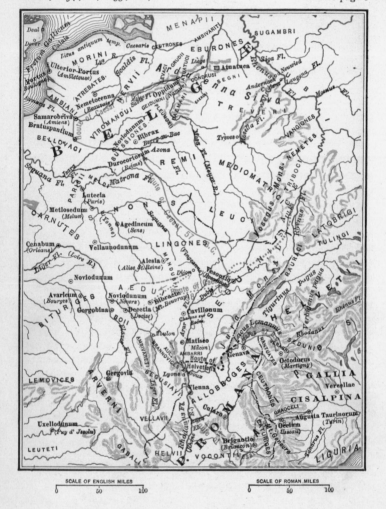

SCALE OF ENGLISH MILES

SCALE OF ROMAN MILES

EXPLANATION

The route of the Helvetians to the Arar is indicated by a broken black line; thence their line of march and Caesar's coincide, to Toulon.

COMMENTARIUS PRIMUS

Geography of Gaul

Divisions and peoples.

1. GALLIA est omnis dīvīsa in partēs trēs, quārum ūnam incolunt Belgae, aliam Aquītānī, tertiam, quī ipsōrum linguā Celtae, nostrā Gallī appellantur. Hī omnēs linguā,

---

Commentārius: 'Commentary.' *273*.[1] **prīmus**: *33, 36*.

1. I. **Gallia**: *2, a*, and *286*. **Gallia omnis**: 'Gaul as a whole,' contrasted with Gaul in the narrower sense, or Celtic Gaul; Celtic Gaul also is often called **Gallia**. *287, b*. **omnis**: *25, a*, and *80, b*. **dīvīsa**: 'divided,' the perfect passive participle of **dīvidō** used as a predicate adj. *148, c*. B. 337, 2; A. 495; H. 640, 3. **in**: 'into.' *124, a*. **partēs**: 'parts.' *17, b*. **trēs**: *37, b*, and *353, c*. **quārum**: 'of which.' *47*. Why genitive? *97, a*. B. 201, 1; A. 346, *a*, 1; H. 442. **ūnam**: sc. *partem*, 'one (part).' *23, a*. Look up the three 'parts' of Gaul on the Map at the end of this book.

2. **incolunt**: 'inhabit.' *55*. **Belgae**: *19, e* ; *287*. **aliam** [partem]: 'another (part),' less precise than *alteram* (*partem*), 'a second (part),' which might have been used. *23, a*. **Aquītānī**: sc. *incolunt*. *89, a*. **tertiam, quī**: = *tertiam partem eī incolunt, quī*, 'a third part is inhabited by those who,' lit. 'those inhabit who.' *164, a*. **ipsōrum**: 'their own'; lit. 'of themselves.' *46*. **ipsōrum linguā**: 'in their own language.' *131, a*. B. 218; A. 409; H. 476.

3. **Celtae**: sc. *appellantur*. *88*, and *287, b*. **nostrā**: *nostrā linguā*, Latin. *157, c*. **appellantur**: 'are called.' *53*. **linguā, īnstitūtīs, lēgibus**: 'in respect to language, institutions, and laws.' *142, a*, and *234, a*. B. 226; A. 418; H. 480.

---

[1] References in Italic type are to the "Companion to Caesar" and "Points to be Noted in Writing Latin," in this book; B., A., and H. refer to the Latin grammars by Bennett, Allen and Greenough, and Harkness, respectively. For other abbreviations consult the list preceding the Vocabulary.

īnstitūtīs, lēgibus inter sē differunt.   Gallōs ab Aquītānīs
5 Garumna flūmen, ā Belgīs Matrona et Sēquana dīvidit.

Hōrum omnium fortissimī sunt Belgae, proptereā quod
ā cultū atque hūmānitāte prōvinciae longissimē absunt,
minimēque ad eōs mercātōrēs saepe commeant, atque ea,
quae ad effēminandōs animōs pertinent, important; proxi-
10 mīque sunt Germānīs, quī trāns Rhēnum incolunt, quibuscum continenter bellum gerunt.

---

4. **inter sē**: 'from one another.' *159*. B. 245; A. 301, *f*; H.
502, 1.   **differunt**: 'differ.' *69, b*.

5. **Garumna**: sc. *dīvidit*, 'separates.'   **flūmen**: *12, e*, and *91, a*.
Derivation? *74, d*.   **Matrona**: *292*.   **dīvidit**: singular number;
why? *173, a*.   B. 255, 3; A. 317, *b*; H. 392, 4.

6. **Hōrum**: *42, b*, and *97, a*.   B. 201, 1; A. 346, *a*, 2; H. 442
fortissimī: 'the bravest.' *27, a*.   **proptereā**: adv. meaning 'on
this account'; closely connected with **quod**, the two words together
being translated 'because.'   Three reasons are given for the bravery
of the Belgians; what are they?

7. **cultū**: 'mode of life,' referring to the outward appearances of
civilization. *20*.   **atque**: *233, a*.   **hūmānitāte**: 'refinement' in
intellectual interests and in feeling. *10, f*.   **prōvinciae**: 'of the
Province.' *94, a*, and *290*.   **longissimē absunt**: 'are furthest
removed.' *34, a*, and *66, a*; also, *183, a*.

8. **mimimē — saepe**: 'very rarely'; lit. 'least often.' *35*.   **eōs**:
44, and *160, b*.   **mercātōrēs**: 'traders' from the Province, especially
from Massilia, followed the course of the Rhone, the Saône, and the
Loire, so that naturally they did not often go so far north as the Belgian
country.   **commeant**: 'make their way to'; lit. 'go and come.' *53*.
ea: 'those things,' object of *important*. *160, c*.   Caesar seems to have
had in mind particularly the importation of wine (II. 15; IV. 2).

9. **ad effēminandōs animōs**: 'to weaken the courage.' *230*, (3).
B. 339, 2; A. 503, 506; H. 628.   **animōs**: *6, a*, and *92, a*.   **pertinent**: 'tend.' *54*.   **important**: 'import.' *53*, and *175, a*.

10. **proximīque sunt**: 'and they are nearest.' *33*, and *233, b*.
Germānīs: why dat.? *108, a*.   B. 192, 1; A. 384; H. 434, 2.
trāns: here 'on the other side of.' *122, a*.   **quibuscum**: *125, c*.

11. **continenter**: 'continually.'   **bellum gerunt**: 'they wage
war.' *6, a*, and *55*.

Quā dē causā Helvētiī quoque reliquōs Gallōs virtūte
praecēdunt, quod ferē cotīdiānīs proeliīs cum Germānīs
contendunt, cum aut suīs fīnibus eōs prohibent, aut ipsī in
eōrum fīnibus bellum gerunt.	15

Figure 27. — Modern road in the Jura Mountains.

In Caesar's time there were only trails, over which the migrating Helvetians with
their carts could not pass; no such barrier protected them from the Germans.

---

12. **Quā dē causā**: 'For this reason.' *167*. B. 251, 6; A. 308, *f*;
H. 510. **quoque**: 'also.' **reliquōs**: 'the rest of the.' *171, a*.
Gallōs: only the inhabitants of Celtic Gaul are meant, as indicated in
l. 3; no comparison with the Belgians and the Aquitanians is implied.
113, a. **virtūte**: 'in valor.' *142, a*. B. 226; A. 418; H. 480.

13. **praecēdunt**: 'excel.' *113, b*. **ferē**: 'almost.' **cotīdiānīs**:
'every day'; lit. 'daily.' *22, b*. **proeliīs**: 'in battle'; lit. 'by means
of battles.' *131, a*. **cum**: the preposition *cum* is distinguished
from the conjunction *cum* only by the sense and the connection.

14. **contendunt**: 'contend.' *55*. **cum**: *185, a*. **aut . . .
aut**: 'either . . . or.' *235, b*. **suīs**: 'their own,' referring to the
Helvetians. *158, a*. **fīnibus**: 'country'; lit. 'boundaries.' *14, b*,
and *127, a*. B. 214, 2; A. 400; H. 464, 1. **eōs**: translate as if
Germānōs, 'the Germans,' in order to avoid using 'them' and 'they'
with reference to two different peoples in the same sentence. **prohibent**: 'are keeping (the Germans) out.' **ipsī**: 'themselves,'
162, a. There is no detailed record of these border raids.

15. **eōrum**: translate as if *Germānōrum*. **fīnibus**: *124, a*.

[Eōrum ūna pars, quam Gallōs obtinēre dictum est,
initium capit ā flūmine Rhodanō; continētur Garumnā
flūmine, Ōceanō, fīnibus Belgārum; attingit etiam ab Sēquanīs et Helvētiīs flūmen Rhēnum; vergit ad septen-
20 triōnēs. Belgae ab extrēmīs Galliae fīnibus oriuntur;
pertinent ad īnferiōrem partem flūminis Rhēnī; spectant
in septentriōnem et orientem sōlem. Aquītānia ā Garumnā
flūmine ad Pȳrēnaeōs montēs et eam partem Ōceanī, quae
est ad Hispāniam, pertinet; spectat inter occāsum sōlis et
25 septentriōnēs.]

The Campaign against the Helvetians.   2–29

Orgetorix, a Helvetian, persuades his countrymen to migrate.

2. Apud Helvētiōs longē nōbilissimus fuit et dītissimus
Orgetorīx. Is, M. Messālā, M. Pīsōne cōnsulibus, rēgnī

16–25. **Eōrum . . . septentriōnēs**: there is reason for believing
that this passage was not written by Caesar but was added after his
time by some one who thought it worth while to give with greater detail
the boundaries of the three divisions of Gaul mentioned by Caesar at
the beginning of the chapter; the style is forced and difficult. If it is
omitted, the transition from the statement about the Helvetians, in lines
12–15, to the activities of the Helvetian leader, Orgetorix, at the beginning of the second chapter, becomes easy and natural. Translation:

'One part of Gaul taken as a whole' (lit. 'of them'), 'which it has been said
the Celts occupy, begins at the river Rhone; it is bounded by the Garonne river,
the Ocean, and the country of the Belgians; on the side where the Sequanians and
Helvetians are it extends also to the river Rhine; it lies to the north. The country
of the Belgians commences at the most distant borders of Celtic Gaul and extends
to the lower part of the river Rhine; it faces north and east. Aquitania extends
from the Garonne river to the Pyrenees mountains and that part of the Ocean
which is off Spain; it faces northwest.'

2. 1. **Apud**: *122, a.*   **longē**: *153, b.*   **nōbilissimus**: 'highest in rank.' *27, a*, and *353, a.*   **dītissimus**: *31.*

2. **Orgetorīx**: *10, c.*   **M.**: = *Mārcō. 19, a.*   **M. . . . cōnsulibus**: = 61 B.C. *144, b,* (1), and *240, a.* B. 227, 1; A. 419, *a*;
H. 489.   **rēgnī**; 'of kingly power,' objective genitive. *6, a*, and *102.*

cupiditāte inductus, coniūrātiōnem nōbilitātis fēcit, et cīvitātī persuāsit, ut dē fīnibus suīs cum omnibus cōpiīs exīrent; *perfacile esse, cum virtūte omnibus praestārent, tōtīus* 5
Galliae imperiō potīrī.

Id hōc facilius eīs persuāsit, quod undique locī nātūrā
Helvētiī continentur: ūnā ex parte flūmine Rhēnō, lātis-

---

3. **cupiditāte**: 'by a desire.' *10, f,* and *135, a.* B. 219; A. 404, *b*;
H. 475, 1.   **inductus**: 'led on.' *226, b,* and *148, b.*   **coniūrātiōnem**: 'conspiracy.' *12, c.*   **nōbilitātis**: here used as a collective
noun, lit. 'of the nobility'; trans. 'among the nobles.' *10, f,* and *92, b.*
fēcit: *57, b.*   **cīvitātī**: *10, f,* and *105.* B. 187, II, *a*; A. 367; H.
426, 2.

4. **persuāsit**: 'persuaded.' *79, b.*   **ut ... exīrent**: 'to go out,'
'to migrate'; kind of clause? *199, a.* B. 295, 1; A. 563; H. 565.
cum omnibus cōpiīs: 'with all (their) effects,' as we say, "bag and
baggage." *137, a.*   **exīrent**: plural because *cīvitātī*, '(his) state,'
to which the unexpressed subject refers, is thought of as if it were
cīvibus, 'the people of (his) state.' *68, b; 173, b,* and *238, h.* B. 254,
4, *a*; H. 389, 1.

5. **perfacile ... potīrī**: indirect discourse, dependent on the idea
of saying in *persuāsit.* *212, a,* and *c,* (5); *213, b.* B. 314, 2; A. 579,
580; H. 641–643.   **perfacile esse**: '(saying) that it was exceedingly easy.' The subject of *esse* is *potīrī*, 'to obtain possession of.'
222, b. Why is *perfacile* neuter? *148, d.*   **virtūte**: *142, a.* B. 226;
A. 418; H. 480.   **omnibus**: *107, a.* B. 187, III, 1; A. 370; H. 429.
praestārent: 'they excelled.' *53,* and *184, a.* B. 286, 2; A. 549;
H. 598.   **tōtīus**: *23, a.*

6. **tōtīus Galliae**: 'of the whole (of) Gaul.' *102.*   **imperiō**:
'sovereignty.' Why ablative? *131, c.* B. 218, 1; A. 410; H. 477.
potīrī: *60,* and *61, a,* (4).

7. **Id**: acc.; 'that (course)'. *117, a,* and *160, c.* B. 176, 2, *a*;
A. 369; H. 426, 6.   **hōc**: 'on this account,' referring to what follows. *135, a,* and *161, a.* B. 219; A. 404; H. 475.   **facilius**: 'the
more easily.' *34, a.*   **eīs**: *44,* and *105.*   **undique**: 'on all sides.'
locī nātūrā: 'by natural features.' *131, a.* How lit.?

8. **continentur**: 'are hemmed in'; why indic.? *183, a.*   **ūnā
ex parte**: 'on one side,' the north side. *126, c.*   **flūmine**: *131, a.*
lātissimō: 'very wide.' *153, a.*

simō atque altissimō, quī agrum Helvētium ā Germānīs
10 dīvidit; alterā ex parte monte Iūrā altissimō, quī est inter
Sēquanōs et Helvētiōs; tertiā, lacū Lemannō et flūmine
Rhodanō, quī prōvinciam nostram ab Helvētiīs dīvidit.

His rēbus fīēbat, ut et minus lātē vagārentur et minus

Figure 28. — Long summit of the Jura range.

This range formed a natural barrier between the country of the Helvetians and that of
the Sequanians, and now carries part of the boundary between France and Switzerland.

---

9. **altissimō**: here 'very deep,' but in l. 10 'very high.'   **quī**:
the antecedent is *Rhēnō*. *163, a*.   **agrum**: here 'territory.'   **ā
Germānīs**: 'from (the territory of) the Germans.' *282*, and *127, c*.

10. **alterā**: for *secundā*, 'second,' as often.   **monte Iūrā**: 'by
the Jura range'; *mōns* refers sometimes to a single mountain, sometimes to a group or chain of mountains, or to a moderate elevation.

11. **tertiā**: sc. *ex parte*.   **lacū**: *20, b*.

12. **Rhodanō**: the part of the Rhone just below Geneva; see Map 1.
prōvinciam: *290*.   **nostram**: i.e. *Rōmānam*. *157, c*.   **Helvētiīs**: *282*. Caesar does not deem it necessary to give the boundary on
the fourth or east side, in the Alps.

13. **His rēbus**: 'Because of these conditions' (lit. 'these things').
135, a.   **fīēbat**: 'it came about.' *70, a*.   **ut . . . possent**: subject of *fīēbat*. *203*, (1). B. 297, 2; A. 569, 1; H. 571, 1.   **et . . .**

facile fīnitimīs bellum īnferre possent; quā ex parte, hominēs bellandī cupidī, magnō dolōre afficiēbantur. Prō multi- 15
tūdine autem hominum et prō glōriā bellī atque fortitūdinis
angustōs sē fīnēs habēre arbitrābantur, quī in longitūdinem
mīlia passuum CCXL, in lātitūdinem CLXXX patēbant.

et: *233, a.* **minus lātē vagārentur**: 'they were more restricted
in their movements,' lit. 'wandered less broadly,' than they wished.
177, a. **minus**: *35.*

14. **fīnitimīs**: '(their) neighbors.' *107, b,* and *154, a.* B. 187, III,
2; A. 370; H. 429, 1. **īnferre**; 'wage.' *69, b.* **possent**: *66, b.*
quā ex parte: 'and on that account.' *167.* **hominēs**: in apposition to the subject of *afficiēbantur,* '(being) men.' *12, b,* and *91, b.*

15. **bellandī**: 'of waging war.' *53,* and *230,* (1). B. 204, 1; A.
349, *a*; H. 451, 1. **cupidī**: 'fond (of).' *22, b.* **magnō dolōre
afficiēbantur** : 'they were sorely' (lit. 'with great vexation') 'troubled.'
57, b. **dolōre**: *11, d,* and *136, b.* **Prō**: 'Considering.' *125, a.*
multitūdine hominum: '(their) population'; how lit.? The number was 263,000 (chap. 29). The Helvetian territory now supports a
population of about 2,250,000.

16. **autem**: *236, b.* **glōriā bellī atque fortitūdinis**: '(their)
reputation for war' (lit. 'of war') 'and for bravery.' *102.*

17. **angustōs fīnēs**: 'too small' (lit. 'narrow') 'territories.' *113, a.*
sē habēre: 'that they had.' *178,* and *213, a.* **arbitrābantur**: 'they
thought,' lit. 'were thinking.' *175, a.* **quī**: i.e. *fīnēs.* **in longitūdinem**: 'in length.' *76.*

18. **mīlia passuum**: 'miles.' Length of the Roman 'pace' and
Roman 'mile'? *243, b.* **mīlia**: *38, a,* and *118, a.* B. 181; A. 425;
H. 417. **passuum**: *20, b,* and *97, a.* **CCXL**: *36,* and *38, b.*
lātitūdinem: 'breadth.' *81.* **CLXXX**: *centum octōgintā,* sc. *mīlia
passuum. 38, b.* As the actual distance across the Helvetian territory was about 80 Roman miles, it has been suggested that Caesar
wrote LXXX, *octōgintā,* which was changed to CLXXX by an error in
copying. **patēbant**: 'extended.' *54.* The territory occupied by
the Helvetians comprised a large portion, or the whole, of the modern
Swiss cantons of Vaud, Neuchâtel, Basel, Freiburg, Bern, Solothurn,
and Aargau. At an earlier period the Helvetians had lived north
of the Rhine, but they had been forced to the south side by the
Germans.

They make preparations; Orgetorix forms a conspiracy.

3. Hīs rēbus adductī, et auctōritāte Orgetorīgis permōtī, cōnstituērunt ea, quae ad proficīscendum pertinērent,
comparāre, iūmentōrum et carrōrum quam maximum numerum coëmere, sēmentēs quam maximās facere, ut in
5 itinere cōpia frūmentī suppeteret, cum proximīs cīvitātibus

---

3.   **1. Hīs rēbus adductī**: 'Prompted by these considerations.'
adductī: agrees with the unexpressed subject of *cōnstituērunt*.   **auctōritāte**: 'by the influence.' *135, a*.   **permōtī**: 'stirred to action.'

2. cōnstituērunt: 'they (i.e. *Helvētiī*) determined'; followed by
comparāre, 'to make ready.' *221, a*. B. 328, 1; A. 457; H. 607, 1.
ea: 'those things'; after *comparāre. 113, a,* and *160, c*.   **ad proficīscendum**: 'for emigration'; lit. 'for setting out.' *230*, (3). B.
338, 3; A. 506; H. 628.   **pertinērent**: subjunctive as giving the
thought of the Helvetians; 'were (as they thought) necessary,' lit.
'pertained (to).' *212, d*. B. 323; A. 592: H. 649, 1.

3. iūmentōrum: 'draft-animals'; horses, mules, and oxen. *97, a*.
carrōrum: two-wheeled 'carts,' drawn largely by oxen. A Helvetian
ox yoke, which was strapped to the horns of the oxen, is shown in Fig. 29.

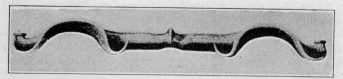

Figure 29. — Helvetian yoke, of wood, found in 1910.
Found near Lake Neuchâtel, with a wooden shield, a spear, the remains of a cart and
the skeleton of the driver, preserved by the water into which he had tumbled with his cart,
perhaps at night.

From the Helvetian cattle the hardy Alpine cattle of Switzerland are
descended.   **quam maximum**: 'the largest possible.' *153, c*. B.
240, 3; H. 159, 2.   **numerum**: 'number.' *113, a*.

4. coëmere: 'to buy up.'   **coëmere, facere, cōnfīrmāre**: after
cōnstituērunt. 221, a.   **sēmentēs quam maximās**: 'as large sow-
ings as possible.' *14, b,* and *153, c*.

5. in itinere: 'on the way.' *18, c*.   **cōpia frūmentī suppeteret**: 'there might be an adequate supply of grain,' lit. 'a supply of
grain might be at hand.' *90, b*.   **suppeteret**: *196, a*. B. 282; A.
531; H. 568.   **proximīs**: 'neighboring,' lit. 'nearest.' *33*.

pācem et amīcitiam cōnfīrmāre. Ad eās rēs cōnficiendās biennium sibi satis esse dūxērunt; in tertium annum pro-fectiōnem lēge cōnfirmant.

Ad eās rēs cōnficiendās Orgetorīx dēligitur. Is sibi lēgātiōnem ad cīvitātēs suscēpit. In eō itinere persuādet 10 Casticō, Catamantāloedis fīliō, Sēquanō, cuius pater rēg-num in Sēquanīs multōs annōs obtinuerat et ā senātū populī Rōmānī amīcus appellātus erat, ut rēgnum in cīvi-

---

6. **pācem et amīcitiam**: '(relations of) peace and friendship.' **cōnfīrmāre**: '(and) to establish.' *234, a.* **Ad . . . cōnficiendās**: gerundive construction, 'to complete these preparations,' lit. 'for those things to be completed.' *230,* (3). B. 339, 2; A. 503; H. 626, 1.

7. **biennium satis esse**: 'that two years would be sufficient.' *212, d,* and *214, a.* **biennium**: *79, b.* **sibi**: 'for them.' *40, b,* and *158, a.* **dūxērunt**: here a verb of thought; 'they reckoned.' *213, a.* **in**: 'for.' **profectiōnem**: '(their) departure.' *157, a.*

8. **cōnfirmant**: historical present; trans. by a past tense, 'they fixed.' *175, b.* Other historical presents which should be translated by a past tense are *dēligitur,* l. 9; *persuādet,* l. 10 and l. 17; *dat,* l. 18; *probat,* l. 19; *cōnfirmat,* l. 23; *dant,* l. 25; *spērant,* l. 26.

9. **Ad . . . cōnficiendās**: 'to carry out these arrangements.' **dēligitur**: 'was chosen.' **sibi — suscēpit**: 'took upon himself.' *104, a.* B. 187, 1; A. 362; H. 424.

10. **lēgātiōnem**, etc.: 'the office of envoy to the states.' *150, d.*

11. **Casticō**: *105.* **Catamantāloedis**: *99.* **fīliō, Sēquanō**: *91, a.* B. 169, 2; A. 282; H. 393. **pater**: *11, b.* **rēgnum**: 'the chief authority'; at this time there was no hereditary or absolute monarchy among the Gauls. *1,* and *289, a.*

12. **annōs**: *118, a.* B. 181, 1; A. 423; H. 417. **obtinuerat**: 'had held.' *79, b.* **senātū populī Rōmānī**: 'the senate of the Roman people,' instead of *senātū populōque,* 'the senate and the Roman people,' because the Roman senate had the right to confer honorary titles on foreign rulers without a popular vote.

13. **amīcus**: 'friend.' *88.* B. 168, 2, *b*; A. 284; H. 393, 8. Such titles were conferred as a recognition of services rendered, or as a means of gaining favor.

tāte suā occupāret, quod pater ante habuerat; itemque
15 Dumnorīgī Aeduō, frātrī Dīviciācī, quī eō tempore prīncipātum in cīvitāte obtinēbat ac maximē plēbī acceptus erat,
ut idem cōnārētur, persuādet, eīque fīliam suam in mātrimōnium dat.

   Perfacile factū esse illīs probat *cōnāta perficere, proptereā*
20 *quod ipse suae cīvitātis imperium obtentūrus esset; nōn*
esse dubium, quīn tōtīus Galliae plūrimum Helvētiī pos-

---

14. **suā**: *157, b.*   **ut . . . occupāret**: 'to seize.' *199, a,* and
177, b.   **quod**: *not* 'because.'   **item**: 'also.'

15. **Dumnorīgī**: *10, c,* and *105.*   **frātrī**: *11, e.*   **Dīviciācī**:
19, d.   **eō tempore**: 'at that time.' *147, a.*   **prīncipātum**: 'the
foremost place'; whether the dominant position of Dumnorix among
the Aeduans was due wholly to his influence, or whether in 61 B.C. he
had also a magistracy, is not indicated.

16. **cīvitāte**: '(his) state,' i.e. the Aeduan state.   **obtinēbat**:
force of the imperfect? *175, a.*   **maximē acceptus**: 'very acceptable.' *30.*   **plēbī**: *108, a.* Our English expression corresponding
with *plēbī acceptus* is 'popular with the masses.'

17. **ut idem cōnārētur**: 'to attempt the same thing'; the construction is similar to that of *ut . . . occupāret* above. *61, a,* (1).   **idem**:
45, and *117, a.*   **eī**: *104, a.*   **in mātrimōnium**: 'in marriage.'

18. **dat**: *67, a,* and *175, b.*

19. **Perfacile . . . possent**: indirect discourse depending on *probat. 213, a.*   **Perfacile**: in predicate after *esse,* as in chap. 2, l. 5.
212, c, (5).   **factū**: 'of accomplishment,' lit. 'in respect to the doing.'
232. B. 340, 2; A. 510, N. 2; H. 635, 1.   **esse**: *214, a.*   **illīs
probat**: 'he (Orgetorix) showed them.' *104, a.*   **cōnāta**: '(their)
undertakings,' *157, a.*   **perficere**: 'to carry through'; subject of
esse. 57, b; 79, b, and *222, b.*

20. **suae**: 'his own,' emphatic. *157, b.*   **imperium**: 'the sovereign power.' *74, b.*   **obtentūrus esset**: 'he was going to seize.'
63. Why subjunctive? *214, a.*   **nōn esse dubium**: 'that there
was no doubt.'

21. **dubium**: in predicate; neuter because the subject of *esse* is a
clause.   **quīn . . . possent**: 'that the Helvetians were the most
powerful (people) in all Gaul,' lit. 'were able the most of the whole (of)
Gaul.' *201, b.* B. 298; A. 558, *a;* H. 595, 1.   **Galliae**: *97, b.* B.

sent; sē suīs cōpiīs suōque exercitū illīs rēgna conciliātūrum cōnfirmat.

Hāc ōrātiōne adductī, inter sē fidem et iūs iūrandum dant; et, rēgnō occupātō per trēs potentissimōs ac firmissi- 25 mōs populōs, tōtīus Galliae sēsē potīrī posse spērant.

The conspiracy is revealed; Orgetorix dies.

4. Ea rēs est Helvētiīs per indicium ēnūntiāta. Mōribus suīs Orgetorīgem ex vinculīs causam dīcere coēgērunt; damnātum poenam sequī oportēbat, ut īgnī cremārētur.

201, 1; A. 346, *a*, 2; H. 442.   **plūrimum**: neuter acc. used substantively. *32*, and *118*, *b*. B. 176, 3, *a*; A. 214, *d*; H. 416, 2.

22. **sē suīs cōpiīs**: 'that he with his own means.' *157*, *b*, and *131*, *a*.   **exercitū**: *not* 'army' but 'armed retinue,' like that with which Orgetorix afterwards overawed the judges, as related in the next chapter.   **illīs**: *104*, *a*.   **illīs rēgna conciliātūrum** [esse]: 'that he would get kingships for them.' *89*, *c*.

23. **cōnfirmat**: 'he (Orgetorix) assured (them).'

24. **Hāc ōrātiōne adductī**: 'Won over by this presentation.' **inter sē**: *159*.   **fidem et iūs iūrandum**: trans. 'an oath-bound pledge of good faith,' lit. 'good faith and oath'; hendiadys. *238*, *d*.

25. **rēgnō occupātō**: 'having seized the supreme power.' *144*, *a*. B. 227, 2; A. 420, 1; H. 489.   **per**: 'with the help of.' *123*, *a*. **potentissimōs ac firmissimōs**: 'very powerful and very firmly established.' *153*, *a*.

26. **populōs**: the Helvetians, the Sequanians, and the Aeduans. **Galliae**: after *potīrī*. *131*, *d*. B. 212, 2; A. 410 *a*; H. 458, 458, 3. **sēsē posse spērant**: 'they hoped that they would be able.' *213*, *a*. **potīrī**: after *posse*. *221*, *a*.

4. 1. **Ea rēs**: 'The matter,' i.e. Orgetorix's scheme; lit. 'that thing.' *160*, *d*.   **Helvētiīs**: why dat.?   **per indicium**: 'through (the agency of) informers'; lit. 'through information.' *92*, *b*, and *123*, *a*.   **est ēnūntiāta**: 'was reported.' *172*, *a*.   **Mōribus suīs**: 'In accordance with their customs,' as distinguished from the Roman procedure. *136*, *c*. B. 220, 3; A. 418, *a*; H. 475, 3.

2. **ex vinculīs**: 'in chains.' *126*, *c*.   **causam dīcere**: 'to plead his case.' *221*, *a*.   **coēgērunt**: 'they compelled.' *79*, *b*.

3. **damnātum**: agrees with *eum* understood as object of *sequī*; 'if

Diē cōnstitūtā causae dictiōnis Orgetorīx ad iūdicium
5 omnem suam familiam, ad hominum mīlia decem, undique
coēgit, et omnēs clientēs obaerātōsque suōs, quōrum mag-

---

condemned.' *209.* B. 337, 2, *b*; A. 496 ; H. 638, 2.   **poenam**:
subject of *sequī*; 'the penalty,' defined by the following *ut*-clause.
oportēbat: *73, a, b.*   **poenam sequī oportēbat**: 'the penalty
would inevitably follow,' lit.
'it was necessary that the
penalty follow.'   **īgnī**: *14, b,*
and *131, a.*   **ut īgnī cremārētur**: 'of being burned
by fire,' lit. 'that he should
be burned by fire.' *203,* (4).
B. 297, 3; A. *561, a,* and
570 ; H. 571, 4. The Gauls
punished some offenses by
burning alive, and sometimes
offered human sacrifices (VI.
16, 19; VII. 4).

4. **Diē cōnstitūtā**: 'On
the day appointed.' *21, a,*
and *147, a.* B. 230; A. 423;
H. 486.   **dictiōnis**: dependent on *Diē*; 'for the
pleading.' *102.*   **iūdicium**:
'the (place of) judgment,'
'the trial.'

5. **familiam**: 'slaves';
lit. 'body of slaves,' taken collectively.   **ad**: adv. modifying *decem,* 'about'; Caesar
often gives a round number
where it is impossible to be
exact.   **hominum**: *12, b,*
and *97, a.*   **mīlia**: appositive of *familiam. 38, a,* and
91, a.

Figure 30. — Gallic standard-bearer.

6. **clientēs** : 'retainers.' *17, c.*   **obaerātōs** : 'debtors.' In Gaul
debtors who were unable to pay might be forced into bondage (VI. 13).

num numerum habēbat, eōdem condūxit; per eōs, nē
causam dīceret, sē ēripuit.

Cum cīvitās, ob eam rem incitāta, armīs iūs suum exsequī
cōnārētur, multitūdinemque hominum ex agrīs magis- 10
trātūs cōgerent, Orgetorīx mortuus est; neque abest
suspīciō, ut Helvētiī arbitrantur, quīn ipse sibi mortem
cōnscīverit.

The Helvetians complete their preparations to migrate.

5. Post eius mortem nihilō minus Helvētiī id, quod
cōnstituerant, facere cōnantur, ut ē fīnibus suīs exeant.

---

7. **eōdem**: 'to the same place,' the place of judgment.   **condūxit**: 'brought,' lit. 'led together.'   **per eōs**: 'with their help,' lit.
'by means of them.' *123, a.*

8. **dīceret**: *196, a.* B. 282; A. 530, 531 ; H. 568.   **nē . . .
ēripuit**: 'he evaded the pleading of his case,' lit. 'he rescued himself
that he might not plead his case'; Orgetorix overawed the judges so
that they did not dare proceed with the trial.

9. **incitāta**: 'aroused.' *148, b.*   **iūs suum**: 'its right' to call
traitors to account.   **exsequī**: 'enforce.' *200, b.*

10. **cōnārētur, cōgerent**: *185, c.* B. 288, I, B; A. 546; H. 600, II,
I. Force of the imperfect tense ?   **hominum**: *98, a.*   **agrīs**: 'the
country.' *7, a,* and *130, a.*   **magistrātūs**: 'the public officials';
here evidently the local officers are meant. *82, b.*

11. **mortuus est**: 'died.' *57, c,* and *176, a.*   **neque abest
suspīciō**: 'and there is ground for suspecting,' lit. 'nor is there lacking
(ground for) suspecting.' *12, c,* and *233, a.*

12. **ut**: meanings of *ut?* See Vocab.   **quīn . . . cōnscīverit**:
'that he committed suicide,' lit. 'that he himself inflicted death upon
himself.' *201, b.* B. 298; A. 558; H. 595, I.   **mortem**: *17, c.*

5. I. **Post**: *122, a.*   **eius**: i.e. *Orgetorīgis.*   **nihilō mīnus**:
'nevertheless'; lit. 'by nothing less.' *140.* B. 223; A. 414 ; H. 479.
id quod: *160, c.*

2. **cōnantur**: *175, b.*   **ut . . . exeant**: explains *id. 203,* (4).
From the fact that, notwithstanding the treason and death of Orgetorix,
the Helvetians carried out the plan of migrating, it is evident that behind
the movement there was a general cause stronger than the influence of

Ubi iam sē ad eam rem parātōs esse arbitrātī sunt, oppida
sua omnia, numerō ad duodecim, vīcōs ad quadringentōs,
5 reliqua prīvāta aedificia incendunt; frūmentum omne,
praeter quod sēcum portātūrī erant, combūrunt, ut, domum
reditiōnis spē sublātā, parātiōrēs ad omnia perīcula subeunda essent; trium mēnsium molita cibāria sibi quemque
domō efferre iubent.

---

any individual. It seems probable that this cause was the pressure of
the Germans, with whom, as stated in chapter 1, the Helvetians were
constantly at war.

3. **Ubi iam**: 'As soon as'; lit. 'When now.'   **rem**: 'undertaking.'   **parātōs**: 'ready.' *148, c.*   **oppida**: 'fortified towns.'
6, a.

4. **numerō**: *142, a*, and *85.* B. 226; A. 418; H. 480.   **ad**:
adverb, as in chap. 4, l. 5.   **vīcōs**: 'villages,' unfortified.   **quadringentōs**: 'four hundred.' *36.*

5. **reliqua**: *171, a.*   **prīvāta aedificia**: 'buildings belonging to
individuals,' not in the walled towns or villages.   **incendunt**: 'they
set fire to.'

6. **praeter quod**: i.e. *praeter id (frūmentum) quod.*   **sēcum**:
'with them.' *125, c.*   **portātūrī erant**: 'they were going to
take.' *63.*   **combūrunt**:
'they burned.' *175, b.*   **domum**: 'home.' *119, b.* B.
182, 1, *b*; A. 427, 2; H.
419, 1.

7. **reditiōnis**: 'of returning.' *12, c*, and *102.*   **spē**:
how declined? *21, b* and *c.*
spē sublātā: 'as a result of
taking away the hope,' lit.
'the hope having been taken
away.' *144, b*, (3).   **perī-
cula**: 'dangers.' *6, a.*   **subeunda**: 'meet,' lit. 'to be met.' *68, b*,
and *230*, (3). B. 339, 2; A. 503; H. 628.

8. **essent**: *196, a.* B. 282; A. 531, 1; H. 568.   **trium**: *37, b.*
mēnsium: *14, b.*   **trium mēnsium**: 'for (lit. 'of') three months.'
100, a.   **molita cibāria**: 'ground rations.' The grain was to be

Figure 31. — Ancient Gallic mill.

Of sandstone. The small grinder was worked
by hand over the grain in the hollow of the bed-
stone, which was about 19 inches long.

Persuādent Rauracīs et Tulingīs et Latobrīgīs, fīnitimīs, 10
utī, eōdem ūsī cōnsiliō, oppidīs suīs vīcīsque exūstīs, ūnā
cum eīs proficīscantur; Boiōsque, quī trāns Rhēnum in-
coluerant et in agrum Nōricum trānsierant Nōreiamque
oppugnārant, receptōs ad sē sociōs sibi ascīscunt.

ground to coarse flour before starting, in contrast with the Roman custom of carrying unground grain on campaigns (*317*); probably the ·
difficulty of carrying the stone mills, in addition to their other effects,
occasioned the order (Fig. 31).   **quemque**: *49, a*, and *170, b*.   **sibi
quemque efferre** : ' that each one for himself should carry away.'   *178*.

9. **domō**: *20, c*, and *130, b*.   B. 229, 1, *b*; A. 427, 1 ; H. 462, 4.
efferre : *69, b*.   B. 331, II ; A. 563, *a* ; H. 614.   **iubent**: ' (and) they
gave orders.'   *200, b*, and *234, a*.   On an allowance of three quarters
of a pound of coarse flour per day for each person, more than 12,000 tons
would be needed to feed 368,000 people (chap. 29) for 90 days.   If each
cart carried a ton, more than 12,000 carts would have been required to
transport the supplies, and perhaps half as many more for other purposes ;
but it is hardly probable that the Helvetians and their allies took so
great a quantity of supplies as the order contemplated.   If we reckon
20 feet to a cart, 18,000 carts in single file would form a line 68 miles long.

10. **Rauracīs** : why dat.?   The Rauraci, Tulingi, and Latobrigi were
apparently north of the Helvetians (Map 1), and particularly exposed to
the attacks and inroads of the Germans ; hence their readiness to join the
Helvetians in migrating.   **et . . . et**: *234, a*.   **fīnitimīs** : '(their)
neighbors.'   *91, a*, and *157, a*.

11. **utī . . . proficīscantur** : trans. by an infinitive, as *ut . . . exīrent* in chap. 2, l. 4.   *199, a*, and *61, a*, (3).   **ūsī** : ' adopting,' or ' to
adopt '; lit. ' having used.'   *61, a*, (3), and *228, a*.   **cōnsiliō** : ' plan.'
131, c.   B. 218, 1 ; A. 410; H. 477.   **oppidīs suīs vīcīsque exūstīs** : ' having burned ' (or ' to burn ') ' their towns and villages,' lit.
' their towns and villages having been burned.'   *144, b*, (2).   B. 227 ;
A. 419; H. 489.   **ūnā**: adv.

12. **eīs**: *Helvētiīs*.   *160, b*, and *137, a*.   **Boiōs**: N. to VI, 24, l. 3.
13. **agrum Nōricum** : ' the territory of the Norici,' corresponding,
in general, with the western part of Austria south of the Danube, between
Bavaria and Hungary.   **trānsierant**: ' had passed over.'   *68, b*.
14. **oppugnārant**: ' had taken ' by storming.   *340*.   Full form ?
64, a, (1).   B. 116, 1 ; A. 181, *a* ; H. 238.   **receptōs sociōs sibi**

Of two possible routes they choose that through the Province.

6. Erant omnīnō itinera duo, quibus itineribus domō
exīre possent : ūnum per Sēquanōs, angustum et difficile,
inter montem Iūram et flūmen Rhodanum, vix quā singulī
carrī dūcerentur; mōns autem altissimus impendēbat, ut
5 facile perpaucī prohibēre possent; alterum per prōvinciam
nostram, multō facilius atque expedītius, proptereā quod

---

ascīscunt: 'they received and associated with themselves' (lit. 'to
themselves') 'as allies.' *228, a.* B. 337, 5 ; A. 496, N. 2 ; H. 639.
sociōs: *115, a.* Cf. N. to IV, 3, l. 4.

6. 1. **Erant**: 'There were.' *90, a.*   **omnīnō**: 'only.'   **duo**:
37, b.   **itineribus**: omit in translation. *165, a.* B. 251, 3 ; A. 307,
a ; H. 399, 1.   **domō**: as in chap. 5, l. 9.

2. **possent**: subj. of characteristic. *194, a.* B. 283 ; A. 535 ;
H. 591, 5.   **ūnum, alterum** (l. 5) : sc. *iter*. *91, c.* B. 169, 5 ; A.
282, *a* ; H. 393, 4.   **per Sēquanōs**: *282.*   **difficile**: 'difficult.' *29.*

3. **inter . . . Rhodanum**: on the right bank of the Rhone. There
was no route across the Jura range practicable for so large a force,
(Fig. 27), while the passage down the left bank of the Rhine, and westward between the Jura and the Vosges Mountains (Map 1), was left out
of consideration, not only (we may assume) because it was less direct,
but also because it was exposed to the attacks of Ariovistus.   **vix**:
'hardly.'   **quā**: 'where'; translate as if the order were *quā vix*.
singulī: 'one at a time.'

4. **dūcerentur**: 'could' (lit. 'would') 'be drawn along'; subj. of
characteristic, the relative adverb *quā* having the force of a relative pronoun. The narrowest point of the route is at the "Mill-race Gorge,"
or Pas de l'Écluse (Fig. 32), 19 Roman miles (about 17½ English miles ;
243, b), below Geneva. See Map 2.   **mōns altissimus**: Mt. Crédo,
now pierced by a tunnel, 2½ miles long, through which passes the railroad
from Geneva to Lyons.   **autem**: 'moreover.' *236, a* and *b*.   **impendēbat**: 'overhung.' *54.*

5. **perpaucī**: 'very few' men, posted on the heights above the road;
see Fig. 32. Force of *per ?* *79, b*, and Vocab.   **prohibēre**: sc. *eōs*.
possent: *197, a*. B. 284, 1 ; A. 537, 1 ; H. 570.   **prōvinciam nostram**: *157, c*, and *290.*

6. **multō**: 'much,' lit. 'by much.' *140.*   **facilius**: *29.*   **expedītius**: 'more convenient.'

inter fīnēs Helvētiōrum et Allobrogum, quī nūper pācātī erant, Rhodanus fluit, isque nōn nūllīs locīs vadō trānsītur.

Extrēmum oppidum Allobrogum est, proximumque Helvētiōrum fīnibus, Genava.   Ex eō oppidō pōns ad Helvētiōs 10 pertinet.   Allobrogibus sēsē vel persuāsūrōs, quod nōndum

Figure 32. — Mill-race Gorge (Pas de l'Écluse), looking down the Rhone.

7. **Allobrogum**: *19, e*.   **nūper**: 'recently,' in 61 B.C., after a revolt; the Allobroges were first conquered by Q. Fabius Maximus, in 121 B.C. (I. 45).   **pācātī erant**: 'had been subdued.'   *53*, and *192*.

8. **fluit**: 'flows.'   **is**: 'it.'   *160, b*.   **nōn nūllīs**: 'some.' *23, a*.   **locīs**: *6, c*, and *145, c*.   **vadō trānsītur**: 'is fordable,' lit. 'is crossed by a ford.'   *134, a*, and *68, c*.

9. **Extrēmum**: 'The most remote,' lit. 'utmost,' from the point of view of Rome.   *33*.

10. **fīnibus**: *108, a*.   B. 192, 1 ; A. 384 ; H. 434, 2.   **pōns**: *17, c*. **Helvētiōs**: *282*.

11. **pertinet**: 'reaches across.'   **Allobrogibus**: *105*.   **vel . . . vel**: *235, b*.   **persuāsūrōs**: sc. *esse*.   *89, c* ; *213, a*, and *214, a*. **nōndum . . . vidērentur**: 'did not yet seem' to the Helvetians; Why is *vidērentur* subjunctive?   *183, a*.

bonō animō in populum Rōmānum vidērentur, exīstimābant,
vel vī coāctūrōs, ut per suōs fīnēs eōs īre paterentur.

Omnibus rēbus ad profectiōnem comparātīs, diem dīcunt,
15 quā diē ad rīpam Rhodanī omnēs conveniant. Is diēs erat
a. d. v. Kal. Apr., L. Pīsōne, A. Gabīniō cōnsulibus.

Caesar hastens to Geneva, and parleys with the Helvetians.

7. Caesarī cum id nūntiātum esset, eōs per prōvinciam
nostram iter facere cōnārī, mātūrat ab urbe proficīscī et,
quam maximīs potest itineribus, in Galliam ulteriōrem

---

12. bonō animō: 'kindly disposed,' lit. 'of kindly feeling'; in
predicate after *vidērentur*. *143, b.* B. 224, 1; A. 415; H. 473, 2.
in: here 'toward.'   **exīstimābant**: 'they believed.'

13. vī: 'by force.' *18, a.*   **coāctūrōs**: i.e. *sēsē* (the Helvetians)
eōs (the Allobroges) *coāctūrōs esse.*   **ut . . . paterentur**: 'to
permit,' substantive clause after *persuāsūrōs (esse), coāctūrōs (esse).*
199, a.   **eōs**: trans. as if *Helvētiōs*; N. to chap. 1, l. 14.   **īre**: *68, a.*

14. Omnibus . . . comparātīs: 'when all preparations had been
completed.' *144, b,* (2). How lit.?   **dīcunt**: 'they appointed.'

15. quā diē: 'on which.' *147, a,* and *165, a.* B. 230; A. 423;
H. 486.   **ad rīpam**: 'on the bank' across from the Province; the
north bank of the Rhone.   **conveniant**: 'they should assemble';
subjunctive of purpose, as if *quā* were *ut eā,* 'that on that day.' *193.*
B. 282, 2; A. 531, 2; H. 590.   **diēs**: gender? *21, a.*

16. a. d. v. Kal. Apr.: *ante diem quīntum Kalendās Aprīlēs,* 'the
fifth day before the Calends of April,' March 28 by our calendar. *241,
a, b.* B. 371, 5; A. 631; H. 754, III, 2.   **L. . . . cōnsulibus**: 58
B.C. *240, a,* and *144, b,* (1).

7. 1. Caesarī: *19, c,* and *353, e.*   **nūntiātum esset**: 'had been
reported.' *185, c.* B. 288, 1, B; A. 546; H. 600, II, 1.   **eōs . . .
cōnārī**: infinitive clause in apposition with *id*; the gist of the report,
in the direct form, was *Helvētiī per prōvinciam nostram iter facere
cōnantur.* *214, a.*

2. mātūrat: 'he hastened.' *255, 256.*   **urbe**: Rome, which by
way of distinction was "*the* city." *17, b.*

3. quam maximīs potest itineribus: stronger than *quam maxi-
mis itineribus*; 'with the utmost possible speed.' *153, c.* How lit.?

contendit et ad Genavam pervenit. Prōvinciae tōtī quam
maximum potest mīlitum numerum imperat (erat omnīnōs
in Galliā ulteriōre legiō ūna); pontem, quī erat ad Genavam,
iubet rescindī.

Ubi dē eius adventū Helvētiī certiōrēs factī sunt, lēgātōs
ad eum mittunt nōbilissimōs cīvitātis, cuius lēgātiōnis Nam-

Galliam ulteriōrem : here including the Province, Caesar's immediate
destination. *286*, and *290.*

4. **ad :** 'to the vicinity of.'
120, a.   **pervenit :** 'came,'
lit. 'comes through.' If, as
Plutarch says, Caesar arrived
at the Rhone on the eighth
day after leaving Rome, he
must have traveled at the
rate of about 100 Roman miles
(about 92 English miles ;
243, b) per day.   **Prōvinciae . . . imperat :** 'he levied
upon the Province.' *106, a.* B.
187, 1 ; A. 369 ; H. 426, 1.

5. **mīlitum :** *10, b.* Legionary soldiers are meant.
(Fig. 33.)

6. **legiō :** this 'legion' was
the tenth, afterwards famous.
307, e.   **ūna :** *23, a.*   **ad :**
'near.'   **pontem . . . rescindī :** 'that the bridge be
broken down.' *200, b.*

8. **adventū :** 'approach.'
20, b.   **certiōrēs factī sunt :**
'were informed,' lit. 'were
made more certain.' *115, c.*
lēgātōs : 'as envoys'; predicate accusative.   *6, a*, and
115, a.

9. **mittunt :** 'sent.' *175, b.*

Figure 33. — Roman legionary soldier.

He has a cuirass, a crested helmet, oval shield,
and pike. Caesar's legionaries had oblong shields.

10 meius et Verucloetius prīncipem locum obtinēbant, quī
dīcerent,

> *Sibi esse in animō sine ūllō maleficiō iter per prōvinciam
> facere, proptereā quod aliud iter habērent nūllum; rogāre,
> ut eius voluntāte id sibi facere liceat.*

15 Caesar, quod memoriā tenēbat, L. Cassium cōnsulem
occīsum exercitumque eius ab Helvētiīs pulsum et sub
iugum missum, concēdendum nōn putābat; neque hominēs
inimīcō animō, datā facultāte per prōvinciam itineris

---

nōbilissimōs: 'the most distinguished men.' *154, a.* **cuius lēgātiōnis**: 'and in this delegation'; lit. 'of which delegation.' *167.*

10. **prīncipem**: 'foremost.' *26, b,* and *10, a.* **quī dīcerent**:
'in order to say.' *193, a.* B. 282, 2; A. 531, 2; H. 590.

12. **Sibi . . . liceat**: *212, a, b,* and *c,* (4). **Sibi esse in animō**:
'that it was their intention'; less freely, 'that they had it in mind,' *Sibi*
being a dative of possession. *111,* and *214, a*; also, *178.* **sine**:
'without.' *125, a.* **ūllō**: *23, a.* **maleficiō**: 'wrong-doing'; we
should say 'without doing any harm.'

13. **facere**: subject of *esse.* *222, b.* **habērent**: *214, a.* **nūllum**: emphatic position. *353, d.* **rogāre**: sc. *sē,* '(and) that they
requested.' *215,* and *234, a.*

14. **eius voluntāte**: 'with his consent.' *138.* **ut . . . liceat**:
'that permission might be granted'; subjunctive also in direct discourse. How lit.? *73, b,* and *199, a.* **facere**: *222, a.*

15. **memoriā**: *131, a.* B. 218; A. 409; H. 476. **memoriā
tenēbat**: 'he remembered.' *183, a.* **L.**: *Lūcium.* *19, a.*

16. **occīsum**: sc. *esse,* 'had been killed.' *89, c,* and *213, a.* **exercitum**: 'army.' *20, a, b,* and *74, b.* **pulsum** [esse]: 'had been
routed.' *178.* **sub iugum**: 'under the yoke,' made by setting two
spears upright and placing a third on them horizontally, as a cross-piece;
under this captured soldiers were made to pass, bending over, as a token
of complete submission and humiliation. The defeat of Cassius by the
Helvetians took place in 107 B.C. *124, a.*

17. **concēdendum nōn putābat**: 'did not think that the request
ought to be granted'; less freely, 'that the concession ought to be made.'
63, and *73, e.* **neque**: trans. as if *et nōn.*

18. **inimīcō animō**: 'of hostile temper.' *143, a.* B. 224; A. 415;
H. 473, 2. **datā facultāte**: = *sī facultās data esset,* 'if opportunity

MAP 2

CAESAR'S LINE OF WORKS ALONG THE RHONE FROM GENEVA TO MILL-RACE GORGE (PAS DE L'ÉCLUSE)

Book I, 8

To face page 20

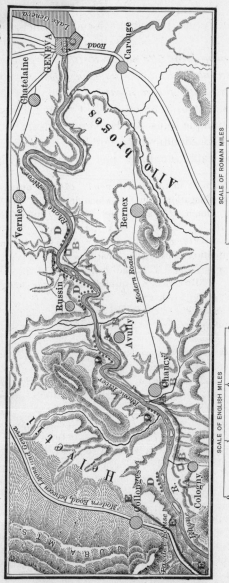

EXPLANATION

A, A. Places where strong fortifications were needed, such as are shown in Figure 34. The lighter red line between these places indicates where less extensive fortifying was required.

B, B̄. Redoubts, *castella* (chap. 8, 1. 6).

C. Site of ancient Geneva, on the south side of the Rhone. The modern city spreads out on both sides of the river.

D, D. Places where the Helvetians probably gathered, in their attempts to force the crossing of the Rhone (chap. 8, ll. 12–16).

E–E. Route of the Helvetian host entering Mill-race Gorge.

faciundī, temperātūrōs ab iniūriā et maleficiō exīstimābat.
Tamen, ut spatium intercēdere posset, dum mīlitēs, quōs 20
imperāverat, convenīrent, lēgātīs respondit,

   Diem sē ad dēlīberandum sūmptūrum; sī quid vellent,
ad Īd. Aprīl. reverterentur.

Caesar prevents the Helvetians from entering the Province.

   8. Intereā eā legiōne, quam sēcum habēbat, mīlitibusque, quī ex prōvinciā convēnerant, ā lacū Lemannō, quī
in flūmen Rhodanum īnfluit, ad montem Iūram, quī fīnēs
Sēquanōrum ab Helvētiīs dīvidit, mīlia passuum XVIIII
mūrum in altitūdinem pedum sēdecim fossamque perdūcit. 5

---

should have been granted.' *144, b,* (4).   **itineris faciundī**: 'of
marching.' *64, b,* and *230,* (1).   How lit.?

   19. **temperātūrōs** [esse]: 'would refrain.' *63.*   **iniūriā**: 'violence.'

   20. **Tamen**: 'Nevertheless.' *236, a.*   **spatium**: trans. as if
tempus, 'time.'   **intercēdere**: 'intervene.' *221, a.*   **dum**: 'until.'

   21. **convenīrent**: 'should assemble.' *190, b.* B. 293, III, 2;
A. 553; H. 603, II, 2.   **respondit**: 'he made answer.'

   22. **Diem**: 'time.'   **sē**: *158, a.*   **dēlīberandum**: 'for consideration.' *230,* (3).   **sūmptūrum** [esse]: 'would take.' *63,* and
214, a.   **quid**: 'anything.' *168.*   **vellent, reverterentur**: 'they
wanted,' 'they should return'; in the direct form, *sī vultis, revertiminī.*
206, (2); *218,* (1), a, and *216.* B. 316; A. 588; H. 642.

   23. **Īd. Aprīl.**: *Īdūs Aprīlēs,* April 13. *241, a, b.*

   8. 1. **Intereā**: 'Meanwhile,' while the more distant troops levied
on the Province were gathering at the Rhone, and the Helvetians were
waiting for Caesar's answer.   **legiōne, mīlitibus**: looked upon as
instrument rather than as agent. *131, b.*   **sēcum**: *125, c.*

   3. **quī . . . īnfluit**: while Caesar's statement is not incorrect, modern geographers consider Lake Geneva as an enlargement of the Rhone,
applying the name "Rhone" also to the principal feeder entering the
lake at the upper end.

   4. **Helvētiīs**: *282.*   **mīlia**: *118, a,* and *243, b*; *38, a.* **XVIIII.**:
ūndēvīgintī. 36, and *38, b.*

   5. **mūrum**: 'a rampart.' *1.*   **in altitūdinem pedum sēdecim**:

Eō opere perfectō, praesidia dispōnit, castella commūnit, quō
facilius, sī, sē invītō, trānsīre cōnārentur, prohibēre possit.

Ubi ea diēs, quam cōnstituerat cum lēgātīs, vēnit, et lēgātī
ad eum revertērunt, negat, sē mōre et exemplō populī
10 Rōmānī posse iter ūllī per prōvinciam dare; et, sī vim
facere cōnentur, prohibitūrum ostendit.

'sixteen feet high.' How lit. ?   **pedum** : *10, b*, and *100, a*.   B. 203,
2 ; A. 345, *b* ; H. 440, 3.   **fossam** : 'trench.'   **perdūcit** : 'he constructed.' *175, b*. For much of the distance between Lake Geneva (Fig.

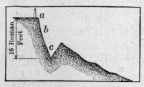

Figure 34. — Section of the
Fortifications along the Rhone.

a. Top of the bluff, with palisade.
b Face of the bluff, cut down.
c. Trench, with dirt thrown out
    toward the river.

35) and Mill-race Gorge (17½ English
miles ; N. to chap. 6, l. 4) the left bank
of the Rhone is steep enough to make
extensive fortifying unnecessary. What
Caesar did was, apparently, to make
the slopes hard to surmount by cutting the
face down from the top for sixteen feet
and throwing the dirt out toward the
river in such a way as to produce the
effect of a rampart and trench (Fig. 34) ;
palisades were probably driven in along
the edge of the bluff. See Map 2.

   6. Eō opere perfectō : 'When this work had been finished.' *13, e,*
and *144, b,* (2).   **praesidia** : 'detachments' of troops.   **dispōnit** :
'he stationed at intervals.' *79, d.*   **castella** : 'redoubts'; their probable location is shown on Map 2.   **commūnit** : 'he strongly fortified.'
quō : why used in place of *ut ?* *193, b.* B. 282, 1, *a* ; H. 568, 7.

   7. sē invītō : 'without his permission,' lit. 'he (being) unwilling.'
144, a.   **cōnārentur** : *177, b*, and *220*. B. 324, 1 ; A. 593 ; H. 652.
prohibēre : sc. *eōs*.

   8. ea diēs : April 13 ; see chap. 7, l. 23.

   9. revertērunt : 'returned.' *79, d.*   **mōre et exemplō** : 'consistently with the settled usage,' lit. 'custom and precedent.' *136, c.*
B. 220, 3 ; H. 475, 3.

   10. iter : 'right of way.'   **ūllī** : here used as a noun, 'to any one.'
vim facere : 'use force.' *18, a.*

   11. cōnentur, [sē eōs] **prohibitūrum** [esse] : in the direct form, *si
cōnābiminī, prohibēbō*. *215* ; *218*, (1), a. B. 314, 1 ; A. 580 ; H. 643.

   12. eā spē dēiectī : 'disappointed in their expectations,' lit. 'cast

Helvētiī, eā spē dēiectī, nāvibus iūnctīs ratibusque complūribus factīs, aliī vadīs Rhodanī, quā minima altitūdō
flūminis erat, nōn numquam interdiū, saepius noctū, sī
perrumpere possent, cōnātī, operis mūnītiōne et mīlitum 15
concursū et tēlīs repulsī, hōc cōnātū dēstitērunt.

Figure 35. — Lake Geneva, ancient Lacus Lemannus.

down from that hope.' *57*, *b*.   **spē**: *127*, *a*.   **nāvibus . . . factīs**:
'joined boats together,' attempting to make a floating bridge, 'and
made a number of rafts,' for poling across.   How lit. ?   *144*, *b*, (2).

13. **aliī**: ' others,' relatively few, compared with the number who tried
to cross in the ways just mentioned.   **vadīs**: *134*, *a*.   **minima**: *32*.

14. **nōn numquam**: 'sometimes.'   **interdiū**: 'by day.'   **saepius**: *35*.   **noctū**: 'at night.'

15. **sī perrumpere possent**: '(to see) whether they could break
through'; after *cōnātī*.   *204*, (4).   B. 300, 3; A. 576, *a*; H. 649, II, 3.
cōnātī: participle, but trans. 'tried.'   *61*, *a*, (1), and *228*, *a*.   **operis
mūnītiōne**: 'by the strength of the fortifications,' i.e. *mūrus*, *fossa*,
castella.   How lit. ?

16. **concursū**: 'by the rapid massing,' at points attacked.   *1*, and
20, *b*.   **tēlīs**: 'by (their) missiles.'   **repulsī**: 'forced back.'
cōnātū: 'they gave up' (lit. 'desisted from') 'the attempt.'   *127*, *a*.
B. 214; A. 402; H. 462.

The Helvetians get leave to go through the country of the Sequanians.

9. Relinquēbātur ūna per Sēquanōs via, quā, Sēquanīs invītīs, propter angustiās īre nōn poterant. Hīs cum suā sponte persuādēre nōn possent, lēgātōs ad Dumnorīgem Aeduum mittunt, ut, eō dēprecātōre, ā Sēquanīs impetrārent.

5 Dumnorix grātiā et largītiōne apud Sēquanōs plūrimum poterat, et Helvētiīs erat amīcus, quod ex eā cīvitāte Orgetorīgis fīliam in mātrimōnium dūxerat, et cupiditāte rēgnī adductus novīs rēbus studēbat, et quam plūrimās cīvitātēs suō beneficiō habēre obstrictās volēbat. Itaque

10 rem suscipit, et ā Sēquanīs impetrat, ut per fīnēs suōs

---

9. 1. Relinquēbātur : 'There was left.' *90, a.*   **ūna via :** 'only the way,' described in chap. 6, ll. 2–5.   **quā :** *134, a.*   **Sēquanōs :** *282.*   **Sēquanīs invītīs :** *144, b, (4).*

2. angustiās : 'the narrowness' of the road through the Mill-race Gorge (Fig. 32).   **Hīs :** *105.*   **suā sponte :** 'by their own influence.' *17, d,* and *157, b.*

3. possent : *184, a,* and *66, b.*

4. eō dēprecātōre : 'through his intercession.' *144, b, (6).* **impetrārent :** 'they might gain their request.' *177, b,* and *196, a.* B. 268, 3 ; A. 485, *e* ; H. 546.

5. grātiā et largītiōne : 'on account of his popularity and lavish giving.' *135, a.*   **plūrimum poterat :** 'had very great influence,' lit. 'was able to a very great degree.' *118, b.* A fuller account of Dumnorix is given in chapter 18, where we learn that he had practical control of the revenues of the Aeduans and was bitterly opposed to Caesar ; a coin struck by Dumnorix is shown in Fig. 42.

6. Helvētiīs : *108, a.* B. 192, 1 ; A. 384 ; H. 434.

7. Orgetorīgis . . . dūxerat : see chap. 3, ll. 15–18, and Notes.

8. novīs rēbus studēbat : 'was eager for a revolution.' *105.* B. 187, II, *a* ; A. 368, 3 ; H. 426, 1. **quam plūrimās :** 'as many . . . as possible.' *153, c.*

9. suō beneficiō obstrictās : 'placed under obligation to himself,' lit. 'bound by his own favor.' **volēbat :** *71.* **Itaque :** 'Accordingly.'

10. rem : 'the negotiation.' **impetrat :** 'obtained a promise.' How lit. ?

Helvētiōs īre patiantur, obsidēsque utī inter sēsē dent, perficit: Sēquanī, nē itinere Helvētiōs prohibeant; Helvētiī,
ut sine maleficiō et iniūriā trānseant.

Caesar, learning of their plan, brings five legions from Italy.

10. Caesarī renūntiātur, Helvētiīs esse in animō per
agrum Sēquanōrum et Aeduōrum iter in Santonum fīnēs
facere, quī nōn longē ā Tolōsātium fīnibus absunt, quae
cīvitās est in prōvinciā. Id sī fieret, intellegēbat magnō
cum perīculō prōvinciae futūrum, ut hominēs bellicōsōs, 5

---

11. **patiantur**: *199, a,* (8).   **obsidēs . . . perficit**: 'and brought
about an exchange of hostages' (lit. 'that they should give') 'between
them.' Hostages were exchanged as a pledge of good faith; if the
agreement were violated, they were liable to be put to death with tortures.
utī . . . dent: after *perficit.* *203,* (3). B. 297, 1; A. 568; H. 571.

12. **Sēquanī, Helvētiī**: in partitive apposition with the subject of
dent; freely, 'the Sequanians (giving hostages).' *91, c.* **itinere**:
127, a. B. 214, 2; A. 400; H. 464. **nē . . . prohibeant, ut . . .
trānseant**: substantive clauses with the subjunctive of purpose, expressing the terms of the agreement for the ratification of which the
exchange of hostages was arranged.

10. 1. **renūntiātur**: 'Word was brought (back) to Caesar,' *re-*
implying that men had been sent out by him and now returned with the
information. *79, d.*   **esse**: subject of *renūntiātur;* cf. chap. 7, ll.
12–14, and Notes.

3. **nōn longē . . . absunt**: the territories of the Santones were
on the west coast, more than 100 miles from the nearest point of the
Province; see Map. If the Helvetians should reach their destination,
they would be further from the Province than when they started; yet
even at that distance they might become dangerous neighbors because
they would no longer be kept on the defensive by the Germans.
quae cīvitās: 'a state which,' the state of the Tolosates. *165, b.*

4. **Id**: the migration to the territory of the Santones, *iter . . . facere.*
fieret . . . futūrum [esse] : in the direct form, *fīet . . . erit. 70, a,*
and *218,* (1), a.

5. **cum**: *136, a.*   **prōvinciae**: 'to' (lit. 'of') 'the Province.'
102.   **ut . . . habēret**: 'to have'; how lit.? *203,* (1). B. 297, 2;
A. 569, 2; H. 571, 1.   **bellicōsōs**: 'warlike.' *75, f.*

populī Rōmānī inimīcōs, locīs patentibus maximēque frūmentāriīs fīnitimōs habēret.

Ob eās causās eī mūnītiōnī, quam fēcerat, T. Labiēnum
lēgātum praefēcit; ipse in Italiam magnīs itineribus con-
10 tendit, duāsque ibi legiōnēs cōnscrībit, et trēs, quae circum
Aquileiam hiemābant, ex hībernīs ēdūcit; et, quā proximum

Figure 36. — A road through the Alps.

6. **inimīcōs**: *91, a*.   **locīs . . . fīnitimōs**: *108, a*, and *115, b*.
B. 192, 1; A. 384; H. 434, 2. Caesar had no reason to interfere with
the passage of the Helvetians through the country of the Sequanians
unless it was clear that Roman interests would be unfavorably
affected by it.   **patentibus**: 'open' to attack, not being protected
by natural barriers.   **frūmentāriīs**: 'productive' of grain. *30*.

8. **mūnītiōnī**: *107, b*, and *74, b*.   **T.**: *Titum. 19, a*.

9. **lēgātum**: 'lieutenant-general,' or 'lieutenant.' *313, a*.   **praefēcit**: 'placed in charge (of).' *57, b*.   **Italiam**: Cisalpine Gaul is
here meant. *283, b*.

10. **duās legiōnēs**: the 11th and 12th.   **cōnscrībit**: 'raised,'
by conscription.   **trēs**: sc. *legiōnēs*, the 7th, 8th, and 9th legions.
circum: 'in the neighborhood of,' lit. 'around'; the winter-quarters
were not in the town. *122, a*.

11. **Aquileiam**: a flourishing Roman colony near the head of the

iter in ulteriōrem Galliam per Alpēs erat, cum hīs quīnque
legiōnibus īre contendit.

Ibi Ceutronēs et Graiocelī et Caturīgēs, locīs superiōribus
occupātīs, itinere exercitum prohibēre cōnantur. Com- 15
plūribus hīs proeliīs pulsīs, ab Ocelō, quod est oppidum
citeriōris prōvinciae extrēmum, in fīnēs Vocontiōrum
ulteriōris prōvinciae diē septimō pervenit; inde in Allobrogum fīnēs, ab Allobrogibus in Segūsiāvōs exercitum
dūcit. Hī sunt extrā prōvinciam trāns Rhodanum prīmī. 20

Adriatic Sea.   **hiemābant**: 'were wintering.'   **hībernīs**: '(their)
winter quarters.'   *127, c,* and *335, a, b.*

12. **ulteriōrem Galliam**: *286.*   **Alpēs**: *291.*   **cum**: *137, b.*

14. **Ibi**: i.e. in the Alps; Caesar's route lay over the pass of Mt.
Genèvre, which is one of the best in the Alps. The roads over all the
Alpine passes are of the same general character. See Map 1, and
Figures 36 and 92.   **locīs superiōribus occupātīs**: 'seized com-
manding heights and.' How lit.?   *144, b,* (2).

15. **itinere**: *127, a.* B. 214, 2; A. 400; H. 464.   **Complūribus
proeliīs**: 'in a number of engagements.' *131, a.*

16. **hīs pulsīs**: 'driving them off.' How lit.?   *144, b,* (2), and
160, b.   **ab**: here 'from.'

17. **citeriōris prōvinciae**: 'nearer' from the viewpoint of Rome.
284.   **extrēmum**: i.e. most westerly.

18. **ulteriōris prōvinciae**: *290.*   **pervenit**: 'passed through.'
175, b.   **inde**: trace on Map 1 Caesar's route from Ocelum.

19. **exercitum**: three trained legions from near Aquileia, and two
legions of recruits just levied in Cisalpine Gaul (the 11th and 12th), with
which was joined the tenth legion, released from guarding the fortification below Geneva; for the campaign against the Helvetians Caesar had
thus 6 legions, aggregating about 22,000 men, besides cavalry. Light-
armed troops, used in the campaign of 57 and afterwards, are not
mentioned in Book I. *307, e.*

20. **trāns Rhodanum**: Caesar probably crossed the Rhone by a
pontoon bridge, a short distance above the junction with the Arar.
The Segusiavi were clients of the Aeduans, hence on good terms with
the Romans. Most of their territory was on the west side of the Rhone,
but they seem to have occupied also the narrow corner between the
Rhone and the Arar.

*The Aeduans, Ambarri and Allobroges entreat Caesar's aid
against the Helvetians, who are ravaging their country.*

11. Helvētiī iam per angustiās et fīnēs Sēquanōrum
suās cōpiās trādūxerant, et in Aeduōrum fīnēs pervēnerant
eōrumque agrōs populābantur. Aeduī, cum sē suaque ab
eīs dēfendere nōn possent, lēgātōs ad Caesarem mittunt
5 rogātum auxilium :

*Ita sē omnī tempore dē populō Rōmānō meritōs esse, ut,
paene in cōnspectū exercitūs nostrī, agrī vāstārī, līberī
eōrum in servitūtem abdūcī, oppida expugnārī nōn dēbuerint.*

---

11. 1. **angustiās** : chap. 9, l. 2, and N. : chap. 6, ll. 2–5, and Notes.
It must have taken Caesar 7 or 8 weeks to go to Cisalpine Gaul, gather
his forces there, and bring them across the Province to the north side of
the Rhone.   Meanwhile the Helvetians with their throng of women and
children and their loaded carts had slowly threaded the narrow Mill-race
Gorge, and had advanced, in all, only about 100 miles.

2. **trādūxerant** : 'had led (across).'   **Aeduōrum fīnēs** : on the
west side of the Arar, which the van of the Helvetian host already had
crossed.   See Map 1.

3. **populābantur** : 'were laying waste.'   *61, a,* (1), and *175, a.*
sua : 'their possessions.'   *154, a.*

4. **possent** : *184, a.*   B. 286, 2 ; A. 549 ; H. 598.

5. **rogātum** : 'to ask for.'   *231, a.*   **auxilium** : 'help.'   *231, b.*

6–8. **Direct form** : Ita (*nōs*) omnī tempore dē populō Rōmānō *meritī
sumus,* ut, paene in cōnspectū exercitūs *tuī,* agrī vāstārī, līberī *nostrī* in servitūtem abdūcī, oppida expugnārī nōn *dēbuerint.*

6. **Ita sē . . . meritōs esse** : '(saying) that they had so (well)
deserved.'   *213, b.*   **omnī tempore** : 'at all times'; with us "every
time" has a different force.   More than 40 years before, in 121 B C., the
Aeduans had by treaty been recognized as *sociī populī Rōmānī,* 'allies of
the Roman people.'   The Romans were first led to intervene in the
affairs of Transalpine Gaul, however, not in the interest of the Aeduans,
but in response to a request of Massilia for protection against the
incursions of Ligurian tribes east of the Rhone ; this was in 155 B.C.
dē : we should say ' of.'

7. **paene** : 'almost.'   **nostrī** : *157, c.*   **vāstārī** : 'to be laid
waste.'   *221, a.*   **līberī eōrum** : 'their children.'

Eōdem tempore, quō Aeduī, Ambarrī, necessāriī et cōnsanguineī Aeduōrum, Caesarem certiōrem faciunt, *sēsē,* 10 *dēpopulātīs agrīs, nōn facile ab oppidīs vim hostium prohibēre.* Item Allobrogēs, quī trāns Rhodanum vīcōs possessiōnēsque habēbant, fugā sē ad Caesarem recipiunt, et dēmōnstrant, *sibi praeter agrī solum nihil esse reliquī.* Quibus rēbus adductus Caesar nōn exspectandum sibi 15 statuit, dum, omnibus fortūnīs sociōrum cōnsūmptīs, in Santonōs Helvētiī pervenīrent.

---

8. **servitūtem**: 'slavery,' the penalty of capture. *10, f.* **abdūcī**: ' (to be) led away.' **expugnārī**: '(to be) taken by assault.' **nōn dēbuerint**: 'ought not.' *197, b.* Why *dēbeant* in the direct form ? *177, b,* and *357, b.*

9. **quō**: *147, a.* **Aeduī**: sc. *lēgātōs mittunt.* **necessāriī**: 'relatives,' including connections by marriage. *154, a,* and *91, a.*

10. **cōnsanguineī**: 'kinsmen,' comprising only blood relations. Notwithstanding their close relationship with the Aeduans, the Ambarri had a separate coinage (Fig. 16).

11. **dēpopulātīs agrīs**: '(their) lands had been ravaged and.' How lit.? *59, b,* and *144, b,* (2). B. 112, *b*; A. 190, *b*; H. 222, 2. **prohibēre**: *214, a,* and *213, a.*

12. **trāns Rhodanum**: i.e. on the north side of the Rhone, probably west of the Mill-race Gorge.

13. **fugā**: *136, b.* **sē recipiunt**: 'made their escape.'

14. **dēmōnstrant**: 'stated.' *175, b.* **sibi . . . nihil esse reliquī**: 'that they had nothing left.' *213, a.* **sibi**: *111.* B. 190; A. 373; H. 430. **agrī solum**: 'the bare ground'; how lit.? **reliquī**: used as a noun, dependent on *nihil. 97, a.* B. 201.

15. **Quibus**: *167.* **nōn exspectandum** [esse] **sibi**: 'that he ought not to wait.' *73, e,* and *89, c.* How lit.? **sibi**: *110.*

16. **dum . . . cōnsumptis**: 'until everything that the allies had should have been destroyed, and.' How lit.? *144, b,* (2).

17. **Santonōs**: 'the (country of) the Santoni'; previously (chap. 10, l. 2), spelled 'Santones.' Caesar was inconsistent in the spelling of this name, which appears in Roman letters on a coin; see Vocab. under *Santones.* The name survives in that of the city Saintes. *19, e,* and *282.* **pervenīrent**: *190, b.* B. 293, III, 2; A. 553; H. 603, II, 2.

Caesar cuts to pieces one division of the Helvetians at the Arar.

12. Flūmen est Arar, quod per fīnēs Aeduōrum et Sēquanōrum in Rhodanum īnfluit, incrēdibilī lēnitāte, ita ut
oculīs, in utram partem fluat, iūdicārī nōn possit.   Id
Helvētiī ratibus ac lintribus iūnctīs trānsībant.

Figure 37. — The Saône at Trévoux, looking upstream.

---

12. 1. Flūmen est Arar: 'There is a river, the Arar.' *90, a.*
Arar: now Saône (pronounced sōn). *18, e.*   **quod:** antecedent?
per fīnēs: for a part of its course the Arar formed the boundary between
the Aeduans and the Sequanians, who engaged in violent strifes over
the right, claimed by both, to levy tolls on passing vessels.   The country
along the Arar furnished the best quality of bacon, which was exported
to Rome.

2. incrēdibilī lēnitāte: 'of incredible sluggishness.' *143, a.* B.
224; A. 415; H. 473, 2.   **incrēdibilī:** *74, f.*

3. oculīs: 'with the eye.' *92, a,* and *131, a.*   **in utram partem:** 'in' (lit. 'into') 'which direction.' *23, a.*   **fluat:** *204,* (3).
B. 300, 1; A. 574; H. 649, II.   **iūdicārī:** '(to) be determined.'
221, a.   **possit:** the subject is the indirect question *in . . . fluat,* but
trans. 'it can not,' etc.   Near Trévoux, 14 miles north of Lyons, the

Ubi per explōrātōrēs Caesar certior factus est, trēs iam 5
partēs cōpiārum Helvētiōs id flūmen trādūxisse, quārtam
ferē partem citrā flūmen Ararim reliquam esse, dē tertiā
vigiliā cum legiōnibus tribus ē castrīs profectus ad eam
partem pervēnit, quae nōndum flūmen trānsierat. — Eōs
impedītōs et inopīnantēs aggressus, magnam partem eōrum 10
concīdit; reliquī sēsē fugae mandārunt atque in proximās
silvās abdidērunt. Is pāgus appellābātur Tigurīnus; nam
omnis cīvitās Helvētia in quattuor pāgōs dīvīsa est.

---

current of the Saône is to-day for a short distance as sluggish as in
Caesar's time (Fig. 37); and here the Helvetians probably crossed the
river.

4. **lintribus iūnctīs** : 'by (means of) small boats fastened together';
the floats thus constructed, as well as the rafts, could be easily poled
across in the still water. *15, a,* and *131, a.*

5. **explōrātōrēs** : 'scouting parties.' *327.* **trēs ... trādūxisse** :
trans. as if *Helvētiōs iam trēs partēs* ('three quarters') *cōpiārum
trāns id flūmen dūxisse.* *114, a.* B. 179, 1 ; A. 395 ; H. 413.

7. **citrā** : 'on this side of,' i.e. the east side. *122, a.* **Ararim** :
18, e. **dē tertiā vigiliā** : *242, d.*

8. **legiōnibus tribus** : about 11,000 men. *137, b.* **castrīs** :
probably not far from Sathonay, east of the Saône, above its junction
with the Rhone. See Map 1. **profectus** : *61, a,* (3).

9. **Eōs** : *160, b.*

10. **impedītōs et inopīnantēs** : 'hampered and off their guard.'
The fighting men, scattered throughout the encampment, were completely
surprised and had no chance to form a line of battle ; the Roman soldiers
plied their savage short swords rapidly and effectively. *322, e.*
aggressus : 'attacking.' *57, c,* and *226, c.*

11. **concīdit** : how different from *concidit ?* **reliquī** : *154, a,* and
171, a. **mandārunt** : = *mandāvērunt* ; lit. 'committed themselves
to flight,' where we should say 'took to flight.' *64, a,* (1). **in** : trans.
'in'; lit. 'into,' on account of the idea of motion in *abdidērunt,* as if we
should say they (went) 'into the neighboring woods' (and) 'concealed
themselves.'

12. **pāgus** : 'canton,' properly a territorial division, here used of
the inhabitants. **Tigurīnus** : *148, a.*

13. **cīvitās** : *288, a.* **dīvīsa** : *148, c.*

Hīc pāgus ūnus, cum domō exīsset, patrum nostrōrum
15 memoriā L. Cassium cōnsulem interfēcerat et eius exercitum sub iugum mīserat. Ita sīve cāsū sīve cōnsiliō deōrum
immortālium, quae pars cīvitātis Helvētiae īnsignem calamitātem populō Rōmānō intulerat, ea prīnceps poenās
persolvit.

20   Quā in rē Caesar nōn sōlum pūblicās, sed etiam prīvātās
iniūriās ultus est, quod eius socerī L. Pīsōnis avum, L.
Pīsōnem lēgātum, Tigurīnī eōdem proeliō, quō Cassium,
interfēcerant.

Caesar, bridging the Arar, crosses.   The Helvetians send envoys.

13. Hōc proeliō factō, reliquās cōpiās Helvētiōrum ut
cōnsequī posset, pontem in Ararī faciendum cūrat atque
ita exercitum trādūcit.

---

14. **domō**: *130, b.* B. 229, 1, *b*; A. 427, 1; H. 462, 4.   **exīsset**:
68, b, and *185, c.*

15. **memoriā**: 'within the memory.' *147, b.* B. 231; A. 423;
H. 487.   **L. Cassium ... mīserat**: see chap. 7, ll. 15–17, and Notes.

16. **sīve ... sīve**: *235, b.*   **cāsū**: 'by chance.' *20, a,* and
135, a.   **deōrum**: *8, d.*

17. **quae pars**: trans. as if *ea pars cīvitātis Helvētiae, quae. 165, c.*
īnsignem: 'notable.' *25, a.*   **calamitātem**: 'disaster.'

18. **populō**: *104, a.*   **prīnceps persolvit**: 'was the first to pay.'
152, b.   **poenās**: *92, a.*

20. **Quā**: *167.*   **nōn sōlum ... sed etiam**: *236, d.*

21. **ultus est**: *61, a,* (3), and *176, a.*   **quod ... interfē-**
cerant: i.e. *quod Tigurīnī, eōdem proeliō quō Cassium* (*interfēcerant*),
interfēcerant Lūcium Pīsōnem lēgātum, avum Lūciī Pīsōnis, eius
(Caesar's) *socerī.* Lucius Calpurnius Piso, consul in 58 B.C., was the
father of Caesar's fourth wife, Calpurnia, whom he had married in the
previous year. *253.*   **socerī**: *7, b.*

22. **proeliō**: *147, b.* B. 230, 2; A. 424, *d*; H. 486, 1.

13. 1. **Hōc proeliō factō**: trans. as if *post hōc proelium.*
144, b, (2).

2. **cōnsequī**: 'to pursue.' *61, a,* (3).   **posset**: *196, a.*   **pontem**
faciendum cūrat: 'he (Caesar) had a bridge built,' i.e. by the me-

Helvētiī, repentīnō eius adventū commōtī, cum id, quod
ipsī diēbus xx aegerrimē cōnfēcerant, ut flūmen trānsīrent, 5
illum ūnō diē fēcisse intellegerent, lēgātōs ad eum mittunt;
cuius lēgātiōnis Dīvicō prīnceps fuit, quī bellō Cassiānō
dux Helvētiōrum fuerat.   Is ita cum Caesare ēgit:

Figure 38. — The Rhone below Geneva.

chanics, *fabrī*, of whom there were a number enrolled in the legions;
it was doubtless a pontoon bridge.   *229, b*, and *310, b*.   B. 337, 8,
b, 2; A. 500, 4; H. 622.   **in**: 'over.'

4. **repentīnō**: 'unexpected.'   **commōtī**: 'alarmed.'   **cum,**
etc.: trans. as if *cum intellegerent illum* (Caesar) *ūnō diē fēcisse* ('had
accomplished') *id quod*, etc.   *178*, and *185, c.*

5. **xx**: *vīgintī*.   *38, b*.   **ut flūmen trānsīrent**: a substantive
clause explaining *id*; trans. 'the crossing of the river.'   *203*, (4).

7. **cuius lēgātiōnis**: 'and of this delegation.'   *167*.   **prīnceps**:
10, b.   **bellō Cassiānō**: 'in the war with Cassius.'   *147, b*.   As the
defeat of Cassius took place in 107 B.C., at the time of which Caesar was
writing, 58 B.C., Divico must have been between 70 and 80 years old.
The Helvetians preferred to avoid a conflict with Caesar, but the tone
of Divico's language made a mutual understanding impossible.

8. **cum Caesare ēgit**: 'treated with Caesar.'   *137, c.*

Sī pācem populus Rōmānus cum Helvētiīs faceret, in eam
10 *partem itūrōs atque ibi futūrōs Helvētiōs, ubi eōs Caesar*
cōnstituisset atque esse voluisset; sīn bellō persequī perse-
verāret, reminīscerētur et veteris incommodī populī Rōmānī
et prīstinae virtūtis Helvētiōrum.

X *Quod imprōvīsō ūnum pāgum adortus esset, cum eī, quī*
15 *flūmen trānsīssent, suīs auxilium ferre nōn possent, nē ob*
eam rem aut suae magnopere virtūtī tribueret aut ipsōs dē-

9–13. **Direct form**: Sī pācem populus Rōmānus cum Helvētiīs *faciet*, in eam partem *ībunt* atque ibi *erunt Helvētiī*, ubi eōs (*tū*) *cōnstitueris* atque esse *volueris;* sīn bellō persequī *persevērābis*, *reminīscere* et veteris incommodī populī Rōmānī et pristinae virtūtis Helvētiōrum.

9. **faceret, itūrōs** [esse], **futūrōs** [esse]: *89, c*, and *218,* (1), a. B. 314, 1 ; A. 589; H. 642, 643.

10. **ubi**: = *in quā*.

11. **cōnstituisset, voluisset**: in the direct form, future perfect indicative ; the tense is influenced by the tense of *ēgit. 177, a.* B. 319, B, *a* ; H. 644, 2. **bellō**: *131, a.* **persequī**: sc. *eōs*, 'to assail (them).' *61, a,* (3), and *221, a.* **persevērāret**: '(Caesar) should continue.'

12. **reminīscerētur**: 'he should remember.' *216.* B. 316; A. 588; H. 642. **veteris**: *26, a.* **incommodī**: the defeat of Cassius. Why genitive? *103, a.* B. 206, 2 ; A. 350, *c* ; H. 454.

13. **prīstinae**: 'old-time.' **virtūtis**: *75, c*, and *81.*

14–21. **Direct form**: Quod imprōvīsō ūnum pāgum adortus *es*, cum eī, quī flūmen *trānsierant*, suīs auxilium ferre nōn possent, *nōlī* ob eam rem aut *tuae* magnopere virtūtī *tribuere*, aut *nōs dēspicere;* (*nōs*) ita ā patribus maiōribusque *nostrīs didicimus*, ut magis virtūte *contendāmus* quam dolō aut īnsidiīs *nītāmur*. Quārē *nōlī committere* ut is locus, ubi *cōnstiterimus* (future perfect), ex calamitāte populī Rōmānī et interneciōne exercitūs nōmen *capiat* aut memoriam *prōdat*.

14. **Quod**: *198, b.* **imprōvīsō**: 'suddenly.' **pāgum**: what canton? see chap. 12. **adortus esset, trānsīssent**: *214, a.*

15. **suīs**: 'to their (countrymen).' *154, a.* **possent**: subjunctive also in the direct form. *185, c.*

16. **rem**: the 'fact' expressed by the clause *Quod . . . adortus esset*. **magnopere**: adv., takes the place of a direct object ; 'that he should not presume overmuch.' **virtūtī**: *104, b.* **tribueret**: *216.* B.

spiceret; sē ita ā patribus maiōribusque suīs didicisse, ut magis virtūte contenderent, quam dolō aut īnsidiīs nīterentur. Quārē nē committeret, ut is locus, ubi cōnstitissent, ex calamitāte populī Rōmānī et internecīōne exercitūs nōmen 20 *caperet aut memoriam prōderet.*

Caesar lays down conditions; the Helvetians scornfully reject them.

14. Hīs Caesar ita respondit :
Eō sibi minus dubitātiōnis darī, quod eās rēs, quās lēgātī

316; A. 588, N. 2 ; H. 642. **aut . . . aut** : *235, a,* and *b.* **ipsōs** : 'them,' i.e. *Helvētiōs. 162, b.*

17. **ita . . . ut** : *197, b.* **maiōribus** : 'forefathers.' *154, a.* **didicisse** : 'had learned.' *178.* **ut . . . contenderent** : 'to fight.' *197, a.* B. 284, 1 ; A. 537, 1 ; H. 570.

18. **magis** : 'rather.' *35.* **quam** [ut] **nīterentur** : '.than to rely upon.' **dolō aut īnsidiīs** : 'deceit or ambuscades.' *131, c.* B. 218, 3 ; A. 431 ; H. 476, 3.

19. **Quārē** : *237, a.* **nē committeret, ut is locus . . . caperet** : ' he should not allow that place to take '; how lit. ? **committeret** : cf. *tribueret,* l. 16. **ubi cōnstitissent** : 'where they should have taken their stand,' in order to fight the Romans.

20. **internecīōne** : 'annihilation.' **exercitūs** : 'of an army,' i.e. Caesar's army. **nōmen** : so the name Bloody Brook, in Massachusetts, commemorates an Indian massacre.

21. **caperet** : *56,* and *203,* (3). B. 297, 1 ; A. 568, N. 1 ; H. 571, 3. **memoriam prōderet** : i.e. *memoriam calamitātis posterīs prōderet* ('transmit').

14. 1. **Hīs** : *lēgātīs Helvētiōrum. 104, b.*

2-7. **Direct form** : Eō *mihi* minus dubitātiōnis *datur,* quod eās rēs, quās *commemorāvistis,* memoriā *teneō,* atque eō gravius *ferō,* quō minus meritō populī Rōmānī *accidērunt;* quī sī alicuius iniūriae sibi cōnscius fuisset, nōn *fuit* difficile cavēre ; sed eō *deceptus est,* quod neque commissum [esse] ā sē *intellegēbat,* quārē timēret, neque sine causā timendum [esse] *putābat.*

2. **Eō** : ' for this reason,' explained by the following *quod*-clause. *135, a,* and *160, c.* **sibi . . . darī** : 'that he had less hesitation,' lit. 'that less of hesitation is given to him.' *97, b.* B. 201, 2 ; A. 346, *a,* 3 ; H. 442. **sibi** : *158, a,* and *104, a.*

Helvētiī commemorāssent, memoriā tenēret, atque eō gravius
ferre, quō minus meritō populī Rōmānī accidissent; quī sī
5 *alicuius iniūriae sibi cōnscius fuisset, nōn fuisse difficile*
cavēre; sed eō dēceptum, quod neque commissum ā sē intelle-
geret, quārē timēret, neque sine causā timendum putāret.

---

3. **commemorāssent**: *64, a,* (1).　**memoriā tenēret**: 'he
remembered.' *131, a.*　**eō gravius ferre, quō minus**: sc. *sē,* 'that
he felt all the more indignant' (lit. 'that he bears them by that the
more heavily'), 'the less.' *140.* B. 223; A. 414, *a*; H. 479.

4. **meritō populī Rōmānī**: 'in accordance with what was due to'
(lit. 'the desert of') 'the Roman people.' *136, c.* B. 220, 3.　**accidissent**: 'they had happened.'
214, a.　**quī**: = *populus Rōmānus,*
'it,' or 'they.' *167.*

5. **alicuius**: from *aliquī. 49, a.*
iniūriae: *102.* B. 204, 1; A.
349, *a*; H. 451, 1.　**sibi**: *109, a.*
fuisse: why *fuit* in the direct
form? *208, b.* B. 304, 3, *a*; A.
437, *a*; H. 583, 3.

6. **cavēre**: 'to take precautions,' lit. 'to be on guard,' against
reprisals, which the Roman people
would have expected if they had in
any way wronged the Helvetians.
eō: as in l. 2.　**dēceptum**:
eum (i.e. *populum Rōmānum*) *de-
ceptum esse,* 'that they had been
deceived.'　**neque . . . putāret**:

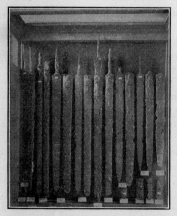

Figure 39.—Rusted Gallic swords
and scabbards, found in France.

'on the one hand they understood that nothing had been done by
them which should cause them to fear, and on the other they thought
that they ought not to be afraid without cause.' How lit.?　**commissum** [esse]: impersonal, but trans. with *neque* as if *et nihil commissum esse.*

7. **timēret**: subjunctive also in the direct form; trans. *quārē*
as if *propter quod. 194, a.* B. 283, 1; A. 535, *a*; H. 591, 4.
timendum [esse]: impersonal, lit. 'it ought not to be feared.'
73, e.

*Quod sī veteris contumēliae oblīvīscī vellet, num etiam
recentium iniūriārum, quod, eō invītō, iter per prōvinciam
per vim temptāssent, quod Aeduōs, quod Ambarrōs, quod 10
Allobrogas vexāssent, memoriam dēpōnere posse?*

*Quod suā victōriā tam īnsolenter glōriārentur, quodque
tam diū sē impūne iniūriās tulisse admīrārentur, eōdem*

8–11. Direct form: Quod sī veteris contumēliae oblīvīscī *volō*, num
etiam recentium iniūriārum, quod, *mē* invītō, iter per prōvinciam per vim
temptāvistis, quod Aeduōs, quod Ambarrōs, quod Allobrogas *vexāvistis*,
memoriam dēpōnere *possum?*

8. Quod: lit. 'as to which,' referring to the thought of the preceding sentence; trans. 'Even.' *118, d.* **veteris**: *28, b.* **contumēliae**: 'indignity,' the destruction of Cassius's army, in 107 B.C. *103, a.*
B. 206, 2; A. 350, *b*; H. 454. **vellet**: *218,* (1), a. **num . . .
posse**: *179, b,* (1).

9. recentium iniūriārum: dependent on *memoriam* in l. 11; 'of
fresh outrages,' specified in the following appositional clauses introduced by *quod,* 'that.' *198, b,* and *214, a.* B. 299, 1, *a*; A. 572; H.
588, 3. **eō**: = *Caesare*; 'in despite of him,' lit. 'he (being) unwilling.' *144, b,* (5). B. 227, 1; A. 419, *a*; H. 489.

10. temptāssent: *64, a,* (1). **quod, quod**: sc. *vexāssent.*
239, a, and *89, a.*

11. Allobrogas: *19, f.* **dēpōnere**: 'put aside.' *221, a.*

12–17. Direct form: Quod *vestrā* victōriā tam īnsolenter *glōriāminī,*
quodque tam diū *vōs* impūne iniūriās tulisse *admīrāminī, eōdem pertinet.
Cōnsuērunt* enim *dī immortālēs,* quō gravius hominēs ex commūtātiōne rērum
doleant, quōs prō scelere eōrum ulcīscī *volunt,* hīs secundiōrēs interdum rēs
et diūturniōrem impūnitātem concēdere.

12. Quod: 'The fact that'; the two clauses introduced by *quod*
stand as subject of *pertinēre. 198, b,* and *214, a.* **suā victōriā**:
'of their victory' over the Romans under Cassius, 107 B.C. *135, a,*
and *81.* **īnsolenter**: 'arrogantly.' *34, a.* **glōriārentur**: 'they
were boasting.' *214, a.*

13. tam . . . tulisse: 'that they so long had kept on perpetrating
wrongs without punishment.' How lit.? **admīrārentur**: 'they
marveled.' *61, a,* (1). **eōdem pertinēre**: 'pointed in the same
direction,' toward impending retribution for the wrongs committed by
the Helvetians.

pertinēre. Cōnsuēsse enim deōs immortālēs, quō gravius
15 *hominēs ex commūtātiōne rērum doleant, quōs prō scelere*
eōrum ulcīscī velint, hīs secundiōrēs interdum rēs et diūturni-
ōrem impūnitātem concēdere.

Cum ea ita sint, tamen, sī obsidēs ab eīs sibi dentur, utī
ea, quae polliceantur, factūrōs intellegat, et sī Aeduīs dē
20 *iniūriīs, quās ipsīs sociīsque eōrum intulerint, item sī Allo-*
brogibus satisfaciant, sēsē cum eīs pācem esse factūrum.

Dīvicō respondit :

Ita Helvētiōs ā maiōribus suīs īnstitūtōs esse, utī obsidēs

---

14. **Cōnsuēsse**: 'are wont.' *64, a*, (2), and *176, b*; also, *214, a*.
deōs: *8, d*.   **quō**: *193, b*. B. 282, 1, *a*; A. 531, 2, *a*; H. 568, 7.
gravius: 'more bitterly.' *34, a*.

15. **ex commūtātiōne rērum**: 'in consequence of reverses.'
How lit.?   **doleant**: 'may suffer.'   **scelere**: 'wickedness.' *13, e*.

16. **ulcīscī**: *223, b*.   **hīs**: 'to those,' antecedent of *quōs* in l. 15.
secundiōrēs rēs: 'a more prosperous estate.'   **diūturniōrem**:
'more prolonged.' *76, b*.

17. **impūnitātem**: 'escape from punishment.' *106, a*.   **con-**
cēdere: after *Cōnsuēsse* in l. 14.   *221, a*, and *113, b*.

18–21. **Direct form**: Cum *haec* ita sint, tamen, sī obsidēs *ā vōbīs mihi*
dabuntur, utī ea, quae *pollicēminī*, *vōs* factūrōs [esse] *intellegam*, et sī
Aeduīs dē iniūriīs, quās ipsīs sociīsque eōrum *intulistis*, item sī Allobrogibus
satisfaciētis, *vōbīscum* pācem *faciam*.

18. **Cum**: 'Although.' *187*. B. 309; A. 549; H. 598.   **ea**:
haec in the direct form. *160, a*.   **tamen**: *236, a*.

19. **ea**: object of *factūrōs* [esse], with which supply *eōs* as subject.
polliceantur: 'they promised.' *61, a*, (2).   **Aeduīs**: dat. after
satisfaciant. 105.   **dē**: 'for.'

20. **ipsīs**: the Aeduans.   **sociīs**: the Ambarri.

21. **satisfaciant**: 'they should make restitution.' *79, b*.

23–25. **Direct form**: Ita *Helvētiī* ā maiōribus suīs *īnstitūtī sunt*, utī obsidēs accipere, nōn dare, cōnsuērint; *huius reī populus Rōmānus est testis*.

23. **Ita īnstitūtōs esse**: 'had inherited such traditions.' How
lit.?   **utī . . . cōnsuērint**: 'that they were accustomed.' *64, a*,
(2), and *197, b*.

accipere, nōn dare, cōnsuērint ; eius reī populum Rōmānum
esse testem.   25

Hōc respōnsō datō, discessit.

The Helvetians resume their march, defeating Caesar's cavalry ;
Caesar follows.

15. Posterō diē castra ex eō locō movent.   Idem facit
Caesar equitātumque omnem, ad numerum quattuor mīlium, quem ex omnī prōvinciā et Aeduīs atque eōrum
sociīs coāctum habēbat, praemittit, quī videant, quās in
partēs hostēs iter faciant.   Quī, cupidius novissimum 5
agmen īnsecūtī, aliēnō locō cum equitātū Helvētiōrum
proelium committunt ; et paucī dē nostrīs cadunt.

Quō proeliō sublātī Helvētiī, quod quīngentīs equitibus

---

25. **esse testem** : 'was a witness'; we should say 'could furnish
testimony.'

26. **Hōc respōnsō datō** : 'after making this reply.' *144, b*, (2).
discessit : 'he (Divico) withdrew.'

15. 1. **Posterō** : 'the following.' *33.*   **movent** : sc. *Helvētiī.*
175, b.   **Idem** : neuter accusative. *45.*

2. **equitātum** : 'his cavalry.' *157, a*, and *309, b.*

4. **coāctum habēbat** : *229, a.*   B. 337, 7 ; A. 497, *b* ; H. 431, 3.
quī videant : 'to see'; how lit. ? *193, a.*   B. 282, 2 ; A. 531, 2 ; H.
590.   **videant** : plural because the subject *quī* is plural, on account
of the idea of *equitēs* in the antecedent *equitātum.*   *164, d*, and *238, h.*
quās in partēs : 'in what direction.'   How lit. ? *48, a.*

5. **faciant** : *204*, (2).   B. 300, 1 ; A. 574 ; H. 649, 11.   **Quī** :
167.   **cupidius** : 'too eagerly.' *153, a.*   **novissimum agmen** :
the 'rear' of the Helvetians.   *27, b*, and *12, e.*

6. **īnsecūtī** : *61, a*, (3).   **aliēnō locō** : 'on unfavorable ground,'
probably too hilly to admit of free movement.   *145, c*, and *6, c.*

7. **dē nostrīs** : trans. as if *nostrōrum.* *97, d.*   From *paucī . . .*
cadunt we infer that the rest made good their escape through flight.
The kind of weapons used by the Helvetians may be inferred from the
spear heads and dart heads shown in Fig. 40.

8. **sublātī** : 'elated'; see *tollō* in the Vocab.   **quīngentīs** : *36.*
equitibus : *131, b.*

tantam multitūdinem equitum prōpulerant, audācius sub-
10 sistere nōn numquam et novissimō agmine proeliō nostrōs
lacessere coepērunt. Caesar suōs ā proeliō continēbat, ac
satis habēbat in praesentiā hostem rapīnīs, pābulātiōnibus
populātiōnibusque prohibēre.

Ita diēs circiter quīndecim iter fēcērunt, utī inter novissi-

---

9. **prōpulerant**: 'had routed'; but the 4000 cavalry of Caesar
were Gauls, only the officers being Romans. **audācius**: 'with greater
boldness.' *34, a.* **subsistere**: 'to halt,' as they were marching.

10. **novissimō agmine**: 'with (their) rear,' attacking the Romans
who were following them. *131, b,* and *152, a.* **proeliō**: *131, a.*
nostrōs: 'our men.' *154, a.*

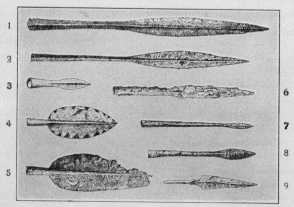

Figure 40. — Gallic spear heads and dart heads.

Of iron, of various types. Nos. 2, 4, 5, 7, and 8 were found in the Helvetian country,
near Lake Neuchâtel ; no. 6 was found on the site of Bibracte.

11. **lacessere**: 'to harass.' **coepērunt**: *72, b.* **suōs**: 'his
soldiers.' *154, a.*

12. **satis habēbat**: 'considered (it) sufficient'; the object of
habēbat is *prohibēre*, and *satis* is used as a predicate accusative. *115,
a.* **in praesentiā**: 'for the present.' **rapīnīs, pabulātiōnibus
populātiōnibusque**: 'from pillaging, foraging, and laying waste' the
country. *92, a,* and *127, a.* B. 214, 2 ; A. 401 ; H. 464.

14. **Ita**: *197, b.* **diēs**: *118, a.* B. 181 ; A. 423 ; H. 417.

mum hostium agmen et nostrum prīmum nōn amplius 15
quīnīs aut sēnīs mīlibus passuum interesset. ——

The Aeduans do not bring grain which they have promised;
Liscus discloses treachery.

16. Interim cotīdiē Caesar Aeduōs frūmentum, quod
essent pūblicē pollicitī, flāgitāre. Nam propter frīgora, nōn
modo frūmenta in agrīs mātūra nōn erant, sed nē pābulī
quidem satis magna cōpia suppetēbat; eō autem frūmentō,
quod flūmine Ararī nāvibus subvexerat, proptereā minus 5
ūtī poterat, quod iter ab Ararī Helvētiī āverterant, ā quibus

---

15. **prīmum** [agmen] : 'van.' *328.*   **amplius** : 'more,' subject of
interesset. 154, a.

16. **quīnīs, sēnīs** : distributive, 'five or six miles' each day. *36.*
mīlibus : *129, a*; *243, b*, and *38, a.* B. 217; A. 406; H. 471. **interesset** : 'intervened.' *66, a.*

16. 1. **Interim** : 'Meanwhile.'   **Aeduōs, frūmentum** : *116, a.*
B. 178, 1, *a*; A. 396; H. 411. **quod essent pollicitī** : 'which (he
said) they had promised'; Caesar the writer presents the statement of
Caesar the commander as if it were quoted from someone else. *214, b.*
B. 323; A. 592, 3; H. 649, 1.

2. **pūblicē** : 'in the name of the state.'   **flāgitāre** : 'kept demanding.' *182.* B. 335; A. 463; H. 610.   **frīgora** : 'cold seasons,' the
spring being later than in Italy. *92, c.*

3. **frūmenta** : the plural is used by Caesar of standing grain; 'crops
of grain.'   **mātūra** : 'ripe.' *81.*   **nē ... quidem** : 'not even.' *237, c.*
pābulī : 'of fodder,' required for the baggage animals as well as the
horses of the cavalry.

4. **autem** : *236, a.*   **frūmentō** : after *ūtī. 131, c.* B. 218, 1; A.
410; H. 477.

5. **flūmine** : *134, a.* B. 218, 9; A. 429, *a*; H. 476. **Ararī** : *18, e.*
subvexerat : 'he had brought up.'

6. **āverterant** : the Helvetians had at first followed the valley of the
Arar (*Saône*) northward, but now 'had turned away from the Arar'
and passed westward into the valley of the Liger (*Loire*), avoiding the
mountainous country opposite the place where they had crossed the
Arar; see Map 1.

discēdere nōlēbat. Diem ex diē dūcere Aeduī; cōnferrī, comportārī, adesse dīcere.

Ubi sē diūtius dūcī intellēxit et diem īnstāre, quō diē
10 frūmentum mīlitibus mētīrī oportēret, convocātīs eōrum prīncipibus, quōrum magnam cōpiam in castrīs habēbat, in hīs Dīviciācō et Liscō, quī summō magistrātuī praeerat,

Figure 41. — Mount Beuvray.

Site of Bibracte, the Aeduan capital, seen from the west. Highest elevation, 2690 feet.

7. **Diem ex diē dūcere**: sc. *eum*, 'were putting him off from day to day.' **Diem**: *118, a*. **dūcere, dīcere**: historical infinitives. *182*. **cōnferrī, comportārī, adesse**: sc. *frūmentum*, 'that (the grain) was being collected' from individuals, 'that it was being brought' to Caesar's headquarters, 'that it was just at hand'; climax, with asyndeton. *238, a*, and *239, d*.

9. **diūtius**: 'too long.' *153, a*. **īnstāre**: 'was near.' *178*, and *213, a*. **diē**: not translated. *165, a*.

10. **frūmentum**: object of *mētīrī*. **mētīrī**: 'to measure out.' *61, a*, (4), and *222, a*. B. 327, 1; A. 454; H. 615. How often did the soldiers receive grain? *317*. **oportēret**: *73, a, b*, and *214, a*. **convocātīs**: 'having called together.' How lit.? *144, b*, (2).

12. **Dīviciācō et Liscō**: sc. *convocātīs*. **summō**: *33*. **magistrātuī**: *107, a*, and *82, b*. **praeerat**: we say 'held.' *66, a*.

quem 'vergobretum' appellant Aeduī, quī creātur annuus
et vītae necisque in suōs habet potestātem, graviter eōs
accūsat, quod, cum neque emī neque ex agrīs sūmī posset, 15
tam necessāriō tempore, tam propinquīs hostibus, ab eīs
nōn sublevētur, praesertim cum, magnā ex parte eōrum
precibus adductus, bellum suscēperit, multō etiam gravius,
quod sit dēstitūtus, queritur.

17. Tum dēmum Liscus, ōrātiōne Caesaris adductus,
quod anteā tacuerat, prōpōnit:

---

13. **vergobretum** : 'vergobret.' *115, a,* and *289, a.* Meaning ?
See Vocab.   **quī** : 'who'; the antecedent is *vergobretum.*   **creā-**
tur : 'is elected.' The seat of government was at Bibracte, which was
securely situated on the top of a mountain (Fig. 41).   **annuus** :
'annually.' *151.*

14. **vītae necisque** : 'of life and death.' *102.*   **in suōs** : 'over
his countrymen.' *154, a.*   **eōs accūsat** : 'he took them to task.' *175, b.*

15. **emī** : 'be purchased.' *55.*   **neque ... neque** : *233, a.*
posset : sc. *frūmentum. 220.*

16. **necessāriō tempore** : 'at so critical a time.' *147, a.*
hostibus : *144, b,* (2).

17. **nōn sublevētur** : with *quod,* 'because (as he said) he received
no help from them,' lit. 'was not helped by them.' *214, b* ; see N. to
chap. 16, l. 1, *quod essent pollicitī.*   **praesertim cum** : 'especially
since.' *184, a, b.*   **magnā ex parte** : 'in great measure.'
eōrum precibus : 'by their entreaties.' *135, a.*

18. **bellum** : 'campaign' against the Helvetians.   **multō** : *140.*
B. 223 ; A. 414 ; H. 471, 10.

19. **sit dēstitūtus** : translate as if pluperfect, 'he had been abandoned'; the time is past relatively to that of **queritur,** which is a historical present, 'he complained.' *177, b,* and *214, b.*

17. 2. **quod** : as antecedent supply *id* with *prōpōnit. 160, c.*
anteā : 'previously.'   **tacuerat** : 'had kept to himself.' How lit.?
prōpōnit : 'brought forward (saying),' i.e. 'declared.' *213, a.*

3–11. **Direct form** : *Nōn nūllī sunt,* quōrum auctōritās apud plēbem plūrimum *valet,* quī prīvātim plūs *possunt* quam ipsī magistrātūs.

Hī sēditiōsā atque improbā ōrātiōne multitūdinem *dēterrent,* nē frūmentum cōnferant, quod (*cōnferre*) *dēbent;* (*dīcunt*) praestāre . . . sint
ēreptūrī.

Esse nōn nūllōs, quōrum auctōritās apud plēbem plūri-
mum valeat, quī prīvātim plūs possint quam ipsī magis-
5 *trātūs.*

Hōs sēditiōsā atque. improbā ōrātiōne multitūdinem
dēterrēre, nē frūmentum cōnferant, quod dēbeant : praestāre,
sī iam prīncipātum Galliae obtinēre nōn possint, Gallōrum
quam Rōmānōrum imperia perferre ; neque dubitāre dēbēre,
10 *quīn, sī Helvētiōs superāverint Rōmānī, ūnā cum reliquā*
Galliā Aeduīs lībertātem sint ēreptūrī.

---

3. **Esse nōn nūllōs** : *that there were some men.* *90, a,* and *212, b*
and *c* ; also *23, a,* and *154, a.*   **plūrimum valeat** : 'carried very
great weight.' *32,* and *118, b.*

4. **prīvātim** : ' as private individuals.' *77.*   **plūs possint** : 'had
more power.' The state of affairs here depicted arose from the feudal
organization of society, which rendered it possible for the great land-
holders to control multitudes of personal adherents. Cf. chap. 4, ll.
4–8 and Book VI, chap. 15. *288, 289.*

6. **sēditiōsā atque improbā ōrātiōne** : ' by seditious and shameless propagandism.' Among the Aeduans there was a strong party
opposed to the Romans.

7. **dēterrēre** : ' were holding back ' by inspiring fear.   **nē . . .
cōnferant** : ' from furnishing.' *201, a.* B. 295, 3 ; A. 558, *b* ; H. 566.
cōnferant : plural because of the idea of plurality in *multitūdinem.*
173, b.   **dēbeant** : ' they were under obligation to furnish ' ; lit.
' owed.'   **praestāre . . . ēreptūrī** : parenthetical indirect discourse,
summarizing the line of argument (*ōrātiōne,* l. 6) by which the anti-
Roman leaders influenced the Aeduan populace ; ' (saying) that it was
better,' etc. *213, a.*

8. **sī iam . . . nōn possint** : ' if they (the Aeduans) could no
longer.' *218,* (1), a. Formerly, for a considerable period, the Aeduans
had been the leading people in Gaul (VI. 13).   **Gallōrum** : ' of
Gauls,' i.e. of Helvetians.

9. **imperia** : plural as referring to the acts of a sovereign power,
trans. ' the rule.'   **perferre** : ' to endure ' ; subject of *praestāre.*
neque dubitāre dēbēre : sc. *sē* ' and they ought not to doubt that.'

10. **superāverint** : ' should have vanquished.' *218,* (1), b, and
219.   **ūnā** : adverb.

11. **Aeduīs** : dative. *109, b.*   B. 188, 2, *d* ; A. 381 ; H. 427.

*Ab eīsdem nostra cōnsilia, quaeque in castrīs gerantur,
hostibus ēnūntiārī ; hōs ā sē coercērī nōn posse.   Quīn etiam,
quod necessāriam rem coāctus Caesarī ēnūntiārit, intellegere
sēsē, quantō id cum perīculō fēcerit, et ob eam causam, quam 15
diū potuerit, tacuisse.*

Privately Caesar learns that Dumnorix is the arch-traitor.

18. Caesar hāc ōrātiōne Liscī Dumnorīgem, Dīviciācī
frātrem, dēsignārī sentiēbat; sed, quod plūribus praesentibus eās rēs iactārī nōlēbat, celeriter concilium dīmittit,

---

sint ēreptūrī: 'they were going to take away' ; subjunctive also in
direct discourse. *201, c,* and *63.*

12–16. **Direct form**: Ab eīsdem *tua* cōnsilia, quaeque in castrīs *geruntur,*
hostibus *ēnūntiantur ; hī ā mē coercērī* nōn *possunt.* Quīn etiam, quod
necessāriam rem coāctus *tibi ēnūntiāvī, intellegō,* quantō id cum perīculō
fēcerim, et ob eam causam, quam diū *potuī, tacuī.*

12. **nostra**: from the Roman point of view. **quaeque . . . gerantur**: 'and whatever is done,' lit. 'and what things are done.'
13. **sē**: Liscus.   **coercērī**: 'be restrained '; Liscus's 'power of
life and death,' which he had as vergobret, was here of no avail.
Quīn etiam: 'moreover.'
14. **quod . . . ēnūntiārit**: *64, a,* (1), and *198, c.*   **coāctus**:
'under compulsion,' by reason of the vehemence of Caesar's com-
plaints (chap. 16, ll. 14-15) and his position as the highest Aeduan
official.
15. **id**: refers to the clause *quod . . . ēnūntiārit.   160, c.*
perīculō: 'danger.' *137, c,* and *84.*   **fēcerit**: trans. as if pluperfect. *204,* (3).   **quam diū**: 'as long as.'
16. **tacuisse**: intransitive, sc. *sē* as subject; 'he had kept silent.'
18. 1. **Dumnorīgem**: *10, c.*   **Dīviciācī**: *19, d,* and *289, c.*
2. **dēsignārī**: 'was meant.' *213, a.*   **sentiēbat**: 'perceived.'
plūribus praesentibus: 'with many persons present.' *144, b,* (2).
3. **rēs**: 'matters,' i.e. the real reasons why the state of the Aeduans
had not made good its promises.   **iactārī**: 'should be discussed.'
223, a.   **celeriter**: 'quickly,' so as to shut off discussion. *34, a.*
concilium: 'the assembly' of leading Aeduans (*prīncipibus,* chap. 16,
l. 11).   **dīmittit**: 'dismissed.'

Liscum retinet. Quaerit ex sōlō ea, quae in conventū
5 dīxerat ; dīcit līberius atque audācius.

Eadem sēcrētō ab aliīs quaerit, reperit esse vēra :

*Ipsum esse Dumnorīgem, summā audāciā, magnā apud
plēbem propter līberālitātem grātiā, cupidum rērum novārum. Complūrēs annōs portōria reliquaque omnia Aeduō-*
10 *rum vectīgālia parvō pretiō redēmpta habēre, proptereā quod,
illō licente, contrā licērī audeat nēmō.*

---

4. **retinet**: '(but) detained.' *238, a*.   **Quaerit ex [eō] sōlō ea,
quae**: '(Caesar) asked him alone about what,' lit. 'those things
which.' *116, c*.   **conventū** : 'the conference.' *1*.

5. **dīcit**: sc. *Liscus*.   **līberius** : 'more freely.' *34, a*.

6. **sēcrētō** : 'privately.' *34, b*.   **reperit** : 'he found.'   **esse
vēra** : sc. *ea*, 'that they (Liscus's statements) were true.' *148, c*.

7-11. **Direct form** : *Ipse est Dumnorīx*, summā audāciā, magnā apud
plēbem propter līberālitātem grātiā, *cupidus* rērum novārum. Complūrēs
annōs portōria reliquaque omnia Aeduōrum vectīgālia parvō pretiō redēmpta
habet, proptereā quod, illō licente, contrā licērī *audet* nēmō.

7. **Ipsum** : in predicate, but trans. 'that in fact it was Dumnorix,'
as Caesar had surmised (l. 2). How lit.? *162, a*. For the indirect
discourse see *212, a–c*.   **summā audāciā** : '(a man) of the utmost
audacity.' *143, a*. B. 224 ; A. 415 ; H. 473, 2.

8. **līberālitātem** : 'lavish giving.'

9. **annōs** : *118, a*.   **portōria** : 'tolls,' levied chiefly, we may
assume, upon goods passing through the country along the roads and
rivers.   **reliqua** : *171, a*.

10. **vectīgālia** : 'revenues' in general ; *vectīgal* (derived from
vectus, participle of *vehō*) means that which is 'brought in' to the
public treasury. *16, d*.   **pretiō** : 'price.' *141*.   **redēmpta habēre** :
trans. as if *redēmisse* '(he) had farmed.' *229, a*. The Aeduan
revenues were "farmed out" as among the Romans ; that is, the privilege of collecting taxes was sold at auction to the highest bidder, who
guaranteed to the state a certain sum, did the collecting through his
agents, and kept for himself all that he could make above the amount
paid into the public treasury and the costs of collection. The "pub-
licans" of the New Testament were collectors of taxes under this system,
which afforded large opportunity for corruption and extortion.

11. **illō licente** : 'when he made a bid.' *61, a*, (2), and *144, a*.

*Hīs rēbus et suam rem familiārem auxisse et facultātēs
ad largiendum magnās comparāsse; magnum numerum
equitātūs suō sūmptū semper alere et circum sē habēre, neque
sōlum domī, sed etiam apud fīnitimās cīvitātēs largiter* 15
*posse, atque huius potentiae causā mātrem in Biturīgibus
hominī illīc nōbilissimō ac potentissimō collocāsse; ipsum
ex Helvētiīs uxōrem habēre, sorōrem ex mātre et propinquās
suās nūptum in aliās cīvitātēs collocāsse.*

---

contrā: here an adverb.   **nēmō**: *12, d.* Since no one dared to
bid against Dumnorix, he could obtain the right to collect the taxes on
terms most favorable to himself. (Fig. 42.)

12–19. **Direct form**: Hīs rēbus et suam
rem familiārem *auxit* et facultātēs ad largiendum magnās *comparāvit*. Magnum numerum equitātūs suō sūmptū semper *alit* et
circum sē *habet;* neque sōlum domī, sed etiam
apud fīnitimās cīvitātēs largiter *potest*, atque
huius potentiae causā mātrem in Biturīgibus
hominī illīc nōbilissimō ac potentissimō *collocāvit; ipse* ex Helvētiīs uxōrem *habet,*
sorōrem . . . *collocāvit.*

Figure 42. — Coin of
Dumnorix.

Silver. Obverse, helmeted head;
inscription DUBNOCOU. Reverse,
warrior carrying a Gallic standard
with the image of a boar, of which
only the lower part is seen; inscription, DUBNOREX.

12. et . . . et: *233, a.*   **rem
familiārem**: 'private fortune.'   **auxisse**: '(he) had increased.'

13. **ad largiendum**: 'for bribery.'   *61, a,* (4), and *230,* (3).
comparāsse: *64, a,* (1).

14. **suō sūmptū**: 'at his own expense.'   **alere**: 'maintained.'
neque: trans. as if *et nōn. 233, a.*

15. **sōlum**: 'only.'   *236, d.*   **domī**: *20, c,* and *146.*   **largiter
posse**: 'had great influence.' How lit.?

16. **huius potentiae causā**: 'to increase this influence.' How lit.?
135, b.   **mātrem**: *11, e.*   **Biturīgibus**: *10, c.*

17. **illīc**: 'of that country.' How lit.?   **collocāsse**: '(he) had
given in marriage.'   **ipsum**: '(he) himself,' Dumnorix.

18. **uxōrem**: 'wife,' a daughter of Orgetorix (chap. 3, l. 17). *13, d.*
sorōrem ex mātre: 'half-sister, on his mother's side.'   **propinquās**: 'his female relatives.'

19. **nūptum in . . . collocāsse**: 'had settled in marriage among
. . .' How lit.? *231, a.* B. 340, 1, *b*; A. 509; H. 633, 1.

20 *Favēre et cupere Helvētiīs propter eam affīnitātem, ōdisse*
etiam suō nōmine Caesarem et Rōmānōs, quod eōrum ad-
ventū potentia eius dēminūta et Dīviciācus frāter in antī-
quum locum grātiae atque honōris sit restitūtus. Sī quid
accidat Rōmānīs, summam in spem per Helvētiōs rēgnī ob-
25 *tinendī venīre; imperiō populī Rōmānī nōn modo dē rēgnō,*
sed etiam dē eā, quam habeat, grātiā dēspērāre.

Reperiēbat etiam in quaerendō Caesar, quod proelium
equestre adversum paucīs ante diēbus esset factum, initium
eius fugae factum ā Dumnorīge atque eius equitibus (nam

20–26. **Direct form:** *Favet* et *cupit* Helvētiīs propter eam affīnitātem,
ōdit etiam suō nōmine Caesarem et Rōmānōs, quod adventū potentia eius
dēminūta [*est*] et Dīviciācus frāter in antīquum locum grātiae atque honōris
est restitūtus. Sī quid accidat Rōmānīs, summam in spem per Helvētiōs
rēgnī obtinendī *veniat;* imperiō populī Rōmānī nōn modo dē rēgnō, sed
etiam dē eā, quam *habet,* grātiā *dēspērat.*

20. **Favēre et cupere:** '(he) favored and wished (success).'
affīnitātem: 'relationship.' **ōdisse:** '(he) hated.' *72, a, b.*

21. **suō nōmine:** 'personally.' How lit.? *135, a.*

22. **dēminūta** [sit]: 'had been lessened.' **in antīquum locum:**
'to his former position,' which the rise of Dumnorix had obscured.
Diviciacus was a man of some culture. Five years previously, in 63 B.C.,
he had visited Rome.

23. **sit restitūtus:** 'had been restored.' **Sī . . . venīre:**
218, (2). **quid:** *49, a,* and *168.*

24. **accidat:** here used of something unfavorable; our expression
"if anything should happen to him," has a similar underlying suggestion. **per:** 'with the help of.' *123, a.* **rēgnī obtinendī:** *230,* (1).

25. **imperiō:** 'under the supremacy.' *138.* **nōn modo . . .**
sed etiam: *236, d.* **dē rēgnō:** 'of the kingship.'

27. **quaerendō:** *230,* (4). **quod,** etc.: 'that (in) the disastrous
cavalry engagement which had taken place'; *proelium* is attracted into
the relative clause, while its proper place in the antecedent clause is
taken by *fugae.*

28. **diēbus:** *140.* **initium:** 'the beginning.'

29. **factum:** sc. *esse.* The implication is that Dumnorix treacherously started with the Aeduan contingent to flee, and that this precipitated a general rout.

equitātuī, quem auxiliō Caesarī Aeduī mīserant, Dumnorīx 30
praeerat), eōrum fugā reliquum esse equitātum perterritum.

*Though convinced of the treachery of Dumnorix, Caesar consults
his brother Diviciacus before taking action.*

19. Quibus rēbus cognitīs, cum ad hās suspīciōnēs cer-
tissimae rēs accēderent, quod per fīnēs Sēquanōrum Helvētiōs trādūxisset, quod obsidēs inter eōs dandōs cūrāsset,
quod ea omnia, nōn modo iniussū suō et cīvitātis, sed etiam
īnscientibus ipsīs, fēcisset, quod ā magistrātū Aeduōrum 5
accūsārētur, satis esse causae arbitrābātur, quārē in eum aut
ipse animadverteret, aut cīvitātem animadvertere iubēret.

Figure 43. — Helvetian spear.
Found near the yoke shown in Figure 29.

---

30. **equitātuī**: *107, a*.   **auxiliō Caesarī**: 'as an aid to Caesar.'
112, b.   B. 191, 2, *b* ; A. 382, 1 ; H. 433, 2.

31. **esse perterritum** : 'had been thrown into a panic.'

19. 1. **Quibus rēbus cognitīs** : 'Having found out these things.'
How lit.?   **suspīciōnēs** : 'grounds for suspicion.'

2. **rēs** : 'facts,' specified in the following *quod*-clauses.   **accēderent** : trans. as if *adderentur*, 'were added.'   **quod . . . accūsārētur** : *198, b*, and *220*.   B. 324, 1 ; A. 593 ; H. 652.

3. **obsidēs dandōs cūrāsset** : 'had effected an exchange of hostages.' *229, b*.   **inter eōs** : between the two peoples, the Sequanians
and the Helvetians.

4. **iniussū suō et cīvitātis** : 'without his own (Caesar's) authorization and that of the state' of the Aeduans. *135, b*.

5. **īnscientibus ipsīs** : 'without their knowledge'; *ipsīs = Caesare
et Aeduīs*. *144, b, (2)*.   **magistrātū Aeduōrum** : Liscus, the vergobret (chap. 16).

6. **satis . . . causae** : *97, b*.   B. 201, 2 ; A. 346, *a*, 4 ; H. 443.
esse : 'that there was.' *90, a*.   **in eum ipse animadverteret** :
'he himself should punish him,' lit. 'should give attention to him.'

7. **animadverteret** : subjunctive also in direct discourse ; *quārē
= propter quam. 194, a*.   **aut . . . aut**: *235, a, b*.

His omnibus rēbus ūnum repugnābat, quod Dīviciācī
frātris summum in populum Rōmānum studium, summam
10 in sē voluntātem, ēgregiam fidem, iūstitiam, temperantiam
cognōverat; nam, nē eius suppliciō Dīviciācī animum
offenderet, verēbātur.

Itaque prius quam quicquam cōnārētur, Dīviciācum ad
sē vocārī iubet et, cotīdiānīs interpretibus remōtīs, per C.
15 Valerium Troucillum, prīncipem Galliae prōvinciae, familiārem suum, cui summam omnium rērum fidem habēbat,
cum eō colloquitur; simul commonefacit, quae, ipsō prae-

---

8. **rēbus**: *105.*   **ūnum**: 'one consideration.'   *154, a.*   **repugnābat**: 'weighed against,' lit. 'contended against.'
  9. **frātris**: *11, e.*   **studium**: 'devotion.' *81.*

Figure 44. — Lance heads found at
Alesia, now in the Museum of
St. Germain.

10. **ēgregiam** : 'remarkable.'
temperantiam : ' self-control. '
238, a, and *81.*

11. **cognōverat**: ' was familiar
with.' *176, b.*   **eius** : trans. as
if *Dumnorīgis*.   **suppliciō** : 'by
the punishment.'

12. **offenderet**: with *nē*, 'that
he might offend.' *202.*   **verēbātur** : 'he was afraid.' *61, a,*
(2).

13. **cōnārētur** : *189, b.*   **Dīviciācum vocārī** : ' that Diviciacus
be summoned.' *223, a.*

14. **cotīdiānīs interpretibus** :
'the ordinary interpreters.' Diviciacus, notwithstanding his visit to
Rome, had evidently not learned to
speak Latin; and Caesar did not

understand Celtic. *10, e.*   **per**: *123, a.*
  15. **Galliae prōvinciae**: *290.*   **familiārem** : 'intimate friend.'
  16. **cui . . . habēbat**: ' in ' (lit. ' to ') 'whom he had the utmost
confidence in ' (lit. ' of ') 'all matters.'
  17. **eō** : Diviciacus.   **colloquitur**: 'he conversed.'   **com-**

sente, in concilió Gallórum dé Dumnorīge sint dicta, et
ostendit, quae séparātim quisque dé eó apud sé dīxerit.
Petit atque hortātur, ut sine eius offēnsióne animī vel ipse 20
dé eó, causā cognitā, statuat, vel cīvitātem statuere iubeat. 〉

*Moved by the pleading of Diviciacus, Caesar pardons Dumnorix,
but warns him.*

20. Dīviciācus, multīs cum lacrimīs Caesarem complexus,
obsecrāre coepit, nē quid gravius in frātrem statueret:

   *Scīre sē, illa esse vēra, nec quemquam ex eó plūs quam sē
dolōris capere, proptereā quod, cum ipse grātiā plūrimum
domī atque in reliquā Galliā, ille minimum propter adulē-* 5

---

monefacit: 'he called to mind.'   **quae**: *48, a,* and *204,* (2).   **ipsō**:
Diviciacus.

19. **séparātim**: 'separately.' *77.*   **quisque**: *49, a.*   **apud sē**:
'in his (Caesar's) presence.' *158, a.*

20. **Petit atque hortātur**: 'He besought and urged (Diviciacus).'
60.   **ut . . . statuat, iubeat**: *199, a.*   **eius**: dependent on
animī: trans., with *sine offēnsióne*, 'without suffering his (Diviciacus's)
feelings to be hurt.' How lit.?   **vel . . . vel**: *235, a, b.*   **ipse . . .
statuat**: lit., 'that he (Caesar) himself pass judgment'; the connection with the preceding *hortātur* shows that the underlying thought
is: 'to permit him (Caesar), having heard the case, to pronounce
judgment on Dumnorix (*dé eó*), or direct the state (of the Aeduans) to
pronounce judgment.'

20. 1. **lacrimīs**: *136, a.*   **complexus**: 'embracing.' *61,
a,* (3), and *226, c.*

2. **obsecrāre**: 'to entreat (him).'   **nē quid gravius statueret**:
'not to take too harsh measures.' How lit.?   **quid**: substantive form.
49, a; *117, a,* and *168.*   **gravius**: *153, a.*   **statueret**: *199, a.*

3. **Scīre sē**: '(saying) that he knew.' *213, b,* and *178.*   **nec
quemquam**: 'and that no one.' *49, a,* and *168.*   **ex eó**: 'on account of that fact.' *160, c.*   **plūs dolōris**: *25, b,* and *97, b.* B.
201, 1; A. 346, *a,* 3; H. 442.

4. **ipse**: Diviciacus.   **grātiā**: *135, à.*   **plūrimum**: sc. *posset.*
118, b.

5. **domī**: i.e. *in Aeduīs.* *20, c,* and *146.*   **ille**: Dumnorix.

scentiam posset, per sē crēvisset; quibus opibus ac nervīs nōn sōlum ad minuendam grātiam, sed paene ad perniciem suam ūterētur.

Sēsē tamen et amōre frāternō et exīstimātiōne vulgī com-
10 *movērī. Quod sī quid eī ā Caesare gravius accidisset, cum ipse eum locum amīcitiae apud eum tenēret, nēminem exīstimātūrum, nōn suā voluntāte factum ; quā ex rē futū-rum, utī tōtīus Galliae animī ā sē āverterentur.*

Haec cum plūribus verbīs flēns ā Caesare peteret,
15 Caesar eius dextram prēndit; cōnsōlātus rogat, fīnem ōrandī faciat; tantī eius apud sē grātiam esse ostendit, utī

---

minimum : *32*, and *118, b*.   **adulēscentiam** : 'his youth.' Dum-norix apparently was considerably younger than Diviciacus.

6. **per sē crēvisset** : '(Dumnorix) had increased (in resources and strength) through his help.' *123, a*.   **quibus** : 'and these.' *167*. **opibus** : 'resources.' Why ablative? *131, c*.

7. **ad minuendam grātiam** : 'to lessen his (Diviciacus's) popu-larity.' *230*, (3).   **perniciem** : 'destruction.'

9. **frāternō** : i.e. *frātris* ; 'by affection for his brother,' we should say.   **exīstimātiōne vulgī** : 'by public opinion.' How lit.? *6, b*.

10. **Quod** : *118, d*.   **eī** : = *Dumnorīgī*.   **ā Caesare** : 'at the hands of Caesar.'   **accidisset** : *218*, (1), b.

11. **cum** : 'while.'   **eum . . . eum** : 'such a relation of friend-ship with Caesar.' How lit.?

12. **nōn factum** [esse] : 'that it was not done,' after *exīstimātūrum* [esse]. *213, a*.   **suā voluntāte** : *136, c*. B. 220, 3; H. 473, 3. **futūrum** [esse] : 'it would come about'; the subject is *utī . . . āverterentur*. *203*, (1).

14. **cum . . . peteret** : *185, c*.   **plūribus verbīs** : 'with very many words ; so we often say, 'at great length.' *138*.   **flēns** : *226, a*, and *227, b*.

15. **dextram** : 'right hand.'   **prēndit** : 'grasped.'   **cōnsōlā-tus rogat** : 'reassuring (Diviciacus) he asked (him).' *61, a*, (1), and *226, c*.

16. **ōrandī** : 'of his pleading.' *230, (1).   **faciat** : 'to make.' *200, a*. B. 295, 8; A. 565, *a*; H. 565, 4.   **tantī . . . esse** : 'that his (Diviciacus's) influence with himself (*sē* refers to Caesar) was so great,' lit. 'of so great account.' *101*. B. 203, 3; A. 417; H. 448, 1.

et reī pūblicae iniūriam et suum dolōrem eius voluntātī
ac precibus condōnet.

Dumnorīgem ad sē vocat, frātrem adhibet; quae in eō
reprehendat, ostendit; quae ipse intellegat, quae cīvitās 20
querātur, prōpōnit; monet, ut in reliquum tempus omnēs
suspīciōnēs vītet; praeterita sē Dīviciācō frātrī condōnāre
dīcit.

Dumnorīgī cūstōdēs pōnit, ut, quae agat, quibuscum
loquātur, scīre possit.   25

Caesar plans to crush the Helvetians by a double surprise.

21. Eōdem diē ab explōrātōribus certior factus, hostēs
sub monte cōnsēdisse mīlia passuum ab ipsīus castrīs octō,

---

17. **et ... et**: *233, a.*   **reī pūblicae**: *102.*   **eius voluntātī**:
'in response to his wishes'; dative of indirect object on account of the
meaning 'give' or 'present' in *con-dōnet*. *104, a.*

18. **condōnet**: 'he would disregard.' *177, b.*

19. **frātrem adhibet**: 'he had the brother (Diviciacus) present.'
238, a.   **quae**: *48, a.*

20. **reprehendat**: 'he objected to.' *204, (2).*   **intellegat**:=
sciat.   **cīvitās**: i.e. of the Aeduans, whose agreement to furnish
grain had been broken.

21. **monet**: 'he warned (Dumnorix).'   **in reliquum tempus**:
'for the future.'

22. **vītet**: 'he should avoid.' *199, a.*   **praeterita**: neuter
plural, 'the past.' *154, a.*   **Dīviciācō frātrī**: dative, but trans.,
'for the sake of Diviciacus, his brother.' *104, a.*

24. **cūstōdēs**: 'watches,' corresponding with the detectives of our
day; for Dumnorix was not imprisoned.   **agat**: *204, (2).*   **quibuscum**: *125, c.*

21. 1. **Eōdem diē**: 'on the same day,' that he had summoned
the council of Gallic leaders in camp (chap. 16, ll. 10–11), and had
had the interviews with Diviciacus and Dumnorix.   **explōrātōribus**: *327.*   **hostēs. . . octō**: *213, a.* The Helvetians were now
in the valley of the Liger (*Loire*), southeast of Bibracte; see Map 1.

2. **sub monte**: 'at the foot of an elevation.' *124, a.*   **cōnsēdisse**: 'had encamped.'   **mīlia passuum**: *118, a,* and *243, a, b.*

quālis esset nātūra montis et quālis in circuitū ascēnsus,
quī cognōscerent, mīsit.   Renūntiātum est, facilem esse.
5   Dē tertiā vigiliā Titum Labiēnum, lēgātum prō praetōre,
cum duābus legiōnibus et eīs ducibus, quī iter cognōverant,

Figure 45. — Typical ridge in France, like that seized by Labienus.

3. **quālis esset**: *204*, (3).   **in circuitū ascēnsus**: 'the ascent
from the opposite side,' lit. 'in the going around.'   Caesar planned a
flank movement, with a surprise attack upon the Helvetians from two
sides at once ; a Roman force, following a circuitous route, would from
the rear secretly ascend the height at the foot of which the Helvetians
were encamped, and charge down upon them from above, while Caesar
with the rest of the army attacked them in front.

4. **cognōscerent**: *193*, *a*.   **mīsit**: sc. *explōrātōrēs* as antecedent of *quī*.   **esse**: sc. *eum* (= *ascēnsum*).

5. **dē tertiā vigiliā**: *242*, *c* and *d*.   **prō praetōre**: when a lieutenant was given a special responsibility, to act outside the presence
of the commander, he was called 'lieutenant in place of the general,' or
as we say 'second in command.'   *313*.

6. **eīs ducibus**: 'with those as guides,' referring to the patrols
previously sent out.

summum iugum montis ascendere iubet; quid suī cōnsiliī
sit, ostendit. Ipse dē quārtā vigiliā eōdem itinere, quō
hostēs ierant, ad eōs contendit equitātumque omnem ante
sē mittit.   10

P. Cōnsidius, quī reī mīlitāris perītissimus habēbātur, et
in exercitū L. Sullae, et posteā in M. Crassī, fuerat, cum
explōrātōribus praemittitur.

Through false information the plan miscarries.

22. Prīmā lūce, cum summus mōns ā Labiēnō tenērētur,
ipse ab hostium castrīs nōn longius mīlle et quīngentīs
passibus abesset, neque, ut posteā ex captīvīs comperit,
aut ipsīus adventus aut Labiēnī cognitus esset, Cōnsidius
equō admissō ad eum accurrit, dīcit *montem, quem ā* 5
Labiēnō occupārī voluerit, ab hostibus tenērī; id sē ā Galli-

---

7. **summum iugum montis** : 'the highest ridge of the elevation,'
which was apparently long and uneven (Fig. 45).   **ascendere** : 'to
ascend.' *81*, and *200, b*.   **quid suī cōnsiliī sit** : 'what his plan
was,' lit. 'what is of his plan.' *94, d*. B. 198, 3 ; A. 343, *b* ; H. 447.

8. **dē quārtā vigiliā** : *242, c, d*.   **itinere, quō** : *134, a*. B. 218,
9 ; A. 429, *a*.

9. **equitātum** : the cavalry were to feel out the enemy. *328*.

11. **reī mīlitāris** : 'in the art of war.' *21, b*, and *102*. B. 204, 1 ;
A. 349, *a* ; H. 451, 1.   **perītissimus** : *153, a*, and *148, c*. This
favorable characterization of Considius is presented as a reason for
having sent so unreliable an officer on so important a reconnoiter.

12. **L. Sullae, M. Crassī** : both of high repute as generals, Sulla
for his services first in the war with Jugurtha in Africa, then in the
Social War, and in the East ; Crassus, for his decisive defeat of Spartacus (chap. 40, l. 17, and N.). *19, a*.   **M. Crassī** : sc. *exercitū*.

22. 1. **Prīmā lūce** : 'At daybreak.' *152, a*. B. 241, 1 ; A. 293 ;
H. 497, 4. As it was now not far from July 1, daybreak was about
four o'clock.   **summus** : *152, a*.

3. **passibus** : *129, a*.   **abesset, cognitus esset** : *185, c*.   **neque** :
233, a.   **captīvīs** : 'prisoners.'   **comperit** : 'he ascertained.'

5. **equō admissō** : *144, b*, (7).   **accurrit** : 'hastened.' How lit. ?

6. **occupārī** : *occupō*, meaning 'seize,' 'take posseʰsion of,' is

cīs armīs atque īnsignibus cognōvisse. Caesar suās cōpiās
in proximum collem subdūcit, aciem īnstruit.

Labiēnus, ut erat eī praeceptum ā Caesare, nē proelium
10 committeret, nisi ipsīus cōpiae prope hostium castra vīsae
essent, ut undique ūnō tempore in hostēs impetus fieret,
monte occupātō, nostrōs exspectābat proeliōque abstinēbat.

Multō dēnique diē per explōrātōrēs Caesar cognōvit, et
montem ā suīs tenērī et Helvētiōs castra mōvisse et Cōn-
15 sidium, timōre perterritum, quod nōn vīdisset, prō vīsō sibi
renūntiāvisse.

Eō diē, quō cōnsuērat intervāllō, hostēs sequitur, et mīlia
passuum tria ab eōrum castrīs castra pōnit.

---

generally much stronger than its English derivative "occupy."   *81.*
voluerit: *214, a.*   **Gallicīs armīs**: *349.*

Figure 46. — Gallic helmets.

7. īnsignibus: ' decorations,'
used especially of the crests of helmets. Two Gallic helmets are
shown in Fig. 46.

8. collem: ' hill.'   *14, b.*
subdūcit: ' led up.'   **aciem īnstruit**: 'drew up a line of battle.'
337, a.

9. erat eī praeceptum: ' he
had been ordered '; lit. ' it had been
ordered to him '; the subject is *nē

proelium committeret.* *73, d,* and *199, b.*   B. 295, 1 ; A. 566 ; H. 565.

10. nisi . . . vīsae essent: *218,* (1), b.   **prope**: ' near.' *122, a.*

11. impetus: ' an attack.' *20, a, b.*   **fieret**: subjunctive of
purpose.

12. nostrōs: the troops with Caesar. *154, a.*   **proeliō**: *127, a.*
B. 214, 2 ; A. 401 ; H. 464.

13. Multō diē: ' Late in the day '; ablative of time.   **per**: *123, a.*

15. timōre: ' fear,' used especially of a cowardly fear. *11, d.*
perterritum: 'thoroughly frightened.' *79, b.*   **quod**: as antecedent supply *id,* object of *renūntiāvisse. 160, c.*   **prō vīsō**: ' as
seen.' *154, a.*

17. quō cōnsuērat intervāllō: = *eō intervāllō, quō sequī cōn-*

committere proelium — join battle
suō — sive — either — or

Caesar turns to go to Bibracte for supplies; the Helvetians attack his marching column on the rear.

23. Postrīdiē eius diēī, quod omnīnō bīduum supererat, cum exercituī frūmentum mētīrī oportēret, et quod ā Bibracte, oppidō Aeduōrum longē maximō et cōpiōsissimō, nōn amplius mīlibus passuum XVIII aberat, reī frūmentāriae prōspiciendum exīstimāvit; iter ab Helvētiīs āvertit ac 5 Bibracte īre contendit.

Ea rēs per fugitīvōs L. Aemiliī, decuriōnis equitum Gallōrum, hostibus nūntiātur. Helvētiī, seu quod timōre perterritōs Rōmānōs discēdere ā sē exīstimārent, eō magis quod prīdiē, superiōribus locīs occupātīs, proelium nōn 10

---

suērat (cōnsuēverat), but trans. 'at the usual interval'; this was five or six miles (chap. 15, ll. 15–16). *138*, and *165, c.*   **mīlia passuum**: *118, a*, and *243, a.*

23. 1. Postrīdiē eius diēī: 'the next day.' *94, c.*   **bīduum supererat**: 'two days remained.' *79, b.*

2. **cum**: trans. freely, 'before.' *185, c.*   **mētīrī**: *61, a*, (4). **oportēret**: *73, a, b.*

3. **Bibracte**: *16, c*, and Vocab.; also Fig. 41.   **oppidō**: *91, a*, and *293, b.*   **longē**: *153, b.*   **cōpiōsissimō**: 'wealthiest.' *75, f.*

4. **mīlibus**: *129, a*, and *243, b.* How many English miles?   **reī frūmentāriae**: 'the supply of grain,' or 'supplies.' *105.*

5. **prōspiciendum** [esse]: 'that he ought to provide for.' How lit.? *73, e.*

6. **Bibracte**: here accusative. *119, a.* B. *182, 1, a*; A. *427, 2*; H. *418.*

7. **fugitīvōs**: 'runaway slaves'; deserters from an army were called *perfugae* (I. 28, l. 4). *74, g.*   **L.**: *19, a.* Lucius Aemilius was a Roman officer in charge of a squad of Gallic horsemen.   **decuriōnis**: 'decurion.' *309, c.*

9. **exīstimārent**: *183, a.* B. *286, 1*; A. *592, 3*; H. *588, II.* **eō magis**: 'all the more on this account,' *eō* being explained by the following *quod*-clause. *135, a.* B. *219*; A. *404*; H. *475.*

10. **prīdiē**: 'on the day before.'   **superiōribus locīs occupātīs**: 'having seized a higher position,' referring to the exploit of Labienus with two legions (chap. 21, ll. 5–8). How lit.? *144, b*, (5).

commīsissent, sīve eō, quod rē frūmentāriā interclūdī posse
cōnfīderent, commūtātō cōnsiliō atque itinere conversō,
nostrōs ā novissimō agmine īnsequī ac lacessere coepērunt.

*Romans and Helvetians prepare for battle, the Romans on
sloping ground. The Helvetians advance.*

24. Postquam id animum advertit, cōpiās suās Caesar
in proximum collem subdūcit equitātumque, quī sustinēret
hostium impetum, mīsit.

Ipse interim in colle mediō triplicem aciem īnstrūxit
5 legiōnum quattuor veterānārum; atque suprā sē in summō
iugō duās legiōnēs, quās in Galliā citeriōre proximē cōn-

---

11. **rē**: *127, a*. **interclūdī**: 'be cut off from.' **posse**: sc.
Rōmānōs.

12. **cōnfīderent**: 'were confident.' **commūtātō, conversō**:
trans. 'having changed,' 'having reversed;' or, 'changing,' 'reversing.'
How lit.? *144, a*, and *239, c*.

13. **ā**: *126, c*. **agmine**: derivation? *74, d*, and Vocab.

24. 1. **Postquam**: 'After.' *188*. **id**: why accusative? *113, c*.

2. **collem**: the hill of Armecy (ar'me-ci), about 16 English miles
southeast of Mt. Beuvray, the site of ancient Bibracte, and not far from
the village of Montmort. See Map 3, **A**. **sustinēret**: *193, a*, and
328. B. 282, 2; A. 531, 2; H. 590.

4. **interim**: 'meanwhile,' while the cavalry were holding back the
enemy; it must have taken Caesar at least two hours to change over
his marching column, which was five or six miles long, into battle lines.
in colle mediō: *152, a*. B. 241, 1; A. 293; H. 497, 4. **triplicem
aciem**: the four legions stood side by side, with the cohorts of each
legion arranged in three lines (*337, a*). The triple line was not
straight, but followed the contour of the hillside, and was about an
English mile in length; see Map 3, **B–B**.

5. **legiōnum**: *98, a*. **veterānārum**: 'veteran.' What four
legions are meant? *307, e*. **suprā sē**: Caesar was near the front.
summō: *152, a*.

6. **legiōnēs . . . cōnscrīpserat**: the 11th and 12th legions; see
chap. 10, ll. 10–11, and *284*. **proximē**: *35*.

scrīpserat, et omnia auxilia collocārī ac tōtum montem
hominibus complērī, et intereā sarcinās in ūnum locum
cōnferrī et eum ab eīs, quī in superiōre aciē cōnstiterant,
mūnīrī iussit.   10

Figure 47. — Site of the battle with the Helvetians.

View from the hill where Caesar's army was posted, looking toward the right. The
hill on which Caesar took up his position, and the height to which the Helvetians retreated,
are similar to this hill in formation and appearance,

---

7. **auxilia**: *308*.   **ac**: 'and (thus).'   **tōtum montem**: 'the
entire upper part' of the hill; see N. to chap. 2, l. 10, *monte Iūrā*.

8. **hominibus**: *131, b*.   **complērī**: 'be completely filled.' By
occupying the gently rounding crest of the hill (cf. Fig. 47) Caesar
strengthened his position in case his battle lines, posted halfway up the
slope, should be forced back.   **intereā**: 'in the meantime,' while
the troops were taking their positions.   **sarcinās**: 'packs.' *330*.

9. **eīs**: the two raw legions mentioned in l. 6.

10. **mūnīrī**: 'be fortified,' by a trench and a rampart formed from
the earth thrown out of the trench. The trench, which for a part of
the distance was double, has been traced by excavations; the earthen
rampart has disappeared. The line of defense thus hastily made on the
highest part of the hill was semicircular in shape (Map 3, **A**).

Helvētiī, cum omnibus suīs carrīs secūtī, impedīmenta in ūnum locum contulērunt; ipsī, cōnfertissimā aciē reiectō nostrō equitātū, phalange factā sub prīmam nostram aciem successērunt.

The Romans charge, forcing the Helvetians back.

25. Caesar, prīmum suō, deinde omnium ex cōnspectū remōtīs equīs, ut, aequātō omnium perīculō, spem fugae tolleret, cohortātus suōs proelium commīsit.

---

11. **secūtī**: *226, c.*   **impedīmenta**: 'baggage.'   After the Helvetian fighting men turned back in order to attack Caesar, the long line of carts turned and came back also and formed a great corral, or laager, probably at the spot marked "Helvetian Corral" on Map 3. *74, d.*

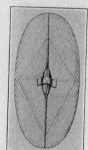

Figure 48. — Gallic shield.

Of wickerwork, with metallic boss; about four and a half English feet in height and twenty-five inches wide. Shown on a life-size statue of a Gallic warrior.

12. **ipsī**: the fighting men, as distinguished from the old men, women, and children with the baggage. **cōnfertissimā aciē**: 'by (their) very close formation.' *131, a.*   **reiectō**: 'hurled back and.' How lit.? *144, b,* (2).

13. **phalange factā**: the Gauls, forming in 'a compact mass,' probably fifteen to twenty men deep, moved forward slowly but with almost irresistible momentum; those in the front rank held their large shields (Fig. 48) so that these would overlap, presenting a firm barrier to the enemy. *18, f.*   **sub**: the Helvetians advanced uphill, and so 'up against' the first line. *124, a.*

14. **successērunt**: 'pressed forward'; see Map 3, **E–E.**

25. 1. **suō**: sc. *equō remōtō. 144, b,* (2). **deinde**: *237, b.*   **omnium equīs**: 'the horses of all' the mounted officers and Caesar's staff, not of the cavalry. According to Plutarch Caesar said that after he had won the victory he should need the horse for the pursuit of the enemy.

2. **aequātō**: 'by equalizing.' *144, b,* (6).

3. **tolleret**: *196, a.*   **cohortātus**: 'having harangued,' or 'harangued and.' It was customary for Roman commanders to address their soldiers just before going into action. *228, a.*

MAP 3

THE BATTLE WITH THE HELVETIANS

Book I, 24–26   To face page 60

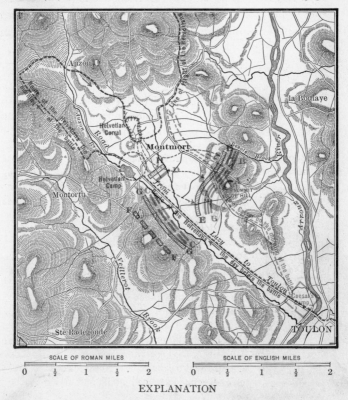

SCALE OF ROMAN MILES   SCALE OF ENGLISH MILES

0   ½   1   ½   2   0   ½   1   ½   2

EXPLANATION

On the day before the battle the Helvetians probably crossed the Arroux at Toulon and encamped near Montmort; a part of the site of the camp is now covered by a pond. Caesar, following, encamped near the Arroux.

A. Semicircular trench hastily dug by the XIth and XIIth legions on the hill (chap. 24, ll. 5–10).

B–B. The four veteran legions in battle order, three lines, first position.

C–C. First and second Roman lines, second position (chap. 25, ll. 21–23).

D. Third Roman line, second position, facing the Boians and Tulingians.

E–E. First position of the Helvetians (chap. 24, ll. 12–14).

F–F. Second position of the Helvetians, on a height (chap. 25, ll. 12–15).

G–G. Third position of the Helvetians, resuming the attack (chap. 25, ll. 18–20).

H. Boians and Tulingians (chap. 25, ll. 15–18).

Mīlitēs, ē locō superiōre pīlīs missīs, facile hostium
phalangem perfrēgērunt. Eā disiectā, gladiīs dēstrictīs in 5
eōs impetum fēcērunt.

Gallīs magnō ad pugnam erat impedīmentō, quod, plūribus
eōrum scūtīs ūnō ictū pīlōrum trānsfīxīs et colligātīs, cum
ferrum sē inflexisset, neque ēvellere neque, sinistrā impedītā,
satis commodē pugnāre poterant, multī ut, diū iactātō brac- 10

---

4. **pīlīs missīs**: 'hurling their pikes,' with precision and terrible
effect, 'from their higher position' on the slope. *322, d*, and *144, b*, (6).

5. **perfrēgērunt**: 'broke up.'   **Eā ... dēstrictīs**: 'Having
thrown this (formation) into disorder they drew their swords and.'
How lit.? *322, (e)*.

6. **impetum fēcērunt**: 'charged.' The first-line soldiers probably
allowed the Helvetians to approach within 60 feet before hurling their
pikes and charging.

7. **Gallīs ... impedīmentō**: 'a great hindrance' (lit. 'for a great
hindrance'), 'to the Gauls.' *112, b*. B. 191, 2, *a*; A. 382, 1; H. 433.
ad pugnam: 'in fighting.'   **erat**: the subject is the following
quod-clause. *198, b*.

8. **scūtīs**: 'shields' (Fig. 48).   **ūnō ictū pīlōrum**: 'by the
blow of a single pike,' we should say. *92, a*.   **trānsfīxīs et colligātīs**: 'pierced and pinned together.' *144, b*, (2).

9. **ferrum**: the 'iron' of the pike (*322, d*) was long enough to
pierce two or more overlapping shields, and was of soft metal, so that it

Figure 49. — The "iron" of a pike.

The pike was carried by one of Caesar's soldiers, and the iron was bent in action; it
was found at Alesia. The length is 22¾ inches, including the barbed point.

would bend easily; the hard barbed point also hindered withdrawal
(Fig. 49).   **sē inflexisset**: 'had become bent.' *185, c*.   **ēvellere**:
'to pull (it) out.'   **sinistrā impedītā**: 'since the left hand,' which
carried the shield, 'was hampered.' *144, b*, (3).

10. **satis commodē**: 'to advantage.' How lit.?   **multī**: emphatic position; subject of *praeoptārent*. *353, d*.   **ut**: 'so that.'
iactātō bracchiō: 'having jerked their arms back and forth' in the
effort to pull the bent pike iron out of their shields. How lit.?
144, b, (2).

chiō, praeoptārent scūtum manū ēmittere, et nūdō corpore
pugnāre. Tandem vulneribus dēfessī, et pedem referre et,
quod mōns suberat circiter mīlle passuum spatiō, eō sē
recipere coepērunt.

15   Captō monte et succēdentibus nostrīs, Boiī et Tulingī,
quī hominum mīlibus circiter XV agmen hostium claudēbant et novissimīs praesidiō erant, ex itinere nostrōs ab

---

11. **praeoptārent**: 'preferred.'   **manū**: *127, a.*   **ēmittere**:
'to drop.'   **nūdō**: 'unprotected' by a shield.   **corpore**: *13, f,*
and *144, b*, (7).

12. **vulneribus**: *13, e*, and *135, a.*   **dēfessī**: 'exhausted.'
pedem referre: 'to fall back.' *69, b*, and *79, d.*

13. **mōns suberat**: 'there was a height near by,' southwest of
the hill of Armecy; see Map 3. *66, a.*   **mīlle**: *38, a.*   **spatiō**:
'at a distance.' *147, c.*   **eō**: adverb.   **sē recipere**: 'to
retreat.'

15. **Captō**: 'reached,' i.e. by the Helvetians; Map 3, **F–F**. *144, b*,
(2).   **Boiī et Tulingī**: see chap. 5, ll. 10–14.

16. **hominum**: *97, a.*   **mīlibus**: *131, a.*   **agmen hostium
claudēbant**: 'were at the end of the enemy's marching column.'

17. **novissimīs** (= *novissimō agminī*), **praesidiō**: *112, b.* B.
191, 2, *a*; A. 382, 1; H. 433.   **ex itinere**: 'directly after marching,' changing from marching order to fighting order as they came up.
In the morning as the long column of emigrants started out, the 15,000
Boians and Tulingians formed the vanguard. When the order passed
along the column to halt and turn back (chap. 23, l. 12), they became
the rearguard, and were several miles away when the battle commenced.
As the host of non-combatants were forming a corral with the carts,
they marched by it and reached the field of battle just as the Romans
were following the retreating Helvetians.   **ab latere apertō**: 'on
the exposed flank.' *126, c.* Since the shield was carried on the left
arm, 'the exposed side' of the soldier was the right side, whence the
expression was carried over to a body of soldiers in action. In the
present instance, the three Roman lines, still retaining, in the confusion
of battle, their distinct formation, were following the stubbornly resisting
Helvetians toward the southwest from their original position, when the
Boians and Tulingians came against them from the west, thus 'attacking' the Romans on the right flank. See Map 3, **H**.

latere apertō aggressī circumvenīre; et, id cōnspicātī, Helvētiī, quī in montem sēsē recēperant, rūrsus īnstāre et
proelium redintegrāre coepērunt.   2c

Rōmānī conversa signa bipertītō intulērunt; prīma et
secunda aciēs, ut victīs ac summōtīs resisteret, tertia, ut
venientēs sustinēret.

The Helvetians are totally defeated.   Caesar pursues the fleeing.

26. Ita ancipitī proeliō diū atque ācriter pugnātum est.
Diūtius cum sustinēre nostrōrum impetūs nōn possent,

---

18. **circumvenīre**: 'to move around them,' so as to fall upon the
Romans in the rear; sc. *coepērunt*.   **cōnspicātī**: 'perceiving.' *226, c.*

19. **rūrsus**: 'again.'   Derivation?   See Vocab.

20. **redintegrāre**: 'to renew,' again assuming the
offensive.   Map 3, **G–G**.

21. **conversa . . . intulērunt**: 'changed front and
advanced in two divisions,' one
division facing straight ahead
(*prīma et secunda aciēs*), the
other (*tertia aciēs*) facing
the Boians and Tulingians.
Strictly speaking, only the third
line changed front (Map 3, **D**);
the first and second lines were
already in position to meet the
new attack of the Helvetians
(Map 3, **C–C**). *228, a,* and
325.

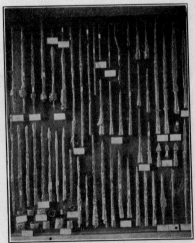

Figure 50.—Roman pike irons, found at
Alesia.

22. **victīs ac summōtīs**:
'those who had been beaten
and driven back.' *154, a,* and
227, a, (4).   **tertia**: sc. *aciēs.   91, c.*

26. 1. **ancipitī proeliō**: 'in two battles,' we should say.   How
lit.? *131, a.*   **ancipitī**: *26, b.*   **diū**: *35.*   **ācriter**: *34, a.*
pugnātum est: *73, d.*

2. **possent**: sc. *hostēs.   185, c.*   B. 288, I, B; A. 546; H. 600, II.

alterī sē, ut coeperant, in montem recēpērunt, alterī ad
impedīmenta et carrōs suōs sē contulērunt.   Nam hōc tōtō
5 proeliō, cum ab hōrā septimā ad vesperum pugnātum sit,
āversum hostem vidēre nēmō potuit.

Ad multam noctem etiam ad impedīmenta pugnātum
est, proptereā quod prō vāllō carrōs obiēcerant et ē locō
superiōre in nostrōs venientēs tēla coniciēbant, et nōn nūllī
10 inter carrōs rotāsque matarās ac trāgulās subiciēbant
nostrōsque vulnerābant.   Diū cum esset pugnātum, im-

---

3. **alterī, alterī**: 'the combatants on one side' (i.e. *Helvētiī*),
'those on the other' (*Boiī et Tulingī*).   How lit.?   *91, c,* and *154, a.*

4. **carrōs**: arranged for defense around the corral (Map 3).   Cf.
chap. 3, l. 3 and N.   **sē contulērunt**: 'retired,' still fighting; there
was no disorderly rout.   **Nam**: *237, a.*

5. **proeliō**: *147, b.*   **cum**: 'although.' *187.*   **hōrā**: *242, a.*
vesperum: 'evening.' *7, b.*

6. **āversum**: 'turned to flight.'   Caesar speaks with evident admiration of the bravery of the enemy.   **nēmō**: *12, d.*

7. **Ad multam noctem**: 'Until late at night.' *17, b,* and *152, a.*
ad: here 'at,' or 'by.'

8. **prō vāllō carrōs obiēcerant**: 'had made a rampart of the
carts' (Fig. 51).   How lit.?
locō superiōre: the top of
the carts.

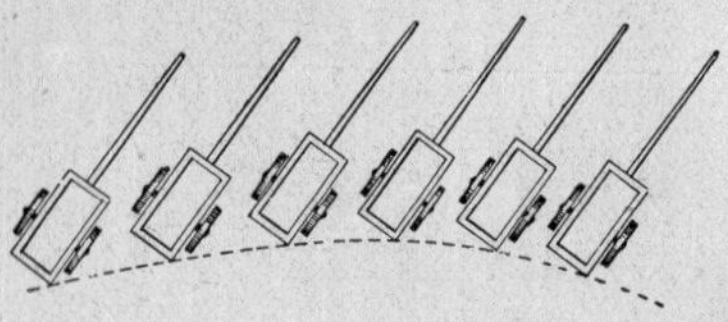

9. **coniciēbant**: 'kept
hurling.' *175, a.*

10. **rotās**: 'wheels.' These
in many cases were doubtless
solid disks of wood, which
Roman weapons would not
pierce.   **matarās ac trāgu-
lās**: 'spears and darts.' *349,* and Fig. 40.   **subiciēbant**: notice
the force of *sub-,* 'kept throwing from below' as the Roman soldiers
attacked the rampart of carts.

Figure 51.—Carts about a corral.

Arrangement of two-wheeled carts to form a
rampart for defense about an encampment.

11. **vulnerābant**: 'were wounding.'   There must have been moon-
light, or at least clear starlight, else the Gauls could not have aimed
their weapons so well.

pedimentīs castrīsque nostrī potītī sunt. Ibi Orgetorīgis
fīlia atque ūnus ē fīliīs captus est.

Ex eō proeliō circiter hominum mīlia cxxx superfuērunt
eāque tōtā nocte continenter iērunt; nūllam partem noctis 15
itinere intermissō, in fīnēs Lingonum diē quārtō pervēnērunt, cum et propter vulnera mīlitum et propter sepul-
tūram occīsōrum nostrī, trīduum morātī, eōs sequī nōn
potuissent.

Caesar ad Lingonas litterās nūntiōsque mīsit, *nē eōs frū-* 20

---

12. **castrīs**: 'encampment,' i.e. the corral. *131, c*. B. 218, 1; A.
410; H. 477. Here were the old men, the women, and the children, of
whom a large number were immediately slaughtered.

13. **ē fīliīs**: trans. as if *fīliōrum*. *97, d*. **captus est**: *172, b*.

14. **cxxx**: *centum trīgintā*. *36*, and *38, b*.

15. **nocte**: *147, c*. **iērunt**: *68, a*. **partem**: *118, a*.

16. **intermissō**: 'breaking.' How lit.? As the survivors seemingly traveled at night only during the first night, the thought in *nūllam*
. . . intermissō is substan-
tially the same as that in *eā*
. . . iērunt; such repetitions
are characteristic of dictated
matter. *275*. **fīnēs Lingonum**: more than fifty miles
north of the battlefield.

17. **cum**: *184, a*. **vulnera mīlitum**: the victory
must have cost the Romans
dearly. Roman soldiers car-
ing for wounded companions
are shown in Fig. 52. **se-
pultūram**: 'burial.'

18. **occīsōrum**: 'the
slain,' chiefly Gauls. *154, a*.

Figure 52. — Care of the wounded.

At the left a legionary, seriously wounded, sits
on a rock and two comrades are helping him to get
up. At the right another sits while his companion
binds up a wound on his leg. Ancient relief.

The number of Gauls that perished in this battle has been estimated by
some as high as 100,000, or even higher. Prompt burial was necessary
for the health of the friendly Aeduans, in whose country Caesar was.

trīduum: 'three days.' *118, a*.

20. **Lingonas**: *19, f*. **litterās**: 'letters.' **nūntiōs**: 'mes-

*mentō nēve aliā rē iuvārent; quī sī iūvissent, sē eōdem locō,
quō Helvētiōs, habitūrum.* Ipse, trīduō intermissō, cum
omnibus cōpiīs eōs sequī coepit.

The Helvetians beg for terms; one division tries to escape.

27. Helvētiī, omnium rērum inopiā adductī, lēgātōs dē
dēditiōne ad eum mīsērunt. Quī cum eum in itinere convēnissent sēque ad pedēs prōiēcissent suppliciterque locūtī
flentēs pācem petīssent, atque eōs in eō locō, quō tum
5 essent, suum adventum exspectāre iussisset, pāruērunt.

Eō postquam Caesar pervēnit, obsidēs, arma, servōs, quī
ad eōs perfūgissent, poposcit. Dum ea conquīruntur et
cōnferuntur, circiter hominum mīlia VI eius pāgī, quī
Verbigenus appellātur, sīve timōre perterritī, nē, armīs

---

sages,' to be delivered orally.   **nē:** ' (saying) that they should not.'
213, b, and *212, a,*   **eōs:** trans. as if *Helvētiōs.*

21. **iuvārent:** 'supply,' lit. 'aid.'   *216.*   B. 316; A. 588; H. 642,
4.   **quī:** *167.*   **iūvissent:** sc. *eōs,* = *Helvētiōs. 218,* (1), b.
sē . . . habitūrum: in full, *sē eōs* (= *Lingonas*) *eōdem locō, quō Helvētiōs habēret, habitūrum esse,* but trans. 'he would consider them in
the same light as the Helvetians.'   *145, c.*

27. 1. **inopiā:** 'lack.'   Why ablative ?   **lēgātōs:** 'envoys.'
2. **dēditiōne:** 'surrender.'   **Quī:** *167.*   **convēnissent:** *113, b.*
3. **sē prōiēcissent:** 'had prostrated themselves.'   **suppliciter:**
'in suppliant fashion.'

4. **flentēs:** *227, b.*   **eōs:** = *Helvētiōs,* not *lēgātōs.*
5. **essent:** See N. to *vellent,* chap. 28, l. 2.   **iussisset:** *185,
c,* and *200, b.*   **pāruērunt:** 'they obeyed.'

6. **postquam:** *188, a.*   **servōs:** 'slaves.'   **quī perfūgissent:**
'who (as he said) had fled.'   *214, b.*

7. **poposcit:** 'he demanded.'   **ea:** comprising *obsidēs, arma,*
(*fugitīvōs*) *servōs* of l. 6; neuter plural under the same rule of agreement as predicate adjectives.   *150, b.*   **conquīruntur:** 'were being
sought for.'   Why present ?   *190, a.*

8. **cōnferuntur:** *69, b.*   **VI:** = *sex.   36.*

9. **perterritī:** with *mīlia. 150, c,* and *238, h.*   **nē:** 'that.'   *202*
armīs trāditīs: 'after giving up their arms.'   *144, b,* (2).

trāditīs, suppliciō afficerentur, sīve spē salūtis inductī, quod 10
in tantā multitūdine dēditīciōrum suam fugam aut occultārī
aut omnīnō ignōrārī posse exīstimārent, prīmā nocte
ē castrīs Helvētiōrum ēgressī ad Rhēnum fīnēsque
Germānōrum contendērunt.

*Caesar deals with the fugitive Verbigens, and sends the rest (except-
ing the Boians) back to the country whence they migrated.*

28. Quod ubi Caesar resciit, quōrum per fīnēs ierant, hīs,
utī conquīrerent et redūcerent, sī sibi pūrgātī esse vellent, imperāvit; reductōs in hostium numerō habuit; reliquōs omnēs,
obsidibus, armīs, perfugīs trāditīs, in dēditiōnem accēpit.

Helvētiōs, Tulingōs, Latobrīgōs in fīnēs suōs, unde erant 5
profectī, revertī iussit; et, quod, omnibus frūgibus āmissīs,

---

10. **salūtis**: 'of safety.' *10, f.*

11. **in tantā multitūdine**: i.e. *cum* ('since') *tanta multitūdō
dēditīciōrum esset.*   **dēditīciōrum**: 'of those who had surrendered.'
occultārī: 'be kept hidden.'

12. **ignōrārī**: 'remain unnoticed.' How lit.?   **exīstimārent**:
183, b.   **prīmā**: *152, a.*

28. 1. **Quod . . . resciit**: 'Now when Caesar found this out,'
referring to the flight of the Verbigens. *167.*   **ubi**: *188, a.*   **quōrum**: precedes its antecedent *hīs*, which is in the dative after *imperāvit.* *105.*

2. **redūcerent**: 'bring (them) back.' *199, a.*   **sibi**: 'in his
sight.' *109, a.* B. 188, 1, N.; A. 376; H. 425, 4.   **pūrgātī**: 'free
from guilt.' How lit.? *221, b.* B. 328, 2; H. 612, 1.   **vellent**: in
indirect discourse as a part of the order; in the direct form, *sī vultis.* *71.*

3. **reductōs**: sc. *eōs,* 'after they had been brought back.' How
lit.? *227, a,* (4).   **in hostium numerō**: 'as enemies.' The 6000
Verbigens were probably massacred, as a terrible warning; but they
may have been sold into slavery.   **reliquōs**: *171, a.*

4. **perfugīs**: 'deserters.'   **accēpit**: *57, a.*

5. **suōs**: *157, b.*   **unde**: = *ē quibus.*   **erant profectī**: *61, a,*
(3).

6. **frūgibus āmissīs**: 'since all the produce of the fields was gone';
no crops had been planted this season. How lit.? *144, b,* (3).

domī nihil erat, quō famem tolerārent, Allobrogibus imperāvit, ut eīs frūmentī cōpiam facerent; ipsōs oppida vīcōsque,
quōs incenderant, restituere iussit.

10 Id eā maximē ratiōne fēcit, quod nōluit, eum locum, unde
Helvētiī discesserant, vacāre, nē propter bonitātem agrōrum
Germānī, quī trāns Rhēnum incolunt, ē suīs fīnibus in
Helvētiōrum fīnēs trānsīrent et fīnitimī Galliae prōvinciae
Allobrogibusque essent.

15 Boiōs, petentibus Aeduīs, quod ēgregiā virtūte erant
cognitī, ut in fīnibus suīs collocārent, concessit; quibus illī
agrōs dedērunt, quōsque posteā in parem iūris lībertātisque
condiciōnem, atque ipsī erant, recēpērunt.

---

7. **domī**: i.e. in their own country. *146.* **erat**: sc. *eīs*.
famem: 'hunger.' *15, b.* **tolerārent**: 'satisfy.' *194, a.*
8. **facerent**: 'furnish.' Why subjunctive? **oppida, vīcōs**:
how many? See chap. 5, ll. 3–4.
9. **quōs**: *163, c.* **incenderant**: when? See chap. 5.
10. **eā maximē ratiōne**: 'especially for this reason.' *161, a.*
nōluit: *71*, and *223, a.* **unde**: = *ē quō.*
11. **vacāre**: 'remain unoccupied.' **bonitātem**: 'good quality.'
76, a.
13. **trānsīrent**: *196, a.* As the Helvetians were now reduced to
about one third of their former number, much of their land must have
been left unoccupied, and was probably soon seized upon by German
immigrants. **prōvinciae**: *290.* The northernmost part of the
Province was held by the Allobroges; see Map I.
15. **Boiōs**: emphatic position; *Aeduīs* (dative after *concessit*),
*petentibus ut Boiōs in fīnibus suīs collocārent, quod (Boiī) ēgregiā
virtūte cognitī erant, (Caesar) concessit.* The Aeduans, hard pressed
in their strifes with the Sequanians, desired an accession of strength.
353, d. **virtūte**: *143, a.*
16. **collocārent**: *199, a.* **concessit**: 'he granted' the request.
quibus: trans. as if *et eīs.* *167.*
17. **quōsque**: = *et eōs.* **posteā**: after the great uprising in
Gaul, narrated in Book VII. **parem . . . atque**: 'the same' (lit.
'like') 'as.' *233, c.* B. 341, I, *c*; A. 324, *c*; H. 657, I, N.

The number of the Helvetians and their allies.

29. In castrīs Helvētiōrum tabulae repertae sunt, litterīs
Graecīs cōnfectae, et ad Caesarem relātae, quibus in tabulīs
nōminātim ratiō cōnfecta erat, quī numerus domō exīsset
eōrum, (quī arma ferre possent, et item sēparātim puerī,
senēs mulierēsque.) Quārum omnium rērum summa erat
capitum Helvētiōrum mīlia CCLXIII, Tulingōrum mīlia XXXVI,
Latobrīgōrum XIIII, Rauracōrum XXIII, Boiōrum XXXII; ex
hīs, quī arma ferre possent, ad mīlia nōnāgintā duo.

---

29. 1. castrīs: the corral, indicated on Map 3.   **tabulae:**
'tablets,' such as those generally used for business documents (Fig.
53). These were of light-colored wood, and made with a rim like that
of a slate. The surface inside the rim was coated with a thin layer of
wax, on which writing was done with a pointed stilus. The writing
appeared on the wood, which showed through wherever the stilus penetrated the wax.   **litterīs Graecīs cōnfectae:** 'written in Greek
characters,' which were used also by the Druids (VI. 14).   On account of

the antiquity of Massilia (*293, a*), the Greek
alphabet must have become familiar to the inhabitants of southern Gaul at an early date.

2. relātae: sc. *sunt. 69, b.*   **tabulīs:**
165, a.

3. nōminātim: 'by name.' *77.*   **ratiō:**
'statement.'   **quī:** *48, b.*   **domō:** *130, b.*
exīsset: *68, b,* and *204,* (2).

4. possent: *194, a.*   **puerī:** 'children.' *7, a.*

5. senēs: *18, b.*   **mulierēs:** *11, c.*
Quārum: *167.*   **rērum:** 'items,' here
used of persons; Caesar was thinking of
the numbers rather than the personality.
summa: 'the aggregate.'

Figure 53.—Writing tablets.
The four tablets contain six
pages for writing, in addition to
the two outside covers.

6. capitum Helvētiōrum: trans. as if *Helvētiōrum*; we say "so
many head" of stock, not of human beings.   **CCLXIII:** *ducenta
sexāgintā tria. 37, b,* and *d,* and *38, b.*   **XXXVI,** etc.: read in the
Latin. *36,* and *37, b.*

8. quī, etc.: i.e. *eī, quī arma ferre possent* (*194, a*), *erant,* etc.
ad: adverb, 'approximately.'

Summa omnium fuērunt ad mīlia CCCLXVIII.

10 Eōrum, quī domum rediērunt, cēnsū habitō, ut Caesar imperāverat, repertus est numerus mīlium C et X.

The Campaign against Ariovistus. 30-54

The Gallic leaders congratulate Caesar, request a conference.

30. Bellō Helvētiōrum cōnfectō, tōtīus ferē Galliae lēgātī, prīncipēs cīvitātum, ad Caesarem grātulātum convēnērunt:

Intellegere sēsē, tametsī prō veteribus Helvētiōrum iniūriīs
populī Rōmānī ab hīs poenās bellō repetīsset, tamen eam rem
5 *nōn minus ex ūsū terrae Galliae quam populī Rōmānī acci-*
disse, proptereā quod eō cōnsiliō, flōrentissimīs rēbus, domōs

---

9. **fuērunt**: plural on account of the influence of the predicate noun *mīlia*. *173, b.*   **ad**: adverb modifying *ccclxviii* (*trecenta duodē-septuāgintā*).

10. **domum**: *119, b.*   **rediērunt**: 'returned.' *68, b.*   **cēnsū**: 'a census.' *80, b.* How many of the Helvetian host failed to return?

30. 1. **Galliae**: Celtic Gaul. *287, b.*

2. **prīncipēs**: *10, b.*   **cīvitātum**: *10, f,* and *288, a,* and *b.* **grātulātum**: *231, a.*

3-11. **Direct form**: *Intellegimus,* tametsī prō veteribus Helvētiōrum iniūriīs populī Rōmānī ab hīs poenās bellō *repetieris,* tamen eam rem nōn minus ex ūsū terrae Galliae quam populī Rōmānī accidisse, proptereā quod eō cōnsiliō, flōrentissimīs rēbus, domōs suās Helvētiī *relīquērunt,* utī tōtī Galliae bellum īnferrent, etc.

3. **Intellegere sēsē, tametsī**: '(Saying) that they understood that, although.' *212, a, b,* and *c,* (1); also *213, b.*   **iniūriīs**: with two genitives, *Helvētiōrum* (95) and *populī* (102); trans. 'wrongs done to the Roman people by the Helvetians.'

4. **poenās**: 'punishment.' *92, a.*   **repetīsset**: = *repetīvisset,* 'had exacted.' *64, a,* (3), and *214, a.*   **rem**: 'achievement.'

5. **ex ūsū terrae**: 'to the advantage of the country.' How lit.? **accidisse**: 'had turned out.'

6. **eō cōnsiliō**: 'with this design,' explained by the following *utī*-clause. *138.*   **flōrentissimīs rēbus**: 'though their circum-

PLATE II   OFFICERS, STANDARD-BEARERS, AND MUSICIANS

1. Commander, *imperator*.   2. Lieutenant-general, *legatus*.
3. Centurion, *centurio*.   4. *Lictor*.   5. Standard-bearers, *signiferi*.
6. Eagle-bearer, *aquilifer*.   7. Trumpeter, *tubicen*.   8. Hornblower, *cornicen*.
9. Eagle, *aquila*.   10. Banner, *vexillum*.

*suās Helvētiī relīquissent, utī tōtī Galliae bellum īnferrent
imperiōque potīrentur, locumque domiciliō ex magnā cōpiā
dēligerent, quem ex omnī Galliā opportūnissimum ac frūctuōsissimum iūdicāssent, reliquāsque cīvitātēs stīpendiāriās* 10
habērent.

Petiērunt, utī sibi concilium tōtīus Galliae in diem certam
indīcere idque Caesaris voluntāte facere licēret; *sēsē habēre
quāsdam rēs, quās ex commūnī cōnsēnsū ab eō petere vellent.* Eā rē permissā, diem conciliō cōnstituērunt et iūre 15
iūrandō, nē quis ēnūntiāret, nisi quibus commūnī cōnsiliō
mandātum esset, inter sē sānxērunt.

---

stances were exceedingly prosperous' (Fig. 54). *144, b,* (5), and
153, a.   **domōs**: *20, c.*

7. **utī . . . habērent**: *196, a,* B. 282, 1; A. 531; H. 568.

8. **imperiō**: *74, b,* and *131, c.*   **domiciliō**: ' for habitation.' *112, a.* B. 191, 1;
A. 382; H. 425, 3.   **cōpiā**: sc. *locōrum.*

9. **opportūnissimum**: ' the most suitable.'   **frūctuōsissimum**: 'the most productive.' *75, f.*

10. **iūdicāssent**: *64, a,* (1).   **stīpendiāriās**: predicative, 'tributary (to
them).' *115, b.*

Figure 54. — Helvetian
coin.

Silver. Reverse, boar. Inscription, NINNO, probably a
name.

12. **Petiērunt, utī sibi . . . licēret**:
' they asked permission.' How lit.?   **sibi**: plural; after *licēret.* *105.*
in: ' for.'

13. **indīcere**: ' to appoint.' *222, a.*   **id**: *160, c.*   **voluntāte**:
138.   **licēret**: *73, b.*   **sēsē habēre**: *213, b.*

14. **ex commūnī cōnsēnsū**: ' in accordance with a general understanding.'   **ab eō**: *116, b.*

15. **permissā**: 'granted.'   **iūre iūrandō**: *13, h.*

16. **nē quis**: ' that no one. How lit.? *49, a,* and *168.*   **ēnūntiāret**: 'should make known (its proceedings).'   **nisi quibus**: i.e.
nisi ut eī ēnūntiārent, quibus . . . mandātum esset (impersonal),
' except those to whom the task should have been assigned.' *73, d.*

17. **inter sē sānxērunt**: ' they mutually bound themselves.'
159.

In secret session they beseech Caesar to defend Gaul against
Ariovistus, Diviciacus stating their case.

31. Eō conciliō dīmissō, īdem prīncipēs cīvitātum, quī
ante fuerant, ad Caesarem revertērunt petiēruntque, ut sibi
sēcrētō, in occultō, dē suā omniumque salūte cum eō agere
licēret. Eā rē impetrātā, sēsē omnēs flentēs Caesarī ad
5 pedēs prōiēcērunt: *Nōn minus sē id contendere et labōrāre,*
nē ea, quae dīxissent, ēnūntiārentur, quam utī ea, quae
vellent, impetrārent, proptereā quod, sī ēnūntiātum esset,
summum in cruciātum sē ventūrōs vidērent.

Locūtus est prō hīs Dīviciācus Aeduus:

---

31. 1. conciliō: where the council of the leading men of Celtic
Gaul was held we are not informed; perhaps at Bibracte.   **Īdem:**
= *eīdem. 45.*

2. fuerant: i.e. with Caesar.   **petiērunt . . . licēret:** as in
chap. 30, l. 12.

3. sēcrētō: 'privately,' as a protection against betrayal.   **in occultō:** 'in a secret place,' as a precaution against spies.   **cum eō:**
137, c.   **agere:** 'to confer.'

4. flentēs: *227, b.*   **Caesarī:** trans. as if *Caesaris. 109, a.*
B. 188, 1, N.; A. 377; H. 425, 4, N.

5–8. Direct form: Non minus id *contendimus* et *labōrāmus,* nē ea, quae
dīxerīmus, ēnūntientur, quam utī ea, quae *velīmus (220), impetrēmus,* proptereā quod, sī ēnūntiātum *erit,* summum in cruciātum *nōs ventūrōs (esse)*
vidēmus.

5. Nōn . . . vidērent: *213, b.*   **sē id contendere et labōrāre:** 'that they strove and toiled (for) this,' explained by the following *nē*-clause. *117, a.*

7. ēnūntiātum esset: impersonal; 'if disclosure should have
been made.'

8. cruciātum: 'torture.'   **ventūrōs:** *89, c.*

10–18. Direct form: Galliae tōtīus factiōnēs *sunt duae;* hārum alterius
prīncipātum *tenent Aeduī,* alterius, *Arvernī.*

Hī cum tantopere dē potentātū inter sē multōs annōs contenderent *(185, c),*
factum *est,* utī ab Arvernīs Sēquanīsque Germānī mercēde arcesserentur.
Hōrum prīmō circiter mīlia xv Rhēnum *trānsiērunt;* posteā quam agrōs et

Galliae tōtīus factiōnēs esse duās; hārum alterius prīn- 10
cipātum tenēre Aeduōs, alterius Arvernōs.

Hī cum tantopere dē potentātū inter sē multōs annōs con-
tenderent, factum esse, utī ab Arvernīs Sēquanīsque Ger-
mānī mercēde arcesserentur. Hōrum prīmō circiter mīlia XV
Rhēnum trānsīsse; posteā quam agrōs et cultum et cōpiās 15
Gallōrum hominēs ferī ac barbarī adamāssent, trāductōs
plūrēs; nunc esse in Galliā ad centum et XX *mīlium*
numerum.

---

cultum et cōpiās Gallōrum hominēs ferī ac barbarī *adamārunt* (=*adamāvē-*
runt), *trāductū sunt* plūrēs; nunc *sunt* in Galliā ad centum et XX mīlium
numerum.

10. **Galliae**: Celtic Gaul. *287, b.* For the indirect discourse
see *212, a* and *c*, (1) ; also *214, a.*   **factiōnēs**: here 'leagues' rather
than 'parties,' because made up of states.   **alterius . . . alterius**:
23, a, b, and *171, b.*   **prīncipātum**: 'headship.' *75, b.*

11. **Arvernōs**: a powerful state, southwest of the country of the
Aeduans. See Map GALLIA.

12. **dē potentātū**: 'for supremacy.'   **annōs**: *118, a.*

13. **factum esse**: the subject is *utī . . . arcesserentur*; trans.
'it had come about.' *203*, (1).   **Sēquanīs**: these entered into alliance with the Arvernians because of their hatred of the Aeduans.   The

strife between the Sequanians and the
Aeduans arose from the fact that the
Arar for a part of its course formed
the boundary between the two states,
and each claimed the exclusive right to
levy tolls on passing vessels. Among
the exports was bacon, which was
highly esteemed in Rome.

Figure 55. — Sequanian coin.

Silver. Reverse, fanciful boar;
inscription, SEQUANOIOTUOS, meaning, perhaps, 'Iotuos, the Sequanian.'

14. **mercēde**: 'for pay.' *141.*
arcesserentur: 'were brought over.'
Finding themselves worsted by the Aeduans, the Sequanians hired
Germans to fight for them (Fig. 55).

15. **trānsīsse**: *113, b.*   **posteā quam**: *188, a,* and *214, a.*

16. **ferī ac barbarī**: 'savage and uncouth.'   **adamāssent**: 'had
formed an eager desire for.' *64, a,* (1). How lit.?   **trāductōs**: *89, c.*

17. **plūrēs**: SC. *Germānōs.*   **esse**: SC. *Germānōs.*

Cum hīs Aeduōs eōrumque clientēs semel atque iterum
20 *armī contendisse; magnam calamitātem pulsōs accēpisse,*
omnem nōbilitātem, omnem senātum, omnem equitātum
āmīsisse. Quibus proeliīs calamitātibusque frāctōs, quī et
suā virtūte et populī Rōmānī hospitiō atque amīcitiā plūri-
mum ante in Galliā potuissent, coāctōs esse Sēquanīs obsidēs
25 *dare nōbilissimōs cīvitātis et iūre iūrandō cīvitātem obstrin-*
gere, sēsē neque obsidēs repetītūrōs, neque auxilium ā populō

19–28. **Direct form** : Cum hīs *Aeduī* eōrumque clientēs semel atque iterum
armīs *contendērunt;* magnam calamitātem *pulsī accēpērunt,* omnem nōbilitātem, omnem senātum, omnem equitātum *āmīsērunt.* Quibus proeliīs
calamitātibusque *frāctī,* quī et suā virtūte et populī Rōmānī hospitiō atque
amīcitiā plūrimum ante in Galliā *potuerant, coāctī sunt* Sēquanīs obsidēs dare
nōbilissimōs cīvitātis et iūre iūrandō cīvitātem obstringere, etc.

19. **clientēs** : 'dependents,' here referring to dependent states.
semel atque iterum : in our idiom, 'time and again.' How lit.?

21. **omnem nōbilitātem,** etc. : the activity of Aeduan men of rank
recorded in Book VII shows that this statement, if accurately reported,
was greatly exaggerated.   **senātum** : *289, b.*   **equitātum** : collective, 'knights,' mentioned last as the broadest term in the enumeration; apparently the 'nobles' were a subdivision of the 'knights,'
preëminent on account of aristocratic birth as well as the possession
of large resources. *288, b.*

22. **frāctōs** : 'crushed'; in agreement with *eōs* understood as subject of *coāctōs esse* and antecedent of *quī.*

23. **hospitiō** : 'relation of hospitality,' less close than the relation
implied in *amīcitia.* Both relations were established by treaties between states; when *hospitium* was established between two states, each
was bound to entertain the other's representatives at public expense.
atque : force? *233, a.*   **plūrimum,** etc. : 'had previously possessed
the greatest power.' *118, b.* See chap. 11, l. 6 and N.

24. **obsidēs** : accusative, 'as hostages.' *115, a.*

25. **nōbilissimōs** : as in chap. 7, l. 8.   **iūre iūrandō** : *13, h.*

26. **sēsē neque repetītūrōs** [esse], etc. : 'that they would neither
try to get back,' etc., the content of the oath; *sēsē . . . essent* would be
in indirect discourse even if the context were in the direct form.
213, b.

*Rōmānō implōrātūrōs, neque recūsātūrōs, quō minus perpetuō
sub illōrum diciōne atque imperiō essent.*

*Ūnum sē esse ex omnī cīvitāte Aeduōrum, quī addūcī nōn
potuerit, ut iūrāret aut līberōs suōs obsidēs daret.   Ob eam* 30
*rem sē ex cīvitāte profūgisse et Rōmam ad senātum vēnisse
auxilium postulātum, quod sōlus neque iūre iūrandō neque
obsidibus tenērētur.*

Sed peius victōribus Sēquanīs quam Aeduīs victīs acci-

---

27. **implōrātūrōs** [esse]: 'solicit.'   **recūsātūrōs** [esse]:
'refuse.'   **quō minus — essent**: 'to be'; how lit.?   *201, a.*   **perpetuō**: 'forever.'   *34, b.*

28. **illōrum**: trans. as if *Sēquanōrum.*   **diciōne**: 'sway.'

29-33. **Direct form**: *Ūnus ego sum,* ex omnī cīvitāte Aeduōrum, quī addūcī nōn *potuerim* (*194, a*), ut *iūrārem* ('to take the oath'; *199, a*) aut
līberōs *meōs* obsidēs (*115, a*) *darem.* Ob eam rem ex cīvitāte *profūgī,* et
Rōmam ad senātum *vēnī* auxilium postulātum, quod sōlus neque iūre iūrandō
neque obsidibus *tenēbar.*

29. **Ūnum sē esse**: 'That he (Diviciacus) was the only one.'

31. **profūgisse**: 'had fled.'   **Rōmam**: *119, a.*   At Rome
Diviciacus met Cicero, who was much interested in him and in what he
had to say about nature; for Diviciacus was a Druid, and the Druids
professed knowledge of the Universe (VI. 14).

32. **postulātum**: 'to demand'; a strong word, justified by the
urgency of the cause and the friendly relations between the Aeduan
state and Rome.   *231, a,* and *b.*

34-44. **Direct form**: Sed peius victōribus Sēquanīs quam Aeduīs victīs
accidit, proptereā quod Ariovistus, rēx Germānōrum, in eōrum fīnibus *cōnsēdit*
(*183, a*), tertiamque partem agrī Sēquanī, quī *est* optimus tōtīus Galliae, *occupāvit;* et nunc dē alterā parte tertiā Sēquanōs dēcēdere *iubet,* proptereā quod,
paucīs mēnsibus ante, Harūdum mīlia hominum XXIIII ad eum *vēnērunt,*
quibus locus ac sēdēs *parentur.*   Paucīs annīs omnēs ex Galliae fīnibus *pellen-
tur,* atque omnēs Germānī Rhēnum *trānsībunt;* neque enim *cōnferendus est
Gallicus* (*ager*) cum Germānōrum agrō, neque *haec cōnsuētūdō* vīctūs cum
illā *comparanda* (*est*).

34. **peius**: 'a worse fate.'   *154, a,* and *32.*   **victōribus**: here an
adjective, 'victorious.'   **victōribus . . . victīs**: *239, c.*

35 *disse, proptereā quod Ariovistus, rēx Germānōrum, in eōrum*
fīnibus cōnsēdisset tertiamque partem agrī Sēquanī, quī
esset optimus tōtīus Galliae, occupāvisset, et nunc dē alterā
parte tertiā Sēquanōs dēcēdere iubēret, proptereā quod, paucīs
mēnsibus ante, Harūdum mīlia hominum XXIIII ad eum vē-
40 *nissent, quibus locus ac sēdēs parārentur.* Futūrum esse

Figure 56. — View across the Rhine valley, in Alsace.

From the site of Ariovistus's camp, Zellenberg (Map 4), looking east toward Ostheim.
In the distance the hills east of the Rhine are visible.

---

35. **rēx**: *91, a.* **Germānōrum**: apparently Swabians (chap. 37,
l. 6). Ariovistus probably crossed the Rhine as early as 72 or 71 B.C.

37. **occupāvisset**: 'had seized,' in the rich level country west of
the Rhine, in modern Alsace. **alterā parte tertiā**: 'a second
third-part.'

38. **dēcēdere**: 'to withdraw.' *200, b.*

39. **mēnsibus**: *140.* B. 223; H. 488, 1. **Harūdum**: *19, e.*

40. **locus ac sēdēs**: 'places of habitation.' How lit.? *15, b.*
parārentur: 'were to be provided.' *193, a.* **Futūrum esse**: 'it
would come about'; the subject is the following *utī*-clause. *203, (1).*

*paucīs annīs, utī omnēs ex Galliae fīnibus pellerentur atque
omnēs Germānī Rhēnum trānsīrent; neque enim cōnferendum esse Gallicum cum Germānōrum agrō, neque hanc
cōnsuētūdinem vīctūs cum illā comparandam.*

Ariovistum autem, ut semel Gallōrum cōpiās proeliō vī- 45
*cerit, quod proelium factum sit Admagetobrigae, superbē
et crūdēliter imperāre, obsidēs nōbilissimī cuiusque līberōs
poscere, et in eōs omnia exempla cruciātūsque ēdere, sī qua*

---

41. **annīs**: *147, a.*   **omnēs**: sc. *Gallī.*

43. **cōnferendum esse**: *229, c.*   **Gallicum**: sc. *agrum.* Caesar
means that the land in Gaul is incomparably better than that in Germany; we usually state such comparisons in the opposite way.

44. **cōnsuētūdinem vīctūs**: 'standard of living.'   **illā**: 'that
(of the Germans).' The civilization of the Gauls was at this time
far superior.   **comparandam**: *89, c.*

45–55. **Direct form**: *Ariovistus* autem, ut semel Gallōrum cōpiās proeliō
vīcit, quod proelium factum *est* Admagetobrigae, superbē et crūdēliter *imperat,* obsidēs nōbilissimī cuiusque līberōs *poscit,* et in eōs omnia exempla
cruciātūsque *ēdit,* sī qua rēs nōn ad nūtum aut ad voluntātem eius facta *est.
Homō est barbarus, īrācundus, temerārius;* non *possunt* eius imperia diūtius
sustinērī. Nisi quid in *tē* populōque Rōmānō *erit* auxiliī, omnibus Gallīs
idem *est* faciendum, quod Helvētiī *fēcērunt,* ut domō ēmigrent, aliud domicilium, aliās sēdēs, remōtās ā Germānīs, petant, fortūnamque, quaecumque
accidat, experiantur.

45. **Gallōrum**: the Aeduans and their allies.   **vīcerit, imperāre,**
etc.: representing perfects and presents in the direct form, used for
vividness; the pluperfect and perfect or imperfect in the direct form
might have been expected, and in translation past tenses should be used.

46. **quod proelium**: 'a battle which.' *165, a.*   **Admagetobrigae**: according to the probable meaning of the Gallic name, 'at
the stronghold of Admagetos'; where the place was we do not know.
The battle was perhaps fought in 61 or 60 B.C. *146.*   **superbē et
crūdēliter**: 'with arrogance and cruelty.'

47. **nōbilissimī cuiusque**: 'of every man of rank.' *170, a.* B.
252, 5, *c*; A. 313, *b*; H. 515, 2.

48. **in**: 'upon.'   **exempla**: 'kinds of punishment,' as warning
examples to others.   **cruciātūs**: 'tortures,' as indicating one kind
of punishment resorted to by Ariovistus.   **ēdere**: 'inflicted.'
qua: *49, a,* and *168.*

rēs nōn ad nūtum aut ad voluntātem eius facta sit.   Homi-
50 *nem esse barbarum, īrācundum, temerārium ; nōn posse eius*
imperia diūtius sustinērī.   Nisi quid in Caesare populōque
Rōmānō sit auxiliī, omnibus Gallīs idem esse faciendum,
quod Helvētiī fēcerint, ut domō ēmigrent, aliud domicilium,
aliās sēdēs, rēmōtās ā Germānīs, petant, fortūnamque, quae-
55 *cumque accidat, experiantur.*

Haec sī ēnūntiāta Ariovistō sint, nōn dubitāre, quīn dē
omnibus obsidibus, quī apud eum sint, gravissimum suppli-
cium sūmat.   Caesarem, vel auctōritāte suā atque exercitūs,
vel recentī victōriā, vel nōmine populī Rōmānī, dēterrēre
60 *posse, nē maior multitūdō Germānōrum Rhēnum trādūcātur,*
Galliamque omnem ab Ariovistī iniūriā posse dēfendere.

---

49. **ad nūtum** : 'at his beck,' at the slightest intimation of his desires.
50. **īrācundum** : 'quick-tempered.'   **temerārium** : 'reckless.'
52. **quid — auxiliī** : 'some help.'   *97, b.*   **Gallīs**, etc. : 'all the Celts would have to do the same thing.'   *110,* and *229, c.*   B. 189, 1 ; A. 374 ; H. 431.   **idem** : subject of *faciendum esse*, explained by the appositive clause *ut . . . experiantur.   203,* (4).
53. **domō** : *130, b.*   **ēmigrent** : 'migrate.'
54. **quaecumque** : indefinite relative ; trans. 'endure whatever fortune might befall them.'   *50, a.*

56–61.   **Direct form** : Haec sī ēnūntiāta Ariovistō *erunt,* nōn *dubitō,* quīn dē omnibus obsidibus, quī apud eum *sint,* gravissimum supplicium sūmat. *Tū,* vel auctōritāte *tuā* atque exercitūs, vel recentī victōriā, vel nōmine populī Rōmānī, dēterrēre *potes,* nē maior multitūdō Germānōrum Rhēnum trādūcātur, Galliamque omnem ab Ariovistī iniūriā *potes* dēfendere.

56. **Haec** : the utterances at the conference, and appeal to Caesar.
nōn dubitāre : sc. *sē,* 'he (Diviciacus) had no doubt.'   **quīn . . .**
sūmat : 'that he (Ariovistus) would inflict.'   *201, c.*   B. 298 ; A. 558, *a* ; H. 595, 1.   **dē** : 'upon.'
58. **exercitūs** : '(that) of his army.'   *157, d.*
59. **dēterrēre nē**, etc. : 'prevent a larger host of Germans from being brought across the Rhine.'   How lit.?   *201, a.*
60. **Rhēnum** : why accusative?   *114, b.*   B. 179, 3 ; A. 395, N. 2 ; H. 413.
61. **Galliam** : as in l. 10.   **Ariovistī** : *95.*

The lot of the Sequanians, showing what might happen to all.

32. Hāc ōrātiōne ab Dīviciācō habitā, omnēs, quī aderant, magnō flētū auxilium ā Caesare petere coepērunt.
Animadvertit Caesar, ūnōs ex omnibus Sēquanōs nihil
eārum rērum facere, quās cēterī facerent, sed trīstēs, capite
dēmissō, terram intuērī. Eius reī quae causa esset, mīrātus, 5
ex ipsīs quaesiit. Nihil Sēquanī respondēre, sed in eādem
trīstitiā tacitī permanēre.

Cum ab hīs saepius quaereret, neque ūllam omnīnō vōcem
exprimere posset, īdem Dīviciācus Aeduus respondit:

Hōc esse miseriōrem et graviōrem fortūnam Sēquanōrum 10

---

32. 2. flētū: 'weeping.' Shedding of tears by men was much
more common among the Gauls and Romans than among us.

3. ūnōs: 'alone.' *23, a.*   **nihil**: 'none.' How lit.?

4. cēterī: *171, a.*   **facerent**: *214, a*, and *213, a.*   **trīstēs**:
'disconsolately.' *151.*   **capite dēmissō**: 'with bowed heads.'
How lit.? *144, b,* (7).

5. intuērī: 'looked upon.'   **quae**: *48, b.*   **esset**: *204,* (2).
mīrātus: *226, c.*

6. quaesiit: *116, c.*   **respondēre, permanēre**: 'answered,'
'remained.' *182.*

7. trīstitiā: 'state of dejection.'   **tacitī**: 'silent.' *148, c.*

8. saepius: 'again and again.' How lit.? *153, a.*   **quaereret**:
185, c, and *116, c.*   **neque**: = *et nōn. 233, a.*   **vōcem**: 'utterance.' *10, c.*

9. exprimere: 'to force out.'   **Aeduus**: an Aeduan is now
speaking for the Sequanians, who were formerly bitter enemies of the
Aeduans.

10–16. Direct form: Hōc *est miserior* et *gravior fortūna* Sēquanōrum
quam reliquōrum, quod sōlī nē in occultō quidem querī neque auxilium implōrāre *audent*, absentisque Ariovistī crūdēlitātem, velut sī cōram *adsit, horrent,*
proptereā quod reliquīs tamen fugae facultās *datur,* Sēquanīs vērō, quī
īntrā fīnēs suōs Ariovistum *recēpērunt,* quōrum oppida omnia in potestāte eius
sunt, omnēs cruciātūs *sunt* perferendī.

10. Hōc: 'On this account,' explained by the following *quod*-clause.
135, a.   **miseriōrem**: 'more wretched.' *22, d.*

*quam reliquōrum, quod sōlī nē in occultō quidem querī neque
auxilium implōrāre audērent, absentisque Ariovistī crūdēlitātem, velut sī cōram adesset, horrērent, proptereā quod
reliquīs tamen fugae facultās darētur, Sēquanīs vērō, quī*
15 *intrā fīnēs suōs Ariovistum recēpissent, quōrum oppida omnia
in potestāte eius essent, omnēs cruciātūs essent perferendī.*

Caesar, for reasons of state, promises his help against Ariovistus.

33. Hīs rēbus cognitīs, Caesar Gallōrum animōs verbīs
cōnfirmāvit pollicitusque est, sibi eam rem cūrae futūram;
*magnam sē habēre spem, et beneficiō suō et auctōritāte adduc-
tum Ariovistum fīnem iniūriīs factūrum.* Hāc ōrātiōne
5 habitā, concilium dīmīsit.

Et secundum ea multae rēs eum hortābantur, quārē sibi

---

11. **nē . . . quidem**: *237, c.*   B. 347; H. 656, 2.
12. **audērent**: *62.*   **absentis**: 'in his absence.'   How lit.?
crūdēlitātem: 'cruelty.'

13. **velut**: 'just as.'   **cōram**: 'in person.'   **adesset**: subjunctive also in the direct form. *210.* B. 307, 1; A. 524; H. 584.
horrērent: 'they shuddered at.'

14. **reliquīs**: 'to the rest' of the Celts. *171, a.*   **tamen**: 'at
any rate,' as a last resource.   **Sēquanīs . . . essent perferendī**:
'the Sequanians . . . had to endure.' How lit.? *229, c,* and *110.* B.
189, 1; A. 374; H. 431.

15. **oppida omnia**: exaggeration; for the Sequanians still held
Vesontio (*Besançon*), which was their strongest fortified place (chap. 38).

16. **omnēs**: as we say, 'all possible.'

33. 2. **sibi . . . futūram** [esse]: 'that this matter should have
his attention.' How lit.? *112, b.*

3. **magnam**, etc.: *213, b.*   **beneficiō suō**: Caesar's kindness
when he was consul (59 B.C.), in helping secure a recognition of
Ariovistus by the Roman senate (*255*); Caesar reminds Ariovistus of
this later (chap. 35, ll. 3–8; chap. 43, ll. 9–15).

4. **iniūriīs**: *104, a.*   **factūrum** [esse]: after *habēre spem,* used
in place of *spērāre. 213, a.*

6. **secundum**: preposition; 'besides those considerations.' *122, a,*
and *160, c.*   **quārē**: trans. as if *propter quās.*   **sibi**: *110.*

eam rem cōgitandam et suscipiendam putāret; in prīmīs,
quod Aeduōs, frātrēs cōnsanguineōsque saepe numerō ā
senātū appellātōs, in servitūte atque diciōne vidēbat Germānōrum tenērī, eōrumque obsidēs esse apud Ariovistum 10
ac Sēquanōs intellegēbat; quod in tantō imperiō populī
Rōmānī turpissimum sibi et reī pūblicae esse arbitrābātur.

Paulātim autem Germānōs cōnsuēscere Rhēnum trānsīre,
et in Galliam magnam eōrum multitūdinem venīre, populō
Rōmānō perīculōsum vidēbat; neque sibi hominēs ferōs ac 15
barbarōs temperātūrōs exīstimābat, quīn, cum omnem Galliam occupāvissent, ut ante Cimbrī Teutonīque fēcissent, in

7. cōgitandam [esse]: 'ought to be taken into consideration.'
putāret: *194, a.*   **in prīmīs**: 'first of all.' How lit.?

8. quod . . . vidēbat: *198, b.*   **frātrēs**: predicate accusative
after *appellātōs*. *88, b.*   **cōnsanguineōs**: 'kin,' implying blood-
relationship, while *frātrēs*, like our "brethren," might be used as a title
implying intimacy of relations without kinship.   The use of the title here
may imply that the Aeduans claimed descent from the Trojans, as did the
Romans, and Caesar himself. *244*, and Fig. 153.   **numerō**: with
saepe, 'repeatedly.' *142, a,* and *85.*

11. quod: '(a state of affairs) which'; the antecedent of *quod* is
the thought expressed by the infinitive clauses depending on *vidēbat*
and *intellegēbat*.   **in . . . Rōmānī**: 'in view of the greatness of the
power of the Roman people.' How lit.?

12. turpissimum: 'exceedingly disgraceful.'   *148, c,* and *153, a.*
sibi: *108, a.*

13. Paulātim, etc.: 'for the Germans gradually to become accustomed'; *Germānōs cōnsuēscere* and *multitūdinem venīre* are the subject of *esse*, 'was,' understood after *vidēbat*. *213, a.*   **autem**: 'moreover.' *236, a.*

15. perīculōsum: 'full of danger.' *148, d* ; *75, f,* and *84.*   **sibi
. . . temperātūrōs** [esse]: 'would hold back,' lit. 'restrain themselves.' *105.*

16. quīn . . . exīrent: 'from passing over.' *201, a.*

17. ut: 'as.' *188, b,* and *214, a.*   **ut . . . fēcissent**: related in
thought with *exīrent* and *contenderent*.   **Cimbrī Teutonīque**: the
terrible hordes of the Cimbrians and Teutons in the closing years of
the second century B.C. swept over Celtic Gaul and passed into the

prōvinciam exīrent atque inde in Italiam contenderent, praesertim cum Sēquanōs ā prōvinciā nostrā Rhodanus dīvi-
20 deret; quibus rēbus quam mātūrrimē occurrendum putābat.

Ipse autem Ariovistus tantōs sibi spīritūs, tantam arrogantiam sūmpserat, ut ferendus nōn vidērētur.

Caesar invites Ariovistus to a conference; he is rebuffed.

34. Quam ob rem placuit eī, ut ad Ariovistum lēgātōs
mitteret, quī ab eō postulārent, utī aliquem locum, medium
utrīusque, colloquiō dēligeret: *Velle sēsē dē rē pūblicā et
summīs utrīusque rēbus cum eō agere.*

5   Eī lēgātiōnī Ariovistus respondit:

Province, whence the Cimbrians made their way into Cisalpine Gaul.
Finally the Teutons were annihilated in a fierce battle at Aquae Sextiae
(now Aix), about 20 miles north of Massilia, by Gaius Marius in
102 B.C.; and a year later the Cimbrians met a similar fate at Vercellae,
in Cisalpine Gaul, northeast of Turin.   See Map GALLIA.

18. **Italiam**: here including Cisalpine Gaul. *283, b.*   **praesertim cum**: *184, b.*

19. **Sēquanōs**: *282.*   **Rhodanus**: '(only) the Rhone,' a slight
protection against an invading host.

20. **quibus rēbus**: 'and these conditions.' *107, a.*   **quam
mātūrrimē**: 'at the earliest possible moment.' *34, a,* and *153, c.*
occurrendum [esse]: sc. *sibi,* 'that he ought to meet.' How lit.?

21. **tantōs spīritūs**: 'such insolent airs.' *20, b.*

22. **arrogantiam**: 'arrogance.'   **ferendus nōn**: 'unbearable.'
How lit.?

34. 1. **placuit eī**: 'he (Caesar) resolved.' How lit.?   **ut ...
mitteret**: with *placuit;* 'to send.' *199, a,* (7).

2. **postulārent**: *193, a.*   **aliquem**: *49, a.*   **medium utrīusque**:
'midway between them.' How lit.? *51,* and *102.*

3. **colloquiō**: 'for a conference.' *112, a.*   **Velle sēsē**: '(stating) that he wished.' *213, b.*

4. **summīs utrīusque rēbus**: 'affairs of the utmost importance to
both.' How lit.?

6–13. **Direct form**: Sī quid *mihi* ā Caesare opus esset, ad eum *vēnissem;*
sī quid ille *mē vult,* illum ad *mē* venīre *oportet.*

*Sī quid ipsī ā Caesare opus esset, sēsē ad eum ventūrum
fuisse; sī quid ille sē velit, illum ad sē venīre oportēre.*

*Praetereā, sē neque sine exercitū in eās partēs Galliae
venīre audēre, quās Caesar possidēret, neque exercitum sine
magnō commeātū atque mōlīmentō in ūnum locum contrahere* 10
posse.

Figure 57.— Pottery found at Bibracte; Museum of St. Germain.

Praetereā, neque sine exercitū in eās partēs Galliae, quās Caesar *possidet*,
venīre *audeō*, neque exercitum sine magnō commeātū atque mōlīmentō in
ūnum locum contrahere *possum*.

Mihi autem mīrum *vidētur*, quid in *meā* Galliā, quam bellō *vīcī*, aut
Caesarī aut omnīnō populō Rōmānō negōtiī *sit.*

6. **Sī . . . fuisse**: *208, c.*   **quid**, etc.: 'he himself had wanted
anything.' How lit.? *132, b.*   **ipsī**: *46.*

7. **quid sē**: 'anything of himself,' Ariovistus. *116, d.*

8. **Praetereā**: 'furthermore.' Ariovistus was seemingly over
near the Rhine, a long distance from Caesar, who was probably in the
vicinity of Bibracte.

9. **possidēret**: 'was occupying.'

10. **commeātū**: 'store of supplies.'   **mōlīmentō**: 'trouble' in

Sibi autem mīrum vidērī, quid in suā Galliā, quam bellō vīcisset, aut Caesarī aut omnīnō populō Rōmānō negōtiī esset.

Caesar through envoys makes demands of Ariovistus, and threatens.

35. Hīs respōnsīs ad Caesarem relātīs, iterum ad eum Caesar lēgātōs cum hīs mandātīs mittit:

Quoniam, tantō suō populīque Rōmānī beneficiō affectus, cum in cōnsulātū suō rēx atque amīcus ā senātū appellātus

---

accumulating supplies as well as in mobilizing his forces; for the army of Ariovistus, so long as it was scattered in small detachments, could live off the country.   **contrahere**: 'bring together.'

12. **mīrum**: 'a cause for wonder.' *148, d.*   **bellō**: *131, a.* **quid . . . esset**: subject of *vidērī*, 'what business either Caesar or,' etc. *204*, (2).

13. **aut . . . aut**: *235, a.*   **Caesarī, populō**: *111.*   **negōtiī**: *97, b.*

35. 2. **hīs mandātīs**: 'this message,' lit. 'these instructions' to the envoys, which were to be presented orally, and are here summarized. *212, c,* (4).

3–8. **Direct form**: Quoniam, tantō *meō* populīque Rōmānī beneficiō affectus, cum in cōnsulātū *meō* rēx atque amīcus ā senātū appellātus *est*, (Ariovistus) hanc *mihi* populōque Rōmānō grātiam *refert*, ut, in colloquium venīre invītātus, *gravētur*, neque dē commūnī rē dīcendum sibi et cognōscendum *putet*, haec *sunt*, quae ab eō *postulō*.

3. **Quoniam**: 'Since.'   **tantō**, etc.: 'although treated with so great kindness by himself and the Roman people.' How lit.? *157, d.*

4. **cōnsulātū suō**: in the previous year; see N. to chap. 33, l. 3. **rēx . . . senātū**: cf. chap. 3, ll. 12–13, and Notes. The truth seems to be that in the strifes between the Aeduans and Ariovistus the Roman Senate thought it the best policy to stand in well with both sides. The Senate therefore continued to profess friendship for the Aeduans, but after they sustained a crushing defeat at Admagĕtos's stronghold (chap. 31, ll. 19–28 and 46) it courted Ariovistus. To what extent Caesar was responsible for the conferring of the titles on Ariovistus in 59 B.C., we do not know.

esset, hanc sibi populōque Rōmānō grātiam referret, ut, in 5
colloquium venīre invītātus, gravārētur, neque dē commūnī
rē dīcendum sibi et cognōscendum putāret, haec esse, quae
ab eō postulāret:

Prīmum, nē quam multitūdinem hominum amplius trāns
Rhēnum in Galliam trādūceret; 10

Deinde, obsidēs, quōs habēret ab Aeduīs, redderet, Sēquanīs-
que permitteret, ut, quōs illī habērent, voluntāte eius reddere
illīs licēret; nēve Aeduōs iniūriā lacesseret, nēve hīs sociīs-
que eōrum bellum īnferret.

Sī id ita fēcisset, sibi populōque Rōmānō perpetuam grā- 15

---

5. **referret**: *183, a,* and *214, a.* **ut . . . gravārētur**: 'that he . . . raised objections'; explaining *grātiam. 203,* (4). **in**: 'to.'

6. **invītātus**: 'when he had been invited.' *227, a.* **neque . . . putāret**: 'and did not consider himself under obligation to discuss, and take under advisement, a matter of mutual interest.' How lit.?

7. **dīcendum** [esse] **sibi**: *73, e,* and *110.* **haec**: *161, a,* and *160, c.*

9–14. **Direct form**: Prīmum, (*postulō*) nē (*Ariovistus*) quam multitūdi-nem hominum amplius trāns Rhēnum in Galliam *trādūcat;*

Deinde, obsidēs, quōs *habet* ab Aeduīs, *reddat,* Sēquanīsque *permittat,* ut (obsidēs), quōs hī habent, voluntāte eius reddere illīs *liceat;* nēve Aeduōs iniūriā *lacessat,* nēve hīs sociīsque eōrum bellum *īnferat.*

9. **Prīmum**: *237, b.* **quam**: *49, a,* and *168.* **hominum**: *98, a.* **amplius**: 'in addition.' How lit.?

10. **trādūceret, lacesseret** (l. 13), **īnferret** (l. 14): *199, a.*

11. **redderet, permitteret**: sc. *ut. 200, a.*

12. **ut . . . licēret**: 'to have his (Ariovistus's) approval in return-ing (to the Aeduans the hostages) which,' etc. How lit.? *199, a,* and *73, a, b.* **voluntāte**: *138.* **reddere**: *67, c,* and *222, a.*

15–21. **Direct form**: Sī id ita *fēcerit* (future perfect), *mihi* (111) popu-lōque Rōmānō *perpetua grātia* atque *amīcitia* cum eō *erit;* sī nōn *impetrābō,* quoniam, M. Messālā, M. Pīsōne cōnsulibus, senātus *cēnsuit,* utī, quīcumque Galliam prōvinciam obtinēret, quod commodō reī pūblicae facere posset, Aeduōs cēterōsque amīcōs populī Rōmānī dēfenderet, Aeduōrum iniūriās nōn *neglegam.*

15. **fēcisset, futūram** [esse]: *218,* (1), b. **perpetuam**: 'lasting.'

*tiam atque amīcitiam cum eō futūram ; sī nōn impetrāret,
sēsē, quoniam, M. Messālā, M. Pīsōne cōnsulibus, senātus
cēnsuisset, utī, quīcumque Galliam prōvinciam obtinēret,
quod commodō reī pūblicae facere posset, Aeduōs cēterōsque*
20 *amīcōs populī Rōmānī dēfenderet, sē Aeduōrum iniūriās nōn
neglēctūrum.*

*Ariovistus replies, claiming prior rights in Gaul and defying
Caesar.*

36. Ad haec Ariovistus respondit :

*Iūs esse bellī, ut, quī vīcissent, eīs, quōs vīcissent, quem
ad modum vellent, imperārent; item populum Rōmānum*

---

17. **M. . . . cōnsulibus** : 61 B.C. *240, a,* and *238, a.*

18. **cēnsuisset** : 'decreed.' *183, a,* and *214, a.*   **utī . . . dēfenderet** : *199, a,* and *177, b.*   **quīcumque** : *50, a.*   **prōvinciam** : 'as a province.' *115, a.*

Figure 58.—Aeduan coin.

Gold. Obverse, Apollo. Reverse, Victory driving a chariot. Copied from a Greek coin of Macedonia ; the Greek name, 'Of Philip,' is retained on the reverse.

19. **quod** : 'so far as.' *194, f.* B. 283, 5 ; A. 535, *d*; H. 591, 3. **commodō reī pūblicae** : 'consistently with the public interest.' *138,* and *102.*   **Aeduōs** : Fig. 58.

20. **sē** : repeated from *sēsē* in l. 17.

21. **neglēctūrum** [esse] : 'he would not leave unnoticed,' a threat sufficiently forceful, although veiled.

36. 2-7. **Direct form** : Iūs *est* bellī, ut, quī *vīcerint* (*220*), eīs, quōs *vīcerint* (*220*), quem ad modum *velint, imperent* (*203, 4*); item *populus Rōmānus* victīs nōn ad alterius praescrīptum, sed ad suum arbitrium, imperāre *cōnsuēvit.* Sī *ego* populō Rōmānō nōn *praescrībō,* quem ad modum suō iūre *ūtātur* (*204, 3*), nōn *oportet* (*73, a*) *mē* ā populō Rōmānō in *meō* iūre impedīrī.

2. **quī** : the antecedent is the implied subject of *imperārent;* 'that those who had conquered should rule over,' etc.   **eīs** : after *imperārent.* *105.*   **quem ad modum** : 'in whatever way,' lit. 'according to which manner ': in full, *ad (eum) modum ad quem.*

victīs nōn ad alterius praescrīptum, sed ad suum arbitrium,
imperāre cōnsuēsse. Sī ipse populō Rōmānō nōn praescrī- 5
beret, quem ad modum suō iūre ūterētur, nōn oportēre sē ā
populō Rōmānō in suō iūre impedīrī.

Aeduōs sibi, quoniam bellī fortūnam temptāssent et armīs
congressī ac superātī essent, stīpendiāriōs esse factōs. Mag-
nam Caesarem iniūriam facere, quī suō adventū vectīgālia 10
sibi dēteriōra faceret. (Aeduīs sē obsidēs redditūrum nōn
esse,' neque hīs neque eōrum sociīs iniūriā bellum illātūrum,
sī in eō manērent, quod convēnisset, stīpendiumque quotan-

---

4. **victīs**: *227, a,* (4).   **ad alterius praescrīptum**: 'according
to the dictates of another.'   How lit.?   *23, b.*   **arbitrium**: 'judgment.'

5. **nōn praescrīberet**: 'should not dictate.'

6. **quem ad modum**: 'in what way'; *quem* is here interrogative.
48, b.   **suō**: 'its own.'   **ūterētur**: 'should exercise.'

7. **suō**: 'his own.'

8–15. **Direct form**: *Aeduī mihi,* quoniam bellī fortūnam *temptāvērunt*
et armīs congressī ac superātī *sunt, stīpendiāriī factī sunt.* Magnam *Caesar*
iniūriam *facit,* quī suō adventū vectīgālia *mihi* dēteriōra *faciat.* Aeduīs
obsidēs nōn *reddam ;* neque hīs neque eōrum sociīs iniūriā bellum *īnferam,*
sī in eō *manēbunt,* quod *convēnit,* stīpendiumque quotannīs *pendent ;* sī
id nōn *fēcerint* (future perfect), longē eīs frāternum nōmen populī Rōmānī
aberit.

9. **congressī** [essent] : 'had contended.'   *57, c.*   **stīpendiāriōs** :
'subject to the payment of tribute.'   *148, c.*   **Magnam** : emphatic
position.   *353, d.*

10. **quī** : 'since he.'   *194, c.*   **suō** : refers to Caesar.   **vectī-**
gālia : see N. to chap. 18, l. 10.

11. **sibi** : refers to Ariovistus.   **dēteriōra** : 'less profitable ';
with Caesar's backing the Aeduans would refuse to pay tribute to
Ariovistus.

12. **iniūriā** : 'wrongfully.'   *136, b.*   B. 220, 2 ; A. 412, *b* ; H.
474, 1.

13. **in . . . convēnisset** : 'they should abide by' (lit. 'in ') 'that
which had been agreed upon.'   **stīpendium** : 'tribute.'   **quotannīs** :
79, b.

nīs penderent; sī id nōn fēcissent, longē eīs frāternum
15 *nōmen populī Rōmānī āfutūrum.*

    Quod sibi Caesar dēnūntiāret, sē Aeduōrum iniūriās nōn neglēctūrum, nēminem sēcum sine suā perniciē contendisse. Cum vellet, congrederētur; intellēctūrum, quid invictī Germānī, exercitātissimī in armīs, quī inter annōs XIIII tēctum
20 *nōn subīssent, virtūte possent.*

Caesar hears further complaints, marches toward Ariovistus.

    37. Haec eōdem tempore Caesarī mandāta referēbantur, et lēgātī ab Aeduīs et ā Trēverīs veniēbant: Aeduī questum, quod Harūdēs, quī nūper in Galliam trānsportātī

---

14. **penderent**: 'should pay'; originally 'weigh out,' a meaning appropriate to the early time when payments were made in uncoined metal. There is a similar development of meaning in the English "pound sterling."   **longē eīs . . . āfutūrum** [esse]: 'would be far from benefiting them.'   **eīs**: dative. *109, b.*   **frāternum . . . Rōmānī**: 'the title of " Brethren of the Roman people."'

16–20. **Direct form**: Quod *mihi* Caesar dēnūntiat, sē Aeduōrum iniūriās nōn neglēctūrum, *nēmō mēcum* sine suā perniciē *contendit*. Cum *volet, congrediātur! Intelleget,* quid invictī Germānī, exercitātissimī in armīs, quī inter annōs XIIII tēctum nōn *subiērunt,* virtūte *possint*. •

16. **Quod . . . dēnūntiāret**: 'As for Caesar's warning to him,' i.e. to Ariovistus. How lit.? *198, c.*   **sē**: Caesar.

17. **suā**: 'his own,' referring to *nēminem*.

18. **congrederētur**: 'let him come on !'   *216.*   B. 316; A. 588; H. 642.   **intellēctūrum**: *eum* (= *Caesarem*) *intellēctūrum esse*. *215*.   **quid Germānī — virtūte possent**: 'what valor the Germans had.' How lit.? *118, b.*   **invictī**: 'unconquered.'

19. **exercitātissimī**: 'most thoroughly trained.'   **inter**: 'during'; with *annōs,* stronger than the simple accusative of time. **XIIII**: *36,* and *38, b.*   **tēctum**: 'roof.'

20. **subīssent**: *113, b.*   **virtūte**: *142, a.*

37. 2. **Aeduī**: sc. *veniēbant*.   **questum**: *231, a,* and *61, a,* (3).

3. **Harūdēs**: chap. 31, ll. 39–40.   **trānsportātī essent**: 'had been brought over' by Ariovistus.

essent, fīnēs eōrum populārentur, *sēsē, nē obsidibus quidem
datīs, pācem Ariovistī redimere potuisse ;* Trēverī autem, 5
*pāgōs centum Suēbōrum ad rīpās Rhēnī cōnsēdisse, quī
Rhēnum trānsīre cōnārentur ; hīs praeesse Nasuam et Cim-
berium frātrēs.*

Quibus rēbus Caesar vehementer commōtus mātūrandum
sibi exīstimāvit, nē, sī nova manus Suēbōrum cum veteribus 10

Figure 59. — The Doubs (Dubis) below Besançon (Vesontio).

4. **populārentur**: 'were (as they said) laying waste.'   *214, b.*
sēsē: '(reporting) that they.'   *213, b.*   **nē obsidibus quidem
datīs**: 'not even by the giving of hostages.'   *144, b,* (6).

5. **Trēverī**: i.e. *Trēverī dīcēbant.*

6. **Suēbōrum**: an account of the ancient Swabians is given in
Book IV, chap. 1.

7. **hīs**: *107, a.*   **praeesse**: *66, a.*   **Nasuam**: *19, d.*

9. **vehementer commōtus**: 'greatly disturbed,' a strong expression. Caesar does not often give us an insight into his feelings,
but the situation now was critical. Why ?   **mātūrandum** [esse]
sibi: 'that he ought to make haste.'   *73, e.*

10. **nē**, etc.: 'that it might not be more difficult to cope with him.'
How lit. ?   *73, c,* and *196, a.*

cōpiīs Ariovistī sēsē coniūnxisset, minus facile resistī posset. Itaque rē frūmentāriā, quam celerrimē potuit, comparātā, magnīs itineribus ad Ariovistum contendit.

*Hearing that Ariovistus has designs on Vesontio, Caesar hastens
thither.*

38. Cum trīduī viam prōcessisset, nūntiātum est eī, Ariovistum cum suīs omnibus cōpiīs ad occupandum Vesontiōnem, quod est oppidum maximum Sēquanōrum, contendere,
trīduīque viam ā suīs fīnibus prōcessisse. Id nē accideret,
5 magnopere sibi praecavendum Caesar exīstimābat.

Namque omnium rērum, quae ad bellum ūsuī erant,

---

11. **sēsē coniūnxisset**: 'should have united.' *218*, (1), b.

12. **quam celerrimē potuit**: 'as quickly as possible.' *153, c.*
comparātā: *144, b*, (2).

13. **magnīs itineribus**: 'by forced marches.' *329*, and *18, c.*
Where Caesar was when the negotiations with Ariovistus were begun,
and whence he started to meet Ariovistus, cannot be determined. It
seems probable that he overtook the survivors of the Helvetians near
the site of Dijon (Map 1); that thence he came back to Bibracte for
the Gallic Council; and that from some point near Bibracte 'the forced
marches' eastward began, as indicated on Map 1.

38. 1. **trīduī**: trans. as if *trium diērum*. Cf. *100, a.*   **viam**:
118, a.

2. **occupandum**: gerundive; the gerund in the accusative would
not have a direct object. *230*, (3).

3. **quod**: why not *quī*, to agree in gender with *Vesontiōnem*? *164,
c*. B. 250, 3; A. 306; H. 396, 2.

4. **suīs fīnibus**: in the country taken from the Sequanians, in
Upper Alsace. But the report was unfounded; for if Ariovistus had
marched as the report indicated he must have reached Vesontio before
Caesar.   **Id**: the seizure of Vesontio by Ariovistus.

5. **sibi praecavendum** [esse]: 'that he ought to take every precaution.' *110*, and *73, e.*

6. **ad**: 'for.'   **ūsuī**: 'useful.' How lit.? *112, a.*

summa erat in eō oppidō facultās, idque nātūrā locī sīc
mūniēbātur, ut magnam ad dūcendum bellum daret facultātem, proptereā quod flūmen Dubis, ut circinō circumductum, paene tōtum oppidum cingit; reliquum spatium, quod 10
est nōn amplius pedum sescentōrum, quā flūmen intermittit,
mōns continet magnā altitūdine, ita, ut rādīcēs montis ex

---

7. **facultās**: 'abundance.' **id**: *oppidum*. **nātūrā locī**: cf.
chap. 2, l. 7, and N.

8. **ad dūcendum bellum**: 'for prolonging the war,' at any rate
till Ariovistus could bring the new Swabian hordes (chap. 37, ll. 6–8) to
his assistance.

9. **ut circinō circumductum**: 'as though drawn around by a
pair of compasses.'

10. **paene cingit**: 'almost encircles.' The Dubis (modern *Doubs*,
'Black River') here bends into the form of a loop, leaving only one
side of the town (*reliquum spatium*)
not surrounded by it; and this
space is taken up by a high hill,
the top of which forms an irregular
plateau (Fig. 60).

11. **pedum sexcentōrum**:
'than six hundred feet' in breadth;
a genitive of measure is here used
instead of a comparative ablative,
quam being omitted after *amplius*.
100, a, and *129, b*. **sexcentōrum**: the distance across the
neck of the loop from the river
to the river again is about 1600
Roman feet; but the distance which
needed to be fortified, measured
across the top of the plateau, was
only 600 feet. **intermittit**:
'leaves a neck' of land. How lit.?

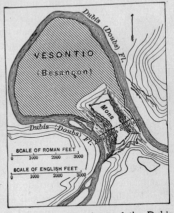

Figure 60. — The loop of the Dubis
(Doubs) at Vesontio.

The high hill is at the neck.

12. **mōns**: N. to chap. 2, l. 10. **altitūdine**: about 400 feet
above the river. *143, a*. B. 224; A. 415; H. 473, 2. **ita,
ut**: *197, b*. **rādīcēs**: object of *contingant*; we should say
'base.'

utrāque parte rīpae flūminis contingant.   Hunc mūrus circumdatus arcem efficit et cum oppidō coniungit.

15   Hūc Caesar magnīs nocturnīs diurnīsque itineribus contendit, occupātōque oppidō ibi praesidium collocat.

Panic seizes Caesar's army on account of fear of the Germans.

39. Dum paucōs diēs ad Vesontiōnem reī frūmentāriae
commeātūsque causā morātur, ex percontātiōne nostrōrum
vōcibusque Gallōrum ac mercātōrum, quī ingentī magnitūdine corporum Germānōs, incrēdibilī virtūte atque exercitā-
5 tiōne in armīs esse praedicābant (saepe numerō sēsē cum

---

13. **contingant**: 'touch.'   **Hunc**: i.e. *hunc montem ;* object of
efficit.   **circumdatus**: 'extended around (it),' at the edge of the
small plateau.   **mūrus**: indicated by a black line in Fig. 60.

14. **arcem efficit**: 'converts (into) a citadel.' *115, a.* Vesontio
was an important city in Roman times, and afterwards ; and Besançon
is now a fortress of the first class.

15. **nocturnīs diurnīsque**: 'by night and by day.' *76, b.* Caesar
probably arrived at Vesontio soon after the middle of August.

39. 1. **ad**: *120, a.* Only a 'garrison' (*praesidium*) was stationed
in the citadel ; the rest of the army were encamped 'near' the town.
reī . . . causā: 'in order to secure grain and (other) supplies.' How
lit.? *135, b.*

2. **morātur**: '(Caesar) was delaying.' *190, a.* **ex percontātiōne**: 'in consequence of the questioning.'

3. **vōcibus**: here 'stories.' *10, c.*   **mercātōrum**: many traders
accompanied the army, to trade with friendly natives as well as to purchase loot from the soldiers and supply them with extras not provided
in the army rations.   **ingentī magnitūdine**: 'of huge size.' *143,
b.* B. 224, 1 ; A. 415 ; H. 473, 2.

4. **corporum**: *92, a,* and *13, f.* Caesar elsewhere (IV, 1) speaks of
the 'huge size' of the Germans, who, by contrast in stature, seemed
larger to the Romans than they would have seemed to us.   **exercitātiōne**: 'practiced skill.'

5. **praedicābant**: 'were declaring.' *84.*   **numerō**: *142, a.*
cum hīs congressōs: 'meeting Germans.' *57, c.* How lit.?

hīs congressōs nē vultum quidem atque aciem oculōrum
dīcēbant ferre potuisse), tantus subitō timor omnem exercitum occupāvit, ut nōn mediocriter omnium mentēs animōsque perturbāret.

Hīc prīmum ortus est ā tribūnīs mīlitum, praefectīs, 10
reliquīsque, quī, ex urbe amīcitiae causā Caesarem secūtī,
nōn magnum in rē mīlitārī ūsum habēbant; quōrum alius
aliā causā illātā, quam sibi ad proficīscendum necessāriam
esse dīceret, petēbat, ut eius voluntāte discēdere licēret;

---

6. **vultum — ferre**: 'to endure the sight of their faces.' How
lit.? Our corresponding phrase is, "to look them in the face." **aciem**:
'fierce look.'

7. **tantus . . . ut**: *197*, *b*. **subitō**: 'suddenly.' **timor**: 'panic';
used of a groundless, cowardly fear.

8. **nōn mediocriter**: 'in no slight degree'; litotes. *239*, *g*.
mentēs animōsque: as we say, 'minds and hearts.'

9. **perturbāret**: 'disturbed.'

10. **ortus est ā**: 'started with.' *61*, *b*. **tribūnīs mīlitum**:
'military tribunes.' *314*. **praefectīs**: not the 'cavalry prefects'
(*309*, *c*), but 'subsidiary officials' in various positions of slight responsibility, chiefly, we may assume, in connection with the light-armed
troops. Caesar's financial and political relations (*251*) made it expedient
for him to furnish military appointments for a number of aristocratic
young mollycoddles, who had had no military experience, but wanted a
taste of it because that was considered the proper thing. These were
in a different class from Publius Crassus, for example, and other young
Romans of high social position with Caesar, who attacked their work
seriously and became excellent officers.

11. **urbe**: Rome. *17*, *b*. **amīcitiae causā**: *135*, *b*. Caesar is
politic as well as polite in ascribing to personal attachment to himself
the presence of these milksops in his army.

12. **nōn magnum**: *239*, *g*. **rē mīlitārī**: 'warfare.' **alius
aliā causā illātā**: '(each) one offering a different excuse.' *171*, *c*.

13. **causā**: *144*, *b*, (2). **quam . . . dīceret**: 'which, as he
said, made it imperative for him to leave.' How lit.? *214*, *b*.

14. **petēbat, ut . . . licēret**: 'begged permission.' *199*, *a*. **voluntāte**: *138*.

15 nōn nūllī pudōre adductī, ut timōris suspīciōnem vītārent,
remanēbant. Hī neque vultum fingere neque interdum
lacrimās tenēre poterant; abditī in tabernāculīs, aut suum
fātum querēbantur aut cum familiāribus suīs commūne
perīculum miserābantur. Vulgō tōtīs castrīs testāmenta
20 obsignābantur.

Figure 61.—The Doubs River above Besançon (Vesontio).

15. **pudōre**: 'by a sense of shame.'

16. **remanēbant**: 'remained' in camp, after the exodus of the
others.　**vultum fingere**: 'to look unconcerned.'　How lit.?

17. **abditī**: 'shutting themselves up.' *174*, and *67, c.*　**tabernāculīs**: 'their tents.' *355, a.*

18. **fātum querēbantur**: 'they were bewailing their fate.'　**familiāribus**: 'intimate friends.'

19. **miserābantur**: 'were despairingly discussing.'　**Vulgō**:
adverb, 'generally.'　**tōtīs castrīs**: 'throughout the camp.' *145, c.*
testāmenta: 'wills.'

20. **obsignābantur**: 'were being made,' as we say; lit. 'were
being sealed,' referring to the process by which wax tablets (Fig. 53),
on which wills were ordinarily written, were sealed up (Fig. 203).

Hōrum vōcibus ac timōre paulātim etiam eī, quī magnum
in castrīs ūsum habēbant, mīlitēs centuriōnēsque, quīque
equitātuī praeerant, perturbābantur. Quī sē ex hīs minus
timidōs exīstimārī volēbant, nōn sē hostem verērī, sed
angustiās itineris et magnitūdinem silvārum, quae inter- 25
cēderent inter ipsōs atque Ariovistum, aut rem frūmentāriam, ut satis commodē supportārī posset, timēre dīcēbant.

Nōn nūllī etiam Caesarī nūntiābant, cum castra movērī ac
signa ferrī iussisset, nōn fore dictō audientēs mīlitēs neque
propter timōrem signa lātūrōs. 30

Caesar deals with the situation in a persuasive address.

40. Haec cum animadvertisset, convocātō cōnsiliō, omniumque ōrdinum ad id cōnsilium adhibitīs centuriōnibus,

---

22. **in castrīs** : 'in the army' is our corresponding phrase. **centuriōnēs** : 'the centurions.' *315, a.* **quīque** : *et* (*eī*) *quī* ; cavalry
prefects and decurions are meant. *309, c.*

23. **Quī ex hīs** : (*eī*) *ex hīs, quī.* *97, d.* **sē . . . exīstimārī** :
223, a.

24. **timidōs** : 'cowardly.' **nōn sē verērī** : 'that they were not
afraid of.'

25. **angustiās** : the gorges in the valley of the Dubis (*Doubs*),
through which the most direct route led northeast to the region where
Ariovistus was (Fig. 61). **silvārum** : there are still extensive forests
on both sides of the upper Doubs.

26. **rem** : object of *timēre*, where a nominative, subject of *posset*,
might have been expected ; prolepsis. *238, g.* B. 374, 5.

27. **ut** : 'that not.' *202.* **supportārī** : 'be brought up.'

29. **signa ferrī** : 'go forward.' How lit.? *324, 325.* **iussisset** :
'should give the order' ; future perfect indicative in the direct form.
214, a. **nōn fore dictō audientēs** : 'would not obey the command ;' like the Scriptural, "Ye will not hearken unto me." How lit.?
dictō : *105.*

40. 2. **ōrdinum** : 'companies.' *12, d.* How many in the six
legions which Caesar now had? *307, c.* **centuriōnibus** : ordinarily only the centurions of first rank, the six centurions of the first cohort

vehementer eōs incūsāvit; prīmum, quod, aut quam in
partem, aut quō cōnsiliō dūcerentur, sibi quaerendum aut
5 cōgitandum putārent:

Ariovistum, sē cōnsule, cupidissimē populī Rōmānī amīci-

---

of each legion, were invited to a war-council. On this occasion all the
centurions of the six legions (360 in number) were brought together,
doubtless with the lieutenants
and other higher officers, not
for deliberation, but for an
address by the commander in
chief (Fig. 62).

3. **vehementer eōs in-
cūsāvit**: 'he severely repri-
manded them.' **quod . . .
putārent**: 'because (as he
told them) they thought.'
214, b. **quam, quō**: *204,*
(2), and *48, b.*

4. **cōnsiliō**: 'plan.'
quaerendum [esse] **aut cōgitandum** [esse]: the subject is the preceding indirect
question; 'that it was their
business to inquire or consider.' How lit.? *73, e.*

6–10. **Direct form**: *Ariovistus, mē* cōnsule, cupidissimē
populī Rōmānī amīcitiam *appe-
tiit;* cūr hunc tam temere
quisquam ab officiō discessūrum
(esse) *iūdicet? Mihi* quidem
persuādētur, cognitīs *meīs* postulātīs atque aequitāte condiciōnum perspectā, eum neque
meam neque populī Rōmānī
grātiam repudiātūrum (esse).

Figure 62. — Centurion.

With a staff, symbol of authority; unhelmeted,
but with ornamented greaves and with military
decorations attached to the cuirass.

6. **Ariovistum**, etc.: *280.*
255, and *144, b,* (2).

sē cōnsule: only a year previously.

*tiam appetīsse; cūr hunc tam temere quisquam ab officiō
discessūrum iūdicāret? Sibi quidem persuādērī, cognitīs
suīs postulātīs atque aequitāte condiciōnum perspectā, eum
neque suam neque populī Rōmānī grātiam repudiātūrum.* 10

*Quod sī, furōre atque āmentiā impulsus, bellum intulisset,
quid tandem verērentur? aut cūr dē suā virtūte aut dē
ipsīus dīligentiā dēspērārent? Factum eius hostis perīculum patrum nostrōrum memoriā, cum, Cimbrīs et Teutonīs
ā Gāiō Mariō pulsīs, nōn minōrem laudem exercitus, quam* 15

---

7. **app°tīsse**: 'strove to secure'; a rhetorical exaggeration. See
chap. 33, l. 3, and chap. 35, l. 4, and Notes.   **temere**: 'recklessly.'
quisquam: *168*, and *49, a*.   **ab officiō**: 'from his obligation' of
allegiance.

8. **iūdicāret**: *179, b*, (2).   **Sibi quidem persuādērī**: 'he at least
was persuaded.' How lit.?   *106, b*.   **cognitīs ... perspectā**:
trans. by a clause commencing with 'after.' *239, c*. Why ablative?

9. **postulātīs**: 'demands.'   **aequitāte**: 'fairness.'   **perspectā**:
'should have been clearly understood.' How lit.?   **eum**: trans. as
if *Ariovistum.*

10. **suam**: *157, d*.   **repudiātūrum** [esse]: 'would reject.'

11-21. **Direct form**: Quod sī (*Ariovistus*), furōre atque āmentiā impulsus,
bellum *intulerit*, quid tandem *vereāminī* (*179, b, 2*)? aut cūr dē *vestrā* virtūte
aut dē *meā* dīligentiā *dēspērētis* (*179, b, 2*)? Factum (*est*) eius hostis perīculum patrum nostrōrum memoriā, cum, Cimbrīs et Teutonīs ā Gāiō Mariō pulsis,
nōn minōrem laudem exercitus, quam ipse imperātor, meritus vidēbātur; factum (*est perīculum*) etiam nūper in Italiā, servīlī tumultū, quōs tamen aliquid
ūsus ac disciplīna, quae ā nōbīs *accēperant, sublevābant*. Ex quō iūdicārī
potest, quantum *habeat* (*204, 3*) in sē bonī cōnstantia, proptereā quod, quōs
aliquamdiū inermōs sīne causā *timuistis*, hōs posteā armātōs ac victōrēs
superāvistis.

11. **Quod**: 'But.' *118, d*.   **furōre ... impulsus**: 'carried
away by rage and madness.'

12. **quid tandem**: 'what, pray.'   **verērentur**: *61, a*, (2).

13. **dīligentiā**: 'careful leadership.'   **Factum** [esse] ... **perīculum**: 'trial had been made of that enemy,' i.e. of the Germans.

14. **memoriā**: *147, b*.   **Cimbrīs, Teutonīs**: N. to chap. 33, l. 17.

15. **laudem**: 'praise.'   *17, c*.

ipse imperātor, meritus vidēbātur; factum etiam nūper in Italiā, servīlī tumultū, quōs tamen aliquid ūsus ac disciplīna, quae ā nōbīs accēpissent, sublevārent. Ex quō iūdicārī posse, quantum habēret in sē bonī cōnstantia, proptereā 20 *quod, quōs aliquamdiū inermōs sine causā timuissent, hōs posteā armātōs ac victōrēs superāssent.*

Dēnique hōs esse eōsdem Germānōs, quibuscum saepe

16. **meritus**: for *meritus esse*; with *vidēbātur*, 'clearly earned.' How lit.? *148, e.* **vidēbātur**: indicative retained from the direct form. *185, b.* **nūper**: fourteen years previously; among the centurions present there were probably a number who had served as soldiers in the war with Spartacus, the term of military service being twenty years. *307, a.*

17. **servīlī tumultū**: = *tumultū servōrum*, 'at the time of the uprising of the slaves,' 73–71 B.C.; referring to the insurrection led by Spartacus, the gladiator, who had a succession of victories for two years, but in 71 B.C. was completely crushed. Caesar implies that among the gladiators and other slaves serving under Spartacus there were many of Germanic origin. **tumultū**: used for *bellum* in case of a sudden war in Italy. Why ablative? *147, b.* **quōs**: *164, b.* B. 251, 2; A. 306, *b*; H. 399, 4. **quōs tamen**, etc.: 'notwithstanding the fact that the experience and training, which they had gained from us, to some extent aided them,' lit. 'whom nevertheless,' etc. **aliquid**: *118, b.*

18. **quae**: neuter. *163, c.* B. 250, 2; A. 305, *a*; H. 398, 1.

19. **quantum**, etc.: 'how great an advantage there is in steadfastness,' lit. 'how much of good steadfastness has in itself.' **bonī**: *97, b.*

20. **aliquamdiū**: 'for a long time.' **inermōs**: 'without arms,' referring to the slaves in the earlier stages of the insurrection, before they were able to supply themselves with weapons. **hōs**: antecedent of *quōs*.

21. **armātōs**: 'equipped with arms.'

22–25. **Direct form**: Dēnique *hī sunt īdem Germānī*, quibuscum saepe numerō Helvētiī congressī, nōn sōlum in suīs, sed etiam in illōrum fīnibus, plērumque *superāvērunt;* quī tamen parēs esse nostrō exercituī nōn *potuērunt.*

22. **Dēnique**: 'Finally,' closing the argument about the Germans. **quibuscum**, etc.: cf. chap. 1, ll. 12–15. *125, c.*

*numerō Helvētiū congressī, nōn sōlum in suīs, sed etiam in
illōrum fīnibus, plērumque superārint; quī tamen parēs esse
nostrō exercituī nōn potuerint.* 25

*Sī quōs adversum proelium et fuga Gallōrum commovē-
ret, hōs, sī quaererent, reperīre posse, diūturnitāte bellī dēfatīgātīs Gallīs, Ariovistum, cum multōs mēnsēs castrīs sē ac
palūdibus tenuisset neque suī potestātem fēcisset, dēspērantēs
iam dē pugnā et dispersōs subitō adortum, magis ratiōne et* 30
*cōnsiliō quam virtūte vīcisse. Cui ratiōnī contrā hominēs
barbarōs atque imperītōs locus fuisset, hāc nē ipsum quidem
spērāre nostrōs exercitūs capī posse.*

---

23. **congressī:** *228, a.*

24. **illōrum:** trans. as if *Germānōrum.* **plērumque superārint:**
superāverint; 'generally defeated (them).' **quī tamen:** 'and they
(the Helvetians) nevertheless.' *236, a.*

26-33. **Direct form:** Sī quōs adversum proelium et fuga Gallōrum *com-
movet, hī, sī* quaerent *(206),* reperīre *poterunt,* diūturnitāte bellī dēfatīgātīs
Gallīs, Ariovistum, cum multōs mēnsēs *(118, a)* castrīs *(131, a)* sē ac palūdibus tenuisset neque suī potestātem fēcisset, *(eōs, = Gallōs)* dēspērantēs iam
dē pugnā et dispersōs subitō adortum *(226, c),* magis ratiōne et cōnsiliō quam
virtūte vīcisse. Cui ratiōnī contrā hominēs barbarōs atque imperītōs locus
fuit, hāc nē *ipse* quidem *spērat* nostrōs exercitūs capī posse.

26. **quōs:** *168,* and *49, a.* **adversum proelium:** 'defeat' at
Admagetos's stronghold; see chap. 31, ll. 45-46. **commovēret:** *172, b.*

27. **diūturnitāte,** etc.: 'when the Gauls had become exhausted by
the length of the war.' *144, b, (2).*

29. **palūdibus:** 'marshes,' added to explain how the encampments
were shut off from approach. *131, a.* **sē tenuisset:** 'had kept
himself secluded.' **neque suī,** etc.: 'and had given (them) no
chance to attack him,' lit. 'no power of himself.' **suī:** *102.*
dēspērantēs . . . vīcisse: i.e. *Ariovistum . . . subitō adortum
(eōs = Gallōs) dēspērantēs iam dē pugnā* ('giving up hope of battle')
et dispersōs ('scattered'), *vīcisse (eōs) ratiōne et cōnsiliō* ('by cunning
and strategy') *magis quam virtūte.*

31. **Cui ratiōnī—hāc:** i.e. *hāc ratiōne, cui,* 'by such cunning'—
'for which.' *165, c.*

32. **imperītōs:** 'unskilled.' **ipsum:** Ariovistus.

33. **capī:** 'be caught.' *56.*

Quī suum timōrem in reī frūmentāriae simulātiōnem
35 *angustiāsque itineris cōnferrent, facere arroganter, cum aut*
dē officiō imperātōris dēspērāre aut praescrībere vidērentur.
Haec sibi esse cūrae; frūmentum Sēquanōs, Leucōs, Lin-
gonēs sumministrāre, iamque esse in agrīs frūmenta mātūra;
dē itinere ipsōs brevī tempore iūdicātūrōs.

40 *Quod nōn fore dictō audientēs neque signa lātūrī dī-*
cantur, nihil sē eā rē commovērī; scīre enim, quibuscumque

34–39. **Direct form:** Quī suum timōrem in reī frūmentāriae simulātiōnem
angustiāsque itineris *cōnferunt, faciunt* arroganter, cum aut dē officiō imperātōris dēspērāre aut praescrībere *videantur (184, a).* Haec *mihi* sunt cūrae;
frūmentum Sēquanī, Leucī, Lingonēs *sumministrant,* iamque *sunt* in agrīs
frūmenta mātūra; de itinere *ipsī* brevī tempore *iūdicābitis.*

Figure 63. — Coin attrib-
uted to the Leuci.

Gold. Reverse, a winged genius
riding on an arrow.

34. **Quī:** i.e. *eī, quī;* see chap. 39,
ll. 23–27.   **suum,** etc.: 'assigned their
fear to a pretended anxiety about supplies.'
How lit.?

35. **arroganter:** 'presumptuously.'

37. **sibi cūrae:** *112, b.* B. 191, 2, *a;*
A. 382, 1; H. 433.   **Leucōs:** Fig. 63.

38. **sumministrāre:** 'were supplying.'
frūmenta: how different from *frūmentum?*
Cf. chap. 16, l. 3 and N.

40–45. **Direct form:** Quod (mīlitēs) nōn fore dictō audientēs neque signa
lātūrī dīcuntur, nihil eā rē *commoveor; sciō* enim, quibuscumque exercitus dictō
audiēns nōn fuerit, aut, male rē gestā, fortūnam dēfuisse, aut, aliquō facinore
compertō, avāritiam esse convictam: *mea innocentia* perpetuā vītā, *fēlicitās*
Helvētiōrum bellō *est perspecta.*

40. **Quod . . . dīcantur:** sc. *mīlitēs;* cf. chap. 39, l. 29. *198, c.*
B. 299, 2.   **signa:** *325.*   **lātūrī** [esse] **dīcantur:** trans. 'it was
said that the soldiers would,' etc. *148, e; 172, d,* and *224, a.*

41. **nihil:** 'not at all.' *118, c.* **scīre:** sc. *sē.* *215.* **quibuscum-**
que: after *dictō audiēns;* these two words express a single concept,
'obedient,' and hence are followed by the dative. *50, a,* and *108, a.*
For an antecedent supply *eīs* after *dēfuisse;* trans. 'that in the case of
any (commanders) whatever who had found their armies mutinous,
either their luck had failed them in consequence of the bad handling of
some enterprise, or,' etc. How lit.?

exercitus dictō audiēns nōn fuerit, aut, male rē gestā, for-
tūnam dēfuisse, aut, aliquō facinore compertō, avāritiam
esse convictam ; suam innocentiam perpetuā vītā, fēlīcitā-
tem Helvētiōrum bellō esse perspectam.   45

Itaque sē, quod in longiōrem diem collātūrus fuisset,
repraesentātūrum et proximā nocte dē quārtā vigiliā castra
mōtūrum, ut quam prīmum intellegere posset, utrum apud
eōs pudor atque officium, an timor, plūs valēret. Quod sī
praetereā nēmō sequātur, tamen sē cum sōlā decimā legiōne 50
itūrum, dē quā nōn dubitāret, sibique eam praetōriam co-
hortem futūram.

---

42. **rē gestā**: *144, b,* (3). **fortūnam**: the Romans were supersti-
tious in avoiding anything that seemed unlucky.

43. **dēfuisse**: *66, a.* **aliquō**: from *aliquī. 49, a.* **facinore**:
'crime.' *13, f,* and *144, b,* (3). **avāritiam**; ' greed,' the underlying
cause of the crimes committed by generals, according to Caesar.

44. **esse convictam**: 'had been clearly proved' against them.
suam: emphatic position. *157, b.* **innocentiam**: 'integrity,'
freedom from the corruption implied in *avāritiam*. **perpetuā
vītā**: 'during his entire life.' *147, c.* B. 231, 1 ; A. 424, *b*; H. 417, 2.
fēlīcitātem; 'good fortune.'

45. **Helvētiōrum bellō**: we say 'war with the Helvetians,' or
'Helvetian campaign.' *147, b.*

46–52. **Direct form**: Itaque, quod in longiōrem diem collātūrus *fuī*,
repraesentābō ; et *hāc* nocte dē quārtā vigiliā castra *movēbō*, ut quam prīmum
intellegere *possim* (*196, a*), utrum apud *mīlitēs* pudor atque officium, an timor,
plūs *valeat* (*204*). Quod sī praetereā nēmō *sequētur* (*218,* I, a), tamen *ego* cum
sōlā decimā legiōne *ibō*, dē quā nōn *dubitō, mihique ea praetōria cohors erit.*

46. **longiōrem**: ' more distant.' **collātūrus fuisset**: 'he had
intended to put off.' *63,* and *69, b.*

47. **repraesentātūrum** [esse] : sc. *id*, antecedent of *quod ;* 'he would
at once do (that).' **dē quārtā vigiliā**: *242, d.*

48. **quam prīmum**: *153, c.* **utrum . . . an**: *204,* (I). B. 300,
4; A. 335 ; H. 380.

49. **plūs valēret**: 'should have the stronger influence' with them.
118, b. **Quod** : *118, d.*

51. **nōn dubitāret**: 'he entertained no doubts.' **praetōriam**

Huic legiōnī Caesar et indulserat praecipuē et propter
virtūtem cōnfīdēbat maximē.

Fear and mutiny give place to enthusiasm.   Caesar advances.

41. Hāc ōrātiōne habitā, mīrum in modum conversae
sunt omnium mentēs, summaque alacritās et cupiditās bellī
gerendī innāta est; prīncepsque decima legiō per tribūnōs
mīlitum eī grātiās ēgit, quod dē sē optimum iūdicium fēcis-
5 set, sēque esse ad bellum gerendum parātissimam cōnfirmāvit. Deinde reliquae legiōnēs cum tribūnīs mīlitum
et prīmōrum ōrdinum centuriōnibus ēgērunt, utī Caesarī
satisfacerent; *Sē neque umquam dubitāsse neque timuisse,
neque dē summā bellī suum iūdicium, sed imperātōris esse*
10 *exīstimāvisse.*

cohortem : 'bodyguard,' to which a general (originally called *praetor*,
see Vocab.) was entitled.

53. **legiōnī**: *105*, and *307*, *e*.   **indulserat**: 'had favored.'
praecipuē: 'especially'; emphatic position. *352*, *a*.

54. **cōnfīdēbat maximē**: 'had the fullest confidence.'

41. 1. **Hāc ōrātiōne habitā**: 'After this address.' How lit.?
144, *b*, (2).   **mīrum in modum**: 'in a wonderful way.'

2. **omnium**: including not only the officers but also the soldiers,
to whom the speech was promptly reported by the centurions.
summa alacritās: 'the utmost enthusiasm.'

3. **innāta est**: 'arose.'   **prīnceps**: adj., 'taking the lead.' How
lit.? *152*, *b*.   **per**: *123*, *a*.   **tribūnos mīlitum**: *314*.

4. **eī grātiās ēgit**: 'conveyed thanks to him.'   **fēcisset**: 'had
passed.'   Why subjunctive? *183*, *a*.

7. **prīmōrum ōrdinum centuriōnibus**: 'the centurions of first
rank,' apparently the six centurions of the first cohort in each legion.
ēgērunt: 'arranged.'   **utī — satisfacerent**: 'to apologize.'
199, *a*.

8. **Sē**: '(declaring) that they.' *213*, *b*.   **dubitāsse**: *64*, *a*, (1).

9. **neque**: trans. as if *et nōn*.   **dē summā bellī iūdicium**:
'the determination of the general plan of campaign.' How lit.?
suum, imperātōris: in predicate after *esse*; 'was not their (business),
but the commander's.' *94*, *d*, and *157*, *d*.

Eōrum satisfactiōne acceptā, et itinere exquīsītō per
Dīviciācum, quod ex Gallīs eī maximam fidem habēbat, ut
mīlium amplius quīnquāgintā circuitū locīs apertīs exercitum dūceret, dē quārtā vigiliā, ut dīxerat, profectus est.
Septimō diē, cum iter nōn intermitteret, ab explōrātōribus 15

Figure 64.— Modern canal in the plain of Alsace near Strassburg.

11. **satisfactiōne**: 'apology.'   **exquīsītō**: 'sought out.'   **per**:
'with the help of.'

12. **eī**: 'in him.' *109, a.*   **maximam fidem**: 'the fullest confidence.'   **ut . . . dūceret**: 'so that he could lead'; explains *itinere. 203,* (4).

13. **mīlium . . . circuitū**: 'although with a detour of more than
fifty miles', in order to avoid the dangerous defiles of the Doubs valley;
see chap. 39, ll. 23–26 and N. (Fig. 61).   **mīlium quīnquāgintā**:
sc. *passuum.* Why genitive? *100, a,* and *129, b.*   **locīs apertīs**:
'through open country,' marching first north, and then northeast,
between the Jura and the Vosegus mountains; see Map 1. *145, c.*

15. **Septimō diē**: Caesar had probably covered about 120 miles
since leaving Vesontio. He was now in the valley of the Rhine, never
previously entered by a Roman general with an army.   **explōrātōribus**: *327.*

certior factus est, Ariovistī cōpiās ā nostrīs mīlibus passuum
quattuor et xx abesse.

Ariovistus suggests a conference, which is arranged.

42. Cognitō Caesaris adventū, Ariovistus lēgātōs ad
eum mittit : *Quod anteā dē colloquiō postulāsset, id per sē
fierī licēre, quoniam propius accessisset, sēque id sine perīculō facere posse exīstimāre.*

5 Nōn respuit condiciōnem Caesar, iamque eum ad sānitātem revertī arbitrābātur, cum id, quod anteā petentī dēnegāsset, ultrō pollicērētur ; magnamque in spem veniēbat,
prō suīs tantīs populīque Rōmānī in eum beneficiīs, cognitīs
suīs postulātīs, fore, utī pertināciā dēsisteret.   Diēs collo-
10 quiō dictus est ex eō diē quīntus.

Interim saepe cum lēgātī ultrō citrōque inter eōs mitterentur, Ariovistus postulāvit, nē quem peditem ad collo-

---

16. **nostrīs** : sc. *cōpiīs*.   **mīlibus** : *147, c.*
17. **xx** : read as *vīgintī*.   *36*, and *38, b.*
   42. 2. **Quod** : the antecedent is *id*. *212, e.*   **postulāsset** (=
postulāvisset), **accessisset** : in translating supply 'Caesar' in order
to avoid using 'he' with reference to two persons.   **per sē** : 'so far
as he was concerned.'
   5. **nōn respuit** : 'did not reject.'   **ad sānitātem** : 'to his
senses.' *157, a.*
   6. **petentī** : sc. *sibi*.   **dēnegāsset** : 'he (Ariovistus) had refused.'
   7. **ultrō** : 'of his own initiative.'   **magnam . . . veniēbat** : 'he
was coming to have great hopes,' we should say.
   8. **prō** : 'in return for.'   **suīs populīque** : *157, d.*   Cf. chap. 35,
ll. 3–4, and Notes.
   9. **fore** : after *spem*, as if Caesar had written *spērābat* ; the subject
is *utī . . . dēsisteret. 225,* and *203, (1).*   **pertināciā** : 'obstinate
course.' *127, a.*   **colloquiō** : *112, a.*
   11. **ultrō citrōque** : 'back and forth' between the headquarters of
the two commanders.   **mitterentur** : *185, c.*
   12. **quem peditem** : 'any foot soldier.' *49, a,* and *10, d.*

quium Caesar addūceret: *Verērī sē, nē per īnsidiās ab eō circumvenīrētur; uterque cum equitātū venīret; aliā ratiōne sēsē nōn esse ventūrum.* 15

Caesar, quod neque colloquium interpositā causā tollī volēbat, neque salūtem suam Gallōrum equitātuī committere audēbat, commodissimum esse statuit, omnibus equīs Gallīs equitibus dētrāctīs, eō legiōnāriōs mīlitēs legiōnis decimae, cui quam maximē cōnfīdēbat, impōnere, ut praesidium 20 quam amīcissimum, sī quid opus factō esset, habēret.

Quod cum fieret, nōn irrīdiculē quīdam ex mīlitibus decimae legiōnis dīxit: *Plūs, quam pollicitus esset, Caesarem facere; pollicitum, sē in cohortis praetōriae locō decimam legiōnem habitūrum, ad equum rescrībere.* 25

---

13. **Verērī sē:** '(saying) that he was afraid.' *213, b.* **nē:** 'that.' *202.*

14. **venīret:** 'should come'; *veniat* in the direct form. *216.* **aliā ratiōne:** 'on any other condition.' *136, c.*

16. **colloquium . . . tollī:** *223, a.* **interpositā causā:** 'by putting forward a pretext.' *144, b, (6).*

17. **Gallōrum equitātuī:** see chap. 15, ll. 1–4.

18. **esse:** the subject is *impōnere*, with *commodissimum*, 'the most expedient (thing),' in predicate. *222, b,* and *148, d.* **Gallīs equitibus:** 'from the Gallic horsemen.' *109, b.*

19. **dētrāctīs:** *144, b, (2).* **eō:** = *in eōs,* 'on them.'

20. **cui:** 'in which.' *105.* **quam:** *153, c.* **impōnere:** 'to mount.'

21. **sī . . . esset:** 'if there should be any need of action.' **quid:** *118, b.* **factō:** *132, a.* B. 218, 2, *c*; A. 411, *a*; H. 477, III.

22. **Quod cum fieret:** 'While this was being done.' *185, c.* **nōn irrīdiculē:** 'not without wit.' *239, g.* **quīdam:** *168.*

23. **Plūs:** object of *facere*; 'was doing more' for the legion.

24. **pollicitum:** 'having promised'; sc. *eum*, referring to Caesar, subject of *rescrībere.* **in,** etc.: 'that he would consider . . . as a body guard.'

25. **ad equum rescrībere:** the phrase has a double meaning, 'enroll as cavalrymen,' "demotion" for a legionary, or 'enroll as knights,' a rank of nobility; in the contrast lies the point of the joke.

Caesar and Ariovistus meet. Caesar justifies his demands.

43. Plānitiēs erat magna et in eā tumulus terrēnus satis grandis. Hīc locus aequō ferē spatiō ā castrīs Ariovistī et Caesaris aberat. Eō, ut erat dictum, ad colloquium vēnē-runt. Legiōnem Caesar, quam equīs dēvexerat, passibus 5 ducentīs ab eō tumulō cōnstituit. Item equitēs Ariovistī parī intervāllō cōnstitērunt. Ariovistus, ex equīs ut collo-querentur et praeter sē dēnōs ut ad colloquium addūcerent, postulāvit.

Figure 65. — Hill of Plettig.

Here the conference between Caesar and Ariovistus probably took place. In the distance are the Vosges mountains.

---

43. 1. Plānitiēs: 'plain' of Alsace, between the Vosges (*Vosegus*) mountains and the Rhine (Fig. 64). *21, a.*   **erat:** *90, a.*   **tumulus terrēnus:** 'an earthy mound,' whose sides, free from rocks and ledges, furnished an easy ascent for horsemen. This is identified by Colonel Stoffel with the hill of Plettig, an elevation of oval shape about 24 miles southwest of Strassburg, between the villages of Epfig and Dambach; it rises in isolation more than 160 feet above the surrounding plain (Fig. 65).

2. aequō ferē spatiō aberat: 'was about equally distant.' How lit.? *147, c.*

3. ut erat dictum: 'as agreed.' How lit.?

4. equīs dēvexerat: 'had brought on horseback,' lit. 'by means of horses.' *131, a.*   **passibus:** *147, c.*

5. ducentīs: *36,* and *37, d.* How many feet in 200 paces? *243, b.*

6. intervāllō: *138.*   **ex equīs:** 'on horseback.' *126, c.*

7. dēnōs: 'ten men each.' *36,* and *85.*   **addūcerent:** *199, a.*

Ubi eō ventum est, Caesar initiō ōrātiōnis sua senātūsque in eum beneficia commemorāvit, quod rēx appellātus 10
esset ā senātū, quod amīcus, quod mūnera amplissimē
missa; quam rem et paucīs contigisse et prō magnīs hominum officiīs cōnsuēsse tribuī docēbat: *illum, cum neque
aditum neque causam postulandī iūstam habēret, beneficiō
ac līberālitāte suā ac senātūs ea praemia cōnsecūtum.*   15

Docēbat etiam, quam veterēs quamque iūstae causae necessitūdinis ipsīs cum Aeduīs intercēderent, quae senātūs
cōnsulta, quotiēns quamque honōrifica, in eōs facta essent,
ut omnī tempore tōtīus Galliae prīncipātum Aeduī tenuis-

---

9. **Ubi eō ventum est**: 'when they (had) come thither.'   *73, d.*
initiō: *147, b.*   **sua senātūsque**: *157, d.*

10. **beneficia**: explained by the appositional *quod*-clauses following; see chap. 35, ll. 3–5 and Notes.   **rēx**: *88, a.*

11. **amīcus**: *89, a.*   **mūnera**: what these 'presents' were, we do
not know.   Gifts considered suitable for a 'king' were a golden crown,
an ivory scepter, a chair of state, and embroidered robes.   **amplissimē**: 'in richest measure.' *34, a.*

12. **missa** [essent]: *214, b.*   **quam rem**: 'and that this recognition.' *167.*   **et . . . et**: *233, a.*   **paucīs**: *105, 154, a.*   **prō
magnīs officiīs**: 'in return for great services.'

13. **docēbat**: 'he stated.'   **illum . . . cōnsecūtum** [esse]:
213, b.

14. **aditum**: '(way of) approach' to the Senate.

15. **suā**: *157, b.*   **praemia**: 'distinctions.'   No special reason
is known why Ariovistus, as implied by Caesar, should have sought the
recognition of Rome.

16. **veterēs**: *26, a.*   **necessitūdinis**: 'of close relationship.'
12, d.

17. **ipsīs**: i.e. *Rōmānīs;* we should say 'existed between the
Romans and the Aeduans.'   **intercēderent**: *204, (3).*   **quae**: *48, b.*

18. **cōnsulta**: 'decrees.'   **quamque**: = *et quam.*   **honōrifica**:
'complimentary.' *31.*   **in eōs facta essent**: 'had been passed
in their behalf.' *204, (2).*

19. **ut**: 'how.' *204, (3).*   **omnī tempore**: see N. to chap. 11,
l. 6.

20 sent, prius etiam quam nostram amīcitiam appetīssent:
*Populī Rōmānī hanc esse cōnsuētūdinem, ut sociōs atque
amīcōs nōn modo suī nihil dēperdere, sed grātiā, dignitāte,
honōre auctiōrēs velit esse; quod vērō ad amīcitiam populī
Rōmānī attulissent, id eīs ēripī quis patī posset?*
25 Postulāvit deinde eadem, quae lēgātīs in mandātīs dederat: *nē aut Aeduīs aut eōrum sociīs bellum īnferret; obsidēs redderet; sī nūllam partem Germānōrum domum
remittere posset, at nē quōs amplius Rhēnum trānsīre
paterētur.*

The attitude of Ariovistus is uncompromising and defiant.

44. Ariovistus ad postulāta Caesaris pauca respondit,
dē suīs virtūtibus multa praedicāvit:

---

20. prius etiam quam: 'even before.'   *189, a,* and *220.*
nostram: *157, c.*

21. hanc: for *hōc. 164, c.*   **ut . . . velit:** 'to desire ;' explaining *hanc. 203,* (4).

22. nōn modo — sed: *236, d.*   **suī nihil dēperdere:** 'should
lose nothing of what they had,' lit. 'of their own.' *97, a,* and *154, a.*
dignitāte: 'in prestige.' *142, a.*

23. auctiōrēs: 'the more abounding.'   **quod . . . posset:** i.e.
quis posset patī id, quod . . . attulissent, eīs ēripī? The reference is
to the power and independence of the Aeduans in former times.

24. attulissent: 'had brought.' *69, b.*   **eīs:** dative, 'from
them.' *109, b.* B. 188, 2, *d* ; A. 381 ; H. 427.   **posset:** *possit*
in the direct form. *179, b,* (2).

25. Postulāvit eadem: 'he made the same demands.' *117, a.*
dederat: 'he had intrusted'; see chap. 35. *67, a.*

26. Nē . . . īnferret, redderet, paterētur: explaining *eadem.*
216. B. 316 ; A. 588 ; H. 642.

28. remittere: 'send back.'   **posset:** *218,* (1), a.   **at:** 'at
any rate.' *236, a.*   **quōs:** *168.*

44. 1. postulāta: 'demands.'   **pauca:** object of *respondit.*
154, a.

2. suīs: emphatic. *157, b.*   **virtūtibus:** 'merits.'   **multa**
praedicāvit: 'had much to say.' *84.* How lit. ?

Trānsīsse Rhēnum sēsē nōn suā sponte, sed rogātum et
arcessītum ā Gallīs; nōn sine magnā spē magnīsque prae-
miīs domum propinquōsque relīquisse; sēdēs habēre in 5
Galliā ab ipsīs concessās, obsidēs ipsōrum voluntāte datōs;
stīpendium capere iūre bellī, quod victōrēs victīs impōnere
cōnsuērint.

Nōn sēsē Gallīs, sed Gallōs sibi bellum intulisse; omnēs
Galliae cīvitātēs ad sē oppugnandum vēnisse ac contrā sē 10
castra habuisse; eās omnēs cōpiās ā sē ūnō proeliō pulsās
ac superātās esse. Sī iterum experīrī velint, sē iterum parā-
tum esse dēcertāre; sī pāce ūtī velint, inīquum esse dē stīpen-
diō recūsāre, quod suā voluntāte ad id tempus pependerint.

3-8. Direct form: *Trānsiī* Rhēnum non *meā* sponte, sed *rogātus* et *ar-*
cessītus ā Gallīs; nōn sine magnā spē magnīsque praemiīs domum propinquōsque *relīquī;* sēdēs *habeō* in Galliā ab ipsīs concessās, obsidēs ipsōrum
voluntāte datōs; stīpendium *capiō* iūre bellī, quod victōrēs victīs impōnere
cōnsuērunt.

3. **rogātum et arcessītum:** 'because he had been asked,' etc.
227, a, (1). B. 337, 2, *f;* A. 496; H. 638, 1.

4. **nōn sine:** *239, g.*

6. **ipsīs:** the Gauls.   **concessās:** 'which had been ceded.'
227, a, (4).   **obsidēs:** i.e. *sē habēre sēdēs et obsidēs. 238, a.*
voluntāte: *138.*

7. **iūre:** 'in accordance with the rights' (lit. 'right') 'of war.' *13,*
g, and *136, c.*   **quod:** the antecedent is *stīpendium.*   **victīs:** 'the
vanquished.'   *227, a,* (4).

9-14. **Direct form:** Nōn *ego* Gallīs, sed *Gallī mihi* bellum *intulērunt;*
omnēs Galliae cīvitātēs ad *mē* oppugnandum *vēnērunt* ac contrā *mē* castra
habuērunt; eae omnēs *cōpiae* ā *mē* ūnō proeliō *pulsae* ac *superātae sunt.* Sī
(*Gallī*) iterum experīrī *volunt,* iterum *parātus sum* dēcertāre; sī pāce ūtī
volunt, inīquum *est* dē stīpendiō recūsāre, quod suā voluntāte adhūc *pepen-*
dērunt.

9. **sēsē Gallīs . . . Gallōs sibi:** *239, b.*

11. **castra habuisse:** 'had fought.'   How lit.?   **ūnō proeliō:**
see chap. 31, l. 46, and N.

12. **parātum dēcertāre:** 'ready to fight it out.'   *148, c,* and *221, c.*

13. **ūtī:** 'to enjoy'; followed by what case?   *131, c.*   **inīquum:**

15 *Amīcitiam populī Rōmānī sibi ōrnāmentō et praesidiō, nōn dētrīmentō, esse oportēre, atque sē hāc spē petīsse. Sī per populum Rōmānum stīpendium remittātur et dēditīcii subtrahantur, nōn minus libenter sēsē recūsātūrum populī Rōmānī amīcitiam, quam appetierit.*

20 *Quod multitūdinem Germānōrum in Galliam trādūcat, id sē suī mūniendī, nōn Galliae impugnandae causā, facere; eius reī testimōnium esse, quod nisi rogātus nōn vēnerit, et quod bellum nōn intulerit, sed dēfenderit.*

'unfair.' Why neuter ? *148, d.*   **dē stīpendiō recūsāre** : 'to refuse to pay the tribute.' How lit.?

14. **suā** : i.e. of the Gauls; they, however, told a different story, as we learn from chap. 31, ll. 34–40.

15–19. **Direct form** : Amīcitiam populī Rōmānī *mihi* ōrnāmentō et praesidiō, nōn dētrīmentō, esse *oportet*, atque (*eam*) hāc spē *petiī.* Sī per populum Rōmānum stīpendium *remittētur* et dēditīcii *subtrahentur*, non minus libenter *recūsābō* (*206*) populī Rōmānī amīcitiam, quam *appetiī.*

15. **sibi ōrnāmentō** : *112, b.* B. 191, 2, *a*; A. 382, 1; H. 433. **ōrnāmentō, etc.** : 'ought to be a source of prestige and a protection, not a loss.'

16. **oportēre** : the subject is *amīcitiam . . . esse.*

17. **per** : *123, a.*

18. **subtrahantur** : 'should be taken from under' his control. The *dēditīcii* were 'prisoners of war,' held as hostages to force the payment of tribute.

20–23. **Direct form** : Quod multitūdinem Germānōrum in Galliam *trādūcō*, id *meī* (*39*) mūniendī (*causā*), nōn Galliae impugnandae causā, *faciō;* eius reī testimōnium *est*, quod nisi rogātus nōn *vēnī*, et quod bellum nōn *intulī*, sed *dēfendī.*

20. **Quod**, etc. : 'In regard to his bringing over,' etc. *198, c.* **multitūdinem** : 120,000, according to chap. 31, l. 17.

21. **suī mūniendī** [causā] : 'in order to protect himself.' *230,* (1).

22. **testimōnium** : 'proof'; in predicate with *esse*, to which the *quod*-clauses stand as subject. **quod** : 'the fact that.' *198, b.* **nisi rogātus** : 'without being asked.'

23. **dēfenderit** : 'had acted on the defensive,' lit. 'warded off (war).'

Sē prius in Galliam vēnisse quam populum Rōmānum.
Numquam ante hōc tempus exercitum populī Rōmānī Galliae 25
prōvinciae fīnibus ēgressum.   Quid sibi vellet?   Cūr in
suās possessiōnēs venīret?   Prōvinciam suam hanc esse
Galliam, sīcut illam nostram.   Ut ipsī concēdī nōn oportēret,
sī in nostrōs fīnēs impetum faceret, sīc item nōs esse inīquōs,
quod in suō iūre sē interpellārēmus.   30

Quod frātrēs ā senātū Aeduōs appellātōs dīceret, nōn sē tam
barbarum neque tam imperītum esse rērum, ut nōn scīret,
neque bellō Allobrogum proximō Aeduōs Rōmānīs auxilium
tulisse, neque ipsōs in hīs contentiōnibus, quās Aeduī sēcum

24-30. **Direct form:** *Ego prius in Galliam* vēnī *quam* populus Rōmānus.
Numquam ante hōc tempus *exercitus* populī Rōmānī Galliae prōvinciae
fīnibus *ēgressus est.*   Quid *tibi vīs?*   Cūr in *meās* possessiōnēs *venīs?*
Prōvincia mea est haec Gallia, sīcut *illa* (*Gallia*) *vestra* (*prōvincia est*).   Ut
mihi concēdī nōn *oporteat,* sī in *vestrōs* fīnēs impetum *faciam* (*207,* I), sīc
item *vōs estis inīquī,* quod *mē* in *meō* iūre *interpellātis.*

24. **Galliam:** Celtic Gaul (*287, b*), as in l. 28; the Province, mentioned in l. 26, as stated elsewhere, had been under Roman control
since 121 B.C.   *290.*

26. **fīnibus:** *127, a.*   **Quid sibi vellet:** 'what did Caesar mean?'
How lit.?   *217, a.*

27. **hanc Galliam:** 'this (part of) Gaul,' toward the Rhine.

28. **Ut:** 'As.'   **ipsī:** *Ariovistō.*   **concēdī nōn oportēret:**
'no concession ought to be made.'   How lit.?

30. **sē interpellārēmus:** 'we were interfering with him.'

31-36. **Direct form:** Quod frātrēs ā senātū Aeduōs appellātōs (*esse*) *dīcis,*
nōn tam *barbarus* neque tam *imperītus* rērum *sum,* ut nōn *sciam,* neque bellō
Allobrogum proximō Aeduōs Rōmānīs auxilium tulisse, neque ipsōs in hīs
contentiōnibus, quās Aeduī *mēcum* et cum Sēquanīs *habuērunt,* auxiliō populī
Rōmānī ūsōs esse.

31. **Quod — dīceret:** 'with reference to his saying.'   **frātrēs:**
88, a.   Cf. chap. 33, l. 8.

32. **imperītum rērum:** 'unversed in affairs.'   *102.*   B. 204, 1 ; A.
349, *a* ; H. 451, 1.   **ut:** *197, b.*

33. **bellō:** only three years before, in 61 B.C.   *147, b.*

34. **ipsōs, Aeduī:** trans. as if *Aeduōs, eī.*   **contentiōnibus:**
struggles.'

35 *et cum Sēquanīs habuissent, auxiliō populī Rōmānī ūsōs
esse.*

*Dēbēre sē suspicārī, simulātā Caesarem amīcitiā, quod
exercitum in Galliā habeat, suī opprimendī causā habēre.
Quī nisi dēcēdat, atque exercitum dēdūcat ex hīs regiōnibus,*
40 *sēsē illum nōn prō amīcō, sed prō hoste, habitūrum. Quod sī
eum interfēcerit, multīs sēsē nōbilibus prīncipibusque populī
Rōmānī grātum esse factūrum (id sē ab ipsīs, per eōrum
nūntiōs, compertum habēre), quōrum omnium grātiam atque
amīcitiam eius morte redimere posset. Quod sī dēcessisset*
45 *et līberam possessiōnem Galliae sibi trādidisset, magnō sē*

37–47. **Direct form :** *Dēbeō* suspicārī, simulātā *tē* amīcitiā, quod exercitum
in Galliā *habēs, meī* opprimendī habēre. Nisi *dēcēdēs*, atque exercitum *dē-
dūcēs* ex hīs regiōnibus, *tē* nōn prō amīcō, sed prō hoste, *habēbō.* Quod sī *te
interfēcerō*, multīs nōbilibus prīncipibusque populī Rōmānī grātum *faciam*
(id ab ipsīs, per eōrum nūntiōs, compertum *habeō*), quōrum omnium grātiam
atque amīcitiam *tuā* morte redimere *possum.* Quod sī *dēcesseris* et līberam
possessiōnem Galliae *mihi trādideris*, magnō *tē* praemiō *remūnerābor* et,
quaecumque bella gerī *volēs*, sīne ūllō *tuō* labōre et perīculō *cōnficiam.*

37. **Dēbēre sē suspicārī :** 'that he had good reason to suspect.'
How lit. ?   **simulātā amīcitiā :** 'under the guise of friendship.'
144, b, (5).

38. **suī opprimendī causā :** 'in order to crush him.' *230,* (1).
habēre : sc. *eum,* 'was keeping (it there).'

39. **Quī :** Caesar. *167.*   **dēdūcat :** 'withdraw.'   **regiōnibus :**
'regions.' *81.*

40. **habitūrum :** sc. *esse.*   **Quod :** 'Moreover.' *118, d.*

42. **grātum :** 'a kindness.'   **id :** 'that fact.' *160, c.*

43. **nūntiōs :** 'agents' rather than 'messengers.'   **compertum
habēre :** trans. as if *comperisse. 229, a.* B. 337, 7; A. 497, *b*; H.
431, 3.   **quōrum omnium :** 'of all of whom.' *97, c.*

44. **eius :** Caesar's. It is not impossible that Ariovistus had been
in communication with Caesar's enemies ; but whether he spoke the truth
or not, he was evidently familiar with the party strifes and jealousies at
this time in Roman politics.   **Quod :** 'On the other hand.' *118, d.*

45. **līberam :** i.e. 'without interference.'   **Galliae :** Celtic Gaul,
as in l. 24.

illum praemiō remūnerātūrum et, quaecumque bella gerī vellet, sine ūllō eius labōre et perīculō cōnfectūrum.

Caesar declines to make any concessions.

45. Multa ā Caesare in eam sententiam dicta sunt, quārē negōtiō dēsistere nōn posset :

Figure 66. — The conference between Caesar and Ariovistus.

46. **illum**: trans. as if *Caesarem*.　　**remūnerātūrum** [esse] : 'he would compensate.' *61, a,* (1).　　**quaecumque**: *50, a*.

47. **eius**: 'on the part of Caesar.' Hòw lit.?　　**cōnfectūrum** [esse] : if Caesar will withdraw, Ariovistus will fight his battles for him. The attitude of Ariovistus seems somewhat less defiant than in his former reply, sent by messengers and summarized in chap. 36. The conference between Caesar and Ariovistus, as conceived by a German designer, is shown in Fig. 66.

45. 1. **in eam sententiam**: lit. 'to this purport'; we should say 'to show.'

2. **negōtiō**: *127, a*.　　**posset**: *204* (3). B. 300, 1 ; A. 574; H. 649, II.

3–8. **Direct form**: Neque *mea* neque populī Rōmānī *cōnsuētūdō patitur*, utī optimē meritōs sociōs *dēseram*, neque *iūdicō*, Galliam potius esse *tuam*

*Neque suam neque populī Rōmānī cōnsuētūdinem patī,
utī optimē meritōs sociōs dēsereret, neque sē iūdicāre,*
5 *Galliam potius esse Ariovistī quam populī Rōmānī. Bellō
superātōs esse Arvernōs et Rutēnōs ā Quīntō Fabiō Maximō,
quibus populus Rōmānus ignōvisset neque in prōvinciam
redēgisset neque stīpendium imposuisset.*

Quod sī antīquissimum quodque tempus spectārī oportēret,
10 *populī Rōmānī iūstissimum esse in Galliā imperium; sī
iūdicium senātūs observārī oportēret, līberam dēbēre esse
Galliam, quam, bellō victam, suīs lēgibus ūtī voluisset.*

---

quam populī Rōmānī. Bellō *superātī sunt Arvernī* et *Rutēnī* ā Quīntō
Fabiō Maximō, quibus populus Rōmānus *ignōvit,* neque (*eōs*) in pro-
vinciam *redēgit,* neque (*eīs*) stīpendium *imposuit.*

3. **Neque,** etc.: *213, b.*   **suam, populī:** *157, d.*

4. **utī ... dēsereret:** after *patī. 199, a,* (6).   **neque:** 'and
not.'

5. **esse Ariovistī:** 'belonged to Ariovistus.' *94, d.* B. 198, 3;
A. 343, *b*; H. 447.   **Bellō:** *131, a.*

6. **Arvernōs, Rutēnōs:** conquered in 121 B.C., but not included
in the Province excepting a small division of the Ruteni, called *Rutēnī
prōvinciālēs* (VII. 7); see Map GALLIA.

7. **quibus:** *105.*   **ignōvisset:** the Romans with good reason
had 'pardoned' them — their country, lying beyond the Cévennes
mountains, could have been held only with the greatest difficulty.
neque ... redēgisset: 'and (whom) it had not reduced.'

9-12. **Direct Form:** Quod sī antīquissimum quodque tempus spectārī
oportet, populī Rōmānī iūstissimum *est* in Galliā imperium; sī iūdicium senātūs observārī *oportet, lībera dēbet* esse *Gallia,* quam, bellō victam, suīs lēgibus
ūtī *voluit.*

9. **antīquissimum quodque tempus:** 'priority of time,' lit.
'each earliest time.' *170, a,* and *49, a.* B. 252, 5, *c*; A. 313, *b*;
H. 515, 2.

11. **observārī:** 'to be regarded.' *357, b.*

12. **victam:** 'although it had been conquered.' *227, a,* (3).
suīs: 'its own,' referring to the subject of *ūtī.*   **voluisset:** i.e.
senātus voluisset.

The conference is abruptly ended by an attack of German cavalry.

46. Dum haec in colloquiō geruntur, Caesarī nūntiātum est, equitēs Ariovistī propius tumulum accēdere et ad nostrōs adequitāre, lapidēs tēlaque in nostrōs conicere. Caesar loquendī fīnem facit sēque ad suōs recēpit suīsque imperāvit, nē quod omnīnō tēlum in hostēs reicerent. 5 Nam etsī sine ūllō perīculō legiōnis dēlēctae cum equitātū proelium fore vidēbat, tamen committendum nōn putābat, ut, pulsīs hostibus, dīcī posset, eōs ab sē per fidem in colloquiō circumventōs.

Posteā quam in vulgus mīlitum ēlātum est, quā arrogantiā 10 in colloquiō Ariovistus ūsus omnī Galliā Rōmānīs interdīxisset, impetumque ut in nostrōs eius equitēs fēcissent, eaque rēs colloquium ut dirēmisset, multō maior alacritās studiumque pugnandī maius exercituī iniectum est.

---

46. 1. **geruntur**: trans. by a past tense. *190, a.*

2. **tumulum**: referred to in chap. 43, l. 1. *123, b.* B. 141, 3; A. 432, *a*; H. 420, 5.   The German cavalry were about a thousand Roman feet from the hill (chap. 43, l. 5), the tenth legion at an equal distance.

3. **adequitāre**: 'were riding up (to).'

5. **nē quod omnīnō tēlum**: 'any missile at all.' *168.*

6. **legiōnis dēlēctae**: mounted on horseback (chap. 42, ll. 16–25); 'to the legion,' we should say. *102.*

7. **committendum** [esse] . . . **eōs**: 'he thought that he ought not to allow it to be said that, if the enemy were routed, they.'   How lit.?

8. **hostibus**: *144, b,* (6).   **per fidem**: 'through a pledge of good faith,' used to entrap them.

10. **Posteā quam**: *188, a.*   **vulgus**: 'rank and file.' *6, b.* **ēlātum est**: *69, b.*   **quā arrogantiā ūsus**: 'with what arrogance.' How lit.? *131, c.*

11. **Galliā**: *127, a.*   **Rōmānīs**: why dative? *109, c.*   **interdīxisset**, etc.: 'had denied to the Romans all right to be in Gaul,' lit. 'from all Gaul.' *204,* (2).

12. **ut**: 'how.'   **fēcissent, dirēmisset**: *204,* (3).

14. **pugnandī**: 'for fighting,' we should say. *230,* (1).   **exercituī**: *107, a.*   **iniectum est**: 'were' (lit. 'was') 'infused.' *172, b.*

*Ariovistus reopens negotiations, but throws Caesar's envoys
into chains.*

47. Bīduō post Ariovistus ad Caesarem lēgātōs mittit:
*Velle sē dē hīs rēbus, quae inter eōs agī coeptae neque per-
fectae essent, agere cum eō; utī aut iterum colloquiō diem
cōnstitueret aut, sī id minus vellet, ē suīs lēgātīs aliquem*
5 *ad sē mitteret.*

Colloquendī Caesarī causa vīsa nōn est, et eō magis,
quod prīdiē eius diēī Germānī retinērī nōn potuerant, quīn
in nostrōs tēla conicerent.   Lēgātum ē suīs sēsē magnō
cum perīculō ad eum missūrum et hominibus ferīs obiec-
10 tūrum exīstimābat.   Commodissimum vīsum est Gāium

---

47. **1.** **Bīduō**: *140.*   **post**: here an adverb.

2-5. **Direct form**: *Volō* dē hīs rēbus, quae inter *nōs* agī coeptae neque
perfectae *sunt, tēcum* agere; (*rogō*) utī aut iterum colloquiō diem *cōnstituās*,
aut, sī id minus *velīs*, ē *tuīs* lēgātīs aliquem ad *mē mittās*.

2. **Velle**, etc.: *212, c,* (4), and *213, b.*   **coeptae** [essent]: *72, b, c.*
3. **utī**, etc.: i.e. *sē rogāre, utī* (*Caesar*) . . . *cōnstitueret;* the idea
of asking is implied in *Velle*, etc.   *199, a.*
4. **minus**: trans. as if *nōn*.   **ē lēgātīs**: *97, d.*   **suīs**: *Caesaris.*   **aliquem**: *49, a.*   Ariovistus wanted Caesar to send not a
messenger but one of his highest officers, probably in order to hold
him as a hostage.
6. **causa vīsa nōn est**: 'there did not seem (to be any) reason.'
90, b.   **et eō magis**: 'especially'; lit. 'and on this account the
more,' *eō* being explained by the following *quod*-clause. *135, a.*
7. **diēī**: *94, c.*   B. 201, 3, *a*; A. 359, *b,* N. 2; H. 446, 5.   **quīn**
. . . **conicerent**: 'from hurling.' *201, a.*   B. 295, 3; A. 558; H.
595, 2.
8. **Lēgātum ē suīs**: 'an envoy from his staff'; one of his officers.
sēsē . . . **missūrum** [esse]: 'that it would be exceedingly hazardous
for him to send to Ariovistus'; how lit.?   **magnō cum perīculō**:
136, a.
10. **vīsum est**, etc.: *vīsum est mittere* (l. 16) *Gāium Valerium
Procillum,* etc.   *222, a.*

Valerium Procillum, C. Valerii Caburī fīlium, summā virtūte et hūmānitāte adulēscentem, cuius pater ā C. Valeriō
Flaccō cīvitāte dōnātus erat, et propter fidem et propter
linguae Gallicae scientiam, quā multā iam Ariovistus
longinquā cōnsuētūdine ūtēbātur, et quod in eō peccandī 15
Germānīs causa nōn esset, ad eum mittere, et ūnā M.
Metium, quī hospitiō Ariovistī ūtēbātur. (Hīs mandāvit,
ut, quae dīceret Ariovistus, cognōscerent et ad sē referrent.)

Quōs cum apud sē in castrīs Ariovistus cōnspexisset,
exercitū suō praesente conclāmāvit: *Quid ad sē venīrent?* 20
an speculandī causā? Cōnantēs dīcere prohibuit et in
catēnās coniēcit.

---

11. **C.** = *Gāī. 19, a.* **Valeriī**: *8, a.* **virtūte**: *143, a.*

12. **hūmānitāte**: 'refinement.' **adulēscentem**: 'a young man.'
C. Valeriō Flaccō: governor of the Province of Gaul in 83 B.C.

13. **cīvitāte**: Roman 'citizenship' was often conferred upon foreigners who had rendered some service. In this case the Gaul *Caburus*
took the First Name and Clan Name of *C. Valerius Flaccus*, to whom he
was indebted for the distinction, and was known as *C. Valerius Caburus. 19, a,* and *b.* **dōnātus erat**: 'had been presented.'

14. **quā multā Ariovistus ūtēbātur**: 'which Ariovistus spoke
fluently'; how lit.?

15. **cōnsuētūdine**: 'practice.' *135, a.* **in eō**: 'in his case.'
peccandī causa: '(any) reason for offering violence,' lit. 'of doing
wrong'; for Procillus was a Gaul.

16. **nōn esset**: 'because (as he thought) there was not.' *183, a.*

17. **ūtēbātur**: 'enjoyed.' Metius may have been received and
entertained by Ariovistus in the course of the negotiations which in
59 B.C. culminated in the recognition of the German ruler by the Roman
Senate (chap. 35, ll. 3–4).

20. **conclāmāvit**: 'he called out loudly.' **Quid**: 'why.' *118, e.*
venīrent: *217, a.*

21. **an speculandī causā**: '(was it) in order to act as spies.'
179, a, (2). How lit.? **Cōnantēs [eōs]**, etc.: 'when they tried to
speak he stopped them,' preventing explanation because he wished his
army to believe that they were spies. *227, a, (5).*

22. **catēnās**: 'chains.'

Ariovistus moves camp so as to cut off Caesar's supplies.

48. Eōdem diē castra prōmōvit et mīlibus passuum sex
ā Caesaris castrīs sub monte cōnsēdit. Postrīdiē eius diēī
praeter castra Caesaris suās cōpiās trādūxit et mīlibus
passuum duōbus ultrā eum castra fēcit eō cōnsiliō, utī frū-
5 mentō commeātūque, quī ex Sēquanīs et Aeduīs supportārētur, Caesarem interclūderet.

Ex eō diē diēs continuōs quīnque Caesar prō castrīs suās
cōpiās prōdūxit et aciem īnstrūctam habuit, ut, sī vellet
Ariovistus proeliō contendere, eī potestās nōn deesset.
10 Ariovistus hīs omnibus diēbus exercitum castrīs continuit,
equestrī proeliō cotīdiē contendit.

---

48. 1. **prōmōvit:** '(Ariovistus) moved forward.'   **mīlibus** :
147, c.   How far by our measurement? *243, a, b.*

2. **Caesaris castrīs** : Caesar's camp is located by Colonel Stoffel
between Gemar and Ostheim, about 35 miles southwest of Strassburg.
See Map 4, LARGE CAMP.   **diēī.** *94, c.*

3. **praeter** . . . **trādūxit**: Ariovistus's line of march, as suggested on
Map 4, probably skirted or traversed the foothills of the Vosges in such
a way that Caesar could not attack him while executing this movement.

4. **castra** : the camp of Ariovistus, probably at the place so marked
on Map 4, was favorably located for defense.   **ūtī** . . . **interclūderet** :
explains *cōnsiliō.* *196, a.*   **frūmentō** : *127, a.* B. 214, 2 ; A. 401 ;
H. 464.   Ariovistus thought that by cutting off Caesar's supplies he could
force Caesar to retire, or else to fight on ground of his own choosing.

5. **quī** : *163, c.*   **supportārētur** : subjunctive by attraction.
220. B. 324, 1 ; A. 593 ; H. 652.

8. **aciem īnstrūctam** : 'his army drawn up' in triple line, as indicated on Map 4, CAESAR'S FIRST POSITION. *337, a.*   **ut** : 'so that.'
vellet : *220.*

9. **eī** . . . **deesset**: 'he did not lack opportunity.'   How lit. ?
197, a, and *239, g.*

10. **diēbus** : *147, c.*   **exercitum** : the German infantry, as we
see from the next line.   **castrīs** : 'within the camp.' *131, a.* B.
218; A. 409; H. 476.

11. **equestrī proeliō** : 'with cavalry skirmishing.'   **contendit** :
238, a.

Genus hōc erat pugnae, quō sē Germānī exercuerant.
Equitum mīlia erant sex, totidem numerō peditēs vēlōcissimī
ac fortissimī, quōs ex omnī cōpiā singulī singulōs suae
salūtis causā dēlēgerant; cum hīs in proeliīs versābantur. ¹⁵
Ad eōs sē equitēs recipiēbant; hī, sī quid erat dūrius, concurrēbant, sī quī, graviōre vulnere acceptō, equō dēciderat,
circumsistēbant; sī quō erat longius prōdeundum aut celerius recipiendum, tanta erat hōrum exercitātiōne celeritās,
ut iubīs equōrum sublevātī cursum adaequārent.   ²⁰

Caesar fortifies a camp beyond Ariovistus, reopening the road.

49. Ubi eum castrīs sē tenēre Caesar intellēxit, nē diūtius commeātū prohibērētur, ultrā eum locum, quō in locō

---

12. **Genus pugnae**: 'The method of fighting.' **hōc**: *161, a*.

13. **erant**: *90, a*. **numerō**: *142, a*, and *85*. **peditēs**: sc.
erant. 10, d. **vēlōcissimī**: 'the fastest.'

14. **quōs**, etc.: 'whom they' (the horsemen) 'had chosen from the
entire force, each one (selecting) a foot-soldier.' How lit.? **singulōs**: agrees with *quōs. 36*.

15. **versābantur**: '(the horsemen) associated themselves.'

16. **eōs, hī**: the foot-soldiers. **sī . . . erat, concurrēbant**:
general condition of fact. *205*, (2). **quid dūrius**: 'unusually
serious difficulty.' *153, a*. How lit.? **concurrēbant**: 'they would
rush to the rescue.'

17. **quī**: 'any one.' *49, a* and *b*. **vulnere**: *13, e*. **equō**:
127, a. **dēciderat**: 'had fallen.' *205*, (4).

18. **circumsistēbant**: 'they would gather round him.' **sī quō**,
etc.: 'if it was necessary to advance in any direction unusually far, or
to retreat with special swiftness.' *73, e*, and *153, a*.

19. **celeritās**: 'swiftness.'

20. **iubīs**: 'by the manes.' **sublevātī**: 'supporting themselves.'
174. **cursum**: 'they kept up with the running' of the horses.
Caesar afterwards employed German horsemen as mercenaries, and they
rendered him very effective service, as at the siege of Alesia (VII. 80).

49. 1. **eum**: Ariovistus. **sē**: object of *tenēre*. **nē . . . prohibērētur**: see chap. 48, ll. 4-6, and Notes. *196, a*.

2. **eum locum**: Map 4, CAMP OF ARIOVISTUS. **locō**: *165, a*.

Germānī cōnsēderant, circiter passūs sexcentōs ab hīs, castrīs idōneum locum dēlēgit aciēque triplicī īnstrūctā ad eum
5 locum vēnit.   Prīmam et secundam aciem in armīs esse,
tertiam castra mūnīre iussit.   Hīc locus ab hoste circiter
passūs sexcentōs, utī dictum est, aberat.

Eō circiter hominum numerō sēdecim mīlia expedīta cum
omnī equitātū Ariovistus mīsit, quae cōpiae nostrōs ter-
10 rērent et mūnītiōne prohibērent.   Nihilō sētius Caesar, ut
ante cōnstituerat, duās aciēs hostem prōpulsāre, tertiam
opus perficere iussit.   Mūnītīs castrīs, duās ibi legiōnēs
relīquit et partem auxiliōrum ; quattuor reliquās in castra
maiōra redūxit.

The Germans, Caesar hears, dare not fight before the new moon.

50.   Proximō diē, īnstitūtō suō, Caesar ē castrīs utrīsque
cōpiās suās ēdūxit, paulumque ā maiōribus castrīs prōgressus aciem īnstrūxit, hostibus pugnandī potestātem
fēcit.

---

4. **castrīs** : *108, a.*   **idōneum** : 'suitable.'   **aciē triplicī** : *337, a.*

6. **castra** : *332.*   This camp on Map 4 is called the 'Small Camp,'
castra minōra, in order to distinguish it from the 'Large Camp,' *castra
maiōra.*   The two camps were not far from two miles apart ; both were
on somewhat higher ground.   Caesar's object in establishing the
smaller camp, which was a little more than half a mile from the Germans, was to keep open the road to Vesontio, and so maintain communication with his base of supplies.   **mūnīre** : 'fortify.'   *333.*

8. **hominum . . . expedīta** : trans. as if *sēdecim mīlia hominum
expedītōrum.*   **expedīta** : 'light-armed.'

9. **quae cōpiae** : 'in order that these forces.'   *193, a.*

10. **Nihilō sētius** : 'Nevertheless,' lit. 'by nothing the less.'   *140.*

11. **duās** : i.e. *prīmam et secundam.*   **prōpulsāre** : 'to ward off.'

13. **reliquās** : sc. *legiōnēs.*   How many men, probably, in the six
legions?   *307, b* and *e.*

50.   1. **īnstitūtō suō** : 'in accordance with his usual practice' (chap.
48, ll. 7-8).   *136, c.*   **utrīsque** : *51.*

3. **aciem** : Map 4, CAESAR'S SECOND POSITION.   **potestātem
fēcit** : 'gave an opportunity.'

MAP 4

THE BATTLE WITH ARIOVISTUS

Book I, 49–53

To face page 120

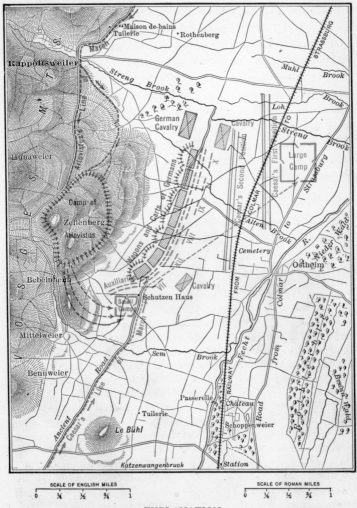

SCALE OF ENGLISH MILES

0   ¼   ½   ¾   1

SCALE OF ROMAN MILES

0   ¼   ½   ¾   1

EXPLANATION

Caesar, marching from the south, encamped north of Modern Ostheim (chap. 48, l. 2). Ariovistus, marching from the north, encamped on Zellenberg.

Ubi nē tum quidem eōs prōdīre intellēxit, circiter merī- 5
diem exercitum in castra redūxit.   Tum dēmum Ariovistus
partem suārum cōpiārum, quae castra minōra oppugnāret,
mīsit.   Ācriter utrimque ūsque ad vesperum pugnātum est.
Sōlis occāsū suās cōpiās Ariovistus, multīs et illātīs et
acceptīs vulneribus, in castra redūxit.   10

Cum ex captīvīs quaereret Caesar, quam ob rem Ariovistus proeliō nōn dēcertāret, hanc reperiēbat causam, quod
apud Germānōs ea cōnsuētūdō esset, ut mātrēs familiae
eōrum sortibus et vāticinātiōnibus dēclārārent, utrum proelium committī ex ūsū esset necne; *eās ita dīcere,*   15

*Nōn esse fās Germānōs superāre, sī ante novam lūnam
proeliō contendissent.*

---

5. **nē . . . quidem**: *237, c.*   **prōdīre**: *68, b.*   **merīdiem**:
'midday.'

7. **quae**: trans. as if *ut ea. 193, a.*

8. **Ācriter — pugnātum est**: 'Fiercely the battle raged.' *73, d.*
utrimque: 'on both sides.'

9. **Sōlis occāsū**: 'At sunset.' *147, a.*

11. **ex**: *116, c.*   **quam ob rem**: 'for what reason.' *204,* (2).
How lit.?

12. **proeliō nōn dēcertāret**: 'would not fight a decisive battle.'
131, a.   How lit.?   Ariovistus had used only a part of his forces (l. 7).
causam: explained by the following appositional *quod*-clause. *198, b.*

13. **esset**: *214, b.*   **mātrēs familiae**: 'matrons,' married women
who were believed to have prophetic powers.

14. **sortibus**: 'by means of lots,' consisting of bits of wood from a
branch of a fruit-bearing tree, which were scattered at random over a
white cloth and then picked up. *17, c.*   **vāticinātiōnibus**: 'prophetic
utterances,' inspired by "eddies of rivers and whirlings and noises of
currents."   **dēclārārent**: *203,* (2).   **utrum . . . necne**: 'whether
. . . or not.' *204,* (1).   B. 300, 4, *a*; A. 335, N; H. 650, 1.

15. **ex ūsū**: 'expedient.'   How lit.?   **eās**, etc.: *213, b.*

16. **Nōn**, etc.: indirect discourse, depending on *dīcere.*   **fās**:
'predestined.'   **superāre**: 'should be victorious.'   **novam lūnam**:
'the new moon' of September 18, 58 B.C., according to modern compu-
tations.   The ancient German superstition about the influence of the

*Taking advantage of their superstition, Caesar forces an
engagement.*

51. Postrīdiē eius diēī Caesar praesidiō utrīsque castrīs,
quod satis esse vīsum est, relīquit; omnēs ālāriōs in cōnspectū hostium prō castrīs minōribus cōnstituit, quod
minus multitūdine mīlitum legiōnāriōrum prō hostium
5 numerō valēbat, ut ad speciem ālāriīs ūterētur; ipse, triplicī īnstrūctā aciē, usque ad castra hostium accessit.

Tum dēmum necessāriō Germānī suās cōpiās castrīs
ēdūxērunt generātimque cōnstituērunt paribus intervāllīs,
Harūdēs, Marcomanōs, Tribocōs, Vangionēs, Nemetēs,
10 Sedusiōs, Suēbōs, omnemque aciem suam raedīs et carrīs
circumdedērunt, nē qua spēs in fugā relinquerētur.   Eō

---

moon still lingers in many places, particularly in respect to commencing
certain farming operations "in the old of the moon."

51. 1. **diēī**: *94, c.*   The date was about September 14.   **praesidiō
utrīsque castrīs**: a dative of purpose and a dative of indirect object;
'as a garrison for each camp,' we should say.   How lit.? *112, a,* and
104, a.

2. **quod**: as antecedent sc. *id,* object of *relīquit.*   **ālāriōs**:
'auxiliaries'; the light-armed troops, called *ālāriī* because usually
stationed on the wings (*ālae*) of an army. *308.*

4. **minus multitūdine valēbat**: 'was weaker in respect to his
force.' How lit.?   **prō**: 'in comparison with.'

5. **ad speciem**: 'for show,' in order to hide from the enemy his
weakness in heavy infantry; Ariovistus would take the *ālāriōs* for
legiōnāriōs.

6. **triplicī aciē**: the front formed by the legions must have been
at least a mile long.   The probable arrangement of the legions in
order of battle is indicated in Map 4; in the rear line only two cohorts
to each legion are shown, for the reason that one cohort was probably
drawn off for the guard duty indicated in l. 1, *praesidiō castrīs. 337, a.*

7. **necessāriō**: 'of necessity.'   **castrīs**: *127, a.*

8. **generātim**: 'by tribes,' the soldiers of each tribe being formed
into a body by themselves.   **intervāllīs**: *138.*

10. **raedīs**: 'with wagons,' probably covered, like gypsy wagons.

11. **circumdedērunt**: 'hemmed in,' on the rear and wings, as indi-

mulierēs imposuērunt, quae in proelium proficīscentēs
passīs manibus flentēs implōrābant, nē sē in servitūtem
Rōmānīs trāderent.

Desperate fighting, hand-to-hand; the Roman left, wavering,
is reënforced.

52. Caesar singulīs legiōnibus singulōs lēgātōs et quaestōrem praefēcit, utī eōs testēs suae quisque virtūtis habēret; ipse ā dextrō cornū, quod eam partem minimē fīrmam
hostium esse animadverterat, proelium commīsit.

Ita nostrī ācriter in hostēs, signō datō, impetum fēcērunt, 5
itaque hostēs repente celeriterque prōcurrērunt, ut spatium
pīla in hostēs coniciendī nōn darētur. Reiectīs pīlīs, comminus gladiīs pugnātum est. At Germānī, celeriter ex
cōnsuētūdine suā phalange factā, impetūs gladiōrum

---

cated in Map 4.   **qua**: *168*.   **Eō**: 'thereon,' upon the wagons and
carts.

12. **mulierēs**: *11, c*.   **proficīscentēs**: sc. *eōs*. *227, a*, (4).

13. **passīs manibus**: 'with outstretched hands.' *144, b*, (2).
flentēs: *227, b*.

52. 1. **singulīs**, etc.: Caesar had six legions (*307, e*). Over each of
five legions he put a lieutenant, and over the sixth he placed the quaestor.
What were the quaestor's ordinary duties ? *313, b*, and *251, b*.

2. **testēs**: 'as witnesses.' *115, a*.   **quisque**: *170, b*.

3. **ā dextrō cornū**: 'on the right wing.' *126, c*.   **eam partem
hostium**: the German left wing, opposite the Roman right.   **minimē
fīrmam**: 'the weakest.'

5. **Ita**: modifies *ācriter*. *34, a*.   **signō**: given on the trumpet.
326, a, (1).

6. **itaque**: = *et ita*.   **repente**: 'suddenly.'   **prōcurrērunt**:
'ran forward.'   **spatium**: trans. as if *tempus*.

7. **pīla**: object of *coniciendī*. *322, d*, and *230*, (1).   **Reiectīs
pīlīs — pugnātum est**: 'they threw aside their pikes and fought.'
How lit.? *144, b*, (2) and *73, d*.   **comminus**: 'at close quarters.'

8. **gladiīs**: *322, e*.   **ex**: 'in accordance with.'

9. **phalange**: 'a compact mass,' like the formation adopted by the
Helvetians; see chap. 24, l. 13, and N.

10 excēpērunt. Repertī sunt complūrēs nostrī, quī in phalanga īnsilīrent et scūta manibus revellerent et dēsuper
vulnerārent.

Cum hostium aciēs ā sinistrō cornū pulsa atque in fugam
conversa esset, ā dextrō cornū vehementer multitūdine
15 suōrum nostram aciem premēbant. Id cum animadvertisset
P. Crassus adulēscēns, quī equitātuī praeerat, quod expedī-

---

10. **excēpērunt**: the Germans apparently did not hurl their javelins
(351) but relied upon their shields and swords; the German sword

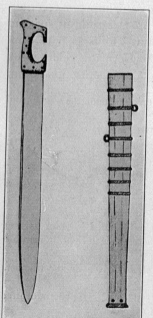

Figure 67. — Ancient German
sword with its wooden scabbard.

was longer than the Roman, and single-
edged (Fig. 67). **complūrēs nostrī**: 'many men on our side.' How
lit.? 97, c. B. 201, 1, b; A. 346, e;
H. 442, 2.

11. **phalanga**: 18, f. **īnsilīrent**:
'leaped (upon).' 194, a. **revellerent**: 'pulled back.' **dēsuper**:
'from above.' In hand-to-hand fighting the Roman soldier, parrying blows
with his own shield, generally tried to
strike with his sword under or around
the shield of the enemy. In this case
the shields of the Germans were inter-
locked in the close formation, and
Caesar's men in their eagerness, as
they rushed on the foe, sprang up,
pulled back the enemy's shields from
the top, and stabbed with their short
swords from above.

13. **ā sinistrō cornū**: 'on their
left wing,' facing the Roman right,
where Caesar was. 126, c.

14. **conversa esset**: why subjunctive? **ā dextrō cornū**: opposite
the Roman left.

16. **P. Crassus**: See Vocab. under *Crassus*, (2). **adulēscēns**:
'young,' so called to distinguish him from his father and from his older
brother, who was afterwards with Caesar in Gaul; see Vocab. under

tior erat quam eī, quī inter aciem versābantur, tertiam aciem labōrantibus nostrīs subsidiō mīsit.

Caesar is victorious. The captive envoys are rescued.

53. Ita proelium restitūtum est, atque omnēs hostēs terga vertērunt neque prius fugere dēstitērunt, quam ad flūmen Rhēnum, mīlia passuum ex eō locō circiter quīn- quāgintā, pervēnērunt. Ibi perpaucī aut, vīribus cōnfīsī, trānāre contendērunt aut, lintribus inventīs, sibi salūtem s repperērunt. In hīs fuit Ariovistus, quī, nāviculam dēli- gātam ad rīpam nactus, eā profūgit; reliquōs omnēs cōn- secūtī equitēs nostrī interfēcērunt.

Crassus, (3). **equitātuī**: *107*. **expedītior**: 'more disengaged,' so that he had an opportunity to look about and see where help was most needed ; the cavalry, which Crassus commanded, was not fighting.

17. **eī**, etc.: the officers of the legions. **inter aciem**: 'in action.' How lit.? **tertiam aciem**: the 'third line' was usually kept as a reserve force till needed. *337, b*.

18. **labōrantibus** : 'who were hard pressed.' *227, a*, (4). **nos- trīs, subsidiō**: *112, b*.

53. 1. **restitūtum est**: the language implies that the Roman left wing was ceasing to fight when the reserves were sent to its aid.

2. **prius quam**: *189, a*. **ad flūmen Rhēnum**: possibly the fleeing Germans followed the valley of the river Ill and came to the Rhine about ' 50 miles ' northeast of the scene of battle. On the other hand a flight and pursuit of 50 miles seem improbable, and it has been suggested that Caesar wrote *quīndecim*, 'fifteen,' instead of *quīnquāgintā*; for the Rhine is about 15 miles east of the supposed battlefield.

4. **vīribus**: *135, a*. B. 219, 1 ; A. 431 ; H. 476, 3. **cōnfīsī**: *62*.

5. **trānāre**: 'to swim across.' **lintribus**: *15, a*.

6. **nāviculam**: 'a small boat.' **dēligātam**: 'tied.'

7. **nactus**: 'coming upon.' *61, a*, (3), and *226, c*. **eā**: 'in it.' *131, a*. Ariovistus seems to have died not long afterwards (V. 29).

8. **equitēs**: what were the uses of the cavalry? *339*. **interfēcē- runt**: the slain numbered 80,000, according to Plutarch.

Duae fuērunt Ariovistī uxōrēs, ūna Suēba nātiōne, quam
10 domō sēcum ēdūxerat, altera Nōrica, rēgis Vocciōnis soror,
quam in Galliā dūxerat, ā frātre missam; utraeque in eā
fugā periērunt.   Duae fīliae; hārum altera occīsa, altera
capta est.

C. Valerius Procillus, cum ā cūstōdibus in fugā, trīnīs
15 catēnīs vinctus, traherētur, in ipsum Caesarem hostēs equitātū īnsequentem incidit.   Quae quidem rēs Caesarī nōn
minōrem quam ipsa victōria voluptātem attulit, quod hominem honestissimum prōvinciae Galliae, suum familiārem
et hospitem, ēreptum ē manibus hostium, sibi restitūtum
20 vidēbat, neque eius calamitāte dē tantā voluptāte et grātulātiōne quicquam fortūna dēminuerat.   Is, sē praesente, dē
sē ter sortibus cōnsultum dīcēbat, utrum īgnī statim necā-

---

9. **Duae uxōrēs**: the Germans ordinarily had but one wife.   **ūna**
[uxor], **altera**: *91, c.*   **nātiōne**: 'by birth.' How lit.? *142, a.*

11. **dūxerat**: i.e. *in mātrimōnium dūxerat*, 'had married.' **utraeque**: *51.*

12. **fīliae**: sc. *fuērunt. 89, a.*   **altera, altera**: *171, b.*   **occīsa**: sc. *est. 89, b.*

14. **Procillus**: see chap. 47, ll. 10–22, and Notes.   **trīnīs**: distributive; 'with three chains.' *37, e.*

15. **vinctus**: 'bound.' Principal parts of *vinciō, vincō,* and *vīvō?*
traherētur: 'was being dragged along.'   **in ... incidit**: 'fell in
the way of.'   **hostēs**: object of *īnsequentem.*

16. **Quae rēs**: 'And this circumstance.' *167.*

17. **voluptātem**: 'pleasure.'   **attulit**: *69, b.*

18. **honestissimum**: 'very honorable'; *honestus,* from *honor,* is
never our "honest."

19. **hospitem**: 'guest-friend.' *10, d.*   **ēreptum** [esse], **restitūtum** [esse]: *213, a.*

20. **neque**: = *et nōn.*   **eius calamitāte**: 'by his' (Procillus's)
'destruction.'   **grātulātiōne**: '(reason for) thankfulness.'

21. **quicquam dēminuerat**: with the negative in *neque,* 'had not
detracted,' lit. 'had not lessened anything at all.' *168,* and *117, a.*
sē praesente: 'in his presence.' How lit.?

22. **ter**: considered among primitive peoples a sacred number; the

rētur an in aliud tempus reservārētur : *sortium beneficiō sē esse incolumem.*

Item M. Metius repertus et ad eum reductus est.　　25

His army in winter quarters, Caesar goes to North Italy.

54. Hōc proeliō trāns Rhēnum nūntiātō, Suēbī, quī ad rīpās Rhēnī vēnerant, domum revertī coepērunt ; quōs ubi, quī proximī Rhēnum incolunt, perterritōs sēnsērunt, īnsecūtī magnum ex hīs numerum occīdērunt.

Caesar, ūnā aestāte duōbus maximīs bellīs cōnfectīs, 5 mātūrius paulō, quam tempus annī postulābat, in hīberna in Sēquanōs exercitum dēdūxit ; hībernīs Labiēnum prae-

---

notion survives in our "three times and out."　　**sortibus cōnsultum** [esse] : 'the lots were consulted'; see chap. 50, l. 14 and N.　How lit.? *73, d,* and *131, a.*　　**utrum . . . an:** *20:,* (1).　　**īgnī:** *14, b.*　　**statim:** *77.*　　**necārētur:** 'should be killed.'

23. **reservārētur:** 'should be saved up.'　　**sē,** etc. : 'that he was unharmed.'

25. **M. Metius:** chap. 47, l. 16.　　**eum:** *Caesarem.*

54. 1. **Suēbī . . . vēnerant:** see chap. 37, ll. 5–8. .

2. **quōs . . . sēnsērunt:** trans. as if *et ubi eī, quī proximī Rhēnum incolunt, eōs* (i.e. *Suēbōs*) *perterritōs (esse) sēnsērunt.*

3. **Rhēnum:** *123, b.*　B. 141, 3 ; A. 432, *a* ; H. 435, 2.

4. **īnsecūtī:** *226, c.*　　**ex hīs:** *97, d.*

5. **aestāte:** 'summer.' *147, a.*　The defeat of the Helvetians took place near the end of June, that of Ariovistus the second week in September.　With not more than 35,000 soldiers, including cavalry and light-armed troops, Caesar in two campaigns completed in a single season, had practically annihilated fighting forces several times as large as his own, and had destroyed, or rendered docile, two hostile populations aggregating several hundred thousand persons.　History affords no more striking instance of a victory of military organization, discipline, and generalship over numbers, barbaric courage, and brute force.

6. **mātūrius:** *34, a.*　　**hīberna:** 'winter quarters.' *335, a,* and *b.*

7. **Sēquanōs:** *282.*　The region in which the battle was fought had probably formed a part of the Sequanian territory but had been ceded to Ariovistus.　　**hībernīs:** probably at Vesontio, which possessed

posuit; ipse in citeriōrem Galliam ad conventūs agendōs
profectus est.

---

great advantages as a military base, as explained in chap. 38.   **prae-
posuit**: 'put in charge of.' *107, b.*

8. **citeriōrem Galliam**: *284.*   **ad conventūs agendōs**: 'to
hold court.' How lit.? The governor of a province from time to time
visited the principal cities in order to preside over provincial courts for
the administration of justice. In Cisalpine Gaul, moreover, Caesar
would be nearer Rome and so enabled to keep in touch with political
conditions there.

Plate III   Roman Soldiers, Infantry and Cavalry

I. Slinger, *funditor*.   2-3. Legionaries, with different types of equipment.
4. Pack, *sarcinae*.   5. Cavalry.

COMMENTARIUS SECUNDUS

Campaign against the Belgians. 1–28

The Belgians form a league against Caesar.

1. CUM esset Caesar in citeriōre Galliā, ita utī suprā
dēmōnstrāvimus, crēbrī ad eum rūmōrēs afferēbantur, litterīsque item Labiēnī certior fīēbat, omnēs Belgās, quam
tertiam esse Galliae partem dīxerāmus, contrā populum
Rōmānum coniūrāre obsidēsque inter sē dare: 5
Coniūrandī hās esse causās: prīmum, quod verērentur,

---

1. 1. **esset**: *185, c.* B. 288, 1, B; A. 546; H. 600, II. **citeriōre**
Galliā: *124, a,* and *284.* **ita utī**: 'just as.' **suprā**: 'above,' in
the last chapter of Book I. We use the word "above" similarly in
referring to the preceding part of a work.

2. **dēmōnstrāvimus**: *156.* B. 242, 3; A. 143, *a*; H. 500, 2.
Caesar the *writer* sometimes speaks in the first person, but always
presents Caesar the *doer* in the third. **crēbrī**: 'frequently'; agrees
with *rūmōrēs,* 'reports,' but has the force of an adverb. *151.* B. 239;
A. 290; H. 497. **afferēbantur**: force of the imperfect? *175, a.*
B. 260, 2; A. 470; H. 534, 3. **litterīs**: *131, a.* B. 218; H. 476.

3. **certior fīēbat**: 'he was informed.' How lit.? **omnēs . . .
dare**: *213, a,* and *214, a.* **Belgās**: *19, e,* and *287, a.* **quam**:
subject accusative with *esse,* = *quōs,* 'who'; attracted to the feminine
singular to agree with *partem* in the predicate. *164, c,* and *282.*

4. **Galliae**: here Transalpine Gaul, as in I, 1, l. 1, referred to in
dīxerāmus. **dīxerāmus**: *214, c.*

5. **coniūrāre**: 'were conspiring,' according to the Roman point of
view. **inter sē dare**: 'were exchanging.' *159.*

6–8. **Direct form**: Coniūrandī *hae sunt causae:* prīmum, quod *verentur,*
nē, omnī pācātā Galliā, ad eōs exercitus noster *addūcātur;* deinde, quod ab
nōn nūllīs Gallīs *sollicitantur.*

6. **Coniūrandī**, etc.: summary of a statement made in a dispatch
from Labienus (l. 2, *litterīs*). *212, c,* (3), and *214, a.* **hās**: 'as fol-

*nē, omnī pācātā Galliā, ad eōs exercitus noster addūcerētur;
deinde, quod ab nōn nūllīs Gallīs sollicitārentur,* partim quī,
ut Germānōs diūtius in Galliā versārī nōluerant, ita populī
¹⁰ Rōmānī exercitum hiemāre atque inveterāscere in Galliā
molestē ferēbant, partim quī mōbilitāte et levitāte animī
novīs imperiīs studēbant; ab nōn nūllīs etiam, quod in
Galliā ā potentiōribus atque eīs, quī ad condūcendōs hominēs facultātēs habēbant, vulgō rēgna occupābantur, quī
¹⁵ minus facile eam rem imperiō nostrō cōnsequī poterant.

---

lows.' *161, a.* **Coniūrandī causās**: explained by the appositional
quod-clauses following. *230,* (1), and *198, b.* **prīmum, deinde**: *237, b.*
7. **nē**: 'that.' *202.* **omnī pācātā Galliā**: = *sī Gallia omnis
pācāta esset. 144, b,* (4). **Galliā**: Celtic Gaul, bordering the Belgian country on the south; the Romans remained in possession of a
considerable portion of Celtic Gaul after the defeat of the Helvetians
and Ariovistus. *287, b.* **ad eōs**, etc.: the fear of a Roman invasion was justified, as the event proved. The "conspiracy" of the Belgians was the natural effort of a spirited people to defend their liberties
against anticipated encroachment. *158, b.* **noster**: *157, c.*

8. **sollicitārentur**: 'were being stirred up.' **partim quī**: 'partly
(by those) who.' Caesar here passes to the direct form of statement,
presenting as facts, on his own authority, details reported by Labienus.

9. **ut**: 'as.' *188, b.* **diūtius**: *153, a.* **Germānōs versārī**:
223, a.

10. **inveterāscere**: 'should become established.'

11. **molestē ferēbant**: 'were seriously objecting.' **mōbilitāte
et levitāte animī**: 'by reason of temperamental instability and fickleness.' How lit.?

12. **novīs imperiīs**: 'a change of rulers.' *105.* How lit.? **nōn
nūllīs**: i.e. powerful nobles; sc. *sollicitābantur.*

13. **ā potentiōribus**: 'by the more powerful.' *154, a.* **ad
condūcendōs hominēs**: 'for hiring men,' i.e. mercenary soldiers.
230, (3).

14. **rēgna occupābantur**: 'the supreme power was seized.' *92, a,*
and *289, c.* **quī**: 'and they.'

15. **eam rem**: 'that object,' the obtaining of supreme power.
imperiō nostrō: 'under our sovereignty.' *138.* B. *221*; A. *412*;
H. *473, 3.* **poterant**: 'would be able.'

He raises two new legions, marches to their territory.

2. Hīs nūntiīs litterīsque commōtus, Caesar duās legiōnēs in citeriōre Galliā novās cōnscrīpsit et initā aestāte,
in ulteriōrem Galliam quī dēdūceret, Q. Pedium lēgātum
mīsit. Ipse, cum prīmum pābulī cōpia esse inciperet, ad
exercitum vēnit.   Dat negōtium Senonibus reliquīsque 5

Figure 68. — Scene in Belgium : the Meuse, below Namur.

2. **1. nūntiīs litterīsque :** cf. I, 26, l. 20, and N.   **duās legiōnēs :** the thirteenth and fourteenth.   Caesar now had eight legions,
numbered VII to XIV.   *307, a, e, f.*

2. **initā aestāte :** 'at the beginning of the warm season,' probably
the latter part of May.   How lit.?   *68, b,* and *144, b,* (1).

3. **ulteriōrem Galliam :** *286.*   **quī [eās] dēdūceret :** 'to lead
them,' probably over the Great Saint Bernard pass.   *193, a.*   B. 282, 2 ;
A. 531, 2 ; H. 590.   **lēgātum :** *313, a.*   Pedius was a son of
Caesar's sister Julia ; see Vocab.

4. **pābulī cōpia :** forage was needed for the numerous draft animals
used for the transportation of military stores, as well as for the horses
of the cavalry and the officers.   **inciperet :** *185, c.*

5. **exercitum :** probably stationed at or near Vesontio ; see Map I.
Dat negōtium : 'He directed.'   *175, b.*   **reliquīs :** *171, a.*

Gallīs, quī fīnitimī Belgīs erant, utī ea, quae apud eōs
gerantur, cognōscant sēque dē hīs rēbus certiōrem faciant.

Hī cōnstanter omnēs nūntiāvērunt, manūs cōgī, exercitum in ūnum locum condūcī. Tum vērō dubitandum nōn
10 exīstimāvit, quīn ad eōs proficīscerētur. Rē frūmentāriā
comparātā, castra movet diēbusque circiter quīndecim ad
fīnēs Belgārum pervenit.

The Remi submit, and give information about the other Belgians.

3. Eō cum dē imprōvīsō celeriusque omnī opīniōne
vēnisset, Rēmī, quī proximī Galliae ex Belgīs sunt, ad eum

---

6. **Belgīs**: *108, a.*   **utī . . . faciant**: *199, a.*

7. **gerantur**: *220.* B. 324; A. 593; H. 652.   **sē**: *158, a.*

8. **cōnstanter**: 'uniformly,' with perfect agreement between the
reports.   **manūs**: 'bodies of troops' among the Belgians.

9. **locum**: why not ablative? *124, a.*   **dubitandum nōn** [esse]:
sc. *sibi*, 'that he ought not to hesitate.' *73, e.*

10. **ad**: 'against.'   **eōs**: *Belgās.*   **proficīscerētur**: *201, c.*
Rē frūmentāriā comparātā: 'Having provided for a supply of
grain.' *144, b,* (2). How lit.?

11. **castra movet**: 'he broke camp.' *175, b.*   **diēbus**: *147, a.*
circiter: adverb with *quīndecim.*   **ad
fīnēs pervenit**: 'he reached the territories.' The probable route is indicated
on Map 1.

Figure 69.—Coin of the Remi.

Bronze. The three heads of the
obverse perhaps belong to a three-
headed divinity ; inscription, REMO.
Reverse, horses and chariot, copied
from a Greek coin.

3. 1. Eō: = *ad fīnēs Belgārum.*
imprōvīsō: ablative singular neuter of
the adjective used as a noun, forming
with **dē** an adverbial phrase like the
English colloquial phrase " of a sudden,"
"all of a sudden," i.e. 'unexpectedly.'
celerius omnī opīniōne: 'more quickly
than any one had expected,' lit., 'than every expectation.' *129, a.* B.
217, 4 ; A. 406; H. 471.

2. **vēnisset**: *185, c.*   **Rēmī**: the name survives in Reims,
modern name of the city occupying the site of the ancient capital of the
Remi, Durocortorum.   **Galliae**: Celtic Gaul. *287, b.* Why dative?
108, a.   **ex Belgīs**: trans. as if *inter Belgās.*

lēgātōs Iccium et Andecumborium, prīmōs cīvitātis, mīsērunt, quī dīcerent :

Sē suaque omnia in fidem atque potestātem populī 5
Rōmānī permittere, neque sē cum reliquīs Belgīs cōnsēnsisse,
neque contrā populum Rōmānum coniūrāsse, parātōsque esse
et obsidēs dare et imperāta facere et oppidīs recipere et frū-
mentō cēterīsque rēbus iuvāre.

Reliquōs omnēs Belgās in armīs esse, Germānōsque, quī 10
cis Rhēnum incolant, sēsē cum hīs coniūnxisse, tantumque esse
eōrum omnium furōrem, ut nē Suessiōnēs quidem, frātrēs

---

3. **lēgātōs** : 'as envoys.' *115, a.*   **prīmōs** : 'the leading men.'
154, a.   **cīvitātis** : of the Remi.

4. **quī dīcerent** : 'to say.' *193, a.*   B. 282, 2 ; A. 531, 2 ; H. 590.

5-9. **Direct form :** *Nōs nostraque* omnia in fidem atque potestātem populī
Rōmānī *permittimus;* neque cum reliquīs Belgīs *cōnsēnsimus,* neque contrā
populum Rōmānum *coniūrāvimus, parātī*que *sumus* et obsidēs dare et imperāta facere et (*tē*) oppidīs recipere et (*tē*) frūmentō cēterīsque rēbus iuvāre.

5. **Sē**, etc. : *212, c,* (3).   **Sē suaque omnia** : 'themselves and
all that they had.' How lit. ?   **in fidem** : 'to the protection.'

6. **permittere** : sc. *sē* as subject. *214, a.*   **neque** : 'and not.'

7. **coniūrāsse** : = *coniūrāvisse. 64, a,* (1).   **parātōs** : adjective,
in predicate.

8. **et, et** : *234, a.*   **dare, facere,** [eum] **recipere,** [eum] **iuvāre** :
after *parātōs. 221, c.*   B. 328, 1 ; A. 460, *b* ; H. 608, 4.   **imperāta**
facere : 'to obey (his) orders.' *157, a.*   **oppidīs** : 'in (their)
towns.' How lit. ? *131, a.*   **frūmentō** : *131, a.*

10-15. **Direct form :** *Reliquī* omnēs *Belgae* in armīs *sunt, Germānī*que,
quī cis Rhēnum *incolunt,* sēsē cum hīs *coniūnxērunt; tantus*que *est* eōrum
omnium *furor,* ut nē Suessiōnēs quidem, frātrēs consanguineōsque *nostrōs,* quī
eōdem iūre et īsdem lēgibus *ūtuntur,* ūnum imperium ūnumque magistrātum
nōbīscum habent, dēterrēre *potuerīmus,* quīn cum hīs cōnsentīrent.

11. **cis Rhēnum** : on the west side of the Rhine ; Caesar writes
from the point of view of the Province.

12. **eōrum omnium** : *Belgārum et Germānōrum.*   **nē — quidem** :
237, c.   **Suessiōnēs** : object of *dēterrēre.* The name survives in
Soissons.

*cōnsanguineōsque suōs, quī eōdem iūre et īsdem lēgibus
ūtantur, ūnum imperium ūnumque magistrātum cum ipsīs*
15 *habeant, dēterrēre potuerint, quīn cum hīs cōnsentīrent.*

Report of the Remi on the history and forces of the Belgians.

4. Cum ab eīs quaereret, quae cīvitātēs quantaeque in
armīs essent et quid in bellō possent, sīc reperiēbat :

*Plērōsque Belgās esse ortōs ā Germānīs, Rhēnumque
antīquitus trāductōs, propter locī fertilitātem, ibi cōnsēdisse,*
5 *Gallōsque, quī ea loca incolerent, expulisse, sōlōsque esse,
quī patrum nostrōrum memoriā, omnī Galliā vexātā, Teu-*

---

13. **suōs** : 'their own,' referring to the Remi.   **iūre** : '(body of)
rights.' *13, g,* and *131, c.*   **īsdem** : *45.*

15. **potuerint** : *197, a, b.*   B. 268, 6 ; A. 485, *c* ;. H. 550.   **quīn**
—**cōnsentīrent** : 'from uniting.' *201, a.*   B. 295, 3, *a* ; A. 558 ; H.
595, 2.

4. 1. **ab eīs** : *116, c.*   **quaereret** : why subjunctive?   **quae** :
48, b.

2. **essent** : *204,* (2).   B. 300 ; A. 574 ; H. 649, II.   **quid—
possent** : 'what strength they had,' lit. 'to what degree they were
able.' *118, b.*   B. 176, 3 ; A. 390, *c* ; H. 409, 1.   **sīc** : 'as follows.'

3–9. **Direct form** : *Plērīque Belgae sunt ortī* ā Germānīs, Rhēnumque antīquitus *trāductī,* propter locī fertilitātem, *hīc cōnsēdērunt,* Gallōsque, quī *haec* loca
*incolēbant, expulērunt ; sōlī*que *sunt,* quī patrum nostrōrum memoriā, omnī
Galliā vexātā, Teutonōs Cimbrōsque intrā suōs fīnēs ingredī prohibuerint
(194, a) ; quā ex rē *fit,* utī eārum rērum memoriā magnam sibi auctōritātem
magnōsque spīritūs in rē mīlitārī *sūmant.*

3. **Plērōsque Belgās** : 'That most of the Belgians.' *97, c.*   **ā
Germānīs** : *128, b.*   The Belgians were of Celtic stock, but had formerly lived on the east side of the Rhine ; hence probably arose the
belief that they were of Germanic origin.   **Rhēnum** : accusative after
trā(ns) in *trāductōs. 114, a.*

4. **antīquitus** : 'in ancient times.'   **fertilitātem** : 'productive-
ness.'   **ibi** : in Gaul.

5. **sōlōs** : in predicate ; 'were the only (people of Gaul) who.'

6. **memoriā** : *147, b.*   **omnī Galliā vexātā** : 'when Gaul as a

*tonōs Cimbrōsque intrā suōs fīnēs ingredī prohibuerint ; quā
ex rē fierī, utī eārum rērum memoriā magnam sibi auctōritātem magnōsque spīritūs in rē mīlitārī sūmerent.*

Dē numerō eōrum omnia sē habēre explōrāta Rēmī dīcē- 10
bant, proptereā quod, propinquitātibus affīnitātibusque
coniūnctī, quantam quisque multitūdinem in commūnī Belgārum conciliō ad id bellum pollicitus sit, cognōverint :

*Plūrimum inter eōs Bellovacōs et virtūte et auctōritāte et
hominum numerō valēre ; hōs posse cōnficere armāta mīlia* 15

---

whole was ravaged' by the Cimbrians and Teutons; see N. to I, 33,
l. 17. *144, b*, (2), and *286.*

7. **ingredī**: 'from entering'; Caesar uses the infinitive with subject-
accusative after *prohibeō. 223, a*, (3).   **quā ex rē**: 'and in consequence of this achievement.' *167.*

8. **fierī, utī . . . sūmerent**: *203*, (1).   **memoriā**: *135, a.*

9. **in rē mīlitārī**: 'in respect to the art of war.'   **sūmerent**:
why imperfect? *177, a.*

10. **eōrum**: *Belgārum.*   **omnia sē habēre explōrāta**: 'that
they possessed complete information.' How lit. ? *229, a.*   B. 337, 7;
A. 497, *b*; H. 431, 3.

11. **proptereā quod**: N. to I, chap. 1, l. 6.   **propinquitātibus
affīnitātibusque**: 'by blood relationships and intermarriages.' *76, a.*

12. **quisque**: 'each' representative, speaking for his state or tribe.
multitūdinem: 'host.'

13. **pollicitus sit**: *204*, (3).   **cognōverint**: *214, a.*

14-17. **Direct form**: Plūrimum inter eōs *Bellovacī* et virtūte et auctōritāte et hominum numerō *valent ; hī
possunt* cōnficere armāta mīlia centum;
pollicitī (sunt) ex eō numerō ēlēcta
sexāgintā, tōtīusque bellī imperium
sibi *postulant.*

Figure 70. — Coin of the Bellovaci.
Gold ; fanciful designs.

14. **Plūrimum**, etc. : *212, c*, (3).
Plūrimum Bellovacōs valēre :
'that the Bellovaci were the most powerful' (Fig. 70).   *118, b.*
virtūte: *135, a.*

15. **cōnficere**: 'muster.' *57, b.*   **armāta mīlia**: trans. as if
mīlia hominum armātōrum.

*centum, pollicitōs ex eō numerō ēlēcta sexāgintā, tōtīusque
bellī imperium sibi postulāre.*

*Suessiōnēs suōs esse fīnitimōs ; fīnēs lātissimōs ferācissi-
mōsque agrōs possidēre. Apud eōs fuisse rēgem nostrā*
20 *etiam memoriā Dīviciācum, tōtīus Galliae potentissimum,
quī cum magnae partis hārum regiōnum, tum etiam Britanniae, imperium obtinuerit ; nunc esse rēgem Galbam ; ad
hunc propter iūstitiam prūdentiamque summam tōtīus bellī
omnium voluntāte dēferrī ; oppida habēre numerō XII, pol-*

16. **pollicitōs :** *89, b.*   **ēlēcta sexāgintā :** sc. *mīlia,* 'sixty (thousand) picked men.'   **tōtīus :** *23, a.*

18–31. **Direct form :** *Suessiōnēs nostrī sunt fīnitimī ; fīnēs lātissimōs
ferācissimōsque agrōs possident.* Apud eōs *fuit rēx* nostrā etiam memoriā
Dīviciācus, tōtīus Galliae *potentissimus,* quī cum magnae partis hārum regiōnum, tum etiam Britanniae, imperium *obtinuit ;* nunc est *rēx Galba ;* ad hunc
propter iūstitiam prūdentiamque *summa* tōtīus bellī omnium voluntāte dēfertur; oppida *habent* numerō XII, *pollicentur* mīlia armāta L; totidem *Nerviī,*
quī maximē ferī inter ipsōs *habentur* longissimēque *absunt ;* XV mīlia Atrebātēs, *Ambiānī* X mīlia, *Morinī* XXV mīlia, *Menapiī* VII mīlia, *Caletī* X mīlia,
Veliocassēs et *Viromanduī* totidem, Atuatucī XVIIII mīlia; Condrūsōs, Eburōnēs, Caerōsōs, Paemānōs, qui ūnō nōmine Germānī appellantur, *arbitrāmur*
posse armāre ad XL mīlia.

18. **suōs fīnitimōs :** 'their neighbors,' neighbors of the Remi.
ferācissimōs : 'very productive.' *27, a,* and *153, a.*

19. **possidēre :** as subject-accusative supply *eōs,* i.e. *Suessiōnēs.*
fuisse 'that there had been.' *90, a.*

20. **Dīviciācum :** not to be confused with Diviciācus the Aeduan
druid, who is mentioned in the next chapter.

21. **cum . . . tum :** 'not only . . . but also,' *186, b.*   **regiōnum :**
dependent on *partis,* which limits *imperium.*   **Britanniae :** not the
whole of Britain — probably only a portion of the island along the
southeast coast. *294.*

22. **esse,** etc.: trans. as if *Galbam esse rēgem. 19, d.*   **ad hunc**
— **dēferrī :** 'that upon him — was conferred.' *69, b.*

23. **prūdentiam :** 'good judgment.'   **summam :** 'the supreme
command.'

24. **voluntāte :** *138.*   **habēre, pollicērī :** sc. *eōs (Suessiōnēs).*
numerō : *142, a,* and *85.*   **XII, L,** etc.: *38, b,* and *36.*

licērī mīlia armāta L; *totidem Nerviōs, quī maximē ferī* 25
inter ipsōs habeantur longissimēque absint; XV *mīlia Atre-*
bātēs, Ambiānōs X *mīlia, Morinōs* XXV *mīlia, Menapiōs* VII
mīlia, Caletōs X *mīlia, Veliocassēs et Viromanduōs totidem,*
Atuatucōs XVIIII *mīlia; Condrūsōs, Eburōnēs, Caerōsōs,*
Paemānōs, quī ūnō nōmine Germānī appellantur, *arbitrārī* 30
sē posse armāre ad XL *mīlia.*

*Caesar, taking hostages from the Remi, crosses the Aisne, and
encamps.*

5. Caesar, Rēmōs cohortātus līberāliterque ōrātiōne prōsecūtus, omnem senātum ad sē convenīre prīncipumque
līberōs obsidēs ad sē addūcī iussit. Quae omnia ab hīs
dīligenter ad diem facta sunt.   35

---

25. **mīlia armāta:** N. to l. 15.   **totidem:** sc. *mīlia armāta pollicērī.*   **Nerviōs:** locate the Nervians, and the other peoples named,
upon Map 1.   **maximē ferī:** in predicate. *30.*

26. **ipsōs:** the Belgians in general, not the Nervians.   **habeantur, absint:** vivid use of the present tense where the imperfect, after
cognōverint, in l. 13, might have been
expected.   **absint:** from the country
of the Remi.   **Atrebātēs:** sc. *pollicērī.*

27. **Ambiānōs:** in the region of
modern *Amiens* (Fig. 71).

29. **XVIIII:** *ūndēvīgintī. 36.*

30. **quī . . . appellantur:** *214, c.*
Germānī: perhaps so called because,
although of Celtic stock, they had been
the last of the Belgians to remove from
the east side of the Rhine to the Belgian country.   **ūnō:** 'a common.'

Figure 71. — Coin of the
Ambiani.

Bronze. Obverse, figure with
uplifted hands, wearing a necklace
and bracelets; perhaps a divinity

31. **sē:** *158, a.*   **ad:** adverb, 'about.'

5. 1. **Rēmōs . . . prōsecūtus:** 'encouraging the Remi and ad-
dressing (them) in gracious words.'   How lit.? *226, c.*

2. **senātum:** *289, b,* and *75, b.*   **prīncipum:** *10, b.*

3. **obsidēs:** 'as hostages.' *88, a.*   **iussit:** 'gave orders (that).'
Quae . . . facta sunt: 'these instructions . . . were carried out.'

4. **dīligenter:** 'carefully.' *34, a.*   **ad diem:** 'promptly.'

5   Ipse, Dīviciācum Aeduum magnopere cohortātus, docet,
quantō opere reī pūblicae commūnisque salūtis intersit,
manūs hostium distinērī, nē cum tantā multitūdine ūnō
tempore cōnflīgendum sit: *Id fierī posse, sī suās cōpiās
Aeduī in fīnēs Bellovacōrum intrōdūxerint et eōrum agrōs*
10 *populārī coeperint.* Hīs mandātīs eum ab sē dīmittit.

Postquam omnēs Belgārum cōpiās in ūnum locum coāctās
ad sē venīre vīdit, neque iam longē abesse, ab eīs, quōs
mīserat, explōrātōribus et ab Rēmīs cognōvit, flūmen Axonam, quod est in extrēmīs Rēmōrum fīnibus, exercitum
15 trādūcere mātūrāvit atque ibi castra posuit. Quae rēs et

---

5. **Dīviciācum** : N. to chap. 4, l. 20, and Book I, chapters
18, 20, 31, etc.

6. **quantō opere**, etc. : 'how important it was for the State and for
their mutual welfare.' How lit.? *103, e.* B. 211, 1 ; A. 355 ; H. 449.
reī pūblicae : *Rōmānōrum.* **commūnis** : of Romans and Aeduans.
intersit : *204,* (3).

7. **manūs distinērī** : subject of *intersit ;* 'that the enemy's forces
be kept apart.' *222, c,* and *79, d.*   **nē . . . cōnflīgendum sit** : 'that
it might not be necessary to fight.' *73, e.*

8. **Id** : refers to *manūs distinērī,* 'that (object).' *213, b,* and
160, c.

9. **in — intrōdūxerint** : 'should have led — into'; future perfect
indicative in the direct form. *218,* (1), b.

11. **coāctās . . . venīre** : 'had been brought together and were
coming.' *228, a.*

12. **vīdit** : more vivid than *intellēxit ;* so we use the word "see" of
things understood but not perceived with the eyes. *188, a.*   **neque** :
trans. as if *et nōn.*   **abesse** : sc. *eās* (= *cōpiās*) ; dependent on *cognōvit.*   **eīs** : with *explōrātōribus.*

13. **explōrātōribus** : *327.*   **flūmen, exercitum** : *114, a.* B.
179, 1 ; A. 395 ; H. 413.   **Axonam** : now *Aisne.* See Map 1.

14. **quod** : the antecedent is *flūmen.*   **extrēmīs fīnibus** : 'the
most remote part of the country.' *152, a.*

15. **ibi castra posuit** : Caesar 'encamped' on the north side of the
Axona, about a mile and a half northeast of the present village of
Berry-au-Bac. See Map 5.   **Quae rēs** : 'Now this movement.' *167.*
et . . . et : *233, d.*

latus ūnum castrōrum rīpīs flūminis mūniēbat et, post eum
quae erant, tūta ab hostibus reddēbat et, commeātūs ab
Rēmīs reliquīsque cīvitātibus ut sine perīculō ad eum portārī possent, efficiēbat.

In eō flūmine pōns erat.   Ibi praesidium pōnit et in 20

Figure 72. — View across the Aisne from the site of Caesar's camp.
The present course of the Aisne is marked by the nearer line of trees.

16. **rīpīs**: *131, a.*   **post . . . reddēbat**: 'made the rear secure
against the enemy.' *331, b.*   How lit.?

17. **quae**: i.e. *ea* (*loca*) *quae.*   **tūta**: *115, b.*   **commeātūs
. . . efficiēbat**: 'made it possible for supplies to be brought,' etc.
203, (3). B. 297, 1 ; A. 568; H. 571, 3.   **commeātūs**: plural
because the supplies were furnished by more than one state.

20. **In**: 'across.'   **pōns**: *17, c.*   **erat**: *90, a.*   **praesidium**:
at **D** on Map 5.   **in alterā parte**: on the south side of the Aisne,
opposite Berry-au-Bac; see Map 5, **C**. Caesar now had both ends of
the bridge well guarded. In consequence he was able to get provisions
from his allies across the river; to set a watch on the Remi, the sincerity
of whose professions of loyalty was not beyond question; and, finally,
to keep open an avenue of retreat in case of disaster (Fig. 72).

alterā parte flūminis Q. Titūrium Sabīnum lēgātum cum
sex cohortibus relinquit; castra in altitūdinem pedum duodecim vāllō fossāque duodēvīgintī pedum mūnīre iubet.

The Belgians attack Bibrax, a town of the Remi.

6. Ab hīs castrīs oppidum Rēmōrum, nōmine Bibrax,
aberat mīlia passuum VIII. Id ex itinere magnō impetū
Belgae oppugnāre coepērunt. Aegrē eō diē sustentātum
est.

5   Gallōrum eadem atque Belgārum oppugnātiō est haec.
Ubi, circumiectā multitūdine hominum tōtīs moenibus, undique in mūrum lapidēs iacī coeptī sunt, mūrusque dēfēnsōribus nūdātus est, testūdine factā portās succendunt

---

22. **sex cohortibus**: about how many men? *307, c.*   **castra**:
Map 5, **A.**   **pedum**: *100, a.* The measurement of twelve feet included both the height of the bank formed by the earth thrown out of
the trench and that of the row of palisades along the outer edge. *333.*
   23. **vāllō**: why ablative?   **duodēvīgintī pedum**: eighteen Roman feet broad, measured across the top; the trench, with sloping sides,
was probably about ten feet deep. Excavations, made in 1862, brought
to light traces of this rampart and trench.

   6. 1. **nōmine**: 'called.' How lit.? *142, a.* B. 226; A. 418; H.
480.   **Bibrax**: the name in Celtic meant 'Beavertown.'

   2. **mīlia passuum VIII**: *118, a;* *100, a,* and *243, b.*   **ex itinere**:
'from the line of march,' attacking the town as soon as they reached it;
see Vocab. under **iter.**

   3. **Aegrē sustentātum est**: 'With difficulty the defense was maintained.'

   5. **eadem atque Belgārum**: 'the same as (that) of the Belgians.'
233, c.   **oppugnātiō**: 'the (method of) storming (fortified places).'
haec: *161, a.*

   6. **Ubi**, etc.: 'When a host of men has been thrown around the
entire (circuit of) fortifications and.' How lit.? *144, b, (2).*   **moenibus**: *104, a.*

   7. **iacī**: *57, b.*   **coeptī sunt**: *72, c.*   **dēfēnsōribus**: 'of its
defenders.' *127, a,* and *74, a.*

   8. **nūdātus est**: 'has been cleared.'   **testūdine factā**: 'having

mūrumque subruunt.   Quod tum facile fīēbat.   Nam cum
tanta multitūdō lapidēs ac tēla conicerent, in mūrō cōnsis- 10
tendī potestās erat nūllī.

Cum fīnem oppugnandī nox fēcisset, Iccius Rēmus,
summā nōbilitāte et grātiā inter suōs, quī tum oppidō praefuerat, ūnus ex eīs, quī lēgātī dē pāce ad Caesarem vēnerant,
nūntium ad eum mittit, *nisi subsidium sibi summittātur, sēsē* 15
diūtius sustinēre nōn posse.

Caesar relieves the town; the Belgians march toward his camp.

7. Eō dē mediā nocte Caesar, īsdem ducibus ūsus, quī
nūntiī ab Icciō vēnerant, Numidās et Crētas sagittāriōs et

---

made a tortoise roof,' in the Roman fashion. *345.*   **testūdine** : *12, d,*
and *144, b,* (2).   **succendunt** : 'they,' the attacking host, 'set on
fire.' *175, c.*

9. **subruunt** : 'undermine.'   **Quod tum** : 'Now this, in the present instance,' referring to the burning of the gates, and undermining of
the walls, of Bibrax.

10. **conicerent** : *173, b,* and *184, a.* B. 254, 4 ; A. 317, *d* ; H. 389, 1.
cōnsistendī : *230,* (1).

11. **nūllī** : trans. as if *nēminī* (*12, d,* and *111*), 'no one was able to
stand.' How lit.?

12. **fīnem oppugnandī fēcisset** : 'had checked the assault.' *185, c.*
How lit.?   **Iccius** : chap. 3, l. 3.

13. **summā nōbilitāte** : *143, a.*   **inter suōs** : 'among his countrymen.' *154, a.*   **oppidō** : *107, a.*   **tum praefuerat** : i.e. *prae-
positus erat et tum praeerat.*

14. **ex eīs** : *97, d.*   **lēgātī** : in predicate after *vēnerant*; 'as envoys.'

15. **nūntium** : here 'a message.'   **nisi** : '(saying) that unless,'
etc. *213, b.*   **sibi** : 'to them,' the beleaguered inhabitants of Bibrax.
summittātur : 'should be sent to their relief.' *218,* (1), a.

16. **sustinēre** : intransitive, 'hold out.'

7. 1. **Eō** : toward Bibrax.   **dē** : *242, d.*   **īsdem** : 'the same
men.' *45,* and *131, c.*   **ducibus** : 'as guides,' predicative. *131, f.*
ūsus : *226, c.*

2. **nūntiī** : construed as *lēgātī* in chap. 6, l. 14.   **Numidās,** etc. :
308.   **Crētas** : *19, f.*   **sagittāriōs** : 'bowmen.'

funditōrēs Baleārēs subsidiō oppidānīs mittit ; quōrum adventū et Rēmīs cum spē dēfēnsiōnis studium prōpugnandī
5 accessit, et hostibus, eādem dē causā, spēs potiundī oppidī
discessit.

Itaque paulisper apud oppidum morātī agrōsque Rēmōrum dēpopulātī, omnibus vīcīs aedificiīsque, quō adīre
potuerant, incēnsīs, ad castra Caesaris omnibus cōpiīs con-
10 tendērunt et ā mīlibus passuum minus duōbus castra posu-

---

3. **funditōrēs**: 'slingers.' *74, a.* Fig. 73 and Fig. 76.   **subsidiō, oppidānīs**: *112, b.*   B. 191, 2 ; A. 382, 1 ; H. 433.   **oppi-**

dānīs: 'the inhabitants of
the town.'   **mittit**: *175, b.*

4. **et . . . et**: *233, a.*
spē dēfēnsiōnis: 'hope of
repelling the assault.'   How
lit. ? *74, b.*   **studium prōpugnandī**: 'eager desire to
take the offensive.'   How
lit. ?

5. **hostibus**: dative, but
trans. 'from the enemy.'
109, b.   **potiundī oppidī**:
64, b, and *230,* (1).

7. **paulisper**: 'for a short
time.'   **morātī**, etc.: sc.
hostēs as subject of *contendērunt*. *61, a,* (1).

8. **vīcīs, aedificiīs**: cf.
Book I, 5, ll. 4, 5 and Notes.
144, b, (2).   **quō**: adverb ;
trans. as if *ad quae.*

9. **omnibus cōpiīs**: *136,
b.* B. 220, 1 ; A. 412 ; H.
473, 3.

Figure 73.—Slinger, supplied with pebbles.   10. **ā . . . duōbus**: 'less
than two miles away,' i.e. 'at'
(lit. 'from') 'a distance of thousands of paces less than two (thousands).'   The Roman point of view differs from ours in such phrases.

ērunt; quae castra, ut fūmō atque īgnibus significābātur, amplius mīlibus passuum VIII in lātitūdinem patēbant.

Caesar adds to the fortifications of his camp, awaits attack.

8. Caesar prīmō et propter multitūdinem hostium et propter eximiam opīniōnem virtūtis proeliō supersedēre statuit; cotīdiē tamen equestribus proeliīs, quid hostis virtūte posset et quid nostrī audērent, perīclitābātur.

Ubi nostrōs nōn esse īnferiōrēs intellēxit, locō prō castrīs 5 ad aciem īnstruendam nātūrā opportūnō atque idōneō, quod is collis, ubi castra posita erant, paululum ex plānitiē ēditus, tantum adversus in lātitūdinem patēbat, quantum

---

11. **quae castra**: 'and this camp,' marked CAMP OF THE BELGIANS on Map 5, while Caesar's camp is at **A**. *167*. **fūmō**: 'by the smoke.' **significābātur**: 'was indicated.' *73, d*.

12. **mīlibus**: why ablative? *129, a*. B. 217, 1; A. 407, *e*; H. 471. VIII: *38, b*, and *36*.

8. 2. **eximiam opīniōnem virtūtis**: 'their extraordinary reputation for bravery.' *102*. **proeliō supersedēre**: 'to refrain from battle.' *127, a*.

3. **equestribus proeliīs**: 'cavalry skirmishes,' as distinguished from a regular engagement, with infantry. **quid . . . posset**: 'what mettle the enemy had.' How lit.? *118, b*. **virtūte**: *142, a*.

4. **perīclitābātur**: 'kept trying to find out.' *175, d*. B. 260, 2; A. 470; H. 534, 3.

5. **locō . . . idōneō**: trans. as if *cum locus* ('since the space') . . . *opportūnus atque idōneus esset*. *144, b*, (3).

6. **ad**, etc.: *230*, (3). **nātūrā**: 'naturally.' How lit.? **atque**: *233, a*.

7. **quod . . . redībat**: explains why the ground in front of the camp was well adapted for forming a line of battle. **ubi**: 'on which.' **castra**: Map 5, **A**. **paululum ēditus**: 'gradually rising.' How lit.?

8. **tantum**, etc.: 'on the side toward the enemy extended in width (far enough to provide) just the amount of space that a line of battle would require.' How lit.? **tantum**: *118, a*. **adversus**: adjective, agreeing with *collis*. **quantum**: correlative with *tantum*, and object of *occupāre*, having *locī* dependent on it.

loci acies instructa occupare poterat, atque ex utraque
10 parte lateris deiectus habebat, et in frontem leniter fastigatus paulatim ad planitiem redibat, ab utroque latere eius
collis transversam fossam obduxit circiter passuum quadringentorum et ad extremas fossas castella constituit ibique
tormenta collocavit, ne, cum aciem instruxisset, hostes, quod
15 tantum multitudine poterant, ab lateribus pugnantes, suos
circumvenire possent.

9. **loci**: trans. as if dependent on *tantum*. *97, a.* The long,
gently sloping hillside, broad enough to afford room for a Roman triple
line, is shown on Map 5, between the Miette brook and the narrowing
crest of the hill southwest of Caesar's camp; six legions are there
shown in order of battle. **ex utraque parte**: = 'on either side,'
the side of the camp toward the river, and the opposite side.

10. **lateris deiectus**: 'steep slopes.' How lit.? *13, e.* **in
frontem**: 'in' (lit. 'into') 'front' of the camp, on the southwest
side. **leniter fastigatus**: 'with gentle slope.' How lit.?

11. **planitiem**: the level ground between the hill and the river
above and below Berry-au-Bac. **redibat**: here 'descended.'

12. **transversam fossam obduxit**: 'he extended a trench crosswise,' that is, at right angles with the length of the hill. Starting from
opposite corners of the camp, Caesar prolonged two lines of intrenchments at right angles to the sides, each about a third of a mile in
length. One ran down the south slope of the hill, toward the Aisne,
the bed of which in Caesar's time is indicated on the plan by the
broken line. The other ran down the north slope, toward the Miette
brook; both are indicated on Map 5 by red lines (**a, b**). At the
ends of these intrenchments he constructed 'redoubts' (**B B**), where
he stationed troops, with military engines. His purpose was to guard
against a flank movement on the part of the enemy, by which they might
reach the rear of the camp, and attack from behind while his forces were
engaged in front. **passuum quadringentorum**: 'four hundred paces'
in length. How lit.? *100, a.* How far by our measurement? *243, b.*

13. **ad extremas fossas**: 'at the ends of the trenches.' *152, a.*
B. 241, 1; A. 293; H. 497, 4. **castella**: Map 5, **B B**.

14. **tormenta**: 'torsioners,' such as were used in siege operations.
343. **instruxisset**: *220.* **quod ... poterant**: 'because they
were so strong in numbers.' Why indicative?

15. **tantum**: *118, b.* **ab lateribus**: 'on the flanks.' *126, c.*

MAP 5

THE BATTLE AT THE AISNE (AXONA)

Book II, 7–10   To face page 144

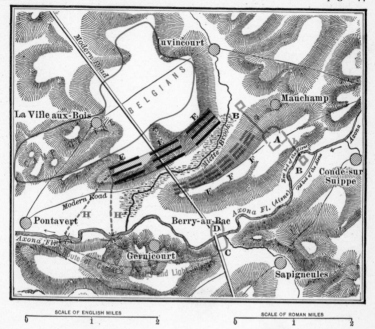

SCALE OF ENGLISH MILES

SCALE OF ROMAN MILES

EXPLANATION

Caesar, marching from the South, encamped on the north or right bank of the Aisne, on a long hill. As the camp was well protected by the streams and the low ground on the west, in order to secure the east side, he ran intrenchments from the corners to both the Aisne and the Miette. The widely extended Belgian camp was on the opposite side of the Miette (chap. 7, ll. 11–12).

A. Caesar's camp (chap. 5, l. 15; chap. 7, l. 9; chap. 8, l. 7).

a, b. Trenches, *fossae* (chap. 8, ll. 11–13).

B, B. Redoubts, *castella* (chap. 8, l. 13).

C. Redoubt at the south end of the bridge, *castellum*, held by Q. Titurius Sabinus (chap. 5, ll. 20–22; chap. 9, l. 11).

D. Guard at the north end of the bridge, *praesidium* (chap. 5, l. 20).

E–E. The Belgians in battle order (chap. 8, l. 20).

F–F. The six legions in battle order (chap. 8, l. 19).

H–H. Probable routes taken by the Belgians to the fords at the Aisne, where they were met by Caesar's light-armed troops and cavalry (chap. 9, ll. 8–15).

Hōc factō, duābus legiōnibus, quās proximē cōnscrīpserat, in castrīs relīctīs, ut, sī quō opus esset, subsidiō dūcī
possent, reliquās VI legiōnēs prō castrīs in aciē cōnstituit.
Hostēs item suās cōpiās ex castrīs ēductās īnstrūxerant. 20

Figure 74. — View toward the Miette from the site of Caesar's camp.
The course of the brook is marked by the trees.   Notice the flat, marshy land (palus)
near the brook.

---

pugnantēs: with *hostēs*.   suōs: 'his men.' *154, a*. A glance at
the Map shows how well designed the trenches were to protect against
an attack upon the right end of the battle line, and block access to the
rear, which was otherwise protected by the river.

17. duābus legiōnibus: the thirteenth and fourteenth, enrolled a
few months before ; see chap. 2, ll. 1–4.   Generally, as in this instance,
Caesar exposed his veterans to the brunt of the battle, leaving recruits,
whose powers had not been fully tested, as a reserve force. *307, d,*
and *f*.

18. relīctīs: *144, b*, (2).   quō: 'at any point.'   esset: *220*.
subsidiō: 'as a reserve force.' *112, a*.

19. aciē: undoubtedly a triple line. *337*.

20. ēductās īnstrūxerant: 'had led forth and drawn up.' *228, a*

The Belgians attempt to cross the Aisne and attack Titurius.

9. Palūs erat nōn magna inter nostrum atque hostium exercitum.   Hanc sī nostrī trānsīrent, hostēs exspectābant; nostrī autem, sī ab illīs initium trānseundī fieret, ut impedī-tōs aggrederentur, parātī in armīs erant.   Interim proeliō
5 equestrī inter duās aciēs contendēbātur.   Ubi neutrī trāns-eundī initium faciunt, secundiōre equitum proeliō nostrīs, Caesar suōs in castra redūxit.

Hostēs prōtinus ex eō locō ad flūmen Axonam contendē-runt, quod esse post nostra castra dēmōnstrātum est.   Ibi,
10 vadīs repertīs, partem suārum cōpiārum trādūcere cōnātī

B. 337, 5 ; A. 496, N. 2 ; H. 639.   For the relative positions of the two armies, see Map 5.

9. 1. **Palūs** : the marshy ground along the Miette brook, indi-cated on Map 5.   In the dry weather of the autumn of 1914 the German army ran first-line and communicating trenches through this marsh, but later these were flooded by the Miette brook.   **erat** : *90, a.* **nostrum,** etc. : ' our army and that of the enemy.' *157, d.*

2. **Hanc** : *palūdem.*   **sī** : ' (to see) whether.' *204,* (4). B. 300, 3 ; A. 576, *a* ; H. 649, II, 3.

3. **nostrī . . . erant** : *nostrī autem parātī in armīs erant, ut, sī ab illīs* (*hostibus*) *initium trānseundī* (*palūdem*) *fieret,* (*eōs,* the enemy engaged in crossing over, hence at a disadvantage) *impedītōs aggrede-rentur.*   **fieret** : *220.* B. 324, 1 ; A. 593 ; H. 652.

4. **aggrederentur** : *57, c.*   Why subjunctive?   **proeliō,** etc. : ' a cavalry engagement continued.'   How lit. ?   *73, d.*

5. **neutrī** : ' neither side '; each side was waiting for the other to assume the offensive.   *23, a.*

6. **secundiōre proeliō** : *144, b,* (5).   B. 227, 2, *c* ; A. 420, 3 ; H. 489, 1.   **nostrīs** : *108, a.*

8. **prōtinus** : ' at once.'   **eō locō** : on the opposite side of the marsh from the Romans.

9. **dēmōnstrātum est** : ' it has been shown '; see chap. 5, ll. 11-19.

10. **vadīs** : shallow places, suitable for fording, are still found in the Aisne, between the mouth of the Miette brook and the village of

sunt, eō cōnsiliō, ut, sī possent, castellum, cui praeerat Q. Titūrius lēgātus, expugnārent pontemque interscinderent; sī minus potuissent, agrōs Rēmōrum populārentur, quī magnō nōbīs ūsuī ad bellum gerendum erant, commeātūque nostrōs prohibērent.

15

Figure 75. — View across the Aisne toward Pontavert.

The water in the foreground is in a canal. The river lies in the gully beyond; there the fight at the ford took place.

Pontavert; for the route of the attacking forces see Map 5, **H H**.

11. eō cōnsiliō: 'with this design,' explained by the appositive *ut*-clauses following. *135, a*, and *203*, (4). **possent**: *220*. **castellum**: on the south bank of the Aisne; Map 5, **C**, and chap. 5, ll. 20–22. The Belgians planned to storm the redoubt from the rear. The attempt was justified, from the military point of view; for the destruction of the bridge would have made Caesar's position extremely difficult.

13. minus: trans. as if *nōn*. **potuissent**: change of tense from *possent*, 'if they could,' to *potuissent* 'if (having made the attempt) they should have been unsuccessful.' **populārentur, prohibērent**: sc. *ut*, the clauses being in apposition with *cōnsiliō*.

14. nōbīs, ūsuī: *112, b*. **commeātū**: *127, a*.

Caesar prevents their crossing; they decide to disperse.

10. Caesar, certior factus ab Titūriō, omnem equitātum et levis armātūrae Numidās, funditōrēs sagittāriōsque pontem trādūcit atque ad eōs contendit. Ācriter in eō locō pugnātum est. Hostēs impedītōs nostrī in flūmine aggressī 5 magnum eōrum numerum occīdērunt; per eōrum corpora reliquōs audācissimē trānsīre cōnantēs multitūdine tēlōrum reppulērunt; prīmōs, quī trānsierant, equitātū circumventōs interfēcērunt.

---

10. 1. certior factus : ' on being informed ' of the attempted movement. **equitātum, pontem :** *114, a.* B. 179, 1 ; A. 395 ; H. 413.

As Caesar's camp was south of the Miette and east of the bridge over the Aisne, he could send his cavalry across the bridge without danger of interference, and from the south side of the Aisne could attack the enemy in the act of crossing.

Figure 76. — Leaden slingshot.

Hurled by soldiers of Octavianus against L. Antonius at the siege of Perusia, 41–40 B.C. Inscription, CAESAR IMP[ERATOR], referring to Octavianus.

2. levis armātūrae : ' of light equipment ' ; trans. ' light-armed.' *308*, and *100, a.* **funditōrēs :** probably provided with leaden bullets, though such are not mentioned by Caesar; slingshots of lead were in use both before and after the Gallic Wars (Fig. 14 and Fig. 76).

3. eōs : *hostēs.* **eō locō :** where the enemy started to cross the river ; marked on Map 5 by crossed swords.

4. pugnātum est : *73, d.* **aggressī :** *226, c.*

5. per : ' over.' The bravery of these Belgians, recorded by Caesar with evident admiration, justifies his characterization at the beginning of Book I (chap. 1, l. 6).

6. cōnantēs : with *reliquōs.* In 1914 this part of the Aisne again became the scene of terrible slaughter. Near Berry-au-Bac French and British troops constructed pontoon bridges in the face of artillery fire accurately directed from the high ground on the north side of the river ; and again the Aisne was choked with corpses.

7. equitātū : *131, b.* **circumventōs interfēcērunt :** ' surrounded and killed.' *228, a.*

Hostēs, ubi et dē expugnandō oppidō et dē flūmine trāns-
eundō spem sē fefellisse intellēxērunt neque nostrōs in 10
locum inīquiōrem prōgredī pugnandī causā vīdērunt, atque
ipsōs rēs frūmentāria dēficere coepit, cōnsiliō convocātō
cōnstituērunt, optimum esse, domum suam quemque revertī,
et, quōrum in fīnēs prīmum Rōmānī exercitum intrōdūxissent, ad eōs dēfendendōs undique convenīrent, ut potius in 15
suīs quam in aliēnīs fīnibus dēcertārent et domesticīs cōpiīs
reī frūmentāriae ūterentur.

Ad eam sententiam cum reliquīs causīs haec quoque
ratiō eōs dēdūxit, quod Dīviciācum atque Aeduōs fīnibus

9. **Hostēs**: the main body of the enemy, which remained inactive
while a detachment (*partem suārum copiārum*, chap. 9, l. 10) tried to
cross the river.　**oppidō**: Bibrax; see chaps. 6 and 7. *230*, (4).

10. **spem sē fefellisse**: 'that they had been disappointed in their
expectations,' lit. 'that their expectation had cheated them.'　**neque**:
trans. as if *et . . . nōn*.　**nostrōs**: the six legions that had been
formed in order of battle and then led back to camp; chap. 8, l. 19,
and chap. 9, ll. 5–7.

11. **locum inīquiōrem**: 'a less favorable position.' How lit.?
pugnandī causā: *230*, (1), and *94*, *b*.

12. **ipsōs**: *hostēs*.　**dēficere**: 'to fail.' *57*, *b*. As the Gauls for
the most part engaged only in short campaigns, their arrangements
for supplies were very defective.　It is a maxim of modern warfare that
"the way to victory lies through the soldier's stomach." Caesar, as all
great generals, paid the most careful attention to the provisioning of his
army. *317*.　**cōnsiliō**: 'a conference' of the leaders.

13. **optimum esse**: 'that it was best.' The subject of *esse* is the
infinitive clause *quemque revertī*, and *optimum* is in predicate. *148*, *d*.
domum suam: 'to his own home.' *119*, *b*.

14. **intrōdūxissent**: *220*. B. 324; A. 593; H. 652.

15. **eōs**: antecedent of *quōrum*; 'to defend that people.' *230*, (3).
convenīrent: sc. *ut*, 'that they should rally.' *199*, *a*, and *200*, *a*.

16. **aliēnīs**: = *aliōrum*, 'of others,' as opposed to **domesticīs**,
'their own.'　**dēcertārent**: *196*, *a*.　**cōpiīs**: 'supplies.' *131*, *c*.

19. **ratiō**: 'consideration,' explained by the appositive clause *quod*
('that') *. . . cognōverant*. *198*, *b*.　**Dīviciācum**, etc.: cf. chap.
5, ll. 5–10.　**fīnibus**: *105*.

20 Bellovacōrum appropinquāre cognōverant.   Hīs persuādērī, ut diūtius morārentur neque suīs auxilium ferrent, nōn
poterat.

The Belgians retreat in disorder; Caesar pursues them with
great slaughter.

11. Eā rē cōnstitūtā, secundā vigiliā magnō cum strepitū ac tumultū castrīs ēgressī, nūllō certō ōrdine neque
imperiō, cum sibi quisque prīmum itineris locum peteret et
domum pervenīre properāret, fēcērunt, ut cōnsimilis fugae
5 profectiō vidērētur.

Hāc rē statim Caesar per speculātōrēs cognitā, īnsidiās
veritus, quod, quā dē causā discēderent, nōndum perspexerat, exercitum equitātumque castrīs continuit.   Prīmā lūce,

---

20. **appropinquāre**: 'were approaching.'   **cognōverant**: 'they
knew.' *176, b.*   **Hīs**: the Bellovaci, whose actual fighting force
probably did not reach the large estimate of 100,000 given by the Remi
(chap. 4, ll. 14–17). *105.*   **Hīs persuādērī**: 'These could not be
persuaded.' How lit.? *106, b.*

21. **ut morārentur**: 'to stay' with the united Belgian host. Caesar's plan of dividing the forces of the Belgians, suggested in chap. 5,
was thus successful.   **neque**: 'and not.'

11. 1. **rē**: 'conclusion,' i.e. to disperse.   **secundā vigiliā**: *242, c,*
and *147, a.*   **strepitū**: 'uproar.' *136, a.*

2. **castrīs**: shown on Map 5. *127, a.*   **nūllō . . . imperiō**:
ablative of attendant circumstance, explaining *magnō . . . tumultū,*
and in turn explained by the causal clause *cum . . . properāret;* 'without a fixed order and without discipline.' *138.*

3. **sibi quisque**: *170, b.*   **prīmum**: 'the foremost.'   **peteret**:
184, a. B. 286, 2 ; A. 549; H. 598.

4. **fēcērunt . . . vidērētur**: 'they made their departure look like
a rout.' How lit.? *203, (3).*   **fugae**: *108, a.*

6. **per**: *123, a.*   **speculātōrēs**: 'spies.' *327.*

7. **veritus**: *226, c.*   **discēderent**: *204, (2).*

8. **castrīs**: *131, a.* Trans. 'in camp.'   **Prīmā lūce**: 'at daybreak.' *152, a.*

cōnfīrmātā rē ab explōrātōribus, omnem equitātum, quī
novissimum agmen morārētur, praemīsit.   Hīs Q. Pedium 10
et L. Aurunculeium Cottam lēgātōs praefēcit; T. Labiēnum
lēgātum cum legiōnibus tribus subsequī iussit.

Hī, novissimōs adortī et multa mīlia passuum prōsecūtī,
magnam multitūdinem eōrum fugientium concīdērunt, cum
ab extrēmō agmine, ad quōs ventum erat, cōnsisterent for- 15
titerque impetum nostrōrum mīlitum sustinērent, priōrēs,
quod abesse ā perīculō vidērentur, neque ūllā necessitāte
neque imperiō continērentur, exaudītō clāmōre perturbātīs
ōrdinibus omnēs in fugā sibi praesidium pōnerent.

Ita sine ūllō perīculō tantam eōrum multitūdinem nostrī 20

---

9. **rē**: 'the fact' that the Belgian host had actually dispersed.
explōrātōribus: *327*.

10. **novissimum agmen**: 'the rear guard' of the retreating Bel-
gians. *27, b*. **morārētur**: *193, a*.   B. 282, 2; A. 531, 2; H. 590.
Hīs: plural from the idea of *equitēs* in *equitātum*. *107, b*.   **Pedium**:
N. to chap. 2, l. 3.

12. **lēgātum**: *313, a*.   **subsequī**: 'to follow closely.'

13. **Hī**: 'These men,' the legionaries under Labienus; the cavalry
had gone ahead to retard the Belgian rear till the Roman infantry could
catch up with it.   **mīlia**: *118, a*.

14. **eōrum fugientium**: 'of them as they fled.'   **cum**, etc.:
sc. *eī*; 'since those (Belgians) at the rear, to whom (the Roman
soldiers) had come, were making a stand.'   How lit.?   **cum**:
184, a.

15. **extrēmō**: *152, a*.   **agmine**: here used not of an orderly
marching column but of a mass of soldiers in flight.   **ventum erat**:
73, d.

16. **priōrēs**: 'those in advance,' the bulk of the retreating host.
154, a, and *33*.

17. **vidērentur**: *220*. B. 324; A. 593; H. 652.   **neque**: 'and
. . . not.'   **necessitāte**: 'compulsion.'

18. **exaudītō clāmōre**: 'when they heard the shouting' behind
them.

19. **ōrdinibus**: 'ranks.'   **sibi**: *109, a*.   **praesidium pōnerent**: 'sought safety.'   How lit.?   **pōnerent**: with *cum* in l. 14.

interfēcērunt, quantum fuit diēī spatium; sub occāsum
sōlis dēstitērunt sēque in castra, ut erat imperātum, recēpērunt.

Noviodunum, besieged by Caesar, surrenders.

12. Postrīdiē eius diēī Caesar, prius quam sē hostēs ex
terrōre ac fugā reciperent in fīnēs Suessiōnum, quī proximī
Rēmīs erant, exercitum dūxit et magnō itinere ad oppidum
Noviodūnum contendit. Id ex itinere oppugnāre cōnātus,
5 quod vacuum ab dēfēnsōribus esse audiēbat, propter lātitūdinem fossae mūrīque altitūdinem, paucīs dēfendentibus, expugnāre nōn potuit. Castrīs mūnītīs, vīneās

---

21. **quantum,** etc.: 'as daylight permitted'; how lit.? **sub**:
'toward.'

22. **ut erat imperātum**: 'in accordance with their orders.' *73, d.*

12. 1. **diēī**: *94, c.* **sē reciperent**: 'could rally.' Why subjunctive? *189, b.*

2. **in fīnēs Suessiōnum**: see Map 1. Having scattered the great
host of united Belgians, Caesar pro-
ceeds to the reduction of the different
states one by one (Fig. 77).

3. **Rēmīs**: *108, a.* **magnō
itinere**: 'by a forced march.' *329.*

4. **Noviodūnum**: = "Newtown"; thought to have been on the
hill of Pommiers, near the modern
city of Soissons. **ex itinere**: see
Vocab. under *iter.* **oppugnāre**: *340.*

Figure 77.— Coin of the
Suessiones.

Bronze. Obverse: a Gallic neck-ring,
torque, is seen on the neck.

5. **vacuum ab**: 'destitute of.'
esse: i.e. *id (oppidum) esse vacuum.* **lātitūdinem fossae**: the
wider the 'moat,' the more difficult the filling of it so as to gain access
to the wall. **lātitūdinem fossae mūrīque altitūdinem**: *239, c.*

6. **paucīs dēfendentibus**: 'though there were but few defending
it.' *144, b, (5).*

7. **Castrīs**: probably on high ground east of Pommiers, where
traces of a Roman camp, thought to date from Caesar's time, have
been discovered. **vīneās agere**: 'to move forward the arbor sheds.'
342, a.

agere, quaeque ad oppugnandum ūsuī erant, comparāre coepit.

Interim omnis ex fugā Suessiōnum multitūdō in oppidum proximā nocte convēnit. Celeriter vīneīs ad oppidum āctīs, aggere iactō turribusque cōnstitūtīs, magnitūdine operum, quae neque vīderant ante Gallī neque audierant, et celeri-

Figure 78. — Hill town in France, having a situation similar to that of Noviodunum.

---

8. **quae**: as antecedent supply *ea*, object of *comparāre*.   **ūsuī**: 'of use.' Why dative? *112, a.*

11. **proximā nocte**: the night following the day on which Caesar reached Noviodunum, encamped, and commenced preparations for besieging the town.   **vīneīs**, etc.: 'arbor sheds,' open at the ends, were rapidly constructed, and placed in parallel rows which began outside the range of the enemy's weapons and were extended to the edge of the moat. *144, b,* (2).

12. **aggere iactō**: 'filling,' carried under the lines of arbor sheds, was 'cast' into the moat so as to level it up and make it possible to roll the towers close to the city wall.   **turribus**: 'towers.' *342, b.* **magnitūdine, celeritāte**: *135, a.*   **operum**: 'siege-works.'

tāte Rōmānōrum permōtī, lēgātōs ad Caesarem dē dēditiōne
15 mittunt et, petentibus Rēmīs, ut cōnservārentur, impetrant.

*The Suessiones submit; Caesar marches against the Bellovaci,
gathered in Bratuspantium.*

13. Caesar, obsidibus acceptīs prīmīs cīvitātis atque
ipsīus Galbae rēgis duōbus fīliīs, armīsque omnibus ex
oppidō trāditīs, in dēditiōnem Suessiōnēs accipit exercitumque in Bellovacōs dūcit.

5 Quī cum sē suaque omnia in oppidum Brātuspantium
contulissent, atque ab eō oppidō Caesar cum exercitū circiter mīlia passuum v abesset, omnēs maiōrēs nātū, ex
oppidō ēgressī, manūs ad Caesarem tendere et vōce significāre coepērunt, sēsē in eius fidem ac potestātem venīre
10 neque contrā populum Rōmānum armīs contendere. Item,
cum ad oppidum accessisset castraque ibi pōneret, puerī
mulierēsque ex mūrō passīs manibus suō mōre pācem ab
Rōmānīs petiērunt.

---

15. **petentibus Rēmīs**: 'at the urgent request of the Remi.' How
lit.?   **ut cōnservārentur**: after *petentibus*, 'that they should be
spared.' *199, a.*

13. 1. **obsidibus**: 'as hostages'; predicative, after *acceptīs*. *88,b.*
prīmīs: 'the foremost men.' *154, a,* and *144, b,* (2).

2. **Galbae**: chap. 4, ll. 22–24.

4. **Bellovacōs**: trans. as if *in fīnēs Bellovacōrum*. *282.*

5. **Quī cum**: 'when they.' *167.*   **suaque omnia**: 'with everything they had.' How lit.? *154, a.*   **oppidum**: 'stronghold'; not
a city but a fortified place of refuge, occupied only in time of danger.

7. **maiōrēs nātū**: 'the old men.' How lit.? *142, a.* B. 226, 1;
A. 418; H. 480.

8. **ēgressī**: 'came out and.' *228, a.*   **tendere**: 'to stretch out.'

9. **in eius fidem**: 'under his protection.' *124, a.*   **venīre**: *213, b.*

10. **neque**: trans. as if *et . . . nōn.*   **contendere**: 'struggle'
any longer.

11. **accessisset**: *185, c.*   **puerī**: 'children,' not 'boys' merely.

12. **passīs manibus**: 'with hands outstretched.' *144, b,* (2).
Principal parts of *pandō* and *patior?*   **mōre**: with *passīs*. *136, a.*

Diviciacus presents the case of the Bellovaci.

14. Prō hīs Dīviciācus (nam post discessum Belgārum, dimissīs Aeduōrum cōpiīs, ad eum reverterat) facit verba :

Bellovacōs omnī tempore in fidē atque amīcitiā cīvitātis Aeduae fuisse ; impulsōs ab suīs prīncipibus, quī dīcerent, Aeduōs, ā Caesare in servitūtem redāctōs, omnēs indignitātēs 5 contumēliāsque perferre, et ab Aeduīs dēfēcisse et populō Rōmānō bellum intulisse. Quī eius cōnsiliī prīncipēs fuissent, quod intellegerent, quantam calamitātem cīvitātī intulissent, in Britanniam profūgisse.

Petere nōn sōlum Bellovacōs, sed etiam prō hīs Aeduōs, 10 ut suā clēmentiā ac mānsuētūdine in eōs ūtātur. Quod sī

---

14. 1. **hīs** : *Bellovacīs.*	**discessum** : 'retreat'; chap. 11, ll. 1–5.

2. **Aeduōrum cōpiīs** : chap. 5, ll. 5–10, and chap. 10, ll. 19–20. **eum** : Caesar.	**facit verba** : 'made a plea.' How lit.?

3–9. **Direct form** : *Bellovacī* omnī tempore in fidē atque amīcitiā cīvitātis Aeduae *fuērunt ; impulsī* ab suīs prīncipibus, quī *dīcēbant,* Aeduōs, ā *tē* in servitūtem redāctōs, omnēs indignitātēs contumēliāsque perferre, et ab Aeduīs *dēfēcērunt* et populō Rōmānō bellum *intulērunt.* Quī eius cōnsiliī prīncipēs *fuerant,* quod *intellegēbant,* quantam calamitātem cīvitātī intulissent (*204, 3*), in Britanniam *profūgērunt.*

3. **Bellovacōs**, etc. : *213, b,* and *212, c,* (1).	**omnī tempore** : N. to I, 11, l. 6.

4. **dīcerent** : 'kept saying.' *175, a.*

5. **in** : 'to.'	**servitūtem** : *10, f.*	**omnēs**, etc. : 'every kind of ill-treatment and insult.' *92, c.*

6. **et . . . et** : *234, a.*	**dēfēcisse** : 'had revolted.' *57, b.*

7. **Quī** : as antecedent supply *eōs* with *profūgisse.*	**prīncipēs** : here = *auctōrēs,* 'advisers.'

10–14. **Direct form** : *Petunt* nōn sōlum Bellovacī, sed etiam prō hīs *Aeduī,* ut *tuā* clēmentiā ac mānsuētūdine in eōs *ūtāris.* Quod sī *fēceris* (future perfect), Aeduōrum auctōritātem apud omnēs Belgās *amplificābis ;* quōrum auxiliīs atque opibus, sī qua bella *incidērunt,* sustentāre *cōnsuērunt* (*176, b*).

10. **petere, ūtātur** : vivid use of present tenses where past tenses might have been expected.

11. **suā** : 'his well-known.' *157, e.*	**clēmentiā** : 'mercifulness,'

*fēcerit, Aeduōrum auctōritātem apud omnēs Belgās ampli-
ficātūrum, quōrum auxiliīs atque opibus, sī qua bella
inciderint, sustentāre cōnsuērint.*

*Caesar makes terms with the Bellovaci and Ambiani, learns about
the Nervians.*

15. Caesar, honōris Dīviciācī atque Aeduōrum causā,
sēsē eōs in fidem receptūrum et cōnservātūrum dīxit; et
quod erat cīvitās magnā inter Belgās auctōritāte atque
hominum multitūdine praestābat, DC ˙obsidēs poposcit.
5 Hīs trāditīs omnibusque armīs ex oppidō collātīs, ab eō
locō in fīnēs Ambiānōrum pervēnit; quī sē suaque omnia
sine morā dēdidērunt.

---

the quality which leads a man to treat with kindness those against
whom he has grounds of offense.   Near the close of his life a temple
was ordered built to 'Caesar's Mercifulness.'   *268*, and Fig. 163.
mānsuētūdine: 'compassionateness,' the quality that makes one able
to realize the sufferings of others.   **in**: 'toward.'   **Quod**: *118, d.*
sī, etc.: *218*, (1), *b.*

13. **sī . . . sustentāre**: 'to carry through any wars that had arisen.'
How lit.?   *168*, and *49, a.*

15. 1. **honōris**: dependent on *causā;* 'out of regard for Diviciacus,' etc.   *94, b.*   **Dīviciācī**: dependent on *honōris.   102.*

2. **in fidem**: as in chap. 13, l, 9.

3. **cīvitās**: *Bellovacōrum.*   **auctōritāte**: 'prestige.'   *143, a.*

4. **multitūdine**: *142, a.*   B. 226;
A. 418; H. 480.   **DC**: *sescentōs.   36.*
The fact that for the sake of his Aeduan
supporters Caesar had spared the Bellovaci did not prevent him from exact-
ing a large number of hostages to bind
them in their pledge of submission.

Figure 79.—A Nervian coin.
Gold, with crude designs.

5. **collātīs**: *69, b.*   **eō locō**: Bratuspantium.   For Caesar's
route, see Map 1.

7. **morā**: 'delay.'   **dēdidērunt**: 'surrendered.'

Eōrum fīnēs Nerviī attingēbant; quōrum dē nātūrā
mōribusque Caesar cum quaereret, sīc reperiēbat:

Nūllum aditum esse ad eōs mercātōribus; nihil patī vīnī 10
reliquārumque rērum ad lūxuriam pertinentium īnferrī,
quod hīs rēbus relanguēscere animōs eōrum et remittī vir-

Figure 80.—A characteristic bit of the country through which Caesar
made his three-day march.

8. **Eōrum**: the Ambiani.   **Nerviī attingēbant**: 'the country
of the Nervians adjoined' (Fig. 79). *282.*   **dē nātūrā**: *116, c.*

10–17. **Direct form**: *Nūllus aditus est* ad eōs mercātōribus; nihil *patiun-*
tur vīnī reliquārumque rērum ad lūxuriam pertinentium īnferrī, quod hīs rēbus
relanguēscere animōs eōrum et remittī virtūtem *exīstimant. Sunt* hominēs
ferī magnaeque virtūtis; *increpitant* atque *incūsant* reliquōs Belgās, quī sē
populō Rōmānō *dēdiderint* patriamque virtūtem *prōiēcerint; cōnfīrmant,* sēsē
neque lēgātōs missūrōs [esse] neque ūllam condiciōnem pācis acceptūrōs
[esse].

10. **Nūllum**, etc.: *212, c,* (3).   **mercātōribus**: *111.*   **nihil
vīnī**: 'no wine.' *97, a.* The Nervii were ancient prohibitionists.
patī: sc. *eōs* as subject. *60.*

11. **ad lūxuriam pertinentium**: 'which contribute to luxurious
living.' How lit.?

12. **rēbus**: *135, a.*   **relanguēscere**: 'becomes weak.'   **ani-**

tūtem exīstimārent ; esse hominēs ferōs magnaeque virtūtis ;
increpitāre atque incūsāre reliquōs Belgās, quī sē populō
15 *Rōmānō dēdidissent patriamque virtūtem prōiēcissent ; cōn-*
firmāre, sēsē neque lēgātōs missūrōs neque ūllam condiciō-
nem pācis acceptūrōs.

*The Nervians, Atrebatians, and Viromanduans await Caesar at
the Sambre.*

16. Cum per eōrum fīnēs trīduum iter fēcisset, inveniēbat ex captīvīs :

Sabim flūmen ā castrīs suīs nōn amplius mīlia passuum x
abesse ; trāns id flūmen omnēs Nerviōs cōnsēdisse adventum-
5 *que ibi Rōmānōrum exspectāre ūnā cum Atrebātibus et Viro-*
manduīs, fīnitimīs suīs (nam hīs utrīsque persuāserant,

---

mōs : *92, a.*   **virtūtem** : 'valor,' the manifestation of courage in
brave deeds.

13. **exīstimārent** : *177, a.*   **magnae virtūtis** : genitive of quality
taking the place of an adjective, hence connected by *-que* with *ferōs*.
100, a.

14. **increpitāre atque incūsāre** : sc. *eōs*, 'that they upbraided
and condemned.'   **reliquōs** : *171, a.*   **quī** : 'because they.' *194, c.*

16. **sēsē**, etc. : indirect discourse after *cōnfirmāre*.   **sēsē** : refers
to *eōs* understood as subject of *cōnfirmāre*.

16. 1. **eōrum** : *Nerviōrum*.   **trīduum** : = *trēs diēs. 118, a.*
īter fēcisset : 'had advanced'; for the route see Map 1, and Fig. 80.
inveniēbat : = *quaerendō cognōscēbat.*

3. **Sabim**, etc. : *212, c, (3).*   **Sabim** : accusative like *turrim.*
14, c.   **mīlia** : why not ablative? *129, b,* and *118, a.*

Figure 81. — Viromanduan
coin.

Bronze, of crude workmanship.
Inscription, SOLLOS (SOLOS).

4. **trāns id flūmen** : they crossed over
to the south side of the Sambre, which
flows in an easterly direction into the
Meuse. *292.*

6. **hīs utrīsque** : 'both these peoples.'
51, and *23, a.* The combined forces of the
Nervians, Atrebatians, and Viromanduans
(Fig. 81) were estimated at 75,000 (chap.
4, ll. 21–28).   **nam**, etc. : *214, c.*

utī eandem bellī fortūnam experīrentur); *exspectārī etiam*
ab hīs Atuatucōrum cōpiās, atque esse in itinere ; mulierēs,
quīque per aetātem ad pugnam inūtilēs vidērentur, in eum
locum coniēcisse, quō propter palūdēs exercituī aditus nōn esset. 10

They plan to surprise him on the march.

17. Hīs rēbus cognitīs, explōrātōrēs centuriōnēsque praemittit, quī locum idōneum castrīs dēligant.   Cum ex dēditīciīs Belgīs reliquīsque Gallīs complūrēs, Caesarem secūtī,
ūnā iter facerent, quīdam ex hīs, ut posteā ex captīvīs
cognitum est, eōrum diērum cōnsuētūdine itineris nostrī 5
exercitūs perspectā, nocte ad Nerviōs pervēnērunt atque
hīs dēmōnstrārunt, *Inter singulās legiōnēs impedīmentō-*
rum magnum numerum intercēdere, neque esse quicquam
negōtiī, cum prīma legiō in castra vēnisset reliquaeque

8. **in itinere** : 'on the way.'   **mulierēs** : object of *coniēcisse.*

9. **quīque** : i.e. *et eōs, quī.*   **per aetātem** : ' by reason of age.'
inūtilēs : predicative, ' useless.'   **eum locum** : 'a place,' perhaps in
the vicinity of the modern city of Mons. *160, d.*

10. **quō** : adverb, = *ad quem.*   **esset** . subjunctive also in the
direct form. *194, a.* B. 283; A. 535; H. 591, 1.

17. 2. **quī . . . dēligant** : 'in order to choose.' *193, a,* and *331, a,*
and *b.*   **ex . . . Gallīs** : after *complūrēs.* *97, d.* B. 201, 1, *a* ; A.
346, *c* ; H. 444.   **dēditīciīs** : the Suessiōnēs (chap. 13, l. 3), the
Bellovaci (chap. 15, l. 2), and the Ambiani (chap. 15, ll. 5–7).

4. **facerent** : *185, c.*   **quīdam** : *168.*   **ut** : *188, b.*

5. **eōrum . . . exercitūs** : 'the marching order of our army in
those days,' the three days when Caesar was advancing into the country
of the Nervians (chap. 16, l. 1). How lit.?

7. **dēmōnstrārunt** : *64, a,* (1).   **impedīmentōrum**, etc.: *311,*
and *74, d.*

8. **numerum** : 'quantity.'   **esse** : the subject is *adorīrī ;* ' and
that there was no difficulty — in attacking.' How lit. ? *222, b.*   **quic-**
quam : *168,* and *49, a.*

9. **negōtiī** : *97, b.*   **castra** : the place selected for a camp ; the camp
would not be fortified till the legions arrived. *332, 333.*   **vēnisset,**
abessent : indicative future perfect, and future, in direct discourse.

10 *legiōnēs magnum spatium abessent, hanc sub sarcinīs
adorīrī; quā pulsā impedīmentīsque dīreptīs, futūrum, ut
reliquae contrā cōnsistere nōn audērent.*

Adiuvābat etiam eōrum cōnsilium, quī rem dēferēbant,
quod Nerviī antīquitus, cum equitātū nihil possent (neque
15 enim ad hōc tempus eī reī student, sed, quicquid possunt,
pedestribus valent cōpiīs), quō facilius fīnitimōrum equitātum, sī praedandī causā ad eōs vēnissent, impedīrent, tenerīs arboribus incīsīs atque īnflexīs, crēbrīsque in lātitūdinem
rāmīs ēnātīs, et rubīs sentibusque interiectīs, effēcerant, ut

---

10. **spatium**: *118, a.*   **sarcinīs**: 'packs.' The plan was to attack the first legion to come up, just as it reached the place chosen for
encampment, before the soldiers could deposit their packs and get themselves into fighting trim.   *330.*

11. **quā**: 'when this' legion.   **dīreptīs**: 'had been plundered.'
How lit.?   **futūrum** [esse]: the subject is *ut . . . audērent* ; 'it
would come about that.'   *203*, (1).

12. **reliquae**: sc. *legiōnēs.*   **contrā**: adverb.   **contrā cōnsistere**: 'to withstand the attack.'

13. **Adiuvābat**: the subject is *quod . . . effēcerant* (l. 19); 'the
plan of those who furnished the information was favored by the fact that
the Nerviī,' etc.   How lit.?   *198, b.*

14. **antīquitus**: 'long ago.'   **cum . . . possent**: 'not being
strong in cavalry.'   How lit.?   *184, a.*   **nihil**: *118, c.*   **neque
enim**: 'and in fact . . . not.'

15. **eī reī student**: 'they give attention to that arm' of the service.
105.   **quicquid . . . cōpiīs**: 'all the strength they have is in infantry.'   How lit.?   **quicquid**: *118, b.*

16. **cōpiīs**: *142, a.*   **quō . . . impedīrent**: *193, b.* B. 282, 1, *a* ;
A. 531, *a* ; H. 568, 7.

17. **praedandī causā**: 'in order to plunder.'   *230*, (1).   **vēnissent**: *220.*

18. **tenerīs . . . īnflexīs**: 'cutting into young trees and bending
them over.'   How lit.?   *144, b*, (2).   **in lātitūdinem**: 'at the sides,'
we should say.

19. **rāmīs ēnātīs**: with *crēbrīs*, 'letting the branches grow thickly.'
151, and *61, a*, (3).   How lit.?   **rubīs**, etc.: 'planting briars and
thorn-bushes in the intervening spaces.'   How lit.?   **effēcerant, ut**

īnstar mūrī hae saepēs mūnīmentum praebērent, quō nōn ²⁰
modo nōn intrārī, sed nē perspicī quidem posset.

Hīs rēbus cum iter agminis nostrī impedīrētur, nōn omittendum sibi cōnsilium Nerviī exīstimāvērunt.

The Romans make camp on a height sloping to the river.

18. Locī nātūra erat haec, quem locum nostrī castrīs
dēlēgerant.

Figure 82. — Hedges, near the river Sambre.

. . . **praebērent**: *203*, (3). By cutting into young trees near the root
they were able to bend these down to a horizontal position without killing them. The stem of the tree would then increase in size very slowly,
but along the trunk branches would grow out, above and on the sides
(*in lātitūdinem*). In the spaces along the line of defense not filled by
trees thus trained, briars and thorn-bushes were planted. The whole
formed a living and impenetrable hedge. Similar hedges are still found
in this region (Figures 82, 83, 87).

20. **īnstar mūrī**: 'like a wall,' lit. 'the likeness of a wall'; *īnstar*,
indeclinable, is in apposition to *mūnīmentum*. *94, b*. **saepēs**:
'hedges.' *15, b*. **mūnīmentum**: 'line of defense.' *74, d*. **praebērent**: 'made.'   **quō**: adverb = *in quod* (*mūnīmentum*); but
trans. with the impersonal *intrārī*, etc., 'which could not only not be
penetrated but not even seen through.' How lit.? *73, d*, and *237, c*.

21. **perspicī**: *79, b*.   **posset**: *220*.

23. **omittendum**: *89, c*, and *73, e*.   **sibi**: *110*.   **cōnsilium**:
'the plan' of attack proposed in ll. 9–12.

18. 1. **haec**: 'as follows.' *161, a*.   **locum**: *165, a*.   **castrīs**:

Collis ab summō aequāliter dēclīvis ad flūmen Sabim,
quod suprā nōmināvimus, vergēbat. Ab eō flūmine parī
5 acclīvitāte collis nāscēbātur adversus huic et contrārius,
passūs circiter CC īnfimus apertus, ab superiōre parte silvestris, ut nōn facile intrōrsus perspicī posset.

Intrā eās silvās hostēs in occultō sēsē continēbant; in
apertō locō secundum flūmen paucae statiōnēs equitum
10 vidēbantur. Flūminis erat altitūdō pedum circiter trium.

A furious attack is made on the Romans while fortifying the camp.

19. Caesar, equitātū praemissō, subsequēbātur omnibus
cōpiīs; sed ratiō ōrdōque agminis aliter sē habēbat, ac

112, a. The site has been identified, on the left or north bank of the
Sambre (*Sabis*), in France, near the Belgian frontier, opposite the city
of Hautmont. Map 6, **A**.

3. **Collis**: on which the camp was laid out.   **ab**, etc.: 'sloping
evenly from the top, descended.' How lit.?

4. **suprā**: chap. 16, l. 3.   **nōmināvimus**: 'we have mentioned by
name.' *156.*   **Ab eō**: 'From the.' *160, d.*   **parī acclīvitāte**:
'with similar upward slope.' *143, a.*

5. **nāscēbātur**: 'arose.'   **adversus huic et contrārius**: 'facing this (hill) and opposite (to it),' on the south side of the Sambre;
the highest part of the second hill is at **B** on Map 6.   **huic**: *108, a.*

6. **passūs**: *118, a.*   **CC**: *ducentōs.* *36.* How far? *243, b.*
īnfimus: 'at the lower edge' of the hill, along the river.   **apertus**:
free from woods.   **ab**, etc.: 'wooded along the upper portion.' *126, c.*

7. **ut**: 'so that.'   **intrōrsus**: 'within.'

9. **apertō locō**: indicated on Map 6, between the river and the
broken line marking the northern limit of the woods.   **secundum**:
preposition, 'along.'   **statiōnēs**: 'pickets.'

10. **vidēbantur**: trans. as passive.   **pedum**: *100, b.*   **trium**:
37, b.

19. 1. **equitātū praemissō**: *328.*   **omnibus cōpiīs**: *137, b.*

2. **ratiō ōrdōque**: 'principle of arrangement,' lit. 'principle and
arrangement.'   **aliter**, etc.: 'were different from what the Belgians.'
How lit.?   **habēbat**: *173, a.* B. 255, 3; A. 317, b; H. 392, 4.
ac: *233, c.*

Belgae ad Nerviōs dētulerant.   Nam quod hostibus appro-
pinquābat, cōnsuētūdine suā Caesar VI legiōnēs expedītās
dūcēbat; post eās tōtīus exercitūs impedīmenta collocārat; 5
inde duae legiōnēs, quae proximē cōnscrīptae erant, tōtum
agmen claudēbant praesidiōque impedīmentīs erant.

Equitēs nostrī, cum funditōribus sagittāriīsque flūmen
trānsgressī, cum hostium equitātū proelium commīsērunt.
Cum sē illī identidem in silvās ad suōs reciperent ac rūrsus 10
ex silvā in nostrōs impetum facerent neque nostrī longius,
quam quem ad fīnem porrēcta loca aperta pertinēbant,
cēdentēs īnsequī audērent, interim legiōnēs VI, quae prīmae vēnerant, opere dīmēnsō castra mūnīre coepērunt.

---

4. **cōnsuētūdine suā**: 'in accordance with his usual practice,' when
in the enemy's country. *136, c*.   **VI**: *38, b*.   The legions were those
numbered 7-12.   **expedītās**: predicative, 'in light order'; without the packs (*sarcinae*), which in such cases were doubtless carried
with the heavy baggage. *115, b*.

5. **impedīmenta**: *311*.   **collocārat**: full form? *64, a*, (1).

6. **duae legiōnēs**: numbered 13 and 14; chap. 2, ll. 1-4.
proximē: *35*.

7. **praesidiō, impedīmentīs**: *112, b*, and *328*. B. 191, 2, *a*; A.
382, 1; H. 433.

9. **trānsgressī**: to the south side of the Sambre.   **cum**: *137, c*.
equitātū: the cavalry (chap. 18, l. 9) must have been furnished by
the Atrebatians and Viromanduans, not by the Nervians (chap. 17,
l. 14).

10. **identidem**: 'repeatedly.'   **suōs**: the enemy's infantry, concealed in the woods (chap. 18, l. 8).   **reciperent**: *175, d*.

11. **neque**: trans. as if *et . . . nōn*.   **longius**: 'further.'

12. **quem ad fīnem**: = *ad eum fīnem ad quem*, 'to the limit to
which.'   **porrēcta**, etc.: 'the stretch of open ground extended.'
How lit.?

13. **cēdentēs**: sc. *eōs* (*hostēs*), object of *īnsequī*; 'as they retreated.'
prīmae vēnerant: 'had been the first to come up.' *152, b*.

14. **opere**: 'the trench-work,' the first work on the fortifications of
the camp. *333*.   **dīmēnsō**: 'having measured off.' How lit.?
144, b, (2), and *59, b*.

15 Ubi prīma impedīmenta nostrī exercitūs ab eīs, quī in
silvīs abditī latēbant, vīsa sunt, quod tempus inter eōs
committendī proeliī convēnerat, ut intrā silvās aciem ōrdinēsque cōnstituerant atque ipsī sēsē cōnfīrmāverant, subitō
omnibus cōpiīs prōvolāvērunt impetumque in nostrōs
20 equitēs fēcērunt. Hīs facile pulsīs ac prōturbātīs, incrēdibilī

Figure 83. — View across the fields in the direction from which Caesar's
baggage was coming.

15. **prīma impedīmenta**: 'the first part of the baggage train.'
Map 6. *152, a.*

16. **vīsa sunt**: passive in meaning.   **quod tempus**: i.e. *tempus*
(in thought an appositive of the clause *Ubi . . . vīsa sunt*, but attracted
into the relative clause) . . . *quod convēnerat*, 'which had been agreed
on.' *165, b.*

17. **committendī proeliī**: dependent on *tempus*, 'for beginning
the battle.' How lit.? *230*, (1).   **ut**: 'just as.'

18. **ipsī sēsē cōnfīrmāverant**: 'had encouraged one another.'

19. **cōpiīs**: *136, b.*   **prōvolāvērunt**: 'they rushed forward.'
nostrōs equitēs: who had crossed the river (ll. 8, 9).

20. **prōturbātīs**: 'scattered in a panic.'   **incrēdibilī**: *74, f.*

MAP 6

THE BATTLE AT THE SAMBRE (SABIS): FIRST PHASE

Book II, 18–22

To face page 164

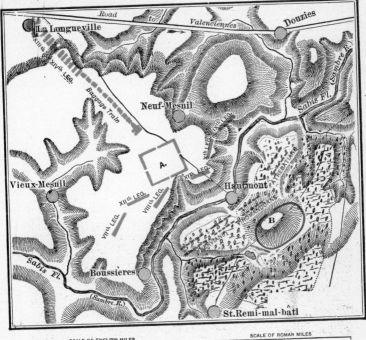

SCALE OF ENGLISH MILES

SCALE OF ROMAN MILES

EXPLANATION

Caesar's army, approaching the Sambre from the north, started to make a camp on a hill overlooking the river. The Belgian forces, comprising Nervians, Viromanduans, and Atrebatians, were lying in wait on the south side.

Supposing that each legion would be followed by its baggage train, the Belgians had planned to attack the first legion and destroy it before the others could come to the rescue, and in like manner to destroy the others one by one. Caesar, however, had placed six legions in light marching order first, then all the baggage, and two legions last, the XIIIth and XIVth; he sent cavalry, bowmen, and slingers in advance of the main column.

When the baggage train came into view, the Belgians hurled back the cavalry, bowmen, and slingers, rushed across the river and charged up the hill.

A. The Roman camp (chap. 18, ll. 1–7), with six legions forming in front.

B. The camp of the Belgians (chap. 26, ll. 10–12)

celeritāte ad flūmen dēcucurrērunt, ut paene ūnō tempore
et ad silvās et in flūmine et iam in manibus nostrīs hostēs
vidērentur. Eādem autem celeritāte adversō colle ad
nostra castra atque eōs, quī in opere occupātī erant, contendērunt.   25

Discipline and training enable the soldiers to meet the emergency.

20. Caesarī omnia ūnō tempore erant agenda : vēxillum prōpōnendum, quod erat īnsigne, cum ad arma concurrī oportēret ; signum tubā dandum ; ab opere revocandī
mīlitēs ; quī paulō longius aggeris petendī causā prōces-

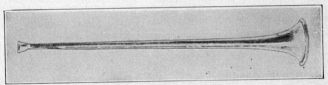

Figure 84. — Roman trumpet, tuba.

21. **dēcucurrērunt**: 'they ran down' the sloping ground between
the edge of the forest and the river.   **ut**: 'so that.'   **tempore**:
'instant.'

22. **ad silvās**: 'near the woods,' whence they had just emerged.
in manibus nostrīs: in our idiom, 'upon us'; how lit.?

23. **adversō colle ... contendērunt**: 'dashed up the hill' on the
north side of the Sambre.   The Belgians may have covered the distance
between the woods on the south side of the Sambre and the site of the
Roman camp in ten minutes; the distance is about two-thirds of an
English mile.

24. **occupātī**: 'engaged.' *148, c.*

20. 1. **Caesarī**: emphatic, hence placed at the beginning. *110,*
and *229, c.*   **vēxillum**: 'the flag.' *324, b,* 3, and Fig. 149.

2. **prōpōnendum, dandum, revocandī**, etc.: sc. *erat, erant.*
229, c.   **ad arma concurrī**: 'to arm.' How lit.? *73, d.*

3. **tubā**: 'with the trumpet'; the signal was to "fall in." *326,*
a, (1). Fig. 84.   **opere** chap. 19, l. 14 and N.   **revocandī**
[erant] : 'had to be recalled.'

4. **quī**: as antecedent sc. *eī (mīlitēs)*, subject of *arcessendī [erant].*

5 serant, arcessendī; aciēs īnstruenda, mīlitēs cohortandī,
signum dandum. Quārum rērum magnam partem temporis brevitās et incursus hostium impediēbat.

His difficultātibus duae rēs erant subsidiō, scientia atque
ūsus mīlitum, quod superiōribus proeliīs exercitātī, quid
10 fierī oportēret, nōn minus commodē ipsī sibi praescrībere,
quam ab aliīs docērī poterant, et quod ab opere singulīsque
legiōnibus singulōs lēgātōs Caesar discēdere, nisi mūnītīs
castrīs, vetuerat. Hī propter propinquitātem et celeritātem
hostium nihil iam Caesaris imperium exspectābant, sed
15 per sē, quae vidēbantur, administrābant.

---

paulō longius: 'a little further' than usual. *140*.   **aggeris**: 'material' for the rampart, in this case probably wood. *230*, (1).

5. **arcessendī** [erant]: 'had to be sent for.'   **cohortandī** [erant]:
N to I, 25, l. 3.

6. **signum dandum** [erat]: 'the signal' for battle 'had to be
given.' *326, c*.   **Quārum**: *167*.

7. **brevitās**: 'the shortness.'   **incursus**: 'the onrush.'   **impediēbat**: *173, a*.

8. **Hīs . . . subsidiō**: 'Two things served to offset these disad-
vantages,' explained by *scientia . . . poterant* and *quod ab opere . . .
vetuerat*. How lit.? *112, b*.

10. **oportēret**: *204*, (2).   **nōn minus**, etc.: 'they were able
(themselves) to determine for themselves . . . just as fitly as others could
instruct them.' How lit.?   **ipsī**: agrees with the subject of *poterant*,
but need not be translated.

11. **quod**, etc.: 'the fact that Caesar had forbidden the several lieutenants to leave the work and their respective legions.' How lit.?
198, b.

12. **discēdere**: *200, b*.   **nisi mūnītīs castrīs**: 'only after the
fortifying of the camp had been completed.'

14. **nihil**: adverbial accusative. *118, c*.

15. **per sē**: 'on their own responsibility.'   **quae vidēbantur**:
i.e. *quae vidēbantur administranda*, 'were taking (the measures) which
the situation seemed to require.' How lit.?   These veterans knew what
to do, when they saw the enemy coming, and did not lose their
heads.

They form hurriedly; under Caesar's encouragement they fight
desperately, against great odds.

21. Caesar, necessāriīs rēbus imperātīs, ad cohortandōs
mīlitēs, quam in partem fors obtulit, dēcucurrit et ad
legiōnem decimam dēvēnit. Mīlitēs nōn longiōre ōrātiōne
cohortātus, quam utī suae prīstinae virtūtis memoriam re-
tinērent neu perturbārentur animō, hostiumque impetum 5
fortiter sustinērent, quod nōn longius hostēs aberant, quam
quō tēlum adigī posset, proeliī committendī signum dedit.
Atque in alteram partem item cohortandī causā profectus
pugnantibus occurrit.

Temporis tanta fuit exiguitās hostiumque tam parātus 10

---

21. 1. **necessāriīs rēbus imperātīs**: 'having given (only) the
indispensable orders.'

2. **quam in partem** : = *in eam partem, in quam;* with *fors obtulit,*
'where chance led,' a statement introduced to explain why Caesar came
first to the tenth legion, which, as the most experienced, had least need
of the general's presence. *69, b.* **dēcucurrit**: Caesar was perhaps
near the northeast corner of the camp (Map 6, **A**) when he started to
rush down the slope to where the troops were forming.

4. **utī . . . sustinērent**: substantive clauses giving the gist of the
words of exhortation. *199, a.*

5. **neu perturbārentur animō**: we should say 'and keep cool.'
How lit.? *142, a,* and *199, d.*

6. **quod . . . aberant**: gives the reason for *signum dedit.* **quam
quō**: 'than (the distance) to which.' *194, b.* B. 283, 2, *a;* A. 571, *a;*
H. 570, 1.

7. **adigī**: 'be thrown.' **signum**: N. to chap. 20, l. 6.

8. **alteram partem**: 'another part' of the hastily formed line;
apparently Caesar went across to the right wing, where the seventh and
twelfth legions were. See Map 6. **profectus**: principal parts of
proficīscor and *prōficiō?*

9. **pugnantibus occurrit**: 'he found (the men already) fighting.'
107, a, and *175, b.*

10. **Temporis . . . exiguitās**: 'So short was the time.' How lit.?
hostium: dependent on *animus.* *233, b,* and *353, d.*

ad dīmicandum animus, ut nōn modo ad īnsignia accommodanda, sed etiam ad galeās induendās scūtīsque tegimenta
dētrahenda tempus dēfuerit. Quam quisque ab opere in
partem cāsū dēvēnīt quaeque prīma signa cōnspexit, ad
15 haec cōnstitit, nē in quaerendīs suīs pugnandī tempus
dīmitteret.

22. Īnstrūctō exercitū, magis ut locī nātūra dēiectusque
collis et necessitās temporis, quam ut reī mīlitāris ratiō
atque ōrdō postulābat, cum dīversae legiōnēs aliae aliā in
parte hostibus resisterent, saepibusque dēnsissimīs, ut ante

---

11. **ad īnsignia accommodanda**: 'for fitting on their decorations,'
particularly the crests, which were taken off from the helmets on the

march. In battle it was important that the crests
be in place, for by differences of these in form
and color the different legions and cohorts could
be distinguished (Fig. 85).

12. **ad galeās induendās**: 'for putting on
their helmets' (Fig. 12). *322, a.*   **scūtīs**,
etc.: 'for drawing the coverings off the shields,'
which were protected by coverings against mois-
ture. *127, a.* B. 214; A. 401; H. 462.

13. **Quam**, etc.: 'Whatever part (of the line)
each (soldier) chanced (to reach as) he came
down from the trench-work, (in that part he
stayed) and.' How lit.?

Figure 85. — Roman
helmet, with crest.

14. **quaeque**: = *et quae*; trans. as if *ad*
('by') *haec signa, quae prīma cōnspexit, cōnstitit*
('he took his stand'). Under ordinary circumstances it was a serious
offense for a soldier to be found in a maniple in which he did not belong.
324, b, (2).

15. **in quaerendīs suīs**: sc. *signīs.*

22. 1. **ut**: 'as.'   **locī**: 'of the ground.'

2. **reī . . . ōrdō**: 'the arrangement approved by military science.'
How lit.?

3. **dīversae**: 'separated.'   **aliae aliā in parte**: fuller expression
of the thought in *dīversae*; 'one at one point, another at another.'
171, c.

4. **dēnsissimīs**: 'very thick.' *153, a.*   **ante**: chap. 17, ll. 13–21.

dēmōnstrāvimus, interiectīs prōspectus impedīrētur, neque 5
certa subsidia collocārī neque, quid in quāque parte opus
esset, prōvidērī, neque ab ūnō omnia imperia administrārī
poterant. Itaque in tantā rērum inīquitāte fortūnae quoque
ēventūs variī sequēbantur.

*Two legions drive the Atrebatians across the river, two force back
the Viromanduans, but two are outflanked by the Nervians.*

23. Legiōnis VIIII et X mīlitēs, ut in sinistrā parte aciēī
cōnstiterant, pīlīs ēmissīs cursū ac lassitūdine exanimātōs
vulneribusque cōnfectōs Atrebātēs (nam hīs ea pars obvēnerat) celeriter ex locō superiōre in flūmen compulērunt
et, trānsīre cōnantēs īnsecūtī, gladiīs magnam partem eōrum 5

---

5. **prōspectus**: 'the view' over the field of battle (Fig. 82).

6. **certa subsidia collocārī** [poterant] : 'could reserves be posted
at fixed points'; the movements of the enemy were so obscured by the
thickets that Caesar could not tell where reserve forces could be posted
to advantage. **certa**: *151.* B. 239; A. 290; H. 497. **quāque**:
from *quisque.* **opus esset**: *132, b.*

7. **prōvidērī**: sc. *poterat.* **ūnō**: 'one person.' **omnia imperia . . . administrārī**: 'all orders . . . be given.'

8. **in tantā rērum inīquitāte**: 'under so disadvantageous conditions.' How lit.? **fortūnae**: dependent on *ēventūs.*

9. **ēventūs variī**: 'various issues.'

23. 1. VIIII, X: *nonae, decimae.* *38, b.* **aciēī**: *21, b.* For the
position of the legions see Map 6.

2. **pīlīs ēmissīs**: 'having hurled their pikes.' *322, d.* **lassitūdine**: 'fatigue,' resulting from the three-quarter mile dash first down-
hill to the river, then across the river, and uphill again to the Roman
line. **exanimātōs**: 'who were out of breath.' *227, a,* (1).

3. **vulneribus cōnfectōs**: 'disabled by wounds,' referring to those
struck by the pikes. **ea pars**: the Roman left wing, which was in
command of Labienus. **obvēnerat**: 'had encountered.'

4. **locō superiōre**: the Romans, being nearer the top of the hill,
were on higher ground. **compulērunt**: 'forced.'

5. **cōnantēs**: sc. *eōs* (*Atrebātēs*), object of *īnsecūtī.*

impedītam interfēcērunt. Ipsī trānsīre flūmen nōn dubitāvērunt et, in locum inīquum prōgressī, rūrsus resistentēs
hostēs, redintegrātō proeliō, in fugam coniēcērunt.

Item aliā in parte dīversae duae legiōnēs, XI et VIII,
10 prōflīgātīs Viromanduīs, quibuscum erant congressae, ex
locō superiōre, in ipsīs flūminis rīpīs proeliābantur.

At tōtīs ferē castrīs ā fronte et ā sinistrā parte nūdātīs,
cum in dextrō cornū legiō XII et, nōn magnō ab eā intervāllō, VII cōnstitisset, omnēs Nerviī cōnfertissimō agmine
15 duce Boduognātō, quī summam imperiī tenēbat, ad eum

---

6. **impedītam**: by the crossing of the river.　**Ipsī**: the soldiers
of the ninth and tenth legions.　**trānsīre**: *201, b.*

7. **locum inīquum**: the 'ground' south of the Sambre, sloping
back from the river and in part covered with woods; Map 7.

8. **hostēs**: object of *cōniēcērunt*.　**redintegrātō proeliō**: 'they
(the Romans) renewed the battle and.' *144, b, (2).*

9. **aliā in parte**: the Roman center, in front of the camp. See
Map 7.　**dīversae**: 'in different places'; not, as ordinarily, forming
a continuous line.

10. **prōflīgātīs Viromanduīs**: 'having driven the Viromanduans.'
quibuscum: *125, c.*　**erant congressae**: *57, c.*

11. **proeliābantur**: 'were continuing the battle.' *175, a.*

12. **ā**: *126, b.*　**nūdātīs**: not only the 8th and 11th legions in
front, but the 9th and 10th legions on the left of the camp, had abandoned their positions to pursue the enemy, leaving the camp 'unprotected' except on the right, where the 12th and 7th legions stood.

13. **cum**: 'since.' *184, a.*　**XII**: *duodecima.*　**nōn**: with *magnō.*
239, g.　**intervāllō**: *138.*

14. **VII**: (*legiō*) *septima.*　**cōnstitisset**: why singular?　**omnēs
Nerviī**: their fighting force was estimated by the Remi at 50,000
(chap. 4, l. 25), but was later reported as 60,000 (chap. 28, l. 8).
cōnfertissimō agmine: a mass formation, like that of the Helvetians
(I, 24, l. 12); called 'column,' *agmen*, rather than 'battle-line,' *aciēs*,
because it was still advancing, not yet having divided in order to
deliver the attack at two points.

15. **duce Boduognātō**: 'led by Boduognatus.' How lit.? *144,
b, (2).*　**summam imperiī**: 'the supreme command.'

locum contendērunt; quōrum pars ab apertō latere legiōnēs
circumvenīre, pars summum castrōrum locum petere coepit.

The Roman camp is taken; seemingly all is lost.

24. Eōdem tempore equitēs nostrī levisque armātūrae
peditēs, quī cum eīs ūnā fuerant, quōs prīmō hostium
impetū pulsōs dīxeram, cum sē in castra reciperent, adversīs

Figure 86. — Open ground along the Sambre, over which the Nervians
advanced; looking toward the site of Caesar's Camp, now in part
covered by woods.

16. **ab apertō latere**: 'on the exposed flank,' the right flank.
legiōnēs: the 7th and 12th.

17. **summum castrōrum locum**: 'the height on which the camp
was.' How lit.?

24. 1. **levis armātūrae peditēs**: slingers and bowmen (chap.
19, l. 8).

2. **cum eīs ūnā**: 'along with them,' the cavalry.

3. **dīxeram**: chap. 19, ll. 15–23.   **reciperent, respexissent**
(l. 7): force of *re-*? *79, d.*   **adversīs**, etc.: 'were meeting the
enemy face to face.' *107, a.*   The Nervians came up so rapidly that they
were already entering the Roman camp at the time when Caesar's cavalry and light-armed troops, which had been routed on the other side

hostibus occurrēbant ac rūrsus aliam in partem fugam petē-
5 bant; et cālōnēs, quī ab decumānā portā ac summō iugō
collis nostrōs victōrēs flūmen trānsisse cōnspexerant, praedandī causā ēgressī, cum respexissent et hostēs in nostrīs
castrīs versārī vīdissent, praecipitēs fugae sēsē mandābant.
Simul eōrum, quī cum impedīmentīs veniēbant, clāmor
10 fremitusque oriēbātur, aliīque aliam in partem perterritī
ferēbantur.

Quibus omnibus rēbus permōtī, equitēs Trēverī, quōrum
inter Gallōs virtūtis opīniō est singulāris, quī auxiliī causā
ā cīvitāte ad Caesarem missī vēnerant, cum multitūdine
15 hostium castra nostra complērī, legiōnēs premī et paene

---

of the Sambre, were just coming back to it again.   The descriptive force
of the imperfects in this chapter adds to the vividness of the picture.

5. **cālōnēs**: 'camp-servants,' chiefly, we may assume, servants of
officers.   **ab decumānā portā**: 'at the rear gate' of the camp,
which, since the hill sloped toward the river, was on the highest part
of the hill.   Map 7, **C, C**.   *334, a.*

6. **nostrōs**: the 9th and 10th legions.   **praedandī**, etc.: they
were leaving the camp by the rear gate to hunt for plunder.

7. **hostēs . . . versārī**: 'that the enemy were moving about.'

8. **praecipitēs**: 'precipitately.'   *151.*   B. 239; A. 290; H. 497.

9. **eōrum, quī**: the drivers of the baggage-train, just coming up;
behind it were the 13th and 14th legions bringing up the rear.   See
Map 7.   **clāmor**: 'shouting.'

10. **fremitus**: 'hubbub.'   **oriēbātur**: *61, b,* and *173, a.*   **aliīque**, etc.: 'some in one direction, others in another.'   *171, c.*

11. **ferēbantur**: 'were rushing.'   *174.*   B. 256, 1; H. 517.

13. **virtūtis opīniō**: 'reputation for courage'; meant of the Treveri as a whole, not merely of the cavalry.   **singulāris**: 'extraordinary.'   The implication is that the Treveran horsemen went away not
by reason of cowardice but because they thought the day hopelessly
lost.   **auxiliī**, etc.: Caesar must have made an agreement with the
Treveri before starting on this campaign.

14. **cīvitāte**: personified, hence with *ā.*   *126, a.*   **cum . . . vīdissent**: *185, c.*

15. **legiōnēs**: the 7th and 12th; see Map 7.

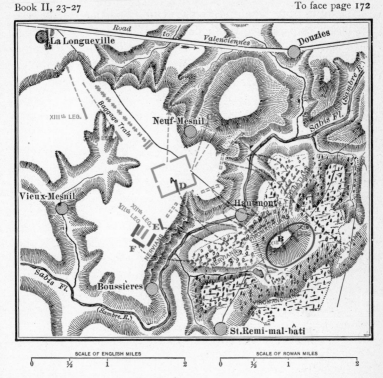

SCALE OF ENGLISH MILES

SCALE OF ROMAN MILES

EXPLANATION

The Atrebatians, having crossed the river, were thrown back by the IXth and X[th] legions, and fled through the woods east of the Belgian camp. The IXth and X[th] legions entered the Belgian camp (**B**), which was on a hill.

In like manner the XIth and VIIIth legions routed the Viromanduans and crossed to the south side of the river in pursuit.

Of the Nervians, one division (**D**) made for the Roman camp (**A**) and entered it; the cavalry, bowmen, and slingers that had taken refuge there fled precipitately (**C**). Other divisions (**E**, **F**) started to surround the VIIth and XIIth legions, which by Caesar's order took up a position rear to rear.

Hearing the noise of battle the baggage train halted, and the XIIIth and XIVth legions hastened to the scene.

Caesar rushed into the front rank, and saved the day.

circumventās tenērī, cālōnēs, equitēs, funditōrēs, Numidās
dīversōs dissipātōsque in omnēs partēs fugere vīdissent,
dēspērātīs nostrīs rēbus, domum contendērunt; Rōmānōs
pulsōs superātōsque, castrīs impedīmentīsque eōrum hostēs
potītōs, cīvitātī renūntiāvērunt.　　　　　　　　　　　　20

*Caesar rushes into the fight, calls centurions by name, directs
the formation of a double front.*

25. Caesar ab x legiōnis cohortātiōne ad dextrum cornū
profectus, ubi suōs urgērī signīsque in ūnum locum collātīs
XII legiōnis cōnfertōs mīlitēs sibi ipsōs ad pugnam esse

---

17. **dīversōs dissipātōsque** : 'separated,' one body of troops from
another, 'and scattered.'

18. **dēspērātīs**, etc. : 'despairing of our victory.' *144, b,* **(3)**.

19. **pulsōs, superātōs** : sc. *esse.*　　**castrīs, impedīmentīs** : after
potītōs [esse]. 131, c.

25. 1. **Caesar**, etc. : subject of a complex sentence which ends
with *possent* in l. 18.

1–18. **Analysis** : The paragraph forms a single complex sentence. The
principal clause has for its subject *Caesar*, with which the participles *profectus*
(l. 2) and *cohortātus* (l. 16) agree; for its predicate it has the verbs *prōcessit*
(l. 15), *iussit* (l. 17). The leading subordinate clause is *ubi . . . vīdit*, which
is so expanded by the introduction of details that *vīdit* is repeated (l. 12) for
clearness. These details are expressed in part by infinitives with subject-accu-
satives dependent on *vīdit*, in part by ablatives absolute, and in part by the
minor clauses *ut . . . posset* (l. 8) and *quod . . . posset* (l. 13).

In translating, the sentence may be broken up into three or four English
sentences; most of the ablatives absolute are best rendered by clauses.

1. **ab . . . cohortātiōne** : = *ab decimā legiōne, quam cohortātus
erat.* Caesar's account of his personal part in this battle, which was
interrupted by his description of the progress of the fighting (chaps.
22–24) is here resumed from chap. 21, ll. 1–9.　　**X** : *38, b,* and *36.*

2. **suōs urgērī** : 'that his men were hard pressed.'　　**signīs** : 'the
standards' of the maniples. *324, b,* (2).

3. **XII** : *duodecimae.* The crowding together of the soldiers of the
12th legion, which exposed them all the more to the missiles of the
enemy, and their consequent losses, were no doubt in part due to their

impedīmentō vīdit, quārtae cohortis omnibus centuriōnibus
5 occīsīs signiferōque interfectō, signō āmissō, reliquārum
cohortium omnibus ferē centuriōnibus aut vulnerātīs aut
occīsīs, in hīs prīmipīlō P. Sextiō Baculō, fortissimō virō,
multīs gravibusque vulneribus cōnfectō, ut iam sē sustinēre
nōn posset, reliquōs esse tardiōrēs et nōn nūllōs ab novis-
10 simīs, dēsertō locō, proeliō excēdere ac tēla vītāre, hostēs
neque ā fronte ex īnferiōre locō subeuntēs intermittere et
ab utrōque latere īnstāre et rem esse in angustō vīdit,

---

lack of experience in fighting; for this legion, raised in 58 B.C. (I, chap.
10, l. 10 and N.), had been in service only a year. During the battle
with the Helvetians it guarded the baggage, having no part in the fray.
sibi . . . impedīmentō: 'were hindering one another in fighting.'
How lit.? *178*, and *112, b*.

4. **quārtae cohortis**: at the front, perhaps at the end of the first
line. *337, a*, and Fig. 186.

5. **signiferō**: 'the standard-bearer.' Each cohort had three standards, of which there were thirty in the legion. Here the reference
probably is to the standard-bearer who carried the standard of the first
maniple of the cohort, which was looked upon as the standard of the
cohort. *324, b*, (2).

7. **prīmipīlō**: 'the first centurion' of the first cohort, hence regarded
as the first centurion of the legion. *315, b*.

8. **multīs gravibusque**: 'many severe wounds.' *152, c*. **cōnfectō**: 'exhausted'; with *prīmipīlō*. Baculus did not die, but lived
to establish the reputation of being one of the bravest, if not the most
brave, among Caesar's men. **ut**: 'so that.'

9. **tardiōrēs**: 'less active,' having lost their initiative. **ab novissimīs**: 'in the rear ranks.' *126, c*.

10. **dēsertō locō . . . excēdere**: 'had abandoned their position
and were withdrawing.' How lit.? **proeliō**: *127, a*. **hostēs,**
etc.: 'that both in front the enemy did not cease coming up — and on
both flanks,' etc.; see Map 7. The Nervians outnumbered the men of
the 12th and 7th legions five or six to one.

11. **neque . . . et**: *233, d*. **ex īnferiōre locō**: 'from the lower
ground' along the river.

12. **rem**, etc.: 'that matters had reached a crisis.' How lit.?
154, a.

neque ūllum esse subsidium, quod summittī posset; scūtō
ab novissimīs ūnī mīlitī dētrāctō, quod ipse eō sine scūtō
vēnerat, in prīmam aciem prōcessit centuriōnibusque 15
nōminātim appellātīs, reliquōs cohortātus, mīlitēs signa īnferre et manipulōs laxāre iussit, quō facilius gladiīs ūtī
possent.

Figure 87. — Typical hedges near the site of the battle at the Sambre.

13. **subsidium**: 'reserve force'; the 13th and 14th legions were
not yet available, because too far off.   **posset**: *194, a.* B. 283, 2;
A. 535, *a*; H. 591, 1.   **scūtō**, etc.: 'snatching a shield from a soldier in the rear rank.' How lit.?   144, *b*, (2).

14. **ūnī**: here 'a,' weaker than 'one'; in English "an" and "one"
were originally the same word. *23, a.*   **mīlitī**: *109, b.* B. 188, 2, *d*;
A. 381; H. 427.   **eō**: adverb.   **sine scūtō**: in battle even commanders may have carried shields, for protection in an emergency.

16. **nōminātim**: Caesar's personal knowledge of his men was
always an important factor in his success.   **signa īnferre**: 'to
advance.' *325.*

17. **manipulōs laxāre**: 'to open up the ranks,' we say; lit. 'to
spread out the companies.'   **quō**: *193, b.* Longfellow in "The

Cuius adventū spē illātā mīlitibus ac redintegrātō animō,
20 cum prō sē quisque in cōnspectū imperātōris etiam in extrēmīs suīs rēbus operam nāvāre cuperet, paulum hostium
impetus tardātus est.

26. Caesar, cum VII legiōnem, quae iūxtā cōnstiterat,
item urgērī ab hoste vīdisset, tribūnōs mīlitum monuit, ut
paulātim sēsē legiōnēs coniungerent et conversa signa in
hostēs īnferrent. Quō factō, cum aliīs aliī subsidium
5 ferrent, neque timērent, nē āversī ab hoste circumvenīrentur, audācius resistere ac fortius pugnāre coepērunt.

*The Romans gain a complete victory, though the enemy fight
with the courage of despair.*

Interim mīlitēs legiōnum duārum, quae in novissimō
agmine praesidiō impedīmentīs fuerant, proeliō nūntiātō,

Courtship of Miles Standish" has portrayed the course of the battle in
verse:

He seized a shield from a soldier,
Put himself straight at the head of his troops, and commanded the captains,
Calling on each by his name, to order forward the ensigns;
Then to widen the ranks, and make more room for their weapons;
So he won the day.

19. **Cuius**: *167.*   **illātā**: *69, b.*   **mīlitibus**: why dative?
20. **prō sē quisque**: *170, b.*   **in extrēmīs suīs rēbus**: 'under
conditions of the utmost peril to himself.'   How lit.?
21. **operam nāvāre**: 'to do his best.'
22. **tardātus est**: 'was checked.'
26. 1. **iūxtā**: the 7th legion was 'near by' the 12th, on the right
wing; see Map 6.
2. **vīdisset**: *185, c.*   **ut ... īnferrent**: 'that the (two) legions
gradually draw together, face about, and advance against the enemy.'
Probably one legion simply took up a position behind the other, facing
in the opposite direction, so that the rear of both was secure. *199, a.*
3. **conversa signa**: *325,* and *228, a.*   B. 337, 2; A. 496, N. 2; H. 639.
5. **ferrent**: *184, a.*   **neque**: trans. as if *et ... nōn.*   **nē**: *202.*
āversī 'in the rear'; the new formation is shown on Map 7.
7. **legiōnum duārum**: the 13th and 14th; see Map 7.

cursū incitātō in summō colle ab hostibus cōnspiciēbantur,
et T. Labiēnus castrīs hostium potītus et ex locō superiōre, 10
quae rēs in nostrīs castrīs gererentur, cōnspicātus, x
legiōnem subsidiō nostrīs mīsit. Quī cum ex equitum et
cālōnum fugā, quō in locō rēs esset, quantōque in perīculō
et castra et legiōnēs et imperātor versārētur, cognōvissent,
nihil ad celeritātem sibi reliquī fēcērunt.   15

27. Hōrum adventū tanta rērum commūtātiō est facta,
ut nostrī, etiam quī vulneribus cōnfectī prōcubuissent,
scūtīs innīxī proelium redintegrārent, cālōnēs, perterritōs
hostēs cōnspicātī, etiam inermēs armātīs occurrerent, equi-

---

9. **cursū incitātō**: 'having quickened their pace'; relation of this
ablative absolute to the preceding?   **summō colle**: 'the top of the
hill' back of the Roman camp. *152, a.*

10. **castrīs**: *131, c.*   **locō superiōre**: the height on which the
Belgian camp was; Map 7, **B**.   Hither Labienus with the 9th and 10th
legions had pursued the Atrebates; chap. 23, ll. 1–8. The probable
lines of flight and pursuit are indicated on Map 7.

11. **quae**: *48, b.*   **gererentur**: *204,* (2).   **cōnspicātus**: as
spy-glasses were not yet invented, Labienus saw with the unaided eye;
the distance from camp to camp across the valley was over a mile.
x: *decimam.*

12. **subsidiō, nostrīs**: *112, b.*   **Quī cum**: 'And when they.'
167.   **Quī**: plural from the idea of *mīlitēs* in *legiōnem.*

13. **quō in locō rēs esset**: 'how matters stood.' How lit.?
204, (2). B. 300, 1 ; A. 574 ; H. 649, 11.

14. **versārētur**: agrees with the nearest subject; trans. 'were.'
172, b, and *204,* (3).

15. **nihil . . . fēcērunt**: 'they made the utmost possible speed,'
more lit. 'left nothing undone in regard to speed.'   **sibi**: *109, a.*
reliquī: predicate genitive.

27. 2. **quī**: (*eī*) *quī.*   **prōcubuissent**: 'had sunk down.' *220.*
B. 324, 1 ; A. 593 ; H. 652.

3. **scūtīs**: *131, c.*   **innīxī**: 'supporting themselves.'   **redintegrārent**: *197, b.*   **perterritōs**: predicative.

4. **inermēs**: with *cālōnēs* ; placed, for the sake of contrast, next to
armātīs ; 'unarmed, rushed against armed (men).'

₅ tēs vērō, ut turpitūdinem fugae virtūte dēlērent, omnibus
in locīs pugnandō sē legiōnāriīs mīlitibus praeferrent.

At hostēs etiam in extrēmā spē salūtis tantam virtūtem
praestitērunt, ut, cum prīmī eōrum cecidissent, proximī
iacentibus īnsisterent atque ex eōrum corporibus pugnā-
₁₀rent; hīs dēiectīs et coacervātīs cadāveribus, quī superessent, ut ex tumulō, tēla in nostrōs conicerent et pīla intercepta remitterent; ut nōn nēquīquam tantae virtūtis
hominēs iūdicārī dēbēret ausōs esse trānsīre lātissimum
flūmen, ascendere altissimās rīpās, subīre inīquissimum
₁₅locum, quae facilia ex difficillimīs animī magnitūdō
redēgerat.

---

5. **vērō**: *236, a*.   **turpitūdinem**: 'disgrace.'   **dēlērent**: 'they
might wipe out.'   **omnibus**, etc.: 'strove to outdo the legionaries at
all points in fighting.'   As an arm of the service cavalry was rated by
the Romans of secondary importance. *309.*

6. **pugnandō**: *230*, (4).   **mīlitibus**: *107, b*.

7. **etiam**, etc.: 'even in utter despair of safety.'

8. **prīmī eōrum**: 'their foremost ranks.' How lit. ? *154, a*.

9. **iacentibus īnsisterent**: 'mounted upon the fallen.' *227, a*, (4).
ex: *126, c*.

10. **coacervātīs cadāveribus**: 'when their bodies had been
heaped' on those of the Nervians that had first fallen.   **quī**: as antecedent supply *eī*, subject of *conicerent*.   **superessent**: *220*.

11. **ut ex tumulō**: 'as from a mound.'   **conicerent**: 'continued
to hurl.'   **pīla intercepta remitterent**: 'picked up and threw back
the pikes,' though these could be of little value as weapons; cf. N. to I,
25, l. 9.   **conicerent, remitterent**: in the same construction as
īnsisterent, pugnārent. *197, b*.

12. **ut**, etc.: a result clause, presenting Caesar's conclusion; 'so
that it ought not to be thought that men of so great valor in vain
dared,' etc.; they fought in a manner worthy of their heroic advance.

13. **ausōs esse**: *62*.   **lātissimum**: Fig. 88. *153, a*.

14. **altissimās**: the banks are steep where the Nervians crossed.

15. **quae**: 'things (referring to the actions expressed in the preceding infinitives) which, in themselves most difficult, their heroic courage
had made easy.' How lit.?   **facilia**: *115, b*.

Caesar spares the remnant of the Nervians.

28. Hōc proeliō factō, et prope ad internecіōnem gente
ac nōmine Nerviōrum redāctō, maiōrēs nātū, quōs ūnā cum
puerīs mulieribusque in aestuāria ac palūdēs coniectōs
dīxerāmus, hāc pugnā nūntiātā, cum victōribus nihil impedītum, victīs nihil tūtum arbitrārentur, omnium, quī 5
supererant, cōnsēnsū lēgātōs ad Caesarem mīsērunt sēque
eī dēdidērunt; et in commemorandā cīvitātis calamitāte, ex

Figure 88. — View on the Sambre, near the site of the battle.

28.　1. **Hōc proeliō factō** : 'Now that this battle was over.'　How
lit.?　**internecіōnem** : 'utter destruction.'　Six years later, however, the Nervians were expected to send a force of 6000 warriors to
Alesia (VII, 75, l. 14).　**gente** : 'stock.'

2. **maiōrēs nātū, puerīs** : Notes to chap. 13, l. 7 and l. 11.

3. **aestuāria** : here 'tidal marshes,' surrounded by salt water at high
tide.　**palūdēs** : 'swamps.'　**coniectōs** : *89, c.*

4. **dīxerāmus** : chap. 16, ll. 8–10.　**cum** : *184, a.*　**nihil impedītum** : 'that there was nothing to oppose.'　How lit.?

5. **victīs** : *227, a,* (4).　**nihil tūtum** : 'no safety,' we should say.
omnium : masculine, dependent on *cōnsēnsū.*

DC ad trēs senātōrēs, ex hominum mīlibus LX vix ad D, quī
arma ferre possent, sēsē redāctōs esse dīxērunt.

10   Quōs Caesar, ut in miserōs ac supplicēs ūsus misericordiā vidērētur, dīligentissimē cōnservāvit suīsque fīnibus
atque oppidīs ūtī iussit et fīnitimīs imperāvit, ut ab iniūriā
et maleficiō sē suōsque prohibērent.

Capture of the Stronghold of the Atuatuci. 29–33

The Atuatuci gather in one stronghold.

29. Atuatucī, dē quibus suprā scrīpsimus, cum omnibus
cōpiīs auxiliō Nerviīs venīrent, hāc pugnā nūntiātā, ex itinere
domum revertērunt; cūnctīs oppidīs castellīsque dēsertīs,
sua omnia in ūnum oppidum, ēgregiē nātūrā mūnītum, con-

---

8. **DC**: *sescentīs* (*senātōribus*). Reckoning the Nervian army at
60,000 (10,000 more than the Remi reported, chap. 4, l. 25), 600 *senātōrēs* would average one to every 100 men. It is possible, therefore,
that the Latin word *senātor* is here applied to a leader of a hundred;
and this suggestion seems to be confirmed by the losses of the *senātōrēs*
in battle.   **D**: *quīngentōs*, modified by *vix*, 'barely.' Exaggeration
on the part of the suppliants was to be expected.   **quī . . . possent**:
subjunctive in the direct form. *194, a.*

10. **in**: 'toward.'   **ūsus**: sc. *esse*. *221, b.* B. 328, 2; A. 582;
H. 612, 1.   **misericordiā**: 'compassion'; cf. chap. 14, l. 11. *131, c.*

12. **ut**, etc.: *199, a.*   **iniūriā et maleficiō**: 'wrong-doing and
ill-treatment' of the weak remnant of the Nervians.

29. 1. **suprā**: chap. 16, ll. 7–8.   **cum**: *185, c.*   **omnibus
cōpiīs**: 19,000 men, if they reached the estimate of the Remi (chap. 4,
l. 29). *136, b.* B. 220, 1; A. 412; H. 473, 3.

2. **auxiliō Nerviīs**: *112, b.*   **ex itinere**: see Vocab., under *iter*.

3. **castellīs**: 'fortresses'; small fortified places, perhaps occupied
only in time of danger.

4. **oppidum**: 'stronghold,' like that of the Bellovaci; see N. to
chap. 13, l. 5. This stronghold is by some located on the hill where
now the citadel of Namur is, at the junction of the Meuse and the
Sambre and across the Sambre from the city of Namur; see Map 8.
Others, considering the hill at Namur too small, prefer, as the site of
the stronghold, the hill of Falhize, which lies on the north bank of the

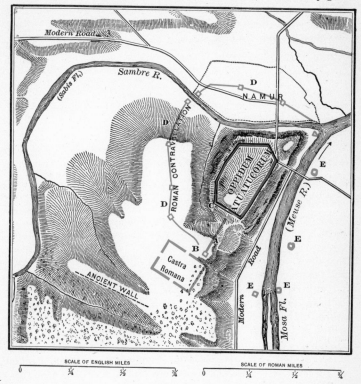

EXPLANATION

The Atuatuci abandoned their towns and gathered in a stronghold protected by steep cliffs except on one side, where there was an easy approach not more than 200 Roman feet wide.

Caesar blockaded the stronghold with a rampart and redoubts. Afterwards he ran an embankment up the inclined approach, and made ready to attack.

A. Incline along which Caesar-constructed his siege embankment, *agger*.

B. General's gate, *porta praetōria*, of Caesar's camp.

C. Upper end of the inclined approach, fortified with a double wall (chap. 29, ll. 8–10) and moat (chap. 32, ll. 9, 10).

D–D. Rampart, *vallum* (chap. 30, l. 3).

E–E. Redoubts, *castella* (chap. 30, l. 4).

tulērunt. Quod cum ex omnibus in circuitū partibus altis- 5
simās rūpēs dēiectūsque habēret, ūnā ex parte lēniter
acclīvis aditus in lātitūdinem nōn amplius ducentōrum
pedum relinquēbātur; quem locum duplicī altissimō mūrō
mūnierant; tum magnī ponderis saxa et praeacūtās trabēs
in mūrō collocābant.   10

Ipsī erant ex Cimbrīs Teutonīsque prōgnātī, quī, cum
iter in prōvinciam nostram atque Italiam facerent, eīs impedīmentīs, quae sēcum agere ac portāre nōn poterant,
citrā flūmen Rhēnum dēpositīs, cūstōdiam ex suīs ac praesidium vi mīlia hominum ūnā relīquērunt. Hī post eōrum 15
obitum multōs annōs ā fīnitimīs exagitātī, cum aliās bel-

Meuse, opposite the town of Huy, 19 miles below Namur.   **ēgregiē**:
'admirably.'

5. **Quod cum**: 'And although this.' *187*, and *167*.   **ex**, etc.:
'on all sides round about.' How lit.?

6. **rūpēs**: 'cliffs.' *15, b*.   **lēniter acclīvis**: 'gently rising.' If
the stronghold was on the hill across from Namur, this narrow 'approach' was on the southwest side.

8. **pedum**: the case is not influenced by *amplius*. *100, a*, and
129, b.   **duplicī**: 'double.' *26, a*.

9. **ponderis**: *100, a*.   **praeacūtās trabēs**: 'beams sharpened
at the ends.' *17, c*.

10. **in**: 'on.'   **collocābant**: 'they were placing,' at the time
(*tum*) when Caesar came up; the change of tense from the pluperfect
(*mūnierant*) is to be noted.

11. **Cimbrīs Teutonīsque**, etc.: see N. to I, chap. 33, l. 17.
prōgnātī: 'descended.' *128, b*.

12. **prōvinciam**: *290*.   **impedīmentīs**: 'cattle and goods';
the use in l. 13 of *agere*, 'drive,' with *portāre*, shows that cattle as
well as portable possessions are here included.

14. **citrā**: on the west side.   **dēpositīs**: with *impedīmentīs*.
cūstōdiam: 'as a guard' of the *impedīmenta*. *115, a*.   **ex suīs**:
i.e. *sex mīlia hominum ex suīs*. *97, d*.   **praesidium**: 'as a garrison.'

15. **Hī**: the 6000 Atuatuci.   **eōrum**: the great host of the Cimbrians and Teutons.

16. **obitum**: 'destruction,' at Aquae Sextiae in 102 B.C. and at

lum īnferrent, aliās illātum dēfenderent, cōnsēnsū eōrum
omnium pāce factā, hunc sibi domiciliō locum dēlēgērunt.

Caesar besieges it ; the Atuatuci ridicule the siege-works.

30. Ac prīmō adventū exercitūs nostrī crēbrās ex oppidō excursiōnēs faciēbant parvulīsque proeliīs cum nostrīs
contendēbant; posteā vāllō pedum XII, in circuitū XV mīlium crēbrīsque castellīs circummūnītī oppidō sēsē con-
5 tinēbant.

Ubi, vīneīs āctīs, aggere exstrūctō, turrim procul cōnstituī
vīdērunt, prīmum irrīdēre ex mūrō atque increpitāre vōci-

Vercellae in 101 B.C.   **exagitātī**: 'harassed.'   **aliās . . . aliās**:
'sometimes . . . sometimes.'

17. **illātum**: sc. *bellum*; 'were repelling attack.'   **eōrum omnium**: 'of them all,' including the Atuatuci and their neighbors.

18. **domiciliō**: *112, a.*   **locum**:
'district' (Fig. 89).

30. 1. **prīmō adventū**: i.e. *prīmō
post adventum tempore*, 'Immediately
after the arrival.' *147, b.*

2. **excursiōnēs**: 'sallies.'   **parvulīs proeliīs**: 'skirmishes.'   How
lit.? *76, c.*

Figure 89. — Coin of the Atuatuci.

Bronze. Obverse, a design suggesting the heads of snakes. Reverse,
horse; inscription, AVAVCIA.

3. **vāllō, castellīs**: these formed
the line of contravallation; see Map 8.

It has been thought strange that, if the site of the stronghold was
opposite Namur, or at Falhize, no mention in this description is made
of the Sambre or the Meuse. The brow of the hill on which the
stronghold stood was so steep and high that perhaps the rivers
hardly entered into Caesar's calculations in planning the contravallation.   **pedum XII**: in height. *38, b,* and *100, a.*   **XV mīlium**:
sc. *pedum*, though Caesar in such cases elsewhere has *passuum*. A
circuit of three Roman miles seems to satisfy the conditions. *243, b.*

4. **circummūnītī**: 'closed in.'   How lit.?   **oppidō**: *131, a.*

6. **vīneīs āctīs**: *342, a.*   **aggere exstrūctō**: '(and) after an
embankment had been built up.' *341.*   **turrim**: *14, b,* and *342, b.*

7. **irrīdēre**: 'they (the Atuatuci) scoffed.' *182.*   **increpitāre
vōcibus**: 'made taunting remarks.'   How lit.? *182,* and *131, a.*

bus, quod tanta māchinātiō ā tantō spatiō īnstituerētur :
*Quibusnam manibus aut quibus vīribus, praesertim hominēs
tantulae statūrae* (nam plērumque omnibus Gallīs prae 10
magnitūdine corporum suōrum brevitās nostra contemptuī
est) *tantī oneris turrim in mūrō sēsē collocāre posse cōnfīderent ?*

Figure 90.— Site of the stronghold at Namur.
Caesar's camp was probably on the hill at the left.

---

8. **quod**, etc. : 'because (as they said) so big an engine,' etc. *214, b.*
B. 286, 1 ; A. 592, 3 ; H. 588, 11. **ā tantō spatiō** : 'so far off' ; i.e.,
'at' (lit. 'from') 'so great a distance.' Cf. N. to chap. 7, l. 10.

9. **Quibusnam . . . cōnfīderent** : *213, b,* and *212, c,* (6). **Quibusnam** : *48, c.* **vīribus** : *18, a.* **hominēs**, etc. : contemptuous,
'(being) men of so small size,' 'such little chaps.' *91, b,* and
100, a.

10. **nam . . . est** : *214, c.* **Gallīs, contemptuī** : both datives,
but trans. 'held in contempt by the Gauls.' How lit. ?

12. **oneris** : 'weight.' *13, e.* The Atuatuci seem to have thought
that the Romans would have to pick up the tower in order to move it.
cōnfīderent : *217, a.* B. 315, 1 ; A. 586 ; H. 642, 3.

*Frightened by the approach of the moveable tower, they sue
for peace; they secretly keep back arms.*

31. Ubi vērō movērī et appropinquāre moenibus vīdērunt, novā atque inūsitātā speciē commōtī, lēgātōs ad
Caesarem dē pāce mīsērunt, quī, ad hunc modum locūtī,

Nōn sē exīstimāre, Rōmānōs sine ope deōrum bellum
5 *gerere, quī tantae altitūdinis māchinātiōnēs tantā celeritāte
prōmovēre possent, sē suaque omnia eōrum potestātī permittere* dīxērunt;

*Ūnum petere ac dēprecārī: sī forte prō suā clēmentiā ac
mānsuētūdine, quam ipsī ab aliīs audīrent, statuisset, Atua-*
10 *tucōs esse cōnservandōs, nē sē armīs dēspoliāret. Sibi omnēs
ferē fīnitimōs esse inimīcōs ac suae virtūtī invidēre; ā quibus sē dēfendere, trāditīs armīs, nōn possent.*

Sibi praestāre, sī in eum cāsum dēdūcerentur, quamvīs

---

31. 1. **movērī**, etc.: sc. *turrim.*   **moenibus**: *105.*   **vīdērunt**:
Atuatucī.

2. **inūsitātā**: 'unwonted.'   **speciē**: 'sight.'   *21, b.*

3. **quī**: subject of *dīxērunt*, l. 7.   **hunc**: 'the following.'   *161, a.*

4. **ope**: 'help.'   **deōrum**: *8, d.*

5. **quī**: 'since they.'   *194, c.*   B. 283, 3, *a*; A. 535, *e*; H. 592.

6. **sē suaque omnia**: 'themselves and all they had.'   How lit.?
eōrum: of the Romans.

8. **Ūnum**: 'one thing (only),' explained by *nē . . . dēspoliāret.*
dēprecārī: 'begged to escape.'   **clēmentiā**, etc.: cf. chap. 14, l. 11,
and N.

9. **audīrent**: 'they kept hearing about'; *audīvissent*, implying a
single instance, would have been less complimentary.   **statuisset,**
etc.: in the direct form, *sī statueris* (future perfect) . . . *nōlī nōs armīs
dēspoliāre.* *218*, (1), b, and *216.*

10. **armīs**: *127, a.*   **Sibi**: after *inimīcōs*, l. 11.

11. **virtūtī**: *105.*   **invidēre**: 'envied.'   **ā**: we say 'against.'

12. **trāditīs armīs**: i.e. *sī arma trādita essent.* *144, b*, (4).   B.
227, 2, *b*; A. 420, 4; H. 575, 9.

13. **praestāre**: 'it was better.'   **eum cāsum**: 'such a condition,'

*fortūnam ā populō Rōmānō patī, quam ab hīs per cruciātum
interfīcī, inter quōs domināri cōnsuēssent.* 15

32. Ad haec Caesar respondit:

*Sē magis cōnsuētūdine suā quam meritō eōrum cīvitātem
cōnservātūrum, sī, prius quam mūrum ariēs attigisset, sē
dēdidissent; sed dēditiōnis nūllam esse condiciōnem nisi
armīs trāditīs. Sē id, quod in Nerviīs fēcisset, factūrum* 5
*fīnitimīsque imperātūrum, nē quam dēditīciīs populī Rō-
mānī iniūriam īnferrent.*

Rē nūntiātā ad suōs, īllī sē, quae imperārentur, facere
dīxērunt. Armōrum magnā multitūdine dē mūrō in fossam,
quae erat ante oppidum, iactā, sīc ut prope summam mūrī 10

---

involving a choice between the mercy of the Romans and the treatment
of their neighbors. **quamvīs fortūnam**: 'any lot whatever.' *49, a.*

14. **ā**: 'at the hands of.' **patī**: subject of *praestāre. 222, b.*

15. **domināri**: 'to exercise dominion.' *61, a*, (1). **cōnsuēssent**: *64, a*, (2).

32. 2. **cōnsuētūdine suā**: 'in accordance with his practice' of
mercifully treating a prostrate foe. *136, c.* **meritō**: *135, a.*

3. **sī**, etc.: in the direct form, *cīvitātem cōnservābō, sī, prius quam
. . . attigerit* (future perfect), *vōs dēdideritis* (future perfect). **ariēs**:
'battering-ram.' It was a rule of war that besieged cities which did not
capitulate before the battering-ram touched the walls, should when
captured be given over to destruction. *10, e*, and *342, c.*

5. **armīs trāditīs**: *144, b*, (2). **id, quod**: *160, c.* **in**: 'in
the case of.' **factūrum**: *89, c.*

6. **nē**, etc.: *199, a.* **quam**: *168,* and *49, a.* **dēditīciīs**: *107, b.*

8. **imperārentur**: *214, a.* **sē facere**: 'that they carried out';
vivid use of the present tense where the future might have been
expected.

9. **multitūdine**: 'quantity'; with *iactā.* **fossam**: Map 8, **C.**

10. **sīc ut**, etc.: *197, b.* **summam . . . altitūdinem**: 'the full
height.' *152, a.* The 'embankment' had been prolonged to the edge
of the moat; the deep space between the end of the 'embankment' and
the 'wall,' from the bottom of the moat up, was nearly filled with
weapons.

aggerisque altitūdinem acervī armōrum adaequārent, et
tamen circiter parte tertiā, ut posteā perspectum est, cēlātā
atque in oppidō retentā, portīs patefactīs, eō diē pāce sunt
ūsī.

*They make a treacherous attack ; are defeated, and sold into
slavery.*

33. Sub vesperum Caesar portās claudī mīlitēsque ex
oppidō exīre iussit, nē quam noctū oppidānī ā mīlitibus
iniūriam acciperent. Illī, ante initō, ut intellēctum est,
cōnsiliō, quod, dēditiōne factā, nostrōs praesidia dēductūrōs
5 aut dēnique indīligentius servātūrōs crēdiderant, partim
cum eīs, quae retinuerant et cēlāverant, armīs, partim
scūtīs ex cortice factīs aut vīminibus intextīs, quae subitō,
ut temporis exiguitās postulābat, pellibus indūxerant,
tertiā vigiliā, quā minimē arduus ad nostrās mūnītiōnēs

---

11. **acervī**: 'heaps.'

12. **cēlātā**: 'concealed.'

13. **patefactīs**: 'thrown open.'.   **pāce sunt ūsī**: 'they kept
quiet'; lit. 'they enjoyed peace.'

33. 1. **Sub**: 'Towards.'   **vesperum**: *7, b.*

2. **nē**, etc.: *196, a.*   **quam**: as in chap. 32, l. 6.   **ā**: as in
chap. 31, l. 14.

3. **ante īnitō — cōnsiliō**: 'having previously formed a plot.' How
lit. ?

4. **praesidia dēductūrōs** [esse]: 'would withdraw the outposts'
from the redoubts and the line of circumvallation, where the Roman
sentries kept watch.

5. **dēnique**: 'at any rate.'   **indīligentius**: 'less carefully.'
153, a.   **servātūrōs** [esse]: 'would maintain (them)' the outposts.

6. **cum**: with *armīs*, and understood with *scūtīs*, l. 7.

7. **cortice**: 'bark.' *98, b.*   **vīminibus intextīs**: '(of) wickerwork,' lit. 'withes interwoven.' Cf. Fig. 48, p. 60.

8. **pellibus**: 'with skins.' The Atuatuci had driven cattle into the
enclosure ; cf. chap. 29, l. 4.

9. **tertiā vigiliā**: *242, c.*   **arduus**: 'steep.' *30.*

ascēnsus vidēbātur, omnibus cōpiīs repente ex oppidō 10
ēruptiōnem fēcērunt.

Celeriter, ut ante Caesar imperāverat, īgnibus significātiōne factā, ex proximīs castellīs eō concursum est, pugnā-
tumque ab hostibus ita ācriter est, ut ā virīs fortibus in
extrēmā spē salūtis inīquō locō, contrā eōs, quī ex vāllō 15
turribusque tēla iacerent, pugnārī dēbuit, cum in ūnā virtūte omnis spēs salūtis cōnsisteret. Occīsīs ad hominum
mīlibus IIII, reliquī in oppidum reiectī sunt.

Postrīdiē eius diēī refrāctīs portīs, cum iam dēfenderet
nēmō, atque intrōmissīs mīlitibus nostrīs, sectiōnem eius 20

---

10. **ascēnsus,** etc.: implies that at the point attacked the Roman
line of contravallation was on ground somewhat above the level of the
plain, so that the enemy, after rushing down from the town, must advance up a height in order to storm the Roman fortifications.   **cōpiīs:**
137, b.

11. **ēruptiōnem:** 'sortie.'

12. **īgnibus:** 'by fire-signals.'   See Plate IV, 2.   **significātiōne:**
'warning.'

13. **eō:** to the point attacked.   **concursum est:** 'the soldiers
rushed.' *73, d.*

14. **ut,** etc.: 'as brave men were bound to fight.'   **in . . . salūtis:** cf. chap. 27, l. 7, and N.

15. **inīquō locō:** *145, c.*   **vāllō:** the Roman line of contravall-
latiоn.

16. **turribus:** stationed at intervals along the line of contravallation, as on the rampart around a camp; cf. Plate IX, 6.   **iacerent:**
194, a. B. 283, 2 ; A. 535 ; H. 591, 1.   **ūnā:** 'alone.'

17. **ad:** adverb, 'about,' modifying *quattuor* (IIII).

19. **diēī:** *94, c.*   **refrāctīs:** 'had been burst in.'   How lit.?
cum: *184, a.*   **iam:** 'any longer.'

20. **intrōmissīs:** 'had been sent in,' lit. 'into,' the stronghold.
sectiōnem ūniversam: 'the booty in one sale,' at auction; in such
cases the buyers who joined in the bid afterwards divided up the purchase among themselves for resale in smaller lots.   Such wholesale
buyers accompanied Roman armies.   In this instance the booty included not only everything that the captured Atuatuci had, but the
people themselves, who were sold into slavery.

oppidī ūniversam Caesar vēndidit.   Ab eīs, quī ēmerant,
capitum numerus ad eum relātus est mīlium LIII.

Successful Closing of the Year. 34, 35

Maritime states in northwestern Gaul submit to Publius Crassus.

34. Eōdem tempore ā P. Crassō, quem cum legiōne
ūnā mīserat ad Venetōs, Venellōs, Osismōs, Coriosolitas,
Esuviōs, Aulercōs, Redonēs, quae sunt maritimae cīvitātēs
Ōceanumque attingunt, certior factus est, omnēs eās
5 cīvitātēs in diciōnem potestātemque populī Rōmānī esse
redāctās.

*German tribes offer submission; the army goes into winter
quarters; a thanksgiving is decreed at Rome.*

35. Hīs rēbus gestīs, omnī Galliā pācātā, tanta huius
bellī ad barbarōs opīniō perlāta est, utī ab eīs nātiōnibus, quae trāns Rhēnum incolerent, lēgātī ad Caesarem

---

21. **vēndidit**: 'sold.'

22. **capitum**: 'of persons'; cf. I, chap. 29, l. 6, and N.   LIII:
quīnquāgintā trium. 38, b, and *36*. Some of the Atuatuci, however,
were still left in the country; cf. V, 38, ll. 1–2, and 39, ll. 9–11.

34. 1. **P.**: *19, a.*   **Crassō**: see Vocab. under *Crassus*, (2).

legiōne ūnā : the 7th, which must
have started for western Gaul soon
after the battle of the Sambre.

2: **Venetōs**: N. to III, 8, l. 3.
Venellōs: for the location of the
Venelli and other peoples mentioned, see Map at the end of this
volume.   **Coriosolitas**: (Fig.
91).   *19, f.*

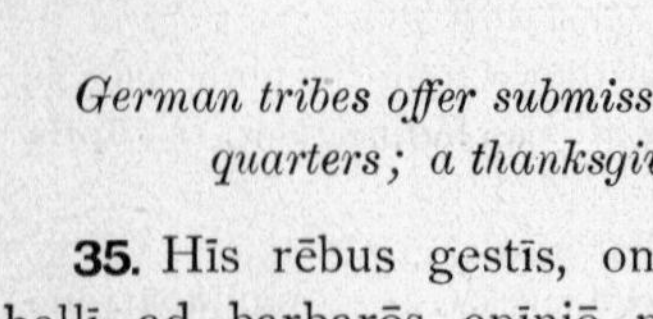

Figure 91. — Coin of the Coriosolites.
Reverse, human-headed horse. Obverse,
a fanciful head.

3. **quae**: *164, c.*   **maritimae**: 'maritime.'

4. **Ōceanum**: the Atlantic; see Vocab.

35. 3. **incolerent**: *220.* B. 324, 1 ; A. 593; H. 652.

mitterentur, quī sē obsidēs datūrās, imperāta factūrās
pollicērentur. Quās lēgātiōnēs Caesar, quod in Italiam 5
Illyricumque properābat, initā proximā aestāte ad sē
revertī iussit.

Ipse, in Carnutēs, Andēs, Turonōs, quaeque cīvitātēs propinquae hīs locīs erant, ubi bellum gesserat, legiōnibus in
hīberna dēductīs, in Italiam profectus est. Ob eāsque rēs 10
ex litterīs Caesaris diērum xv supplicātiō dēcrēta est, quod
ante id tempus accidit nūllī.

---

4. **sē**: feminine, taking the gender of *nātiōnibus*; hence *datūrās*
and *factūrās* (sc. *esse*) are feminine.

5. **pollicērentur**: *193, a.*   **Quās**: *167.*   **Italiam**: here including Cisalpine Gaul. *283, b.*

6. **Illyricum**: *298.*

8. **Carnutēs**, etc.: *282.* See Map.   **quaeque cīvitātēs**: *et in
eās cīvitātēs quae. 165, c.*

10. **hīberna**: *335, b.*   **eāsque**: *233, b.*

11. **ex**: 'after receipt of.'   **litterīs**: 'dispatches' to the Roman
Senate, reporting his victories.   **supplicātiō**: 'solemn thanksgiving,' services of prayer to avert misfortune as well as giving of thanks
to the gods for victory. Usually such services lasted only three or four
days; the longest previous 'thanksgiving' was of twelve days, decreed
after Pompey had brought to a close the war with Mithridates.   **quod**:
sc. *id*, referring to the fact stated in the preceding clause.

12. **nūllī**: = *nēminī. 12, d.*

COMMENTARIUS TERTIUS

Operations in the Alps. 1-6

Caesar stations Galba with a small force in the Alps.

1. Cum in Italiam proficīscerētur Caesar, Ser. Galbam,
cum legiōne XII et parte equitātūs, in Nantuātēs, Veragrōs
Sedūnōsque mīsit, quī ā fīnibus Allobrogum et lacū Lemannō et flūmine Rhodanō ad summās Alpēs pertinent.
5 Causa mittendī fuit, quod iter per Alpēs, quō magnō cum
perīculō magnīsque cum portōriīs mercātōrēs īre cōnsuērant, patefierī volēbat. Huic permīsit, sī opus esse arbitrārētur, utī in hīs locīs legiōnem hiemandī causā collocāret.

---

1. 1. proficīscerētur: Caesar 'was starting' on the trip referred
to in II, chap. 35, l. 10. *185, c*. The events of Book III, as a whole,
belong to the year 56 B.C.; but the uprising of the Alpine tribes, narrated in chapters 1-6, took place in the latter part of the autumn and
early winter of B.C. 57. **Italiam**: Cisalpine Gaul. *283, b*. **Ser.**
= *Servium*. *19, a*. **Galbam**: see Vocab. under Galba, (1).

2. **XII**: *duodecimā*. *38, b*. Caesar had eight legions, numbered 7 to
14 inclusive. **Nantuātēs**: *282*. Locate the states mentioned on Map 1.

4. **summās Alpēs**: 'the highest part of the Alps.' *152, a*.

5. **mittendī**: *230*, (1). **iter**: 'route' to Italy, over the pass now
known as the Great St. Bernard, where the famous hospice is. By this
route Napoleon I in May, 1800, made his venturesome "crossing of the
Alps," with an army of 36,000 men. (Fig. 92.)

6. **perīculō**: the danger arose not so much from the precipitous
way over the mountains as from the hostility of the natives. These
lived in part by plundering and by levying tolls on the goods of traders
going over the pass. **portōriīs**: N. to I, 18, l. 9.

7. **patefierī**: 'be kept open'; the subject is *iter. 70, c*, and *223, a*.
Huic: Galba. **opus esse**: 'that it was necessary.' **arbitrārētur**:
arbitrāberis in the unattracted form. *220*.

8. **legiōnem**, etc.: the 12th legion had suffered so severely in the

Galba locates his winter quarters in Octodurus.

Galba, secundīs aliquot proeliīs factīs castellīsque complūribus eōrum expugnātīs, missīs ad eum undique lēgātīs[10]
obsidibusque datīs et pāce factā, cōnstituit cohortēs duās in

Figure 92. — The Great St. Bernard Pass and the famous hospice.

battle of the Sambre (II, chap. 25), that Caesar would hardly have stationed it at so difficult a post if he had anticipated serious opposition.
collocāret: *199, a.*

9. **proeliīs,** etc.: the abiatives absolute indicate successive events,
and should be rendered by clauses. First come the engagements, then
the taking of strongholds; later, the sending of envoys, then the giving
of hostages; finally, the ratification of peace.

11. **cohortēs duās:** how many men? *307, c.*   **in Nantuātibus:** perhaps where St. Maurice now is, on the upper Rhone. *282.*

Nantuātibus collocāre et ipse, cum reliquīs eius legiōnis
cohortibus, in vīcō Veragrōrum, quī appellātur Octodūrus,
hiemāre; quī vīcus, positus in valle, nōn magnā adiectā
15 plānitiē, altissimīs montibus undique continētur.　Cum hīc
in duās partēs flūmine dīviderētur, alteram partem eius vīcī
Gallīs concessit, alteram, vacuam ab hīs relīctam, cohortibus
ad hiemandum attribuit.　Eum locum vāllō fossāque mū-
nīvit.

There is a sudden uprising of the mountaineers.

2.　Cum diēs hībernōrum complūrēs trānsīssent, frūmentumque eō comportārī iussisset, subitō per explōrātōrēs
certior factus est, ex eā parte vīcī, quam Gallīs concesserat,
omnēs noctū discessisse, montēsque, quī impendērent, ā
5 maximā multitūdine Sedūnōrum et Veragrōrum tenērī.

---

12. reliquīs cohortibus: doubtless the two strongest cohorts were
detailed for the separate post; how many men the remaining eight contained it is difficult to estimate.

13. vīcō: how different from *oppidum?*　　**Octodūrus**: near Martigny; see Map I, and Fig. 93.

14. quī: *167.*　**valle**: 'valley.'　　**nōn magnā**: *239, g.*　**adiectā**:
'adjoining.'　How lit.?

16. flūmine: the Dranse, which flows into the Rhone, from the
south, at the point where the Rhone turns northwest toward Lake
Geneva.　　**alteram . . . alteram**: *171, b.*

17. vacuam: predicative, after *relīctam;* Galba expelled the inhabitants from the part of Octodurus which was on the west bank of the
Dranse, and turned the dwellings into winter quarters.　*88, b.*

2. 1. hībernōrum: 'of the (life in) winter quarters.'　**trānsīssent**: *68, b,* and *185, c.*

2. eō: to the part of the town used for winter quarters.　**iussisset**:
sc. *Galba.*　　**explōrātōrēs**: *327.*

3. concesserat: *214, c.*　The Gauls occupied the part of the town
on the east bank.

4. impendērent: *214, a.*　　**ā**: with the ablative of agent because
of the idea of *hominēs* in *multitūdō.　126, b.*

Id aliquot dē causīs acciderat, ut subitō Gallī bellī reno-
vandī legiōnisque opprimendae cōnsilium caperent: prīmum, quod legiōnem, neque eam plēnissimam, dētrāctīs
cohortibus duābus et complūribus singillātim, quī commeātūs petendī causā missī erant, absentibus, propter paucitā- 10
tem dēspiciēbant; tum etiam, quod propter inīquitātem locī;
cum ipsī ex montibus in vallem dēcurrerent et tēla conicerent, nē prīmum quidem impetum suum posse sustinērī
exīstimābant.

Accēdēbat, quod suōs ab sē līberōs abstrāctōs obsidum 15

Figure 93.—Valley of the Dranse.
View near Martigny. The tower belongs to the ruined castle of Batiaz.

6. **Id**: explained by the clause *ut . . . caperent*. *203*, (4). **reno-
vandī**: 'of renewing.' *230*, (1).

8. **neque eam plēnissimam**: 'and that lacking its full strength';
the reason is explained by the following ablatives absolute. How lit. ?
161, c.

9. **complūribus**: sc. *mīlitibus*. **singillātim**: 'as individuals,'
not sent out as cohorts or maniples. **commeātūs**, etc.: *230*, (1).

11. **tum etiam**: *deinde* is more common as correlative with *prīmum*.
237, b.

12. **ipsī**: *Gallī*. **dēcurrerent**: 'should rush down.'

15. **quod . . . dolēbant**: subject of *Accēdēbat*; 'There was the

nōmine dolēbant, et Rōmānōs nōn sōlum itinerum causā,
sed etiam perpetuae possessiōnis culmina Alpium occupāre
cōnārī et ea loca fīnitimae prōvinciae adiungere sibi persuāsum habēbant.

•   *Galba, calling a council, decides not to retreat.*

3. Hīs nūntiīs acceptīs, Galba, cum neque opus hībernōrum mūnītiōnēsque plēnē essent perfectae, neque dē frūmentō reliquōque commeātū satis esset prōvīsum, quod,
dēditiōne factā obsidibusque acceptīs, nihil dē bellō timen-
5 dum exīstimāverat, cōnsiliō celeriter convocātō, sententiās
exquīrere coepit.

Quō in cōnsiliō, cum tantum repentīnī perīculī praeter

---

further consideration that,' etc.   *198, b.*   B. 299, 1; A. 572; H. 588, 3.
abstrāctōs: 'had been taken away.'   *89, c,* and *223, a,* (2).

16. **nōmine**: 'under the name.'   *136, b.*   **itinerum causā**: cf.
chap. 1, ll. 5–7.

17. **culmina**: 'summits,' commanding the passes.   *12, e.*

18. **prōvinciae**: *107, b,* and *290.*   **adiungere**: 'annex.'   **sibi
persuāsum habēbant**, etc.: 'were convinced that the Romans were
trying,' lit. 'had persuaded themselves', etc.   *229, a.*   B. 337,7; A. 497,
b.   **persuāsum**: predicative, in agreement with the infinitive clause
Rōmānōs . . . cōnārī, object of *habēbant.*   *148, d.*

3. 1. **neque . . . neque**: 'not . . . and not.'   **opus hībernōrum,
mūnītiōnēs**: 'the work on the winter quarters,' in general, including
as the most important item, 'the fortifications' (chap. 1, l. 18).   Cf.
I, 31, l. 48, *exempla cruciātūsque,* and N.

2. **plēnē**: 'quite.'   **perfectae**: agreement?   *172, b.*   **dē**: 'for.'

3. **satis esset prōvīsum**: 'sufficient provision had been made.'

4. **nihil . . . timendum** [esse]: 'that he had no occasion to
fear hostilities.'   How lit.?   *73, e.*

5. **cōnsiliō**: doubtless of the centurions; cf. I, 40, ll. 1–2.
sententiās exquīrere: 'to ask for opinions' regarding the best course
to pursue.

7. **Quō**: *167.*   **tantum repentīnī perīculī**: 'so great danger
suddenly;' lit. 'so much of sudden danger.'   *97, b.*   **praeter opīniōnem**; 'contrary to expectation.'

opīniōnem accidisset ac iam omnia ferē superiōra loca
multitūdine armātōrum complēta cōnspicerentur, neque
subsidiō venīrī neque commeātūs supportārī, interclūsīs 10
itineribus, possent, prope iam dēspērātā salūte nōn nūllae
eius modī sententiae dīcēbantur, ut, impedīmentīs relīctīs
ēruptiōne factā, īsdem itineribus, quibus eō pervēnissent,
ad salūtem contenderent. Maiōrī tamen partī placuit, hōc
reservātō ad extrēmum cōnsiliō, interim reī ēventum experīrī 15
et castra dēfendere.

The mountaineers, superior in numbers, make a furious attack.

4. Brevī spatiō interiectō, vix ut eīs rēbus, quās cōn-
stituissent, collocandīs atque administrandīs tempus darētur, hostēs ex omnibus partibus, signō datō, dēcurrere,
lapidēs gaesaque in vāllum conicere.

Nostrī prīmō integrīs vīribus fortiter repugnāre neque 5
ūllum frūstrā tēlum ex locō superiōre mittere, et quae-

---

9. complēta [esse] : participle here used as a predicate adjective.
221, b.   neque subsidiō venīrī : sc. *posset* 'and help could not
come.' How lit.? *73, d,* and *112, a.*

10. interclūsīs itineribus : *144, b,* (3).

12. eius modī : ' of the following purport.' *100, a.*   ut, etc. :
203, (4).

13. īsdem : *45.*   itineribus : *134, a.*   pervēnissent : *220.*

14. ad salūtem : ' to (a place of) safety.'   Maiōrī partī
placuit : 'the majority decided.' *73, c.*

15. ad extrēmum : 'to the last.' *154, a.*   ēventum experīrī :
'to await the outcome.'

4. 1. Brevī spatiō interiectō : 'After a brief interval.'   How
lit.?   ut : 'so that.'   rēbus — collocandīs : *230,* (2).   cōnsti-
tuissent : *220.*

3. dēcurrere, conicere : *182.*   B. 335 ; A. 463 ; H. 610.

4. gaesa : Gallic 'javelins.' *349,* and Fig. 40.

5. integrīs : 'unimpaired.' *22, f,* and *80, b* ; also, *135, a.*
neque ūllum tēlum : ' and no missile.'

6. frūstrā : ' in vain.'   ex locō superiōre : the rampart of the
camp ; chap. i, l. 18.   quaecumque : *50, a,* and *192.*

cumque pars castrōrum nūdāta dēfēnsōribus premī vidēbātur, eō occurrere et auxilium ferre; sed hōc superārī, quod
diūturnitāte pugnae hostēs dēfessī proeliō excēdēbant, aliī
10 integrīs vīribus succēdēbant. Quārum rērum ā nostrīs
propter paucitātem fierī nihil poterat, ac nōn modo dēfessō
ex pugnā excēdendī, sed nē sauciō quidem eius locī, ubi
cōnstiterat, relinquendī ac suī recipiendī facultās dabātur.

The Romans, forced to extremities, resolve upon a sally.

5. Cum iam amplius hōrīs sex continenter pugnārētur
ac nōn sōlum vīrēs, sed etiam tēla nostrōs dēficerent, atque
hostēs ācrius īnstārent languidiōribusque nostrīs vāllum
scindere et fossās complēre coepissent, rēsque esset iam
5 ad extrēmum perducta cāsum, P. Sextius Baculus, prīmī

---

7. **dēfēnsōribus** : *127, a,* and *74, a.*

8. **eō** : = *in eam partem* ; ' to that part they rushed.'   **ferre** :
182.   **hōc superārī**: ' on this account they were at a disadvantage.'
How lit.? *135, a.*

9. **dēfessī**: '(when) exhausted.'   **proeliō** : *127, a.*   **aliī** :
'(and) others.' *238, a.*

10. **vīribus** : *143, a.*   **succēdēbant** : ' were taking their places.'
rērum : dependent on *nihil*. *97, a.*

11. **nōn modo** : trans. as if *nōn modo nōn ;* 'not only not to one
(who was) exhausted,' i.e. one on the Roman side. *236, d,* and *154,
a.* B. 343, 2, *a* ; A. 288 ; H. 495.

12. **excēdendī**: dependent on *facultās*.   **sauciō** : 'to one (who
was) wounded.' *154, a,* and *237, c.*   **locī — relinquendī** : *230,* (1).

13. **suī recipiendī** : ' of looking after himself.'

5. 1. **Cum iam — pugnārētur** : 'When fighting had been going
on.' *175, f,* and *73, d.*   **hōrīs** : *129, a.*

3. **ācrius** : *34, a.*   **languidiōribus nostrīs** : ' as our men became weaker.' How lit.? *144, b,* (3).   **vāllum scindere** : ' to destroy the rampart' by pulling up the palisades along the outer edge.'

4. **fossās** : plural because the parts of the moat on the four sides
are thought of as separate trenches.

5. **ad extrēmum cāsum** : ' to the last crisis.'   **P. Sextius
Baculus, prīmī pīlī centuriō** : II, 25, l. 8, and Note. *315, b.*

pīlī centuriō, quem Nervicō proeliō complūribus cōnfectum
vulneribus dīximus, et item C. Volusēnus, tribūnus mīlitum,
vir et cōnsiliī magnī et virtūtis, ad Galbam accurrunt atque
ūnam esse spem salūtis docent, sī, ēruptiōne factā, extrēmum auxilium experīrentur.　　　　　　　　　　　　　　10

Itaque, convocātīs centuriōnibus, celeriter mīlitēs certiōrēs
facit, paulisper intermitterent proelium ac tantum modo
tēla missa exciperent sēque ex labōre reficerent; post, datō
signō, ex castrīs ērumperent atque omnem spem salūtis in
virtūte pōnerent.　　　　　　　　　　　　　　　　　　15

The Romans win; but Galba withdraws to the Province.

6. Quod iussī sunt, faciunt, ac subitō, omnibus portīs
ēruptiōne factā, neque cognōscendī, quid fieret, neque suī

---

6. **proeliō**: *147, b.*　　　**Nervicō**: 'with the Nervians,' we should
say. The battle had taken place not long before this time; see II,
chapters 19–28.

7. **Volusēnus**: the suggestion was evidently made first by Baculus to his ranking officer, Volusēnus, who hurried with him to Galba.
tribūnus: *314.*

8. **cōnsiliī magnī**: 'of excellent judgment.'　　*100, a.*

9. **ūnam spem**: 'that the only hope.'　　　**factā**: 'by making,' etc.
144, b, (6).　　　**extrēmum auxilium**: 'the last resource.'

11. **centuriōnibus**: how many ordinarily in 8 cohorts?　*315, b.*
mīlitēs certiōrēs facit: 'he directed the soldiers,' through the centurions.

12. **intermitterent proelium**: 'to stop fighting.'　*216.*　B. 316;
A. 588: H. 642.　　　**tantum modo**, etc.: 'only to parry,' with their
shields, 'the missiles hurled' by the enemy, in order to save their
strength for the sortie.

14. **ērumperent**: 'to burst forth,' suddenly assuming the offensive.
216.

6. 1. **Quod**, etc.: *id, quod facere iussī sunt, faciunt. 160, c.*
portīs: *134, a,* and *334, a.*　B. 218, 9; A. 429, *a*; H. 476.

2. **suī colligendī**: 'of collecting their forces,' scattered on all
sides of the camp, in order to resist the four mass attacks launched from
the four gates.　*154, b.*　B. 339, 5; A. 504, *c*; H. 626, 3.

colligendī hostibus facultātem relinquunt. Ita, commūtātā
fortūnā, eōs, quī in spem potiundōrum castrōrum vēnerant,
5 undique circumventōs intercipiunt; et ex hominum mīlibus
amplius xxx, quem numerum barbarōrum ad castra vēnisse
cōnstābat, plūs tertiā parte interfectā, reliquōs perterritōs in
fugam coniciunt ac nē in locīs quidem superiōribus cōnsistere patiuntur. Sīc, omnibus hostium cōpiīs fūsīs armīsque
10 exūtīs, sē in castra mūnītiōnēsque suās recipiunt.

Quō proeliō factō, quod saepius fortūnam temptāre Galba
nōlēbat, atque aliō sē in hīberna cōnsiliō vēnisse memine-
rat, aliīs occurrisse rēbus vīderat, maximē frūmentī commeātūsque inopiā permōtus, posterō diē, omnibus eius vīcī

---

4. **eōs — circumventōs intercipiunt**: 'they surrounded and slew
those.' *228, a.*   **potiundōrum**: *64, b.*

5. **ex**, etc.; i.e. *plūs tertiā parte, ex amplius trīgintā hominum
mīlibus, numerō barbarōrum* ('of natives') *quem ad castra vēnisse
cōnstābat, interfectā.*   **ex**: *97, d.*

6. **amplius, plūs**: *129, b.*   **numerum**: *165, b.*   It seems
hardly credible that a force of more than 30,000 men, attacking under
conditions very favorable to themselves, could have been beaten off
even by a Roman force less than one tenth as large; perhaps the estimate of the number of the enemy was exaggerated.

7. **plūs tertiā parte interfectā**: on this basis the Roman soldiers
on the average accounted for three to five Gauls apiece.

8. **locīs superiōribus**: the heights round about; see chap. 1, l. 15.

9. **fūsīs**: 'routed.'   **armīsque exūtīs**: 'and bereft of their
arms,' which they dropped in their hasty flight.   **armīs**: *127, a.*

11. **Quō proeliō factō**: 'After this battle.' How lit.?   **saepius**:
'too often.' *153, a.*

12. **aliō — cōnsiliō**: 'with one design,' stated in chap. 1, ll. 5–8.
138, and *171, c.*

13. **aliīs occurrisse rēbus**: '(but) that he had found conditions
different,' implying the impossibility of carrying out the original design
with the force at his disposal.

14. **eius vīcī**: Octodurus, of which the part assigned to the natives,
as well as that occupied by the Romans (chap. 1, ll. 15–18), was now
burned.

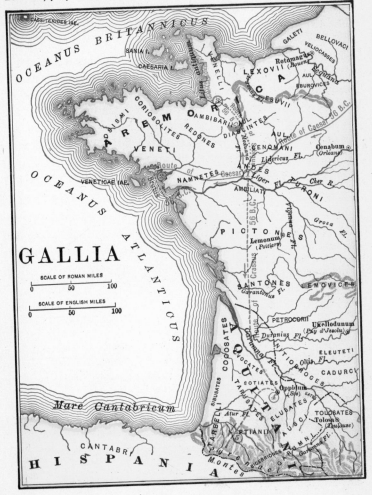

EXPLANATION

1. Base whence Caesar sent Sabinus north and Crassus south.   2. Sea-fight with the Venetans (chap. 13–15).   3. Battle of Sabinus (17–19).   4. Battle of Crassus with the Sotiates (20–22).   5. Final victory of Crassus (23–26).

aedificiīs incēnsīs, in prōvinciam revertī contendit, ac, nūllō 15
hoste prohibente aut iter dēmorante, incolumem legiōnem
in Nantuātēs, inde in Allobrogēs, perdūxit, ibique hiemāvit.

Campaign against the Venetans.   7–16

*Crassus, wintering near the Ocean, sends to the nearest states
for grain.*

7. Hīs rēbus gestīs, cum omnibus dē causīs Caesar
pācātam Galliam exīstimāret, superātīs Belgīs, expulsīs
Germānīs, victīs in Alpibus Sedūnīs, atque ita initā hieme
in Īllyricum profectus esset, quod eās quoque nātiōnēs
adīre et regiōnēs cognōscere volēbat, subitum bellum in 5
Galliā coörtum est.

Eius bellī haec fuit causa.   P. Crassus adulēscēns cum
legiōne VII proximus mare Ōceanum in Andibus hiemābat.
Is, quod in hīs locīs inopia frūmentī erat, praefectōs
tribūnōsque mīlitum complūrēs in fīnitimās cīvitātēs frū- 10
mentī commeātūsque petendī causā dīmīsit; quō in numerō

---

16. **iter dēmorante**: 'delaying his march.'   *61, a,* (1).   **in-
colūmem**: predicative, 'in safety.'

7. 1. **cum**: 'although.'   *187.*   **omnibus dē causīs**: with
exīstimāret, 'had every reason to think.'   How lit.?

2. **pācātam** : sc. *esse.*   **Galliam**: *287, b.*   **superātīs Belgīs**: II, chapters 1–33.   **expulsīs Germānīs**: I, chapters 30–54.

3. **Sedūnīs**: of the Alpine tribes the Seduni, as the most important, are alone mentioned.   **initā hieme**: 'at the beginning of
winter.'   How lit.?   *68, b,* and *144, b,* (1).

4. **Īllyricum**: *298,* and *255.*   See II, 35, l. 6.

6. **coörtum est**: 'broke out.'   How lit.?   *61, b.*

7. **haec**: 'as follows.'   *161, a.*   **adulēscēns**: cf. I, 52, l. 16,
and N., and Vocab. under *Crassus,* (2).

8. **VII**: *septimā.*   *38, b.*   **proximus**, etc.: 'very near the
Ocean'; lit. 'very near the sea,' more specifically designated as 'the
Ocean' to distinguish it from the Mediterranean sea.   *123, b.*

9. **praefectōs**: 'subsidiary officers' ; cf. I, 39, l. 10, and N.

10. **tribūnōs mīlitum**: *314.*   **complūrēs**: with *cīvitātēs.*

est T. Terrasidius missus in Esuviōs, M. Trebius Gallus in
Coriosolitas, Q. Velānius cum T. Sīliō in Venetōs.

The Venetans detain his representatives and lead a revolt.

8. Huius est cīvitātis longē amplissima auctōritās omnis
ōrae maritimae regiōnum eārum, quod et nāvēs habent
Venetī plūrimās, quibus in Britanniam nāvigāre cōnsuērunt,
et scientiā atque ūsū rērum nauticārum reliquōs antecēdunt,
5 et in magnō impetū maris atque apertō, paucīs portibus interiectīs, quōs tenent ipsī, omnēs ferē, quī eō marī ūtī
cōnsuērunt, habent vectīgālēs.   Ab hīs fit initium retinendī
Sīliī atque Vēlāniī, quod per eōs suōs sē obsidēs, quōs
Crassō dedissent, recuperātūrōs exīstimābant.

---

13. **Coriosolitas:** *19, f.*, and *282.*   Locate, on Map 9, the peoples
mentioned.
   8. 1. **Huius cīvitātis:** of the Venetans.   **omnis ōrae,** etc.:
trans. as if *omnium cīvitātum ōrae maritimae eārum regiōnum.*
   2. **et. . . et** (l. 4) . . . **et** (l. 5): *233, d.*
   3. **in — nāvigāre :** 'to make the voyage to.'   The Venetans
had developed an extensive carrying business between Gaul and
Britain; Britain was less advanced than Gaul in most respects but was
regarded as the center of Druidism (VI, 13, ll. 34–37).   **Britanniam:**
294.   **cōnsuērunt:** *64, a,* (2), and *176, b.*
   4. **scientiā:** *142, a.*   **rērum nauticārum,** 'nautical matters.'
antecēdunt: 'excel.'
   5. **in,** etc.: 'since the violence of the open sea is great, with harbors
few and far between.'   How lit.?
   6. **omnēs:** object of *habent.*   **eō marī:** the modern Bay of Biscay.   *16, b,* and *131, c.*
   7. **vectīgālēs:** 'subject to tribute'; predicative.   *115, a, b.*   On
account of the violence of the sea, and the fewness of the harbors, navi-
gators were obliged to take refuge in the harbors of the Venetans, who
mulcted them in tolls.   **Ab hīs,** etc.: 'These took the first step by
detaining,' etc.   How lit.?
   8. **per eōs:** as an exchange.   *123, a.*   **suōs,** etc.: *sē recuperātūrōs
[esse] suōs obsidēs.*
   9. **dedissent:** *214, a.*   **recuperātūrōs** [esse]: 'would get back.'

Hōrum auctōritāte fīnitimī adductī — ut sunt Gallōrum 10
subita et repentīna cōnsilia — eādem dē causā Trebium
Terrasidiumque retinent; et celeriter, missīs lēgātīs, per
suōs prīncipēs inter sē coniūrant, nihil, nisi commūnī cōnsiliō, āctūrōs eundemque omnēs fortūnae exitum esse lātūrōs; reliquāsque cīvitātēs sollicitant, ut in eā lībertāte, quam 15
ā maiōribus accēperint, permanēre, quam Rōmānōrum servitūtem perferre mālint.   Omnī ōrā maritimā celeriter ad
suam sententiam perductā, commūnem lēgātiōnem ad

Figure 94. — View of the Loire river, with the town of Decize and its
medieval castle.

10. **Hōrum auctōritāte**: 'by their example.'   **ut,** etc.: 'consistently with the practice of the Gauls, to form plans suddenly and
without reflection.'   How lit.?   The fickleness of the Gauls is more
than once alluded to by Caesar; see N. to chap. 19, l. 20.

13. **inter sē**: *159.*   **nihil,** etc.: *sē nihil āctūrōs esse . . . lātūrōs
esse. 213, b.*

14. **eundem**: *45.*   **exitum**: 'issue.'

15. **reliquās**: *171, a.*   **ut . . . mālint**: *199, a,* and *71.*

16. **accēperint**: *220.*   **quam**: '(rather) than.'

P. Crassum mittunt: *sī velit suōs recuperāre, obsidēs sibi*
20 *remittat.*

Caesar orders ships built — the coast states prepare for war.

9. Quibus dē rēbus Caesar ā Crassō certior factus, quod
ipse aberat longius, nāvēs interim longās aedificārī in
flūmine Ligerī, quod īnfluit in Ōceanum, rēmigēs ex prōvinciā īnstituī, nautās gubernātōrēsque comparārī iubet.
5 Hīs rēbus celeriter administrātīs, ipse, cum prīmum per
annī tempus potuit, ad exercitum contendit.

Venetī reliquaeque item cīvitātēs, cognitō Caesaris adventū, simul quod, quantum in sē facinus admīsissent,
intellegēbant, lēgātōs — quod nōmen ad omnēs nātiōnēs
10 sānctum inviolātumque semper fuisset — retentōs ab sē et
in vincula coniectōs, prō māgnitūdine perīculī bellum
parāre et maximē ea, quae ad ūsum nāvium pertinent,

---

19. **sī**, etc.: in the direct form, *sī vīs tuōs recuperāre, obsidēs nōbīs
remitte. 218*, (1), a, and *216.*

9. 2. **longius:** 'too far away.' Caesar was probably in Cisalpine
Gaul; for the revolt of the Venetans came to a head in the early spring,
and in April of 56 B.C. Caesar met Pompey and Crassus at Luca. *256,*
and *153, a.*   **nāvēs longās:** 'galleys.' *346, a.*   **interim:** 'meanwhile,' pending his return to the army.   **aedificārī:** 'be built.'

3. **Ligerī:** *18, e.* See Maps 9 and 10.   **quod,** etc.: explains
why, although the Venetans were strong on the ocean, the ships were
ordered built on the Loire (Fig. 94).   **rēmigēs:** 'rowers.'

4. **nautās:** 'sailors.'   **gubernātōrēs:** 'steersmen,' who managed
the rudders. *346, b,* and *84.* The fighting on these ships was to be
done by legionaries (chap. 14, l. 9).

5. **cum,** etc.: 'as soon as the season of the year permitted.' How
lit.? *185, b.* Caesar probably rejoined the army in May.

8. **in sē . . . admīsissent:** 'they had committed'; *sē* refers to the
subject of *admīsissent.* How lit. ? *204,* (3).

9. **lēgātōs . . . coniectōs** [esse]: explains *quantum . . . admīsissent;* 'in that envoys had been,' etc.   **quod nōmen:** 'a title
which,' the title of envoy or ambassador. *165, b.*   **ad:** 'among.'

10. **sānctum inviolātumque:** 'sacred and inviolable.'

prōvidēre īnstituunt, hōc maiōre spē, quod multum nātūrā
locī cōnfīdēbant.

Pedestria esse itinera concīsa aestuāriīs, nāvigātiōnem 15
impedītam propter īnscientiam locōrum paucitātemque
portuum sciēbant, neque nostrōs exercitūs propter inopiam
frūmentī diūtius apud sē morārī posse cōnfīdēbant; *ac iam
ut omnia contrā opīniōnem acciderent, tamen sē plūrimum
nāvibus posse, Rōmānōs neque ūllam facultātem habēre nā-* 20
*vium, neque eōrum locōrum, ubi bellum gestūrī essent, vada,
portūs, īnsulās nōvisse;* ac longē aliam esse nāvigātiōnem
in conclūsō marī atque in vastissimō atque apertissimō
Ōceanō perspiciēbant.

Hīs initīs cōnsiliīs, oppida mūniunt, frūmenta ex agrīs in 25
oppida comportant, nāvēs in Venetiam, ubi Caesarem prīmum esse bellum gestūrum cōnstābat, quam plūrimās

---

13. **īnstituunt**: *175, b.*　　**hōc**: 'on this account.'　　**spē**: *138.*
multum cōnfīdēbant: 'had much confidence.' *118, b.*　　**nātūrā**:
135, a.

15. **Pedestria**, etc.: 'that the land routes were cut by inlets of the
sea,' making progress of an army difficult; see Map 10.　　**nāvigātiōnem**: 'navigation,' by the Romans; sc. *esse. 81.*

16. **īnscientiam locōrum**: 'lack of knowledge of the country.'

17. **neque**: trans. as if *et . . . nōn.*

18. **ac . . . nōvisse**: a brief summary in indirect discourse; 'and
(they believed) that,' etc. *212, c, (6).*

19. **ut**: with *iam,* 'even granting that.'　　**acciderent**: subjunctive also in direct discourse. *191, b.* B. 308; A. 527, *a*; H. 586, II.
plūrimum posse: cf. I, 3, l. 21 and N.

21. **ubi**: = *in quibus.*　　**gestūrī essent**: *63.*

22. **īnsulās**: 'islands.'　　**longē aliam . . . atque**: 'far different
. . . from what it was.' *233, c.*

23. **in conclūsō marī**: 'on a land-locked sea,' referring to the
Mediterranean.　　**vastissimō, apertissimō**: 'illimitable, unconfined.'
How lit. ?

25. **frūmenta**: unthreshed 'grain,' just ripening in the fields,
hurriedly cut and transported into the towns; N. to I, 16, l. 3. The
time was near the beginning of July.

possunt, cōgunt.   Sociōs sibi ad id bellum Osismōs, Lexo-
viōs, Namnetēs, Ambiliatōs, Morinōs, Diablintēs, Menapiōs
30 ascīscunt; auxilia ex Britanniā, quae contrā eās regiōnēs
posita est, arcessunt.

*Caesar considers it equally important to check this uprising
and to distribute his forces so as to prevent revolts elsewhere.*

10. Erant hae difficultātēs bellī gerendī, quās suprā
ostendimus, sed multa tamen Caesarem ad id bellum inci-
tābant: iniūria retentōrum equitum Rōmānōrum, rebelliō
facta post dēditiōnem, dēfectiō datīs obsidibus, tot cīvitā-
5 tum coniūrātiō, in prīmīs nē, hāc parte neglēctā, reliquae
nātiōnēs sibi idem licēre arbitrārentur.

Itaque cum intellegeret, omnēs ferē Gallōs novīs rēbus
studēre et ad bellum mōbiliter celeriterque excitārī, omnēs
autem hominēs nātūrā lībertātī studēre et condiciōnem ser-

---

28. **Sociōs**: 'as allies.' *115, a.*   **Osismōs**, etc.: locate these
states on the Map at the end of this volume.

30. **auxilia**, etc.: help furnished to his enemies by the Britons
gave Caesar a pretext later for invading the island (IV, chap. 20).

10. 1. **Erant**: *90, a.*   **suprā**: chap. 9.

3. **iniūria**, etc.: 'the wrong done by the detention of Roman
knights,' referring to the envoys (chap. 8, ll. 7–12), who, as the other
tribunes in Caesar's army, had the rank of *equitēs*. *228, b.* B. 337, 6;
A. 497; H. 636, 4.   **equitum**: *96.*   **rebelliō**: 'renewal of war.'

4. **dēfectiō**: 'revolting.'   **datīs obsidibus**: *144, b, (5).*

5. **nē . . . arbitrārentur**: the clause is in the same construction
as *iniūria, rebelliō*, etc., in apposition with *multa*; '(the fear) that,' etc.
202.   **hāc parte neglēctā**: 'if this part (of Gaul),' etc. *144, b, (4).*

6. **idem**: subject accusative with *licēre*; 'the same course.'
licēre: *73, b.*

7. **cum**: *184, a.*   **novīs rēbus studēre**: 'were eager for a
change of rule.' *105.*

8. **mōbiliter**: 'easily.'   **excitārī**: 'were stirred.'

9. **nātūrā lībertātī studēre**: 'have a natural desire for liberty.'
How lit.?

vitūtis ōdisse, prius quam plūrēs cīvitātēs cōnspīrārent, 10
partiendum sibi ac lātius distribuendum exercitum putāvit.

11. Itaque T. Labiēnum lēgātum in Trēverōs, quī proximī
flūminī Rhēnō sunt, cum equitātū mittit. Huic mandat,
Rēmōs reliquōsque Belgās adeat atque in officiō contineat,
Germānōsque, quī auxiliō ā Belgīs arcessītī dīcēbantur, sī
per vim nāvibus flūmen trānsīre cōnentur, prohibeat. 5

P. Crassum, cum cohortibus legiōnāriīs XII et magnō
numerō equitātūs, in Aquītāniam proficīscī iubet, nē ex hīs
nātiōnibus auxilia in Galliam mittantur ac tantae nātiōnēs
coniungantur.

Q. Titūrium Sabīnum lēgātum cum legiōnibus tribus in 10
Venellōs, Coriosolitas Lexoviōsque mittit, quī eam manum
distinendam cūret.

D. Brūtum adulēscentem classī Gallicīsque nāvibus, quās

---

10. **ōdisse:** *72, b,* and *176, b.*   **prius quam:** with the subjunctive also in direct discourse. *189, b.*   **cōnspīrārent:** 'should
league together.'

11. **partiendum** [esse], etc.: 'that he ought to divide up his army
and distribute (it) more widely,' in order to hold all parts of the country in check. *73, e.*

11. 1. **Trēverōs:** see Map at the end of the volume. *282.*
proximī: here followed by the dative. *108, a.*

3. **adeat:** sc. *ut.* *200, a,* and *199, a.*   **in officiō:** 'in allegiance.'

4. **auxiliō:** *112, a.*   **arcessītī** [esse] : *148, e.*

5. **cōnentur:** *220.* B. 324; A. 593; H. 652.

6. **XII:** *duodecim ;* Crassus had a legion and two cohorts of infantry.

7. **Aquītāniam:** *287, c.*

8. **Galliam:** Celtic Gaul. *287, b.* As the Aquitanians were of
different stock, their relations with their Celtic neighbors seem ordinarily not to have been intimate.

11. **quī . . . cūret:** 'in order to keep their forces at a distance.'
How lit. ? *193, a.*

12. **distinendam:** *79, d,* and *229, b.* B. 337, 8, *b,* 2 ; H. 622.

13. **D.:** *19, a.*   **classī:** 'fleet,' built on the Loire (chap. 9,
ll. 2–5).   **Gallicīs nāvibus:** used as supply ships.

ex Pictonibus et Santonīs reliquīsque pācātīs regiōnibus con-
15 venīre iusserat, praeficit et, cum prīmum possit, in Venetōs
proficīscī iubet.   Ipse eō pedestribus cōpiīs contendit.

The capture of strongholds of the Venetans proves fruitless.

12. Erant eius modī ferē sitūs oppidōrum, ut, posita in
extrēmīs lingulīs prōmunturiīsque, neque pedibus aditum
habērent, cum ex altō sē aestus incitāvisset (quod bis

Figure 95. — A tongue of land, on the Venetan coast.

This tongue of land, projecting westward, is seen across the inlet as one looks northward
from Le Croisic (Map 10).

15. **possit**: Indicative in the direct form.

16. **eō**: *in Venetōs.*   **cōpiīs**: *137, b.*

12. 1. **eius modī . . . ut**: 'of such a character that.' *100, b,*
and *197, b.*   **sitūs**: 'locations.'

2. **extrēmīs**, etc.: 'at the ends of tongues of land,' relatively
low, 'and promontories,' high points of land, projecting into the sea.
(Fig. 95).   *152, a.*   **pedibus**: 'by land.' How lit.? *131, a.*
aditum: i.e. for an attacking army.

3. **cum**, etc.: 'when the tide had rushed in from the deep.' How
lit. ?   **quod**: 'which,' referring to the preceding clause ; hence
neuter.   **bis**, etc.: On July 1 in Quiberon Bay the sun rises at 4.12
and sets at 7.48, while the tide reaches high-water mark at 5 A.M.
and 5.25 P.M. ; there are thus two tides in the one day. The interval
between the forenoon and afternoon tides, in general, is less than the
length of the summer days when Caesar was in this region; hence

accidit semper hōrārum XII spatiō), neque nāvibus, quod,
rūrsus minuente aestū, nāvēs in vadīs afflictārentur. 5

Ita utrāque rē oppidōrum oppugnātiō impediēbātur; ac
sī quandō, magnitūdine operis forte superātī, extrūsō marī
aggere ac mōlibus atque hīs oppidī moenibus adaequātīs,
suīs fortūnīs dēspērāre coeperant, magnō numerō nāvium
appulsō, cuius reī summam facultātem habēbant, omnia sua 10

Caesar's form of statement, as Professor Oliphant has shown (American
Journal of Philology, 1916, p. 297).

4. **accidit**: 'happened.' **hōrārum**: the long 'hours,' of the
summer days. *242, a.* **spatiō**: 'within the period.' *147, c.*
rūrsus minuente aestū: 'at ebb tide.' How lit.?

5. **afflictārentur**: ' would be stranded,' in case they should be
over the shallow places when the tide went out.

6. **utrāque rē**: 'by both conditions,' both the rising and the ebbing of the tide. How lit.?

7–11. **Explanation**: Starting from the nearest point of land which at
high tide remained above water, the Romans prolonged toward the town two
massive parallel embankments, or dikes, working whenever the tide would
allow, since at high tide the inclosed space would be under water. Having
prolonged their dikes almost to the city, quickly, when the tide was low, they
filled in the last stretch and shut out the water from both sides, thus giving a
dry avenue of approach between the dikes from the adjacent country to the
town. But by the time they were ready to attack, using each embankment
as an *agger (341)*, the townspeople had already taken ship and departed
"bag and baggage." See Map 10, **A**.

7. **quandō**: 'at any time.' **operis**: $=$ *mūnītiōnum*, explained by
what follows. **superātī**: agrees with *oppidānī*, understood as subject
of *coeperant*. **extrūsō marī**: 'when the sea had been shut out.' *144,
b, (2).*

8. **aggere ac mōlibus**: 'by massive dikes'; hendiadys. How
lit.? *238, d.* B. 374, 4; A. 640; H. 751, 3, N. 1. **hīs**, etc.: 'when
these had been built up to a level with the walls.' **moenibus**:
107, a.

9. **fortūnīs**: dative. *109, a.*

10. **appulsō**: 'having brought up' to the threatened town. How
lit.? **cuius reī**: instead of *quārum*; we should say, 'of which they
had the greatest abundance.' How lit.?

dēportābant sēque in proxima oppida recipiēbant; ibi sē
rūrsus īsdem opportūnitātibus locī dēfendēbant.

Haec eō facilius magnam partem aestātis faciēbant, quod
nostrae nāvēs tempestātibus dētinēbantur, summaque erat
15 vastō atque apertō marī, magnīs aestibus, rārīs ac prope
nūllīs portibus, difficultās nāvigandī.

Advantages of the sea-going Venetan ships over Roman galleys.

13. Namque ipsōrum nāvēs ad hunc modum factae
armātaeque erant: carīnae aliquantō plāniōrēs quam no-
strārum nāvium, quō facilius vada ac dēcessum aestūs exci-
pere possent; prōrae admodum ērēctae, atque item puppēs,
5 ad magnitūdinem fluctuum tempestātumque accommodātae;
nāvēs tōtae factae ex rōbore ad quamvīs vim et contumēliam

---

11. **dēportābant**: repeated action, 'they would carry off.' *175, d.*
12. **īsdem**: *45.*   **opportūnitātibus**: 'advantages.'   **dēfendēbant**: *175, d.*

14. **tempestātibus dētinēbantur**: 'were held back,' in the Loire
(chap. 9, ll. 1–4), 'by storms.'   **summa . . . difficultās**: *353, d.*

15. **vastō**, etc.: *144, b, (3).*   There is an implied contrast with the
more sheltered and almost tideless waters of the Mediterranean.
rārīs ac prope nūllīs: 'infrequent, in fact, almost entirely lacking.'
How lit.?

13. 1. **Namque ipsōrum**: closely connected with the preceding;
'And (the Venetans have not the same difficulty in navigating these
waters) for their.'   **hunc**: 'the following.'

2. **armātae**: 'equipped.'   **carīnae**: 'keels'; sc. *erant.*   **aliquantō plāniōrēs**: 'considerably flatter,' so that the ships were more
flat-bottomed than the Roman galleys.   **quam**: 'than (those).'

3. **quō**: *193, b.*   **dēcessum**: 'the ebbing.'

4. **prōrae**, etc.: 'the prows were very high'; sc. *erant* in this and
the following clauses.   **puppēs**: 'sterns.'

5. **fluctuum**: 'of sea-waves.'   **accommodātae**: 'adapted.'

6. **tōtae**: 'wholly.' *151.*   **rōbore**: 'oak.' *13, f.*   **quamvīs**:
'no matter how great,' lit. 'any you please.' *49, a.*   **vim et contumēliam**: 'violence and buffeting.' *230, (3).*

MAP 10

SEA-FIGHT WITH THE VENETANS

Book III, 7–16   To face page 208

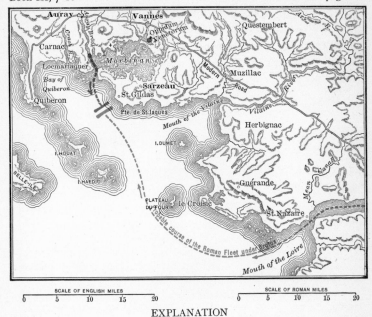

SCALE OF ENGLISH MILES   SCALE OF ROMAN MILES

EXPLANATION

Caesar's fleet was built on the Loire (Liger, chap. 9, ll. 2–4), and placed in command of Brutus. From the mouth of the Loire it followed a northerly course till it met the Venetan fleet (chap. 14).

MAP 10, **A**

OPERATIONS AGAINST A VENETAN TOWN
(III, 12)

a. Mainland.

b. Stronghold, *oppidum*, surrounded by water at high tide.

c. Parallel dikes over land submerged except at low tide. The dikes, or embankments, were high enough to keep out the water at high tide.

SCALE OF MILES

MAP 10, **A**

perferendam; trānstra, ex pedālibus in altitūdinem trabibus,
cōnfīxa clāvīs ferreīs digitī pollicis crassitūdine; ancorae
prō fūnibus ferreīs catēnīs revinctae; pellēs prō vēlīs alū-
taeque tenuiter cōnfectae, sīve propter līnī inopiam atque 10
eius ūsūs īnscientiam, sīve eō, quod est magis vērī simile,
quod tantās tempestātēs Ōceanī tantōsque impetūs ven-
tōrum sustinērī ac tanta onera nāvium regī vēlīs nōn satis
commodē posse arbitrābantur.

Cum hīs nāvibus nostrae classī eius modī congressus 15
erat, ut ūnā celeritāte et pulsū rēmōrum praestāret; reliqua
prō locī nātūrā, prō vī tempestātum illīs essent aptiōra et

---

7. **trānstra**, etc.: 'the cross-timbers, (made) of beams a foot
thick' (lit. 'in height'), were 'fastened (to the sides) with iron bolts of
the thickness of a thumb.'   **trabibus**: *17, c.*

8. **crassitūdine**: *143, a.*   **ancorae**: 'anchors,' like those in use
to-day.

9. **prō**: 'instead of.'   **fūnibus**: 'ropes.' As the Romans used
only cables of rope, the chain cables of the Venetans seemed noteworthy.   **revinctae**: were 'held.'   **pellēs**: 'hides.'   **vēlīs**:
'sails' of canvas.

10. **alūtae tenuiter cōnfectae**: 'leather dressed thin.'   **sīve**
. . . **sīve**: *235, a, b.*   **līnī**: 'flax.'

11. **eius**: *līnī.*   **eō**: 'on this account,' explained by *quod* (l. 12)
. . . *arbitrābantur. 135, a.*   **quod**: relative, refers to the thought
of the following *quod*-clause.   **vērī**: *108, b.*

12. **impetūs**: 'gusts.'

13. **tanta onera nāvium**: trans. 'so heavy vessels.' How lit.?
onera: *13, e.*   **regī**: 'be managed.'   **vēlīs**: 'with (canvas)
sails.'

15. **nostrae classī congressus**: 'the encounter of our fleet.'
How lit.?   *111.*   **eius modī**: 'such.' How lit.?   *100, b.*

16. **erat**: 'would be.'   **ūnā**: 'only.'   **pulsū rēmōrum**: 'pro-
pulsion by oars,' which gave to the galley a rapidity and freedom of
movement comparable with that of a modern steamship.   **reliqua**:
'other conditions.'   *154, a.*

17. **prō**: 'in regard to.'   **illīs**: the Venetan ships.   **aptiōra**:
'better suited.'

accommodātiōra. Neque enim hīs nostrae rōstrō nocēre
poterant (tanta in eīs erat fīrmitūdō), neque propter altitū-
20 dinem facile tēlum adigēbātur, et eādem dē causā minus
commodē cōpulīs continēbantur.

Accēdēbat, ut, cum saevīre ventus coepisset et sē ventō
dedissent, et tempestātem ferrent facilius et in vadīs cōnsisterent tūtius et, ab aestū relīctae, nihil saxa et cautēs
25 timērent; quārum rērum omnium nostrīs nāvibus cāsus
erat extimēscendus.

Caesar's fleet, commanded by Brutus, arrives ; desperate sea-
fight.

14. Complūribus expugnātīs oppidīs, Caesar, ubi intellēxit, frūstrā tantum labōrem sūmī, neque hostium fugam,
captīs oppidīs, reprimī neque eīs nocērī posse, statuit exspectandam classem.

---

18. **hīs**: *105.* **nostrae**: sc. *nāvēs.* **rōstrō**: 'by ramming,'
lit. 'with the beak.' *346, c*, and *347.* **nocēre**: 'do injury.'

19. **fīrmitūdō**: 'solidity.'

20. **tēlum adigēbātur**: 'could a missile be thrown up' on to them.
The galleys were built relatively low, and light.

21. **cōpulīs continēbantur**: 'could they be held with grappling
hooks,' thrown out from a galley to catch and hold a hostile ship so
that the Romans could board it. *347.*

22. **Accēdēbat, ut**: 'There was the further advantage, that.'
203, (1). **saevīre**: 'to blow a gale.' How lit.? **sē ventō de-**
dissent: 'they ran before the wind.' *220.* How lit.?

23. **ferrent**: 'they would weather.' **cōnsisterent**: 'would ride.'

24. **tūtius**: *34, b.* **aestū**: personified, hence with *ab. 126, b.*
relīctae: the Venĕtan ships, being flat-bottomed, when left by the
tide settled easily and safely on the ground. **nihil**: = emphatic
nōn. 118, c. B. 176, 2, *b*; A. 390, *d*, and N. 2 ; H. 416, 2.

25. **nāvibus**: *110*, and *239, h.* B. 189, 1 ; A. 374; H. 431.
cāsus, etc. : 'the occurrence was greatly to be feared.' *229, c.*

14. 3. **captīs**, etc. : 'could be checked by taking the towns.' *144,*
5, (6). **eīs nocērī posse**: 'harm could be done them.' *106, 5,*
and *105.* **exspectandam**: in full, *sibi exspectandam esse.*

Quae ubi convēnit ac prīmum ab hostibus vīsa est, 5
circiter ccxx nāvēs eōrum, parātissimae atque omnī genere
armōrum ōrnātissimae, profectae ex portū nostrīs adversae
cōnstitērunt; neque satis Brūtō, quī classī praeerat, vel
tribūnīs mīlitum centuriōnibusque, quibus singulae nāvēs
erant attribūtae, cōnstābat, quid agerent aut quam ratiōnem 10
pugnae īnsisterent. Rōstrō enim nocērī nōn posse cognōverant; turribus autem excitātīs, tamen hās altitūdō pup-
pium ex barbarīs nāvibus superābat, ut neque ex īnferiōre

---

5. **Quae**: *167.*   **convēnit**: 'arrived.'

6. **ccxx**: *ducentae et vīgintī. 38, b,* and *36.*   **parātissimae**:
'fully ready.' *153, a.*   **genere**: *133.*

7. **armōrum**: 'of equipment,' including everything needed to make
a ship ready for action.   **ōrnātissimae**: 'completely fitted out.'
ex portū, etc.: the sea-fight probably took
place in the bay of Quiberon, Caesar's army
being drawn up in sight on the heights of
St. Gildas. The courses of the fleets may
be traced on Map 10.

8. **neque . . . cōnstābat**: 'and it was
not quite clear to Brutus,' etc. After the
Gallic war Brutus, as an official of the
Roman mint, struck a coin commemorating
Gallic victories (Fig. 96). *73, c.*

9. **tribūnīs**, etc.: the legionaries on the
Roman galleys were under their regular
officers. How many galleys participated in
the battle we do not know.

Figure 96. — Coin of
Decimus Brutus.

Silver, denarius; struck in
49 or 48 B.C. Oval Gallic
shield and round shield between
two Gallic war trumpets;
inscription, ALBINUS BRUTI
F[ILIUS], 'Albinus, son of
Brutus.'

Decimus Brutus was named
Albinus after A. Postumius
Albinus, who adopted him.

10. **quid agerent**: 'what they were to
do.' *217, b.* B. 315, 3; A. 587; H. 642, 3.

11. **Rōstrō**: as in chap. 13, l. 18.
nocērī: sc. *eīs*, the enemy's ships.

12. **turribus excitātīs**: 'even though
the towers had been erected' on the Roman
ships. *144, b, (5),* and *346, d.*

13. **ex**: 'on.' *126, c.*   **īnferiōre locō**: the decks and towers
of the Roman vessels.

locō satis commodē tēla adigī possent et missa ā Gallīs
15 gravius acciderent.

Ūna erat magnō ūsuī rēs praeparāta ā nostrīs, falcēs
praeacūtae īnsertae affīxaeque longuriīs, nōn absimilī fōrmā
mūrālium falcium. Hīs cum fūnēs, quī antemnās ad mālōs
dēstinābant, comprehēnsī adductīque erant, nāvigiō rēmīs
20 incitātō, praerumpēbantur. Quibus abscīsīs, antemnae necessāriō concidēbant; ut, cum omnis Gallicīs nāvibus spēs
in vēlīs armāmentīsque cōnsisteret, hīs ēreptīs, omnis ūsus
nāvium ūnō tempore ēriperētur.

Reliquum erat certāmen positum in virtūte, quā nostrī
25 mīlitēs facile superābant, atque eō magis, quod in cōnspectū
Caesaris atque omnis exercitūs rēs gerēbātur, ut nūllum

---

14. **adigī possent**: cf. chap. 13, l. 20, and N.   **missa**: sc. *tēla*.
15. **gravius**: 'with greater force,' because thrown from a considerable height down upon the decks of the galleys.
16. **magnō ūsuī**: 'very useful.' How lit. ? *112, a*.   **praeparāta**: 'made ready beforehand.'   **falcēs**, etc. : 'hooks sharpened at
the ends, let into (the ends of) long poles and fastened to (them).'
falcēs: *17, c*, and *91, a*.
17. **nōn**, etc. : = *fōrmā nōn absimilī fōrmae mūrālium falcium,*
'of a shape not unlike that of wall hooks.' *143, a*, and *238, b*.
18. **mūrālium falcium**: used on long poles to pull stones out of
walls. *342, c*.   **Hīs**: *131, a*.   **cum**: 'whenever.' *186, a*. B. 288,
B, 3; H. 601, 4.   **antemnās**: 'sail-yards.'   **mālōs**: 'masts.'
19. **dēstinābant**: 'fastened.'   **adductī erant**: 'had been
pulled taut.'   **nāvigiō incitātō**: 'when the ship,' that had caught its
hook in the enemy's rigging, 'was driven forward,' etc. *144, b*, (2).
20. **praerumpēbantur**: 'they were severed.'   **abscīsīs**: 'cut off.'
21. **concidēbant**: 'fell down.'   **cum**: *184, a*.   **Gallicīs nāvibus**: 'in the case of the Gallic ships'; dative. *109, a*. B. 188, 1, N.;
A. 376; H. 425, 4, N.
22. **armāmentīs**: 'rigging'; they had no oars.   **ūsus**: 'control.'
23. **ūnō**: trans. as if *eōdem*.
24. **Reliquum**: emphatic position. *353, d*.   **certāmen**: 'contest.'   **erat positum in**: 'depended on.' How lit.?
26. **rēs**: 'the struggle.'   **gerēbātur**: force of the imperfect?

paulō fortius factum latēre posset; omnēs enim collēs ac
loca superiōra, unde erat propinquus dēspectus in mare,
ab exercitū tenēbantur.

Roman courage, ingenuity, and good luck win the day.

15. Dēiectīs, ut dīximus, antemnīs, cum singulās bīnae
ac ternae nāvēs circumsteterant, mīlitēs summā vī trānscendere in hostium nāvēs contendēbant.   Quod postquam
barbarī fierī animadvertērunt, expugnātīs complūribus nāvibus, cum eī reī nūllum reperīrētur auxilium, fugā salūtem ₅
petere contendērunt.

Ac iam conversīs in eam partem nāvibus, quō ventus

---

27. **paulō fortius**: 'unusually brave,' lit. 'a little braver (than
usual).'   **factum**: 'deed.'   **latēre**: 'be unobserved.'   **collēs**,
etc.: heights of St. Gildas; see Map 10.

28. **dēspectus in mare**: 'view over the sea,' *dē* implying a view
from an elevation.

15. 1. **cum**: *186, a.*   **singulās**, etc.: 'two or' (lit. 'and')
'three galleys had surrounded a single ship' of the enemy.   We are not
to suppose that Caesar's fleet outnumbered that of the Venetans; the
Romans simply concentrated their forces on one vessel at a time, instead of engaging the whole line of the enemy at once.   **singulās**:
sc. *nāvēs*.   **bīnae**: *36*.

3. **trānscendere in**: 'to board,' in the nautical sense.   **contendēbant**: 'would hasten.'   *175, d.*   B. 260, 2; A. 470; H. 534, 3.
Quod: trans. as if *et hoc*.

5. **eī auxilium**: 'no remedy,' i.e. counter-tactic, 'was discovered
against this,' the boarding of their vessels by the legionaries.

5-6. **Historical Significance**: "Thus was this naval battle," says
Mommsen (History of Rome, Vol. V, p. 57) — "so far as historical knowledge reaches, the earliest fought on the Atlantic Ocean — just like the engagement at Mylae two hundred years before, notwithstanding the most
unfavorable circumstances, decided in favor of the Romans by a lucky invention suggested by necessity."

7. **quō**: trans. as if *in quam*.   **ventus ferēbat**: 'the wind was
blowing,' we should say.

ferēbat, tanta subitō malacia ac tranquillitās exstitit, ut sē
ex locō movēre nōn possent. Quae quidem rēs ad negōtium
10 cōnficiendum maximē fuit opportūna; nam singulās nostrī
cōnsectātī expugnāvērunt, ut perpaucae ex omnī numerō
noctis interventū ad terram pervēnerint, cum ab hōrā ferē
IIII ūsque ad sōlis occāsum pugnārētur.

The captive Venetans are sold into slavery as a warning.

16. Quō proeliō bellum Venetōrum tōtīusque ōrae maritimae cōnfectum est. Nam cum omnis iuventūs, omnēs
etiam graviōris aetātis, in quibus aliquid cōnsiliī aut dignitātis fuit, eō convēnerant, tum, nāvium quod ubīque fuerat,
5 in ūnum locum coēgerant; quibus āmissīs, reliquī neque
quō sē reciperent, neque quem ad modum oppida dē-

---

8. **malacia ac tranquillitās:** 'calm and stillness.'   **exstitit:**
'ensued'; in the latter part of summer a morning wind in these regions
is usually followed by a calm in the afternoon. *176, a,* and *173, a.*

9. **nōn possent:** relying entirely on sails, the Venetans were help-
less when the wind failed them.   **rēs:** 'circumstance.'

10. **singulās:** 'one by one'; sc. *nāvēs.*

11. **cōnsectātī:** 'pursuing.' *226, c.*   **numerō:** *97, d.*

12. **interventū:** 'because of the coming.' *135, a.*   **cum:**
'although.' *187.*   **hōrā quārtā:** a little before ten o'clock by our
reckoning; the battle took place toward the end of summer, before the
autumnal equinox. *242, a,* and *b.*

16. 2. **cum . . . tum:** *186, b.* B. 290, 2; H. 657, 4, N. 1.

3. **graviōris:** 'more advanced.'   **aliquid . . . dignitātis:**
'any weight of judgment or influence.' *97, b.*

4. **fuit:** *90, a.*   **eō:** to the country of the Venetans.   **nāvium
quod:** i.e. *id nāvium, quod eīs ubīque fuerat,* 'all the ships that they
had had anywhere.' *97, b.*

5. **quibus:** including men as well as ships.   **reliquī:** 'those
who survived.' How lit.?   **neque,** etc.: 'had (in mind) neither a
place to which they might make their escape, nor any means by which
they might defend,' etc. How lit.?

6. **reciperent,** etc.: indirect question; it would have the subjunctive
also as a direct question. *217, b.*

fenderent, habēbant. Itaque sē suaque omnia Caesarī
dēdidērunt.

In quōs eō gravius Caesar vindicandum statuit, quō
dīligentius in reliquum tempus ā barbarīs iūs lēgātōrum 10
cōnservārētur. Itaque, omnī senātū necātō, reliquōs sub
corōnā vēndidit.

Expedition of Sabinus against the Venellans. 17–19

Sabinus encamps in the country of the Venelli and pretends fear.

17. Dum haec in Venetīs geruntur, Q. Titūrius Sabīnus
cum eīs cōpiīs, quās ā Caesare accēperat, in fīnēs Venellōrum pervēnit.

Hīs praeerat Viridovīx ac summam imperiī tenēbat

---

7. **suaque omnia**: 'and all they had.' How lit. ?

9. **eō . . . quō**: 'on this account . . . in order that.' *193, b.*
gravius vindicandum [esse]: 'that a severer punishment ought to
be inflicted.' How lit. ?

10. **in reliquum tempus**: 'for the future.' **iūs lēgātōrum**:
'the rights of ambassadors,' whose persons, from the beginning of
civilized life, have been considered inviolable.

11. **omnī**, etc.: 'killed all the senate and.' How lit. ? *144, b, (2),*
and *289, b.* **sub corōnā**: 'into slavery'; lit. 'under the wreath,' referring to the wreath placed on the heads of captives sold at auction.
We can hardly suppose that the entire population was sold into slavery;

Figure 97. — Venellan coin.
Gold; reverse, fanciful lion turning its
head toward a wheel.

yet these maritime states were so reduced in strength that they afterwards
gave Caesar no trouble.

17. 1. **Venetīs**: *282.* **geruntur**:
trans. by a past tense. *190, a.*

2. **eīs cōpiīs**: three legions, as
related in chap. 11, ll. 10–12. **in
fīnēs Venellōrum**: the probable route
of Sabinus is shown on Map 9.

4. **Viridovīx**: *19, d.* **summam imperiī**: 'the chief command.'
How lit. ? Viridovix not only commanded the forces of the Venellans
(Fig. 97) but was commander in chief of all the forces raised by the
revolting states.

5 eārum omnium cīvitātum, quae dēfēcerant, ex quibus exercitum magnāsque cōpiās coēgerat; atque hīs paucīs diēbus
Aulercī Eburovīcēs Lexoviique, senātū suō interfectō, quod
auctōrēs bellī esse nōlēbant, portās clausērunt sēque cum
Viridovīce coniūnxērunt; magnaque praetereā multitūdō
10 undique ex Galliā perditōrum hominum latrōnumque convēnerat, quōs spēs praedandī studiumque bellandī ab agrī
cultūrā et cotīdiānō labōre sēvocābat.

Sabīnus idōneō omnibus rēbus locō castrīs sēsē tenēbat,
cum Viridovīx contrā eum duōrum mīlium spatiō cōnsēdis-
15 set cotīdiēque, prōductīs cōpiīs, pugnandī potestātem faceret, ut iam nōn sōlum hostibus in contemptiōnem Sabīnus
venīret, sed etiam nostrōrum mīlitum vōcibus nōn nihil
carperētur; tantamque opīniōnem timōris praebuit, ut iam

5. **exercitum**: 'an army,' trained and equipped, as distinguished
from **cōpiās**, 'forces' hastily levied and organized.

6. **hīs paucīs diēbus**: 'within the few days' after the arrival of
Sabinus. *147, a*, and *160, d*.

7. **Aulercī Eburovīcēs**: one name; see Map 9.

8. **auctōrēs**: 'favorers'; why nominative? *221, b*.   **nōlēbant**:
plural because *senātū* is thought of as *senātōribus*. *173, b*.   **portās
clausērunt**: the shutting of city gates on the approach of an army
was a virtual declaration of war.

10. **perditōrum**: 'desperate.'   **latrōnum**: 'bandits.'

12. **agrī cultūrā**: 'farming.'   **sēvocābat**: lured away. How
lit. ? *79, d*.

13. **omnibus rēbus**: 'in all respects.' *142, a*.   **locō**: *145, c*.
castrīs: *131, a*. The camp of Sabinus was probably near the small
river Sée, in the southern part of the Venellan territory (Map 9).

14. **cum**: *187*.   **duōrum**, etc.: '(only) two miles away.'
spatiō: *147, c*.

16. **ut**: 'so that.'   **hostibus**: 'in the eyes of the enemy.'
109, a. B. 188, 1, N.; A. 377; H. 425, 4, N.   **contemptiōnem**:
'contempt.'

17. **nōn nihil**: 'rather sharply.' How lit.? *118, c*.

18. **carperētur**: 'was criticized.'   **opīniōnem**: 'impression.'
81.   **praebuit**: 'produced.'

Plate **IV**   Weapons, Standards, and Roman Camp

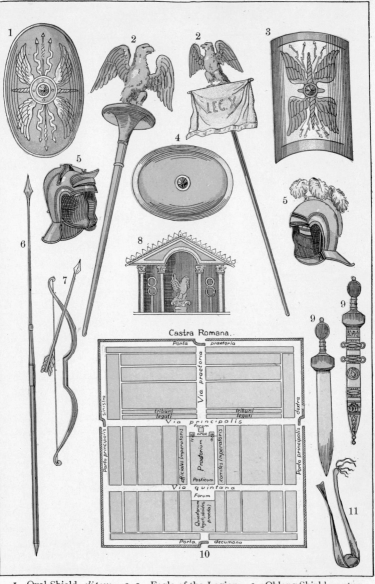

Castra Romana.

1. Oval Shield, *clipeus*.   2, 2. Eagle of the Legion.   3. Oblong Shield, *scutum*.
4. Light Shield, *parma*.   5, 5. Cavalry Helmet, *cassis*.   6. Pike, *pilum*.
7. Bow, *arcus ;* Arrow, *sagitta*.   8. Shrine for the Eagle, *sacellum*.
9, 9. Sword, *gladius ;* Scabbard, *vagina*.   10. Roman Camp.
11. Sling, *funda*.

ad vāllum castrōrum hostēs accēdere audērent. Id eā dē
causā faciēbat, quod cum tantā multitūdine hostium, prae- 20
sertim eō absente, quī summam imperiī tenēret, nisi aequō
locō aut opportūnitāte aliquā datā, lēgātō dīmicandum nōn
exīstimābat.

By a ruse he leads the enemy to attack him.

18. Hāc cōnfirmātā opīniōne timōris, idōneum quendam
hominem et callidum dēlēgit, Gallum, ex eīs, quōs auxiliī
causā sēcum habēbat. Huic magnīs praemiīs pollicitātiōnibusque persuādet, utī ad hostēs trānseat, et, quid fierī
velit, ēdocet.   5

Quī ubi prō perfugā ad eōs vēnit, timōrem Rōmānōrum
prōpōnit; quibus angustiīs ipse Caesar ā Venetīs premātur,
docet, neque longius abesse, quīn proximā nocte Sabīnus
clam ex castrīs exercitum ēdūcat et ad Caesarem auxiliī
ferendī causā proficīscātur. Quod ubi audītum est, con- 10
clāmant omnēs, occāsiōnem negōtiī bene gerendī āmit-
tendam nōn esse; ad castra īrī oportēre.

---

19. **Id**: the holding of the Roman soldiers in camp.

21. **eō absente, quī**: 'in the absence of him (Caesar) who.'
144, b, (3).   **tenēret**: *214, a.*   **nisi**: i.e. *nisi dīmicāret.*
aequō locō: 'advantageous position'; sc. *datō. 144, b,* (2).

22. **dīmicandum** [esse], etc.: 'a lieutenant ought not,' etc. *110.*

18. 2. **callidum**: 'tactful.'   **ex eīs**: *97, d.*

5. **velit, premātur** (l. 7): *204,* (2).   **ēdocet**: 'explained.' *175, b.*

6. **Quī, Quod** (l. 10): *167.*   **prō perfugā**: 'as if a deserter.'
vēnit: *188, a.*

8. **neque**, etc.: *neque longius abesse proximā nocte, quīn . . . proficīscātur,* 'and that no later than the following night Sabinus would
stealthily lead,' etc. *201, b.* B. 298; A. 558; H. 595, 1.

11. **occāsiōnem**, etc.: 'the chance to score a notable success.'
How lit.?

12. **īrī**, etc.: 'that they ought to attack the camp.' How lit.? *68,
d,* and *73, d.* B. 138, IV; A. 208, *d*; H. 302, 6.

Multae rēs ad hōc cōnsilium Gallōs hortābantur: superiōrum diērum Sabīnī cunctātiō, perfugae cōnfīrmātiō, inopia
15 cibāriōrum, cui reī parum dīligenter ab eīs erat prōvīsum,
spēs Veneticī bellī, et quod ferē libenter hominēs id, quod
volunt, crēdunt.

Hīs rēbus adductī, nōn prius Viridovīcem reliquōsque
ducēs ex conciliō dīmittunt, quam ab hīs sit concessum,
20 arma utī capiant et ad castra contendant. Quā rē concessā,
laetī, ut explōrātā victōriā, sarmentīs virgultīsque collēctīs,
quibus fossās Rōmānōrum compleant, ad castra pergunt.

He surprises them, and wins a decisive victory.

19. Locus erat castrōrum ēditus et paulātim ab īmō
acclīvis circiter passūs mīlle. Hūc magnō cursū contendērunt, ut quam minimum spatiī ad sē colligendōs armandōs-
que Rōmānīs darētur, exanimātīque pervēnērunt.

---

14. **superiōrum**: 'preceding.'   **cunctātiō**: 'inaction.' *91, a,*
and *74, b.*   **cōnfīrmātiō**: 'the assurance.'
16. **quod . . . crēdunt**: appositive of *rēs. 198, b,* and *175, c.*
ferē: 'as a rule.' Caesar's keen insight into human nature was an
important factor in his success.
18. **prius —— quam —— sit concessum**: 'until permission had
been granted.' *189, b.* B. 292; H. 605, 1.
21. **laetī**: 'joyfully.' *151.* **ut explōrātā victōriā**: 'as if victory
were (already) assured.'   **sarmentīs**: 'brushwood,' cut from trees.
virgultīs: 'fascines,' bundles of shoots and bushes tied together for
convenience in handling.   **collēctīs**: 'they gathered and.' How
lit.?
22. **quibus . . . compleant**: trans. as if *ut eīs . . . compleant.*
193, a, and *131, a.*
19. 1. **Locus**: 'site.'   **ab īmō**: 'from the bottom' of the hill.
154, a.
2. **passūs**: *118, a.*   **Hūc**: up the slope to the camp.   **magnō
cursū**: 'at full speed.'
3. **quam minimum spatiī**: 'as little time as possible.' *97, b,* and
153, c.

Sabīnus, suōs hortātus, cupientibus signum dat. Im- 5
pedītīs hostibus propter ea, quae ferēbant, onera, subitō
duābus portīs ēruptiōnem fierī iubet. Factum est opportūnitāte locī, hostium īnscientiā ac dēfatīgātiōne, virtūte
mīlitum et superiōrum pugnārum exercitātiōne, ut nē ūnum
quidem nostrōrum impetum ferrent ac statim terga ver- 10
terent. Quōs impedītōs integrīs vīribus mīlitēs nostrī cōnsecūtī, magnum numerum eōrum occīdērunt; reliquōs
equitēs cōnsectātī, paucōs, quī ex fugā ēvāserant, relīquērunt.

Sīc, ūnō tempore, et dē nāvālī pugnā Sabīnus et dē 15
Sabīnī victōriā Caesar certior factus est, cīvitātēsque
omnēs sē statim Titūriō dēdidērunt. Nam ut ad bella
suscipienda Gallōrum alacer ac prōmptus est animus, sīc
mollis ac minimē resistēns ad calamitātēs perferendās
mēns eōrum est. 20

---

5. **hortātus**: N. to I, 25, l. 3. *226, c.* **cupientibus**: sc. *eīs.*

7. **duābus portīs**: sc. *castrōrum*; probably the gates on the right
and left sides of the camp. *334, a,* and *134, a.* **Factum est**: 'the
result was.' How lit.? **opportūnitāte**: *135, a.*

8. **īnscientia**: 'lack of skill.' **dēfatīgātiōne**: 'exhaustion.'

10. **ferrent**: sc. *hostēs.* *203,* (1). **ac**: 'but.' *234, b.*

11. **vīribus**: *135, a,* and *18, a.* **cōnsecūtī**: *226, c.*

12. **reliquōs**: 'the rest' of the Gauls not slain by the legionaries.

13. **equitēs** := *equitēs nostrī.* **paucōs**: '(only) a few.' *154, a.*

17. **Titūriō**: for the full name see chap. 11, l. 10. *19, b.* **ut**:
'just as.' The subjugation of these states was now complete; the submission reported the previous year (II. 34) had been only nominal.

18. **alacer**: 'impetuous.' *24.* **prōmptus**: 'ready.' **animus**:
'temperament.'

19. **mollis**: 'yielding.' **resistēns**: adjective; with *minimē,* 'not
at all capable of resistance.' Caesar again comments on the fickleness
of the Gauls (cf. III. 8, ll. 10–11, and 10, ll. 7–8; IV, 5, ll. 5–13). 'At
the beginning of a battle,' says Livy, 'the fighting of the Gauls is more
than that of men; at the end, less than that of women.'

20. **mēns**: 'character.'

Conquest of Aquitania by Crassus. 20-27

Crassus, entering Aquitania, meets a force of the Sotiates.

20. Eōdem ferē tempore P. Crassus, cum in Aquītāniam
pervēnisset, quae, ut ante dictum est, tertiā pars Galliae
est, cum intellegeret, in eīs locīs sibi bellum gerendum, ubi
paucīs ante annīs L. Valerius Praecōnīnus lēgātus, exercitū
5 pulsō, interfectus esset, atque unde L. Mānlius prōcōnsul,
impedīmentīs āmissīs, profūgisset, nōn mediocrem sibi
diligentiam adhibendam intellegēbat.

Itaque rē frūmentāriā prōvīsā, auxiliīs equitātūque com-

---

20. **1. P. Crassus**: with twelve cohorts and a large body of cavalry
(chap. 11, ll. 6-9). The
cavalry would have been of no
use to Caesar in the campaign
against the Venetans, but
could be employed by Crassus
to advantage in the moun-
tainous regions of Aquitania
(Fig. 98).

3. cum: *184, a.* **gerendum**: sc. *esse.* **ubi**:
= *in quibus.*

4. paucīs ante annīs:
twenty-two years before, in
78 B.C. In that year Prae-
cŏninus, mentioned only here,
and Lucius Manlius, pro-
consul of the Province, were
routed by Hirtuleius, the
quaestor of Sertorius. Cf.
chap. 23, l. 11, and N. *140*.

5. unde: = *ē quibus.*
L.: *19, a.*

6. nōn mediocrem: 'no
ordinary.' *239, g.* **sibi**:
110.

Figure 98. — Cavalryman.

This cavalryman has helmet and spear; his
sword is not shown.

parātō, multīs praetereā virīs fortibus Tolōsā et Carcasōne
et Narbōne, quae sunt cīvitātēs Galliae prōvinciae fīnitimae 10
hīs regiōnibus, nōminātim ēvocātīs, in Sōtiātium fīnēs
exercitum intrōdūxit. Cuius adventū cognitō Sōtiātēs,
magnīs cōpiīs coāctīs, equitātūque, quō plūrimum valēbant,
in itinere agmen nostrum adortī, prīmum equestre proelium
commīsērunt; deinde, equitātū suō pulsō atque īnsequenti- 15
bus nostrīs, subitō pedestrēs cōpiās, quās in convallę in
īnsidiīs collocāverant, ostendērunt.   Hī, nostrōs disiectōs
adortī, proelium renovārunt.

In a fierce fight he defeats them and captures their city.

21. Pugnātum est diū atque ācriter, cum Sōtiātēs,
superiōribus victōriīs frētī, in suā virtūte tōtīus Aquītāniae
salūtem positam putārent, nostrī autem, quid sine imperātōre et sine reliquīs legiōnibus, adulēscentulō duce, efficere
possent, perspicī cuperent; tandem cōnfectī vulneribus 5
hostēs terga vertērunt.   Quōrum magnō numerō interfectō,

---

9. **virīs fortibus** : soldiers who, having served their time (20 years),
were living in the Province. *307, a.*   **Tolōsā** : *127, a,* and *293, a.*

11. **nōminātim** : requests to reënter the service were sent to the
veterans individually.   **ēvocātīs** : 'called out.'   **Sōtiātium** : see
Map 9.   *19, e.*

13. **equitātū** : with *adortī. 131, a.*   **quō** : *142, a.*   **plūrimum** :
118, b.

15. **equitātū**, etc. : apparently the flight of the cavalry was a ruse,
to draw the pursuing Romans into the valley (*convalle*) where the infantry of the Sotiates was in ambush.

17. **Hī** : referring to *pedestrēs cōpiās* of l. 16.   Why masculine ?

21. 2. **victōriīs** : *131, e.*   B. 218, 3 ; A. 431, *a* ; H. 476, 1.   **frētī** :
'relying on.'

3. **putārent** : *184, a.*   **quid . . . possent** : subject of *perspicī.*
204, (2).

4. **adulēscentulō duce** : 'with a youth as leader,' referring to
Crassus.   *144, b,* (2).

Crassus ex itinere oppidum Sōtiātium oppugnāre coepit.
Quibus fortiter resistentibus, vīneās turrēsque ēgit.

Illī, aliās ēruptiōne temptātā, aliās cunīculīs ad aggerem
10 vīneāsque āctīs (cuius reī sunt longē perītissimī Aquītānī,
proptereā quod multīs locīs apud eōs aerāriae sectūraeque
sunt), ubi dīligentiā nostrōrum nihil hīs rēbus prōficī posse
intellēxērunt, lēgātōs ad Crassum mittunt, sēque in dēditiōnem ut recipiat, petunt.   Quā rē impetrātā, arma trādere
15 iussī faciunt.

Adiatunnus with a devoted band makes a sortie, is captured.

22. Atque in eā rē omnium nostrōrum intentīs animīs,
aliā ex parte oppidī Adiatunnus, quī summam imperiī tenē-

---

7. **ex itinere**: Vocab. under *iter*.   **oppidum**: identified with Sos,
the name of which is derived from *Sotiātes*.   **oppugnāre**: Crassus
tried to take the town by sudden storming.   *340.*

8. **Quibus**: *167.*   **vīneās, turrēs**: appliances for besieging.
342, a and *b.*

9. **aliās . . . aliās**: ' at one time . . . at another.'   **cunīculīs**:
'tunnels,' underground passageways from which the Roman works could
be undermined, so that they would fall in, or could be set on fire.

10. **cuius reī**: 'an operation,' the driving of tunnels, 'in which.'
102, and *165, b.*

11. **locīs**: *145, c.*   **aerāriae**: 'copper mines.'   **sectūrae**:
'excavations,' probably open cuts from which iron ore was taken, as

Figure 99.— Coin of the
Sotiates.

Bronze, struck by Adiatunnus.
Obverse, REX ADIETUANUS EF; reverse, wolf with the word, SOTIOTA.

distinguished from the more elaborate tunnels of the copper mines.   Remains of
ancient copper and iron mines have been
found in the region of the Sotiates, and
mining operations are still carried on there.

12. **sunt**: *90, a.*   **dīligentiā**: *135, a.*
hīs rēbus: ' by these devices.'   *131, a.*

22. 1. **in**: 'upon.'   **intentīs animīs**: 'while the attention was fixed.'
How lit.?   *144, b,* (2).

2. **Adiatunnus**: a coin has been found bearing his name (Fig. 99)
in Roman letters; the spelling of the name is not the same as that

bat, cum DC dēvōtīs, quōs illī 'solduriōs' appellant — quōrum haec est condiciō, utī omnibus in vītā commodīs ūnā
cum eīs fruantur, quōrum sē amīcitiae dēdiderint; sī quid 5
hīs per vim accidat, aut eundem cāsum ūnā ferant aut sibi
mortem cōnscīscant (neque adhūc hominum memoriā repertus est quisquam, quī, eō interfectō, cuius sē amīcitiae
dēvōvisset, mortem recūsāret) — cum hīs Adiatunnus ēruptiōnem facere cōnātus, clāmōre ab eā parte mūnītiōnis 10
sublātō, cum ad arma mīlitēs concurrissent vehementerque
ibi pugnātum esset, repulsus in oppidum tamen, utī eādem
dēditiōnis condiciōne ūterētur, ā Crassō impetrāvit.

Proceeding further, Crassus finds a formidable army.

23. Armīs obsidibusque acceptīs, Crassus in fīnēs
Vocātium et Tarusātium profectus est.   Tum vērō barbarī,
commōtī, quod oppidum et nātūrā locī et manū mūnītum
paucīs diēbus, quibus eō ventum erat, expugnātum cognō-

---

given by Caesar, and E F at the end may be for E— F[ilius], in imitation of Roman usage.   **summam imperiī**: chap. 17, l. 4, and N.

3. **DC**: *sescentīs*. 38, *b*.   **dēvōtīs**: 'faithful followers.'   **solduriōs**: 'the vow-beholden.'   **quōrum**, etc. : 'the terms of whose
association are these.'   How lit.?

4. **utī . . . fruantur**: *203*, (4).   **commodīs**: *131*, *c*.   B. 218,
1 ; A. 410 ; H. 477, 1.

5. **amīcitiae**: dative.   **dēdiderint**: *220*.   **sī quid**, etc. : cf.
I, 18, l. 24, and N.

6. **vim**: 'violence.'   **eundem cāsum ūnā**: 'the same fate at the
same time.'   **ferant**: sc. *ut*.   **sibi**, etc. : cf. I, 4, l. 12, and N.

7. **adhūc**: 'up to this time.'   **memoriā**: *147*, *b*.

9. **recūsāret**: *194*, *a*.   B. 283, 2 ; A. 535, a ; H. 591, 1.   **hīs**: = *dēvōtīs* in l. 3, resuming the narrative interrupted by the long explanation.

12. **utī**, etc. : *199*, *a*.   **eādem**: 'the same' as the rest.

23. 3. oppidum: *oppidum Sōtiātium*, chap. 21, l. 7.   **manū**: the
natural defenses of the town had been strengthened by fortifications.

4. **quibus**: 'after,' lit. 'within which.'   *147*, *a*.   **ventum erat**:
73, *d*.   **expugnātum**: sc. *esse*.

5 verant, lēgātōs quōque versus dīmittere, coniūrāre, obsidēs
inter sē dare, cōpiās parāre coepērunt. Mittuntur etiam
ad eās cīvitātēs lēgātī, quae sunt citeriōris Hispāniae fīnitimae Aquītāniae; inde auxilia ducēsque arcessuntur.
Quōrum adventū magnā cum auctōritāte et magnā
10 hominum multitūdine bellum gerere cōnantur. Ducēs
vērō eī dēliguntur, quī ūnā cum Q. Sertōriō omnēs annōs
fuerant summamque scientiam reī mīlitāris habēre exīsti-
mābantur. Hī cōnsuētūdine populī Rōmānī loca capere,
castra mūnīre, commeātibus nostrōs interclūdere īnstituunt.
15 Quod ubi Crassus animadvertit, suās cōpiās propter
exiguitātem nōn facile dīdūcī, hostem et vagārī et viās
obsidēre et castrīs satis praesidiī relinquere, ob eam causam
minus commodē frūmentum commeātumque sibi suppor-

---

5. **quōque versus**: 'in all directions.'

7. **citeriōris Hispāniae**: _94 d_, and _296_.　　**fīnitimae**: agrees
with _quae_.

9. **adventū**: _147, b_.　　**magnā**, etc.: to be taken closely with
adventū.　　**auctōritāte**: 'prestige.'

10. **hominum**: _98, a_.　　**Ducēs**: in predicate. _88, a_.

11. **Q. Sertōriō**: a military leader of the popular party in the first
Civil War at Rome, the war between Marius and Sulla. After the
death of Marius, and Sulla's return to Rome, Sertorius organized an
army in Spain, and held his own against the government for ten years,
till at length he was treacherously assassinated, in 72 B.C.　　**omnēs
annōs**: 'during all (those) years,' 82–72 B.C., when Sertorius had an
army in the field.

13. **loca capere**: 'to choose locations' for encampment. The
Aquitanians were in this respect in advance of the Gauls, who did not
begin to fortify their camps till four years later (VII, 29, ll. 16–18).

15. **Quod**: 'Now — this (fact),' explained by the following infinitive clauses.

16. **dīdūcī**: 'spread out,' so as to cope at all points with the
numerically superior enemy.　　**hostem**, etc.: '(but) that the enemy
both roamed,' at will 'and.'

17. **et**: 'and (still).'　　**castrīs**: of the enemy.　　**praesidiī**:
_97, b_.

tārī, in diēs hostium numerum augērī, nōn cunctandum
exīstimāvit, quīn pugnā dēcertāret. Hāc rē ad cōnsilium 20
dēlātā, ubi omnēs idem sentīre intellēxit, posterum diem
pugnae cōnstituit.

Forming battle order, he waits, then attacks the enemy's camp.

24. Prīmā lūce prōductīs omnibus cōpiīs, duplicī aciē
īnstitūtā, auxiliīs in mediam aciem coniectīs, quid hostēs
cōnsiliī caperent, exspectābat. Illī, etsī propter multitūdinem et veterem bellī glōriam paucitātemque nostrōrum
sē tūtō dīmicātūrōs exīstimābant, tamen tūtius esse arbitrā- 5
bantur, obsessīs viīs, commeātū interclūsō, sine ūllō vulnere
victōriā potīrī, et, sī propter inopiam reī frūmentāriae
Rōmānī sēsē recipere coepissent, impedītōs in agmine et

---

19. **in diēs** : 'day by day.'   **nōn cunctandum** [esse] : sc. *sibi*,
'that he ought not to delay.'

20. **quīn**, etc. : ' to fight a decisive battle.' How lit.? *201, b.*

21. **omnēs idem sentīre** : ' that all held the same opinion.' *117, a.*

24. 1. **duplicī aciē** : not so strong as the customary triple line, but
necessary here because the Roman force was so greatly outnumbered
by the enemy. *337.*   **duplicī** : *26, a.*

2. **auxiliīs** : the auxiliary troops were usually stationed upon the
wings ; in this instance they were placed at the middle of the line because Crassus did not have confidence in them (chap. 25, ll. 3–4).
quid cōnsiliī : ' what plan.' *97, b.*

3. **caperent** : ' would adopt.' *204,* (2).   **exspectābat** : ' was
waiting (to see).'   **multitūdinem** : estimated at 50,000 (chap. 26,
l. 16).

4. **paucitātem** : the whole force under the command of Crassus
(chap. 11, ll. 6–7 ; chap. 20, ll. 8–12) can hardly have amounted to
10,000 men.

5. **tūtō** : *34, b.*   **tūtius** : predicative with *esse*, of which the subject is *potīrī* (l. 7). *222, b,* and *148, d.*

6. **obsessīs viīs** : 'having blocked the roads (and).' How lit.?
238, a.

8. **sēsē recipere** : ' to retreat.'   **impedītōs** : sc. *eōs* [*Rōmānōs*].

sub sarcinīs īnfīrmiōrēs animō adorīrī cōgitābant. Hōc
10 cōnsiliō probātō ab ducibus, prōductīs Rōmānōrum cōpiīs,
sēsē castrīs tenēbant.

Hāc rē perspectā Crassus, cum suā cunctātiōne atque
opīniōne timōris hostēs nostrōs mīlitēs alacriōrēs ad pug-
nandum effēcissent, atque omnium vōcēs audīrentur,
15 *exspectārī diūtius nōn oportēre, quīn ad castra īrētur,*
cohortātus suōs, omnibus cupientibus, ad hostium castra
contendit.

He learns that the enemy's rear gate is not well guarded.

25. Ibi cum aliī fossās complērent, aliī, multīs tēlīs
coniectīs, dēfēnsōrēs vāllō mūnītiōnibusque dēpellerent,
auxiliārēsque, quibus ad pugnam nōn multum Crassus
cōnfīdēbat, lapidibus tēlīsque sumministrandīs et ad ag-
5 gerem caespitibus comportandīs speciem atque opīniōnem

---

9. **sarcinīs**: *330*.   **īnfīrmiōrēs animō**: 'less courageous.' How
lit. ? *142, a*.   **cōgitābant**: 'they were proposing.'

13. **opīniōne**: 'impression.'   **hostēs**: nominative.

14. **omnium**: i.e. *omnium mīlitum*.   **vōcēs**: 'remarks.'

15. **exspectārī**, etc.: '(to the effect) that they ought not to delay
further to attack the camp.' How lit.? *213, b*.   **īrētur**: *68, d*,
73, d, and *201, b*.

16. **omnibus cupientibus**: *144, b*, (3).   **ad hostium castra**: this
is the only attack of the Romans on a fortified camp recorded in the
Gallic War.

25. 1. **aliī . . . aliī**: *mīlitēs Rōmānī. 171, b*.   **fossās**: as in
chap. 5, l. 4.

2. **vāllō**: constructed in the Roman fashion (chap. 23, ll. 13–14).
127, a, and *333*.

3. **auxiliārēs**: chap. 24, l. 2 and N.   **quibus**: dative. *105*.

4. **lapidibus . . . comportandīs**: 'by bringing,' etc., ablatives of
means. *230*, (4).   **ad aggerem**: sc. *faciundum*. The rampart of
the enemy's camp was so high that the Romans began to make a sloping
mound up to it, like the *agger* used in besieging a town.

5. **caespitibus**: 'sods.' *10, d*.   **speciem . . . pugnantium**:
'the appearance and impression of combatants.'

pugnantium praebērent; cum item ab hostibus cōnstanter
ac nōn timidē pugnārētur tēlaque ex locō superiōre missa
nōn frūstrā acciderent, equitēs, circumitīs hostium castrīs,
Crassō renūntiāvērunt, nōn eādem esse dīligentiā ab decumānā portā castra mūnīta facilemque aditum habēre.   10

Surprising the enemy by a rear attack, he routs them.

26. Crassus, equitum praefectōs cohortātus, ut magnīs
praemiīs pollicitātiōnibusque suōs excitārent, quid fierī
velit, ostendit.

Illī, ut erat imperātum, ēductīs eīs cohortibus, quae, prae·
sidiō castrīs relīctae, intrītae ab labōre erant, et longiōre 5
itinere circumductīs, nē ex hostium castrīs cōnspicī possent,
omnium oculīs mentibusque ad pugnam intentīs, celeriter
ad eās, quās dīximus, mūnītiōnēs pervēnērunt, atque, hīs
prōrutīs, prius in hostium castrīs cōnstitērunt, quam plānē
ab hīs vidērī aut, quid reī gererētur, cognōscī posset.   10

---

7. **locō superiōre**: the top of the rampart of the camp; the camp
lay in a plain (chap. 26, l. 16).

8. **circumitīs hostium castrīs**: 'having ridden about the enemy's
camp.' *334, a.*

9. **ab decumānā portā**: 'on the side of the rear gate.' *126, c.*

26. 1. **equitum praefectōs**: *309, c.*   **ut**, etc.: *199, a.*

2. **suōs**: the cavalrymen, on whom the success of the surprise
depended.

4. **Illī**: the cavalry prefects, who guided cohorts of infantry to the
rear of the enemy's camp. It is possible that the cavalrymen took the
legionaries with them on their horses in order to transport them quickly
thither by a roundabout way.   **praesidiō castrīs**: *112, b.*

5. **intrītae**: 'unfatigued.'   **longiōre**: *153, a.*

7. **omnium**: *hostium.*   **oculīs**, etc.: *144, b,* (2).

8. **eās — mūnītiōnēs**: at the rear of the enemy's camp; chap. 25,
ll. 9-10.

9. **prōrutīs**: 'demolished.'   **prius — quam**: *189, b.*   **plānē**:
'clearly.'

10. **vidērī**: sc. *possent*, 'they could be seen.'   **quid**, etc.: 'what
was going on.' How lit.?

Tum vērō, clāmōre ab eā parte audītō, nostrī, redintegrātīs vīribus, quod plērumque in spē victōriae accidere
cōnsuēvit, ācrius impugnāre coepērunt. Hostēs undique
circumventī, dēspērātīs omnibus rēbus, sē per mūnītiōnēs
15 dēicere et fugā salūtem petere contendērunt. Quōs equitātus apertissimīs campīs cōnsectātus, ex mīlium L numerō,
quae ex Aquītāniā Cantabrīsque convēnisse cōnstābat, vix
quārtā parte relīctā, multā nocte sē in castra recēpit.

Crassus receives the submission of other Aquitanian states.

27. Hāc audītā pugnā, maxima pars Aquītāniae sēsē
Crassō dēdidit obsidēsque ultrō mīsit; quō in numerō
fuērunt Tarbellī, Bigerriōnēs, Ptiāniī, Vocātēs, Tarusātēs,
Elusātēs, Gatēs, Auscī, Garumnī, Sibusātēs, Cocosātēs;
5 paucae ultimae nātiōnēs, annī tempore cōnfīsae, quod hiems
suberat, hōc facere neglēxērunt.

---

11. **clāmōre**, etc.: from the shouting at the rear of the camp the
Romans fighting in front knew that the attack there was in progress,
and were inspired to greater efforts.

12. **quod**: relative, refers to the thought in *redintegrātīs vīribus*;
trans., with *plērumque*, 'as generally.'

14. **dēspērātīs omnibus rēbus**: 'in utter despair.' How lit.?
per: 'over.'

16. **apertissimīs**: 'wide and open.' Cf. *153, a*.   **campīs**: *145, c*.
cōnsectātus: *226, c*.

17. **quae**: subject accusative of *convēnisse*; the antecedent is
mīlium.

18. **multā nocte**: 'late at night.' *152, a*.

27. 2. **quō in numerō**: we should say 'in the number of whom,'
'among whom.'

3. **Tarbellī**, etc.: see Map 9. The Tarbelli have left a trace of their
name in modern Tarbes; the Bigerriones, in Bagnères de Bigorre, a
watering-place in the Pyrenees; the Elusates, in Eauze; the Ausci, in
Auch; the Sibusates, in Saubusse.

5. **paucae ultimae nātiōnēs**: i.e. *paucae nātiōnēs, quae ultimae
erant*; 'a few remote peoples.'   **tempore**: *135, a*. B. 219, 1;
A. 431; H. 476, 3.

Expedition of Caesar against the Morini and the Menapii. 28, 29

Caesar proceeds against the Morini and the Menapii.

28. Eōdem ferē tempore Caesar, etsī prope exācta iam aestās erat, tamen, quod, omnī Galliā pācātā, Morinī Mena-piīque supererant, quī in armīs essent neque ad eum umquam lēgātōs dē pāce mīsissent, arbitrātus id bellum celeriter cōnficī posse, eō exercitum dūxit; quī longē aliā 5 ratiōne ac reliquī Gallī bellum gerere coepērunt. Nam quod intellegēbant, maximās nātiōnēs, quae proeliō conten-dissent, pulsās superātāsque esse, continentēsque silvās ac palūdēs habēbant, eō sē suaque omnia contulērunt.

---

28. 1. Eōdem ferē tempore: 'About the same time' that Crassus completed the reduction of Aquitania, perhaps in the latter part of August. The narrative of Caesar's own military operations, inter-rupted at chap. 16, is here resumed. **prope exācta:** 'almost over.'

2. omnī Galliā: 'Gaul as a whole.'

3. supererant, etc.: 'were the only remaining (peoples) that were.' The Morini and Menapii were more backward than most of the Gauls, but were good fighters (Fig. 100). **essent:** *194, a.* **neque:** trans. as if *et nōn.*

4. arbitrātus: *226, c.*

5. exercitum dūxit: the distance traversed in the march from the sea-coast of the country of the Venetans could hardly have been less than 400 English miles. **quī:** 'but they.' *167.* **longē,** etc.: 'in a way far different from that of the rest of the Gauls.' How lit.? *233, c.*

Figure 100. — Coin of the Morini.

Gold, but of rude workmanship, par-ticularly in the fanciful representation of a horse appearing disjointed.

8. continentēs: 'continuous.'

9. habēbant: coördinate with *intellegēbant*; sc. *quod.* **eō:** *in eās [silvās ac palūdēs].*

10   Ad quārum initium silvārum cum Caesar pervēnisset
castraque mūnīre īnstituisset, neque hostis interim vīsus
esset, dispersīs in opere nostrīs, subitō ex omnibus partibus
silvae ēvolāvērunt et in nostrōs impetum fēcērunt. Nostrī
celeriter arma cēpērunt eōsque in silvās reppulērunt et,
15 complūribus interfectīs, longius impedītiōribus locīs secūtī,
paucōs ex suīs dēperdidērunt.

Hiding in forests, favored by rains, they elude him.

29. Reliquīs deinceps diēbus Caesar silvās caedere īnstituit et, nē quis inermibus imprūdentibusque mīlitibus ab
latere impetus fierī posset, omnem eam māteriam, quae
erat caesa, conversam ad hostem collocābat et prō vāllō ad
5 utrumque latus exstruēbat. Incrēdibilī celeritāte magnō
spatiō paucīs diēbus cōnfectō, cum iam pecus atque extrēma impedīmenta ā nostrīs tenērentur, ipsī dēnsiōrēs
silvās peterent, eius modī sunt tempestātēs cōnsecūtae, utī

---

13. **ēvolāvērunt** : 'rushed forth.' How lit. ?

15. **longius** : 'too far.' *153, a.*   **impedītiōribus locīs** : 'in places
(that were) much obstructed' by trees and marshes.

29. 1. **deinceps** : 'without interruption.'   **caedere** : 'to cut
down.'

2. **quis** : *49, a.*   **imprūdentibus** : 'off their guard.' *144, b, (2).*

3. **māteriam** : 'timber,' here used of untrimmed trees.

4. **conversam**, etc. : 'turned toward the enemy and laid in order
and built up as a rampart.' How lit. ? As the Romans advanced they
felled trees, and placed them, with the tops outwards, at either side of
the space which they cleared, thus forming an effective defense against
the lurking foe.

6. **cōnfectō** : 'cleared.'   **iam . . . tenērentur** : 'were already in
our hands.'   **pecus** : 'cattle.' *13, f.*   **extrēma impedīmenta** :
'the rear of their baggage-train.' *152, a.*

7. **ipsī** : the people themselves, as distinguished from their possessions ; as Caesar cut his way through the woods, they retreated further
and further into the forest fastnesses. *238, a.*

opus necessāriō intermitterētur et continuātiōne imbrium
diūtius sub pellibus mīlitēs continērī nōn possent.   10

Itaque vāstātīs omnibus eōrum agrīs, vīcīs aedificiīsque
incēnsīs, Caesar exercitum redūxit et in Aulercīs Lexoviīs-
que, reliquīs item cīvitātibus, quae proximē bellum fēcerant,
in hībernīs collocāvit.

---

9. **continuātiōne**: 'continuation.' *135*, *a*, and *81*.   **imbrium**:
'rainstorms.' *15*, *c*.

10. **sub pellibus**: 'in tents.'   How lit.? *335*, *a*.

12. **Aulercīs**, etc.: see Map 9.   **Lexoviīs**: chap. 11, ll. 10–12.

13. **reliquīs cīvitātibus**: Venetans (chapters 12–16), Venellans
(17–19), and Sotiates (20–27).

COMMENTARIUS QUARTUS

Destruction of the Usipetes and Tencteri. 1–15

Pressed by the Suebi, the Usipetes and Tencteri enter Gaul.

1. Eā, quae secūta est, hieme, quī fuit annus Cn. Pompeiō, M. Crassō cōnsulibus, Usipetēs Germānī et item Tencterī magnā cum multitūdine hominum flūmen Rhēnum trānsiērunt, nōn longē ā marī, quō Rhēnus īnfluit. Causa 5 trānseundī fuit, quod, ab Suēbīs complūrēs annōs exagitātī, bellō premēbantur et agrī cultūrā prohibēbantur.

Customs, hardihood, and prowess of the Suebi.

Suēbōrum gēns est longē maxima et bellicōsissima Germānōrum omnium. Hī centum pāgōs habēre dīcuntur, ex

---

1. 1. hieme: *12, a*, and *147, a*.   **quī**: in agreement not with the antecedent *hieme*, but with the predicate noun *annus*. *164, c*. B. 250, 3; A. 306; H. 396, 2.   **annus**: 55 B.C.; Pompey and Crassus entered upon their consulship January 1 of that year. The winter of 56–55 B.C., according to the calendar in use, fell wholly in 55 B.C.; for the old Roman calendar, which was still used, had fallen so far behind, that January 1 of the official year came on November 30 of the solar year. A corrected calendar was introduced later by Julius Caesar.

    2. cōnsulibus: *240, a*.   **Germānī**: appositive of both *Usipetēs* and *Tencterī*.

    4. quo: = *in quod*. The horde of Usipetes and Tencteri is thought to have crossed the Rhine near Xanten or Emmerich, below Cologne, in the region where the Rhine receives the Lippe as tributary. (Map 11, and Fig. 101.)

    5. trānseundī: *68, b*.   **Suēbīs**: ancestors of the modern Swabians; see Map at the end of this volume.   **annōs**: *118, a*.

    6. premēbantur: force of Imperfect? *175, a*.   **cultūrā**: *127, a*.

MAP 11

Operations of 55 and 54 B.C.

Books IV, V.

To face page 232

SCALE OF ENGLISH MILES   SCALE OF ROMAN MILES
0   50   100   0   50   100

EXPLANATION

MAP 11

1, 2. Winter quarters, 56–55 B.C. (III.29).

3. Expedition into Germany, 55 B.C. (IV. 19).

4. March into Britain, 54 B.C. (V. 21).

MAP 11, A

Heavy broken red line, route of main fleet in 55 B.C. (IV. 23).

Light broken red lines, route of transports with cavalry, part driven back, part driven down the channel (IV. 28).

Unbroken red line, route of fleet in 54 B.C. (V. 8).

MAP 11, A

Detail of Caesar's crossings to Britain.

quibus quotannīs singula mīlia armātōrum bellandī causā
ex fīnibus ēdūcunt.   Reliquī, quī domī mānsērunt, sē atque 10
illōs alunt; hī rūrsus in vicem annō post in armīs sunt, illī
domī remanent.   Sīc neque agrī cultūra nec ratiō atque
ūsus bellī intermittitur.   Sed prīvātī ac sēparātī agrī apud
eōs nihil est, neque longius annō remanēre ūnō in locō
colendī causā licet.   15

Figure 101. — A typical landscape on the Lower Rhine.

9. **singula mīlia** : 'a thousand each'; if each clan furnished a
thousand warriors, the armed force of the Swabians must have reached
a total of 100,000 men.   **bellandī** : *230*, (1).

10. **ex fīnibus ēdūcunt** : invasion of neighboring territory is implied.   **quī domī mānsērunt** : 'who (each year) have remained at
home.'

11. **illōs** : 'the others,' those in the field.   **hī, illī** : 'the latter,'
'the former.'   *161, b.*   **in vicem** : 'in turn.'   **annō** : *140*.

12. **ratiō . . . bellī** : 'the pursuit of war in theory and practice.'
How lit.?

13. **intermittitur** : *173, a.*   **prīvātī ac sēparātī** : 'assigned to
an individual and marked off' by boundaries; the land was held in
common.   **agrī nihil** : 'no land.'   *97, a.*

14. **annō** : *129, a.*   **remanēre** : *222, a.*

15. **colendī causā** : 'in order to till the soil.'   How lit.? Changes

Neque multum frūmentō, sed maximam partem lacte
atque pecore vīvunt, multumque sunt in vēnātiōnibus;
quae rēs, et cibī genere et cotīdiānā exercitātiōne et lībertāte vītae, quod, ā puerīs nūllō officiō aut disciplīnā assuē-
20 factī, nihil omnīnō contrā voluntātem faciunt, et vīrēs alit
et immānī corporum magnitūdine hominēs efficit. Atque
in eam sē cōnsuētūdinem addūxērunt, ut, locīs frīgidissimīs,
neque vestītūs praeter pellēs habeant quicquam, quārum
propter exiguitātem magna est corporis pars aperta, et
25 laventur in flūminibus.

2. Mercātōribus est aditus magis eō, ut, quae bellō
cēperint, quibus vēndant, habeant, quam quō ūllam rem ad

---

of location were doubtless made each year in order to obtain the best
results from the primitive farming.

16. **frūmentō**: ablative of means; trans. with *vīvunt*, 'they live
on grain.' How lit.?   **partem**: *118, c.*   **lacte**: 'milk.' *10, g.*

17. **pecore**: *13, f.*   **multum sunt in**: 'devote much time to.'
How lit.?   **vēnātiōnibus**: 'hunting,' we should say. *92, a.*

18. **quae rēs**: 'this circumstance,' their devotion to hunting. *167.*
et cibī genere: 'both by reason of the kind of food' obtained by
hunting. *135, a.*

19. **ā puerīs**: 'from childhood.' How lit.?   **officiō**: ablative;
'habituated to no obligation or training.' How lit.? *139.*

20. **et . . . et**: *233, a.*   **vīrēs**: *18, a.*

21. **immānī**: 'huge.'   **hominēs**: predicate accusative, with *eōs*
understood as object of *efficit.* Cf. I, 39, l. 4 and N.

22. **in**, etc.: 'they have trained themselves to.' How lit.?   **locīs
frīgidissimīs**: '(even) in the coldest places.' *145, c.*

23. **neque vestītūs — quicquam**: 'no clothing.' How lit.?
neque . . . et: *233, d.*   **habeant**: *203*, (4).   **quicquam**: *49, a.*

25. **laventur**: 'to bathe.' How lit.? *174.*

2. 1. **Mercātōribus**, etc.: *Mercātōribus est aditus (ad Suēbōs)
magis eō* ('on this account'), *ut (eōs) habeant quibus vēndant (ea),
quae bellō cēperint, quam*, etc.

2. **cēperint**: *220.* [eōs] **quibus vēndant**: 'those to whom they
may sell'; purchasers for their booty are meant. *194, a.*   **quam
quō**: = *quam eō quod*, 'than for the reason that.' *183, c.*

sē importārī dēsīderent.   Quīn etiam iūmentīs, quibus
maximē Gallī dēlectantur quaeque impēnsō parant pretiō,
Germānī importātīs nōn ūtuntur, sed quae sunt apud eōs 5
nāta, parva atque dēfōrmia, haec cotīdiānā exercitātiōne,
summī ut sint labōris, efficiunt.

Equestribus proeliīs saepe ex equīs dēsiliunt ac pedibus
proeliantur, equōsque eōdem remanēre vēstigiō assuēfē-
cērunt, ad quōs sē celeriter, cum ūsus est, recipiunt; neque 10
eōrum mōribus turpius quicquam aut inertius habētur, quam
ephippiīs ūtī.   Itaque ad quemvīs numerum ephippiātōrum
equitum quamvīs paucī adīre audent.

---

3. **dēsīderent**: 'desire.'   **iūmentīs**: with *ūtuntur* (*131*, *c*);
emphatic by position.   Horses alone are meant. *353*, *d*.

4. **maximē dēlectantur**: 'have very great pleasure.'   How lit.?
impēnsō pretiō: 'at an extravagant price.' *141*.   **parant**: 'obtain.'   So great was the interest of the
Gauls in horses that they developed
choice breeds, and Gallic horses were
in demand in Rome.   The horse
figures prominently on Gallic coins
(Fig. 102).

6. **dēfōrmia**: 'unsightly.'

7. **summī labōris**: '(capable) of
the greatest endurance.' *100*, *b*. B.
203, 5; A. 345; H. 447.   **sint**:
203, (3).

Figure 102. — Coin of the
Treverans.

Gold. Fanciful design on the obverse.
Reverse: horse galloping, wheel, star;
above, the letter V.

8. **dēsiliunt**: 'leap down.'   **pedibus**: 'on foot.'   Why ablative?

9. **eōdem vēstigiō**: 'on the same spot' where they have been left.
145, *c*.

10. **cum ūsus est**: 'when it is necessary.' *186*, *a*.   **neque —
quicquam**: *168*.

11. **eōrum mōribus**: 'according to their view.'   How lit.? *136*,*c*.
inertius: 'more unmanly.'   **habētur**: 'is regarded.'

12. **ephippiīs**: 'saddle-cloths,' padded, spread over the horse's
back, and taking the place of our saddles.   **quemvīs**: *49*, *a*.
ephippiātōrum: 'riding with saddle-cloths.'

13. **quamvīs paucī**: 'however few' in number.

Vīnum omnīnō ad sē importārī nōn patiuntur, quod eā rē
15 ad labōrem ferendum remollēscere hominēs atque effē-
minārī arbitrantur.

3. Pūblicē maximam putant esse laudem, quam lātissimē
ā suīs fīnibus vacāre agrōs; hāc rē significārī, magnum
numerum cīvitātum suam vim sustinēre nōn posse. Itaque
ūnā ex parte ā Suēbīs circiter mīlia passuum c agrī vacāre
5 dīcuntur.

Ad alteram partem succēdunt Ubiī, quōrum fuit cīvitās
ampla atque flōrēns, ut est captus Germānōrum; eī paulō
sunt eiusdem generis cēterīs hūmāniōrēs, proptereā quod
Rhēnum attingunt, multumque ad eōs mercātōrēs ventitant,
10 et ipsī propter propinquitātem Gallicīs sunt mōribus assuēfactī. Hōs cum Suēbī, multīs saepe bellīs expertī, propter

---

14. **Vīnum**, etc.: cf. II, 15, ll. 10–13.   **rē**: *135, a.*

15. **remollēscere**: ' lose their vigor.'

3. 1. **Pūblicē**: 'for a people.' How lit.?   **laudem**: *88, a.*
quam: *153, c.*

2. **vacāre agrōs**: subject of *esse.*   **significārī**: the subject is the
infinitive clause following.

4. **ūnā ex parte**: ' on one side.' The east side is meant, and the
country left vacant was probably Bohemia, from which the Boii had
withdrawn; cf. I, 5, ll. 12–14. The name *Boii* survives in "Bohemia."
Suēbīs: *282.*   **mīlia**: *118, a.*   **c**: *38, b,* and *36.*   **agrī**:
nominative plural. *172, d.*

6. **Ad alteram partem**: ' On the opposite side,' toward the Rhine.
How lit.?   **fuit**: the past tense implies that the condition described
no longer exists.

7. **ut est captus Germānōrum**: 'according to the German
standard.' How lit.?

8. **eiusdem generis cēterīs**: i.e. than the rest of the Germans.
129, a.   **hūmāniōrēs**: ' more civilized.'

9. **multum ventitant**: ' freely come and go.' *78, a.*

10. **sunt**, etc.: ' have become familiar with,' etc. Caesar gives an
interesting comparison between Gallic and German customs later (VI,
chapters 11–24). *139.*

11. **expertī**: ' although they had tried.' How lit.? *227, a, (3).*

amplitūdinem gravitātemque cīvitātis fīnibus expellere nōn
potuissent, tamen vectīgālēs sibi fēcērunt ac multō humiliōrēs infirmiōrēsque redēgērunt.

By strategy the Usipetes and Tencteri overcome the Menapii.

4. In eādem causā fuērunt Usipetēs et Tencterī, quōs
suprā dīximus, quī complūrēs annōs Suēbǫrum vim sustinuērunt; ad extrēmum tamen, agrīs expulsī et multīs locīs
Germāniae triennium vagātī, ad Rhēnum pervēnērunt, quās
regiōnēs Menapiī incolēbant.   Hī ad utramque rīpam 5
flūminis agrōs, aedificia vīcōsque habēbant; sed, tantae
multitūdinis aditū perterritī, ex eīs aedificiīs, quae trāns
flūmen habuerant, dēmigrāvērunt et cis Rhēnum, dispositīs
praesidiīs, Germānōs trānsīre prohibēbant.

Illī, omnia expertī, cum neque vī contendere propter 10
inopiam nāvium neque clam trānsīre propter cūstōdiās

---

12. **gravitātem**: here 'power of resistance.'   **cīvitātis**: of the
Ubii.   **fīnibus**: *127, a.*

13. **vectīgālēs**: predicate accusative; 'made (them) tributary.'
115, b.   **multō**, etc.: 'caused them to become much less prominent
and powerful.'   How lit.?

4. 1. **eādem causā**: 'the same condition' of subjection to the
Swabians.

2. **suprā**: chap. 1, ll. 1–6.   **annōs**: *118, a.*

3. **ad extrēmum**: 'finally.'   **multīs locīs**: 'over many parts.'
145, c.

4. **triennium**: used instead of *trēs annōs.*   **quās regiōnēs**: '(to)
the districts which '; in full, *ad eās regiōnēs quās. 165, c.*

6. **aedificia, vīcōs**: cf. Notes to I, 5, ll. 4, 5.   **tantae multitūdinis**: reported as 430,000 (chap. 15, l. 8).

7. **trāns flūmen**: on the east side of the Rhine; Caesar writes from
the point of view of one in Gaul.

8. **dēmigrāvērunt**: 'they moved away.'

9. **Germānōs trānsīre**: 'the Germans from crossing.' *223, a,* (3).

10. **Illī**: *Germānī.*   **omnia expertī**: 'having tried every expedient.'   How lit.?   **vī contendere**: 'to force a passage.'

Menapiōrum possent, revertī sē in suās sēdēs regiōnēsque
simulāvērunt et, trīduī viam progressī, rūrsus revertērunt
atque, omnī hōc itinere ūnā nocte equitātū cōnfectō, īnsciōs
15 inopīnantēsque Menapiōs oppressērunt, quī, dē Germānōrum discessū per explōrātōrēs certiōrēs factī, sine metū
trāns Rhēnum in suōs vīcōs remigrāverant. Hīs interfectīs nāvibusque eōrum occupātīs, prius quam ea pars
Menapiōrum, quae citrā Rhēnum erat, certior fieret, flūmen
20 trānsiērunt atque, omnibus eōrum aedificiīs occupātīs, reliquam partem hiemis sē eōrum cōpiīs aluērunt.

Caesar fears the effect of this victory upon the fickle Gauls.

5. Hīs dē rēbus Caesar certior factus et īnfirmitātem
Gallōrum veritus, quod sunt in cōnsiliīs capiendīs mōbilēs
et novīs plērumque rēbus student, nihil hīs committendum
exīstimāvit.

5 Est enim hōc Gallicae cōnsuētūdinis, utī et viātōrēs,
etiam invītōs, cōnsistere cōgant et, quid quisque eōrum dē

---

13. **trīduī**: trans. as if *trium diērum*. *100, a.*   **viam** : *117, b.*

14. **omnī hōc itinere cōnfectō** : 'covered the entire distance —
and.' How lit.? *144, b,* (2).   **equitātū** : *131, a.*   **īnsciōs** : 'being in ignorance' of what the Germans were doing.

17. **trāns** : to the east side.   **remigrāverant** : 'had moved back.'

19. **fieret** : *189, b.* B. 292, 1, *b*; A. 551, *b*; H. 605, II.

21. **partem** : *118, a.*   **eōrum** : the Menapii on the west side of
the Rhine.   **eōrum cōpiīs** : 'with their supplies.'

5. 1. **īnfirmitātem** : 'fickleness.' Cf. III, 19, ll. 17–20, and Notes.

3. **nihil hīs committendum** [esse] : 'that no reliance whatever
ought to be placed on them.' *73, e.*   **nihil** : = emphatic *nōn*. *118, c.*
B. 176, 2, *b*; A. 390, *d*, N. 2 ; H. 416, 2.

5. **Est . . . cōgant** : 'For it is a custom of the Gauls to compel,'
etc. How lit.?   **cōnsuētūdinis** : *100, b.*   **utī cōgant, quaerant,
circumsistat, cōgat** : explain *hōc. 203,* (4).   **viātōrēs** : 'travelers,' on country roads.

6. **invītōs** : *151.*   **cōgant** : the subject is supplied in thought from
Gallicae, as if it were *Gallōrum.*   **quid** : *204,* (2).   **eōrum** : *97, a.*

quāque rē audierit aut cognōverit, quaerant, et mercātōrēs
in oppidīs vulgus circumsistat, quibusque ex regiōnibus
veniant quāsque ibi rēs cognōverint, prōnūntiāre cōgat.
Hīs rēbus atque audītiōnibus permōtī, dē summīs saepe 10
rēbus cōnsilia ineunt, quōrum eōs in vēstīgiō paenitēre
necesse est, cum incertīs rūmōribus serviant et plērīque ad
voluntātem eōrum ficta respondeant.

Figure 103. — Falls of the Rhine at Schaffhausen.

7. **quāque**: *49, a.* **audierit**: *64, a,* (3).

8. **vulgus**: *6, b.* **quibusque**: = *quibus* (*48, b*) + *-que.*

9. **quāsque**: = *quās* + *-que.* *204,* (2). **prōnūntiāre**: '(them)
to declare.'

10. **rēbus atque audītiōnibus**: 'reports and mere hearsay.'
How lit.? **summīs**: 'of the utmost importance.'

11. **quōrum**: 'of which they must immediately repent.' How lit.?
103, c. B. 209, 1; A. 354, *b*; H. 457. **paenitēre**: subject of *est.*
73, a.

12. **incertīs**: 'indefinite.' **serviant**: 'they subject themselves.'
184, a. **plērīque**: 'most men,' when questioned. **ad**, etc.: 'make
up answers to gratify them.' How lit.?

He resolves to fight the Usipetes and Tencteri.

6. Quā cōnsuētūdine cognitā, Caesar, nē grăviōrī bellō occurreret, mātūrius, quam cōnsuĕrat, ad exercitum profi-cīscitur. Eō cum vēnisset, ea, quae fore suspicātus erat, facta cognōvit ; missās lēgātiōnēs ab nōn nūllīs cīvitātibus 5 ad Germānōs invītātōsque eōs, utī ab Rhēnō discēderent ; *omniaque, quae postulāssent, ab se fore parāta.* Quā spē adductī, Germānī lātius iam vagābantur et in fīnēs Eburō-num et Condrūsōrum, quī sunt Trēverōrum clientēs, per-vēnerant.

10 Prīncipibus Galliae ēvocātīs, Caesar ea, quae cognōverat, dissimulanda sibi exīstimāvīt eōrumque animīs permulsīs et cōnfīrmātīs, equitātūque imperātō, bellum cum Germānīs gerere cōnstituit.

---

6. 1. **graviōrī** : 'quite serious,' in case the fickle Gauls and the Germans should unite against him. *153, a.* **bellō** : *107, a.*

2. **mātūrius** : 'earlier' in the spring, perhaps in the first part of April. *34, a.* **exercitum** : divided up for winter quarters, among the Lexovii and other states, in the autumn of 56 B.C. (III, 29, ll. 12–14) ; now probably brought together again, near the lower Seine, in advance of Caesar's arrival.

3. **Eō** : *ad exercitum.* **fore** : 'would take place.'

4. **facta, missās, invītātōs** : sc. *esse.*

5. **utī**, etc. : i.e. to proceed toward the interior of Gaul in order to help drive the Romans out.

6. **omniaque** : 'and (with the promise) that everything.' *213, b.* **postulāssent** : future perfect indicative in the direct form. *64, a,* (1). **fore parāta** : a substitute for the future infinitive passive. **Quā spē** : 'by this prospect.' *167.*

8. **Eburōnum, Condrūsōrum**, etc. : see Map at the end of the volume.

11. **dissimulanda** [esse] : 'ought to be kept secret.' **permul-sīs** : 'having soothed.' How lit.?

13. **cōnstituit** : here not 'determined,' but 'announced his inten-tion' ; he had previously made up his mind.

He marches near; the Germans parley, assert their rights in Gaul, and request lands.

7. Rē frūmentāriā comparātā equitibusque dēlēctīs, iter in ea loca facere coepit, quibus in locīs esse Germānōs audiēbat. Ā quibus cum paucōrum diērum iter abesset, lēgātī ab hīs vēnērunt, quōrum haec fuit ōrātiō :

Germānōs neque priōrēs populō Rōmānō bellum īnferre, 5 *neque tamen recūsāre, sī lacessantur, quīn armīs contendant, quod Germānōrum cōnsuētūdō sit ā maiōribus trādita, quīcumque bellum īnferant, resistere neque dēprecārī.*

Haec tamen dīcere, vēnisse invītōs, ēiectōs domō ; sī suam grātiam Rōmānī velint, posse eīs ūtilēs esse amīcōs ; vel 10 *sibi agrōs attribuant vel patiantur eōs tenēre, quōs armīs possēderint : sēsē ūnīs Suēbīs concēdere, quibus nē dī quidem*

---

7. 2. **iter facere :** 'to march.'　　**locīs :** *165, a.*

3. **quibus :** 'these (places).'　*167.*　　**diērum :** *100, a.*　　**iter :** *118, a,* and *243, c.*

4. **quōrum,** etc. : 'whose plea was as follows.'　*161, a.*

5. **Germānōs,** etc. : 'that the Germans did not take the lead in making war . . . and that, nevertheless, they would not refuse to fight.' How lit.?　**priōrēs :** *152, b.*

6. **lacessantur :** present, used for greater vividness, where a past tense might have been expected. *218,* (1), *a.*　　**contendant :** subjunctive also in the direct form. *201, a.*

8. **quīcumque :** *50, a.*　　**resistere :** sc. *eīs* (*105*), as antecedent of *quīcumque. 79, d.*　　**neque dēprecārī :** 'and not to beg for mercy.'

9–14. **Direct form :** Haec tamen *dīcimus,* (*nōs*) vēnisse invītōs, ēiectōs domō; sī (*vōs Rōmānī*) *nostram* grātiam *vultis, possumus vōbīs* ūtilēs esse amīcōs; vel *nōbīs* agrōs *attribuite* (*216*) vel *patiminī* (*nōs*) eōs (*agrōs*) tenēre, quōs armīs *possēdimus ;* ūnīs Suēbīs *concēdimus,* quibus nē dī quidem immortālēs parēs esse *possint* (*194, a*); *reliquus* quidem in terrīs est *nēmō,* quem nōn superāre *possimus.*

9. **dīcere, vēnisse, posse, tenēre** (l. 11) : sc *sē. 215.*　　**ēiectōs :** 'because they had been driven forth.' *227, a,* (1).　　**domō :** *127, a.*

12. **possēderint :** from *possīdō.*　　**ūnīs :** 'alone.' *23, a.*　　**dī :** *8, d,* and *237, c.*　　**concēdere :** 'admitted inferiority.'

immortālēs parēs esse possent; reliquum quidem in terrīs
esse nēminem, quem nōn superāre possint.

Caesar insists that they go back to Germany; parleying continues.

8. Ad haec Caesar, quae vīsum est, respondit; sed exitus
fuit ōrātiōnis :

 Sibi nūllam cum hīs amīcitiam esse posse, sī in Galliā
remanērent; neque vērum esse, quī suōs fīnēs tuērī nōn
5 *potuerint, aliēnōs occupāre; neque ūllōs in Galliā vacāre*
agrōs, quī darī, tantae praesertim multitūdinī, sine iniūriā
possint; sed licēre, sī velint, in Ubiōrum fīnibus cōnsīdere,
quōrum sint lēgātī apud sē et dē Suēbōrum iniūriīs queran-
tur et ā sē auxilium petant; hōc sē Ubiīs imperātūrum.

 9. Lēgātī haec sē ad suōs relātūrōs dīxērunt et, rē dēlī-
berātā, post diem tertium ad Caesarem reversūrōs; intereā
nē propius sē castra movēret, petiērunt. Nē id quidem

---

13. **reliquum nēminem** : ' no one else.' *12, d.*   **in terrīs** : ' on
earth '; why is *terrīs* plural?

 8. 1. vīsum est : sc. *respondēre.* Caesar does not give the whole
of his answer, which perhaps followed the same line of argument as his
statement to Ariovistus (I, chap. 45).

 3. **Sibi**, etc. : in the direct form, *Mihi nūlla cum vōbīs amīcitia esse*
potest, ' I can have no friendly relations with you.' *111*, and *212, c*, (1).

 4. **vērum** : consistent with what is true, ' a fair thing.' **quī** : for
antecedent supply *eōs* as subject-accusative with *occupāre.*

 5. **aliēnōs** : sc. *fīnēs;* ' of others.'

 7. **possint**, etc. : the present tense is used for the sake of vividness.
licēre : sc. *eīs. 73, a, b.*

 8. **apud sē** : ' with him.' **Suēbōrum iniūriīs** : chap. 3, ll. 6–14.

 9. **hōc**, etc. : ' that he would order the Ubii (to allow them to do)
this,' lit. ' he would command this to the Ubii.' Caesar could ' order '
the Ubii because he held hostages from that people (chap. 16, ll. 19–20).

 9. 2. post diem tertium : ' in three days,' i.e. ' the next day but
one '; in such expressions the Romans included the days with which a
period began and ended.

 3. **propius sē** : *123, b.* **movēret** : *199, a.*

Caesar ab sē impetrārī posse dīxit. Cognōverat enim, magnam partem equitātūs ab eīs, aliquot diēbus ante, prae- 5 dandī frūmentandīque causā ad Ambivaritōs trāns Mosam missam; hōs exspectārī equitēs atque eius reī causā moram interpōnī arbitrātur.

Figure 104. — Along the Meuse, below Namur.

Women are unloading clay from a canal boat.

4. **ab**: 'from.'

5. **diēbus**: *140*. B. 223; A. 424, *f*; H. 488, 1.

6. **frūmentandī causā**: 'to forage.' How lit.? **trāns**: 'across' to the west side of the Meuse (Fig. 104); the main body, and Caesar, were on the east side, between the Meuse and the Rhine.

7. **hōs exspectārī**, etc.: in order that an attack with all their forces might be made upon the Romans. **reī**: the return of the cavalry.

Description of the Rhine region.

[**10.** Mosa prōfluit ex monte Vosegō, quī est in fīnibus Lingonum, et parte quādam ex Rhēnō receptā, quae appellātur Vacalus, īnsulam efficit Batāvōrum, neque longius ab eō mīlibus passuum LXXX in Ōceanum īnfluit.

5 Rhēnus autem oritur ex Lepontiīs, quī Alpēs incolunt, et longō spatiō per fīnēs Nantuātium, Helvētiōrum, Sēquanōrum, Mediomatricōrum, Tribocōrum, Trēverōrum citātus fertur et, ubi Ōceanō appropinquāvit, in plūrēs diffluit partēs, multīs ingentibusque īnsulīs effectīs, quārum pars 10 magna ā ferīs barbarīsque nātiōnibus incolitur (ex quibus sunt, quī piscibus atque ōvīs avium vīvere exīstimantur), multīsque capitibus in Ōceanum īnfluit.]

---

10. 1–12. On account of certain difficulties and inconsistencies in this chapter many think that it was not written by Caesar, but added later by some one who wished to supply a geographical background for this part of the narrative ; the Meuse, for example, does not rise in the Vosges mountains, and the Rhine could hardly have flowed through the country of the Nantuates. Nevertheless the rapid current of the Rhine is referred to, which is particularly noticeable in the upper part of its course, as at Schaffhausen (Fig. 103) ; and we cannot assume that Caesar had accurate knowledge of regions so far from those which he himself had visited.

If the chapter is omitted, there is an easy transition from chap. 9 to chap. 11. Translation : —

'The Meuse rises in the Vosges mountains, which are in the country of the Lingones; receiving from the Rhine an affluent, which is called the Waal, it forms (with this) the island of the Batavians, and not further from this than eighty miles it flows into the Ocean.

'The Rhine, moreover, rises in the country of the Lepontii, who dwell in the Alps, and in a long course flows rapidly through the territories of the Nantuates, the Helvetians, the Sequanians, the Mediomatrici, the Triboci, and the Treverans; where it approaches the Ocean it divides up into several branches, forming many large islands. Of these (islands) a considerable portion are inhabited by wild and savage tribes, some of whom are believed to live on fish and birds' eggs. (The Rhine) flows into the Ocean through many mouths.'

The parleying, Caesar concludes, is continued merely to gain time.

11. Caesar cum ab hoste nōn amplius passuum XII mīlibus abesset, ut erat cōnstitūtum, ad eum lēgātī revertuntur;
quī in itinere congressī magnopere, nē longius prōgrederētur, ōrābant. Cum id nōn impetrāssent, petēbant, utī ad
eōs equitēs, quī agmen antecessissent, praemitteret eōsque 5
pugnā prohibēret, sibique ut potestātem faceret in Ubiōs
lēgātōs mittendī; *quōrum sī prīncipēs ac senātus sibi iūre
iūrandō fidem fēcisset, eā condiciōne, quae ā Caesare ferrētur, sē ūsūrōs* ostendēbant; *ad hās rēs cōnficiendās sibi
trīduī spatium daret.*   1C

Haec omnia Caesar eōdem illō pertinēre arbitrābātur, ut,
trīduī morā interpositā, equitēs eōrum, quī abessent, reverterentur; tamen *sēsē nōn longius mīlibus passuum IIII,
aquātiōnis causā, prōcessūrum eō diē* dīxit; *hūc posterō diē*

---

11. 1. cum ab hoste, etc.: after denying the request of the Germans (chap. 9, l. 3), Caesar evidently had marched toward them.
XII : *38, b,* and *36.*   **mīlibus :** *129, a.*

2. ut erat cōnstitūtum : the agreement was that the envoys
should return in three days (chap. 9, l. 2). *73, d.*

3. congressī : sc. *cum eō*, 'meeting him.' *57, c*, and *226, c.*
prōgrederētur : *199, a.*

5. antecessissent : *220,* and *328.*   **praemitteret :** here without
an object; with *ad eōs equitēs,* 'that he send forward to,' etc.

6. pugnā : *127, a.*   **sibi,** etc.: 'that he would give them permission to send.' How lit.?

8. iūre iūrandō fidem fēcisset : 'should have bound themselves
by an oath.' *13, h.* How lit.?   **fēcisset :** agrees with the nearer
subject. *172, b.*   **eā,** etc.: 'that they would accept the terms proposed by Caesar.' *131, c.* How lit.?

10. daret : *dā* in the direct form. *216.*

11. eōdem illō pertinēre : 'had the same end in view.' How
lit.? **ut,** etc. : explaining *eōdem illō.* *199, a.*

12. abessent : *220.* Cf. chap. 9, ll. 4–8.

14. aquātiōnis causā : 'in order to get water.' *94, b.*   **hūc :** to
the place where he was at the time of the conference.

15 *quam frequentissimī convenīrent, ut dē eōrum postulātīs*
cognōsceret.

Interim ad praefectōs, quī cum omnī equitātū antecesserant, mittit, quī nūntiārent, nē hostēs proeliō lacesserent et,
sī ipsī lacesserentur, sustinērent, quoad ipse cum exercitū
20 propius accessisset.

The German cavalry surprises and routs the cavalry of Caesar.

12. At hostēs, ubi prīmum nostrōs equitēs cōnspexērunt,
quōrum erat v mīlium numerus, cum ipsī nōn amplius DCCC
equitēs habērent, quod eī, quī frūmentandī causā erant
trāns Mosam profectī, nōndum redierant, nihil timentibus
5 nostrīs, quod lēgātī eōrum paulō ante ā Caesare discesserant atque is diēs indūtiīs erat ab hīs petītus, impetū factō
celeriter nostrōs perturbāvērunt; rūrsus hīs resistentibus,
cōnsuētūdine suā ad pedēs dēsiluērunt, subfossīsque equīs

---

15. **quam frequentissimī**: 'in as great numbers as possible.'
153, c.   **convenīrent**: *convenīte* in the direct form.   *216.*

17. **praefectōs**: *309, c.*   **equitātū**: *137, a.*

18. **quī nūntiārent**: '(men) to convey the order.' *193, a.*

19. **sustinērent**: sc. *ut.* *200, a.* The Roman cavalry were ordered
to act on the defensive.

20. **accessisset**: subjunctive also in the direct form. *190, c.*
B. 293, III, 2 ; A. 553; H. 603, II, 2.

12. 1. **ubi prīmum**: *188, c.*   **nostrōs equitēs**: the Roman
cavalry had apparently advanced in the direction of the German camp.

2. **v mīlium**: *309, b*, and *100, a.*   **cum**: *187.*   DCCC: *octin-*
gentōs. 38, b, and *36.*

3. **equitēs**: *129, b.*   **eī . . . profectī**: chap. 9, ll. 4–8.

6. **indūtiīs**: 'for a truce.' *112, a.* Caesar explains why his cavalry were caught off their guard.   **impetū factō**: 'charged and.'
How lit.? *144, b,* (2).

7. **hīs**: the Roman cavalry.

8. **cōnsuētūdine**: *136, c.*   **suā**: *157, b.*   **ad pedēs**: 'to the
ground,' we should say. *10, b.*   **dēsiluērunt**: from their horses.
subfossīs . . . dēiectīs: 'stabbed the horses (of our cavalry) underneath and dismounted quite a number of our men and.' How lit.?

complūribusque nostrīs dēiectīs, reliquōs in fugam coniēcērunt atque ita perterritōs ēgērunt, ut nōn prius fugā dēsis- 10
terent, quam in cōnspectum agminis nostrī vēnissent.

Bravery of the Aquitanian, Piso, in the skirmish.

In eō proeliō ex equitibus nostrīs interficiuntur IIII et LXX,
in hīs vir fortissimus, Pīsō Aquītānus, amplissimō genere
nātus, cuius avus in cīvitāte suā rēgnum obtinuerat, amīcus

Figure 105. — The slopes of the Rhine Valley.

9. **reliquōs**: sc. *nostrōs*. **fugam**: the flight of the Gallic cavalry, as in a previous instance (I, 18, ll. 27–31), may have been stimulated by treachery among the native leaders.

11. **agminis**: the main force. **vēnissent**: subjunctive by attraction. *189, a,* and *220.*

12. **ex equitibus**: *97, d.* **IIII et LXX**: *quattuor et septuāgintā. 38, b.* The result of the skirmish showed the superiority of the
German over the Gallic cavalry. Caesar afterwards hired German
horsemen, and made much use of them (VII, 80, l. 20 and N.).

13. **Pīsō**: a Roman name, probably conferred on some Aquitanian
with the Roman citizenship; cf. I, chap. 47, l. 13 and N. **genere**:
128, a. B. 215; A. 403, 2, *a*; H. 469, 2.

14. **amīcus**: cf. I, 3, l. 13 and N. *88, a.*

15 ā senātū nostrō appellātus. Hīc cum frātrī, interclūsō ab
hostibus, auxilium ferret, illum ex perīculō ēripuit, ipse, equō
vulnerātō, dēiectus, quoad potuit, fortissimē restitit; cum
circumventus, multīs vulneribus acceptīs, cecidisset, atque
id frāter, quī iam proeliō excesserat, procul animadvertisset,
20 incitātō equō sē hostibus obtulit atque interfectus est.

The German leaders come to offer apology; Caesar detains them.

13. Hōc factō proeliō Caesar neque iam sibi lēgātōs
audiendōs neque condiciōnēs accipiendās arbitrābātur ab
eīs, quī per dolum atque īnsidiās, petītā pāce, ultrō bellum
intulissent; exspectāre vērō, dum hostium cōpiae augēren-
5 tur equitātusque reverterētur, summae dēmentiae esse iūdicābat; et, cognitā Gallōrum īnfīrmitāte, quantum iam apud
eōs hostēs ūnō proeliō auctōritātis essent cōnsecūtī, sentiēbat;
quibus ad cōnsilia capienda nihil spatiī dandum exīstimābat.

---

17. **dēiectus**: 'although thrown' from his horse, he continued to
fight on foot. *227, a*, (3).   **potuit**: *190, c.*

19. **id**: 'that (mishap).'   **proeliō**: *127, a.*

20. **incitātō equō**: 'urging his horse forward.' How lit.?   **sē
hostibus obtulit**: 'he hurled himself upon the enemy.' Many instances of individual bravery and devotion are recorded by Caesar.

13. 1. **Hōc factō proeliō**: 'After this battle.' How lit.?

2. **audiendōs**: *89, c.*   **ab**: 'from'; Caesar had arranged to take
up their proposals (chap. 11, ll. 14–15) on the following day.

3. **per dolum atque īnsidiās**: 'craftily and treacherously.' How
lit.?   **ultrō**: 'without provocation.' How lit.?   **bellum intulissent**: 'had made an attack.'

4. **exspectāre**: subject of *esse. 222, b.*   **dum**: 'until,' with the
subjunctive also in the direct form. *190, b.* B. 293, III, 2 ; A. 553; H.
603, II, 2.

5. **summae dēmentiae esse**: 'that it was the height of folly.'
How lit.? *100, b.*

6. **īnfīrmitāte**: cf. chap. 5, ll. 1–3.   **quantum — auctōritātis**:
'how great prestige.' *97, b,* and *204,* (3).

8. **quibus**: trans. as if *et eīs.*   **ad**, etc.: *230,* (3).   **nihil spatiī**:
'no time.' *97, a.*

His cōnstitūtīs rēbus et cōnsiliō cum lēgātīs et quaestōre commūnicātō, nē quem diem pugnae praetermitteret, 10
opportūnissima rēs accidit, quod postrīdiē eius diēī māne,
eādem et simulātiōne et perfidiā ūsī, Germānī frequentēs,
omnibus prīncipibus maiōribusque nātū adhibitīs, ad eum
in castra vēnērunt, simul, ut dīcēbātur, suī pūrgandī causā,
quod contrā, atque esset dictum et ipsī petīssent, proelium 15
prīdiē commīsissent, simul ut, sī quid possent, dē indūtiīs
fallendō impetrārent. Quōs sibi Caesar oblātōs gāvīsus,
illōs retinērī iussit; ipse omnēs cōpiās castrīs ēdūxit equitātumque, quod recentī proeliō perterritum esse exīstimābat,
agmen subsequī iussit.   20

---

9. **cōnsiliō**: 'determination,' explained by the appositive clause
nē . . . praetermittet, 'not to let slip any chance to fight,' lit. 'any
day of battle.'   **cum — commūnicātō**: 'after he had imparted
to.' How lit.? *137, c*.   **quaestōre**: *313, b*.

11. **diēī**: *94, c*.   **māne**: 'early in the morning.'

12. **eādem**: 'the same' as before.   **perfidiā**: 'treachery.'   To
justify his own course Caesar accuses the Germans of bad faith. But
if they did not mean what they said, why did so many of them trust
themselves in Caesar's power? The collision on the previous day may
have been precipitated by hotheads, without the approval of the leaders
of the German host.

14. **simul — simul**: 'both — and.'   **suī pūrgandī causā**: 'in
order to clear themselves.' *154, b*, and *230*, (1). B. 339, 5; A. 504,
c; H. 626, 3.

15. **quod**, etc.: 'because, contrary to what had been said.'   **contrā**: adverb.   **atque**: *233, c*.

16. **commīsissent**: '(as they admitted) they had started the
battle.' *183, a*.   **sī quid possent**: 'if in any degree possible.'
How lit.? *118, b*.   **dē**: 'in the matter of.'

17. **fallendō**: 'by playing false.'   **Quōs**: *167*.   **oblātōs** [esse]:
69, b.   **gāvīsus**: 'rejoicing.' *62*, and *226, e*.

20. **agmen subsequī**: 'to follow the main force,' i.e. to bring up
the rear, instead of leading the van, as the cavalry usually did. *328*.

Surprising the leaderless German host, he utterly destroys it.

14. Aciē triplicī īnstitūtā et celeriter VIII mīlium itinere cōnfectō, prius ad hostium castra pervēnit, quam, quid agerētur, Germānī sentīre possent. Quī omnibus rēbus subitō perterritī, et celeritāte adventūs nostrī et discessū
5 suōrum, neque cōnsiliī habendī neque arma capiendī spatiō datō, perturbantur, cōpiāsne adversus hostem dūcere, an castra dēfendere, an fugā salūtem petere praestāret.

Quōrum timor cum fremitū et concursū significārētur, mīlitēs nostrī, prīstinī diēī perfidiā incitātī, in castra irrūpē-
10 runt. Quō locō, quī celeriter arma capere potuērunt, pau-lisper nostrīs restitērunt atque inter carrōs impedīmentaque proelium commīsērunt; at reliqua multitūdō puerōrum mulierumque (nam cum omnibus suīs domō excesserant

---

14. 1. **Aciē triplicī**: *337, a.* **VIII**: *38, b.* **itinere**: the army probably marched in three parallel columns, which deployed as they neared the camp of the enemy. The country must have been open and fairly level to admit of the rapid execution of the movement.

2. **prius . . . quam . . . possent**: *189, b.* B. 292, 1, *b*; A. 551, *b*; H. 605, II. **hostium castra**: a corral protected by carts, like that of the Helvetians (I, 26, l. 8).

4. **et — et**: 'both — and.' *233, a.*

5. **suōrum**: the German leaders who had gone to Caesar and were held by him under guard. **cōnsiliī . . . capiendī**: gerundive and gerund in coördinate construction; trans. 'for,' etc. *230, (1).* **spa-tiō**: *tempore.*

6. **perturbantur**: 'were (too) confused (to decide).' **ne . . . an . . . an**: 'whether . . . or . . . or.' *204, (1).* **dūcere**: *222, a.*

8. **Quōrum**: *167.* **cum**: *185, c.*

9. **prīstinī diēī**: 'of the previous day.' **irrūpērunt**: 'burst into.'

10. **Quō locō**: *castrīs Germānōrum.*

11. **restitērunt**: sc. *eī,* antecedent of *quī.* **inter carrōs**, etc.: cf. I, 26, ll. 7–11.

12. **at**: *236, a.* **reliqua**, etc.: 'the rest of the host (consisting) of women and children.' *98, a.*

13. **cum**: N. to l, 1, l. 13. **excesserant**: i.e. *Usipetēs et Tencterī.*

Rhēnumque trānsierant) passim fugere coepit ; ad quōs
cōnsectandōs Caesar equitātum misit.　　　　　　　　15

15. Germānī, post tergum clāmōre audītō, cum suōs interficī vidērent, armīs abiectīs signīsque mīlitāribus relīctīs,
sē ex castrīs ēiēcērunt, et cum ad cōnfluentem Mosae et

Figure 106.— The Moselle at Beilstein ; ruins of the castle at the right.

14. **quōs** : the antecedent is *multitūdō*. *164, d.* Caesar's conduct
in detaining the German leaders, who had come to him under a flag of
truce, and then attacking and pursuing the leaderless host without
mercy, seems treacherous and unlike his ordinary procedure. When
afterwards his friends proposed, in the Roman senate, a thanksgiving
for the victory, Cato urged that Caesar be delivered up to those whom
he had treacherously entrapped, as an atonement for the wrong. Not
much weight should be attached to this as a judgment on Caesar's course,
however, for debates in the Roman senate, as in our own, were colored
by political and personal antagonisms.

15. 1. **Germānī** : the warriors who armed for defense when the camp
was attacked (chap. 14, l. 10).　　**clāmōre** : ' the shrieking ' of the
women and children, part of whom were cut down by the legionaries
entering the camp, part by the cavalry after they had fled from the camp.

3. **cōnfluentem** : ' confluence.'　　**Mosae** : probably the Moselle
(Fig. 106) is here meant, not the Meuse ; *Mosellae* may have been

Rhēnī pervēnissent, reliquā fugā dēspērātā, magnō numerō
5 interfectō, reliquī se in flūmen praecipitāvērunt atque ibi
timōre, lassitūdine, vī flūminis oppressī periērunt. Nostrī
ad ūnum omnēs incolumēs, perpaucīs vulnerātīs, ex tantī
bellī timōre, cum hostium numerus capitum CCCCXXX mīlium fuisset, sē in castra recēpērunt.

10　　Caesar eīs, quōs in castrīs retinuerat, discēdendī potestātem fēcit. Illī, supplicia cruciātūsque Gallōrum veritī,
quōrum agrōs vexāverant, remanēre sē apud eum velle
dīxērunt. Hīs Caesar lībertātem concessit.

First Expedition into Germany.　16–19

Caesar resolves to cross the Rhine and enter Germany.

16. Germānicō bellō cōnfectō, multīs dē causīs Caesar
statuit sibi Rhēnum esse trānseundum; quārum illa fuit

---

written and changed to *Mosae* in copying. It seems probable that the
German camp was south of the Moselle and that the fleeing warriors
came to the region of Coblenz, which lies in the angle formed by the
Moselle as it enters the Rhine.

4. **reliquā**, etc.: 'abandoning hope of further flight.' How lit.?
144, b, (2).

5. **flūmen**: the Rhine, at Coblenz.

6. **lassitūdine**: in consequence of the fighting and running.

7. **ad ūnum**: 'to a man.'　**incolumēs**: 'in safety.'　**ex . . .
cum**: 'notwithstanding (their) apprehension of a hard campaign,
since.' *184, a.* How lit.?

8. **capitum . . . fuisset**: 'had amounted to 430,000'; cf. N. to I,
29, l. 6. *100, b.*　**CCCCXXX**: = *quadringentōrum trīgintā.* *38, b,*
and *36.* If, as among the Helvetians, one fourth were fighting-men,
the Usipetes and Tencteri mustered an army of more than 130,000
The number seems greatly exaggerated.

11. **veritī**: *61, a,* (2), and *226, c.*

13. **lībertātem**: 'leave' to stay. They probably entered his service as mercenaries.

16. 2. **quārum**: *97, a.*　**illa**: *161, a.*

iūstissima, quod, cum vidēret Germānōs tam facile impellī,
ut in Galliam venīrent, suīs quoque rēbus eōs timēre voluit,
cum intellegerent, et posse et audēre populī Rōmānī exer- 5
citum Rhēnum trānsīre.

Accessit etiam, quod illa pars equitātūs Usipetum et
Tencterōrum, quam suprā commemorāvī praedandī frūmentandīque causā Mosam trānsīsse neque proeliō inter-
fuisse, post fugam suōrum sē trāns Rhēnum in fīnēs 10
Sugambrōrum recēperat sēque cum eīs coniūnxerat.   Ad
quōs cum Caesar nūntiōs mīsisset, quī postulārent, eōs,
quī sibi Galliaeque bellum intulissent, sibi dēderent,
respondērunt:

Populī Rōmānī imperium Rhēnum fīnīre ; sī, sē invītō, 15
Germānōs in Galliam trānsīre nōn aequum exīstimāret, cūr
suī quicquam esse imperiī aut potestātis trāns Rhēnum
postulāret?

---

3. **iūstissima:** 'the most weighty.'   **quod . . . voluit:** explains *illa [causa].*

4. **ut . . . venīrent:** 'to come.'   *199, a.*   **suīs quoque rēbus:**
'for their own interests also.'

5. **cum:** *cum* temporal has here a conditional force also; 'in
case.'

7. **Accessit etiam quod:** 'There was the further reason that.'
198, a, and *b.*

8. **suprā:** chap. 9, ll. 4-8.   **commemorāvī:** cf. *dēmōnstrāvi-*
mus, II, 1, l. 2, and N.

12. **quōs:** *Sugambrōs.*   **postulārent:** *193, a.*

13. **dēderent:** *200, a.*   B. 295, 8; A. 565, *a*; H. 562, I, N.

15. **imperium Rhēnum fīnīre:** i.e. *Rhēnum* (subject accusative)
esse fīnem ('limit') *imperiī.*   **sē invītō:** N. to I, 8, l. 7.

16. **aequum:** 'right'; in predicate, neuter, accusative, in agreement with the infinitive clause *Germānōs trānsīre,* which stands as
object of *exīstimāret.*

17. **suī,** etc.: 'that anything beyond the Rhine was under his
authority or power.'   *94, d.*

18. **postulāret:** with *cur,* 'why should he claim.'   *217, a.*

Ubiī autem, quī ūnī ex Trānsrhēnānīs ad Caesarem
20 lēgātōs mīserant, amīcitiam fēcerant, obsidēs dederant,
magnopere ōrābant, ut sibi auxilium ferret, quod graviter
ab Suēbīs premerentur:

*Vel, sī id facere occupātiōnibus reī pūblicae prohibērētur,
exercitum modo Rhēnum trānsportāret ; id sibi ad auxilium*
25 *spemque reliquī temporis satis futūrum.   Tantum esse
nōmen atque opīniōnem eius exercitūs, Ariovistō pulsō et
hōc novissimō proeliō factō, etiam ad ultimās Germānōrum
nātiōnēs, utī opīniōne et amīcitiā populī Rōmānī tūtī esse
possint.*

30   Nāvium magnam cōpiam ad trānsportandum exercitum
pollicēbantur.

He builds a bridge across the Rhine.

17. Caesar hīs dē causīs, quās commemorāvī, Rhēnum
trānsīre dēcrēverat; sed nāvibus trānsīre neque satis tūtum esse arbitrābātur, neque suae neque populī Rōmānī

---

19. **ūnī**: 'alone.' *23, a.*   **ex Trānsrhēnānīs**: 'of the peoples
across the Rhine.' *97, d.*

20. **mīserant, fēcerant, dederant**: *234, a,* and *238, a.*

21. **quod . . . premerentur**: *183, a.*

23. **Vel**: *213, b,* and *235, a.*   **id facere**: 'from doing that.'
223, a, (3).   **occupātiōnibus reī pūblicae**: 'by the requirements
of public business.'

24. **exercitum, Rhēnum**: *114, a.*   **trānsportāret**: *216.*   **id**:
'that (movement).'   **ad . . . temporis**: 'for (present) help and
(for) hope in respect to the future.'   How lit.?

26. **opīniōnem**: 'reputation.'   **eius**: 'his,' i.e. *Caesaris.*   **Ariovistō pulsō**: 'in consequence of the defeat of Ariovistus,' related in
Book I.   How lit.?   *144, b,* (3).

17. 2. trānsīre: *222, b.*   **tūtum**: predicative. *148, d.*   Caesar
was always careful to have the country in the rear of his army well
secured, not only for the transportation of supplies but also to make a
retreat safe in case of necessity.

3. **suae, populī**: *157, d.*

dignitātis esse statuēbat. Itaque, etsī summa difficultās
faciendī pontis prōpōnēbātur propter lātitūdinem, rapiditā- 5
tem altitūdinemque flūminis, tamen id sibi contendendum,
aut aliter nōn trādūcendum exercitum, exīstimābat.

Ratiōnem pontis hanc īnstituit :

Tigna bīna sēsquipedālia, paulum ab īmō praeacūta,
dīmēnsa ad altitūdinem flūminis, intervāllō pedum duōrum 10
inter sē iungēbat. Haec cum, māchinātiōnibus immissa
in flūmen, dēfīxerat fistūcīsque adēgerat, nōn sublicae modō

---

4. **dignitātis**, etc. : ' would be inconsistent with the prestige.' *94, d.*
How lit.?　**etsī** : *191, a.*

5. **lātitūdinem** : between 1300 and 1600 feet in the region where
Caesar built the bridge, that is, near Neuwied, between Coblenz and An-
dernach (Map 11, facing p. 232).　**rapiditātem** : ' swiftness.' *76, a.*

6. **id**, etc. : sc. *esse*, ' that he ought to make every effort (to accomplish) this.'

7. **aut** : *235, a.*

8. **Ratiōnem**, etc. : ' the plan of the bridge (which) he devised
(was) as follows.' *161, a.* How lit.?

9. **Tigna bīna** : ' a pair of logs,' to be driven into the river bed and
used as posts to support the bridge ; see Plates V and VI, **a a.** *36.*
sēsquipedālia : ' a foot and a half thick.' *79, b.*　**ab īmō** : ' at the
lower end.' *154, a*, and *126, c.*

10. **dīmēnsa** : passive ; with *ad*, etc., ' measured off to correspond
with the depth of the river,' the longer piles for use near the middle,
the shorter for driving nearer the banks. How lit.? *59, b.*　**intervāllō**, etc. : ' two feet apart.' How lit. ? *138.*

11. **inter sē** : ' together.' *159.*　**iungēbat** : sc. *Caesar* ; the object is *Tigna*. The two logs of each pair were apparently fastened
together on the bank, before they were driven into the river bed.
māchinātiōnibus immissa : ' had let down by mechanical appliances,'
rafts equipped with suitable tackle. How lit.? *228, a.*

12. **dēfīxerat**, etc. : ' had planted these firmly and driven [them]
home with pile-drivers,' in the case of each pair ; the pluperfect with
cum implies repeated action. *186, a.* B. 288, 3 ; H. 539, 2.　**nōn
sublicae modō** : ' not like an (ordinary) pile,' because ordinarily piles
are driven in perpendicularly, while these pairs were driven with a slant.
How lit. ?

dērēctē ad perpendiculum, sed prōnē ac fastīgātē, ut secundum nātūram flūminis prōcumberent, hīs item contrāria
15 duo ad eundem modum iūncta, intervāllō pedum quadrāgēnum ab īnferiōre parte, contrā vim atque impetum flūminis conversa, statuēbat.

Haec utraque, īnsuper bipedālibus trabibus immissīs,
quantum eōrum tignōrum iūnctūra distābat, bīnīs utrimque
20 fībulīs ab extrēmā parte distinēbantur; quibus disclūsīs

---

13. **dērēctē**: 'straight up and down.'   **ad perpendiculum**:
'according to a plumb-line.'   **prōnē ac fastīgātē**: 'leaning forward
with a decided slant.'   How lit.?   **secundum**: 'in conformity with.'
122, a.

14. **nātūram flūminis**: 'the direction of the current.'   *74, d.*
hīs contrāria: 'opposite these.'   *108, a.*   Plates V, VI, a′ a′.

15. **duo**: sc. *tigna; bīna* might have been used.   **ad eundem
modum**: 'in the same manner.'   *45.*   **quadrāgēnum**: 'forty' Roman feet in each case.   *22, c.*   The distance must have been measured
on the surface of the water.   Plate V, A.

16. **ab īnferiōre parte**: 'on the lower side,' i.e. downstream from
the first pair.   **contrā**, etc.: 'against the violent rushing of the current.'   How lit.?   As the first pair of posts slanted downstream, so the
second pair slanted upstream.   Plate V, A, a a′.

18. **Haec utraque . . . distinēbantur**: 'the two pairs' of posts
'were held apart.'   *51.*   **īnsuper**: 'above.'   **bipedālibus**, etc.:
'after a beam having the thickness of two feet, corresponding with the
space between the posts' (of each pair), 'had been let in.'   How lit.?
The heavy crossbeam, or sill, is marked, b b on Plates V, VI.

19. **quantum**: representing the idea of measure in *bipedālibus*; accusative.   *118, a.*   **bīnīs . . . parte**: 'by a pair of braces on each
side' (i.e. with each pair of posts), 'at the very end' of the sill.   What
these 'pairs of braces' were it is not easy to understand.   If of wood,
they may have been like those represented in the Plates V and VI, c c;
for with such braces the greater the pressure the more closely the
structure would have been bound together.   If the braces were of iron
— a less probable supposition because of the amount of iron required,
— the arrangement must have been altogether different.

20. **quibus . . . revinctīs**: i.e. *tignīs;* 'now that these' (the two
pairs of posts, one pair above and one below) 'were kept' (at the proper

PLATE V   CAESAR'S BRIDGE ACROSS THE RHINE, SECTIONS

Lib. IV, 17

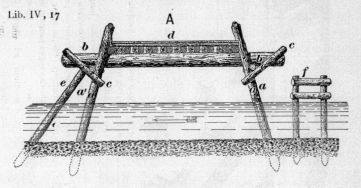

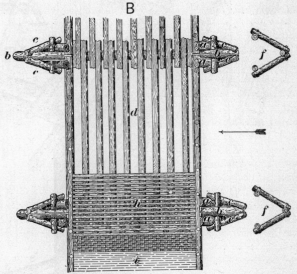

A. Cross-section.

B. The Bridge seen from above.

PLATE VI

CAESAR'S BRIDGE ACROSS THE RHINE

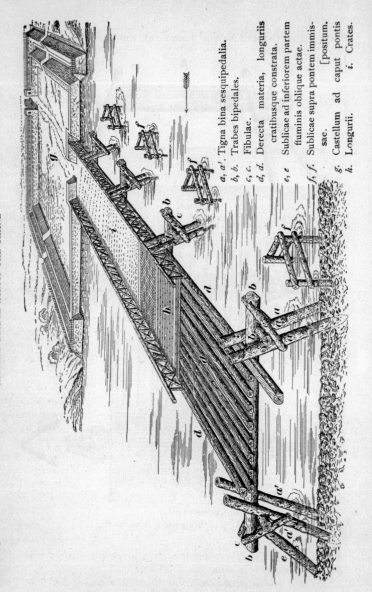

a, a'. Tigna bina sesquipedalia.
b, b. Trabes bipedales.
c, c. Fibulae.
d, d. Derecta materia, longuriis cratibusque constrata.
e, e. Sublicae ad inferiorem partem fluminis oblique actae.
f, f. Sublicae supra pontem immissae. [positum.
g. Castellum ad caput pontis
h. Longurii. i. Crates.

atque in contrāriam partem revinctīs, tanta erat operis
firmitūdō atque ea rērum nātūra, ut, quō maior vīs aquae
sē incitāvisset, hōc artius illigāta tenērentur.

Haec dērēctā māteriā iniectā contexēbantur ac longuriīs
crātibusque cōnsternēbantur; ac nihilō sētius sublicae et 25
ad īnferiōrem partem flūminis oblīquē agēbantur, quae, prō
ariete subiectae et cum omnī opere coniūnctae, vim flūminis

---

distance) 'apart, and were braced in opposite directions,' the lower posts
slanting upstream, the upper posts slanting downstream.   How lit.?
144, b, (3).

22. **ea rērum nātūra**: 'such the character of the structure' as a
whole.   How lit.?   **quō**, etc.: 'the greater the force of the water
rushing against it.'   *220.*   How lit.?   **quō . . . hōc**: *140.*   B. 223;
A. 414, *a*; H. 471, 10.

23. **hōc**, etc.: 'the more closely they' (the opposite pairs of posts,
tigna) 'were tied and held together.'   **illigāta**: *228, a.*

24. **Haec**: 'These piers,' each pier formed by fastening the sill, two
feet thick, securely to the pair of posts at either end.   **dērēctā**: 'in
the direction of the bridge.'   How lit.?   **māteriā iniectā**: 'by laying timber,' i.e. girders, **d** on the Plates; these were, of course, at right
angles with the direction of the current.   *92, b,* and *144, b,* (6).   **contexēbantur**: 'were joined.'   As the bridge was designed to carry a
moving load of cavalry and draft animals as well as infantry, and was
obviously built hastily of rough timbers, with a wide margin of safety, we
may suppose that the length of the girders between the sills was not more
than 25 English feet, possibly not more than 20 feet; the number of piers
was probably between sixty and seventy.   **longuriīs**: 'joists,' laid on
the girders, in the direction of the current; marked **h** on the Plates.

25. **crātibus**: 'wickerwork,' woven of supple branches, laid over
the joists and taking the place of the planks on a modern bridge;
marked **i** on the Plates.   **cōnsternēbantur**: 'were covered.'   **nihilō sētius**: 'nevertheless,' in order still further to assure the safety
of the bridge.   *140.*   **et**: 'also.'

26. **ad**, etc.: 'on the down-stream side.'   How lit.?   **oblīquē
agēbantur**: 'were driven with a slant'; these piles, slanting upstream,
braced the piers against the force of the current; marked **e** on the
Plates.   **quae**: 'in order that they.'   *193, a.*

27. **prō ariete subiectae**: 'set below as props.'   *10, e.*   How lit.?

exciperent; et aliae item suprā pontem mediocrī spatiō, ut,
sī arborum truncī sīve nāvēs dēiciendī operis causā essent
30 ā barbarīs missae, hīs dēfēnsōribus eārum rērum vīs minuerētur, neu pontī nocērent.

*Entering Germany, he finds some tribes submissive ; but the
Sugambrians flee.*

18. Diēbus x, quibus māteria coepta erat comportārī,
omnī opere effectō, exercitus trādūcitur. Caesar, ad utramque partem pontis firmō praesidiō relīctō, in fīnēs Sugambrōrum contendit.

5   Interim ā complūribus cīvitātibus ad eum lēgātī veniunt;
quibus, pācem atque amīcitiam petentibus, līberāliter respondit obsidēsque ad sē addūcī iubet. At Sugambrī ex

---

28. **aliae**: *aliae sublicae agēbantur*, marked **f f** on the Plates.
These vertical piles protected the bridge against floating logs or other
objects in the current liable to damage it.   **mediocrī spatiō**: 'a
short distance.' *140*.

29. **truncī**: 'tree-trunks.' *81*.   **nāvēs**: barges loaded with stones
or earth are probably meant.   **operis**: 'the structure.' *230*, (1).
essent missae: *220*.

30. **hīs dēfēnsōribus**: ablative absolute, = *hīs dēfendentibus*, *hīs*
being personified; trans. 'by these defenses.'   **eārum rērum**: tree-
trunks and weighted barges.

31. **neu**: 'and not'; lit. 'or not.' *196*, *b*.

18. 1. **Diēbus X, quibus**: 'Within ten days after.' *147*, *a*.
comportārī: *72*, *c*. The rapidity and skill with which the bridge was
built bear witness to Caesar's genius in practical affairs as well as to
the efficiency of his engineers and mechanics. *310*, *b*.

3. **partem**: we should say 'end.'   **praesidiō relīctō**: 'having
left,' etc. *144*, *b*, (2). Plate VI, **g**.   **Sugambrōrum**: the German
end of the bridge led into the country of the Ubians; north of the
Ubians were the Sugambrians. See Map at the end of the volume.

6. **quibus**: dative.   **līberāliter respondit**: 'be returned a gracious answer.' How lit.? *175*, *b*.

7. **At**: *236*, *a*.   **ex**: 'immediately after.'

eō tempore, quō pōns īnstituī coeptus est, fugā comparātā, hortantibus eīs, quōs ex Tencterīs atque Usipetibus apud sē habēbant, fīnibus suīs excesserant suaque omnia expor- 10 tāverant sēque in sōlitūdinem ac silvās abdiderant.

He ravages the country of the Sugambrians, encourages the Ubians, and returns to Gaul.

19. Caesar, paucōs diēs in eōrum fīnibus morātus, omnibus vīcīs aedificiīsque incēnsīs frūmentīsque succīsīs, sē in fīnēs Ubiōrum recēpit; atque hīs auxilium suum pollicitus, sī ab Suēbīs premerentur, haec ab eīs cognōvit:

Suēbōs, posteā quam per explōrātōrēs pontem fierī compe- 5 rissent, mōre suō conciliō habitō, nūntiōs in omnēs partēs dīmīsisse, utī dē oppidīs dēmigrārent, līberōs, uxōrēs suaque omnia in silvīs dēpōnerent, atque omnēs, quī arma ferre possent, ūnum in locum convenīrent; hunc esse dēlēctum

---

8. **eō**: 'the.' *160, d.*　　**fugā comparātā**: 'taking to flight.' How lit.?

9. **hortantibus eīs**: 'at the instigation of those.'　From chap. 15, ll. 1–6, it might be inferred that few of the Tencteri and the Usipetes escaped besides cavalry (chap. 16, ll. 7–11).

11. **exportāverant**: 'had carried away.'　　**in**: cf. N. to I, 12, l. 11; 'into the recesses of the forests.'

19. 1. **eōrum**: *Sugambrōrum.*　　**morātus**: *226, c.*

2. **vīcīs**, etc.: cf. I, 5, ll. 4–5 and Notes.　　**frūmentīs succīsīs**: 'cut down the standing grain and.'　How lit.?　*144, b, (2).*

4. **sī . . . premerentur**: indirect, from the idea of "saying" in *pollicitus*; future indicative in the direct form.　*213, b.*

5. **posteā quam**: with the indicative in the direct form.　*188, a.*

6. **mōre**: *136, c.*　　**nūntiōs**: 'messengers.'

7. **utī**, etc.: '(directing the people) to move away from the strongholds,' etc.; the substantive clauses give the gist of the instructions conveyed by the messengers.　*199, a.*

9. **hunc**: predicative after *dēlēctum esse*, with which *locum* is to be supplied as subject; 'that there had been chosen, as this (mustering point). a place.'

10 *medium ferē regiōnum eārum, quās Suēbī obtinērent ; hīc*
Rōmānōrum adventum exspectāre atque ibi dēcertāre cōn-
stituisse.

Quod ubi Caesar comperit, omnibus eīs rēbus cōnfectīs,
quārum rērum causā trādūcere exercitum cōnstituerat, ut
15 Germānīs metum iniceret, ut Sugambrōs ulcīscerētur, ut
Ubiōs obsidiōne līberāret, diēbus omnīnō XVIII trāns Rhēnum cōnsūmptīs, satis et ad laudem et ad ūtilitātem prōfectum arbitrātus, sē in Galliam recēpit pontemque rescidit.

First Expedition to Britain. 20–38

Caesar resolves to invade Britain ; he lacks information.

20. Exiguā parte aestātis reliquā, Caesar, etsī in hīs
locīs, quod omnis Gallia ad septentriōnēs vergit, mātūrae
sunt hiemēs, tamen in Britanniam proficīscī contendit, quod,

---

10. **medium ferē**: 'nearly (at) the center.'   **regiōnum**: *102.*

11. **exspectāre**: sc. *eōs (Suēbōs)*.   **ibi**: 'at that point.'

13. **Quod**: 'this fact.' *167.*   **eīs rēbus cōnfectīs**: 'having
accomplished the objects,' explained by the appositive *ut*-clauses following. *144, b,* (3). In reality Caesar accomplished very little by the
march into Germany. The formal enumeration which follows seems
intended to justify an expedition barren of tangible results.

14. **rērum**: *165, a.*   **ut**, etc.: *199, a.*

16. **obsidiōne**: 'from oppression '; the Ubii had been forced to pay
tribute to the Swabians (chap. 3, ll. 11–14). *127, a.*   **ut . . . lībe-**
rāret: 'to free.'   **XVIII**: *38, b,* and *36.*

17. **prōfectum** [esse]: the subject is *satis. 57, b.*

20. 1. **Exiguā . . . reliquā**: ablative absolute; 'As a small part,'
etc.; it was now near the end of July.

2. **omnis Gallia**: cf. I, 1, l. 1, and N.   **ad . . . vergit**: 'lies
toward the north,' in relation to the latitude of Italy; cf. Map 12.

3. **Britanniam**: *294.*   **quod . . . intellegēbat**: the aid given
by the Britains to the Venetans (III, 9, ll. 30–31) and to the other
Gauls, as for example to refugees from the Bellovaci (II, 14, ll. 3–9),
seems to have been of slight account; it furnished, however, a plausible
pretext for the invasion of Britain.

omnibus ferē Gallicīs bellīs, hostibus nostrīs inde sumministrāta auxilia intellegēbat et, sī tempus annī ad bellum ge- 5
rendum dēficeret, tamen magnō sibi ūsuī fore arbitrābātur,
sī modo īnsulam adīsset, genus hominum perspexisset, loca,
portūs, aditūs cognōvisset; quae omnia ferē Gallīs erant
incognita. Neque enim temere, praeter mercātōrēs, illō

Figure 107.— Foot of chalk cliffs north of Dover, at low tide.

---

4. **bellīs**: *147, b.*   **inde**: *ē Britanniā.*   **sumministrāta**: sc.
esse.

6. **dēficeret**: 'was insufficient.'   **sibi ūsuī fore**: *112, b.*   **arbitrābātur**: *183, a.*

7. **adīsset**: *adīret* might have been expected; Caesar conceives of
the expedition as an accomplished fact. *218, (1), b.*

8. **aditūs**: 'approaches'; points, outside the regular harbors, where
a landing could be made.   **quae omnia ferē**: 'for nearly all of
these things.' *167, and 97, c.*

9. **incognita**: the Venetans at least must have been informed about
Britain (III, 8, ll. 1–3), but they had been well-nigh exterminated; and
it was not to be expected that Gauls having the knowledge desired by
Caesar would be free in imparting it to him.   **Neque enim —
quisquam**: 'for no one.' *168.*   **temere**: 'without good reason';
only traders and students of Druidic theology (VI, 13, ll. 34–37) had
occasion to go to Britain.   **illō**: adverb.

10 adit quisquam, neque eīs ipsīs quicquam praeter ōram
maritimam atque eās regiōnēs, quae sunt contrā Galliās,
nōtum est.

Itaque vocātīs ad sē undique mercātōribus, neque quanta
esset īnsulae magnitūdō, neque quae aut quantae nātiōnēs
15 incolerent, neque quem ūsum bellī habērent aut quibus
īnstitūtīs ūterentur, neque quī essent ad maiōrem nāvium
multitūdinem idōneī portūs, reperīre poterat.

*He sends Volusenus to Britain and makes preparations ; he re-
ceives British envoys, and sends Commius also to Britain.*

21. Ad haec cognōscenda, prius quam perīculum faceret, idōneum esse arbitrātus C. Volusēnum cum nāvī longā
praemittit.　Huic mandat, ut, explōrātīs omnibus rēbus, ad
sē quam prīmum revertātur.

5　Ipse cum omnibus cōpiīs in Morinōs proficīscitur, quod
inde erat brevissimus in Britanniam trāiectus.　Hūc nāvēs

---

10. **neque . . . quicquam** : 'and nothing.'　　**eīs** : *108, a.*

11. **Galliās** : plural because referring to the different divisions ; we
should say, 'the (several) parts of Gaul.'

15. **incolerent** : sc. *eam. 204,* (2) and (3).　　**quem** : *48, b.*
ūsum bellī : 'methods of warfare.'　How lit.?

16. **ad . . . multitūdinem** : i.e. for a fleet, whose requirements
were very different from those of trading vessels coming to port singly
or in small numbers.

21. 1. **prius . . . faceret** : 'before making the attempt.' *189, b.*

2. **idōneum** : adj. in predicate ; trans. 'a suitable person.'　　**nāvī
longā** : *346, a.*

3. **praemittit** : sc. *eum.*　　**ut**, etc. : *199, a.*

4. **quam prīmum** : *153, c.*

6. **inde** : 'from their country.'　How lit.?　See Map 11.　　**in Britanniam** : after *trāiectus. 150, d.*　　**trāiectus** : 'passage.'　　**Hūc** :
to the vicinity of modern Boulogne.

7. **quam — classem** : = *eam classem, quam. 165, c.*　B. 251, 4, *a* ;
A. 307, *b* ; H. 399, 3.

undique ex finitimīs regiōnibus et, quam superiōre aestāte
ad Veneticum bellum effēcerat classem, iubet convenīre.

Interim, cōnsiliō eius cognitō et per mercātōrēs perlātō
ad Britannōs, ā complūribus insulae cīvitātibus ad eum 10
lēgātī veniunt, quī polliceantur obsidēs dare atque imperiō
populī Rōmānī obtemperāre. Quibus audītīs, līberāliter
pollicitus hortātusque, ut in eā sententiā permanērent, eōs
domum remittit; et cum eīs ūnā Commium, quem ipse,
Atrebātibus superātīs, rēgem ibi cōnstituerat, cuius et vir- 15
tūtem et cōnsilium probābat et quem sibi fidēlem esse
arbitrābātur, cuiusque auctōritās in hīs regiōnibus magnī
habēbātur, mittit. Huic imperat, quās possit, adeat cīvitā-
tes hortēturque, ut populī Rōmānī fidem sequantur, sēque
celeriter eō ventūrum nūntiet.   20

Volusēnus, perspectīs regiōnibus omnibus, quantum eī
facultātis darī potuit, quī nāvī ēgredī ac sē barbarīs committere nōn audēret, quīntō diē ad Caesarem revertitur,
quaeque ibi perspexisset, renūntiat.

---

8. **ad Veneticum bellum**: III, 11, ll. 13–16, and chaps. 14, 15.

11. **polliceantur**: *193, a.*   **dare**: i.e. *sē datūrōs esse. 178.*
imperiō obtemperāre: 'submit to the authority.' *105.*

15. **Atrebātibus**: conquered in the battle at the Sambre, two years
previously (II, 23, ll. 1–8).   **rēgem**: *115, a.*   **ibi**: among the
Atrebatians.   **virtūtem et cōnsilium**: 'energy and discretion.'

16. **probābat**: 'he appreciated.'   **fidēlem**: 'loyal.' Afterwards
Commius was disloyal to Caesar; cf. VII, chap. 75, ll. 22–26.

17. **magnī habēbātur**: 'was considered great,' lit. 'of great
(value).' *101.* B. 203, 3; A. 417; H. 448, 1.

18. **possit**: sc. *adīre.* Why subjunctive? *220.*   **adeat**: *200, a.*
B. 295, 8; A. 565, *a*; H. 565, 4.

19. **populī . . . sequantur**: 'fix their confidence in the Roman
people.' How lit.? *199, a.*   **sē**: Caesar.

21. **quantum facultātis**: 'so far as opportunity.' *97, b.*

22. **quī**: 'since he.' *194, c.*   **nāvī**: *14, b,* and *127, a.*

Opportunely he receives the submission of the Morini.   He assembles a fleet.

22. Dum in hīs locīs Caesar nāvium parandārum causā morātur, ex magnā parte Morinōrum ad eum lēgātī vēnērunt, quī sē dē superiōris temporis cōnsiliō excūsārent, quod, hominēs barbarī et nostrae cōnsuētūdinis imperītī, 5 bellum populō Rōmānō fēcissent, sēque ea, quae imperāsset, factūrōs pollicērentur.

Hōc sibi Caesar satis opportūnē accidisse arbitrātus, quod neque post tergum hostem relinquere volēbat neque bellī gerendī propter annī tempus facultātem habēbat neque 10 hās tantulārum rērum occupātiōnēs Britanniae antepōnendās iūdicābat, magnum eīs numerum obsidum imperat. Quibus adductīs, eōs in fidem recēpit.

Nāvibus circiter LXXX onerāriīs coāctīs contrāctīsque,

---

22. 1. **hīs locīs**: in the country of the Morini, probably in the vicinity of modern Boulogne.

2. **morātur**: *190, a.*   B. 293, 1 ; A. 556 ; H. 533, 4.

3. **quī sē . . . excūsārent, pollicērentur**: 'to offer excuse,' lit. 'excuse themselves,' etc. *193, a.*   **dē . . . cōnsiliō**: 'for their conduct the previous season,' 56 B.C. (III, chap. 28).

4. **quod . . . fēcissent**: 'because (as they said) they had made.' *183, a.*   **hominēs barbarī**: '(being) uncivilized people.' *91, b.* **cōnsuētūdinis**: sing., but trans.. 'usages'; the reference is particularly to the Roman practice of treating with consideration peoples that submitted to Roman rule. *102.*

5. **imperāsset**: *64, a,* (1), and *214, a.*

9. **annī tempus**: it was already August, too late in the season to enter upon an extended campaign.   **neque**, etc.: 'and he judged that the exactions of so trivial affairs ought not to have precedence over (the invasion of) Britain.' How lit.?

10. **hās**: *160, d.*   **tantulārum**: *76, c.*   **Britanniae**: *107, a.*

13. **Nāvibus onerāriīs**: 'transports'; these were sailing vessels, while the galleys were propelled by oars. *346, a.*   **LXXX**: *octōgintā. 38, b.*   **coāctīs contrāctīsque**: 'pressed into service and brought together' in a single harbor.

quot satis esse ad duās trānsportandās legiōnēs exīstimābat,
quod praetereā nāvium longārum habēbat, quaestōrī, lēgā- 15
tīs praefectīsque distribuit. Hūc accēdēbant XVIII onerāriae nāvēs, quae ex eō locō ā mīlibus passuum VIII ventō
tenēbantur, quō minus in eundem portum venīre possent;
hās equitibus distribuit.

Reliquum exercitum Q. Titūriō Sabīnō et L. Auruncu- 20
leiō Cottae lēgātīs in Menapiōs atque in eōs pāgōs Morinōrum, ā quibus ad eum lēgātī nōn vēnerant, dūcendum
dedit; P. Sulpicium Rūfum lēgātum cum eō praesidiō,
quod satis esse arbitrābātur, portum tenēre iussit.

---

14. **quot**: 'as many as.'   **duās legiōnēs**: the 7th and the 10th.
The smallness of the force is consistent with Caesar's statement that
the purpose of the expedition was not conquest but the obtaining of
information.   If the two legions, after three years of hard fighting, contained each about 3600 men (*307*, *b*) fit for service, the total of 7200
men divided up among the 80 transports would have averaged 90 men
to a ship.   The vessels were not large; and the supplies, not merely
provisions but tents and other equipment, must have taken up much room.

15. **quod nāvium longārum**: 'the galleys which'; lit. 'what of
long ships.'   *97*, *b*.   **quaestōrī**: *313*, *b*.

16. **praefectīs**: 'subsidiary officers.'   The galleys seem also to
have carried slingers, bowmen, and artillery (chap. 25).   **Hūc accēdēbant**: 'In addition to this number there were.'   How lit.?   *90*, *b*.

17. **eō locō**: portus Itius, now Boulogne; see Map 11.   **ā**: 'off.'
The small harbor eight Roman miles up the coast, where the 18 transports were detained, is now called Ambleteuse.   Map 11 **A**.

18. **quō minus**: 'so that . . . not.'   *201*, *a*.   **eundem portum**:
portus Itius.

19. **equitibus**: the cavalry contingents of the two legions, 500 or
600 horsemen in all.   *309*, *a*.   **equitibus distribuit**: the horsemen
could more easily go across the country to the smaller harbor (chap.
23, ll. 2–3).

20. **Reliquum exercitum**: five legions, if we assume that one
legion was assigned to duty at the harbor; for Caesar had eight legions
in all, and only two were required for the expedition.

21. **in — dūcendum**: 'for operations against.'   How lit ?   *229*, *b*.

23. **eō praesidiō, quod**: = *tantō praesidiō, quantum*.

Caesar sails to Britain, and makes preparation to land.

23. Hīs cōnstitūtīs rēbus, nactus idōneam ad nāvigandum tempestātem, tertiā ferē vigiliā solvit equitēsque in
ulteriōrem portum prōgredī et nāvēs cōnscendere et sē
sequī iussit. Ā quibus cum paulō tardius esset adminis-
5 trātum, ipse hōrā diēī circiter quārtā cum prīmīs nāvibus
Britanniam attigit, atque ibi in omnibus collibus expositās
hostium cōpiās armātās cōnspexit.

Cuius locī haec erat nātūra, atque ita montibus angustīs
mare continēbātur, utī ex locīs superiōribus in lītus tēlum
10 adigī posset. Hunc ad ēgrediendum nēquāquam idōneum

---

23. 1. **nactus**: *61, a*, (3), and *226, c.*

2. **tempestātem**: 'weather.' As might be inferred from its derivation from *tempus*, 'time,' *tempestās* may imply good or bad weather
according to the connection. We use "time" similarly in "a good
time," "a bad time." **tertiā ferē vigiliā**: 'about the third watch';
indefinite because the embarkation must have taken two or three hours.
242, c. **solvit**: sc. *nāvēs*, 'got under way,' from Boulogne. The
date was probably August 26.

3. **ulteriōrem portum**: Ambleteuse, northeast of Boulogne (chap.
22, l. 17). **prōgredī**: i.e. by land. **nāvēs cōnscendere**: 'to
embark.'

4. **quibus**: 'them,' the cavalry. *167.* **paulō tardius**: 'with a
little too much delay,' probably due to the difficulty of getting the horses
aboard. *153, a.* **esset administrātum**: 'the orders were carried
out.' How lit.? *73, d.*

5. **hōrā quārtā**: the beginning of 'the fourth hour' on August 26
in the latitude of Dover by Roman reckoning was about 8.30 A.M. by
our time. *242, b.*

6. **Britanniam attigit**: 'reached Britain,' near Dover; see Map
11. **expositās**: 'arrayed.'

8. **haec**: 'such.' **ita**, etc : 'the sea was so closely bordered by
abrupt cliffs'; *angustīs*, lit. 'narrow,' implies sharp outlines, as seen
from the sea, and an abrupt descent. The chalk cliffs neai Dover run
almost straight up from the water's edge. (See Figures 107, 108, 110,
and Plate VIII.)

9. **locīs superiōribus**: the top of the cliffs. **lītus**: 'shore.' *13, f.*

locum arbitrātus, dum reliquae nāvēs eō convenīrent, ad hōram nōnam in ancorīs exspectāvit.

Interim lēgātīs tribūnīsque mīlitum convocātīs, et quae ex Volusēnō cognōvisset, et quae fierī vellet, ostendit, monuitque, ut reī mīlitāris ratiō, maximē ut maritimae rēs 15 postulārent, ut, cum celerem atque īnstabilem mōtum habērent, ad nūtum et ad tempus omnēs rēs ab eīs admi-

Figure 108. — St. Margaret's Bay, passed by Caesar in his search for a landing place.

11. **convenīrent**: *190, b.* B. 293, III, 2 ; A. 553 ; H. 603, II, 2.

12. **hōram nōnam**: the beginning of the ninth hour was about 2.20 P.M. by our time. *242, b.* **in ancorīs**: 'at anchor.' The ancient anchors were like those of to-day.

13. **tribūnīs mīlitum**: *314.* **et . . . et**: *233, a.* **quae**: *204*, (2). The information derived from Volusenus was probably to the effect that there was a good landing place further up the coast.

15. **ut . . . postulārent**: 'as military practice, above all, as marine service required.' *220.* How lit.?

16. **ut . . . omnēs**, etc.: after *monuit*; 'that all orders be executed.' *199, a.* **cum**, etc.: 'since (these conditions) involved quick and unsteady movement.'

17. **ad nūtum**: 'on the instant.' How lit.? **ad tempus**: 'at the (right) time.'

nistrārentur. Hīs dīmissīs, et ventum et aestum ūnō tempore nactus secundum, datō signō et sublātīs ancorīs,
20 circiter mīlia passuum VII ab eō locō prōgressus, apertō
ac plānō lītore nāvēs cōnstituit.

The legionaries attempt to land; the Britons resist fiercely.

24. At barbarī, cōnsiliō Rōmānōrum cognitō, praemissō
equitātū et essedāriīs, quō plērumque genere in proeliīs
ūtī cōnsuērunt, reliquīs cōpiīs subsecūtī, nostrōs nāvibus
5 ēgredī prohibēbant.

Erat ob hās causās summa difficultās, quod nāvēs propter
magnitūdinem, nisi in altō, cōnstituī nōn poterant; mīlitibus
autem, ignōtīs locīs, impedītīs manibus, magnō et gravī
onere armōrum oppressīs, simul et dē nāvibus dēsiliendum
10 et in fluctibus cōnsistendum et cum hostibus erat pugnan-
dum, cum illī, aut ex āridō aut paulum in aquam prōgressī,

---

19. **secundum**: 'favorable,' both wind and tide bearing toward the
northeast.

20. **eō locō**: Dover.　　**prōgressus**: *226, c.*　　**apertō ac plānō
lītore**: between Walmer and Deal, about seven miles northeast of
Dover. *145, c.*

21. **nāvēs cōnstituit**: 'he ran the ships aground.' How lit.?

24. 2. **essedāriīs**: 'chariot-fighters,' described in chap. 33.　　**quō
genere**: 'a type (of warrior) which.' *165, b.*

3. **cōpiīs**: the Britons followed by land, as near the shore as possible. *137, b.*　　**nāvibus ēgredī**: 'from disembarking.' *223, a,* and
127, a.

5. **Erat**: *90, a.*　　**hās**: refers to what follows. *161, a.*

6. **in altō**: 'in deep (water).' *154, a.*　　**cōnstituī**: 'be grounded,'
so as to remain firm.　　**mīlitibus . . . dēsiliendum** [erat]: 'the
soldiers . . . had to jump down.' How lit.? *73, e,* and *110.*

7. **ignōtīs locīs**: '(being) on unfamiliar ground.' How lit.? *145, c.*

8. **oppressīs**: agrees with *mīlitibus;* 'weighed down.'　　**et . . .
et . . . et**: *238, f.*

10. **cum**: 'while.' *187.*　　**illī**: *Britannī.*　　**ex āridō**: 'from
dry land.'

omnibus membrīs expedītīs, nōtissimīs locīs, audācter tēla
conicerent et equōs īnsuēfactōs incitārent.   Quibus rēbus
nostrī perterritī, atque huius omnīnō generis pugnae imperītī, nōn eādem alacritāte ac studiō, quō in pedestribus ūtī
proeliīs cōnsuērant, ūtēbantur.   15

*The standard-bearer of the Tenth leaps overboard, bidding the
others follow.*

25. Quod ubi Caesar animadvertit, nāvēs longās, quārum
et speciēs erat barbarīs inūsitātior et mōtus ad ūsum ex-

---

11. **nōtissimīs locīs**: 'thoroughly acquainted with the ground.
How lit.?   *153, a*, and *144, b*, (2).
audācter, etc.: the British were provided with weapons much like those
of the Gauls (Fig. 109).

12. **īnsuēfactōs**: 'trained' to go
into the water.

13. **generis**: with *imperītī*.   *102.*
B. 204, 1 ; A. 349, *a* ; H. 451, 1.

14. **eādem** : *150, a.*   **quō** :
163, c.   **pedestribus** : i.e. *terres-
tribus,* 'on land.'

15. **ūtēbantur** : 'were displaying.'

25. 1. **Quod** : 'Now . . . this.'
167.   **animadvertit** : *188, a.*

2. **speciēs** : 'appearance.'   *80, b.*
inūsitātior : 'less familiar.'   Oar-
driven galleys were not so well
adapted to withstand the buffetings
of northern waters as solidly built
sailing vessels, such as those of the
Venetans (III, chap. 13–14).   **ad
ūsum** : i.e. *ad nāvigandum;* 'the
movement was more easily controlled.'   How lit.?   The galleys
could be driven faster, and in any
direction.

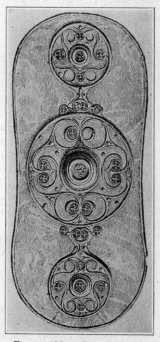

Figure 109. — British shield.
Of bronze, enamelled; found in the
Thames, near London.

peditior, paulum removērī ab onerāriīs nāvibus et rēmīs
incitārī et ad latus apertum hostium cōnstituī, atque inde
5 fundīs, sagittīs, tormentīs hostēs prōpellī ac summovērī
iussit; quae rēs magnō ūsuī nostrīs fuit. Nam, et nāvium
figūrā et rēmōrum mōtū et inūsitātō genere tormentōrum
permōtī, barbarī cōnstitērunt ac paulum modo pedem rettu-
lērunt.

10 Atque nostrīs mīlitibus cunctantibus, maximē propter altitūdinem maris, quī decimae legiōnis aquilam ferēbat, obtestātus deōs, ut ea rēs legiōnī fēlīciter ēvenīret, 'Dēsilīte,'
inquit, 'commīlitōnēs, nisi vultis aquilam hostibus
prōdere; ego certē meum reī pūblicae atque
15 imperātōrī officium praestiterō.'

---

4. **ad latus apertum**: 'over against the exposed flank,' the
right flank of the enemy. The galleys were to be placed parallel with
the shore.   **inde**: = *ē nāvibus longīs*.

5. **fundīs**: 'with slings,' which hurled slingshots of lead when this
material was available; such slingshots were sometimes inscribed (N. to
II, 10, l. 2.).   **sagittīs**: 'arrows.' *308*.   **tormentīs**: 'artillery';
our word "artillery" was applied to engines of war, whose propelling
force was derived from tension, before it came to be restricted to cannon,
which derive their propelling force from explosives. The *'torsioners'*
used on the galleys were probably small catapults, which Caesar elsewhere calls 'scorpions' (*343*, *a*).

6. **quae rēs**: 'and this manoeuver.'   **ūsuī**: *112*, *b*.

7. **figūrā**: the galleys were relatively long, narrow, and low.

8. **paulum modo**: 'just a little,' from the water's edge.

10. **altitūdinem**: the sailing vessels which had been run aground
on the sandy bottom formed a line, irregular because of the variation in
depth, at least two thirds of a mile long; the water where the bows
were driven into the sand was probably up to the soldiers' necks.

11. **quī**: as antecedent sc. *is*, subject of *inquit*.   **aquilam**:
'eagle.' *324*, *b*, (1).   **obtestātus**, etc.: 'praying the gods that his
effort might turn out fortunately for the legion.' *199*, *a*.

13. **commīlitōnēs**: 'fellow-soldiers.' *93*.   **vultis**: *71*.

14. **ego**: *87*, *b*.   **certē**: 'at any rate.'

15. **praestiterō**: *176*, *c*.

Hōc cum vōce magnā dīxisset, sē ex nāvī prōiēcit atque
in hostēs aquilam ferre coepit.   Tum nostrī, cohortātī inter
sē, nē tantum dēdecus admitterētur, ūniversī ex nāvī
dēsiluērunt.   Hōs item ex proximīs prīmī nāvibus cum
cōnspexiṣent, subsecūtī hostibus appropinquārunt.   2c

Finally the Romans force the enemy back, and land.

26. Pugnātum est ab utrīsque ācriter.   Nostrī tamen,
quod neque ōrdinēs servāre neque fīrmiter īnsistere neque
signa subsequī poterant, atque alius aliā ex nāvī, quibuscumque signīs occurrerat, sē aggregābat, magnopere perturbābantur; hostēs vērō, nōtīs omnibus vadīs, ubi ex 5
lītore aliquōs singulārēs ex nāvī ēgredientēs cōnspexerant,
incitātīs equīs impedītōs adoriēbantur, plūrēs paucōs circumsistēbant, aliī ab latere apertō in ūniversōs tēla coniciēbant.

---

16. **cum**: *185, c.*   **vōce**: *136, b.*   **magnā**: 'loud.'

17. **cohortātī inter sē**: *159* and *226, c.*

18. **dēdecus**: 'disgrace,' the loss of the eagle of the legion.   *13, f.*
ūniversī: 'all together.'

20. **subsecūtī**: 'they followed and.' How lit.? *228, a.*   **appropinquārunt**: *64, a,* (1).

26. 1. **Pugnātum**, etc.: 'sharp fighting was kept up by both sides.'
How lit.?   **utrīsque**: *51.*

2. **ōrdinēs servāre**: 'to keep the ranks.'   **fīrmiter īnsistere**:
'to get a firm footing.'

3. **signa**: *324, b,* (2).   **alius**, etc.: 'one from this ship, another
from that.' *171, c.*   **quibuscumque . . . aggregābat**: 'they were
joining any standards that they had fallen in with.' How lit.? *50, a.*

6. **singulārēs**: 'one by one.'   **cōnspexerant**: *188, d.*

7. **incitātīs equīs**: 'urging their horses forward.' *144, b,* (2).
adoriēbantur: 'they would attack.' *175, d.*   **plūrēs paucōs**:
plūrēs hostēs paucōs Rōmānōs.

8. **ab latere apertō**: 'on the exposed flank,' the right side, unprotected by a shield.   **ūniversōs**: 'groups of soldiers,' contrasted with
the individuals referred to in l. 6.

10 Quod cum animadvertisset Caesar, scaphās longārum
nāvium, item speculātōria nāvigia, mīlitibus complērī iussit
et, quōs labōrantēs cōnspexerat, hīs subsidia summittēbat.
Nostrī, simul in āridō cōnstitērunt, suīs omnibus cōnsecūtīs,
in hostēs impetum fēcērunt atque eōs in fugam dedērunt;
15 neque longius prōsequī potuērunt, quod equitēs cursum
tenēre atque īnsulam capere nōn potuerant. Hōc ūnum
ad prīstinam fortūnam Caesarī dēfuit.

The Britons offer to submit, and return Commius to Caesar.

27. Hostēs proeliō superātī, simul atque sē ex fugā
recēpērunt, statim ad Caesarem lēgātōs dē pāce mīsērunt; obsidēs sēsē datūrōs, quaeque imperāsset, factūrōs
pollicitī sunt. Ūnā cum hīs lēgātīs Commius Atrebās
5 vēnit, quem suprā dēmōnstrāveram ā Caesare in Britanniam praemissum. Hunc illī ē nāvī ēgressum, cum ad
eōs ōrātōris modō Caesaris mandāta dēferret, comprehen-
derant atque in vincula coniēcerant; tum, proeliō factō,

---

10. **scaphās**: 'small boats,' carried on the galleys.

11. **speculātōria nāvigia**: 'scouting vessels,' smaller and lighter
than the galleys, without a beak, and designed for rapid movement.

13. **in āridō**: 'on dry ground.' *154, a.* **cōnstitērunt**:
188, a.

15. **neque**: 'but . . . not.' **equitēs**: still at Ambleteuse (chap.
23, l. 4).

16. **īnsulam capere**: 'to make the island.' **Hōc**, etc.: 'in this
respect only was Caesar's usual good fortune incomplete.' How lit.?

27. 2. **recēpērunt**: *188, a.* **statim**: *77.* **lēgātōs**: 'envoys.'

3. **datūrōs**: *89, c.* **quaeque**, etc.: i.e. *et ea, quae imperāvisset,
factūrōs esse. 214, a.*

5. **suprā**: chap. 21, ll. 14–20. **dēmōnstrāveram**: cf. II, 1, l. 2,
and N.

7. **ōrātōris modō**: 'in the character of an envoy,' lit. 'of a pleader.'
80, b.

8. **proeliō factō**: i.e. *post hōc proelium. 144, b, (2).*

remīsērunt.   In petendā pāce eius reī culpam in multitūdinem contulērunt et, propter imprūdentiam ut ignōscerē- 10
tur, petīvērunt.

Caesar questus, quod, cum ultrō, in continentem lēgātīs
missīs, pācem ab sē petīssent, bellum sine causā intulissent,
ignōscere sē imprūdentiae dīxit obsidēsque imperāvit;

Figure 110. — Cliffs on the English coast, north of Dover.

9. **remīsērunt**: sc. *eum*.   **eius reī**: i.e. *quod Commius, ōrātor
Caesaris, comprehēnsus atque in vincula coniectus erat.*

10. **imprūdentiam**: 'lack of knowledge.'   **ignōscerētur**: sc.
sibi, 'that pardon be granted them.' *199, a,* and *106, b.*

12. **questus**: *226, c.*   **quod . . . intulissent**: 'because (as
he said) they had,' etc. *183, a.* B. 286, 1; A. 540; H. 588, II.   **continentem**: 'the continent,' Gaul.

13. **petīssent**: *187.*   **sine causā**: from the Roman point of view;
but the Romans would have considered the defence of the shores of
Italy against an armed force a most noble action. Thus conditions
alter opinions. In 1916 many Mexicans considered the presence of the
American punitive expedition in Mexico as a hostile invasion.

14. **ignōscere sē**: 'that he would pardon.'   **imprūdentiae**: *105.*

15 quōrum illī partem statim dedērunt, partem, ex longinqui-
ōribus locīs arcessītam, paucīs diēbus sēsē datūrōs dīxērunt.
Intereā suōs remigrāre in agrōs iussērunt, prīncipēsque
undique convenīre et sē cīvitātēsque suās Caesarī commendāre coepērunt.

The ships with the cavalry are prevented from landing by a storm.

28. Hīs rēbus pāce cōnfirmātā, post diem quārtum,
quam est in Britanniam ventum, nāvēs XVIII, dē quibus
suprā dēmōnstrātum est, quae equitēs sustulerant, ex
superiōre portū lēnī ventō solvērunt.

5   Quae cum appropinquārent Britanniae et ex castrīs vidērentur, tanta tempestās subitō coorta est, ut nūlla eārum
cursum tenēre posset, sed aliae eōdem, unde erant profectae, referrentur, aliae ad īnferiōrem partem īnsulae, quae

---

16. **arcessītam**: i.e. *cum ea* (*pars*) *arcessīta esset.* *227, a,* (1).

17. **suōs**: 'their people'; the demobilization of the British host
was ordered.   **iussērunt**: sc. *eī*, the British envoys.

18. **convenīre**: *ad Caesarem.*   **Caesarī commendāre**: 'to put
under Caesar's protection.'

28. 1. **Hīs rēbus**: the giving of hostages, the demobilization of
the British host, and the presence of British leaders in Caesar's camp.
post — quam: = *quārtō diē postquam,* 'three days after' by our reckoning; cf. chap. 9, l. 2, and N.

2. **est ventum**: *73, d.*

3. **suprā**: chap. 22, ll. 16-19.   **sustulerant**: 'had taken on
board.'

4. **superiōre portū**: Ambleteuse.   **lēnī ventō**: 'with a light
breeze,' blowing north or northeast. *138.*   **solvērunt**: 'sailed.'

5.   **ex castrīs**: Caesar's camp was on rising ground, not far from
the shore, so that it commanded a wide view of the sea.   **vidērentur**: trans. as passive.

6. **tempestās**: 'storm,' a northeaster. Cf. N. to chap. 23, l. 2.

7. **aliae . . . aliae**: *171, b.*   **eōdem**, etc.: Ambleteuse.

8. **referrentur**: sc. *ut.*   **ad . . . occāsum**: southwest from
Caesar's landing-place. See Map 11, **A.**

est propius sōlis occāsum, magnō suō cum perīculō dēicerentur; quae, tamen ancorīs iactīs, cum fluctibus complē- 10
rentur, necessāriō adversā nocte in altum prōvectae continentem petiērunt.

The fleet on the British shore is wrecked by a high tide.

29. Eādem nocte accidit, ut esset lūna plēna, quī diēs
maritimōs aestūs maximōs in Ōceanō efficere cōnsuēvit,
nostrīsque id erat incognitum. Ita ūnō tempore et longās
nāvēs, quibus Caesar exercitum trānsportandum cūrāverat,
quāsque in āridum subdūxerat, aestus complēbat, et one- 5
rāriās, quae ad ancorās erant dēligātae, tempestās afflictā-
bat, neque ūlla nostrīs facultās aut administrandī aut
auxiliandī dabātur.

Complūribus nāvibus frāctīs, reliquae cum essent — fūni-

---

9. **propius** : *123, b.* B. 141, 3; A. 432, *a*; H. 420, 5.   **suō** : 'to
themselves.' How lit.?   **dēicerentur** : 'were driven.' *57, b.*

10. **quae . . . cum** : 'nevertheless they anchored and when they.'
How lit.? *167,* and *144, b,* (2).

11. **adversā nocte** : 'in the face of the night,' a form of expression
transferred from space (as *adversō colle, 134, a*) to time.   **in altum
prōvectae** : 'they put out to sea and.' How lit.? *226, c,* and *228, a.*

29. 1. **eādem nocte** : the night of August 30, as determined by
astronomical calculations.   **accidit . . . plēna** : 'it happened to be
full moon.' How lit.?   **quī diēs** : 'and this date.'

2. **aestūs . . . incognitum** : the rise and fall of the tide in the
Mediterranean, as in our Great Lakes, is hardly perceptible. Caesar's
men had learned of the existence of tides in the Ocean the previous
year (III, chap. 12); what they had failed to notice was the coinci-
dence of the highest tides with the time of the full moon. At Dover
the highest tide rises about 19 feet; at Boulogne, 25 feet.

4. **exercitum**, etc. : 'had had the army brought over.' *229, b.*

7. **administrandī** : 'of managing' the vessels, the crews being on
shore.

8. **auxiliandī** : by getting men on to the ships.

9. **fūnibus . . . āmissīs** : 'on account of the loss of,' etc. *144,
b,* (3).

10 bus, ancorīs reliquīsque armāmentīs āmissīs — ad nāvigandum inūtilēs, magna, id quod necesse erat accidere, tōtīus
exercitūs perturbātiō facta est. Neque enim nāvēs erant
aliae, quibus reportārī possent, et omnia deerant, quae ad
reficiendās nāvēs erant ūsuī, et quod omnibus cōnstābat,
15 hiemārī in Galliā oportēre, frūmentum in hīs locīs in
hiemem prōvīsum nōn erat.

The Britons, learning of the disaster, secretly plan a revolt.

30. Quibus rēbus cognitīs, prīncipēs Britanniae, quī post
proelium ad Caesarem convēnerant, inter sē collocūtī, cum
equitēs et nāvēs et frūmentum Rōmānīs deesse intellegerent, et paucitātem mīlitum ex castrōrum exiguitāte cognōs-
5 cerent, quae hōc erant etiam angustiōra, quod sine impedīmentīs Caesar legiōnēs trānsportāverat, optimum factū
esse dūxērunt, rebelliōne factā, frūmentō commeātūque nostrōs prohibēre et rem in hiemem prōdūcere; quod, hīs

---

11. **magna**: with *perturbātiō*; emphatic. *353, d.* **id**, etc.: 'as
was bound to happen.' How lit.? *160, c.*

12. **perturbātiō**: 'commotion.' **Neque**, etc.: 'for there were
no other ships.' *90, a.* How lit.?

13. **reportārī**: 'be carried back.' **possent**: *194, a.*

14. **ūsuī**: trans. as if *ūtilia*. *112, a.* **cōnstābat**, etc.: 'it was
clear that they would have to winter.' How lit.?

15. **hīs locīs**: in Britain. **in hiemem**: 'for the winter.' *12, a.*
Rations had been taken for only a limited stay in Britain.

30. 2. **inter sē collocūtī**: *159.* B. 245, 1; A. 301, *f*; H. 502, 1.

5. **quae erant**: 'which was.' **hōc etiam angustiōra**: 'even
smaller (than usual for two legions) for this reason,' explained by the
quod-clause. **impedīmentīs**: left in Gaul. *311.*

6. **optimum factū esse**: 'that the best thing to do was.' How
lit.? **optimum**: in predicate, after *esse*. *148, d.* **factū**: *232.*

7. **dūxērunt**: 'decided'; the subject is *prīncipēs* in l. 1. **rebelliōne factā**: 'renewing hostilities.' How lit? *144, b, (2).* **frūmentō**: *127, a.*

8. **rem**: 'their operations.' **hīs**, etc.: 'if these (invaders) should
be,' etc. *144, b, (4).*

superātīs aut reditū interclūsīs, nēminem posteā bellī īnferendī causā in Britanniam trānsitūrum cōnfīdēbant.　　10

Itaque, rūrsus coniūrātiōne factā, paulātim ex castrīs
discēdere ac suōs clam ex agrīs dēdūcere coepērunt.

Caesar, anticipating trouble, gathers supplies and hastens repairs
on the ships.

31. At Caesar, etsī nōndum eōrum cōnsilia cognōverat,
tamen et ex eventū nāvium suārum, et ex eō, quod obsidēs
dare intermīserant, fore id, quod accidit, suspicābātur.

Itaque ad omnēs cāsūs subsidia comparābat.　Nam et
frūmentum ex agrīs cotīdiē in castra cōnferēbat et, quae 5
gravissimē afflīctae erant nāvēs, eārum māteriā atque aere
ad reliquās reficiendās ūtēbātur et, quae ad eās rēs erant
ūsuī, ex continentī comportārī iubēbat.　　Itaque, cum

---

9. **reditū**: 'return.' *127, a.*　　**posteā**: 'in the future.'

11. **paulātim**: one or two at a time.　That the British leaders were
assembled in the Roman camp is
clear from ll. 1–2.

31. 1. **cognōverat**: 'was familiar
with.' *176, b.*

2. **ex . . . suārum**: 'from what
had happened to his ships.'　How
lit.?　　**ex eō, quod**: 'from the fact
that.' *198, b.*

4. **ad . . . comparābat**: 'he was
providing for every emergency.'

5. **frūmentum**: from the new
harvest.　Later a head of wheat on
British coins became an appropriate
symbol of the island's staple crop
(Fig. 111).　　**quae . . . nāvēs, eārum**: = *eārum nāvium, quae.*
165, c.

Figure 111. — British coin.

Gold, struck within a century after
Caesar's invasions.　Inscription, CAMU-
[LODUNI], CUNO[BELINI], 'of Cunobelinus, at Camulodunum,' modern Col-
chester.

Cunobelinus was a British ruler, better
known under the name Cymbeline.

7. **quae**: as antecedent sc. *ea*, subject-accusative with *comportārī.*
ad eās rēs: 'for that purpose.'

summō studiō ā mīlitibus administrārētur, XII nāvibus
10 āmissīs, reliquīs ut nāvigārī commodē posset, effēcit.

The Britons make a treacherous attack, using war-chariots.

32. Dum ea geruntur, legiōne ex cōnsuētūdine ūnā
frūmentātum missā, quae appellābātur VII, neque ūllā ad id
tempus bellī suspīciōne interpositā, cum pars hominum in
agrīs remanēret, pars etiam in castra ventitāret, eī, quī prō
5 portīs castrōrum in statiōne erant, Caesarī nūntiāvērunt,
pulverem maiōrem, quam cōnsuētūdō ferret, in eā parte
vidērī, quam in partem legiō iter fēcisset. Caesar id, quod
erat, suspicātus, aliquid novī ā barbarīs initum cōnsiliī,
cohortēs, quae in statiōnibus erant, sēcum in eam partem

---

9. **summō studiō**: 'with the utmost enthusiasm.' **administrārētur**: 'the work was carried on.' *184, a.*

10. **reliquīs**, etc.: sc. *nāvibus* (*131, a*); 'he made it possible to
utilize the others fairly well for navigation.' How lit.? *203, (3)*.

32. 1. **geruntur**: *190, a.* **legiōne**: with *missā*.

2. **frūmentātum**: 'to get grain,' from the fields. *231, a.* VII:
septima. 38, a, and *36.* **neque**, etc.: 'without any suspicion of
hostilities up to that time.' How lit.?

3. **hominum**: *Britannōrum. 98, a.*

4. **ventitāret**: 'came frequently,' a frequentative from *veniō. 78, a.*
eī: *mīlitēs.*

5. **portīs castrōrum**: *334, a.* **in statiōne**: 'on guard.' *81.*

6. **pulverem**: '(a cloud of) dust.' *13, g.* **quam**, etc.: 'than
usual.' *197, c.* **parte**: 'direction.'

7. **quam in partem**: 'in which.' *165, a.* **quod erat**: 'which
was actually the case.'

8. **suspicātus**: *226, c.* **aliquid**, etc.: 'some new scheme had
been worked up.' How lit.? **aliquid**: *168,* and *49, a.* **initum**:
sc. *esse. 68, b* and *c.* **cōnsiliī**: *97, b.*

9. **cohortēs**: probably four in number, one at each of the four
gates of the camp. How many men? *307, c.* **in statiōnibus**:
'on guard'; plural because each gate was thought of as a separate
post.

proficīscī, ex reliquīs duās in statiōnem cohortēs succēdere, 10
reliquās armārī et cōnfestim sēsē subsequī iussit.

Cum paulō longius ā castrīs prōcessisset, suōs ab hostibus premī atque aegrē sustinēre et, cōnfertā legiōne, ex
omnibus partibus tēla conicī animadvertit. Nam quod,
omnī ex reliquīs partibus dēmessō frūmentō, pars ūna erat 15
reliqua, suspicātī hostēs, hūc nostrōs esse ventūrōs, noctū
in silvīs dēlituerant; tum dispersōs, dēpositīs armīs, in
metendō occupātōs subitō adortī, paucīs interfectīs reliquōs, incertīs ōrdinibus, perturbāverant, simul equitātū
atque essedīs circumdederant.   20

---

10. **reliquīs**: six cohorts, of the 10th legion. The four cohorts
on guard went with Caesar; two stood guard in their place, and the
last four cohorts of the legion were ordered to arm and follow Caesar
as soon as they could. *307, c.*   **in statiōnem succēdere**: 'to relieve guard.'

11. **armārī**: 'to arm,' lit. 'to arm themselves.' *174.*   **cōnfestim**: 'with all haste.'

12. **paulō longius**: 'some little distance.' *153, a.*   **suōs**: the
men of the 7th legion.

13. **aegrē sustinēre**: 'were holding their own with difficulty.'
cōnfertā legiōne: 'since the legion was crowded together.' *144, b,* (3).
The more closely the men stood the more effective were the missiles of
the enemy surrounding them.

14. **conicī**: sc. *in eam. 57, b.*

15. **dēmessō**: 'cut.' *144, b.* (3).   **ūna**: 'only one.'

17. **dēlituerant**: 'had hidden.'   **dispersōs, occupātōs**: sc.
eōs (= *nostrōs* of l. 16), object of *adortī.*   **dēpositīs armīs**: 'having laid aside their weapons.'

18. **in metendō**: 'in reaping.' *230,* (4).   **adortī**: *226, c.*

19. **incertīs ōrdinibus**: 'since their ranks were in disorder,' a
proper formation being impossible under the circumstances.

20. **essedīs**: 'with war chariots.' Scythed war chariots, with a
long sharp blade projecting from each end of the axle, were in use in
Oriental countries, but the British chariots to which Caesar refers were
apparently without scythes. Remains of chariot wheels have been found
in the graves of warriors.

The way the Britons use war-chariots in battle.

33. Genus hōc est ex essedīs pugnae :

Prīmō per omnēs partēs perequitant et tēla coniciunt,
atque ipsō terrōre equōrum et strepitū rotārum ōrdinēs plērumque perturbant; et cum sē inter equitum turmās īnsi-
5 nuāvērunt, ex essedīs dēsiliunt et pedibus proeliantur.

Aurīgae interim paulātim ex proeliō excēdunt, atque ita
currūs collocant, ut, sī illī ā multitūdine hostium premantur,
expedītum ad suōs receptum habeant.

---

33.   1. **ex essedīs**: with *pugnae*. *150, d.* B. 353, 5, N.

2. **per . . . perequitant**: sc. *essedāriī*; 'they' (the chariot-
fighters) 'ride everywhere.' Each chariot (Fig. 112) carried a driver

and one fighter. As the drivers
dashed against the enemy, the
men in the chariots sprang out
and fought on foot. The chariots
meanwhile withdrew a little
from the thick of the fight, so
that the drivers could see how
the battle was going. If they
saw their warriors defeated in
any part of the line they swiftly
drove thither, took on board
those hard pressed, and quickly
passed beyond the reach of
danger.

Figure 112. — British war chariot.

3. **terrōre equōrum**: 'fright caused by the horses'; subjective
genitive. *95.*   **ōrdinēs**: 'the ranks' of the enemy.

4. **sē . . . īnsinuāvērunt**: 'they have penetrated'; the British
cavalry were so deployed as to leave spaces through which the chariots
could be driven against the enemy.

5. **pedibus**: 'on foot.' *131, a.*

6. **Aurīgae**: 'the drivers.'   **ita . . . ut**: *197, b.*

7. **illī**: the chariot-fighters.   **premantur**: *220.*

8. **ad suōs**: 'to their own lines,' we should say.   **receptum**: 'a
retreat.'

Ita mōbilitātem equitum, stabilitātem peditum in proeliīs
praestant; ac tantum ūsū cotīdiānō et exercitātiōne efficiunt, 10
utī in dēclīvī ac praecipitī locō incitātōs equōs sustinēre
et brevī moderārī ac flectere, et per tēmōnem percurrere et
in iugō īnsistere, et sē inde in currūs citissimē recipere cōnsuērint.

Caesar brings aid; the Britons prepare to attack the camp.

34. Quibus rēbus perturbātīs nostrīs, novitāte pugnae,
tempore opportūnissimō Caesar auxilium tulit; namque eius
adventū hostēs cōnstitērunt, nostrī sē ex timōre recēpērunt.
Quō factō, ad lacessendum hostem et ad committendum
proelium aliēnum esse tempus arbitrātus, suō sē locō con- 5
tinuit et, brevī tempore intermissō, in castra legiōnēs redūxit.

Dum haec geruntur, nostrīs omnibus occupātīs, quī erant
in agrīs reliquī, discessērunt. Secūtae sunt continuōs com-

---

9. **stabilitātem**: 'steadiness.'   **peditum**: *10, d.*

10. **praestant**: 'exhibit'; sc. *essedāriī*.   **tantum . . . efficiunt**:
'they become so expert.' How lit.?

11. **incitātōs equōs sustinēre**: 'to keep control of their horses
at full gallop.' How lit.?

12. **brevī**: for *brevī tempore,* 'in an instant.'   **moderārī**: 'to
check.'   **flectere**: 'to turn.'   **per**, etc.: 'to run along the
pole.'

13. **iugō**: yokes were used with horses as well as cattle; see Fig. 29,
p. 8.   **citissimē**: 'with the utmost quickness.' *34, b.*

34. 1. **rēbus**: ablative of means.   **nostrīs**: dative after *tulit.*
154, a.   **novitāte**: 'strangeness.' *135, a.*

4. **Quō factō**: 'Though this had been accomplished,' referring
to the effects of Caesar's arrival. *144, b,* (5).

5. **aliēnum**: 'unfavorable.'   **suō**: 'favorable,' to himself. How
lit.?

7. **nostrīs**, etc.: while the Romans were busy repairing ships and
strengthening their defenses, the Britons 'withdrew' from the open
country, gathering for attack.   **quī**: as antecedent, sc. *eī* as subject
of *discessērunt.*

plūrēs diēs tempestātēs, quae et nostrōs in castrīs conti-
10 nērent et hostem ā pugnā prohibērent.

   Interim barbarī nūntiōs in omnēs partēs dīmīsērunt paucitātemque nostrōrum mīlitum suīs praedicāvērunt et, quanta
praedae faciendae atque in perpetuum suī līberandī facultās
darētur, sī Rōmānōs castrīs expulissent, dēmōnstrāvērunt.
15 Hīs rēbus celeriter magnā multitūdine peditātūs equitātūsque coāctā, ad castra vēnērunt.

Caesar repels the attack on the camp and pursues the Britons.

   35. Caesar, etsī idem, quod superiōribus diēbus acciderat,
fore vidēbat, ut, sī essent hostēs pulsī, celeritāte perīculum
effugerent, tamen nactus equitēs circiter xxx, quōs Commius
Atrebās, dē quō ante dictum est, sēcum trānsportāverat,
5 legiōnēs in aciē prō castrīs cōnstituit. Commissō proeliō
diūtius nostrōrum mīlitum impetum hostēs ferre nōn potuērunt ac terga vertērunt. Quōs tantō spatiō secūtī, quantum cursū et vīribus efficere potuērunt, complūrēs ex eīs

---

   9. **quae . . . continērent**: *194, a.* B. 283; H. 591, 2.

   13. **praedae faciendae**: 'of securing booty.'   **in perpetuum**:
'forever.'   **suī**: *154, b.* B. 339, 5; A. 504, *c*; H. 626, 3.

   14. **darētur**: *204*, (3).   **expulissent**: *218*, (1), *b.*

   15. **Hīs rēbus**: 'by means of these statements.' How lit.?   **equitātūs**: apparently including also the *essedāriī*, the close connection of
whom with the cavalry has already been noted.

   35. 1. idem: subject of *fore*, explained by the appositive clause *ut
. . . effugerent. 203*, (4).

   3. **effugerent**: 'they would escape from.'   **nactus**: *61, a*, (3),
and *226, c.*   **xxx**: a squad (*turma*). *38, b*, and *309, c.*

   4. **ante**: chap. 21, 14-20. The 30 horsemen were too few to be of
service except in scouting or in following up a fleeing enemy.

   6. **diūtius**: 'very long.' *153, a.*

   7. **ac**: 'but.' *234, b.*   **tantō spatiō**, etc.: 'so far as their speed
and strength allowed.' How lit.? *147, c.*   **secūtī**, etc.: sc.
nostrī.

   8. **complūrēs**: accusative. **ex eīs**: *97, d.*

occīdērunt; deinde, omnibus longē lātēque aedificiīs incēnsīs,
sē in castra recēpērunt.　　　　　　　　　　　　　　　　10

The Britons sue for peace.　Caesar sails back to Gaul.

36. Eōdem diē lēgātī, ab hostibus missī, ad Caesarem dē
pāce vēnērunt. Hīs Caesar numerum obsidum, quem
ante imperāverat, duplicāvit, eōsque in continentem addūcī
iussit, quod, propinquā diē aequinoctiī, īnfīrmīs nāvibus
hiemī nāvigātiōnem subiciendam nōn exīstimābat.　　5

Ipse, idōneam tempestātem nactus, paulō post mediam
noctem nāvēs solvit; quae omnēs incolumēs ad continentem
pervēnērunt, sed ex eīs onerāriae duae eōsdem portūs, quōs
reliquae, capere nōn potuērunt, et paulō īnfrā dēlātae sunt.

Legionaries from two transports are attacked by the Morini.

37. Quibus ex nāvibus cum essent expositī mīlitēs circiter
ccc atque in castra contenderent, Morinī, quōs Caesar, in

---

36. 2. **Hīs**: with *duplicāvit;* kind of dative? *109, a.*　　**quem**, etc.:
see chap. 27, ll. 12-19.

3. **duplicāvit**: 'doubled.'

4. **propinquā diē aequinoctiī**: 'since the season of the equinox
was near at hand,' a period when storms are unusually prevalent. *144,*
b, (3). The equinox fell on September 26, and Caesar probably left
Britain at least a week before that date. He had been on the island about
three weeks, and had hardly been able to go out of sight of the seashore.

5. **hiemī**, etc.: 'that the voyage ought to run the risk of stormy
weather.' How lit.?

8. **eōsdem portūs**: probably Boulogne and Ambleteuse.

9. **reliquae**: 'as the rest'; sc. *nāvēs cēpērunt.*　　**capere**: 'make.'
paulō īnfrā: i.e. southwest. Whether the two transports made some
harbor, or were stranded on the beach, Caesar does not say.

37. 1. **Quibus nāvibus**: 'these vessels,' the two transports mentioned in l. 8 of the preceding chapter.　　**essent expositī**: 'had
been landed.'

2. **ccc**: *trecentī,* averaging about 150 men to a ship.　　**castra**:
probably constructed by Publius Sulpicius Rufus for the protection of

Britanniam proficīscēns, pācātōs relīquerat, spē praedae
adductī prīmō nōn ita magnō suōrum numerō circumste-
5 tērunt ac, sī sēsē interficī nōllent, arma pōnere iussērunt.
Cum illī, orbe factō, sēsē dēfenderent, celeriter ad clāmōrem
hominum circiter mīlia vi convēnērunt. Quā rē nūntiātā,
Caesar omnem ex castrīs equitātum suīs auxiliō mīsit.

Interim nostrī mīlitēs impetum hostium sustinuērunt atque
10 amplius hōrīs quattuor fortissimē pūgnāvērunt; et, paucīs
vulneribus acceptīs, complūrēs ex hīs occīdērunt. Posteā
vērō quam equitātus noster in cōnspectum vēnit, hostēs,
abiectīs armīs, terga vertērunt magnusque eōrum numerus
est occīsus.

---

the harbor at *portius Itius*, Boulogne; cf. chap. 22, ll. 23–24.
Morinī, etc.: belonging to the part of the Morini who had given
hostages to Caesar just before he sailed for Britain; cf. chap. 22, ll. 1–12.

4. **nōn ita magnō**: 'not very large.'   **circumstetērunt**: sc. *eōs*,
'the three hundred.'

5. **sī . . . nōllent, pōnere**: in the direct form, *sī . . . nōn vultis*,
pōnite.   **pōnere**: here = *dēpōnere*, 'lay down.'

6. **orbe factō**: 'formed a circle and'; how lit.? *144, b*, (2).
The 'circle' formed by soldiers for defense was hollow and corresponded with our "hollow square." *338.*   **ad clamōrem:** 'on
(hearing) the shouting' of the attacking Morini. In Gaul news was
transmitted quickly by shouting across the country (VII, 3, ll. 8–13).

7. **hominum**: i.e. *Morinōrum*; dependent on *mīlia*. *98, a.*   **vi**:
sex. The number is probably exaggerated; in any case it evidences a
much denser population in this region than is implied for the regions
penetrated in the expedition against the Morini and Menapii the
previous year; cf. III, chap. 28–29.

8. **omnem equitātum**: including probably the cavalry that had
embarked in the 18 transports but had failed to reach Britain (chap.
22, ll. 16–19), as well as the contingent left with Sulpicius (chap. 22,
ll. 23–24); the rest must have gone with Titurius Sabinus and Cotta.
(chap. 22, ll. 20–22).

12. **Posteā quam**: *188, a.*   **vērō**: *236, a.*

Caesar inflicts punishment upon the Morini and Menapii.

38. Caesar posterō diē T. Labiēnum lēgātum cum eīs legiōnibus, quās ex Britanniā redūxerat, in Morinōs, quī rebelliōnem fēcerant, mīsit. Quī cum propter siccitātēs palūdum, quō sē reciperent, nōn habērent (quō perfugiō superiōre annō fuerant ūsī), omnēs ferē in potestātem 5 Labiēnī pervēnērunt.

At Q. Titūrius et L. Cotta lēgātī, quī in Menapiōrum fīnēs legiōnēs dūxerant, omnibus eōrum agrīs vastātīs, frū-mentīs succīsīs, aedificiīs incēnsīs, quod Menapiī sē omnēs in dēnsissimās silvās abdiderant, sē ad Caesarem recēpērunt. 10

Winter quarters in Belgium. Thanksgiving decreed at Rome.

Caesar in Belgīs omnium legiōnum hīberna cōnstituit. Eō duae omnīnō cīvitātēs ex Britanniā obsidēs mīsērunt, reliquae neglēxērunt.

---

38. 1. **T. Labiēnum**: he had probably accompanied Caesar to Britain.

3. **Quī cum**: ' And since they.' *184, a.* **siccitātēs**: plural be-cause there was dryness in a number of marshes; trans. 'dryness.' *92, c.*

4. **quō**, etc.: ' (a place) to which they might escape.' *194, a.* **quō perfugiō**: i.e. *perfugium, quō,* ' the refuge which.' *165, b.*

5. **superiōre annō**: 56 B.C.; cf. III, chap. 28–29.

7. **Menapiōrum**: N. to III, 28, l. 3, and Fig. 113.

10. **in**, etc.: cf. I, 12, l. 11 and N.

13. **reliquae neglēxērunt**: *obsidēs mittere.* The expedition to Britain, as that into Germany, was followed by no tangible results; but great fame was thereby won by the daring general for having opened up to his fellow-countrymen new and extensive regions. Hence the thanksgiving

Figure 113.— Coin of the Menapii.

Gold, of very crude workmanship. The attribution to the Menapii is not certain.

Hīs rēbus gestīs, ex litterīs Caesaris diērum xx sup-
15 plicātiō ā senātū dēcrēta est.

---

decreed at Rome, obtained by his friends for Caesar in the face of all
the opposition that his enemies could stir up (N. to chap. 14, l. 14).

14. **supplicātiō**: cf. II, 35, ll. 10-12. This 'thanksgiving' was
to be 5 days longer than the one decreed at the end of 57 B.C.,
though that was the longest known up to that time.

PLATE VII   MILITARY DEVICES

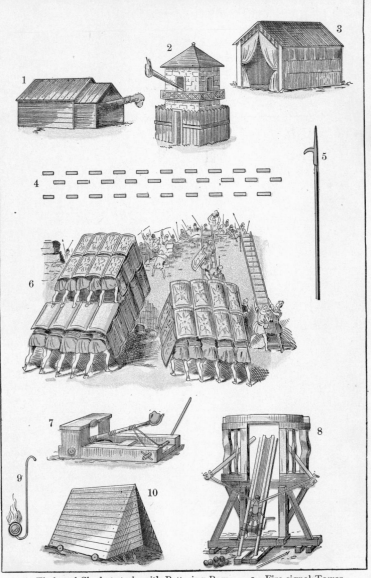

1. Timbered Shed, *testudo*, with Battering Ram.   2. Fire-signal Tower.
3. Tent, *tabernaculum*.   4. Order of Battle.   5. Wall Hook, *falx muralis*.
6. Turtle-shell roof, *testudo*.   7. Onager.   8. *Ballista*.
9. *Glans fusili ex argilla* (V. 43).   10. Turtle-shell shed, *testudo*.

COMMENTARIUS QUINTUS

Second Expedition to Britain. 1–23

Caesar orders ships built, and quiets disturbances in Illyricum.

1. L. Domitiō, Ap. Claudiō cōnsulibus, discēdēns ab hībernīs Caesar in Italiam, ut quotannīs facere cōnsuērat, lēgātīs imperat, quōs legiōnibus praefēcerat, utī, quam plūrimās possent, hieme nāvēs aedificandās veterēsque reficiendās cūrārent.   5

Figure 114. — View across Belgium's fertile fields.

Caesar usually chose the site of his winter quarters with reference to the grain supply.

1. 1. **L. Domitiō, Ap. Claudiō cōnsulibus :** 54 B.C. *240, a,* and *234, a.*

2. **hībernīs :** in Belgium (IV, chap. 38).   **Italiam :** *283, b.*

287

Eārum mōdum fōrmamque dēmōnstrat. Ad celeritātem
onerandī subductiōnēsque paulō facit humiliōrēs, quam
quibus in nostrō marī ūtī cōnsuēvimus, atque id eō magis,
quod propter crēbrās commūtātiōnēs aestuum minus
10 magnōs ibi fluctūs fierī cognōverat; ad onera ac multitūdinem iūmentōrum trānsportandam paulō lātiōrēs, quam
quibus in reliquīs ūtimur maribus. Hās omnēs āctuāriās
imperat fierī, quam ad rem humilitās multum adiuvat.
Ea, quae sunt ūsuī ad armandās nāvēs, ex Hispāniā ap-
15 portārī iubet.

Ipse, conventibus Galliae citeriōris perāctīs, in Īllyricum
proficīscitur, quod ā Pīrustīs fīnitimam partem prōvinciae
incursiōnibus vāstārī audiēbat. Eō cum vēnisset, cīvitātibus mīlitēs imperat certumque in locum convenīre iubet.
20 Quā rē nūntiātā, Pīrustae lēgātōs ad eum mittunt, quī doceant, nihil eārum rērum pūblicō factum cōnsiliō, sēsēque
parātōs esse dēmōnstrant omnibus ratiōnibus dē iniūriīs
satisfacere. Perceptā ōrātiōne eōrum, Caesar obsidēs
imperat eōsque ad certam diem addūcī iubet; nisi ita fē-
25 cerint, sēsē bellō cīvitātem persecūtūrum dēmōnstrat. Eīs
ad diem adductīs, ut imperāverat, arbitrōs inter cīvitātēs
dat, quī lītem aestiment poenamque cōnstituant.

---

7. **onerandī**: 'of loading.'   **subductiōnēs**: 'beaching.' *92, a.*
humiliōrēs: 'shallower.'   **quam quibus**: i.e. *quam eae [nāvēs]
sunt, quibus.*

9. **commūtātiōnēs aestuum**: cf. IV, 29, l. 2, and N.

11. **lātiōrēs**: predicative; sc. *eās facit.*

12. **āctuāriās**: predicative, 'for rapid movement,' with the use of
oars as well as sails.

13. **humilitās**: 'lowness' of the deck above the water.

14. **Hispāniā**: *296.*   **apportārī**: 'be brought.'

16. **perāctīs**: 'finished.'   **Īllyricum**: *298.*

18. **incursiōnibus**: 'raids.'

26. **arbitrōs**: 'referees.' *7, c,* and *80, b.*

27. **lītem**: 'the (matter of) damages.'

Proceeding to Gaul he finds ships ready, visits the Treverans.

2. Hīs cōnfectīs rēbus conventibusque perāctīs, in citeriōrem Galliam revertitur atque inde ad exercitum proficīscitur. Eō cum vēnisset, circûmitīs omnibus hībernīs,
singulārī mīlitum studiō in summā omnium rērum inopiā
circiter DC eius generis, cuius suprā dēmōnstrāvimus, nāvēs, 5
et longās XXVIII, invenit īnstrūctās, neque multum abesse
ab eō, quīn paucīs diēbus dēdūcī possint. Collaudātīs
mīlitibus atque eīs, quī negōtiō praefuerant, quid fierī velit,
ostendit, atque omnēs ad portum Itium convenīre iubet,
quō ex portū commodissimum in Britanniam trāiectum 10
esse cognōverat, circiter mīlium passuum XXX ā continentī;
huic reī, quod satis esse vīsum est mīlitum, relīquit.

Ipse cum legiōnibus expedītīs IIII et equitibus DCCC in
fīnēs Trēverōrum proficīscitur, quod hī neque ad concilia
veniēbant neque imperiō pārēbant, Germānōsque Trāns- 15
rhēnānōs sollicitāre dīcēbantur.

By means of hostages he binds Indutiomarus to keep the peace.

3. Haec cīvitās longē plūrimum tōtīus Galliae equitātū
valet magnāsque habet cōpiās peditum, Rhēnumque, ut
suprā dēmōnstrāvimus, tangit.

In eā cīvitāte duo dē prīncipātū inter sē contendēbant,
Indutiomārus et Cingetorīx; ē quibus alter, simul atque dē 5
Caesaris legiōnumque adventū cognitum est, ad eum vēnit,
sē suōsque omnēs in officiō futūrōs neque ab amīcitiā

---

2. 5. DC : *sescentās.*　　**cuius** : *cuius generis nāvēs*; trans. *cuius*
as if *quod.*　　**suprā** : in chap. I.

6. **longās** : i.e. *nāvēs duodētrīgintā. 346, a.*　　**neque,** etc. : 'and
that in a few days they would be about ready to launch.' How lit.?

7. **Collaudātīs** : 'warmly commending.'　　How lit.?

12. **huic reī** : 'for this purpose.'　　**quod mīlitum** : 'so many
soldiers as.'　　*97, b.*

3. 3. **suprā** : III, II, ll. 1–2.　　**tangit** : 'extends to'; lit. 'touches.'

populī Rōmānī dēfectūrōs cōnfīrmāvit, quaeque in Trēverīs
gererentur, ostendit.

10 At Indutiomārus equitātum peditātumque cōgere, eīsque,
quī per aetātem in armīs esse nōn poterant, in silvam
Arduennam abditīs, quae, ingentī magnitūdine, per mediōs
fīnēs Trēverōrum ā flūmine Rhēnō ad initium Rēmōrum
pertinet, bellum parāre īnstituit. Sed posteā quam nōn
15 nūllī prīncipēs ex eā cīvitāte, et familiāritāte Cingetorīgis
adductī et adventū nostrī exercitūs perterritī, ad Caesarem
vēnērunt et dē suīs prīvātim rēbus ab eō petere coepērunt,
quoniam cīvitātī cōnsulere nōn possent, veritus, nē ab
omnibus dēsererētur, Indutiomārus lēgātōs ad Caesarem
20 mittit :

Sēsē idcircō ab suīs discēdere atque ad eum venīre
nōluisse, quō facilius cīvitātem in officiō continēret, nē
omnis nōbilitātis discessū plēbs propter imprūdentiam lābe-
rētur; itaque cīvitātem in suā potestāte esse, sēque, sī Caesar
25 *permitteret, ad eum in castra ventūrum, et suās cīvitātisque*
fortūnās eius fideī permissūrum.

4. Caesar, etsī intellegēbat, quā dē causā ea dīcerentur,
quaeque eum rēs ab īnstitūtō cōnsiliō dēterrēret, tamen, nē
aestātem in Trēverīs cōnsūmere cōgerētur, omnibus ad
Britannicum bellum rēbus comparātīs, Indutiomārum ad
5 sē cum CC obsidibus venīre iussit. Hīs adductīs, in eīs fīliō
propinquīsque eius omnibus, quōs nōminātim ēvocāverat,
cōnsōlātus Indutiomārum hortātusque est, utī in officiō

---

11. **per aetātem** : 'by reason of age.'   **in armīs esse** : i.e. *arma*
ferre.

21. **Sēsē**, etc. : ' (saying) that he.'   **idcircō** : 'on this account.'

23. **imprūdentiam** : 'lack of foresight.'   **lāberētur** : 'fall away,'
becoming disloyal.

4. 2. **ab īnstitūtō cōnsiliō** : 'from (carrying out) the plan (which
he had) formed.'

6. **ēvocāverat** : sc. *Caesar*.

manēret; nihilō tamen sētius, prīncipibus Trēverōrum ad
sē convocātīs, hōs singillātim Cingetorīgī conciliāvit; quod
cum meritō eius ab sē fierī intellegēbat, tum magnī interesse 10
arbitrābātur, eius auctōritātem inter suōs quam plūrimum
valēre, cuius tam ēgregiam in sē voluntātem perspexisset.

Id factum graviter tulit Indutiomārus, suam grātiam
inter suōs minuī, et, quī iam ante inimīcō in nōs animō
fuisset, multō gravius hōc dolōre exārsit.　　　　　　　　15

Caesar gathers his forces at portus Itius.

5. Hīs rēbus cōnstitūtīs, Caesar ad portum Itium cum
legiōnibus pervenit.

Ibi cognōscit, LX nāvēs, quae in Meldīs factae erant,
tempestāte reiectās cursum tenēre nōn potuisse atque
eōdem, unde erant profectae, revertisse; reliquās parātās 5
ad nāvigandum atque omnibus rēbus īnstrūctās invenit.

Eōdem equitātus tōtīus Galliae convenit, numerō mīlium
quattuor, prīncipēsque ex omnibus cīvitātibus; ex quibus
perpaucōs, quōrum in sē fidem perspexerat, relinquere in
Galliā, reliquōs obsidum locō sēcum dūcere dēcrēverat, 10
quod, cum ipse abesset, mōtum Galliae verēbātur.

---

9. **quod cum**, etc.: 'and not only did he understand that he was
doing this in accordance with what Cingetorix deserved.' How lit.?
186, b.

10. **eius**: *Cingetorīgis. 19, d.*　　**magnī**: *103, d.*

14. **quī**: 'although he.' *187.* B. 283, 3, *b*; H. 593, 2.

15. **gravius ... exārsit**: 'on account of this grievance he became
much more indignant.' How lit.?

5. 3. **nāvēs**, etc.: these vessels had to be taken down the Marne
and the Seine to the Channel, then north to Boulogne (portus Itius);
see Map 11.

7. **numerō**: *142, a,* and *85.*　　**mīlium**: dependent on *equitātus.*
100, a, and *309, b.*

11. **abesset**: *185, c.*

Dumnorix attempts to elude Caesar's vigilance, and is slain.

6. Erat ūnā cum cēterīs Dumnorīx Aeduus, dē quō
ante ā nōbīs dictum est. Hunc sēcum habēre in prīmīs
cōnstituerat, quod eum cupidum rērum novārum, cupidum
imperiī, magnī animī, magnae inter Gallōs auctōritātis
5 cognōverat. Accēdēbat hūc, quod in conciliō Aeduōrum
Dumnorīx dīxerat, sibi ā Caesare rēgnum cīvitātis dēferrī;
quod dictum Aeduī graviter ferēbant, neque recūsandī aut
dēprecandī causā lēgātōs ad Caesarem mittere audēbant.
Id factum ex suīs hospitibus Caesar cognōverat.
10 Ille omnibus prīmō precibus petere contendit, ut in
Galliā relinquerētur, partim quod, īnsuētus nāvigandī, mare
timēret, partim quod religiōnibus impedīrī sēsē dīceret.
Posteā quam id obstinātē sibi negārī vīdit, omnī spē impe-
trandī adēmptā, prīncipēs Galliae sollicitāre, sēvocāre sin-
15 gulōs hortārīque coepit, utī in continentī remanērent; metū
territāre:
*Nōn sine causā fierī, ut Gallia omnī nōbilitāte spoliārē-
tur; id esse cōnsilium Caesaris, ut, quōs in cōnspectū
Galliae interficere verērētur, hōs omnēs in Britanniam trā-
20 ductōs necāret;* fidem reliquīs interpōnere, iūs iūrandum
poscere, ut, quod esse ex ūsū Galliae intellēxissent, commūnī cōnsiliō administrārent.

---

6. 2. **ante**: I, chap. 16–20. Dumnorix had always opposed Caesar.
3. **eum**: sc. *esse. 289, c.*
6. **sibi . . . dēferrī**: contrary to the constitution of the Aeduans,
who elected a Vergobret annually; see I, 16, ll. 12–14.
11. **īnsuētus nāvigandī**: 'unused to sailing.' *230*, (1).
12. **religiōnibus**: 'by religious scruples.'   **dīceret**: *183, b.*
13. **obstinātē**: 'persistently.'
14. **sēvocāre**: 'to call aside,' for secret conference. *79, d.*
16. **territāre**: sc. *eōs;* 'he worked upon their fears (saying).' *182*,
and *213, b.* How lit.?
17. **spoliārētur**: 'was being stripped,' by taking the leading men
to Britain.

Haec ā complūribus ad Caesarem dēferēbantur.

7. Quā rē cognitā Caesar, quod tantum cīvitātī Aeduae
dignitātis tribuēbat, coercendum atque dēterrendum, quibuscumque rēbus posset, Dumnorīgem statuēbat; quod
longius eius āmentiam prōgredī vidēbat, prōspiciendum,
nē quid sibi ac reī pūblicae nocēre posset. Itaque diēs 5
circiter xxv in eō locō commorātus, quod Cōrus ventus
nāvigātiōnem impediēbat, quī magnam partem omnis
temporis in hīs locīs flāre cōnsuēvit, dabat operam, ut in
officiō Dumnorīgem continēret, nihilō tamen sētius omnia
eius cōnsilia cognōsceret; tandem idōneam nactus tem- 10
pestātem mīlitēs equitēsque cōnscendere nāvēs iubet.

At, omnium impedītīs animīs, Dumnorīx cum equitibus
Aeduōrum ā castrīs, īnsciente Caesare, domum discēdere
coepit. Quā rē nūntiātā, Caesar, intermissā profectiōne
atque omnibus rēbus postpositīs, magnam partem equitātūs 15
ad eum īnsequendum mittit retrahīque imperat; sī vim
faciat neque pāreat, interficī iubet, nihil hunc, sē absente,
prō sānō factūrum arbitrātus, quī praesentis imperium
neglēxisset. Ille autem revocātus resistere ac sē manū
dēfendere suōrumque fidem implōrāre coepit, saepe clā- 20
mitāns, līberum sē līberaeque esse cīvitātis. Illī, ut erat
imperātum, circumsistunt hominem atque interficiunt; at
equitēs Aeduī ad Caesarem omnēs revertuntur.

---

7. 3. **posset**: sc. *eum coercēre et dēterrēre.*

4. **prōspiciendum**: sc. *esse statuēbat.*

6. **eō locō**: portus Itius, Boulogne.   **commorātus**: 'while waiting.'   **Cōrus**: 'from the northwest.'

8. **dabat operam**: 'was taking pains.'

10. **tempestātem**: cf. IV, 23, l. 2, and N.

16. **retrahī**: sc. *eum,* 'that he be brought back.'

18. **prō sānō**: 'like a man in his senses.' How lit.?   **praesentis**: sc. *suī,* i.e. *Caesaris.*

20. **clāmitāns**: 'crying out.' *78, a.*

Caesar sails to Britain, lands, and captures a stronghold.

8. Hīs rēbus gestīs, Labiēnō in continentī cum III legiōnibus et equitum mīlibus duōbus relīctō, ut portūs tuērētur et rem frūmentāriam prōvidēret, quaeque in Galliā gererentur, cognōsceret, cōnsiliumque prō tempore 5 et prō rē caperet, ipse cum V legiōnibus et parī numerō equitum, quem in continentī relīquerat, ad sōlis occāsum nāvēs solvit.

Et lēnī Āfricō prōvectus, mediā circiter nocte ventō intermissō, cursum nōn tenuit et, longius dēlātus aestū, ortā 10 lūce sub sinistrā Britanniam relīctam cōnspexit. Tum, rūrsus aestūs commūtātiōnem secūtus, rēmīs contendit, ut eam partem īnsulae caperet, quā optimum esse ēgressum superiōre aestāte cognōverat. Quā in rē admodum fuit mīlitum virtūs laudanda, quī vectōriīs gravibusque nāvigiīs, 15 nōn intermissō rēmigandī labōre, longārum nāvium cursum adaequārunt.

Accessum est ad Britanniam omnibus nāvibus merīdiānō ferē tempore, neque in eō locō hostis est vīsus; sed, ut posteā Caesar ex captīvīs cognōvit, cum magnae manūs 20 eō convēnissent, multitūdine nāvium perterritae, quae cum annōtinīs prīvātīsque, quās suī quisque commodī causā

---

8. 4. **prō . . . rē**: 'as conditions at the time might require.' How lit.?

5. **parī**: trans. as if *eōdem*.

8. **Āfricō**: 'southwest wind.' Caesar probably sailed about July 6.

11. **aestūs**, etc.: the change of course is shown on Map 11, **A**.

12. **caperet**: 'reach.'

14. **laudanda**: 'praiseworthy.' **vectōriīs**, etc.: 'heavy transports.'

15. **rēmigandī**: 'of rowing'; the transports were provided with oars, in addition to the usual sails (Fig. 202, in Vocab.).

17. **merīdiānō tempore**: 'midday.'

21. **annōtinīs**: sc. *nāvibus*, 'ships of the previous year.'

Between Dover and Deal. The cliff is here about 400 feet high. At the top is the lighthouse of South Foreland.

fēcerat, amplius DCCC ūnō erant vīsae tempore, ā lītore
discesserant ac sē in superiōra loca abdiderant.

9. Caesar, expositō exercitū et locō castrīs idōneō captō,
ubi ex captīvīs cognōvit, quō in locō hostium cōpiae cōnsē-
dissent, cohortibus x ad mare relīctīs et equitibus CCC, quī
praesidiō nāvibus essent, dē tertiā vigiliā ad hostēs contendit, eō minus veritus nāvibus, quod in lītore mollī atque 5
apertō dēligātās ad ancorās relinquēbat; eī praesidiō nāvibusque Q. Ātrium praefēcit. Ipse, noctū prōgressus mīlia
passuum circiter XII, hostium cōpiās cōnspicātus est.

Illī, equitātū atque essedīs ad flūmen prōgressī, ex locō
superiōre nostrōs prohibēre et proelium committere coepē- 10
runt. Repulsī ab equitātū sē in silvās abdidērunt, locum
nactī ēgregiē et nātūrā et opere mūnītum, quem domesticī
bellī, ut vidēbātur, causā iam ante praeparāverant; nam
crēbrīs arboribus succīsīs omnēs introitūs erant praeclūsī.
Ipsī ex silvīs rārī prōpugnābant, nostrōsque intrā mūni- 15
tiōnēs ingredī prohibēbant. At mīlitēs legiōnis septimae,
testūdine factā et aggere ad mūnītiōnēs adiectō, locum
cēpērunt eōsque ex silvīs expulērunt, paucīs vulneribus
acceptīs. Sed eōs fugientēs longius Caesar prōsequī
vetuit, et quod locī nātūram ignōrābat, et quod, magnā 20

---

22. DCCC: *octingentae;* with *quae,* 'of which more than 800.' *97, c,*
and *129, b.*

9. 3. quī . . . essent: 'to guard the ships.' How lit.? *193, a,*
and *112, b.*

5. nāvibus: dative.   mollī: affording good anchorage.

9. essedīs: see IV, chap. 33 and Notes.   flūmen: the Great
Stour; see Map II.

14. omnēs, etc.: 'all the entrances were obstructed.'

15. rārī prōpugnābant: 'in small bodies were hurling missiles.'
How lit.? The British stronghold was perhaps near Canterbury.

16. prohibēbant: 'were trying to prevent.' *175, e,* and *223, a.*

17. testūdine: *345.*   aggere: probably made of tree trunks.
341.

parte diēī cōnsūmptā, mūnītiōnī castrōrum tempus relinquī
volēbat.

*A storm shatters the fleet; Caesar orders repairs, returns
inland.*

10. Postrīdiē eius diēī māne tripertītō mīlitēs equitēsque
in expedītiōnem mīsit, ut eōs, quī fūgerant, persequerentur.
Hīs aliquantum itineris prōgressīs, cum iam extrēmī essent
in prōspectū, equitēs ā Q. Ātriō ad Caesarem vēnērunt,
5 quī nūntiārent, superiōre nocte maximā coortā tempestāte,
prope omnēs nāvēs afflīctās atque in lītus ēiectās esse,
quod neque ancorae fūnēsque subsisterent, neque nautae
gubernātōrēsque vim tempestātis patī possent; itaque ex
eō concursū nāvium magnum esse incommodum acceptum.

11. Hīs rēbus cognitīs, Caesar legiōnēs equitātumque
revocārī atque in itinere resistere iubet, ipse ad nāvēs revertitur; eadem ferē, quae ex nūntiīs litterīsque cognōverat, cōram perspicit, sīc ut, āmissīs circiter XL nāvibus,
5 reliquae tamen reficī posse magnō negōtiō vidērentur.

Itaque ex legiōnibus fabrōs dēligit et ex continentī aliōs
arcessī iubet; Labiēnō scrībit, ut, quam plūrimās posset,
eīs legiōnibus, quae sint apud eum, nāvēs īnstituat. Ipse,

---

10. 1. **tripertītō**: 'in three columns.'

2. **in expedītiōnem**: 'for a rapid march,' with light equipment.

3. **aliquantum itineris**: 'some distance.'   How lit.?   **extrēmī**:
'the rear' of the Roman force was just visible to those in camp.

11. 2. **in itinere resistere**: to beat off the enemy, without halting
for a pitched battle.

3. **nūntiīs**: 'messengers,' mounted (chap. 10, l. 4).   **litterīs**:
'dispatch,' from Quintus Atrius.

5. **negōtiō**: 'trouble.'

6. **fabrōs**: 'mechanics.' *7, c,* and *310, b.*

8. **eīs legiōnibus**: 'with (the help of) the legions,' at portus Itius
160, d.

etsī rēs erat multae operae ac labōris, tamen commodissimum esse statuit, omnēs nāvēs subdūcī et cum castrīs ūnā 10
mūnītiōne coniungī. In hīs rēbus circiter diēs x cōnsūmit,
nē nocturnīs quidem temporibus ad labōrem mīlitum intermissīs.

Subductīs nāvibus castrīsque ēgregiē mūnītīs, eāsdem
cōpiās, quās ante, praesidiō nāvibus relinquit, ipse eōdem, 15
unde redierat, proficīscitur. Eō cum vēnisset, maiōrēs iam
undique in eum locum cōpiae Britannōrum convēnerant,
summā imperiī bellīque administrandī commūnī cōnsiliō
permissā Cassivellaunō; cuius fīnēs ā maritimīs cīvitātibus flūmen dīvidit, quod appellātur Tamesis, ā marī circiter 20
mīlia passuum LXXX. Huic superiōre tempore cum reliquīs cīvitātibus continentia bella intercesserant; sed, nostrō
adventū permōtī, Britannī hunc tōtī bellō imperiōque prae-
fēcerant.

The Britons and their island.

12. Britanniae pars interior ab eīs incolitur, quōs nātōs
in īnsulā ipsā memoriā prōditum dīcunt; maritima pars ab
eīs, quī praedae ac bellī īnferendī causā ex Belgiō trānsiē-

---

9. **rēs**, etc.: 'it was a wearisome and laborious undertaking.'
How lit.? *100, b.*

10. **subdūcī**: the ships were built so that they could be beached;
chap. 1, ll. 6–10.

15. **eōdem**, etc.: the British stronghold, near modern Canterbury
(chap. 9, ll. 11–19).

20. **Tamesis**: only the upper Thames formed the boundary of the
territories ruled by Cassivellaunus. *14, c.* **marī**: at the point
where Caesar landed, near Deal.

12. 1. **quōs**, etc.: *quōs nātōs [esse]* is subject of *prōditum [esse]*;
'who, they say, according to tradition, originated in the island itself.'
How lit.? *294.*

2. **dīcunt**: *172, c.* Several ancient peoples considered themselves
"autochthones," sprung from the soil in the region in which they
dwelt.

runt (quī omnēs ferē eīs nōminibus cīvitātum appellantur,
5 quibus ortī ex cīvitātibus eō pervēnērunt), et, bellō illātō,
ibi permānsērunt atque agrōs colere coepērunt. Hominum
est īnfīnīta multitūdō crēberrimaque aedificia ferē Gallicīs
cōnsimilia, pecorum magnus numerus. Ūtuntur aut aere
aut nummō aureō, aut tāleīs ferreīs ad certum pondus ex-
10 āminātīs, prō nummō.

Nāscitur ibi plumbum album in mediterrāneīs regiōnibus,

---

4. **quī,** etc.: there was, for example, a British tribe called *Atrebātēs.*

6. **Hominum,** etc.: 'The population is beyond number.' How lit.?

Figure 115. — British gold coin.

Probably in circulation in Caesar's time. Obverse, curious patterns; reverse, conventional horse, star, chariot wheel.

7. **aedificia:** sc. *sunt.* **Gallicīs** [aedificiīs]: large round huts of timbers and wickerwork, with conical thatched roofs.

8. **aere:** 'bronze,' bronze coins. The earliest British bronze coins yet discovered date from a few years after Caesar's time.

9. **nummō aureō:** 'gold coins,' we should say. Gold coins began to be struck in Britain at least a hundred years before Caesar's invasions (Fig. 115). **tāleīs ferreīs:** 'iron bars.' **ad,** etc.: 'weighed to a certain standard,' lit. 'weight.' The iron currency bars that have been found represent several different weights, the heaviest being twice as heavy as the second, and so on.

11. **Nāscitur:** 'is found.' **plumbum album:** 'tin,' which began to be exported from Cornwall as early as the ninth century, B.C. **mediterrāneīs:** 'inland.' The Cornish tin mines were in

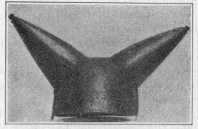

Figure 116. — British helmet.

Of bronze; found in the Thames at London.

reality near the sea, but they were a long distance from Caesar's landing-place.

in maritimīs ferrum, sed eius exigua est cōpia; aere ūtuntur importātō. Māteria cuiusque generis, ut in Galliā, est,
praeter fāgum atque abietem.

Leporem et gallīnam et ānserem gustāre fās nōn putant; 15
haec tamen alunt animī voluptātisque causā. Loca sunt
temperātiōra quam in Galliā, remissiōribus frīgoribus.

13. Īnsula nātūrā triquetra, cuius ūnum latus est contrā
Galliam. Huius lateris alter angulus, quī est ad Cantium,
quō ferē omnēs ex Galliā nāvēs appelluntur, ad orientem
sōlem, īnferior ad merīdiem spectat. Hōc latus pertinet
circiter mīlia passuum D.   5

---

12. **ferrum**: iron mines were worked in Sussex from the prehistoric
period to the nineteenth century.   **aere**: some bronze seems to have
been imported into Britain (Fig. 125), but most of the bronze objects
found in Britain were made there, from native mixtures of the component
metals (Fig. 116).

14. **fāgum**: 'beech.' *5, b.*   Caesar seems to have been mistaken
in saying that the beech was not found in Britain; but his opportunities
for direct observation were limited.   **abietem**: 'fir.' *10, e.*

15. **Leporem**, etc.: 'hare, chicken, and goose.' The origin of the
superstition it is difficult to understand; for the hare, cf. Levit. XI. 6.
13, g, and *234, a.*   **ānserem**: *11, c.*   **gustāre**: 'to taste.'

16. **haec alunt**: 'they raise these.'   **animī**, etc.: 'for pastime
and amusement.'   **Loca**: 'the region.' *6, c.*   **sunt temperātiōra**:
'has a milder climate.' How lit.?

17. **remissiōribus frīgoribus**: 'the cold being less severe.' How
lit.? *92, c*, and *13, f.*

13. 1. **nātūrā**: 'in shape'; lit. 'by nature.'   **triquetra**: 'triangular.'   **contrā**: 'opposite.'

2. **alter angulus**: 'one corner.'   **ad Cantium**: 'by Kent' (Map
12, **A**); the boundaries of Kent in Caesar's time are not known with
exactness.

3. **quō**: refers to *angulus.*   **appelluntur**: 'come to land.' How
lit.?   **ad orientem sōlem**: 'toward the east.' How lit.?

4. **īnferior** [angulus]: see Map 12, **B**.   **ad merīdiem**: 'toward
the south.'

5. **D**: *quīngentōrum*; how many English miles in 500 Roman miles?
243, a, b.

Alterum vergit ad Hispāniam atque occidentem sōlem;
quā ex parte est Hibernia, dīmidiō minor, ut exīstimātur,
quam Britannia, sed parī spatiō trānsmissūs, atque ex
Galliā est in Britanniam.　In hōc mediō cursū est īnsula,
10 quae appellātur Mona; complūrēs praetereā minōrēs subiectae īnsulae exīstimantur; dē quibus īnsulīs nōn nūllī
scrīpsērunt, diēs continuōs xxx sub brūmā esse noctem.
Nōs nihil dē eō percontātiōnibus reperiēbāmus, nisi certīs
ex aquā mēnsūrīs breviōrēs esse quam in continentī noctēs

---

6. **Alterum** [latus], etc.: 'The second side has a westerly trend,
toward Spain.' How lit.?　Caesar's erroneous belief that Spain extended north nearly to Britain was shared by his contemporaries, and
even by some writers after his time.　See Map 12.

7. **quā ex parte**: 'and on this side.'　　**dīmidiō minor**: 'a half
smaller.' How lit.?　*140.*

8. **Britannia**: sc. *est.*　　**parī**, etc.: '(reached by) a passage just
as long as that from Gaul to Britain.' How lit.?　　**parī spatiō**: descriptive ablative, taking the place of an adjective, and coördinated with
minor by *sed.*　　**trānsmissūs**: genitive, depending on *spatiō.*　　**atque**:
233, c.

9. **In . . . cursū**: 'half way across,' between Britain and Ireland.
How lit.?　*152, a.*

10. **Mona**: see Map 12.　　**subiectae** [esse], etc.: 'are thought
to lie off (the coast on this side).'

11. **īnsulae**: probably the Hebrides are referred to.　**nōn nūllī
scrīpsērunt**: perhaps Greek writers, whose works have perished, are
meant.

12. **sub brūmā**: 'about the winter solstice.'　The statement regarding a period of thirty days without the sun is not true of the
Hebrides or of the other islands near Scotland.

13. **Nōs**: *156.*　　**percontātiōnibus**: 'through　inquiries.'
certīs, etc.: 'by exact measurements (made) with a water-clock.'
How lit.?　A water-clock, *clepsydra*, was used in a Roman camp, especially to mark the watches.　*242, e.*

14. **ex aquā**: with *mēnsūrīs. 150, d.*　　**breviōrēs**: Caesar's observations were made in summer; in winter the nights would of course
be longer.

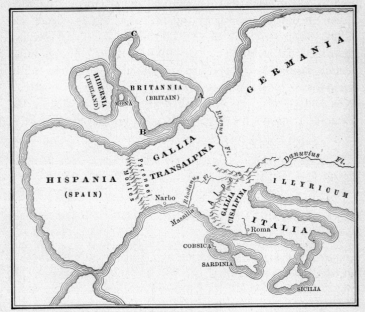

EXPLANATION

In view of the meagerness of Caesar's information, his statement about the geography of Britain is surprisingly near the truth in essential particulars. In this respect it compares favorably with the statements of modern travelers and explorers in regard to regions of which they have seen only a small part.

He knew that the Island was triangular in shape, and in his two expeditions he had himself seen a portion of the coast facing Gaul (chap. 13, l. 1). He could easily believe that one corner (**A**) faced east, another (**B**) toward the south. His language implies that he had a vague idea of a projection eastward (**C**) at the northern extremity (l. 18). He knew the location, and approximately the size, of Ireland (l. 7).

Caesar, as other ancients, found it more difficult to estimate distances north and south than east and west. He fell easily into the error of supposing that the northern end of Spain extended so far that it lay west of the southern part of Britain (l. 6); and his conception of the relative positions of the two Gauls, Italy and Illyricum, was probably very nearly as represented.

The strait between Italy and Sicily, now Strait of Messina, is called by Caesar *Fretum* (C. II, l. 3).

vidēbāmus. Huius est longitūdō lateris, ut fert illōrum 15
opīniō, DCC mīlium.

Tertium est contrā septentriōnēs; cui partī nūlla est
obiecta terra, sed eius angulus lateris maximē ad Germā-
niam spectat. Hōc mīlia passuum DCCC in longitūdinem
esse exīstimātur.　　　　　　　　　　　　　　　　　　　20

Ita omnis īnsula est in circuitū vīciēs centum mīlium
passuum.

14. Ex hīs omnibus longē sunt hūmānissimī, quī Cantium incolunt, quae regiō est maritima omnis, neque multum ā Gallicā differunt cōnsuētūdine. Interiōrēs plērīque
frūmenta nōn serunt, sed lacte et carne vīvunt pellibusque
sunt vestītī.　　　　　　　　　　　　　　　　　　　　　5

Omnēs vērō sē Britannī vitrō īnficiunt, quod caeru-

---

15. **ut**, etc. : 'according to their idea,' i.e. of the Britons.　How lit.?

16. **DCC**: *septingentōrum*.　　**mīlium** : *100, b.*

17. **Tertium** [latus] : cf. *ūnum* (l. 1), and *alterum* (l. 6).

19. **Hōc** : *hōc latus*.　　**DCCC** : *octingenta*.

21. **vīciēs centum** : 'two thousand.' How lit.? Caesar's estimate
is nearer the truth than might have been expected; no Roman is
known to have sailed around the island until more than a century after
Caesar's time, in 84 A.D.

14. 1. **hīs omnibus** : the Britons. *97, d.* **hūmānissimī** : 'most
civilized.'

2. **omnis** : 'wholly.' *151.* **neque** : 'and . . . not.'

3. **Interiōrēs plērīque** : 'Those living in the interior, for the most
part.'

4. **serunt** : 'sow.' **lacte** : cf. IV, 1, l. 16. *131, a.* **carne** :
'meat.' *18, a.*

5. **sunt vestītī** : 'clothe themselves.' *174.* Caesar was misinformed about the life of the inland tribes of Britain. It has been
proved by discoveries that, long before his time, at least the more progressive raised crops and had woolen and linen clothes.

6. **sē vitrō īnficiunt** : 'stain themselves with woad,' a plant from
the leaves of which is made a dye resembling indigo in color.
caeruleum colōrem : 'a bluish color.' *80, b.*

leum efficit colōrem, atque hōc horridiōrēs sunt in pugnā
aspectū; capillōque sunt prōmissō.

The Britons fight fiercely, but Caesar defeats them.

15. Equitēs hostium essedāriīque ācriter proeliō cum
equitātū nostrō in itinere cōnflīxērunt, ita tamen, ut nostrī
omnibus partibus superiōrēs fuerint atque eōs in silvās col-
lēsque compulerint; sed, complūribus interfectīs, cupidius
5 īnsecūtī nōn nūllōs ex suīs āmīsērunt.

At illī, intermissō spatiō, imprūdentibus nostrīs atque
occupātīs in mūnītiōne castrōrum, subitō sē ex silvīs ēiēcērunt, impetūque in eōs factō, quī erant in statiōne prō
castrīs collocātī, ācriter pugnāvērunt; duābusque missīs
10 subsidiō cohortibus ā Caesare, atque hīs prīmīs legiōnum
duārum, cum hae perexiguō intermissō locī spatiō inter sē
cōnstitissent, novō genere pugnae perterritīs nostrīs, per
mediōs audācissimē perrūpērunt sēque inde incolumēs
recēpērunt. Eō diē Q. Laberius Dūrus, tribūnus mīlitum,
15 interficitur. Illī, plūribus summissīs cohortibus, repelluntur.

16. Tōtō hōc in genere pugnae, cum sub oculīs omnium

---

7. **hōc**: 'on this account.'   **horridiōrēs aspectū**: 'rather wild-
looking'; similar was the use of war-paint by the American Indians.
How lit.? *142, a.*

8. **capillō**, etc.: 'they let their hair grow long.' How lit.?

15. 1. **Equitēs**, etc.: cf. IV, 33, and Notes. The narrative,
interrupted by the description of Britain, is here resumed from chap.
II.

10. **atque**, etc.: 'and those the first.' *161, c.*

11. **perexiguō**: 'very small.' *79, b.*   **inter sē**: 'apart.'

12. **novō**, etc.: the two cohorts had evidently not been on the first
expedition.   **per mediōs**: between the cohorts.

16. 1. **genere**, etc.: 'throughout the engagement, with fighting of
this sort.' How lit.?   **sub oculīs omnium**: i.e. *in cōnspectū
omnium.*

ac prō castrīs dīmicārētur, intellēctum est, nostrōs propter
gravitātem armōrum, quod neque īnsequī cēdentēs possent
neque ab signīs discēdere audērent, minus aptōs esse ad
huius generis hostem; equitēs autem magnō cum perīculō 5
proeliō dīmicāre, proptereā quod illī etiam cōnsultō plērumque cēderent et, cum paulum ab legiōnibus nostrōs remō-
vissent, ex essedīs dēsilīrent et pedibus disparī proeliō
contenderent. Accēdēbat hūc, ut numquam cōnfertī, sed

Figure 117. — Scene in a Roman camp.

Left to right: background, captives, foreground, legionary in marching order; cavalry
officer; legionaries, one with head bandaged in consequence of a wound; Roman standards; three captured standards, one in the left hand of a military tribune, the other two
lying on the ground; commander-in-chief, lictors, second in command, and horn blowers.

2. **intellēctum est**: 'it was evident.' How lit.?

6. **illī**, etc.: 'they,' the Britons, 'would fall back purposely.'

8. **disparī proeliō**: 'in battle with the advantage on their side,'
because Caesar's Gallic cavalry were no match for warriors fighting on
foot. How lit.?

9. **Accēdēbat hūc**: 'There was the further fact that.' **cōnfertī**: 'in close formation'

10 rārī magnīsque intervāllīs proeliārentur statiōnēsque dispositās habērent, atque aliōs aliī deinceps exciperent, integrī-
que et recentēs dēfatīgātīs succēderent.

17. Posterō diē procul ā castrīs hostēs in collibus cōnstitērunt, rārīque sē ostendere et lēnius, quam prīdiē, nostrōs equitēs proeliō lacessere coepērunt. Sed merīdiē,
cum Caesar, pābulandī causā, III legiōnēs atque omnem
5 equitātum cum C. Trebōniō lēgātō mīsisset, repente ex
omnibus partibus ad pābulātōrēs advolāvērunt sīc, utī ab
signīs legiōnibusque nōn absisterent.

Nostrī, ācriter in eōs impetū factō, reppulērunt neque
fīnem sequendī fēcērunt, quoad, subsidiō cōnfīsī, equitēs,
10 cum post sē legiōnēs vidērent, praecipitēs hostēs ēgērunt;
magnōque eōrum numerō interfectō, neque suī colligendī
neque cōnsistendī, aut ex essedīs dēsiliendī, facultātem
dedērunt.

Ex hāc fugā prōtinus, quae undique convēnerant, auxilia
15 discessērunt, neque post id tempus umquam summīs
nōbīscum cōpiīs hostēs contendērunt.

---

10. **rārī**: 'in small bodies.'   **statiōnēs**: here 'reserves.'

11. **aliōs**, etc.: 'were relieving one another in turn.' *171, b.*

12. **dēfatīgātīs**: *227, a,* (4).

17. 4. **pābulandī causā**: 'to forage.' Three legions and the
cavalry made a foraging party of extraordinary size.

6. **pābulātōrēs**: 'foragers.'   **advolāvērunt**: 'rushed upon.'
How lit.?   **ab . . . absisterent**: 'they did not hold back from the
standards of the legions,' lit. 'and the legions'; the Britons even
charged upon the legionaries, formed in order of battle. *238, d,* and
324, b, (2).

9. **quoad**: *190, c.*   **subsidiō**: 'on the support (of the legions).'
135, a.

10. **cum**: *184, a.*   **praecipitēs**: accusative, 'head over heels.'
151.

11. **suī colligendī**: *154, b.*   B. 339, 5; A. 504, *c*; H. 626, 3.

14. **Ex**: 'after.'   **auxilia**: *auxilia Britannōrum.*

With great dash Caesar's men force the passage of the Thames.

18. Caesar, cognitō cōnsiliō eōrum, ad flūmen Tamesim in fīnēs Cassivellaunī exercitum dūxit; quod flūmen ūnō omnīnō locō pedibus, atque hōc aegrē, trānsīrī potest. Eō cum vēnisset, animadvertit, ad alteram flūminis rīpam magnās esse cōpiās hostium īnstrūctās. Rīpa autem erat 5 acūtīs sudibus praefīxīs mūnīta, eiusdemque generis sub aquā dēfīxae sudēs flūmine tegēbantur.

Hīs rēbus cognitīs ā captīvīs perfugīsque, Caesar, prae- missō equitātū, cōnfestim legiōnēs subsequī iussit. Sed eā celeritāte atque eō impetū mīlitēs iērunt, cum capite 10 sōlō ex aquā exstārent, ut hostēs impetum legiōnum atque equitum sustinēre nōn possent rīpāsque dīmitterent ac sē fugae mandārent.

Cassivellaunus harasses Caesar's army on the march.

19. Cassivellaunus, ut suprā dēmōnstrāvimus, omnī dēpo- sitā spē contentiōnis, dīmissīs ampliōribus cōpiīs, mīlibus circiter IIII essedāriōrum relīctīs, itinera nostra servābat; paulumque ex viā excēdēbat locīsque impedītīs ac silvestri-

---

18. 1. **cōnsiliō**: the 'plan' of the Britons, revealed in chap. 19.

3. **locō**: *145, c.*   **hōc**: sc. *locō.*

6. **acūtīs sudibus**: 'with sharp stakes.'   **praefīxīs**: 'driven in front,' at the water's edge.

10. **cum**, etc.: 'though they were in water up to the chin.' How lit.? Caesar crossed the Thames from the south to the north side; precisely where he crossed, is not known. See Map 11.

19. 2. **contentiōnis**: 'of a general engagement.'   **ampliōribus cōpiīs**: 'the greater part of his forces.'

3. **IIII**: *quattuor.* It is not possible to determine whether Caesar means that Cassivellaunus kept in the field 4000 chariot-drivers, each having a chariot and accompanied by a warrior (N. to IV, 33, l. 2), mak- ing a force of 8000 men, or whether in *essedāriōrum* both drivers and warriors are included; in the latter case there would be 2000 chariots, each with two men, making a total of 4000 men.

5 bus sēsē occultābat, atque eīs regiōnibus, quibus nōs iter
factūrōs cognōverat, pecora atque hominēs ex agrīs in
silvās compellēbat; et, cum equitātus noster, līberius praedandī vāstandīque causā, sē in agrōs effūderat, omnibus
viīs sēmitīsque essedāriōs ex silvīs ēmittēbat, et magnō cum
10 perīculō nostrōrum equitum cum eīs cōnflīgēbat atque hōc
metū lātius vagārī prohibēbat.

Relinquēbātur, ut neque longius ab agmine legiōnum
discēdī Caesar paterētur, et tantum in agrīs vāstandīs
incendiīsque faciendīs hostibus nocērētur, quantum labōre
15 atque itinere legiōnāriī mīlitēs efficere poterant.

*The Trinovantes and other peoples submit. Caesar takes
Cassivellaunus' stronghold.*

20. Interim Trinovantēs, prope fīrmissima eārum regiōnum cīvitās, ex quā Mandubracius adulēscēns, Caesaris
fidem secūtus, ad eum in continentem vēnerat (cuius pater
in eā cīvitāte rēgnum obtinuerat interfectusque erat ā
5 Cassivellaunō, ipse fugā mortem vītāverat), lēgātōs ad
Caesarem mittunt pollicenturque, sēsē eī dēditūrōs atque
imperāta factūrōs; petunt, ut Mandubracium ab iniūriā
Cassivellaunī dēfendat, atque in cīvitātem mittat, quī
praesit imperiumque obtineat. Hīs Caesar imperat obsidēs
10 XL frūmentumque exercituī Mandubraciumque ad eōs

---

8. **sē effūderat:** 'had dashed forth.' **omnibus,** etc.: 'by all
the roads and passage-ways,' well known to the Britons. *134, a.*

10. **equitum:** *102.* **hōc metū:** 'from fear of this' danger.

11. **vagārī:** sc. *nostrōs.*

13. **discēdī:** i.e. *equitibus,* 'that (the cavalry) should leave,' etc.
tantum — nocērētur: 'that so great harm be done.' How lit.?

14. **labōre atque itinere:** 'by toilsome marching.' *238, d.*

20. 2. **Caesaris fidem secūtus:** 'attaching himself to Caesar.'
How lit.?

8. **Cassivellaunī:** 'at the hands of Cassivellaunus.' *95.* **quī:**
193, a.

mittit. Illī imperāta celeriter fēcērunt, obsidēs ad numerum
frūmentumque mīsērunt.

21. Trinovantibus dēfēnsīs atque ab omnī mīlitum iniūriā
prohibitīs, Cēnimagnī, Segontiācī, Ancalitēs, Bibrocī, Cassī,
lēgātiōnibus missīs, sēsē Caesarī dēdunt.

Ab hīs cognōscit, nōn longē ex eō locō oppidum Cassivellaunī abesse, silvīs palūdibusque mūnītum, quō satis 5
magnus hominum pecorisque numerus convēnerit.　Oppidum autem Britannī vocant, cum silvās impedītās vāllō
atque fossā mūniērunt, quō, incursiōnis hostium vītandae
causā, convenīre cōnsuērunt.

Eō proficīscitur cum legiōnibus.　Locum reperit ēgregiē 10
nātūrā atque opere mūnītum; tamen hunc duābus ex partibus oppugnāre contendit.　Hostēs, paulisper morātī, mīlitum
nostrōrum impetum nōn tulērunt sēsēque aliā ex parte
oppidī ēiēcērunt.　Magnus ibi numerus pecoris repertus,
multīque in fugā sunt comprehēnsī atque interfectī.　　15

An attack on the naval camp is repulsed.　Cassivellaunus yields.

22. Dum haec in hīs locīs geruntur, Cassivellaunus ad
Cantium, quod esse ad mare suprā dēmōnstrāvimus, quibus
regiōnibus IIII rēgēs praeerant, Cingetorīx, Carvilius, Taximagulus, Segovax, nūntiōs mittit atque hīs imperat, utī,

---

21. 2. **Cēnimagnī,** etc.: some of these small states are located on
the Map at the end of this volume.

4. **eō locō**: where Caesar met the envoys.　　**oppidum**: 'the
stronghold of Cassivellaunus' is thought to have been in the vicinity
of St. Albans.

6. **Oppidum vocant**: 'call (it) a stronghold.' Several fortified enclosures of extreme antiquity, intended not for permanent habitation
but only for refuge and defense in time of danger, have been found in
England.

22. 1. **in hīs locīs**: in the region of St. Albans.

2. **suprā**: chap. 14, ll. 1-3.

5 coāctīs omnibus cōpiīs, castra nāvālia dē imprōvīsō adoriantur atque oppugnent. Hī cum ad castra vēnissent, nostrī,
ēruptiōne factā, multīs eōrum interfectīs, captō etiam nōbilī
duce Lugotorīge, suōs incolumēs redūxērunt.

Cassivellaunus, hōc proeliō nūntiātō, tot dētrīmentīs
10 acceptīs, vāstātīs fīnibus, maximē etiam permōtus dēfectiōne cīvitātum, lēgātōs per Atrebātem Commium dē dēditiōne ad Caesarem mittit. Caesar, cum cōnstituisset
hiemāre in continentī propter repentīnōs Galliae mōtūs,
neque multum aestātis superesset, atque id facile extrahī
15 posse intellegeret, obsidēs imperat et, quid in annōs
singulōs vectīgālis populō Rōmānō Britannia penderet,
cōnstituit; interdīcit atque imperat Cassivellaunō, nē Man-
dubraciō neu Trinovantibus noceat.

Caesar returns to the coast, finds ships ready, sails to Gaul.

23. Obsidibus acceptīs, exercitum redūcit ad mare, nāvēs
invenit refectās. Hīs dēductīs, quod et captīvōrum magnum numerum habēbat et nōn nūllae tempestāte dē-
perierant nāvēs, duōbus commeātibus exercitum reportāre
5 īnstituit. Ac sīc accidit, utī ex tantō nāvium numerō tot
nāvigātiōnibus neque hōc neque superiōre annō ūlla omnīnō nāvis, quae mīlitēs portāret, dēsīderārētur, at ex eīs,

---

5. **castra nāvālia**: see chap. 11, ll. 8–13.

8. **Lugotorīge**: *10, c.*   **incolumēs**: predicative.

14. **id**, etc.: 'and that this could easily be wasted,' lit. 'drawn out,'
in profitless negotiations.

15. **quid — vectīgālis**: *97, b.*   **in annōs singulōs**: 'each year.'

17. **interdīcit**, etc.: 'laid the strictest injunctions on Cassivellaunus.' How lit. ? *175, b.*

23. 2. **refectās**: 'repaired'; cf. chapters 10, 11.   **dēductīs**:
'launched,' lit. 'drawn down' to the water, from the fortified enclosure
(*castra nāvālia*, chap. 22, l. 5) in which they had been guarded and
repaired.

4. **duōbus commeātibus**: 'in two trips.' *136, b.*

quae inānēs ex continentī ad eum remitterentur, et priōris
commeātūs, expositīs mīlitibus, et quās posteā Labiēnus
faciendās cūrāverat, numerō LX, perpaucae locum caperent, 10
reliquae ferē omnēs reicerentur.

Quās cum aliquamdiū Caesar frūstrā exspectāsset, nē
annī tempore ā nāvigātiōne exclūderētur, quod aequinoctium suberat, necessāriō angustius mīlitēs collocāvit ac,
summā tranquillitāte cōnsecūtā, secundā initā cum solvisset 15
vigiliā, prīmā lūce terram attigit omnēsque incolumēs nāvēs
perdūxit.

Division of the Army for the Winter.   24, 25

Grain being scarce, Caesar for the winter divides his army.

24. Subductīs nāvibus conciliōque Gallōrum Samarobrīvae perāctō, quod eō annō frūmentum in Galliā, propter
siccitātēs, angustius prōvēnerat, coāctus est aliter ac superiōribus annīs exercitum in hībernīs collocāre legiōnēsque in
plūrēs cīvitātēs distribuere.   Ex quibus ūnam, in Morinōs 5
dūcendam, C. Fabiō lēgātō dedit, alteram in Nerviōs Q.
Cicerōnī, tertiam in Esuviōs L. Rōsciō ; quārtam in Rēmīs
cum T. Labiēnō in cōnfīniō Trēverōrum hiemāre iussit ;

---

8. **et**, etc. : ‘both (the ships used) in the first trip, (sent back) after
the soldiers had been landed, and (other ships) which.’

10. **locum caperent** : ‘reached their destination,’ Britain.

12. **Quās** : ‘these’ ships, sent from the continent. *167.*

13. **aequinoctium** : Caesar must have left Britain shortly after the
middle of September, having been two months or more on the island.

14. **necessāriō angustius** : ‘of necessity rather closely.’ *153, a.*

24. 1. **Subductīs** : cf. chap. 1, ll. 6–7.   **Samarobrīvae** : *4, a.*

3. **siccitātēs** : cf. IV, 38, l. 3, and N.   **aliter ac** : *233, c.*

6. **dūcendam**, etc. : ‘to be led into the country of the Morini.’
229, b.

8. **in cōnfīniō Trēverōrum** : ‘on the Treveran frontier.’ The
site of Labienus’s camp is indicated on Map 11.

trēs in Bellovacīs collocāvit: hīs M. Crassum et L.
10 Munātium Plancum et C. Trebōnium lēgātōs praefēcit.

Ūnam legiōnem, quam proximē trāns Padum cōnscrīpserat, et cohortēs v in Eburōnēs, quōrum pars maxima est
inter Mosam ac Rhēnum, quī sub imperiō Ambiorīgis et
Catuvolcī erant, mīsit. Hīs mīlitibus Q. Titūrium Sabī-
15 num et L. Aurunculeium Cottam lēgātōs praeesse iussit.

Ad hunc modum distribūtīs legiōnibus, facillimē inopiae
reī frūmentāriae sēsē medērī posse exīstimāvit. Atque
hārum tamen omnium legiōnum hīberna praeter eam,
quam L. Rōsciō in pācātissimam et quiētissimam partem
20 dūcendam dederat, mīlibus passuum c continēbantur. Ipse
intereā, quoad legiōnēs collocātās mūnītaque hīberna cognōvisset, in Galliā morārī cōnstituit.

*Tasgetius murdered, Caesar transfers Plancus to the country of
the Carnutes.*

25. Erat in Carnutibus, summō locō nātus, Tasgetius,
cuius maiōrēs in suā cīvitāte rēgnum obtinuerant. Huic
Caesar prō eius virtūte atque in sē benevolentiā, quod in
omnibus bellīs singulārī eius operā fuerat ūsus, maiōrum
5 locum restituerat. Tertium iam hunc annum rēgnantem,
inimīcī palam, multīs ex cīvitāte auctōribus, interfēcērunt.

Dēfertur ea rēs ad Caesarem. Ille veritus, quod ad

---

9. **M. Crassum**: quaestor; see Vocab. under *Crassus*, (3).

11. **trāns Padum**: north of the Po, in Cisalpine Gaul; Caesar
writes from the point of view of one in Rome.

16. **inopiae—medērī**: 'to remedy the shortage' (Fig. 114). *106, b.*

20. **c**: *centum*. Caesar perhaps means that no two camps were
more than 100 Roman miles apart; if so, his estimate is somewhat
under the truth. *81.*

25. 1. **summō locō nātus**: 'of the highest rank by birth.' *128, a.*

3. **virtūte**: 'efficiency.'   **in sē benevolentiā**: 'loyalty to himself.' *150, d.*

7. **quod**, etc.: 'because a large number were implicated.' How lit.?

plūrēs pertinēbat, nē cīvitās eōrum impulsū dēficeret, L.
Plancum cum legiōne ex Belgiō celeriter in Carnutēs pro-
ficīscī iubet ibique hiemāre, quōrumque operā cognōverat 10
Tasgetium interfectum, hōs comprehēnsōs ad sē mittere.

Interim ab omnibus lēgātīs quaestōreque, quibus legiōnēs
trādiderat, certior factus est, in hīberna perventum locumque esse mūnītum.

Attacks of the Gauls upon Caesar's Winter Camps

1. Destruction of the force under Sabinus and Cotta by Ambiorix, 26-37

Ambiorix attacks the camp of Sabinus and Cotta, parleys.

26. Diēbus circiter xv, quibus in hīberna ventum est,
initium repentīnī tumultūs ac dēfectiōnis ortum est ab
Ambiorīge et Catuvolcō; quī cum ad fīnēs rēgnī suī Sabīnō
Cottaeque praestō fuissent frūmentumque in hīberna com-
portāvissent, Indutiomārī Trēverī nūntiīs impulsī, suōs con- 5
citāvērunt, subitōque oppressīs lignātōribus, magnā manū
ad castra oppugnātum vēnērunt.

Cum celeriter nostrī arma cēpissent vāllumque ascendissent, atque ūnā ex parte, Hispānīs equitibus ēmissīs,
equestrī proeliō superiōrēs fuissent, dēspērātā rē, hostēs 10

---

11. **comprehēnsōs,** etc. : 'to take into custody and send to him.'
228, a.

26. 1. **Diēbus . . . quibus :** 'About fifteen days after.'

3. **Ambiorīge et Catuvolcō :** chap. 24, ll. 13–14. *19, d,* and *10, c.*
Sabīnō, etc. : 'had met Sabinus and Cotta,' whom they came to meet
at the Eburonian frontier (*ad fīnēs rēgnī suī*). How lit.?

5. **Trēverī :** genitive.   **suōs :** the Eburones.

6. **lignātōribus :** 'wood foragers,' soldiers detailed to get wood
(Fig. 136, p. 402).   **manū :** *137, b.*

8. **vāllum :** the camp of Sabinus and Cotta was perhaps on the site
of modern Limburg ; see Map 11.

suōs ab oppugnātiōne redūxērunt. Tum suō mōre con-
clāmāvērunt, utī aliquī ex nostrīs ad colloquium prōdīret :

*Habēre sēsē, quae dē rē commūnī dīcere vellent, quibus
rēbus contrōversiās minuī posse spērārent.*

27. Mittitur ad eōs colloquendī causā C. Arpineius,
eques Rōmānus, familiāris Q. Titūriī, et Q. Iūnius ex
Hispāniā quīdam, quī iam ante, missū Caesaris, ad Ambiorīgem ventitāre cōnsuērat ; apud quōs Ambiorīx ad hunc
5 modum locūtus est :

*Sēsē prō Caesaris in sē beneficiīs plūrimum eī cōnfitērī
dēbēre, quod, eius operā, stīpendiō līberātus esset, quod Atua-
tucīs, fīnitimīs suīs, pendere cōnsuēsset, quodque eī et fīlius
et frātris fīlius ā Caesare remissī essent, quos Atuatucī,
10 obsidum numerō missōs, apud sē in servitūte et catēnīs tenu-
issent ; neque id, quod fēcerit dē oppugnātiōne castrōrum, aut
iūdiciō aut voluntāte suā fēcisse, sed coāctū cīvitātis, suaque
esse eius modī imperia, ut nōn minus habēret iūris in sē
multitūdō, quam ipse in multitūdinem.*

15 *Cīvitātī porrō hanc fuisse bellī causam, quod repentīnae
Gallōrum coniūrātiōnī resistere nōn potuerit. Id sē facile
ex humilitāte suā probāre posse, quod nōn adeō sit imperītus
rērum, ut suīs cōpiīs populum Rōmānum superārī posse
cōnfīdat. Sed esse Galliae commūne cōnsilium ; omnibus
20 hībernīs Caesaris oppugnandīs hunc esse dictum diem, nē*

12. **aliquī**: *49, a.*

14. **contrōversiās** : 'the questions at issue.'

27. 2. **Q. Titūriī**: Q. Titūrius Sabinus, called *Sabinus* in l. 3 of
chap. 26, and elsewhere. Cf. chap. 24, l. 14. *19, a–c.*

3. **missū Caesaris** : 'sent by Caesar.' How lit. ?

6. **Sēsē**, etc. : *Sēsē cōnfitērī, prō Caesaris beneficiīs in sē, (sē) eī
plūrimum dēbēre. 213, b.*

8. **eī**: for *sibi,* referring to Ambiorix.

12. **iūdiciō**: *138.*   **coāctū cīvitātis** : 'forced by his state.'
How lit. ?   **suaque, etc.** : 'and that the conditions of his authority
were such.'

qua legiō alterī legiōnī subsidiō venīre posset.   Nōn facile
Gallōs Gallīs negāre potuisse, praesertim cum dē recuperandā
commūnī lībertāte cōnsilium initum vidērētur.

Quibus quoniam prō pietāte satisfēcerit, habēre nunc sē
ratiōnem officiī prō beneficiīs Caesaris; monēre, ōrāre Titū- 25
rium prō hospitiō, ut suae ac mīlitum salūtī cōnsulat.   Mag-
nam manum Germānōrum conductam Rhēnum trānsīsse;
hanc affore bīduō.   Ipsōrum esse cōnsilium, velintne prius
quam fīnitimī sentiant, ēductōs ex hībernīs mīlitēs aut ad
Cicerōnem, aut ad Labiēnum, dēdūcere, quōrum alter mīlia 30
passuum circiter L, alter paulō amplius ab eīs absit.   Illud
sē pollicērī et iūre iūrandō cōnfīrmāre, tūtum sē iter per suōs
fīnēs datūrum.   Quod cum faciat, et cīvitātī sēsē cōnsulere,
quod hībernīs levētur, et Caesarī prō eius meritīs grātiam
referre. 35

Hāc ōrātiōne habitā, discēdit Ambiorīx.

Cotta refuses to receive advice from Ambiorix, an enemy;
Sabinus trusts him.

28. Arpineius et Iūnius, quae audiērunt, ad lēgātōs
dēferunt.   Illī, repentīnā rē perturbātī, etsī ab hoste ea

---

23. **initum**: sc. *esse.*

24. **Quibus**, etc.: 'Since he had done his duty by them and by his
country,' in attacking the Roman camp.   Duty to one's country is here
expressed by *pietāte*; cf. Fig. 25.   How lit.?   **habēre**, etc.: 'he
recognized (his) obligation.'   How lit.?

27. **conductam**: i.e. *conductam mercēde*; 'mercenaries.'

28. **Ipsōrum esse cōnsilium**: 'They (the Roman officers) were
to decide.'   How lit.?   *94, d.*   **velintne**: *204,* (1).

33. **Quod cum faciat**: 'in doing this.'   **cīvitātī**: *105.*

34. **hībernīs levētur**: 'it would be relieved of the winter encampment.'   *127, a,* and *335, b.*   **grātiam referre**: 'and would show
his gratitude.'   This wily and lying speech lured the Roman force to
its destruction.

28. 2. **etsī . . . dīcēbantur**: implies Caesar's disapproval of the
consideration afforded to Ambiorix's statement.

dīcēbantur, tamen nōn neglegenda exīstimābant, maximēque hāc rē permovēbantur, quod cīvitātem ignōbilem atque
5 humilem Eburōnum suā sponte populō Rōmānō bellum
facere ausam vix erat crēdendum.

Itaque ad cōnsilium rem dēferunt, magnaque inter eōs
exsistit contrōversia. L. Aurunculeius complūrēsque tri-
būnī mīlitum et prīmōrum ōrdinum centuriōnēs nihil
10 temere agendum, neque ex hībernīs iniussū Caesaris dis-
cēdendum exīstimābant; quantāsvīs Gallōrum, magnās
etiam cōpiās Germānōrum sustinērī posse, mūnītīs hībernīs,
docēbant:

Rem esse testimōniō, quod prīmum hostium impetum,
15 *multīs ultrō vulneribus illātīs, fortissimē sustinuerint; rē*
frūmentāriā nōn premī; intereā et ex proximīs hībernīs
et ā Caesare conventūra subsidia; postrēmō, quid esse levius
aut turpius, quam, auctōre hoste, dē summīs rēbus capere
cōnsilium?

29. Contrā ea Titūrius *sērō factūrōs* clāmitābat, *cum*
maiōrēs manūs hostium, adiūnctīs Germānīs, convēnissent,
aut cum aliquid calamitātis in proximīs hībernīs esset
acceptum.

---

4. **ignōbilem**: 'obscure' (Fig. 118.)
6. **ausam** [esse]: *62.*   **vix erat crēdendum**: 'was hardly
credible.'   How lit.?
9. **prīmōrum ōrdinum centuriōnēs**: cf. I, 41, l. 7 and N.

11. **quantāsvīs**: *copiās*; 'any force
of Gauls,' no matter how great.

15. **rē**, etc.: 'that there was no
difficulty about supplies.'   How lit.?

17. **quid esse**: *217, c.*

18. **auctōre hoste**: 'on the advice
of an enemy.'   *144, b,* (2).

Figure 118.— Coin of the
Eburones.

Gold.   The curved designs on the obverse perhaps represent boar's tusks.

29. 1. **sērō**: 'too late.'   **factū-**
rōs: *sē factūrōs esse.*   **clāmitābat**:
'kept protesting loudly.'   *78, a.*

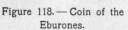

Brevem cōnsulendī esse occāsiōnem.   Caesarem, sē arbi- 5
trārī, profectum in Italiam ; neque aliter Carnutēs interfici-
endī Tasgetiī cōnsilium fuisse captūrōs, neque Eburōnēs, sī
ille adesset, tantā contemptiōne nostrī ad castra ventūrōs
esse.

Sēsē nōn hostem auctōrem, sed rem spectāre : subesse 10
Rhēnum ; magnō esse Germānīs dolōrī Ariovistī mortem et
superiōrēs nostrās victōriās; ārdēre Galliam, tot contumēliīs
acceptīs, sub populī Rōmānī imperium redāctam, superiōre
glōriā reī mīlitāris exstinctā.   Postrēmō, quis hōc sibi per-
suādēret, sine certā spē Ambiorīgem ad eius modī cōnsilium 15
dēscendisse ?

Suam sententiam in utramque partem esse tūtam : sī
nihil esset dūrius, nūllō cum perīculō ad proximam legiōnem
perventūrōs ; sī Gallia omnis cum Germānīs cōnsentīret,
ūnam esse in celeritāte positam salūtem.   Cottae quidem 20
atque eōrum, quī dissentīrent, cōnsilium quem habēre exi-
tum ? in quō sī nōn praesēns perīculum, at certē longinquā
obsidiōne famēs esset timenda.

---

6. **Italiam** : *283, b.*   **interficiendī**, etc. : chap. 25.

7. **sī adesset . . . ventūrōs esse** : *218*, (3).

8. **nostrī** : *155.*   **ad**, etc. : i.e. *castra oppugnātūrōs esse.*

10. **Sēsē**, etc. : 'that he had regard not for the enemy as adviser,
but for (the facts of) the situation.'

11. **Germānīs, dolōrī** : *112, b.*   **Ariovistī mortem** : nothing
is known about the death of Ariovistus, who was last mentioned in
Book I, chap. 53.

12. **victōriās** : over Ariovistus (I, 30–54), the Usipetes and Tencteri
(IV, 1–15), and the expedition into Germany in the previous year (IV,
16–19).   **ārdēre** : ' was ablaze.'

14. **exstinctā** : 'obscured.'   **quis**, etc. : *217, a.*

15. **ad . . . dēscendisse** : ' had resorted to.'

17. **in utramque partem** : 'for either alternative.'   **sī . . . dūrius** :
'if nothing serious should happen.' How lit.?

20. **ūnam — salūtem** : 'their only safety.'   *353, d.*

21. **dissentīrent** : 'disagreed with him.'   **habēre** : *217, c.*

*After heated argument Sabinus persuades Cotta to accept Ambi-
orix's guarantees of safety and leave the camp.*

30. Hāc in utramque partem disputātiōne habitā, cum ā
Cottā prīmīsque ōrdinibus ācriter resisterētur,
'Vincite,' inquit, 'sī ita vultis,' Sabīnus, et id clāriōre
vōce, ut magna pars mīlitum exaudīret; 'neque is sum,'
5 inquit, 'quī gravissimē ex vōbīs mortis perīculō terrear.
Hī sapient; sī gravius quid acciderit, abs tē ratiōnem reposcent; quī, sī per tē liceat, perendinō diē, cum proximīs
hībernīs coniūnctī, commūnem cum reliquīs bellī cāsum
sustineant, nōn, reiectī et relēgātī longē ā cēterīs, aut ferrō
10 aut fame intereant.'

31. Cōnsurgitur ex cōnsiliō; comprehendunt utrumque
et ōrant, nē suā dissēnsiōne et pertināciā rem in summum
perīculum dēdūcant; *facilem esse rem, seu maneant, seu
proficīscantur, sī modo ūnum omnēs sentiant ac probent;*
5 *contrā in dissēnsiōne nūllam sē salūtem perspicere.*

Rēs disputātiōne ad mediam noctem perdūcitur. Tandem dat Cotta, permōtus, manūs; superat sententia Sabīnī.
Prōnūntiātur, prīmā lūce itūrōs.

---

30. 1. **in utramque partem** : 'on both sides.' **disputātiōne** :
'discussion.'

2. **ōrdinibus** : = *centuriōnibus*. **ācriter resisterētur** : 'vigorous opposition was still offered.'

3. **Vincite** : 'Have your own way.' **et id** : *161, c.* **clāriōre
vōce** : 'raising his voice.' How lit.?

5. **ex vōbīs** : *97, d.* **terrear** : *194, a.*

6. **Hī sapient** : 'These,' the soldiers, spoken with a gesture, 'will
understand.' **sī**, etc. : *206,* (4).

7. **sī . . . liceat** : 'if you would consent.' **perendinō diē** : 'day
after tomorrow.'

9. **relēgātī** : 'treated as outlaws.'

31. 1. **Cōnsurgitur** : 'all stood up.' How lit.? **comprehendunt** :
by the hand. **utrumque** : Sabinus and Cotta.

2. **dissēnsiōne** : 'disagreement.'

7. **dat — manūs** : 'yielded'; Sabinus was the senior officer.

Cōnsūmitur vigiliīs reliqua pars noctis, cum sua quisque
mīles circumspiceret, quid sēcum portāre posset, quid ex 10
īnstrūmentō hībernōrum relinquere cōgerētur.   Omnia ex-
cōgitantur, quārē nec sine perīculō maneātur et languōre
mīlitum et vigiliīs perīculum augeātur.

Prīmā lūce sīc ex castrīs proficīscuntur, ut quibus esset
persuāsum, nōn ab hoste, sed ab homine amīcissimō cōn- 15
silium datum, longissimō agmine maximīsque impedīmentīs.

Figure 119. — Looking down into a depression thought by some to be
the valley where the ambuscade took place.

10. **quid**: '(to see) what.'

11. **īnstrūmentō**: 'outfit.'   **Omnia,** etc.: 'Every reason was
thought of (to prove to themselves) both why they could not remain
without danger and (why) the danger would be increased by the exhaustion of the soldiers resulting from (unrelieved) watches.'   How
lit.?

14. **ut . . . persuāsum**: 'like men convinced,' i.e. *ut* ('as') *eī,
quibus persuāsum esset* (subjunctive of characteristic).

16. **longissimō**, etc.: with disregard of every precaution.

The Roman force, enticed into a defile, is treacherously attacked.

32. At hostēs, posteā quam ex nocturnō fremitū vigili-
īsque dē profectiōne eōrum sēnsērunt, collocātīs īnsidiīs
bipertītō in silvīs opportūnō atque occultō locō ā mīlibus
passuum circiter duōbus, Rōmānōrum adventum exspectā-
5 bant; et cum sē maior pars agminis in magnam convallem
dēmīsisset, ex utrāque parte eius vallis subitō sē ostendērunt
novissimōsque premere et prīmōs prohibēre ascēnsū atque,
inīquissimō nostrīs locō, proelium committere coepērunt.

33. Tum dēmum Titūrius, quī nihil ante prōvīdisset,
trepidāre et concursāre cohortēsque dispōnere, haec tamen
ipsa timidē atque ut eum omnia dēficere vidērentur ; quod
plērumque eīs accidere cōnsuēvit, quī in ipsō negōtiō cōn-
5 silium capere cōguntur.

At Cotta, quī cōgitāsset, haec posse in itinere accidere,
atque ob eam causam profectiōnis auctor nōn fuisset, nūllā
in rē commūnī salūtī deerat ; et in appellandīs cohortan-
dīsque mīlitibus imperātōris, et in pugnā mīlitis, officia
10 praestābat. Cum propter longitūdinem agminis nōn facile
per sē omnia obīre et, quid quōque locō faciendum esset,

---

32. 3. **bipertītō** : 'at two points,' on opposite sides of a depression
through which the road ran (Fig. 119).   **ā** : 'off' ; N. to II, 8, l. 10.

5. **sē . . . dēmīsisset** : 'had passed down.'   **convallem** :
'defile.'

7. **novissimōs**, etc. : the enemy crowded toward those in the rear
and checked the advance of those in front.

33. 1. **quī** : 'since he.' *194, c.* B. 283, 3, *a* ; A. 535, *e* ; H. 592.

2. **trepidāre** : 'was greatly agitated.' *182.*   **concursāre** : 'rushed
from place to place.'

3. **ut,** etc. : '(in such a way) that all (his resources) seemed to fail
him.'   **quod** : *id, quod.*

4. **in ipsō negōtiō** : 'in the emergency.'

7. **auctor** : 'in favor of.' How lit.?

11. **omnia obīre** : 'to look after everything.'

prōvidēre possent, iussērunt prōnūntiārī, ut impedīmenta
relinquerent atque in orbem cōnsisterent.

Quod cōnsilium, etsī in eius modī cāsū reprehendendum
nōn est, tamen incommodē accidit; nam et nostrīs mīliti- 15
bus spem minuit et hostēs ad pugnam alacriōrēs effēcit,
quod nōn sine summō timōre et dēspērātiōne id factum
vidēbātur. Praetereā accidit, quod fierī necesse erat, ut
vulgō mīlitēs ab signīs discēderent, quaeque quisque eōrum
cārissima habēret, ab impedīmentīs petere atque arripere 20
properāret, clāmōre et flētū omnia complērentur.

34. At barbarīs cōnsilium nōn dēfuit. Nam ducēs
eōrum tōtā aciē prōnūntiārī iussērunt, nē quis ab locō
discēderet : *illōrum esse praedam atque illīs reservārī,
quaecumque Rōmānī relīquissent; proinde omnia in vic-
tōriā posita exīstimārent.*   5

Nostrī, tametsī ab duce et ā fortūnā dēserēbantur, tamen
omnem spem salūtis in virtūte pōnēbant, et quotiēns quaeque cohors prōcurrerat, ab eā parte magnus numerus hostium cadēbat. Quā rē animadversā Ambiorīx prōnūntiārī
iubet, ut procul tēla coniciant neu propius accēdant et, 10
quam in partem Rōmānī impetum fēcerint, cēdant (levitāte

---

12. **iussērunt prōnūntiārī** : ' they,' Cotta and Sabinus, ' gave orders
that the word be passed.'

13. **relinquerent** : ' that (the men) should abandon.'   **orbem** :
' circle,' corresponding with our hollow square. *338.*

14. **reprehendendum nōn est** : ' it is not to be criticized.'

15. **incommodē accidit** : ' turned out unfortunately.'   **mīlitibus** :
109, a.

17. **nōn sine** : *239, g.*   **dēspērātiōne** : ' despair.'

20. **cārissima** : ' most dear,' predicative ; *petere ab impedīmentīs
(ea) quae quisque cārissima habēret.*   **habēret** : *220.*   **arripere** :
' carry off,' before the enemy should loot the abandoned baggage.

34. 1. **cōnsilium** : ' presence of mind,' contrasted with the confusion and panic on the Roman side.

10. **coniciant** : ' that (his men) hurl.'

armōrum et cotīdiānā exercitātiōne nihil eīs nocērī posse),
rūrsus sē ad signa recipientēs īnsequantur.

35. Quō praeceptō ab eīs dīligentissimē observātō, cum
quaepiam cohors ex orbe excesserat atque impetum fēcerat, hostēs vēlōcissimē refugiēbant.   Interim eam partem
nūdārī necesse erat et ab latere apertō tēla recipere.
5 Rūrsus, cum in eum locum, unde erant ēgressī, revertī
coeperant, et ab eīs, quī cesserant, et ab eīs, quī proximī
steterant, circumveniēbantur; sīn autem locum tenēre
vellent, nec virtūtī locus relinquēbātur, neque ab tantā
multitūdine coniecta tēla cōnfertī vītāre poterant.

10 Tamen, tot incommodīs cōnflīctātī, multīs vulneribus
acceptīs, resistēbant, et magnā parte diēī cōnsūmptā, cum ā
prīmā lūce ad hōram octāvam pugnārētur, nihil, quod ipsīs
esset indignum, committēbant.   Tum T. Balventiō, quī
superiōre annō prīmum pīlum dūxerat, virō fortī et mag-
15 nae auctōritātis, utrumque femur trāgulā trāicitur; Q.

---

12. **nihil**, etc.: '(saying that) no harm could be done to them.'

13. **sē**: object of *recipientēs*; '(the Romans) returning to their
standards,' to the place in the circle whence they had made a charge.

35. 1. **praeceptō**: 'order.'   **eīs**: *barbarīs*.

2. **quaepiam**: 'any.' *49, a.*

3. **refugiēbant**: 'would rush back in flight.' *175, d.*   **eam
partem**: the charging cohort.

4. **ab latere apertō**: 'on the exposed side,' the right side, unprotected by a shield. *126, c.*

5. **eum locum**: in the circle.   **ēgressī**, etc.: sc. *mīlitēs*.

7. **locum tenēre**: in the circle, without charging.

10. **cōnflīctātī**: 'although harassed.'

12. **hōram octāvam**: *242, a.*   **pugnārētur**: *184, a.*   **ipsīs
indignum**: 'unworthy of them.' *142, b.*

13. **T. Balventiō**: *109, a.*

14. **superiōre**, etc.: Balventius had been the first centurion of the
legion the year before; he was now serving probably as a veteran volunteer (*ēvocātus*). *316.*

15. **auctōritātis**: 'influence.' *100, a.*   **femur**: 'thigh.' *18, d.*

Lūcānius, eiusdem ōrdinis, fortissimē pugnāns, dum circumventō fīliō subvenit, interficitur; L. Cotta lēgātus, omnēs
cohortēs ōrdinēsque adhortāns, in adversum ōs fundā
vulnerātur.

Sabinus and others surrender to Ambiorix, and are cut down.

36. Hīs rēbus permōtus, Q. Titūrius, cum procul Ambiorīgem suōs cohortantem cōnspexisset, interpretem suum,
Cn. Pompeium, ad eum mittit rogātum, ut sibi mīlitibusque
parcat.   Ille appellātus respondit:

Sī velit sēcum colloquī, licēre; spērāre, ā multitūdine im- 5
petrārī posse, quod ad mīlitum salūtem pertineat; ipsī vērō
nihil nocitum īrī, inque eam rem sē suam fidem interpōnere.

Ille cum Cottā sauciō commūnicat, sī videātur pugnā ut
excēdant et cum Ambiorīge ūnā colloquantur; *spērāre, ab*
eō dē suā ac mīlitum salūte impetrārī posse.   Cotta sē ad 10
armātum hostem itūrum negat, atque in eō persevērat.

37. Sabīnus, quōs in praesentiā tribūnōs mīlitum circum
sē habēbat, et prīmōrum ōrdinum centuriōnēs, sē sequī

---

16. **eiusdem ōrdinis**: 'of the same rank,' a first centurion.   **circumventō**: 'who had been surrounded.' *227, a,* (4).

17. **fīliō subvenit**: 'came to the rescue of his son.' *175, b.*

18. **ōrdinēs**: here 'centuries.'   **in adversum ōs**: 'full in the
face.'   **fundā**: by a sling-shot.

36. 2. **cohortantem**: *228, c.*   **interpretem**: *10, e.*

4. **parcat**: 'to spare.' *199, a.*

5. **impetrārī**, etc.: 'that the request might be granted, so far as the
safety of the soldiers was concerned.'

6. **quod**: the antecedent is implied in *impetrārī. 194, f.*   **ipsī**:
Titurius Sabinus.   **vērō**: *236, a.*

7. **nocitum īrī**: future infinitive passive; 'that no harm should be
done.' *54,* and *73, d.*

8. **Ille**: Titurius Sabinus.   **videātur**: *204,* (4).

10. **dē**, etc.: 'for their own safety and that of the soldiers.' *157, d.*

37. 1. **quōs tribūnōs**: *eōs tribūnōs, quōs.*   **in praesentiā**: 'at
the time.'

iubet et, cum propius Ambiorīgem accessisset, iussus arma
abicere, imperātum facit suīsque, ut idem faciant, imperat.
5 Interim, dum dē condiciōnibus inter sē agunt longiorque
cōnsultō ab Ambiorīge īnstituitur sermō, paulātim circumventus interficitur.

*Cotta dies heroically fighting. The soldiers spared by the day's
slaughter at night end their own lives.*

Tum vērō suō mōre 'Victōriam' conclāmant atque ululātum tollunt impetūque in nostrōs factō ōrdinēs perturbant.
10 Ibi L. Cotta pugnāns interficitur cum maximā parte
mīlitum.

Reliquī sē in castra recipiunt, unde erant ēgressī. Ex
quibus L. Petrosidius aquilifer, cum magnā multitūdine
hostium premerētur, aquilam intrā vāllum prōiēcit; ipse
15 prō castrīs fortissimē pugnāns occīditur. Illī aegrē ad
noctem oppugnātiōnem sustinent; noctū ad ūnum omnēs,
dēspērātā salūte, sē ipsī interficiunt.

---

3. **Ambiorīgem**: *123, b.*

Figure 120. — Statue of Ambiorix.

6. **sermō**: 'talk.' *12, b.*

8. **mōre**: *136, c.*   **ululātum**:
'yell,' a kind of war whoop.

13. **aquilifer**: 'eagle bearer.'
324, b, (1).   **cum**: 'although.'

16. **ad ūnum**: 'to a man.'
They probably killed one another.

17. **sē ipsī**: *162, c.* The
number of Roman soldiers that
perished was probably above 5000.
We are told that when Caesar
heard of this disaster he vowed
that he would cut neither hair nor
beard till he had wreaked vengeance on Ambiorix and the Eburones. Ambiorix is now regarded
by some as a national hero, as a

Paucī, ex proeliō ēlāpsī, incertīs itineribus per silvās ad
T. Labiēnum lēgātum in hīberna perveniunt atque eum dē
rēbus gestīs certiōrem faciunt.　　　20

2. Heroic defence of Cicero's camp against the Nervians.
38–45

A fierce attack, inspired by Ambiorix, is made on Cicero's camp.

38. Hāc victōriā sublātus, Ambiorīx statim cum equitātū
in Atuatucōs, quī erant eius rēgnō fīnitimī, proficīscitur;
neque noctem neque diem intermittit, peditātumque sēsē
subsequī iūbet. Rē dēmōnstrātā Atuatucīsque concitātīs,
posterō diē in Nerviōs pervenit hortāturque, nē suī in per- 5
petuum līberandī atque ulcīscendī Rōmānōs prō eīs, quās
accēperint, iniūriīs occāsiōnem dīmittant; *interfectōs esse
lēgātōs duōs magnamque partem exercitūs interīsse* dēmōnstrat; *nihil esse negōtiī, subitō oppressam legiōnem,
quae cum Cicerōne hiemet, interficī;* sē ad eam rem pro- 10
fitētur adiūtōrem.　Facile hāc ōrātiōne Nerviīs persuādet.

39. Itaque cōnfestim dīmissīs nūntiīs ad Ceutronēs,
Grudiōs, Levācōs, Pleumoxiōs, Geidumnōs, quī omnēs sub
eōrum imperiō sunt, quam maximās possunt manūs, cōgunt,
et dē imprōvīsō ad Cicerōnis hīberna advolant, nōndum ad
eum fāmā dē Titūriī morte perlātā.

---

defender of his people's liberties against Roman aggression; a statue
has been erected in his honor at Tongres (Fig. 120).
　38. 4. **Rē**: 'what had been done.'　　**concitātīs**: 'stirred up.'
144, b, (2).
　5. **nē**, etc.: 'not to lose the chance.'　　**suī**: *154, b.*
　8. **lēgātōs duōs**: Sabinus and Cotta.　　**magnam partem**: in
reality about one fifth of Caesar's legionaries.
　9. **nihil**, etc.: 'that it would be no trouble suddenly to crush the
legion . . . and destroy it.'　How lit.?　*97, a,* and *228, a.*
　10. **sē**, etc.: 'he promised his coöperation.'　How lit.?　*115, a.*
　39. 1. **Ceutronēs**, etc.: small Belgic peoples, clients of the Nervii.
　3. **eōrum**: *Nerviōrem.*　　**quam maximās**: *153, c.*

Huic quoque accidit, quod fuit necesse, ut nōn nūllī
mīlitēs, quī lignātiōnis mūnītiōnisque causā in silvās discessissent, repentīnō equitum adventū interciperentur.
Hīs circumventīs, magnā manū Eburōnēs, Nerviī, Atu-
10 atucī atque hōrum omnium sociī et clientēs legiōnem
oppugnāre incipiunt.   Nostrī celeriter ad arma concurrunt,
vāllum cōnscendunt.   Aegrē is diēs sustentātur, quod
omnem spem hostēs in celeritāte pōnēbant atque, hanc
adeptī victōriam, in perpetuum sē fore victōrēs cōnfīdēbant.

40. Mittuntur ad Caesarem cōnfestim ā Cicerōne litterae,
magnīs prōpositīs praemiīs, sī pertulissent; obsessīs omnibus viīs, missī intercipiuntur.   Noctū ex eā māteriā, quam
mūnītiōnis causā comportāverant, turrēs admodum cxx
5 excitantur; incrēdibilī celeritāte, quae deesse operī vidēbantur, perficiuntur.

Hostēs posterō diē, multō maiōribus coāctīs cōpiīs, castra
oppugnant, fossam complent.   Eādem ratiōne, quā prīdiē,
ā nostrīs resistitur.

---

6. **Huic**: Cicero; the probable location of his camp is indicated
on Map 11.   **quod**: for *id, quod.*

7. **lignātiōnis**, etc.: 'to get timber for the fortification' of the
camp (Fig. 136).   How lit.?   **discessissent**: *220.*

12. **vāllum cōnscendunt**: they stood on the rampart, behind the
palisades (*vāllī*).   *333.*

13. **hanc adeptī victōriam**: = *sī hanc victōriam adeptī essent.*
227, a, (2).

40. 1. **Mittuntur**: emphatic position.   *353, a.*   **ad Caesarem**:
at Samarobriva.

2. **sī pertulissent**: *sī nūntiī eās litterās pertulissent.*

3. **missī**: 'those who had been sent.'   *227, a, (4).*

4. **turrēs**: *333.*   **admodum**: 'fully.'   **cxx**: *centum vīgintī.*
Unless the camp were larger than would seem to have been required
for a single legion, the 120 towers must have been about 40 feet apart;
if so, men on the towers could defend the short spaces between with
any kind of missile.   Ordinarily such towers were about 80 feet apart.

5. **excitantur**: 'were erected.'

Hōc idem reliquīs deinceps fit diēbus.   Nūlla pars noc- 10
turnī temporis ad labōrem intermittitur; nōn aegrīs, nōn
vulnerātīs facultās quiētis datur.   Quaecumque ad proximī
diēī oppugnātiōnem opus sunt, noctū comparantur; multae
praeūstae sudēs, magnus mūrālium pīlōrum numerus īnstituitur; turrēs contabulantur, pinnae lōrīcaeque ex crātibus 15
attexuntur.

Ipse Cicerō, cum tenuissimā valētūdine esset, nē nocturnum quidem sibi tempus ad quiētem relinquēbat, ut
ultrō mīlitum concursū ac vōcibus sibi parcere cōgerētur.

*The crafty parleying, which was Sabinus's undoing, has no
effect on Cicero.*

41. Tunc ducēs prīncipēsque Nerviōrum, quī aliquem sermōnis aditum causamque amīcitiae cum Cicerōne habēbant,
colloquī sēsē velle dīcunt.   Factā potestāte, eadem, quae
Ambiorīx cum Titūriō ēgerat, commemorant: *Omnem
Galliam esse in armīs ; Germānōs Rhēnum trānsisse ; Cae-* 5
saris reliquōrumque hīberna oppugnārī.

Addunt etiam dē Sabīnī morte ; Ambiorīgem ostentant

---

12. **vulnerātīs**: *227, a,* (4).   **facultās quiētis**: 'chance to rest.'
How lit.?   *10, e.*   **Quaecumque**: *50, a.*

14. **praeūstae sudēs**: 'stakes hardened at the ends by burning';
the stock of ordinary weapons had given out.   **mūrālium pīlōrum**:
'of wall-pikes'; heavy pikes, to be hurled from the towers.

15. **contabulantur**: 'were provided with floors.'   **pinnae**: 'battlements.'   **lōrīcae ex crātibus**: 'breastworks of wattle,' made by
interweaving branches, and put up as screens to protect the soldiers in
the towers.   *98, b,* and *150, d.*

16. **attexuntur**: 'were attached,' lit. 'woven,' 'to the towers.'

17. **cum**: *187.*   **tenuissimā valetūdine**: 'in very delicate
health.'   *143, a.*

41. 1. **sermōnis aditum**: 'pretext for an interview.'

7. **ostentant**, etc.: 'they pointed to Ambiorix in order to inspire
credence.'

fideī faciundae causā. *Errāre eōs* dīcunt, *sī quicquam ab
hīs praesidiī spērent, quī suīs rēbus diffīdant ;*

10 *Sēsē tamen hōc esse in Cicerōnem populumque Rōmānum
animō, ut nihil nisi hīberna recūsent, atque hanc inveterāscere cōnsuētūdinem nōlint ; licēre illīs per sē incolumibus
ex hībernīs discēdere et, quāscumque in partēs velint, sine
metū proficīscī.*

15 Cicerō ad haec ūnum modo respondit :

*Nōn esse cōnsuētūdinem populī Rōmānī, accipere ab hoste
armātō condiciōnem ; sī ab armīs discēdere velint, sē adiū-
tōre ūtantur lēgātōsque ad Caesarem mittant ; spērāre, prō
eius iūstitiā, quae petierint, impetrātūrōs.*

The Nervians besiege the camp. Fire rages among the huts.

42. Ab hāc spē repulsī, Nerviī vāllō pedum x et fossā
pedum xv hīberna cingunt. Haec et superiōrum annōrum
cōnsuētūdine ā nōbīs cognōverant et, quōsdam dē exercitū
nactī captīvōs, ab hīs docēbantur ; sed nūllā ferrāmentōrum
5 cōpiā, quae esset ad hunc ūsum idōnea, gladiīs caespitēs

---

8. **faciundae** : *64, b.*   **Errāre** : 'were deluding themselves.'
eōs : Cicero and his men.   **quicquam praesidiī** : 'any help at all.'
49, a.

9. **hīs** : the Romans in the other camps.   **quī**, etc. : 'who were
in desperate straits.' How lit.?   *62,* and *135, a.*

10. **hōc esse — animō** : 'had this feeling.' How lit.?   *143, b.*

12. **cōnsuētūdinem** : 'custom' of imposing winter camps upon
them.   **per sē** : 'so far as they,' the Nervii, 'were concerned.'

17. **armātō** : 'in arms.'   **ab armīs discēdere** : in our idiom,
'to lay down their arms.'   **sē**, etc. : 'they might utilize him as
mediator.' *131, f.*

18. **spērāre** : sc. *sē*, Cicero.

42. 1. **spē** : 'hope' of cozening Cicero.   **pedem x** : in height.

2. **pedum xv** : in width, at the top.   *100, a.*

4. **nūllā**, etc. : 'having no stock of iron tools.' *144, b,* (3).

5. **esset** : *194, a.*   **caespitēs** : *10, d.*

circumcīdere, manibus sagulīsque terram exhaurīre cōgē-
bantur.

Quā quidem ex rē hominum multitūdō cognōscī potuit;
nam minus hōrīs tribus mīlium passuum III in circuitū
mūnītiōnem perfēcērunt. Reliquīs diēbus turrēs ad alti- 10
tūdinem vāllī, falcēs testūdinēsque, quās īdem captīvī docu-
erant, parāre ac facere coepērunt.

43. Septimō oppugnātiōnis diē, maximō coortō ventō,
ferventēs fūsilī ex argillā glandēs fundīs et fervefacta
iacula in casās, quae mōre Gallicō strāmentīs erant tēctae,
iacere coepērunt. Hae celeriter īgnem comprehendērunt
et ventī magnitūdine in omnem locum castrōrum distu- 5
lērunt. Hostēs maximō clāmōre, sīcutī partā iam atque
explōrātā victōriā, turrēs testūdinēsque agere et scālīs
vāllum ascendere coepērunt.

At tanta mīlitum virtūs atque ea praesentia animī fuit

---

6. **circumcīdere**: 'cut'; lit. 'cut around.'　　**sagulīs**: 'in their
cloaks.' *348*, and *131*, *a*.　　**exhaurīre**: 'to take out.'

10. **turrēs**: movable 'towers.'　　**ad**: 'proportioned to.'

11. **falcēs**: large 'hooks' for pulling down the palisade.　　**testūdinēs**: 'turtle-shell sheds,' probably less solid than those built by the
Romans. *342*, *a*.

43. 2. **ferventēs**, etc.: 'red-hot balls of kneaded clay,' which would
not crack to pieces when heated. Experiments have shown that red-
hot balls of clay the size of one's fist when thrown will retain their heat
long enough to ignite straw. *98*, *b*.　　**fervefacta iacula**: 'burning javelins.'

3. **casās**: 'huts.' *335*, *b*.　　**strāmentīs**: 'with thatch.'

5. **ventī magnitūdine**: 'by reason of the force of the wind.'
distulērunt: *hae casae ignem distulērunt*, the huts being looked upon
as agents. Probably the high wind carried bits of burning thatch all
over the camp. *239*, *h*.

6. **sīcutī**: 'just as if.'

7. **agere**: 'to move up.' The Gauls were using Roman methods
of attack. *342*, *a* and *b*.　　**scālīs**: 'with scaling-ladders.' *342*, *d*.

9. **At**: *236*, *a*.　　**ea praesentia animī**: 'such their presence of
mind.'

10 ut, cum undique flammā torrērentur maximāque tēlōrum
multitūdine premerentur, suaque omnia impedīmenta
atque omnēs fortūnās cōnflagrāre intellegerent, nōn modo
dēmigrandī causā dē vāllō dēcēderet nēmō, sed paene nē
respiceret quidem quisquam, ac tum omnēs ācerrimē for-
15 tissimēque pugnārent.

Hīc diēs nostrīs longē gravissimus fuit; sed tamen hunc
habuit ēventum, ut eō diē maximus numerus hostium vulnerārētur atque interficerētur, ut sē sub ipsō vāllō cōnstī-
pāverant recessumque prīmīs ultimī nōn dabant.

20 Paulum quidem intermissā flammā, et quōdam locō turrī
adāctā et contingente vāllum, tertiae cohortis centuriōnēs
ex eō, quō stābant, locō recessērunt suōsque omnēs remō-
vērunt, nūtū vōcibusque hostēs, sī introīre vellent, vocāre
coepērunt; quōrum prōgredī ausus est nēmō. Tum ex omnī
25 parte lapidibus coniectīs dēturbātī, turrisque succēnsa est.

---

10. **cum** : *187.*   **flammā torrērentur** : 'they were being scorched
by the flames.' *92, b.*

12. **cōnflagrāre** : 'were on fire.'

13. **dēmigrandī causā** : 'in order to withdraw' temporarily to
rescue his valuables or get a brief respite.   **paene,** etc. : 'but hardly
any one even looked around.'

14. **tum** : emphatic, 'then,' above all other times.

18. **ut** : 'since.'   **sub,** etc. : 'had crowded together close up to
the rampart.'

19. **recessum . . . dabant** : 'those behind would not give those in
front a chance to draw back.'

20. **intermissā flammā** : the Gauls dared not risk moving forward
the wooden towers while the flames were at their height.   **locō** : *145, c.*

22. **recessērunt** : 'drew back.'

23. **sī** : *204,* (4).   **introīre** : 'to come inside.'

25. **lapidibus** : the supply of ordinary weapons had given out.
Practice in hurling the pike enabled Roman soldiers to throw stones
effectively.   Both pike-hurling and stone-throwing find a parallel in the
throwing of hand grenades in the Great War.   **dēturbātī** : sc. *sunt* ;
'they were forced back in disorder.'

Brave deeds of two rival centurions, Pullo and Vorenus.

44. Erant in eā legiōne fortissimī virī, centuriōnēs, quī
prīmīs ōrdinibus appropinquārent, T. Pullō et L. Vorēnus.
Hī perpetuās inter sē contrōversiās habēbant, uter alterī
anteferrētur, omnibusque annīs dē locō summīs simultātibus
contendēbant.   5

Ex hīs Pullō, cum ācerrimē ad mūnītiōnēs pugnārētur,
'Quid dubitās,' inquit, 'Vorēne? aut quem locum tuae pro-
bandae virtūtis exspectās? hīc diēs dē nostrīs contrōversiīs
iūdicābit.'

Haec cum dīxisset, prōcēdit extrā mūnītiōnēs, quaeque 10
pars hostium cōnfertissima est vīsa, in eam irrumpit.

Nē Vorēnus quidem sēsē tum vāllō continet, sed, omnium veritus exīstimātiōnem, subsequitur.

Mediocrī spatiō relīctō, Pullō pīlum in hostēs immittit
atque ūnum ex multitūdine prōcurrentem trāicit; quō per- 15
cussō et exanimātō, hunc scūtīs prōtegunt hostēs, in illum
ūniversī tēla coniciunt neque dant prōgrediendī facultātem.
Trānsfīgitur scūtum Pullōnī et verūtum in balteō dēfīgitur.

---

44. 1. **Erant**: *90, a.*   **quī**, etc.: 'who were nearing the first
rank,' the position of centurion of first rank. *194, a,* and *315, a.*

4. **anteferrētur**, etc.: 'should have the preference over the other,'
as the better man. *69, b,* and *204,* (3).   **omnibus annīs**: 'year in
year out.'   **dē locō**: 'for advancement.'   **summīs simultātibus**:
'with the utmost bitterness.'

6. **ācerrimē — pugnārētur**: 'the fighting was the very hottest.'

7. **Quid**: 'Why.' *118, e.*   **locum**: 'opportunity.'

11. **eam**: *eam partem. 165, c.*   **irrumpit**: 'he rushed.'

14. **Mediocrī spatiō relīctō**: 'At a moderate distance,' perhaps
four or five rods from the enemy.

15. **quo**: refers to the wounded Gaul, who, as *prōtegunt* implies,
was not killed; trans. as if *et hōc,* 'and since he was made breathless
by the blow.' How lit.?

16. **prōtegunt**: 'protected.'   **illum**: Pullo.

18. **Pullōnī**: *109, a.*   **verūtum**: the same 'dart' that pierced
Pullo's shield.   **balteō**: 'sword-belt.' *322, e.*

Āvertit hīc cāsus vāgīnam et gladium ēdūcere cōnantī
20 dextram morātur manum, impedītumque hostēs circumsistunt. Succurrit inimīcus illī Vorēnus et labōrantī
subvenit.

Ad hunc sē cōnfestim ā Pullōne omnis multitūdō convertit; illum verūtō trānsfīxum arbitrantur. Vorēnus
25 gladiō rem comminus gerit atque, ūnō interfectō, reliquōs
paulum prōpellit; dum cupidius īnstat, in locum dēiectus
īnferiōrem concidit. Huic rūrsus circumventō subsidium
fert Pullō, atque ambō incolumēs, complūribus interfectīs,
summā cum laude sēsē intrā mūnītiōnēs recipiunt.
30 Sīc fortūna in contentiōne et certāmine utrumque versāvit, ut alter alterī inimīcus auxiliō salūtīque esset, neque
diiūdicārī posset, uter utrī virtūte anteferendus vidērētur.

Word of Cicero's desperate plight finally reaches Caesar.

45. Quantō erat in diēs gravior atque asperior oppugnātiō, et maximē quod, magnā parte mīlitum cōnfectā

---

19. **vāgīnam**: 'scabbard.'   **cōnantī**: sc. *eī*, 'as he' (lit. 'to
him') 'was attempting.'

20. **impedītum**: sc. *eum*.

21. **Succurrit illī**: 'ran to his rescue.' How lit.?   **inimīcus**:
'adversary.'

25. **rem comminus gerit**: 'engaged in close fighting.' *175, b.*

26. **in**, etc.: 'stumbling' (lit. 'thrown down') 'into a hollow.'

28. **ambō**: 'both.' *37, c.*

30. **contentiōne et certāmine**: 'in contest and combat.'
utrumque versāvit: 'shifted (the positions of) both.'

31. **alter alterī**: *171, b.*   **alterī, auxiliō**: *112, b.*

32. **diiūdicārī**: 'be determined.'   **utrī**: 'to the other.' *23, a,*
and *107, a.*   **virtūte**, etc.: 'should seem worthy to be considered
superior in point of valor.' *142, a.*

45. 1. **Quantō**, etc.: 'The harder and more violent — the more
frequently dispatches.' How lit.? *140.* B. 223; A. 414, *a*; H. 471,
10.   **in diēs**: 'day by day.'

2. **maximē quod**: 'chiefly because.'   **cōnfectā**: 'enfeebled.'

vulneribus, rēs ad paucitātem dēfēnsōrum pervēnerat,
tantō crēbriōrēs litterae nūntiīque ad Caesarem mittēban-
tur; quōrum pars, dēprehēnsa, in cōnspectū nostrōrum 5
mīlitum cum cruciātū necābātur.

Erat ūnus intus Nervius, nōmine Verticō, locō nātus
honestō, quī ā prīmā obsidiōne ad Cicerōnem perfūgerat
suamque eī fidem praestiterat.   Hīc servō spē lībertātis
magnīsque persuādet praemiīs, ut litterās ad Caesarem 10
dēferat.   Hās ille in iaculō illigātās effert et, Gallus inter
Gallōs sine ūllā suspīciōne versātus, ad Caesarem pervenit.
Ab eō dē perīculīs Cicerōnis legiōnisque cognōscitur.

3. Crushing defeat of the beleaguering Gauls by Caesar. 46-52

*Caesar makes hurried preparations, and proceeds by forced
marches to relieve Cicero.*

46. Caesar, acceptīs litterīs hōrā circiter ūndecimā diēī,
statim nūntium in Bellovacōs ad M. Crassum quaestōrem
mittit, cuius hīberna aberant ab eō mīlia passuum XXV;
iubet mediā nocte legiōnem proficīscī celeriterque ad sē
venīre.   Exit cum nūntiō Crassus.   Alterum ad C. Fabium 5

---

5. **dēprehēnsa**: 'caught.'

7. **ūnus**: 'one,' the only Nervian.   **intus**: in the camp.   **locō,**
etc.: 'of good family.'   *128, a.*

8. **ā prīmā obsidiōne**: 'soon after the beginning of the siege.'
152, a.

11. **in iaculō illigātās**: 'tied in a javelin.'   The javelin may have
been split; the dispatch, written on papyrus, may have been put between the parts, the javelin then being tied with cords as if acciden-
tally split and repaired.   **inter Gallōs versātus**: 'mingling with
Gauls.'

13. **Ab eō — cognoscitur**: *Caesar ab eō cognōscit.*

46. 1. **Caesar**: at Samarobrīva.   **hōrā ūndecimā**: about 5 P.M.;
it was now early autumn.   *242, a* and *b.*

5. **Alterum**: sc. *nūntium.*   **C. Fabium**: chap. 24, ll. 5-6.

lēgātum mittit, ut in Atrebātium fīnēs legiōnem addūcat,
quā sibi iter faciendum sciēbat. Scrībit Labiēnō, sī reī
pūblicae commodō facere posset, cum legiōne ad fīnēs
Nerviōrum veniat. Reliquam partem exercitūs, quod
10 paulō aberat longius, nōn putat exspectandam; equitēs
circiter cccc ex proximīs hībernīs cōgit.

47. Hōrā circiter tertiā ab antecursōribus dē Crassī adventū certior factus, eō diē mīlia passuum xx prōcēdit.
Crassum Samarobrīvae praeficit legiōnemque eī attribuit,
quod ibi impedīmenta exercitūs, obsidēs cīvitātum, litterās
5 pūblicās frūmentumque omne, quod eō, tolerandae hiemis
causā, dēvexerat, relinquēbat. Fabius, ut imperātum erat,
nōn ita multum morātus, in itinere cum legiōne occurrit.

Labiēnus, interitū Sabīnī et caede cohortium cognitā,
cum omnēs ad eum Trēverōrum cōpiae vēnissent, veritus
10 nē, sī ex hībernīs fugae similem profectiōnem fēcisset,
hostium impetum sustinēre nōn posset, praesertim quōs

---

6. **ut**: '(directing him) to.' *199, a.* Caesar would have to march
through the country of the Atrebatians (Fig. 121) in order to reach
Cicero's camp, in the country of the
Nervians. See Map 11.

7. **reī pūblicae commodō**: 'consistently with the public interest.'
138.

9. **veniat**: *216.* **Reliquam partem exercitūs**: chap. 24, ll. 7, 10.

Figure 121.— Coin of the
Atrebatians.

Gold. Obverse, crude head, with
mark on right cheek. Reverse, fanciful horse, and crescent.

47. 1. **antecursōribus**: 'advance
guard' of Crassus.

3. **Crassum**, etc.: Caesar left Samarobriva before Crassus arrived.

4. **impedīmenta**: *311.* **litterās pūblicās**: 'state documents,'
such as dispatches and accounts.

7. **nōn ita**, etc.: 'with very little delay.' How lit.? **occurrit**:
sc. *Caesarī.*

11. **praesertim quōs**, etc.: 'especially since he knew that they.'
184, b.

recentī victōriā efferrī scīret, litterās Caesarī remittit,
quantō cum perīculō legiōnem ex hībernīs ēductūrus esset;
rem gestam in Eburōnibus perscrībit; docet, omnēs equitātūs peditātūsque cōpiās Trēverōrum III mīlia passuum 15
longē ab suīs castrīs cōnsēdisse.

48. Caesar, cōnsiliō eius probātō, etsī opīniōne trium
legiōnum dēiectus ad duās redierat, tamen ūnum commūnis
salūtis auxilium in celeritāte pōnēbat.   Vēnit magnīs itineribus in Nerviōrum fīnēs.

Ibi ex captīvīs cognōscit, quae apud Cicerōnem gerantur, 5
quantōque in perīculō rēs sit.   Tum cuidam ex equitibus
Gallīs magnīs praemiīs persuādet, utī ad Cicerōnem epistulam dēferat.

Hanc Graecīs cōnscrīptam litterīs mittit, nē, interceptā
epistulā, nostra ab hostibus cōnsilia cognōscantur.   Sī ad- 10
īre nōn possit, monet, ut trāgulam cum epistulā ad āmmentum dēligātā intrā mūnītiōnem castrōrum abiciat.   In
litterīs scrībit, sē cum legiōnibus profectum celeriter affore;
hortātur, ut prīstinam virtūtem retineat.

Gallus, perīculum veritus, ut erat praeceptum, trāgulam 15
mittit.   Haec cāsū ad turrim adhaesit, neque ā nostrīs bīduō

---

13. **quantō**, etc. : ʻ (explaining) how dangerous it would be for him
to withdraw the legion.ʼ   How lit.?   *204*, (3).

14. **rem gestam** : ʻwhat had taken place,ʼ referring to the destruction of the force under Sabinus and Cotta.

48. 1. **opīniōne**, etc. : ʻ disappointed in his expectation of (having)
three legions he had been reduced to two,ʼ the legion which he had had
at Samarobrīva, and the one under Fabius that had joined him.

3. **magnīs itineribus** : *329*.

7. **epistulam** : ʻletter.ʼ

9. **Graecīs litterīs** : in Greek characters, not Greek words ; some of
the Nervians apparently could read Latin.

11. **adīre** : ʻto reach ʼ the camp.   **ammentum** : ʻthongʼ attached
to a javelin and used in throwing.

16. **turrim** : *14, b.*   **adhaesit** : ʻstuck.ʼ   **neque** : ʻand not.ʼ

animadversa, tertiō diē ā quōdam mīlite cōnspicitur, dēmpta
ad Cicerōnem dēfertur. Ille perlēctam in conventū mīlitum recitat maximāque omnēs laetitiā afficit. Tum fūmī
20 incendiōrum procul vidēbantur; quae rēs omnem dubitā-
tiōnem adventūs legiōnum expulit.

*Caesar approaching, the Gauls turn from Cicero's camp to attack
him.*

49. Gallī, rē cognitā per explōrātōrēs, obsidiōnem relinquunt, ad Caesarem omnibus cōpiīs contendunt. Haec
erant armāta circiter mīlia LX.

Cicerō, datā facultāte, Gallum ab eōdem Verticōne, quem
5 suprā dēmōnstrāvimus, repetit, quī litterās ad Caesarem
dēferat; hunc admonet, iter cautē dīligerenterque faciat;
perscrībit in litterīs, hostēs ab sē discessisse omnemque ad
eum multitūdinem convertisse. Quibus litterīs circiter
mediā nocte Caesar allātīs suōs facit certiōrēs eōsque ad
10 dīmicandum animō cōnfīrmat.

Posterō diē, lūce prīmā, movet castra; et circiter mīlia
passuum IIII prōgressus, trāns vallem magnam et rīvum
multitūdinem hostium cōnspicātur. Erat magnī perīculī rēs,

---

17. **dēmpta**: 'was taken down and.' *228, a.*

18. **perlēctam — recitat**: sc. *eam*; 'after he had read it through
he read it aloud.' *227, a.*

19. **afficit**: 'filled.'   **fūmī incendiōrum**: of burning villages,
set on fire as Caesar's relieving force passed through; the plural implies
more than one fire.

49. 1. **rē**: 'the fact' of Caesar's approach.   **per**: *123, a.*

4. **Gallum**, etc.: 'asked the same Vertico . . . for another Gaul.'
116, b.

5. **suprā**: chap. 45, ll. 7–12.   **quī**, etc.: *193, a.*

6. **hunc**, etc.: 'warned him' (Caesar) 'to proceed with caution.'
200, a.

12. **rīvum**: 'brook,' flowing in a 'wide valley.'

13. **Erat**, etc.: 'It was extremely hazardous.' How lit.?

tantulīs cōpiīs inīquō locō dīmicāre ; tum, quoniam obsidiōne līberātum Cicerōnem sciēbat, aequō animō remittendum 15
dē celeritāte exīstimābat. Cōnsēdit et, quam aequissimō
potest locō, castra commūnit, atque haec, etsī erant exigua
per sē, vix hominum mīlium VII, praesertim nūllīs cum
impedīmentīs, tamen angustiīs viārum, quam maximē potest,
contrahit, eō cōnsiliō, ut in summam contemptiōnem hosti- 20
bus veniat. Interim, speculātōribus in omnēs partēs dīmissīs,
explōrat, quō commodissimē itinere vallem trānsīre possit.

Caesar, encamped, pretends ~~. . . . . the Gauls~~ on, routs them.

50. Eō diē, parvulīs equ~~. . . . . . .~~clīs ad aquam factīs,
utrīque sēsē suō locō contin~~. . . .~~Gallī, quod ampliōrēs
cōpiās, quae nōndum convēn~~. . .~~nt, exspectābant ; Caesar,
sī forte timōris simulātiōne hostēs in suum locum ēlicere
posset, ut citrā vallem prō castrīs proeliō contenderet ; sī 5
id efficere nōn posset, ut, explōrātīs itineribus, minōre cum
perīculō vallem rīvumque trānsīret.

Prīmā lūce hostium equitātus ad castra accēdit proeli-
umque cum nostrīs equitibus committit. Caesar cōnsultō
equitēs cēdere sēque in castra recipere iubet ; simul ex 1c

---

15. **aequō**, etc.: 'that without anxiety he could slacken his pace.'
How lit.?

17. **haec**: object of *contrahit*; 'this' camp, 'although it was,' etc.

18. **vix**, etc.: ' (containing) barely 7000 men '; the two legions
with Caesar averaged hardly 3500 men each. *100, b,* and *307, b.*

19. **angustiīs**, etc.: ' by making the passages as narrow as possible.'
334, b, and Fig. 185.

20. **cōnsiliō**: *138.*   **hostibus**: trans. as if *hostium. 109, a.*

50. 1. **ad aquam**: 'by the water,' the brook mentioned chap. 49,
l. 12.

3. **Caesar**, etc.: *Caesar [sē continet suō locō] ut, sī . . . posset,
citrā vallem . . . contenderent.*

4. **suum locum**: 'a position favorable to himself.' *157, e.*
ēlicere: 'to entice.'

omnibus partibus castra altiōre vāllō mūnīrī portāsque
obstruī atque in hīs administrandīs rēbus quam maximē
concursārī et cum simulātiōne agī timōris iubet.

51. Quibus omnibus rēbus hostēs invītātī cōpiās trādūcunt aciemque inīquō locō cōnstituunt; nostrīs vērō etiam
dē vāllō dēductīs, propius accēdunt et tēla intrā mūnītiōnem ex omnibus partibus coniciunt praecōnibusque cir-
5 cummissīs prōnūntiārī iubent :

Seu quis, Gallus seu Rōmānus, velit ante hōram tertiam
ad sē trānsīre, sine perīculō licēre ; post id tempus nōn fore
potestātem.

Ac sīc nostrōs contempsērunt, ut, obstrūctīs in speciem
10 portīs singulīs ōrdinibus caespitum, quod eā nōn posse
intrōrumpere vidēbantur, aliī vāllum manū scindere, aliī
fossās complēre inciperent.

Tum Caesar, omnibus portīs ēruptiōne factā equitātūque
ēmissō, celeriter hostēs in fugam dat, sīc utī omnīnō pug-
15 nandī causā resisteret nēmō, magnumque ex eīs numerum
occīdit atque omnēs armīs exuit.

Caesar, joining Cicero, praises him and his men.

52. Longius prōsequī veritus, quod silvae palūdēsque
intercēdēbant neque etiam parvulō dētrīmentō illōrum

---

12. **obstruī**: 'be blocked up.'

13. **concursārī**: 'that the men rush about.' *73, d.*   **agī**: 'go
through their motions.' How lit.?

51. 1. **cōpiās trādūcunt**: *cōpiās rīvum trādūcunt. 114; a.*

4. **praecōnibus**, etc.: 'they sent criers around' the camp, 'directing that the announcement be made.' How lit.?

9. **in speciem**: 'for show.' The barriers in the gates, of turf and
only the breadth of a sod in thickness, seemed solid but were easily
pushed over from the inside.

10. **eā — intrōrumpere**: 'to break in that way,' through the gates.

14. **omnīnō — nēmō**: 'no one at all.'

52. 2. **neque . . . relinquī**: 'and that no opportunity was left
for (inflicting) even a trifling loss upon them.' How lit.?

locum relinquī vidēbat, omnibus suīs incolumibus eōdem
diē ad Cicerōnem pervēnit.

Īnstitūtās turrēs, testūdinēs mūnītiōnēsque hostium ad- 5
mīrātur; prōductā legiōne, cognōscit, nōn decimum quemque esse reliquum mīlitem sine vulnere; ex hīs omnibus
iūdicat rēbus, quantō cum perīculō et quantā cum virtūte
rēs sint administrātae. Cicerōnem prō eius meritō legiōnemque collaudat; centuriōnēs singillātim tribūnōsque 10
mīlitum appellat, quōrum ēgregiam fuisse virtūtem testimōniō Cicerōnis cognōverat.

Dē cāsū Sabīnī et Cottae certius ex captīvīs cognōscit.
Posterō diē, cōntiōne habitā, rem gestam prōpōnit, mīlitēs
cōnsōlātur et cōnfirmat; quod dētrīmentum culpā et teme- 15
ritāte lēgātī sit acceptum, hōc aequiōre animō ferundum
docet, quod, beneficiō deōrum immortālium et virtūte eōrum expiātō incommodō, neque hostibus diūtina laetitia
neque ipsīs longior dolor relinquātur.

---

5. **turrēs**, etc.: chap. 42, ll. 10–11, and Notes.

6. **prōductā**: 'drawn up' for review.　　**nōn**, etc.: 'that not one
soldier in ten had escaped unwounded.' How lit.? *170, a.*

9. **rēs**, etc.: 'the operations ' for defence 'were handled.'　　**eius
meritō**: Cicero's heroic defence is famous in military annals.

11. **appellat**: 'he addressed' in complimentary terms.

13. **certius**: an earlier report had come from Labienus (chap. 37).

14. **cōntiōne**: 'an assembly.'　　**rem**, etc.: 'set forth what had
happened.'

15. **quod dētrīmentum**: *id dētrīmentum, quod.*　　**culpā et
temeritāte**: 'through the culpable rashness.' *238, d.*

16. **hōc**: 'on this account.'　　**aequiōre animō**: 'with the greater
tranquillity.'

18. **expiātō**: 'atoned for.'

53–58. Summary. A report of the relief of Cicero's camp was quickly
conveyed to Labienus, encamped on the Treveran border (Map 11); but
notwithstanding this victory Cæsar found it increasingly difficult to prevent
revolts. Finally Indutiomarus and the Treverans made an attack on Labienus,
who first feigned fear, then surprised and routed them. Indutiomarus was slain.

COMMENTARIUS SEXTUS

Second Expedition into Germany. 9-29

Caesar bridges the Rhine, crosses, makes terms with the Ubii.

9. Caesar, postquam ex Menapiīs in Trēverōs vēnit, duābus dē causīs Rhēnum trānsīre cōnstituit; quārum ūna erat, quod Germānī auxilia contrā sē Trēverīs mīserant, altera, nē ad eōs Ambiorīx receptum habēret. Hīs cōn-
5 stitūtīs rēbus, paulum suprā eum locum, quō ante exercitum trādūxerat, facere pontem īnstituit. Nōtā atque īnstitūtā ratiōne, magnō mīlitum studiō, paucīs diēbus opus efficitur. Fīrmō in Trēverīs ad pontem praesidiō relīctō, nē quis ab hīs subitō mōtus orerētur, reliquās cōpiās equitātumque
10 trādūcit.

Ubiī, quī ante obsidēs dederant atque in dēditiōnem vē-nerant, pūrgandī suī causā ad eum lēgātōs mittunt, quī doceant, neque auxilia ex suā cīvitāte in Trēverōs missa neque ab sē fidem laesam; petunt atque ōrant, ut sibi

---

1-8. Summary. Early in 53 B.C. Caesar heard that the Nervians and several other peoples were preparing for war. By sudden movements he forced the Nervians, Senones, and Menapians to sue for peace, and marched into the country of the Treverans, who had meanwhile been defeated by Labienus.

9. 4. **Ambiorīx**: cf. N. to V, 37, l. 17.

5. **ante**: in 55 B.C.; see IV, 17–19, and Notes.

6. **Nōtā . . . studiō**: 'Since the plan (of such a bridge) was familiar and had been tried, (and) the soldiers worked with much enthusiasm.' How lit.?

9. **orerētur**: *61, b.*

12. **suī**: *154, b,* and *230,* (1). **quī doceant**: *193, a.*

14. **fidem laesam** [esse] : ' (their) pledge had been violated.'

MAP 13

OPERATIONS OF 53 AND 52 B.C.

Books VI, VII.

To face page 338

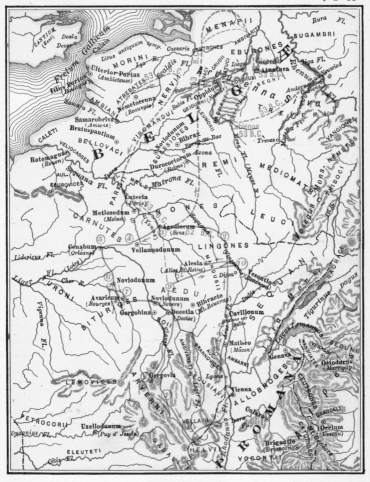

EXPLANATION

1. March into the Arvernian country, 52 B.C. (VII. 8).   2. Winter quarters (VII. 9).   3. Base, 52 B.C. (VII. 10).   4. Vellaunodunum captured (VII. 11). 5. Cenabum destroyed (VII. 11).   6. Noviodunum captured (VII. 12).   7. Avaricum destroyed (VII. 14–28).   8. Gergovia blockaded (VII. 36 ff.).   9. Junction with Labienus (VII. 62).   10. Defeat of Vercingetorix (VII. 67).

parcat, nē commūnī odiō Germānōrum innocentēs prō no- 15
centibus poenās pendant; sī amplius obsidum velit darī,
pollicentur. Cognitā Caesar causā reperit, ab Suēbīs auxilia missa esse; Ubiōrum satisfactiōnem accipit, aditūs
viāsque in Suēbōs perquīrit.

He finds it impossible to reach the Suebi.

10. Interim paucīs post diēbus fit ab Ubiīs certior, Suēbōs omnēs in ūnum locum cōpiās cōgere atque eīs nātiōnibus, quae sub eōrum sint imperiō, dēnūntiāre, ut auxilia
peditātūs equitātūsque mittant. Hīs cognitīs rēbus, rem
frūmentāriam prōvidet, castrīs idōneum locum dēligit; 5
Ubiīs imperat, ut pecora dēdūcant suaque omnia ex agrīs
in oppida cōnferant, spērāns, barbarōs atque imperītōs
hominēs, inopiā cibāriōrum adductōs, ad inīquam pugnandī
condiciōnem posse dēdūcī; mandat, ut crēbrōs explōrātōrēs in Suēbōs mittant, quaeque apud eōs gerantur, co- 10
gnōscant.

Illī imperāta faciunt et, paucīs diēbus intermissīs, referunt:
Suēbōs omnēs, posteā quam certiōrēs nūntiī dē exercitū
Rōmānōrum vēnerint, cum omnibus suīs sociōrumque cōpiīs,
quās coēgissent, penitus ad extrēmōs fīnēs sē recēpisse; 15
silvam esse ibi īnfīnītā magnitūdine, quae appellātur
Bacēnis; hanc longē intrōrsus pertinēre et, prō nātīvō mūrō

---

15. **commūnī odiō**: 'indiscriminate hatred.'   **innocentēs**, etc.:
'the innocent for the guilty.' *81.*

16. **amplius obsidum**: 'more hostages.' *97, b.* B. 201, 2; A.
346, *a*, 3; H. 442.

19. **Suēbōs**: *282.* **perquīrit**: 'made careful inquiry about.'

10. 2. **in ūnum locum**, etc.: cf. IV, 19, ll. 5–12.

9. **crēbrōs**: 'a great many.' The scouts were of course Ubians;
cf. chap. 29, l. 1.

15. **extrēmōs fīnēs**: 'the most remote part of their country.'
152, a.

17. **prō nātīvō mūrō**: 'as a natural barrier.'

*obiectam, Cheruscōs ab Suēbīs Suēbōsque ab Cheruscīs
iniūriīs incursiōnibusque prohibēre ; ad eius silvae initium*
20 *Suēbōs adventum Rōmānōrum exspectāre cōnstituisse.*

The customs of the Gauls and Germans contrasted.
11–28.

Political conditions in Gaul ; motives for leadership.

11. Quoniam ad hunc locum perventum est, nōn aliēnum
esse vidētur, dē Galliae Germāniaeque mōribus et, quō
differant hae nātiōnēs inter sēsē, prōpōnere.

In Galliā nōn sōlum in omnibus cīvitātibus atque in
5 omnibus pāgīs partibusque, sed paene etiam in singulīs
domibus factiōnēs sunt, eārumque factiōnum prīncipēs
sunt, quī summam auctōritātem eōrum iūdiciō habēre exīstimantur, quōrum ad arbitrium iūdiciumque summa
omnium rērum cōnsiliōrumque redeat.

---

18. **ab** : ' on the part of.'
19. **iniūriīs**, etc. : ' protected . . . from destructive raids.' *238, d,*
and *127, a.*
11. 1. Quoniam, etc. : ' Since we have reached this point ' in the
narrative. *73, d.*   **aliēnum** : ' out of place.' The digression which
follows was introduced to gratify Roman readers, who were eager to
have information about the new countries ; it is regarded by historians
as a source of information of prime importance regarding political institutions and conditions of life in Northern Europe in antiquity. Cf. N.
at end of chap. 23.
2. **dē — prōpōnere** : ' to give an account of.'   **quō** : ' in what
respect,' introduces an indirect question.
5. **partibus** : ' districts.' *289, c.*
6. **domibus** : *20, c.*   **factiōnēs** : ' party divisions.'
7. **eōrum** : *Gallōrum.*   **iūdiciō** : *138.*
8. **quōrum** : refers to (*eī*) *quī . . . exīstimantur ;* ' so that the
final decision in respect to all affairs and projects is referred to their
arbitrament and judgment.' How lit. ? *194, a.*

Idque eius reī causā antīquitus īnstitūtum vidētur, nē 10
quis ex plēbe contrā potentiōrem auxiliī egēret; suōs enim
quisque opprimī et circumvenīrī nōn patitur, neque, aliter
sī faciat, ūllam inter suōs habet auctōritātem.   Haec eadem
ratiō est in summā tōtīus Galliae; namque omnēs cīvitātēs
dīvīsae sunt in duās partēs.   15

12. Cum Caesar in Galliam vēnit, alterius factiōnis prīncipēs erant Aeduī, alterius Sēquanī.   Hī cum per sē minus
valērent, quod summa auctōritās antīquitus erat in Aeduīs
magnaeque eōrum erant clientēlae, Germānōs atque Ariovistum sibi adiūnxerant eōsque ad sē magnīs iactūrīs pol- 5
licitātiōnibusque perdūxerant.

Proeliīs vērō complūribus factīs secundīs, atque omnī
nōbilitāte Aeduōrum interfectā, tantum potentiā antecesserant, ut magnam partem clientium ab Aeduīs ad sē trādū-

---

10. **Id — īnstitūtum** [esse] **vidētur**: 'that practice seems to
have become established.'   **eius reī causā**: 'with this object in
view,' referring to the clause *nē . . . egēret.*   How lit.?   *161, a.*

11. **auxiliī**: *127, d.*   **egēret**: 'lack.'

12. **quisque**: 'each (leader).'   **neque . . . faciat, habet**:
207, (2).

14. **ratiō**, etc.: 'This same condition holds true of the whole of
Gaul.'   How lit.?

15. **dīvīsae**: *148, c.*   **partēs**: 'groups,' explained in chap. 12.

12. 1. **Cum**: '(At the time) when.'   *185, b.*   **alterius**: *23, b,*
and *171, b.*

2. **Hī**: 'The latter.'   Previously the Arvernians had held a position
of leadership; cf. I, 31, ll. 10–28.

4. **clientēlae**: 'dependencies,' states acknowledging the sovereignty
of the Aeduans.

5. **eōs ad sē . . . perdūxerant**: 'had won them over.'   **iactūrīs**: 'pecuniary sacrifices.'

7. **omnī nōbilitāte**: cf. I, 31, l. 21 and N.

8. **tantum — antecesserant**: 'they had so far outstripped (the
Aeduans).'

9. **clientium**: dependent states are here meant.

10 cerent obsidēsque ab eīs prīncipum fīliōs acciperent, et
pūblicē iūrāre cōgerent, nihil sē contrā Sēquanōs cōnsiliī
initūrōs, et partem fīnitimī agrī per vim occupātam possidērent Galliaeque tōtīus prīncipātum obtinērent. Quā
necessitāte adductus, Dīviciācus, auxiliī petendī causā,
15 Rōmam ad senātum profectus, īnfectā rē redierat.

Adventū Caesaris factā commūtātiōne rērum, obsidibus
Aeduīs redditīs, veteribus clientēlīs restitūtīs, novīs per
Caesarem comparātīs, quod ei, quī sē ad eōrum amīcitiam
aggregāverant, meliōre condiciōne atque aequiōre imperiō
20 sē ūtī vidēbant, reliquīs rēbus eōrum grātiā dignitāteque
amplificātā, Sēquanī prīncipātum dīmīserant.

In eōrum locum Rēmī successerant; quōs quod adae-
quāre apud Caesarem grātiā intellegēbātur, eī, quī propter
veterēs inimīcitiās nūllō modō cum Aeduīs coniungī pote-
25 rant, sē Rēmīs in clientēlam dicābant. Hōs illī dīligenter

---

11. **pūblicē**: 'for the state.'   **iūrāre**: as subject sc. *eōs*, i.e.
Aeduōrum prīncipēs.   **nihil — cōnsiliī**: 'no scheme.' *97, a.*

12. **occupātam possidērent**: 'seized . . . and retained in their
possession.' *228, a.*

14. **Dīviciācus**, etc.: the statement of Diviciacus himself on this
point is summarized by Caesar, I, 31, ll. 29–33.

15. **īnfectā rē**: 'without accomplishing his purpose.' How lit.?

16. **Adventū**: *147, b.*   **factā**, etc.: the ablatives absolute are
best translated by clauses. *144, b,* (2) and (3).   **commūtātiōne
rērum**: 'a complete change of relations.'

17. **Aeduīs**: dative.   **novīs**: sc. *clientēlīs*.

18. **comparātīs**: for the Aeduans.   **sē**, etc.: 'had joined themselves to them as allies.' How lit.?

20. **sē ūtī**: 'that they enjoyed.'   **reliquīs rēbus**: 'in all other
respects' also.

22. **quōs . . . intellegēbātur**: 'and since it was understood that
they (the Remi) stood equally high in Caesar's favor.' How lit.?

24. **inimīcitiās**: 'enmities.'   **coniungī**: *174.*

25. **Rēmīs**, etc.: 'attached themselves as dependents to the Remi.'
How lit.?

tuēbantur ; ita et novam et repente collēctam auctōritātem
tenēbant.   Eō tum statū rēs erat, ut longē prīncipēs habē-
rentur Aeduī, secundum locum dignitātis Rēmī obtinērent.

The two ruling classes, and the common people, in Gaul.

13. In omnī Galliā eōrum hominum, quī aliquō sunt
numerō atque honōre, genera sunt duo ; nam plēbēs paene
servōrum habētur locō, quae nihil audet per sē, nūllī adhi-
bētur cōnsiliō. Plērīque, cum aut aere aliēnō aut magnitūdine tribūtōrum aut iniūriā potentiōrum premuntur, sēsē 5
in servitūtem dicant nōbilibus ; quibus in hōs eadem omnia
sunt iūra, quae dominīs in servōs.

Sed dē hīs duōbus generibus alterum est druidum,
alterum equitum.

*The Druids: their power as priests and judges, their organiza-
tion, their teachings about the soul.*

Illī rēbus dīvīnīs intersunt, sacrificia pūblica ac prīvāta 10
prōcūrant, religiōnēs interpretantur ; ad hōs magnus adu-

---

26. **repente collēctam** : 'suddenly acquired,' in the brief period
since the defeat of Ariovistus, five years before.

13. 1. **aliquō**, etc. : 'are of any account and (receive) recognition.'
How lit.? *143, b.*

3. **servōrum locō** : 'as slaves.' *288, b.*   **nūllī cōnsiliō** : 'to no
consultation.' *23, a.*

4. **aere aliēnō** : 'by debt.'   How lit.?

5. **tribūtōrum** : 'of the taxes.'   **sēsē**, etc. : 'attach themselves as
bondmen.' How lit.?

6. **quibus**, etc. : 'and these have over them.' *167,* and *111.*

7. **quae**, etc. : sc. *sunt ;* 'as masters (have) over slaves.'

8. **alterum** [genus] : *171, b.*   **druidum** : '(that of) the Druids,'
a priesthood possessing great power in Gaul and Britain. Very little
is known of the Druids in Caesar's time beyond what he tells us in this
book.

10. **Illī**, etc. : 'the former have charge of the services of worship.'
sacrificia — prōcūrant : 'regulate the sacrifices.'

11. **religiōnēs interpretantur** : 'settle religious questions.' *238, a.*

lēscentium numerus disciplīnae causā concurrit, magnōque
hī sunt apud eōs honōre. Nam ferē dē omnibus contrōversiīs pūblicīs prīvātīsque cōnstituunt et, sī quod est
15 facinus admissum, sī caedēs facta, sī dē hērēditāte, dē
fīnibus contrōversia est, īdem dēcernunt, praemia poe-
nāsque cōnstituunt; sī quī, aut prīvātus aut populus, eōrum
dēcrētō nōn stetit, sacrificiīs interdīcunt.

Haec poena apud eōs est gravissima. Quibus ita est
20 interdictum, hī numerō impiōrum ac scelerātōrum habentur,
hīs omnēs dēcēdunt, aditum eōrum sermōnemque dēfugiunt, nē quid ex contāgiōne incommodī accipiant, neque
hīs petentibus iūs redditur neque honōs ūllus commūnicātur.

25 Hīs autem omnibus druidibus praeest ūnus, quī summam
inter eōs habet auctōritātem. Hōc mortuō aut, sī quī ex
reliquīs excellit dignitāte, succēdit, aut, sī sunt plūrēs

---

12. **disciplīnae causā** : 'in order to receive instruction.' How lit.?
81.

13. **hī** : the Druids. **eōs** : *Gallōs*.

14. **quod** : adjective form. *49, a,* and *168*.

15. **facta** : sc. *est*. **hērēditāte** : 'an inheritance.'

16. **fīnibus** : here 'boundaries.' **īdem dēcernunt** : 'they likewise render judgment.'

17. **quī** : substantive form; 'any (party)' to a controversy, 'whether
. . . or,' etc. *49, a.*

18. **dēcrētō** : 'decision.' *138.* **sacrificiīs interdīcunt** : 'they
exclude (the offender) from the sacrifices.' *127, a.*

19. **Quibus** : dative; 'on whom such an interdict has been laid.'

20. **numerō**, etc. : 'as wicked and crime-polluted men.' How lit.?

21. **hīs** : dative; 'these all men avoid.' *109, b.* **dēfugiunt** :
'shun.'

22. **contāgiōne** : 'contact' with the excommunicated.

23. **petentibus** : 'though they may seek (justice).' **honōs** : *13, a,*
and *b.*

26. **Hōc mortuō** : 'When he' (the arch-Druid) 'dies.' *160, b.*

27. **excellit** : 'is preëminent.' *205*, (1). **dignitāte** : 'in standing.' *142, a.*

parēs, suffrāgiō druidum, nōn numquam etiam armīs, dē prīncipātū contendunt.

Hī certō annī tempore in fīnibus Carnutum, quae regiō ₃₀ tōtīus Galliae media habētur, cōnsīdunt in locō cōnsecrātō. Hūc omnēs undique, quī contrōversiās habent, conveniunt eōrumque dēcrētīs iūdiciīsque pārent.

Disciplīna in Britanniā reperta atque inde in Galliam trānslāta esse exīstimātur, et nunc, quī dīligentius eam rem ₃₅ cognōscere volunt, plērumque illō discendī causā proficīscuntur.

14. Druidēs ā bellō abesse cōnsuērunt neque tribūta ūnā cum reliquīs pendunt, mīlitiae vacātiōnem omniumque rērum habent immūnitātem. Tantīs excitātī praemiīs, et suā sponte multī in disciplīnam conveniunt et ā parentibus propinquīsque mittuntur.   ₅

Magnum ibi numerum versuum ēdiscere dīcuntur. Itaque annōs nōn nūllī vīcēnōs in disciplīnā permanent.

---

28. **parēs**: i.e., *parēs dignitāte.*   **suffrāgiō**: ' by vote.'

30. **quae regiō**: ' a region which.'   *165, b.*   **Carnutum**: Fig. 122.

31. **cōnsīdunt**: ' hold a meeting.'   **locō cōnsecrātō**: the ' hallowed spot' was probably a sacred grove.   *145, a.*

34. **Disciplīna**: ' The system' of the Druids.   **reperta, trānslāta**: *221, b.*   It is not now possible to determine the truth of the tradition recorded by Caesar, that Druidism originated in Britain.

35. **dīligentius**: ' with special thoroughness.'   **eam rem**: ' the system.'   *160, d.*

14. 2. **ūnā cum reliquīs**: ' at the same rate as the rest'; the Druids paid taxes at a lower rate than ordinary citizens, or were not legally bound to pay taxes at all.   **pendunt**: N. to I, 36, l. 14. **mīlitiae**: *80, b.*   **vacātiōnem**, etc.: ' exemption from' (lit. ' of') ' military service and freedom from all (public) burdens.'   *81.*

4. **in disciplīnam**: ' to receive instruction,' from the Druids.   How lit.?   **parentibus**: *81.*

5. **mittuntur**: sc. *multī*; so to-day many "are sent" to school.

6. **versuum**: ' lines'; the metrical form was probably adopted to facilitate memorizing.   **ēdiscere**: ' to learn by heart.'

7. **vīcēnōs**: *36.*   **in disciplīnā**: ' under instruction.'

346 Caesar's Gallic War [B.C. 53

Neque fās esse exīstimant ea litterīs mandāre cum in
reliquīs ferē rēbus, pūblicīs prīvātīsque ratiōnibus, Graecīs
10 litterīs ūtantur. Id mihi duābus dē causīs īnstituisse
vidētur, quod neque in vulgus disciplīnam efferrī velint,
neque eōs, quī discunt, litterīs cōnfīsōs, minus memoriae
studēre ; quod ferē plērīsque accidit, ut praesidiō litterārum
dīligentiam in perdiscendō ac memoriam remittant.
15   In prīmīs hōc volunt persuādēre, nōn interīre animās,
sed ab aliīs post mortem trānsīre ad aliōs; atque hōc
maximē ad virtūtem excitārī putant, metū mortis neglēctō.

---

8. **ea**: the teachings set forth in verse. **litterīs**: 'to writing,' we
should say. **cum**: 'although.' *187*.

9. **ratiōnibus**: 'accounts,' inclu led under *rēbus* but added as a
concrete example ; trans. 'as in,' etc. **Graecīs litterīs**: 'Greek

Figure 122. — Coin of the
Carnutes.

Bronze. Obverse, head, Venus ;
inscription, PIXTILOS, a name. Reverse, lion-headed griffin holding down
a man ; inscription, PИX or PILX.

characters,' used in writing the Gallic
languages (cf. I, 29, l. 1). Gallic coins
occasionally had inscriptions in the Latin
alphabet, in imitation of Roman coins
(Fig. 122).

11. **quod . . . velint**: 'because (as
it has been suggested) they do not wish
to have their body of teachings spread
abroad among the common people,' who
would remain in subjection to the druidi-
cal priesthood only so long as they
should be kept in ignorance. *183, a*.

12. **discunt**: vivid use of the indicative ; cf. *220*. **litterīs**: *135, a*.
minus — studēre: 'pay too little heed.'

13. **quod**: 'and this.' *167*. **praesidiō litterārum**: 'through
reliance upon written records.' How lit. ?

14. **perdiscendō**: 'learning by heart.' *230*, (4). The truth of
this statement is unquestioned.

15. **animās**: 'the soul,' as life-principle ; the doctrine of transmigration of souls, or metempsychosis, was widely accepted in antiquity, and
is held to-day by the Buddhists. *92, a*.

16. **aliīs, aliōs**: *171, b*, and *154, a*. **hōc**: 'by this (belief).'

17. **excitārī**: impersonal ; 'men are spurred on.' **metū**, etc.:
144, b, (3).

Multa praetereā dē sīderibus atque eōrum mōtū, dē mundī
ac terrārum magnitūdine, dē rērum nātūrā, dē deōrum immortālium vī ac potestāte disputant et iuventūtī trādunt. 20

The knights : their warlike occupation, and their retainers.

15. Alterum genus est equitum. Hī, cum est ūsus
atque aliquod bellum incidit (quod ferē ante Caesaris adventum quotannīs accidere solēbat, utī aut ipsī iniūriās īnferrent aut illātās prōpulsārent), omnēs in bellō versantur,
atque eōrum ut quisque est genere cōpiīsque amplissimus, 5
ita plūrimōs circum sē ambactōs clientēsque habet. Hanc
ūnam grātiam potentiamque nōvērunt.

Superstitions of the Gauls ; their human sacrifices.

16. Nātiō est omnis Gallōrum admodum dēdita religiōnibus, atque ob eam causam, quī sunt affectī graviōribus
morbīs quīque in proeliīs perīculīsque versantur, aut prō
victimīs hominēs immolant aut sē immolātūrōs vovent, ad-
ministrīsque ad ea sacrificia druidibus ūtuntur, quod, prō 5
vītā hominis nisi hominis vīta reddātur, nōn posse deōrum

---

18. **Multa — disputant**: 'They treat many subjects.' **sīderibus**: 'heavenly bodies.' **mundī**: 'the universe.'

19. **terrārum**: for *orbis terrārum*, 'the earth.'

15. 1. **Alterum**: cf. chap. 13, l. 8. **cum**: 'whenever.' *186, a.*

2. **aliquod**: *49, a.* **incidit**: 'breaks out.' **quod**: 'and this.'

5. **eōrum**, etc. : 'each knight has about him the greatest number
of vassals and retainers that his social position and resources will war-
rant.' How lit.? A notable example is Orgetorix (I, 4, ll. 4-7).

6. **Hanc**, etc. : 'This (numerousness of retinue) is the only sign of
influence and power that they recognize.' How lit.? *176, b.*

16. 1. **omnis**: 'as a whole.' **dēdita**: 'devoted.' *148, c.* **religiōnibus**: 'religious observances.'

3. **morbīs**: 'diseases.' **prō victimīs**: 'as victims.'

4. **immolant**: 'offer up.' **sē immolātūrōs**: i.e. *sē immolātūrōs
esse hominēs prō victimīs.* **vovent**: 'vow.' **administrīs**: 'as
officiating priests.' *7, c,* and *131, f.*

immortālium nūmen plācārī arbitrantur; pūblicēque eiusdem generis habent īnstitūta sacrificia.

Aliī immānī magnitūdine simulācra habent, quōrum con-
10 texta vīminibus membra vīvīs hominibus complent; quibus
succēnsīs, circumventī flammā exanimantur hominēs.

Supplicia eōrum, quī in fūrtō aut latrōciniō aut aliquā
noxiā sint comprehēnsī, grātiōra dīs immortālibus esse
arbitrantur; sed cum eius generis cōpia dēfēcit, etiam ad
15 innocentium supplicia dēscendunt.

The gods worshipped by the Gauls.

17. Deōrum maximē Mercurium colunt. Huius sunt
plūrima simulācra; hunc omnium inventōrem artium fe-

---

7. **nūmen**: 'majesty;' lit. 'nod.'   **plācārī**: 'be appeased.'

8. **habent īnstitūta**: 229, a. B. 337, 7; A. 497, b; H. 431, 3.
sacrificia: human sacrifices were offered at times in Eastern lands (cf.,
for example, 2 Kings, iii. 27), and in ancient Mexico; and even at Rome
an instance of human sacrifice is reported as late as 216 b. c.

9. **simulācra**: 'images' of wickerwork, having some resemblance
to the human form.

10. **vīvīs**: 'living.'   **quibus**: *et eīs* (*simulācrīs*).

12. **Supplicia**: *92, a*.   **fūrtō**: 'theft.'   **latrōciniō**: 'highway
robbery.'

13. **noxiā**: 'crime.'   **grātiōra**: 'more acceptable.'

15. **dēscendunt**: 'resort.'

17. 1. **Deōrum**: dependent on *maximē*. *97, e*.   **Mercurium**:
in the case of Mercury and the other gods mentioned, Caesar gives the
name of the Roman divinity whose attributes and functions seemed to
him to correspond most nearly with those of the Gallic divinity; the
Gallic names were of course not known to Roman readers.

2. **simulācra**: since the Gauls began making statues only after the
Roman conquest, it has been suggested that the 'images' of Mercury
referred to here were the huge upright stones (menhirs) of which several
groups must have been seen by Caesar in Gaul (Fig. 123), and that these
were associated in some way with the worship of the Gallic divinity
identified by him with this god. Pillars of a certain type were sacred
to Hermes, the Greek god corresponding with Mercury.   **inventōrem**:
80, b.   **artium**: 'arts.' *81*.   **ferunt**: *172, c*.

runt, hunc viārum atque itinerum ducem, hunc ad quaestūs pecūniae mercātūrāsque habēre vim maximam arbitrantur; post hunc, Apollinem et Mārtem et Iovem et Minervam. 5

Dē hīs eandem ferē, quam reliquae gentēs, habent opīniōnem : Apollinem morbōs dēpellere, Minervam operum atque artificiōrum initia trādere, Iovem imperium caelestium tenēre, Mārtem bella regere.

Huic, cum proeliō dīmicāre cōnstituērunt, ea, quae bellō 10 cēperint, plērumque dēvovent; cum superāvērunt, animālia capta immolant reliquāsque rēs in ūnum locum cōnferunt.

Figure 123. — Sacred stones called Menhirs.

Probably thought by Caesar to be images of Mercury. These Menhirs are near that part of the west coast where Caesar and his army witnessed the sea-fight with the Venetans (III, 14, l. 25). In the background is a modern windmill.

---

3. **viārum** : Mercury is 'guide for roads' in that he points out the road, and 'for journeys' because he accompanies the traveler on the way.   **quaestūs** : 'acquisition.' *92, a.*

4. **mercātūrās** : 'commercial transactions.'

7. **Apollinem**, etc. : the infinitive clauses are appositional.   *12, d.*
operum, etc. : 'imparts the elements of the trades and crafts.'

8. **caelestium** : 'the gods' as dwellers in the sky (*caelum*).

11. **cēperint** : subjunctive in implied indirect discourse, for the future perfect indicative.   **cum superāvērunt** : *post victōriam.*
animālia : *16, b,* and *80, b.*

Multīs in cīvitātibus hārum rērum exstrūctōs tumulōs locīs
cōnsecrātīs cōnspicārī licet; neque saepe accidit, ut
15 neglēctā quispiam religiōne aut capta apud sē occultāre
aut posita tollere audēret, gravissimumque eī reī supplicium
cum cruciātū cōnstitūtum est.

18. Gallī sē omnēs ab Dīte patre prōgnātōs praedicant
idque ab druidibus prōditum dīcunt. Ob. eam causam
spatia omnis temporis nōn numerō diērum, sed noctium
fīniunt; diēs nātālēs et mēnsium et annōrum initia sīc ob-
5 servant, ut noctem diēs subsequātur.

Strange customs of the Gauls.

In reliquīs vītae īnstitūtīs hōc ferē ab reliquīs differunt,
quod suōs līberōs, nisi cum adolēvērunt, ut mūnus mīlitiae

---

13. **tumulōs**: such piles of booty would after a time rot down and
be covered with vegetation, presenting the appearance of a mound.

15. **quispiam**: *49, a.*   **capta**: neuter plural, accusative. *227,
a*, (4).   **apud sē**: 'in his possession.'

16. **posita tollere**: 'to take away what had been deposited' as an
offering to the gods, as Achan did (Joshua, chap. 7, verses 20–22).
supplicium, etc.: like the terrible doom of Achan (Josh. 7, 23–26).

18. 1. **Dīte patre**: Caesar identifies the Gallic divinity with a
Roman god of the Underworld known in earlier times as 'Father Dis'
(*Dīs pater*), later generally called Pluto. *128, b.*

2. **Ob eam causam**: because sprung from the god of the Underworld, the realm of darkness and night.

4. **fīniunt**: 'measure.' The ancient Germans also reckoned time
by the number of nights; traces of this reckoning remain in our words
"fortnight" (= fourteen nights) and "sennight" (= seven nights, i.e.
a week).   **diēs nātālēs**: 'birthdays.'

5. **ut**, etc.: instead of saying "the first day of the month," as we do,
the Gauls said 'the first night of the month,' 'the first night of the year,'
'birthnight,' etc. Primitive peoples find it more difficult to keep track of
time by days than by nights because it is easier to note the changes of
the moon than of the sun. So Indians reckoned time by "moons."

6. **hōc**: *142, a.*   **ab reliquīs**: 'from all other people.' *171, a.*

7. **adolēvērunt**: 'have grown up.'   **mūnus mīlitiae**: 'military
service.'

sustinēre possint, palam ad sē adīre nōn patiuntur, fīlium-
que puerīlī aetāte in pūblicō in cōnspectū patris assistere
turpe dūcunt.   10

19. Virī, quantās pecūniās ab uxōribus dōtis nōmine
accēpērunt, tantās ex suīs bonīs, aestimātiōne factā, cum
dōtibus commūnicant. Huius omnis pecūniae coniūnctim
ratiō habētur frūctūsque servantur; uter eōrum vītā supe-
rāvit, ad eum pars utrīusque cum frūctibus superiōrum 5
temporum pervenit.

Virī in uxōrēs, sīcutī in līberōs, vītae necisque habent
potestātem; et cum pater familiae, illūstriōre locō nātus,

---

8. **sē**: only the fathers are referred to, as shown by l. 9.

9. **puerīlī aetāte**: 'while in the age of childhood.' How lit.?
143, a.

10. **turpe**: predicative, 'consider it disgraceful for a son . . . to appear.' On public occasions the Gauls would appear armed; it was
thought in bad form for an armed man to have with him, in a public
place, a son who was not also armed.

19. 1. **Virī**: 'husbands'; German *Mann* is similarly used.   **pecūniās**: 'property' in general; trans. as if *tantās pecūniās, quantās*.
dōtis nōmine: 'as dowry.' *17, c.*

2. **bonīs**: 'possessions.'   **aestimātiōne factā**: 'making an estimate of value.' *144, b, (2).*

3. **commūnicant**: 'set aside.' From his own property the husband set aside an amount equal to the dower received with the wife.
The income from this common fund, or estate, was saved up and
added to the principal; when the husband or wife died the whole
went to the survivor.   **coniūnctim**, etc.: 'a joint account is kept.'
How lit.?

4. **frūctūs**: 'income.' *92, a.*   **uter**: 'whichever,' husband or
wife.   **vītā**: *142, a.*

5. **utrīusque**: 'of both.' *51.* The custom could have prevailed
only among the higher classes, on account of the abject poverty of the
common folk (chap. 13, ll. 2–4).

7. **in**: 'over.'   **vītae**, etc.: among the early Romans also the
father had 'the power of life and death' over his household.

8. **pater familiae**: 'the head of a family.'   **illūstriōre locō
nātus**: 'of higher rank.' *128, a.*

dēcessit, eius propinquī conveniunt et, dē morte sī rēs in
10 suspīciōnem vēnit, dē uxōribus in servīlem modum quaesti-
ōnem habent et, sī compertum est, īgnī atque omnibus tormentīs excruciātās interficiunt.

Fūnera sunt prō cultū Gallōrum magnifica et sūmptuōsa;
omniaque, quae vīvīs cordī fuisse arbitrantur, in īgnem īn-
15 ferunt, etiam animālia, ac paulō suprā hanc memoriam servī

---

9. **dē**, etc.: 'if suspicion has arisen regarding (the cause of) death.'
How lit.?

10. **uxōribus**: the plural implies the existence of polygamy among
the higher classes in Gaul.   **in**, etc.: 'an examination like that of
slaves,' under torture. How
lit.? Roman law and custom
sanctioned the torture of
slaves on the death of a
master under suspicious circumstances.

11. **compertum est**: impersonal, '(their guilt) has
been proved.'   **īgnī**, etc.:
'agonize and kill them with
fire and every instrument of
torture.' *228, a*, and *205* (3).

13. **Fūnera**: 'funerals.'
13, e.   **prō cultū**: 'considering the civilization,'
which in art as in life seemed
to the Roman crude (Fig.
124).   **magnifica**: 'splendid.' *31.*   **sūmptuōsa**:
'costly.' *75, f.*

14. **cordī fuisse**: 'were
dear.' How lit.? *10, g*, and
112, b.   **īgnem**: of the
funeral pyre. The ashes were
sometimes buried in wooden

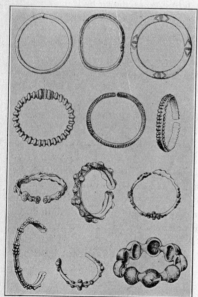

Figure 124. — Gallic bronze bracelets.

Bronze bracelets and neck rings were popular
ornaments in ancient Gaul.

buckets adorned with bronze ornaments (Fig. 125; wood restored).

15. **suprā hanc memoriam**: 'before our time.' How lit.?

et clientēs, quōs ab eīs dīlēctōs esse cōnstābat, iūstīs fūne-
bribus cōnfectīs, ūnā cremābantur.

Their precautions in dealing with rumors affecting public safety.

20. Quae cīvitātēs commodius suam rem pūblicam administrāre exīstimantur, habent lēgibus sānctum, sī quis
quid dē rē pūblicā ā fīnitimīs rūmōre aut fāmā accēperit,
utī ad magistrātum dēferat nēve cum quō aliō commūnicet,
quod saepe hominēs temerāriōs atque imperītōs falsīs rū- 5
mōribus terrērī et ad facinus impellī et dē summīs rēbus
cōnsilium capere cognitum est.

Magistrātūs, quae vīsa sunt, occultant, quaeque esse ex
ūsū iūdicāvērunt, multitūdinī prōdunt. Dē rē pūblicā nisi
per concilium loquī nōn concēditur.   10

---

16. **dīlēctōs esse**: 'were loved.'   **iūstīs,** etc.: 'on the completion of the regular funeral rites.'

17. **ūnā**: 'at the same time,' with the body of the master. The
burning of favorite dependents on their master's funeral pyre was probably
intended to continue their service for
him in the other world. Interment without burning was also in vogue in Gaul.

20. 1. **Quae cīvitātēs**: i.e. *eae
cīvitātēs, quae.*   **rem pūblicam**:
'public affairs.'

2. **habent,** etc.: 'have it ordained
by law that if anybody has heard anything.' *49, a.*

3. **dē rē pūblicā**: 'touching the
public interest.' How lit.?

4. **nēve**: 'and not.'   **quō**: *49, a.*

5. **falsīs**: 'baseless.' *83, a.* Cf.
IV, 5, ll. 5–13.

8. **vīsa sunt**: i.e. *vīsa sunt occul-
tanda,* 'which they have thought best to
conceal.'   **quaeque**: *et (ea) quae.*

Figure 125.— Bucket in which
burnt human bones were found;
imported from Gaul into Britain
in Caesar's time.

10. **per concilium**: 'at an assem-
bly' duly convoked, lit. 'through (the medium of) an assembly.' Very
few states could have enforced this regulation for any length of time.

Altogether different are the beliefs and customs of the Germans.

21. Germānī multum ab hāc cōnsuētūdine differunt.
Nam neque druidēs habent, quī rēbus dīvīnīs praesint, neque sacrificiīs student. Deōrum numerō eōs sōlōs dūcunt,
quōs cernunt et quōrum apertē opibus iuvantur, Sōlem et
5 Vulcānum et Lūnam; reliquōs nē fāmā quidem accēpērunt.

Vīta omnis in vēnātiōnibus atque in studiīs reī mīlitāris
cōnsistit; ā parvīs labōrī ac dūritiae student.

The Germans do not take to farming, and have no private land.

22. Agrī cultūrae nōn student, maiorque pars eōrum
vīctūs in lacte, cāseō, carne cōnsistit. Neque quisquam
agrī modum certum aut fīnēs habet propriōs; sed magistrātūs ac prīncipēs in annōs singulōs gentibus cognātiōnibus-
5 que hominum, quīque ūnā coiērunt, quantum et quō locō

---

21. 1. **Germānī**, etc.: 'The German mode of life and government
differs greatly from that described.' How lit.? *238, b.*

2. **druidēs**: there were priests among the Germans, but they did
not form a dominant class, as the Druids did in Gaul. **rēbus dīvīnīs**: chap. 13, l. 10, and N. **praesint**: *193, a.* B. 282, 2; A. 531, 2.

3. **Deōrum**, etc.: the religion of the Germans in Caesar's time was
a primitive nature-worship.

5. **Vulcānum**: god of fire. **Lūnam**: the host of Ariovistus dared
not fight before the new moon (I, 50, ll. 11–17). **reliquōs**: sc. *deōs.*

6. **vēnātiōnibus**: 'hunting' *92, a.* **in**, etc.: 'in warlike
pursuits.'

7. **ā parvīs**: 'from childhood.' **dūritiae**: 'hardship.'

22. 2. **lacte**: *10, g.* **cāseō**: 'cheese.' **carne**: *18, a.*

3. **fīnēs propriōs**: 'lands of his own'; there was no private own-
ership of land. Cf. IV, 1, ll. 13–15.

4. **in annōs singulōs**: 'each year.' **gentibus**: 'clans.' **cog-
nātiōnibus**: 'those connected by blood,' groups of families.

5. **quīque**, etc.: 'and (to those) who have joined together,' asso-
ciating themselves for the purpose. **quantum — agrī**, etc.: 'as much
land as they deem proper, and in whatever place (they think best).'

vīsum est agrī, attribuunt, atque annō post aliō trānsīre cōgunt.

Eius reī multās afferunt causās : nē, assiduā cōnsuētūdine captī, studium bellī gerendī agrī cultūrā commūtent; nē lātōs fīnēs parāre studeant, potentiōrēsque humiliōrēs 10 possessiōnibus expellant; nē accūrātius ad frīgora atque aestūs vītandōs aedificent; nē qua oriātur pecūniae cupiditās, quā ex rē factiōnēs dissēnsiōnēsque nāscuntur; ut animī aequitāte plēbem contineant, cum suās quisque opēs cum potentissimīs aequārī videat.   15

Their ambitions are military; but they protect a guest.

23. Cīvitātibus maxima laus est, quam lātissimē circum sē, vāstātīs fīnibus, sōlitūdinēs habēre.   Hōc proprium virtūtis exīstimant, expulsōs agrīs fīnitimōs cēdere, neque quemquam prope audēre cōnsistere; simul hōc sē fore tūtiōrēs arbitrantur, repentīnae incursiōnis timōre sublātō.   5

Cum bellum cīvitās aut illātum dēfendit aut īnfert, magis-

---

6. **vīsum est:** sc. *eīs (magistrātibus ac prīncipibus).*   **annō :** *140.*   Cf. IV, 1, ll. 9–13.   **aliō :** adverb, 'to another place.'

8. **Eius reī causās :** 'explanations of this practice,' defined by the *nē*-clauses and *ut*-clause following.   **assiduā,** etc.: 'captivated by the attractiveness of permanent residence.'   How lit.?

9. **cultūrā :** *139.*   A. 417, b; H. 478, 4.

11. **accūrātius :** 'with too great pains.'   **frīgora :** *92, c.*

13. **dissēnsiōnēs :** 'dissensions.'   *81.*   **nāscuntur :** indicative as expressing the view of the writer; cf. *220.*

14. **animī aequitāte :** 'in a state of contentment.'   How lit.? **cum,** etc.: 'each one seeing.'

15. **cum potentissimīs :** *cum opibus potentissimōrum.   238, b.*

23. 1. **maxima laus :** 'the highest distinction.'   **quam :** *153, c.*

2. **proprium virtūtis :** 'a proof of valor.'   How lit.?   *102.*   Cf. IV, 3, ll. 1–5.

3. **neque quemquam :** 'and that no one.'   *168,* and *49, a.*

5. **incursiōnis :** 'raid.'   **timōre :** *144, b,* (3).

6. **bellum illātum dēfendit :** 'repels an attack that has been made.'

trātūs, quī eī bellō praesint et vītae necisque habeant
potestātem, dēliguntur. In pāce nūllus est commūnis
magistrātus, sed prīncipēs regiōnum atque pāgōrum inter
10 suōs iūs dīcunt contrōversiāsque minuunt.

Latrōcinia nūllam habent īnfāmiam, quae extrā fīnēs
cuiusque cīvitātis fīunt, atque ea iuventūtis exercendae ac
dēsidiae minuendae causā fierī praedicant. Atque ubi quis
ex prīncipibus in conciliō dīxit, *sē ducem fore, quī sequī*
15 *velint, profiteantur,* cōnsurgunt eī, quī et causam et hominem probant, suumque auxilium pollicentur atque ā multitūdine collaudantur; quī ex hīs secūtī nōn sunt, in
dēsertōrum ac prōditōrum numerō dūcuntur, omniumque
hīs rērum posteā fidēs dērogātur.

---

7. **praesint**: *193, a.* B. 282, 2; A. 531, 2; H. 590.

8. **commūnis**: 'common' to a whole people or tribe.

9. **prīncipēs**, etc.: 'the head men of divisions and districts.' Nothing is known about the details of the German civil administration in
Caesar's time; these probably varied somewhat among the different
peoples.

10. **iūs dīcunt**: 'administer justice.'

11. **Latrōcinia**: 'marauding expeditions' outside their own borders
have generally been considered by barbarous peoples as not merely
permissible but even praiseworthy.   **habent**: 'involve.'   **īnfāmiam**: 'disgrace.'

13. **dēsidiae**: 'indolence.'   **praedicant**: 'they (the Germans)
declare.'   **quis**: *49, a.*

14. **ducem**: 'leader' of an expedition or raid.   **quī**: as antecedent supply *eī*, subject of *profiteantur*.

15. **profiteantur**: 'that they . . . are to volunteer.' *216.*

17. **ex hīs**: 'of those' who have offered to follow. In this volun-
tary relation between the chieftain as leader and his followers lies the
origin of the peculiar relation between lord and vassal in the Middle
Ages.

18. **dēsertōrum**, etc.: 'as deserters and traitors.' *81.*   **omnium
rērum fidēs**: 'confidence in all matters,' not merely in respect to warlike prowess.

19. **hīs**: dative. *109, b.*   **dērogātur**: 'is withdrawn.'

Hospitem violāre fās nōn putant; quī quācumque dē 20
causā ad eōs vēnērunt, ab iniūriā prohibent, sānctōs habent,
hīsque ōmnium domūs patent vīctusque commūnicātur.

The Gauls, once superior to the Germans, are now inferior.

24. Ac fuit anteā tempus, cum Germānōs Gallī virtūte
superārent, ultrō bella īnferrent, propter hominum multitūdinem agrīque inopiam trāns Rhēnum colōniās mitterent.
Itaque ea, quae fertilissima Germāniae sunt, loca, circum
Hercyniam silvam, quam Eratosthenī et quibusdam Graecīs 5

---

20. **Hospitem violāre**: 'to maltreat a guest.'   **quī**: as antecedent supply *eōs*, object of *prohibent*.   **quācumque**: *50, a.*

References. The statements in chapters 22 and 23 about the institutions
of the early Germans are of particular interest; for they reveal the application, in a crude way, of principles of government the fuller outworking of
which in the feudal system and in the English Constitution have had much to
do with shaping the political history of Europe, and even of America. References are: Stubbs, Constitutional History of England, vol. I., chaps. 1 and
2; Taylor, Origin and Growth of the English Constitution, book I., chaps.
1, 2; Adams, Civilization during the Middle Ages, chap. 5; Hallam, View
of the State of Europe during the Middle Ages, chap. 2.

24. 2. **īnferrent, mitterent**: *238, a.*
3. **trāns Rhēnum**; the Gauls in earlier times had not only held extensive regions east of the Rhine, but
had pressed far down into Italy, giving
to Cisalpine Gaul its name. The
Boii (as noted elsewhere) gave their
name to "Bohemia," and coins struck
by different branches of the Boii,
east of the Rhine and in northern
Italy, have been found (Fig. 126 and
Vocab. under **Boiī**).   **colōniās**: *81.*
4. **fertilissima**: 'most productive.'
81.   **loca**: accusative.

Figure 126. — Coin of the Boii.

Silver; probably struck east of the
Rhine, while the Boii still dwelt there.
Reverse, serpent with a lion's head.

5. **Hercyniam silvam**: see Vocab.   **Eratosthenī**: see Vocab.
quibusdam: *168.*   **Graecīs**: it is not now possible to determine to
what Greek writers Caesar refers.

fāmā nōtam esse videō, quam illī Orcyniam appellant,
Volcae Tectosagēs occupāvērunt atque ibi cōnsēdērunt;
quae gēns ad hōc tempus hīs sēdibus sēsē continet summamque habet iūstitiae et bellicae laudis opīniōnem.

10 Nunc, quod in eādem inopiā, egestāte, patientiā, quā
ante, Germānī permanent, eōdem vīctū et cultū corporis
ūtuntur, Gallīs autem prōvinciārum propinquitās et trānsmarīnārum rērum nōtitia multa ad cōpiam atque ūsūs
largītur, paulātim assuēfactī superārī multīsque victī proeliīs,
15 nē sē quidem ipsī cum illīs virtūte comparant.

The Hercynian forest, and the wonderful animals found in it.

25. Huius Hercyniae silvae, quae suprā dēmōnstrāta
est, lātitūdō VIIII diērum iter expedītō patet; nōn enim

---

6. **videō** : Caesar evidently had before him the works of the Greek
writers referred to. He probably kept at his headquarters copies of
writings that he thought might be in any way useful in his campaigns.

7. **Volcae Tectosagēs** : see Vocab. under *Tectosagēs.*

8. **quae gens** : 'and that people.'   **ad . . . continet** : 'to this
day continues to maintain itself,' a Gallic outpost, as it were, on German
soil.   **summam** : *353, d.*

9. **bellicae**, etc. : 'reputation for . . . prowess in war.'

10. **in**, etc. : 'in the (same condition of) poverty, privation, (and)
endurance as before.' *234, a.*

12. **prōvinciārum** : the two provinces, Cisalpine Gaul and "the
Province" in Transalpine Gaul.   **trānsmarīnārum**, etc. : 'familiarity
with products brought across the sea,' which entered Gaul chiefly
through the port of Massilia. How lit.? *293, a.*

13. **multa** : 'many articles,' not contributing to the "simple life."
ad . . . largītur : 'supply in abundance for common use.' How lit.?

15. **ipsī** : *Gallī.*   **illīs** : trans. as if *Germānīs.*

25. 1. **suprā** : chap. 24, l. 5.

2. **lātitūdō** : 'breadth,' from north to south.   **VIIII**, etc. : *243, c.*
expedītō : 'for an unencumbered (traveler),' who might average 20
miles a day; if so, the 'nine days' journey' would be a rough equivalent of 180 miles.

aliter fīnīrī potest, neque mēnsūrās itinerum nōvērunt. Oritur ab Helvētiōrum et Nemetum et Rauracōrum fīnibus, rēc-
tāque flūminis Dānuviī regiōne pertinet ad fīnēs Dācōrum 5
et Anartium; hinc sē flectit sinistrōrsus, dīversīs ā flūmine
regiōnibus, multārumque gentium fīnēs propter magnitūdinem attingit; neque quisquam est huius Germāniae, quī
sē aut adīsse ad initium eius silvae dīcat, cum diērum iter
LX prōcesserit, aut, quō ex locō oriātur, accēperit; multaque 10
in eā genera ferārum nāscī cōnstat, quae reliquīs in locīs
vīsa nōn sint; ex quibus quae maximē differant ā cēterīs
et memoriae prōdenda videantur, haec sunt.

26. Est bōs cervī figūrā, cuius ā mediā fronte inter aurēs
ūnum cornū exsistit, excelsius magisque dērēctum hīs, quae

---

3. **neque,** etc.: 'and (the people) have no system of measuring distances,' by paces and miles (*243, a*) such as the Romans had. How
lit.? **Oritur:** sc. *ea. (Hercynia silva).*

4. **fīnibus:** 'frontiers.' **rēctā,** etc.: 'following the line of the
Danube it extends' How lit.?

5. **regiōne:** *136, b.*

6. **sinistrōrsus:** 'to the left' of the Danube, spreading out northward, toward the Carpathian Mountains. **dīversīs,** etc.: 'in a direction away from the river.' *92, a.*

8. **huius Germāniae:** 'of this (part of) Germany,' the western part.

9. **initium:** the eastern limit. **dīcat:** *194, a.* **cum:** *187.*

11. **ferārum:** 'wild animals.' **quae:** 'such as.' *194, a.* **reliquīs locīs:** 'any other places.'

12. **ex quibus quae:** *et ex eīs (ea) quae.*

13. **memoriae:** dative; trans., 'seem worthy of mention.' How
lit.? **haec:** *161, a.*

26. 1. **Est:** *90, a.* **bōs,** etc.: 'an ox having the form of a stag.'
Caesar is describing the reindeer, with which the American caribou is
closely related. As a descriptive term *bōs* was applied also to the elephant, one name of which was *Lūca bōs,* 'Lucanian cow.' *18, a.*
figūrā: *143, a.* **mediā:** *152, a.* **aurēs:** 'ears.' *82, c.*

2. **ūnum cornū:** reindeer and caribou shed their antlers each year,
and Caesar's informant may have seen a reindeer which had lost one
antler, but had not yet shed the other. In the Provincial Museum at

nōbīs nōta sunt, cornibus; ab eius summō sīcut palmae
rāmīque lātē diffunduntur. Eadem est fēminae marisque
5 nātūra, eadem fōrma magnitūdōque cornuum.

Figure 127. — Caribou with one horn.
In the Provincial Museum at Victoria, British Columbia.

Victoria, British Columbia, there is a degenerate caribou which, when
shot, had only one antler (Fig. 127).   **excelsius**, etc. : 'higher and
straighter.'   *30*, and *129, a.*

3. **ab eius summō** : 'at the end of the antler.' How lit.?   **sīcut**,
etc. : 'hands' (i.e. with fingers extended) 'and branches, as it were,
are widely spread out.' The aptness of the description, and the comparison with the deer-horns familiar to the Romans (*nōbīs nōta sunt*),
suggest that Caesar had probably obtained an antler of a reindeer
The error of placing a single antler at the middle of the forehead of
the reindeer may be due to an interpreter's misunderstanding; if so,
the error is certainly no more remarkable than that mistranslation of
Exodus (chapter 34, verse 29), which led Michael Angelo to put horns
on his famous statue of Moses.

4. **fēminae**, etc. : 'the natural characteristics of the male and the
female.'   **maris** : *13, g.*

5. **eadem**, etc. : here again Caesar was misinformed; the antlers of
the female reindeer are somewhat smaller than those of the male.

27. Sunt item, quae appellantur alcēs. Hārum est cōnsimilis caprīs figūra et varietās pellium, sed magnitūdine paulō antecēdunt mutilaeque sunt cornibus et crūra sine nōdīs articulīsque habent, neque quiētis causā prōcumbunt, neque, sī quō afflīctae cāsū concidērunt, ērigere sēsē aut 5 sublevāre possunt.

Hīs sunt arborēs prō cubīlibus; ad eās sē applicant, atque ita, paulum modo reclīnātae, quiētem capiunt. Quārum ex vēstīgiīs cum est animadversum ā vēnātōribus, quō sē recipere cōnsuērint, omnēs eō locō aut ab rādīcibus subru- 10

---

27. 1. **alcēs**: 'moose.' The American moose closely resembles the European elk, to which Caesar refers; the American elk belongs to a different genus.

2. **caprīs**: i.e. *figūrae* (dative) *caprārum*, ' (like) that of goats'; brachylogy. *238, b.* **varietās**: 'mottled appearance.'

3. **antecēdunt**: 'they surpass (the reindeer).' **mutilae**, etc.: 'their horns present a broken appearance' (Fig. 128). How lit.? **cornibus**: *142, a.* **crūra**: 'legs.' *13, g.*

4. **nōdīs articulīsque**: 'nodes and joints.' In this statement Caesar reflects the condi-

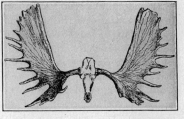

Figure 128.—Horns of a Moose.

tion of scientific knowledge in his time. The even more marvelous unicorn found a place in a textbook of Natural History as late as the fourteenth century. In England down to the nineteenth century the belief was still current that elephants have no joints in their legs. **quiētis**: *10, e.*

5. **afflīctae**: 'thrown down.' **ērigere**, etc.: 'to assume a standing position, or raise themselves up.'

7. **sunt prō cubīlibus**: 'serve as resting-places.' **ad**, etc.: 'they lean up against these.'

8. **reclīnātae**: 'leaning to one side'; lit. 'leaned back.'

9. **cum**: *185, b.* **vēnātōribus**: 'hunters.' *74, a.*

10. **omnēs**: with *arborēs. 353, d.* **ab**: 'at.' *126, c.*

unt aut accīdunt arborēs, tantum, ut summa speciēs eārum
stantium relinquātur. Hūc cum sē cōnsuētūdine reclīnā-
vērunt, īnfīrmās arborēs pondere afflīgunt atque ūnā ipsae
concidunt.

28. Tertium est genus eōrum, quī ūrī appellantur. Hī
sunt magnitūdine paulō īnfrā elephantōs, speciē et colōre et
figūrā taurī. Magna vīs eōrum est et magna vēlōcitās,
neque hominī neque ferae, quam cōnspexērunt, parcunt.
5 Hōs studiōsē foveīs captōs interficiunt. Hōc sē labōre
dūrant adulēscentēs atque hōc genere vēnātiōnis exercent,
et quī plūrimōs ex hīs interfēcērunt, relātīs in pūblicum
cornibus, quae sint testimōniō, magnam ferunt laudem.
Sed assuēscere ad hominēs et mānsuēfierī nē parvulī quidem
10 exceptī possunt.

Amplitūdō cornuum et figūra et speciēs multum ā nostrō-

---

11. **accīdunt**: 'cut into.'   **tantum**, etc.: '(only) so much that
the trees retain perfectly the appearance of standing firmly.' How lit.?

12. **Hūc**: *in hās arborēs.*   **cōnsuētūdine**: *136, c.* This wonderful story may have originated in a distorted account of a kind of pitfall, made by covering a deep hole with timber so weakened by notches
that a heavy animal passing above would break through.

28. 1. **ūrī**: 'wild cattle,' now extinct; sometimes confused with the
aurochs, or European buffalo, of which a few herds still exist in game
preserves. The 'wild cattle' had spreading horns, like those of our
Texas cattle, and it is thought that they represented the primitive stock
from which our domestic cattle are descended. The last specimen died
in 1627.

2. **elephantōs**: 'the elephant.' *92, a.*   **speciē**: *143, a.*   **colōre**: *80, b.*

3. **taurī**: i.e. of a domestic 'bull.'

4. **parcunt**: 'spare'; they attack indiscriminately. *105.*

5. **studiōsē**: 'diligently.'   **foveīs**: 'by means of pitfalls.'   **captōs**: *228, a.*   **sē dūrant**: 'they develop hardihood.' How lit.?

7. **relātīs**, etc.: 'publicly exhibiting the horns as a trophy.'

8. **sint**: *193, a.*   **testimōniō**: *112, a.*

9. **assuēscere**, etc.: 'become domesticated.'   **mānsuēfierī**: 'be
tamed.'   **nē**, etc.: 'not even if very young when caught.'

rum boum cornibus differt.   Haec studiōsē conquīsīta ab .
labrīs argentō circumclūdunt atque in amplissimīs epulīs
prō pōculīs ūtuntur.

Caesar returns to Gaul, cuts down the farther end of the bridge.

29. Caesar, postquam per Ubiōs explōrātōrēs comperit,
Suēbōs sēsē in silvās recēpisse, inopiam frūmentī veritus,
quod, ut suprā dēmōnstrāvimus, minimē omnēs Germānī agrī
cultūrae student, cōnstituit nōn prōgredī longius; sed, nē
omnīnō metum reditūs suī barbarīs tolleret atque ut eōrum 5
auxilia tardāret, reductō exercitū, partem ultimam pontis,
quae rīpās Ubiōrum contingēbat, in longitūdinem pedum
CC rescindit, atque in extrēmō ponte turrim tabulātōrum
IV cōnstituit praesidiumque cohortium XII, pontis tuendī
causā, pōnit magnīsque eum locum mūnītiōnibus fīrmat.   10

Eī locō praesidiōque C. Volcācium Tullum adulēscentem
praefēcit.

---

12. **conquīsīta**: 'collect and.' *228, a.*   **āb labrīs**, etc.: 'mount
them with silver at the rim.' How lit.?

13. **in amplissimīs epulīs**: 'at their more elaborate feasts.' The
principal beverage was beer.

14. **ūtuntur**: sc. *hīs*; 'use them as drinking cups.' Such drinking
horns continued in use in the Middle Ages; in later times horns of
cattle were made into "powderhorns," the use of which in this country
continued till after the Revolutionary War. Drinking horns were used
also by the early Greeks.

29. 1. **Caesar**, etc.: the narrative, broken off at chapter 10, is here
resumed.

3. **suprā**: chap. 22, ll. 1–2; cf. IV, 1, ll. 12–15.

8. **in extrēmō ponte**: 'on the end of the bridge,' in the river, 200
Roman feet from the east bank. The bridge here probably crossed
a small island, which furnished a secure foundation for the tower.
tabulātōrum iv: 'four stories high.' How lit.? *100, a.*

10. **mūnītiōnibus**: of a fortified enclosure at the end of the bridge,
on the west bank.

COMMENTARIUS SEPTIMUS

Beginning of a General Uprising; First Movements. 1-10

The Gauls secretly plan a general uprising.

1. Quiētā Galliā, Caesar, ut cōnstituerat, in Italiam ad conventūs agendōs proficīscitur. Ibi cognōscit dē P. Clōdiī caede; dē senātūsque cōnsultō certior factus, ut omnēs iūniōrēs Italiae coniūrārent, dīlēctum tōtā prōvinciā habēre 5 īnstituit.

Eae rēs in Galliam Trānsalpīnam celeriter perferuntur. Addunt ipsī et affingunt rūmōribus Gallī, quod rēs poscere

---

1-10. The Circumstances. During the sixth year of the Gallic War (53 B.C.) the restlessness of the conquered states became increasingly manifest, but all attempts to revolt were sternly repressed by Caesar. After his return from the second expedition into Germany (VI, 29), Caesar devoted himself particularly to the chastisement of the Eburones, but narrowly escaped the loss of a legion, which was stationed at Atuatuca in command of Quintus Cicero and was attacked by a force of marauding Sugambrians (VI, 30-44).

Before the close of the winter 53-52 B.C. the Gauls began to organize a general rebellion. The earlier part of the Seventh Book, which is devoted to the events of 52 B.C., deals with the first movements of the Gauls and with Caesar's counter-movements, which were characterized by amazing quickness of decision, energy, and despatch.

1. 1. **Quiētā Galliā**: the "calm before the storm." *144, b*, (3). **Italiam**: Cisalpine Gaul. *283, b*. **ad**, etc.: N. to I, 54, l. 8.

2. **P. Clōdiī**: killed in January, 52 B.C., in an encounter with his personal enemy, T. Annius Milo. Riots ensued at Rome, and the Senate ordered out all men throughout Italy capable of bearing arms.

4. **iūniōrēs**: men between the ages of 17 and 46. **coniūrārent**: 'should together take the oath' that they would obey the consuls. **dīlēctum**: 'levy.' *307, a*. **prōvinciā**: = *citeriōre prōvinciā*. *284*.

7. **Addunt et affingunt**: 'added to (the facts) and embellished (them) with rumors.' *175, b*. **quod**: = *id quod*, explained by *retinērī . . . posse*; "the wish" was "father to the thought." **rēs**: 'the condition of affairs.'

PLATE IX   APPLIANCES FOR SIEGE AND DEFENSE

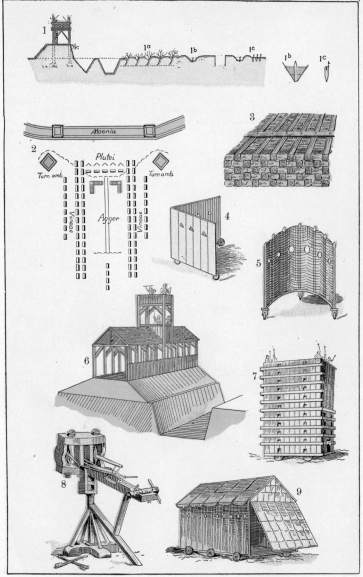

1. Caesar's Works before Alesia (VII. 72, 73): 1a, *Cippi*; 1b, *Lilia*; 1c, *Stimuli*.
2. *Agger*, etc. (VII. 24).   3. Gallic City Wall (VII. 23).
4, 5. Movable Breastworks, *plutei*.
6. Rampart of Camp, with Passageway and Towers.
7. Movable Tower, *turris ambulatoria*.   8. Catapult, *catapulta*.
9. Sapper's Hut, *vinea*.

vidēbātur, retinērī urbānō mōtū Caesarem neque in tantīs dissēnsiōnibus ad exercitum venīre posse.

Hāc impulsī occāsiōne, quī iam ante sē populī Rōmānī 10 imperiō subiectōs dolērent, līberius atque audācius dē bellō cōnsilia inīre incipiunt. Indictīs inter sē prīncipēs Galliae conciliīs silvestribus ac remōtīs locīs querunter dē Accōnis morte; hunc cāsum ad ipsōs recidere posse dēmōnstrant; miserantur commūnem Galliae fortūnam; omnibus pollici- 15 tātiōnibus ac praemiīs dēposcunt, quī bellī initium faciant et suī capitis perīculō Galliam in lībertātem vindicent. In prīmīs ratiōnem esse habendam dīcunt, prius quam eōrum clandestīna cōnsilia efferantur, ut Caesar ab exercitū inter-
clūdātur: 20

*Id esse facile, quod neque legiōnēs audeant, absente im-
perātōre, ex hībernīs ēgredī, neque imperātor sine praesidiō
ad legiōnēs pervenīre possit; postrēmō in aciē praestāre
interficī, quam nōn veterem bellī glōriam lībertātemque,
quam ā maiōribus accēperint, recuperāre.* 25

The Carnutes lead in revolt, massacre the Romans in Cenabum.

2. Hīs rēbus agitātīs, profitentur Carnutēs, sē nūllum perīculum commūnis salūtis causā recūsāre, prīncipēsque

---

8. **urbānō mōtū:** 'the disturbances in the city,' in Rome.

9. **dissēnsiōnibus:** 'strifes.'

10. **quī:** 'since they.' *194, c.* **ante:** adverb.

13. **Accōnis:** a leader in uprisings the previous year (VI, 4, 44).

14. **ad ipsōs recidere:** 'might fall upon themselves.'

15. **omnibus pollicitātiōnibus:** 'by every sort of promise.'

17. **suī,** etc.: 'at the risk of their lives would assert the freedom of Gaul.' How lit.?

18. **ratiōnem esse habendam:** 'that a plan should be devised.'

22. **hībernīs:** 6 legions at Agedincum (3, Map 13), 2 among the Lingones (2, Map 13), and 2 near the Treveran frontier.

2. 1. profitentur: at a meeting of representatives of Gallic states.

2. prīncipēs, etc.: 'that they will be the first of all to make war.'

ex omnibus bellum factūrōs pollicentur et, quoniam in
praesentiā obsidibus cavēre inter sē nōn possint, nē rēs
5 efferātur, at iūre iūrandō ac fidē sanciātur, petunt, collātīs
mīlitāribus signīs, quō mōre eōrum gravissima caerimōnia
continētur, nē, factō initiō bellī, ab reliquīs dēserantur.
Tum, collaudātīs Carnutibus, datō iūre iūrandō ab omnibus, quī aderant, tempore eius reī cōnstitūtō, ā conciliō
10 discēditur.

3. Ubi ea diēs vēnit, Carnutēs, Cotuātō et Conconneto-
dumnō ducibus, dēspērātīs hominibus, Cēnabum signō datō
concurrunt cīvēsque Rōmānōs, quī negōtiandī causā ibi
cōnstiterant, in hīs C. Fūfium Citam, honestum equitem
5 Rōmānum, quī reī frūmentāriae iussū Caesaris praeerat,
interficiunt bonaque eōrum dīripiunt.

Celeriter ad omnēs Galliae cīvitātēs fāma perfertur.
Nam ubi quae maior atque illūstrior incidit rēs, clāmōre
per agrōs regiōnēsque significant; hunc aliī deinceps ex-

---

3. **quoniam,** etc.: 'since at the time they could not bind one another for mutual protection by an exchange of hostages.'

5. **fidē**: 'a pledge of honor.'   **sanciātur**: sc. *ut;* 'that (the
compact) be ratified.' *199, a.*   **collātīs signīs**: 'by placing their
standards close together,' signifying inviolable alliance for war.

6. **mōre eōrum**: 'in accordance with their custom.' *136, c.*   **gravissima**: 'most solemn.'

9. **eius reī**: the commencing of hostilities.

10. **discēditur**: 'they went away.' *73, d,* and *175, b.*

3. 1. **diēs**: the 'day' appointed for commencing hostilities. *21, a.*

2. **dēspērātīs**: here an adjective.   **Cēnabum**: Map 13. *119, a.*

3. **negōtiandī**: the Roman citizens engaged in business in Gallic
cities were chiefly money-lenders who furnished capital for various enter-
prises, and dealers in supplies, particularly of grain; cf. p. xxviii.

6. **interficiunt**: the massacre of the Roman citizens, well organized
in advance, took place at daybreak (l. 11).

8. **quae**: 'any.' *168.*   **clāmōre**: 'by shouting.'

9. **per agrōs regiōnēsque**: 'across the country.' How lit.?
hunc [clāmōrem], etc.: 'others in turn take up the shouting.'

cipiunt et proximīs trādunt, ut tum accidit.   Nam quae 10
Cēnabī oriente sōle gesta essent, ante prīmam cōnfectam
vigiliam in fīnibus Arvernōrum audīta sunt, quod spatium
est mīlium passuum circiter CLX.

The Arverni revolt, under the leadership of Vercingetorix.

4. Similī ratiōne ibi Vercingetorīx, Celtillī fīlius, Arvernus, summae potentiae adulēscēns, cuius pater prīncipātum
tōtīus Galliae obtinuerat et ob eam causam, quod rēgnum
appetēbat, ā cīvitāte erat interfectus, convocātīs suīs
clientibus facile incendit.   Cognitō eius cōnsiliō, ad arma 5
concurritur.   Prohibētur ā Gobannitiōne, patruō suō, reliquīsque prīncipibus, quī hanc temptandam fortūnam nōn
exīstimābant; expellitur ex oppidō Gergoviā; nōn dēstitit
tamen, atque in agrīs habet dīlēctum egentium ac perditōrum.   10

Hāc coāctā manū, quōscumque adit ex cīvitāte, ad suam
sententiam perdūcit; hortātur, ut commūnis lībertātis causā

---

11. **Cēnabī**: *146.*   **gesta essent**: adversative, 'although these
things had been done.' *194, d.*   **ante ... vigiliam**: *228, b,* and *242, c.*

12. **quod spatium**: 'a distance which.'   Perhaps men had been
posted in advance along the roads leading from Cenabum, in readiness
to transmit the news; otherwise the population must have been so dense
over the country that neighbors were within hailing distance.   *165, b.*

4. 1. **ibi**: in the country of the Arvernians; Map 13.

2. **prīncipātum tōtīus Galliae**: 'a position of leadership throughout the Celtic country,' on account of his influence.   *287, b.*

3. **eam**: *161, a.*   **causam**: explained by the *quod*-clause.

5. **clientibus**: a feudal following, like that of Orgetorix (I, 4).

6. **ad arma concurritur**: 'they rushed to arms.'   How lit.?   *73, d.*
patruō: 'uncle,' on his father's side.

7. **hanc**, etc.: 'that fortune ought not to be tempted in this way';
cf. Fig. 198.   How lit.?

11. **quōscumque**, etc.: 'all the men of his state whom he approached.'   *50, a.*

arma capiant, magnīsque coāctīs cōpiīs adversāriōs suōs, ā
quibus paulō ante erat ēiectus, expellit ex cīvitāte.   Rēx
15 ab suīs appellātur.   Dīmittit quōque versus lēgātiōnēs;
obtestātur, ut in fidē maneant.

Vercingetorix wins over many states, including the Bituriges.

Celeriter sibi Senonēs, Parīsiōs, Pictonēs, Cadūrcōs, Turonōs, Aulercōs, Lemovīcēs, Andōs reliquōsque omnēs,
quī Ōceanum attingunt, adiungit; omnium cōnsēnsū ad
20 eum dēfertur imperium.   Quā oblātā potestāte, omnibus
hīs cīvitātibus obsidēs imperat, certum numerum mīlitum
ad sē celeriter addūcī iubet, armōrum quantum quaeque
cīvitās domī quodque ante tempus efficiat, cōnstituit; in
prīmīs equitātuī studet.

25 Summae dīligentiae summam imperiī sevēritātem addit;
magnitūdine suppliciī dubitantēs cōgit.   Nam, maiōre commissō dēlīctō, īgnī atque omnibus tormentīs necat, leviōre
dē causā auribus dēsectīs, aut singulīs effossīs oculīs, domum
remittit, ut sint reliquīs documentō et magnitūdine poenae
30 perterreant aliōs.

5. Hīs suppliciīs celeriter coāctō exercitū, Lucterium
Cadūrcum, summae hominem audāciae, cum parte cōpiārum in Rutēnōs mittit; ipse in Biturīgēs proficīscitur.

---

13. **adversāriōs** : 'opponents,' such as Gobannitio.

16. **obtestātur** : 'he adjured (his allies),' through his envoys.

22. **ārmōrum quantum**, etc. : 'how great a supply of arms each
state should furnish.' *97, b.*

23. **domī** : 'of its own manufacture,' lit. 'at home.' *146.*   **quod,**
etc. : 'and before what time'; Vercingetorix fixed the date for delivery.

26. **dubitantēs** : 'those who hesitated' to join him. *227, a, (4).*

27. **dēlīctō** : 'offence.'   **necat**: sc. *eum quī id commīserat.*

28. **leviōre dē causā** : i.e. *sī quī levius peccāvērunt.*   **auribus,**
etc. : 'he cut off their ears, or gouged out one eye, and.' *144, b, (2).*

29. **documentō** : 'a warning.' *112, b.*

5. 3. **Rutēnōs**, etc. : Vercingetorix (Figures 18, 145) proceeds
with great energy against the states friendly to Caesar.

Eius adventū Biturīgēs ad Aeduōs, quōrum erant in fidē, lēgātōs mittunt subsidium rogātum, quō facilius hostium 5 cōpiās sustinēre possint.

Aeduī dē cōnsiliō lēgātōrum, quōs Caesar ad exercitum relīquerat, cōpiās equitātus peditātusque subsidiō Biturīgibus mittunt. Quī cum ad flūmen Ligerim vēnissent, quod Biturīgēs ab Aeduīs dīvidit, paucōs diēs ibi morātī neque 10 flūmen trānsīre ausī, domum revertuntur lēgātīsque nostrīs renūntiant, sē Biturīgum perfidiam veritōs revertisse, quibus id cōnsiliī fuisse cognōverint, ut, sī flūmen trānsissent, ūnā ex parte ipsī, alterā Arvernī sē circumsisterent. Id eāne dē causā, quam lēgātīs prōnūntiārunt, an perfidiā 15 adductī fēcerint, quod nihil nōbīs cōnstat, nōn vidētur prō certō esse pōnendum.

Biturīgēs eōrum discessū statim sē cum Arvernīs coniungunt.

Caesar leaves Cisalpine Gaul, proceeds to Narbo, in the Province.

6. Hīs rēbus in Italiam Caesarī nūntiātīs, cum iam ille urbānās rēs virtūte Cn. Pompeī commodiōrem in statum

---

4. **quōrum**, etc.: 'in whose allegiance they were.' The Aeduans were at the head of one league of Gallic states, the Arvernians of the other (I, 31, ll. 10–28).

5. **rogātum**: *231, a.* **hostium**: the Arvernian army.

7. **lēgātōrum**: these had been left 'with the army' when it was placed in winter quarters at the end of 53 B.C. *313, a.*

9. **Biturīgibus**: *19, e,* and *112, b.* **Quī**: *167.* **Ligerim**: *18, e.*

11. **ausī**: *62.* **domum**: *20, c,* and *119, b.*

12. **veritōs**: *61, a,* (2), and *227, a,* (1). **quibus**, etc.: 'having found out that the Bituriges had the design.' *97, b,* and *214, a.*

15. **-ne . . . an**: *204,* (1). B. 162, 4; A. 335; H. 380.

16. **fēcerint**: the object is *Id.* **nihil**: adverbial accusative. *118, c.* **nōbīs**: *156.* **prō certō**: 'as certain.' *154, a.*

6. 1. **Italiam**: Caesar was in Cisalpine Gaul. *283, b,* and *256.*

2. **urbānās rēs**: 'affairs in the city,' Rome; see chap. 1, ll. 2–9, and Notes. **virtūte**: 'through the energetic action.' The break between Caesar and Pompey did not come till two years later. *258.*

pervēnisse intellegeret, in Trānsalpīnam Galliam profectus
est.

5 Eō cum vēnisset, magnā difficultāte afficiēbātur, quā
ratiōne ad exercitum pervenīre posset. Nam sī legiōnēs
in prōvinciam arcesseret, sē absente in itinere proeliō dīmi-
cātūrās intellegēbat; sī ipse ad exercitum contenderet, nē
eīs quidem eō tempore, quī quiētī vidērentur, suam salūtem
10 rēctē committī vidēbat.

7. Interim Lucterius Cadūrcus in Rutēnōs missus eam
cīvitātem Arvernīs conciliat. Prōgressus in Nitiobrogēs
et Gabalōs, ab utrīsque obsidēs accipit et, magnā coāctā
manū, in prōvinciam Narbōnem versus irruptiōnem facere
5 contendit.

Quā rē nūntiātā, Caesar omnibus cōnsiliīs antevertendum
exīstimāvit, ut Narbōnem proficīscerētur. Eō cum vēnisset, timentēs cōnfīrmat, praesidia in Rutēnīs prōvinciālibus,
Volcīs Arecomicīs, Tolōsātibus circumque Narbōnem, quae
10 loca hostibus erant fīnitima, cōnstituit, partem cōpiārum
ex prōvinciā supplēmentumque, quod ex Italiā addūxerat,
in Helviōs, quī fīnēs Arvernōrum contingunt, convenīre
iubet.

---

5. **magnā**, etc.: 'he experienced great difficulty in devising a plan
for reaching his army.' How lit. ?

6. **posset:** *204*, (2).   **legiōnēs:** see chap. 1, l. 22, ánd N.

8. **ipse:** alone, or with only a small military escort.

9. **eō tempore:** 'at so critical a time.' How lit.?

7. 1. **Rutēnōs:** *282.*   **missus:** chap. 5, ll. 1–3.

2. **Nitiobrogēs, Gabalōs:** west, and east, of the Ruteni; see
Map GALLIA.

4. **versus:** 'in the direction of.' *123, c.*   **irruptiōnem:** 'raid.'

6. **omnibus**, etc.: 'that setting out for Narbo should precede all
(forming of) plans.' How lit. ?

8. **prōvinciālibus:** a part of the Ruteni were in the Province.

9. **quae loca:** (*in*) *locīs quae. 165, c.*

11. **supplēmentum:** 'raw contingent'; cf. chap. 1, ll. 3–5.

Caesar crosses the Cévennes through deep snow, surprising the Arverni.

8. Hīs rēbus comparātīs, repressō iam Lucteriō et remōtō, quod intrāre intrā praesidia perīculōsum putābat, in
Helviōs proficīscitur. Etsī mōns Cebenna, quī Arvernōs
ab Helviīs disclūdit, dūrissimō tempore annī altissimā nive
iter impediēbat, tamen, discussā nive in altitūdinem pedum 5
sex atque ita viīs patefactīs summō mīlitum sūdōre, ad
fīnēs Arvernōrum pervēnit. Quibus oppressīs inopīnantibus, quod sē Cebennā ut mūrō mūnitōs existimābant,
ac nē singulārī quidem umquam hominī eō tempore annī
sēmitae patuerant, equitibus imperat, ut, quam lātissimē 10
possint, vagentur et quam maximum hostibus terrōrem
īnferant.

Celeriter haec fāmā ac nūntiīs ad Vercingetorīgem perferuntur; quem perterritī omnēs Arvernī circumsistunt
atque obsecrant, ut suīs fortūnīs cōnsulat neu sē ab hos- 15
tibus dīripī patiātur, praesertim cum videat omne ad sē
bellum trānslātum. Quōrum ille precibus permōtus, castra
ex Biturīgibus movet in Arvernōs versus.

---

8. **1. Hīs,** etc. : 'Having completed these preparations.'

2. intra praesidia : 'within the (chain of) garrisons' by which
Caesar had secured the western frontier of the Province.   **perīculōsum** : *75, f ; 84,* and *148, d.*   **putābat** : sc. *Lucterius.*

3. proficīscitur : sc. *Caesar.*

4. dūrissimō tempore : 'the most inclement season.'

5. discussā nive : 'the snow was cleared away' in the pass by
which he crossed the Cévennes. Cf. Map 13, (1). *144, b,* (2).

6. summō sūdōre : 'with the utmost effort.' *136, b.* How lit. ?

9. nē, etc. : 'not even for one man alone,' not to speak of an army.

10. sēmitae : mountain 'trails.'   **patuerant** : 'were passable.'

13. fāmā : 'by report ;' less definite than **nūntiīs,** 'by messages.'

15. suīs : 'their own.'   **neu** : *199, d.*

16. cum : *184, b.*   **omne** : *353, d.*

18. in . . . versus : *123, c.*   **Arvernōs** : *282.*

Caesar assembles his legions; he leaves two at Agedincum and
starts for Gorgobina, besieged by Vercingetorix.

9. At Caesar, bīduum in hīs locīs morātus, quod haec
dē Vercingetorīge ūsū ventūra opīniōne praecēperat, per
causam supplēmentī equitātūsque cōgendī ab exercitū discēdit, Brūtum adulēscentem hīs cōpiīs praeficit; hunc
5 monet, ut in omnēs partēs equitēs quam lātissimē perva-
gentur: *Datūrum sē operam, nē longius trīduō ā castrīs
absit.*

Hīs cōnstitūtīs rēbus, suīs inopīnantibus, quam maximīs
potest itineribus, Viennam pervenit. Ibi nactus recentem
10 equitātum, quem multīs ante diēbus eō praemīserat, neque
diurnō neque nocturnō itinere intermissō, per fīnēs Aeduōrum in Lingonēs contendit, ubi duae legiōnēs hiemābant,
ut, sī quid etiam dē suā salūte ab Aeduīs inīrētur cōnsiliī,
celeritāte praecurreret. Eō cum pervēnisset, ad reliquās
15 legiōnēs mittit priusque omnēs in ūnum locum cōgit, quam
dē eius adventū Arvernīs nūntiārī posset.

Hāc rē cognitā, Vercingetorīx rūrsus in Biturīgēs exercitum redūcit, atque inde profectus Gorgobinam, Boiōrum

---

9. **1.** **haec dē Vercingetorīge**: 'these movements on the part of
Vercingetorix.'

2. **ūsū ventūra** [esse]: 'would take place;' lit., 'would come in
experience.' *142, a*. **opīniōne praecēperat**: 'had conjectured.'

3. **per causam**, etc.: 'making a pretext of bringing together his
new force,' etc. How lit.?

6. **Datūrum** [esse] . . . **absit**: said as a blind, to prevent information regarding his plans from reaching the enemy.

9. **nactus**, etc.: 'finding his cavalry refreshed.'

12. **duae legiōnēs**: see (2) on Map 13.

13. **quid**, etc.: 'any design involving his personal safety.' *97, b*;
353, d.

14. **celeritāte**: 'by quickness of movement.' **praecurreret**:
'that he might forestall (it).'

16. **nūntiārī posset**: 'any report could reach.' *73, d*; *189, b*.

18. **Boiōrum**, etc.: I, 28, ll. 15–18; also, N. to VI, 24, l. 3.

oppidum, quōs ibi, Helvēticō proeliō victōs, Caesar collocāverat Aeduīsque attribuerat, oppugnāre īnstituit.   20

10. Magnam haec rēs Caesarī difficultātem ad cōnsilium
capiendum afferēbat: sī reliquam partem hiemis ūnō locō
legiōnēs continēret, nē, stīpendiāriīs Aeduōrum expugnātīs, cūncta Gallia dēficeret, quod nūllum amīcīs in eō
praesidium vidēret positum esse; sī mātūrius ex hībernīs 5
ēdūceret, nē ab rē frūmentāriā dūrīs subvectiōnibus labō-
rāret.

---

10. **1.** **haec rēs**: 'This movement' of Vercingetorix.

3. nē, etc.: if Caesar failed to protect the Gauls pledged to his
interest, he would soon find them enemies.

Figure 129. — Low ground northeast of Bourges, ancient Avaricum.

4. cūncta Gallia: 'the whole of Gaul.'   **amīcīs**: 'for those
(who were) friendly (to him).'   **eō**: Caesar.

6. ēdūceret: sc. *legiōnēs*.   **ab**: 'in respect to.'   **dūrīs subvectiōnibus**: 'on account of difficulties of transportation,' caused by
the bad state of the roads toward the end of winter.

Praestāre vīsum est tamen omnēs difficultātēs perpetī,
quam, tantā contumēliā acceptā, omnium suōrum volun-
10 tātēs aliēnāre. Itaque cohortātus Aeduōs dē supportandō
commeātū, praemittit ad Boiōs, quī dē suō adventū doceant,
hortenturque, ut in fidē maneant atque hostium impetum
magnō animō sustineant. Duābus Agedincī legiōnibus
atque impedīmentīs tōtīus exercitūs relictīs, ad Boiōs pro-
15 ficiscitur.

The Siege and Destruction of Avaricum. 23–31

The ingenious construction of Gallic city walls.

23. Mūrī autem omnēs Gallicī hāc ferē fōrmā sunt.
Trabēs dērēctae, perpetuae in longitūdinem paribus inter-
vāllīs, distantēs inter sē bīnōs pedēs, in solō collocantur.
Hae revinciuntur intrōrsus et multō aggere vestiuntur; ea

---

9. **tantā contumēliā acceptā**: 'by acquiescing in so great an
indignity' as the capture of Gorgobina by Vercingetorix would be.
suōrum: 'who were loyal to him.' **voluntātēs**: 'the good will.

11. **quī**, etc.: '(messengers) to explain.' *193, a.*

14. **tōtīus exercitūs**: ten legions, besides auxiliary troops. *308.*

11–22. Summary. Caesar in rapid succession captures Vellaunodunum,
Cenabum, and Noviodunum (4, 5, and 6 on Map 13), and marches toward
Avaricum (7 on Map 13). This city the Gauls, contrary to the advice of Vercingetorix, resolve to defend. Caesar besieges it, and Vercingetorix is unable
to gain any advantage over him.

23. 2. Trabēs, etc.:
beams at right angles to the
course of the wall were laid
in a row two feet apart along
the entire length of the wall.

4. **revinciuntur intrōr-
sus**: 'are made fast inside'
the wall, probably by means
of crossbeams parallel with
the line of the wall, as indicated in Plate IX, 3. **vestiuntur**: 'are covered.'

Figure 130. Section of works at
Avaricum.

a, a. Roman agger, with a tower on the raised
front facing the Gallic wall, and a higher movable
tower further back.

b. Section of Gallic wall surmounted by a tower.

MAP 14
THE SIEGE OF AVARICUM

Book VII, 15–28

To face page 374

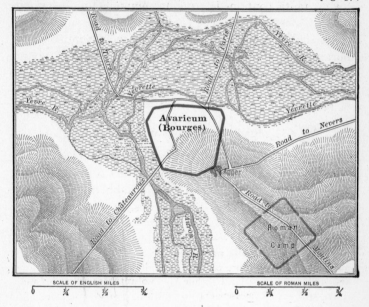

SCALE OF ENGLISH MILES

SCALE OF ROMAN MILES

EXPLANATION

The city of Avaricum, on the site of modern Bourges, was situated at the confluence of two streams, now called Yèvre and Auron, and was protected by marshes on three sides. It was surrounded by a strong wall (outlined in blue), and was reckoned by its inhabitants the most beautiful city in Gaul.

Caesar encamped on the higher ground on the side of the city free from marshes. Selecting a favorable point of approach he commenced the construction of a huge embankment, agger, consisting of two parallel dikes, or viaducts, terminating in a long embankment near the wall and parallel with it.

The siege embankment, composed largely of timber, was in part destroyed by fire, and the city was finally taken by assault.

autem, quae dīximus, intervālla grandibus in fronte saxīs 5
efferciuntur.

His collocātīs et coagmentātīs, alius īnsuper ōrdō
additur, ut idem illud intervāllum servētur nēque inter sē
contingant trabēs, sed, paribus intermissīs spatiīs, singulae
singulīs saxīs interiectīs artē contineantur. Sīc deinceps 10
omne opus contexitur, dum iūsta mūrī altitūdō expleātur.

The Gauls set the agger on fire and make a fierce attack.

24. His tot rēbus impedītā oppugnātiōne, mīlitēs, cum
tōtō tempore frīgore et assiduīs imbribus tardārentur,
tamen continentī labōre omnia haec superāvērunt et diēbus xxv aggerem lātum pedēs cccxxx, altum pedēs LXXX
exstrūxērunt.   5

Cum is mūrum hostium paene contingeret, et Caesar
ad opus cōnsuētūdine excubāret mīlitēsque hortārētur,
nē quod omnīnō tempus ab opere intermitterētur, paulō
ante tertiam vigiliam est animadversum, fūmāre aggerem,
quem cunīculō hostēs succenderant, eōdemque tempore, 10

---

5. **fronte**: the outside of the wall; the large stones tightly fitted
the spaces between the ends of the beams.

6. **efferciuntur**: 'are closely packed.'

7. **coagmentātīs**: 'fastened together.'

8. **idem illud intervāllum**: two feet.   **inter**, etc.: 'touch one
another.' *159*.

9. **singulae**, etc.: 'the individual (beams) are held in position by
tightly fitting a stone between' each two.   How lit.?

11. **iūsta**: 'proper.'   **expleātur**: 'is reached.'   *190, b.*

24. 1. **oppugnātiōne**: *340.*   **cum**: 'although.'

2. **tempore**: *147, c.*   **frīgore**: it was still winter, probably in
March (chap. 32, l. 4).   **assiduīs**: 'continual.' *81.*

4. **CCCXXX**: *trecentōs et trīgintā*, measured where the siege bank
faced the wall (Map 14, and Fig. 130).   **LXXX**: *octōgintā.*   The unusual height is explained by the existence of a gully in front of the wall.

7. **excubāret**: 'was watching.'

9. **fūmāre aggerem**: 'that the siege embankment was smoking.'

10. **cunīculō**: 'by means of a countermine,' run out underneath.

tōtō mūrō clāmōre sublātō, duābus portīs ab utrōque
latere turrium ēruptiō fīēbat; aliī facēs atque āridam
māteriem dē mūrō in aggerem ēminus iaciēbant, picem
reliquāsque rēs, quibus īgnis excitārī potest, fundēbant,
15 ut, quō prīmum occurrerētur aut cui reī ferrētur auxilium,
vix ratiō inīrī posset.

Tamen, quod īnstitūtō Caesaris duae semper legiōnēs
prō castrīs excubābant plūrēsque, partītīs temporibus, erant
in opere, celeriter factum est, ut aliī ēruptiōnibus resisterent,
20 aliī turrēs redūcerent aggeremque interscinderent, omnis
vērō ex castrīs multitūdō ad restinguendum concurreret.

An instance of extraordinary bravery.

25. Cum in omnibus locīs, cōnsūmptā iam reliquā
parte noctis, pugnārētur semperque hostibus spēs victōriae
redintegrārētur, eō magis, quod deūstōs pluteōs turrium
vidēbant nec facile adīre apertōs ad auxiliandum animad-

---

11. **portīs**: *134, a.*   **ab utrōque latere**: 'on both sides' of the
siege embankment, designated by the movable towers now at the corners
(Plate IX, 2).

12. **facēs**: 'firebrands.'   *17, c.*   **āridam**: *81.*

15. **ut**, etc.: 'so that it was hardly possible to decide at what point
a counter-attack should first be made, or to what part reinforcements
should be sent.' How lit.?

17. **īnstitūtō**, etc.: *136, c.* The legionaries on duty worked in shifts.

20. **turrēs**, etc.: they first drew back the towers, so as to remove
these beyond the reach of the flames, then cut the siege embankment
in two in order to confine the fire to the part already burning.

21. **ad restinguendum**: 'to put out (the fire).'   *230, (3).*

25. 2. **hostibus**: *109, a.* B. 188, 1, N.; A. 377; H. 425, 4, N.

3. **deūstōs**, etc.: sc. *esse,* 'that the breastworks of the towers were
burned'; these were wooden screens, probably protected by hides, on
the front of the towers.

4. **nec**, etc.: sc. *mīlitēs;* 'and that it was not easy for the men
exposed' to the enemy's missiles 'to come forward to help' in putting
out the fire. The artillery was placed in the towers, which were there-

vertēbant, semperque ipsī recentēs dēfessīs succēderent 5
omnemque Galliae salūtem in illō vēstīgiō temporis positam arbitrārentur, accidit, īnspectantibus nōbīs, quod, dignum memoriā vīsum, praetereundum nōn exīstimāvimus.

Quīdam ante portam oppidī Gallus per manūs sēbī ac
picis trāditās glēbās in īgnem ē regiōne turris prōiciēbat; 10
scorpiōne ab latere dextrō trāiectus exanimātusque, concidit. Hunc ex proximīs ūnus iacentem trānsgressus, eōdem
illō mūnere fungēbātur; eādem ratiōne, ictū scorpiōnis, exanimātō alterō, successit tertius, et tertiō quārtus, nec prius
ille est ā prōpugnātōribus vacuus relīctus locus, quam, 15
restīnctō aggere atque omnī ex parte summōtīs hostibus,
fīnis est pugnandī factus.

The defenders, despairing, plan to flee, but are thwarted.

26. Omnia expertī Gallī, quod rēs nūlla successerat,
posterō diē cōnsilium cēpērunt ex oppidō profugere, hor-
tante et iubente Vercingetorīge. Id silentiō noctis cōnātī,

---

fore special objects of attack ; the towers were finally saved, perhaps by
throwing earth against the parts that caught fire.

5. **ipsī**: 'on their side.'   **recentēs, dēfessīs**: *227, a,* (4).

7. **accidit**: sc. *id;* 'there happened, under my own observation,
(something) which.' How lit.? *156.*   **dignum**: predicative, after
vīsum. 142, b.

9. **per**, etc.: 'lumps of tallow and pitch passed from hand to hand,'
till they reached the Gaul who threw them. The siege embankment,
built of green timber and earth and stones, did not burn readily.

10. **ē regiōne turris**: 'directly in a line with one of the towers' on
the siege embankment, hence within range. How lit.?

11. **scorpiōne**, etc.: 'his right side pierced with a (bolt from a)
scorpion.' How lit.? *343, a.*

12. **Hunc**, etc.: 'stepping over him as he lay.'

14. **tertiō**: *ictū scorpiōnis exanimātō tertiō (Gallō), successit
quārtus (Gallus).*   **prius . . . . quam**: *189, a.*

15. **prōpugnātōribus**: 'defenders.'   **vacuus**: predicative.

nōn magnā iactūrā suōrum sēsē effectūrōs spērābant, prop-
5 tereā quod neque longē ab oppidō castra Vercingetorīgis
aberant, et palūs perpetua, quae intercēdēbat, Rōmānōs ad
īnsequendum tardābat.

Iamque hōc facere noctū apparābant, cum mātrēs
familiae repente in pūblicum prōcurrērunt flentēsque prō-
10 iectae ad pedēs suōrum omnibus precibus petiērunt, nē sē
et commūnēs līberōs hostibus ad supplicium dēderent, quōs
ad capiendam fugam nātūrae et vīrium īnfīrmitās impedīret.
Ubi eōs in sententiā perstāre vīdērunt, quod plērumque in
summō perīculō timor misericordiam nōn recipit, conclāmāre
15 et significāre dē fugā Rōmānīs coepērunt.

Quō timōre perterritī Gallī, nē ab equitātū Rōmānōrum
viae praeoccupārentur, cōnsiliō dēstitērunt.

In a final assault the Romans capture Avaricum, sparing none.

27. Posterō diē Caesar, prōmōtā turrī perfectīsque operi-
bus, quae facere īnstituerat, magnō coörtō imbrī, nōn
inūtilem hanc ad capiendum cōnsilium tempestātem arbitrātus, quod paulō incautius cūstōdiās in mūrō dispositās
5 vidēbat, suōs quoque languidius in opere versārī iussit et,

---

26. 4. nōn māgnā : 'no great.' *239, g.*

6. et : correlative with *neque. 233, a.*   palūs : cf. chap. 19, ll. 1–10.

7. tardābat : 'would delay.'

8. apparābant : 'they were preparing.'

10. prōiectae : 'casting themselves.'   suōrum : 'of their (husbands).'

14. nōn, etc. : 'knows no pity.' *177, c,* and *175, c.*

16. Quō, etc. : 'frightened by this' (giving of notice to the Romans)
'and fearing that.' How lit.?

17. praeoccupārentur : 'be seized in advance.' *202.*

27. 2. imbrī : *15, c.*   nōn inūtilem : *239, g.*

4. incautius : 'rather carelessly.' *153, a.*

5. languidius : 'quite lazily' according to appearances, in order to
deceive the enemy.

quid fierī vellet, ostendit. Legiōnēs intrā vīneās in occultō expedītās cohortātus, ut aliquandō prō tantīs labōribus frūctum victōriae perciperent, eīs, quī prīmī mūrum ascendissent, praemia prōposuit mīlitibusque signum dedit.

Illī subitō ex omnibus partibus ēvolāvērunt mūrumque 10 celeriter complēvērunt.

28. Hostēs, rē novā perterritī, mūrō turribusque dēiectī, in forō ac locīs patentiōribus cuneātim cōnstitērunt, hōc animō, ut, sī quā ex parte obviam venīrētur, aciē īnstrūctā dēpugnārent. Ubi nēminem in aequum locum sēsē dēmittere, sed tōtō undique mūrō circumfundī vīdērunt, veritī, nē 5 omnīnō spēs fugae tollerētur, abiectīs armīs ultimās oppidī partēs continentī impetū petīvērunt, parsque ibi, cum angustō exitū portārum sē ipsī premerent, ā mīlitibus, pars iam ēgressa portīs ab equitibus est interfecta. Nec fuit quisquam, quī praedae studēret. Sīc, et Cēnabī caede et 10 labōre operis incitātī, nōn aetāte cōnfectīs, nōn mulieribus, nōn īnfantibus pepercērunt.

Dēnique ex omnī numerō, quī fuit circiter mīlium XL, vix DCCC, quī, prīmō clāmōre audītō, sē ex oppidō ēiēcerant, incolumēs ad Vercingetorīgem pervēnērunt. Quōs ille 15 multā iam nocte silentiō ex fugā excēpit, et veritus, nē qua

---

9. **praemia** : *318.*   **signum** : *326, b.*

28. 1. **turribus** : on the walls of Avaricum (chap. 22, l. 9).   *127, a.*

2. **cuneātim** : 'in wedge-shaped masses.' *77.*

3. **sī**, etc. : 'if an attack should be made from any quarter.' How lit.?

4. **dēpugnārent** : 'they would fight it out.'

5. **circumfundī** : impersonal, 'that they' (the Romans) 'distributed themselves thickly.' How lit.? *174.*

8. **ā mīlitibus** : sc. *interfecta est.*

10. **quisquam** : *168.*   **studēret** : *194, a.*   **Cēnabī** : *146.*

11. **nōn**, etc. : *239, a.*   **aetāte cōnfectīs** : 'the aged.' How lit.?

15. **Vercingetorīgem** : In Fig. 131 a modern designer represents

in castrīs ex eōrum concursū et misericordiā vulgī sēditiō
orerētur, procul in viā dispositīs familiāribus suīs prīncipibusque cīvitātum, disparandōs dēdūcendōsque ad suōs
20 cūrāvit, quae cuique cīvitātī pars castrōrum ab initiō
obvēnerat.

Figure 131. — Vercingetorix viewing the burning of Avaricum.

Vercingetorix with a group of Gallic soldiers as viewing from a distance
the burning of Avaricum after the slaughter of the inhabitants.

     17. **sēditiō** : 'mutiny.'

     18. **orerētur** : *61, b*.   **procul**, etc.: 'he stationed personal rep-
resentatives and leading men of the (different) states along the road at
a distance' from the camp, in order to intercept the fugitives, '(and).'

     19. **disparandōs**, etc.: 'he had them' (the fugitives) 'divided up
and conducted in each case to the men of their own state, (who were)
in the part of the camp that had from the first been assigned to that
state.' How lit.?   The 10,000 defenders of Avaricum had been drawn
from different states (chap. 21, l. 6). *229, b*.

     "It is probable," says Desjardins, "that if the orders of the Gallic

The Siege of Gergovia.   36–51

Caesar arrives at Gergovia and fortifies two camps.

36. Caesar ex eō locō quīntīs castrīs Gergoviam pervēnit equestrīque eō diē proeliō levī factō, perspectō urbis sitū, quae, posita in altissimō monte, omnēs aditūs difficilēs habēbat, dē oppugnātiōne dēspērāvit, dē obsessiōne nōn prius agendum cōnstituit, quam rem frūmentāriam expedīsset.   5

At Vercingetorīx, castrīs prope oppidum positīs, mediocribus circum sē intervāllīs sēparātim singulārum cīvitātum

---

chief had been obeyed, and Avaricum had been burned, as he wished to have it, Caesar and his army would have had the lot of Napoleon after the burning of Moscow."

29–35. Summary. Vercingetorix, calling together the Gallic leaders, reminded them that at the outset he had opposed the defense of Avaricum, and encouraged them with the hope of ultimate victory. He undertook to win over the remaining states that had not yet joined in the revolt, and levied more troops.

Representative Aeduans appealed to Caesar to settle a dispute between two claimants for the office of Vergobret; he proceeded to Decetia (*Decize*), ascertained the facts, and gave the office to Convictolitavis. He sent four legions north under Labienus, and himself led six legions southward into the Arvernian country. He marched first along the east bank of the Elaver (*Allier*), Vercingetorix marching on the opposite side; by a clever ruse (p. xv) he crossed the river behind Vercingetorix, who proceeded rapidly toward Gergovia, Caesar following (Map 13)

36. 1. eō locō: the place where Caesar encamped after crossing the Elaver (*Allier*).   **quīntīs castrīs**: 'in five marches,' encampments being counted as marches because at the close of each day's march a camp was fortified. *147, c,* and *331, a.*   **Gergoviam**: *119, a.*

2. equestrī, etc.: Vercingetorix had reached Gergovia first.

3. monte, etc.: Gergovia lay on a high, narrow plateau, accessible only from the south and southeast. See Map 15.

4. oppugnātiōne, obsessiōne: *340.*

5. expedīsset: 'had arranged for.' *189, b.*

6. castrīs . . . positīs: on an elevated terrace, adjoining the town on the south; marked GALLIC ENCAMPMENT on Map 15.

7. sēparātim: the soldiers of each state had a separate camp.

cōpiās collocāverat, atque omnibus eius iugī collibus occupātīs, quā dēspicī poterat, horribilem speciem praebēbat:
10 prīncipēsque eārum cīvitātum, quōs sibi ad cōnsilium
capiendum dēlēgerat, prīmā lūce cotīdiē ad sē convenīre
iubēbat, seu quid commūnicandum, seu quid administran-
dum vidērētur; neque ūllum ferē diem intermittēbat, quīn
equestrī proeliō, interiectīs sagittāriīs, quid in quōque esset
15 animī ac virtūtis suōrum, perīclitārētur.

Erat ē regiōne oppidī collis sub ipsīs rādīcibus montis,
ēgregiē mūnītus atque ex omnī parte circumcīsus; quem sī
tenērent nostrī, et aquae magnā parte et pābulātiōne līberā
prohibitūrī hostēs vidēbantur. Sed is locus praesidiō ab
20 hīs nōn nimis fīrmō tenēbātur. Tamen silentiō noctis
Caesar, ex castrīs ēgressus, prius quam subsidiō ex oppidō
venīrī posset, dēiectō praesidiō, potītus locō, duās ibi
legiōnēs collocāvit fossamque duplicem duodēnum pedum

---

8. **eius iugī collibus**: 'the minor elevations of the height,' the
points of vantage on the mountain, about and below the town. *160, d.*

9. **quā**, etc.: 'where a view over the plain could be had.' How
lit.? *73, d.* **horribilem**: 'formidable.' *81.*

13. **neque**, etc.: 'and he allowed hardly a day to pass without trying.' *201, a.*

14. **interiectīs sagittāriīs**: 'placing archers among (the cavalry).'
How lit.? **quid**, etc.: i.e. *quid animī ac virtūtis (97, b) in quōque
suōrum (97, a) esset (204, 2).*

16. **ē regiōne oppidī**: 'directly opposite the town,' on the south.
collis: White Rock (*La Roche Blanche*), near the village of the same
name (Map 15).

17. **mūnītus**: principally by nature. **circumcīsus**: 'precipitous.'

18. **aquae**, etc.: the Gauls probably obtained water from the Auzon.

19. **hostēs**: accusative. **ab hīs**: *ab hostibus.*

21. **castrīs**: marked LARGE CAMP on Map 15. **subsidiō**, etc.:
'before relief could come.' How lit.? *73, d,* and *112, a.*

22. **locō**: *131, c.* **ibi**: on White Rock.

23. **fossam**, etc.: 'two (parallel) trenches, each 12 feet wide.' How
lit.? According to the excavations, which have brought to light many

ā maiōribus castrīs ad minōra perdūxit, ut tūtō ab repentīnō hostium incursū etiam singulī commeāre possent. 25

Figure 132. — Gergovia.

East end of the plateau of Gergovia and upper half of slope down toward White Rock,
as seen from an elevation just above the village of Jussat.

traces of Caesar's works near Gergovia, the hastily dug trenches were
hardly more than six feet wide. **duodēnum**: *22, c.*

24. **minōra** [castra] : on White Rock, marked SMALL CAMP on
Map 15. As this contained two legions, in the large camp there must
have been stationed four legions besides the cavalry and auxiliaries.

37–45. Summary. Leading Aeduans, including Convictolitavis, turned
against Caesar, and a body of 10,000 Aeduan soldiers, sent to serve under him,
was moved to defection. Caesar by prompt action won back the allegiance
of the soldiers, but in his absence from Gergovia the Gauls fiercely attacked
both camps. The Aeduan revolt was temporarily checked.

Anticipating more serious trouble, however, Caesar began to plan how he
could withdraw from Gergovia, and reunite his forces, without giving the
impression that he was fleeing from the enemy. In order to frighten the
Gauls he resolved to make a feint assault. He sent part of his forces around,
as if to threaten an exposed point west of the town (**D** on Map 15), thus
drawing off the Gauls from their encampment, which he prepared to attack
in force.

46. Mūrus oppidī ā plānitiē atque initiō ascēnsus rēctā
regiōne, sī nūllus ānfrāctus intercēderet, MCC passūs
aberat; quicquid hūc circuitūs ad molliendum clīvum
accesserat, id spatium itineris augēbat. Ā mediō ferē
5 colle in longitūdinem, ut nātūra montis ferēbat, ex grandibus saxīs VI pedum mūrum, quī nostrōrum impetum tardāret, praedūxerant Gallī atque, īnferiōre omnī spatiō vacuō
relīctō, superiōrem partem collis, ūsque ad mūrum oppidī,
dēnsissimīs castrīs complēverant.

10 Mīlitēs, datō signō, celeriter ad mūnītiōnem perveniunt
eamque trānsgressī trīnīs castrīs potiuntur; ac tanta fuit
in castrīs capiendīs celeritās, ut Teutomatus, rēx Nitio-
brogum, subitō in tabernāculō oppressus, ut merīdiē con-

---

46. 1. **plānitiē**, etc.: the lower ground at the right of the Small
Camp and just above the Parallel Trenches; **E** on Map 15.   **rēctā
regiōne**: 'in a straight line.'

2. **sī**, etc.: 'if there should be no deviation.' How lit.?   **ānfrāctus**:
79, d.   MCC: *mīlle ducentōs*, somewhat more than an English mile.
38, a, b, and 243, b.

3. **quicquid . . . augēbat**: 'the distance to be traversed was increased by every detour (made) in order to render (the ascent of) the
slope easy.' How lit.? The wall of Gergovia lay almost 1000 feet
above the point where the legions started.

4. **Ā**, etc.: 'about halfway up the height.' 126, c, and 152, a.

5. **in**, etc.: 'following the long side of the mountain as the contour
permitted.' How lit.?

6. **mūrum**: marked WALL 6 FEET HIGH on Map 15.   **tardāret**:
193, a.

7. **īnferiōre spatiō**: the sloping mountain side below the wall.
vacuō: predicative. 148, c.

8. **superiōrem partem collis**: GALLIC ENCAMPMENT on Map 15.

9. **dēnsissimīs castrīs**: 'with camps (standing) close together';
each camp contained the troops of a single state, in accordance with
the arrangement described in chap. 36, ll. 6–8. 153, a.

11. **trīnīs castrīs**: 'three camps.' 37, e, and 131, c.

13. **conquiēverat**: 'he was having a nap'; lit. 'had taken complete
rest.'

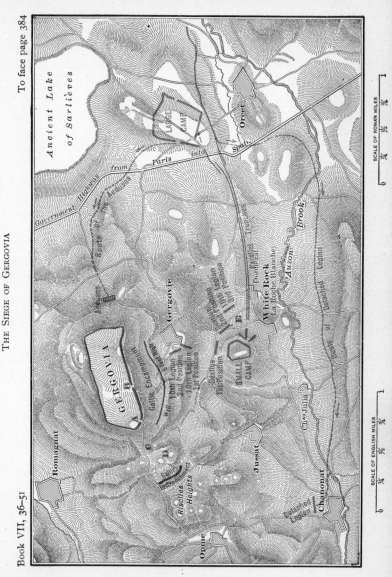

MAP 15

THE SIEGE OF GERGOVIA

Book VII, 36-51

To face page 384

quiēverat, superiōre corporis parte nūdā, vulnerātō equō,
vix sē ex manibus praedantium mīlitum ēriperet.   15

Flushed with victory, the soldiers do not retreat as ordered.

47. Cōnsecūtus id, quod animō prōposuerat, Caesar
receptuī canī iussit, legiōnisque x, quācum erat, continuō
signa cōnstituit.   At reliquārum legiōnum mīlitēs, nōn
exaudītō sonō tubae, quod satis magna vallēs intercēdēbat,
tamen ā trībūnīs mīlitum lēgātīsque, ut erat ā Caesare 5
praeceptum, retinēbantur ; sed, ēlātī spē celeris victōriae et
hostium fugā et superiōrum temporum secundīs proeliīs,
nihil adeō arduum sibi esse exīstimāvērunt, quod nōn vir-
tute cōnsequī possent, neque fīnem prius sequendī fēcērunt
quām mūrō oppīdī portīsque appropinquārunt.   10

Tūm vērō, ex omnibus urbis partibus ortō clāmōre, quī
longius aberant, repentīnō tumultū perterritī, cum hostem
intrā portās esse exīstimārent, sēsē ex oppidō ēiēcērunt.
Mātrēs familiae dē mūrō vestem argentumque iactābant
et, pectore nūdō prōminentēs, passīs manibus obtestābantur 15

47. I. **id**, etc. : 'what he had in mind,' that is, to give the enemy
a good scare by a bold dash, so as to be able to retire from Gergovia
without discredit.

2. **receptuī**, etc. : 'gave orders that the recall be sounded.' *326, c.*
How lit.? *112, a,* and *73, d.*

3. **signa cōnstituit** : 'brought to a halt the standards.' *324, b,* (2).
nōn exaudītō : 'though they did not hear.' How lit.? *144, b,* (5).

4. **tubae** : *326, a,* (1).   **vallēs** : a depression in the slope, just
west of the village of Gergovie ; Caesar with the tenth legion was east
of this depression (Map 15, 10th LEGION, 1st POSITION).

6. **retinēbantur** : 'an attempt was being made . . . to hold the
soldiers . . . back.' How lit.? *175, e.*

10. **portīs** : probably at the points marked **A** and **B** on Map 15.

12. **longius**, etc. : the Gauls who were some distance inside the
wall.   **hostem** : the Romans.

14. **vestem** : 'clothing.'   **argentum** : 'silver.'

15. **pectore** : 'breast.'   **prōminentēs** : 'leaning forward.'   **passīs manibus** : N. to II, 13, l. 12.

Rōmānōs, ut sibi parcerent neu, sīcut Avaricī fēcissent, nē
ā mulieribus quidem atque īnfantibus abstinērent; nōn
nūllae dē mūrō per manūs dēmissae sēsē mīlitibus trādēbant.

L. Fabius, centuriō legiōnis VIII, quem inter suōs eō diē
20 dīxisse cōnstābat, excitārī sē Avaricēnsibus praemiīs neque
commissūrum, ut prius quisquam mūrum ascenderet, trēs
suōs nactus manipulārēs atque ab eīs sublevātus, mūrum
ascendi†; hōs ipse rūrsus singulōs exceptāns in mūrum
extulit.

The Gauls rally and attack the Romans.

48. Interim eī, quī ad alteram partem oppidī, ut suprā
dēmōnstrāvimus, mūnītiōnis causā convēnerant, prīmō
exaudītō clāmōre, inde etiam crēbrīs nūntiīs incitātī, oppidum ā Rōmānīs tenērī, praemissīs equitibus magnō cursū
5 eō contendērunt.

Eōrum ut quisque prīmus vēnerat, sub mūrō cōnsistēbat
suōrumque pugnantium numerum augēbat. Quōrum cum
magna multitūdō convēnisset, mātrēs familiae, quae paulō
ante Rōmānīs dē mūrō manūs tendēbant, suōs obtestārī et
10 mōre Gallicō passum capillum ostentāre līberōsque in cōnspectum prōferre coepērunt.

---

16. **neu,** etc.: 'and not refuse to spare even women.' How lit.?
199, d.   **Avaricī**: *146.*   **fēcissent**: *220.*

18. **dēmissae**: 'being let down' outside the wall.

20. **Avaricēnsibus praemiīs**: 'the prizes (offered) at Avaricum';
see chap. 27, ll. 6–9.   **neque**, etc.: 'and that he was not going to
let any one scale the wall ahead of him.' How lit.?

22. **suōs manipulārēs**: 'men of his maniple.'

23. **hōs singulōs exceptāns**: 'taking hold of them, one at a time.'

48. 1. **eī**: *Gallī.*   **alteram partem**: see chap. 44, l. 11.   **suprā**:
chap. 44, ll. 10–16, and chap. 45, ll. 13–14.

6. **Eōrum**, etc.: 'In succession as each came up.'   **sub mūrō**:
'at the foot of the wall,' on the outside.

10. **passum capillum**: 'their hair disheveled.'

11. **prōferre**: 'to bring out.'   *69, b.*

Erat Rōmānīs nec locō nec numerō aequa contentiō;
simul et cursū et spatiō pugnae dēfatīgātī, nōn facile recentēs atque integrōs sustinēbant.

49. Caesar cum inīquō locō pugnārī hostiumque cōpiās
augērī vidēret, praemetuēns suīs, ad T. Sextium lēgātum,
quem minōribus castrīs praesidiō relīquerat, mīsit, ut cohortēs ex castrīs celeriter ēdūceret et sub īnfimō colle ab
dextrō latere hostium cōnstitueret, ut, sī nostrōs locō dēpul- 5
sōs vīdisset, quō minus līberē hostēs īnsequerentur, terrēret.

Ipse, paulum ex eō locō cum legiōne prōgressus, ubi
cōnstiterat, ēventum pugnae exspectābat.

The Romans fight stubbornly, though against overwhelming odds.

50. Cum ācerrimē comminus pugnārētur, hostēs locō et
numerō, nostrī virtūte cōnfīderent, subitō sunt Aeduī vīsī
ab latere nostrīs apertō, quōs Caesar ab dextrā parte aliō
ascēnsū, manūs distinendae causā, mīserat.

Hī similitūdine armōrum vehementer nostrōs perterruē- 5
runt, ac tametsī dextrīs umerīs exsertīs animadvertēbantur,

---

13. **spatiō**: 'duration.'　　**nōn**, etc.: 'they could not easily hold
out against.'

49. 2. **praemetuēns suīs**: 'becoming anxious about his men.'

4. **sub īnfimō colle**: 'at the foot of the hill' on which the small
camp was; see Map 15, SEXTIUS, 1st POSITION.

5. **locō dēpulsōs**: 'forced from their position.'

6. **quō**, etc.: 'deter the enemy from pursuing them further.' How
lit.? *201, a.*

7. **prōgressus**, etc.: see Map 15, 10th LEGION, 2d POSITION.

50. 1. **hostēs**: sc. *cōnfīderent*.　　**locō**: *135, a.*

2. **Aeduī**, etc.: see chap. 45, ll. 24–25; Map 15, AEDUANS.

4. **manūs**, etc.: 'to separate the (enemy's) forces' by a diversion.

5. **similitūdine armōrum**: 'from the likeness of their arms' to
those of the hostile Gauls.

6. **dextrīs**, etc.: 'it was noticed that they had their right shoulders
bare.' How lit.? *172, d*; also *191, a.*

quod īnsigne pācātōrum esse cōnsuērat, tamen id ipsum
suī fallendī causā mīlitēs ab hostibus factum exīstimābant.

Eōdem tempore L. Fabius centuriō, quīque ūnā mūrum
10 ascenderant, circumventī atque interfectī, mūrō praecipitā-
bantur.

The heroic self-sacrifice of Marcus Petronius.

M. Petrōnius, eiusdem legiōnis centuriō, cum portās excīdere cōnātus esset, ā multitūdine oppressus ac sibi dē-
spērāns, multīs iam vulneribus acceptīs, manipulāribus
15 suīs, quī illum secūtī erant,

'Quoniam,' inquit, 'mē ūnā vōbīscum servāre nōn possum, vestrae quidem certē vītae prōspiciam, quōs, cupiditāte
glōriae adductus, in perīculum dēdūxī. Vōs, datā facultāte,
vōbīs cōnsulite.'

20 Simul in mediōs hostēs irrūpit duōbusque interfectīs reliquōs ā portā paulum summōvit. Cōnantibus auxiliārī
suīs,

'Frūstrā,' inquit, 'meae vītae subvenīre cōnāminī, quem
iam sanguis vīrēsque dēficiunt. Proinde abīte, dum est
25 facultās, vōsque ad legiōnem recipite.'

Ita pugnāns, post paulum concidit ac suīs salūtī fuit.

---

7. **quod,** etc.: 'the customary sign indicating those at peace.' How
lit.?

8. **suī**: *154, b.* B. 339, 5; A. 504, *c*; H. 626, 3.

12. **eiusdem legiōnis**: the 8th; see chap. 47, l. 19.   **excīdere**:
'to hew down.'

14. **manipulāribus**: dative after *inquit*.

16. **Quoniam,** etc.: *211, b,* (2).   **mē**: *158, b.*   **vōbīscum**:
125, c.

17. **vestrae vītae, quōs**: 'for the lives of you, whom.' How lit.?
92, b, and *164, b.*

23. **meae vītae, quem**: i. e. *vītae meī* (genitive), *quem.*

25. **vōs**: object of *recipite.* *158, b.*

26. **ac,** etc.: 'and saved his men.' How lit.? *112, b.*

The Romans retire, with severe losses.

51. Nostrī, cum undique premerentur, XLVI centuriōnibus āmissīs, dēiectī sunt locō. Sed intolerantius Gallōs
īnsequentēs legiō X tardāvit, quae prō subsidiō paulō aequiōre locō cōnstiterat. Hanc rūrsus XIII legiōnis cohortēs
excēpērunt, quae, ex castrīs minōribus ēductae, cum T. 5
Sextiō lēgātō cēperant locum superiōrem. Legiōnēs, ubi
prīmum plānitiem attigērunt, īnfestīs contrā hostēs signīs
cōnstitērunt. Vercingetorīx ab rādīcibus collis suōs intrā
mūnītiōnēs redūxit.

Eō diē mīlitēs sunt paulō minus DCC dēsīderātī. 10

---

51. 1. **XLVI**: *quadrāgintā sex.* As the centurions led their men,
the percentage of casualties was proportionately much higher than
among the common soldiers (l. 10).

2. **dēiectī sunt locō**: 'were forced down from their position.'
intolerantius: 'with considerable violence.'

3. **paulō aequiōre locō**: see Map 15, 10th LEGION, 3d POSITION.

6. **locum superiōrem**: see Map 15, SEXTIUS, 2d POSITION.

7. **īnfestīs**, etc.: 'they halted and faced the enemy.' How lit.?
325, and *144*, *b*, (2). That the soldiers, swept down the slope by an
overwhelming force, rallied even when supported by the 10th and 13th
legions, is all the more remarkable in view of the severe losses among
their officers.

10. **DCC**: *septingentī.* *129*, *b*. If the losses among the common
soldiers had been in proportion to those among the centurions, the
number would have been considerably above two thousand.

52–56. Summary. Caesar addressed his soldiers, rebuking them for not
obeying the order to halt, but nevertheless paying a tribute to their bravery.
Afterwards he drew up in battle order, but Vercingetorix did not come down
to fight. Caesar retired from Gergovia, and recrossed the Elaver (*Allier*), to
the east side.

Two prominent Aeduans, who had heretofore been loyal to Caesar, now
left him, and joined their countrymen in declaring for Vercingetorix; they
destroyed Caesar's supplies at Noviodunum (*Nevers*), burning the town.
Caesar pushed rapidly northward, and forded the Liger (*Loire*) in the face
of the enemy.

General Uprising, with Vercingetorix in Command. 63–68

The Aeduans lead; Vercingetorix assumes command.

63. Dēfectiōne Aeduōrum cognitā, bellum augētur.
Lēgātiōnēs in omnēs partēs circummittuntur; quantum
grātiā, auctōritāte, pecūniā valent, ad sollicitandās cīvitātēs
nītuntur; nactī obsidēs, quōs Caesar apud eōs dēposuerat,
5 hōrum suppliciō dubitantēs territant. Petunt ā Vercingetorīge Aeduī, ut ad sē veniat ratiōnēsque bellī gerendī
commūnicet. Rē impetrātā contendunt, ut ipsīs summa
imperiī trādātur, et, rē in contrōversiam dēductā, tōtīus
Galliae concilium Bibracte indīcitur.

10 Eōdem conveniunt undique frequentēs. Multitūdinis
suffrāgiīs rēs permittitur; ad ūnum omnēs Vercingetorīgem
probant imperātōrem.

Ab hōc conciliō Rēmī, Lingonēs, Trēverī āfuērunt: illī,

57–62. Summary. While Caesar was engaged in the operations about
Gergovia and in checking the first attempts of the revolting Aeduans, Labienus
with four legions advanced from Agedincum (modern *Sens*) toward the northwest and captured Metlosedum (*Melun;* Map 13). Thence he proceeded to
the neighborhood of Lutecia, a town of the Parisii on an island in the Seine,
which forms the heart of modern Paris (Fig. 133). He defeated the Parisii
and their allies in battle, and marching south rejoined Caesar (at 9 on Map 13).

63. 1. **Dēfectiōne Aeduōrum**: the Aeduans, after much dissension, had finally cast in their lot
with Vercingetorix.

2. **circummittuntur**: 'were
sent in all directions' by the
Aeduans. **quantum**, etc.: 'to
the limit of their influence.'

5. **dubitantēs territant**: cf.
chap. 4, ll. 25–30 and NN.

6. **ratiōnēs**, etc.: 'work out
the plan of campaign with (them).'

Figure 133. — Coin of the Parisii.
Gold. Fanciful designs.

9. **Bibracte**; *145, b,* and *16, c.* See Fig. 41, p. 42.

11. **ad ūnum**: 'to a man'; the vote was unanimous.

13. **illī**; 'the former,' including both the Remi and the Lingones.

quod amīcitiam Rōmānōrum sequēbantur; Trēverī, quod
aberant longius et ā Germānīs premēbantur, quae fuit 15
causa, quārē tōtō abessent bellō et neutrīs auxilia mitterent.

Magnō dolōre Aeduī ferunt sē dēiectōs prīncipātū,
queruntur fortūnae commūtātiōnem et Caesaris in sē indulgentiam requīrunt, neque tamen, susceptō bellō, suum
cōnsilium ab reliquīs sēparāre audent.   Invītī summae 20
speī adulēscentēs, Eporēdorīx et Viridomārus, Vereinge-
torīgī pārent.

64. Ille imperat reliquīs cīvitātibus obsidēs itemque eī
reī cōnstituit diem; omnēs equitēs, xv mīlia numerō, celeriter convenīre iubet.   Peditātū, quem anteā habuerit, sē
fore contentum dīcit, neque fortūnam temptātūrum aut in
aciē dīmicātūrum;   5

Sed, quoniam abundet equitātū, perfacile esse factū frū-
mentātiōnibus pābulātiōnibusque Rōmānōs prohibēre; aequō
modo animō sua ipsī frūmenta corrumpant aedificiaque in-
cendant, quā reī familiāris iactūrā perpetuum imperium
lībertātemque sē cōnsequī videant.   10

---

16. **tōtō bellō**: *147, c.*   **abessent**: 'they held aloof.'

17. **sē dēiectōs** [esse] **prīncipātū**: 'that they had been forced
out of their position of leadership'; cf. VI, 12, ll. 27–28.

19. **indulgentiam**: 'favor.'   **requīrunt**: 'they greatly missed.'

20. **Invītī**: 'Unwillingly.'   *151.*
summae speī: 'of the greatest promise.' *100, a.*

64. 1. **Ille**: Vercingetorix.   **eī**
reī: the delivery of the hostages to him.

3. **Peditātū**: *135, a.* B. 219, 1.

4. **neque . . . videant**: the policy
of Vercingetorix was to avoid a decisive
battle with infantry.

6. **frūmentātiōnibus**: 'from getting grain.'

9. **quā . . . iactūrā**: 'since by
this sacrifice of property.'

Figure 134. — Coin of the
Senones.

Bronze. Fanciful designs taken
from animals; reverse, wolf and boar.
On the obverse, four Greek letters,
ΑΓΗΔ, abbreviation of Agedillus or
some similar name.

Hīs cōnstitūtīs rēbus, Aeduīs Segusiāvīsque, quī sunt
fīnitimī prōvinciae, x mīlia peditum imperat; hūc addit
equitēs DCCC. Hīs praeficit frātrem Eporēdorīgis bellum-
que īnferrī Allobrogibus iubet. Alterā ex parte Gabalōs
15 proximōsque pāgōs Arvernōrum in Helviōs, item Rutēnōs
Cadūrcōsque ad fīnēs Volcārum Arecomicōrum dēpopu-
landōs mittit. Nihilō minus clandestīnīs nūntiīs lēgātiōni-
busque Allobrogas sollicitat, quōrum mentēs nōndum ab
superiōre bellō resēdisse spērābat. Hōrum prīncipibus pe-
20 cūniās, cīvitātī autem imperium tōtīus prōvinciae pollicētur.

Caesar takes account of his forces, sends for German cavalry.

65. Ad hōs omnēs cāsūs prōvīsa erant praesidia cohortium duārum et vīgintī, quae, ex ipsā coācta prōvinciā ab
L. Caesare lēgātō, ad omnēs partēs oppōnēbantur. Helvii
suā sponte cum fīnitimīs proeliō congressī pelluntur et,
5 C. Valeriō Donnotaurō, Cabūrī fīliō, prīncipe cīvitātis,
complūribusque aliīs interfectīs, intrā oppida mūrōsque
compelluntur. Allobrogēs, crēbrīs ad Rhodanum dispositīs praesidiīs, magnā cūrā et dīligentiā suōs fīnēs tuentur.
Caesar, quod hostēs equitātū superiōrēs esse intellegē-
10 bat et, interclūsīs omnibus itineribus, nūllā rē ex prōvinciā
atque Italiā sublevārī poterat, trāns Rhēnum in Germā-
niam mittit ad eās cīvitātēs, quās superiōribus annīs pācā-
verat, equitēsque ab hīs arcessit et levis armātūrae peditēs,

---

12. **prōvinciae**: *290.*   **hūc**: for *hīs*, 'to these.'
15. **Helviōs**: west of the Rhone; see Map GALLIA.
19. **superiōre bellō**: the uprising of the Allobroges in 61 B.C.
65. 1. **Ad hōs omnēs cāsūs**: 'To meet all these conditions.'
3. **ad . . . oppōnēbantur**: 'were posted to secure every point.'
5. **Cabūrī fīliō**: see I, 47, ll. 10-13.   **prīncipe**: 'first magistrate.'
6. **intrā**, etc.: 'into their fortified towns and behind walls.'
10. **interclūsīs**, etc.: 'since all the roads were blocked.'
12. **eās cīvitātēs**: the Ubii were friendly to Caesar (IV, 16, ll.
19-20); what other German states are here referred to we do not know.
superiōribus annīs: 55 and 53 B. C. (IV, 16-19, and VI, 9-28).

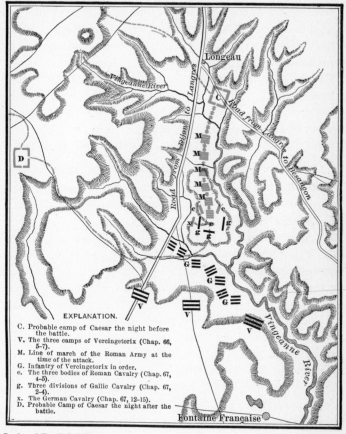

EXPLANATION.

C. Probable camp of Caesar the night before
the battle.
V. The three camps of Vercingetorix (Chap. 66,
5–7).
M. Line of march of the Roman Army at the
time of the attack.
G. Infantry of Vercingetorix in order.
e. The three bodies of Roman Cavalry (Chap. 67,
4–5).
g. Three divisions of Gallic Cavalry (Chap. 67,
2–4).
x. The German Cavalry (Chap. 67, 12–15).
D. Probable Camp of Caesar the night after the
battle.

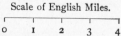

Scale of English Miles.

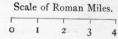

Scale of Roman Miles.

EXPLANATION

Vercingetorix drew up his infantry in front of his three camps, on the bank of
a river, and ordered his cavalry to attack Caesar's army, which was marching
toward the river on the opposite side.

Caesar's legionaries, though surprised, held their own until finally the German
cavalry in Caesar's employ hurled back the Gallic cavalry, which suffered complete
defeat.

quī inter eōs proeliārī cōnsuērant. Eōrum adventū, quod
minus idōneīs equīs ūtēbantur, ā tribūnīs mīlitum reliquīs- 15
que equitibus Rōmānīs atque ēvocātīs equōs sūmit Ger-
mānīsque distribuit.

Vercingetorix encamps near Caesar, addresses his troops.

66. Intereā, dum haec geruntur, hostium cōpiae ex
Arvernīs equitēsque, quī tōtī Galliae erant imperātī, conveniunt. Magnō hōrum coāctō numerō, cum Caesar in Sēquanōs per extrēmōs Lingonum fīnēs iter faceret, quō
facilius subsidium prōvinciae ferrī posset, circiter mīlia 5
passuum x ab Rōmānīs trīnīs castrīs Vercingetorīx cōnsēdit, convocātīsque ad concilium praefectīs equitum,
vēnisse tempus victōriae dēmōnstrat :

Fugere in prōvinciam Rōmānōs Galliāque excēdere. Id
sibi ad praesentem obtinendam lībertātem satis esse ; ad 10
reliquī temporis pācem atque ōtium parum prōficī ; maiōri-
bus enim coāctīs cōpiīs reversūrōs neque fīnem bellandī
factūrōs.

Proinde in agmine impedītōs adoriantur. Sī peditēs suīs

14. **quī . .   cōnsuērant**: in the manner previously described (I,
48, ll. 12–20). Caesar had previously had a division of German cavalry.

15. **minus idōneīs equīs**: cf. IV, 2, ll. 3–7, and p. xxviii.

66. 1. **dum**, etc.: while Caesar was collecting forces from the
Province and from Germany. *190, a.*

4. **extrēmōs Lingonum fīnēs**: 'the most distant (part of the)
country of the Lingones'; i.e. the southeastern part, 'most distant' from
Agedincum, chief city of the Senones (Fig. 134), which was Caesar's
principal base for the operations of 52 B.C. See Map 13.

6. **trīnīs castrīs**: marked **V, V, V**, on Map 16, which represents
the location as fixed by Napoleon, about 40 miles northeast of Dijon.
The battle was probably fought north of Dijon, and much nearer; but
Napoleon's plan indicates the relative positions clearly. **trīnīs**: *37, e.*

9. **Fugere**, etc.: *213, b.*   **Id**: the retreat to the Province.

12. **reversūrōs** [esse] : sc. *Rōmānōs.*

14. **impedītōs**: sc. *eōs* (= *Rōmānōs*). If the legionaries, thus caught
at a disadvantage, should attempt to defend the baggage-train, their

*15 auxilium ferant atque in eō morentur, iter facere nōn posse ;
sī, id quod magis futūrum cōnfīdat, relīctīs impedīmentīs
suae salūtī cōnsulant, et ūsū rērum necessāriārum et dignitāte spoliātum īrī. Nam dē equitibus hostium, quīn nēmō
eōrum prōgredī modo extrā agmen audeat, nē ipsōs quidem
20 dēbēre dubitāre.*

*Id quō maiōre faciant animō, cōpiās sē omnēs prō castrīs
habitūrum et terrōrī hostibus futūrum.*

Conclāmant equitēs, sānctissimō iūre iūrandō cōnfīrmārī
oportēre, nē tēctō recipiātur, nē ad līberōs, nē ad parentēs,
25 nē ad uxōrem aditum habeat, quī nōn bis per agmen hostium perequitārit.

The cavalry of Vercingetorix is defeated by Caesar's cavalry.

67. Probātā rē atque omnibus iūre iūrandō adāctīs,
posterō diē, in trēs partēs distribūtō equitātū, duae sē aciēs
ab duōbus lateribus ostendunt, ūna ā prīmō agmine iter
impedīre coepit. Quā rē nūntiātā, Caesar suum quoque
5 equitātum, tripertītō dīvīsum, contrā hostem īre iubet.

Pugnātur ūnā omnibus in partibus. Cōnsistit agmen ;
impedīmenta intrā legiōnēs recipiuntur. Sī quā in parte

---

retreat would be stopped ; if they should abandon the baggage-train and
try to defend only themselves, they would be cut off from their supplies.

18. **dignitāte spoliātum īrī**: 'would be despoiled of their prestige.'   **hostium**: the Romans.

21. **Id faciant**: 'That they might make the attack.'   How lit.?

23. **iūre iūrandō**: explained by the *nē*-clauses following. Cf. p.
446, ll. 16–19, and N. *13, h.*

24. **recipiātur**: cf. *quī* in l. 25, '(the man) who.'

67. 1. **iūre iūrandō**: the oath given in ll. 23–26 above.

2. **duae aciēs, ūna** [aciēs]: the three divisions of Gallic cavalry,
marked g, g, g, on Map 16.

3. **lateribus, prīmō agmine**: 'flanks,' 'van,' of the Romans.

5. **equitātum, tripertītō dīvīsum**: marked e, e, e, on Map 16.

7. **impedīmenta**, etc.: each legion formed a hollow square (*orbis*,
338) about its baggage (*328*). Caesar was surprised.

nostrī labōrāre aut gravius premī vidēbantur, eō signa īnferrī Caesar aciemque cōnstituī iubēbat; quae rēs et hostēs
ad īnsequendum tardābat et nostrōs spē auxiliī cōn- 10
fīrmābat.

Tandem Germānī ab dextrō latere summum iugum nactī
hostēs locō dēpellunt; fugientēs ūsque ad flūmen, ubi Vercingetorīx cum pedestribus cōpiīs cōnsēderat, persequuntur
complūrēsque interficiunt.   Quā rē animadversā, reliquī, 15
nē circumīrentur, veritī, sē fugae mandant.   Omnibus
locīs fit caedēs.

Trēs nobilissimī Aeduī captī ad Caesarem perdūcuntur :
Cotus, praefectus equitum, quī contrōversiam cum Con-
victolitāvī proximīs comitiīs habuerat, et Cavarillus, quī 20
post dēfectiōnem Litaviccī pedestribus cōpiīs praefuerat,
et Eporēdorīx, quō duce ante adventum Caesaris Aeduī
cum Sēquanīs bellō contenderant.

Vercingetorix and his army take refuge at Alesia.

68. Fugātō omnī equitātū, Vercingetorīx cōpiās suās,
ut prō castrīs collocāverat, redūxit prōtinusque Alesiam,
quod est oppidum Mandubiōrum, iter facere coepit celeriterque impedīmenta ex castrīs ēdūcī et sē subsequī iussit.

Caesar, impedīmentīs in proximum collem dēductīs, duā- 5
bus legiōnibus praesidiō relīctīs, secūtus hostēs, quantum
diēī tempus est passum, circiter III mīlibus ex novissimō
agmine interfectīs, alterō diē ad Alesiam castra fēcit.

Perspectō urbis sitū perterritīsque hostibus, quod equitātū,
quā maximē parte exercitūs cōnfīdēbant, erant pulsī, adhor- 10
tātus ad labōrem mīlitēs circumvāllāre īnstituit.

---

12. **Germānī**: from the favorable position which they had reached
on the height (**x** on Map 16) the German cavalry charged the Gallic
cavalry with irresistible momentum. Cf. chap. 70, ll. 5–10 ; 80, ll. 19–22.

14. **pedestribus copiīs**: Map 16, **G, G, G**.

68. 6. **legiōnibus**: abl. abs. with *relīctīs*.   **praesidiō**: *112, a*.

8. **alterō diē**: = *posterō diē*, ' the next day.'   Cf. Map 13.

The Siege and Fall of Alesia. 69-90

Caesar commences to surround Alesia with a line of works.

69. Ipsum erat oppidum Alesia in colle summō, admodum ēditō locō, ut nisi obsidiōne expugnārī nōn posse
vidērētur. Cuius collis rādīcēs duo duābus ex partibus
flūmina subluēbant.

5   Ante oppidum plānitiēs circiter mīlia passuum III in longitūdinem patēbat; reliquīs ex omnibus partibus collēs,
mediocrī interiectō spatiō, parī altitūdinis fastīgiō oppidum
cingēbant.

Sub mūrō, quae pars collis ad orientem sōlem spectābat,
10 hunc omnem locum cōpiae Gallōrum complēverant fossamque et māceriam in altitūdinem VI pedum praedūxerant.

Eius mūnītiōnis, quae ab Rōmānīs īnstituēbātur, circuitus

---

69. 1. Alesia, etc.: Alesia was situated on the top of an oval hill
now called *Mont Auxois*, a part of which is occupied by the village of
Alise-Ste-Reine (see Map 17).   The highest point is more than 500
feet above the beds of the small streams on either side (Fig. 135).
The accuracy of Caesar's description has been attested by discoveries
made in the course of excavations in 1862–65, and since 1900.

Various objects found at Alesia are reproduced in this book; see
Figures 44, 49, 50, 138, 144, 190; cf. also Fig. 1.

2. **obsidiōne**: *340*.

4. **flūmina**: the *Ose* and the *Oserain*.   **subluēbant**: 'washed.'

5. **plānitiēs**: 'the plain' of *Les Laumes* (pronounced lā lōm).

7. **spatiō**: the average distance between the height of Alesia and
the tops of the surrounding hills is about a mile.   **parī**, etc.: 'having
a like elevation.'   How lit.?

9. **Sub mūrō**, etc.: ' Below the wall,' on the side facing the east.

10. **hunc omnem locum**: 'all the space.' *160, d.*

11. **māceriam**: 'wall of loose stones,' without mortar; Map 17.

13. **Eius mūnītiōnis**: ' of the line of investment,' a series of
fortified camps, between which at intervals were the 'redoubts,'
castella.

xi mīlia passuum tenēbat.   Castra opportūnīs locīs erant
posita ibique castella xxiii facta; quibus in castellīs interdiū 15
statiōnēs pōnēbantur, nē qua subitō ēruptiō fieret; haec
eadem noctū excubitōribus ac fīrmīs praesidiīs tenēbantur.

The Gauls attempt to stop the work, and are driven back.

70. Opere īnstitūtō fit equestre proelium in eā plānitiē, quam, intermissam collibus, tria mīlia passuum in lon-

Figure 135. — The hill of Alesia, as seen from the southeast.

14. **tenēbat**: 'extended.'   **Castra**: plural.   The infantry camps
are those marked **A, B, C, D** on Map 17; the camps marked **G, H, I, K**
were probably occupied by cavalry.

16. **statiōnēs**: 'outposts.'

17. **excubitōribus ac fīrmīs praesidiīs**: 'by strong garrisons of
men in bivouac,' sleeping under arms in the open; the redoubts were
fortified enclosures without tents.   *238 d.*

70. 2. **intermissam collibus**: 'free from hills,' lit. 'left off by
hills.'

gitūdinem patēre suprā dēmōnstrāvimus.   Summā vī ab
utrīsque contenditur.

5 Labōrantibus nostrīs Caesar Germānōs summittit legiōnēsque prō castrīs cōnstituit, nē qua subitō irruptiō ab
hostium peditātū fīat.   Praesidiō legiōnum additō, nostrīs
animus augētur; hostēs, in fugam coniectī, sē ipsī multitūdine
impediunt atque angustiōribus portīs relīctis coartantur.
10 Germānī ācrius ūsque ad mūnītiōnēs persequuntur.   Fit
magna caedēs; nōn nūllī, relīctīs equīs, fossam trānsīre et
māceriam trānscendere cōnantur.

Paulum legiōnēs Caesar, quās prō vāllō cōnstituerat,
prōmovērī iubet.   Nōn minus, quī intrā mūnītiōnēs erant,
15 Gallī perturbantur; venīrī ad sē cōnfestim exīstimantēs, ad
arma conclāmant; nōn nūllī, perterritī, in oppidum irrumpunt.
Vercingetorīx iubet portās claudī, nē castra nūdentur.
Multīs interfectīs, complūribus equīs captīs, Germānī sēsē
recipiunt.

---

3. suprā: chap. 69, ll. 5-8.   Summā, etc.: 'Both sides fought
with their utmost strength.'   How lit. ?

5. Labōrantibus: 'hard pressed.'   How lit.?   Germānōs:
mercenaries, consisting of cavalry, and light-armed troops, trained to
fight with them, brought from Germany to offset the superiority of
Vercingetorix in cavalry (chap. 65, ll. 9-17).

6. castrīs: plural, as in chap. 69, l. 14.   irruptiō: 'attack.'

7. Praesidiō: 'support.'   nostrīs: 109, a.

9. portīs, etc.: 'gate-openings' in the wall of loose stones (chap. 69,
ll. 10-11; a, b, c, on Map 17), '(which had been) left rather narrow';
it is not probable that gates had been placed in the openings.   coartantur: 'were jammed together.'   352, a.

13. prō vāllō: probably the rampart of the infantry camps alone
(A, B, C, D, on Map 17) is meant.

15. venīrī: trans. 'that the Romans were coming.'   73, d.

17. portās: here 'gates' of the town, through which panic-stricken
Gauls rushed, in the effort to escape from their threatened camp into
the city.   castra: on the east side of Alesia, between the city wall
and the wall of loose stones.

*Vercingetorix summons all Gaul to the rescue, and apportions
the available provisions.*

71. Vercingetorīx, prius quam mūnītiōnēs ab Rōmānīs
perficiantur, cōnsilium capit, omnem ab sē equitātum noctū
dīmittere. Discēdentibus mandat, ut suam quisque eōrum
cīvitātem adeat omnēsque, quī per aetātem arma ferre
possint, ad bellum cōgant. Sua in illōs merita prōpōnit 5
obtestāturque, ut suae salūtis ratiōnem habeant, neu sē,
optimē dē commūnī lībertāte meritum, hostibus in cruciātum
dēdant. Quod sī indīligentiōrēs fuerint, mīlia hominum
dēlēcta LXXX ūnā sēcum interitūra dēmōnstrat; *ratiōne
initā, sē exiguē diērum* XXX *habēre frūmentum, sed paulō* 10
etiam longius tolerārī posse parcendō.

Hīs datīs mandātīs, quā erat nostrum opus intermissum,
secundā vigiliā silentiō equitātum dīmittit. Frūmentum
omne ad sē referrī iubet; capitis poenam eīs, quī nōn pāruerint, cōnstituit; pecus, cuius ˙magna erat cōpia ā Man- 15
dubiīs compulsa, virītim distribuit; frūmentum parcē et

---

71. 2. **perficiantur**: *189, b.* B. 292; A. 551, *b*, N. 2; H. 605, 1.

3. **Discēdentibus**: sc. *eīs* (*equitibus*), implied in the preceding
equitātum.

4. **omnēs**: object of *cōgant.* **per aetātem**: 'by reason of age.'

7. **meritum**: participle; 'who had rendered most excellent service
in behalf of their common liberty.' How lit.?

8. **Quod**: *118, d.* **indīligentiōrēs**: 'too remiss.'

9. **ratiōne initā**: '(he said that), having made calculation.' *213, b.*

10. **diērum** XXX: '(to last) 30 days.' How lit.? *100, a.*

11. **parcendō**: 'by reducing the rations,' we should say. How
lit.? *230,* (4).

12. **erat**, etc.: 'there was a break in our line of works,' the contravallation, which there had not been time to complete.

13. **secundā vigiliā**: *242, c.* **Frūmentum omne**: in the city;
Vercingetorix put the inhabitants under martial law.

14. **capitis poenam**: 'the penalty of death.' **pāruerint**: subjunctive in implied indirect discourse, as part of the notice given to the
Alesians.

paulātim mētīrī īnstituit. Cōpiās omnēs, quās prō oppidō
collocāverat, in oppidum recipit. Hīs ratiōnibus auxilia
Galliae exspectāre et bellum administrāre parat.

Description of the inner line of Caesar's siege works.

72. Quibus rēbus cognitīs ex perfugīs et captīvīs, Caesar
haec genera mūnītiōnis īnstituit.

Fossam pedum xx dērēctīs lateribus dūxit, ut eius fossae
solum tantundem patēret, quantum summae fossae labra
5 distārent. Reliquās omnēs mūnītiōnēs ab eā fossā pedēs
cccc redūxit, hōc cōnsiliō, quoniam tantum esset necessāriō
spatium complexus, nec facile tōtum opus corōnā mīlitum
cingerētur, nē dē imprōvīsō aut noctū ad mūnītiōnēs multitūdō hostium advolāret, aut interdiū tēla in nostrōs, operī
10 dēstinātōs, conicere possent.

Hōc intermissō spatiō, duās fossās xv pedēs lātās, eādem

---

17. **prō oppidō** : in the encampment on the east side.

72. 2. **haec** : 'the following.' *161, a.*   **mūnītiōnis** : 'works,'
together forming the contravallation, the purpose of which was to hem
in Vercingetorix and protect Caesar's forces against attack from within
(Map 17, CONTRAVALLATION). *92, b.*

3. **Fossam**, etc. : 'a trench twenty feet (in width), with vertical
sides,' much harder for an enemy to fill and cross than the ordinary
triangular trench (*333*) ; it ran across the plain west of the town, between the Ose and the Oserain (Map 17, TRENCH 20 FEET WIDE).

4. **solum**, etc. : 'the bottom was as broad as the distance between
the edges at the top.' How lit.?

6. **cccc** : *quadringentōs.* The distance, as shown by excavation,
averages so much more than 400 Roman feet, that it has been suggested
that Caesar intended to write *passūs* or *passibus.*   **hōc**, etc. : i.e. *hōc
cōnsiliō, nē, quoniam . . . cingerētur, dē imprōvīsō . . . possent.*
esset — complexus, cingerētur : *220.*

7. **nec**, etc. : 'and the whole line of works could not easily be
manned with a continuous cordon of soldiers.' How lit.?

11. **spatiō** : refers to *pedēs cccc* above.   **duās fossās** : Map 17,
where it will be observed that the outer trench ran only to the edges
of the plain, while the inner trench was continued around the town,

MAP 17

THE SIEGE OF ALESIA

Book VII, 69–90

To face page 400

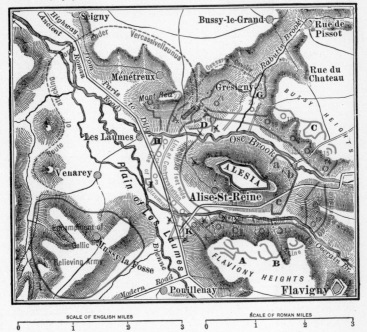

SCALE OF ENGLISH MILES

SCALE OF ROMAN MILES

EXPLANATION

Caesar's lines of works about Alesia encompassed a circuit of 11 Roman miles on the inside, 14 miles on the outside.

In the plain west of the city, and at other points where required, there were two systems of defenses, one to protect Caesar's men against the attacks of Vercingetorix in the city, the other as a defense against the relieving army.

Camps of infantry were probably located at **A, B, C, D**; of cavalry, at **G, H, I, K**. The redoubts, castella (chap. 69), are numbered 1 to 23.

On the west, along the edge of the plain, a trench, or moat, 20 feet wide, with vertical sides, was constructed (chap. 72, ll. 3–5). Further west, in this order, 'goads,' stimulī; 'wolf-holes,' līlia; 'boundary posts,' cippī; two V-shaped 'trenches,' fossae; 'rampart,' agger, and 'palisade,' vallus, with a 'breastwork,' lōrīca, and 'battlements,' pinnae; also 'towers,' turrēs, at intervals of 80 feet. These defenses formed the LINE OF CONTRAVALLATION (chap. 72–73).

The same defenses, in a reverse series, the 'goads' being furthest outside, the rampart inside, formed the LINE OF CIRCUMVALLATION (chap. 74).

altitūdine, perdūxit; quārum interiōrem campestribus ac dēmissīs locīs aquā, ex flūmine dērīvātā, complēvit.

Post eās aggerem ac vāllum XII pedum exstrūxit. Huic lōrīcam pinnāsque adiēcit, grandibus cervīs ēminentibus ad 15 commissūrās pluteōrum atque aggeris, quī ascēnsum hostium tardārent, et turrēs tōtō opere circumdedit, quae pedēs LXXX inter sē distārent.

---

forming a part of the contravallation.   **eādem altitūdine**: of the same depth, 8 or 9 feet; these trenches were V-shaped.

12. **īnteriōrem**: sc. *fossam*.   **campestribus**: 'in the plain.'

13. **dēmissīs**: 'low.'   **flūmine**: the Oserain.   **dērīvātā**: 'drawn.' Silt, evidencing the action of running water, was found in the inner trench.

14. **Post eās**: 'Behind these,' on the side away from the town. **aggerem**: 'bank,' made of the earth thrown out of the nearer trench. **vāllum**: masculine, 'palisade,' like the palisade of a camp (*333*). **XII pedum**: measured from the surface of the ground beside the 'bank' to the top of the 'palisade.'   **Huic**: singular because the 'bank' and the 'palisade' are thought of as forming one fortification; 'to this rampart.'

15. **lōrīcam**: a 'breastwork,' made by weaving supple branches closely together on the exposed side of the palisade.   **pinnās**: 'battlements,' covered with wickerwork and projecting above the palisade, behind which the soldiers could find shelter after hurling their weapons over the palisade.   **cervīs**: 'stags,' large limbs of trees and tops of young trees, from which the foliage and twigs had been removed, the branches being stripped of their bark and sharpened; these were planted along the bank at the foot of the palisade, projecting outwards over the trench and towards the town (Plate IX, 1, the projecting branches at the foot of the tower).   **ēminentibus**: 'projecting.'

16. **ad commissūrās**, etc.: 'along the line where the wood construction was fitted to the bank,' *pluteōrum* here including the 'palisade' (*vāllus*), the 'breastwork' (*lōrīca*), and the 'battlements' (*pinnās*). How lit.?

17. **tardārent**: *193*, *a*.   **opere**: 'the line of works.'   **quae**, etc.: *194*, *a*.

18. **pedēs LXXX**: artillery was mounted in the towers (chap. 81, ll. 14–15; chap. 82, ll. 1–5); the spaces between the towers could be

73. Erat eōdem tempore et māteriārī et frūmentārī et
tantās mūnītiōnēs fierī necesse, dēminūtīs nostrīs cōpiīs, quae
longius ā castrīs prōgrediēbantur; ac nōn numquam opera
nostra Gallī temptāre atque ēruptiōnem ex oppidō plūri-
5 bus portīs summā vī facere cōnābantur. Quārē ad haec
rūrsus opera addendum Caesar putāvit, quō minōre numerō
mīlitum mūnītiōnēs dēfendī possent.

Itaque, truncīs arborum aut admodum fīrmīs rāmīs
abscīsīs, atque hōrum dēlibrātīs ac praeacūtīs cacūminibus,
10 perpetuae fossae quīnōs pedēs altae dūcēbantur. Hūc illī
stīpitēs dēmissī, et ab īnfimō revinctī, nē revellī possent,

---

covered also by hand-thrown missiles, in case the enemy should burst
through the palisade.

73. 1. Erat — necesse : as subject *māteriārī* (Fig. 136) and
frūmentārī are coördinated with *mūnītiōnēs fierī*; 'it was necessary
both to get timber and to secure grain and
to carry on the construction of these extensive fortifications.' How lit.?

2. **dēminūtīs**, etc.: 'with (consequent)
weakening of our forces.' How lit.?

3. **longius :** the supplies of timber and
grain near the camp were soon exhausted.

6. **addendum** [esse] : 'that an addition
ought to be made.' *73, e.*

8. **admodum fīrmīs rāmīs :** 'very
large limbs,' probably not less than four
or five inches in diameter.

9. **hōrum**, etc.: 'the ends (of their
branches) barked and sharpened to a point.'

10. **perpetuae :** 'continuous,' running
parallel with the rampart, at the points
where needed, on the side toward the town.
quīnōs : distributive; 'each five feet deep.'

Figure 136. — A Roman
soldier cutting timber.

36.   **Hūc :** 'Into these,' the parallel trenches.   **illī stīpitēs :** 'the
stocks' of trees, prepared as described. *160, d.*

11. **revinctī :** 'fastened down'; how the stocks were fastened at
the bottom we do not know.   **ab īnfimō :** *126, c,* and *154, a.*

ab rāmīs ēminēbant. Quīnī erant ōrdinēs, coniūnctī inter
sē atque implicātī; quō quī intrāverant, sē ipsī acūtissimīs
vāllīs induēbant. Hōs cippōs appellābant.

Ante hōs, oblīquīs ōrdinibus in quīncuncem dispositīs, 15
scrobēs in altitūdinem trium pedum fodiēbantur, paulātim
angustiōre ad īnfimum fastīgiō. Hūc teretēs stīpitēs feminis crassitūdine, ab summō praeacūtī et praeūstī, dēmittē-
bantur ita, ut nōn amplius digitīs IIII ex terrā ēminērent;
simul, cōnfīrmandī et stabiliendī causā, singulī ab īnfimō 20
solō pedēs terrā exculcābantur; reliqua pars scrobis ad

---

12. **ab**, etc.: 'had their branches' (these having been barked
and sharpened) 'projecting' above the ground. How lit.? *126, c.*
Quīnī ōrdinēs: 'five rows,' one in 'each (trench)'; cf. Plate IX, 1.

13. **implicātī**: 'interwoven,' the parallel trenches being near together.   **quō**, etc.: 'and any who tried to enter these' rows of
branches, corresponding with the barbed wire entanglements of modern
fortifications. How lit.?

14. **vāllīs**: 'points.'   **sē induēbant**: 'would pierce themselves.'
cippōs: 'boundary posts,' jestingly named from their resemblance to
the firmly set stocks of trees and posts used by surveyors to mark
boundaries, especially in regions where boundary posts of stone were
hard to procure.   **appellābant**: 'the soldiers called.' *172, c.*

15. **Ante**: 'In front of,' on the side toward the town.   **oblīquīs**,
etc.: 'in slanting rows having a quincuncial arrangement.' How lit.?

16. **scrobēs**: 'holes.'   **fodiēbantur**: 'were dug.' *57, b.*

17. **angustiōre**, etc.: 'the side gradually narrowing toward the
bottom,' like a funnel. How lit.?   **Hūc**: 'Into these.'   **teretēs**:
'smooth.'   **feminis crassitūdine**: 'of the thickness of a thigh.'
18, d, and *143, a.*

18. **ab**, etc.: 'sharpened at the top and hardened (at the point) by
burning.'

19. **amplius**, etc.: 'more than four finger-breadths,' about equivalent to three inches. *243, a.*

20. **stabiliendī**, etc.: 'to give them a solid setting.' How lit.?
singulī, etc.: 'earth was packed about them by treading, to the depth
of a foot from the bottom,' lit. 'feet in each case from the bottom were
trodden with earth.' Cf. Figures 1 and 2.

occultandās īnsidiās vīminibus ac virgultīs integēbātur.
Huius generis octōnī ōrdinēs ductī ternōs inter sē pedēs
distābant. Id, ex similitūdine flōris, līlium appellābant.
25 Ante haec tāleae, pedem longae, ferreīs hāmīs īnfīxīs,
tōtae in terram īnfodiēbantur, mediocribusque intermissīs spatiīs, omnibus locīs disserēbantur, quōs stimulōs
nōminābant.

Caesar completes a similar outer line of works.

74. Hīs rēbus perfectīs, regiōnēs secūtus quam potuit
aequissimās prō locī nātūrā, XIIII mīlia passuum complexus

---

22. **īnsidiās**: 'the pitfall.' **integēbātur**: 'was covered up.'

23. **octōnī ōrdinēs**: 'eight rows in each case,' wherever the wolf-
holes were used; they were not needed at all points
of the contravallation.

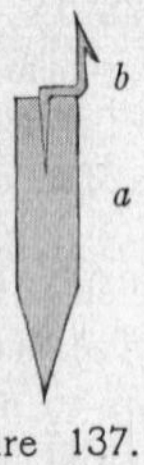

24. **flōris**: *13, c.* **līlium**: 'lily,' the name being
suggested by the appearance of the stalk of the lily
rising from its funnel-shaped
circlet of leaves; now "wolf-
pit" or "wolf-hole.".

25. **tāleae**: 'blocks'
(Fig. 137). **ferreīs**, etc.:
'with barbed hooks, of iron,
set in.'

26. **infodiēbantur**, etc.:
'were buried in the earth,'
only the barbed iron pro-
jecting. How lit.?

27. **disserēbantur**: 'were planted here
and there.' Several of the irons have been
found (Fig. 138). **stimulōs**: 'goads,' so
called from the likeness of the projecting points
to the sharp end of a goad.

Figure 137. — A
"goad," stimulus.

a. Wooden block,
talea, in which the
barbed hook was set.

b. Barbed hook, of
iron.

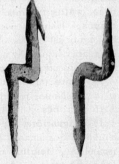

Figure 138. — Barbed
hooks.

Barbed iron hooks, found
at Alesia. The wooden blocks
had rotted away.

74. 1. **regiōnēs**, etc.: 'following a course
over the most nearly level stretches that the configuration of the country
afforded.' How lit.?

2. **complexus**: participle; 'he embraced (a circuit of) fourteen
miles and.' *228, a.*

parēs eiusdem generis mūnītiōnēs, dīversās ab hīs, contrā
exteriōrem hostem perfēcit, ut nē magnā quidem multitūdine, sī ita accidat, mūnītiōnum praesidia circumfundī pos- 5
sent ; ac nē cum perīculō ex castrīs ēgredī cōgātur, diērum
xxx pābulum frūmentumque habēre omnēs convectum
iubet.

The Gauls gather a great army for the relief of Alesia.

75. Dum haec ad Alesiam geruntur, Gallī, conciliō prīncipum indictō, nōn omnēs, quī arma ferre possent, ut
cēnsuit Vercingetorīx, convocandōs statuunt, sed certum
numerum cuique cīvitātī imperandum, nē, tantā multitūdine cōnfūsā, nec moderārī nec discernere suōs nec frūmen- 5
tandī ratiōnem habēre possent.

Imperant Aeduīs atque eōrum clientibus, Segusiāvīs,
Ambivaretīs, Aulercīs Brannovīcibus, mīlia xxxv ; parem

---

3. **parēs** : 'corresponding.' **dīversās** : 'facing in the opposite
direction' from the inner line of works ; see Map 17, CIRCUMVALLATION.

4. **exteriōrem hostem** : a relieving force. A view of a section
of the outer works is shown in Fig. 1. **multitūdine** : sc. *hostium.*

5. **sī**, etc. : *sī magna multitūdō veniat.* **circumfundī** : 'be
completely surrounded.'

6. **ex castrīs ēgredī** : in order to secure forage and grain.

7. **xxx** : cf. chap. 71, l. 10,
and N. **omnēs** : 'all' his forces.
convectum : 'collected.' *229, a.*

75. 1. **ad** : *120, a.* **Gallī**,
etc. : in response to the appeal
of Vercingetorix (chap. 71).

4. **nē**, etc. : ' (fearing) that . . .
they would not be able either to
manage (it) or . . . or.' **tantā**,
etc. : ' if so enormous a host should
be massed together.' *144, b,* (4).

Figure 139. — Coin of the Aulerci
Cenomani.

Gold. Reverse, human headed horse
galloping over a prostrate man. The driver
above holds a branch, perhaps of mistletoe.

5. **frūmentandī**, etc. : 'to make systematic provision for supplying
grain.'

7. **clientibus** : 'dependent states.'

numerum Arvernīs, adiūnctīs Eleutetīs, Cadūrcīs, Gabalīs,
10 Vellaviīs, qui sub imperiō Arvernōrum esse cōnsuērunt;
Sēquanīs, Senonibus, Biturīgibus, Santonīs, Rutēnīs, Carnutibus duodēna mīlia; Bellovacīs x; totidem Lemovīci-
bus; octōna Pictonibus et Turonīs et Parīsiīs et Helvētiīs;
sēna Andibus, Ambiānīs, Mediomatricīs, Petrocoriīs, Ner-
15 viīs, Morinīs, Nitiobrogibus; quīnque mīlia Aulercīs Cēnomanīs; totidem Atrebātibus; IIII Veliocassīs; Aulercīs
Eburovīcibus III; Rauracīs et Boiīs bīna: xxx ūniversīs
cīvitātibus, quae Ōceanum attingunt quaeque eōrum cōnsuētūdine Aremoricae appellantur, quō sunt in numerō
20 Coriosolitēs, Redonēs, Ambibariī, Caletēs, Osismī, Venetī,
Lexoviī, Venellī.

Ex hīs Bellovacī suum numerum nōn complēvērunt, quod
sē suō nōmine atque arbitriō cum Rōmānīs bellum gestūrōs dīcerent neque cuiusquam imperiō obtemperātūrōs;
25 rogātī tamen ā Commiō, prō eius hospitiō duo mīlia ūnā
mīsērunt.

---

12. **duodēna mīlia**: 'twelve thousand each,' or 72,000 for these
six states. The total levy, amounting to 287,000 men, shows that after
six years of war the population of Gaul must have been considerably
larger than is ordinarily supposed. The population, in Caesar's time,
of the territory west of the Rhine has been estimated as high as "20 to
30 millions."

15. **Aulercīs Cēnomanīs**: Fig. 139.

21. **Venellī**: in the list of revolting states we do not find the
Remi and the Lingones, who remained friendly, nor the Treverans,
who were pressed by the Germans (chap. 63, ll. 13–17), nor the
Aquitanïan states.

22. **numerum**: 'contingent.'   **quod . . . dīcerent**: *183, b.*

23. **suō**, etc.: 'on their own responsibility and in their own way.'
How lit.?

25. **prō eius hospitiō**: 'in consideration of their relations of hospitality with him'; N. to I, 31, l. 23.   **ūnā**: 'at the same time'
with the other states.

*Commius, Viridomarus, Eporedorix, and Vercassivellaunus are
placed in command of the Gallic army of relief.*

76. Huius operā Commiī, ut anteā dēmōnstrāvimus,
fidēlī atque ūtilī superiōribus annīs erat ūsus in Britanniā
Caesar; quibus ille prō meritīs cīvitātem eius immūnem
esse iusserat, iūra lēgēsque reddiderat atque ipsī Morinōs
attribuerat.   Tanta tamen ūniversae Galliae cōnsēnsiō fuit 5
lībertātis vindicandae, et prīstinae bellī laudis recuperandae,
ut neque beneficiīs neque amīcitiae memoriā movērentur,
omnēsque et animō et opibus in id bellum incumberent.

Coāctīs equitum mīlibus VIII et peditum circiter CCL,
haec in Aeduōrum fīnibus recēnsēbantur, numerusque 10
inībātur, praefectī cōnstituēbantur; Commiō Atrebātī,

---

76. 1. **Commiī**: after the final defeat of the Gauls Commius seems
to have established himself as a ruler in Britain, and to have left sons
who were rulers, who issued coins in
imitation of Roman coins struck near
the beginning of the Empire.   Three
sons of Commius are named on coins,
Verica or Virica, Tincommius, and
Eppillus (*294*, and Fig. 140).

3. **quibus**, etc.: trans. as if *et
prō hīs meritīs*.   **cīvitātem**: the
Atrebates.   **immūnem**: 'free from
tribute.'   Apparently, as implied also
by *iūra lēgēsque reddiderat*, the Atrebates had become a dependency of
some other state.

Figure 140.   British coin, struck
by a son of Commius.

Gold; dated about the beginning of
the Christian era.   Inscription: VIR
[ICA] REX COM[MI] F[ILIUS], 'Virica,
king, son of Commius.'

4. **ipsī**: to Commius; the Morini had been hard to manage.

5. **Tanta**, etc.: 'So strong was the common purpose of entire Gaul
to recover its liberty.'

7. **movērentur**: the subject is implied in *Galliae*; 'men were influenced.'

8. **-que**: 'but.'   *234, b*.   **incumberent**: 'were devoting themselves.'

10. **recēnsēbantur**: 'were reviewed'; we say 'mobilized.'

Viridomārō et Eporēdorīgī Aeduīs, Vercassivellaunō Ar-
vernō, cōnsobrīnō Vercingetorīgis, summa imperiī trāditur.
Hīs dēlēctī ex cīvitātibus attribuuntur, quōrum cōnsiliō
15 bellum administrārētur.

Omnēs alacrēs et fidūciae plēnī ad Alesiam proficīscuntur;
neque erat omnium quisquam, quī aspectum modo tantae
multitūdinis sustinērī posse arbitrārētur, praesertim ancipitī
proeliō, cum ex oppidō ēruptiōne pugnārētur, forīs tantae
20 cōpiae equitātūs peditātūsque cernerentur.

*The Gallic force in Alesia faces starvation; Critognatus pro-
poses to sustain life by eating the non-combatants.*

77. At eī, quī Alesiae obsidēbantur, praeteritā diē,
quā auxilia suōrum exspectāverant, cōnsūmptō omnī
frūmentō, īnsciī, quid in Aeduīs gererētur, conciliō coāctō
dē exitū suārum fortūnārum cōnsultābant. Ac variīs dic-
5 tīs sententiīs, quārum pars dēditiōnem, pars, dum vīrēs
suppeterent, ēruptiōnem cēnsēbat, nōn praetereunda ōrātiō
Critognātī vidētur propter eius singulārem et nefāriam
crūdēlitātem.

Hīc, summō in Arvernīs ortus locō et magnae habitus
10 auctōritātis,

---

13. **cōnsobrīnō**: 'cousin.'   **summa imperiī**: the commander-
in-chief, Vercingetorix, was shut up in Alesia.

14. **dēlēctī**: 'men chosen'; delegates, forming a kind of general
staff.   **quōrum cōnsiliō**: 'in accordance with whose counsel.'
193, a.

16. **fidūciae**: 'confidence.'   **ad**: 'for.' *120, a.*

18. **ancipitī proeliō**: 'with fighting on two sides.'

19. **forīs**: 'on the outer side.'

77. 1. **Alesiae**: *146.*   **praeteritā diē**: the limit of 30 days had
passed (chap. 71, l. 10). *21, a.*

6. **suppeterent**: subjunctive in implied indirect discourse. *214, b.*

7. **vidētur**, etc.: sc. *mihi*; 'the speech of Critognatus should not,
I think, be passed over.'   **nefāriam**: 'atrocious.'

9. **locō**: *128, a.*   **magnae auctōritātis**: *100, b.*

'Nihil,' inquit, 'dē eōrum sententiā dictūrus sum, quī
turpissimam servitūtem dēditiōnis nōmine appellant; neque
hōs habendōs cīvium locō neque ad concilium adhibendōs
cēnseō. Cum hīs mihi rēs sit, quī ēruptiōnem probant;
quōrum in cōnsiliō, omnium vestrum cōnsēnsū, prīstinae 15
residēre virtūtis memoria vidētur. Animī est ista mollitia,
nōn virtūs, paulisper inopiam ferre nōn posse. Quī sē
ultrō mortī offerant, facilius reperiuntur, quam quī dolōrem
patienter ferant.

Figure 141.— Alise-Ste-Reine, the modern city on the site of Alesia.
The point against the sky-line at the left is the statue of Vercingetorix (Fig. 142).

11. **Nihil**, etc.: *211, b*, (3), and *280*.

14. **Cum**, etc.: 'Let me deal (only) with those.' *180, b*.

15. **omnium**, etc.: 'according to the common feeling of you all.'
97, c, and *138*.

16. **residēre — vidētur**: 'is seen to linger.'   **ista**: for *istud*, addressed to those who would risk all by an immediate sortie, explained
by the appositional infinitive clause *paulisper . . . posse*; 'that is lack
of resolution on your part.' *160, a*, and *e*.

18. **offerant**: *194, a*.   **reperiuntur**: sc. *eī*.   **quam**: *quam eī*.

20 'Atque ego hanc sententiam probārem (tantum apud mē
dignitās potest), sī nūllam praeterquam vītae nostrae iactūram fierī vidērem ; sed in cōnsiliō capiendō omnem Galliam
respiciāmus, quam ad nostrum auxilium concitāvimus.
Quid, hominum mīlibus LXXX ūnō locō interfectīs, propin-
25 quīs cōnsanguineīsque nostrīs animī fore exīstimātis, sī
paene in ipsīs cadāveribus proeliō dēcertāre cōgentur?
Nōlīte hōs vestrō auxiliō exspoliāre, quī vestrae salūtis
causā suum perīculum neglēxērunt, nec stultitiā ac temeritāte vestrā aut animī imbēcillitāte omnem Galliam prōster-
30 nere et perpetuae servitūtī subicere.

'An, quod ad diem nōn vēnērunt, dē eōrum fidē cōn-
stantiāque dubitātis? Quid ergō? Rōmānōs in illīs
ulteriōribus mūnītiōnibus animīne causā cotīdiē exercērī
putātis? Sī illōrum nūntiīs cōnfirmārī nōn potestis, omnī
35 aditū praesaeptō, hīs ūtiminī testibus, appropinquāre eōrum

---

20. **ego**: *87, b.*   **hanc sententiam**: in favor of a sortie.   **tantum**, etc. : 'so great weight does the standing (of its advocates) carry
with me.'

21. **iactūram**: 'loss'; *nūllam iactūram praeterquam vītae nostrae
(iactūram).*

23. **respiciāmus**: *180, a.*   **concitāvimus**: 'we have summoned.'

24. **Quid — animī**: 'what feelings.'   **mīlibus LXXX**: the number
of the army of Vercingetorix, not counting the inhabitants of Alesia
(chap. 71, l. 9).

27. **Nōlīte — exspoliāre**: 'do not rob.'   *181, b.*   **auxiliō**: *127, a.*
quī, etc.: the relieving force.

28. **stultitiā**, etc.: 'by your folly and rashness or weakness of resolution, utterly cast down.'

31. **An**: *179, a,* (2).   B. 162, 4, *a* ; A. 335, *b*; H. 380, 3.   **vēnērunt**: *176, a.*

33. **animī causā**: 'for the sake of amusement.'   **-ne**: *179, a,* (1).
exercērī: 'are exerting themselves.' *174.*

34. **illōrum**: the Gallic forces on the way.

35. **praesaeptō**: 'shut off.'   **hīs**: the Romans.

adventum; cuius reī timōre exterritī, diem noctemque in
opere versantur.

'Quid ergō meī cōnsiliī est? Facere, quod nostrī maiōrēs nēquāquam parī bellō Cimbrōrum Teutonumque fēcērunt; quī in oppida compulsī ac similī inopiā subāctī, 40
eōrum corporibus, quī aetāte ad bellum inūtilēs vidēbantur,
vītam tolerāvērunt neque sē hostibus trādidērunt. Cuius
reī sī exemplum nōn habērēmus, tamen lībertātis causā
īnstituī et posterīs prōdī pulcherrimum iūdicārem.

'Nam quid illī simile bellō fuit? Dēpopulātā Galliā, 45
Cimbrī, magnāque illātā calamitāte, fīnibus quidem nostrīs
aliquandō excessērunt atque aliās terrās petiērunt; iūra,
lēgēs, agrōs, lībertātem nōbīs relīquērunt. Rōmānī vērō
quid petunt aliud aut quid volunt, nisi, invidiā adductī,
quōs fāmā nōbilēs potentēsque bellō cognōvērunt, hōrum 50
in agrīs cīvitātibusque cōnsīdere atque hīs aeternam iniungere servitūtem? Neque enim umquam aliā condiciōne
bella gessērunt. Quod sī ea, quae in longinquīs nātiōnibus
geruntur, ignōrātis, respicite fīnitimam Galliam, quae, in

---

38. **Quid**, etc.: 'What, then, is my proposal?'   **Facere**: i.e.
meum cōnsilium est facere.

39. **Cimbrōrum**: 'with the Cimbrians' and Teutons; N. to I, 33, l. 17.

40. **subāctī**: 'reduced to straits.'

42. **Cuius**, etc.: 'And if we had no precedent for such a course.'
How lit.?

44. **īnstituī**: sc. *exemplum*, 'that a precedent be established.'
pulcherrimum: 'a most noble thing.' *28, a.*

45. **quid**, etc.: 'what resemblance had that war to the present
one?' How lit.?   **Dēpopulātā**: *59, b.*

49. **invidiā**: 'envy.'

50. **fāmā nōbilēs potentēsque bellō**: *239, c.*

51. **iniungere**: 'to fasten upon,' as a yoke is fastened upon
oxen.

52. **aliā condiciōne**: 'on (any) other principle.'

54. **fīnitimam Galliam**: 'the neighboring (part of Gaul).'
152, a.

55 prōvinciam redācta, iūre et lēgibus commūtātīs, secūribus
subiecta, perpetuā premitur servitūte.'

*The residents of Alesia with wives and children are driven
outside the walls; Caesar refuses to receive them.*

78. Sententiīs dictīs, cōnstituunt, ut eī, quī valētūdine
aut aetāte inūtilēs sint bellō, oppidō excēdant, atque omnia
prius experiantur, quam ad Critognātī sententiam dēscen-
dant ; *Illō tamen potius ūtendum cōnsiliō, sī rēs cōgat atque
5 auxilia morentur, quam aut dēditiōnis aut pācis subeundam
condiciōnem.*

Mandubiī, quī eōs oppidō recēperant, cum līberīs atque
uxōribus exīre cōguntur. Hī, cum ad mūnītiōnēs Rōmānōrum accessissent, flentēs omnibus precibus ōrābant, ut
10 sē in servitūtem receptōs cibō iuvārent. At Caesar,
dispositīs in vāllō cūstōdiīs, recipī prohibēbat.

The cavalry of the Gallic army of relief attacks fiercely, is repulsed.

79. Intereā Commius reliquīque ducēs, quibus summa
imperiī permissa erat, cum omnibus cōpiīs ad Alesiam
perveniunt et, colle exteriōre occupātō, nōn longius mīlle
passibus ab nostrīs mūnītiōnibus cōnsīdunt.

---

55. **secūribus** : 'the axes' of the lictors, symbols of authority; see
Plate II, 4.

78. 1. **valētūdine** : 'by reason of health.'

5. **subeundam** [esse] **condiciōnem** : 'submit to terms.'

7. **Mandubiī** : the inhabitants of Alesia and those who had fled
into the city from the surrounding country.

10. **sē — receptōs** : 'receive them — and.' *228, a.*

11. **recipī** : sc. *eōs*. Cast out by Vercingetorix and rejected by
Caesar, the women and children and men unfit for war perished miser-
ably in the spaces between the town walls and the Roman contravallation. Caesar's army at the time was suffering from lack of supplies
(C. III, 47, ll. 16-21). *223, a.*

79. 1. **Commius** : chap. 76, l. 1.   **ducēs** : chap. 76, ll. 11-13.

3. **colle exteriōre** : southwest of Alesia; see Map 17, ENCAMP-
MENT OF GALLIC RELIEVING ARMY.

Posterō diē, equitātū ex castrīs ēductō, omnem eam
plānitiem, quam in longitūdinem tria mīlia passuum patēre
dēmōnstrāvimus, complent, pedestrēsque cōpiās, paulum
ab eō locō abditās, in locīs superiōribus cōnstituunt.

Erat ex oppidō Alesiā dēspectus in campum. Concurrunt, hīs auxiliīs vīsīs; fit grātulātiō inter eōs atque 10
omnium animī ad laetitiam excitantur. Itaque, prōductīs
cōpiīs, ante oppidum cōnsīdunt et proximam fossam crātibus atque aggere explent sēque ad ēruptiōnem atque omnēs
cāsūs comparant.

80. Caesar, omnī exercitū ad utramque partem mūnītiōnum dispositō, ut, sī ūsus veniat, suum quisque locum
teneat et nōverit, equitātum ex castrīs ēdūcī et proelium
committī iubet. Erat ex omnibus castrīs, quae summum
undique iugum tenēbant, dēspectus, atque omnēs mīlitēs 5
intentī pugnae prōventum exspectābant.

Gallī inter equitēs rārōs sagittāriōs expedītōsque levis
armātūrae interiēcerant, quī suīs cēdentibus auxiliō suc-
currerent et nostrōrum equitum impetūs sustinērent.
Ab hīs complūrēs, dē imprōvīsō vulnerātī, proeliō ex- 10
cēdēbant.

---

6. **plānitiem**, etc.; see chap. 69, ll. 5–8.

8. **abditās**: 'drew back and.' *228, a.*

9. **Concurrunt**: 'They' (the Gauls in the town) 'rushed together.'

12. **proximam fossam**: the trench nearest the city; " TRENCH
20 FEET WIDE " on Map 17.

80. 1. **utramque**, etc.: both the inner and the outer lines of works.

3. **castrīs**: the cavalry camps were probably those marked **G, H,
I, K** on Map 17.

4. **castrīs**, etc.: the infantry camps (**A, B, C, D**), in which were
the *mīlitēs*.

6. **prōventum**: 'issue.'

7. **inter equitēs**, etc.: N. to chap. 18, l. 4.

8. **quī**, etc.: 'in order that these might furnish support.' *193, a,*
and *112, a.*

10. **complūrēs**: of Caesar's cavalry.

Cum suōs pugnā superiōrēs esse Gallī cōnfīderent et nostrōs multitūdine premī vidērent, ex omnibus partibus et eī, quī mūnītiōnibus continēbantur, et hī, quī ad auxilium
15 convēnerant, clāmōre et ululātū suōrum animōs cōnfīrmābant. Quod in cōnspectū omnium rēs gerēbātur neque rēctē aut turpiter factum cēlārī poterat, utrōsque et laudis cupiditās et timor ignōminiae ad virtūtem excitābat.

Cum ā merīdiē prope ad sōlis occāsum dubiā victōriā
20 pugnārētur, Germānī ūnā in parte cōnfertīs turmīs in hostēs impetum fēcērunt eōsque prōpulērunt; quibus in fugam coniectīs, sagittāriī circumventī interfectīque sunt. Item ex reliquīs partibus nostrī, cēdentēs ūsque ad castra īnsecūtī, suī colligendī facultātem nōn dedērunt.

25 At eī, quī ab Alesiā prōcesserant, maestī, prope victōriā dēspērātā, sē in oppidum recēpērunt.

---

13. **nostrōs**: *equitēs*; the infantry did not go into action.

14. **mūnītiōnibus**: of the town.

15. **ululātū**: N. to V, 37, l. 8. If upwards of 200,000 men were shouting and shrieking at once, the noise in the Roman lines across the plain, where the sounds from both sides met, must have been terrific; even the noise at one of the great football games would furnish no standard of comparison. The Romans under arms in the camps were probably silent, awaiting a signal for action.

16. **rēs gerēbātur**: 'the engagement was going on.'

17. **rēctē**, etc.: 'and no brave or cowardly action.' How lit.?

18. **ignōminiae**: 'disgrace.' *81*.

19. **Cum**, etc.: 'After the battle had been raging . . . with victory in doubt.' How lit.?

20. **Germānī**: the German cavalry rendered effective service on several critical occasions (chap. 67, ll. 12–15, and 70, ll. 5–12).

22. **sagittāriī**, etc.: among the cavalry; they had not yet learned to keep up with the horsemen by taking hold of the horses' manes, as the Germans did (I, 48, ll. 18–20).

23. **cēdentēs**: 'the enemy in retreat.' How lit.? *227, a, (4)*.

24. **suī**: *154, b*. B. 339, 5; A. 504, *c*; H. 626, 3.

25. **maestī**: 'in sadness.' *151*.

A second attack, by night, is equally unsuccessful.

81. Ūnō diē intermissō, Gallī, atque hōc spatiō magnō crātium, scālārum, harpagōnum numerō effectō, mediā nocte silentiō ex castrīs ēgressī, ad campestrēs mūnītiōnēs accēdunt. Subitō clāmōre sublātō, quā significātiōne, quī in oppidō obsidēbantur, dē suō adventū cognōscere pos- 5 sent, crātēs prōicere, fundīs, sagittīs, lapidibus nostrōs dē vāllō prōturbāre reliquaque, quae ad oppugnātiōnem pertinent, parant administrāre. Eōdem tempore, clāmōre exaudītō, dat tubā signum suīs Vercingetorix atque ex oppidō ēdūcit.   10

Nostrī, ut superiōribus diēbus suus cuique erat locus attribūtus, ad mūnītiōnēs accēdunt; fundīs lībrīlibus sudi-

---

81. 1. **hōc spatiō**: 'during this interval.' *147, c.*

2. **scālārum** : 'ladders.' **harpagōnum**: 'grappling-hooks,' for pulling down the Roman breastworks and palisades. *12, c.*

3. **campestrēs** : west of the town, and nearest the Gallic encampment.

4. **quā significātiōne**: *ut eā significātiōne,* 'that by this sign.' *193, a.*

5. **obsidēbantur**: vivid use of the indicative. Cf. *220.*

7. **vāllō**: of the circumvallation, running from the Ose to Flavigny Heights.   **prōturbāre**: 'dislodge.'

9. **dat tubā signum**: Vercingetorix had adopted the Roman system of signals. *326,*

Figure 142. — Statue of Vercingetorix at Alesia.

a, (1), and II, 20, l. 3.

12. **fundīs lībrīlibus**: 'pound-weight slings'; whether these were

busque, quās in opere disposuerant, ac glandibus Gallōs
prōterrent. Prōspectū tenebrīs adēmptō, multa utrimque
ᵏ⁵ vulnera accipiuntur. Complūra tormentīs tēla cōniciuntur.
At M. Antōnius et C. Trebōnius lēgātī, quibus hae partēs
ad dēfendendum obvēnerant, quā ex parte nostrōs premī
intellēxerant, hīs auxiliō ex ulteriōribus castellīs dēductōs
summittēbant.

82. Dum longius ā mūnītiōne aberant Gallī, plūs multitūdine tēlōrum prōficiēbant; posteā quam propius successērunt, aut sē stimulīs inopīnantēs induēbant aut in
scrobēs dēlātī trānsfodiēbantur aut ex vāllō ac turribus
5 trāiectī pīlīs mūrālibus interībant. Multīs undique vulneribus acceptīs, nūllā mūnītiōne perruptā, cum lūx appe-
teret, veritī, nē ab latere apertō ex superiōribus castrīs
ēruptiōne circumvenīrentur, sē ad suōs recēpērunt.

At interiōrēs, dum ea, quae ā Vercingetorīge ad ērup-
10 tiōnem praeparāta erant, prōferunt, priōrēs fossās explent,

---

slingshots of stone weighing about a Roman pound, or stones of a pound
weight hurled with the help of a cord attached to them, we do not
know; Balearic slingers were trained to hurl stones weighing a pound.
85. **sudibus**; 'stakes,' with pointed ends hardened by fire, for use as
javelins (*praeūstae sudēs;* cf. V, 40, l. 14 and N.).

13. **disposuerant**: 'had piled at intervals,' as reserve ammunition.
79, d. **glandibus**: probably leaden 'bullets' ; N. to II, 10, l. 2.

14. **prōterrent**: 'drove back.' **tenebrīs**: 'by the darkness';
the attack began at midnight (l. 2). **multa,** etc.: the soldiers could
not parry the blows with their shields because they could not see the
missiles coming.

16. **M. Antōnius**: the first mention of Mark Antony by Caesar.
hae partēs: 'this portion' of the fortifications, in the plain.

82. 3. **stimulīs**, etc.: chap. 73, ll. 25–28, and Notes.

4. **scrobēs**: chap. 73, ll. 15–24. **dēlātī**: 'stumbling.' How
lit.? **trānsfodiēbantur**: 'were impaled.' *57, b.*

5. **trāiectī**, etc. : 'transfixed by wall pikes'; N. to V, 40, l. 14.

7. **superiōribus castrīs**: on Flavigny Heights; marked **A, B.**

9. **interiōrēs**: the Gallic army in Alesia.

10. **priōrēs fossās**: precisely what trenches are meant we do

diūtius in hīs rēbus administrandīs morātī, prius suōs discessisse cognōvērunt, quam mūnītiōnibus appropinquārent.
Ita rē īnfectā in oppidum revertērunt.

The Gauls plan a surprise, and make a last desperate assault.

83. Bis magnō cum dētrīmentō repulsī, Gallī, quid agant,
cōnsulunt; locōrum perītōs adhibent; ex hīs superiōrum
castrōrum sitūs mūnītiōnēsque cognōscunt.

Erat ā septentriōnibus collis, quem propter magnitūdinem circuitūs opere circumplectī nōn potuerant nostrī; 5

Figure 143. — A characteristic bit of the slope at Alesia.
On the south side, near the top, facing Flavigny Heights.

not know; evidently not the same as *proximam fossam*, chap. 79,
l. 12.

13. **rē īnfectā**: 'without accomplishing their purpose.'

83. 1. **Bis . . . repulsī**: first in an attack with cavalry (chap. 80),
then in an attack with infantry (chap. 81–82).

2. **locōrum**, etc.: 'they brought in men who knew the ground.'
How lit.? *102*.

4. **ā septentriōnibus**: 'on the north.'   **collis**: Mont Réa.

necessāriō paene inīquō locō et lēniter dēclīvī castra fēcerant. Haec C. Antistius Rēgīnus et C. Canīnius Rebilus
lēgātī cum duābus legiōnibus obtinēbant.

Cognitīs per explōrātōrēs regiōnibus, ducēs hostium LX
10 mīlia ex omnī numerō dēligunt eārum cīvitātum, quae
maximam virtūtis opīniōnem habēbant; quid quōque pactō
agī placeat, occultē inter sē cōnstituunt; adeundī tempus
dēfīniunt, cum merīdiēs esse videātur. Hīs cōpiīs Vercassivellaunum Arvernum, ūnum ex IIII ducibus, propinquum
15 Vercingetorīgis, praeficiunt.

Ille ex castrīs prīmā vigiliā ēgressus, prope cōnfectō sub
lūcem itinere, post montem sē occultāvit, mīlitēsque ex
nocturnō labōre sēsē reficere iussit. Cum iam merīdiēs
appropinquāre vidērētur, ad ea castra, quae suprā dēmōn-
20 strāvimus, contendit; eōdemque tempore equitātus ad campestrēs mūnītiōnēs accēdere et reliquae cōpiae prō castrīs
sēsē ostendere coepērunt.

Vercingetorix attacks the Roman works on the inner side.

84. Vercingetorīx, ex arce Alesiae suōs cōnspicātus, ex
oppidō ēgreditur; crātēs, longuriōs, mūsculōs, falcēs reliquaque, quae ēruptiōnis causā parāverat, prōfert.

---

6. **lēniter dēclīvī**: 'gently sloping' toward the city; hence offering an advantage to a force attacking from the north.   **castra**: **D** on
Map 17.

11. **virtūtis opīniōnem**: 'reputation for courage.'   **quid**, etc.:
'what plan they would deem it best to carry out, and in what way.'

12. **adeundī**, etc.: 'they fixed as the hour of attack.'

14. **IIII ducibus**: 'the four commanders' named in chap. 76,
ll. 11–13.

16. **sub lūcem**: 'toward daybreak.'

17. **itinere**: shown on Map 17, ROUTE OF ATTACKING FORCE
UNDER VERCASSIVELLAUNUS.   **post montem**: behind Mont Réa.

19. **castra**: marked **D**; described in lines 4–8.

20. **campestrēs**: chap. 72, l. 12, and N.

84. 2. **longuriōs**: 'poles,' sharpened at the end, for thrusting;

Pugnātur ūnō tempore omnibus locīs, atque omnia temptantur; quae minimē vīsa pars fīrma est, hūc concurritur. 5
Rōmānōrum manus tantīs mūnītiōnibus distinētur nec facile
plūribus locīs occurrit. Multum ad terrendōs nostrōs valet
clāmor, quī post tergum pugnantibus exsistit, quod suum
perīculum in aliēnā vident virtūte cōnstāre; omnia enim
plērumque, quae absunt, vehementius hominum mentēs 10
perturbant.

Caesar surveys the field, meets crises wherever they arise.

85. Caesar idōneum locum nactus, quid quāque in parte
gerātur, cognōscit; labōrantibus subsidium summittit.

Utrīsque ad animum occurrit, ūnum esse illud tempus,
quō maximē contendī conveniat: Gallī, nisi perfrēgerint
mūnītiōnēs, dē omnī salūte dēspērant; Rōmānī, sī rem 5
obtinuerint, fīnem labōrum omnium exspectant.

Maximē ad superiōrēs mūnītiōnēs labōrātur, quō Vercassivellaunum missum dēmōnstrāvimus. Inīquum locī ad

---

much ·longer than the ordinary javelin. **mūsculōs**: 'mousies';
Vercingetorix had adopted the Roman siege appliances (*342, a*).
falcēs: *falcēs mūrālēs;* N. to chap. 22, l. 4. *342, c*, and Figure 188.

6. **nec**, etc.: 'could not easily meet (the enemy) at several points
(at the same time).'

8. **post tergum pugnantibus**: 'at the rear of the men in action';
the shouting of those fighting on the outer line of works was heard
by those defending the inner line, and *vice versa.* *109, a.*

10. **absunt, perturbant**: *175, c.*

85. 1. **locum**, etc.: Caesar's post of observation was probably on
the Flavigny Heights, at the point marked with a cross on Map 17.

3. **Utrīsque**, etc.: 'To both sides came the conviction, that now
was the time for a supreme final effort.' How lit.?

5. **sī**, etc.: 'if they could (only) maintain their position, looked
forward to.'

8. **dēmōnstrāvimus**: chap. 83, ll. 9–20. **Inīquum**, etc.: 'The
unfavorable ground' (above the camp marked **D**), 'sloping downwards' (cf. chap. 83, l. 6), 'proved a serious factor.' How lit.?

dēclīvitātem fastīgium magnum habet mōmentum. Aliī
10 tēla coniciunt, aliī, testūdine factā, subeunt; dēfatīgātīs in
vīcem integrī succēdunt. Agger, ab ūniversīs in mūnītiōnem coniectus, et ascēnsum dat Gallīs et ea, quae in terrā
occultāverant Rōmānī, contegit; nec iam arma nostrīs nec
vīrēs suppetunt.

86. Hīs rēbus cognitīs, Caesar Labiēnum cum cohortibus VI subsidiō labōrantibus mittit; imperat, sī sustinēre
nōn possit, dēductīs cohortibus ēruptiōne pugnet; id, nisi
necessāriō, nē faciat.

5   Ipse adit reliquōs; cohortātur, nē labōrī succumbant;
omnium superiōrum dīmicātiōnum frūctum in eō diē atque
hōrā docet cōnsistere.

---

10. **testūdine factā**: 'formed a turtle-shell roof' (in the Roman
fashion) 'and.' *144, b*, (2), and *338, 345*.

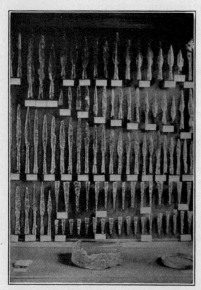

Figure 144. — Heads and butts of lances found at Alesia.

11. **Agger**: 'earth'; no
regular siege embankment was
made.

12. **ea, quae**, etc.: chap.
73, ll. 8–28.

13. **contegit**: 'covered
up.'

86. 2. **labōrantibus**: the
troops under Antistius Reginus
and Caninius Rebilus, in the
fiercely assaulted camp at **D**.

3. **dēductīs**, etc.: 'to draw
off the cohorts (from the engagement) and make a sortie.'
A similar tactic had saved the
day for Galba at Octodurus
(III, 5, ll. 8–15).

5. **Ipse**: 'in person.' **reliquōs**: the other divisions
besides that to which Labienus
had been sent.

6. **dīmicātiōnum**: 'com-
bats.'

The attack of Vercingetorix is repulsed.

Interiōrēs, dēspērātīs campestribus locīs propter magnitūdinem mūnītiōnum, loca praerupta ascēnsū temptant;
hūc ea, quae parāverant, cōnferunt.   Multitūdine tēlōrum 10
ex turribus prōpugnantēs dēturbant, aggere et crātibus
fossās explent, falcibus vāllum ac lōrīcam rescindunt.

87. Mittit prīmō Brūtum adulēscentem cum cohortibus
Caesar, post cum aliīs C. Fabium lēgātum; postrēmō ipse,
cum vehementius pugnārētur, integrōs subsidiō addūcit.

A charge and a flank movement on the north rout the enemy.

Restitūtō proeliō ac repulsīs hostibus, eō, quō Labiēnum
mīserat, contendit; cohortēs IIII ex proximō castellō dēdū- 5
cit, equitum partem sē sequī, partem circumīre exteriōrēs
mūnītiōnēs et ā tergō hostēs adorīrī iubet.

Labiēnus, postquam neque aggerēs neque fossae vim
hostium sustinēre poterant, coāctīs ūnā XI cohortibus, quās

---

8. **Interiōrēs**: as in chap. 82, l. 9.

9. **loca**, etc.: 'places with a steep ascent' (lit. 'steep in respect to
ascent'), along the side of Flavigny Heights, which it had not been
thought necessary to provide with defenses as elaborate as those in
the plain of Les Laumes.

10. **ea, quae**, etc.: see chap. 84, ll. 2–3.

11. **prōpugnantēs**, etc.: 'forced back (our) men (who were) fighting from the towers.'

12. **falcibus**: chap. 84, l. 2.   **vāllum, lōrīcam**: chap. 72,
ll. 14–15.

87. 1. **Mittit**: to the point attacked by Vercingetorix.   **cohortibus**: the number is not given.

4. **Restitūtō**, etc.: reënforced, the men defending the ramparts
attacked by Vercingetorix rallied and beat him off.

6. **partem circumīre**: sc. *equitum*.   The division of cavalry ordered
to execute the flank movement probably started from the camp at **G**;
Map 17, ROUTE OF CAESAR'S CAVALRY.

8. **aggerēs**: here 'ramparts,' at camp **D**.

10 ex proximīs praesidiīs dēductās fors obtulit, Caesarem per
nūntiōs facit certiōrem, quid faciendum exīstimet. Accelerat Caesar, ut proeliō intersit.

88. Eius adventū ex colōre vestītūs cognitō, quō īnsignī
in proeliīs ūtī cōnsuērat, turmīsque equitum et cohortibus
vīsīs, quās sē sequī iusserat, ut dē locīs superiōribus haec
dēclīvia et dēvexa cernēbantur, hostēs proelium commit-
5 tunt.

Utrimque clāmōre sublātō, excipit rūrsus ex vāllō atque
omnibus mūnītiōnibus clāmor.

Nostrī, omissīs pīlīs, gladiīs rem gerunt.

Repente post tergum equitātus cernitur; cohortēs aliae
10 appropinquant.

Hostēs terga vertunt; fugientibus equitēs occurrunt.
Fit magna caedēs.

Sedulius, dux et prīnceps Lemovīcum, occīditur; Vercassivellaunus Arvernus vīvus in fugā comprehenditur;

---

10. **praesidiīs**: detachments under arms at the redoubts; cf. chap.
69, l. 17, and N.

11. **Accelerat**: 'hastened.'

88. 1. **colōre**: scarlet.   **vestītūs**: cloak (*palūdāmentum*).
321.   **cognitō**: by the enemy.   **īnsignī**: 'as a distinguishing mark.'

3. **locīs superiōribus**: Mont Réa.   **haec dēclīvia et dēvexa**:
'these descending slopes,' on the northwest side of Flavigny Heights,
down which Caesar passed, on horseback, in full view of the enemy.

4. **committunt**: with the division under Labienus just coming into
action.

6. **Utrimque**, etc.: the extraordinary vividness of the following description is due in part to the brevity of the sentences, some of which
a writer of less restraint would have expanded into paragraphs; to the
omission of connectives (*238, a*), and to the sparing use of adjectives.
excipit — clāmor: 'the cheering was taken up' by those not in the
action. How lit.? *353, a.*

8. **omissīs pīlīs**: the legionaries were charging up hill, so that
pikes could not be hurled to advantage.

9. **tergum**: sc. *hostium.*   **equitātus**: from camp **G.**   **cohortēs aliae**: the fresh cohorts with Caesar (l. 2).

signa mīlitāria LXXIIII ad Caesarem referuntur; paucī ex 15
tantō numerō sē incolumēs in castra recipiunt.

Cōnspicātī ex oppidō caedem et fugam suōrum, dēspērātā salūte, cōpiās ā mūnītiōnibus redūcunt.

Fit prōtinus, hāc rē audītā, ex castrīs Gallōrum fuga.
Quod nisi crēbrīs subsidiīs ac tōtīus diēī labōre mīlitēs 20
essent dēfessī, omnēs hostium cōpiae dēlērī potuissent.
Dē mediā nocte missus equitātus novissimum agmen cōnse-
quitur; magnus numerus capitur atque interficitur, reliquī
ex fugā in cīvitātēs discēdunt.

Vercingetorix surrenders.

89. Posterō diē Vercingetorīx, conciliō convocātō, id
bellum sē suscēpisse nōn suārum necessitātum, sed commūnis lībertātis causā dēmōnstrat, et quoniam sit fortūnae
cēdendum, ad utramque rem sē illīs offerre, seu morte suā
Rōmānīs satisfacere seu vīvum trādere velint.   5

Mittuntur dē hīs rēbus ad Caesarem lēgātī. Iubet arma
trādī, prīncipēs prōdūcī. Ipse in mūnītiōne prō castrīs
cōnsēdit; eō ducēs prōdūcuntur. Vercingetorīx dēditur,
arma prōiciuntur.

---

15. **signa mīlitāria**: see Figures 30 and 42.

16. **numerō**: 60,000 (chap. 83, l. 9).

17. **Cōnspicātī ex oppidō**: brief for *eī, quī in oppidō sunt, cōnspicātī*, etc.

20. **Quod**: *118, d.*   **nisi**, etc.: *208, a*, (2).   **crēbrīs subsidiīs**: 'with frequent (service in) supporting forces.'

22. **Dē mediā nocte**: *242, d.*

89. 4. **ad utramque rem**: 'for either alternative' (Fig. 145).

7. **Ipse**: Caesar.

8. **Vercingetorīx**, etc.: Vercingetorix, as we learn from Plutarch, having
arrayed himself in splendid armor, mounted a horse adorned with trappings,
passed slowly out from Alesia, and rode around Caesar sitting to receive the
prisoners; then, halting before Caesar, he sprang from his horse, laid off his
armor, and without a word seated himself at the feet of his conqueror,
"every inch a king!"

10   Reservātīs Aeduīs atque Arvernīs, sī per eōs cīvitātēs
recuperāre posset, ex reliquīs captīvīs tōtī exercituī capita
singula praedae nōmine distribuit.

For six years after this Vercingetorix was confined in a Roman prison.*
At length, in 46 B.C., he was led along the streets of Rome to grace Caesar's

great triumph; then, in accordance with Roman
custom, "while his conqueror was offering
solemn thanks to the gods on the summit of
the Capitol, Vercingetorix was beheaded at its
foot as guilty of high treason against the
Roman nation" (Fig. 145).

Thus ended the career of the greatest of the
Gauls, the first national hero of France.

10. **Reservātīs**, etc.: afterwards 20,000
prisoners were returned to the Aeduans and
Arvernians (chap. 90, l. 5). **sī**: '(to see)
whether.' *204*, (4). B. 300, 3; A. 576, *a*;
H. 649, 3.

11. **capita singula**, etc.: each soldier
in Caesar's army received a prisoner as his
share of the booty (*318*); the number was
probably not far from 50,000. On receipt

Figure 145. — Vercin-
getorix.

Denarius, struck while Vercingetorix was in prison, in
Rome. He is represented with
pointed beard and flowing hair,
and with a chain about his neck.
Behind the head is a shield.

of Caesar's dispatches announcing the victory, a thanksgiving of 20
days was declared at Rome (chap. 90, ll. 17–18).

Historical Significance of the Siege of Alesia. Caesar's devices for ren-
dering impassable his lines of defense at Alesia, in ingenuity and adaptation to
the purpose for which they were intended, have never been excelled in the
annals of military engineering.

Caesar's success, again, well illustrates the superiority of generalship, discipline, persistency, and hard work over vastly greater numbers, even in the face
of every disadvantage of position and surroundings.

For the Gauls the fall of Alesia was the crowning disaster of a hopeless
struggle. They staked all on the relief of the city, and lost. But if Caesar
had here suffered complete defeat, probably Gaul would long have remained
unconquered, and the course of European history would have been changed.

The siege of Alesia may well rank among the decisive military operations
of the world.

* Doubtless the Mamertine Prison; for which see the editor's Select Orations
and Letters of Cicero, p. 115 and N. to p. 115, 15.

PLATE X   BUST OF CAESAR AT NAPLES

Truly a wonderful man was Caius Julius Caesar.
Better be first, he said, in a little Iberian village
Than be second in Rome; and I think he was right when he said it.
    LONGFELLOW, *Courtship of Miles Standish.*

SELECTIONS FROM CAESAR'S CIVIL WAR

The Second Sea-fight off Massilia. II. 3-7

The Massilian fleet is reënforced by ships sent by Pompey.

3. Interim L. Nāsidius, ab Cn. Pompeiō cum classe
nāvium xvi, in quibus paucae erant aerātae, L. Domitiō
Massiliēnsibusque subsidiō missus, fretō Siciliae, imprū-
dente atque inopīnante Cūriōne, pervehitur, appulsīsque
Messānam nāvibus atque, inde propter repentīnum terrōrem 5

3–7. The circumstances. On his way to Spain in April, 49 B.C. (*259*)
Caesar sought the allegiance of Massilia (*293, a*), but the Massilians decided
to cast in their lot with Pompey. Caesar directed Trebonius to besiege the
city and Decimus Brutus, who had won the sea-fight with the Venetans, to
destroy their formidable fleet. In June, when his ships were ready, Brutus
took up a position at the island opposite Massilia (Map 18); the much larger
Massilian fleet came out to fight, but proved to be no match for Brutus, who
sank some ships, captured others, and drove the rest back into the harbor.

The second sea-fight, even more disastrous to the Massilians, took place in
July; it is described in the following chapters.

3. 1. L. Nāsidius: apparently the same as Q. Nasidius named on
coins (Figures 146 and 160). **Pompeiō:** Pompey, having fled from
Italy (*259*), was on the east side of the Adriatic, in Macedonia (*299*).

2. aerātae: 'sheathed with copper,' particularly the beaks (*346, c*).
L. Domitiō: at Massilia. The enemies of Caesar had arranged the
appointment of Domitius to succeed Caesar in Gaul in 49 B.C., and he
had helped the Massilians in the first sea-fight. *112, b.*

3. fretō: 'strait,' between Italy and Sicily; Map 12. *134, a.*

4. Cūriōne: Curio was engaged in crushing the Pompeian party in
Sicily, whence, in August of 49, he crossed over to Africa. *12, c.*
pervehitur: 'sailed along.' How lit. ? **appulsīs,** etc.: he landed
at Messana, now Messina.

prīncipum ac senātūs fugā factā, nāvem ex nāvālibus eōrum
dēdūcit.

Hāc adiūnctā ad reliquās nāvēs, cursum Massiliam versus
perficit, praemissāque clam nāviculā, Domitium Massilēn-
sēsque dē suō adventū certiōrēs facit, eōsque magnopere
hortātur, ut rūrsus cum Brūtī classe, additīs suīs auxiliīs,
cōnfligant.

4. Massiliēnsēs, post superius incommodum, veterēs ad
eundem numerum ex nāvālibus prōductās nāvēs refēcerant
summāque industriā armāverant (rēmigum, gubernātōrum
magna cōpia suppetēbat) piscātōriāsque adiēcerant atque
contēxerant, ut essent ab ictū tēlōrum rēmigēs tūtī; hās
sagittāriīs tormentīsque complēvērunt.

Tālī modō īnstrūctā classe, omnium seniōrum, mātrum
familiae, virginum precibus et flētū excitātī, extrēmō tempore cīvitātī subvenīrent, nōn minōre animō ac fīdūciā,
quam ante dīmicāverant, nāvēs cōnscendunt. Commūnī
enim fit vitiō nātūrae, ut invisitātis atque incognitīs rēbus
magis cōnfīdāmus vehementiusque exterreāmur; ut tum

6. **nāvālibus**: 'shipyards.'   **eōrum**: of the Messanians.

9. **nāviculā**: a small sailing vessel, faster than the fleet.

4. 1. **superius incommodum**: the first sea-fight, described C. I.
56-58.

2. **eundem numerum**: 'the same number,' 17, as in the first sea-
fight; Nasidius, counting the ship seized at Messana, also had 17 ships.

4. **piscātōriās** [nāvēs]: 'fishing-smacks.'

5. **contēxerant**: 'had covered (them)' with decks, to protect the
rowers underneath; the fishing-smacks, like those of the Mediterranean
to-day, were open.

7. **seniōrum**: 'older men,' unfit for military or naval service.

8. **virginum**: *12, d*.   **extrēmō tempore**: 'in utmost peril.'

9. **subvenīrent**, etc.: '(begging) them to help the state'; the idea
of asking is implied in *precibus*. *200, a*.

10. **Commūnī**, etc.: 'For it is a common failing of human nature
that we are swayed by unseen and unknown factors to overconfidence
and to too great fear.' How lit. ? *135, a*, and *203*, (1).

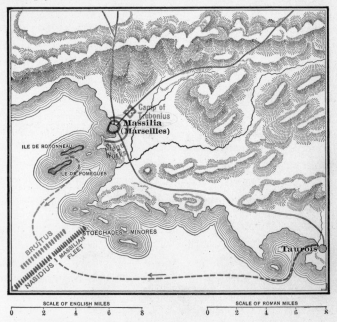

EXPLANATION

Nasidius, admiral of Pompey, had come to Taurois with 17 galleys. Here he was joined by the Massilian fleet, consisting of an equal number of galleys and some protected fishing-smacks.

To oppose this formidable squadron Brutus had only 18 galleys, some of which, newly built, could be less easily maneuvered than the ships of the enemy. His rowers, too, were inferior to those of the enemy, lacking experience.

Nevertheless Brutus left his anchorage, near an island opposite the harbor of Massilia, and led his fleet in the direction of Taurois.

In the battle an attempt to ram Brutus's flagship from opposite sides disabled two of the enemy's ships by collision. Brutus's men showed themselves specially skillful in the seizing of hostile ships by grappling-hooks and boarding, with hand-to-hand fighting. The fleet of Nasidius fled.

On the land side Massilia was shut in by the siege works of Trebonius, whose camp was on high ground on the northwest side of the city (chap. 5, l. 8).

accidit.   Adventus enim L. Nāsidii summā spē et voluntāte cīvitātem complēverat.

Nactī idōneum ventum, ex portū exeunt et Tauroënta, 15
quod est castellum Massiliēnsium, ad Nāsidium perveniunt;
ibique nāvēs expediunt rūrsusque sē ad cōnflīgendum
animō cōnfīrmant et cōnsilia commūnicant.   Dextra pars
attribuitur Massiliēnsibus, sinistra Nāsidiō.

Brutus, in command of Caesar's fleet, comes out to join battle.

5. Eōdem Brūtus contendit, auctō nāvium numerō.
Nam ad eās, quae factae erant Arelāte per Caesarem,
captīvae Massiliēnsium accesserant VI.   Hās superiōribus
diēbus refēcerat atque omnibus rēbus īnstrūxerat.   Itaque

---

13. **voluntāte**: ' eagerness ' to fight.

15. **idōneum ventum**: from the north; see Map 18.   **Tau-roënta**: *18, g*, and *119, a.*

16. **castellum**: Tauroīs was a fortified port.   Nasidius had stopped there, instead of proceeding to Massilia, in order not to expose his fleet, in passing the islands, to the risk of an attack by Brutus; Map 18.

17. **expediunt**: ' made ready for action.' *175, b.*

18. **animō**: *142, a.*   **cōnsilia commūnicant**: ' worked out together their plan ' of battle.   **pars**: ' formation.'

5. 1. **contendit**: from his naval base, at the island opposite Massilia.

2. **Arelāte**: *140, b.*   **per Caesarem**: ' on Caesar's order '; 12 galleys were built at Arelas (C. I. 36), and in the first sea-fight these alone formed the fleet of Brutus.

3. **captīvae**: sc. *nāvēs*; ' captured ' in the first sea-fight.   In all, Brutus now had 18 galleys as against 34 galleys and the protected fishing-smacks in the combined fleet of the Massilians and Nasidius.

Figure 146. — Coin of
Quintus Nasidius.

Silver, denarius, struck 38–36 B.C.   Galley with beak, oars, and sail. The pilot stands on the prow; at the stern sits the helmsman, controlling a large steering-paddle thrust down into the sea. For obverse see Fig. 160.

5 suōs cohortātus, quōs integrōs superāvissent, ut victōs
contemnerent, plēnus speī bonae atque animī, adversus eōs
proficīscitur.

The inhabitants of Massilia offer prayers for victory.

Facile erat, ex castrīs C. Trebōniī atque omnibus superiōribus locīs, prōspicere in urbem, ut omnis iuventūs, quae
10 in oppidō remānserat, omnēsque superiōris aetātis cum
līberīs atque uxōribus ex pūblicīs locīs cūstōdiīsque aut
mūrō ad caelum manūs tenderent aut templa deōrum immortālium adīrent et, ante simulācra prōiectī, victōriam ab
dīs exposcerent.

15 Neque erat quisquam omnium, quīn in eius diēī cāsū
suārum omnium fortūnārum ēventum cōnsistere exīstimāret. Nam et honestī ex iuventūte, et cuiusque aetātis
amplissimī, nōminātim ēvocātī atque obsecrātī atque nāvēs cōn-
scenderant, ut, sī quid adversī accidisset, nē ad cōnandum
20 quidem sibi quicquam reliquī fore vidērent; sī superāvis-

---

5. **suōs,** etc.; *suōs cohortātus ut (eōs), quōs integrōs* ('at their full
strength') *superāvissent, victōs* ('as beaten') *contemnerent. 199, a.*

8. **castrīs**: on the northwest side of the city; Map. 18.

9. **ut**: 'how.' *204, (3).* **quae,** etc.: cf. *220.*

10. **superiōris aetātis**: 'of more advanced age.'

11. **cūstōdiīs**: 'watch stations,' where watchmen were on duty.

12. **ad . . . tenderent**: in the attitude of prayer.

13. **simulācra**: 'images' of the gods. *74, d.* **prōiectī**: 'casting themselves down.' *174.*

14. **exposcerent**: 'were imploring.' *204, (3).*

15. **quīn**: = *quī nōn. 195.* **in . . . cāsū**: 'upon the issue.'

16. **ēventum cōnsistere**: 'that the destiny . . . rested.'

17. **honestī ex iuventūte**: 'the youth of good family.' How
lit.? *97, d.*

18. **amplissimī**: 'the most prominent men,' the leading men of the
city.

19. **adversī, reliquī**: *97, b.* **nē, . . . fore**: 'that even the
possibility of making another attempt would be cut off.' How lit.?

sent, vel domesticīs opibus vel externīs auxiliīs dē salūte
urbis cōnfīderent.

The Massilians and their allies, the Albici, fight desperately.

6. Commissō proeliō, Massiliēnsibus rēs nūlla ad virtūtem dēfuit; sed memorēs eōrum praeceptōrum, quae paulō
ante ab suīs accēperant, hōc animō dēcertābant, ut nūllum
aliud tempus ad cōnandum habitūrī vidērentur et, quibus in
pugnā vītae perīculum accideret, nōn ita multō sē reliquō- 5
rum cīvium fātum antecēdere exīstimārent, quibus, urbe
captā, eadem esset bellī fortūna patienda.

Dīductīsque nostrīs paulātim nāvibus, et artificiō gubernātōrum et mōbilitātī nāvium locus dabātur; et sī quandō
nostrī, facultātem nactī, ferreīs manibus iniectīs, nāvem 10
religāverant, undique suīs labōrantibus succurrēbant.
Neque vērō coniūnctī Albicī comminus pugnandō dēficiēbant neque multum cēdēbant virtūte nostrīs.

---

21. **externīs**: 'foreign.' **dē**, etc.: 'they confidently expected
to assure the safety of the city' against Trebonius.

6. 1. **Commissō proeliō**: 'After the engagement had begun.'
The probable formation in battle order is indicated on Map 18.

4. **habitūrī vidērentur**: sc. *sibi*, 'it seemed to them that they were
going to have.' **quibus . . . accideret**: 'if they should risk their
lives.' How lit.?

6. **exīstimārent**: *203*, (4). **urbe captā**: *144, b*, (4).

7. **eadem fortūna**: they expected an indiscriminate slaughter, like
that at Avaricum (VII. 28), if the city should be taken.

8. **Dīductīs**, etc.: the gradual drawing apart of Brutus's fleet in
the course of the engagement gave to the Massilian steersmen, who
were very skillful, a favorable opportunity to manœuver their ships,
which were seasoned and more easily handled than the new battleships of Brutus. **gubernātōrum**: *84*.

10. **ferreīs**, etc.: 'had thrown grappling-hooks upon a ship and
held it fast.' *144, b*, (2), and *346, d*.

12. **coniūnctī Albicī**: 'the Albici serving with (them),' as marines.
pugnandō: dative after *dēficiēbant*; trans. 'fail in hand-to-hand fighting,' when Brutus's men boarded a Massilian ship.

Simul ex minōribus nāvibus magna vīs ēminus missa
15 telōrum multa nostrīs dē imprōvīsō, imprūdentibus atque
impedītīs, vulnera inferēbant. Cōnspicātaeque nāvēs trirēmēs duae nāvem D. Brūtī, quae ex īnsignī facile agnōscī
poterat, duābus ex partibus sēsē in eam incitāvērunt. Sed
tantum, rē prōvīsā, Brūtus celeritāte nāvis ēnīsus est, ut
20 parvō mōmentō antecēderet. Illae adeō graviter inter sē
incitātae cōnflīxērunt, ut vehementissimē utraque ex concursū labōrārent, altera vērō, praefrāctō rōstrō, tōta collabe-
fieret. Quā rē animadversā, quae proximae eī locō ex
Brūtī classe nāvēs erant, in eās impedītās impetum faciunt
25 celeriterque ambās dēprimunt.

Brutus wins the victory; grief fills the city.

7. Sed Nāsidiānae nāvēs nūllī ūsuī fuērunt celeriterque
pugnā excessērunt; nōn enim hās aut cōnspectus patriae
aut propinquōrum praecepta ad extrēmum vītae perīculum
adīre cōgēbant; itaque ex eō numerō nāvium nūlla dēsīde-
5 rāta est. Ex Massiliēnsium classe v sunt dēpressae, IIII

---

14. **minōribus nāvibus**: the protected fishing-smacks (chap. 4,
ll. 4–6).

16. **inferēbant**: *173, b.*　　**Cōnspicātae**: 'sighting'; the ships
are personified. *226, c,* and *239, h.*　　**nāvēs trirēmēs**: 'triremes.'
346, a.

17. **īnsignī**: a red banner. *346, d.*　　**agnōscī**: 'be recognized.'

18. **duābus ex partibus**: 'from opposite sides.' *347.*

19. **tantum, etc.**: 'Brutus, seeing what would happen, by a quick
movement of his ship just managed, by a narrow margin, to drive
ahead,' so that the two attacking ships rammed each other. How lit.?

22. **praefrāctō, etc.**: 'had had its beak broken off and was quite
shattered.' *346, c,* and Fig. 146.

25. **dēprimunt**: 'sunk.'

7. 1. **Nāsidiānae**: 'of Nasidius.'　　**-que**: 'but.' *234, b.*

2. **hās** [nāvēs]: personification, as in chap. 6, l. 16.

4. **eō numerō nāvium**: i.e. *numerō eārum nāvium,* 17 (chap. 3,
ll. 1–7).

Plate XI   An Ancient Sea-fight between Galleys

A bireme, with two banks of oars, is ramming a quinquereme, with five banks. Fighting-tops were used in the later Roman days, but not in Caesar's time.

The boat in the foreground, with one bank of oars on each side and deck along the middle, would pass very well for one of the protected fishing-smacks used by the Massilians, enlarged (C. III. 4).

captae, ūna cum Nāsidiānīs profūgit; quae omnēs citeriōrem Hispāniam petīvērunt.

At ex reliquīs ūna, praemissa Massiliam huius nūntiī
perferendī grātiā, cum iam appropinquāret urbī, omnis sēsē
multitūdō ad cognōscendum effūdit; et, rē cognitā, tantus
lūctus excēpit, ut urbs ab hostibus capta eōdem vēstīgiō
vidērētur.

Massiliēnsēs tamen nihilō sētius ad dēfēnsiōnem urbis
reliqua apparāre coepērunt.

Heroic Endurance of Caesar's Soldiers before Dyrrachium.
III. 47–49, 53

Caesar with a smaller army shuts Pompey up at Dyrrachium.

47. Erat nova et inūsitāta bellī ratiō, cum tot castellōrum numerō tantōque spatiō et tantīs mūnitiōnibus et tōtō
obsidiōnis genere, tum etiam reliquīs rēbus.

---

6. **captae**: sc. *sunt nāvēs*. The losses of Brutus are not reported.
quae omnēs: *97, c*.   **citeriōrem Hispāniam**: *296*.

10. **multitūdō**: 'population.'   **ad cognōscendum**: 'to learn the
news.'

11. **lūctus excēpit**: 'lamentation followed.'   **capta**: *148, e*.
eōdem vēstīgiō: 'at that moment.' How lit.?

47–53. Caesar before Dyrrachium. When, early in 49 B.C., Pompey fled
with his army from Italy (*259*), he established his base in the region of
Dyrrachium, now *Durazzo* (Map 19). Here he had easy communication by
sea with coastal regions, and by land also with Greece and the wealthy provinces of the Orient (*261*). Before the end of 49 Caesar had vanquished
Pompey's forces in Spain and had received the capitulation of Massilia; in
January, 48 B.C. (Unreformed Calendar; *241, c*), he landed an army at
Palaeste (Map 19), and took possession of Apollonia. By the middle of
April, 48, military operations were concentrated at Dyrrachium, where Caesar,
though he had a smaller army, shut Pompey in by an extended line of works
on the land side.

After a long and bitter struggle Caesar was obliged to retire from before
Dyrrachium; but the difficulties of the undertaking served only to bring out
in clearer light the loyalty and endurance of his soldiers.

47. 1. **inūsitāta**: 'unprecedented.'   **cum**, etc.: 'considering
not only the great number of redoubts.' How lit.?   **castellōrum**:

Nam quīcumque alterum obsidēre cōnātī sunt, perculsōs
5 atque īnfirmōs, hostēs adortī, aut proeliō superātōs aut aliquā offēnsiōne permōtōs, continuērunt, cum ipsī numerō
equitum mīlitumque praestārent; causa autem obsidiōnis
haec ferē esse cōnsuēvit, ut frūmentō hostēs prohibērent.
At tum integrās atque incolumēs cōpiās Caesar īnferiōre
10 mīlitum numerō continēbat, cum illī omnium rērum cōpiā
abundārent; cotīdiē enim magnus undique nāvium numerus conveniēbat, quae commeātum supportārent, neque
ūllus flāre ventus poterat, quīn aliquā ex parte secundum
cursum habērent. Ipse autem, cōnsumptīs omnibus longē
15 lātēque frūmentīs, summīs erat in angustiīs.

*His men, half-starved, say they will live on bark rather than let
Pompey escape.*

Sed tamen haec singulārī patientiā mīlitēs ferēbant.
Recordābantur enim eadem sē superiōre annō in Hispāniā
perpessōs, labōre et patientiā maximum bellum cōnfēcisse,
meminerant ad Alesiam magnam sē inopiam perpessōs,

the number of redoubts in Caesar's lines we do not know; Pompey,
hemmed in by Caesar, built 24 for defense.

2. **spatiō**: the area included between Caesar's lines and the sea exceeded 20 square miles.   **mūnītiōnibus**: Caesar's lines extended 17
Roman miles. For about two thirds of the distance they ran along
higher ground; for the rest, on lower ground, where parallel trenches
and ramparts were constructed, 600 feet apart.

3. **reliquīs rēbus**: 'other conditions.'

4. **quīcumque**, etc.: 'commanders who heretofore have attempted
to blockade an opponent.' How lit.?   **perculsōs**: 'demoralized';
the reason is given in *aut . . . permōtōs.*

5. **aliquā offēnsiōne**: 'by some other reverse.'

10. **illī**: the soldiers of Pompey, whose fleets controlled the sea.

15. **frūmentīs**: here 'stores of grain.'

17. **Recordābantur**: 'They recalled the fact.' *259.*   **eadem**:
object of *perpessōs*; 'having experienced the same hardships.'

multō etiam maiōrem ad Avaricum, maximārum gentium 20
victōrēs discessisse. Nōn illī hordeum, cum darētur, nōn
legūmina recūsābant; pecus vērō, cuius reī summa erat ex
Ēpīrō cōpia, magnō in honōre habēbant.

48. Est etiam genus rādīcis inventum ab eīs, quī fuerant
in vallibus, quod appellātur chara, quod admixtum lacte
multum inopiam levābat.

Id ad similitūdinem pānis efficiēbant. Eius erat magna
cōpia. Ex hōc effectōs pānēs, cum in colloquiīs Pompeiānī 5
famem nostrīs obiectārent, vulgō in eōs iaciēbant, ut spem
eōrum minuerent.

49. Iamque frūmenta mātūrescere incipiēbant, atque
ipsa spēs inopiam sustentābat, quod celeriter sē habitūrōs
cōpiam cōnfīdēbant; crēbraeque vōcēs mīlitum in vigiliīs
colloquiīsque audiēbantur, prius sē cortice ex arboribus
vīctūrōs, quam Pompeium ē manibus dīmissūrōs . . . 5

---

20. **maiōrem** : sc. *inopiam perpessōs* (VII. 17).

21. **hordeum** : 'barley,' not considered a fair substitute for wheat
in the soldier's rations. *317.*

22. **legūmina** : 'pulse,' including beans, lentils, etc. **pecus,**
etc. : Caesar's soldiers counted it a hardship to have fresh meat as the
staple of diet.

23. **Ēpīrō** : mountainous, well adapted for raising cattle.

48. 2. **vallibus** : numerous ravines cut the surface of the higher
ground on which Caesar extended his lines. **chara** : probably a
species of arum, the tubers of which contained starch but were bitter to
the taste and had to be mixed with milk, or cooked with milk, to make
them edible. **admixtum** : 'mixed.' *139.*

4. **Id,** etc. : 'This they made into a kind of bread.' How lit.?

5. **pānēs** : 'loaves.' **colloquiīs** : the opposing lines were within
calling distance. **Pompeiānī** : 'the soldiers of Pompey.'

6. **famem,** etc. : 'would taunt our men with hunger.'

49. 1. **frūmenta** : 'fields of grain.' The blockade of Pompey
dragged on from April to July.

3. **crēbrae** : *151.* **vigiliīs** : when on guard duty at night.

4. **cortice,** etc. : 'that they would live on bark off the trees.' Cf.
IV, 1, l. 16, and N. **ex** : *150, d.*

One day's fighting before Dyrrachium.

53. Ita ūnō diē VI proeliīs factīs, tribus ad Dyrrachium, tribus ad mūnītiōnēs, cum hōrum omnium ratiō habērētur, ad duo mīlia numerō ex Pompeiānīs cecidisse reperiēbāmus, ēvocātōs centuriōnēsque complūrēs (in eō fuit numerō Valerius Flaccus, L. fīlius, eius, quī praetor Asiam obtinuerat); signaque sunt mīlitāria sex relāta.

Nostrī nōn amplius XX omnibus sunt proeliīs dēsīderātī.

The extraordinary bravery of Scaeva, centurion, and his men.

Sed in castellō illō nēmō fuit omnīnō mīlitum, quīn vulnerārētur, quattuorque ex ūnā cohorte centuriōnēs oculōs āmīsērunt.

Et cum labōris suī perīculīque testimōnium afferre vellent, mīlia sagittārum circiter XXX, in castellum coniecta,

---

49-53. Summary. Pompey's water supply was cut off by Caesar, so that his troops were obliged to dig wells, which proved to be inadequate; the baggage-animals died, and there was much sickness among the soldiers. Pompey finally ordered an attack upon several of Caesar's redoubts at the same time, in order that reënforcements might not be sent from one to the other.

53. 1. **ūnō diē**: the day on which Pompey attacked several redoubts at the same time; the offensive cost him heavily. **Dyrrachium**: near the upper end of the area hemmed in by Caesar, on a peninsula projecting into the Adriatic sea.

4. **ēvocātōs**: *316*.

5. **L.**: *Lūciī.* *8, a.* **eius**: sc. *Valeriī Flaccī.* This Lucius Valerius Flaccus was praetor in the year of Cicero's Consulship, 63 B.C. **Asiam**: the province Asia. *302, c.* **obtinuerat**: ex-praetors, as well as ex-consuls, went out as governors of provinces.

6. **signa mīlitāria**: of Pompey, 'brought back' by Caesar's men. *324, b, (2).*

7. **XX**: *vigintī.* *129, b.* **omnibus proeliīs**: *147, b.*

8. **castellō illō**: apparently a redoubt held by the eighth cohort of the sixth legion.

12. **in castellum coniecta**: 'that had been shot against the redoubt.'

Caesarī numerāvērunt, scūtōque ad eum relātō Scaevae,
centuriōnis, inventa sunt in eō forāmina cxx.   Quem Caesar, ut erat dē sē meritus et dē rē pūblicā, dōnātum mīlibus 15
cc . . . atque ab octāvīs ōrdinibus ad prīmipīlum sē trādūcere prōnūntiāvit (eius enim operā castellum magnā ex
parte cōnservātum esse cōnstābat) cohortemque posteā
duplicī stipendiō, frūmentō, veste, cibāriīs mīlitāribusque
dōnīs amplissimē dōnāvit.   20

Caesar's Treatment of Two "Grafters."   III. 59–61

Two "grafters," Gauls, are found in Caesar's cavalry.

59. Erant apud Caesarem in equitum numerō Allobrogēs duo, frātrēs, Roucillus et Egus, Adbucillī fīliī, quī
prīncipātum in cīvitāte multīs annīs obtinuerat, singulārī
virtūte hominēs, quōrum operā Caesar omnibus Gallicīs

---

13. **numerāvērunt**: 'they counted out.'   **scūtō**, etc.: Scaeva, we
are elsewhere told, held his post, at the gate of the redoubt, to the end
of the engagement, though one eye was put out and he was wounded in
shoulder and thigh (Suetonius, *Caesar*, 68).

14. **forāmina**: 'holes,' made by arrows.   Scaeva must have parried
with marvelous steadiness and quickness.   **Quem**: trans. as if *et
eum*.

15. **dōnātum**, etc.: filling the gap in the text as Meusel suggests
we may read, *dōnātum* (*228, a*) *mīlibus ducentīs sēstertium* (see Vocab.)
prō cōntiōne laudāvit, 'presented him with 200,000 sesterces and praised
him before the assembly of the soldiers.'   The value of the gift exceeded
$8000 in our money.

16. **ab**, etc.: 'announced his promotion from the rank of centurion
in the eighth cohort to the position of first centurion.'   How lit.?

18. **cohortem**: all the men of the cohort had their pay doubled,
besides receiving other gifts and decorations.   *318.*

59. 1. **Erant**, etc.: the incidents related in chapters 59–61 took
place while Caesar was still before Dyrrachium.   *90, a.*   **in equitum
numerō**: 'among the cavalry,' apparently a contingent raised among
the Allobroges.

3. **annīs**: *147, c.*   **singulārī virtūte**: *143, a.*

5 bellīs optimā fortissimāque erat ūsus. Hīs domī ob hās
causās amplissimōs magistrātūs mandāverat atque eōs extrā
ōrdinem in senātum legendōs cūrāverat, agrōsque in Galliā,
ex hostibus captōs, praemiaque reī pecūniāriae magna tri-
buerat, locuplētēsque ex egentibus fēcerat.

10 Hī propter virtūtem nōn sōlum apud Caesarem in honōre erant, sed etiam apud exercitum cārī habēbantur;
sed, frētī amīcitiā Caesaris, et stultā ac barbarā arrogantiā
ēlātī, dēspiciēbant suōs, stīpendiumque equitum fraudābant
et praedam omnem domum āvertēbant. Quibus illī rēbus
15 permōtī, ūniversī Caesarem adiērunt palamque dē eōrum
iniūriīs sunt questī, et ad cētera addidērunt, falsum ab eīs
equitum numerum dēferrī, quōrum stīpendium āverterent.

Caesar disciplines them privately.

60. Caesar, neque tempus illud animadversiōnis esse
exīstimāns, et multa virtūtī eōrum concēdēns, rem tōtam
distulit; illōs sēcrētō castīgāvit, quod quaestuī equitēs

---

5. **bellīs**: 'campaigns.' **domī**: in their own country. *146.*

6. **amplissimōs**: 'highest.' **extrā ōrdinem**: 'out of due
course.'

7. **senātum**: sc. *Allobrogum. 289, b.* **legendōs**: *229, b.*

8. **praemia reī pecūniāriae**: 'rewards in money.'

12. **amīcitiā**: *131, e.* **stultā**: 'stupid.'

13. **dēspiciēbant**: 'looked down upon their fellow-countrymen.'
fraudābant: 'were appropriating.'

14. **domum āvertēbant**: they turned aside to private use what
should have been divided up among all. **illī**: the aggrieved cavalrymen.

17. **equitum**, etc.: by turning in a 'fictitious number of cavalrymen' they drew pay for soldiers who did not exist. **āverterent**:
193, a.

60. 1. **neque**, etc.: 'that that (time) was not the (proper) time
for punishment.' *94, d.*

3. **quaestuī**, etc.: 'they made booty of the cavalrymen.' *112, a.*

habērent, monuitque, ut ex suā amīcitiā omnia exspectārent
et ex praeteritīs suīs officiīs reliqua spērārent.   5

Resentful, they borrow money, buy horses, go over to Pompey.

Magnam tamen haec rēs illīs offēnsiōnem et contemptiōnem ad omnēs attulit, idque ita esse cum ex aliōrum
obiectātiōnibus, tum etiam ex domesticō iūdiciō atque animī
cōnscientiā intellegēbant. Quo pudōre adductī, et fortasse
nōn sē līberārī, sed in aliud tempus reservārī, arbitrātī, dis- 10
cēdere ab nōbīs et novam temptāre fortūnam novāsque
amīcitiās experīrī cōnstituērunt.

Et cum paucīs collocūtī clientibus suīs, quibus tantum
facinus committere audēbant, prīmum cōnātī sunt praefectum equitum, C. Volusēnum, interficere, ut posteā, bellō cōn- 15
fectō, cognitum est, ut cum mūnere aliquō perfūgisse ad
Pompeium vidērentur ; postquam id facinus difficilius vīsum
est, neque facultās perficiendī dabātur, quam maximās
potuērunt pecūniās mūtuātī, proinde ac sī suīs satisfacere
et fraudāta restituere vellent, multīs coēmptīs equīs ad 20

---

5. **praeteritīs suīs officiīs** : 'his good offices in the past.'

7. **ad omnēs** : 'before all.'   **id**, etc. : 'and that this was so.'

8. **obiectātiōnibus** : 'reproaches.'   **domesticō iūdiciō** : 'the
judgment (of those) of their own household.'   **animī cōnscientiā** :
' (their own) conscience.'

10. **līberārī** : sc. *poenā.*

13. **cum**, etc. : 'after conferring with a few of their clients.' How
lit. ?

14. **committere** : 'to entrust (the knowledge of).'   **praefectum
equitum** : *309, c.*

15. **C. Volusēnum** : he had distinguished himself in the Gallic
war ; cf. III, 5, ll. 7–10.

16. **mūnere aliquō** : 'some service' rendered, to commend them
to Pompey.

18. **quam**, etc. : 'having borrowed the largest sums of money that
they could.'

20. **fraudāta** : 'the embezzled funds.'   **vellent** : *210.*

Pompeium trānsiērunt cum eīs, quōs suī cōnsiliī participēs
habēbant.

61. Quōs Pompeius, quod erant honestō locō nātī et
īnstrūctī līberāliter, magnōque comitātū et multīs iūmentīs
vēnerant, virīque fortēs habēbantur et in honōre apud Caesarem fuerant, quodque novum id, et praeter cōnsuētūdinem,
5 acciderat, omnia sua praesidia circumdūxit atque ostentāvit.
Nam ante id tempus nēmō, aut mīles aut eques, ā Caesare
ad Pompeium trānsierat, cum paene cotīdiē ā Pompeiō ad
Caesarem perfugerent, vulgō vērō in Ēpīrō atque Aetōliā
cōnscrīptī mīlitēs, eārumque regiōnum omnium, quae ā
10 Caesare tenēbantur.

Last Operations about Dyrrachium. III. 64

*Bravery of a dying standard-bearer in a panic of Caesar's
troops.*

64. Hōc tumultū nūntiātō, Mārcellīnus cohortēs . . .
subsidiō nostrīs labōrantibus summittit ex castrīs; quae,

---

21. **suī cōnsiliī participēs**: 'as associates in the plot.' How lit. ?
26, b, and *115, b*.

61. 1. **Quōs**: object of *circumdūxit*. *167*.   **locō**: *128, a*.

2. **īnstrūctī līberāliter**: 'generously supplied,' as explained in the
next clause.   **comitātū**: 'retinue.' Cf. chap. 84, ll. 20–23.

4. **novum**, etc.: 'as something new and without precedent.'

5. **circumdūxit**: with two accusatives. *114, a*.

8. **perfugerent**: 'men were deserting.' *187*.   **vulgō**: 'in large
numbers.'

9. **mīlitēs**: sc. *perfugerent*.   **eārum regiōnum**: sc. *mīlitēs*.

64. 1. **tumultū**: 'sudden attack' at one end of Caesar's line of
works, near the sea; two cohorts of the ninth legion, on guard duty,
were driven back.   **cohortēs**: a word, giving the number of the
cohorts sent as reënforcement, has been lost.

2. **subsidiō nostrīs**: *112, b*.   **castrīs**: one of Caesar's camps,
in charge of the quaestor Marcellinus and near the point of attack.
quae, etc.: 'but these (cohorts), when they saw our men fleeing.'
How lit. ?

MAP 19

OPERATIONS OF THE YEAR 48 B.C.

To face page 438

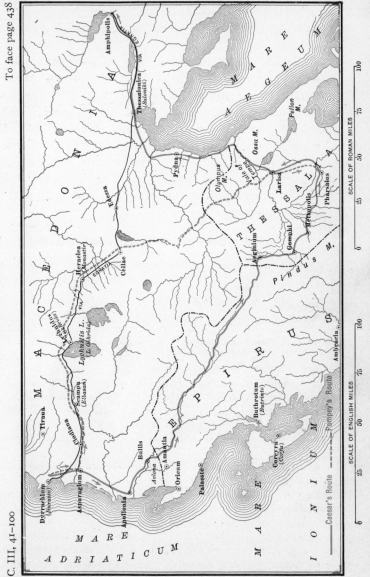

SCALE OF ENGLISH MILES

SCALE OF ROMAN MILES

——— Caesar's Route
- - - - - Pompey's Route

fugientēs cōnspicātae, neque illōs suō adventū cōnfīrmāre
potuērunt, neque ipsae hostium impetum tulērunt.   Itaque
quodcumque addēbātur subsidiō, id, correptum timōre fugi- 5
entium, terrōrem et perīculum augēbat; hominum enim
multitūdine receptus impediēbātur.

In eō proeliō cum gravī vulnere esset affectus aquilifer
et ā vīribus dēficerētur, cōnspicātus equitēs nostrōs,
'Hanc ego,' inquit, 'et vīvus multōs per annōs magnā 10
dīligentiā dēfendī et nunc moriēns, eādem fidē Caesarī
restituō.   Nōlīte, obsecrō, committere, quod ante in exercitū Caesaris nōn accidit, ut reī mīlitāris dēdecus admittā-
tur, incolumemque ad eum dēferte.'

Hōc cāsū aquila cōnservātur, omnibus prīmae cohortis 15
centuriōnibus interfectīs praeter prīncipem priōrem.

---

5. **quodcumque**, etc. : 'every additional detachment sent as reënforcement, seized by the panic of those in flight, (only) increased.'
How lit.?

8. **aquilifer** : 'eagle-bearer,' always accompanying the first cohort
of a legion.   *324, b,* (1).

9. **ā vīribus dēficerētur** : 'his strength began to fail.'   How lit.?
equitēs : perhaps belonging to the cavalry detachment of the ninth
legion.   *309, a.*

10. **Hanc** : *hánc aquilam.   211, a, b,* (3).

12. **Nōlīte**, etc. : 'Do not permit the incurring of a military disgrace.'   How lit.?   *181, b.*

14. **incolumen** : sc. *hanc aquilam.*   The cavalrymen heeded his
plea, and took the eagle.   -**que** : *234, b.*   **dēferte** : *69, b.*

15. **Hōc cāsū** : the appearance of the cavalrymen at the opportune
moment.

16. **prīncipem priōrem** : 'the first centurion of the second maniple.'
315, b.

65–83. Dyrrachium to Pharsalus.   While at Dyrrachium (*261*) Caesar
sent Domitius Calvinus with two legions eastward into Macedonia in order to
check the advance of Scipio (father of Pompey's fifth and last wife, Cornelia),
who was bringing an army westward to Pompey.

Forced finally to withdraw from Dyrrachium, Caesar fell back on Apollonia
(Map 19); thence he marched southeast, effected a junction with Domitius at

The Battle of Pharsalus.　III. 82–99

Caesar draws up his army near Pompey's camp, tests his cavalry.

84. Rē frūmentāriā praeparātā cōnfīrmātīsque mīlitibus, et satis longō spatiō temporis ā Dyrrachīṇīs proeliīs intermissō, quō satis perspectum habēre mīlitum animum vidērētur, temptandum Caesar exīstimāvit, quidnam Pompeius 5 prōpositī aut voluntātis ad dīmicandum habēret. Itaque exercitum ex castrīs ēdūxit aciemque īnstrūxit, prīmō suīs locīs paulōque ā castrīs Pompeī longius, continentibus vērō diēbus, ut prōgrederētur ā castrīs suīs collibusque Pompeiānīs aciem subiceret. Quae rēs in diēs cōnfīrmā-10 tiōrem eius exercitum efficiēbat.

Aeginium in Thessaly (*301*, and Map 19), and led the united army to Gomphi, which, because its gates were closed, he stormed and gave over to looting. From Gomphi Caesar marched by way of Metropolis to the vicinity of Pharsalus, where he encamped, in a plain rich with ripening harvests, resolved there to await the coming of Pompey (Map 20).

Pompey, taking a northerly route (Map 19) by way of Heraclea (modern *Monastir*), joined the army of Scipio with his own, entered Thessaly from the north, and encamped not far from Caesar (Map 20).

84. 1. **Rē**, etc.: trans. by clauses commencing with 'when.' **cōnfīrmātīs**: 'encouraged.'

2. **satis**, etc.: 'a sufficiently long period had elapsed since the engagements at Dyrrachium to enable him to assure himself of the spirit of his soldiers.' How lit.?

3. **perspectum**: *229, a.*　**vidērētur**: sc. *sibi*. *194, a.*

4. **temptandum** [esse]: sc. *sibi;* 'that he ought to find out.' **quidnam**: etc.: 'what intention or desire.' *48, c*, and 97, *b*.]

7. **suīs locīs**: 'in a position favorable to himself,' in front of his own camp.　**castrīs Pompeī**: on an elevation, east of Caesar's camp (Map 20). *8, b.*　**continentibus**: 'successive.'

8. **ut**: *ita īnstrūxit ut;* trans. 'in such a way that he moved forward.' **collibus**, etc.: 'pushed his line up to the hills occupied by Pompey.'

9. **rēs**: the fact that Pompey did not offer battle when Caesar's line moved up near him.　**cōnfīrmātiōrem**: 'more confident.'

Superius tamen īnstitūtum in equitibus, quod dēmōnstrāvimus, servābat, ut, quoniam numerō multīs partibus
esset īnferior, adulēscentēs atque expedītōs ex antesignānīs, ēlēctīs ad pernīcitātem armīs, inter equitēs proeliārī
iubēret, quī cotīdiānā cōnsuētūdine ūsum quoque eius ¹⁵
generis proeliōrum perciperent.

Hīs erat rēbus effectum, ut equitēs mīlle, etiam apertiōribus locīs, VII mīlium Pompeiānōrum impetum, cum adesset ūsus, sustinēre audērent, neque magnopere eōrum
multitūdine terrērentur.   Namque etiam per eōs diēs proe- ²⁰
lium secundum equestre fēcit, atque ūnum Allobrogem ex
duōbus, quōs perfūgisse ad Pompeium suprā docuimus,
cum quibusdam interfēcit.

---

11. **Superius īnstitūtum**: 'the former arrangement.'   **dēmōnstrāvimus**: in chapter 75; there Caesar relates how he interspersed
400 light-armed footmen among his cavalry which, thus strengthened,
defeated Pompey's cavalry with much slaughter.

12. **numerō**: sc. *equitum*. *142, a*.   **multīs partibus**: 'much.'
How lit.? *140*.

13. **expedītōs**: 'with light equipment,' in place of the heavy
weapons ordinarily carried by the legionary.   **antesignānīs**: in each
legion the 'men before the standards' formed a select contingent
of the best fighters who were charged to protect the standards and
in battle were posted in the parts of the line that were in front of the
standards.

14. **ēlēctīs**, etc.: 'with arms selected for quickness of movement.'

15. **quī**: 'in order that they.' *193, a*.   **quoque**, etc.: 'in that
kind of fighting also,' as well as in the methods in which they were
trained as legionaries. The interspersing of agile footmen among
cavalry Caesar had learned from the Germans (I, 48, ll. 12–20); in the
latter part of the Gallic War Caesar had employed German horsemen
(N. to VII, 70, l. 5).

17. **apertiōribus locīs**: 'on more open ground,' where Pompey's
much larger force of cavalry could be deployed to the best advantage.
145, c.

18. **cum adesset ūsus**: 'when the necessity presented itself.' *220*.

22. **duōbus**: Roucillus and Egus.   **suprā**: chapters 59–61.

*Pompey remains stationary; finally, as Caesar breaks camp, he
advances.*

85. Pompeius, quī castra in colle habēbat, ad īnfimās
rādīcēs montis aciem īnstruēbat, semper, ut vidēbātur,
exspectāns, sī inīquīs locīs Caesar sē subiceret.

Caesar, nūllā ratiōne ad pugnam ēlicī posse Pompeium
5 exīstimāns, hanc sibi commodissimam bellī ratiōnem iūdi-
cāvit, utī castra ex eō locō movēret semperque esset in
itineribus, haec spectāns, ut movendīs castrīs plūribusque
adeundīs locīs commodiōre rē frūmentāriā ūterētur ; simul-
que in itinere ut aliquam occāsiōnem dīmicandī nancīsce-
10 rētur, et īnsolitum ad labōrem Pompeī exercitum cotīdiānīs
itineribus dēfatīgāret.

Hīs cōnstitūtīs rēbus, signō iam profectiōnis datō, taber-
nāculīsque dētēnsīs, animadversum est, paulō ante, extrā
cotīdiānam cōnsuētūdinem longius ā vāllō esse aciem Pompeī
15 prōgressam, ut nōn inīquō locō posse dīmicārī vidērētur.
Tum Caesar apud suōs, cum iam esset agmen in portīs,

---

85. 2. **montis**: 'elevation.'   **aciem**: Map 20, POMPEY'S FIRST
POSITION.   **īnstruēbat**: on successive days. *175, d.*

3. **exspectāns**: 'waiting (to see) whether Caesar would move close
up to the unfavorable ground.' *204*, (4).

4. **ēlicī**: 'be lured forth.' *57, b.*

5. **bellī ratiōnem**: 'plan of campaign.'

7. **in itineribus**: 'on the march.'   **haec spectāns**: 'having
this in view.'   **movendīs castrīs**: 'by constantly moving his camp.'
230, (4).

10. **īnsolitum ad labōrem**: 'not used to hard work.'

12. **Hīs**, etc.: Caesar probably reached his decision on August 8,
and gave orders to break camp early the next morning.

13. **dētēnsīs**: 'struck.'   **paulō**, etc.: the movement of Pompey's
line, 'contrary to his daily practice,' was noticed 'a little before' the
packing and loading of the tents was completed.

15. **ut**, etc.: 'so that it seemed possible to fight in a not disadvantageous position,' the advantages being more nearly equalized by Pom-

' Differendum est,' inquit, ' iter in praesentiā nōbīs, et dē proeliō cōgitandum, sīcut semper dēpoposcimus. Animō sīmus ad dīmicandum parātī; nōn facile occāsiōnem posteā reperiēmus; '

cōnfestimque expedītās cōpiās ēdūcit.

Pompey believed that his cavalry alone would win the battle.

86. Pompeius quoque, ut posteā cognitum est, suōrum omnium hortātū, statuerat proeliō dēcertāre. Namque etiam in cōnsiliō superiōribus diēbus dīxerat, *Prius quam concurrerent aciēs, fore, utī exercitus Caesaris pellerētur.* Id cum essent plērīque admīrātī,

' Sciō mē,' inquit, ' paene incrēdibilem rem pollicērī; sed ratiōnem cōnsiliī meī accipite, quō fīrmiōre animō in proelium prōdeātis. Persuāsī equitibus nostrīs (idque mihi factūrōs cōnfirmāvērunt), ut, cum propius sit accessum,

---

pey's advance further into the plain from his camp on higher ground. *73, d,* and *239, g.*

18. **dēpoposcimus**: ' we have earnestly desired.' How lit.? **Animō**: ' in spirit.'

21. **expedītās**: ' in fighting trim '; lit. ' unencumbered,' having laid aside the burdens which they had started to carry on the march.

86. 2. **hortātū**: ' in consequence of the urging.' *135, a.*

3. **cōnsiliō**: a meeting of officers. **superiōribus diēbus**: from *in posterum diem* (l. 16) we are led to infer that the meeting of officers took place on August 8, the day before the battle.

4. **concurrerent**: present subjunctive in the direct form. *189, b.* **aciēs**: the two opposing lines, Caesar's and Pompey's. **fore,** etc.: *203,* (1).

6. **Sciō,** etc.: Fig. 147. *211, b,* (3).

7. **ratiōnem cōnsiliī meī**: ' the explanation of my plan.' **quō,** etc.: *193, b.*

8. **Persuāsī**: a   Pompey had only to ' persuade ' the cavalry to carry out the move   — and the battle would be won!

9. **cum,** etc.:   the lines have drawn nearer.' How lit.? *73, d.*

10 dextrum Caesaris cornū ab latere apertō aggrederentur, et,
circumventā ā tergō aciē, prius perturbātum exercitum
pellerent, quam ā nobīs tēlum in hostem iacerētur.

'Ita sine perīculō legiōnum, et paene sine vulnere, bellum
cōnficiēmus. Id autem difficile nōn est, cum tantum equi-
15 tātū valeāmus.'

Simul dēnūntiāvit, ut essent animō parātī in posterum
diem et, quoniam fieret dīmicandī potestās, ut saepe
rogitāvissent, nē suam neu reliquōrum opīniōnem fal-
lerent.

Figure 147. — Pompey.

Marble bust in the Jacobsen Museum, Copenhagen; from a photograph courteously furnis[...]
by the Director of the Museum.

10. **ab latere apertō**: N.
to I, 25, l. 17. Pompey's huge
force of cavalry was to outflank Caesar's line of infantry
and attack it from the rear.
The outflanking was planned
for Caesar's right wing because
his left would be protected by
the river Enipeus (cf. Map
20).

11. **perturbātum**: 'throw
his army into confusion and.'
228, a.

14. **cum**, etc.: 'since we
are so much stronger in cavalry.' Pompey's horsemen
numbered 7000, Caesar's 1000.
184, a.

16. **dēnūntiāvit**: 'he en-
joined (them).'

18. **nē**, etc.: 'and not dis-
appoi[...]is own expectation
or t['s if] [...]e others.' *157, d.*
[...]ment[...] : senators and
['wher] [...]s of standing who
[...] [...]ompey. **falle-**

*Even Labienus, over-confident, had expressed his contempt for
Caesar's troops.*

87 Hunc Labiēnus excēpit et, cum Caesaris cōpiās
dēspiceret, Pompeī cōnsilium summīs laudibus efferret,

'Nōlī,' inquit, 'exīstimāre, Pompeī, hunc esse exercitum,
quī Galliam Germāniamque dēvīcerit. Omnibus interfuī
proeliīs neque temere incognitam rem prōnūntiō. 5

'Perexigua pars illīus exercitūs superest; magna pars
dēperiit (quod accidere tot proeliīs fuit necesse), multōs
autumnī pestilentia in Italiā cōnsūmpsit, multī domum
discessērunt, multī sunt relīctī in continentī.

'An nōn audīstis, ex eīs, quī per causam valētūdinis re- 10

---

87. 1. Labienus: Labienus had gone over to the side of Pompey
and had already shown himself an implacable enemy of Caesar. So
long as he was under the direction of Caesar he was an efficient officer,
displaying military talents of a high order. When, however, he came
to act more independently he showed lack of insight, as in the present
instance; and he failed to realize the expectations of his new friends.
excēpit: 'followed,' in speaking. **cum . . . dēspiceret**: 'dis-
paraging.' *185, c.*

3. **Nōlī**: *181, b.* **Pompeī**: *8, c.* B. 25, 1; A. 49, *c*; H.
83, 5.

4. **dēvīcerit**: 'subdued.' The statement is an exaggeration, to
heighten the effect; Germany was far from being subdued. There is
similar exaggeration in the following statement, that Labienus took part
in all the battles in Gaul and Germany.

5. **neque**, etc.: 'and I am not recklessly asserting something that
I do not know.' How lit.?

6. **Perexigua pars**: 'An exceedingly small remnant.'

7. **dēperiit**: 'has been destroyed.' **quod**: = *id quod.* *160, c.*

8. **autumnī pestilentia**: 'the autumn sickness,' fevers, from which,
in the autumn of 49 B.C., Caesar's army had suffered in Apulia and the
region of Brundisium (C. III, 2).

9. **in continentī**: in Italy.

10. **An**: *179, a,* (2). B. 162, 4, *a*; A. 335, *b*; H. 380, 3. **audīstis**:
64, a, (3).

mānsērunt, cohortēs esse Brundisiī factās? Hae cōpiae,
quās vidētis, ex dīlēctibus hōrum annōrum in citeriōre
Galliā sunt refectae, et plērīque sunt ex colōniīs Trāns-
padānīs. Ac tamen, quod fuit rōboris, duōbus proeliīs
15 Dyrrachīnīs interiit.'

Haec cum dīxisset, iūrāvit, sē nisi victōrem in castra nōn
reversūrum, reliquōsque, ut idem facerent, hortātus est.

Hōc laudāns, Pompeius idem iūrāvit; nec vērō ex reliquīs
fuit quisquam, quī iūrāre dubitāret.

20 Haec tum facta sunt in cōnsiliō, magnaque spē et laetitiā
omnium discessum est; ac iam animō victōriam praecipiē-
bant, quod dē rē tantā et ā tam perītō imperātōre nihil
frūstrā cōnfīrmārī vidēbātur.

---

11. **cohortēs**, etc.: 'that (whole) cohorts at Brundisium have been
made up of those who were left behind on account of sickness.' *146*.

12. **hōrum annōrum**: i.e. of the last two years, since the outbreak
of the Civil War.   **citeriōre Galliā**: *284*.

13. **sunt refectae**: 'have been recruited.'

14. **quod fuit rōboris**: 'all the (real) strength there was' in
Caesar's army; the small nucleus of veterans which, after the reductions
mentioned, Labienus thought that Caesar had been able to bring across
the Adriatic. *97, b.*

15. **interiit**: how badly mistaken Labienus was, he afterwards
learned to his sorrow; the brunt of the fighting at Pharsalus was borne
by Caesar's veterans.

16. **iūrāvit**, etc.: the oath was not unlike that taken by the Gauls
under Vercingetorix (VII, 66, ll. 23–26; 67, l. 1); the result was in
both cases the same. Similar, too, was the proclamation of General
Ducrot, addressed to his soldiers in beleaguered Paris November 28, 1870,
when he was trying to break through the Prussian "ring of iron" about
the city. "For myself," the proclamation says, "I am fully resolved,
I make my oath before you and before the entire nation, that I will re-
enter Paris either dead or victorious; you may see me fall, but you will
not see me retreat." Vercingetorix and his officers, Pompey, Labienus,
Ducrot — all alike survived overwhelming defeat.

21. **omnium**: including, besides the officers, prominent civilians.

22. **tam perītō imperātōre**: Labienus.   **nihil**, etc.: sc. *sibi*; 'they

Caesar notes the arrangement of Pompey's line of battle.

88. Caesar, cum Pompeī castrīs appropinquāsset, ad hunc modum aciem eius instrūctam animum advertit:

Erant in sinistrō cornū legiōnēs duae, trāditae ā Caesare initiō dissēnsiōnis ex senātūs cōnsultō; quārum ūna prīma, altera tertia appellābātur. In eō locō ipse erat Pompeius. 5
Mediam aciem Scīpiō cum legiōnibus Syriacīs tenēbat. Ciliciēnsis legiō coniūncta cum cohortibus Hispānīs, quās

---

thought that confident assurances were not given without good grounds.' How lit.?

88. 2. **hunc**: *161, a.*   **animum advertit**: *113, c.*

3. **trāditae**: 'which had been handed over (to him).' *227, a,* **(4).**

4. **initiō dissēnsiōnis**: 'at the beginning of the strife,' in 50 B.C. *147, b.* **ex senātūs cōnsultō**: 'in accordance with a decree of the Senate.' *258.* **prīma, tertia**: predicative. A legion transferred to another commander received a new number. Pompey's 'First Legion' had been *legio VI* in Caesar's army, and his 'Third Legion' had been Caesar's *legio XV*; both legions entered the service of Caesar in 53 B.C. *307, g.*

5. **eō locō**: Pompey's left wing, facing Caesar's right.

6. **legiōnibus Syriacīs**: two legions that had been serving in Syria, that Scipio had conducted to Pompey in Macedonia.

7. **Ciliciēnsis**: 'from Cilicia'; this was a veteran legion. **quās . . . docuimus**: the passage here referred to has

Figure 148. — Legionary's cuirass.

Pompey's soldiers had the same armor and weapons as Caesar's; there was no such disparity in equipment as there had been between Caesar's soldiers and the Gauls.

trāductās ab Āfrāniō docuimus, in dextrō cornū erant collocātae. Hās fīrmissimās sē habēre Pompeius exīstimābat.

10　Reliquās inter aciem mediam cornuaque interiēcerat
numerōque cohortēs CX explēverat. Haec erant numerō
mīlia XLV; ēvocātōrum circiter duo, quae ex beneficiāriīs
superiōrum exercituum ad eum convēnerant, quae tōtā
aciē disperserat.

15　Reliquās cohortēs VII castrīs propinquīsque castellīs praesidiō disposuerat. Dextrum cornū eius rīvus quīdam impedītīs rīpīs mūniēbat; quam ob causam cūnctum equitātum,
sagittāriōs funditōrēsque omnēs sinistrō cornū adiēcerat.

Caesar arranges his troops in order of battle.

89. Caesar, superius īnstitūtum servāns, X legiōnem in
dextrō cornū, nōnam in sinistrō collocāverat, tametsī erat

---

been lost. Afranius and Petreius commanded forces of Pompey in
Spain, but were conquered by Caesar in 49 B.C.

8. erant collocātae: the subject grammatically is *legiō*, but in
thought the 'Spanish cohorts' also are included, as if *legiō et Hispānae
cohortēs* had been written. *173, b.*

9. Hās: the five legions mentioned, and the Spanish cohorts; 'that
these were the strongest legions which he had.' How lit.?

10. Reliquās: sc. *legiōnēs* (Fig. 148).

11. numerō, etc.: Pompey had 110 cohorts, the equivalent of
11 legions, in his battle line (Map 20); these comprised 47,000 regular
soldiers, besides cavalry and light-armed troops.

12. ēvocātōrum: 'veteran volunteers.' *316.*　**duo**: sc. *mīlia-
erant*.　**beneficiāriīs**: 'privileged soldiers'; see Vocab.

13. superiōrum exercituum: 'of (his) former armies,' as in the
war with Mithridates.

15. castellīs: marked **A A A** on Map 20.

16. rīvus quīdam: probably the Enipeus; see Map 20.　**impedītīs rīpīs**: 'with banks hard to cross.'

89. 1. superius īnstitūtum: 'his earlier arrangement' of having
the tenth legion in the place of honor on the right wing, as in the battle
with Ariovistus, eleven years before (Map 4).　**X**: *decimam. 38, b.*

2. erat, etc.: 'it had been greatly reduced in strength.' *191, a.*

MAP 20

THE BATTLE OF PHARSALUS

To face page 448

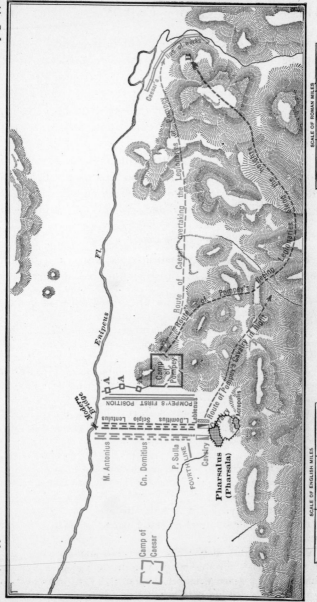

A. Redoubts, built by Pompey (chap. 88, l. 15).   B. Height on which Pompey's soldiers halted (chap. 97, l. 12).

Dyrrachīnīs proeliīs vehementer attenuāta, et huic sīc
adiūnxerat octāvam, ut paene ūnam ex duābus efficeret,
atque alteram alterī praesidiō esse iusserat.   5

Cohortēs in aciē LXXX cōnstitūtās habēbat, quae summa
erat mīlium XXII; cohortēs VII castrīs praesidiō relīquerat.
Sinistrō cornū Antōnium, dextrō P. Sullam, mediae aciēī
Cn. Domitium praeposuerat. Ipse contrā Pompeium
cōnstitit.   10

Simul hīs rēbus animadversīs, quās dēmōnstrāvimus,
timēns, nē ā multitūdine equitum dextrum cornū circumvenīrētur, celeriter ex tertiā aciē singulās cohortēs dētrāxit

---

5. **alterī**: sc. *legiōnī;* 'that the one (legion) should support the
other.' *23, a,* and *112, b.*

6. LXXX: *36.*   **quae summa**: trans. as if *quārum summa* (cf.
I, 29, l. 5).

7. **mīlium XXII**: Caesar's 80 cohorts, 8 legions (Map 20), containing a total of only 22,000
men, averaged less than 300
men to a cohort; Pompey's 110
cohorts averaged above 400 men
each. *100, b,* and *307, b, c.*

8. **cornū**: dative. *20, b.*
Antōnium: Mark Antony.

9. **contrā Pompeium**:
Caesar was with the tenth legion
on the right wing, facing Pompey's left wing, where Pompey
was (chap. 88, l. 5).

11. **hīs rēbus**: Pompey's
disposition of forces, especially
the massing of cavalry and light
infantry over against Caesar's
right wing (chap. 88, ll. 17-18);
Caesar saw at a glance that
a flanking movement was in-

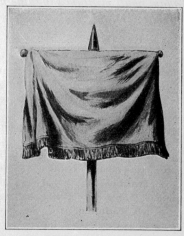

Figure 149. — Banner, vēxillum.

tended, and with amazing quickness of decision devised a means to
resist it.

13. **tertiā aciē**: *337.*

atque ex hīs quārtam īnstituit equitātuīque opposuit, et,
15 quid fierī vellet, ostendit, monuitque eius diēī victōriam in
eārum cohortium virtūte cōnstāre.

Simul tertiae aciēī imperāvit, nē iniussū suō concurreret;
sē, cum id fierī vellet, vēxillō signum datūrum.

*Caesar briefly addresses his soldiers and gives the signal
to attack.*

90. Exercitum cum mīlitārī mōre ad pugnam cohortā-
rētur suaque in eum perpetuī temporis officia praedicāret,
in prīmīs commemorāvit:

Testibus sē mīlitibus ūtī posse, quantō studiō pācem
5 *petīsset; quae per Vatīnium in colloquiīs, quae per A. Clō-*
dium cum Scīpiōne ēgisset, quibus modīs ad Ōricum cum
Libōne dē mittendīs lēgātīs contendisset. Neque sē um-
quam abūtī mīlitum sanguine neque rem pūblicam alterutrō
exercitū prīvāre voluisse.

14. **quārtam** [aciem] : this line was made up of eight cohorts, less
than 3000 men ; see Map 20, FOURTH LINE.

18. **vēxillō** : used generally to give the signal 'to arms' (II, 20,
l. 2, and Fig. 149) ; in this instance, to order a division into action.
324, b, (3).

90. 1. **mīlitārī mōre** : 'in accordance with military custom' ; N. to
I, 25, l. 3. *136, c*.

2. **sua**, etc. : 'was setting forth his kindnesses to it, an unbroken
series' (lit. 'of unbroken time'). *100, a*.

4. **Testibus**, etc. : 'that he could call upon his soldiers to bear
witness.' How lit.? *131, f*, and *212, c*, (2).

5. **per Vatīnium**, etc. : the efforts made by Caesar to arrange
terms of peace through the agency of Publius Vatininus and Aulus
Clodius are narrated in chapters 19 and 57 of Book III.

7. **dē**, etc. : 'had endeavored to arrange the sending of envoys' for
a peace conference ; cf. C. III, 16–17. *204*, (3).

8. **abūtī** : 'waste.' *131, c*.   **alterutrō** : *51*.

9. **exercitū** : *127, a*. B. 214 ; H. 462.   **prīvāre** : 'deprive.'

Hāc habitā ōrātiōne, exposcentibus mīlitibus et studiō 10
pugnae ārdentibus, tubā signum dedit.

With heroic words, Crastinus leads the charge.

91. Erat Crāstinus, ēvocātus, in exercitū Caesaris, quī
superiōre annō apud eum prīmum pīlum in legiōne x dūxerat, vir singulārī virtūte.   Hīc, signō datō,

'Sequiminī mē,' inquit, 'manipulārēs meī quī fuistis, et
vestrō imperātōrī, quam cōnsuēvistis, operam date.   Ūnum 5
hōc proelium superest; quō cōnfectō, et ille suam dignitātem, et nōs nostram lībertātem recuperābimus.'

Simul respiciēns Caesarem,

'Faciam,' inquit, 'hodiē, imperātor, ut aut vīvō mihi aut
mortuō grātiās agās.'   10

Haec cum dīxisset, prīmus ex dextrō cornū prōcucurrit,
atque eum ēlēctī mīlitēs circiter cxx voluntāriī sunt prōsecūtī.

---

10. **ōrātiōne**: the words must have been repeated several times,
probably by Caesar himself, riding along the line; no single utterance
could have been heard over so extended a front.   **exposcentibus**:
sc. *signum*.   Caesar's watchword in this battle was VENUS VICTRIX,
'Venus Bringer of Victory.'   He vowed a temple to this goddess if he
should be victorious, and afterwards fulfilled his vow by erecting a
temple to Venus in Rome.   *244.*

11. **ārdentibus**: a strong word; 'burning.'   **tubā**, etc.: *326, a,*
(1), and *b.*   The date was August 9, unreformed calendar.   *261,*
and *241, c.*

91. 1. **Crāstinus**: *76, b.*   **ēvocātus**: *316.*

2. **pīlum**: from *pīlus*; see Vocab., and *315, b.*   **x**: *38, b.*

4. **manipulārēs**, etc.: 'who were the men of my maniple' (when
I was first centurion).

6. **quō cōnfectō**: 'when this is over.'   How lit.?   **dignitātem**:
'his position' in the state; sc. *recuperābit.*

7. **nostram lībertātem**: jeopardized by Pompey.

9. **Faciam**, etc.: 'General, you will to-day have occasion to thank
me, living or dead.'   How lit.?   *203, (3).*

12. **voluntāriī**: 'who were serving as volunteers'; like Crastinus,
they were 'veterans,' *ēvocātī.*

Caesar's veterans halt to take breath, hurl themselves on the foe.

92. Inter duās aciēs tantum erat relīctum spatiī, ut satis esset ad concursum utrīusque exercitūs. Sed Pompeius suīs praedīxerat, ut Caesaris impetum exciperent, nēve sē locō movērent aciemque eius distrahī paterentur; idque
5 admonitū C. Triāriī fēcisse dīcēbātur, ut prīmus excursus vīsque mīlitum īnfringerētur aciēsque distenderētur, atque in suīs ōrdinibus dispositī dispersōs adorīrentur; leviusque cāsūra pīla spērābat, in locō retentīs mīlitibus, quam sī ipsī immissīs tēlīs occurrissent; simul fore, ut, duplicātō cursū,
10 Caesaris mīlitēs exanimārentur et lassitūdine cōnficerentur.

Quod nōbīs quidem nūllā ratiōne factum ā Pompeiō vidētur, proptereā quod est quaedam animī incitātiō atque

---

92. 1. tantum spatiī: '(only) so much space'; probably about 100 *passūs*, somewhat less than 500 English feet. *97, b*, and *243, b*. **ut**, etc.: 'as to enable each army to charge.' How lit.? *197, b.*

3. praedīxerat, etc.: 'had given orders in advance' (i.e. not to countercharge when they saw the enemy advancing but) 'to await Caesar's attack and not to move from their position.' *199, d.*

4. aciem, etc.: 'his line to become disordered,' as his soldiers should rush forward in the charge.

5. prīmus, etc.: 'that the initial vigor of attack of (Caesar's) soldiers might be lessened.' How lit.?

7. dispositī dispersōs: sc. *suī* (i.e. *Pompeiānī mīlitēs*) *eōs* (*Caesaris mīlitēs*); 'that his own men with ranks in perfect order might fall upon them when in confusion.' How lit.? **levius cāsūra** [esse]: 'would fall with less effect,' than if his soldiers should charge against them as they were hurled.

8. in, etc.: 'if his soldiers should be held in position.' *144, b,* (4).

9. duplicātō cursū: 'having twice as far to run' in the charge, covering the whole distance between the two armies instead of half the distance.

10. exanimārentur, etc.: 'would get out of breath and be weakened by fatigue.'

11. Quod: 'Now this.' *167.* **nūllā ratiōne**: 'quite without reason.' How lit.? *135, a.* **factum**: sc. *esse.*

12. est, etc.: 'all men have by nature a kind of latent capacity for being spurred to action, and this is kindled by the heat of battle.' How lit.?

alacritās nātūrāliter innāta omnibus, quae studiō pugnae incenditur. Hanc nōn reprimere, sed augēre imperātōrēs dēbent; neque frūstrā antīquitus īnstitūtum est, ut signa 15 undique concinerent clāmōremque ūniversī tollerent; quibus rēbus et hostēs terrērī et suōs incitārī exīstimāvērunt.

93. Sed nostrī mīlitēs, signō datō, cum īnfestīs pīlīs prōcucurrissent atque animum advertissent nōn concurrī ā Pompeiānīs, ūsū perītī ac superiōribus pugnīs exercitātī, suā sponte cursum repressērunt et ad medium ferē spatium cōnstitērunt, nē cōnsūmptīs vīribus appropinquārent; par- 5 vōque intermissō temporis spatiō, ac rūrsus renovātō cursū, pīla mīsērunt celeriterque, ut erat praeceptum ā Caesare, gladiōs strīnxērunt.

Neque vērō Pompeiānī huic reī dēfuērunt. Nam et tēla missa excēpērunt et impetum legiōnum tulērunt et ōrdinēs 10 cōnservārunt, pīlīsque missīs, ad gladiōs rediērunt.

---

15. **signa**: 'signals' with the trumpet. *326, a, b.*

16. **undique concinerent**: 'should in all parts (of the line) sound at the same time.'   **ūniversī**: '(the soldiers) in a body.'

17. **quibus rēbus**: 'and by these means.'   **exīstimāvērunt**: as subject supply *antīquī*, 'men of the olden time.'

93. 1. **cum**: *185, c.*   **īnfestīs pīlīs**: 'with pikes raised,' ready for hurling. How lit.?

2. **nōn concurrī**, etc.: 'that no advance was made by the soldiers of Pompey,' who had been ordered to stand still and let Caesar's soldiers come on.

4. **ad medium ferē spatium**: 'about half-way between' the two armies. These experienced soldiers covered nearly the distance of our 100-yard dash, stopped of their own accord to take breath, ran again a like distance and hurled their pikes, then 'drew their swords.' Pompey had again miscalculated, in assuming that Caesar's men would allow themselves to be exhausted by a charge of twice the ordinary length.

9. **Neque**, etc.: 'And in truth the soldiers of Pompey did not fail to meet this movement.' How lit.?   **tēla**: the pikes hurled by Caesar's men.

10. **excēpērunt**: with their shields.   **ōrdinēs**: 'ranks.'

Caesar's cavalry is defeated; his fourth line routs Pompey's cavalry and attacks Pompey's left wing in the rear.

Eōdem tempore equitēs ab sinistrō Pompeī cornū, ut erat imperātum, ūniversī prōcucurrērunt, omnisque multitūdō sagittāriōrum sē prōfūdit. Quōrum impetum noster equi-
15 tātus nōn tulit, sed paulātim locō mōtus cessit; equitēsque Pompeī hōc ācrius īnstāre et sē turmātim explicāre aciem- que nostram ab latere apertō circumīre coepērunt.

Quod ubi Caesar animum advertit, quārtae aciēī, quam īnstituerat, cohortibus dedit signum.
20 Illae celeriter prōcucurrērunt īnfestīsque signīs tantā vī in Pompeī equitēs impetum fēcērunt, ut eōrum nēmō cōn- sisteret, omnēsque conversī nōn sōlum locō excēderent, sed prōtinus incitātī fugā montēs altissimōs peterent. Quibus .summōtīs, omnēs sagittāriī funditōrēsque dēstitūtī, inermēs,
25 sine praesidiō, interfectī sunt.

---

12. **Equitēs**, etc.: see chap. 86, ll. 8–15 ; chap. 88, ll. 17–18. Pom- pey's cavalry was commanded by Labienus, who soon forgot his oath (chap. 87, ll. 16–17). See Map 20.

14. **sē prōfūdit**: 'rushed forward.'

16. **hōc**: *135, a.* **sē turmātim explicāre**: 'to deploy by squad- rons.' The cavalry had charged in close formation ; it now deployed by squadrons in order the more easily to execute the flanking movement ordered by Pompey. *309, c.*

18. **aciēī**: dependent on *cohortibus ;* see chap. 89, ll. 14–16, and Map 20, FOURTH LINE.

20. **īnfestīs signīs**: *325.* Cavalry are at a disadvantage in with- standing a charge of infantry.

2? **-que**: 'but.' *234, b.* **conversī**: 'wheeling about.' How lit. ?

23. **incitātī fugā**: 'scurrying in flight.' How lit. ? Their probable course is shown on Map 20, ROUTE OF POMPEY'S CAVALRY IN FLIGHT.

24. **dēstitūtī**: by the flight of the cavalry. **inermēs**: without de- fensive weapons.

25. **sine praesidiō**: in the open plain, without a rampart to shield them.

Eōdem impetū cohortēs sinistrum cornū, pugnantibus etiam tum ac resistentibus in aciē Pompeiānīs, circumiērunt eōsque ā tergō sunt adortae.

Caesar's third line enters the action; Pompey's infantry gives way, and Pompey flees to his camp.

94. Eōdem tempore tertiam aciem Caesar, quae quiēta fuerat et sē ad id tempus locō tenuerat, prōcurrere iussit. Ita cum recentēs atque integrī dēfessīs successissent, aliī autem ā tergō adorīrentur, sustinēre Pompeiānī nōn potuērunt atque ūniversī terga vertērunt.   5

Sed Pompeius, ut equitātum suum pulsum vīdit atque eam partem, cui maximē cōnfīdēbat, perterritam animum advertit, aliīs diffīsus aciē excessit prōtinusque sē in castra equō contulit et eīs centuriōnibus, quōs in statiōne ad praetōriam portam posuerat, clārē, ut mīlitēs exaudīrent,   10

---

26. **Eōdem impetū**: 'Continuing their movement.' How lit.? **cohortēs**: of the fourth line.   **sinistrum cornū**: of Pompey.

27. **Pompeiānīs**: Pompey's legionaries; his cavalry and light-armed troops were already disposed of.

28. **ā tergō**: by forming a fourth line, notwithstanding his inferior numbers, Caesar was enabled not only to defeat Pompey's plan to outflank him but to turn the tables and outflank Pompey.

94. 1. **tertiam aciem**: the third line had been ordered to await Caesar's signal with the red banner (chap. 89, ll. 17-18).

3. **recentēs atque integrī**: the soldiers of Caesar's third line. **dēfessīs**: the soldiers of the first and second lines, fighting against superior numbers, until now without reënforcements. *337, b.*   **aliī**: Caesar's fourth line.

6. **ut**: *188, a.*   **atque**: 'and (thus).'   **eam partem**: the cavalry.

8. **aliīs diffīsus**: 'losing confidence in his other troops.' *62*, and *105.*   **aciē**: *127, a.*   **sē equō contulit**: 'rode on horseback.' How lit.?   *131, a.*

10. **praetōriam portam**: here the west gate of the camp (Map 20). *334, a.*   **clārē**: 'in a loud voice.'

'Tuēminī,' inquit, 'castra et dēfendite dīligenter, sī quid dūrius acciderit. Ego reliquās portās circumeō et castrōrum praesidia cōnfīrmō.'

Haec cum dīxisset, sē in praetōrium contulit, summae
15 reī diffīdēns et tamen ēventum exspectāns.

*Caesar takes Pompey's camp, finding many evidences
of luxury.*

95. Caesar, Pompeiānīs ex fugā intrā vāllum compulsīs, nūllum spatium perterritīs darī oportēre exīstimāns, mīlitēs cohortātus est, ut beneficiō fortūnae ūterentur castraque oppugnārent. Quī, etsī magnō aestū fatīgātī — nam ad
5 merīdiem rēs erat perducta — tamen, ad omnem labōrem animō parātī, imperiō pāruērunt.

Castra ā cohortibus, quae ibi praesidiō erant relīctae, industriē dēfendēbantur, multō etiam ācrius ā Thrācibus barbarīsque auxiliīs. Nam quī ex aciē refūgerant mīlitēs,
10 et animō perterritī et lassitūdine cōnfectī, dīmissīs plērīque

---

11. **Tuēminī**: *61, a,* (2).   **sī**, etc.: 'if any unusual difficulty presents itself.' How lit.? *206.*

13. **cōnfīrmō**: 'encourage'; vivid use of the present tense.

14. **praetōrium**: 'general's quarters.' *334, b.*   **summae**: dative, with *reī,* genitive, depending on it; 'distrustful of the final issue.' How lit.?

95. 1. **vāllum**: of Pompey's camp; his men had been forced back to the elevation on which the camp was, and up the slope (Map 20).

3. **ut**, etc.: 'to take advantage of fortune's favor.'

4. **magnō aestū**: in the plain of Pharsalus the heat in summer is intense.

5. **rēs**: 'the struggle.'   **tamen**, etc.: notwithstanding the physical exhaustion of Caesar's soldiers, their grit did not fail them.

7. **cohortibus**: 7 in number, for the camp and redoubts (chap. 88, ll. 15–16).

9. **barbarīsque auxiliīs**: 'and (other) barbarian auxiliary troops.' **Nam**: '(The defense was left to these) for.'

10. **dīmissīs**, etc.: 'in most cases throwing away.' How lit.?

armīs signīsque mīlitāribus, magis dē reliquā fugā quam dē
castrōrum dēfēnsiōne cōgitābant.

Neque vērō diūtius, quī in vāllō cōnstiterant, multitūdinem tēlōrum sustinēre potuērunt, sed, cōnfectī vulneribus,
locum reliquērunt, prōtinusque omnēs, ducibus ūsī centuri- 15
ōnibus tribūnīsque mīlitum, in altissimōs montēs, quī ad
castra pertinēbant, cōnfūgērunt.

96. In castrīs Pompeī vidēre licuit trichilās strūctās,
magnum argentī pondus expositum, recentibus caespitibus
tabernācula cōnstrāta, L. etiam Lentulī et nōn nūllōrum
tabernācula prōtēcta hederā, multaque praetereā, quae
nimiam lūxuriam et victōriae fīdūciam dēsignārent; ut 5
facile exīstimārī posset, nihil eōs dē ēventū eius diēī timuisse, quī nōn necessāriās conquīrerent voluptātēs. At hī

---

13. **qui**: as antecedent sc. *eī*, subject of *potuērunt*.

15. **ducibus**, etc.: 'having as their leaders' (in flight) 'the centurions and military tribunes,' who ought to have rallied the demoralized
troops and continued the battle; bitter sarcasm, veiled under a form
of expression that on the surface is complimentary. *131, f.*

16. **montēs**, etc.: see Map 20, ROUTE OF POMPEY'S FLEEING
LEGIONARIES.

96. 1. **licuit**: *73, b.* **trichilās strūctās**: 'arbors that had been
built,' covered with branches having their leaves on, as a protection
against the sun. These did not take the place of the tents, but were
used for dining; in summer well-to-do Romans made much use of
arbors shaded with branches or vines.

2. **argentī**: 'silver plate.' **expositum**: 'set out' on tables, in
readiness for dinner. **recentibus**, etc.: 'tents carpeted with fresh
turf.'

3. **L. Lentulī**: mentioned by name because of his prominence; he
had been consul the previous year.

4. **prōtēcta hederā**: 'decked with ivy,' trailed along the sides, to
keep out the heat.

5. **dēsignārent**: 'evidenced.' The unsoldierly camp life of Pompey's aristocratic civilian contingent is known from other sources. *194, a.*

7. **nōn necessāriās voluptātēs**: 'needless indulgences.' *239, g.*
At: *236, a.*

miserrimō ac patientissimō exercituī Caesaris lūxuriam
obiciēbant, cui semper omnia ad necessārium ūsum dē-
10 fuissent!

Pompey flees from the camp, reaches the sea, takes ship.

Pompeius, cum iam intrā vāllum nostrī versārentur,
equum nactus, dētrāctīs īnsignibus imperātōriīs, decumānā
portā sē ex castrīs ēiēcit prōtinusque equō citātō Lārīsam
contendit.

15 Neque ibi cōnstitit, sed eādem celeritāte, paucōs suōs
ex fugā nactus, nocturnō itinere nōn intermissō, comitātū
equitum xxx ad mare pervēnit nāvemque frūmentāriam
cōnscendit, saepe, ut dīcēbātur, querēns tantum sē opīniōnem fefellisse, ut, ā quō genere hominum victōriam spē-
20 rāsset, ab eō initiō fugae factō, paene prōditus vidērētur.

---

8. **miserrimō**: *28, a.*   **patientissimō**: 'most long-suffering.'
27, a.

9. **cui**, etc.: 'although it had lacked everything.' *194, d.*

12. **equum nactus**: the language implies that Pompey did not
wait to get his own mount but jumped on the first horse he could find.
61, a, (3), and *226, c.*   **īnsignibus imperātōriīs**: the distinguishing marks of his rank as commander, particularly his scarlet mantle
(*palūdāmentum*), which he replaced by a traveler's cloak. *321.*   **decumānā portā**: in this case the east gate (Map 20). *334, a,* and *134, a.*

13. **equō citātō**: 'urging his horse forward.' *144, b,* (7).   **Lārīsam**: see Map 19. The distance from Pharsalus to Larisa is about
25 English miles.

15. **paucōs suōs**: among Pompey's companions in flight was
Lucius Lentulus (l. 3) who likewise met death in Egypt (C. III. 104).

17. **mare**: at the mouth of the Peneus, about 25 miles northeast of
Larisa; in the latter part of his flight Pompey passed through the famous
Vale of Tempe, which runs back from the sea between Mt. Olympus
and Mt. Ossa (Map 19); see Fig. 209, in Vocab.

18. **sē**, etc.: 'that he had been so grievously disappointed in his
expectations'; *sē* is object of *fefellisse*. How lit.?

19. **ā quō**, etc.: 'that it almost seemed as if he had been betrayed,

Caesar completes the victory, taking many captives.

97. Caesar, castrīs potītus, ā mīlitibus contendit, nē, in praedā occupātī, reliquī negōtiī gerendī facultātem dīmitterent. Quā rē impetrātā, montem opere circummūnīre īnstituit.

Pompeiānī, quod is mōns erat sine aquā, diffīsī eī locō, 5 relictō monte, ūniversī iugīs eīs Lārīsam versus sē recipere coepērunt. Quā rē animadversā, Caesar cōpiās suās dīvīsit partemque legiōnum in castrīs Pompeī remanēre iussit, partem in sua castra remīsit, IIII sēcum legiōnēs dūxit commodiōreque itinere Pompeiānīs occurrere coepit, 10 et, prōgressus mīlia passuum VI, aciem īnstrūxit.

Quā rē animadversā, Pompeiānī in quōdam monte cōnstitērunt. Hunc montem flūmen subluēbat.

---

since the rout was started by that division of men (the cavalry), from whom.' How lit.? *148, e; 172, d,* and *165, c.*

97. 1. castrīs: *131, c.*   **mīlitibus:** the soldiers immediately on capturing the camp began to plunder it.   **contendit:** 'urged and demanded,' not *imperat;* see N. to chap. 98, l. 7. *199, a.*

2. **reliquī,** etc.: 'the opportunity to finish up the business in hand.' How lit.?

3. **Quā rē impetrātā:** 'Having carried his point.' That under the circumstances Caesar's soldiers left off looting in order to resume fighting, is evidence not only of his power to maintain discipline but also of their loyalty to him.   **montem:** 'elevation'; see chap. 95, l. 16. **opere:** the usual trench and rampart.

6. **iugīs eīs:** 'along the ridges,' connecting the heights. *134, b,* and *160, d.*   **Lārīsam versus:** 'in the direction of Larisa.' Their course was first toward the northeast, to find a place where they could cross the Enipeus; Map 20, ROUTE OF POMPEY'S FLEEING LEGIONARIES.

10. **commodiōre itinere:** Caesar passed over the height on which was Pompey's camp and followed the more level ground along the river, being thus enabled to head off the fleeing legionaries who were traversing the high ground; Map 20, ROUTE OF CAESAR OVERTAKING THE LEGIONARIES OF POMPEY.

12. **quōdam monte:** marked **B** on Map 20.

13. **flūmen:** Enipeus.

Caesar, mīlitēs cohortātus, etsī tōtius diēī continentī
15 labōre erant cōnfectī noxque iam suberat, tamen mūnītiōne flūmen ā monte sēclūsit, nē noctū aquārī Pompeiānī
possent. Quō perfectō opere, illī dē dēditiōne, missīs
lēgātīs, agere coepērunt. Paucī ōrdinis senātōriī, quī sē
cum hīs coniūnxerant, nocte fugā salūtem petīvērunt.

98. Caesar prīmā lūce omnēs eōs, quī in monte cōnsēderant, ex superiōribus locīs in plānitiem dēscendere
atque arma prōicere iussit. Quod ubi sine recūsātiōne
fēcērunt, passīsque palmīs, prōiectī ad terram, flentēs, ab eō
5 salūtem petīvērunt, cōnsōlātus cōnsurgere iussit, et pauca
apud eōs dē lēnitāte suā locūtus, quō minōre essent timōre,
omnēs cōnservāvit; mīlitibusque suīs commendāvit, nē quī
eōrum violārētur, neu quid suī dēsīderārent. Hāc adhibitā
dīligentiā, ex castrīs sibi legiōnēs aliās occurrere et eās,

---

15. **mūnītiōne**: Map 20, CAESAR'S LINE OF WORKS.

16. **sēclūsit**: 'shut off.' *79, d.*   **aquārī**: 'to obtain water.'

18. **ōrdinis senātōriī**: 'of senatorial rank.' These men, having
bitterly opposed Caesar, feared his vengeance even more than the soldiers did.

98. 3. **Quod**: trans. as if *et id.*   **recūsātiōne**: 'protest.'

4. **passīs palmīs**: 'with their palms outstretched,' in supplication.
prōiectī ad terram: 'casting themselves upon the ground.' *174.*
ab eō: *116, b.*

5. **cōnsurgere iussit**: sc. *eōs*, 'he bade them rise.'

6. **quō**, etc.: 'in order to allay their fears.' How lit.? *143, b.*

7. **nē**: '(urging) that.'   **quī**: *49, a,* and *168.*   **commendāvit**
[eōs]: not *imperāvit*; in a time of so great excitement and strain
Caesar could more easily control his men through a request than by a
command.

8. **violārētur**: 'be harmed.'   **neu**: *199, d.*   **suī**: genitive,
singular, neuter; 'anything that belonged to them,' lit. 'anything of
their own.' *97, b,* and *154, a.*   **Hāc adhibitā dīligentiā**: 'Having
given this matter careful attention.' How lit.?

9. **sibi occurrere**: with *iussit*, 'he ordered other legions to join
him.'

quās sēcum dūxerat, in vicem requiēscere atque in castra 10 revertī iussit, eōdemque diē Lārīsam pervēnit.

The losses, on both sides.   Death of the brave Crastinus.

99. In eō proeliō nōn amplius CC mīlitēs dēsīderāvit, sed centuriōnēs, fortēs virōs, circiter XXX āmīsit.

Interfectus est etiam, fortissimē pugnāns, Crāstinus, cuius mentiōnem suprā fēcimus, gladiō in ōs adversum. coniectō. Neque id fuit falsum, quod ille, in pugnam prōficīscēns, 5 dīxerat. Sīc enim Caesar exīstimābat, eō proeliō excellentissimam virtūtem Crāstinī fuisse, optimēque eum dē sē meritum iūdicābat.

---

10. **quās**, etc.: these legions had been fighting, marching, fortifying, or on guard duty, continuously for twenty-four hours.   **requiēscere:** 'to take rest.'

11. **Lārīsam pervēnit:** a march of 25 English miles, on the day after the battle, in very hot weather — no mean accomplishment. *329.*

99. 1. **CC:** *ducentōs. 129, b.* B. 217, 3; A. 407, *c*; H. 471, 4.

2. **centuriōnēs**, etc.: cf. N. to VII, 51, l. 1.

3. **suprā:** chap. 91. **gladiō**, etc.: 'having received a sword-thrust directly in the face.'

6. **excellentissimam**, etc.: 'that the valor of Cras-

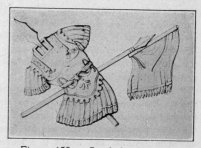

Figure 150. — Symbols of Victory.

Cuirass, two spears, and a banner, suggesting victory over a civilized nation.   From a relief.

tinus was the most extraordinary' of all.   "The army bore witness," says Appian, "how, like one inspired, running to each rank he performed prodigies of valor.   And when, after search, he was found among the dead, Caesar put military decorations upon him, and buried them with him, and built for him a separate tomb near the common burial-place where many were interred."

Ex Pompeiānō exercitū circiter mīlia xv cecidisse vidē-
10 bantur, sed in dēditiōnem vēnērunt amplius mīlia XXIIII
(namque etiam cohortēs, quae praesidiō in castellīs fuerant,
sēsē Sullae dēdidērunt), multī praetereā in fīnitimās
cīvitātēs refūgērunt; signaque mīlitāria ex proeliō ad
Caesarem sunt relāta CLXXX et aquilae VIIII.

15 L. Domitius ex castrīs in montem refugiēns, cum vīrēs
eum lassitūdine dēfēcissent, ab equitibus est interfectus.

---

9. **vidēbantur**, etc.: the expression suggests a rough estimate; the number of prisoners is more definitely stated, since they were accurately counted.

14. **aquilae VIIII**: the eagles of all but two of Pompey's 11 legions fell into Caesar's hands, a sweeping victory (Fig. 150). The most graphic description of the battle of Pharsalus in English literature is in chap. 21 of *A Friend of Caesar*, by W. S. Davis.

15. **L. Domītius**: N. to chap. 3, l. 2.

Historical Significance of the Battle of Pharsalus. "In none (of the world's decisive battles)," says Warde Fowler, "have the contending forces in a world-wide revolution been so exactly focussed in two armies on a single battle-field. On one side the disunion, selfishness, and pride of the last survivors of an ancient oligarchy, speculating before the event on the wealth or office that victory was to bring them; on the other, the absolute command of a single man, whose clear mental vision was entirely occupied with the facts and issues that lay before him that day.

"The one host was composed in great part of a motley crowd from Greece and the East, representing that spurious Hellenic civilisation that for a century had sapped the vigour of Roman life; the other was chiefly drawn from the Gallic populations of Italy and the West, fresh, vigorous, intelligent, and united in devotion and loyalty to a leader whom not even defeat could dishearten.

"With Pompeius was the spirit of the past, and his failure did but answer to the failure of a decaying world; with Caesar was the spirit of the future, and his victory marks the moment when humanity could once more start hopefully upon a new line of progress."

SELECTIONS FOR SIGHT READING

1. The Pig's Last Will and Testament

Testāmentum Porcellī.

Incipit testāmentum porcellī.

M. Grunnius Corocotta, porcellus, testāmentum fēcit.
Quoniam manū meā scrībere nōn potuī, scrībendum dictāvī.

Magīrus, cocus, dīxit :

'Venī hūc, ēversor domī, solivertiātor, fugitīve porcelle, 5
et hodiē tibi dirimō vitam.'

Corocotta, porcellus, dīxit :

'Sī qua fēcī, sī qua peccāvī, sī qua vāscella pedibus meīs

---

1. 1. Incipit: '(Here) begins.' **testāmentum** : in our legal
phrase, 'the last will and testament.' The Pig's Will, the author of
which is unknown, afforded amusement to many generations of Roman
schoolboys.   **porcellus, -ī**, m., 'pig.' *75, a.*

2. **M. Grunnius Corocotta**, gen. **Mārcī Grunniī Corocottae**,
m., 'Marcus Grunter Bristleback.'   All the names of the Will are made
up, and their meaning, although obvious to a Roman, can be only ap-
proximated in translation.

3. **scrībendum** : gerundive, 'for writing'; sc. *testāmentum*.
dictō, -āre, -āvī, -ātus, [frequentative of **dīcō**, *78, a*], 1, 'dictate.'

4. **Magīrus, -ī**, [μάγειρος], m., 'Chef'; Greek word meaning 'cook,'
here used as a name.   **cocus, -ī**, m., 'cook.'

5. **ēversor, -ōris**, [**ēvertō**], m., 'overturner.'   **solivertiātor,
-ōris**, [**solum**, 'ground,' **vertō**], m., a made-up word, 'rooter.'

6. **hodiē** : adv., 'to-day.'   **dirimō** : colloquial present instead of
the future.

8. **qua** : 'anything,' lit. 'anythings.'   **peccō, -āre, -āvī, -ātus**, 1,
'transgress,' 'do mischief.'   **qua peccāvī** : 'have done any mischief.'
qua : 'any.'   **vāscellum, -ī**, n., 'dish.'

cōnfrēgī, rogō, domine coce, vītam petō, concēde rogantī.'

10　Magīrus, cocus, dīxit :

'Trānsī, puer, affer mihi dē cocīnā cultrum, ut hunc por-
cellum faciam cruentum.'

Porcellus comprehenditur ā famulīs, ductus, sub diē XVI
kal. lucernīnās, ubi abundant cȳmae, Clībanātō et Pipe-
15　rātō cōnsulibus.　Et ut vīdit, sē moritūrum esse, hōrae
spatium petiit, et cocum rogāvit, ut testāmentum facere
posset.

Clāmāvit ad sē suōs parentēs, ut dē cibāriīs suīs aliquid
dīmitteret eīs.　Quī ait :

20　'Patrī meō, Verrīnō Lārdīnō, dō, lēgō darī glandis modiōs XXX; et mātrī meae, Veturīnae Scrōfae, dō, lēgō darī
Lacōnicae silīginis modiōs XL; et sorōrī meae Quirīnae, in

---

9. cōnfringō, -ere, cōnfrēgī, -frāctus, 3, 'smash,' 'break to
pieces.'　dominus, -ī, m., 'master.'　rogantī: sc. *mihi*.

11. puer : the cook's helper.　cocīna, -ae, f., 'kitchen.'　culter,
-trī (7, c), m., 'butcher-knife.'

12. cruentus, -a, -um, adj., 'bloody'; here, 'all bloody.'

13. famulus, -ī, m., 'servant.'

14. lucernīnus, -a, -um, adj., a made-up word, 'of candle-light';
the expression 'the kalends of candle-light' humorously suggests the
beginning of the long winter nights — the season when spring pigs
(and turkeys) are in demand.　cȳma, -ae, f., 'young cabbage.'
Clībanātus, -ī, [clībanus, 'baking-pan '], m., 'Roastingpan.'　Pipe-
rātus, -ī, [piper, 'pepper '], m., 'Blackpepper.'

18. clāmō, -āre, -āvī, -ātus, 1, 'call.'

19. dīmitteret eīs : 'bestow upon them.'　Quī ait : 'And he said.'

20. Verrīnus Lārdīnus, -ī -ī, [verrēs, 'boar,' lārdum, 'bacon '],
m., 'Boar Bacon.'　lēgō, -āre, -āvī, -ātus, 1, 'appoint.'　lēgō
darī : 'I bequeath,' lit. 'I appoint to be given '; legal formality and re-
dundancy of expression.　glandis : singular where we use the plural ;
'of acorns.'　modius, -ī, m., 'peck.'

21. Veturīna Scrōfa, -ae -ae, 'Dame Hogg.'

22. Lacōnicus, -a, -um, adj. 'Lacedaemonian.'　silīgō, -inis, f.
'white wheat.'　Quirīna, -ae, f., 'Squealy.'　in : 'at.'

23. vōtum : 'wedding.'　hordeum, -ī, n., 'barley.'

cuius vōtum interesse nōn potuī, dō, lēgō darī hordeī
modiōs xxx.

'Et dē meīs vīsceribus dabō, dōnābō, sūtōribus saetās, 25
rīxōribus capitīnās, surdīs auriculās, causidicīs et verbōsīs
linguam, isiciāriis femora, cursōribus et vēnātōribus tālōs,
latrōnibus ungulās.

'Et nec nōminandō cocō lēgātō dimittō popiam et pīstillum, quae mēcum attuleram, dē Tebeste ūsque ad Ter- 30
geste ; liget sibi collum dē reste.

'Et volō mihi fierī monumentum, aureīs litterīs scrīptum,

M · GRUNNIUS · COROCOTTA · PORCELLUS

VIXIT · ANNĪS · DCCCC XC VIIII · ET · S

QUOD · SĪ · SĒMISSEM · VĪXISSET   35

MILLE · ANNOS · IMPLESSET

---

25. **vīscus, -eris,** (*13, e*), n., 'flesh.'   **sūtor, -ōris,** m., 'shoe-
maker.'   **saeta, -ae,** f., 'bristle,' used by cobblers in the waxed
end of their threads.
26. **rīxor, -ōris,** m., 'quarreler.'   **capitīna, -ae,** [**caput**], f.,
'head-meat,' suggesting our word "headcheese."   **surdus, -a, -um,**
adj., 'deaf.'   **auricula, -ae,** [diminutive of **auris**], f., 'ear'; the
hearing of pigs is very keen.   **causidicus, -ī,** [**causa, dīcō**], m.,
'pleader.'   **verbōsus, -ī,** [**verbum**], m., 'talkative person.'
27. **isiciārius, -ī,** m., 'sausage-maker.'   **cursor, -ōris,** [**currō**], m.,
'runner.'   **tālus, -ī,** m., 'knucklebone.'
28. **ungula, -ae,** f., 'hoof.'
29. **nec nōminandō** : 'unspeakable.'   **lēgātum, -ī,** n., 'legacy';
here dative of purpose.   **popia, -ae,** f., 'soup-ladle.'   **pīstillum, -ī,**
n., 'pestle' of a mortar.
30. **dē**, etc. : like "from Dan to Beersheba."   **Tebeste, -is,** n., 'Tebeste,' a city in Numidia, now Tébessa.   **Tergeste, -is,** n., now Trieste.
31. **ligō, -āre, -āvī, -ātus,** 1, 'bind.'   **collum, -ī,** n., 'neck.'
dē : we should say 'with.'   **restis, -is,** f., 'rope'; the cook is ex-
horted to hang himself.
32. **monumentum, -ī,** [**moneō** ; *74, d*], n., 'monument.'
34. **S** : for **sēmisse,** abl.   **sēmis, sēmissis,** m., 'half.'

'Optimī amātōrēs meī, vel cōnsulēs vītae, rogō vōs, ut
cum corpore meō bene faciātis, bene condiātis dē bonīs
condīmentīs nucleī, piperis et mellis, ut nōmen meum in
40 sempiternum nōminetur.

'Meī dominī vel cōnsobrīnī meī, quī in mediō testāmentō
interfuistis, iubēte signārī.'

　　　　　　　Lārdiō signāvit.
　　　　　　　Ofellicus signāvit.
45　　　　　　Cȳminātus signāvit.
　　　　　　　Lūcānicus signāvit.
　　　　　　　Tergillus signāvit.
　　　　　　　Celsīnus signāvit.
　　　　　　　Nūptiālicus signāvit.

50　Explicit testāmentum porcellī, sub diē XVI kal. lucernīnās,
Clībanātō et Piperātō cōnsulibus, fēlīciter.

---

35. **quod** : 'but.'　　**sēmissem** : 'half' of a year.

36. **impleō, -ēre, implēvī, -ētus**, 2, 'fill out'; satirical in respect
to the veracity of inscriptions on tombstones.

37. **amātor, -ōris,** [amō], m., 'lover.'　　**meī** : 'of me.'　　**cōnsulēs** : translate as if *cōnsulentēs;* double meaning, 'ye who have regard
for (my) life,' 'ye who are fond of good living.'

38. **condiō, -īre, -īvī, -ītus**, 4, word of double meaning: 'em-
balm' from the pig's point of view, 'season' from the point of view of
the 'lovers' of roast pig.　　**condiātis** : sc. *id*.　　**dē** : 'with.'

39. **condīmentum, -ī,** [condiō], n., 'seasoning.'　　**nucleus, -ī,** m.,
'nut-meat.'　　**piper, -eris,** n., 'pepper.'　　**mel, mellis,** n., 'honey.'

40. **sempiternus, -a, -um,** [semper], adj., 'everlasting'; neuter
as noun, **in sempiternum,** 'forever and ever.'

41. **Meī dominī** : title of respect; 'good sirs.'　　**cōnsobrīnus, -ī,**
m., 'cousin.'　　**in mediō testāmentō** : i.e. 'at the making of my
will.'

42. **signō, -āre, -āvī, -ātus,** [signum], 1, 'affix a seal'; **signārī,**
'that the seals be affixed.' Each of the seven witnesses of a will was
supposed to stamp his signet in the wax covering the ends of the
string with which the tablets were tied together (Fig. 203).

43–49. **Lārdiō** : 'Fatbacon.'　　**Ofellicus** : 'Tidbit.'　　**Cȳmi·**

clever sayings

2. Witticisms attributed to Cicero

On Lentulus, his son-in-law.

little
son-in-law scanty

Cicerō cum Lentulum, generum suum, exiguae statūrae
hominem, longō gladiō accīnctum vīdisset,
arm
'Quis,' inquit, 'generum meum ad gladium alligāvit?'

On Piso, a son-in-law, who walked effeminately.

walked
Cicerō, cum Pīsō gener eius mollius incēderet, fīlia autem
concitātius, ait fīliae : 'Ambulā tamquam vir!'   5

On a portrait of his brother Quintus, larger than life.

Nec Q. Cicerōnī frātrī circā similem mordācitātem pepercit. Nam cum in eā prōvinciā, quam ille rēxerat, vīdisset

---

nātus : 'Youngcabbager.'   **Lūcānicus** : 'Porksausager.'   **Tergillus** :   'Porkrind.'   **Celsīnus** : 'Porkpie.'   **Nūptiālicus** :
'Weddingporker,' suggesting a dish in favor for wedding-feasts.

50. **explicō, -āre, explicuī, explicitus,** [ex + plicō], 1, 'unroll,'
as a book written in the form of a scroll.   **Explicit** : in full, *explicitum
est*, lit. 'is unrolled'; we should say, 'Here ends.' The form of expression, while not suitable for the tablets on which wills were written, is
appropriate for the scroll-shaped book in which the Pig's Will is represented as being recorded (Figures 166 and 191).

51. **fēlīciter** : 'happily,' a word of good omen, often added at the
end of a writing.

2. 2. **accingō, -cingere, -cīnxī, -cīnctus,** [ad + cingō], 3, 'gird
on,' 'arm.'

3. **alligō, -āre, -āvī, -ātus,** [ad + ligō], 1, 'tie (to).'

4. **molliter,** [mollis], adv., 'lazily.'

5. **concitātē,** [concitātus, participle of concitō], adv., 'energetically.'   **ambulō, -āre, -āvī,** 1, 'walk.'   **tamquam,** [tam +
quam], adv., 'just as.'   **vir** : '(your) husband (does).'

6. **circā** : 'in the use of'; lit. 'around.'   **mordācitās, -ātis,**
[mordāx], f., 'sharpness' of speech.   **pepercit** : sc. *M. Cicero.*

7. **rēxerat** : 'had governed'; Quintus Cicero was governor of the
province of Asia (*302, c*) for three years, before he became a lieutenant
of Caesar in Gaul.

clipeātam imāginem eius, ingentibus līniāmentīs, ūsque ad
pectus ex mōre pīctam (erat autem Quīntus ipse statūrae
10 parvae), ait :

'Frāter meus dīmidius maior est quam tōtus.'

On a certain foppishness of Caesar's attire.

In Caesarem quoque mordācitās Cicerōnis dentēs suōs
strīnxit. Nam prīmum post victōriam Caesaris interrogā-
tus, cūr in ēlectiōne partis errāsset, respondit: 'Praecinctūra
15 mē dēcēpit,' iocātus in Caesarem, quī ita togā praecingēbā-
tur, ut trahendō laciniam velut mollis incēderet.

On Caesar's enlargement of the Senate.

Cicerō aliās facilitātem Caesaris in allēgandō senātū
irrīsit palam. Nam cum ab hospite suō, P. Malliō, rogārē-

---

8. **clipeātus,** -a, -um, [**clipeus**], adj., 'shield-shaped,' i.e. 'oval,'
like the *clipeus.*   **imāgō,** -inis, f., 'portrait.'   **līniāmentum,** -ī, n.,
'feature.'   **ūsque,** etc.: the painted portrait resembled a bust.

9. **ex mōre :** 'in the usual fashion.'   **pingō,** -ere, pīnxī, pīctus,
3, 'paint.'

11. **Frāter meus dīmidius :** 'the half of my brother.'

12. **dentēs suōs strīnxit :** 'showed its teeth,' we should say.

13. **victōriam :** at Pharsalus; Cicero had joined the party of
Pompey.

14. **ēlectiō,** -ōnis, [**ēligō**], f., 'choice.'   **praecinctūra,** -ae, [**praecingō**], f., 'manner of dress,' referring to the effeminate way that Caesar draped his toga.

15. **iocor,** -ārī, -ātus, 1, dep., 'jest.'   **toga,** -ae, f., 'toga,' the
principal outer garment worn by Roman men.   **praecingō,** -cingere,
-cīnxī, -cīnctus, [**prae + cingō**], 3, 'gird about.' The passive is
here used in a middle sense; 'would wrap his toga about him in such
a way,' lit. 'would so wrap himself up with his toga.'

16. **lacinia,** -ae, f., 'end' of a toga ; 'by letting the end of his toga
drag,' instead of carefully tucking it in.

17. **facilitās,** -ātis, [**facilis**], f., 'ready compliance.'   **allēgō,**
-āre, -āvī, -ātus, 1, 'depute'; 'in appointing (men to) the Senate.'

18. **P. Mallius,** gen. **Publiī Malliī,** m., a friend of Cicero.

tur, ut decuriōnātum prīvignō eius expedīret, assistente
frequentiā, dīxit :   20
  ‘ Rōmae, sī vīs, habēbit ; Pompeiīs difficile est.’

A play upon words.

Nē illa quidem (ōrātōribus conveniunt), quae Cicerōnī
aliquandō, sed nōn in agendō, excidērunt, ut dīxit, cum is
candidātus, quī cocī fīlius habēbātur, cōram eō suffrāgium ab aliō peteret :   25
  ‘ Ego, quoque, tibi favēbō.’

To Vatinius, Caesar’s friend, anticipating a compliment.

Vatīnius, pedibus aeger, cum vellet vidērī commodiōris valētūdinis factus et dīceret, sē iam bīna mīlia
ambulāre :
  ‘ Diēs enim,’ inquit *Cicero*, ‘ longiōrēs sunt.’   30

---

19. **decuriōnātus, -ūs**, m., ‘membership in a town council,’ probably at Pompeii, near which Cicero had a countryseat.   **prīvignus, -ī,**
m., ‘step-son.’   **expedīret** : ‘help to secure.’

20. **frequentia, -ae, [frequēns],** f., ‘crowd.’

21. **Rōmae** : locative. *146.*   **Pompeiīs** : ‘at Pompeii.’ *145, b.*

22. **illa** : ‘those (sayings).’   **ōrātōribus conveniunt** : ‘are
proper for an orator.’   **Cicerōnī — excidērunt** : ‘fell from the lips
of Cicero.’ *109, b.*

23. **in agendō** : ‘while arguing ’ in court.

24. **candidātus, -ī, [candidus,** ‘white ’], m., ‘candidate.’   **cocī** :
gen. of **cocus**, ‘cook,’ pronounced as if spelled **quoquus.**   **cōram** :
here a preposition with the ablative ; ‘in his presence.’

26. **quoque** : either the adverb, or the vocative of *quoquus = cocus.*

27. **pedibus aeger** : Vatinius had the gout.

28. **commodiōris valētūdinis factus** [esse] : ‘to have improved
in health,’ lit. ‘to have become of better health.’   **bīna mīlia** [pas-
suum] : ‘two miles (a day).’

30. **enim** : ‘(Of course), for.’

On the consulship of Vatinius, which lasted a few days.

In cōnsulātū Vatīniī, quem paucīs diēbus gessit, notābilis Cicerōnis urbānitās circumferēbātur:

'Magnum ostentum,' inquit, 'annō Vatīniī factum est, quod illō cōnsulātū nec brūma nec vēr nec aestās nec autumnus fuit.'

Querentī deinde Vatīniō, quod gravātus esset, domum ad sē īnfīrmātum venīre, respondit:

'Voluī in cōnsulātū tuō venīre, sed nox mē comprehendit.'

On the consulship of Caninius Rebilus, formerly a lieutenant of Caesar, which lasted only a few hours, at the end of 45 B.C.

'Hōc cōnsecūtus est Rebilus, ut quaererētur, quibus cōnsulibus cōnsul fuerit.'

'Vigilantem habēmus cōnsulem Canīnium, quī in cōnsulātū suō somnum nōn vīdit.'

Retorts for persons who lie about their age.

Redarguimus interim apertē, ut Cicerō Vibium Curium, multum dē annīs aetātis suae mentientem:

---

31. **notābilis, -e,** [**nota**], adj., 'remarkable.'

32. **urbānitās, -ātis,** [**urbānus**], f., 'pleasantry'; trans. 'witticism.'　　**circumferō, -ferre, -tulī, -lātus,** [**circum + ferō**], 3, 'carry around'; here 'circulate.'

33. **ostentum, -ī,** [**ostendō**], n., 'marvel.'

36. **gravātus esset:** 'because (as he said, Cicero) had been unwilling.'　　**domum ad sē:** 'to his house to (see) him.'

37. **īnfīrmō, -āre, -āvī, -ātus,** [**īnfīrmus**], 1, 'enfeeble.'　　**īnfīrmātum:** 'when he was laid up.'

40. **ut quaererētur:** 'that the question should be raised.'　　**quibus cōnsulibus:** 'in whose consulship.'

42. **vigilāns, -antis** [**vigilō,** 'keep awake'], adj. of double meaning, 'watchful' and 'wakeful.'

44. **redarguō, -ere, -uī,** 3, 'show up'; 'we show up (people).'　　**interim:** 'sometimes.'　　**Vibius Curius, -ī -ī,** m., an acquaintance of Cicero's; sc. *redarguit.*

'Tum ergō, cum ūnā dēclāmābāmus, nōn erās nātus!'

Interim et simulātā assēnsiōne, ut īdem, Fabiā Dolā-
bellae dīcente *trigintā sē annōs habēre*,

'Vērum est,' inquit, 'nam hōc illam iam vigintī annīs
audiō!'

50

On a man from Africa, who wished to pass as an aristocrat.

Octāvius, quī nātū nōbilis vidēbātur, Cicerōnī recitantī
ait: 'Nōn audiō, quae dīcis.'

Ille respondit: 'Certē solēbās bene forātās habēre aurēs!'

Hōc eō dictum, quia Octāvius Libys oriundus dīcēbātur,
quibus mōs est aurem forāre.

55

3. Legal Maxims

Fundamental maxims of right conduct.

Iūris praecepta sunt haec: honestē vivere, alterum nōn
laedere, suum cuique tribuere.

Definition of justice.

Iūstitia est cōnstāns et perpetua voluntās iūs suum cuique tribuendī.

---

45. **mentior, -īrī, -ītus,** 4, dep., 'lie.'
46. **dēclāmō, -āre,** etc., [dē + clāmō], 1, 'practice declamation.'
47. **assēnsiō, -ōnis,** f., 'agreement.'   **īdem**: Cicero; subject of
inquit.   **Fabia, -ae,** f., wife of Dolabella.   **Dolābella, -ae,** m.,
P. Cornelius Dolabella, who was born in 70 B.C., and was prominent
in Roman politics at the time of the Civil War.
48. **trigintā,** etc.: 'that she was thirty years old.'
49. **hōc,** etc.: sc. *dicere*; 'I've been hearing her say that.'
53. **forō, -āre, -āvi, -ātus,** 1, 'bore'; of the ear, 'pierce.'
54. **Libys, -yos,** m., 'a Libyan'; 'was said to be a Libyan by birth.'
55. **quibus**: *et eīs*, the Libyans.
3. 1. **honestē,** [honōs]: adv., 'honorably.'
2. **suum cuique**: 'to each what belongs to him.'
3. **cōnstāns, -tis,** adj., 'unvarying.'   **voluntās**: 'determination.'
iūs suum cuique: 'to each his due.'
4. **tribuendī**: translate as if an infinitive.

The principal is responsible for his agent.

5 Quī facit per alium, facit per sē.

The plea, " I did not know the law," is not valid.

Ignōrantia lēgis nēminem excūsat.

We cannot confer upon another ampler rights than we ourselves possess.

Nēmō plūs iūris in alium trānsferre potest quam ipse habet.

A single crime, a single punishment.

Nēmō dēbet bis pūnīrī prō ūnō dēlīctō.

In heated argument men lose sight of the truth.

10 Nimium altercandō vēritās āmittitur.

4. Fables

In union lies safety; in discord, weakness.

In eōdem prātō pāscēbantur trēs bovēs in maximā concordiā, et sīc ab omnī ferārum incursiōne tūtī erant. Sed discidiō inter illōs ortō, singulī ā ferīs petītī et laniātī sunt. Fābula docet, quantum bonī sit in concordiā.

Circumstances may make cowards brave.

5 Haedus, stāns in tēctō domūs, lupō praetereuntī male-

---

6. ignōrantia, -ae, f., 'ignorance.'

9. pūniō, -īre, -īvī, -ītus, 4, 'punish.'

10. altercor, -ārī, -ātus, [alter], 1, dep., 'dispute.' vēritās, -ātis, [vērus], f., 'truth.'

4. 1. prātum, -ī, n., 'meadow.' pāscor, -ī, pāstus, 3, dep., 'feed.' concordia, -ae, f., 'harmony.'

3. discidium, -ī, n., 'discord.' laniō, -āre, etc., 1, 'tear to pieces.'

4. fābula, -ae, f., 'fable.'

5. haedus, -ī, m., 'kid.' lupus, -ī, m., 'wolf.' maledīcō, -dīcere, -dīxī, -dictus, 3, 'rail at.'

dīxit. Cui lupus, 'Nōn tū,' inquit, 'sed tēctum mihi male-
dīcit.'
Saepe locus et tempus hominēs timidōs audācēs reddit.

The dog in the manger.

Canis iacēbat in praesēpī bovēsque lātrandō ā pābulō
arcēbat. Cui ūnus boum, 'Quanta ista,' inquit, 'invidia 10
est, quod nōn pateris, ut eō cibō vescāmur, quem tū ipse
capere nec possīs!

Haec fābula invidiae indolem dēclārat.

" Who will put the bell on the cat ?"

Mūrēs aliquandō habuērunt cōnsilium, quō modō sibi ā
fēle cavērent. Multīs aliīs prōpositīs, omnibus placuit, ut 15
eī tintinnābulum annecterētur; sīc enim ipsōs sonitū ad-
monitōs eam fugere posse. Sed cum iam inter mūrēs
quaererētur, quī fēlī tintinnābulum annecteret, nēmō repertus est.

Fābula docet, in suādendō plūrimōs esse audācēs, sed in 20
ipsō perīculō timidōs.

He who urges others on, shares the responsibility.

Tubicen ab hostibus captus, 'Nē mē,' inquit, 'interficite;
nam inermis sum, neque quicquam habeō praeter hanc
tubam.'

---

9. **canis, -is,** m., 'dog.'   **praesēpe, -is,** n., 'manger.'   **lātrō,
-āre, -āvī,** 1, 'bark.'

10. **arceo, -ēre, -uī,** 2, 'keep (from).'   **invidia, -ae,** f., 'meanness.'

11. **vescor, -ī,** 3, dep., 'eat.'

13. **indolēs, -is,** f., 'true nature.'

14. **mūs, mūris,** m., 'mouse.'

15. **fēlis, -is,** f., 'cat.'

16. **tintinnābulum, -ī,** n., 'bell.'   **annectō, -nectere, -nexuī,
-nexus,** 3, 'tie (to).'   **sonitus, -ūs,** m., 'sound.'

20. **suādeō, -ēre, -sī,** 2, 'advise.'

22. **tubicen, -inis,** m., 'trumpeter.'

25 At hostēs, 'Propter hōc ipsum,' inquiunt, 'tē interimē-
mus, quod, cum ipse pugnandī sis imperītus, aliōs ad
pugnam incitāre solēs.'

Fābula docet, nōn sōlum maleficōs esse pūniendōs, sed
etiam eōs, quī aliōs ad male faciendum irritent.

5. The First Psalm

Beātus vir, quī nōn abiit in cōnsiliō impiōrum,
    et in viā peccātōrum nōn stetit,
    et in cathedrā pestilentiae nōn sēdit;
sed in lēge Dominī voluntās eius,
5   et in lēge eius meditābitur diē ac nocte.
Et erit tamquam lignum, quod plantātum est secus dēcur-
        sūs aquārum,
    quod frūctum suum dabit in tempore suō,
et folium eius nōn dēfluet,
    et omnia, quaecumque faciet, prosperābuntur.

---

25. **inquiunt**: from *inquam*; 'say.'   **interimō, -imere, -ēmī,
-ēmptus**, 3, 'kill.'

28. **maleficus, -ī**, m., 'evildoer.'

29. **irritō, -āre, -āvī, -ātus**, 1, 'stir up.'

5. 1 **Beātus, -a, -um**, adj., 'happy,' 'blessed.'   **impius, -a, -um,
[in- + pius]**, adj., 'wicked,' 'ungodly'; as a noun, **impius, -ī**, m.,
'wicked man.'

2. **peccātor, -ōris, [peccō]**, m., 'sinner.'

3. **cathedra, -ae, [καθέδρα]**, f., 'chair,' 'seat.'   **pestilentia, -ae,
[pestilēns**, 'unwholesome'], f., 'plague'; here 'they that are a plague,'
'the scornful.'   **sedeō, -ēre, sēdī**, sup. **sessum**, 2, 'sit.'

4. **Dominus, -ī**, m., 'Lord.'   **voluntās** : sc. *est*.

5. **meditor, -ārī, -ātus**, 1. dep., 'reflect,' 'meditate.'

6. **lignum, -ī**, n., 'wood,' 'tree.'   **plantō, -āre, -āvī, -ātus,
[planta**, 'a plant'], 1, 'plant.'   **secus**, prep., 'along,' 'beside.'
dēcursus, -ūs, [dēcurrō], m., 'course' of a brook or stream, 'river.'

8. **folium, -ī**, n., 'leaf.'   **dēfluō, -fluere, -flūxī, [dē + fluō]**, 3,
'flow away'; of a leaf, 'fade,' 'wither.'

9. **prosperō, -āre, -āvī, -ātus, [prosper**, 'favorable'], 1, 'succeed,'
'prosper.'

Nōn sīc impiī, nōn sīc;   10
 sed tamquam pulvis, quem prōicit ventus ā faciē terrae.
Ideō nōn resurgent impiī in iūdiciō,
 neque peccātōrēs in conciliō iūstōrum;
quoniam nōvit Dominus viam iūstōrum,
 et iter impiōrum perībit.   15

6. The Twenty-third Psalm

Dominus regit mē, et nihil mihi deerit.
 In locō pāscuae ibi mē collocāvit;
super aquam refectiōnis ēducāvit mē,
 animam meam convertit.
Dēdūxit mē super sēmitās iūstitiae propter nōmen suum.   5
Nam, et sī ambulāverō in mediō umbrae mortis,
 nōn timēbō mala, quoniam tu mēcum es:
virga tua et baculus tuus, ipsa mē cōnsōlāta sunt.
Parāstī in cōnspectū meō mēnsam, adversus eōs quī trību-
 lant mē:

---

10. **impiī** : sc. *sunt*.

11. **faciēs, -ēī**, f., 'face.'

12. **resurgō, -ere, resurrēxī, resurrēctus**, [re- + **surgō**], 3, 'rise again,' 'stand.'

13. **iūstus, -ī**, [**iūstus, -a, -um**], m., 'just man,' 'righteous man.'

6. 2. **pāscua, -ae**, f., 'pasturage,' 'pasture.'

3. **refectiō, -ōnis**, [**reficiō**], f., 'refreshing.'   **ēducō, -āre, -āvī, -ātus**, [ē + **ducō**, from **dux**], 1, 'rear'; 'support,' 'nourish.'

5. **iūstitiae** : 'righteousness.'

6. **et** : 'even.'   **ambulō, -āre, -āvī**, 1, 'walk.'   **umbra, -ae**, f., 'shadow.'

8. **virga, -ae**, f., a slender branch, 'rod.'   **baculus, -ī**, m., 'staff.'
ipsa : neuter plural as referring to both *virga* and *baculus* (cf. *163, c*); emphatic 'they.'

9. **mēnsa, -ae**, f., 'table.'   **trībulō, -āre**, 1, 'thresh'; 'afflict,' 'torment.'

10   impinguāstī in oleō caput meum,
     et calix meus inēbriāns quam praeclārus est!
Et misericordia tua subsequetur mē omnibus diēbus vītae
     meae,
     et ut inhabitem in domō Dominī in longitūdinem diērum.

---

10. **impinguō, -āre, -āvī, -ātus,** [in + pinguis], 1, 'make fat';
'anoint.'   **in**: 'with.'   **oleum, -ī,** n., 'oil' of the olive.

11. **calix, -icis,** m., 'cup.'   **inēbriō, -āre,** 1, 'fill full'; 'overflow.'   **praeclārus, -a, -um,** [prae + clārus], adj., 'glorious,'
'splendid.'

13. **inhabitō, -āre, -āvī,** [in + habitō], 1, 'dwell in,' 'dwell.'
in longitūdinem diērum: 'forever.'

A COMPANION TO CAESAR

FIGURE 151. — The Goddess of Victory bearing a Gallic
war trumpet, in commemoration of a victory over
Gauls. From a relief at Pompeii.

ESSENTIALS OF LATIN GRAMMAR FOR THE STUDY OF CAESAR

INFLECTIONS

NOUNS

1. The Latin language has no article. In translating into English, the definite article *the*, or the indefinite article *a*, should be supplied with nouns in the different cases as the sense may require.

FIRST DECLENSION

2. *a.* The Nominative Singular of nouns of the First Declension ends in -**ă**.

b. Nouns of the First Declension are nearly all of the Feminine Gender; a few nouns referring to males are masculine, as **nauta**, *sailor* (III. 9); **Cotta**, a man's name (C. I. 6).

3. An example of the First Declension is: **via** (stem **viā**-), F., *way* (I. 9):

SINGULAR

CASE		MEANING	TERMINATION
Nom.	via	*a way, the way*	-ă
Gen.	viae	*of a way, of the way*	-ae
Dat.	viae	*to or for a way, or the way*	-ae
Acc.	viam	*a way, the way*	-am
Voc.	via	*O way!*	-ă
Abl.	viā	*from, by, in a way or the way*	-ā

PLURAL

CASE		MEANING	TERMINATION
Nom.	viae	*ways, the ways*	-ae
Gen.	viārum	*of ways, of the ways*	-ārum
Dat.	viīs	*to or for ways, or the ways*	-īs
Acc.	viās	*ways, the ways*	-ās
Voc.	viae	*O ways!*	-ae
Abl.	viīs	*from, by, in ways, or the ways*	-īs

4. *a.* Besides the six cases of the First Declension there is a rare Locative Case, of which the Singular is exactly like the Genitive, as **Samarobrīvae**, *at Samarobriva* (V. 24).

b. The Greek Name **Achillās** (C. III. 104) is of the First Declension, and declined as follows: *Nom.* **Achillās**, *Gen.* **Achillae**, *Dat.* **Achillae**, *Acc.* **Achillam**, *Voc.* **Achillā** or **Achilla**, *Abl.* **Achillā**.

SECOND DECLENSION

5. *a.* The Nominative Singular of the Second Declension ends in -um for Neuter Nouns and -us, -er, -ir for all others.

b. Nouns of the Second Declension in -us, -er, and -ir are generally Masculine. Feminine are most names of Trees and Plants, as **fāgus**, *beech* (V. 12), and most names of Countries, Islands, and Cities, as **Aegyptus**, *Egypt* (C. III. 104).

6. *a.* Examples of Nouns of the Second Declension in -us and -um are **lēgātus** (I. 7) and **bellum** (I. 1):

lēgātus (stem **lēgāto-**), m.,   **bellum** (stem **bello-**), n., *war*
     envoy, lieutenant

SINGULAR

		TERMINATION		TERMINATION
Nom.	lēgāt**us**	-us	bell**um**	-um
Gen.	lēgāt**ī**	-ī	bell**ī**	-ī
Dat.	lēgāt**ō**	-ō	bell**ō**	-ō
Acc.	lēgāt**um**	-um	bell**um**	-um
Voc.	lēgāt**e**	-e	bell**um**	-um
Abl.	lēgāt**ō**	-ō	bell**ō**	-ō

PLURAL

Nom.	lēgāt**ī**	-ī	bell**a**	-a
Gen.	lēgāt**ōrum**	-ōrum	bell**ōrum**	-ōrum
Dat.	lēgāt**īs**	-īs	bell**īs**	-īs
Acc.	lēgāt**ōs**	-ōs	bell**a**	-a
Voc.	lēgāt**ī**	-ī	bell**a**	-a
Abl.	lēgāt**īs**	-īs	bell**īs**	-īs

b. Caesar uses the Neuter **vulgus** in the Nominative (IV. 5), Genitive **vulgī** (I. 20), and the Accusative **vulgus** (I. 46).

c. Caesar uses **locus, -ī**, m., *place*, with a Neuter Plural declined thus: *Nom.* **loca**, *Gen.* **locōrum**, *Dat.* **locīs**, *Acc.* **loca**, *Abl.* **locīs**.

d. The Second Declension has a rare Locative Case, of which the Singular is like the Genitive; as **Cavillōnī**, *at Cavillonum* (VII. 90).

7. *a.* Examples of Nouns of the Second Declension in -er and -ir are **puer**, *boy* (I. 29), **ager**, *field* (I. 4), and **vir**, *man* (II. 25):

puer (stem **puero-**),   **ager** (stem **agro-**),   **vir** (stem **viro-**),
     m., *boy*   m., *field*   m., *man*

SINGULAR

				TERMINATION
Nom.	puer	ager	vir	——
Gen.	puer**ī**	agr**ī**	vir**ī**	-ī
Dat.	puer**ō**	agr**ō**	vir**ō**	-ō
Acc.	puer**um**	agr**um**	vir**um**	-um
Voc.	puer	ager	vir	——
Abl.	puer**ō**	agr**ō**	vir**ō**	-ō

PLURAL

				TERMINATION
Nom.	puerī	agrī	virī	-ī
Gen.	puerōrum	agrōrum	virōrum	-ōrum
Dat.	puerīs	agrīs	virīs	-īs
Acc.	puerōs	agrōs	virōs	-ōs
Voc.	puerī	agrī ·	virī	-ī
Abl.	puerīs	agrīs	virīs	-īs

b. Declined like **puer** are **socer**, M., *father-in-law* (I. 12), **gener**, M., *son-in-law* (V. 56), **vesper**, M., *evening* (I. 26), **līberī**, M., plural only, *children* (I. 11), and compounds of -**fer** and -**ger**, as **signifer**, *standard-bearer* (II. 25).

c. Like **ager** is **arbiter**, -**trī**, M., *referee* (V. 1); also **faber**, -**brī**, M., *mechanic*, *Gen.* Plural generally **fabrum** (V. 11), **administer**, -**trī**, M., *helper* (VI. 16), **culter**, -**trī**, M., *butcher-knife* (p. 464).

8. *a.* In Caesar's time nouns of the Second Declension in -**ius** and -**ium** formed the Genitive Singular in -**ī** (not -**iī**), retaining the accent on the penult of words of more than two syllables even when this was short; thus, **fīlī**, **Vale′rī**, **negō′tī**, **impe′rī**. Afterwards Common Nouns in -**ius**, and many Proper Names in -**ius**, were written with the Genitive in -**iī**, and for the sake of consistency such Genitives are frequently printed with -**iī** to-day, as **cōnsiliī** (I. 21), **Valeriī** (I. 47).

b. The Genitive of **Pompeius** is written with -**ī**, **Pompe′ī** (VII. 6, C. III. 84), as are also the Genitives of some other Proper Names in -**ius**.

c. The Vocative of **fīlius** and of Proper Names in -**ius** ends in -**ī** (not -**ie**), the accent remaining on the penult of vocatives containing more than two syllables; thus: **Pompe′ī** (C. III. 87).

d. The declension of **deus**, M., *god* (I. 12), is irregular:

SINGULAR		PLURAL	
Nom.	deus		dī, deī, diī
Gen.	deī		deōrum, deum
Dat.	deō		dīs, deīs, diīs
Acc.	deum		deōs
Voc.	deus		dī, deī, diī
Abl.	deō		dīs, deīs, diīs

THIRD DECLENSION

9. In the Third Declension are comprised nouns with stems ending in a consonant (mute stems, liquid stems, nasal stems, and -**s** stems), nouns with stems ending in -**i**, nouns with mixed stems, and nouns of irregular declension. The stem rarely appears unchanged in the Nominative, but may usually be recognized in the Genitive.

10. *a.* Mute Stems may end in a Labial, **p, b**; in a Guttural, **c, g**; or in a Dental, **t, d.** In Guttural Stems the **-s** of the case ending in the Nominative unites with the **c** or **g** of the stem, producing **x**; thus **dux** for **duc-s**, in which the stem is **duc-**, the termination **-s**; and **rēx** for **rēg-s**.

b. Examples of nouns with mute stems are **prīnceps** (I. 13), **rēx** (I. 31), **pēs** (I. 8), **mīles** (I. 7), **virtūs** (I. 1) and **caput** (I. 29):

prīnceps (stem in oblique cases **prīncip-**), M., *leader, leading man*

rēx (stem **rēg-**), M., *king*

pēs (stem in oblique cases **ped-**), M., *foot*

SINGULAR

				TERMINATION
Nom.	prīnceps	rēx	pēs	-s
Gen.	prīncipis	rēgis	pedis	-is
Dat.	prīncipī	rēgī	pedī	-ī
Acc.	prīncipem	rēgem	pedem	-em
Voc.	prīnceps	rēx	pēs	-s
Abl.	prīncipe	rēge	pede	-e

PLURAL

Nom.	prīncipēs	rēgēs	pedēs	-ēs
Gen.	prīncipum	rēgum	pedum	-um
Dat.	prīncipibus	rēgibus	pedibus	-ibus
Acc.	prīncipēs	rēgēs	pedēs	-ēs
Voc.	prīncipēs	rēgēs	pedēs	-ēs
Abl.	prīncipibus	rēgibus	pedibus	-ibus

mīles (stem in oblique cases **mīlit-**), M., *soldier*

virtūs (stem in oblique cases **virtūt-**), F., *valor, virtue*

caput (stem in oblique cases **capit-**), N., *head*

SINGULAR

Nom.	mīles	virtūs	caput
Gen.	mīlitis	virtūtis	capitis
Dat.	mīlitī	virtūtī	capitī
Acc.	mīlitem	virtūtem	caput
Voc.	mīles	virtūs	caput
Abl.	mīlite	virtūte	capite

PLURAL

Nom.	mīlitēs	virtūtēs	capita
Gen.	mīlitum	virtūtum	capitum
Dat.	mīlitibus	virtūtibus	capitibus
Acc.	mīlitēs	virtūtēs	capita
Voc.	mīlitēs	virtūtēs	capita
Abl.	mīlitibus	virtūtibus	capitibus

c. Like **rēx** are declined Gallic Proper Names in **-rīx**, as, in Singular only, **Orgetorīx**, *Gen.* **Orgetorīgis** (I. 2), and **Dumnorīx**,

-rīgis (I. 3), and, in Plural only, **Biturīgēs, Biturīgum** (I. 18) ; also **dux, ducis,** M., *leader* (I. 13), **pāx, pācis,** F., *peace* (I. 3), **pix, picis,** F., *pitch* (VII. 22), and **vōx, vōcis,** F., *voice, utterance* (I. 32).

d. Like **mīles** in Declension are **eques, equitis,** M., *horseman* (I. 15), **pedes, peditis,** M., *foot-soldier* (I. 42); and **caespes,** M., *sod* (III. 25), **comes,** M., *companion* (VI. 30), **hospes,** M., *guest-friend* (I. 53), **stīpes,** M., *tree-trunk* (VII. 73).

e. **Quiēs,** F., *repose* (V. 40), is declined **quiēs, quiētis, quiētī,** etc. ; but **ariēs,** M., *battering-ram* (II. 32), **abiēs,** F., *fir-tree* (V. 12), **interpres,** M., *interpreter* (I. 19), **seges,** F., *grainfield* (VI. 36) have -**ĕtis** in the Genitive and are declined **ariēs, arietis, arietī, arietem,** etc.

f. Like **virtūs** are **salūs, salūtis,** F., in Singular only, *safety* (I. 27), **servitūs, servitūtis,** F., *slavery* (I. 11) ; here also belong the Feminine Nouns whose Nominative ends in -**tās**, as **cīvitās, cīvitātis,** *state* (I. 2), **aestās, aestātis,** *summer* (I. 54).

g. Lacking the Dental in the Nominative are the Neuters **cor, cordis,** *heart* (VI. 19), and **lac, lactis,** *milk* (IV. 1).

11. *a.* Liquid stems end in -**l** or -**r**.

b. Examples of nouns with liquid stems are **cōnsul** (I. 2), **victor** (I. 31) and **pater** (I. 3) :

cōnsul (stem **cōnsul-**), M.,   **victor** (stem **victōr-**), M.,   **pater** (stem **patr-**),
         consul   *victor*   M., *father*

SINGULAR

Nom.	cōnsul	victor	pater
Gen.	cōnsulis	victōris	patris
Dat.	cōnsulī	victōrī	patrī
Acc.	cōnsulem	victōrem	patrem
Voc.	cōnsul	victor	pater
Abl.	cōnsule	victōre	patre

PLURAL

Nom.	cōnsulēs	victōrēs	patrēs
Gen.	cōnsulum	victōrum	patrum
Dat.	cōnsulibus	victōribus	patribus
Acc.	cōnsulēs	victōrēs	patrēs
Voc.	cōnsulēs	victōrēs	patrēs
Abl.	cōnsulibus	victōribus	patribus

c. Like **consul** are **sōl, sōlis,** M., *sun* (I. 1), **exsul, exsulis,** M., *exile* (V. 55), **sāl, salis,** M., *salt* (C. II. 37) ; also some -**r** stems, as **Caesar, Caesaris,** M., *Caesar* (*19, c*) ; **agger, aggeris,** M., *mound* (II. 20), **ānser, -eris,** M., *goose* (V. 12), **mulier, mulieris,** F., *woman* (I. 29), **arbor, arboris,** F., *tree* (II. 17).

d. Like **victor** are declined Masculine nouns of Agency in -tor, as **mercātor**, -ōris, *trader* (I. 1), **dēprecātor**, -ōris, *intercessor* (I. 9); and Abstract nouns in -or, as **timor**, -ōris, M., *fear* (I. 22).

e. Like **pater** are declined **frāter**, **frātris**, M., *brother* (I. 3), and **māter**, **mātris**, F., *mother* (I. 18).

12. *a.* Nasal Stems end in -n, excepting in **hiems**, **hiemis**, F., *winter* (IV. 1), of which the stem ends in -m.

b. Examples are **sermō** (V. 37), **homō** (I. 2) and **nōmen** (I. 13):

	sermō (stem **sermōn**-), M., *conversation*	**homō** (stem **homin**-), M., *man*	**nōmen** (stem **nomin**-), N., *name*
	SINGULAR		
Nom.	sermō	homō	nōmen
Gen.	sermōnis	hominis	nōminis
Dat.	sermōnī	hominī	nōminī
Acc.	sermōn**em**	homin**em**	nōmen
Voc.	sermō	homō	nōmen
Abl.	sermōn**e**	homin**e**	nōmin**e**
	PLURAL		
Nom.	sermōn**ēs**	homin**ēs**	nōmin**a**
Gen.	sermōn**um**	homin**um**	nōmin**um**
Dat.	sermōn**ibus**	homin**ibus**	nōmin**ibus**
Acc.	sermōn**ēs**	homin**ēs**	nōmin**a**
Voc.	sermōn**ēs**	homin**ēs**	nōmin**a**
Abl.	sermōn**ibus**	homin**ibus**	nōmin**ibus**

c. Like **sermō** are declined **harpagō, harpagōnis**, M., *grappling-hook* (VII. 81); **latrō, latrōnis**, M., *bandit* (III. 17); **Dīvicō, Dīvicōnis**, M., (I. 13; in Singular only); and nouns in -iō, as **suspīciō, suspīciōnis**, F., *suspicion* (I. 4), **coniūrātiō**, -ōnis, F., *league* (I. 2), **Cūriō, Cūriōnis**, M., (C. II. 3; in Singular only).

d. Like **homō** are declined **ōrdō, ōrdinis**, M., *rank* (I. 40); **necessitūdō**, -inis, F., *close connection* (I. 43); **testūdō, testūdinis**, F., *testudo* (II. 6); **nēmō**, *Dat.* **nēminī**, *Acc.* **nēminem** (the place of the *Gen.* and *Abl.*, and sometimes the *Dat.*, being supplied by *Gen.* **nūllīus**, *Abl.* **nūllō**, *Dat.* **nūllī**, from **nūllus**), M., *no one*; **Apollo, Apollinis**, M., (VI. 17, in Singular only); **sōlitūdō, sōlitūdinis**, F., *wilderness* (IV. 18); and **virgō**, -inis, F., *maiden* (C. II. 4).

e. Like **nōmen** are declined other Neuters in -men, as **flūmen, flūminis**, *river* (I. 1), **agmen, agminis**, *column* (I. 15), and **certāmen**, -inis, *contest* (III. 14).

13. *a.* The -s- of -s Stems becomes **r** between vowels in the oblique cases. In **honōs**, **-r** generally appears also in the Nominative; **-r** is always found in the Nominative of **rūmor** and many other nouns of this class.

b. Examples of nouns with **-s** stems are **mōs** (I. 4), **honōs** (VI. 13), or **honor**, and **genus** (I. 48) :

mōs (oblique stem **mōr-**), M., *custom*	**honōs, honor** (oblique stem **honōr-**), M., *honor*	**genus** (oblique stem **gener-**), N., *race*
	SINGULAR	

Nom.	mōs	honōs *or* honor	genus
Gen.	mōris	honōris	generis
Dat.	mōrī	honōrī	generī
Acc.	mōrem	honōrem	genus
Voc.	mōs	honor	genus
Abl.	mōre	honōre	genere

	PLURAL	
Nom.	mōrēs	honōrēs	genera
Gen.	mōrum	honōrum	generum
Dat.	mōribus	honōribus	generibus
Acc.	mōrēs	honōrēs	genera
Voc.	mōrēs	honōrēs	genera
Abl.	mōribus	honōribus	generibus

c. Like **mōs** is declined **flōs**, M., *flower* (VII. 73).

d. Like **honor** are **soror, sorōris**, F., *sister* (I. 18), **uxor, uxōris**, F., *wife* (I. 18).

e. Like **genus** are declined the Neuters **fūnus, fūneris**, *funeral* (VI. 19); **latus, lateris**, *side* (I. 25); **mūnus, mūneris**, *gift* (I. 43); **onus, oneris**, *burden, load* (II. 30); **opus, operis**, *work* (I. 8); **scelus, sceleris**, *crime* (I. 14); **vulnus, vulneris**, *wound* (I. 25), etc.

f. Similar in declension to **genus**, but having a different vowel before the Endings of the Oblique Cases, are the Neuters **corpus, corporis**, *body* (I. 25); **dēdecus, -oris**, *disgrace* (IV. 25); **facinus, -oris**, *evil deed* (I. 40); **frīgus, frīgoris**, *cold* (I. 16); **lītus, lītoris**, *shore* (IV. 23); **pectus, pectoris**, *breast* (VII. 47); **pecus, pecoris**, *cattle* (III. 29); **tempus, temporis**, *time* (I. 16); and **rōbur, rōboris**, *oak* (III. 13).

g. Among other Nouns of the Third Declension with Nominative in **-s** and Genitive in **-ris** are the Masculine **pulvis, pulveris**, *dust* (*Acc.* **pulverem**, IV. 32), **lepus, leporis**, *hare* (*Acc.* **leporem**, V. 12), **mās, maris**, *male* (*Gen.* VI. 26) ; and the Neuters **iūs, iūris** (I. 4; *Nom.* Plural **iūra**, VI. 13), **aes, aeris**, *copper* (IV. 31), **crūs, crūris**, *leg* (VI. 27), and **ōs, ōris**, *mouth, face* (V. 35; *Acc.* Plural **ōra**, VI. 39).

h. **iūs iūrandum**, N., *oath* (I. 3), is thus declined, in the Singular :

Nom. iŭs iūrandum, *Gen.* iūris iūrandī, *Dat.* iūrī iūrandō, *Acc.* iŭs iūrandum, *Abl.* iūre iūrandō.

14. *a.* The Nominative Singular of Masculine and Feminine nouns with -i Stems ends ordinarily in **-is,** the Genitive Plural always in **-ium.**

b. Examples of Masculine and Feminine -i Stems with Nominative Singular in **-is** are **turris** (II. 30), **ĭgnis** (I. 4) and **hostis** (I. 21) :

turris (stem **turri-**), F., *tower*   **ĭgnis** (stem **ĭgni-**), M., *fire*   **hostis** (stem **hosti-**), C., *enemy*

SINGULAR

				TERMINATION
Nom.	turris	ĭgnis	hostis	-is
Gen.	turris	ĭgnis	hostis	-is
Dat.	turrī	ĭgnī	hostī	-ī
Acc.	turrim or -em	ĭgnem	hostem	-im, -em
Voc.	turris	ĭgnis	hostis	-is
Abl.	turrī or -e	ĭgnī or -e	hoste	-e, -ī

PLURAL

Nom.	turrēs	ĭgnēs	hostēs	-ēs
Gen.	turrium	ĭgnium	hostium	-ium
Dat.	turribus	ĭgnibus	hostibus	-ibus
Acc.	turrīs or -ēs	ĭgnīs or -ēs	hostīs or -ēs	-īs, -ēs
Voc.	turrēs	ĭgnēs	hostēs	-ēs
Abl.	turribus	ĭgnibus	hostibus	-ibus

c. Like **turris,** but in the Singular only, is **Sabis, -is,** *Acc.* **-im,** M., *the Sambre* (II. 16) ; also **Tamesis, -is,** *Acc.* **-im,** M., *the Thames* (V. 11, 18).

15. *a.* The Nominative Singular of some nouns with -i Stems ends in **-ēs,** of a few others in **-er.** Examples are **caedēs** (V. 47) and **linter** (I. 12) :

caedēs (stem **caedi-**), F., *slaughter*   **linter** (stem **lintri-**), F., *skiff*

	SINGULAR	PLURAL		SINGULAR	PLURAL
Nom.	caedēs	caedēs		linter	lintrēs
Gen.	caedis	caedium		lintris	lintrium
Dat.	caedī	caedibus		lintrī	lintribus
Acc.	caedem	caedēs or -īs		lintrem	lintrēs, -īs
Voc.	caedēs	caedēs		linter	lintrēs
Abl.	caede	caedibus		lintrī or -e	lintribus

b. Like **caedēs** are declined the Feminine Nouns **cautēs, cautis,** *jagged rock* (III. 13), **mōlēs, mōlis,** *dike* (III. 12), **rūpēs, -is,** *cliff* (II. 29), **sēdēs, -is,** *abode* (I. 31), **saepēs, -is,** *hedge* (II. 17), **alcēs, -is,** *moose* (VI. 27) ; also **famēs, -is,** *hunger* (I. 28), which, however, has **famē** in the Ablative Singular (VII. 20).

c. Like **linter** is **imber, imbris,** M., *rainstorm* (III. 29).

16. *a.* The Nominative Singular of Neuter nouns with -i Stems ends in -e, -al, and -ar; the Ablative Singular ends in -ī, the Genitive Plural in -ium.

b. Examples of neuter nouns with -i Stems are **mare** (III. 7) and **animal** (VI. 17):

mare (stem **mari-**), N.,　　**animal** (stem **animāli-**), N.,
　　sea　　　　　　　　　　　*animal*

	SINGULAR	PLURAL	SINGULAR	PLURAL	TERMINATIONS	
					SINGULAR	PLURAL
Nom.	mare	maria	animal	animālia	-e or wanting	-ia
Gen.	maris	marium	animālis	animālium	-is	-ium
Dat.	marī	maribus	animālī	animālibus	-ī	-ibus
Acc.	mare	maria	animal	animālia	-e or wanting	-ia
Voc.	mare	maria	animal	animālia	-e or wanting	-ia
Abl.	marī	maribus	animālī	animālibus	-ī	-ibus

c. **Bibracte**, N., is declined thus: *Nom.* **Bibracte**, *Gen.* **Bibractis**, *Dat.* **Bibractī**, *Acc.* **Bibracte**, *Abl.* **Bibracte**; no Plural.

d. Like **animal** is **vectīgal, -ālis** (I. 18).

17. *a.* The declension of nouns with Mixed Stems in the Singular conforms to that of Mute Stems, in the Plural to that of -i Stems.

b. Examples of nouns with Mixed Stems are **mōns** (I. 1), **pars** (I. 1), **nox** (I. 26) and **urbs** (I. 39):

	mōns (stem **mont-**), M., *height*	**pars** (stem **part-**), F., *part*	**nox** (stem **noct-**), F., *night*	**urbs** (stem **urb-**), F., *city*
	SINGULAR			
Nom.	mōns	pars	nox	urbs
Gen.	montis	partis	noctis	urbis
Dat.	montī	partī	noctī	urbī
Acc.	montem	partem	noctem	urbem
Voc.	mōns	pars	nox	urbs
Abl.	monte	parte	nocte	urbe
	PLURAL			
Nom.	montēs	partēs	noctēs	urbēs
Gen.	montium	partium	noctium	urbium
Dat.	montibus	partibus	noctibus	urbibus
Acc.	montēs, -īs	partēs, -īs	noctēs, -īs	urbēs, -īs
Voc.	montēs	partēs	noctēs	urbēs
Abl.	montibus	partibus	noctibus	urbibus

c. Among Nouns with Mixed Stems used by Caesar are **pōns, pontis**, M., *bridge* (I. 6); **cliēns, clientis**, M., *retainer* (I. 4); **parēns, -entis**, M. and F., *parent* (V. 14); **falx, falcis**, F., *sickle, hook* (III. 14); **fax, facis**, F., *torch* (VII. 24); **glāns, glandis**, F., *acorn,* *slingshot* (V. 43); **dōs, dōtis**, F., *dowry* (VI. 19); **fraus, fraudis**, F., *deception* (VII. 40); **frōns, frontis**, F., *front* (II. 8); **laus, laudis**, F., *praise* (I. 40); **līs, lītis**, F., *damages* (V. 1); **mors, mortis**, F., *death* (I. 5); **nix, nivis**, F., *snow* (VII. 8); **plēbs, plēbis**, F., *people* (I. 3); **trabs, trabis**, F., *beam* (II. 29); **sors, sortis**, F., *lot* (I. 50); **stirps, stirpis**, F., *stock* (VI. 34).

d. Defective is the noun with the stem **spont-**, which has only a Genitive, **spontis**, and Ablative, **sponte** (I. 9).

18. *a.* The declension of the nouns **vīs** (I. 6), **bōs** (VI. 26), **carō** (V. 14), and **Iuppiter** (VI. 17), is exceptional, not conforming to any of the types which have been given:

vīs (stems **vi-, vīr-**), F., *force*	**bōs** (stem **bov-**), C., *ox, cow*	**carō** (stem **carn-**), F., *flesh*	**Iuppiter** (stem **iov-**, + **pater** in the Nom.), M., *Jupiter*

SINGULAR

Nom. vīs	bōs	carō	Iuppiter
Gen. ——	bovis	carnis	Iovis
Dat. ——	bovī	carnī	Iovī
Acc. vim	bovem	carnem	Iovem
Voc. vīs	bōs	carō	Iuppiter
Abl. vī	bove	carne	Iove

PLURAL

Nom. vīrēs	bovēs	carnēs	
Gen. vīrium	boum or bovum	carnium	
Dat. vīribus	bōbus or būbus	carnibus	
Acc. vīrēs	bovēs	carnēs	
Voc. vīrēs	bovēs	carnēs	
Abl. vīribus	bōbus or būbus	carnibus	

b. **Senex**, M., *old man* (I. 29), stem **seni-** in oblique cases, is declined thus: **senex, senis, senī, senem, senex, sene; senēs, senum, senibus, senēs, senēs, senibus.**

c. **Iter**, N., *journey, route* (I. 3), has a stem **itiner-** in the oblique cases: **iter, itineris, itinerī, iter, iter, itinere; itinera, itinerum, itineribus, itinera, itinera, itineribus.**

d. **Femur**, N., *thigh*, in the oblique cases has two stems, **femor-** and **femin-**, thus: *Nom.* **femur**, *Gen.* **femoris** or **feminis** (VII. 73), etc.

e. **Arar**, M., *the Arar* (I. 12, 13, 16), is declined thus: **Arar, Araris, Ararī, Ararim, Arar, Ararī**; similar is **Liger, Ligeris**, M., *the Liger* (III. 9).

f. **phalanx**, F., *mass formation, mass*, is declined thus: *Nom.* **phalanx** *Gen.* **phalangis**, *Dat.* **phalangī**, *Acc.* **phalangem** or **phalanga**, *Abl.* **phalange.**

g. **Taurois**, F., *Taurois*, is thus declined : **Taurois**, *Gen.* **Tauro-**
ëntis, *Acc.* **Tauroënta** (C. II. 4).

NAMES OF THE FIRST, SECOND, AND THIRD DECLENSIONS

19. *a.* Of the Second Declension are all Roman First Names (**prae-**
nōmina) used by Caesar, and in reading the text the name should be
supplied, in the proper case form, from the abbreviation. The First
Names are **Aulus**, *Gen.* **Aulī** (abbreviation **A.**), **Appius** (**Ap.**), **Gāius**
(abbreviation **C.**, an old form of **G.**), **Decimus** (**D.**), **Gnaeus** (**Cn.**),
Lūcius (**L.**), **Mārcus** (**M.**), **Pūblius** (**P.**), **Quīntus** (**Q.**), **Servius**
(**Ser.**), and **Titus** (**T.**).

b. The Clan Names (**nōmina**), ending in -ius (as **Iūlius, Tullius**),
are of the Second Declension.

c. The Family Names or Surnames (**cognōmina**) are partly of the
First Declension, as **Galba** (**Servius Sulpicius Galba**) ; of the Sec-
ond, as **Baculus** (**Pūblius Sextius Baculus**); and of the Third,
as **Caesar** (*11, c*), the full name being declined thus : *Nom.* **Gāius**
Iūlius Caesar, *Gen.* **Gāī Iūlī Caesaris** or **Gāiī Iūliī Caesaris** (*8, a*),
Dat. **Gāiō Iūliō Caesarī**, *Acc.* **Gāium Iūlium Caesarem**, *Voc.* **Gāī**
Iūlī Caesar (*8, c*), *Abl.* **Gāiō Iūliō Caesare**.

d. The names of Gauls or Germans are generally of the Second
Declension, as **Dīviciācus**, **-ī**, or of the Third, as **Dumnorīx**, *Gen.*
Dumnorīgis; of the First Declension are **Galba** (II. 4, 13) and
Nasua (I. 37), as well as the Numidian names **Juba**, **Saburra** (C.
II. 38).

e. The names of Foreign Peoples are ordinarily declined in the
Plural only. A few are of the First Declension, as **Belgae**, **-ārum**
(I. 1) ; the rest are of the Second Declension, as **Helvētiī**, **-ōrum**
(I. 1), or of the Third, as **Allobrogēs**, **-um** (I. 6).

f. In the Accusative Plural of names of foreign peoples Caesar
sometimes has the Greek ending -as instead of -ēs; as **Allobrogas**
(I. 14), **Crētas** (II. 7), **Coriosolitas** (II. 34).

FOURTH DECLENSION

20. *a.* Nouns of the Fourth Declension ending in -us are generally
Masculine, nouns ending in -ū are Neuter; **domus, manus,** and **Īdūs**
(Plural) are Feminine.

b. Examples of nouns of the Fourth Declension are **frūctus** (VI. 19)
and **cornū** (I. 52) :

frūctus (stem **frūctu-**) M., *fruit*   **cornū** (stem **cornu-**), N., *horn*

	SINGULAR	PLURAL	SINGULAR	PLURAL
Nom.	frūctus	frūctūs	cornū	cornua
Gen.	frūctūs	frūctuum	cornūs	cornuum
Dat.	frūctuī	frūctibus	cornū	cornibus
Acc.	frūctum	frūctūs	cornū	cornua
Voc.	frūctus	frūctūs	cornū	cornua
Abl.	frūctū	frūctibus	cornū	cornibus

c. **Domus** (stem **domu-**), f., *house*, has also a stem **domo-** of the Second Declension, from which are formed a Locative Singular, **domī**, *at home* (I. 18, 20, etc.), an Ablative Singular, **domō**, *from home*, (I. 5, 6, etc.), an Accusative Plural, **domōs** (I. 30), and some forms not used by Caesar.

d. Many nouns of the Fourth Declension are defective, being used only in the Ablative Singular, as **iniussū** (I. 19), **iussū** (VII. 3), **nātū** (II. 13).

FIFTH DECLENSION

21. *a.* Nouns of the Fifth Declension end in -**ēs**, and are Feminine except **diēs**, *day*, and **merīdiēs**, *midday* (I. 50), which are Masculine; but **diēs** is usually Feminine when referring to a certain day (as I. 4, 8, 30), or to *time* in general.

b. Examples of nouns of the Fifth Declension are:

diēs (stem **diē-**), M., *day*   **rēs** (stem **rē-**), F., *thing*

	SINGULAR	PLURAL	SINGULAR	PLURAL
Nom.	diēs	diēs	rēs	rēs
Gen.	diēī	diērum	reī	rērum
Dat.	diēī	diēbus	reī	rēbus
Acc.	diem	diēs	rem	rēs
Voc.	diēs	diēs	rēs	rēs
Abl.	diē	diēbus	rē	rēbus

c. In the Genitive and Dative Singular -**ēī** becomes -**eī** when a consonant precedes, as in **reī** (I. 21); so **speī** (VII. 63, C. II. 5).

ADJECTIVES

22. *a.* In Adjectives of the First and Second Declensions the Masculine is declined like **lēgātus** (*6, a*), **puer** (*7, a*), or **ager** (*7, a*), the Feminine like **via** (*3*), and the Neuter like **bellum** (*6, a*).

b. Declined like **lēgātus**, **via**, **bellum**, are many Adjectives, as **bonus, bona, bonum**, *good:*

| | SINGULAR | | | PLURAL | |
MASCULINE	FEMININE	NEUTER	MASCULINE	FEMININE	NEUTER
Nom. bon**us**	bon**a**	bon**um**	bon**ī**	bon**ae**	bon**a**
Gen. bon**ī**	bon**ae**	bon**ī**	bon**ōrum**	bon**ārum**	bon**ōrum**
Dat. bon**ō**	bon**ae**	bon**ō**	bon**īs**	bon**īs**	bon**īs**
Acc. bon**um**	bon**am**	bon**um**	bon**ōs**	bon**ās**	bon**a**
Voc. bon**e**	bon**a**	bon**um**	bon**ī**	bon**ae**	bon**a**
Abl. bon**ō**	bon**ā**	bon**ō**	bon**īs**	bon**īs**	bon**īs**

c. Distributive adjectives are declined like **bonus** except that in the Genitive Plural they have -**um** instead of -**ōrum**, as **quadrāgēnum** (IV. 17).

d. A few Adjectives are declined like **puer, via, bellum**, as **miser, misera, miserum**, *wretched* (I. 32):

| | SINGULAR | | | PLURAL | |
MASCULINE	FEMININE	NEUTER	MASCULINE	FEMININE	NEUTER
Nom. miser	misera	miser**um**	miser**ī**	miser**ae**	miser**a**
Gen. miser**ī**	miser**ae**	miser**ī**	miser**ōrum**	miser**ārum**	miser**ōrum**
Dat. miser**ō**	miser**ae**	miser**ō**	miser**īs**	miser**īs**	miser**īs**
Acc. miser**um**	miser**am**	miser**um**	miser**ōs**	miser**ās**	miser**a**
Voc. miser	miser**a**	miser**um**	miser**ī**	miser**ae**	miser**a**
Abl. miser**ō**	miser**ā**	miser**ō**	miser**īs**	miser**īs**	miser**īs**

e. Like **miser** are declined **asper** (V. 45), **līber** (I. 44), and **tener** (II. 17).

f. Declined like **ager, via, bellum**, are most adjectives in -**er**, as **aeger, aegra, aegrum**, *sick* (V. 40), **integer** (III. 4), etc.:

| | SINGULAR | | | PLURAL | |
MASCULINE	FEMININE	NEUTER	MASCULINE	FEMININE	NEUTER
Nom. aeger	aegra	aegr**um**	aegr**ī**	aegr**ae**	aegr**a**
Gen. aegr**ī**	aegr**ae**	aegr**ī**	aegr**ōrum**	aegr**ārum**	aegr**ōrum**
Dat. aegr**ō**	aegr**ae**	aegr**ō**	aegr**īs**	aegr**īs**	aegr**īs**
Acc. aegr**um**	aegr**am**	aegr**um**	aegr**ōs**	aegr**ās**	aegr**a**
Voc. aeger	aegr**a**	aegr**um**	aegr**ī**	aegr**ae**	aegr**a**
Abl. aegr**ō**	aegr**ā**	aegr**ō**	aegr**īs**	aegr**īs**	aegr**īs**

23. *a.* Six Adjectives in -**us** (**ūnus**, *one;* **sōlus**, *alone;* **tōtus**, *whole;* **alius**, *other;* **ūllus**, *any;* **nūllus**, *none*) and three in -**er** (**alter**, *the other;* **ūter**, *which (of two)?* and **neuter**, *neither*), have -**īus** (or -**ius**) in the Genitive and -**ī** in the Dative Singular of all genders, and lack the Vocative; the Plural is regular. They are thus declined in the Singular:

| | SINGULAR | | | PLURAL | |
MASCULINE	FEMININE	NEUTER	MASCULINE	FEMININE	NEUTER
Nom. alius	alia	aliud	alter	altera	alterum
Gen. [alīus	alīus	alīus]	alterīus	alterīus	alterīus
Dat. aliī	aliī	aliī	alterī	alterī	alterī
Acc. alium	aliam	aliud	alterum	alteram	alterum
Abl. aliō	aliā	aliō	alterō	alterā	alterō

Nom. tōtus	tōta	tōtum	uter	utra	utrum
Gen. tōtīus	tōtīus	tōtīus	utrīus	utrīus	utrīus
Dat. tōtī	tōtī	tōtī	utrī	utrī	utrī
Acc. tōtum	tōtam	tōtum	utrum	utram	utrum
Abl. tōtō	tōtā	tōtō	utrō	utrā	utrō

b. The Genitive Singular of **alter** is generally **alterius**, instead of **alterīus**; and **alterius** is ordinarily used in place of the Genitive **alīus**.

24. Some Adjectives of the Third Declension have three endings in the Nominative Singular, others two, and others only one. Adjectives with three endings are declined like **ācer, ācris, ācre,** *sharp* (C. III. 72):

| | SINGULAR | | | PLURAL | |
MASCULINE	FEMININE	NEUTER	MASCULINE	FEMININE	NEUTER
Nom. ācer	ācris	ācre	ācrēs	ācrēs	ācria
Gen. ācris	ācris	ācris	ācrium	ācrium	ācrium
Dat. ācrī	ācrī	ācrī	ācribus	ācribus	ācribus
Acc. ācrem	ācrem	ācre	ācrēs, -īs	ācrēs, -īs	ācria
Voc. ācer	ācris	ācre	ācrēs	ācrēs	ācria
Abl. ācrī	ācrī	ācrī	ācribus	ācribus	ācribus

25. *a.* Adjectives of the Third Declension with two endings are in part formed on -i Stems, like nouns, and in the Positive Degree, as **fortis, forte,** *strong* (II. 33); in part they are Comparatives formed on -s Stems (*13, a*), as **fortior, fortius,** *stronger* (III. 14), **melior, melius,** *better* (VI. 12): .

| | SINGULAR | | PLURAL | |
MASCULINE AND FEM.	NEUTER	MASCULINE AND FEM.	NEUTER
Nom. fortis	forte	fortēs	fortia
Gen. fortis	fortis	fortium	fortium
Dat. fortī	fortī	fortibus	fortibus
Acc. fortem	forte	fortēs or -īs	fortia
Voc. fortis	forte	fortēs	fortia
Abl. fortī	fortī	fortibus	fortibus

SINGULAR		PLURAL	
MASCULINE AND FEM.	NEUTER	MASCULINE AND FEM.	NEUTER
Nom. melior	melius	meliōrēs	meliōra
Gen. meliōris	meliōris	meliōrum	meliōrum
Dat. meliōrī	meliōrī	meliōribus	meliōribus
Acc. meliōrem	melius	meliōrēs or -īs	meliōra
Voc. melior	melius	meliōrēs	meliōra
Abl. meliōre	meliōre	meliōribus	meliōribus

b. **Plūs**, *more*, is defective, in the Singular having only the neuter forms, *Nom.* **plūs**, *Gen.* **plūris**, *Acc.* **plūs**, *Abl.* **plūre**; the Plural is declined *Nom.* **plūrēs**, **plūra**, *Gen.* **plūrium**, **plūrium**, *Dat.* **plūribus**, **plūribus**, *Acc.* **plūrēs** or **plūrīs**, **plūra**, *Abl.* **plūribus**, **plūribus**.

26. *a.* With Adjectives of the Third Declension having one ending in the Nom. Singular are included also present participles. Examples are **duplex**, *double* (II. 29), **regēns**, *ruling*, and **vetus**, *old* (1. 13):

SINGULAR		PLURAL	
MASCULINE AND FEM.	NEUTER	MASCULINE AND FEM.	NEUTER
Nom. duplex	duplex	duplicēs	duplicia
Gen. duplicis	duplicis	duplicium	duplicium
Dat. duplicī	duplicī	duplicibus	duplicibus
Acc. duplicem	duplex	duplicēs or -īs	duplicia
Voc. duplex	duplex	duplicēs	duplicia
Abl. duplicī	duplicī	duplicibus	duplicibus

SINGULAR		PLURAL	
MASCULINE AND FEM.	NEUTER	MASCULINE AND FEM.	NEUTER
Nom. regēns	regēns	regentēs	regentia
Gen. regentis	regentis	regentium	regentium
Dat. regentī	regentī	regentibus	regentibus
Acc. regentem	regēns	regentēs or -īs	regentia
Voc. regēns	regēns	regentēs	regentia
Abl. regente (participle) regentī (adjective)	regente (participle) regentī (adjective)	regentibus	regentibus

SINGULAR		PLURAL	
MASCULINE AND FEM.	NEUTER	MASCULINE AND FEM.	NEUTER
Nom. vetus	vetus	veterēs	vetera
Gen. veteris	veteris	veterum	veterum
Dat. veterī	veterī	veteribus	veteribus
Acc. veterem	vetus	veterēs	vetera
Voc. vetus	vetus	veterēs	vetera
Abl. vetere	vetere	veteribus	veteribus

b. The Adjective **prīnceps, -cipis** (I. 7) is declined like the Noun (*10, b*); the Adjectives **anceps, ancipitis** (I. 26), **particeps, -cipis**, (C. III. 60), and **praeceps, -cipitis** (II. 24), also have additional syllables in the oblique cases.

COMPARISON OF ADJECTIVES

27. *a.* Examples of the Regular Comparison of Adjectives, and of participles used as Adjectives, are:

POSITIVE	COMPARATIVE	SUPERLATIVE
altus, -a, -um, *high*	altior, altius, *higher*	altissimus, -a,-um, *very high, highest*
antīquus, -a, -um, *ancient*	antīquior, -ius	antīquissimus
fortis, -e, *brave*	fortior, fortius	fortissimus
nōbilis, -e, *noble*	nōbilior, nōbilius	nōbilissimus
ferāx, *fertile*	ferācior, ferācius	ferācissimus
potēns, *able*	potentior, potentius	potentissimus
apertus, *open, exposed*	apertior, apertius	apertissimus

b. **Novus**, *new*, lacks the Comparative, but has a Superlative, **novissimus**, *last* (I. 15).

28. *a.* Examples of Adjectives in **-er**, with Comparative in **-ior** and Superlative in **-rimus**, are:

asper, -ra, -rum, *rough*	asperior, -ius	asperrimus, -a, -um
celer, -eris, -ere, *swift*	celerior, -ius	celerrimus
crēber, -bra, -brum, *frequent*	crēbrior, crēbrius	crēberrimus
pulcher, -chra, -chrum, *beautiful*	pulchrior, -ius	pulcherrimus

b. **Vetus**, *Gen.* **veteris**, *old*, *Sup.* **viterrimus**, lacks the Comparative.

29. Six Adjectives in **-ilis** have **-limus** in the Superlative: **facilis, difficilis, gracilis, humilis, similis, dissimilis**:

facilis, -e, *easy*	facilior, facilius	facillimus, -a, -um
difficilis, -e, *difficult*	difficilior, -ius	difficillimus
humilis, -e, *low*	humilior, -ius	humillimus
similis, -e, *like*	similior, -ius	simillimus•

30. Some Adjectives form the Comparative and the Superlative by prefixing **magis**, *more*, and **maximē**, *most*, as **magis dērēctum**, *straighter* (VI. 26), and **maximē acceptus**, *very acceptable* (I. 3), **maximē frūmentāriīs**, *exceedingly fertile* (I. 10), **maximē ferī**, *most barbarous* (II. 4).

31. The Adjectives **dīves** or **dīs**, *rich* (I. 2), **honōrificus**, *complimentary* (I. 43), and **magnificus**, *splendid* (VI. 19) are thus compared:

dīves or dīs	dīvitior or dītior	dīvitissimus or dītissimus
honōrificus	honorificentior	honorificentissimus
magnificus	magnificentior	magnificentissimus

32. Several common Adjectives are irregular in Comparison :

bonus, -a, -um, *good*	melior, melius, *better*	optimus, -a, -um, *best*
malus, *bad*	peior, peius, *worse*	pessimus, *worst*
parvus, *small*	minor, minus, *less*	minimus, *least*
magnus, *great*	maior, maius, *greater*	maximus, *greatest*
multus, *much*	plūs, gen. plūris (25, b)	plūrimus, *most*

33. Several Adjectives lack the Positive, though the Stem appears in Prepositions and Adverbs; others have a Positive only in a limited or special use. Examples are :

(citrā, *on this side*)	citerior, citerius, *on this side, hither*	citimus, -a, -um, *nearest*
(ultrā, *beyond*)	ulterior, ulterius, *farther*	ultimus, *farthest*
(intrā, *within*)	interior, interius, *inner*	intimus, *inmost*
(prope, *near*)	propior, propius, *nearer*	proximus, *nearest*
(dē, *down*)	dēterior, dēterius, *inferior*	dēterrimus, *worst*
(prae, prō, *before*)	prior, prius, *former*	prīmus, *first*
posterus, *following*	posterior, *later*	postrēmus, *latest, last*
īnferus, *below*	īnferior, īnferius, *lower*	{ īnfimus, ⎫ *lowest* ⎰ { īmus, ⎭
superus, *above*	superior, superius, *higher*	{ suprēmus, *last* { summus, *highest*
exterus, *foreign* ⎱ (C. III. 43) ⎰	exterior, *outer*	extrēmus, *outermost*

ADVERBS

34. *a.* Adverbs regularly formed from Adjectives have the Positive in -ē (-ĕ in **facile**) or -ter, the Comparative in -ius, and the Superlative in -ē :

POSITIVE	COMPARATIVE	SUPERLATIVE
amplē (amplus), *fully*	amplius, *more fully*	amplissimē, *most fully*
aegrē (aeger), *ill*	aegrius	aegerrimē
mātūrē (mātūrus), *early*	mātūrius	mātūrrimē
facile (facilis), *easily*	facilius	facillimē
fortiter (fortis), *bravely*	fortius	fortissimē
audācter (audāx), *boldly*	audācius	audācissimē
ācriter (ācer), *fiercely*	ācrius	ācerrimē

b. Some Adverbs formed from Adjectives end in -ō (-ŏ in **cito**), as **continuō, subitō, prīmō**; such, with Comparative and Superlative, are :

crēbrō (crēber), *frequently*	crēbrius	crēberrimē
tūtō (tūtus), *safely*	tūtius	tūtissimē
cito (citus), *quickly*	citius	citissimē

c. A few Adverbs formed from Adjectives end in -um (Acc. Singular Neuter), as **multum (multus)**, *much* (III. 9); in -tim, as **prīvātim (prīvātus)**, *privately* (I. 17); and in -tus, as **antīquitus (antīquus)**, *in ancient times* (II. 4).

35. The following Adverbs have irregularities in Formation or in Comparison :

bene, *well*	melius, *better*	optimē, *best*
male, *ill*	peius, *worse*	pessimē, *worst*
magnopere, *greatly*	magis, *more*	maximē, *most*
multum, *much*	plūs, *more*	plūrimum, *most*
nōn multum, } parum, } *little*	minus, *less*	minimē, *least*
nūper, *recently*	—	nūperrimē, *most recently, very recently*
diū, *long*	diūtius, *longer*	diūtissimē, *longest*
saepe, *often*	saepius, *oftener*	saepissimē, *most often, oftenest*
prope, *near*	propius, *nearer*	proximē, *nearest, next*
—	potius, *rather*	potissimum, *especially, above all*
satis, *enough*	satius, *better*	
—	prius, *before*	prīmum, *first*

NUMERALS

36. The Roman Notation, and Cardinal, Ordinal, and Distributive Adjectives are presented in the following list:

ROMAN NOTATION	CARDINALS	ORDINALS	DISTRIBUTIVES
I.	ūnus, ūna, ūnum,	prīmus, *first*	singulī, *one by one*
II.	duo, duae, duo	secundus, *second*	bīnī, *two each*
III.	trēs, tria, *three*	tertius, *third*	ternī, trīnī, *three by three, three each*
IIII, or IV. }	quattuor, *four*	quārtus, *fourth*	quaternī, *four by four, four each*
V.	quīnque, *five*	quīntus, *fifth*	quīnī, *five by five, five each*
VI.	sex, *six*	sextus, *sixth*	sēnī, *six by six, six each*
VII.	septem, *seven*	septimus, *seventh*	septēnī, *by sevens, seven each*
VIII.	octō, *eight*	octāvus, *eighth*	octōnī, *by eights, eight apiece*
VIIII, or IX. }	novem, *nine*	nōnus, *ninth*	novēnī, *nine each*
X.	decem, *ten*	decimus, *tenth*	dēnī, *ten each*
XI.	ūndecim, *eleven*	ūndecimus, *eleventh*	ūndēnī, *eleven each*
XII.	duodecim, *twelve*	duodecimus, *twelfth*	duodēnī, *twelve each*
XIII.	tredecim, *thirteen*	tertius decimus, *thirteenth*	ternī dēnī, *thirteen each*
XIIII, or XIV. }	quattuordecim, *fourteen*	quārtus decimus, *fourteenth*	quaternī dēnī, *fourteen each*
XV.	quīndecim, *fifteen*	quīntus decimus, *fifteenth*	quīnī dēnī, *fifteen each*
XVI.	sēdecim, *sixteen*	sextus decimus, *sixteenth*	sēnī dēnī, *sixteen each*

ROMAN NOTATION	CARDINALS	ORDINALS	DISTRIBUTIVES
XVII.	septendecim, *seventeen*	septimus decimus, *seventeenth*	septēnī dēnī, *seventeen each*
XVIII.	duodēvīgintī, *eighteen*	duodēvīcēsimus, *eighteenth*	duodēvīcēnī, *eighteen each*
XVIIII, or XIX.	ūndēvīgintī, *nineteen*	ūndēvīcēsimus, *nineteenth*	ūndēvīcēnī, *nineteen each*
XX.	vīgintī, *twenty*	vīcēsimus, *twentieth*	vīcēnī, *twenty each*
XXI.	{ vīgintī ūnus, ūnus et vīgintī, *twenty-one*	vīcēsimus prīmus, ūnus et vīcēsimus, *twenty-first*	vīcēnī singulī, singulī et vīcēnī, *twenty-one each* }
XXII.	{ vīgintī duo, duo et vīgintī, *twenty-two*	vīcēsimus secundus, alter et vīcēsimus, *twenty-second*	vīcēnī bīnī, bīnī et vīcēnī, *twenty-two each* }
XXX.	trīgintā, *thirty*	trīcēsimus, *thirtieth*	trīcēnī, *thirty each*
XXXX, or XL.	quadrāgintā, *forty*	quadrāgēsimus, *fortieth*	quadrāgēnī, *forty each*
L.	quīnquāgintā, *fifty*	quīnquāgēsimus, *fiftieth*	quīnquāgēnī, *fifty each*
LX.	sexāgintā, *sixty*	sexāgēsimus	sexāgēnī, *sixty each*
LXX.	septuāgintā, *seventy*	septuāgēsimus, *seventieth*	septuāgēnī, *seventy each*
LXXX.	octōgintā, *eighty*	octōgēsimus, *eightieth*	octōgēnī, *eighty each*
LXXXX, or XC.	nōnāgintā, *ninety*	nōnāgēsimus, *ninetieth*	nōnāgēnī, *ninety each*
C.	centum, *one hundred*	centēsimus *one hundredth*	centēnī, *one hundred each*
CI.	{ centum ūnus, centum et ūnus, *one hundred and one*	centēsimus prīmus, centēsimus et prīmus, *hundred and first*	centēnī singulī, *one hundred and one each* }
CC.	ducentī, -ae, -a, *two hundred*	ducentēsimus, *two hundredth*	ducēnī, *two hundred each*
CCC.	trecentī, -ae, -a, *three hundred*	trecentēsimus, *three hundredth*	trecēnī, *three hundred each*
CCCC.	quadringentī, *four hundred*	quadringentēsimus, *four hundredth*	quadringēnī, *four hundred each*
D.	quīngentī, *five hundred*	quīngentēsimus, *five hundredth*	quīngēnī, *five hundred each*
DC.	sescentī, *six hundred*	sescentēsimus, *six hundredth*	sescēnī, *six hundred each*
DCC.	septingentī, *seven hundred*	septingentēsimus, *seven hundredth*	septingēnī, *seven hundred each*
DCCC.	octingentī, *eight hundred*	octingentēsimus, *eight hundredth*	octingēnī, *eight hundred each*
DCCCC.	nōngentī, *nine hundred*	nōngentēsimus, *nine hundredth*	nōngēnī, *nine hundred each*
M.	mīlle, *thousand*	mīllēsimus, *thousandth*	singula mīlia, *a thousand each*
MM.	duo mīlia, *two thousand*	bis mīllēsimus, *a two thousandth*	bīna mīlia, *two thousand each*

37. *a.* **Ūnus** is declined like **tōtus** (*23, a*).

b. **Duo** (I. 48) and **trēs** (I. 1) are declined thus:

Nom.	duo	duae	duo	trēs	tria
Gen.	duōrum	duārum	duōrum	trium	trium
Dat.	duōbus	duābus	duōbus	tribus	tribus
Acc.	duōs, duo	duās	duo	trēs, trīs	tria
Abl.	duōbus	duābus	duōbus	tribus	tribus

c. Like **duo** is declined **ambō** (V. 44), excepting -**ō** instead of -**o**.

d. **Ducentī, -ae, -a** (I. 43) and the other words for *hundreds* to **nōngentī, -ae, -a** (C. III. 71) are declined like the Plural of **bonus**, but the Genitive Plural generally ends in -**um**.

e. When Plural Nouns, which generally have a Singular Meaning, are used with a Plural Meaning, a Numeral in agreement must be Distributive; with such Nouns **trīnī** is always used instead of **ternī**. Thus, **trīnīs catēnīs**, *with three chains* (I. 53).

38. *a.* **Mīlle** (I. 22) in the Singular is used as an Indeclinable Adjective. In the Plural it is used as a Substantive and thus declined:

Nom. mīlia   *Gen.* mīlium   *Dat.* mīlibus   *Acc.* mīlia   *Abl.* mīlibus

b. The Roman numerical symbols are frequently used in place of Ordinal as well as Cardinal Adjectives. In reading Latin the proper form of the Adjective should be supplied; thus **ducenta quadrāgintā** should be read for CCXL in **mīlia passuum** CCXL (I. 2); **decimā** for X in **legiōne** X (C. III. 91).

PRONOUNS

39. *a.* The Personal Pronouns of the First and Second Person are declined as follows:

	SINGULAR	PLURAL	SINGULAR	PLURAL
Nom.	ego, *I*	nōs, *we*	tū, *thou*	vōs, *you*
Gen.	meī	nostrum, nostrī	tuī	vestrum, vestrī
Dat.	mihi	nōbīs	tibi	vōbīs
Acc.	mē	nōs	tē	vōs
Voc.	——	——	tū	vōs
Abl.	mē	nōbīs	tē	vōbīs

b. The place of a Personal Pronoun of the Third Person is taken by the demonstratives (*160, a* and *b*).

40. *a.* In the oblique cases the Pronouns of the First and Second Person may be used in a Reflexive sense, as **vōs recipite**, lit. *take yourselves back*, *retreat* (VII. 50); **meī**, may mean *of myself*, **tibi**, *to* or *for thyself*, *yourself*, etc.

b. The Reflexive Pronoun of the Third Person has no separate forms for the three genders, and is declined in Singular and Plural alike, as follows:

> Gen. **suī**, *of himself, of herself, of itself, of themselves*
> Dat. **sibi**, *to or for himself, herself, itself, themselves*
> Acc. **sē** or **sēsē**, *himself, herself, itself, themselves*
> Abl. **sē** or **sēsē**, *with, or by, himself, herself, itself, themselves*

41. The Possessive Pronouns are declined like Adjectives. They are: **meus, mea, meum,** *my;* **noster, nostra, nostrum,** *our;* **tuus, tua, tuum,** *thy;* **vester, vestra, vestrum,** *your;* and **suus, sua, suum,** *his, her, its, their.* **Suus** is used only in a Reflexive sense.

42. *a.* The Demonstrative Pronouns are **hīc,** *this, such;* **iste,** *that of yours, that;* **ille,** *that, such;* **is,** *that, he, such,* and **īdem,** *the same.*

b. **Hīc,** *this, such,* is declined thus:

	SINGULAR			PLURAL		
	MASCULINE	FEMININE	NEUTER	MASCULINE	FEMININE	NEUTER
Nom.	hīc	haec	hōc	hī	hae	haec
Gen.	huius	huius	huius	hōrum	hārum	hōrum
Dat.	huic	huic	huic	hīs	hīs	hīs
Acc.	hunc	hanc	hōc	hōs	hās	haec
Abl.	hōc	hāc	hōc	hīs	hīs	hīs

43. *a.* The Demonstrative Pronoun **ille,** *that, such,* is declined as follows:

	SINGULAR			PLURAL		
	MASCULINE	FEMININE	NEUTER	MASCULINE	FEMININE	NEUTER
Nom.	ille	illa	illud	illī	illae	illa
Gen.	illīus	illīus	illīus	illōrum	illārum	illōrum
Dat.	illī	illī	illī	illīs	illīs	illīs
Acc.	illum	illam	illud	illōs	illās	illa
Abl.	illō	illā	illō	illīs	illīs	illīs

b. The Demonstrative Pronoun **iste, ista, istud,** *that of yours, that,* is declined like **ille.**

44. The Demonstrative Pronoun **is,** *that, he, such,* is thus declined:

	SINGULAR			PLURAL		
	MASCULINE	FEMININE	NEUTER	MASCULINE	FEMININE	NEUTER
Nom.	is	ea	id	eī, iī,	eae	ea
Gen.	eius	eius	eius	eōrum	eārum	eōrum
Dat.	eī	eī	eī	eīs, iīs	eīs, iīs	eīs, iīs
Acc.	eum	eam	id	eōs	eās	ea
Abl.	eō	eā	eō	eīs, iīs	eīs, iīs	eīs, iīs

45. The Demonstrative Pronoun **īdem,** *the same,* is declined as follows:

	SINGULAR			PLURAL		
	MASCULINE	FEMININE	NEUTER	MASCULINE	FEMININE	NEUTER
Nom.	īdem	eadem	idem	eīdem, iīdem, *or* īdem	eaedem	eadem
Gen.	eiusdem	eiusdem	eiusdem	eōrundem	eārundem	eōrundem
Dat.	eīdem	eīdem	eīdem	eīsdem, iīsdem, *or* īsdem	eīsdem, iīsdem, *or* īsdem	eīsdem, iīsdem, *or* īsdem
Acc.	eundem	eandem	idem	eōsdem	eāsdem	eadem
Abl.	eōdem	eādem	eōdem	eīsdem, iīsdem, *or* īsdem	eīsdem, iīsdem, *or* īsdem	eīsdem, iīsdem, *or* īsdem

46. The Intensive Pronoun **ipse**, *self*, is thus declined:

	SINGULAR			PLURAL		
	MASCULINE	FEMININE	NEUTER	MASCULINE	FEMININE	NEUTER
Nom.	ipse	ipsa	ipsum	ipsī	ipsae	ipsa
Gen.	ipsīus	ipsīus	ipsīus	ipsōrum	ipsārum	ipsōrum
Dat.	ipsī	ipsī	ipsī	ipsīs	ipsīs	ipsīs
Acc.	ipsum	ipsam	ipsum	ipsōs	ipsās	ipsa
Abl.	ipsō	ipsā	ipsō	ipsīs	ipsīs	ipsīs

47. The Relative Pronoun **quī**, *who, which*, is declined as follows:

	SINGULAR			PLURAL		
	MASCULINE	FEMININE	NEUTER	MASCULINE	FEMININE	NEUTER
Nom.	quī	quae	quod	quī	quae	quae
Gen.	cuius	cuius	cuius	quōrum	quārum	quōrum
Dat.	cui	cui	cui	quibus	quibus	quibus
Acc.	quem	quam	quod	quōs	quās	quae
Abl.	quō	quā	quō	quibus	quibus	quibus

48. *a.* The Substantive Interrogative Pronoun is **quis, quid**, *who? what?* It is declined as follows:

	SINGULAR		PLURAL		
	MASC. AND FEM.	NEUTER	MASCULINE	FEMININE	NEUTER
Nom.	quis	quid	quī	quae	quae
Gen.	cuius	cuius	quōrum	quārum	quōrum
Dat.	cui	cui	quibus	quibus	quibus
Acc.	quem	quid	quōs	quās	quae
Abl.	quō	quō	quibus	quibus	quibus

b. The Adjective Interrogative Pronoun is **quī, quae, quod**, *what?* as **quī numerus**, *what number?* (I. 29). It is declined like the Relative Pronoun (*47*).

c. Interrogative **quis** and **quī** may be strengthened by -**nam**, as **quibusnam manibus**, *by what hands, pray?* (II. 30).

49. *a.* The Indefinite Pronouns follow the Declension of the Relative and Interrogative Pronouns, but only the Pronominal Part of the Compounds is declined. The following Indefinite Pronouns are used by Caesar, in both Substantive and Adjective forms:

SUBSTANTIVE FORMS			ADJECTIVE FORMS			
MASC. AND FEM.	NEUT.		MASC.	FEM.	NEUT.	
quis *or* quī (Masc.)	quid	{ *any one, anything*	quī *or* quis *Nom.* and *acc.* Pl. Neut., quae *or* qua	quae *or* qua	quod	} *any*
aliquis aliquī (V. 26)	aliquid	{ *some one, something*	aliquī	aliqua	aliquod	} *any*
quispiam	quidpiam	{ *some one, some-thing*	quispiam	quaepiam	quodpiam	} *some*
quisquam	quicquam	{ *any one, anything at all*	quisquam		quicquam	} *any (rare)*
(Plural lacking.)			(Plural lacking.)			
quisque	quidque	{ *each one, each thing*	quisque	quaeque	quodque	} *each*
quīvīs quaevīs quidvīs *acc.* quem- quam- quid- vīs vīs vīs		{ *any one, anything you please*	quīvīs quaevīs quodvīs *acc.* quemvīs quamvīs quod-vīs			} *any you please*
quīdam quaedam quiddam *acc.* quen- quan- quid-dam dam dam		} *a certain person, or thing*	quīdam quaedam quoddam *acc.* quen- quan- quod-dam dam dam			} *a cer-tain*

b. The Indefinite Pronoun **quis, quī,** is used by Caesar only after **sī, nisī, seu, nē, neu,** and **ubi.**

50. *a.* The Indefinite Relative **quīcumque, quaecumque, quodcumque,** *whoever, whatever,* the first part **quī-** being declined like the relative **quī,** is used both as an Adjective and as a Substantive; as **quaecumque bella,** *whatever wars* (I. 44), **quīcumque bellum īnferant,** *whoever,* or *no matter who, should wage war* (IV. 7).

b. The parts of the Indefinite Relative **quisquis, quidquid** or **quicquid,** *whoever, whatever,* are both declined like **quis** (*48*), but only **quisquis, quicquid** (II. 17), and **quōquō** are in common use.

51. Caesar uses two compounds of **uter** (*23, a*) with the force of Indefinite Pronouns, **uterque, utraque, utrumque** (**utrīusque,** *etc.*), *each of two,* Plural *both, the two;* and **alteruter, alterutra, alterutrum,** *one or the other,* as **alterutrō exercitū,** *the one or the other army* (C. III. 90).

VERBS [1]

52. The verb **sum** is inflected as follows:

PRINCIPAL PARTS:

PRES. INDICATIVE   PRES. INFINITIVE   PERF. INDICATIVE   FUT. PART. (Perf. Part. lacking)

sum   **esse**   **fuī**   **futūrus**

INDICATIVE MOOD

SUBJUNCTIVE

PRESENT TENSE

PRESENT

SINGULAR	PLURAL	SINGULAR	PLURAL
sum, *I am*	**sumus**, *we are*	**sim**	**sī**mus
es, *thou art*	e**stis**, *you are*	**sī**s	**sī**tis
est, *he (she, it) is*	**sunt**, *they are*	**sit**	**sint**

IMPERFECT

IMPERFECT

eram, *I was*	e**rāmus**, *we were*	**essem**	es**sēmus**
e**rās**, *thou wast*	e**rātis**, *you were*	es**sēs**	es**sētis**
e**rat**, *he was*	e**rant**, *they were*	**esset**	**essent**

FUTURE

e**rō**, *I shall be*	e**rimus**, *we shall be*
e**ris**, *thou wilt be*	e**ritis**, *you will be*
e**rit**, *he will be*	e**runt**, *they will be*

PERFECT

PERFECT

fuī, *I have been, I was*	f**uimus**, *we have been, we were*	**fuerim**	**fuerīmus**
fuistī, *thou hast been, you were*	**fuistis**, *you have been, you were*	**fuerīs**	**fuerītis**
fuit, *he has been, he was*	**fuērunt**, } *they have been, they were* **fuēre**, }	**fuerit**	**fuerint**

PLUPERFECT

PLUPERFECT

fueram, *I had been*	**fuerāmus**, *we had been*	**fuissem**	**fuissēmus**
fuerās, *thou hadst, you had, been*	**fuerātis**, *you had been*	**fuissēs** **fuisset**	**fuissētis** **fuissent**
fuerat, *he had been*	**fuerant**, *they had been*		

FUTURE PERFECT

fuerō, *I shall have been*	**fuerimus**, *we shall have been*
fueris, *thou wilt have been*	**fueritis**, *you will have been*
fuerit, *he will have been*	**fuerint**, *they will have been*

---

[1] Since the Principal Parts of all the Verbs in the Latin Text of this book are given in the Vocabulary, it has not been thought necessary to extend this outline by presenting either a List of Verbs or a discussion of the Stems.

IMPERATIVE		INFINITIVE

IMPERATIVE

Pres. es, *be thou* este, *be ye*
Fut. estō, *thou* estōte, *ye shall be*
    shalt be suntō, *they shall be*
  estō, *he shall be*

INFINITIVE

Pres. esse, *to be*
Perf. fuisse, *to have been*
Fut. futūrus esse, *or* fore,
    to be about to be

PARTICIPLE

Fut. futūrus, *about to be*

FIRST CONJUGATION

53. Verbs of the First Conjugation are inflected like **amō,** *I love.*

PRINCIPAL PARTS:

PRES. INDICATIVE	PRES. INFINITIVE	PERF. INDICATIVE	PERF. PASS. PARTICIPLE
Active. amō	amāre	amāvī	amātus

	PRES. INDICATIVE	PRES. INFINITIVE	PERF. INDICATIVE
Passive. amor	amārī		amātus sum

ACTIVE VOICE
INDICATIVE MOOD
PRESENT TENSE

SINGULAR	PLURAL
amō, *I love*	amāmus, *we love*
amās, *you love*	amātis, *you love*
amat, *he loves*	amant, *they love*

IMPERFECT

amābam, *I was loving*	amābāmus, *we were loving*
amābās, *you were loving*	amābātis, *you were loving*
amābat, *he was loving*	amābant, *they were loving*

FUTURE

amābō, *I shall love*	amābimus, *we shall love*
amābis, *thou wilt, you will, love*	amābitis, *you will love*
amābit, *he will love*	amābunt, *they will love*

PERFECT

amāvī, *I have loved, I loved*	amāvimus, *we have loved, we loved*
amāvistī, *you have loved, you loved*	amāvistis, *you have loved, you loved*
amāvit, *he has loved, he loved*	amāvērunt, -ēre, *they have loved, they loved*

PASSIVE VOICE
INDICATIVE MOOD
PRESENT TENSE

SINGULAR	PLURAL
I am loved, etc.	
amor	amāmur
amāris *or* -re	amāminī
amātur	amantur

IMPERFECT

I was loved, etc.

amābar	amābāmur
amābāris *or* -re	amābāminī
amābātur	amābantur

FUTURE

I shall be loved, etc.

amābor	amābimur
amāberis, *or* -re	amābiminī
amābitur	amābuntur

PERFECT

I have been loved or *I was loved,* etc.

amātus (-a, -um) sum	amātī (-ae, -a) sumus
amātus es	amātī estis
amātus est	amātī sunt

ACTIVE VOICE	PASSIVE VOICE

INDICATIVE MOOD   ## INDICATIVE MOOD

PLUPERFECT

amāveram, *I had loved,* amāverāmus, *we had loved*
amāverās, *you had loved* amāverātis, *you had loved*
amāverat, *he had loved* amāverant, *they had loved*

PLUPERFECT

I had been loved, etc.

amātus erām [1]	amātī erāmus
amātus erās	amātī erātis
amātus erat	amātī erant

FUTURE PERFECT

amāverō, *I shall have loved* amāverimus, *we shall have loved*
amāveris, *you will have loved* amāveritis, *you will have loved*
amāverit, *he will have loved* amāverint, *they will have loved*

FUTURE PERFECT

I shall have been loved

amātus erō [1]	amātī erimus
amātus eris	amātī eritis
amātus erit	amātī erunt

SUBJUNCTIVE   ## SUBJUNCTIVE

PRESENT   ### PRESENT

SINGULAR	PLURAL	SINGULAR	PLURAL
I may love, let us love, etc.		*I may be loved,* etc.	
amem	amēmus	amer	amēmur
amēs	amētis	amēris, *or* -re	amēminī
amet	ament	amētur	amentur

IMPERFECT   ### IMPERFECT

I might love		*I might be loved*	
amārem	amārēmus	amārer	amārēmur
amārēs	amārētis	amārēris, *or* -re	amārēminī
amāret	amārent	amārētur	amārentur

PERFECT   ### PERFECT

I may have loved		*I may have been loved*	
amāverim	amāverīmus	amātus sim [2]	amātī sīmus
amāveris	amāverītis	amātus sīs	amātī sītis
amāverit	amāverint	amātus sit	amātī sint

PLUPERFECT   ### PLUPERFECT

I might have loved		*I might have been loved*	
amāvissem	amāvissēmus	amātus essem [2]	amātī essēmus
amāvissēs	amāvissētis	amātus essēs	amātī essētis
amāvisset	amāvissent	amātus esset	amātī essent

---

[1] In the Perfect Passive fuī, fuistī, fuit, *etc.,* are sometimes used for sum es, est, *etc.,* and fueram, fuerās, fuerō, *etc.,* for eram, erō, *etc.*

[2] Here fuerim, fuerīs, fuissem, *etc.,* are sometimes used for sim, essem, *etc.*

ACTIVE VOICE		PASSIVE VOICE	

IMPERATIVE

IMPERATIVE

Pres. amā, *love thou* amāte, *love ye*
Fut. amātō, *thou shalt love* amātōte, *ye shall love*
 amātō, *he shall love* amantō, *they shall love*

SINGULAR

Pres. amāre, *be thou loved*
Fut. amātor, *thou shalt be loved*
 amātor, *he shall be loved*

PLURAL

Pres. amāminī, *be ye loved*
Fut. amantor, *they shall be loved*

INFINITIVE

INFINITIVE

Pres. amāre, *to love*
Perf. amāvisse, *to have loved*
Fut. amātūrus esse, *to be about to love*

Pres. amārī, *to be loved*
Perf. amātus esse, *to have been loved*
Fut. amātum īrī, *to be about to be loved*

PARTICIPLE

PARTICIPLE

Pres. amāns, *loving* (*Gen.* amantis)
Fut. amātūrus, *about to love*

Perfect. amātus, *loved, having been loved*
Gerundive. amandus, *to be loved, worthy to be loved*

GERUND

SUPINE

Gen. amandī, *of loving*
Dat. amandō, *for loving*
Acc. amandum, *loving* *Acc.* amātum, *to love*
Abl. amandō, *by loving* *Abl.* amātū, *to love, to be loved*

SECOND CONJUGATION

54. Verbs of the Second Conjugation are conjugated like **moneō**, *I advise.*

PRINCIPAL PARTS :

PRES. INDICATIVE	PRES. INFINITIVE	PERF. INDICATIVE	PERF. PASS. PARTICIPLE
Active. moneō	monēre	monuī	monitus

PRES. INDICATIVE	PRES. INFINITIVE	PERF. INDICATIVE	
Passive. moneor	monērī	monitus sum	

ACTIVE VOICE		PASSIVE VOICE	

INDICATIVE MOOD

INDICATIVE MOOD

PRESENT TENSE

PRESENT TENSE

SINGULAR	PLURAL	SINGULAR	PLURAL
I advise, etc.		*I am advised,* etc.	
moneō	monēmus	moneor	monēmur
monēs	monētis	monēris or -re	monēminī
monet	monent	monētur	monentur

ACTIVE VOICE		PASSIVE VOICE	

INDICATIVE MOOD

INDICATIVE MOOD

IMPERFECT

I was advising, or *I advised*, etc.

monēbam	monēbāmus
monēbās	monēbātis
monēbat	monēbant

IMPERFECT

I was advised, etc.

monēbar	monēbāmur
monēbāris, *or* -re	monēbāminī
monēbātur	monēbantur

FUTURE

I shall advise

monēbō	monēbimus
monēbis	monēbitis
monēbit	monēbunt

FUTURE

I shall be advised

monēbor	monēbimur
monēberis, *or* -re	monēbiminī
monēbitur	monēbuntur

PERFECT

I have advised, or *I advised*

monuī	monuimus
monuistī	monuistis
monuit	monuērunt, *or* -ēre

PERFECT

I have been advised, I was advised

monitus sum	monitī sumus
monitus es	monitī estis
monitus est	monitī sunt

PLUPERFECT

I had advised

monueram	monuerāmus
monuerās	monuerātis
monuerat	monuerant

PLUPERFECT

I had been advised

monitus eram	monitī erāmus
monitus erās	monitī erātis
monitus erat	monitī erant

FUTURE PERFECT

I shall have advised

monuerō	monuerimus
monueris	monueritis
monuerit	monuerint

FUTURE PERFECT

I shall have been advised

monitus erō	monitī erimus
monitus eris	monitī eritis
monitus erit	monitī erunt

SUBJUNCTIVE

SUBJUNCTIVE

PRESENT

I may advise, let us advise, etc.

moneam	moneāmus
moneās	moneātis
moneat	moneant

PRESENT

I may be advised, etc.

monear	moneāmur
moneāris, *or* -re	moneāminī
moneātur	moneantur

IMPERFECT

I might advise, you would advise

monērem	monērēmus
monērēs	monērētis
monēret	monērent

IMPERFECT

I might be advised

monērer	monērēmur
monērēris, *or* -re	monērēminī
monērētur	monērentur

ACTIVE VOICE

SUBJUNCTIVE

PERFECT

I may have advised, etc.

monuerim	monuerīmus
monuerīs	monuerītis
monuerit	monuerint

PLUPERFECT

I might have advised, you would have advised, etc.

monuissem	monuissēmus
monuissēs	monuissētis
monuisset	monuissent

IMPERATIVE

Pres. monē, *advise thou*	monēte, *advise ye*
Fut. monētō, *thou shalt advise*	monētōte, *ye shall advise*
monētō, *he shall advise*	monentō, *they shall advise*

INFINITIVE

Pres. monēre, *to advise*	
Perf. monuisse, *to have advised*	
Fut. monitūrus esse, *to be about to advise*	

PARTICIPLE

Pres. monēns, *advising* (*Gen.* monentis)	
Fut. monitūrus, *about to advise*	

PASSIVE VOICE

SUBJUNCTIVE

PERFECT

I may have been advised, etc.

monitus sim	monitī sīmus
monitus sīs	monitī sītis
monitus sit	monitī sint

PLUPERFECT

I might have been advised

monitus essem	monitī essēmus
monitus essēs	monitī essētis
monitus esset	monitī essent

IMPERATIVE

Pres. monēre, *be thou advised*	monēminī, *be ye advised*
Fut. monētor, *thou shalt be advised*	
monētor, *he shall be advised*	monentor, *they shall be advised*

INFINITIVE

Pres. monērī, *to be advised*	
Perf. monitus esse, *to have been advised*	
Fut. monitum īrī, *to be about to be advised*	

PARTICIPLE

Perfect, monitus, *advised, having been advised*	
Gerundive, monendus, *to be advised, worthy to be advised*	

GERUND

Gen. monendī, *of advising*	
Dat. monendō, *for advising*	
Acc. monendum, *advising*	
Abl. monendō, *by advising,*	

SUPINE

Acc. monitum, *to advise*	
Abl. monitū, *to advise, to be advised*	

THIRD CONJUGATION

55. Verbs of the Third Conjugation are inflected like **regō**, *I rule.*

PRINCIPAL PARTS:

	PRES. INDICATIVE	PRES. INFINITIVE	PERF. INDICATIVE	PERF. PASS. PARTIC.
Active.	regō	regere	rēxī	rēctus

	PRES. INDICATIVE	PRES. INFINITIVE	PERF. INDICATIVE
Passive.	regor	regī	rēctus sum

ACTIVE VOICE

INDICATIVE MOOD

PRESENT TENSE

I rule, etc.

SINGULAR	PLURAL
regō	regimus
regis	regitis
regit	regunt

IMPERFECT

I was ruling, or *I ruled*

regēbam	regēbāmus
regēbās	regēbātis
regēbat	regēbant

FUTURE

I shall rule

regam	regēmus
regēs	regētis
reget	regent

PERFECT

I have ruled, or *I ruled*

rēxī	rēximus
rēxistī	rēxistis
rēxit	rēxērunt, *or* -ēre

PLUPERFECT

I had ruled

rēxeram	rēxerāmus
rēxerās	rēxerātis
rēxerat	rēxerant

FUTURE PERFECT

I shall have ruled

rēxerō	rēxerimus
rēxeris	rēxeritis
rēxerit	rēxerint

PASSIVE VOICE

INDICATIVE MOOD

PRESENT TENSE

I am ruled, etc.

SINGULAR	PLURAL
regor	regimur
regeris *or* -re	regiminī
regitur	reguntur

IMPERFECT

I was ruled

regēbar	regēbāmur
regēbāris, *or* -re	regēbāminī
regēbātur	regēbantur

FUTURE

I shall be ruled

regar	regēmur
regēris, *or* -re	regēminī
regētur	regentur

PERFECT

I have been ruled, or *I was ruled*

rēctus sum	rēctī sumus
rēctus es	rēctī estis
rēctus est	rēctī sunt

PLUPERFECT

I had been ruled

rēctus eram	rēctī erāmus
rēctus erās	rēctī erātis
rēctus erat	rēctī erant

FUTURE PERFECT

I shall have been ruled

rēctus erō	rēctī erimus
rēctus eris	rēctī eritis
rēctus erit	rēctī erunt

ACTIVE VOICE		PASSIVE VOICE	
SUBJUNCTIVE		SUBJUNCTIVE	

PRESENT
I may rule, let us rule, etc.

SINGULAR	PLURAL
regam	regāmus
regās	regātis
regat	regant

PRESENT
I may be ruled, etc.

SINGULAR	PLURAL
regar	regāmur
regāris, *or* -re	regāminī
regātur	regantur

IMPERFECT
I might rule, you would rule, etc.

regerem	regerēmus
regerēs	regerētis
regeret	regerent

IMPERFECT
I might be ruled, you would be ruled

regerer	regerēmur
regerēris, *or* -re	regerēminī
regerētur	regerentur

PERFECT
I may have ruled

rēxerim	rēxerīmus
rēxerīs	rēxerītis
rēxerit	rēxerint

PERFECT
I may have been ruled

rēctus sim	rēctī sīmus
rēctus sīs	rēctī sītis
rēctus sit	rēctī sint

PLUPERFECT
I might have ruled, you would have ruled

rēxissem	rēxissēmus
rēxissēs	rēxissētis
rēxisset	rēxissent

PLUPERFECT
I might have been ruled, you would have been ruled

rēctus essem	rectī essēmus
rēctus essēs	rectī essētis
rēctus esset	rectī essent

IMPERATIVE

Pres.	rege, *rule thou*	regite, *rule ye*
Fut.	regitō, *thou shalt rule*	regitōte, *ye shall rule*
	regitō, *he shall rule*	reguntō, *they shall rule*

IMPERATIVE

Pres.	regere, *be thou ruled*	regiminī, *be ye ruled*
Fut.	regitor, *thou shalt be ruled*	
	regitor, *he shall be ruled*	reguntor, *they shall be ruled*

INFINITIVE   PARTICIPLE

	INFINITIVE		PARTICIPLE
Pres.	regere, *to rule*	Pres.	regēns, *ruling* (Gen. regentis)
Perf.	rēxisse, *to have ruled*		
Fut.	rēctūrus esse, *to be about to rule*	Fut.	rēctūrus, *about to rule*

INFINITIVE   PARTICIPLE

	INFINITIVE	PARTICIPLE
Pres.	regī, *to be ruled*	Perfect, rēctus, *ruled, having been ruled*
Perf.	rēctus esse, *to have been ruled*	Gerundive regendus, *to be ruled, deserving to be ruled*
Fut.	rēctum īrī, *to be about to be ruled*	

ACTIVE VOICE

GERUND	SUPINE
Gen. **regendī**, *of ruling*	
Dat. **regendō**, *for ruling*	
Acc. **regendum**, *ruling*	*Acc.* **rēctum**, *to rule*
Abl. **regendō**, *by ruling*	*Abl.* **rēctū**, *to rule, to be ruled*

56. Verbs in **-iō** of the Third Conjugation have in the present system forms in which **-i-** is followed by a vowel; these forms are like the corresponding forms of the Fourth Conjugation. An example is **capiō**, *I take.*

PRINCIPAL PARTS:

	PRES. INDICATIVE	PRES. INFINITIVE	PERF. INDICATIVE	PERF. PASS. PARTIC.
Active.	capiō	capere	cēpī	captus

	PRES. INDICATIVE	PRES. INFINITIVE	PERF. INDICATIVE	
Passive.	capior	capī	captus sum	

ACTIVE VOICE		PASSIVE VOICE	
INDICATIVE MOOD		**INDICATIVE MOOD**	
PRESENT TENSE		PRESENT TENSE	
SINGULAR	PLURAL	SINGULAR	PLURAL
capiō	capimus	capior	capimur
capis	capitis	caperis, *or* -re	capiminī
capit	capiunt	capitur	capiuntur
IMPERFECT		IMPERFECT	
capiēbam	capiēbāmus	capiēbar	capiēbāmur
capiēbās	capiēbātis	capiēbāris	capiēbāminī
capiēbat	capiēbant	capiēbātur	capiēbantur
FUTURE		FUTURE	
capiam	capiēmus	capiar	capiēmur
capiēs	capiētis	capiēris	capiēminī
capiet	capient	capiētur	capientur
PERFECT		PERFECT	
cēpī	cēpimus	captus sum	captī sumus
cēpistī	cēpistis	captus es	captī estis
cēpit	cēpērunt *or* -ēre	captus est	captī sunt
PLUPERFECT		PLUPERFECT	
cēperam	cēperāmus	captus eram	captī erāmus
cēperās	cēperātis	captus erās	captī erātis
cēperat	cēperant	captus erat	captī erant
FUTURE PERFECT		FUTURE PERFECT	
cēperō	cēperimus	captus erō	captī erimus
cēperis	cēperitis	captus eris	captī eritis
cēperit	cēperint	captus erit	captī erunt

ACTIVE VOICE		PASSIVE VOICE	
SUBJUNCTIVE		**SUBJUNCTIVE**	
PRESENT		PRESENT	
SINGULAR	PLURAL	SINGULAR	PLURAL
capiam	capiāmus	capiar	capiāmur
capiās	capiātis	capiāris, *or* -re	capiāminī
capiat	capiant	capiātur	capiantur
IMPERFECT		IMPERFECT	
caperem	caperēmus	caperer	caperēmur
caperēs	caperētis	caperēris	caperēminī
caperet	caperent	caperētur	caperentur
PERFECT		PERFECT	
cēperim	cēperīmus	captus sim	captī sīmus
cēperis	cēperītis	captus sīs	captī sītis
cēperit	cēperint	captus sit	captī sint
PLUPERFECT		PLUPERFECT	
cēpissem	cēpissēmus	captus essem	captī essēmus
cēpissēs	cēpissētis	captus essēs	captī essētis
cēpisset	cēpissent	captus esset	captī essent

IMPERATIVE			IMPERATIVE	
Pres.	cape	capite	*Pres.* capere	capiminī
Fut.	capitō	capitōte	*Fut.* capitor	
	capitō	capiuntō	capitor	capiuntor

INFINITIVE	PARTICIPLE	INFINITIVE	PARTICIPLE
Pres. capere	*Pres.* capiēns	*Pres.* capī	
Perf. cēpisse	(*Gen.* capientīs)	*Perf.* captus esse	*Perf.* captus
Fut. captūrus esse	*Fut.* captūrus	*Fut.* captum īrī	*Ger.* capien-dus

GERUND		SUPINE	
Gen.	capiendī		
Dat.	capiendō		
Acc.	capiendum	*Acc.*	captum
Abl.	capiendō	*Abl.*	captū

57. *a.* Inflected like **capiō** are its Compounds, **accipiō, con-cipiō, dēcipiō, excipiō, incipiō, percipiō, praecipiō, recipiō,** and **suscipiō.**

b. The following verbs in -iō, inflected like **capiō,** are used by Caesar: **cupiō,** *ardently desire, wish well to* (I. 18, etc.); **faciō,** *do, make,* and its Compounds **afficiō, cōnficiō, dēficiō, efficiō, īnficiō, perficiō, praeficiō, prōficiō, reficiō** and **sufficiō;** **ēliciō,** *entice* (V. 50), **fodiō,** *dig* (VII. 73) and its Compounds **effodiō** (VII. 4), **īnfodiō** (VII. 73), **subfodiō** (IV. 12), **trānsfodiō** (VII. 82); **fugiō,** *run away,* and its Compounds **cōnfugiō, dēfugiō, effugiō, perfugiō, prōfugiō,** and **refugiō**; **iaciō,** *throw,* and its Compounds **abiciō, coniciō, dēiciō, disiciō, ēiciō, iniciō, obiciō, prōiciō, reiciō,** and **subiciō**; **pariō,** *bring forth, gain* (C. III. 82); two Compounds of **quatiō,** *shake,* **discutiō** (VII. 8) and **percutiō** (V. 44); five Compounds of **rapiō,** *seize,* **arripiō** (V. 33), **corripiō, dīripiō, ēripiō** and **praeripiō**; **sapiō,** *have sense* (V. 30); **alliciō,** *attract* (V. 55, VII. 31); and Compounds of **speciō,** *look,* **cōnspiciō, dēspiciō, perspiciō, prōspiciō,** and **respiciō.**

c. Similar in inflection to the Passive of **capiō** are the following Deponent Verbs in **-ior** used by Caesar: **patior,** *suffer* (inflected below, *60*), and its Compound **perpetior** (C. III. 47); **morior,** *die* (I. 4, etc.); and the following Compounds of **gradior,** *step:* **aggredior, congredior, dēgredior, dīgredior, ēgredior, ingredior, praegredior, prōgredior,** and **regredior.**

FOURTH CONJUGATION

58. Verbs of the Fourth Conjugation are inflected like **audiō,** *I hear.*

PRINCIPAL PARTS:

	PRES. INDICATIVE	PRES. INFINITIVE	PERF. INDICATIVE	PERF. PASS. PARTIC.
Active.	audiō	audīre	audīvī	audītus
	PRES. INDICATIVE	PRES. INFINITIVE	PERF. INDICATIVE	
Passive.	audior	audīrī	audītus sum	

ACTIVE VOICE

INDICATIVE MOOD

PRESENT TENSE

I hear, etc.

SINGULAR	PLURAL
audiō	audīmus
audīs	audītis
audit	audiunt

IMPERFECT

I was hearing, or *I heard*

audiēbam	audiēbāmus
audiēbās	audiēbātis
audiēbat	audiēbant

FUTURE

I shall hear

audiam	audiēmus
audiēs	audiētis
audiet	audient

PASSIVE VOICE

INDICATIVE MOOD

PRESENT TENSE

I am heard, etc.

SINGULAR	PLURAL
audior	audīmur
audīris, *or* -re	audīminī
audītur	audiuntur

IMPERFECT

I was heard

audiēbar	audiēbāmur
audiēbāris, *or* -re	audiēbāminī
audiēbātur	audiēbantur

FUTURE

I shall be heard

audiar	audiēmur
audiēris, *or* -re	audiēminī
audiētur	audientur

<table>
<tr><td>

ACTIVE VOICE

INDICATIVE MOOD

PERFECT

I have heard, or I heard

audīvī	audīvimus
audīvistī	audīvistīs
audīvit	audīvērunt, *or* -ēre

PLUPERFECT

I had heard

audīveram	audīverāmus
audīverās	audīverātis
audīverat	audīverant

FUTURE PERFECT

I shall have heard

audīverō	audīverimus
audīveris	audīveritis
audīverit	audīverint

</td><td>

PASSIVE VOICE

INDICATIVE MOOD

PERFECT

I have been heard, or I was heard

audītus sum	audītī sumus
audītus es	audītī estis
audītus est	audītī sunt

PLUPERFECT

I had been heard

audītus eram	audītī erāmus
audītus erās	audītī erātis
audītus erat	audītī erant

FUTURE PERFECT

I shall have been heard

audītus erō	audītī erimus
audītus eris	audītī eritis
audītus erit	audītī erunt

</td></tr>
</table>

SUBJUNCTIVE

PRESENT

I may hear, let us hear, etc.

SINGULAR	PLURAL
audiam	audiāmus
audiās	audiātis
audiat	audiant

IMPERFECT

I might hear, you would hear

audīrem	audīrēmus
audīrēs	audīrētis
audīret	audīrent

PERFECT

I may have heard

audīverim	audīverīmus
audīverīs	audīverītis
audīverit	audīverint

PLUPERFECT

I might have heard, you would have heard

audīvissem	audīvissēmus
audīvissēs	audīvissētis
audivisset	audīvissent

SUBJUNCTIVE

PRESENT

I may be heard, let us be heard, etc.

SINGULAR	PLURAL
audiar	audiāmur
audiāris, *or* -re	audiāminī
audiātur	audiantur

IMPERFECT

I might be heard, you would be heard

audīrer	audīrēmur
audīrēris, *or* -re	audīrēminī
audīrētur	audīrentur

PERFECT

I may have been heard

audītus sim	audītī sīmus
audītus sīs	audītī sītis
audītus sit	audītī sint

PLUPERFECT

I might have been heard, you would have been heard

audītus essem	audītī essēmus
audītus essēs	audītī essētis
audītus esset	audītī essent

ACTIVE VOICE		PASSIVE VOICE	
IMPERATIVE		**IMPERATIVE**	

Pres. audī, *hear thou*　　audīte, *hear ye*　　*Pres.* audīre, *be thou heard*　　audīminī, *be ye heard*

Fut. audītō, *thou shalt hear*　　audītōte, *ye shall hear*　　*Fut.* audītor, *thou shalt be heard*

　　audītō, *he shall hear*　　audiuntō, *they shall hear*　　audītor, *he shall be heard*　　audiuntor, *they shall be heard*

INFINITIVE	**PARTICIPLE**	**INFINITIVE**	**PARTICIPLE**

Pres. audīre, *to hear*　　*Pres.* audiēns, *hearing (Gen.* audientis)　　*Pres.* audīrī, *to be heard*　　*Perf.* audītus, *heard, having been heard*

Perf. audīvisse, *to have heard*　　　　*Perf.* audītus esse, *to have been heard*

Fut. audītūrus esse, *to be about to hear*　　*Fut.* audītūrus, *about to hear*　　*Fut.* audītum īrī, *to be about to be heard*　　*Ger.* audiendus, *to be heard, worthy to be heard*

GERUND	**SUPINE**

Gen. audiendī, *of hearing*

Dat. audiendō, *for hearing*

Acc. audiendum, *hearing*　　*Acc.* audītum, *to hear*

Abl. audiendō, *by hearing*　　*Abl.* audītū, *to hear, to be heard*

DEPONENT VERBS

59. *a.* The forms of Deponent Verbs are generally Passive, while the meaning is Active.

b. The Passive meaning is found in the Gerundive of Deponent Verbs, and sometimes in the Perfect Participle; as dīmēnsō, *measured off* (II. 19); dēpopulātīs, *having been ravaged* (I. 11).

c. Deponent Verbs have in the Active form a Future Infinitive, Present and Future Participles, Gerund, and Supine.

60. Deponent Verbs in the four conjugations are inflected, as **hortor**, *urge* (I. 19); **vereor**, *fear* (I. 19); **sequor**, *follow* (I. 22), and **patior**, *suffer, allow* (I. 6, 9); **largior**, *give freely* (I. 18):

INDICATIVE MOOD

	FIRST CONJUGATION	SECOND CONJUGATION	THIRD CONJUGATION	THIRD CONJ. IN -ior	FOURTH CONJUGATION
Pres.	hortor	vereor	sequor	patior	largior
	hortāris, -re	verēris, -re	sequeris, -re	pateris, -re	largīris, -re
	hortātur	verētur	sequitur	patitur	largītur
	hortāmur	verēmur	sequimur	patimur	largīmur
	hortāminī	verēminī	sequiminī	patiminī	largīminī
	hortantur	verentur	sequuntur	patiuntur	largiuntur
Imp.	hortābar, *etc.*	verēbar, *etc.*	sequēbar, *etc.*	patiēbar, *etc.*	largiēbar, *etc.*
Fut.	hortābor	verēbor	sequar	patiar	largiar
Perf.	hortātus sum	veritus sum	secūtus sum	passus sum	largītus sum
Plup.	hortātus eram	veritus eram	secūtus eram	passus eram	largītus eram
F. P.	hortātus erō	veritus erō	secūtus erō	passus erō	largītus erō

SUBJUNCTIVE

Pres.	horter	verear	sequar	patiar	largiar
Imp.	hortārer	verērer	sequerer	paterer	largīrer
Perf.	hortātus sim	veritus sim	secūtus sim	passus sim	largītus sim
Plup.	hortātus essem	veritus essem	secūtus essem	passus essem	largītus essem

IMPERATIVE

Pres.	hortāre	verēre	sequere	patere	largīre
Fut.	hortātor	verētor	sequitor	patitor	largītor

INFINITIVE

Pres.	hortārī	verērī	sequī	patī	largīrī
Perf.	hortātus esse	veritus esse	secūtus esse	passus esse	largītus esse
Fut.	hortātūrus esse	veritūrus esse	secūtūrus esse	passūrus esse	largītūrus esse

PARTICIPLES

Pres.	hortāns	verēns	sequēns	patiēns	largiēns
Fut.	hortātūrus	veritūrus	secūtūrus	passūrus	largītūrus
Perf.	hortātus	veritus	secūtus	passus	largītus
Ger.	hortandus	verendus	sequendus	patiendus	largiendus

GERUND

Gen.	hortandī	verendī	sequendī	patiendī	largiendī
Dat.	hortandō	verendō	sequendō	patiendō	largiendō
Acc.	hortandum	verendam	sequendum	patiendum	largiendum
Abl.	hortandō	verendō	sequendō	patiendō	largiendō

SUPINE

Acc.	hortātum	veritum	secūtum	passum	largītum
Abl.	hortātū	veritū	secūtū	passū	largītū

61. *a.* Of the Deponent Verbs used by Caesar, besides those previously mentioned, the most important are:

(1) First Conjugation, **arbitror**, *think* (I. 4), **cohortor**, *urge on* (I. 25), **cōnor**, *attempt* (I. 3), **cōnsector**, *pursue* (III. 19), **cōnsōlor**, *reassure* (I. 20), **cōnspicor**, *catch sight of* (I. 25), **cunctor**, *delay* (III. 23), **dominor**, *hold sway* (II. 31), **frūmentor**, *get supplies* (IV. 9), **glōrior**, *boast* (I. 14), **grātulor**, *congratulate* (I. 30), **interpretor**, *expound* (VI. 13); **mīror**, *wonder* (I. 32) and **admīror** (I. 14); **miseror**, *lament* (I. 39); **moror**, *delay* (I. 39), and **dēmoror** (III. 6); **pābulor**, *get fodder* (V. 17), **populor**, *lay waste* (I. 11), and **dēpopulor**, *completely lay waste* (II. 7); **recordor**, *recall* (C. III. 72), **remūneror**, *compensate* (I. 44), and **speculor**, *spy out* (I. 47).

(2) Second Conjugation, **fateor**, *acknowledge* (C. III. 20), and its Compounds **cōnfiteor** (V. 27) and **profiteor** (VI. 23); **liceor**, *bid* (I. 18), and **polliceor**, *promise* (I. 14); **mereor**, *earn* (I. 40); **tueor**, *protect* (IV. 8), and **intueor**, *look upon* (I. 32); **vereor**, *be afraid* (I. 19).

(3) Third Conjugation, **complector**, *embrace* (I. 20), **dēfetīscor**, *become exhausted* (VII. 88); **fruor**, *enjoy* (III. 22); **lābor**, *slip, fall away* (V. 3), and **ēlābor**, *escape* (V. 37); **loquor**, *speak* (I. 20); **nāscor**, *be born, rise* (II. 18), and **ēnāscor**, *grow out* (II. 17); **nancīscor**, *obtain* (I. 53); **nītor**, *strive, rely on* (I. 13), and **innītor**, *lean upon* (II. 27); **oblīvīscor**, *forget* (I. 14), **proficīscor**, *set out* (I. 3), **queror**, *complain* (I. 16); the Compounds of **sequor**, **cōnsequor**, **exsequor**, **īnsequor**, **persequor**, **prōsequor**, **subsequor**; **reminīscor**, *remember* (I. 13), **ulcīscor**, *avenge* (I. 12); and **ūtor**, *use, adopt* (I. 5).

(4) Fourth Conjugation, **experior**, *try* (I. 31), **largior**, *give freely, bribe* (I. 18); **mētior**, *measure* (I. 16), and **dīmētior**, *measure off* (II. 19, IV. 17); **partior**, *divide* (III. 10), and **potior**, *become master of* (I. 3).

b. To the Fourth Conjugation belongs the Deponent **orior**, *rise*, with its Compounds **adorior**, *attack* (I. 13) and **coörior**, *arise* (III. 7); but Caesar uses certain forms of **orior** which are like those of Deponents in -ior of the Third Conjugation, as **oritur** (VI. 25) and **orerētur** (Imperfect Subjunctive; VI. 9, VII. 28).

62. Semi-Deponent Verbs have a Perfect System Passive in form but Active in meaning; they are **audeō** (I. 18), **fīdō** (C. III. 111) with its compounds **cōnfīdō** (I. 23) and **diffīdō** (V. 41); **gaudeō** (IV. 13), and **soleō** (VI. 15):

> **audeō, audēre, ausus sum,** *dare.*
> **fīdō, fīdere, fīsus sum,** *trust.*
> **gaudeō, gaudēre, gāvīsus sum,** *rejoice.*
> **soleō, solēre, solitus sum,** *be wont.*

PERIPHRASTIC CONJUGATION

63. The Periphrastic Conjugation has an Active and a Passive form, made up by combining the Future Active Participle and the Future Passive Participle, or Gerundive, with the verb **sum**, thus:

ACTIVE PERIPHRASTIC CONJUGATION

INDICATIVE MOOD	SUBJUNCTIVE MOOD
Pres. **amātūrus (-a, -um) sum,** *I am about to love*	*Pres.* **amātūrus sim,** *I may be about to love*
Imp. **amātūrus eram,** *I was about to love*	*Imp.* **amātūrus essem,** *I might be about to love*
Fut. **amātūrus erō,** *I shall be about to love*	*Perf.* **amātūrus fuerim,** *I may have been about to love*
Perf. **amātūrus fuī,** *I have been, was, about to love*	*Plup.* **amātūrus fuissem,** *I might have been about to love*
Plup. **amātūrus fueram,** *I had been about to love*	
Fut. P. **amātūrus fuerō,** *I shall have been about to love*	

INFINITIVE

Pres. **amātūrus esse,** *to be about to love*
Perf. **amātūrus fuisse,** *to have been about to love*

PASSIVE PERIPHRASTIC CONJUGATION

INDICATIVE	SUBJUNCTIVE
Pres. **amandus (-a, -um) sum,** *I am to be loved, I must be loved*	*Pres.* **amandus sim,** *I may have to be loved*
Imp. **amandus eram,** *I had to be loved*	*Imp.* **amandus essem,** *I might have to be loved*
Fut. **amandus erō,** *I shall have to be loved*	*Perf.* **amandus fuerim,** *I may have had to be loved*
Perf. **amandus fuī,** *I have had to be loved, had to be loved*	*Plup.* **amandus fuissem,** *I might have had to be loved*
Plup. **amandus fueram,** *I had deserved to be loved*	
Fut. P. **amandus fuerō,** *I shall have had to be loved*	

INFINITIVE

Pres. **amandus esse,** *to have to be loved*
Perf. **amandus fuisse,** *to have had to be loved*

64. *a.* Perfects in **-āvī**, **-ēvī**, and **-īvī**, and other tenses formed from the same stems, are sometimes contracted by the loss of **-vi-** or **-ve-** before **-s-** or **-r-**; Perfects in **-īvī** lose the **-v-** before **-r-** but retain the vowel.   Examples are:

(1) **oppugnārant** (I. 5) for **oppugnāverant**; **adamāssent** (I. 31) for **adamāvissent**; **commemorāssent** (I. 14) for **commemorāvissent**; **superārint**, Perfect Subjunctive (I. 40) for **superāverint**; **superāssent** (I. 40) for **superāvissent**.

(2) **cōnsuērunt** (III. 8, etc.) for **cōnsuēvērunt**; **cōnsuērint** (I. 44, etc.) for **cōnsuēverint**; **cōnsuēsse** (I. 14) for **cōn-suēvisse**.

(3) **audiērunt** (V. 28) for **audīvērunt**; **audierit** (IV. 5) for **audīverit**; **audierant** (II. 12, VI. 37) for **audīverant**; **audīssent** (VII. 62) for **audīvissent**; **audīstis** (C. III. 87) for **audīvistis**.

b. The Future Passive Participle, or Gerundive, sometimes has the ending **-undus** instead of **-endus**, as **faciundī** (I. 7), **potiundī** (II. 7).

IRREGULAR VERBS

65. Of the Irregular Verbs Caesar most frequently uses **sum**, **dō**, **eō**, **ferō**, **fīō**, **volō** and certain compounds.

66. *a.* Of the compounds of **sum** Caesar uses **absum**, **adsum**, **dēsum**, **intersum**, **possum**, **praesum**, **prōsum**, **subsum**, and **supersum**.   These are inflected like **sum** (*52*), excepting **possum**; but in **prō-sum** (**prōfuisse**, VI. 40) the preposition has the form **prōd-** before vowels, as **prōdest**.

b. **Possum**, *I am able*, is inflected as follows:

PRINCIPAL PARTS:

	possum	posse	potuī	

INDICATIVE MOOD		SUBJUNCTIVE MOOD	

	SINGULAR	PLURAL		SINGULAR	PLURAL
Pres.	possum	possumus	*Pres.*	possim	possīmus,
	potes	potestis		possīs	possītis,
	potest	possunt		possit	possint
Imp.	poteram, pote-rās, *etc.*	poterāmus -erātis, *etc.*	*Imp.*	possem	possēmus
				possēs	possētis
Fut.	poterō, poteris, *etc.*	poterimus		posset	possent
			Perf.	potuerim	potuerīmus
Perf.	potuī, potuistī, *etc.*	potuimus		potuerīs	potuerītis
				potuerit	potuerint
Plup.	potueram, po-tuerās, *etc.*	potuerāmus	*Plup.*	potuissem	potuissēmus
				potuissēs	potuissētis
Fut. P.	potuerō, potue-ris, *etc.*	potuerimus		potuisset	potuissent

INFINITIVE	PARTICIPLE
Pres. posse	*Pres.* potēns (*used as an adjective*)
Perf. potuisse	*Gen.* potentis

67. *a.* **Dō, dare,** *give,* has **-a-** instead of **-ā-** in the Present System except in the Second Person of the Present Indicative and the Present Imperative. The inflection of the Perfect System (**dedī,** *etc.*), is regular.

PRINCIPAL PARTS:

dō   dare   dedī   datus

ACTIVE VOICE

INDICATIVE MOOD		SUBJUNCTIVE MOOD	
Pres.	dō	damus	*Pres.*	dem	dēmus
	dās	datis		dēs	dētis
	dat	dant		det	dent
Imp.	dabam, *etc.*	dabāmus	*Imp.*	darem	darēmus
Fut.	dabō, *etc.*	dabimus		darēs	darētis
Perf.	dedī, *etc.*	dedimus		daret	darent
Plup.	dederam, *etc.*	dederāmus	*Perf.*	dederim, *etc.*	dederīmus, *etc.*
Fut. P.	dederō, *etc.*	dederimus	*Plup.*	dedissem, *etc.*	dedissēmus, *etc.*

IMPERATIVE		INFINITIVE	PARTICIPLE
Pres.	dā	date	*Pres.* dare	dāns
Fut.	datō	datōte	*Perf.* dedisse	
	datō	dantō	*Fut.* datūrus esse	datūrus

GERUND	SUPINE
dandī, *etc.*	datum, datū

b. The Passive of **dō** has **-a-** instead of **-ā-,** as **darī, datur, dabar, dabor, darer, datus,** *etc.;* the First Person of the Present Indicative Passive is not in use.

c. The compounds of **dō** are of the Third Conjugation except **circumdō,** which is inflected like **dō.**

68. *a.* **Eō, īre,** *go,* is thus inflected:

PRINCIPAL PARTS:

eō   īre   iī (īvī)   itum (est)

INDICATIVE MOOD		SUBJUNCTIVE MOOD	
Pres.	eō	īmus	*Pres.*	eam	eāmus
	īs	ītis		eās	eātis
	it	eunt		eat	eant
Imp.	ībam, *etc.*	ībāmus	*Imp.*	īrem	īrēmus
Fut.	ībō, *etc.*	ībimus		īrēs	īrētis
Perf.	iī	iimus		īret	īrent
	īstī *or* iistī	īstis *or* iistis	*Perf.*	ierim	ierīmus
	iit	iērunt *or* iēre		ieris	ierītis
Plup	ieram, *etc.*	ierāmus		ierit	ierint
Fut. P.	ierō, *etc.*	ierimus	*Plup.*	īssem, *etc.*	īssēmus, *etc.*

IMPERATIVE		INFINITIVE	PARTICIPLE	
Pres. ī	īte	*Pres.* īre	*Pres.* iēns	*Gen.* euntis
Fut. ītō	ītōte	*Perf.* īsse		
ītō	euntō	*Fut.* itūrus esse	*Fut.* itūrus	*Gerundive* eundum
		Pass. īrī		

GERUND	SUPINE
eundī, eundō, *etc.*	itum, itū

b. Caesar uses the Compounds **abeō, adeō, coeō** (VI. 22), **exeō,
ineō, obeō, prōdeō, redeō, subeō,** and **trānseō,** inflected like **eō.**

c. Transitive compounds of **eō** are used also in the Passive, as
numerus inībātur, *the number was cast up* (VII. 76); **initā aestāte,**
at the beginning of summer (II. 2); **trānsītur,** *is crossed* (I. 6).

d. Impersonal Passive forms of **eō** are **īrī** (III. 18), **īrētur** (III. 24).

69. *a.* **Ferō, ferre,** *bear, carry,* is inflected as follows:

PRINCIPAL PARTS:

Active.	**ferō**	**ferre**	**tulī**	**lātus**
Passive.	**feror**	**ferrī**		**lātus sum**

ACTIVE VOICE

INDICATIVE MOOD

	SINGULAR	PLURAL
Pres.	ferō	ferimus
	fers	fertis
	fert	ferunt
Imp.	ferēbam, *etc.*	ferēbāmus
Fut.	feram	ferēmus
Perf.	tulī	tulimus
Plup.	tuleram	tulerāmus
Fut. P.	tulerō	tulerimus

SUBJUNCTIVE MOOD

Pres.	feram	ferāmus
	ferās	ferātis
	ferat	ferant
Imp.	ferrem	ferrēmus
	ferrēs	ferrētis
	ferret	ferrent
Perf.	tulerim	tulerīmus
Plup.	tulissem	tulissēmus

IMPERATIVE

Pres.	fer	ferte
Fut.	fertō	fertōte
	fertō	feruntō

PASSIVE VOICE

INDICATIVE MOOD

	SINGULAR	PLURAL
Pres.	feror	ferimur
	ferris	feriminī
	fertur	feruntur
Imp.	ferēbar	ferēbāmur
Fut.	ferar	ferēmur
Perf.	lātus sum	lātī sumus
Plup.	lātus eram	lātī erāmus
Fut. P.	lātus erō	lātī erimus

SUBJUNCTIVE MOOD

Pres.	ferar	ferāmur
	ferāris, *or* -re	ferāminī
	ferātur	ferantur
Imp.	ferrer	ferrēmur
	ferrēris	ferrēminī
	ferrētur	ferrentur
Perf.	lātus sim	lātī sīmus
Plup.	lātus essem	lātī essēmus

IMPERATIVE

Pres.	ferre	feriminī
Fut.	fertor	
	fertor	feruntor

ACTIVE VOICE   PASSIVE VOICE

INFINITIVE   PARTICIPLE   INFINITIVE   PARTICIPLE

Pres. ferre   *Pres.* ferēns   *Pres.* ferrī
Perf. tulisse   (*Gen.* ferentis)   *Perf.* lātus esse   *Perf.* lātus
Fut. lātūrus   *Fut.* lātūrus   *Fut.* lātum īrī   *Ger.* ferendus
        esse   *or* ferundus

         GERUND   SUPINE

Gen. ferendī
Dat. ferendō
Acc. feren-   *Acc.* lātum
        dum
Abl. ferendō   *Abl.* lātū

b. Caesar uses the Compounds, **afferō, anteferō, conferō, dēferō, differō, efferō, īnferō, offerō, perferō, praeferō, prōferō** and **referō,** which are inflected like **ferō.**

70. *a.* **Fīō,** *become* (with -ī- except in **fit** and before **-e-**), is used as the Passive of **faciō,** with the meaning *be made, be done.* It is inflected as follows:

PRINCIPAL PARTS: **fīō**   **fierī**   **factus sum**

INDICATIVE MOOD   SUBJUNCTIVE MOOD

SINGULAR   PLURAL   SINGULAR   PLURAL

Pres. fīō   fīmus   *Pres.* fīam   fīāmus
         fīs   fītis   fīās   fīātis
         fit   fīunt   fīat   fīant
Imp. fīēbam, *etc.* fīēbāmus   *Imp.* fierem   fierēmus
Fut. fīam   fīēmus   fierēs   fierētis
Perf. factus sum   factī sumus   fieret   fierent
Plup. factus eram factī erāmus *Perf.* factus sim factī sīmus
Fut. P. factus erō factī erimus *Plup.* factus essem factī essēmus

IMPERATIVE

Pres. fī   fīte

INFINITIVE   PARTICIPLE

Pres. fierī
Perf. factus esse   *Perf.* factus
Fut.   factum īrī   *Ger.* faciendus

b. Of compounds of **fīō** Caesar uses **cōnfierī** (VII. 58) and **collabefierī** (C. II. 6).

c. Compounds of **facio** with Prepositions have their own Passive forms; so **cōnfecta erat**, *had been made* (I. 29); **patefierī**, *be kept open* (III. 1).

71. **Volō**, *I wish*, and its compounds **nōlō**, *I am unwilling*, and **mālō**, *I prefer*, are inflected as follows:

PRINCIPAL PARTS:

volō	velle	voluī
nōlō	nōlle	nōluī
mālō	mālle	māluī

INDIC.	SUBJ.	INDIC.	SUBJ.	INDIC.	SUBJ.
PRESENT	PRESENT	PRESENT	PRESENT	PRESENT	PRESENT
volō	velim	nōlō	nōlim	mālō	mālim
vīs	velīs	nōn vīs	nōlīs	māvīs	mālīs
vult	velit	nōn vult	nōlit	māvult	mālit
volumus	velīmus	nōlumus	nōlīmus	mālumus	mālīmus
vultis	velītis	nōn vultis	nōlītis	māvultis	mālītis
volunt	velint	nōlunt	nōlint	mālunt	mālint

IMPERFECT		IMPERFECT		IMPERFECT	
volēbam, *etc.*	vellem	nōlēbam	nōllem	mālēbam	māllem

FUTURE	FUTURE	FUTURE
volam, *etc.*	nōlam	mālam

PERFECT		PERFECT		PERFECT	
voluī, *etc.*	voluerim	nōluī	nōluerim	māluī	māluerim

PLUPERFECT		PLUPERFECT		PLUPERFECT	
volueram	voluissem	nōlueram	nōluissem	mālueram	māluissem

FUTURE PERFECT	FUTURE PERFECT	FUTURE PERFECT
voluerō, *etc.*	nōluerō	māluerō

IMPERATIVE

Pres.	nōlī	nōlīte
Fut.	nōlītō	nōlītōte
	nōlītō	nōluntō

INFINITIVE	INFINITIVE	INFINITIVE
Pres. velle	nōlle	mālle
Perf. voluisse	nōluisse	māluisse

PARTICIPLE

Pres. volēns	nōlēns	—

DEFECTIVE VERBS

72. *a.* Caesar uses one or more forms of each of the following Defective Verbs : **inquam**, *I say*, which he uses only in direct quotations, in the Third Person Singular Indicative Present, **inquit**, *he says, says he;* **coepī**, *I have begun, I began*, which belongs chiefly to the Perfect System ; **meminī**, *I remember.* and **ōdī**, *I hate*, which are Perfect in form, but Present in meaning.

b. **Coepī, meminī** and **ōdī** are inflected as follows :

INDICATIVE MOOD

Perf.	coepī, *etc.*	meminī	ōdī
Plup.	coeperam	memineram	ōderam
Fut.P.	coeperō	meminerō	ōderō

SUBJUNCTIVE MOOD

coeperim	meminerim	ōderim
coepissem	meminissem	ōdissem

IMPERATIVE

Sing.	mementō
Plur.	mementōte

INFINITIVE

Perf.	coepisse	meminisse	ōdisse
Fut.	coeptūrus esse		ōsūrus esse

PARTICIPLE

Perf.	coeptus, *begun*	ōsus
Fut.	coeptūrus	ōsūrus

c. The Passive forms of **coepī** are used with the Passive Infinitive, as **lapidēs iacī coeptī sunt**, *stones began to be thrown* (II. 6).

IMPERSONAL VERBS

73. *a.* Of the Impersonal Verbs Cæsar oftenest uses **licet**, *it is permitted* (I. 7) and **oportet**, *it is necessary, it behooves* (I. 4) ; he has also **paenitet**, *it makes sorry* (IV. 5) and **pudet**, *it makes ashamed* (VII. 42).

b. The Impersonal **licet** is inflected as follows :

INDICATIVE

Pres.	licet, *it is permitted*
Imp.	licēbat, *it was permitted*
Fut.	licēbit, *it will be permitted*
Perf.	licuit, *it has been permitted or it was permitted*
Plup.	licuerat, *it had been permitted*
Fut. P.	licuerit, *it will have been permitted*

SUBJUNCTIVE

Pres.	liceat, *it may be permitted*
Imp.	licēret, *it might be permitted*
Perf.	licuerit, *it may have been permitted*
Plup.	licuisset, *it might have been permitted*

INFINITIVE

Pres.	licēre, *to be permitted*
Perf.	licuisse, *to have been permitted.*

c. Cæsar uses Impersonally the Third Person Singular of a number of Verbs, among which are **accēdit**, *it is added, there is the further fact that* (III. 13); **accidit**, *it happens, it turns out* (I. 31); **cōnstat**, *it is certain* (III. 6); **interest**, *it is important* (II. 5); **placet**, *it pleases* (I. 34); and **praestat**, *it is better* (I. 17).

d. Cæsar uses Impersonally the Passive of several Intransitive Verbs, making prominent the action rather than the doer; as **pugnā-tur**, *fighting goes on*, lit. *it is fought* (VII. 67, 84); **pugnātum est**, *fighting went on* (I. 26); **Ubi eō ventum est**, *when (they) had come thither*, lit. *when it was come thither*, the *coming* being made prominent (I. 43).

e. Verbs are often used impersonally in the Passive Periphrastic Conjugation, denoting Obligation or Necessity (*229, c*); as, **reī frū-mentāriae prōspiciendum [esse]**, *that he should provide for supplies*, lit. *that it ought to be provided for supplies* by him (I. 23).

WORD FORMATION

74. The following classes of words are derived from Verbs:

a. Nouns with the Suffix -**tor** denoting the agent, as **vic-tor**, (I. 31), *victor*, from **vincō**; **dēfēn-sor** (II. 6; for **dēfend-tor**, as **dēfēn-sus** for **dēfend-tus**), *defender*, from **dēfendō**.

b. Nouns with the Suffixes -**tiō** (-**siō**), -**tus**, -**tūra**, -**ium**, denoting an action or the result of an action, as **coniūrā-tiō** (I. 2), *a swearing together, league* (**coniūrō**); **mūnī-tiō** (I. 10), *a fortifying, a fortification* conceived as a result of fortifying (**mūniō**); **adven-tus** (I. 22), *arrival* (**adveniō**); **exerci-tus** (I. 13), *army*, conceived as a product of *training* (**exerceō**); **armā-tūra** (II. 10), *equipment* (**armō**); **imperium** (I. 3), *command, sovereignty* (**imperō**); **iūdic-ium** (I. 4), *judgment, trial* (**iūdicō**).

c. Nouns with the Suffix -**or**, denoting a condition or state, as **tim-or** (I. 22), *fear* (**timeō**).

d. Nouns with the Suffixes -**men** or -**mentum**, -**ulum**, -**bulum**, -**crum**, denoting process, means, or result, as **flū-men** (I. 12), *stream, river*, conceived as *a flowing* or *current* (**fluō**); **impedī-mentum** (I. 25), *hindrance* (**impediō**), pl. **impedīmenta** (I. 24), *baggage*, conceived as an aggregation of hindrances; **vinc-ulum** (I. 4), *bond, chain*, conceived as a means of binding (**vinciō**); **pā-bulum** (I. 16), *fodder*, conceived as a means of feeding (**pāscō**); **simulā-crum** (VI. 16), *image*, conceived as something *made like* something else (**simulō**, *make like*).

e. Adjectives with the Suffix -**āx**, denoting a quality or tendency, as **ferāx** (II. 4), *productive, fertile* (**ferō**, *bear*).

f. Adjectives with the Suffixes -**ilis** and -**bilis**, denoting passive qualities, or capacity, as **fac-ilis** (I. 6), *easy*, i.e. capable of being done or made (**faciō**); **mō-bilis** (IV. 5), *easily moved, changeable* (**moveō**); **incrēdibilis** (I. 12), *incredible* (negative **in-** + **crēdibilis**, *capable of being believed*, from **crēdō**).

g. A few Adjectives in -**tīvus**, as **cap-tīvus** (I. 50), *captive* (**capiō**), **fugi-tīvus** (I. 23), *fugitive* (**fugiō**).

75. The following classes of words are derived from Nouns:

a. Diminutive Nouns, ending in -**lus** (Fem. -**la**, Neut. -**lum**), and in -**ulus**, -**olus**, -**culus**, etc., as **arti-culus** (VI. 27), *joint* (**artus**);

tabella (C. III. 83), *voting tablet* (tabula) ; porcellus, *pig*, dim. from porculus, *young hog, pig*, which is itself a dim. from porcus, *hog*, (p. 463).

b. Nouns with the Suffix -ātus, denoting an official position or body, as cōnsul-ātus (I. 35), *consulship* (cōnsul) ; magistrātus (I. 4), *magistracy, magistrate* (magister) ; senātus (I. 3), *senate* (senex).

c. A few Abstract Nouns in -tās and -tūs, as cīvi-tās (I. 2), *citizenship, state* (cīvis) ; vir-tūs (I. 1), *valor.* (vir).

d. Adjectives with the Suffix -eus, denoting material, as aureus (V. 12), *of gold* (aurum) ; ferreus (III. 13), *of iron* (ferrum).

e. Adjectives with the Suffixes -ius, -icus, -cus, -ānus, -īnus, -nus, -ālis, -īlis, -ārius, -āris, -īvus, meaning *connected with, belonging to, from*, etc., as patr-ius (II. 15), *of a father, ancestral* (pater) ; bell-icus (VI. 24), *of war* (bellum) ; Gall-icus (I. 31), *Gallic* ; Germān-icus (IV. 16), *Germanic* ; urb-ānus (VII. 1), *of a city, of the city* (urbs) ; Rōm-ānus, *of Rome* (Rōma) ; Lat-īnus, *of Latium, Latin* ; nāv-ālis (III. 19), *naval* (nāvis) ; legiōn-ārius (I. 51), *of a legion, legionary* (legiō) ; cōnsul-āris (C. III. 82), *consular* ; aest-īvus (VI. 4), *of summer.*

f. Adjectives with the suffix -ōsus, denoting fullness, as perīcu-lōsus (I. 33), *full of danger* (perīculum) ; bellic-ōsus (I. 10), *warlike* (bellic-us, bellum).

g. Denominative Verbs, of the different conjugations, as cūrō, -āre (I. 19), *care for, take care* (cūra) ; laudō, -āre (C. III. 87), *praise* (laus, laudis) ; tribuō, -ere (I. 13), *assign* (tribus) ; fīniō, -īre (IV. 16), *limit* (fīnis) ; partior, -īrī (III. 10), *divide* (pars, partis).

76. *a.* Derived from Adjectives are Abstract Nouns with the Suffixes -tia, -ia, -tās, and -tūdō, denoting quality or condition, as dūri-tia (VI. 21), *hardness* (dūrus) ; audāc-ia (I. 18), *boldness* (audāx) ; grāt-ia (I. 9), *favor* (grātus) ; cupidi-tās (I. 2), *desire* (cupidus) ; forti-tūdō (I. 2), *bravery* (fortis).

b. Derived from Adverbs are several Adjectives in -urnus, -turnus, -tinus, referring to Time, as diū-turnus (I. 14), *long-continued* (diū), and diū-tinus (V. 52), *protracted* (diū) ; so Crāstinus (C. III. 91), like the English name *Morrow*, from crās-tinus, *of to-morrow* (crās).

c. A few Adjectives have a Diminutive in -ulus ; as tantulus, *so small*, from tantus (IV. 22).

77. Adverbs[1] are sometimes formed from the Stem of the Perfect Passive Participle with the suffix -im, as stat-im (I. 53), *immediately*

---

[1] The formation of Adverbs from Adjectives is treated under Adverbs, *34, 35.*

(**status, stō**) ; and from nouns, with the ending **-tim** (or **-im**), as **virī-tim** (VII. 71), *man by man* (**vir**), and **part-im** (II. 1), *partly*, which was originally an Accusative of **pars**.

78. Verbs derived from Verbs are :

a. Frequentatives, expressing repeated or intensive action; frequentatives derived from Verbs of the First Conjugation end in -**itō**, as **clāmitō** (V. 7), *cry out loudly, shout* (**clāmō**) ; others end in -**tō** or -**sō**, as **iactō** (I. 25), *toss about, cast* (**iaciō**), **concursō** (V. 33), *rush hither and yon, rush about* (**concurrō**).

b. Inchoatives, or Inceptives, expressing the beginning of an action or state, a becoming; they end in -**scō**, preceded by -**ā**-, -**ē**-, or -**ī**-, as **mātūrēscō** (VI. 29), *become ripe* (**mātūrō**).

79. *a.* In the first part of a Compound Word the final vowel of the Stem of a Noun or Adjective is dropped before a vowel, and becomes -**i**- before a consonant, while in the case of consonant Stems -**i**- is often inserted; in the second part vowel changes frequently appear. Thus **signi-fer** (II. 25), *standard-bearer* (for **signo-fer**, **signum** + **fer**- in **ferō**) ; **prīn-ceps** (I. 30), *leader,* i.e. *taking foremost place* (for **prīmo-cap-s, prīmus** + **cap**- in **capiō**); **ampli-ficō** (II. 14), *enlarge* (for **amplo-fac-ō, amplus** + **fac**- in **faciō**).

b. The first part of a Compound is often a Preposition or other indeclinable word, as **per-ficiō** (I. 3), *carry through* (**per** + **faciō**) ; **in-iussū** (I. 19), *without orders* (negative **in**- + **iussū**) ; **bi-enn-ium** (I. 3), (*period of*) *two years* (for **bi-anno-ium, bis** + **annus** + suffix -**ium**) ; **quotannīs** (I. 36), *annually* (**quot** + Ablative of **annus**).

c. Compounds originating in phrases are sometimes declinable, as **prō-cōnsul**, *proconsul*, Abl. **prō-cōnsule** (VI. 1) ; sometimes indeclinable, as **ob-viam**, *in the way* (VII. 12, 28).

d. The following indeclinable prefixes are found only in Compound Words:

amb-, am-, (an-), *about*, as in **ān-frāctus** (VII. 46), *curve.*

com-, co- (old form of **cum**, *with*), *with, together ;* see under **cum** in Vocabulary.

dis-, appearing also as **dir-, dī-**, *apart*, as in **dis-cēdō** (I. 16), *go apart;* **dir-imō** (I. 46), *take apart, break off ;* **dī-mītto** (I. 18), *send about, send off.*

in-, = *un-, not,* as in **incertus** (IV. 5) ; to be carefully distinguished from the preposition **in** in composition.

por-, *forth, forward,* as in **por-rigō** (II. 19), *extend.*

re-, red-, *back,* as in **re-maneō** (I. 39), *stay behind ;* **red-eō** (I. 29), *return.*

sē-, sēd-, *apart*, as in **sē-parō** (VII. 63), *separate*, **sēd-itiō** (VII. 28), *mutiny.*

THE DERIVATION OF ENGLISH WORDS FROM THE LATIN[1]

80. *a.* Very many of the Words in the English Language in common use are derived, indirectly or directly, from the Latin.

The percentage of classical Latin words that have been taken over into English directly,[2] however, is exceedingly small; the people whose name survives in the word " English " reached Britain too late for any direct contact with classical Latin. But in the Middle Ages a modified Latin was spoken and written by educated men all over Europe; and classical Latin authors continued to be read, less in the Middle Ages, but extensively after the Revival of Learning. Meanwhile the Latin spoken by the common people in Italy, France, Spain, and other countries conquered by the Romans, had developed into the Romance languages, French, Italian, Spanish and kindred tongues; and after the Norman Conquest, in the eleventh century, French was both spoken and written in England. Thus it happens that words of Latin origin have come down into the English of to-day. in various ways, some through the writings and speech of those who read classical Latin, a great many through mediæval Latin, but far the greatest number through the Romance languages, particularly French.

b. Some Latin words appear in English in their Latin forms, though they may have passed through other forms and may now have a different meaning; as " arbor " (II. 17), " census " (I. 29), " color " (V. 14), " duplex " (II. 29), " senator " (II. 28), " victor " (I. 31), and " omnibus," meaning originally *for all*, from the Dative Plural Masculine of **omnis** (I. 1).

81. Many Latin Words appear in English with slight change of spelling, as " cent " from **centum** (I. 37), " condition " from **condiciō** (I. 28) through a late spelling **conditiō**; " difficulty " from **difficultās**

---

[1] Classes in Caesar find it a useful exercise to make, on separate slips or cards, a list of Latin words in each lesson having English derivatives, adding the words derived from them. The Latin words from time to time can be classified, in groups corresponding with the numbered paragraphs *80–85*, the words in each group being arranged in alphabetical order.

[2] The editor is indebted to Professor O. F. Emerson, of Western Reserve University, for helpful suggestions.

(II. 20), "fort" from **fortis** (I. 48), "future" from **futūrus** (I. 10), the Future Participle associated with **sum**; "office" from **officium** (I. 40), "senate" from **senātus** (I. 3), and "victory" from **victōria** (I. 53); "false" from **falsus** (VI. 20), and "pedal" from **pedālis** (III. 13), which goes back to **pēs**, Gen. **pedis**, *foot* (I. 25); "admire" from **admīror** (I. 14), "ascend" from **ascendō** (I. 21), "accept" from **accipiō** (I. 14) through the Frequentative **acceptō**, *accept*, which is formed from **acceptus** (I. 48), Participle of **accipiō**.

82. *a.* Some English Words have been formed from Latin Words by Analogy of Latin or French Words already in the language. Examples are "magistracy" and "classical."

b. "Magistracy" goes back to **magistrātus** (I. 4). From **magistrātus** came "magistrate," to which the suffix "-cy" was added from Analogy to the English nouns of Latin origin ending in "-cy"[1]; this suffix represents the Latin termination **-tia**, as in "clemency," from **clēmentia** (II. 14). With the addition of the suffix "-cy" the last two letters of "magistrate" disappeared; hence "magistracy."

c. "Classical" comes from the Adjective **classicus**, *first class*, which goes back to **classis**, *a class*, though in Caesar **classis** (III. 14, etc.) has only the meaning *fleet*, as a class or division of military forces. From **classicus** comes "classic"; the suffix "-al" was added from Analogy to the English Words which are derived from the Latin Adjectives ending in **-ālis**, as "social" from **sociālis** (ultimately from **socius**, *fellow, ally*, I. 5), "hospital" from **hospitālis** (ultimately from **hospes**, Gen. **hospitis**, *guest-friend*, I. 53), and "legal" from **lēgālis** (ultimately from **lēx**, **lēgis**, *law*, I. 1). Similarly, "aural" is derived from **auris**, *ear* (VI. 26), "continual" from **continuus** (I. 48), and "senatorial" from **senātōrius** (C. III. 83), the suffix "-al" replacing the Latin terminations.

83. *a.* Some English Words are formed from Words of ultimate Latin origin by the addition of a suffix of English origin. Thus "falsehood" comes from "false" (Latin **falsus**, VI. 20) with the suffix "-hood" denoting quality; "citizenship" from "citizen," which goes back ultimately to Latin **cīvis** (VII. 77), with the suffix "-ship" denoting state or office; "instantly" from "instant" (Latin **īnstāns**, Gen. **īnstantis**, Present Participle of **īnstō**, I. 16), and "nobly" from "noble" (Latin **nōbilis**, I. 2), by addition of the suffix "-ly," which has the same origin as the English word "like."

---

[1] This suffix has no connection with a similar suffix of Greek origin found in "democracy" and a few other English words.

b. A few English Words are formed from Latin Words by the addition of an English suffix of Greek origin; as "jurist" from **iūs**, Gen. **iūris** (I. 4) with the suffix "-ist," which represents a Greek termination denoting the agent; "Caesarism," "nihilism," "terrorism" from **Caesar** (I. 7), **nihil** (I. 11), and **terror** (II. 12) with the suffix "-ism," also of Greek origin, implying doctrine or practice.

84. Many Latin Words, especially those that have come into English through the French, have undergone so great changes that their Latin origin is not at once perceived, though it can always be traced through intermediate forms. Such are "captaincy," from "captain," which is ultimately derived from **caput** (I. 29), *head*, with the suffix "-cy" (*82, b*); "city," from **cīvitās** (I. 2); "lieutenant," from **locum tenēns** (Present Participle of **teneō**, *hold*), one holding another's office or place; "madam," "Madonna," from **mea domina**, Feminine corresponding to the Masculine **meus dominus** (Dative **dominīs**, VI. 13); "governor" from **gubernātor** (III. 9); "peril" from **perīculum** (I. 17), and "perilous" from **perīculōsus** (I. 33), "preach" from **praedicō** (I. 44), and "receive" from **recipiō** (I. 5).

85. A few common abbreviations represent Latin Words; as "no." in "no. 9," where "no." stands not for "number" but for **numerō** (I. 5), the Ablative of **numerus**. Also, the symbols for English money, £ s. d., now read as "pounds, shillings, pence," are derived from Latin words: £ = **lībra**, a *pound* in weight, whence **lībrīlis**, *weighing a pound* (VII. 81); s. = **solidus**, a Roman gold coin; and d. = **dēnārius**, a Roman silver coin, translated *penny*, though its value as silver was originally between fifteen and twenty cents in our currency. **Solidus**, the name of the coin, came from the Adjective **solidus**, from which our word "solid" is derived; it survives in our word "soldier" as "one having pay" for military service. **Dēnārius** came from **dēnī**, *ten each* (I. 43) because it originally contained ten of the monetary units called **as**, and **as** survives in our word "ace."

Our abbreviation "Mr." is for "Master," but "Master" is of Latin origin, being derived from **magister** (C. III. 43).

86. The value of the contribution which the English language has received from the Latin cannot be measured in percentages of words. The words of English origin which we use are largely concrete, and well fitted to express fundamental ideas; but we are indebted to the Latin for a very large proportion of the words employed in the arts, science and education, which fit the English language to be the vehicle of expression for a constantly developing civilization.

SYNTAX

SUBJECT AND PREDICATE

87. *a.* A Noun or Pronoun, or an Adjective taking the place of a Noun, when used as the Subject of a Finite Verb is in the Nominative Case; as, **lēgātī revertērunt**, *the envoys returned* (I. 8); **integrī dēfessīs succēderent**, *fresh men were relieving the exhausted* (VII. 41).

b. A Personal Pronoun used as a Subject is expressed only when there is emphasis or contrast; as, **Dēsilīte, commīlitōnēs, nisi vultis aquilam hostibus prōdere**; **ego certē meum . . . officium praestiterō**, *Leap down, comrades, unless you want to abandon your eagle to the enemy; I at any rate shall have done my duty.* Here **ego** is emphatic, but the subject of the Plural Verbs is not emphatic, and hence is not expressed (IV. 25).

c. Instead of a Noun or other Substantive word an Infinitive or a Clause may be used as the Subject of a Verb; as, **Commodissimum vīsum est Gāium Valerium Procillum . . . mittere**, *It seemed most expedient to send Gaius Valerius Procillus,* where **mittere** is the subject of **vīsum est** (I. 47).

88. *a.* A Predicate Noun, in the same case as the Subject, is used with **sum** and the Passives of Verbs of *calling, choosing, making, esteeming,* and the like; as, **Dīvicō prīnceps fuit**, *Divico was the leading man* (I. 13); **quī . . . Gallī appellantur**, *who are called Gauls* (I. 1); **ducēs eī dēliguntur**, *those are chosen* (*as*) *leaders* (III. 23).

b. A Predicate Noun after Passive Participles is similarly used; as, **obsidibus acceptīs prīmīs cīvitātis**, *having received the foremost men of the state as hostages,* lit. *the foremost men of the state having been received as hostages* (II. 13).

89. *a.* A Verb is sometimes omitted when it can easily be supplied from the context; as, **aciēs** (I. 25), where **intulit** is to be supplied.

b. Forms of **sum** are often omitted in the compound tenses; as, **occīsa** (I. 53) for **occīsa est**, *was killed.*

c. In the Future Active and Perfect Passive Infinitive, and also in the Present Passive Infinitive of the Periphrastic Conjugation, **esse** is frequently omitted; as, **conciliātūrum** (I. 3) for **conciliātūrum esse**; **itūrōs atque futūrōs** (I. 13) for **itūrōs esse atque futūrōs esse**; **lātūrī** for **lātūrī esse** (I. 40); **occīsum . . . pulsum . . . missum** (I. 7) for **occīsum esse . . . pulsum esse . . . missum esse**; **exspectandum** (I. 11) for **exspectandum esse**.

90. *a.* In certain connections **est, erat**, etc., may best be translated *there is, there was*, etc., with the Subject following; as, **Flūmen est Arar**, *There is a river, the Arar* (I. 12); **Erant itinera duo**, *There were two routes* (I. 6).

b. Occasionally *there* may be used in like manner in translating other verbs than **sum**; as, **Relinquēbātur ūna via**, *There remained only the route* (I. 9).

NOUNS

91. *a.* Nouns used as Appositives, whether in the Nominative or in the Oblique cases, agree in case with the Nouns to which they belong; as, **Ariovistus, rēx Germānōrum**, *Ariovistus, king of the Germans* (I. 31); **ā Bibracte, oppidō** (Ablative) **Aeduōrum**, *from Bibracte, a town of the Aeduans* (I. 23).

b. Nouns in Predicate Apposition sometimes agree with an unexpressed Subject, which is implied in the Verb; as, **hominēs . . . (eī) afficiēbantur**, *(being) men . . . they were sorely troubled* (I. 2).

c. A Noun referring to a Part may be in Apposition to a Noun expressing the Whole (Partitive Apposition); as, **itinera duo : unum** (iter), **alterum** (iter), *two routes : the one (route) . . . , the other . . .* (I. 6).

92. *a.* A Plural Noun is often used in Latin where English usage prefers the Singular; as, **ad effēminandōs animos**, *to weaken the courage* (I. 1).

b. An Abstract Noun is sometimes used in Latin where English usage expects a Concrete Plural Noun; as, **coniūrātiōnem nōbilitātis**, *a conspiracy of the nobles*, lit. *of the nobility* (I. 2).

c. Abstract Nouns are sometimes used in the Plural to denote instances of the Quality; as; **ad frīgora atque aestūs vītandōs**, *to avoid heat and cold* (VI. 22).

THE VOCATIVE CASE

93. The Vocative Case is used only in Direct Address; as, **Quid dubitās, Vorēne**? *Vorenus, why do you hesitate?* (V. 44).

THE GENITIVE CASE

94. *a.* In the Possessive Genitive the idea of Possession or of Close Connection is generally prominent; as, **fīnēs Sēquanōrum,** *the territory of the Sequanians, the Sequanians' country* (I. 8); **ā hūmāni- tāte prōvinciae,** *from the refinement of the Province* (I. 1).

b. The Possessive Genitive is used idiomatically with **causā, grātiā** and **īnstar**; as, **auxiliī causā,** *as an auxiliary force,* lit. *for the sake of support* (II. 24); **suī pūrgandī grātiā,** *in order to clear them- selves* (VII. 43); **īnstar mūrī mūnīmentum,** *a barrier like a wall,* lit. *the image of a wall* (II. 17).

c. A Genitive, perhaps Possessive in Origin, is used with **prīdiē** and **postrīdiē**; as, **prīdiē eius diēī,** *the day before that day, on the previous day* (I. 47); **postrīdiē eius diēī,** *the next day* (II. 12).

d. With **sum** and **fīō** the Possessive Genitive is used Predicatively with the meaning (*the business*) *of, belonging to,* etc.; as, **neque sē iūdicāre Galliam potius esse Ariovistī quam populī Rōmānī,** *and he judged that Gaul did not belong to Ariovistus* (lit. *was not Ario- vistus's*) *any more than to the Roman people* (I. 45).

95. The Subjective Genitive designates the Person or Agent whose act or feeling is expressed in the Noun on which the Genitive de- pends; as, **ab Ariovistī iniūriā,** *from the wrongdoing of Ariovistus* (I. 31); **terrōre equōrum,** *the fright caused by the horses,* lit. *of the horses* (IV. 33).

96. The Appositional Genitive defines or explains the Noun on which it depends; as, **iniūria retentōrum equitum,** *the wrong (com- mitted by) detaining the knights,* the detaining of the knights being the wrong expressed in **iniūria** (III. 10).

97. *a.* The Partitive Genitive, or Genitive of the Whole, designates the Whole of which a Part is expressed in the Noun, Pronoun, Adjec- tive, or Numeral on which it depends; as, **quārum ūnam (partem),** *of which* (i. e. *three parts*) *one* (*part*) (I. 1); **mīlia passuum CCXL,** *two hundred and forty miles,* lit. *two hundred and forty thousands of paces* (I. 2); **prīmōs cīvitātis,** *the first* (*men*) *of the state* (II. 3); **nihil reliquī . . . fēcērunt,** *they spared no effort,* lit. *nothing of the rest* (II. 26).

b. The Part on which the Genitive of the Whole depends may be indefinitely expressed by the Singular Neuter of a Pronoun or of an Adjective, used substantively, or by the Adverb **satis** used substan- tively; as, **quid negōtiī,** *what business,* lit. *what of business* (I. 34);

quid suī cōnsiliī sit, *what his plan was* (I. 21); aliquid novī cōnsiliī, *some new scheme or other* (IV. 32); quantum bonī, *how great
good* (I. 40); plūs dolōris, *more suffering* (I. 20); tōtīus Galliae
plūrimum possent, *were the most powerful of all Gaul* (I. 3); satis
causae, *sufficient ground*, lit. *enough of cause* (I. 19).

c. In the English phrase *all of these* there is no Partitive idea, because *these* and *all* refer to the same whole. Such phrases are not
expressed in Latin by the Partitive Genitive but by words agreeing
in Case; as, Hī omnēs, *all these* (I. 1); complūrēs nostrī, *a large
number of our men* (I. 52); omnium vestrum, *of all of you, of you
all* (VII. 77).

d. Caesar sometimes uses dē or ex with the Ablative instead of
the Genitive of the Whole; so regularly with quīdam and words
referring to Number. Thus, quīdam ex hīs, *some of these* (II. 17);
paucī dē nostrīs, *a few of our men* (I. 15).

e. A Genitive of the Whole may be used with an Adverb in the
Superlative Degree; as Deōrum maximē Mercurium colunt, *of the
gods they worship Mercury above all others* (VI. 17).

98. *a.* A variety of the Genitive of the Whole is the Genitive of
Material, which is used to designate the Material or Units included
in the Noun on which it depends; as, multitūdinem hominum, *a
force of men*, lit. *a multitude (made up) of men* (I. 4); aciem legiōnum quattuor, *a line (consisting) of four legions* (I. 24).

b. The Material of which anything is made is expressed by the
Ablative with ex; as, scūtīs ex cortice factīs, *with shields made of
bark* (II. 33).

99. The Genitive is used to express Origin; as, Catamantāloedis
fīliō, *son of Catamantaloedes* (I. 3).

100. *a.* The Genitive of Quality and the Genitive of Measure are
modified by Adjectives or Numerals; as, hominēs magnae virtūtis,
men of great valor (II. 15); mūrum in altitūdinem pedum sēdecim,
a rampart sixteen feet high, lit. *to the height of sixteen feet* (I. 8)

b. The Genitive of Quality and Genitive of Measure may be used
predicatively; as, Erant eius modī sitūs oppidōrum, *The strongholds were so situated*, lit. *the situations of the strongholds were of such a
character* (III. 12).

101. The Neuter Genitives magnī, tantī, and some others are used
predicatively, without a Noun, to express Indefinite Value; as, magnī
habēbātur, *was considered of great weight* (IV. 21); tantī, *of so great
account* (I. 20).

102. The Objective Genitive is used with Nouns to denote the Object toward which Action or Feeling is directed, and with Adjectives to limit their application; as, **reī pūblicae** (Genitive) **iniūriam,** *the wrong done to the state* (I. 20); **rēgnī cupiditāte inductus,** *led by desire of kingly power* (I. 2); **imperītum rērum,** *unversed in affairs* (I. 44); **alicuius iniūriae cōnscius,** *conscious of any wrong-doing* (I. 14).

103. *a.* Caesar uses **reminīscor** and **oblīvīscor** with a Genitive of the thing remembered or forgotten; as, **reminīscerētur incommodī,** *he should recall the disaster* (I. 13); **contumēliae oblīvīscī,** *to be forgetful of an affront* (I. 14).

b. A Genitive of the Charge is used with Verbs of Accusing and Condemning; as, **prōditiōnis īnsimulātus,** *accused of treachery* (VII. 20); **capitis damnārent,** *should condemn* (*to loss*) *of civil rights,* lit. *of head* (C. III. 83).

c. Caesar uses the impersonal **paenitet** with the Accusative of the Person repenting and the Genitive of the Object of Repentance; as, **quōrum eōs paenitēre necesse est,** *of which they of necessity repent,* lit. *of which it is necessary that it repent them* (IV. 5).

d. Caesar uses **interest** with a Genitive Neuter to express the degree of concern; as, **magnī interesse arbitrābātur,** *he thought that it was of great importance* (V. 4).

e. With **interest** Caesar uses a Genitive of the Interest concerned; as, **reī pūblicae commūnisque salūtis intersit** (Historical Present), *it concerned the State and their mutual welfare* (II. 5).

THE DATIVE CASE

104. *a.* The Dative of the Indirect Object is used with Transitive Verbs which have a Direct Object in the Accusative, or an Infinitive Clause as Object, and also with the Passive of such Verbs; as, **dat** (Historical Present) **negōtium Senonibus,** *He assigned the task to the Senones* (II. 2); **nostrīs — dabātur,** *was given to our men* (IV. 29).

b. With such Verbs the place of the Direct Object may be taken by an Adverb or a Clause; as, **nē suae magnopere virtūtī tribueret,** *that he should not presume over-much upon his valor* (I. 13).

105. The Dative of the Indirect Object is used with many Intransitive Verbs meaning *persuade, trust, distrust; command, obey, serve, resist; pardon, spare; please, displease, favor, indulge; approach; envy, threaten, rebuke,* and some others; as, **persuādet Casticō,** *he persuades Casticus* (I. 3), that is, *he prevails upon Casticus.* The Roman point of view in these verbs is somewhat different from that of the English, which with corresponding verbs generally uses a Direct Object.

The following are among the Intransitive Verbs thus used with the Dative by Caesar:

accidit, *happens to* (I. 18); **appropinquō**, *approach* (II. 10); **cēdō**, *yield to* (VII. 89); **concēdō**, *acknowledge inferiority to* (IV. 7); **cōnfīdō**, *trust* (I. 42); **cōnsulō**, *look out for* (VI. 31); **contingit**, *it falls to the lot of* (I. 43); **crēdō**, *intrust* (VI. 31); **cupiō**, *wish well to* (I. 18).

dēspērō, *despair of* (III. 12); **diffīdō**, *lose confidence in* (VI. 38); **ēvenit**, *it turns out* (IV. 25); **faveō**, *favor* (VI. 7); **ignōscō**, *pardon* (I. 45); **imperō**, *command* (I. 28); **indulgeō**, *treat with favor* (I. 40); **invideō**, *envy, be jealous of* (II. 31).

licet, *it is permitted* (I. 30); **medeor**, *remedy* (V. 24); **noceō**, *do injury to* (III. 13); **obtemperō**, *submit to* (IV. 21); **parcō**, *spare* (VI. 28); **pāreō**, *obey* (VI. 13); **persuādeō**, *persuade* (I. 2); **placet**, *it pleases* (I. 34); **prōspiciō**, *arrange for* (I. 23); **prōsum**, *be of benefit to* (VI. 40).

repugnō, *contend against* (I. 19); **resistō**, *oppose* (I. 25); **satisfaciō**, *make restitution* (I. 14); **serviō**, *be the slave of* (IV. 5), *devote one's self to* (VII. 34); **studeō**, *be eager for* (I. 9), *give attention to* (II. 17); **temperō**, *restrain* (I. 33).

106. *a.* A few Intransitive Verbs are also used Transitively by Caesar, and govern the Accusative; examples are, **impūnitātem concēdere**, *grant escape from punishment* (I. 14); **mīlitēs, quōs imperāverat**, *the soldiers that he had levied* (I. 7).

b. Verbs which take the Dative of the Indirect Object are in the Passive used only Impersonally; as, **Sibi persuādērī**, *That the conviction was forced upon him, that he was persuaded* (I. 40).

107. *a.* The Dative of the Indirect Object is used after many Verbs compounded with the Prepositions **ad, ante, com-** (for **cum**), **in, inter, ob, prae, sub,** and **super;** as, **omnibus praestārent**, *they excelled all* (I. 2).

b. Transitive Verbs compounded with these Prepositions may have both a Direct and an Indirect Object, the Dative depending not on the Preposition but on the Compound; as, **fīnitimīs bellum īnferre**, *to wage war on their neighbors* (I. 2).

108. *a.* The Dative is used after Adjectives meaning *agreeable, friendly, hurtful, hostile, like, unlike, near, subject, obedient, suitable, appropriate,* and many others; as, **plēbī acceptus**, *acceptable to the people* (I. 3); **proximī Germānīs**, *next to the Germans* (I. 1); **locum idōneum castrīs**, *a place suitable for a camp* (II. 17).

b. **Similis** is used with the Genitive when referring to an inner or complete resemblance, as, **vērī simile**, *probable,* lit. *having the likeness* *of truth* (III. 13); otherwise with the Dative; as, **fugae similis**, *like a rout* (V. 53).

109. *a.* The Dative of Reference designates the Person or Interest affected by the action or state expressed in a Verb, or in a Clause as a whole; it should be translated with *to, for, of, from, in,* or left untranslated, according to the meaning of the clause in which it appears, and the requirements of English idiom. Thus, **iniūriae sibi cōnscius fuisset,** *had been conscious of wrong-doing,* lit. *had been conscious, to itself, of wrong-doing* (I. 14); **sī sibi pūrgātī esse vellent,** *if they wanted to clear themselves in his sight,* lit. *to clear themselves with reference to himself* (I. 28); **sēsē Caesarī ad pedēs prōiēcērunt,** *prostrated themselves at Caesar's feet,* lit. *in relation to Caesar* (I. 31).

b. A Dative of Reference is used with Verbs of *taking away,* especially those compounded with **ab, dē,** and **ex** (sometimes called Dative of Separation); thus, **Aeduīs lībertātem sint ēreptūrī,** *that they were going to take away liberty from the Aeduans,* lit. *that as regards the Aeduans, they are,* etc. (I. 17); **scūtō ūnī mīlitī dētrāctō,** *snatching a shield from a soldier,* lit. *to a soldier,* the Dative expressing the point of view of the soldier (II. 25); **longē eīs āfutūrum,** *would be far from benefiting them,* lit. *would be far away with reference to them* (I. 36).

c. A Dative of Reference is used with **interdīcō,** which may take also the Ablative of the Thing; as, **Galliā Rōmānīs interdīxisset,** *had denied to the Romans any rights in Gaul,* lit. *from Gaul* (I. 46).

110. The Dative is used with the Passive Periphrastic Conjugation to express Agency; as, **omnibus Gallīs idem esse faciendum,** *that all the Celts would have to do the same thing* (I. 31); **Caesarī omnia erant agenda,** *Caesar had to see to everything* (II. 20).

111. The Dative is used with the Verb **sum** to denote Possession; as, **Mercātōribus est aditus,** *Traders have access* (IV. 2); **quid . . . Caesarī . . . negōtiī esset,** *what business Caesar . . . had* (I. 34).

112. *a.* The Dative is used with Verbs to denote the Purpose or Tendency of an action; as, **locum domiciliō dēligerent,** *might select a place for a permanent habitation* (I. 30); **locum castrīs dēligit** (Historical Present), *selected a place for a camp* (VII. 16 and often); **Diēs colloquiō dictus est,** *a day was appointed for a conference* (I. 42).

b. **Sum** and several other Verbs may have two Datives, a Dative of Purpose or Tendency and a Dative of Reference; as, **sibi eam rem cūrae futūram,** *that this matter should have his attention,* lit. *should be to him for a care* (I. 33); **cum auxiliō Nerviīs venīrent,** *when they were*

coming to the assistance of the Nervians, lit. *for an aid to the Nervians*
(II. 29).

THE ACCUSATIVE CASE

113. *a.* The Direct Object of a Transitive Verb is in the Accusative Case; as, **frūmentum combūrunt** (Historical Present), *they burned the grain* (I. 5).

b. Caesar uses as Transitive Verbs several Intransitives compounded with **ad, ante, circum, com-, in, ob, prae, praeter, sub,** and **trāns**; as, **sī īnsulam adīsset,** *if he should have visited the island* (IV. 20); **reliquōs antecēdunt,** *surpass the rest* (III. 8); **eum convēnissent,** *had met him* (I. 27); **sē grātiam initūrōs [esse],** *that they would gain favor* (VI. 43); **initā hieme,** *at the beginning of winter,* lit. *winter having been begun* (III. 7); **tēctum nōn subīssent,** *had not found shelter under a roof,* lit. *had not passed under a roof* (I. 36); **tantam virtūtem praestitērunt,** *displayed so great valor* (II. 27).

c. Caesar uses both **animadvertō** and **animum advertō** with the Accusative of the Direct Object conceived as the object of the mental action expressed by the Compound; thus, **id animum advertit,** *he noticed that* (I. 24); **haec animadvertisset,** *had noticed this* (I. 40).

114. *a.* Transitive Verbs compounded with **trāns** or **circum** may have two Accusatives, one dependent on the Verb, the other on the Preposition; as, **trēs partēs cōpiārum Helvētiōs id flūmen trādūxisse,** *that the Helvetians had taken three-fourths of their forces across the river* (I. 12), **partēs** being the object of **dūcere,** while **flūmen** is governed by **trāns**.

b. In the Passive the Object of the Verb used with two Accusatives becomes a Subject, while the Accusative governed by the Preposition remains; as, **nē maior multitūdō Rhēnum trādūcātur,** *that no greater host be brought across the Rhine* (I. 31).

115. *a.* Verbs of *making, choosing, regarding, giving, sending, having, calling, showing,* and some others, may have two Accusatives, one a Direct Object, the other a Predicate Accusative; as, **quem rēgem cōnstituerat,** *whom he had made king* (IV. 21); **quem 'vergobretum' appellant Aeduī,** *which the Aeduans call Vergobret* (I. 16).

b. In the construction of Verbs of *making, choosing, calling,* etc., with two Accusatives, the Predicate Accusative may be an Adjective; as, **utī . . . cīvitātēs stīpendiāriās habērent,** *that they might have states tributary to them* (I. 30).

c. In the Passive of Verbs of *making, choosing, calling,* etc., the

Direct Object of the Active is made the Subject and the Predicate
Accusative becomes a Predicate Nominative; as, **quī Celtae appellantur,** *who are called Celts* (I. 1); **Helvētiī certiōrēs factī sunt,**
the Helvetians were informed, where **certiōrēs,** an adjective in the
comparative degree, is predicative (I. 7).

116. *a.* Verbs of *asking, demanding, teaching* may have two Accusatives, one of the Person, the other of the Thing; as, **Aeduōs frūmentum flāgitāre,** *kept pressing the Aeduans for the grain* (I. 16).

b. With Verbs of *asking* and *demanding,* the Person may be expressed by the Ablative with a Preposition, the Thing asked by an
Accusative or by a Clause; as, **abs tē ratiōnem reposcent,** *they will
demand an accounting from you* (V. 30); **cum ab eīs quaereret quae
cīvitātēs . . . essent,** *making inquiry of them what states were . . .*
(II. 4).

c. With **quaerō** the Person may be expressed by the Ablative with
ab or **ex;** as, **quaerit ex sōlō ea,** *asked,* lit. *asks, (him) alone about
those things* (I. 18); the Accusative of the Thing may be replaced by
an Ablative with **dē;** as, **quōrum dē nātūrā cum quaereret,** *making
inquiry about the character of whom* (II. 15).

d. **Volō** is sometimes used like a Verb of *asking,* with two Accusatives; as, **sī quid** (Accusative) **ille sē** (Accusative) **velit,** *if he
(Caesar) wished anything of him* (I. 34).

117. *a.* With both Intransitive and Transitive Verbs Caesar sometimes uses a Neuter Pronoun as an Accusative of Result produced, to
carry forward or qualify the meaning; as, **Id eīs persuāsit,** *he persuaded them (to adopt) that (course),* lit. *he persuaded that to them* (I. 2);
hōc facere, *to do this* (III. 27).

b. The Accusative of Result may be a Noun of kindred meaning
with the Verb (Cognate Accusative); thus, **tūtam vītam vīvere,** *to
live a safe life.*

118. *a.* The Accusative is used to express Extent and Duration;
as, **mīlia passuum XVIIII** (for **undēvīgintī**), *nineteen miles* (I. 8);
multōs annōs, *many years* (I. 3); **magnam partem aestātis,** *during
a great part of the summer* (III. 12); **trīduī viam prōcessisset,** *had
advanced a three days' march* (I. 38).

b. Indefinite Extent or Degree may be expressed with certain
Verbs by the Neuter Accusative of Pronouns, or of Adjectives used
substantively; as, **quicquid possunt,** *whatever strength they have,* lit.
to whatever degree they are able (II. 17); **quid Germānī virtūte possent,** *what mettle the Germans had,* lit. *to what degree the Germans were*

able in respect to bravery (I. 36); **quōrum auctōritās plūrimum valeat** (Historical Present), *whose influence carried very great weight*, lit. *is strong to the highest degree* (I. 17); **sī quid** (Accusative) **opus esset,** *if there should be any need*, lit. *need to any extent* (I. 42).

c. Extent is expressed by the Accusative of **nihil,** and also by **partem** (Accusative of **pars**) used indefinitely, a construction often called Adverbial Accusative ; as, **nihil Caesaris imperium exspectābant,** *were not waiting at all for Caesar's orders,* lit. *to extent of nothing, to no extent* (II. 20); **maximam partem lacte atque pecore vīvunt,** *they live mostly on milk and meat,* where **partem** is used indefinitely, not being limited to a definite idea, as it is when a Genitive is dependent upon it (IV. 1).

d. Caesar uses **quod,** Singular Neuter of the Relative **quī,** as an Adverbial Accusative before **sī, nisi,** and **ubi,** where it may be translated *now, moreover, but, and,* or *even,* lit. *as to which;* as, **Quod sī . . . vellet,** *even if he were willing* (I. 14); **Quod sī quid . . .** *Now if anything* (I. 20).

e. Caesar uses **quid,** Singular Neuter of the Interrogative **quis,** as an Adverbial Accusative with the meaning *why ?* lit. *as to what thing ?* Thus, **Quid dubitās,** *Why do you hesitate ?* (V. 44).

119. *a.* Names of Towns or Small Islands are put in the Accusative to express the Limit of Motion; as, **Bibracte īre contendit** (Historical Present), *he made haste to go to Bibracte* (I. 23).

b. In like manner **domum,** the Accusative of **domus,** is used to express Limit of Motion; as, **quī domum rediērunt,** *who returned home* (I. 29).

120. *a.* The Accusative of names of towns is used with **ad** to express *to the vicinity of, in the neighborhood of;* as, **ad Genavam pervenit,** *he proceeded to the vicinity of Geneva* (I. 7) ; **Caesar . . . ad Alesiam castra fēcit,** *Caesar encamped in the neighborhood of Alesia* (VII. 68); but Caesar has **Vercingetorīx . . . Alesiam iter facere coepit,** *Vercingetorix began to march to Alesia,* without **ad,** because Vercingetorix fled to the town itself for refuge, **Alesiam** here expressing the Limit of Motion (VII. 68).

b. In such phrases as **ad oppidum Noviodūnum** (II. 12) the Name of the Town is in the Accusative, not because expressing a Limit of Motion, but as an appositive of **oppidum.**

121. The Subject of the Infinitive is in the Accusative; as, **diem īnstāre,** *that the day was at hand* (I. 16).

122. *a.* Caesar uses the following Prepositions with the Accusa-

tive only: **ad**, *to;* **adversus**, *against;* **ante**, *before;* **apud**, *near, with,
among;* **circā**, *around* (C only); **circiter**, *about;* **circum**, *around;*
cis, *on this side of;* **citrā**, *on this side of;* **contrā**, *against;* **ergā**,
towards; **extrā**, *outside of;* **infrā**, *below;* **inter**, *between;* **intrā**, *within;*
iuxtā, *near;* **ob**, *on account of;* **penes**, *in the possession of;* **per**,
through; **post**, *after;* **praeter**, *excepting;* **prope**, *near;* **propter**, *on
account of;* **secundum**, *along, after, besides, according to ;* **suprā**, *above;*
trāns, *across, on the other side of;* **ultrā**, *beyond;* **versus**, *toward.*

b. Several of these Prepositions are used by Caesar also as Adverbs;
as, **contrā**, *in opposition* (I. 18); **suprā**, *above* (II. 18).

123. *a.* With Nouns referring to Persons Caesar often uses **per**
with the Accusative to express the Means through which something
is done, as distinguished from Direct Agency, which is expressed by
the Ablative with **ab** ; as, **per eōs**, *with their help,* lit. *by means of them*
(I. 4).

b. Caesar uses also **propius**, *nearer,* the Comparative of **prope**, and
proximus, *next,* the Superlative of **propior**, with the Accusative; as,
propius sē, *nearer to themselves* (IV. 9); **quī proximī Rhēnum incolunt**, *who dwell next to the Rhine* (I. 54).

c. **Versus** follows its Noun, and is sometimes used in a separable
Compound with **ad** and **in** ; as, **Metlosēdum versus**, *towards Metlosedum* (VII. 61); **ad Oceanum versus**, *towards the Ocean* (VI. 33).

124. *a.* The Prepositions **in** and **sub** are used with the Accusative
to denote Motion, with the Ablative to denote Rest; as, **in partēs
trēs**, *into three parts* (I. 1); **in eōrum fīnibus**, *in their country* (I. 1) ;
sub iugum missum, *sent under the yoke* (I. 7); **sub aquā**, *under
water* (V. 18).

b. **Super** is used ordinarily with the Accusative, but occasionally
with the Ablative.

THE ABLATIVE CASE

125. *a.* Caesar uses the following Prepositions with the Ablative :
ā, or **ab, abs**, *away from, by;* **cum**, *with;* **dē**, *down from, concerning;*
ex or **ē**, *out from, out of;* **prae**, *before;* **prō**, *in front of, for, considering, as ;* **sine**, *without.*

b. The form **abs** appears only in **abs tē** (V. 30). **Ab** and **ex** are
regularly used before vowels and **h** ; **ā** and **ē**, before consonants, but
before consonants **ab** and **ex** are also used.

c. With the Ablative of the Personal, Reflexive, and Relative Pronouns **cum** is ordinarily joined; thus **nōbīscum**, *with us* (V. 17);

sēcum, *with him* (I. 8), *with himself* (I. 36); **quibuscum**, *with whom* (I. 1).

126. *a.* Direct Agency with the Passive is expressed by **ā, ab**, with the Ablative; as, **ab Helvētiīs pulsum**, *routed by the Helvetians* (I. 7).

b. Caesar sometimes uses an Abstract or Collective Noun with **ā, ab**, to express Agency; as, **ā multitūdine**, *by a host* (III. 2).

c. Caesar often uses **ā, ab**, and sometimes **ex**, to indicate a Local Relation, where we use *on*, *in*, or *at*; as, **ā dextrō cornū**, *on the right wing*, lit. *from (the point of view of) the right wing* (I. 52); **ā novissimō agmine**, *on the rear* (I. 23); **ā fronte**, *in front* (II. 23).

127. *a.* An Ablative of Separation without a Preposition is regularly used by Caesar with many Verbs meaning *keep from, refrain from; withdraw from; strip, deprive of; free from; lack, be without;* as, **proeliō abstinēbat**, *was refraining from battle* (I. 22); **eā spē dēiectī**, *deprived of this hope* (I. 8).

The most important of the Verbs thus used by Caesar are:

abstineō, *refrain from;* **careō**, *be without* (VI. 38); **dēiciō**, *cast down from;* **dēsistō**, *desist from, leave off* (I. 8); **egeō**, *lack* (C. III. 32); **emittō**, *let go from* (I. 25); **excēdō**, *withdraw from, leave* (II. 25); **exuō**, *strip* (III. 6); **interclūdō**, *cut off* (I. 23).

levō, *relieve from* (V. 27); **līberō**, *free from* (IV. 19); **nūdō**, *clear* (II. 6); **prohibeō**, *keep from* (I. 1); **spoliō**, *rob of, despoil* (V. 6), and **exspoliō**, *rob* (VII. 77).

b. With several of these Verbs the idea of Separation may be expressed by a Preposition; as, **ab oppidīs vim hostium prohibēre**, *to defend the towns against the violence of the enemy*, lit. *to hold back the violence of the enemy from the towns* (I. 11).

c. With other Verbs the Ablative of Separation is regularly accompanied by a Preposition; as, **exercitum dēdūcat ex hīs regiōnibus**, *leads his army out of these regions* (I. 44).

d. Caesar uses **egeō** with the Genitive also: **nē quis . . . auxiliī egēret**, *that not any one be without help* (VI. 11).

128. *a.* A variety of the Ablative of Separation is the Ablative of Source, or Origin, which Caesar uses with **nātus**, participle of **nāscor**, and **ortus**, participle of **orior**; as, **amplissimō genere nātus**, *sprung from most illustrious stock* (IV. 12); **summō ortus locō**, *born to the highest station in life*, lit. *risen from the highest place* (VII. 77).

b. Origin is more broadly stated with Prepositions; as, **quibus ortī ex cīvitātibus**, *tribes from which they (were) descended* (V. 12);

ortōs ā Germānīs, *descendants* (lit. *descended*) *from the Germans* (II.
4); **ab Dīte patre prōgnātōs**, *descendants from Father Dis* (VI. 18).

129. *a.* The Ablative of Comparison is used by Caesar after
Comparative Adjectives and Adverbs; as, **paulō cēterīs hūmāniōrēs**, **cēterīs** being used instead of **quam cēterī (sunt)**, *a little
more civilized than the rest* (IV. 3); **nōn amplius quīnīs aut sēnīs
mīlibus passuum**, *not more than five or six miles each day* (I. 15);
celerius omnī opīniōne, *more quickly than any one had anticipated*,
lit. *than every expectation* (II. 3).

b. In a few instances Caesar uses **amplius, longius**, and **minus**
as if in place of **amplius quam, longius quam, minus quam**, without influence upon the construction of the Noun following; as,
nōn amplius pedum sescentōrum (Genitive of Measure), *not more
than six hundred feet* (I. 38); **neque longius mīlia** (Accusative of
Extent) **passuum VIII**, *and not further than eight miles* (V. 53);
mīlitēs sunt paulō minus DCC dēsīderātī, *almost seven hundred
men were lost*, lit. *by a small degree less than* 700 (VII. 51).

130. *a.* The Place Whence is regularly expressed by the Ablative
with a Preposition, generally **ex** or **dē**; as, **ex agrīs**, *from the country*
(I. 4).

b. **Domō**, Ablative of **domus**, is used in the Ablative of the Place
Whence without a Preposition; as, **domō exīre**, *to go out from home*
(I. 6).

131. *a.* The Ablative is used to denote Means or Instrument; as,
gladiīs partem eōrum interfēcērunt, *killed a part of them with
swords* (II. 23); **proeliīs contendunt**, *they contend in battle*, lit. *by
means of battles* (I. 1); **memoriā tenēbat**, *he remembered*, lit. *held by
means of memory* (I. 7).

b. The Ablative of Means may denote persons as well as things;
as, **quīngentīs equitibus**, *with five hundred horsemen* (I. 15).

c. Caesar uses the Ablative of Means with **ūtor, abūtor, fruor,
fungor, nītor, innītor**, and ordinarily with **potior**; thus **ephippiīs
ūtī**, *to use saddle-cloths*, lit. *to assist themselves by means of saddle-cloths*
(IV. 2); **impedīmentīs potītī sunt**, *obtained possession of the baggage*,
that is *made themselves masters by means of the baggage* (I. 26).

d. Caesar uses **potior** also with the Genitive; as, **tōtīus Galliae
potīrī**, *to become masters of the whole* (*of*) *Gaul* (I. 3).

e. Caesar uses an Ablative of Means with **frētus**, *relying on*, lit.
supported by; as, **victōriīs frētī**, *relying on their victories* (III. 21).

f. The Ablative with **ūtor** is sometimes accompanied by a Predicate Ablative, the construction resembling that of two Accusatives after verbs of *having* (*115, a*); thus **īsdem ducibus ūsus,** *employing the same men as guides* (II. 7).

132. *a.* **Opus est,** *there is need,* is used with the Ablative of the Thing needed, which may be expressed by a Perfect Passive Participle; thus, **sī quid opus factō esset,** *if anything should require action,* lit. *if there should be need of* (*something*) *done, to any extent* (I. 42).

b. With **opus est** the Thing needed may be expressed by a Neuter Pronoun in the Nominative; as, **sī quid** (Subject) **ipsī ā Caesare opus esset,** *if he himself had wanted anything of Caesar,* lit. *if anything were necessary to himself from Caesar* (I. 34); **quid . . . opus esset,** *what was necessary* (II. 22); **Quaecumque opus sunt,** *Whatever is* (lit. *whatever things are*) *necessary* (V. 40).

133. The Ablative of Means is used with a few Adjectives; as, **nāvēs . . . omnī genere armōrum ōrnātissimae,** *ships completely fitted out with every kind of equipment* (III. 14).

134. *a.* Caesar uses the Ablative of the Way by Which with several words referring to Natural Features and Military Operations; as, **adversō colle,** *up the hill,* lit. *by the hill facing them* (II. 19); **quod flūmine subvexerat,** *which he had brought up the river,* lit. *by means of the river* (I. 16); **duābus portīs ēruptiōnem fierī,** *that a sally be made from* (lit. *by*) *two gates* (III. 19).

The words thus used are:

collis, flūmen; fretum (C. II. 3); **iter,** especially in **magnīs itineribus,** *by forced marches* (I. 37); **iugum** (C. III. 97); **pōns** (C. I. 55); **porta, vadum** (I. 6, 8), and **via** (V. 19).

b. The Ablative of the Way by Which is sometimes used indefinitely with words referring to Distance; as, **tantō spatiō secūtī quantum efficere potuērunt,** *following so great a distance* (lit. *by so great a space*) *as they were able to cover* (IV. 35).

135. *a.* An Ablative denoting Cause is used with many Verbs and Adjectives, particularly those which express *pleasure, pain, trust, distrust, boastfulness,* and the like; as, **annī tempore cōnfīsae,** *trusting in the time of year,* lit. *confident because of the time of year* (III. 27); **Quod suā victōriā glōriārentur,** *the fact that they were boasting of* (lit. *by reason of*) *their victory* (I. 14).

b. In some phrases the force of the Ablative of Cause has become obscured, as in **causā** and **grātiā,** *for the sake of,* with the Genitive, and in **iussū, iniussū,** and the like; as, **auxiliī causā,** *as an auxiliary force,* lit. *for the sake of support* (III. 18; II. 24); **iussū Caesaris,** *by* *(reason of)* Caesar's orders (VII. 3); **iniussū suō et cīvitātis,** *without his own authorization and (that) of the state,* i.e. because of un-authorization (I. 19).

136. *a.* The Ablative of Manner (answering the question "How?") is used by Caesar with **cum,** especially when the Noun is modified by an Adjective; as, **cum cruciātū necābātur,** *was put to death with torture* (V. 45); **multīs cum lacrimīs,** *with many tears* (I. 20).

b. The Ablative of Manner is often used without a Preposition; as, **et mente et animō,** *with heart and soul* (VI. 5).

c. In certain connections Caesar uses an Ablative with the meaning *in accordance with;* as, **Mōribus suīs,** *in accordance with their customs* (I. 4); **cōnsuētūdine populī Rōmānī,** *in accordance with the practice of the Roman people* (III. 23).

137. *a.* The Ablative is used with **cum** to express Accompaniment; as, **cum suīs omnibus cōpiīs,** *with all his forces* (I. 38).

b. An Ablative of Accompaniment referring to Military Operations, when qualified by an Adjective, may be used without **cum;** but if the modifier is a Numeral, **cum** must be used. Thus, **omnibus cōpiīs contendērunt,** *they hastened with all their forces* (II. 7); **cum duābus legiōnibus,** *with two legions* (I. 21).

c. The use of **cum** with the Ablative of Accompaniment is much broader than the meaning *together with.* Examples are: **cōnstituerat cum lēgātīs,** *had appointed with the envoys* (I. 8); **cōnsiliō cum lēgātīs commūnicātō,** *having imparted his determination to his lieutenants* (IV. 13); **cum Caesare ēgit,** *treated with Caesar* (I. 13); **cum illā (cōnsuētūdine) comparandam,** *to be compared with that manner of life* (I. 31).

138. An Ablative of Attendant Circumstance is used by Caesar with an Adjective, Pronominal Adjective, or Genitive as modifying word, and without a Preposition; as, **paribus intervāllīs,** *at equal intervals* (I. 51); **imperiō nostrō,** *under our sovereignty* (II. 1); **commodō reī pūblicae,** *with advantage to* (lit. *of*) *the State* (I. 35); **Caesaris voluntāte,** *with Caesar's approval* (I. 30).

139. The Ablative is used with certain Verbs meaning *exchange, mix,* and *accustom;* thus, **nē studium bellī gerendī agrī cultūrā commūtent,** *that they may not exchange their devotion to aggressive warfare for farming* (VI. 22); **nūllō officiō aut dīsciplīnā assuēfactī,** *habituated to* (lit. *familiarized with*) *no obligation or training* (IV. 1); **admixtum lacte,** *mixed with milk* (C. III. 48).

140. The Ablative of Degree of Difference is used with Comparatives, and with Adverbs or Phrases implying Comparison; as, **paulō longius**, *a little further*, lit. *further by a little* (II. 20); **paucīs ante diēbus**, *a few days before* (I. 18); **mīlibus passuum duōbus ultrā eum**, *two miles beyond him*, lit. *beyond him by two miles* (I. 48).

141. The Ablative of Price is used by Caesar only in indefinite expressions; thus, **parvō pretiō redēmpta**, *purchased at a low price* (I. 18); **impēnsō pretiō**, *at a high price* (IV. 2); **quantō dētrīmentō**, *at how great a loss* (VII. 19); **levī mōmentō**, *of slight account* (VII. 39).

142. *a.* The Ablative of Specification (answering the question "In respect to what?") is used with Verbs and Adjectives and the Adverb **saepe**; as, **cum virtūte omnibus praestārent**, *since they surpassed all in valor* (I. 2); **Suēba nātiōne**, *a Sueban by birth* (I. 53); **numerō ad duodecim**, *about twelve in number*, lit. *in number about twelve* (I. 5); **saepe numerō**, *frequently*, lit. *often in respect to number* (I. 33).

b. The Ablative of Specification is used with **dignus** and **indignus**; as, **nihil, quod ipsīs esset indignum, committēbant**, *they did nothing that was unworthy of them*, lit. *in respect to themselves* (V. 35).

143. *a.* The Descriptive Ablative, or Ablative of Quality, is modified by an Adjective or, more rarely, by a Noun in the Genitive; as, **hominēs inimīcō animō**, *men of unfriendly (attitude of) mind* (I. 7).

b. The Descriptive Ablative may be used predicatively; as, **ingentī magnitūdine Germānōs esse**, *that the Germans were of huge size* (I. 39); **sunt speciē . . . taurī**, *they have* (lit. *are of*) *the appearance of a bull* (VI. 28).

144. *a.* The Ablative Absolute consists of a Noun or Pronoun in the Ablative with a Participle, Adjective, or Noun in the same case, and is loosely related with the rest of the sentence; as, **rēgnō occupātō**, *having seized the governing power*, lit. *the governing power having been seized* (I. 3).

b. The Ablative Absolute may express Time, Attendant Circumstance, Cause, Condition, Concession, Means, or Manner, and may often be translated by a clause; thus:

(1) Time: **M. Messālā, M. Pīsōne cōnsulibus**, *in the consulship of Marcus Messala and Marcus Piso*, lit. *Marcus Messala, Marcus Piso (being) consuls* (I. 2).

(2) Attendant Circumstance: **convocātīs eōrum prīncipibus**, *having called together their leading men* (I. 16); **captō monte et succēdentibus nostrīs**, *after they had reached the height and our men were coming up* (I. 25).

(3) Cause: **omnibus frūgibus āmissīs**, *since all the produce of the fields was gone*, lit. *all . . . having been lost* (I. 28).

(4) Condition: **datā facultāte**, *if opportunity should have been granted* (I. 7).

(5) Concession or Opposition: **superiōribus locīs occupātīs**, *though the higher positions had been seized* (I. 23).

(6) Means: **eō dēprecātōre**, *through his intercession*, lit. *he (being) intercessor* (I. 9).

(7) Manner: **equō admissō**, *with (his) horse at top speed*, lit. *his horse having been let go* (I. 22).

145. *a.* The Place Where is regularly expressed by the Ablative with a Preposition; as, **in eōrum fīnibus**, *in their territories* (I. 1).

b. Names of Towns, excepting those in the Singular of the First and Second Declensions, are put in the Ablative of the Place Where, without a Preposition; as, **Bibracte**, *at Bibracte* (VII. 90).

c. The Noun **locus**, Singular and Plural, is often used in the Ablative of the Place Where without a Preposition, as are also several other Nouns when modified by an Adjective, particularly **tōtus**; thus, **aliēnō locō**, *on unfavorable ground*, lit. *in an unfavorable place* (I. 15); **tōtīs castrīs**, *throughout the camp*, lit. *in the whole camp* (I. 39); **eōdem vēstīgiō**, *in the same spot* (IV. 2).

146. With Names of Towns of the First and Second Declensions, Singular, Place Where is expressed by the Locative; as, **Cēnabī**, *at Cenabum* (VII. 14); also **domī**, Locative of **domus**, *at home* (I. 18).

147. *a.* The Time When, and Time Within Which anything happens, may be denoted by the Ablative without a Preposition; as, **diē quārtō**, *on the fourth day* (I. 26); **paucīs annīs**, *within a few years* (I. 31).

b. Words that have only an indirect reference to Time are sometimes put in the Ablative of Time When or Within Which; as, **patrum nostrōrum memoriā**, *within the memory of our fathers* (I. 12); **initiō ōrātiōnis**, *at the beginning of his statement* (I. 43).

c. Intervals of Space and Duration of Time are sometimes expressed by the Ablative, especially when modified by an Adjective or Genitive; as, **mīlibus passuum sex**, *six miles (distant)*, lit. *by six thousands of paces* (I. 48); **tōtā nocte iērunt**, *all night long they went on* (I. 26).

ADJECTIVES

148. *a.* Adjectives and Participles, whether Attributive or Predicative, agree in Gender, Number, and Case with the Noun or Pronoun to which they belong.

b. Attributive Adjectives and Participles stand in direct relation with a Noun or Pronoun; as, **fortissimō virō** (Abl.), *a very brave man* (II. 25); **Is, rēgnī cupiditāte inductus,** *He, led on by a desire of kingly power* (I. 2).

c. Predicate Adjectives, and Participles in Predicate used as Adjectives, are connected with a Noun or Pronoun through a Verb or Participle; as, **fortissimī sunt Belgae,** *the Belgians are the bravest* (I. 1); **quī perītissimus habēbātur,** *who was considered highly skilled* (I. 21); **Gallia est dīvīsa,** *Gaul is divided,* the Perfect Passive Participle of **dīvidō** being used as an Adjective; if **est dīvīsa** were here a Perfect Passive tense, it would have to be translated *has been divided* or *was divided* (I. 1).

d. A Predicate Adjective or Participle limiting an Infinitive or Clause is Neuter; as, **perfacile esse . . . potīrī,** *that it was exceedingly easy* (or, *a very easy thing*) *to obtain possession of,* **perfacile** being the Predicate after **esse,** to which **potīrī** stands as subject (I. 2).

e. A Participle forming part of an Infinitive may agree with the Subject of the Principal Verb; as, **meritus** [esse] **vidēbātur,** *was seen to have earned* (I. 40).

149. Demonstrative and other Pronouns used like Adjectives agree with the word to which they belong; as, **eō tempore,** *at that time* (I. 3); **quā arrogantiā,** *what presumption* (I. 46); **id ipsum,** *that very thing* (VII. 50).

150. *a.* An Attributive Adjective used with two or more Nouns regularly agrees with the Nearest; as, **eādem alacritāte ac studiō,** *the same eagerness and enthusiasm* (IV. 24).

b. A Predicate Adjective used with two or more Nouns is regularly Plural; when the Nouns are of Different Genders, the Adjective is generally Masculine if Persons are referred to, Neuter if only Things or Abstract Qualities are denoted, though even in this case the agreement may be with the nearer substantive; as, **frāter et soror eōrum bonī sunt,** *their brother and sister are good;* **et mūrus et porta alta erant,** *both the wall and the gate were high;* **ut bracchia atque umerī . . . līberī esse possent,** *that their arms and shoulders might be free* (VII. 56).

c. An Adjective or Participle may agree with a Noun in Sense, without regard to Grammatical Gender or Number; as, **hominum mīlia** (Neuter) **VI, perterritī** (Masculine), *six thousand (of) men, thoroughly frightened* (I. 27).

d. A Noun, particularly a Noun with Verbal Force, is sometimes modified by a prepositional phrase; as, **lēgātiōnem ad cīvitātēs**, *the office of envoy to the states* (I. 3).

151. Adjectives are sometimes used in Latin where in English an Adverb or a Phrase is required; as, **laetī . . . ad castra pergunt** (Historical Present), *joyfully . . . they advanced against the camp* (III. 18); **viātōrēs etiam invītōs cōnsistere cōgant**, *they oblige travelers, even against their will, to stop* (IV. 5).

152. *a.* Certain Adjectives often designate a part of that to which they refer; as, **in colle mediō**, *halfway up the hill* (I. 24); **prīmā nocte**, *in the first part of the night* (I. 27); **summus mōns**, *the top of the height* (I. 22).

The Adjectives thus used by Caesar are **extrēmus** (as II. 5); **īnfimus** (II. 18); **medius**; **multus** (I. 22); **novissimus**, in **novissimum agmen** (I. 15 and often), *the rear of a* marching *column* as the *latest part* of a column to pass a given point; **prīmus** and **summus**.

b. The Adjectives **prīnceps, prior, prīmus** are sometimes used by Caesar to designate *the first to* do or experience something; as, **prīnceps poenās persolvit**, *was the first to pay the penalty* (I. 12); **neque priōrēs bellum īnferre**, *did not take the lead in waging war*, where **prior** is used because only two peoples, the Germans and the Romans, are referred to (IV. 7).

c. The Adjective **multus** and another Adjective agreeing with the same Noun are joined by **et** or **-que**; as, **multīs gravibusque vulneribus**, *many severe wounds* (II. 25).

153. *a.* The Comparative and Superlative of both Adjectives and Adverbs sometimes have shades of meaning best expressed in English by *too, rather, very, exceedingly,* or *highly,* and the like, with the Positive; as, **paulō fortius**, *unusually brave,* lit. *a little braver* than usual (III. 14); **lātissimō atque altissimō**, *very wide and very deep* (I. 2).

b. A Superlative is sometimes modified by an Adverb; as, **longē nōbilissimus**, *far the highest in rank* (I. 2).

c. The highest possible degree is expressed by **quam** with the Superlative, as **quam maximum numerum**, *as great a number as possible, the greatest possible number* (I. 3); **quam celerrimē potuit**, *as quickly as possible* (I. 37); **quam prīmum**, *as soon as possible* (I. 40).

154. *a.* Adjectives and Participles are used as Substantives, frequently in the Plural, less often in the Singular; as, **vērī** (Neuter) **simile,** *probable,* lit. *like truth* (III. 13); **nostrī,** *our men* (I. 52); **novissimīs** (Masculine), *for the rear,* lit. *for those last* (I. 25); **sua,** *their possessions* (I. 11); **prō vīsō,** *as seen,* lit. *for (that which was) seen* (I. 22).

b. Caesar uses the Genitive Singular Neuter **suī** with a collective force in the Gerundive Construction, and in such cases it should be translated as if plural; as, **suī colligendī facultātem,** *opportunity of collecting their forces,* lit. *of collecting themselves* (III. 6).

PRONOUNS

155. The Genitives **meī, nostrī, tuī,** and **vestrī** (*39, a*) are regularly Objective, **nostrum** and **vestrum** being used in other relations; as, **tantā contemptiōne nostrī,** *with so great contempt for us* (V. 29); **omnium vestrum,** *of you all* (VII. 77).

156. The Plural is often used for the Singular of the Pronoun of the First Person, just as in our "editorial we"; thus Caesar when referring to himself as writer often uses a Plural Verb, as, **ut ante dēmōnstrāvimus,** *as we have previously shown* (II. 22).

157. *a.* The Possessive Pronouns are expressed only when required for the sake of Clearness, Emphasis, or Contrast; in translating they must be supplied in accordance with English idiom; as, **Cōnsidius, equō admissō,** *Considius with (his) horse at top speed* (I. 22).

b. When expressed for Clearness, and unemphatic, the Possessive Pronoun follows its Noun, as, **in cīvitāte suā,** *in his state* (I. 3); when used for Emphasis or Contrast, the Possessive Pronoun precedes its Noun, as, **meum officium,** *MY duty* (IV. 25).

c. Caesar often uses **noster** to designate that which is Roman; as, **nostram amīcitiam,** *our friendship* (I. 43).

d. A Possessive Pronoun and a Genitive are sometimes coördinated in construction; as, **suō populīque Rōmānī beneficiō,** *with his own kindness and that of the Roman people,* that is, *kindness of himself and of the Roman people* (I. 35).

e. **suus** may mean *his characteristic, his well-known;* as **suā clēmentiā,** *his well-known clemency* (II. 14).

158. *a.* The Reflexive Pronoun of the Third Person, **sē,** and the corresponding Possessive **suus,** refer to the Subject of the Verb; in a Subordinate Clause they may refer to the Subject of the Principal Clause (Indirect Reflexive). Thus, **sē ēripuit,** *he rescued himself*

(I. 4); **legiō . . . eī grātiās ēgit, quod dē sē optimum iūdicium fēcisset,** *the legion . . . conveyed thanks to him because he had passed an extremely favorable opinion on it* (I. 41).

b. In the Pronouns of the First and Second Persons the regular forms are sometimes Reflexive, as, **mē servāre nōn possum,** *I cannot save myself* (VII. 50); so also *is,* as **eōs,** *themselves* (II. 1).

c. In translating into Latin the English Possessives 'his,' ' her,' 'its,' ' their,' when referring to the subject of the Verb must be rendered by forms of the Reflexive **suus.**

159. The Reciprocal Relation is expressed by **inter sē** (lit. *among themselves*), which must be translated in accordance with the requirements of English idiom; as, **inter sē dant,** *they gave* (lit. *give*) *to one another* (I. 3); **inter sē differunt,** *they differ from one another* (I. 1); **inter sē collocūtī,** *having conferred with one another* (IV. 30); **cohortātī inter sē,** *urging one another on* (IV. 25); **inter sē contenderent,** *they strove together* (I. 31); **inter sē,** referring to two persons, *with each other* (V. 44).

160. *a.* The Demonstrative Pronoun **hīc,** *this,* refers to something near the speaker or the subject of thought; **iste,** *that of yours,* to something near the person addressed; **ille,** *that,* to something more remote; and **is,** *that,* to something thought of in a less definite relation. Thus: **Hīc pāgus,** *This canton* (I. 12); **Animī est ista mollitia,** *That is lack of resolution on your part* (VII. 77); **illī simile bellō,** *like that war* with the Cimbrians and Teutons (VII. 77); **Is diēs,** *That day* just referred to (I. 6).

b. Caesar frequently uses the Demonstrative **is,** less frequently **hīc** and **ille,** where the English has a Personal Pronoun of the Third Person; as, **ad eōs,** *to them* (I. 1); **cur hunc quisquam discessūrum iūdicāret,** *why should any one suppose that he* (Ariovistus) *would withdraw* (I. 40); **illum ūnō diē fēcisse . . . ,** *that he* (Caesar) *had in one day accomplished* (I. 13).

c. Caesar frequently uses the Neuter Singular and Neuter Plural of **hīc, ille,** and **is** with the meaning *this* (*thing*), *that* (*thing*), *it, these things, those things;* a Noun may sometimes be supplied in translation. Thus, **id quod,** *that which* (I. 5); **Id eīs persuāsit,** *he persuaded them* (*to*) *that course* (I. 2); **illa esse vēra,** *that those statements were true* (I. 20).

d. A Demonstrative Pronoun is sometimes used in Latin where English usage prefers an Article; thus, **Ea rēs,** *The matter,* lit. *that thing* (I. 4); **eum locum,** *a place* (II. 16).

e. A Demonstrative Pronoun used as Subject is regularly attracted into agreement with a Noun in the Predicate; as **Animī est ista mollitia**, for **istud est animī mollitia**, *that is lack of resolution on your part* (VII. 77).

161. *a.* The Demonstratives **hīc** and **ille** sometimes refer to what follows; as, **hōc facilius . . . quod**, *the more easily on this (account) because* (I. 2); **multīs dē causīs . . . quārum illa fuit iūstissima, quod**, *for many reasons, of which this was the most weighty, that* (IV. 16).

b. Caesar sometimes uses **hīc** and **ille** in contrast, with the meaning *the latter* (that last mentioned) and *the former* (that previously mentioned); as, **Reliquī . . . sē atque illōs alunt ; hī rūrsus annō post in armīs sunt, illī domī remanent**, *The rest support themselves and those* in the field; *the latter after one year are again in arms, the former remain at home* (IV. I).

c. A Conjunction followed by **is** or **hīc** may express an Emphatic Characterization; as, **legiōnem, neque eam plēnissimam** (sc. **legiōnem**), *the legion, and that lacking its full strength*, lit. *and that not most full* (III. 2).

162. *a.* The Intensive Pronoun **ipse** with Nouns and Pronouns has the meaning *self, very;* as, **ipsī magistrātūs**, *the magistrates themselves* (I. 17); **ipsum esse Dumnorīgem**, *that Dumnorix was the very man* (I. 18); **in ipsīs rīpīs**, *on the very banks* (II. 23).

b In Subordinate Clauses **ipse** may be used as an Indirect Reflexive referring to the Principal Subject, or to avoid ambiguity; as, **Ariovistus respondit, sī quid ipsī ā Caesare opus esset**, *Ariovistus answered that if he himself had wanted anything of Caesar*, lit. *if anything were necessary to himself from Caesar* (I. 34).

c. Contrasted pronouns are often placed in proximity; as, **sē ipsī interficiunt**, *they all killed one another*, lit. *they themselves slay themselves* (V. 37).

163. *a.* A Relative Pronoun agrees with its Antecedent in Gender and Number, but its Case depends upon its construction in the clause to which it belongs; as, **trēs (legiōnēs**, Fem., Acc.), **quae** (Fem., Pl., Nom.) **. . . hiemābant**, *three legions which were wintering* (I. 10).

b. A Relative referring to two or more Antecedents of the same Gender and Number agrees with them in Gender, but in Number may agree with the nearest Antecedent, or be Plural; as, **prō suā clēmentiā ac mānsuētūdine, quam audīrent**, *in accordance with his forbearance and graciousness, of which they were hearing* (II. 31);

fīlius et frātris fīlius, . . . quōs . . . , *his son and his brother's son, whom* . . . (V. 27).

c. A Relative referring to two or more Antecedents of different Gender or Number may agree with the nearest Antecedent, or be Masculine Plural in case one Antecedent denotes a man, Feminine Plural in case one Antecedent denotes a woman and the others things, or Neuter Plural in case only things are denoted; thus, **frūmentō** (Neut.) **commeātūque, quī** (M., Sing.), *grain and (other) supplies which* . . . (I. 48); **mātrēs familiae** . . . **petiērunt, nē sē** (Fem.), **et līberōs dēderent, quōs** . . . , *the matrons besought not to give up themselves and the children whom* (VII. 26); **ūsus ac disciplīna, quae** (Neuter Plural) . . . , *experience and training, which* . . . (I. 40).

164. *a.* The Antecedent of a Relative Pronoun is sometimes omitted; as, (**eī incolunt**) **quī,** *those inhabit who* (I. 1).

b. Caesar sometimes uses a Relative referring to an implied Antecedent; as, **servīlī tumultū, quōs** . . . , as if he had said **tumultū servōrum, quōs** . . . , *in the uprising of the slaves, whom* . . . (I. 40).

c. A Noun in Predicate attracts a Relative Pronoun standing as subject into agreement with it; as, **Belgās, quam** (for **quōs**) **tertiam esse Galliae partem dīxerāmus,** *the Belgians who, we had said, form* (lit. *are*) *a third of Gaul* (II. 1).

d. A Plural Relative may refer for its Antecedent to a Singular Collective Noun which suggests Plurality; as, **equitātum** . . . **quī videant,** *cavalry* . . . *to see,* lit. *who should see* (I. 15).

165. *a.* An Antecedent is sometimes repeated in a Relative Clause, and should be translated only once; as, **itinera duo, quibus itineribus,** *two routes by which* (I. 6), not *by which routes.*

b. An Appositional Antecedent is sometimes incorporated in a Relative Clause, and should be translated; as, **quod tempus convēnerat,** *the time which had been agreed on* (II. 19).

c. An Antecedent is often incorporated in a Relative Clause; as, **Cui ratiōnī,** . . . **hāc,** *By the cunning,* . . . *for which* (I. 40).

166. Caesar uses the Neuter of a Relative or Demonstrative Pronoun, sometimes both a Demonstrative and a Relative, referring to a Clause or Thought as a whole; as, **supplicātiō dēcrēta est, quod** . . . , *a thanksgiving was decreed, (a distinction) which* . . . (II. 35); **magna, id quod necesse erat accidere, perturbātiō facta est,** *a great commotion, as was bound to be the case, ensued* (IV. 29).

167. A Relative is often used in Latin at the beginning of a Clause or Sentence where English idiom requires a Demonstrative, with or without a connective; as, **Quā dē causā,** *And for this reason, For this reason* (I. 1); **Quī . . . proelium committunt** (Historical Present), *They* (or *And they*) *. . . joined battle* (I. 15).

168. Of the Indefinite Pronouns, Caesar uses **quīdam,** *a certain,* in respect to persons or things distinctly thought of but not described; **aliquis,** *some, any, somebody,* of persons or things referred to in a general way; **quis** and **quī,** *any, some,* still more vaguely, with **sī, nisi, seu, nē,** and **ubi;** and **quisquam,** *any at all,* in Interrogative or Negative Clauses or in a Clause following a Comparative; as, **quāsdam rēs,** *certain things* (I. 30); **quīdam ex mīlitibus,** *a certain one* (or *one*) *of the soldiers* (I. 42); **alicuius iniūriae,** *of any wrong-doing* (I. 14); **sī quid vellent,** *if they wanted anything* (I. 7); **Cur quisquam iūdicāret,** *Why should any one suppose* (I. 40); **prius quam quicquam cōnārētur,** *before taking any measures,* lit. *before he should attempt anything at all* (I. 19).

169. Caesar uses the Indefinite Distributive Pronoun **uterque,** *each of two,* in the Plural as well as the Singular; as, **utrīsque castrīs,** *for each camp* (I. 51); **ab utrīsque,** *by those on each side* (IV. 26).

170. *a.* Caesar sometimes uses the Indefinite Distributive Pronoun **quisque,** *each,* with a Superlative to designate a Class, or with a Numeral Ordinal to indicate a Proportion; thus, **nōbilissimī cuiusque līberōs,** *the children of every man of high rank* (I. 31); **decimum quemque mīlitem,** *one soldier in ten,* lit. *each tenth soldier* (V. 52).

b. Caesar uses **quisque,** *each,* in close connection with **sē** and **suus;** as, **cum sibi quisque . . . peteret,** *when each one was seeking for himself* (II. 11); **utī eōs testēs suae quisque virtūtis habēret,** *that each might have them as witnesses of his own valor* (I. 52).

171. *a.* Of the Pronominal Adjectives, **cēterī** (Plural) means *the other, the rest* besides those mentioned; **reliquī,** *the rest* in the sense *those remaining* after some are taken; as, **Aeduōs cēterōsque amīcōs populī Rōmānī,** *the Aeduans and the other friends of the Roman people* (I. 35); **reliquōs Gallōs,** *the rest of the Gauls,* after the Helvetians have been singled out (I. 1).

b. Caesar repeats **alter** and **alius** in a Correlative Relation; as, **hārum altera occīsa, altera capta est,** *of these* (*daughters*) *one was killed, the other captured* (I. 53); **aliae** (**nāvēs**) *. . .* **aliae . . . ,** *some* (*ships*) *. . . others* (IV. 28); **alterī — alterī,** *the latter — the former* (VII. 17).

c. Caesar repeats **alius** with the sense *one . . . one, another . . . another;* as, **legiōnēs aliae aliā in parte resisterent,** *legions were offering resistance, one at one point, another at another* (II. 22).

VERBS

AGREEMENT, MOODS AND TENSES, QUESTIONS

172. *a.* A Finite Verb agrees with its Subject in Number and Person; in compound forms of the Verb the Participle must agree with the Subject also in Gender. Thus, **Orgetorīx dēligitur**, *Orgetorix is chosen* (I. 3); **Ea rēs est ēnūntiāta**, *The matter* (lit. *that thing*) *was made known* (I. 4).

b. When a Verb is used with more than one Subject, it may agree with the nearest Subject, or be Plural; as, **fīlia et ūnus ē fīliīs captus est**, *a daughter and one of the sons were taken captive* (I. 26); **Nammeius et Verucloetius . . . obtinēbant**, *Nammeius and Verucloetius held* (I. 7).

c. Verbs are sometimes used in the Third Person Plural with an implied indefinite subject, as, **dīcunt**, *they say* (V. 12).

d. A verb in Latin is sometimes used with a Personal Subject where the English prefers the Impersonal Construction with " it "; as, **Quod nōn fore dictō audientēs . . . dīcantur**, *As to the fact that it was said that they would not be obedient*, lit. *that they are said not to be about to be*, etc. (I. 40).

173. *a.* When two Subjects express a single idea, the Verb may be Singular; as, **Matrona et Sēquana dīvidit**, *the Marne and the Seine separate . . .*, the two rivers being thought of as forming one boundary (I. 1).

b. A Plural Verb may be used with a Singular Noun, or with an unexpressed Subject representing a Singular Noun, where the sense suggests Plurality; as, **cum tanta multitūdō lapidēs conicerent**, *when so great a host were hurling stones* (II. 6).

174. Caesar rarely uses a Passive Verb or Participle in a Reflexive Sense; as, **sublevātī**, *supporting themselves* (I. 48); **armārī**, *to arm themselves* (IV. 32).

175. *a.* The Present, Imperfect, and Future Tenses represent an action as going on in Present, Past, or Future Time; as, **eōrumque agrōs populābantur**, *and were laying waste their country* (I. 11).

b. In vivid narration Caesar often thinks of past events as in progress and uses the Present Indicative (Historical Present). In translating the Historical Present a past tense should generally be used; as, **dīcit līberius**, *he spoke* (lit. *speaks*) *more freely* (I. 18).

c. The Present is used in statements true at all times (Universal Present), and statements about Customs; as, **hominēs id, quod [crēdere] volunt, crēdunt**, *men readily believe what they wish to believe* (III. 18).

d. The Imperfect may be used of Repeated or Customary Action; as, **perīclitābātur**, *he kept trying* (II. 8); **adoriēbantur . . . circumsistēbant . . . coniciēbant**, *would attack . . . would surround . . . would hurl* (IV. 26).

e. The Imperfect is sometimes used of Attempted Action (Conative Imperfect); as, **nostrōs intrā mūnītiōnēs ingredī prohibēbant**, *were trying to prevent our men from getting inside the fortification* (V. 9).

f. The Imperfect with **iam**, used of an action already in progress for a considerable period, should be translated with a Progressive Pluperfect; as, **Cum iam amplius hōrīs sex pugnārētur**, *when fighting had now been going on more than six hours* (III. 5).

176. *a.* Caesar generally uses the Historical Perfect, as **discessit**, *he withdrew* (I. 14); very rarely he uses the Perfect in the sense of the English Present Perfect, as **nōn vēnērunt**, *they have not come* (VII. 77).

b. The Perfect and Pluperfect of **nōscō, cognōscō, cōnsuēscō** express a state resulting from action, and are generally best translated by the Present and Imperfect; as, **nōvērunt**, *they are familiar with*, lit. *have come to know* (VI. 15); **īre cōnsuērant**, *were accustomed* (*had become accustomed*) *to go* (III. 1). The Perfect and Pluperfect of **meminī** and **ōdī** also are translated by the Present and Imperfect.

c. The Latin Future Perfect is used with great precision, where frequently in English a Future or Present Tense might be employed; as, **meum officium praestiterō**, *I shall have done my duty*, where we should ordinarily say, *I shall do my duty* (IV. 25).

177. *a.* In the Sequence of Tenses a Primary Tense (Present, Future, or Future Perfect [1]) in the Principal Clause is ordinarily followed by a Primary Tense in the Subordinate Clause; and a Secondary Tense (Imperfect, Perfect, or Pluperfect [2]) of the Principal

---

[1] The Primary Tenses of the Indicative, referring to Present and Future Time, are the Present, Future, and Future Perfect. The Primary Tenses of the Subjunctive are the Present and Perfect. Cf. *354* (p. 642).

[2] The Secondary Tenses of the Indicative, referring to Past Time, are the Imperfect, Perfect, and Pluperfect. The Secondary Tenses of the Subjunctive are the Imperfect and Pluperfect.

Clause by a past tense in the Subordinate Clause. Thus, **Mercātō-ribus est aditus ut, quae bellō cēperint, quibus vēndant, habeant,** *Traders have access (to them) . . . that they may have purchasers for the things that they have captured in war,* lit. *that they may have (those) to whom they may sell (those things) which they have taken in war* (IV. 2); **equitātumque, quī sustinēret impetum, mīsit,** *and he sent his cavalry to sustain the attack* (I. 24).

b. A Historical Present in the Principal Clause is sometimes followed by a Primary Tense, sometimes by a Secondary Tense, in the Subordinate Clause; as, **diem dīcunt, quā diē . . . conveniant,** *they set a day on which they were* (lit. *are*) *to come together* (I. 6); **pontem, quī erat ad Genavam, iubet rescindī,** *he gave* (lit. *gives*) *orders that the bridge, which was near Geneva, be cut down* (I. 7).

c. A verb in a Subordinate Clause containing a Statement of Fact or a General Truth may be in the Present Tense even though the verb of the Principal Clause is in a Past Tense; as, **eīs persuāsit, quod Helvetiī . . . continentur,** *he persuaded them, because the Helvetians are hemmed in . . .* (I. 2).

178. The Tenses of the Infinitive in Indirect Discourse express time relative to that of the Verbs on which they depend, the Present Infinitive expressing the same time as the Governing Verb; the Perfect Infinitive, time earlier than that of the Governing Verb; and the Future Infinitive, time later than that of the Governing Verb. Thus, **nōn sē hostem verērī . . . dīcēbant,** *were saying that they did not fear the enemy* (I. 39); **illum fēcisse intellegerent,** *they understood that he had done* (1. 13); **Caesar . . . sēsē eōs . . . cōnservātūrum [esse] dīxit,** *Caesar said that he would spare their lives* (II. 15).

179. *a.* Direct Questions in Latin are introduced by Question Words and are of two kinds:

> (1) Single Questions, introduced by Interrogative Pronouns and Adverbs, or by the Enclitic -**ne** attached to the emphatic word of the question and asking for information, by **nōnne** implying the answer "Yes," or **num** implying the answer "No." Thus: **quem locum . . . exspectās?** *what (kind of a) chance are you waiting for* (V. 44)? **Audīsne?** *Do you hear?* **Nōnne audīs?** *Do you not hear?* **Num audīs?** *You don't hear, do you?*
>
> (2) Double Questions, which ordinarily have **utrum** or the Enclitic -**ne** in the First Member, and **an,** *or,* or **annōn,** *or not,* in the second; as, **utrum officium, an timor, plūs valet,** *Is sense*

of duty, or cowardice, stronger? The First Member of a Double Question may be omitted, **An** alone introducing the second; as, **An . . . dubitātis?** *Do you have (any) doubt* (VII. 77)?

b. In Indirect Discourse Caesar uses Rhetorical Questions, implying a Negative Answer, Doubt, or Perplexity; these in the Direct Form would have had the Indicative, or the Deliberative Subjunctive. Thus:

(1) Indicative in the Direct Form: **num . . . memoriam dēpōnere posse?** *could he lay aside the recollection?* As a Direct Question: **Num . . . memoriam dēpōnere possum,** *can I put aside the recollection?* implying the answer "No"; as when we say "How can I do that?" meaning, emphatically, "I cannot do that" (I. 14).

(2) Deliberative Subjunctive in the Direct Form: **cūr quisquam . . . iūdicāret,** *why should any one infer?* in the Direct form, **cūr iūdicet?** (I. 40); **neque satīs Brūtō . . . centuriōnibusque . . . cōnstābat, quid agerent,** *and Brutus and the centurions . . . did not quite know what to do,* lit. *and it was not quite clear to Brutus and the centurions . . . what they should do;* as a Direct Question, **Quid agāmus?** *What are we to do?* (III. 14).

180. *a.* Caesar rarely uses the Subjunctive in the First Person to express an Exhortation (Hortatory Subjunctive); as, **hōs latrōnēs interficiāmus,** *let us kill these bandits* (VII. 38); **sīmus parātī,** *let us be ready* (C. III. 85).

b. Caesar rarely uses the Subjunctive in the Third Person to express a Command (Jussive Subjunctive); as, **Cum hīs mihi rēs sit,** *let me deal* (lit. *let the issue be to me*) *with those* (VII. 77).

c. A Wish Capable of Realization is expressed by the Present Subjunctive, often with **utinam;** as, **utinam redeant,** *may they return!*

d. A Wish Incapable of Realization is expressed in Present Time by **utinam** with the Imperfect Subjunctive and in Past Time by **utinam** with the Pluperfect Subjunctive; as, **utinam adessent,** *oh that they were here* (but they are not); **utinam redīssent,** *oh that they had come back* (but they did not).

181. *a.* Caesar rarely uses the Imperative, in Direct Quotations, as **Dēsilīte,** *Jump down* (IV. 25).

b. Caesar uses the Imperatives **nōlī, nōlīte** with the Infinitive to express Prohibition; as, **Nōlīte hōs vestrō auxiliō exspoliāre**, *Do not* (lit. *be unwilling to*) *rob them of your assistance* (VII. 77).

182. Caesar rarely uses an Infinitive in a Principal Clause in the place of an Imperfect or Perfect Indicative (Historical Infinitive), the Subject being in the Nominative; as, **Caesar Aeduōs frūmentum flāgitāre**, *Caesar kept pressing the Aeduans for the grain* (I. 16); **hostēs . . . signō datō dēcurrere**, *the enemy at a given signal rushed down* (III. 4).

CAUSAL AND TEMPORAL CLAUSES, RELATIVE CLAUSES, CLAUSES OF PURPOSE AND RESULT

183. *a.* In Causal Clauses introduced by **quod** and **quoniam** Caesar uses the Indicative when the reason is stated as that of Caesar the Writer, the Subjunctive when the reason is presented as some one else's. Thus, **Dumnorīx . . . Helvētiīs erat amīcus, quod . . . dūxerat**, *Dumnorix was friendly to the Helvetians, because he had taken . . .*, the **quod**-clause containing Caesar's explanation of the reason why Dumnorix favored the Helvetians (I. 9); **eī grātiās ēgit, quod optimum iūdicium fēcisset**, *thanked him because* (as the delegation said) *he had passed a most favorable judgment*, the **quod**-clause here having the Subjunctive because it presents the reason given by the delegation for the expression of thanks (I. 41).

b. In Causal Clauses Caesar sometimes uses the Subjunctive of a Verb of Saying or Thinking to introduce a statement of a reason ascribed to some one else; as, **Bellovacī suum numerum nōn complēvērunt, quod sē suō nōmine . . . bellum gestūrōs dīcerent**, *the Bellovaci did not furnish their full contingent because, as they said, they were going to wage war on their own account . . .* (VII. 75).

c. The Subjunctive introduced by **nōn quod**, *not because*, or **quam quō** (= **quam eō quod**), *than because*, may be used to express an alleged or assumed reason; as, **quam quō . . . dēsīderent**, *than because they desire* (IV. 2).

184. *a.* A Causal Clause introduced by **cum**, *since*, has its verb in the Subjunctive; as, **cum . . . persuādēre nōn possent**, *since they were not able to persuade* (I. 9).

b. Caesar sometimes uses the adverb **praesertim**, *especially*, to make prominent the Causal Idea in a Clause introduced by **cum**; as, **praesertim cum eōrum precibus adductus bellum suscēperit**, *especially* *since, in response to* (lit. *prevailed upon by*) *their entreaties, he had under-taken the campaign* (I. 16).

185. *a.* **Cúm** Temporal, *when*, referring to the Present or Future is used with the Indicative; as, **cum . . . premuntur,** *when they are overwhelmed* (VI. 13).

b. With **cum** Temporal, *when*, and **cum prīmum,** *as soon as*, refer-ring to Past Time, Caesar uses the Indicative when the force of **cum** is purely Temporal; as, **cum . . . exercitus . . . meritus (esse) vidēbātur,** *when the army clearly earned*, lit. *was seen to have earned* (I. 40); **cum prīmum potuit,** *as soon as he could* (III. 9).

c. With **cum** Temporal, *when*, and **cum prīmum,** *as soon as*, refer-ring to Past Time, Caesar uses the Subjunctive when an idea of Circumstance, Condition, or Cause is involved; as, **cum ferrum sē īnflexisset,** *when* (i.e. *when and because*) *the iron had become bent*, lit. *had bent itself* (I. 25); **cum prīmum pābulī cōpia esse inciperet,** *as soon as* (*and because*) *there began to be plenty of forage* (II. 2).

186. *a.* Caesar sometimes uses **cum** Temporal or **ubi** with the Indicative to denote recurrent action; as, **cum ūsus est,** *whenever it is necessary* (IV. 2).

b. Caesar sometimes uses **cum** Temporal correlatively with the Adverb **tum** in the sense *not only . . . but also, but, both . . . and;* as, **cum omnis iuventūs . . . convēnerant, tum nāvium quod ubīque fuerat,** *not only* (lit. *when*) *had all the youth . . . assembled but* (lit. *then*) *all the ships they had* (III. 16).

187. Caesar sometimes uses **cum** Adversative, *although, while*, with the Subjunctive; as, **cum ea ita sint,** *although this* (lit. *those things*) *is true* (I. 14).

188. *a.* Caesar uses the Temporal Conjunctions **ubi, ut,** *when*, **postquam,** *after*, **posteā quam** (written as two words) *after that, after*, and **simul atque, simul,** *as soon as*, with the Indicative, usually in the Perfect Tense. Thus, **Quod ubi Caesar resciit,** *When Caesar found this out* (I. 28); **postquam Caesar pervēnit,** *after Caesar arrived* (I. 27); **simul atque sē recēpērunt,** *so soon as they rallied* (IV. 27).

b. The conjunction **ut,** *as*, introducing a comparison, is used with the Indicative; as, **ut . . . nōluerant, ita,** *as they had been unwilling so . . .* (II. 1).

c. **ubi prīmum,** *as soon as* (lit. *when first*), is used with the Perfect Indicative; as, **ubi prīmum nostrōs equitēs cōnspexērunt,** *as soon as they saw our horsemen* (IV. 12).

d. The Pluperfect Indicative with **ubi** may denote a Repeated Action; as, **ubi . . . cōnspexerant**, *whenever they saw*, lit. *when they had seen* (IV. 26).

189. *a.* Caesar uses **prius quam**, *until, before*, with the Indicative to denote an actual occurrence or a fact; as, **neque prius fugere dē-stitērunt quam ad flūmen Rhēnum . . . pervēnērunt**, *and they did not stop their flight until they reached the river Rhine* (I. 53).

b. Caesar uses **prius quam** and **ante quam**, *sooner than, before*, with the Subjunctive, implying Expectancy or Purpose in an action; as, **prius quam sē hostēs reciperent**, *before the enemy could rally* (II. 12).

190. *a.* Caesar uses **dum** Temporal in the sense of *while* with the Indicative Historical Present; in the sense of *so long as, while*, with the Indicative Present, Imperfect, and Perfect. Thus, **Dum ea conquī-runtur**, *while those things were* (lit. *are*) *being sought out* (I. 27); **Dum longius aberant Gallī**, *so long as the Gauls were further away* (VII. 82).

b. Caesar uses **dum**, *until*, with the Subjunctive to denote Intention or Expectancy; as, **dum . . . Helvētiī pervenīrent**, *until the Helvetians should reach* (I. 11).

c. Caesar uses **quoad** in the Temporal sense of *so long as, until*, with the Indicative; in the sense of *until* denoting Intention or Expectancy, with the Subjunctive. Thus, **quoad potuit**, *so long as he could* (IV. 12); **quoad ipse propius . . . accessisset**, *until he himself should have come up nearer* (IV. 11).

191. *a.* Caesar uses the Adversative Conjunctions **etsī, tametsī**, *although*, with the Indicative; as, **etsī . . . vidēbat**, *although he saw* (I. 46).

b. Concessive **ut**, meaning *granted that, although*, is followed by the Subjunctive; as, **ut omnia contrā opīniōnem accidant**, *granted that everything turn out contrary to expectation* (in Indirect Form III. 9).

192. Relative Clauses, introduced by a Relative or General Relative Pronoun, have their Verb in the Indicative unless an idea of Purpose, Characteristic, Cause, Result, or Condition is involved; as, **Allobrogum, quī nūper pācātī erant**, *of the Allobroges, who had lately been subdued* (I. 6); **quaecumque pars castrōrum . . . premī vidēbātur**, *whenever any part* (lit. *whatever part*) *of the camp seemed to be hard pressed* (III. 4).

193. *a.* A Relative Clause of Purpose may be introduced by **quī** (= **ut is**, *in order that he*), or by the Relative Adverbs **quō** (= **ut**

eō), quā (= ut eā), and has its Verb in the Subjunctive; as, **lēgātōs mittunt** (Historical Present) **nōbilissimōs cīvitātis . . . quī dīcerent**, *they sent as envoys the citizens of highest rank to say*, lit. *who should say* (I. 7); **quō gravius hominēs . . . doleant**, *in order that men may more bitterly suffer* (I. 14). Cf. *355* (p. 643).

b. In Relative Clauses of Purpose **quō** is generally used with a Comparative; as, **quō facilius . . . possit**, *that he might* (lit. *may*) *be able the more easily* (I. 8).

194. *a.* A Relative Clause with the Subjunctive, introduced by a Relative Pronoun or Relative Adverb, may characterize an Indefinite Antecedent (Clause of Characteristic); as, **itinera duo, quibus itineribus . . . exīre possent**, *two routes by which they could go out*, i.e. two routes of such a character that by them they could go out (I. 6); **nihil [eīs] erat quō famem tolerārent**, *they had nothing with which they could satisfy hunger* (I. 28).

b. A Clause of Characteristic may be used after a Comparative; as, **nōn longius aberant quam quō tēlum adigī posset**, *were already within range*, lit. *not further away than* (the distance) *to which a dart could be thrown* (II. 21).

c. A Relative Clause with the Subjunctive may have a Causal Force; as, **Catuvolcus . . . dētestātus Ambiorīgem, quī eius cōnsiliī auctor fuisset, . . . sē exanimāvit**, *cursing Ambiorix, since he* (lit. *who*) *had been the originator of that scheme, Catuvolcus killed himself* (VI. 31).

d. A Relative Clause with the Subjunctive may have an Adversative Force; as, **Cicerō, quī . . . mīlitēs in castrīs continuisset**, *Cicero, although he had kept the soldiers in camp* (VI. 36).

e. A Relative Clause with the Subjunctive may have a Conditional Force; as **quī . . . vidēret** *if one should look at* (VII. 19).

f. A Restrictive Clause may be introduced by the Relative **quod** and have the Subjunctive; as, **quod . . . posset**, *so far as he might be able*, (lit. *that*) *which*, etc. (I. 35).

195. A Relative Clause of Result may be introduced by **quī** (= **ut is**, *so that he*), or **quīn** (= **quī nōn, quae nōn, quod nōn**), and has its Verb in the Subjunctive; as, **Nēmō est tam fortis, quīn reī novitāte perturbētur**, *No one* (*of them*) *was so strong that he was not upset by the unexpectedness of the occurrence* (VI. 39).

196. *a.* Clauses of Purpose in Caesar are most often introduced by **ut, utī**, *in order that, that*, or **nē**, *in order that not, lest*, and have their Verb in the Subjunctive; as, **ut spatium intercēdere posset,**

in order that a period of time might (lit. *might be able to*) *intervene* (I. 7) ; **Id nē accideret,** *in order that this might not happen* (I. 38).

b. In Clauses of Purpose Caesar uses **nē . . . nēve (neu)** in the sense of *that not . . . nor,* and **ut (utī) . . . nēve (neu)** in the sense of *that . . . and that not,* with the Subjunctive; as, **ut . . . eārum rērum vīs minuerētur, neu pontī nocērent,** *that the force of these things might be lessened and that they might not damage the bridge* (IV. 17).

197. *a.* Clauses of Result are most often introduced by **ut** or **utī,** *so that, that* (negative **nōn**), and have their Verb in the Subjunctive; as, **ut perpaucī prohibēre possent,** *so that a very few* (*men*) *could stop them* (I. 6); **ut . . . iūdicārī nōn possit,** *that it cannot be determined* (I. 12).

b. Clauses of Result are often preceded by a word of Measure or Quality, **tam, tantus, ita, sīc,** etc.; as, **tanta rērum commūtātiō est facta, ut nostrī . . . proelium redintegrārent,** *so great a change was brought about that our* (*men*) *renewed the fight* (II. 27) ; **sīc mūniēbātur, ut magnam . . . daret facultātem,** *was so fortified that it afforded a great resource* (I. 38).

c. A Clause of Result with the Subjunctive may be introduced by **quam** after a Comparative, with or without **ut**; as, **pulverem maiōrem, quam cōnsuētūdō ferret,** *a cloud of dust greater than usual* lit. *greater than* (*so that*) *an ordinary condition would bring it* (IV. 32).

SUBSTANTIVE CLAUSES

198 *a.* Substantive Clauses are used as Subject of a Verb, as Object of a Verb, and in other Relations similar to those in which Nouns are used.

b. A Substantive Clause introduced by **quod,** meaning *the fact that, that,* has its Verb in the Indicative, and may stand as Subject, or Predicate, or Object of a Verb, or in Apposition. Thus, **magnō erat impedīmentō, quod . . . neque . . . poterant,** *A great hindrance . . . was the fact that they were able neither to . . .* the **quod**-clause being the Subject of **erat** (I. 25) ; **causa mittendī fuit quod . . . volēbat,** *the reason for sending was the fact that he wanted . . .* the **quod**-clause being in Predicate (III. 1) ; **multae rēs . . . in prīmīs quod . . . vidēbat,** *many circumstances, first of all the fact that he saw . . .* the **quod**-clause being in Apposition with **rēs** (I. 33).

c. A Substantive Clause introduced by **quod,** meaning *As to the fact that, As regards the fact that,* may have the force of an Accusative or Ablative of Specification. Thus, **quod . . . ēnūntiārit,** ' *As to the* fact that he had reported'; in the direct form, **quod ēnūntiāvī**, *as to the fact that I have reported* (I. 17).

199. *a.* Substantive Clauses with the Subjunctive introduced by **ut**, or **utī**, *that*, and **nē**, *that not*, are used after Verbs of *Commanding, Urging, Reminding, Asking, Persuading, Conceding* and *Permitting, Deciding, Striving;* the Subjunctive may often best be translated by an Infinitive. Thus, **Allobrogibus imperāvit, ut . . . cōpiam facerent**, *ordered the Allobroges to furnish* (lit. *that they should furnish*) *a supply* . . . (I. 28); **persuādet** (Historical Present) **Casticō . . . ut rēgnum . . . occupāret**, *persuaded Casticus to seize the kingly power* (I. 3).

Such Verbs and Phrases used by Caesar are :

(1) Commanding : **imperō**, *order;* **interdīcō**, *enjoin* (VII. 40); **mandō**, *command* (I. 47) ; **negōtium dō**, *assign the task* (II. 2) ; **praecipiō**, *enjoin, direct* (I. 22) ; **dēnūntiō**, *enjoin,* (C. III. 86); **praedīcō**, *order in advance* (C. III. 92).

(2) Urging : **cohortor**, *encourage* (II. 21) ; **hortor**, *urge* (I. 19) ; **sollicitō**, *press* (III. 8).

(3) Reminding : **admoneō**, *admonish* (V. 49) ; **moneō**, *warn* (I. 20).

(4) Asking : **dēprecor**, *beg to escape* (II. 31) ; **ōrō**, *beg* (IV. 16) ; **obsecrō**, *beseech* (I. 20) ; **obtestor**, *pray* (IV. 25) ; **petō**, *ask earnestly* (I. 28) ; **postulō**, *demand* (I. 34) ; **rogō**, *ask* (I. 7).

(5) Persuading : **addūcō**, *prevail upon* (I. 31) ; **persuadeō**, *persuade;* **impellō**, *incite* (IV. 16).

(6) Conceding and Permitting : **concēdō**, *grant* (III. 18) ; **patior**, *suffer, allow* (I. 45) ; **permittō**, *permit* (I. 35).

(7) Deciding : **cēnseō**, *decree* (I. 35) ; **cōnstituō**, *determine* (II. 10) ; **placuit**, *it pleased* (I. 34) ; **sanciō**, *bind* (I. 30).

(8) Striving : **agō**, *arrange* (I. 41) ; **contendō**, *strive* (I. 31) ; **dō operam**, *take pains* (V. 7) ; **impetrō**, *obtain one's request* (I. 9) ; **labōrō**, *put forth effort* (I. 31).

b. Such Verbs are sometimes used impersonally in the Passive, the Substantive Clause taking the place of a Subject; as **erat eī praeceptum, nē proelium committeret**, *he had been ordered not to join battle*, lit. *it had been ordered to him that he should not*, etc. (I. 22).

c. With such Verbs the Substantive Clause is sometimes replaced by the Infinitive, with or without a Subject Accusative; as, **loquī concēditur**, *permission is given to speak* (VI. 20) ; **Hās [nāvēs] āctuāriās imperat** (Historical Present) **fierī**, *he ordered that these (ships) be built for fast movement* (V. 1).

d. As a Negative Connective between Substantive Subjunctive Clauses Caesar uses **nēve** (before vowels and **h**) and **neu** (before consonants), with the meaning *and that . . . not, or that . . . not.*

200. *a.* In Substantive Clauses with **ut** after **admoneō, cōhortor, cōnstituō, imperō, mandō, nūntiō,** *order,* **postulō,** *demand,* and **rogō,** *ask,* and a few phrases, the **ut** is sometimes omitted; as, **rogat** (Historical Present), **fīnem ōrandī faciat,** *asked him to make an end of his pleading* (I. 20).

b. **Iubeō,** *order, bid,* and **vetō,** *forbid,* are regularly used by Caesar with the Infinitive and Subject Accusative; **cōnor,** *attempt,* with the Infinitive; as, **quemque efferre iubent,** *they gave* (lit. *give*) *orders that each person carry away* . . . (I. 5); **exsequī cōnārētur,** *attempted to enforce* (I. 4).

201. *a.* Substantive Clauses with the Subjunctive introduced by **nē,** *that not,* **quō minus,** *that not* (lit. *by which the less*), and **quīn,** *that not,* are used after Verbs of *Hindering, Preventing,* and *Refusing;* the Conjunction often may best be rendered by *from* with a Participle. Thus, **hōs . . . dēterrēre nē frūmentum cōnferant,** *these through fear were holding back* (*the people*) *from furnishing the grain* (I. 17); **retinērī nōn potuerant quīn . . . tēla conicerent,** *could not be restrained from hurling darts* (I. 47).

Such Verbs used by Caesar are:

dēterreō, *hold back through fear;* **recūsō,** *refuse* (I. 31); **retineō,** *restrain;* **temperō,** *restrain one's self* (I. 33); **teneō,** *hold back* (IV. 22); **terreō,** *frighten* (VII. 49).

b. Substantive Clauses with the Subjunctive introduced by **quīn** are used also after general expressions of Doubt and Negation, **quīn** being translated *that.* Thus, **nōn esse dubium, quīn . . .,** *that there was no doubt that* (I. 3); **neque abest suspīciō . . . quīn,** *and there is ground for suspecting that,* lit. *and there is not lacking suspicion that* (I. 4).

c. After **dubitō,** meaning *doubt,* Caesar uses a Substantive Clause with **quīn** and the Subjunctive; after **dubitō,** *hesitate,* generally the Infinitive, rarely a clause with **quīn.** Thus, **nōn dubitāre quīn . . . sūmat,** *he did not doubt that he* (Ariovistus) *would inflict* (I. 31); **trānsīre flūmen nōn dubitāvērunt,** *did not hesitate to cross the river* (II. 23); **dubitandum nōn exīstimāvit quīn . . . proficīscerētur,** *thought that he ought not to hesitate to set out* (II. 2).

202. Substantive Clauses with the Subjunctive introduced by **ut** and **nē** are used after Verbs of Fearing; after such Verbs **ut** is to be translated *that not,* and **nē,** *that,* or *lest.* Thus, **nē . . . offenderet verēbātur,** *was afraid that he might offend* (I. 19); **ut . . . supportārī posset, timēre dīcēbant,** *were saying that they feared that* (*the supply of grain*) *could not be brought up* (I. 39).

203. Clauses of Result introduced by **ut** or **utī** and **ut nōn** are used as Substantive Clauses in four ways:

(1) As the Subject of Impersonal Verbs; thus, **fīēbat ut . . . va-gārentur,** *it came about that they wandered* (I. 2); **Accēdēbat ut . . . tempestātem ferrent,** *There was the additional fact that they weathered the storm* (III. 13).

The more important Impersonal Forms thus used by Caesar are **accēdēbat**; **accidit,** *it happened* (IV. 29); **fit** (C. II. 4); **fīēbat**; **factum est** (III. 19); **factum esse** (I. 31), **fierī** (II. 4); **īnstitūtum est,** *the custom became fixed* (C. III. 92); **Relinquēbātur,** *the result was,* lit. *it was left* (V. 19); and the Future Infinitive of **sum** in both forms, **futūrum esse** (I. 10, 20, 31), and **fore** (I. 42).

(2) As Predicate or Appositive with **cōnsuētūdō est** and **iūs est**; thus, **ea cōnsuētūdō esset, ut mātrēs familiae . . . dē-clārārent,** *there was the custom that the matrons should declare* (I. 50).

(3) As Object after Verbs of Action and Accomplishment; thus, **committeret ut is locus . . . nōmen caperet.** lit. *bring it about that the place . . . should assume a name* (I. 13); **com-meātūs ut . . . portārī possent, efficiēbat,** *made it possible for supplies to be brought,* lit. *was accomplishing that supplies could be brought* (II. 5).

The Verbs thus used by Caesar are **committō, efficiō, perficiō** (I. 9).

(4) As Appositive of a Noun or Neuter Pronoun whose meaning the **ut**-clause defines; thus, **poenam, ut īgnī cremārētur,** *the penalty of being burned by fire,* lit. *that he should be burned by fire* (I. 4); **id, quod cōnstituerant . . . ut ē fīnibus suīs exeant,** *that which they had resolved upon, a migration from their country,* lit. *that they should go out from their territories* (I. 5).

204. Indirect Questions are used as Substantive Clauses after Expressions of Inquiry, Narration, Deliberation, and Uncertainty, and have the Subjunctive. The following types of Indirect Questions are used by Caesar:

(1) Introduced by the Interrogative Particles **-ne** (V. 27), **num** (I. 14) in Single Questions; in Double Questions, by the Correlative Particles **utrum . . . an,** *whether . . . or* (I. 40); **utrum . . . necne,** *whether . . . or not,* **necne** representing **annōn** of the Direct Form (I. 50); **-ne . . . an,** *whether . . .*

or (VI. 31); -ne . . . an . . . an, *whether . . . or . . . or* (IV. 14);
-ne . . . -ne, *whether . . . or* (VII. 14); and **an** alone, **utrum**
being omitted, *or* (VII. 15). Thus, **cōnsultum [esse]**,
utrum īgnī statim necārētur an . . . reservārētur, *that
counsel was taken whether he should at once be put to death by
burning, or saved up* for another occasion (I. 53).

(2) Introduced by an Interrogative Pronoun; as, **Dumnorīgī cūstōdēs pōnit** (Historical Present), **ut, quae agat, quibuscum
loquātur, scīre possit** (*Caesar*), *set guards over Dumnorix,
in order to be able to know what* (lit. *what things*) *he did, with
whom he talked* (I. 20).

(3) Introduced by Pronominal Adjectives, and Adverbs used Inter-
rogatively; as, **in utram partem fluat,** *in which direction it
flows* (I. 12). Adjectives and Adverbs thus used by Caesar
are **quālis,** *of what sort* (I. 21); **quam** with an Adjective,
how (I. 43); **quantus,** *how great* (I. 17); **quem ad modum,**
in what way (I. 36); **uter,** *which ;* **cūr,** *why* (I. 40); **quārē,**
wherefore, why (I. 45); **quō,** *whither* (III. 16); **quot,** *how
many* (VII. 19); **quotiēns,** *how often* (I. 43); **unde,** *whence*
(V. 53); **ut, how** (I. 43).

(4) Introduced by **sī,** *if, whether,* after Verbs of Effort and Expectation; as, **sī perrumpere possent, cōnātī,** *trying* (*to see*)
whether they could break through (I. 8).

CONDITIONAL SENTENCES

205. Caesar has General Conditions of the First Type (Conditions
of Fact) introduced by **sī,** *if,* with the Indicative in both Protasis and
Apodosis, the Protasis implying Customary or Repeated Action; **sī** is
almost equivalent to *whenever.* Thus:

(1) Present Tense in both Protasis and Apodosis : **sī quī ex reliquīs excellit, succēdit,** *if anyone of the rest is preëminent, he
becomes the successor* of the arch-druid (VI. 13).

(2) Imperfect Tense in both Protasis and Apodosis : **sī quid erat
dūrius, concurrēbant,** *if there was unusually serious difficulty*
(lit. *if there was anything rather hard*) *they would rush to the
rescue* (I. 48).

(3) Perfect Tense in the Protasis, Present in the Apodosis : **sī
compertum est, interficiunt,** *if the fact* (*of crime*) *has been
established, they kill* (VI. 19).

(4) Pluperfect Tense in the Protasis, Imperfect in the Apodosis: **sī quī . . . equō dēciderat, circumsistēbant,** *if anyone had fallen from his horse, they would gather around him* (I. 48).

206. Caesar has Specific Conditions of the First Type (Conditions of Fact) introduced by **sī,** *if,* or **nisi,** *unless,* with the Indicative in the Protasis, and the Indicative, Imperative, or Hortatory Subjunctive in the Apodosis. Thus:

(1) Present Indicative in both Protasis and Apodosis: **Cuius sī vōs paenitet, vestrum vōbīs beneficium remittō,** *if you regret this, I give you back your favor* (C. II. 32).

(2) Present Indicative in the Protasis, Present Imperative in the Apodosis: **Dēsilīte . . . nisi vultis aquilam hostibus prōdere,** *jump down, unless you wish to abandon your eagle to the enemy* (IV. 25).

(3) Present Indicative in the Protasis, Hortatory Subjunctive in the Apodosis: **Sī quid in nōbīs animī est, persequāmur mortem,** *if we have any vestige of courage in us, let us avenge the death* (VII. 38).

(4) Future Perfect Indicative in the Protasis, Future Indicative or Imperative in the Apodosis: **sī gravius quid acciderit, ratiōnem reposcent,** *if any disaster shall befall them* (lit. *anything rather heavy shall have happened*), *they will demand an accounting* (V. 30); **Tuēminī castra, et dēfendite, sī quid dūrius acciderit,** *guard the camp, and defend it in case of any trouble,* lit. *if anything rather hard shall have happened* (C. III. 94).

207. Caesar has conditions of the Second Type (Conditions of Possible Realization), introduced by **sī,** *if,* **nisi,** *unless,* or **sīn,** *but if,* with the Subjunctive in the Protasis, and the Potential Subjunctive, or the Indicative (emphasizing the situation as an actual one) in the Apodosis; thus:

(1) Present Subjunctive in both Protasis and Apodosis: **quī, sī per te liceat, . . . cum reliquīs bellī cāsum sustineant,** *if they should have your permission, they would share the fortune of war with the rest* (V. 30).

(2) Present Subjunctive in the Protasis, Present Indicative in the Apodosis: **neque, aliter sī faciat, ūllam habet auctōritātem,** *and if (a leading man) does* (lit. *should do*) *otherwise, he has no influence at all* (VI. 11).

(3) Imperfect Subjunctive in the Protasis, Imperfect Indicative in the Apodosis: **sī continēre ad signa manipulōs vellet, locus ipse erat praesidiō barbarīs,** *if he desired to keep his companies with the standards, the very (character of the) region was a protection to the natives* (VI. 34).

208. *a.* Caesar has Conditions of the Third Type (Conditions Contrary to Fact), introduced by **sī,** *if,* or **nisi,** *unless,* with the Subjunctive in both Protasis and Apodosis, the Imperfect referring to Present Time, the Pluperfect to Past Time. Thus:

(1) Imperfect: **ego hanc sententiam probārem . . . sī nūllam praeterquam vītae nostrae iactūram fierī vidērem,** *I should approve this view if I saw that no (loss) was involved except the loss of our own lives,* implying that the speaker did not approve the view, and that other loss was involved (VII. 77).

(2) Pluperfect: **nisi . . . mīlitēs essent dēfessī, omnēs hostium cōpiae dēlērī potuissent,** *if the soldiers had not been exhausted . . ., the entire forces of the enemy might have been wiped out,* implying that the soldiers were exhausted, and that many of the enemy escaped (VII. 88).

b. The Indicative is used in the Apodosis of Conditions Contrary to Fact when there is present an idea of Necessity, Propriety, or Possibility; as, **sī populus Rōmānus alicuius iniūriae sibi cōnscius fuisset, nōn fuit difficile cavēre,** *if the Roman people had been conscious of any wrongdoing it would not have been* (lit. *was not*) *difficult (for them) to take precautions* (from the Indirect Form in I. 14).

c. The Imperfect Subjunctive, referring to Past Time, may be used in Conditions Contrary to Fact, if a lasting state of affairs is implied; as, **sī quid mihi ā Caesare opus esset, ad eum vēnissem,** *If I had wanted (or now wanted) anything of Caesar, I should have come to him* (from the Indirect Form in I. 34).

209. In the Protasis of a Conditional Sentence an Ablative Absolute, a Participle, or other form of expression implying a Condition, may be used in place of the clause with **sī**; as, **datā facultāte,** taking the place of **sī facultās data esset,** *if an opportunity should have been granted,* in the Direct Form, **sī facultās data erit** (I. 7); **damnātum (eum),** *him, if condemned,* **damnātum** taking the place of **sī damnātus esset** (I. 4).

210. Caesar has Conditional Clauses of Comparison with the Subjunctive introduced by **velut sī, quasi,** and **proinde ac sī.** Thus: **quod . . . absentis Ariovistī crūdēlitātem velut sī cōram adesset, horrērent,** that is . . . **velut horrērent, sī cōram adesset, horrērent,** *because they dreaded Ariovistus's cruelty when he was away just as (they would dread it) if he were present* (I. 32) ; **Quasi vērō cōnsiliī sit rēs,** *As if indeed it were a matter of choice,* i.e. *as it would be, if it should be a matter of choice* (VII. 38) ; **proinde ac sī . . . vellent,** *just as if they proposed* (C. III. 60).

DIRECT AND INDIRECT QUOTATION AND INDIRECT DISCOURSE

GENERAL STATEMENT

211. *a.* Caesar presents the language of another person in two ways, either in Direct Quotation, or in Indirect Quotation, a form of Indirect Discourse.

b. In Direct Quotation Caesar quotes :

(1) Words spoken directly to him, as the brave words of Crastinus just before going into action at the battle of Pharsalus (C. III. 91).

(2) Words reported to him, presumably by his officers ; as the exhortation of the unnamed standard-bearer of the Tenth Legion when landing on the British shore, if this was spoken outside of Caesar's hearing (IV. 25), and the challenge of Pullo to Vorenus (V. 44).

(3) Words or Speeches, sometimes in dialects foreign to Caesar, which he presents in his own language, but throws into the form of Direct Quotation in order to enhance the effect ; such are the words of the Eburonian captive to the Sugambrian leaders (VI. 35), and the speech of the cold-blooded Critognatus at the war council in Alesia (VII. 77) ; also the words of the dying eagle-bearer (C. III. 64), and the remarks of Pompey and Labienus before Pharsalus (C. III. 86, 87).

212. *a.* In Indirect Quotation, or Indirect Discourse in the narrower sense, Caesar in most cases aims to present, not a word-for-word reproduction of what was said or written, but a summary, as brief as possible, of the main points. For example, in order to move to action the other prominent Helvetians, and carry through the negotiations with Casticus and Dumnorix, Orgetorix must have had many conferences, extending over a considerable period of time; yet the gist of the argument by which, according to Caesar, he persuaded the whole Helvetian nation to migrate, is given in ten words of Indirect Discourse (I. 2), while the gist of the argument by which Casticus and Dumnorix were induced to join him in forming a triumvirate of usurpation is summarized in thirty-one words (I. 3).

b. The kind of Summary found in the longer passages of Caesar's Indirect Discourse has a parallel in the condensed reports of addresses in the newspapers. A reporter, sent to prepare a synopsis of a lecture an hour in length, on the Moon, might on his return to the newspaper office find his space reduced, by pressure of matter, to sixty words; he might nevertheless summarize the main points thus:

" The lecturer said *that the moon is nearly two hundred and thirty-nine thousand miles from the earth ; that under the telescope it has the appearance of a dead planet; that most careful observations have failed to detect the presence of air or water; and that, notwithstanding the moon's brightness, due to reflection, its surface must be as cold as ice.*"

c. In a manner somewhat similar, but with marvelous clearness and cogency in view of the degree of condensation, Caesar in Indirect Discourse presents summarizing statements, or outlines, including —

(1) Conferences with Gallic and German leaders, conducted, no doubt haltingly, through interpreters, as with Divico (I. 13, 14), Liscus and other Aeduans (I. 17, 18), the Gallic delegation (I. 30–33), and Ariovistus (I. 43–45).

(2) His own addresses; as the speech with which he quelled an incipient mutiny (I. 40), and his exhortation to his soldiers at Pharsalus (C. III. 90).

(3) Reports made to him; as by Labienus (II. 1) and the envoys of the Remi (II. 3. 4).

(4) Requests and replies, messages and instructions; as the request of the Helvetian envoys, and Caesar's answer (I. 7); the plea of the Aeduans (I. 11), Caesar's message to the Lingones (I. 26), messages to and from Ariovistus (I. 34–36, 47).

(5) Arguments; as the arguments of Orgetorix (I. 2, 3), and of disloyal natives (II. 17).

(6) Brief reports, explanations or speeches, presented in some cases with little or no condensation, as the hurried report of Considius (I. 22), the apology of the soldiers (I. 41), the joke by the soldier of the Tenth Legion (I. 42), and the taunt of the Atuatuci as translated into Latin (II. 30).

d. Indirect Discourse in a broader sense includes all statements in the Indirect Form after words of Thought as well as Speech; as, **biennium satis esse dūxērunt,** *they reckoned that two years would be sufficient* (I. 3).

e. In the Latin text of this book the more important Indirect Quotations and Summaries are printed in Italic Type.

213. *a.* Indirect Discourse is introduced by a Verb or other Expression of *Saying, Perceiving, Ascertaining, Thinking, Knowing,* or *Remembering;* as, **sē . . . condōnāre dīcit** (Historical Present) *he said that he would pardon* (I. 20).

Such Verbs and Expressions used by Caesar are:

ago, *present a case* (I. 13); **animadvertō,** *notice* (I. 32); **arbitror,** *think* (I. 2); **audiō,** *hear* (IV. 7); **cēnseō,** *decide, think* (VII. 21); **certiōrem faciō,** *inform* (I. 11); **certior fit,** *is informed* (I. 12); **clāmitō,** *cry out* (V. 7), **cogitō,** *think* (V. 33); **cognōscō,** *learn* (I. 22); **commemorō,** *relate* (IV. 16); **comperiō,** *ascertain* (IV. 19); **conclāmō,** *shout* (III. 18); **cōnfīdō,** *be confident, trust* (III. 9); **cōnfīrmō,** *assure* (I. 3); **coniectūram capiō,** *infer* (VII. 35); **cōnspiciō,** *see* (II. 24); **cōnstat,** *it is agreed* (III. 6); **cōnstituō,** *resolve* (II. 10); **contendō,** *insist* (VI. 41); **crēdō,** *believe* (II. 33).

dēmōnstrō, *show, prove* (I. 11); **dēnūntiō,** *threaten* (I. 36); **dīcō,** *say;* **diffīdō,** *lose confidence* (VI. 36); **discō,** *learn* (VII. 54); **doceō,** *explain* (I. 43); **dūcō,** *reckon* (I. 3); **exīstimō,** *reckon, think* (I. 6); **faciō verba,** *make a plea* (II. 14); **intellegō,** *understand* (I. 16); **inveniō,** *find out* (II. 16); **iūdicō,** *judge* (I. 45); **iūrō,** *swear* (VI. 12); **loquor,** *speak, say* (II. 31).

meminī, *remember* (III. 6); **memoriā teneō,** *hold in memory, remember* (I. 7); **mihi persuāsum habeō,** *am convinced* (III. 2); **moneō,** *explain* (C. III. 89); **negō,** *declare that . . . not* (I. 8); **nūntiō,** *announce* (II. 2); **nūntium mittō,** *send word* (II. 6); **ostendō,** *make plain* (I. 8); **perscrībō,** *write fully* (V. 49); **perspiciō,** *perceive* (III. 9); **polliceor,** *promise* (I. 33); **praedicō,** *declare* (I. 39); **prō explōrātō habeō,** *consider certain* (VI. 5); **probō,** *show, prove* (I. 3); **profiteor,** *declare* (VII. 2); **prōnūntiō,** *announce* (V. 56); **próvideō,** *foresee* (VII. 39); **putō,** *think* (IV. 3).

recordor, *recall* (C. III. 47); **referō,** *report* (VI. 10); **renūntiō,** *bring (back) report* (I. 10); **reperiō,** *find out, ascertain* (I. 18); **respondeō,** *answer* (I. 14); **sciō,** *know* (I. 20); **scrībō,** *write* (V. 13); **sentiō,** *perceive* (I. 18); **spem habeō,** *have hope that* (I. 33); **significō,** *give intimation* (II. 13); **simulō,** *pretend* (IV. 4); **spērō,** *hope* (I. 3); **statuō,** *determine* (I. 42); **suspicor,** *suspect* (I. 44); **testibus ūtor,** *take as witnesses that* (VII. 77); **videō,** *see* (I. 33); **voveō,** *vow* (VI. 16).

b. The Verb of Saying, on which Indirect Discourse depends, is sometimes not expressed, but implied in the Context; as, **Caesarem complexus obsecrāre coepit . . . scīre sē,** *throwing his arms around Caesar began to beseech* (*him, saying*) *that he knew* (I. 20).

RULES FOR INDIRECT DISCOURSE

214. *a.* In Indirect Discourse the Principal Statements, corresponding with the Principal Clauses of Direct Discourse, are expressed by the Subject Accusative and the Infinitive; Subordinate Clauses have the Subjunctive. Thus, **Cōnsuēsse deōs immortālēs ... quōs prō scelere eōrum ulcīscī velint, hīs secundiōrēs interdum rēs, et diūturniōrem impūnitātem, concēdere,** *The immortal gods are wont to grant a more prosperous estate meanwhile, and longer freedom from punishment, to those whom they desire to punish for their wickedness;* in the Direct Form **cōnsuēsse deōs** would become **consuērunt dī,** and **velint** in the Subordinate Clause would be **volunt,** the other words remaining unchanged, and the sentence would read **Cōnsuērunt dī immortālēs ... quōs prō scelere eōrum ulcīscī volunt, hīs secundiōrēs interdum rēs et diūturniōrem impūnitātem concēdere** (I. 14).

b. A Subordinate Clause containing an implied quotation may have the Subjunctive; as, **frūmentum, quod essent pollicitī,** *the grain which (as he said) they had promised* (I. 16).

c. In Indirect Discourse a Subordinate or Parenthetical Clause, presenting a Statement of Fact which is not necessarily a part of the Indirect Discourse, may have the Indicative; as, **Condrūsōs ... Paemānōs, quī Germānī appellantur,** *that the Condrusi ... and the Paemani, who are called Germans* (II. 4).

215. The Subject Accusative in Indirect Discourse is sometimes omitted when it is easily understood from the Context, especially when it refers to the same person as the Subject of the Verb on which the Indirect Discourse depends; as, **scīre,** for **sē scīre,** *that he knew* (I. 40, l. 41); **prohibitūrum ostendit,** for **sē prohibitūrum esse ostendit** (Historical Present), *he showed that he would prevent them* (I. 8).

216. Commands expressed in Direct Quotation by the Imperative, or by the Jussive Subjunctive, in Indirect Discourse have the Subjunctive, the Negative being **nē.** Thus, **reminīscerētur,** *let him remember,* which in the Direct Form would be Imperative, **reminīscere,** *remember* (I. 13); **nē ... tribueret,** *that he should not presume,* the Direct Form being **nōlī tribuere** (I. 13).

217. *a.* Ordinary Questions in Indirect Discourse have the Subjunctive; as, **Cūr in suās possessiōnēs venīret,** *Why did he (Caesar) come into his possessions?* in the Direct Form this would be,

Cūr in meās possessiōnēs venīs? *Why do you come into my possessions* (I. 44)?

b. Deliberative Questions in Indirect Discourse retain the Subjunctive, but the Tense is governed by that of the Verb on which the Indirect Discourse depends (*177, a, b*); thus, **Quid agāmus?** *What are we to do?* after a Past Tense in Indirect Discourse becomes **Quid agerent;** as, **neque satis . . . cōnstābat, quid agerent,** *and it was not quite clear . . . what they should do* (III. 14).

c. Rhetorical Questions in Indirect Discourse have the Infinitive (*179, b*); as, **quid esse levius,** *what is more capricious,* implying that nothing could be more capricious (V. 28).

218. An Apodosis of a Conditional Sentence containing a Statement is expressed in Indirect Discourse by the Accusative and Infinitive, containing a Command, by the Subjunctive; the Protasis, containing the Condition, has the Subjunctive, as follows:

(1) *a.* In the First Type (Conditions of Fact), the Tense of the Infinitive in Indirect Discourse corresponds with the Tense of the Apodosis in the Direct Form, while the Tense of the Protasis, introduced by **sī** or **sīn**, is governed by that of the Verb on which the Indirect Discourse depends (*177, a, b*). Thus, **Is ita cum Caesare ēgit: sī pācem populus Rōmānus cum Helvētiīs faceret, in eam partem itūrōs [esse] atque ibi futūrōs [esse] Helvētiōs, ubi eōs Caesar cōnstituisset atque esse voluisset,** *He took up (the matter) with Caesar thus: If the Roman people would make peace with the Helvetians, they would go wherever Caesar should have appointed and wished them to be, and would there remain;* in the Direct Form, **Sī pācem populus Rōmānus cum Helvētiīs faciet, in eam partem ībunt atque ibi erunt Helvētiī, ubi eōs tū cōnstitueris** (Future Perfect Indicative) **atque esse volueris** (I. 13).

b. In the Protasis of the First Type a Perfect or Pluperfect Subjunctive in Indirect Discourse may represent a Future Perfect Indicative in the Direct Form; as, **Quod sī fēcerit** (Perfect Subjunctive), **Aeduōrum auctōritātem amplificātūrum [esse],** *If he should do this, he would increase the prestige of the Aeduans;* in the Direct Form, **Quod sī fēceris** (Future Perfect Indicative) **Aeduōrum auctōritātem amplificābis,** *If you will do* (lit. *shall have done*) *this, you will increase the prestige of the Aeduans* (II. 14).

(2) In the Second Type (Conditions of Possible Realization) the
Infinitive in Indirect Discourse represents the Subjunctive
of the Direct Form; the Tense of the Present Subjunctive in
the Protasis is Present after a Present Tense, but Imperfect
in case the Indirect Discourse follows a Past Tense. Thus,
after a Present Tense, **Sī quid accidat Rōmānīs, summam
in spem . . . venīre,** *if any (disaster) should befall the Romans,
he would entertain the highest expectation,* lit. *would come into the
highest hope*; in the Direct Form, **sī quid accidat Rōmānīs, summam in spem veniat** (I. 18).

(3) In the Third Type (Conditions Contrary to Fact) in Indirect
Discourse the Perfect Infinitive of the Active Periphrastic
Conjugation corresponds to the Active Pluperfect Subjunctive
in the Apodosis of the Direct Form, while a Passive Pluperfect Subjunctive in the Apodosis is represented by **futūrum
fuisse** (Impersonal) **ut . . .** with a Passive Imperfect Subjunctive, the Protasis being in the Subjunctive; as, **neque
Eburōnēs, sī ille adesset, (fuisse) ventūrōs,** *nor would the
Eburones have come if he (had been and) were at hand* (V. 29;
cf. *208, c*); **nisi nūntiī essent allātī, exīstimābant plērīque
futūrum fuisse, utī (oppidum) amitterētur,** *if news had
not been brought, most people were of the opinion that the town
would have been lost,* in the Direct Form, **nisi nuntiī essent
allātī, oppidum amissum esset** (C. III. 101).

219. The Apodosis of a Conditional Sentence is sometimes incorporated in a Substantive Clause introduced by **ut, nē,** or **quīn.** Thus,
**ut, sī vellet Ariovistus proeliō contendere, eī potestās non dē-
esset,** *in order that, if Ariovistus wished to contend in battle, opportunity
might not be lacking to him,* in the Direct Form, **Sī . . . volet . . . nōn
deerit** (I. 48); **neque dubitāre debēre quīn, sī Helvētiōs superāverint** (Perfect Subjunctive) **Rōmānī . . . Aeduīs lībertātem
sint ēreptūrī,** *and that they ought not to doubt that, if the Romans should
have overpowered the Helvetians, they were going to take away liberty from
the Aeduans,* in the Direct Form, **sī Helvētiōs superāverint** (Future
Perfect Indicative) **Rōmānī . . . ēreptūrī sunt** (I. 17).

220. The Verb of a clause subordinate to a clause having its Verb in
the Subjunctive, or in the Infinitive, is ordinarily put in the Subjunctive
(Subjunctive by Attraction); as, **utī frūmentō commeātūque, quī
. . . supportārētur, Caesarem interclūderet,** *that he might cut Caesar
off from the grain and other supplies which were being brought up* (I. 48).

THE INFINITIVE

221. *a.* Caesar uses the Infinitive after many Verbs to complete the Meaning (Complementary Infinitive); as, . . . **exīre possent**, *they were able to go out*, **exīre** filling out the sense which with **possent** alone would be incomplete (I. 6).

b. A Participle, Adjective or Noun in Predicate with a Complementary Infinitive is attracted to the case of the Subject of the Verb on which the Infinitive depends; as, **pūrgātī esse vellent**, *they should wish to be guiltless* (I. 28).

c. Caesar has the Infinitive after certain Participles used as Adjectives; as, **parātum** (Accusative) **dēcertāre**, *ready to fight it out* (I. 44).

222. *a.* An Infinitive may be the Subject of an Impersonal Verb, or of other Verbs used Impersonally; as, **Maiōrī partī placuit . . . dēfendere**, *The majority decided* (lit. *to the greater part it was pleasing*) *to defend* . . . (III. 3); **Commodissimum vīsum est . . . mittere**, *It seemed most expedient to send*, **mittere** being the Subject of **vīsum est** (I. 47).

b. An Infinitive is sometimes used as the Subject of an Infinitive, especially in Indirect Discourse; as, **commodissimum esse statuit . . . impōnere**, *he decided that the most expedient* (*thing*) *was to place . . . on*, **impōnere** being the Subject of **esse** used impersonally (I. 42).

c. An Infinitive used as Subject may have a Subject Accusative; as, **intersit** (Historical Present) **manūs distinērī**, *it was important that the forces be kept apart* (II. 5).

223. *a.* Caesar uses the Accusative with the Infinitive not only after words of Speech and Thought (Indirect Discourse, *212, d*), but also after Words expressing *Will* or *Desire*, *Feeling*, *Permission* and *Prevention*, *Persuasion*, *Command*, *Training* and *Compulsion;* as, **eās rēs iactārī nōlēbat**, *he was unwilling that those matters should be discussed* (I. 18); **eōs īre paterentur**, *would allow them to go* (I. 6).

Such Words used by Caesar are:

(1) Expressing Will or Desire: **dēsīderō**, *desire* (IV. 2); **mālō**, *prefer* (C. III. 80); **nōlō**, *be unwilling;* **studeō**, *be eager* (C. I. 4); **vōlō**, *wish* (I. 13).

(2) Expressing Feeling: **admīror**, *be surprised* (I. 14); **doleō**, *grieve* (III. 2); **gaudeō**, *rejoice* (IV. 13); **glōrior**, *boast* (C. I. 4); **queror**, *complain* (C. III. 96; usually followed by a **quod** clause); **magnō dolōre ferō**, *feel deeply chagrined* (VII. 63); **molestē ferō**, *feel irritation* (II. 1).

(3) Expressing Permission or Prevention: **patior**, *suffer, allow* (sometimes followed by an **ut**-clause) ; **prohibeō**, *prevent . . . from* (II. 4, etc.).

(4) Expressing Command, Training, or Compulsion: **iubeō**, *order* (I. 5) ; **vetō**, *forbid* (II. 20) ; **assuēfaciō**, *train* (IV. 2) ; **cōgō**, *force* (I. 4).

b. **Cupiō, mālō, nōlō, studeō,** and **volō** frequently have the Infinitive without a Subject Accusative (Complementary Infinitive) ; as, **ulcīscī velint,** *may wish to punish* (I. 14).

224. *a.* When Verbs which, in the Active Voice, have the Accusative and Infinitive, are used in the Passive, a Subject Nominative may take the place of the Accusative, the Infinitive remaining the same ; in translating, the English Impersonal construction should often be used. Thus, **nōn fore dictō audientēs . . . dīcantur,** *that it is said they will not be obedient to the command,* lit. *that they are said not to be about to be obedient* (I. 40).

b. The Accusative and the Infinitive may stand as the Subject of an Impersonal Verb, or of other Verbs used Impersonally ; as, **poenam sequī oportēbat,** *the penalty would inevitably follow,* lit. *that the penalty follow, was inevitable* (I. 4) ; **Nōn esse fās Germānōs superāre,** *That it was not right for the Germans to conquer,* **Germānōs superāre** being the Subject of **esse** used Impersonally (I. 50).

225. The place of the Future Infinitive may be taken by **fore** or **futūrum esse** and a clause with **ut** and the Subjunctive ; as, **fore, utī pertināciā dēsisteret,** *that he would desist from his obstinate course,* lit. *that it would be that he would desist* (I. 42).

PARTICIPLES

226. *a.* The Time denoted by a Present Participle is the same as that of the Principal Verb ; as, **flēns peteret,** *with tears* (lit. *weeping*) *he was entreating* (I. 20).

b. The Time denoted by a Perfect Participle is prior to that of the Principal Verb ; as, **cupiditāte inductus,** *led on* (lit. *having been led*) *by a desire* (I. 2).

c. Caesar sometimes uses Perfect Participles of Deponent and Semi-deponent Verbs where English usage prefers a Present Participle ; as, **Caesarem complexus,** *embracing Caesar,* lit. *having embraced* (I. 20**).** Examples are :

arbitrātus, *thinking* (III. 28) ; **complexus** ; **commorātus,** *delaying* (V. 7) ; **cōnfīsus,** *trusting* (I. 53) ; **cōnsōlātus,** *comforting* (I. 20) ; **diffīsus,** *distrusting* (VI. 38) ; **gāvīsus,** *rejoicing* (IV. 13) ; **mīrātus,** *wondering* (I. 32) ; **secūtus,** *following* (I. 24) ; **ūsus,** *using* (II. 7) ; **veritus,** *fearing* (II. 11).

227. *a.* A Participle is often used to express concisely an idea which might have been expanded into a Clause, particularly an idea of *Cause, Condition, Opposition, Characterization,* or *Description.* Thus:

(1) Expressing Cause: **sē, Biturīgum perfidiam veritōs, rever-tisse,** *that they, fearing the treachery of the Bituriges, had come back,* that is, *that they had come back because they feared the treachery of the Bituriges* (VII. 5).

(2) Expressing Condition: **hanc adeptī victōriam, in perpe-tuum sē fore victōrēs cōnfīdēbant,** *having won this victory, they were confident that they would be victorious for all time,* **adeptī** being equivalent to **sī adeptī essent** (V. 39).

(3) Expressing Opposition: **in colloquium venīre invītātus,** *although invited to come to a conference* (I. 35).

(4) Expressing Characterization or Description: **victīs, venientēs,** *those beaten, those coming up,* meaning *those who had been beaten, those who were coming up* (I. 25).

(5) Expressing Time: **cōnantēs,** *when they were attempting* (I. 47).

b. A Participle may express Manner or Circumstance; as, **flēns peteret,** *with tears* (lit. *weeping*) *he was entreating* (I. 20); **pugnāns interficitur,** *is killed while fighting* (V. 37).

228. *a.* Caesar sometimes uses a Perfect Participle in agreement with the Subject or the Object of a Verb where English usage prefers a coördinate clause. Thus, **Persuādent** (Historical Present) **Rauracīs . . . utī, eōdem ūsī cōnsiliō, . . . cum eīs proficīscantur,** *Persuaded the Rauraci . . . to adopt the same plan, and set out with them,* lit. *that, having used the same plan, they should set out* (I. 5); **Boiōs . . . receptōs ad sē sociōs sibi ascīscunt,** *they received and associated with themselves the Boians,* lit. *the Boians, having been received . . . they associated* (I. 5).

b. Caesar sometimes uses a Perfect Passive Participle in agreement with a Noun where the Participle has the main idea and is best trans-lated by a Noun; as, **ante prīmam cōnfectam vigiliam,** *before the end of the first watch,* lit. *before the first watch having been completed* (VII. 3).

c. Caesar sometimes uses a Participle in agreement with the Object of a Verb to depict an Action or a Situation more vividly. Thus, **aliquōs ex nāvī ēgredientēs cōnspexerant,** *had seen some (soldiers) disembarking,* is more vivid than **aliquōs . . . ēgredī,** *that some (sol-diers) were disembarking* (IV. 26).

229. *a.* **Habeō** with a Perfect Passive Participle in agreement with its Object may have almost the force of a Perfect or Pluperfect tense; as, **quem . . . coāctum habēbat,** *which he had collected,* lit. *which, having been collected, he was having* (I. 15).

b. Caesar uses the Future Passive Participle (Gerundive) in agreement with the Object of Certain Verbs to express Purpose or Accomplishment; as, **pontem faciendum cūrat** (Historical Present), *he had a bridge built, he attended to the building of a bridge,* lit. *cared for a bridge to be built* (I. 13).

The verbs thus used are **cūrō,** *arrange, provide;* **dō,** *give* (IV. 22); and **trādō,** *deliver* (VI. 4).

c. The Future Passive Participle combined with the forms of **sum** in the Passive Periphrastic Conjugation (*63*) is often used to express Obligation, Necessity, or Propriety; as, **revocandī [erant] mīlitēs,** *the soldiers had to be called back* (II. 20). Cf. *357, a* and *b* (p. 643).

GERUND AND GERUNDIVE CONSTRUCTION

230. In place of the Gerund, Caesar more often uses the Gerundive Construction, with the Noun in the case in which the Gerund might have been put, and the Gerundive agreeing with it. His use of the Gerund and of the Gerundive Construction is as follows:

(1) Genitive after Nouns and Adjectives, and with **causā** and **grātiā** expressing Purpose: **bellandī cupidī,** *desirous of waging war* (I. 2); **Galliae impugnandae causā,** *in order to attack Gaul* (I. 44). Cf. *355* (p. 643).

(2) Dative after Verbs (Gerundive Construction only): **vix ut eīs rēbus . . . collocandīs . . . tempus darētur,** *barely time (enough) was given for making those arrangements,* lit. *for those things to be arranged* (III. 4).

(3) Accusative after **ad** to express Purpose: **ad dēlīberandum,** *for consideration* (I. 7); **Ad eās rēs cōnficiendās,** *To complete these preparations,* lit. *for these things to be accomplished* (I. 3). Cf. *355* (p. 643).

(4) Ablative of Means without a Preposition, and Ablative with the Prepositions **in** or **dē**: **fallendō,** *by practising deception* (IV. 13); **in quaerendō,** *on making inquiry* (I. 18); **dē expugnandō oppidō,** *in regard to storming the stronghold* (II. 10).

THE SUPINES

231. *a.* The Supine in -**um** is used, chiefly after Verbs of Motion, to express Purpose; as, **ad Caesarem grātulātum convēnērunt**, *came to Caesar to offer congratulations* (I. 30). Cf. *355* (p. 643).

b. The Supine in -**um** may be followed by a Direct Object, or by a Clause; as, **lēgātōs mittunt** (Historical Present) **rogātum auxilium**, *sent envoys to ask for help* (I. 11); **questum, quod Harūdēs . . . fīnēs eōrum populārentur**, *to make complaint because the Harudes were laying waste their country* (I. 37).

232. Caesar uses the Supine in -**ū** after a few adjectives to denote in What Respect their Meaning is to be taken; as, **Perfacile factū**, *very easy of accomplishment*, lit. *very easy in respect to the doing* (I. 3).

The Adjectives thus used by Caesar are **horridus** (V. 14), **optimus** (IV. 30), and **perfacilis** (I. 3, VII. 64).

CONJUNCTIONS

233. *a.* Of the Copulative Conjunctions Caesar uses **et**, *and*, **et . . . et**, *both . . . and*, *on the one hand . . . on the other*, to express simple connection; -**que**, *and*, -**que . . . -que**, *both . . . and*, to express a closer connection; **atque** or **ac**, *and also*, *and indeed*, *and*, to express a close connection and also make that which follows slightly more prominent; and **neque** or **nec**, *and . . . not*, **neque** (or **nec**) . . . **neque** (or **nec**), *neither . . . nor*, *not . . . and not;* **et . . . neque**, *both . . . and not;* **neque** or **nec . . . et**, *and not . . . and*, to express a connection with a negative idea.

b. The enclitic Conjunction -**que**, *and*, is attached to the word introduced by it, or to the first word of a Phrase or Clause which it introduces, excepting a Prepositional Phrase; -**que** introducing a Prepositional Phrase may be attached to the first word after the Preposition. Thus, **ob eāsque rēs**, *and on account of these things* (II. 35).

c. After words expressing Similarity, or the Opposite, **atque** or **ac** has the force of *than*, *as;* as, **in parem . . . condiciōnem atque ipsī erant**, *into the same condition . . . as themselves*, lit. *as (and) they themselves were* (I. 28).

d. Caesar uses the conjunctions **et**, -**que**, **atque**, **ac**, and **neque** in various combinations, sometimes joining more than two members; as, **et . . . que** (III. 11), -**que . . . et** (II. 22), **et . . . atque** (I. 15), **atque . . . et** (II. 8), **atque . . . -que** (VI. 11), **neque . . . atque**

(II. 10), **neque . . . et** (II. 25), **-que . . . -que . . . -que** (I. 30),
ac . . . atque . . . -que (III. 5), **et . . . atque . . . et . . . et
. . . et** (IV. 33).

234. *a.* When more than two words stand in the same relation,
the Copulative Conjunction may be expressed with all, or omitted
with all, or the last two words may be joined by **-que**; in each case
English usage generally prefers " and " between the last two words.
Thus, **Rauracīs et Tulingīs et Latobrīgīs,** *the Rauraci, Tulingi, and
Latobrigi* (I. 5) ; **linguā, īnstitūtīs, lēgibus,** *in respect to language, institutions, and laws* (I. 1) ; **puerī, senēs mulierēsque,** *children, old men,
and women* (I. 29).

b. Sometimes, especially after a negative expression, Caesar uses
et, -que, and **atque** or **ac,** where English usage prefers *but;* as,
portūs . . . capere nōn potuērunt, et paulō īnfrā dēlātae sunt,
could not make the harbors but were carried a short distance below (IV. 36).

235. *a.* Of the Disjunctive Conjunctions Caesar uses **aut,** *or,* to
connect alternatives that cannot, in most cases, both be true at the
same time; **vel,** *or,* negative **nēve** or **neu,** *or not, and not,* to connect
alternatives between which there might be a choice; and **sīve** or **seu,**
or if, to connect alternatives involving a condition. Thus, **quīnīs aut
sēnīs mīlibus passuum,** *five or six miles* each day (I. 15) ; **Brūtō . . .
vel tribūnīs,** *to Brutus or the tribunes* (III. 14).

b. The Disjunctive Conjunctions are often used in pairs, as **aut . . .
aut,** *either . . . or* (I. 1), **vel . . . vel,** *either . . . or* (I. 6), **sīve
. . . sīve,** *whether . . . or, either . . . or* (I. 12).

236. *a.* Of the Adversative Conjunctions Caesar uses **at,** *but, at any
rate,* to express Contrast or Restriction ; **autem,** *however, on the other
hand, moreover,* to express Contrast or Addition ; **sed,** *but,* to correct
or limit a Preceding Statement; **tamen,** *nevertheless, yet,* to emphasize
the importance of something that follows in opposition to a Preceding Statement; and **vērō,** *in fact, but in truth,* to emphasize a contrast
with a Preceding Statement.

b. The Adversative Conjunctions **autem** and **vērō** are regularly
placed after the First Word of a Clause.

c. The Adversative Conjunction **tamen** sometimes stands after the
First Word of a Clause.

d. Caesar uses correlatively **nōn sōlum . . . sed etiam,** *not only . . .
but also;* **nōn modo . . . sed etiam,** *not only . . . but also;* **nōn
modo . . . sed,** *not only . . . but;* **nōn modo nōn . . . sed nē . . .
quidem,** *not only not . . . but not even.*

e. In **nōn modo . . . nē** — **quidem** Caesar uses **nōn modo** as equivalent to **nōn modo nōn**, when a verb appears only in the second member; as **nōn modo dēfessō . . . sed nē sauciō quidem**, *not only not to one (who was) exhausted . . . but even to a wounded man* (III. 4).

237. *a.* Of the Conjunctions denoting Logical Relations Caesar uses chiefly **itaque**, *accordingly* (lit. *and so*), to introduce a statement of a fact or situation naturally resulting from what preceded; **proinde**, *hence*, to introduce a Command; **nam** or **enim**, *for*, to introduce an Explanation of a Preceding Statement; and **quārē**, *wherefore, and therefore*, to introduce a Logical Consequence, or a Command.

b. In presenting a succession of points Caesar often uses **prīmum**, *first*, and **deinde**, *then, in the second place*; sometimes, also, **dēnique** *in fine*, to introduce the conclusion of an argument.

c. In the Adverbial Phrase **nē . . . quidem**, *not even*, the word or phrase emphasized is placed between the two words; as, **nē pabulī quidem**, *not even of fodder* (I. 16).

FIGURES OF SPEECH

238. Caesar uses the following Grammatical Figures:

a. *Asyndeton* (a-sin′de-ton),[1] the omission of a Conjunction where a Connective might have been used; as, **loca, portūs, aditūs cognōvisset**, *should have become acquainted with the natural features, the harbors (and) the approaches* (IV. 20); **L. Pīsōne, A. Gabīniō cōnsulibus**, *in the Consulship of Lucius Piso (and) Aulus Gabinius* (I. 6).

b. *Brachylogy* (bra-kil′ọ-ji), a condensed form of expression; as, **cōnsimilis caprīs figūra**, *shape like (that of) goats*, that is, **figūra cōnsimilis figūrae** (Dative) **caprārum** (VI. 27).

c. *Ellipsis* (ĕ-lip′sis), the omission of words essential to the meaning; as, **Duae fīliae**, for **Duae fīliae fuērunt**, *There were two daughters* (I. 53).

d. *Hendiadys* (hen-dī′ạ-dis), the use of two Nouns with a Connective where a noun with a Modifying Genitive or Adjective might have been expected; as, **fidem et iūs iūrandum**, *a pledge of good faith bound by an oath*, lit. *good faith and oath* (I. 3).

e. *Parenthesis* (pạ-ren′the-sis), the insertion of an Independent Sentence or phrase, interrupting the Construction; as, **quam maximum potest mīlitum numerum imperat (erat . . . legiō ūna)**,

---

[1] The key to the Pronunciation is given at the beginning of the Vocabulary.

pontem . . . iubet (Historical Present), **rescindī,** *he levied as many soldiers as possible (there was only one legion, altogether, in further Gaul) and gave orders that the bridge be cut down* (I. 7).

f. Polysyndeton (pol-i̯-sin'de̯-ton), the use of more Conjunctions than the sense requires; as, **Ceutronēs et Graiocelī et Caturīgēs,** *the Ceutrones, the Graioceli, and the Caturiges* (I. 10).

g. Prolepsis (prō-lep'sis), or *Anticipation,* the use of a Noun as Object in a clause preceding that in which it naturally belongs as Subject; as, **rem frūmentāriam, ut supportārī posset, timēre,** *that they feared that the supply of grain could not be brought up,* lit. *they feared the supply of grain, that it . . .* (I. 39).

h. Synesis (sin'e̯-sis), construction according to the Sense, without regard to the Grammatical Form; as, **cīvitātī persuāsit, ut . . . exīrent,** *persuaded the (people of his) state to go out,* lit. *persuaded his state that they should go out* (I. 2).

239. Caesar uses the following Rhetorical Figures:

a. Anaphora (an-af'o̯-ra̯), the Repetition of the same word at the beginning of Successive Phrases or Clauses; as, **nōn aetāte cōnfectīs, nōn mulieribus, nōn īnfantibus pepercērunt,** *they spared not the aged, not the women, not the children* (VII. 28).

b. Antithesis (an-tith'e-sis), the juxtaposition of contrasted expressions in like order; as, **Nōn sēsē Gallīs, sed Gallōs sibi, bellum intulisse,** *He did not make war on the Gauls, but the Gauls on him* (I. 44).

c. Chiasmus (kī-as'mus), an arrangement of contrasted words in inverse order; as, **fāmā nōbilēs potentēsque bellō,** *in reputation notable, and powerful in war* (VII. 77).

d. Climax (klī'max), an arrangement of words, phrases, or clauses with gradual increase of interest or vigor of expression to the end; as, **cōnferre, comportarī, adesse,** *that it was being collected, was on the way, was at hand* (I. 16).

e. Euphemism (ū'fe̯-mizm), the use of a mild expression in order to avoid a word of bad omen; as, **sī quid accidat Rōmānīs,** *if anything should happen to the Romans,* meaning *if any disaster should befall the Romans* (I. 18).

f. Hyperbaton (hī-per'ba-ton), the arrangement of words in unusual order, as the separation of words that belong together, such as the insertion of one or more words between the parts of an Ablative Absolute; thus, **simulātā Caesarem amīcitiā,** *that Caesar under the pretense of friendship,* the usual order being **Caesarem, simulātā amīcitiā** (I. 44, l. 37).

g. Litotes (lit′o̭-tēz), the Affirmation of an idea through the Negation of its Opposite; as, **neque tam imperītum esse rērum ut nōn scīret,** *and he was not so unversed in affairs as not to know,* meaning *that he was so worldly wise that he very well knew* (I. 44, l. 32).

h. Personification (pėr-son′i̭-fi̭′ka̅′shun), the representation of something inanimate or abstract as endowed with Life and Action; as **Cōnspicātae nāvēs trirēmēs duae nāvem D. Brūtī,** *Two triremes, sighting the ship of Decimus Brutus* (C. II. 6).

EXPRESSIONS RELATING TO TIME

240. *a.* The Roman year (**annus**) is usually dated by the consuls in office, their names being given in the Ablative Absolute with

Figure 152. — A Roman Calendar.

Of marble. Above the name of each month is a sign of the zodiac associated with it: Capricorn with January, Aquarius with February, Pisces with March, Aries with April, Taurus with May, and Gemini with June.

cōnsulibus; as, **Cn. Pompeiō, M. Crassō cōnsulibus,** *in the consulship of Gnaeus Pompey and Marcus Crassus* (IV. 1), 55 B.C.

b. In Caesar's time the year commenced on January 1, and the months were named (**mēnsis**) **Iānuārius, Februārius, Mārtius** (originally the first month of the year), **Aprīlis, Maius, Iūnius, Quīnctīlis** (from **quīnque**; named the *fifth* month when the year began with March), **Sextīlis** (**sex**), **September, Octōber, November, December** (the *tenth* month, reckoning March as the first). Afterwards **Quīnctīlis** was changed to **Iūlius** (our *July*) in honor of Julius Caesar, and **Sextīlis** to **Augustus** (our *August*) in honor of the Emperor Augustus.

241. *a.* Dates in the month were reckoned backward from three points, the mode of reckoning being similar to that which we use when we say " Four days yet before the New Moon." These points, designated by Plural Feminine Nouns, are *the Calends,* **Kalendae,**

the *first* day of the month; *the Nones*, **Nōnae** (ninth before the Ides), the *seventh* day of March, May, July, and October, the *fifth* day of other months; and *the Ides* (**Īdūs**), the *fifteenth* day of March, May, July, and October, the *thirteenth* of other months.

b. In giving dates the days at the beginning and end of a given period were both included, and abbreviations were employed. Thus, **a. d. v. Kal. Apr.** (I. 6), in full would be **ante diem quīntum Kalendās Aprīlēs**, which is translated as if it were (**diēs**) **quīntus ante Kalendās Aprīlēs**, *the fifth* (*day*) *before the Calends of April;* since March had 31 days, we start from April 1 and count back:

DAY I	DAY II	DAY III	DAY IV	DAY V
April 1	March 31	March 30	March 29	March 28

and so we find the fifth day, which is March 28 according to our method of writing dates.

c. In 46 B.C. the Calendar was reformed by Julius Caesar by virtue of his authority as Supreme Pontiff (*252*), and since that year it has undergone slight change. As the dates of the Gallic War and of the Civil War are prior to 46 B.C., they fall in the period of the Unreformed Calendar, when there was much confusion. Thus, the twenty-eighth day of March of the Unreformed Calendar in 58 B.C. (I. 6) is considered by some to be the same as March 24 of our Calendar; by others, the same as March 25; by others still, as April 16 of our Calendar.

242. *a.* The day from sunrise to sunset was divided into twelve hours, **hōrae**, which varied in length according to the season of the year, and were numbered 1–12; thus, **hōra septima**, *the seventh hour* (I. 26). Since the sixth hour ended at noon, the seventh hour at the equinoxes would correspond exactly with the hour between twelve and one o'clock according to our reckoning; at other times the seventh hour would end after, or before, one o'clock.

b. The method of reducing the Roman hours to our system of reckoning may be illustrated by the following problem:

Question. "What, approximately, is our equivalent of the fourth Roman hour in the last week of August in the region of Dover, England ?"

Answer. In the region of Dover in the last week in August the sun rises about 5 o'clock and sets about 7. The length of the day is therefore about 14 hours by our reckoning. Since the Romans divided the full day into 12 equal hours, we divide 14 by 12 and have $1\frac{1}{6}$, that is, the Roman hour in this problem = $1\frac{1}{6}$ of our hours. At the beginning of the fourth Roman hour 3 Roman hours have passed; $3 \times 1\frac{1}{6} = 3\frac{1}{2}$, that is, at the beginning of the fourth Roman hour $3\frac{1}{2}$ of our hours have passed since sunrise. As sunrise is reckoned about 5 o'clock by our time, we add 3½ to 5, making 8.30; that is, 8.30 A.M., by our reckoning from midnight, will approximately represent the beginning of the fourth hour of the day by Roman reckoning under the conditions of the problem.

c. In military usage the night was divided into four watches of three hours each: **prīma vigilia**, *first watch* (VII. 3), commencing at sunset, 6 to 9 o'clock by Roman reckoning; **secunda vigilia** (II. 11), ending at midnight, 9 to 12 o'clock; **tertia vigilia** (II. 33), commencing at midnight, 12 to 3 o'clock A.M.; **quārta vigilia** (I. 21), ending at sunrise, 3 to 6 o'clock A.M., by Roman reckoning.

d. Caesar uses the Preposition **dē** in certain expressions of time with the meaning *just after, in the course of;* as **dē mediā nocte**, *just after midnight* (II. 7); **dē tertiā vigiliā**, *soon after the beginning of the third watch* (I. 12), which lasted from midnight to 3 A. M.

e. When the sun was not visible, recourse might be had to water clocks, **ex aquā mensūrae** (V. 13), for the measurement of time.

EXPRESSIONS RELATING TO LENGTH AND DISTANCE

243. *a.* Of the terms denoting measurement Caesar uses **digitus**, *finger-breadth* (VII. 73); **pēs**, *foot* (I. 8), which measured approximately .97 of the English foot; **passus**, *pace* (I. 49); and **mīlle passūs**, *mile*, Plural **mīlia passuum**, *miles* (I. 2). The **passus** contained two ordinary steps (**gradus**), and measured the distance between the points where the same heel is lifted and touches the ground again.

b. The relations of the units of measurement, and their modern equivalents, are as follows:

			ENGLISH FEET	METERS
	1 digitus	= .728 inch	=	.0185
16 digitī	= 1 pēs	= 11.65 inches	=	.296
2½ pedēs	= 1 gradus	= 2 feet 5⅛ inches	=	.74
2 gradūs	= 1 passus	= 4 feet 10¼ inches	=	1.48
1000 passūs =	mīlle passūs	= 4854 feet	=	1480.00

Since the Roman foot was approximately .97 of the English foot in length, the Roman mile, 4854 English feet in length, was 426 feet shorter than the English mile of 5280 feet; 12 English miles are a little more than the equivalent of 13 Roman miles.

c. Long distances may be loosely expressed by **iter** (Accusative) with the Genitive; as, **novem diērum iter**, *a nine days' journey* (VI. 25).

GAIUS JULIUS CAESAR

LIFE OF CAESAR

244. "My aunt Julia," said Julius Caesar in an address in
68 B.C. at the funeral of his aunt, wife of the famous Marius,
"My aunt Julia on her mother's side traced her ancestry back
to kings, on her father's side to the immortal gods. For those
who bear the name Marcius Rex, her mother's family, are
descended from Ancus Marcius;[1] from Venus the Julii are
sprung, and to that clan our family
belongs. In our stock therefore are
blended the sacred authority of kings,
whose power is greatest among men,
and a right to the reverence due to
the gods, under whose power kings
themselves are."

Whatever the truth may be about
the origin of the Julian clan (*gens*),
in these proud words the man who was
destined to become its most distinguished representative asserted, un-
mistakably, its aristocratic standing.
Twenty years afterwards, when Caesar

Figure 153. — Aeneas fleeing from Troy.

Silver coin, denarius, struck in
the East soon after the battle
of Pharsalus.   Inscription,
CAESAR.

had the authority to strike coins, he gave a visible expression
to the popular belief in the Trojan origin of the Julii, from
Venus and Anchises; stamped upon a denarius (*85*) Aeneas
appears, in the flight from burning Troy, carrying his aged
father Anchises upon his left shoulder and in his right hand
the sacred image, the Palladium, which, men said, had fallen
from heaven (Fig. 153).

[1] The fourth king of Rome, following Tullus Hostilius.

245. Toward the end of the Republic the Caesar family far outstripped the other families of the Julian gens in prominence. In the two centuries immediately preceding the Christian era it furnished a full score of names sufficiently distinguished to find mention in biographical dictionaries two thousand years afterwards. Of the father of Julius Caesar, however, nothing important is of record except his sudden death, at Pisa, when he was putting on his shoes.

246. Gaius Julius Caesar was born on July 12, in the year 100 B.C.; he was thus six years younger than Pompey and the orator Cicero. It is assumed that his birthplace was Rome. His mother was Aurelia, a Roman matron of the highest type. She not only watched over the education of her son — and Julius was the only son — with great care, but followed his career with solicitude, and on one occasion at least rendered him a notable service. She was not spared, however, to see her son at the head of the State, or to be harrowed by civil war; she died when Caesar was in Gaul.

Figure 154. — A Roman Boy

Portrait of a Roman boy, probably connected with the Caesar family. From a bronze statue of the first century B.C., in the Metropolitan Museum, New York.

We know nothing about the education of the young Julius, except that he had as private teacher, at his own home, Antonius Gnipho, a distinguished rhetorician, who had studied at Alexandria and was well versed in Greek. We may assume that the youth received the usual training of the time in Greek as well as in declamation, numbers, and music; for Greek was then the foundation of liberal studies.

At the age of twelve Caesar's face must remotely, at least, have resembled that of the Roman boy whose portrait is preserved in the lifelike bronze statue acquired in 1914 by the Metropolitan Museum in New York (Fig. 154).

247. The only career deemed suitable for a young patrician was in the service of the State, either through public office, or through service in the field, as occasion might require. We do not understand how high-born Caesars were first led to espouse the cause of the common people and champion the interests of the masses as opposed to the aristocracy, which believed in the government of the many by the few and had its stronghold in the Senate; but when Julius was old enough to take an active interest in public affairs, his uncle by marriage, Marius, was leader of the popular or democratic party, which was then dominant. Marius died in 86 B.C., and was succeeded by Cornelius Cinna as democratic leader.

248. The daughter of this Cinna, Cornelia, in 83 B.C. became Caesar's wife. To them was born a daughter Julia who, in 59 B.C., in her early twenties, became the fourth wife of Pompey.

249. In 82 B.C. Sulla returned from a series of victories in the East and restored the power of the Senate, wreaking vengeance upon political enemies. There was a reign of terror. Cinna had been killed, and Sulla ordered Caesar to divorce his wife, Cinna's daughter. This Caesar refused, at the risk of his life. In disguise he made his escape to the mountains. He was tracked by Sulla's emissaries, one of whom found him; he purchased his life with a large bribe. After a time, through influential friends, pardon was obtained from Sulla, who is said to have granted it with the warning that in young Caesar there were many Mariuses.

Advancement in Rome, however, was blocked so long as Sulla lived. Caesar went East and joined the army. At the siege of Mytilene, on the island of Lesbos, in 80 B.C., he was awarded the Civic Crown for conspicuous bravery. This crown, though made of oak leaves, represented a military distinction rarely conferred, and most highly esteemed. It was given only to the soldier who had saved the life of a Roman citizen in battle, had killed his adversary, and held the position where the rescue was made, without retreating. There is a good representation of a Civic Crown on a coin of the Emperor Augustus (Fig. 155).

Figure 155.—Civic Crown, corona civica.

Silver coin of Augustus, denarius, struck in 16 or 15 B.C. The crown, of oak leaves, is tied with a fillet Inscription, OB CIVIS SERVATOS, 'on account of the saving of citizens.'

250. Returning to Rome, after Sulla's death (78 B.C.), Caesar brought charges of extortion in provincial management first against Gnaeus Dolabella, who had been proconsul in Macedonia, and afterwards against Gaius Antonius, who had plundered Greece; at that time the bringing of delinquent officials to justice was a common way of introducing one's self to public notice. Though both Dolabella and Antonius seem to have escaped punishment, Caesar showed marked oratorical power, and in prosecuting them attracted favorable attention.

Wishing to perfect himself in oratory, in 76 Caesar started for Rhodes, to study under Apollonius Molo, the most eminent teacher of the art. In the Eastern Mediterranean the pirates were still active; near Miletus his ship was captured, and he was held a prisoner on an island for thirty-eight days, until his retinue could return and bring to the pirates a ransom of fifty talents, more than fifty thousand dollars. As a captive he showed himself merry and sociable; and he jokingly told his captors that some day he would come back and crucify them. Being released, he at once manned ships at Miletus, attacked the pirates suddenly, and captured most of them. True to his word, he crucified them, but ordered their throats cut first — Suetonius adds, as an example of Caesar's humaneness — in order to spare needless suffering. The quickness of action, daring, and success of this adventure reveal in Caesar at the age of twenty-four the qualities that characterized his entire career.

251. *a.* During the next sixteen years Caesar followed the usual course of political promotion, neglecting no means by which he might increase his popularity. He bestowed gifts with a free hand, assumed the debts of bankrupt young nobles who had squandered their inheritance, gave largesses to the people. When his own means were exhausted, he borrowed large sums at high rates of interest, with the design of obtaining reimbursemen. from the spoils of office. According to Plutarch his indebtedness, before he held a single office, had reached the enormous sum of thirteen hundred talents, about a million and a half of dollars.

Figure 156. — Ancient trophy, of marble.

Now on the Capitoline hill in Rome, badly weatherworn; by some thought to be one of the very trophies set up by Marius and restored by Julius Caesar.

This is an imitation of the trophies which were made on battle-fields by fastening shields, helmets, and other weapons of the enemy to trunks of trees, or posts.

b. In 68 B.C. Caesar was quaestor, and accompanied Antistius Vetus to Spain. Here his duties were chiefly financial ; the provincial quaestor had charge of the military stores and supervised the keeping of accounts for the provincial governor. This was doubtless a good business training for Caesar, which he turned to excellent use later in his administration in Gaul.

c. In 65 B.C. Caesar was curule aedile, with Bibulus as colleague; the curule aediles had charge of the streets and public buildings, the markets, and the celebration of the public games. In this office, by extravagant expenditures on games and public improvements, he raised the enthusiasm of the populace to the highest pitch. He even dared by night to set up in the Capitol the statue of Marius, and trophies of victories in the Jugurthine and Cimbrian wars, which had been thrown down by Sulla seventeen years before; and the people wept for joy at the revival of old memories (Fig. 156). He secured so many gladiators for public shows that the Senate became alarmed, on account of the presence of so great an armed force, and passed a law restricting the number; but he nevertheless exhibited three hundred and twenty pairs, all resplendent in silver armor. Caesar's political methods were not unlike those of his contemporaries, but he excelled them in daring and foresight — and succeeded.

Figure 157. — Symbols of Caesar's office, as Supreme Pontiff.

Middle, axe used in sacrifices, with wolf's head above.

Right, priest's cap, with point (apex), and bands for tying under the chin.

Left, sprinkler for holy water, and underneath, wine-ladle.

Silver coin, denarius, struck by Caesar in Gaul, probably in 50 B.C. Obverse in Fig. 164.

252. It has been believed by many that Caesar was connected with the Catilinarian conspiracy of 65 B.C., if not also with that of 63; but the evidence is meager. Much more important was his election, in 63 B.C., after a bitter contest, to the office of Supreme Pontiff, Pontifex Maximus. The tenure of this office was for life. As the head of the college of pontiffs, then fifteen in number, the Supreme Pontiff was virtually the head of the Roman religious system. He decided questions relating to religious law and usage, and he had charge of the

Calendar; the priests of Jupiter and of other divinities, as well as the Vestal Virgins, were under his jurisdiction. The first coin struck by Caesar in Gaul on one side bears the symbols of his sacred office (Fig. 157), the ax for striking victims in offering sacrifice, the close-fitting cap, with point of olive wood, worn by certain priests, the brush-shaped sprinkler for holy water, and the ladle for dipping up wine, for use in pouring libations.

253. In 62 B.C. Caesar held the office of praetor, in the discharge of which, amid scenes of violence, he carried himself with firmness and dignity; the functions of the praetor were judicial, and in stormy times the administration of justice is doubly difficult. The next year he was propraetor in Further Spain, where he won distinction by subduing several tribes along the Atlantic in Gallaecia and Lusitania. Returning to Rome in the summer of 60, with abundant means of satisfying his creditors, he was decreed a public thanksgiving for his victories, and was soon elected consul for the year 59.

In the year of his consulship, 59, Caesar married Calpurnia, familiar to readers of Shakespeare's "Julius Caesar"; she was the daughter of Calpurnius Piso (I. 12), and was Caesar's fourth wife. For his first wife, Cossutia, was divorced before he married Cornelia, his second wife (*248*), who had died before his quaestorship; and Pompeia, whom Caesar married in 67 B.C., as his third wife, was divorced six years later.

254. For some years Pompey had been the most conspicuous Roman. His successes in the campaign against the pirates and the war with Mithridates, and his conquest of Syria and Palestine, had made him the national hero (Fig. 147). But in the qualities needful for a political leader he was quite lacking; so that even from his own party, the aristocratic, he was unable to win either the recognition he desired or the privileges to which he was entitled. More than once the Senate snubbed him outright. Here Caesar saw an opportunity. Relying on his own popularity, he proposed to Pompey that they work in harmony, and by uniting their influence accomplish what either might desire. Pompey agreed; and with these two, Crassus, the wealthiest man of Rome, was joined, making a political coalition really supreme, which is known as the First Triumvirate. It had no official existence; it was simply a political ring, of only three members but of unlimited power. It was to cement this union that Pompey, then a widower for the third time, married Caesar's daughter Julia (*248*), who was less than half his age.

255. During his consulship, in 59, among other measures Caesar caused a law to be passed regarding the division of the

Figure 158. — Goddess of Concord.

Silver coin, denarius, struck about 53 B.C. to symbolize the harmony between the members of the Triumvirate. Inscription, CONCORDIAI = *Concordiae*, 'To Concord.'

public lands, which, though bitterly opposed by the Senate, pleased the people greatly. With his aid, too, Pompey gained the favors previously denied. While consul he seems to have used his influence with the Senate to secure a recognition of Ariovistus, the German ruler, with whom he afterwards fought (I. 33, 35, 40).

At the close of his consulship, as it was the custom to give to ex-consuls the charge of provinces, Caesar easily obtained for five years the government of both Cisalpine Gaul (*284*) and Illyricum (*298*), together with the part of Transalpine Gaul previously subdued, which in this book is called the Province (*290*).

256. Caesar was soon engaged in the conquest of Transalpine Gaul beyond the Province. The first summer (58 B.C.) he drove back to their homes the Helvetians, who had attempted to migrate from the country now called Switzerland, to the west of Gaul; and he annihilated the army of the German king, Ariovistus. The following year he subdued the Belgic States in the north.

The third campaign (56 B.C.) was against the peoples of northwest Gaul, that had leagued together to resist Caesar. In April

of this year at Luca, near the southern border of Cisalpine Gaul,
Caesar had renewed his compact with Pompey and Crassus, who
agreed to see to it that his command should be extended for
five years longer (Fig. 158). A part of every winter except one
(54–53), he spent in Cisalpine Gaul, so as to be near Rome and
retain his influence in home politics ; it was contrary to law that
a provincial governor having an army should enter Italy while
in office.

In 55 B.C. Caesar chastised several German tribes and bridged
the Rhine ; then he crossed over to Britain. The campaign of

the next summer (54) was principally
against the Britons, part of whom he
reduced to nominal subjection. In the
fall a division of his army in Belgium,
under the command of Sabinus and
Cotta, was cut off by a sudden uprising
of the enemy.

In 53 Caesar had to face an extensive
rebellion of the Gallic states, which,
however, he speedily crushed. But the
next year almost all Gaul rose against
him, and under the leadership of Vercingetorix taxed his powers to the
utmost. He finally prevailed ; and
after the fall of Alesia (52 B.C.), the
strength of the Gauls was forever
broken.

In the eighth campaign, summer of
51, the states that had not submitted

Figure 159. — Symbols of
victories over the Gauls.

Middle, trophy, draped ; at
the top, a Gallic helmet, horned.

Hanging from the trophy at
the left is an oval shield ; at the
right, a Gallic war-trumpet.

Behind the war-trumpet is
a sacrificial axe, above which
is the head of an animal.

Gold coin, aureus, struck by
Caesar in Rome in 49 B.C.

were one by one reduced to complete subjection. The following
spring, in 50 B.C., Caesar left his army and went into Cisalpine
Gaul. Here he resolved to remain till the expiration of his
command in 49, returning to Transalpine Gaul only for a
short time during the summer to review the troops.

257. Caesar's Gallic victories are symbolically portrayed on
several coins. On one (Fig. 159), we see in the middle a trophy,

draped ; on the top is a Gallic helmet, with a bull's horns. Suspended on one side of the trophy is an oval shield ; opposite is a Gallic war trumpet, with the mouth carved to represent the head of a serpent ; then, nearer the edge of the coin, a sacrificial ax. The base of the trophy divides the victor's name, CAESAR. A trophy appears less distinctly on another coin of Caesar, but at the foot is Vercingetorix, sitting, with his hands tied behind him ; his head is turned toward the left as he looks upward (cf. Fig. 161).

258. During Caesar's absence in Gaul, in 55 B.C., Crassus undertook a campaign of conquest against the Parthians, in the Far East ; he was defeated and killed in 53 B.C. The triumvirate was thus brought to an end, and with it speedily ended the coöperation between Caesar and Pompey.

Figure 160. — Pompey the Great.

Silver coin struck by Pompey's admiral, Nasidius, some years after his death. The trident, the dolphin, and the inscription NEPTUNI, 'Of Neptune,' refer to the fleet of his son, Sextus Pompey. Cf. Fig. 146.

Pompey began to view Caesar's successes with distrust and alarm. He entered into alliance again with the aristocracy. In 50 B.C. the Senate in Pompey's interest passed a decree that he and Caesar should each give up a legion for service in the East. Since 53 Caesar had had one of Pompey's legions ; this was now demanded back. Caesar let it go, and one of his own too, without a complaint, although the intent of the whole action was evidently to weaken his forces. As it was not lawful for him to proceed in person to Rome, he stationed himself in Ravenna, the town of Cisalpine Gaul nearest the boundary of Italy (*283*), on the east side ; thence he sent agents and friends to the City to negotiate for him, to try to offset the influence now openly brought to bear against him, but the negotiations were fruitless.

Pompey (Fig. 160) and the Senate both hated and feared Caesar. A decree was passed that he should disband his army by a certain date, or be considered an outlaw. In the state of public affairs at the time, this was simply to wrest from him the fruits of his hard-won successes, without leaving him even a guaranty of his personal safety. Caesar hesitated. The Senate voted further, that the consuls should "provide that the state receive no hurt," which is like a proclamation of martial law in our day.

259. This action of the Senate was virtually a declaration of war against Caesar, inspired by the jealousy of his opponent. With one legion he at once (in January, 49 B.C.) crossed the Rubicon, the boundary of his province (*283*), and marched south. Soon all Italy was in his power; Pompey, the Senate, and their followers had fled to Macedonia, on the east side of the Adriatic (*299*).

After arranging matters at Rome to suit himself, in April, 49 B.C., Caesar went to Spain, where lieutenants devoted to Pompey, Afranius and Petreius, had a strong army. They were soon crushed, the main force being captured near Ilerda in August of 49. On his return from Spain to Italy, Massilia (*Marseilles*), which had closed its gates to him on the way out, and had been besieged with great energy in his absence by Trebonius, gave itself into his hands; its fleet had been destroyed, in two engagements, by Decimus Brutus (p. 425).

260. Operations in Africa in 49 were not so fortunate; for the force dispatched under Curio to defeat the followers of Pompey in Africa, led by Varus, was utterly destroyed through the aid of the wily Numidian king, Juba.

261. At the end of 49 Caesar had control of all Roman territories west of the Adriatic; the provinces east of the Adriatic, however, were in the hands of Pompey, who was mobilizing forces in Macedonia obviously for a descent upon Italy from across the sea; in consequence Caesar also now gathered his forces on the east side of the Adriatic. For some months, in the earlier part of 48, the armies of Pompey and Caesar faced each other near Dyrrachium (*Durazzo*); but Caesar was obliged to withdraw into the interior. The decisive battle was fought August 9, 48 B.C., near the city of Pharsalus, in Thessaly. Caesar's forces numbered about twenty-two thousand men, with one thousand cavalry ; Pompey had forty-seven thousand infantry, seven thousand cavalry, and some light-armed troops. But superior generalship and the courage of desperation won the day against overwhelming odds. The Senatorial forces were entirely routed. Pompey fled to Egypt, where he was treacherously murdered.

262. Caesar also went with a small force to Egypt, where, in Alexandria, he became involved in the Alexandrine War. For a time this war occasioned him great difficulty because of his inability to secure reënforcements ; but finally Mithridates of Pergamum came to his assistance with an army, marching down through Cilicia and Syria to Egypt. By April of 47 B.C. Caesar had the country under complete control ; but he himself is said to have fallen a victim to the charms of the young and beautiful Egyptian princess, Cleopatra.

263. Leaving Cleopatra and a younger brother on the Egyptian throne, Caesar in June proceeded through Syria north to Pontus, where at Zela he easily crushed the rebellious King Pharnaces, reporting the quick victory to a friend in the laconic message, vēnī, vīdī, vīcī. He soon afterwards returned to Rome.

264. Caesar had only three months in Rome before he was obliged to take the field against the Pompeian forces, now gathered in Africa under the leadership of Scipio and Labienus. In January, 46, he landed with a small army near Hadrumetum, southeast from Carthage, where he maintained his position until sufficient forces could be brought over. At the battle of Thapsus, April 6, 46 B.C., he won a complete victory over the Pompeians and Juba, who was still helping them.

265. Caesar was now everywhere master. In accordance with legal forms he promulgated several laws of great benefit to the people. He reformed the calendar also (*241*, *c*). In August of 46 in Rome Caesar celebrated his great triumph. On four different days triumphal processions wound along the

Sacred Way through the Forum and up the Capitoline Hill,
displaying to the astonished multitudes the spoils of victories
in Gaul, Egypt, and Pontus, and over Juba in Africa.
Treasure amounting to 65,000 talents (more than $70,000,000)
was carried in the procession; and a conspicuous figure was
the Gallic commander-in-chief, Vercingetorix, who had been
kept in prison six years awaiting this event.   In honor of the

triumph twenty-two thousand tables
were spread for the feasting of the
populace, and games and gladiatorial
shows were given with a magnificence
previously unheard of.

266. In 45 B.C. a large army was
collected against Caesar in Spain, commanded by the two sons of Pompey.
Caesar marched against it, and at the
battle of Munda (March 17) totally
defeated it.   On a coin struck in Spain
in 45, and perhaps put into circulation
in order to pay his soldiers, Caesar
commemorates Spanish as well as
Gallic victories (Fig. 161).   A large
trophy supports, in the middle, a coat
of mail, above which is a helmet; on
either side is a spear (disproportion-
ately short), then a shield, and a war-

Figure 161. — Commemo-
ration of Gallic and
Spanish victories.

Middle, trophy with Gallic
and Spanish arms; cuirass,
helmet, two spears, two oval
shields, two trumpets.

Below, at right, Vercingetorix, seated, with hands bound
behind him; at left, Hispania,
personified, weeping.

Silver coin, denarius, struck
by Caesar in Spain in 45 B.C.

trumpet.   At the foot, on the right, is a seated captive, with
his hands tied behind him and face turned backward, looking
up, his hair streaming down; this we may safely identify as
Vercingetorix.   At the left sits a female figure, weeping, a
personification of Hispania.

267. On Caesar's return to Rome the Senate, whose members were now mainly of his own choosing, loaded him with
honors.   By conferring upon him all the important offices,
especially the dictatorship in life tenure, it centered the whole
authority in his hands.   Finally it ordered his portrait struck

on coins, from which previously faces of living men had been
excluded (Fig. 162), and decreed that statues of him should be

placed in the temples of the gods in
Rome.

268. Caesar's use of absolute power
was marked by unexpected clemency
towards former opponents; in recognition of this the Senate shortly before
his death ordered a temple built and
dedicated to 'Caesar's Mercifulness,'
personified as a divinity (Fig. 163).

Figure 162. — Caesar.

Silver coin, denarius, struck
in Rome in 44 B.C.

Obverse, head of Caesar
with laurel wreath. Inscription:
CAESAR, DICT[ATOR] PER-
PETUO, 'Dictator for Life.'

He contemplated large projects for the
public weal; nevertheless his foresight
and breadth of view counted for nothing in the bitter hatred of his political
enemies. A conspiracy was formed to
take his life. On March 15, 44 B.C.,
as Caesar had just entered the hall where the Senate met,
near Pompey's Theater, he was set
upon with daggers, and fell, pierced
by twenty-three wounds, at the foot of
a statue of his vanquished rival.

Though the assassination of Caesar
was commemorated by a coin (Fig.
167), the plans of the murderers all
miscarried. It is said that not one of
them died a natural death; and before
many years Caesar's nephew and heir,
Octavianus, afterwards called Augustus, was Emperor of the Roman world.

Figure 163. — Temple of
Caesar's Mercifulness.

Front of the Temple, with
four columns, and double doors
closed. Inscription, CLEMEN-
TIAE CAESARIS, 'To the Mercifulness of Caesar.'

Silver coin, denarius, struck
in 44 B.C.

269. Caesar was tall and of commanding presence. His features were
angular and prominent. He had a
fair complexion, with keen black eyes.
In later years he was bald; at no time of life did he wear a
beard. Suetonius says that among all the honors conferred

upon Caesar by the Senate and the People none was more acceptable to him than the privilege of wearing at all times a laurel crown, by which his baldness was concealed (Fig. 162). Though endowed with a constitution naturally by no means robust, he became inured to hardship, and exhibited astonishing powers of endurance. In matters of dress he was particular to the verge of effeminacy.

270. Of all the Romans Caesar was without doubt the greatest. In him the most varied talents were united with a restless ambition and tireless energy. While deliberate and far-seeing in forming his plans, in carrying them out he often acted with a haste that seemed like recklessness. He could occasion scenes of the most shocking cruelty; yet none could be more forgiving, or more gracious in granting pardon. Apparently believing, with the Epicurean philosophy, that death ends all and life is worth living only for the pleasure to be gotten out of it, he mingled freely with the dissolute society of Rome; yet when it was time for action he spurned indulgences, gave himself to the severest toil, and endured privations without a murmur.

In regard to all these things, however, we may say that Caesar's faults were those he shared in common with his age; his genius belongs to all ages. Chateaubriand declares that Caesar was the most complete man of all history; for his genius was transcendent in three directions — in politics, in war, and in literature.

THE NAME CAESAR

271. Roman surnames, which in many cases became family names, were generally derived from some personal characteristic or association. For the name **Caesar** scholars in antiquity suggested four derivations, of which one was, that the first of the Julii to bear the name Caesar received it because he was born with a thick *head of hair*, **caesariēs**; another was, that it came from the color of the eyes, *bluish gray*, **caesius**.

There was also a tradition that the first Julius to be called Caesar had killed an elephant and received the name from the

Figure 164. — Elephant trampling upon a serpent-headed Gallic war-trumpet.

Silver coin, denarius, struck by Caesar in Gaul, probably in 50 B.C.

The reverse of the same coin is shown in Fig. 157.

word for elephant in the language of the Mauri, in Africa, from whose country elephants came. This derivation seems to have commended itself to Julius Caesar; for on a coin struck by him in Gaul (Fig. 164), we see, over his name, an elephant trampling upon a Gallic war trumpet with a serpent's head, symbolizing his utter defeat of the Gauls and conquest of the country.

To the end of the Empire Roman emperors adopted the name Caesar as a title; and it survives in two imperial titles of modern times, "Kaiser," of Germany and Austria, and "Czar," of Russia. What an impress the life of Julius Caesar made upon the world — not merely to leave a heritage of influence in government and literature, but to transmit his very name across the ages as a designation of the highest authority recognized among men !

THE PORTRAITS OF CAESAR

272. After Caesar became supreme, almost innumerable likenesses of him must have been made. Statues of him were ordered set up in all cities, as well as in the temples of Rome; his features were not only stamped on coins but engraved upon gems (Fig. 165).

Figure 165. — Caesar.

Gem. Behind is an augur's staff, symbolic of his priestly authority.

Of the numerous extant busts and statues bearing Caesar's name, however, only a few can be considered authentic.

Though two of the best of these, a colossal bust at Naples and a large statue in Rome, have been somewhat restored, the expression of face has not been materially affected; a bust in the British Museum, representing Caesar at a somewhat later period of life, is singularly well preserved.

In the statue in Rome (shown in the frontispiece of this book, Plate I) Caesar appears as a commander. To judge from the manner of treatment, both this statue and the bust at Naples (Plate X) were made near the end of the first century A.D., but copied from earlier works.

CAESAR'S COMMENTARIES

273. The Commentaries of Caesar were not designed to be a biographical work, nor yet, strictly speaking, a military history. They were rather, as the title *Commentaries of Deeds*, **Commentāriī Rērum Gestārum**, implies, an informal record of events.

For **commentārius** comes from **commentor**, a verb used by speakers with the meaning *make preparation* for a speech by gathering material and preparing outlines; whence **līber commentārius**, or **commentārius**, *commentary*, came to designate a collection of materials for future use.

Figure 166. — A Case for Books.

With cover and straps for carrying. In the case are seven rolls, volumina, corresponding with the number of the Commentaries on the Gallic War. A writing tablet leans against the case.

Had Caesar intended that the Commentaries should be a formal history, the matter, in accordance with the universal custom of antiquity, would have been arranged in such a way that the books would be of about the same length; but he grouped his material by years, without regard to the length of the divisions, and we find that the first book, or Commentary, is as long as the second and third combined, while the seventh is almost as long as the second, third, and fourth taken together. Approximate uniformity in the length of the books comprised in a literary work was usual on account of convenience in handling, since each book formed a separate roll; hence the name for the *roll* or *book*, **volūmen** (from **volvō**, *roll up*), which survives in our word "volume" (Fig. 166).

274. Nevertheless it is evident that the Commentaries were not prepared as a diary, for private use, but written at one time and intended for circulation. We are safe in believing that Caesar intended through them not only to give to the public an authoritative account of the important events treated, but also to supply to historians of the period a collection of authentic material on which they might draw; hence, perhaps, the peculiar restraint under which he refers to himself in the third person, a practice as rare in narratives of the kind in antiquity as it is to-day; hence, also, presumably, the frequent use of indirect discourse near the beginning, while in the later books the style is more often enlivened, as generally in Greek and Latin historical works, by direct quotation (*211, b*).

275. The Seven Commentaries of the Gallic War were probably composed soon after the fall of Alesia, in the winter of 52–51 B.C.; they were probably taken down from dictation and circulated through the multiplication of copies from the original copy or copies sent from Gaul to Rome in 51.

276. The Civil War was seemingly incomplete at the time of Caesar's death; only two Commentaries, narrating the events of 49 and 48 B.C., were finished. Later the first Commentary, dealing with the events of 49, was divided into two books, the other remaining undivided; consequently in manuscripts and editions the Civil War now appears in three books, the first and second being devoted to the events of 49, the third to those of 48 B.C.

277. A gap of two years was left between the Commentaries of the Gallic War, covering the period 58–52 B.C., and those of the Civil War, covering the years 49 and 48. This was filled by Aulus Hirtius, who added to the Gallic War an eighth book narrating briefly the events of 51 and 50 B.C. in Gaul. Other writers afterwards extended the Civil War also by adding narratives of Caesar's military operations in Egypt, Africa, and Spain.

278. Notwithstanding Caesar's aim in composing the Commentaries as source books rather than finished works, the clearness, conciseness, and vigor of his style, and the importance of the matter, have given them a place in the first rank of historical writings. Of the Commentaries on the Gallic War Cicero wrote (*Brut.* lxxv. 262):

Figure 167. — Coin commemorating the assassination of Caesar.

"They are worthy of all praise. They are unadorned, straightforward, and elegant, every embellishment being stripped off as a garment. Caesar desired, indeed, to furnish others, who might wish to write history, with

Struck by an officer of Marcus Junius Brutus. A "cap of liberty" appears between two daggers. Inscription : EID · MAR, for EIDIBUS MARTIIS, 'On the Ides of March.'

material upon which they might draw; and perhaps men without good taste, who like to deck out facts in tawdry graces of expression, may think that he has rendered a service to historians by providing them with raw material, but he has deterred men of sound sense from trying to improve on the Commentaries in literary expression. For in history a pure and brilliant conciseness of style is the highest attainable beauty."

279. The question has been much discussed whether or not in the Commentaries Caesar warped the truth in self-justification. No one will deny that he had a complete command of the facts, and that, when the Commentaries on the Gallic War were published, there were many officers and men who would instantly have detected untruths and condemned them. Caesar seems to have been too large a man to condescend to misrepresentation even in narrating his own defeats, as at Gergovia and Dyrrachium ; while there may have been occasional lapses of memory in respect to details, we have no reason to question the substantial accuracy of the Commentaries as historical documents.

The Commentaries themselves convey no impression of exaggeration. Plutarch, who had at hand other sources of information, no longer extant, thus summarizes the results of the Gallic war:

"Caesar was engaged in the Gallic war less than ten years. In that time he captured more than eight hundred towns, brought into submission three hundred peoples, fought against three million foes, killed a million, and took a million prisoners."

Caesar took part in thirty battles.

CAESAR AS AN ORATOR

280. As an orator Caesar was rated second only to Cicero. His orations have perished; but apart from other evidence a favorable judgment of Caesar's oratorical style might be formed from the speech which he puts into the mouth of Critognatus (VII. 77), and the outline of the argument by which he quelled an incipient mutiny (I. 40).

THE GEOGRAPHY OF CAESAR'S COMMENTARIES

INTRODUCTORY

281. The Geography of the Commentaries on the Gallic War touches Italy, Cisalpine Gaul, Illyricum, and Transalpine Gaul; that of the Civil War touches also Spain, Macedonia, Epirus and Thessaly, Asia Minor, Syria, Egypt, and Africa.

282. Caesar frequently uses the name of a people for that of the country inhabited by them, where English usage expects the word "country" or "land" or an equivalent; as **quī agrum Helvētium ā Germānīs dīvidit**, *which separates the Helvetian territory from that of the Germans*, lit. *from the Germans* (I. 2); **ūnum per Sēquanōs**, *one (route) through the country of the Sequanians*, lit. *through the Sequanians* (I. 6).

ITALY AND CISALPINE GAUL

283. Caesar uses **Italia**, *Italy*, in two senses:

a. Italy in the narrower sense as a political unit (C. I. 6), Italy proper, having as its northern boundary on the east side the small river Rubicon, on the west the lower course of the river Auser, and between the two rivers a line running a short distance south of Luca (modern *Lucca*).

b. Italy in the geographical sense (I. 10), designating the entire peninsula as far as the Alps, and including Cisalpine Gaul in addition to Italy proper.

284. Cisalpine Gaul is designated by Caesar as **Cisalpīna Gallia** (VI. 1), **Gallia citerior**, *Hither Gaul* (I. 24), and **citerior prōvincia**, *the nearer province* (I. 10). It comprised the great drainage area of the **Padus**, *Po* (V. 24), extending from Italy proper to the Alps. The entire region was brought under

Roman domination in the second century B.C., but Cisalpine
Gaul was not joined with Italy politically till the reign of
Augustus.

285. Of the cities of Cisalpine Gaul Caesar mentions two,
Aquileia (I. 10), at the head of the Adriatic Sea, chief city
of the Cisalpine Veneti, who gave their name to modern
"Venice"; and **Ocelum** (I. 10), in the extreme western part.

TRANSALPINE GAUL

286. Transalpine Gaul is designated by Caesar as **Trānsalpīna Gallia** (VII. 6), **Gallia Trānsalpīna** (VII. 1); **Gallia ulterior**
(I. 7), and **ulterior Gallia** (I. 10), *Further Gaul;* or simply **Gallia,**

Figure 168. — Conquered
Gaul, personified.

Behind the head is a Gallic
war-trumpet. Denarius, 48 B.C.

Gaul (I. 1). It extended from the
Alps and the Rhine to the Atlantic
Ocean, comprising the countries now
known as France and Belgium, the
German possessions west of the Rhine,
and the greater part of Switzerland
and Holland. In this book where
" Gaul " stands alone, *Transalpine Gaul*
is meant. (See Map inside back cover).

After the conquest, **Gallia** as a subject country was personified as a female
figure, sometimes with the characteristic Gallic war-trumpet, as on a coin
struck in Rome in 48 B.C. (Fig. 168); here only the head
is shown, with long hair, dishevelled, the war-trumpet being
behind the head.

287. On account of differences in speech, and other characteristics, Caesar describes Transalpine Gaul as divided into
three parts:

a. The land of the Belgians, Belgium, in the northeast, extending from the rivers **Sēquana**, *Seine*, and **Matrona**, *Marne*,
to the river **Rhēnus**, *Rhine*. The Belgium described by Caesar
was much larger than the modern country. The ancient Bel-

gian stock survives in the Walloons.   The language was mostly
Celtic.

b. The land of the Galli, the Celtic country, Celtic Gaul, ex-
tending from the *Seine* and *Marne* to the river **Garumna**,
Garonne. This part is often called **Gallia** (I. 1, l. 20; I. 30).
The numerous dialects of Celtic Gaul belonged to the great
Celtic family, which has modern representatives in Armoric,
spoken in Brittany, and the Welsh language.

c. The land of the Aquitanians, Aquitania, extending from
the Garonne River to the Pyrenees. The language of the
Aquitanians seems to have been related to the Basque.

288. *a.* The three divisions of Gaul were made up of many
small *states,* **cīvitātēs,** each of which had its own political
organization. A number of the states had their own coinage
in gold and other metals; but the coins were mostly imita-
tions of those struck by Greek states and Rome.

b. In Celtic Gaul the governing power was in the hands of
two classes, the knights and the Druid priests; the condition
of the common people was not much above slavery (VI. 13).

289. *a.* Government in Gaul was administered by *magistrates,* **magistrātūs,** chosen by the dominant classes, such as
the Vergobrets (I. 16); a few of the more backward states
had *kings,* **rēgēs,** as Galba, king of the Suessiones (II. 4), and
Commius, king of the Atrebates (IV. 21).

b. In some states there was a *council of elders,* **senātus**
(II. 5).

c. Politically Gaul in Caesar's time was in a condition of
unrest. Usurpations of power and changes of rulers were
frequent (II. 1). Not only in the different states but in the
subdivisions of states, and even in powerful families, there
were party divisions (VI. 11), from which strifes of great bitterness arose. A conspicuous example is the irreconcilable
antagonism between the brothers Diviciacus and Dumnorix (I.
18), of whom the former did everything possible to advance
Caesar's interests (II. 5, 10), while the latter, as leader of an
anti-Roman party among the Aeduans, sought in all ways to

thwart Caesar, until finally he was killed, while resisting capture, by Caesar's cavalry (V. 7).

290. The southeastern part of Gaul, not specified in Caesar's threefold division, had been conquered by the Romans and organized into a province in 121 B.C. This was the only part of Transalpine Gaul that properly came under Caesar's jurisdiction when he went out as governor in 58 B.C. (*255*). It is designated by Caesar as **Gallia prōvincia** (I. 19) or **prōvincia Gallia** (I. 53), *the Gallic Province ;* as **ulterior prōvincia**, *the Further Province* (I. 10), **prōvincia nostra**, *our Province* (I. 2), or simply **prōvincia**, *the Province* (I. 1).

291. Of the mountains of Gaul the most important are: **Alpēs**, *the Alps* (I. 10), of which the western and southern portion, the French and the Swiss Alps, were known to Caesar; **mōns Cebenna**, *the Cévennes* (VII. 8), in Southern Gaul; **mōns Iūra**, *the Jura Mountains* (I. 2), extending from the Rhone below Geneva northeast to the Rhine; **mōns Vosegus**, *the Vosges* (IV. 10), west of the Rhine and north of the Jura range; **Pȳrēnaeī montēs**, *the Pyrenees*, on the border toward Spain (I. 1).

292. The more important rivers of Gaul mentioned by Caesar are: **Rhodanus**, *the Rhone* (I. 2), which flows through **lacus Lemannus**, *Lake Geneva* (I. 2), and empties into the Mediterranean; **Arar**, *Saône* (I. 12), a tributary of the Rhone, which it enters from the north; **Sēquana**, *the Seine* (I. 1); **Matrona**, *Marne* (I. 1), a tributary of the *Seine*, which it enters from the east; **Axona**, *Aisne* (II. 5), a tributary of the *Oise*, which in turn flows into the *Seine* from the northeast, below the confluence with the Marne; **Rhēnus**, *Rhine* (I. 1); **Garumna**, *Garonne* (I. 1); **Liger**, *Loire* (III. 9), the largest river of Gaul, flowing into the Bay of Biscay; **Mosa**, *Meuse* (IV. 9), in northeastern Gaul; **Sabis**, *Sambre*, a tributary of the *Meuse*, which it enters from the west (II. 16).

293. The cities of Gaul in Caesar's time were situated on or near a coast, on a river, or on the top of a high mountain. The more noteworthy were:

a. In the Province: **Massilia**, *Marseilles* (C. II. 3), founded by Greeks from Phocaea about 600 B.C., a prosperous city, which retained its Greek character, carried on an extensive commerce, and became an important civilizing influence (Fig. 169); **Narbo**, *Narbonne* (III. 20), on the river Atax not far from the sea, colonized by the Romans in 118 B.C.; **Tolōsa**, *Toulouse* (III. 20), on the Garonne river; **Genava**, *Geneva* (I. 6), on **lacus Lemannus**, *Lake Geneva* (I. 2).

Figure 169. — Coin of Massilia.

Silver. Obverse, head of Artemis with earrings and necklace; reverse, lion, prowling, with abbreviation of the Greek name above, and crescent in front.

b. In Celtic Gaul: **Agedincum**, *Sens* (VI. 44); **Alesia**, *Alise-Sainte-Reine* (VII. 68); **Avaricum**, *Bourges* (VII. 13); **Bibracte**, on *Mt. Beuvray* (I. 23); **Cēnabum**, *Orléans* (VII. 3); **Decetia**, *Decize* (VII. 33); **Gergovia** (VII. 36); **Lutecia Parīsiōrum**, *Paris* (VI. 3); **Vesontiō**, *Besançon* (I. 38).

c. In Belgium: **Bibrax** (II. 6) near the *Aisne;* **Dūrocortorum**, *Reims* (VI. 44); **Noviodūnum** of the Suessiones, near *Soissons* (II. 12); **Samarobrīva**, *Amiens* (V. 24).

BRITAIN, GERMANY, AND SPAIN

294. Caesar uses **Britannia**, *Britain* (II. 4), to designate the island of Great Britain, including modern England, Scotland, and Wales. He was the first Roman general to invade the island, whose inhabitants he found similar to those of Celtic Gaul in language and institutions, but not so far advanced in civilization (Fig. 170). His two expeditions, in 55 and 54 B.C., had slight apparent effect, but they stimulated commerce and prepared the way for the introduction of Roman wares and customs (Fig. 140). The subjugation of Britain by the Romans began in 43 A.D.

Figure 170. — Early British Coin.

Silver, of crude workmanship; probably in circulation in Caesar's time.

295. Caesar uses **Germānia**, *Germany* (IV. 4), to designate a country of indefinite extent east of the Rhine and north of the Danube. He came into contact only with the German peoples near the Rhine. His two expeditions across the Rhine, in 55 and 53 B.C., produced slight effect; the Romans never conquered more of Germany than a narrow strip along the Rhine and the Danube.

296. Ancient *Spain*, **Hispānia**, included modern Spain and Portugal. After the Roman Conquest, about 200 B.C., it was divided into two provinces, **citerior Hispānia**, *Hither Spain* (III. 23), including the northern and eastern part of the peninsula, and **ulterior Hispānia**, *Further Spain* (C. I. 38), on the south and west.

297. Caesar sometimes uses **Hispānia**, *Spain*, to designate the peninsula as a whole (V. 1); sometimes the plural, **Hispāniae**, *the Spains* (C. III. 73), referring to the two Spanish provinces.

ILLYRICUM, MACEDONIA, EPIRUS, AND THESSALY

298. **Illyricum** was a narrow province that bordered Cisalpine Gaul for a short distance at the head of the Adriatic Sea, and extended down the east side of the Adriatic as far as the river **Drilo**, *Drin*. It included parts of modern Albania, Montenegro, Herzegovina, Dalmatia, Croatia, and Istria. It came under Roman control about 167 B.C.

299. Belonging, in Caesar's time, to the province of **Macedonia**, was a strip of coast between Illyricum and Epirus with the important cities **Apollōnia** (C. III. 75), about five miles from the sea, and **Dyrrachium**, *Durazzo* (C. III. 53), on the coast (Map 19).

300. **Ēpīrus** was the northernmost division of Greece on the west side; it occupied a part of modern Albania. It was conquered by the Romans in 168 B.C. (Map 19).

Towns of Epirus mentioned by Caesar are **Būthrōtum** (C. III. 16) and **Ōricum** (C. III. 90), both on the coast (Map 19).

301. **Thessalia**, *Thessaly*, in northeastern Greece, corresponded roughly with the division of modern Greece called by the same name. Towns of Thessaly mentioned by Caesar are **Gomphī** (C. III. 80), **Lārīsa**, *Larissa* (C. III. 96), and **Metropolis** (C. III. 80). Cf. Map 19.

ASIA, SYRIA, EGYPT, AND AFRICA

302. The Romans used **Asia** in three senses, designating :

(*a*.) The continent Asia, as we use the name to-day.

(*b*.) The western projection of the continent, between the Mediterranean and the Black Sea ; called **Asia Minor** in order to distinguish it from the mass of the continent as a whole.

(*c*.) The Roman province **Asia**, which was organized in 129 B.C. The Roman province Asia included only the western part of Asia Minor, with the countries Caria, Lydia, Mysia, and Phrygia. Caesar uses Asia (C. III. 53) to designate the Roman province, not Asia Minor or the continent.

303. At the time of the Civil War **Bithȳnia**, including a part of Pontus (C. III. 3), and **Cilicia** in Asia Minor (C. III. 102) were already organized as separate provinces.

304. **Syria** (C. III. 103), including **Phoenicia** and **Palestine**, was conquered by Pompey and became a Roman province about 64 B.C. At Jerusalem Pompey profaned the Holy of Holies in the Temple by entering it, but he refrained from carrying off the treasure. The treasure, however, a few years later fell a prey to Crassus, who, on his way to attack the Parthians (*258*), delayed in Jerusalem in order to rob the Temple.

305. **Aegyptus**, *Egypt* (C. III. 104), at the time of the Civil War was an independent kingdom. It was not made subject to Rome till 29 B.C. Its principal city, **Alexandrīa**, *Alexandria* (C. III. 103), was founded by Alexander the Great, who gave to it his name.

306. Caesar uses **Africa** (C. II. 37) to designate, not the continent, but the comparatively small Roman province of *Africa*, which was organized after the destruction of Carthage in 146 B.C. After the battle of Thapsus and the death of Juba (*262*) Caesar

made another province out of the Kingdom of Numidia, which
adjoined the province Africa on the south and west, and after
his death was added to it.

Figure 171. — Africa, personified as a goddess.

As a headdress she wears the spoils of an elephant, with trunk and tusks projecting
above and broad ears falling beside the neck; over the right shoulder we see, projecting,
the bow of the hunting goddess, Artemis, and the club of Hercules; underneath is the
rattle, sistrum, sacred to Isis.

On her right shoulder is a lion, while an asp rises threateningly above her right hand,
facing a panther that stands on the fruits gathered in the fold of her robe; these creatures
and the fruits symbolize the wild life and fertility of the Province.   Relief on a silver plate.

Africa was personified as a female figure, wearing as a headdress the spoils of an elephant (Fig. 171).

THE ROMAN ART OF WAR IN CAESAR'S TIME

I. COMPOSITION OF THE ARMY

307. The legion. — *a.* The *legion*, **legiō** (I. 7), in Caesar's time was composed exclusively of Roman citizens. Probably Caesar's *legionary soldiers*, **legiōnāriī** (C. III. 63) or simply **mīlitēs** (I. 7), were mainly volunteers who were willing to enlist for the regular term of twenty years on account of the certainty of the pay, and of provision for their old age in case they lived beyond the period of service. However, citizens between the ages of seventeen and forty-six were liable to be called out by a *levy*, **dīlectus** (C. I. 6), at any time. Romans of the upper classes who wished to serve in the army, or found themselves unable to evade conscription, were employed as officers, or attached to the bodyguard of the commander.

b. The normal strength of a legion at the end of the Republic was 6000 men; but the average number of men in Caesar's legions probably did not exceed 3600 in the Gallic War, and 3000 in the Civil War.

c. The legion was divided into ten *cohorts*, **cohortēs** (III. 1), averaging, in Caesar's army, about 360 men each; the cohort was divided into three *maniples*, **manipulī** (II. 25), of 120 men; the maniples into two *centuries* or *companies*, **ōrdinēs** (I. 40). In legions having a full complement of men each century would contain 100; in Caesar's army the number could hardly have averaged more than 60.

d. The legions that had seen long service, apparently not less than nine or ten years, were called *veteran*, **legiōnēs veterānae** (I. 24); the rest, *last levied*, or *raw*, **legiōnēs proximē cōnscrīptae** (I. 24), or **legiōnēs tīrōnum** (C. III. 28). The legions were designated by number.

e. In the first year of the Gallic War Caesar had four veteran legions, numbered VII., VIII., IX., — these three apparently brought from the vicinity of Aquileia (I. 10), — and X.; the tenth legion was in the Province at the time of his arrival in Gaul (I. 7). After Caesar learned that the Helvetians proposed to go through the country of the Sequanians and Aeduans he hastily raised in Cisalpine Gaul two legions (I. 10), which were numbered XI. and XII. With these six legions he gained two of his most brilliant victories, over the Helvetians and over Ariovistus.

f. In the second year of the war Caesar raised two new legions in Cisalpine Gaul (II. 2), numbered XIII. and XIV., so that he now had four veteran and four raw legions, eight in all.

g. In the fifth year (54 B.C.) the XIVth legion and half of another were annihilated in the ambuscade set by Ambiorix (V. 26–37). At the beginning of the next year Caesar raised two more legions in Cisalpine Gaul, one replacing the lost XIVth (VI. 32), the other numbered XV., and besides obtained a legion from Pompey, which was numbered VI. (VI. 1; VIII. 54). In the last two years of the war he had thus ten legions (VII. 34), numbered VI. to XV. inclusive. It appears probable that the whole force of legionary soldiers engaged in the siege of Alesia fell short of forty thousand.

308. The infantry auxiliaries. — In addition to the legions, a Roman army contained bodies of infantry and cavalry drawn from allied and subject peoples, or hired outright from independent nations, called *auxiliaries* or *auxiliary troops*, **auxilia** (I. 24). These in some cases retained their native dress, equipment, and mode of fighting, in others were armed and trained after the Roman fashion (Fig. 172). To the former class belong the *light-armed troops*, **levis armātūrae peditēs** (II. 24), including as special classes the slingers (Plate III. 1), and bowmen. In the Gallic War Caesar availed himself of the help of *slingers*, **funditōrēs**, from the Balearic Islands (II. 7), *bowmen*, **sagittāriī**, from Crete and from Numidia (II. 7), and light-armed German troops (VII. 65). He utilized also contingents from the Gallic States that he subdued (III. 18, VIII. 10). In 52 B.C. he had a force of ten thousand Aeduans (VII. 34). Caesar, as other Roman writers, is generally not careful to state the exact number of the auxiliary troops; they were regarded as relatively unimportant. The officers of the auxiliaries, both infantry and cavalry, were Romans. Auxiliary troops posted on the wing of an army might be called *wing-men*, **ālāriī** (I. 51).

309. The cavalry. — *a.* A troop of cavalry usually accompanied each legion. While the evidence is not conclusive, it is probable that in the latter part of the Gallic War, if not from the beginning, Caesar had contingents of cavalry in connection with his legions, averaging 200 to 300 men each. These horsemen were foreigners, serving for pay; they were drawn

Figure 172. — Light-armed soldier.

from Spain, *Spanish horsemen*, **Hispānī equitēs** (V. 26), from Germany, *German horsemen*, **Germānī equitēs** (VII. 13), and from Gaul.

b. Apart from the legionary contingents, Caesar had a force of cavalry raised from the Gallic States subject or friendly to

Rome, which was reckoned as a single body, numbering under ordinary circumstances about 4000 (I. 15; V. 5), or 5000 men (IV. 12).

c. The cavalry was divided into *squads* or *squadrons*, **turmae,** of about 30 horsemen; such a squad went with Commius to Britain (IV. 35). Probably the squad contained three *decuries,* **decuriae,** of 10 men each, under the command of *decurions,* **decuriōnēs** (I. 23). The higher officers were called *cavalry prefects,* **praefectī equitum** (III. 26). See Plate III, 5.

310. The non-combatants. — *a.* There were two classes of non-combatants, slaves employed for menial services, and free men, or freedmen. In the former class were included the officers' servants and *camp servants,* **cālōnēs** (II. 24), as well as the drivers and *muleteers* with the heavy baggage, **mūliōnēs** (VII. 45); in the latter class were citizens or others who were allowed to accompany the army but were obliged to find quarters outside of the camp, as the *traders,* **mercātōrēs** (VI. 37).

b. The *mechanics,* **fabrī** (V. 11), were not enrolled as a separate corps, but were drawn from the ranks of the legionary soldiers whenever needed.

311. The baggage train. — Each legion had a separate baggage train. The heavy *baggage,* **impedīmenta** (II. 19), comprised tents, hand-mills for grinding grain, artillery, extra weapons, and other military stores, as well as supplies of food. In the enemy's country for better defense the baggage trains of a number of legions might be formed into a single column (II. 19). From the baggage of the legion, or heavy baggage, the baggage of the soldiers, carried in individual *packs,* **sarcinae,** should be clearly distinguished (Fig. 6).

II. THE OFFICERS

312. The general was properly called *leader,* **dux,** until he had won a victory; after the first victory he had a right to the title **imperātor,** *commander* or *general* (I. 40). Caesar used the title Imperator from the time that he defeated the Helvetians, in 58 B.C., until his death (I. 40, etc.).

313. *a.* Next in rank came the *lieutenant*, or *lieutenant-general*, **lēgātus** (I. 10), who was frequently placed by Caesar in command of separate legions, or of corps containing more than one legion. When acting in the absence of the general the lieutenant became *lieutenant in the general's place*, **lēgātus prō praetōre** (I. 21), and exercised unusual authority. The title "lieutenant general" would more accurately define the military position of Labienus, for example, than that of "lieutenant" as the word is used in the United States and England.

b. The *quaestor*, **quaestor** (I. 52), was charged with the care of the military chest and the supplies, but was sometimes clothed with purely military authority, and assumed the functions of a lieutenant. The quaestor and the lieutenants belonged to the staff of the general, and had with him the distinction of a *body-guard*, **cohors praetōria** (I. 40), composed of picked soldiers and of young men of rank who wished to acquire military experience.

314. The *military tribunes*, **trībūnī mīlitum** (I. 39), numbered six to a legion. In Caesar's army the tribunes appear to have received appointment for personal rather than military reasons; and they were intrusted with subordinate services, such as the leading of troops on the march, the command of detachments smaller than a legion (cf. VI. 39), the securing of supplies (III. 7), and the oversight of the watches. Only one military tribune, Gaius Volusenus (III. 5), is mentioned by Caesar in terms of praise.

315. *a.* In marked contrast with the higher officers, who were of good social position, were the captains, or *centurions*, **centuriōnēs, ōrdinēs** (V. 30). These were often of the humblest origin; they were promoted from the ranks simply on account of bravery and efficiency. At the drill, on the march, and in battle, they were at the same time the models and the leaders of the soldiers.

b. As each century had a centurion, there were 2 centurions in each maniple (distinguished as *first*, **prior**, and *second*, **pos-**

terior), 6 in each cohort, and 60 in the legion. The first in rank was the *first centurion* (of the first maniple) *of the first cohort*, **prīmipīlus** (II. 25). The first centurion of the second maniple of a cohort was called **prīnceps prior** (C. III. 64).

316. Below the centurions, but ranking above the common soldiers, were the privileged soldiers, who were relieved from picket duty as well as work on fortifications and other manual labor. Such were the *veteran volunteers*, **ēvocātī** (C. III. 53), soldiers who had served their full time but had reënlisted at the general's request; the musicians, and the *standard-bearers*, **signiferī**.

III. PROVISIONING AND PAY OF THE SOLDIERS

317. Caesar was careful to have ample supplies always at hand.

The care of the stores was in the hands of the quaestor, with his staff. Not bread or flour, but *grain*, **frūmentum** (I. 16), usually wheat, was served out to the soldiers for rations. This they themselves ground with *hand-mills*, **molae maṇuālēs**, and prepared for food by boiling into a paste or by making into bread without yeast.

The grain was portioned out every fifteen days, and on the march each soldier carried his share in a sack. The amount furnished does not seem large when we reflect that the men lived almost exclusively on a vegetable diet. The allowance for the fifteen days was two Roman *pecks*, **modiī**, about half a bushel by our measure. As the weight of this was not far from thirty pounds, the soldier had about two pounds per day. On difficult or forced marches extra rations were served out.

If the soldier desired to do so he could trade off his grain for bread, or buy other articles of food from the numerous *traders*, **mercātōrēs** (I. 39), who accompanied the army and had a flourishing business. When wheat was scarce, *barley*, **hordeum** (C. III. 47), was substituted. Rations of barley were frequently served out also instead of wheat as a punishment for slight

offenses. In traversing an enemy's country fresh meat was
often secured.

318. The wages of the Roman soldier were very small, but
in successful campaigns the men had a share of the *booty*,
praeda (C. III. 97), consisting largely of captives, who were
sold as slaves (VII. 89).   These were bought up on the spot by
the traders, and thus readily turned into cash.   Sometimes
Caesar gave money realized from the sale of booty ; thus after
the conquest of the Bituriges in 51 B.C. the soldiers received
200 sesterces (about $8.00) apiece, the centurions a much
larger sum (VIII. 4).   As other *rewards*, **praemia** (V. 58), the
commander could make special *gifts*, **mīlitāria dōna** (C. III. 53),
such as disk-shaped *decorations* of metal for the breast, **phalerae**
(Fig. 62), clothing, and double pay (C. III. 53).

When convicted of cowardly or disgraceful conduct the
soldier was deprived of his weapons and driven from the
camp, or in extreme cases put to death ; officers and privileged
soldiers might be reduced in rank, as were certain standard-
bearers after an engagement before Dyrrachium (C. III. 74).

319. At the close of his period of service, twenty years, or
on reaching his fiftieth year, the soldier who had served well
was entitled to an *honorable discharge*, **missiō honesta**, or **missiō**
(C. I. 86), together with an allotment of land, or a payment of
money.

IV. THE DRESS AND EQUIPMENT

320. The legionary soldier wore a thick woolen undergar-
ment, *tunic*, **tunica**, reaching nearly to the knees (cf. C. III. 44).

His *cloak*, **sagum** (C. I. 75), which
served also as a blanket, was likewise of undyed wool, and fastened
by a *clasp*, **fībula**, on the right
shoulder, so as not to impede the
movement of the right arm.   The
soldier's *shoes*, **caligae** (Fig. 173),
were like a sandal, but had heavy

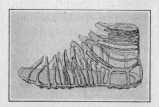

Figure 173. — Soldier's shoe.

Figure 174.— Legionary's helmet, galea, without the crest.

soles which were fastened on by straps over the foot and instep.

321. The *cloak* of the commander, **palū-dāmentum**, differed from that of the soldier only in being more ample, of finer quality, and ornamented; it was ordinarily scarlet in color (VII. 88).

322. The weapons of the legionary were in part offensive, in part defensive.

As defensive *weapons*, **arma**, he had :

a. A *helmet*, **galea** (Fig. 174), ornamented with a *crest*, **crista** (Plate III, 3; Fig. 33). On the march the helmet was hung on a cord which passed through the ring at the top and around the soldier's neck. The crest was fastened on before going into action.

b. A *cuirass*, or *coat of mail*, **lōrīca**, of leather, or of leather strengthened with strips of metal, or of metal (Figures 148, 150).

c. A *shield*, ordinarily rectangular, **scūtum** (II. 25; Fig. 175; Plate IV, 3), but in some cases oval, **clipeus** (Plate IV, 1), made of two layers of boards fastened together, strengthened on the outside by layers of linen or of leather, and at the edges by a rim of metal. At the middle of the outside was an iron knob, **umbō**, used in striking.

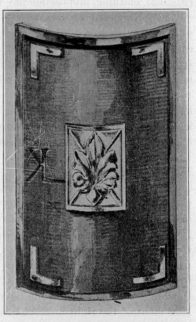

Figure 175.— Roman oblong shield, scutum.

On the march the shield was protected from the wet by a leather *covering*, **tegimentum** (II. 21). In battle it was held on the left arm (Fig. 33).

The offensive weapons of the legionary were:

d. A *pike*, **pīlum** (I. 25), a heavy and formidable javelin. It

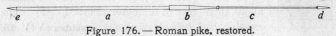

Figure 176. — Roman pike, restored.

a. Wooden shaft.

b. Iron collar, strengthening the end of the wooden shaft where the iron is fitted in.

c. The "iron," ferrum ; of soft iron, easily bent.

d. Hard barbed point, of iron.

e. Iron shoe, making it possible to stick the pike into the ground, so that it would stand upright, without frazzling the wood.

consisted of a shaft of wood about four feet long, into the end of which was fitted a small iron shaft, **ferrum** (I. 25), with a pointed head, which projected two feet beyond the end of the wood (see Figures 49, 50, 176, and Plate IV, 6). The weight of the whole was not far from ten or eleven pounds. Pikes could be thrown only about 75 feet; but they were hurled with such skill and force that the first hurling often decided the battle.

e. A *sword*, **gladius** (I. 25), called *Spanish sword*, **gladius Hispānus**, because made according to a pattern brought from Spain after the Second Punic War. The Spanish sword was short, broad, two-edged, and pointed, better adapted for stabbing than for slashing, though used for both purposes (Plate IV, 9). It was kept in a *scabbard*, **vāgīna** (V. 44), fastened to a *belt*, **balteus** (V. 44), which was passed over the left shoulder (Plate III, 3, and Fig. 177); this brought the sword on the right side, so that it was not in the way of the shield.

f. In the time of the Empire, and probably

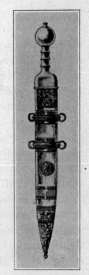

Figure 177. — Spanish sword, in the scabbard.

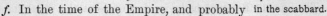

also in Caesar's day, officers carried a *dagger*, **pugiō**, which was attached to a belt running around the waist (Fig. 178).

323. The dress and equipment of the light-armed soldiers varied greatly (Fig. 172, and Plate III, 1; Pl. IV, 7, 11).

They, as well as the cavalry, seem generally to have had a light round or oval *shield*, **parma**, about three feet in diameter (Plate IV, 4). The cavalry had *helmets* of metal, **cassidēs** (VII. 45, Figure 179), light lances for hurling, and a longer sword than that used by the infantry (Figure 98, and Plate III, 5).

V. THE STANDARDS

Figure 178. — Roman dagger.

324. *a.* While the ancient battle lacked the noise and smoke of cannon and of other death-dealing devices of modern war, great clouds of dust were raised and obscured the movements of the combatants; the standards, or ensigns, were consequently more numerous, and had a relatively more important place, than flags have to-day.

b. The ensigns of Caesar's army were :

(1) The *eagle* of the legion, **aquila** (IV. 25), of silver, carried in battle on the end of a pole by the *eagle-bearer*, **aquilifer** (V. 37). In camp it was kept in a little *shrine*, **sacellum** (Plate IV, 8). It was the standard of the legion as a

Figure 179. — Cavalryman's helmet, cassis.

whole; the eagle with extended wings borne aloft seemed to signify that the bird sacred to Jupiter, god of victory, was ready to lead the legion to success; and the loss of the eagle was the deepest disgrace that could be incurred (IV. 25; V. 37; C. III. 64). See Fig. 180, and Plate IV, 2.

The ancient Persians had a golden eagle as the royal standard; and to-day the eagle appears among the emblems of several European countries, and of the United States.

(2) The *standards*, **signa** (II. 21), one to each maniple, carried by *standard-bearers*, **signiferī** (II. 25; Fig. 187). These varied in appearance. One type, known from a coin struck in 49 B.C. (Fig. 180), had small streamers attached to the end of the pole, underneath which were two crescents (perhaps for good luck), one just above the other; below these were two disks of metal, **phalerae**, no doubt presented to the maniple for meritorious conduct, and last of all a square plate of metal, indicating by a letter the place of the maniple (**H =** **hastātī, P = prīncipēs**). In some cases figures of animals appeared.

There was no separate standard for the cohort.

Figure 180. — Standards.

Denarius, struck in 49 B.C.; eagle between two standards. Inscription, L · LENT[ULUS], C · MARC[ELLUS] COS, 'Lucius Lentulus and' Gaius Marcellus, Consuls.'

(3) The *banners*, **vēxilla**, rectangular flags of different sizes used for a variety of purposes (Fig. 149). A large red flag was the special ensign of the commander (II. 20). Smaller banners were used by special detachments not formed of regular maniples (VI. 36), or attached to the standards of the maniples.

325. On the march the standard was at the front, in battle some distance behind the front, of the maniple.

From the immediate association of the manipular standards with military movements arose several idiomatic expressions used by Caesar. Such are:

signa ferre, *to go forward* (I. 39).

signa inferre, *to advance* (II. 26).

signa convertere, *to face about* (I. 25).

ad signa convenīre, *to assemble* (VI. 1).

infestīs signīs, *in battle formation,* lit. *with hostile standards* (VII. 51; C. III. 93).

VI. THE MUSICAL INSTRUMENTS

326. *a.* The musical instruments were:

(1) The *trumpet*, **tuba** (II. 20), about three feet long, with

Figure 181. — Horn, with crosspiece by which it was carried.

a funnel-shaped opening (Fig. 84, and Plate II, 7); it had a deep tone, and was sounded by the *trumpeters*, **tubicinēs** (VII. 47).

(2) The *horn*, **cornū**, a large curved instrument, with a shriller note (Fig. 181, and Plate II. 8).

(3) The *shell trumpet*, **būcina**, perhaps resembling the large shells in use in modern times about Naples as dinner horns (Fig. 182); such at least is Triton's **būcina** described by Ovid (Met. I, 333–338).

The shell trumpet was used especially in camp for giving the signals to change the watches (C. II. 35).

b. As the maniple was the unit of military movement, signals were addressed to the *standard-bearers*, **signiferī**.

c. The order "to advance" or "to fall back" was conveyed by the general to the *trumpeters*, **tubicinēs** (cf. VII. 47); their signal was taken up by the *horn-blowers*, **corni-**

Figure 182. — Modern shell trumpet, with iron mouthpiece.

It has a deep tone which can be heard a long distance. From Boscoreale, near Pompeii.

cinēs, of whom there was one to each maniple. The notes of the instruments could be heard above the din of battle much more clearly than the spoken words of the officers.

VII. THE ARMY ON THE MARCH

327. When in an enemy's country Caesar maintained an exceedingly efficient information service. Parties of mounted *patrols*, **explōrātōrēs** (I. 21), scoured the country; and their observation was supplemented by single *scouts* or *spies*, **speculātōrēs** (II. 11), who gathered information wherever they could (Fig. 183).

Figure 183. — Scout, speculator.

328. The army advanced ordinarily in three divisions. At the *front*, **prīmum agmen** (VII. 67), came the cavalry, with perhaps a division of light-armed troops, sent ahead to feel out the enemy (I. 15), and in case of attack, to hold him at bay until the rest of the army could prepare for action (II. 19).

Next came the main force, each legion being accompanied by its baggage train; but when there was danger of attack the legions marched in single column, with the baggage of the whole army united (II. 19).

The *rear*, **novissimum agmen**, might in case of danger be formed of part of the legionary force, the baggage being between the rear and the main body (II. 19).

329. The regular *day's march*, **iūstum iter**, was from six to seven hours long. The start was usually made at sunrise; but in emergencies the army got under way at midnight, or two or three o'clock in the morning. The distance ordinarily traversed was about 15 or 16 English miles; on a *forced march*, **iter magnum** (II. 12), a much greater distance might be made, as 25 or 30 English miles (VII. 41). Caesar's forced marches manifested astonishing powers of endurance on the part of his soldiers. Rivers were often crossed by fording; in such operations the ancient army had the advantage over the modern, because it carried no ammunition that would be spoiled by the water (V. 18, VII. 56).

330. On the march the soldier carried his rations, his cooking utensils, his arms, blanket, and one or two *rampart stakes*, or *palisades*, **vallī**; palisades for defense were carried by dragoons as late as the seventeenth century.

The luggage was done up in tight *bundles* or *packs*, **sarcinae** (Plate III, 4), which were fastened to forked poles, and raised over the shoulder (Fig. 6). This arrangement was introduced by Marius, in memory of whom soldiers so equipped were called *Marius's mules*, **mūlī Mariānī**. The helmet was hung by a cord from the neck, the other weapons disposed of in the most convenient way. When it rained, the oblong *shields*, **scūta** (*322*, *c*), could be put over the head like a roof.

VIII. THE ARMY IN CAMP

331. *a.* A camp was fortified at the close of every day's march. When the army was still on the march, men were sent

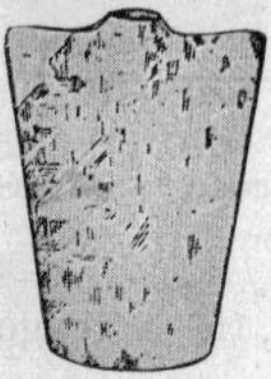

Figure 184. — Roman spade.

Of iron; such, with wooden handles, were used by Caesar's soldiers.

forward to choose a suitable location for a camp and measure it off.

b. Whenever possible, a site for the camp was selected on a slight elevation, with abundance of water, and of wood for fuel, near at hand. The proximity of a dense forest or overhanging mountain was avoided, that a favorable opportunity of attack might not be given to the enemy. Sometimes the rear or one side was placed parallel with a river (II. 5).

332. The camp was usually rectangular (see Maps 3, 4, 6, 20); in a few cases there were camps of irregular shapes, adapted to the nature of the ground (Maps 5, 15). The size of the camp varied according to the size of the force.

333. In fortifying a camp, first an embankment was thrown up on all four sides; for digging the soldiers used spades, or trenching tools, like those in use to-day (Figures 3, 4, 184).

Outside of this embankment was a trench, usually triangular in section (V-shaped), from which the earth for the embankment was taken (Fig. 185, and Plate IV, 10). On the outer

Figure 185. — Bird's-eye view of a Roman Camp.

Plainly seen are the trench or moat, and the rampart, with its stockade, on which are battlements; gates, with towers at each side; the general's quarters, and the rows of tents.

edge of the embankment a row of strong *rampart stakes* or *palisades*, **vallī**, was driven firmly in, forming a *stockade*. The *rampart*, **vallum** (II. 5), thus made, was several feet high and wide enough so that the soldiers could stand on it behind the palisades. The *trench*, or *moat*, **fossa** (II. 8), was from twelve to eighteen feet wide (II. 5) and from seven to ten feet deep. When the army expected to remain in the same place for a long time, as in *winter quarters*, **hīberna** (I. 54), or a *stationary camp*, **castra statīva** (C. III. 30), sometimes *towers*, **turrēs** (V. 40), were added at brief intervals, and the intervening spaces further protected by a roof (Plate IX, 6).

The labor of fortifying a camp was prodigious.

334. *a.* The camp had four gates (Plate IV, 10). That in the direction of the advance, toward the enemy, was called the *general's gate*, **porta praetōria** (C. III. 94), the one opposite to this, at the rear, *the decuman gate*, **porta decumāna** (II, 24); the gates on the right and left side respectively, as one faced the front, *main right gate*, **porta prīncipālis dextra**, and *main left gate*, **porta prīncipālis sinistra**. The last two were connected by the *main street*, **via prīncipālis**. The entrances were made more easily defensible by an approach so laid out that an enemy attempting to enter would expose the right, or unprotected side (Fig. 185).

b. Inside the rampart, between it and the tents, a vacant space two hundred feet wide was left on all sides. The remaining room in the enclosure was systematically divided, so that every maniple, decuria, and body of light-armed troops knew its place and could find its quarters at once. The *general's quarters*, **praetōrium** (C. III. 94), was near the middle of the camp; near it was an open space where he could address his troops from a *platform*, **suggestus** (VI. 3). Access to all parts of the camp was made by means of *passageways*, **viae** (V. 49).

335. *a.* The *tents*, **tabernācula** (I. 39), were of leather (Plate VII, 3); hence **sub pellibus**, lit. *under hides*, means *in tents* (III. 29). Each was calculated to hold ten men; but a centurion seems generally to have had more room to himself than the soldiers.

b. The *winter quarters*, **hīberna**, were made more comfortable by the substitution of straw-thatched *huts*, **casae** (V. 43), for tents.

c. In a hostile country a strong guard was kept before the gates of the camp (IV. 32). In the earlier times, and probably in Caesar's army, the password, admitting to the camp, was different each night; it was written on slips of wood, which were given by the commander to the military tribunes, and passed by these to the men on duty.

336. Many Roman camps became the nucleus of permanent

settlements, which survive in cities to-day. A marked instance is the city of *Chester*, England, the name of which is derived from **castra**; so *Rochester* comes from **Rodolphī castra**.

IX. THE ARMY IN BATTLE ARRAY

337. *a.* When the Roman force was far outnumbered by the enemy, the legionary soldiers might be arranged in a *double line*, **duplex aciēs** (III. 24), or even in a *single line*, **aciēs simplex**,

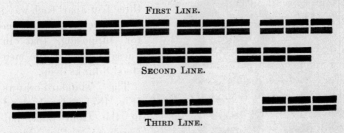

FIRST LINE.

SECOND LINE.

THIRD LINE.

Figure 186. — Acies triplex.

One legion in triple line formation, showing the arrangement of the ten cohorts, and of the three maniples and six centuries in each cohort.

Four cohorts are shown in the first line, three in the second, and three in the third.

In each cohort the three maniples stand side by side. Each maniple is represented as divided into two centuries, one century being behind the other.

The men in each maniple probably stood 8 ranks deep, each century being formed in 4 ranks.

as at the battle of Ruspina, near Hadrumetum (*264*). But under ordinary circumstances Caesar drew up his legions in a *triple line*, **triplex aciēs**, as in the battles with the Helvetians, Ariovistus, and the Usipetes and Tencteri. This arrangement was probably as follows (Fig. 186):

(1) Four cohorts of each legion stood in the first line; about 160 feet behind them stood three cohorts; and ordinarily the remaining three cohorts of the legion were posted still farther back as a reserve. At the battle of Pharsalus there were only two cohorts in Caesar's third line (as indicated on Map 20), one cohort from each legion having been drawn off to form a

fourth line; and there were probably only two cohorts in the third line at the battle with Ariovistus (Map 4), one cohort from each legion being required for guard duty at the camps.

Figure 187. — Standard-bearer.

This standard-bearer belongs to a time somewhat later than Caesar; whether Caesar's standard-bearers wore bearskins on their heads or not, we do not know.

(2) In each cohort the three maniples stood side by side, one of the centuries in each maniple being behind the other.

The soldiers in each battle line stood about three feet apart each way; and there is some reason for supposing that in Caesar's cohorts the men stood 8 ranks deep.

The standard-bearers (Fig. 187) did not stand in the front rank, but were protected by soldiers selected for their agility and strength, *the men before the standards*, **antesignānī** (C. III. 84).

b. As the first line went into action the second followed closely behind; as the men of the first fell or withdrew exhausted, those of the second pressed forward and took their places; in case of need the third line advanced and in like manner relieved the combined first and second. In the battle with the Helvetians the whole third line faced about and repelled an attack on the rear (Map 3).

338. When circumstances required it, soldiers were massed in serried ranks, as in a wedge-shaped column, *wedge*, **cuneus** (VI. 40), or under a *turtle-shell roof*, **testūdō** (used by the Gauls, VII. 85). For defense sometimes a force was formed into a *circle*, **orbis**, corresponding with our hollow square (IV. 37).

339. The place of the light-armed troops and cavalry was ordinarily at first in front of the triple line, or on the wings. They opened the engagement by skirmishing, prevented flank movements of the enemy, drew the brunt of the attack if the legions wished to take another position, and were employed in various other ways as occasion demanded. The cavalry were utilized especially to cut down the fleeing.

X. OPERATIONS AGAINST FORTIFIED PLACES

340. The taking of walled towns was accomplished either by *sudden storming* without long preparation, **repentīna oppugnātiō** (C. III. 80), or **oppugnātiō** (VII. 36); by *siege blockade*, **obsidiō** (VII. 69), or **obsessiō** (VII. 36), which aimed to repel all attempts of the enemy to escape or secure supplies, and to reduce him by starvation, as at Alesia (VII. 69–90); or by *siege and storming*, **longinqua oppugnātiō** (C. III. 80), with the help of appliances to break down the enemy's fortifications and gain admission to the city, as at Avaricum (VII. 16–28).

In storming a city the forces rushed forward, tried to batter down the gates, fill up the moat, and mount the walls with ladders.

341. The siege was begun by extending a line of works, in case the nature of the site allowed, entirely around the place to be reduced. Then a *siege embankment*, or *mole*, **agger**, a wide roadway of timber and earth, was begun outside the reach of the enemy's weapons; it was gradually prolonged toward the city wall, and raised until at the front the top was on a level with the wall, or even higher.

342. *a.* The workmen at the front were protected by movable *breastworks*, **plutei** (cf. Plate IX, 4, 5), or by *arbor-sheds*, or *sappers' huts,* **vīneae** (II, 12 ; see Plate IX, 9), made of timber or of thick wickerwork, with rawhides stretched over the outside as a protection against fire. Rows of arbor-sheds were placed along the sides of the mole to afford passageways to the front (Plate IX, 2); a long arbor-shed was called a *mousie,* **mūsculus** (VII. 84 ; C. II. 10). A sappers' shed with a sloping roof of strong boards specially adapted for use in undermining a wall was called a *turtle-shell shed,* **testūdō** (Plate VII, 10).

b. Movable towers, **turrēs ambulātōriae** (II. 12, 31), to be filled with soldiers, were built out of range of the enemy's missiles

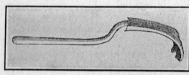

Figure 188. — Wall hook.

Iron head of a wall hook, found in the remains of the Gallic wall at Besançon, ancient Vesontio.

and brought up near the walls, usually on the siege embankment, which sloped gently from the rear up to the wall (Plate IX, 7 ; Plate XII).

c. In the lowest story of the movable tower, or under a separate roof, was the *battering ram,* **ariēs** (II. 32), an enormous beam with a metallic head which was swung against the walls with terrific force (Plate VII, 1). The attacking force tried also to pry stones out of the walls with *wall hooks,* **falcēs** (**mūrālēs**), light poles with a strong iron hook at the end (VII. 22 ; Fig. 188), and clear the walls of defenders by means of *artillery* of the *torsioner* type, **tormenta.**

d. Walls and ramparts were mounted by means of *scaling ladders,* **scālae** (V. 43).

343. For throwing heavy missiles the Romans had *torsioners,* **tormenta** (VII. 81), so named from the method of developing the force required for hurling ; **tormentum** is derived from **torqueō,** *twist.* This was obtained by twisting with great tension strong ropes of hair (Fig. 189), which were suddenly released by means of a trigger ; the force was utilized for the shooting of missiles by a mechanism of which there were three principal types :

a. The *catapult,* **catapulta** (Plate IX, 8), for shooting large arrows or darts. A small catapult is called *scorpion*, **scorpiō**, by Caesar (VII. 25).

b. The *ballista*, **ballista** (Plate VII, 8), which cast stones; the trough was sharply inclined, while that of the catapult was nearly horizontal. The ballista is not mentioned by Caesar.

Figure 189. — Head of a catapult, restored. In the Museum of St. Germain, near Paris.

a, a. Tightly twisted ropes.

b, b. Arms, to which are attached the cords connected with the trigger. The methods of loading and discharging artillery of this kind are easily understood from the figures shown in Plate VII, 8, and Plate IX, 8.

c. The *wild ass*, **onager** (Plate VII, 7), which hurled stones, but was probably not used in Caesar's time.

Where the ground allowed, the walls were undermined and tunnels run under the town.

344. The besieged met mines by counter-mines. With great hooks they tried to catch the head of the battering ram and hold it, or let down masses of wood or wickerwork along the

side of the wall to deaden the force of the blow, or drew
the wall hooks over into the city with windlasses (VII. 22).
By frequent *sallies*, **ēruptiōnēs** (VII. 22), they endeavored
to destroy the works of the besiegers, drove the workmen
from their posts, and hurled firebrands into the sheds and
towers.

345. Owing to the amount of wood used in siege works the
danger from fire was great. Once even the siege embankment
was burned (VII. 24). When a breach had been made in the
wall, or a gate battered down, an attack was begun wherever
it was thought possible to force an entrance. The siege embankment and towers were connected with the top of the wall
by means of planks and beams thrown across (Plate XII).
Detachments of soldiers, holding their oblong shields close
together above their heads, formed a *turtle-shell roof*, **testūdō**,
under which they marched up close to the walls and tried to
scale them, or entered the breach (Plate VII, 6).

XI. THE ROMAN BATTLESHIPS.

346. *a.* The *battleships* or *galleys*, **nāvēs longae** (III. 9), of
Caesar's time were propelled mainly by oars; they had only
one mast, and generally one large sail (Fig. 146). There were
usually three rows or banks of oars, hence the name *trireme*,
nāvis trirēmis (C. II. 6) or **trirēmis** (C. III. 101), but sometimes vessels with two banks of oars were used, *bireme*, **birēmis**
(C. III. 40), and even five banks, *quinquereme*, **quīnquerēmis**
(C. III. 101). The rowers kept time to the sound of a horn or
click of a hammer.

b. The *rudders*, **gubernācula**, were not like those of to-day,
but consisted of two large paddles thrust down into the sea,
one on each side of the stern (Fig. 146); they were controlled
by the *steersman*, **gubernātor** (III. 9). The anchor was like
those of our own time.

c. At the prow, near the water line, was the ship's *beak*,
rōstrum (III. 13), consisting of one or more sharp metal-

PLATE XII

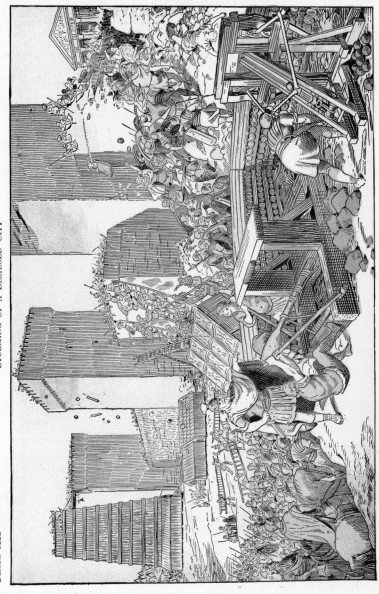

pointed beams projecting in front, for use in ramming a hostile ship (Figures 24, 146). When the galleys were not in use they might be drawn up on the shore (IV. 29).

d. Before the galley went into action the sail was rolled up and the mast taken down; a *tower,* **turris** (III. 14), was raised on the front part of the ship, from which missiles could be hurled over into a vessel near at hand; *grappling-hooks,* **ferreae manūs** (lit. *iron hands;* C. II. 6), were provided, by which the opposing ship might be seized, and a movable bridge that could be thrown across in boarding.

e. For the carrying of his troops Caesar used *transports,* **onerāriae nāvēs** (IV. 22), which were broader and slower than the galleys (Fig. 202, in the Vocabulary); these were accompanied by galleys as escort (V. 8).

f. The admiral's ship, or flag-ship, was distinguished by a red *banner,* **vēxillum,** resembling that used by the general on land (*324, b, 3*).

347. The naval tactics of the Romans consisted mainly in either propelling a vessel with great force against a rival and crushing the side by ramming, or in catching hold of the hostile craft with grappling-hooks, pulling alongside, springing over on it, and settling the conflict with a hand-to-hand fight (Plate XI). In the sea-fight with the Venetans, who had only sailing vessels, the Roman sailors crippled the enemy's ships by cutting down the sail yards; the legionaries on the galleys then boarded the Venetan ships and despatched the crews (III. 13–15).

Galleys were used on the Mediterranean until the beginning of the nineteenth century.

XII. DRESS AND EQUIPMENT OF THE GAULS AND GERMANS

348. The Gauls wore trousers, **brācae,** which the Romans considered barbaric. The Gallic military *cloak,* **sagulum** (V. 42), was apparently smaller than that of the Roman soldiers.

Figure 190. — Gallic sword and sheath.

Found at Alesia. The handle has rusted away.

349. The Gallic infantry were protected by large oblong or oval shields, of wood or metal (called by Caesar, **scūta,** I. 25 ; Figures 19, 48, and 131), and by helmets of metal on which sometimes horns, and even wheels, appeared (Figures 46 and 131).

The offensive weapons of the Gauls were a long sword (Figures 39 and 190), and several types of missile for throwing (Figures 40, 43), as *javelins,* **gaesa** (III. 4), *spears,* **matarae** (I. 26), and *darts,* **trāgulae** (I. 26), or **verūta** (V. 44).

350. The Gallic standard, in many cases at least, was an image of a boar mounted on a pole (Figures 30, 42).

Signals in Gallic armies were given on a curved *war-trumpet,* **carnyx**, which terminated in the head of an animal or serpent (Figures 19, 151).

351. The clothing of the Germans was largely of skins (IV. 1), but the more advanced wore trousers, like the Gauls, and confined their long hair in a kind of knot (Fig. 66).

The principal weapons of the Germans were a shield and spear, and a long sword with a single edge (Fig. 67).

EXERCISES IN LATIN COMPOSITION

Forty Exercises reprinted, by permission, from
Latin Composition, by Bernard M. Allen and John L. Phillips,
of Phillips Academy, Andover, Massachusetts.

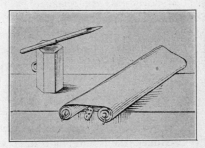

Figure 191. — Roman inkstand, reed pen, and book partly
unrolled, with title on a small tag attached at the end.
From an ancient wall painting.

POINTS TO BE NOTED IN WRITING LATIN

ORDER OF WORDS IN LATIN

352. Normal Order. *a.* When the emphasis is evenly distributed in a Latin sentence, the Subject comes first, the Predicate last, and the Modifiers of the Predicate precede the Verb in this order: Indirect Object, Direct Object, Adverb or Adverbial Phrase; as, **Is sibi lēgātiōnem ad cīvitātēs suscēpit,** *he took upon himself the misson of envoy to the states* (I. 3).

b. Genitives, Adjectives, Possessive Pronouns, and Ordinal Numerals when unemphatic follow their Nouns; as **glōriā bellī,** *reputation for war* (I. 2); **cupiditāte rēgnī,** *by desire of kingly power* (I. 9); **locīs patentibus maximēque frūmentāriīs,** *open and exceedingly productive country* (I. 10); **fīliam suam,** *his daughter* (I. 3); **diē quārtō,** *on the fourth day* (I. 26).

c. The Demonstrative Pronouns **hīc, iste, ille, is,** the Intensive **ipse,** and Adjectives indicating quantity or position when unemphatic precede their Nouns; as, **Hīs rēbus,** *by these conditions* (I. 3); **ipse imperātor,** *the general himself* (I. 40); **trēs populōs,** *three peoples* (I. 3); **magnum numerum,** *a great number* (I. 4); **extrēmum oppidum,** *the furthest town* (I. 6); **superiōre aciē,** *the upper line* (I. 24).

353. Order according to Emphasis. *a.* For the sake of emphasis the Normal Order of words in the sentence may be reversed, the Subject being placed last; as, **Apud Helvētiōs longē nōbilissimus fuit et dītissimus Orgetorīx,** *Among the Helvetians Orgetorix was far the highest in rank, and wealthiest* (I. 2).

b. Genitives, Adjectives, Possessive Pronouns, and Ordinal Numerals when emphatic precede their Nouns; as, **rēgnī cupiditāte,** *by desire of kingly power* (I. 2); **inimīcō animō,** *of hostile disposition* (I. 7); **decima legiō,** *the tenth legion* (I. 41).

c. When emphatic, the Demonstratives **hīc, iste, ille, is,** the Intensive **ipse** and Adjectives indicating quantity or position follow their nouns; as, **in īnsulā ipsā,** *in the island itself* (V. 12); **Galliae tōtīus,** *of entire Gaul* (I. 31); **partēs trēs,** *three parts* (I. 1); **locīs superiōribus,** *the higher places* (I. 10).

d. For the sake of emphasis words belonging together in construction are often separated; as, **aliud iter habērent nūllum,** *they had*

641

no other way (I. 7); **magnō ad pugnam erat impedīmentō**, *was a great hindrance* (I. 25).

e. An important word in a clause may be made emphatic by placing it before the conjunction introducing the clause; as **Diū cum esset pugnātum**, *When the fighting had continued a long time* (I. 26).

THE SEQUENCE OF TENSES

354. In writing Latin the Sequence of Tenses should be particularly noted when a Subjunctive is required in a Dependent Clause. For convenience of reference the statement of the grammar (*177, a*) is here supplemented by a tabular outline:

PRIMARY SEQUENCE

rogat	quid faciam	*He asks, is asking*	*what I am*
rogābit	(incomplete ac-	*He will ask*	*doing.*
rogāverit	tion)	*He will have asked*	
rogat	quid fēcerim	*He asks, is asking*	*what I did,*
rogābit	(completed ac-	*He will ask*	*or have*
rogāverit	tion)	*He will have asked*	*done.*

SECONDARY SEQUENCE

rogābat	quid facerem	*He asked, was asking*	*what I*
rogāvit	(incomplete ac-	*He asked*	*was do-*
rogāverat	tion)	*He had asked*	*ing.*
rogābat	quid fēcissem	*He asked, was asking*	*what I*
rogāvit	(completed ac-	*He asked*	*had*
rogāverat	tion)	*He had asked*	*done.*

TABLE ILLUSTRATING SEQUENCE OF TENSES

	MAIN VERB	FOLLOWED BY SUBJUNCTIVE	
		Referring to the Same or Later Time	Referring to Previous Time
PRIMARY TENSES	Present Future Future Perfect	Present	Perfect
SECONDARY TENSES	Imperfect Perfect Pluperfect	Imperfect	Pluperfect

WAYS OF EXPRESSING PURPOSE

355. Purpose in Latin may be expressed in five ways:

By the use of **ut** with the Subjunctive (*196, a*);

By the use of a Relative with the Subjunctive (*193, a*);

By **ad** with the Accusative of the Gerund or the Gerundive Construction (*230, 3*);

By **causā** with the Genitive of the Gerund or the Gerundive Construction (*230, 1*);

By the Supine in **-um** (*231, a and b*).

"MAY," "MIGHT," AND "MUST," "OUGHT" IN LATIN

356. *a.* "May" and "might" often appear in clauses expressing Purpose, which are translated into Latin by **ut** with the Subjunctive; as, "in order that they might be more ready," **ut parātiōrēs essent** (I. 5). *196, a.*

b. "May" and "might" may also express Permission and be best translated by **licet** with the Dative of the Person and the Infinitive; as, "We may discuss with him," **nōbīs cum eō agere licet,** lit. 'it is permitted to us,' etc. *73, b,* and *222, a.*

357. *a.* "Must" implies Necessity, and is translated by the Passive Periphrastic conjugation (*73, e,* and *229, c*), or by **necesse est** with the Infinitive, or Infinitive with Subject-Accusative, the Infinitive with **necesse est** being the Subject of **est**; as, 'as was bound to happen,' **quod necesse erat accidere,** lit. 'which was necessary to happen,' **quod accidere** being the subject of **erat** (IV. 29).

b. "Ought," implying Obligation or Propriety, is translated either by the Passive Periphrastic conjugation (*73, e,* and *229, c*), by **oportet** and the Present Infinitive with Subject Accusative (*73, a*), or by **dēbeō** with a Present Infinitive; since "ought" is a defective verb, past time is expressed in English by the Past Infinitive with "ought," while in Latin past time is expressed by the Principal Verb and only the Present Infinitive is used.   Thus:

PRESENT TIME "They ought to fight bravely"	**fortiter pugnāre dēbent** **eōs fortiter pugnāre oportet** **eīs fortiter pugnandum est**
PAST TIME "He ought to have sent hostages"	**obsidēs mittere dēbuit** **eum obsidēs mittere oportuit** **obsidēs eī mittendī erant**

LESSON I

PRONOUNS

Personal. *39*, *a* and *b*; *87*, *a* and *b*; *155, 156*. B. 242; A. 295; H. 500.

Demonstrative and Intensive. *42–45, 46*; *160–162*; B. 246–249; A. 296–298; H. 505–507.

Reflexive. *40*, *a* and *b*; *158*, *a* and *b*; *159*. B. 244; A. 299, and 300, 1, 2; H. 502–504.

Book I. 1, 2. 1. These often carry on war with them. 2. That river separates all these from the Belgians. 3. We call you Gauls. 4. They call themselves Celts. 5. The Helvetians carry on war with the Germans, and fight in their territory. 6. They all differ from one another. 7. The Belgians inhabit this part of Gaul, and call themselves the bravest of all. 8. Their boundaries are narrow in proportion to the number of men.

LESSON II

PRONOUNS — *Continued*

Relative. *47*; *163*, *a* and *b*. B. 250, 251; A. 304–306, and 308, *a*; H. 510.

Possessive. *41*; *157*, *a–c*, *158*, *c*. B. 243; A. 302, *a*, *c*, *d*, *e*; H. 501.

Book I. 3, 4. 1. Casticus had been called our friend. 2. He will seize the royal power in his own state. 3. Diviciacus, who held the leadership, was a brother of Dumnorix. 4. They will establish peace with those states which are nearest. 5. They were influenced by his speech, and gave a pledge to one another. 6. His father held the royal power for many years. 7. He will take all his clients with him to the trial. 8. Dumnorix, to whom he gave his daughter in marriage, was very powerful. 9. You attempted the same thing in your state.

LESSON III

PRONOUNS — *Continued*

Interrogative. *48, a* and *b*. B. 90; A. 148, 152; H. 511.
Indefinite. *49, a* and *b*; *168*. B. 252; A. 309–314; H. 512–515.
Direct Questions. *179, a*. B. 162; A. 330–333; H. 378.
Ablative of Agent and Means. *126, a*; *131, a, b*, and *c*. B. 216; A. 405;
H. 468, and 1.

Book I. 5, 6. 1. Were all the towns and villages burned by the Helvetians? 2. Certain[1] of the Rauraci adopted the same plan, and started out with them. 3. If there is any road by which we can[2] go from home, we will burn all our towns and villages. 4. What did they try to do when[3] they went out from home? 5. They cannot persuade their neighbor, can they, to attempt to do this? 6. They permitted them to go through their territory.

[1] *certain;* **quīdam** and numerals take **ex** with the Ablative instead of the Partitive Genitive. *97, d*.

[2] *can;* note mood in text. *194, a*.

[3] *when;* use **ubi**. Note construction in text.

LESSON IV

REVIEW

Book I. 7, 8. Lake Geneva empties into the Rhone, which is a river in Gaul between the (country of the) Sequanians[1] and the (country of the) Allobroges. Caesar built a rampart ten feet high from this lake to the Jura mountains, which separate the (country of the) Helvetians from the (country of the) Sequanians. When this rampart was finished, he fortified redoubts; and after stationing[2] garrisons, he was able very easily to stop those who tried to cross over. The Helvetians were intending to march through the Province because they could not go by any other route; and so[3] they fastened many boats together, and made rafts by which they crossed the Rhone at its shallowest point.

[1] *282*. [2] *after stationing;* use Ablative Absolute. *144, a* and *b*.

[3] *and so*, **itaque**. *237, a*.

LESSON V

Indirect Questions. *204.* B. 300; A. 573, 574; H. 649, II.
Sequence of Tenses. *177, a,* and *354.* B. 267, 268; A. 482–484; H. 543–545.

Book I. 9, 10.   1. He does not understand why they are sending envoys.   2. He announced what[1] the Helvetians were planning.   3. They found out why he had enrolled two legions.   4. Did Caesar know whether Dumnorix was a friend of the Helvetians or not?   5. Caesar knew what[1] was being done by the Helvetians.   6. He does not know whether they obtained their request.   7. Can he find out why they led their legions out from winter quarters?   8. I asked him whether Caesar was passing the winter there, or had gone into Gaul.

[1] *what,* plural.

LESSON VI

Subjunctive of Purpose. *196, a, b,* and *193, a, b.* B. 282; A. 531; H. 568, 590.
Constructions of Place. *119, a, b,* and *120, a; 130, a* and *b; 145, a, b, c; 146.* B. 182, 228, 229, 232; A. 426, 427; H. 418, and 4, 419, 1, and 461, 462, 483, 484.

Book I. 11, 12.   1. The Aeduans, in order to defend themselves and their possessions, asked help of[1] Caesar.   2. They sent an army to keep off the attack of the enemy.   3. They had nothing left at home.   4. When the Tigurini had gone out from home, they sent Cassius's army under the yoke.   5. He will cross the river in order to be able to judge in which direction it flows.   6. Caesar inflicted a great disaster on this state, with the design of avenging[2] his personal wrongs.   7. He will send envoys to Rome to ask help.

[1] *ask of,* **petō**, with *ab* and Ablative. *116, b.*
[2] *with the design of avenging;* in Latin, *with this design that he might avenge.*

LESSON VII

REVIEW

Book I. 13. Caesar led his army across the Arar, so that he might follow up the forces of the Helvetians. His sudden arrival alarmed them, and they sent envoys to him to make peace, for[1] they could not understand how[2] he had crossed the river so quickly.[3] Divico was the leader of this embassy, and he asked Caesar where he wished the Helvetians to go. He inquired if Caesar remembered the former valor[4] of the Helvetians, and the destruction of the army which had crossed from the Roman Province[5] into their territory.

[1] *for*, **nam**.   [2] *how*, **quem ad modum**.   [3] *quickly*, **celeriter**.
[4] *valor*; note case after **reminīscor** in text.
[5] *province*, **prōvincia**.

LESSON VIII

Subjunctive of Result. *197*, *a* and *b*. B. 284; A. 537; H. 570.
Ablative of Means. *131*, *a*. B. 218; A. 409; H. 476.
Dative of Possession. *111*. B. 190; A. 373; H. 430.

Book I. 14, 15. 1. They boasted so insolently that Caesar could not put aside the memory of the injuries.   2. Caesar had less doubt because he remembered what the envoys had mentioned.   3. They will march in such a way that we cannot attack them.   4. By this battle he kept the enemy from foraging.   5. The gods had granted prosperity to them for so long that they were grieved at the change of circumstances.   6. The number of the enemy is so large that they cannot drive them back.   7. He stationed men to see in what direction the enemy were marching.

LESSON IX

Indirect Discourse: Simple Declarative Sentences. *212, d; 213, a* and *b; 214, a; 178.* B. 313, 314, 1, 2, and 317; A. 579–582, 584; H. 642, 644.

Partitive Genitive. *97, a, b, c,* and *d.* B. 201, 1, 2; A. 346, *a, c*; H. 440, 5, and 441–443.

Book I. 16, 17. 1. Caesar said that the grain in the fields was not ripe. 2. He knew that many of their chiefs had been called together to complain about the leadership of the Aeduans. 3. For this reason he thought Caesar would take away liberty from the Gauls.[1] 4. Day after day he declared that the Aeduans were not collecting the grain. 5. They have a large supply of grain, which they can use if Caesar undertakes[2] the war. 6. He said that he thought we knew with how great danger he had reported our plans.

[1] *Gauls;* note case in text.
[2] *undertakes;* what time is referred to?

LESSON X

REVIEW

Book I. 18. Caesar realized that Liscus referred to Dumnorix, and that these matters had been discussed very freely and boldly; but because Dumnorix was in charge of the cavalry and was utterly reckless,[1] he wished him to favor the Romans. After dismissing[2] the council he asked many questions,[3] and discovered that for several years Dumnorix had been enlarging his private property and had very great power both at home and among the Helvetians. Caesar knew that Dumnorix, by means of this power, could restore himself to his former position of influence, and that he had amassed so much[4] wealth that he entertained hopes of getting the royal power. He learned also that Dumnorix and his horsemen had started the flight of the cavalry a few days before.

[1] *utterly reckless;* in Latin, *of supreme recklessness.*
[2] *after dismissing;* use Ablative Absolute. *144, a* and *b.*
[3] *questions;* omit, and use neuter adjective as a noun.
[4] *so much,* **tantus.**

LESSON XI

INDIRECT DISCOURSE

Complex Sentences. *214, a; 218; 158, a; 354.* B. 314, 1 and 318; A. 580, and 585, *a*; H. 643.

Prepositions. *122, a; 124, a; 125, a.* B. 141, 142, 143; A. 220, *a, b, c*; H. 420, 2 and 3, and 490, 2.

Book I. 19, 20. 1. He knew that everything [1] which was said to him was true. 2. Caesar hoped not to hurt (that he should not hurt) the feelings of Diviciacus, if he should punish his brother. 3. We all know that Procillus was a man in whom [2] he had great confidence. 4. Diviciacus thought that Caesar would punish Dumnorix because he had led an army through the territory of the Sequanians. 5. He will order Diviciacus to be called to him, in order that he may tell him what he knows. 6. Caesar replied that he would tell what had been said in the council.

[1] *everything;* in Latin, *all things.*
[2] *in whom;* use the Dative.

LESSON XII

ABLATIVE ABSOLUTE

Ablative Absolute. *144, a* and *b.* B. 227; A. 419, 420; H. 489.

Book I. 21, 22. 1. Caesar, having sent ahead all his cavalry, ordered Labienus to climb to the summit of the mountain. 2. While our men were seizing this mountain, the Helvetians moved camp. 3. After seizing the mountain, Labienus did not begin battle, but waited for Caesar. 4. Caesar led his forces to the nearest hill, but did not make an attack on the enemy. 5. When they had pitched camp three miles from Caesar's camp, the enemy refrained from battle.

LESSON XIII

REVIEW

Book I. 23, 24. On the following day it was announced to the enemy that Caesar had changed his route and gone to Bibracte, which was the richest city of the Helvetians, to provide for grain. The Helvetians thought that he was withdrawing because he was frightened, and attacked him in the rear; but Caesar, after leading his forces to the nearest hill and drawing up his line of battle, stationed two legions on the top of the ridge, and collected the packs in [1] one place. The Helvetians, following with all their baggage, formed a phalanx close by [2] the line of battle of the Romans.

[1] *in;* in Latin, *into.* *124, a.*   [2] *close by,* **sub,** with the Ablative.

LESSON XIV

Substantive Clauses with Verbs of *Commanding, Urging, Reminding, Persuading,* and *Permitting.* *199, a; 200, b; 223, a,* (1) and (4). B. 294, 295, 1, 2, and 296, 1; A. 563; H. 564, 565, 568.
   Ablative of Accompaniment. *137, a, b,* and *c.* B. 222; A. 413; H. 473, and 474, 2, N. 1.

_____

Book I. 25, 26. They threw away their shields, and fought with the enemy with swords.   2. Caesar ordered the soldiers to make an attack on the Helvetians with drawn swords.   3. Having noticed this, he bade the cavalry surround the enemy and renew the battle.   4. He urges them to retreat to the mountain with their baggage and carts.   5. We persuaded them not to help the soldiers with wagons or anything else.   6. They fought a long time near the baggage, and got possession of the camp and the horses.

LESSON XV

Substantive Clauses with Verbs of *Asking* **and** *Fearing*. *199, a,* and *202.* B. 295, 1, and 296, 2; A. 563, 564; H. 565, 567.

Book I. 27, 28. 1. Caesar demanded that they should await his [1] arrival in that place.   2. The Helvetians feared that Caesar would ask that they surrender their arms. 3. They begged Caesar not to regard them as enemies. 4. He will ask that envoys be sent to him.   5. He was afraid that the Germans might cross into the territory of the Helvetians.   6. Caesar asked the Helvetians to return to their own territory, so that the lands [2] might not be unoccupied. 7. They urge him to accept their surrender.[3]   8. They fear that they may not be able to conceal their flight.

[1] *his*, indirect reflexive. *158, a.*   [2] *lands*, **agrī**.
[3] *accept their surrender;* note the text.

LESSON XVI

REVIEW

Book I, 29, 30. The soldiers found records in the camp showing [1] the number of Helvetians who could bear arms. These had gone out from home with all the women and children.   Caesar ordered his men to make an enumeration of those who had returned home, and the total was about 120,000. The envoys of the Gauls, who had come to Caesar, feared that he would inflict punishment on their states, but nevertheless asked him not to take possession of all Gaul.   This war had turned out to the advantage of Gaul, and they begged Caesar that they might be permitted to appoint a council, and to ask of him the things which they wished.[2]   This request was granted, and they agreed together not to disclose anything except with Caesar's consent.

[1] *showing;* in Latin, *which showed.*
[2] *wished;* use Subjunctive, Subordinate Clause in implied Indirect Discourse. *214, b.*

LESSON XVII

Ablative of Separation or Source. *127, a, b,* and *c.* B. 214, 215; A. 400–402, and 403, 1; H. 461–465, 467.

Ablative of Comparison. *129, a* and *b.* B. 217; A. 406 and 407, *a*; H. 471.

Ablative of Degree of Difference. *140.* B. 223; A. 414; H. 479.

Book I. 31 (*first half*).   1. They asked back their hostages from the Sequanians, and sought aid of the Roman people. 2. The Germans are much fiercer than the Gauls,[1] and covet their lands.   3. Diviciacus fled from his state, and came to Rome many years before.   4. The Aeduans are less powerful in Gaul than the Sequanians, being weakened by great disasters. 5. We are working to induce[2] Diviciacus to give his children as hostages to the Germans.   6. About a thousand of the Germans crossed the Rhine, and contended in arms with the Aeduans and their dependents.

[1] *than the Gauls;* express in two ways.   [2] *to induce, 196, a.*

LESSON XVIII

Substantive Clauses of Result. *203.* B. 297; A. 568, 569; H. 571.

Ablative of Manner. *136, a* and *b.* B. 220; A. 412; H. 473, 3.

Ablative of Accordance. *136, c.* B. 220, 3; A. 418, *a*; H. 475, 3.

Book I. 31 (*latter half*).   1. The result was that they could not longer endure his cruelty.   2. He will cause a place to be prepared for the Harudes.   3. He saw that the best part of entire Gaul would be occupied by Ariovistus.   4. All these things were done with the greatest injustice.   5. He says that they will not be able to drive the Germans from the Gallic territory.   6. The cruelty of Ariovistus caused them to seek another home.   7. It happened that a larger number of Germans crossed the Rhine.

LESSON XIX

REVIEW

Book I. 32, 33.   The lot of the Sequanians was much more unhappy than (that) of the others, because the cruelty of Ariovistus had caused them to fear him in his absence, and they did not dare to seek aid from Caesar.

Therefore[1] when Caesar asked why they did not do what the others did, it happened that they made no answer,[2] but remained silent.   Diviciacus finally told what the reason was. Caesar promised to put an end to the outrages of Ariovistus, and dismissed the council.   The Roman Province was separated by the Rhone from the territory of the Sequanians, and Caesar thought it would be dangerous to the Roman people (for) the Germans to cross from their own boundaries into Gaul.

[1] *therefore*, **itaque.**
[2] *made no answer;* in Latin, *answered nothing.*

LESSON XX

Verbs of Hindering, Preventing, Doubting. *201, a, b,* and *c.* B. 295, 3, and 298; A. 558; H. 568, 8, and 595, 1, 2, and 596, 2.
Ablative of Time. *147, a* and *b.* B. 230, 231; A. 423; H. 486, 487.
Accusative of Extent. *118, a.* B. 181; A. 423, 425; H. 417.

Book I. 34, 35. 1. They could not be restrained from sending envoys to Caesar.   2. In three days he will advance many miles.   3. There was no doubt that these replies had been brought back to Caesar.   4. He talked[1] with him a large part of the day about very important matters. 5. Caesar demanded of him that he prevent a large number from being led across the Rhine.   6. This river was half a mile (five hundred paces) wide.[2]

[1] *talked,* **agō.**   [2] *36,* and *243, a* and *b.*

LESSON XXI

Dative with Special Verbs. *105.* B. 187, II; A. 367; H. 426.
Dative with Compounds. *107, a* and *b*. B. 187, III; A. 370; H. 429.

Book I. 36. 1. The Germans rule those whom they conquer, as they wish.   2. We do not prescribe to you how you shall pay the tax.   3. I shall not make war on their allies unjustly.   4. They could not be persuaded to return the hostages.   5. No one had resisted him without his own destruction.   6. They put him in command [1] of the conquered. 7. He ordered [2] them not to make the revenues less.   8. He will persuade them to do what he wishes.   9. They had been ordered [2] to do all these things.

[1] *put in command,* **praeficiō.**
[2] *ordered;* use **imperō** in one sentence, and **iubeō** in the other.

LESSON XXII

REVIEW

Book I. 37, 38. The Harudes, who had lately come into Gaul, could not be kept from laying waste the lands of the Aeduans. The latter resisted bravely for many days, and did not doubt that Caesar was hurrying by forced marches against the Swabians, commanded by Nasua,[1] in order to prevent them from crossing the Rhine. Caesar thought that he ought to advance as quickly as possible to seize Vesontio, and after getting ready a grain supply, he hastened to that town with all his forces. The town is almost surrounded by a river of great width, which touches the base of a mountain six hundred feet high. Caesar fortified this town with a very high wall, so that a great opportunity was given to prolong the war, and having stationed a garrison there, he advanced a three days' march toward Ariovistus.

[1] *commanded by Nasua;* in Latin, *whom Nasua commanded.*

LESSON XXIII

Gerund and Gerundive. *230.* B. 338, 339; A. 501–507; H. 623–631.

Supine. *231, 232.* B. 340; A. 509; H. 633.

Active Periphrastic Conjugation. *63.* B. 115; A. 193–195, and 498, *a*; H. 236, 531.

Passive Periphrastic Conjugation. *63, 73, e,* and *229, c.* B. 115, and 337, 8, *b*, 1; A. 193, 194, 196, and 500, 2; H. 237, and 621, 1, 2.

Dative of Agent. *110.* B. 189, 1; A. 374, *a*; H. 431.

Book I. 39. 1. One assigned one reason for departing, another another. 2. He remained in camp for the sake of avoiding suspicion. 3. Caesar intended to delay a few days near Vesontio. 4. Caesar sent some of his men to bring up the grain.[1] 5. We shall have to break camp in a few days. 6. He said that he was going to report this to Caesar. 7. Having sealed their wills, they remained in their tents to lament the common danger. 8. The Germans, with whom they were going to contend, had[2] incredible valor.

[1] *to bring up the grain;* write in five ways. *355.*
[2] *had;* in Latin, *were of.*

LESSON XXIV

MAY, MIGHT, MUST, OUGHT

May, Might. *356, a* and *b.* B. 327, 1; A. 565, N. 1, 2; H. 564, 2.

Must, Ought. *357, a* and *b.* B. 115, 270, 2, and 337, 8, *b*, 1; A. 194, 196, 486, *a,* and 500, 2; H. 237, 618, 2, and 621, 1, 2.

Book I. 40 (*first half*). 1. Caesar ought[1] to summon to the council the centurions of all ranks. 2. A centurion is not allowed to inquire by what plan he is being led. 3. Caesar said he did this in order that Ariovistus might not reject his friendship. 4. This he should not have said (= ought not to have said). 5. After learning their plans, you may stay in camp if you wish. 6. The Romans did not need to fear that these unarmed men would conquer them.[2]

[1] *ought;* write in three ways. *357, b.*   [2] *them, 158, a.*

LESSON XXV

REVIEW

Book I. 40 (*latter half*).   Caesar urged the Roman soldiers
not to despair in regard to grain, which was then already ripe
in the fields.   He told them that they ought not to be disturbed by the narrow roads, and that they were not permitted
to dictate to the commander concerning his duties.   He desired to know as soon as possible whether the soldiers were
going to be [1] obedient to his command or not, and so he ordered
them to move camp on the next night.   He had the greatest
confidence in the tenth legion, and did not [2] doubt that they
would follow [3] him,[4] and do what [5] had to be done.

[1] *were going to be*, etc., *63*, and *204*, (1).   [2] *and . . . not*, **neque.**
[3] *follow*, *201*, *b*.   [4] *him*, *158*, *a*.
[5] *what*; in Latin, = *those things which.*

LESSON XXVI

Temporal Clauses with *Ubi, Ut, Postquam, Simul atque.*   *188*, *a*.   B. 287,
1; A. 543; H. 602.

Temporal Clauses with *Cum, Cum primum.*   *185*, *a*, *b*, *c*.   B. 288, 1, and
289; A. 545-547; H. 600, 601.

Ablative with Certain Deponents.   *131*, *c*.   B. 218, 1; A. 410; H. 477.

Book I. 41, 42.   1. When Caesar had delivered this speech,
the military tribunes thanked him.   2. As soon as Ariovistus
learned of Caesar's arrival, he promised many things of his
own accord.   3. After getting possession of the horses, he
put on them his bravest soldiers.   4. When he saw that
Ariovistus wished a conference, he decided not to use the
Gallic horsemen.   5. As soon as they came, they said that the
enemy's forces were twenty miles away.

LESSON XXVII

Temporal Clauses with *Prius quam.*   *189, a* and *b.*   B. 291, 292;   A. 551; H. 605.

Temporal Clauses with *Dum* and *Quoad.*   *190, a, b,* and *c.*   B. 293;   A. 553–556; H. 603, 604, 1.

Ablative of Specification.   *142, a* and *b.*   B. 226;   A. 418;   H. 480.

Ablative of Cause.   *135, a* and *b.*   B. 219;   A. 404;   H. 475.

Book I. 43.   1. Caesar stationed the legion two hundred paces from the mound, before he came to the conference. 2. While he was making war on their allies, a part of the Germans crossed the Rhine.   3. The Aeduans had held the leadership before Ariovistus came into Gaul.   4. They had been able to secure these gifts through his kindness.   5. They did not send back the hostages until[1] he demanded them. 6. They were his allies, and for this reason he made these demands.   7. He waited[2] until they should seek our friendship.

[1] *until, 190, b.*   [2] *wait,* **exspectō.**

LESSON XXVIII

REVIEW

Book I. 44 (*first half*).   After Ariovistus was summoned by the Gauls, he crossed the Rhine, and took possession of the settlements which the Gauls had granted him. When they made war upon him, they were routed in one battle, and after being defeated, paid tribute and enjoyed peace. While this was going on, Caesar was marching to attack Ariovistus, and wished to come into Gaul before he[1] should impose tribute on all the states. As soon as he came there, he pitched camp, and waited[2] until Ariovistus should reply to his demands. The latter[3] was ready to fight if Caesar wished to, but Caesar made objection about the tribute, which up to this time had been paid willingly by the Gauls.

[1] *he,* **ille.**   [2] *wait,* **exspectō.**   [3] *the latter,* here **ille.**

LESSON XXIX

Causal Clauses with *Quod, Quia, Quoniam.*   *183,* a and b. B. 286, 1;
A. 540; H. 588.
 Causal Clauses with *Cum.*   *184,* a and b. B. 286, 2; A. 549; H. 598.
 Dative with Adjectives.   *108,* a and b. B. 192; A. 383–385; H. 434.

———

Book I. 44 (*latter half*).   1. He withdrew his army into
those regions, because they were nearest the province (of) Gaul.
2. Since the Aeduans had been called brothers by the senate,
they ought to have enjoyed the assistance of the Romans.
3. Ariovistus complained because we had made an attack on
his territories.   4. The friendship of the Roman people was
pleasing to the Aeduans, since they did not wish to be overwhelmed.   5. Since he has withdrawn from Gaul, we shall
consider him as a friend, and not as an enemy.

LESSON XXX

Adversative or Concessive Clauses.   *187,* and *191,* a and b. B. 308, and
309, 2, 3; A. 527, 549; H. 585, 586, 598.
 Genitive with Adjectives.   *102.* B. 204, 1; A. 349, a; H. 450, 451.

———

Book I. 45, 46.   1. Although Fabius conquered the Aver-
nians, he did not reduce them to a province.   2. Since the
horsemen were hurling weapons against our men, Caesar
stopped speaking.[1]   3. Although the soldiers were eager for
the battle, Caesar ordered them not to make an attack.
4. Even if Gaul is free, still it cannot use its own laws.
5. When this had been announced to Caesar, he ordered his
men to return to camp.   6. Although they are ignorant of
the custom of the Roman people, he will not pardon them.

———

[1] *stopped speaking;* note the expression in the text.

LESSON XXXI

REVIEW

Book I. 47. Ariovistus sent a messenger to Caesar, to ask that he should a second time appoint a day for a conference. Although the matters which they had begun to discuss the day before had not been finished, Caesar was unwilling to go himself, or to send envoys and expose them to so great danger. However,[1] because he desired to know what Ariovistus would say (was going to say),[2] it seemed best to him to send Valerius Procillus and Marcus Mettius. When they had come to Ariovistus in[3] camp, and were attempting to speak, he called out that they were spies, and threw them into chains. Caesar ought not to have sent these men to Ariovistus, since there was no reason for a conference, and he knew that the danger to[4] them would be great.

[1] *however,* **autem,** the second word of its clause.   *236, a* and *b.*
[2] *would say, 63.*
[3] *in,* **in** with accusative.   *124, x.*
[4] *to ;* in Latin, *of.*

LESSON XXXII

Subjunctive of Characteristic.   *194, a.*   B. 283, 1, 2; A. 535, *a, b*; H. 591, 1, 2, 4, 5.
  Ablative of Description.   *143, a* and *b.*   B. 224; A. 415; H. 473, 2.
  Genitive of Quality and Measure.   *100, a* and *b.*   B. 203; A. 345; H. 440, 3.

Book I. 48, 49.   1. A place about six hundred paces long was picked out, suitable for two legions.   2. The forces of Ariovistus are the only ones which can keep our troops from supplies.   3. The Germans were very swift and of great courage, and terrified our men.   4. There is no army in all Gaul that can overcome the forces of the Romans.   5. They were (men) of so great swiftness that they equaled the speed of the horses.   6. They were cut off from grain and supplies by a river two hundred feet in width.[1]

[1] *Two hundred feet in width ;* express in two ways.

LESSON XXXIII

Exhortations, and Jussive Subjunctive. *180*, *a* and *b*.　B.　273–275;　A. 439;　H. 559, 1, 2.

　　Commands and Prohibitions. *181*, *a* and *b*.　B. 276, *b*;　A. 450;　H. 561, 1.

　　Wishes. *180*, *c* and *d*.　B. 279;　A. 441;　H. 558.

　　Dative of Purpose; Two Datives. *112*, *a* and *b*.　B. 191, 1, 2;　A. 382; H. 425, 3, and 433.

Book I. 50, 51.　1. Let us lead out the troops from camp, and draw up our line of battle.　2. Would that we had not given them an opportunity for fighting !　3. Caesar left the auxiliaries as a protection for the smaller camp.　4. O that they would not deliver us into slavery !　5. Do not fight before the new moon, if you wish to conquer.　6. Let him not use the auxiliaries for a show.　7. Would that it were not ordained that the Germains should conquer !

LESSON XXXIV

Conditions. *205–209*.　B. 301–304, 1;　A. 515–517;　H. 574–579.

Book I. 52.　1. If the enemy should suddenly make an attack on our men, they would not be able to hurl their javelins. 2. They would have sent the lieutenant to our assistance, if they had noticed this.　3. If Caesar were in command of the troops, they would not be in difficulty.　4. I shall not begin battle on the left wing, unless I see that that part of the line is the strongest.　5. They said that if they leaped upon the enemy from above, they would put them to flight.　6. Do not throw your javelins against the enemy, unless they make an attack upon you.　7. Had he not put a lieutenant in charge of our men, they would have been routed.

LESSON XXXV

REVIEW

Book I. 53, 54. When the battle had been renewed, the enemy were put to flight, and fled to the river. A few, who trusted in their strength, swam across. There were some who crossed over in boats which they found, but the rest were put to death by our cavalry. Ariovistus himself would have been killed, if he had not found a skiff fastened to the shore, and sought safety in it.

While he was following the enemy, Caesar fell in with Valerius Procillus, whom the guards were dragging along. Having rescued him, Caesar said: "I should have little pleasure in this victory, if you were now in the hands of the enemy. Would that the other envoys, whom I sent to Ariovistus, had also been restored to me! Let us hope that they may be found and brought back."

LESSON XXXVI

REVIEW

Causal and Concessive Clauses (Lessons XXIX and XXX).

Book IV. 27, 28. As soon as the hostages, whom the enemy sent to Caesar, did what he had ordered, he pardoned them, and begged them not to make war on him without good cause. Although he pardoned their ignorance, he complained because they had thrown Commius the Atrebatian into chains, and had not sent him back. Since part of the hostages which they promised were at a distance, he ordered them to be sent to the continent in a few days. (The ships in which the cavalry were carried approached Britain, but could not hold their course because a great storm suddenly came up and carried them back to the continent.)

LESSON XXXVII

REVIEW

Clauses of Result, and Substantive Clauses of Result (Lessons VIII and XVIII).

Book IV. 29–31. 1. It happened that the tides were very high on that night because there was a full moon.   2. He caused those things which were of use to be brought from the continent.   3. We must keep them from supplies, and prolong the affair until winter.   4. The tide was so[1] high that it filled the ships which had been drawn up on dry land.   5. Although they were going to pass the winter in Gaul, they had made no provision for grain.   6. The ships are so damaged by the storm that they cannot be repaired.   7. He brought it about that no one afterwards crossed to Britain to bring on war.   8. It happened that everything was lacking which was useful for carrying on war.

[1] *so,* **tam.**

LESSON XXXVIII

REVIEW

Exhortations, Commands, Prohibitions and Wishes (Lesson XXXIII).

Book IV. 32, 33. 1. Let part of the legion march in that direction in which the dust was seen.   2. Would that Caesar had suspected the plans of the barbarians, and attacked them when their arms were laid aside !   3. It was reported to the general that the cohorts which were on guard had started in the same direction.   4. If the enemy attack you, throw your weapons quickly ; let the cavalry dismount and fight on foot.   5. Do not be disturbed by the noise of the chariots, for if hard pressed, you will have an easy retreat.   6. The Britons fight with chariots, and daily practice makes them able to do many things with their horses at full speed.

LESSON XXXIX

REVIEW

Purpose Clauses, and Substantive Clauses after Certain Verbs (Lessons VI, XIV, and XV).

Book IV. 34, 35. 1. Caesar will keep his men in camp that they may not be attacked by the enemy. 2. The barbarians sent messengers in all directions to tell what had happened. 3. Storms followed for so many days[1] that the enemy were kept from a battle. 4. Caesar feared that the same thing would happen. 5. They urged the rest, who were in the fields, to depart. 6. Disturbed by the strange sort of fighting, they begged Caesar to send aid to them. 7. They gathered a large number of cavalry and infantry, in order that they might the more easily[2] drive the Romans from the camp. 8. He ordered them to burn the buildings far and near, and return to camp. 9. Having killed many, they prevented the rest from escaping.[3]

[1] *days, 118, a.* [2] *easily,* **facile**. [3] *from escaping, 201, a, and 223, a, (3).*

LESSON XL

REVIEW

Conditions (Lesson XXXIV).

Book IV. 36–38. If Caesar had not sailed on that night, the hostages which he ordered would have been brought to him, but the equinox was near, and he thought if he hastened he would arrive safely at the continent. After finding a suitable place, he disembarked some three hundred men, who started for the camp, but were surrounded by the Morini, who said, "Lay down your arms if you do not wish to be killed. If Caesar and his cavalry were here, they would defend you, but you cannot withstand our attack and will be all killed unless he comes to your assistance." But after those who said this saw that our cavalry were coming, they quickly turned and fled.

LIST OF ILLUSTRATIONS[1]

---

[1] Stereopticon slides of all illustrations and maps in this book can be supplied to teachers and schools at cost; inquiry should be addressed to the *Latin Department, University of Michigan, Ann Arbor, Michigan.*

[2] The three series of wall plates, L. Gurlitt's *Anschauungstafeln zu Caesar*, S. Cybulski's *Tabulae quibus antiquitates Graecae et Romanae illustrantur*, and Ad. Lehmann's *Kulturgeschichtliche Bilder* (cf. Fig. 117), are imported by G. E. Stechert and Company, New York, and A. J. Nystrom and Company, Chicago.

[3] The designs reproduced in the illustrations from Cybulski's *Tabulae* were prepared by Dr. Martin Fickelscherer.   They are based chiefly upon evidence drawn from monuments later than Caesar's time, yet in most respects the designs are correct for the military equipment of Caesar's army.

[4] The photographs designated " G. R. S. " were made by Mr. George R. Swain.

---

[1] Casts of Roman coins engraved for this book were kindly furnished by the British Museum, through the courtesy of Mr. G. F. Hill.

670   List of Illustrations

List of Illustrations 671

PAGE

VOCABULARY

In the preparation of this Vocabulary Meusel's *Lexicon Caesarianum* has been of greatest service; Lodge's *Vocabulary of High School Latin* has also been helpful. For the less obvious Latin etymologies Walde's *Lateinisches Etymologisches Wörterbuch* (second edition) has generally been followed; for the English derivatives, *The Century Dictionary* and *The New English Dictionary*.

For the Key to the English Pronunciation of Proper Names, and in other matters of English pronunciation, the Editor was indebted to Professor George Hempl.

ABBREVIATIONS

A list of Abbreviations is given on the following page.

ENGLISH PRONUNCIATION OF PROPER NAMES

After each Proper Name in the Vocabulary a Key to the English Pronunciation is given, thus:

Matrona, -ae, f., (Mat′ rǫ-na̤)

The English long vowels (so called) have above them a macron or some mark indicative of quality; the short stressed vowels have no mark at all; the obscure unstressed vowels have a dot under them, thus:

ā as in 'f*a*te.'	e̤ as in 'hat*e*d.' *	o̤ as in 'dem*o*crat.' *
a " " 'f*a*t.'	é " " 'h*er*.'	ū " " '*u*se.'
a̤ " " 'id*ea*.' *	I " " 'p*i*ne.'	u " " '*u*p.'
ä " " '*a*rm.'	i " " 'p*i*n.'	ṳ " " 'sing*u*lar.' *
â " " '*a*ll.'	i̤ " " 'un*i*ty.' *	ṳ " " 'circ*u*s.' *
ē " " 'm*e*.'	ō " " 'n*o*.'	Ū " " 'r*u*de.'
e " " 'm*e*t.'	o " " 'n*o*t.'	U " " 'f*u*ll.'

The chief stress, or accent, is indicated by ′, the secondary by ″; but the secondary stress is not marked when separated from another stress by a single intervening unstressed syllable, for in that case one naturally puts it in the proper place.

---

* The obscure unstressed vowels are in effect very much alike, but they differ slightly according to the character of the adjoining consonants. They are most correctly sounded when one glides over them rapidly and naturally.

ABBREVIATIONS

References to the Gallic War are printed thus: I. 7 (Book I, chapter 7); to the Civil War, C. I. 7.

English Derivatives of Latin words are inserted at the end of the definitions, set off by a half-bracket, thus: [accuse.

* Implies that the form before which it stands is hypothetical.

abl.	= *ablative.*	inf.	= *infinitive.*
abs.	= *absolute.*	intens.	= *intensive.*
acc.	= *accusative.*	inter.	= *interrogative.*
adj.	= *adjective.*	interj.	= *interjection.*
adv.	= *adverb, adverbial.*	intr.	= *intransitive.*
C.	= *Bellum Civile,* Caesar's	irr.	= *irregular.*
	Civil War.	l., ll.,	= *line, lines.*
causat.	= *causative.*	lit.	= *literally.*
chap.	= *chapter.*	m.	= *masculine.*
comp.	= *comparative.*	n., neut.	= *neuter.*
conj.	= *conjunction.*	N.	= *note.*
dat.	= *dative.*	nom.	= *nominative.*
decl.	= *declension.*	num.	= *numeral.*
def.	= *defective.*	ord.	= *ordinal.*
dem.	= *demonstrative.*	p., pp.	= *page, pages.*
dep.	= *deponent.*	part.	= *participle.*
dim.	= *diminutive.*	pass.	= *passive.*
distrib.	= *distributive.*	patr.	= *patronymic.*
e.g.	= *exempli gratia = for ex-*	pers.	= *person, personal.*
	ample.	pf.	= *perfect.*
et al.	= *et alibi = and elsewhere.*	pl.	= *plural.*
et seq.	= *et sequentia = and what*	pos.	= *positive.*
	follows.	pred.	= *predicate.*
etc.	= *et cetera = and so forth.*	prep.	= *preposition.*
excl.	= *exclamation.*	pres.	= *present.*
f.	= *feminine.*	pron.	= *pronoun.*
freq.	= *frequentative.*	reflex.	= *reflexive.*
fut.	= *future.*	rel.	= *relative.*
gen.	= *genitive.*	semi-dep.	= *semi-deponent.*
i.e.	= *id est = that is.*	sing.	= *singular.*
imp.	= *imperative.*	subj.	= *subjunctive.*
impers.	= *impersonal.*	sup.	= *superlative.*
impf.	= *imperfect.*	trans.	= *translate,* or *translation.*
inch.	= *inchoative.*	v.	= *verb.*
indecl.	= *indeclinable.*	voc.	= *vocative.*
indef.	= *indefinite.*	1, 2, 3, 4 with verbs = 1st, 2d, 3d, or
indic.	= *indicative.*	4th conjugation.

2

VOCABULARY

A

A., with proper names, = *Aulus*.

a. d. = ante diem.

ā, ab, abs, prep. with abl., *from, away from, out of; at, on; of agency, with the passive voice, by, on the part of; of time, from, since, after.* ab utrōque latere, *on both sides.* ā parvīs, *from childhood* (vi. 21).

abditus, -a, -um, [part. of abdō], adj., *concealed, secluded.* vi. 34.

abdō -dere, -didī, -ditus, [ab + dō], 3, *put away, remove; conceal.* sē abdere, *to hide one's self.*

abdūcō, -dūcere, -dūxī, -ductus, [ab + dūcō], 3, *withdraw; lead away, take off* (I. 11). [abduct.

abeō, -īre, -iī, -itūrus, [ab + eō], irr., *go away, depart.* vi. 43; vii. 50.

abesse, see absum.

abiciō, -icere, -iēcī, -iectus, [ab + iaciō], 3, *throw away, throw down; hurl* (v. 48). [abject.

abiēs, -ietis, f., *fir tree, spruce.* v. 12.

abiungō, -iungere, -iūnxī, -iūnctus, [ab + iungō], 3, *unyoke; separate, part* (vii. 56).

abscīdō, -cīdere, -cīdī, -cīsus, [abs + caedō], 3, *cut off* (III. 14); *lop off, cut away* (VII. 73).

absēns, [part. of absum], adj., *absent.* sē absente, *in his absence.* [absent

absimilis, -e, [ab + similis], adj., *unlike.*

absistō, -sistere, -stitī, [ab + sistō], 3, *withdraw, go away.*

abstineō, -tinēre, -tinuī, -tentus, [abs + teneō], 2, *hold back; re-*

frain *from* (i. 22); *spare, give quarter* (vii. 47). [abstain.

abstrahō, -trahere, -trāxī, -trāctus, [abs + trahō], 3, *drag away, drag off, take away by force.* [abstract.

absum, -esse, āfuī, āfutūrus, [ab + sum], irr., *be distant, be absent* or *away from; be wanting, be lacking.* longē abesse, *to be far away.* ā bellō abesse, *to be exempt from military service* (vi. 14). tōtō bellō abessent, *they took no part in the entire war* (VII. 63).

abundō, -āre, -āvī, -ātus, [ab + undō, from unda, *wave*], 1, *overflow; abound in; be well provided with* (VII. 14, 64). [abundant.

abūtor, -ūtī, -ūsus, [ab + ūtor], 3, dep., *use up, misuse; waste* (C. III. 90). [abuse.

ac, see atque.

accēdō, -cēdere, -cessī, -cessūrus, [ad + cēdō], 3, *come to, draw near, approach; be added.* [accede.

accelerō, -āre, -āvī, -ātus, [ad + celerō, from celer], 1, *make haste, hasten.* VII. 87. [accelerate.

acceptus, -a, -um, comp. -ior, sup. -issimus, [part. of accipiō], adj., *acceptable, welcome, dear.* i. 3.

accidō, -cidere, -cidī, [ad + cadō], 3, *fall* (III. 14, 25) ; *happen, occur, turn out; befall, fall to the lot of.* Impers., accidit, *it happens.* [accident.

accīdō, -cīdere, -cīdī, -cīsus, [ad + caedō], 3, *cut into.* vi. 27.

accipiō, -cipere, -cēpī, -ceptus, [ad + capiō], 3, *take to one's self;*

3

receive, accept; hear of, learn; incur (vii. 17). [accept.

acclīvis, -e, [ad, cf. clīvus], adj., sloping; up-hill, rising.

acclīvitās -tātis, [acclīvis], f., upward slope, ascent. ii. 18. [acclivity.

Accō, -ōnis, m., (ak′ ō), a leader among the Senones. vi. 4, 44; vii. 1.

accommodātus, -a, -um, comp. -ior, sup. -issimus, [part. of accommodō], adj., suited, adapted. III. 13. [accommodate.

accommodō, -āre, -āvī, -ātus, [ad + commodō, from commodus], 1, adjust, put on. ii. 21.

accūrātē, comp. -ius, sup. -issimē, [accūrātus], adv., carefully. Comp., with greater pains (vi. 22).

accurrō, -currere, -cucurrī, or -currī, -cursum est, [ad + currō], 3, run to (iii. 5), hasten to (i. 22).

accūsō, -āre, -āvī, -ātus, [ad + causā], 1, call to account, find fault with; reproach, accuse. [accuse.

ācer, ācris, ācre, comp. ācrior, sup. ācerrimus, adj., sharp; of fighting, fierce (C. III. 72). [acrid.

acerbē, comp. acerbius, sup. acerbissimē, [acerbus], adv., bitterly. sī acerbius inopiam ferrent, if they found the scarcity too severe (vii. 17).

acerbitās, -tātis, [acerbus], f., bitterness, sourness; pl., sufferings (vii. 17). [acerbity.

acerbus, -a, -um, comp. -ior, sup. -issimus, [ācer], adj., bitter, harsh.

ācerrimē, see ācriter.

acervus, -ī, m., heap, pile. ii. 32.

Achillās, -ae, ['Αχιλλάς, 'Αχιλλεύς], m., Achillas (a-kil′ as), an official under the young King Ptolemy of Egypt in 49 B.C., one of the slayers of Pompey. C. III. 104.

aciēs, -ēī, f., edge; of the eye, keen look (i. 39); of an army, line of battle. line, army in battle array, battle.

acquīrō, -quīrere, -quīsīvī, -quīsītus, [ad + quaerō], 3, get in addition; gain further (vii. 59). [acquire.

ācriter, comp. ācrius, sup. ācerrimē, [ācer], adv., sharply, fiercely, with vigor, courageously. cum ācriter resisterētur, when a vigorous resistance was offered (v, 30).

āctuārius, -a, -um, [agō], adj., easily driven, swift. nāvis āctuāria, swift vessel, driven by oars as well as sails. v. 1. [actuary.

āctus, see agō.

Acūtius, -ī, m., Acutius Rufus (a-kū′ sh(y)ŭs rū′ fŭs), a partizan of Pompey. C. III. 83.

acūtus, -a, -um, comp. -ior, sup. -issimus, [part. of acuō, sharpen], adj., sharpened, sharp. [acute.

ad, prep. with acc., to, towards, up to; of place, in the vicinity of, at, near to, by, in the presence of, among, on; of time, till, to, up to, until; of purpose, especially with the gerundive constr., for, in order to, for the purpose of, in; of other relations, with regard to, according to, in respect to, in consequence of, as to, in; with words of number, with adverbial force, about. ad hunc modum, after this manner. ad ūnum, to a man. ad exercitum manēre, to remain with the army (v. 53). ad virtūtem, in respect to valor. (C. II. 6).

adāctus, see adigō.

adaequō, -āre, -āvī, -ātus, [ad + aequō], 1, make equal to, bring up to a level with (III. 12); be equal to, keep up with (i. 48), keep abreast of (v. 8). [adequate.

adamō, -āre, -āvī, -ātus, [ad + amō], 1, *conceive a love for, covet,* i. 31.

Adbucillus, -ī, m., (ad-bū-sil′ us), an Allobrogian, father of Roucillus and Egus. C. III. 59.

addō, -dere, -dĭdī, -ditus, [ad + dō], 3, *add, join to; lay on* (vii. 23). [add.

addūcō, -dūcere, -dūxī, -ductus, [ad + dūcō], 3, *lead to, bring, bring up* to a place; *lead, draw; induce, prevail upon.* [adduce.

adēmptus, see adimō.

adeō, -īre, -iī, -itum est, [ad + eō], irr., *go to, come near, draw near, approach; reach, visit.*

adeō, [ad + eō, from is], adv., *so far, to such a degree; so, so much.*

adeptus, see adipīscor.

adequitō, -āre, -āvī, [ad + equitō, from eques], 1, *ride towards; ride up to* (i. 46).

adhaerēscō, -haerēscere, -haesī, [ad + haerēscō], 3, *stick, adhere; remain clinging* (v. 48).

adhibeō, -hibēre, -hibuī, -hibitus, [ad + habeō], 2, *hold toward; bring forward, bring in, call in, summon, admit; use, employ.*

adhortor, -ārī, -ātus, [ad + hortor], 1, dep., *encourage, rally, exhort, rouse, urge.*

adhūc, [ad + hūc], adv., *hitherto, until now, as yet.* iii. 22.

adiaceō, -iacēre, -iacuī, [ad + iaceō], 2, *lie near, border upon, be adjacent.* vi. 33. [adjacent.

Adiatunnus, -ī, m., (ā′′ dĭ-a-tun′ us), a leader of the Sotiates. iii. 22.

adiciō, -icere, -iēcī, -iectus, [ad + iaciō], 3, *throw to, hurl; throw up; join to, add.*

adigō, -igere, -ēgī, -āctus, [ad + agō], 3, *drive* (*to*), *drive in; of*
missiles, *cast, hurl* (*to*); *of piles, drive home* (iv. 17); *of a tower, move up* (v. 43); *of an oath, bind* (vii. 67, C. I. 76).

adimō, -imere, -ēmī, -ēmptus, [ad + emō], 3, *take away* (v. 6, C. I. 7); *cut off* (vii. 81).

adipīscor, -ipīscī, -eptus, [ad + apīscor, *reach*], 3, dep., *gain, obtain, secure.* v. 39. [adept.

aditus, -ūs, [adeō], m., *approach, access; way of approach, means of access;* pl. *landing-places* (IV. 20).

adiūdicō, -āre, -āvī, -ātus, [ad + iūdicō], 1, *award* by judicial decision, *adjudge.* VII. 37. [adjudicate.

adiungō, -iungere, -iūnxī, -iūnctus, [ad + iungō], 3, *join to, attach; add, unite with; annex.* [adjunct.

adiūtor, -ōris, [adiuvō], m., *helper, confederate* (v. 38); *mediator* (v. 41).

adiuvō, -iuvāre, -iūvī, adiūtus, [ad + iuvō], 1, *help, assist, support; render assistance, be of assistance.* [adjuvant.

Admagetobriga, -ae, f., (ad′′ mă-je-tob′ rĭ-ga), a place in Gaul. i. 31.

administer, -trī, [ad + minister], m., *assistant, helper; officiating priest* (VI. 16).

administrō, -āre, -āvī, -ātus, [ad + ministrō], 1, *render assistance; manage, carry on, administer; arrange for, get ready; of orders, execute, carry out.* [administer.

admīror, -ārī, -ātus, [ad + mīror], 1, dep., *wonder at, be surprised at; admire.* [admire.

admisceō, -ēre, admiscuī, admixtus, [a + misceō], 2, *mingle with, mix with.* C. III. 48. [admix.

admittō, -mittere, -mīsī, -missus, [ad + mittō], 3, *let go; admit, receive; become guilty of, commit; incur* (IV. 25, C. III. 64). **facinus admittere** *to commit a crime.* **ad-**

missīs equīs, *with their horses at top speed*, lit. *let go* (C. II. 34). [admit.

admodum, [ad + acc. of modus], adv., lit. *up to the measure; quite, very;* with numbers, *fully, at least.*

admoneō, -ēre, -uī, -itus, [ad + moneō], 2, *warn.* [admonish.

admonitus, -ūs, [admoneō], m., *suggestion, advice.* C. III. 92.

adnō, -nāre, [ad + nō, *swim*], 1, *swim to.* C. II. 44.

adolēscō, -olēscere, -olēvī, -ultus, [ad + olēscō, *grow*], 3, *grow up, reach maturity.* vi. 18. [adolescent.

adorior, -orīrī, -ortus, [ad + orior], 4, dep., *fall upon, attack, assail.*

adortus, pf. part. of **adorior,** *having attacked, attacking.*

adsum, -esse, affuī, [ad + sum], irr., *be at hand, be present; assist, help* (vii. 62).

adulēscēns, -entis, [adolēscō], adj., *young.* As noun, m., *young man, youth.*

adulēscentia, -ae, [adulēscēns], f., *youth.* i. 20 ; C. II. 38. [adolescence.

adulēscentulus, -ī, [dim. of adulēscēns], m., *very young man, stripling.* iii. 21.

adventus, -ūs, [adveniō], m., *coming, approach, arrival.* [advent.

adversārius, -a, -um, [adversor], adj., *opposed.* As noun, adversārius, -ī, m., *opponent, enemy.* [adversary.

adversus, -a, -um, sup. -issimus, [part. of advertō], adj., *turned towards, fronting, in front, facing, opposite; unfavorable, adverse, unsuccessful.* adversō flūmine, *up the stream* (vii. 60). in adversum ōs, *full in the face* (v. 35). rēs adversae, *misfortune, disasters* (vii. 30). [adverse.

adversus, [advertō], prep. with acc. only, *opposite to ; against* (iv. 14).

advertō, -tere, -tī, -sus, [ad + vertō], 3, *turn to, direct.* animum advertō, *notice, observe.* [advert.

advocō, -āre, -āvī, -ātus, [ad + vocō], 1, *call.* vii. 52. [advocate.

advolō, -āre, -āvī, [ad + volō, *fly*], 1, *fly to ; hasten to, rush upon.*

aedificium, -ī, [aedificō], n., *building.* [edifice.

aedificō, -āre, -āvī, -ātus, [aedēs, *building,* + FAC, in faciō], 1, *build, construct.*

Aeduus, -a, -um, adj., *Aeduan.* As noun, Aeduus, -ī, m., *an Aeduan ;* pl., *Aeduans, the Aedui,* (ed'ū-ī or ej' u-ī), a Gallic people, between the upper waters of the Sequana (*Seine*) and the Liger (*Loire*), in alliance with the Romans before Caesar's arrival in Gaul and prominent throughout the Gallic War.

aeger, -gra, -grum, adj., *sick.* As noun, aegrī, -ōrum, m., pl., *the sick* (v. 40, C. III. 75).

aegerrimē, see aegrē.

aegrē, comp. aegrius, sup. aegerrimē, [aeger], adv., *with difficulty, scarcely, hardly.* aegerrimē, *with the greatest difficulty* (i. 13).

Aegyptus, -ī, [Αἴγυπτος], f., *Egypt.* C. III. 104.

Aemilius, -ī, m., *Lucius Aemilius* (ę-mil' į-ųs), a decurion in charge of a squad of Gallic cavalry. i. 23.

aequāliter, [aequālis, *equal*], adv., *evenly, uniformly.* ii. 18.

aequinoctium, -ī, [aequus + nox], n., *equinox.* iv. 36; v. 23. [equinox.

aequitās, -tātis, [aequus], f., *evenness; justness, fairness.* animī aequitās, *contentment* (vi. 22). [equity.

aequō, -āre, -āvī, -ātus, [aequus], 1, *equalize, make equal.* [equate.

aequus, -a, -um, comp. **aequior,** sup. **aequissimus,** adj., *level, even, flat; fair, just, equitable; like, equal; favorable, advantageous.* **aequō animō,** *with tranquil mind, without anxiety.*

aerāria, -ae, [aerārius, *of copper*], f., *copper mine.* iii. 21.

aerārium, -ī, [aerārius, *of copper*], n., *the public treasury* in Rome, *the treasury.* C. I. 6.

aerātus, -a, -um, [aes, through *aerō, -āre], adj., *sheathed with copper* or *bronze.* C. II. 3.

aes, aeris, n., *copper; bronze,* an alloy of copper and tin; *money.* **aes aliēnum,** (lit., *another's money*), *debt* (vi. 13).

aestās, -tātis, f., *warm season, summer.*

aestimātiō, -ōnis, [aestimō], f., *valuation, appraisement.* [estimation.

aestimō, -āre, -āvī, -ātus, [aes], 1, *value, appraise, estimate; regard, consider.* [estimate.

aestīvus, -a, -um, [aestās], adj., *of summer.*

aestuārium, -ī, [aestus], n., *place overflowed at high tide, (salt) marsh.* ii. 28; iii. 9. [estuary.

aestus, -ūs, m., *heat; tide.*

aetās, -tātis, f., *age, time of life; old age.* **aetāte cōnfectus,** *advanced in years.* **puerīlis aetās,** *age of childhood.* **per aetātem,** *by reason of age.*

aeternus, -a, -um, [for *aeviternus, from aevum], adj., *everlasting, perpetual.* vii. 77. [eternal.

Aetōlia, -ae, [Αἰτωλία], f., (ē-tō'li-a), a province of Greece, south of Epirus. C. III. 61.

afferō, -ferre, attulī, allātus, [ad + ferō], irr., *bring, convey, deliver; bring forward, allege; produce, cause, occasion.* [afferent.

afficiō, -ficere, -fēcī, -fectus, [ad + faciō], 3, *do something to, treat, use; visit with, afflict, trouble, weaken, impair; treat* with kindness, *place under obligation* (i. 35; vii. 37); *visit* with punishment (I. 27); *fill* with joy (v. 48). [affect.

affīgō, -fīgere, -fīxī, -fīxus, [ad + fīgō], 3, *fasten to.* iii. 14. [affix.

affingō, -fingere, -finxī, -fictus, [ad + fingō], 3, *fashion;* of a report, *embellish* (vii. 1).

affīnitās, -tātis, [affīnis, from ad + fīnis], f., *relationship* by marriage, *kinship, connection.* [affinity.

affīrmātiō, -ōnis, [affīrmō], f., *assurance.* vii. 30. [affirmation.

affīxus, see **affīgō.**

afflīctō, -āre, -āvī, -ātus, [freq. of afflīgō], 1, *shatter, damage* (iv. 29); *strand, wreck* (iii. 12).

afflīgō, -flīgere, -flīxī, -flīctus, [ad + flīgō, *strike*], 3, *dash against; throw down, knock down; shatter, damage.* [afflict.

affore (= **affutūrus esse**), future infinitive of **adsum.**

Āfrānius, -ī, m., *Lucius Afranius,* (a-frā' ni-ŭs), a lieutenant of Pompey defeated by Caesar in Spain in 49 B.C. C. III. 83, 88.

Āfrica, -ae, f., (af' ri-ka), the Roman province of Africa. C. II. 37.

Āfricus, -a, -um, [Āfrica], adj., *of Africa.* As noun, **Āfricus, -ī,** m. (originally sc. **ventus**), *southwest wind* (v. 8).

āfuisse, āfutūrus, see **absum.**

Agedincum, -ī, n., (aj-e-ding' kŭm), chief city of the Senones, now *Sens.*

ager, agrī, m., *land* under cultivation, *field, territory, domain;* pl. *lands, territory, country, the country.*

agger, -geris, [aggerō, ad + gerō], m., *that which is brought to* a place, *material for an embankment, filling* of earth and timber; *earth; embankment, mound, dike; rampart.* aggerem exstruere, *to build a rampart* (vii. 72). multō aggere, *with much earth* (vii. 23).

aggredior, -gredī, -gressus, [ad + gradior, *walk, go*], 3, dep., *approach; go against, attack, fall upon.* [aggressive.

aggregō, -āre, -āvī, -ātus, [ad + gregō, from grex, *flock*], 1, *bring together, join.* sē aggregāre, *to place one's self with* (iv. 26), *to join one's self to* (vi. 12). [aggregate.

agitō, -āre, -āvī, -ātus, [freq. of agō], 1, *drive onward, impel; stir up, discuss* (vii. 2). [agitate.

agmen, -minis, [agō], n., *army on the march, marching column; line of march.* agmen claudere, *to bring up the rear* (I. 25, II. 19). novissimum agmen, *the rear.* prīmum agmen, *the van.* in agmine, *on the march* (iii. 24, VII. 66).

agnōscō, -ere, agnōvī, [ad + gnōscō], 3, *recognize.* C. II. 6.

agō, agere, ēgī, āctus, 3, *set in motion, drive, move forward; direct, conduct, guide; incite, urge; press forward, chase, pursue; drive off* as plunder, *rob; do, act, transact, perform; manage, carry on, accomplish; treat, discuss, confer, plead with;* of time, *spend, pass, live;* of court, *hold;* of sheds and towers, *bring up.* grātiās agere, *to thank.* [act.

alacer, -cris, -cre, comp. alacrior, adj., *lively; eager, in high spirits.*

alacritās, -tātis, [alacer], f., *liveliness; enthusiasm.* [alacrity.

ālārius, -a, -um, [āla, *wing*], adj., *of the wing.* As noun, alāriī, -ōrum, m., pl., *auxiliary troops* posted on the wings, *wing-men.*

Albicī, -ōrum, m., pl., (al′ bi̯-sī), a

small warlike people living north of Massilia. C. II. 6.

albus, -a, -um, adj., *white.* plumbum album, *tin* (v. 12). [album.

alcēs, -is, f., *moose,* European *elk.* vi. 27.

Alesia, -ae, f., (a̯-lē′ sh[y]a̯ *or* a̯-lē′ zh [y]a̯), chief city of the Mandubians, now *Alise-Sainte-Reine.* vii. 68-90.

Alexandrīa, -ae, [Ἀλεξάνδρεια], f., (al-eg-zan′ dri̯-a̯), capital of Egypt. C. III. 103, 104.

ali-, the form of alius in composition.

aliās, [alius], adv., *at another time.* aliās . . . aliās, *at one time . . . at another, sometimes . . . sometimes, now . . . now.* [alias.

aliēnō, -āre, -āvī, -ātus, [aliēnus], 1, *alienate, estrange.* aliēnātā mente, *deprived of reason* (vi. 41) [alienate.

aliēnus, -a, -um, [alius], adj., *belonging to another, another's; strange, foreign; unsuitable, unfavorable, disadvantageous.* As noun, aliēnissimī, -ōrum, sup., m., pl., *entire strangers* (vi. 31). [alien.

aliō, [alius], adv., *to another place, elsewhere.* vi. 22.

aliquamdiū, [aliquī, diū], adv., *for some time, for a while.*

aliquandō, [alī- + quandō], adv., *at some time or other, sometime; at length* (vii. 27, 77).

aliquantus, -a, -um, [ali- + quantus], adj., *some, considerable.* Neut., aliquantum, as noun, *a little, somewhat.* aliquantum itineris, *some distance* (v. 10).

aliquī, aliqua, aliquod, [ali- + quī], indefinite pronominal adj., *some, any, some other.*

aliquis (rarely aliquī), aliqua, aliquid, nom. and acc. pl., n., aliqua, [ali- + quis], indefinite pron., *some one, any one, anybody;* pl., *some, any*

Neut., aliquid, *something, somewhat, anything.* aliquid calamitātis, *some disaster* (v. 29).

aliquot [ali- + quot], num. adj., indecl., *some, several.*

aliter, [alis, alius], adv., *otherwise, differently.* aliter ac, *otherwise than, different from what.*

alius, -a, -ud, dat. aliī, adj., *another, some other, other, different, else,* alius . . . alius, *one . . . another, the one . . . the other ;* pl., aliī . . . aliī, *some . . . other ;* often as noun, alius, *another,* aliī, *others.* longē alius atque, *very different from.*

allātus, see afferō.

allicīō, -licere, -lexī, [ad + laciō *entice*], 3, *attract, allure.*

Figure 192. — Coin of the Allobroges.

Silver. Reverse, horned animal galloping; underneath, a wheel.

Allobrogēs, -um, (acc. Allobrogas, i. 14, vii. 64), m., pl., (a-lob′rō-jēz), a Gallic people in the northeastern part of the Province. Acc. sing., Allobrogem, *an Allobrogian* (C. III. 84). Fig. 192.

alō, alere, aluī, altus, 3, *nourish, increase ; maintain, keep ; rear, foster, raise.*

Alpēs, -ium, 3, f., pl., *Alps,* general term for the mountains separating Cisalpine Gaul from Transalpine Gaul and Germany.

alter, -era, -erum, gen. alterīus or alterius, adj., often with the force of a noun, *one of two, the other, another ; second.* alter . . . alter,

the one . . . the other. **alterī** . . . alterī, *the one division, the one party . . . the other.* [alter.

alternus, -a, -um, [alter], adj., *in turn, alternate.* vii. 23. [alternate.

alteruter, -tra, -trum, pronominal adj., *either of two.* C. III. 90.

altitūdō, -inis, [altus], f., *height, depth ;* of a beam, *thickness* (iii. 13). [altitude.

altus, -a, -um, comp. -ior, sup. -issimus, [part. of alō], adj., *high, deep.* As noun, altum, -ī, n., *the deep, the open sea.*

alūta, -ae, f., *soft leather.* iii. 13.

am-, see ambi-.

ambactus, -ī, m., *vassal, dependant.* vi. 15.

Ambarrī, -ōrum, m., pl., (am-bar′rī), a people east of the Arar (*Saône*), near its junction with the Rhone. i. 11, 14.

ambi-, **amb-**, **am-**, **an-**, prep. found only in composition, *round about, around.*

Ambiānī, -ōrum, m., pl., (am-bi-ā′nī), a small state in Belgic Gaul. Fig. 193.

Figure 193. — Coin of the Ambiani.

Gold. Crude imitation of a Greek coin with a head of Hercules and a four-horse chariot. Underneath the chariot, imitation of the Greek name, "Of Philip."

Ambibariī, -ōrum, m., pl. (am-bi-bā′rī-ī), a small state on the northwest coast of Gaul. vii. 75.

Ambiliatī, -ōrum, m., pl., (am″bi-li′a-tī), a small state in Central Gaul. iii. 9.

Ambiorīx, -īgis, m., (am-bī′ o̧-ri̧ks), a leader of the Eburones, who destroyed the Roman force under Sabinus and Cotta, and inspired the attack on Cicero's camp.

Ambivaretī, -ōrum, m., pl., (am-bi̧-var′ ȩ-tī), a people in Central Gaul, clients of the Aeduans.

Ambivaritī, -ōrum, m., pl. (am-bi̧-var′i̧-tī), a small state in Belgic Gaul. IV. 9.

ambō, -ae, -ō, [cf. **ambi-**], adj., often used as noun, *both*. v. 44, C. II. 6.

āmentia, -ae, [**āmēns**, from **ā** + **mēns**], f., *madness, folly*.

āmmentum, -ī, n., *thong, strap*, for hurling a dart. v. 48.

amīcitia, -ae, [**amīcus**], f., *friendship;* of a state, *friendship, alliance*.

amīcus, -a, -um, comp. -ior, sup. -issimus, [**amō**], adj., *friendly, faithful, well-disposed*. [amicable.

amīcus, -ī, [**amō**], m., *friend, ally*.

āmittō, -mittere, -mīsī, -missus, [**ā** + **mittō**], 3, *send away; let go, let slip, lose*.

amor, -ōris, [**amō**], m., *affection, love*.

amplificō, -āre, -āvī, -ātus, [**amplus** + **faciō**], I, *make large, increase, extend*. [amplify.

amplitūdō, -inis, [**amplus**], f., *breadth, size; greatness, dignity*. [amplitude.

amplius, [comp. of **amplē**, from **amplus**], sup. **amplissimē**, adv., *more, further*.

amplus, -a, -um, comp. -ior, sup. -issimus, adj., *large* in extent, *great, extensive; distinguished, splendid, noble, prominent*. As noun, **amplius**, comp., n., *more*. **amplius obsidum**, *more hostages* (vi. 9). [ample.

an, inter. conj., *or, or rather, or indeed*. **-ne ... an**, or **utrum ... an**, *whether . . . or*.

an-, see **ambi-**.

Anartēs, -ium, m., pl., (an-är′ tēz), a tribe on the Tibiscus (*Theiss*), in Dacia (*Hungary*).

Ancalitēs, -um, m., pl., (an-cal′ i̧-tēz), a British tribe. v. 21.

anceps, -cipitis, [**an-** + **CAP** in **caput**], adj., *two-headed, twofold, double*. **anceps proelium**, *battle on two fronts*.

ancora, -ae, [ἄγκυρα], f., *anchor*. **in ancorīs**, *at anchor*. [anchor.

Andecumborius, -ī, m., (an′′ dȩ-co̧m-bō′ ri̧-u̧s), a leader among the Remi.

Andēs, -ium, or **Andī**, -ōrum, m., pl., (an′ dēz, or an′ dī), a Gallic people north of the Liger (*Loire*).

ānfrāctus, -ūs, [**an-**, cf. **frangō**], m., *curve* in a path or road, *bend, turn*. vii. 46.

angulus, -ī, m., *corner*. v. 13. [angle.

angustē, comp. -ius, sup. -issimē, [**angustus**], adv., *closely, in close quarters; scantily, sparingly*.

angustiae, -arum, [**angustus**], f., pl., *narrow place, narrow part, defile, narrowness; straits, difficulties, perplexity; scarcity*.

angustus, -a, -um, comp. -ior, sup. -issimus, [cf. **angō**, *squeeze*], adj., *contracted, narrow, close*. Neut. as noun, **angustum**, -ī, *crisis* (ii. 25).

anima, -ae, f., *breath; soul, life* (vi. 14). [animate.

animadversiō, -ōnis, [**animadvertō**], f., *consideration; punishment* (C. III. 60). [animadversion.

animadvertō, -tere, -tī, -sus, [**animus** + **advertō**], 3, *turn the mind to, attend to; notice, observe, perceive*. **in eum animadvertō**, *inflict punishment upon him*, as we say "attend to him." I. 19. [animadvert.

animal, -ālis, [anima], n., *living being, animal.* vi. 17, 19. [animal.

animus, -i, m., *soul, mind, consciousness; disposition, feelings; courage, spirit, temper, resolution.* **esse in animō,** *to intend.* [animus.

annōtinus, -a, -um, [annus], adj., *of the year before, last year's.* v. 8.

annus, -ī, m., *year.* [annual.

annuus, -a, -um, [annus], adj., *of a year, yearly, annual.* i. 16. [annuity.

ānser, -eris, m., *goose.* v. 12.

ante, adv. and prep. :

(1) As adv., *in front; before, previously.* **ante quam,** *before.* **paulō ante,** *a little while before, a short time previously.* **paucīs ante diēbus,** *a few days before.*

(2) As prep. with acc., *before, in front of, in advance of.*

anteā, [ante + eā], adv., *previously, before, formerly.*

antecēdō, -cēdere, -cessī, [ante + cēdō], 3, *go in advance, outstrip; anticipate* (C. III. 6); *surpass, excel.* [antecedent.

antecursor, -ōris, [antecurrō], m., lit., *fore-runner;* pl., *advance guard, vanguard* (v. 47).

anteferō, -ferre, -tulī, -lātus, [ante + ferō], irr., *carry in front; place before, prefer* (v. 44).

antemna, -ae, f., *sail-yard.* [antennae.

antepōnō, -pōnere, -posuī, -positus, [ante + pōnō], 3, *place before; prefer, value above* (iv. 22).

antesignānus, -ī, [ante signum], m., *one in front of a standard;* pl., **antesignānī**, -ōrum, *soldiers before the standards* (C. III. 84).

antevertō, -tere, -tī, [ante + vertō], 3, *place before, take precedence.*

antīquitus [antīquus], adv., *in former times, long ago, anciently.*

antīquus, -a, -um, comp. -ior, sup. -issimus, [ante], adj., *old, former, old-time, ancient.* [antique.

Antistius, -ī, m., *Gaius Antistius Reginus* (an-tis' tĭ-ŭs rḗ-jī' nŭs), a lieutenant of Caesar.

Antōnius, -ī, m., *Marcus Antonius,* (mär' kŭs an-to' nĭ-ŭs), *Mark Antony* (born 83, died 30 B.C.), a lieutenant of Caesar in Gaul in 52 and 51 B.C., and afterwards in the Civil War ; member of the Second Triumvirate, and rival of Octavianus. vii. 81; C. III. 89.

aperiō, -perīre, -peruī, -pertus, 4, *open, uncover.* vii. 22. [aperient.

apertē, -ius, -issimē, [apertus], adv., *openly, clearly, manifestly.*

apertus, -a, -um, comp. -ior, sup. -issimus, [part. of aperiō], adj., *open, uncovered ; exposed, unprotected.* **loca aperta,** *open country.* **latus apertum,** *open flank, exposed flank.*

Apollō, -inis, m., (a-pol' ō), a divinity worshiped by the Greeks and Romans, identified by Caesar with a Gallic deity. vi. 17.

Apollōnia, -ae, ['Απολλωνία], f., (ap-ọ-lō' nĭ-a), a city in the Roman province of Macedonia, near the Adriatic Sea, about fifty miles south of Dyrrachium. C. III. 75.

apparō, -āre, -āvī, -ātus, [ad + parō], 1, *prepare, make ready, get ready.* [apparatus.

appellō, -pellere, -pulī, -pulsus, [ad + pellō], 3, *drive to, bring in ;* of ships, *make for, put in, land.*

appellō, -āre, -āvī, -ātus, 1, *address, accost, call to, appeal to ; call by name, name.* [appellate.

appetō, -petere, -petīvī, or -iī, -petītus, [ad + petō], 3, *strive after, seek; approach, draw near.* [appetite.

Appius, -ī, m., (ap' ĭ-ŭs), a Roman
first name.

applicō, -plicāre, -plicāvī or -plicuī,
-plicātus, [ad + plicō], *fold, join.*
sē applicāre ad, *to lean against*
(vi. 27). [applicant.

apportō, -āre, -āvī, -ātus, [ad +
portō], I, *carry to, bring.* v. I.

approbō, -āre, -āvī, -ātus, [ad +
probō], I, *approve, favor.* [approve.

appropinquō, -āre, -āvī, -ātum est,
[ad + propinquō], I, *approach,
come near, draw near.*

appulsus, see appellō.

Apr., = Aprīlis. i. 6.

Aprīlis, -e, adj., *of April.*

aptus, -a, -um, comp. -ior, sup. -issi-
mus, adj., *fitted, adapted, suited;
suitable, appropriate, ready.* [apt.

apud, prep. with acc. only, *at, with,
near, close to, by; among, in the
presence of.*

aqua, -ae, f., *water.* [aqueous.

aquātiō, -ōnis, [aquor], f., *obtaining
water.* iv. II.

aquila, -ae, f., *eagle;* as an eagle of
silver or gold on the end of a pole
formed the chief ensign of the legion,
eagle, standard. [aquiline.

Aquileia, -ae, f., (ak-wĭ-lē' yą), a city
at the head of the Adriatic Sea. I. 10.

aquilifer, -erī, [aquila + ferō], m.,
bearer of the eagle, eagle-bearer.

Aquītānia, -ae, f., (ak-wĭ-tā' nĭ-ą),
one of the three main divisions of
Gaul.

Aquītānus, -a, -um, adj., *of Aquitania.* As noun, Aquītānus, -ī,
m., *Aquitanian* (iv. 12); pl., *Aquitanians, Aquitani,* (ak-wĭ-tā' nī),
inhabitants of Aquitania. i. I; iii.
21.

aquor, -ārī, -ātus, [aqua], I, dep.,
obtain water, get water. C. III. 97.

Arar, -aris, acc. -im, m., *Arar* (ā' rạr)
River, now *Saône* (sōn). It rises in

the Vosges (vōzh) Mts., and flows
southward into the Rhone.

arbiter, -trī, m., *witness; referee,
commissioner* (v. I). [arbiter.

arbitrium, -ī, [arbiter], n., *decision,
arbitrament; authority.*

arbitror, -ārī, -ātus, [arbiter], I,
dep., *think, consider, believe.* [arbi-
trate.

arbor, -oris, f., *tree.* [arbor-vitae.

arcessō, -sere, -sīvī, -sītus, 3, *cause
to come, fetch; send for, summon,
call in, invite.*

ārdeō, -ēre, ārsī, ārsūrus, 2, *be on
fire; be ablaze, be aroused; be eager,
desire ardently.* [ardent.

Arduenna, -ae, f., (är-dū-en' ną), *the
Ardennes,* a forest-covered range of
hills in the northeastern part of
France, extending also into Belgium.

arduus, -a, -um, adj., *steep, high;
hard, difficult.* [arduous.

Arecomicī, -ōrum, m., pl., (ar-ę-
kom' ĭ-sī), a division of the Volcae,
in the Province.

Arelās, -ātis, f., (är' ę-lạs), a town in
Southern Gaul, on the Rhone, north
of Massilia; now *Arles.* C. II. 5.

Aremoricus, -a, -um, [Celtic, a r ē =
ad, + mori, = mare, ' by the s e a'],
adj., *Aremorican,* name applied to a
group of small states along the
northwest coast of Gaul (**Aremoricae cīvitātēs**).

argentum, -ī, n., *silver* (vi. 28); *sil-
ver-ware* (vii. 47 ; C. III. 96). [ar-
gent.

argilla, -ae, f., *clay.* v. 43. [argilla-
ceous.

āridus, -a, -um, sup. -issimus, [āreō,
be dry], adj., *dry.* As noun, āridum, -ī, n., *dry land, shore.* [arid.

ariēs, -ietis, m., *ram; battering-ram;
prop, buttress* (iv. 17). [Aries.

Arīminum, -ī, n., (ą-rim' ĭ-nųm), a
town in Italy on the Adriatic, the

northernmost city in Italy proper; now *Rimini.* C. 1. 8.

Ariovistus, -ī, m., (ā'' rĭ-ọ-vis' tụs), a German king, defeated by Caesar, 58 B.C.

Aristius, -ī, m., *Marcus Aristius,* (ạ-ris' tĭ-ụs), a military tribune. vii. 42, 43.

arma, -ōrum, n., pl., *implements; implements of war, arms, armor, weapons;* of a ship, *equipment, tackle* (iii. 14). **ad arma concurrere,** *to rush to arms.* [arms.

armāmenta, -ōrum, [armō], n., pl., *implements; equipment;* of a ship, *rigging.* [armament.

armātūra, -ae, [armō], f., *armor, equipment.* **levis armātūrae pedĭtēs,** *light infantry.* **levis armātūrae Numidae,** *light-armed Numidians* (ii. 10). [armature.

armātus, -a, -um, sup. **armātissimus,** [part. of **armō**], adj., *armed, in arms, equipped.* As noun, **armātī,** -ōrum, m., pl., *armed men, warriors, soldiers.*

armō, -āre, -āvī, -ātus, [arma], 1, *provide with weapons, arm;* of a ship, *equip, fit out.* [arm.

Arpineius, -ī, m., *Gaius Arpineius,* (är-pĭ- nē' yụs), a Roman knight, envoy of Caesar to Ambiorix. v. 27, 28.

arripiō, -ripere, -ripuī, -reptus, [ad + rapiō], 3, *lay hold of, snatch.* v. 33.

arroganter, comp. -ius, [arrogāns], adv., *presumptuously, arrogantly.*

arrogantia, -ae, [arrogāns], f., *presumption, insolence.* [arrogance.

ars, artis, f., *skill; art, science* (vi. 17). [art.

artē, comp. artius, sup. artissimē, [artus], adv., *closely, tightly.*

articulus, -ī, [dim. of artus, *joint*], m., *joint, knuckle.* vi. 27. [article.

artificium, -ī, [artifex, *artist*], n., *an art, trade; skill; craft, cunning.* [artifice.

artus, -a, um, comp. -ior, sup. **artissimus,** adj., *close;* of woods, *dense* (vii. 18).

Arvernus, -a, -um, adj., *of the Arverni, Arvernian.* As noun, **Arvernī,** -ōrum, m., pl., *Arvernians, the Averni,* (är -vėr' nĭ), a powerful people about the upper part of the Elaver (*Allier*); their chief city, Gergovia, was unsuccessfully besieged by Caesar. Fig. 194.

Figure 194. — Arvernian coin.

Gold. Obverse, Apollo. Reverse, two-horse chariot, copied from a coin of Philip, father of Alexander the Great ; Greek name, "Of Philip," misspelled.

arx, arcis, f., *citadel, stronghold.*

ascendō, -scendere, -scendī, -scēnsus, [ad + scandō, *climb*], 3, *ascend, climb up ; mount.* [ascend.

ascēnsus, -ūs, [ascendō], m., *ascent, climbing ; approach.*

ascīscō, asciscere, ascīvī, ascītus, [ad + scīscō, *approve*], 3, *admit* to association with one's self, *accept.*

Asia, -ae, ['Ασία], f., the Roman province *Asia,* (ā' sh[y]ạ, *or* ā' zh[y]ạ), including Phrygia, Lydia, Caria, and Mysia in Asia Minor. C. III. 53.

aspectus, -ūs, [aspiciō, *look at*], m., *appearance, sight, look.* [aspect.

asper, -era, -erum, comp. -ior, sup. -rimus, adj., *rough, uneven ; fierce, violent* (v. 45).

assiduus, -a, -um, [ad + SED, SID, in sedeō, *sit*], adj.,*continuous,constant, incessant.* [assiduous.

assistō, -ere, astitī, [ad + sistō], 3, *stand near, stand by; appear* (vi. 18). [assist.

assuēfaciō, -facere, -fēcī, -factus, [assuētus + faciō], 3, *accustom, habituate, familiarize, train.*

assuēscō, -suēscere, -suēvī, -suētus, [ad + suēscō, *become accustomed*], 3, *become accustomed to.* **assuēscere ad hominēs,** *to become domesticated* (VI. 28).

at, conj., *but, yet, but yet, at least.*

atque, ac, [ad + -que], conj. :
   (1) Copulative, *and, and also, and even, and in particular.*
   (2) Comparative, after words of likeness or unlikeness, *as, than.* **idem atque, par atque,** *the same as.*

Atrebās, -ātis, m., *an Atrebatian;* pl., *Atrebatians, the Atrebates,* (at-re̜-bā′ tēz), a Belgic people.

Ātrius, -ī, m., *Quintus Atrius* (ā′tri̜us), an officer in Caesar's army. v. 9, 10.

attenuō, -āre, -āvī, -ātus, [ad + tenuō from tenuis], 1, *make thin; weaken, reduce in strength* (C. III. 89). [attenuate.

attexō, -ere, -texuī, attextus, [ad + texō], 3, *weave to, join on.* v. 40.

Attiānus, -a, -um, [Attius], adj., *of Attius,* referring to P. Attius Varus. C. II. 34.

attingō, -tingere, -tigī, -tāctus, [ad + tangō], 3, *touch upon, touch; reach;* of territorial divisions, *border on, extend to, adjoin.*

Attius, -ī, m., *P. Attius Varus* (at′ i̜-us vā′ rus), a lieutenant of Pompey in Africa. C. II. 34.

attribuō, -uere, -uī, -ūtus, [ad + tribuō], 3, *assign, allot.* [attribute.

attulī, see afferō.

Atuatuca, -ae, f., (at-ū̜-at′ ū̜-ka̜), a stronghold in the territory of the Eburones.

Atuatucī, -ōrum, m., pl., (at-ū̜-at′ ū̜-sī), a warlike people on the left bank of the Meuse, descended from the Cimbrians and Teutons.

auctor, -ōris, [augeō], m., *originator, instigator; adviser, promoter, favorer.* [author.

auctōritās, -tātis, [auctor], f., *influence, weight; prestige, authority, power.* [authority.

auctus, -a, -um, comp. **auctior,** [augeō], adj.,*increased; rich.* i. 43.

audācia, -ae, [audāx], f., *boldness, daring, recklessness.* [audacity.

audācter, comp. **audācius,** sup. **audācissimē,** [audāx], adv., *boldly, courageously, fearlessly.*

audeō, audēre, ausus sum, 2, semidep., *venture, dare, risk; attempt.*

audiō, -īre, -īvī or **-iī, -ītus,** 4, *hear, listen to; hear of.* Present participle as Adj. in **dictō audiēns esse,** *to be obedient to the word of command, to obey.* [audience.

audītiō, -ōnis, [audiō], f., *report, rumor, hearsay.* [audition.

augeō, augēre, auxī, auctus, 2, semi-dep., *increase, enlarge, augment, add to.*

Aulercus, -ī, m., *an Aulercan* (vii. 57); pl., *the Aulerci* (â-lèr′ sī), a people of Central Gaul, of which Caesar mentions three branches, **Brannovīcēs** (vii. 75), **Cēnomanī** (vii. 75), and **Eburovīcēs** (iii. 17, vii. 75).

Aulus, -ī, m., (â′ lus), a Roman first name.

aureus, -a, -um, [aurum], adj., *of gold, golden.* v. 12. [oriole.

aurīga, -ae, [aurea, *bridle,* + agō], m., *charioteer, driver.* iv. 33.

auris, -is, f., *ear*. [aural.

Aurunculeius, -i, m., *Lucius Aurunculeius Cotta*, (â'' ṛung-kū-lē' yụs
kot' ạ), a lieutenant of Caesar, killed
by the Eburones.

Auscī, -ōrum, m., pl., (â' sī), a people
in the eastern part of Aquitania.
iii. 27.

ausus, see audeō.

aut, conj., *or*.   **aut** . . . **aut**, *either
. . . or*.   **aut** . . . **aut** . . . **aut**,
either . . . or . . . or.

autem, conj., *but, however, on the
contrary ; and now, moreover*.

autumnus, -ī, m., *autumn*. [autumn.

auxiliāris, -e, [auxilium], adj., *auxiliary*.   As noun, **auxiliārēs**,
-ium, m., pl., *auxiliary troops,
auxiliaries* (iii. 25).   [auxiliar.

auxilior, -ārī, -ātus, [auxilium], 1,
dep., *render aid, assist, help*.

auxilium, -ī, [cf. augeō], n., *help,
aid, assistance ; relief, remedy, resource*.   Pl., **auxilia**, *auxiliary
troops, auxiliaries, allied forces*.

Avaricēnsis, -e, adj., *of Avaricum,
at Avaricum*.   VII. 47.

Avaricum, -ī, n., (ạ-var' ị-kụm), largest and most strongly fortified city of
the Bituriges, now *Bourges;* besieged
and taken by Caesar, the inhabitants
put to the sword.

avāritia, -ae, [avārus, *greedy*], f.,
greed, covetousness.   [avarice.

āvehō, -vehere, -vexī -vectus,
[ā + vehō], 3, *carry off, carry
away*.

āversus, -a, -um, sup. āversissimus,
[part of āvertō], adj., *turned away ;
behind, in the rear*.   [averse.

āvertō, -tere, -tī, -sus, [ā + vertō],
3, *turn away, turn aside, avert ;
divert, alienate, estrange*.   [avert.

avis, -is, f., *bird*.   iv. 10.   [aviation.

avus, -ī, m., *grandfather*.

Axona, -ae, f., (aks' ọ-nạ), a river in

the southern part of Belgic Gaul,
now *Aisne*.

B

Bacēnis, -is, (sc. silva), f., (bạ-
sē' nịs), a forest in Germany.   vi. 10.

Baculus, -ī, m., *Publius Sextius Baculus*, (bac' ū-lụs), one of the bravest
of Caesar's centurions.   He distinguished himself in the battle with the
Nervians (II. 25) ; his advice saved
the day when Galba was attacked in
the Alps (III. 5) ; and his heroic resistance checked a surprise attack on
Cicero's camp (VI. 38).

Bagradās, or **Bagrada**, -ae, m.,
(bag' rạ-dạs), an important river of
Roman Africa, now *Medjerda*.   C.
II. 38.

Baleārēs, -ium, [= βαλιαρεὶς, *slingers*], m., pl., (bạl-ẹ-ā'rēz), natives of
the Balearic Islands, off the east coast
of Spain; famous as slingers.   ii. 7.

balteus, -ī, m., *belt, sword-belt*.

Balventius, -ī, m., *Titus Balventius*,
(bạl-ven' sh[y]-ụs), a brave centurion.   v. 35.

barbarus, -a, -um, [= βάρβαρος], adj.,
*foreign, strange ; rude, savage, un-
civilized*.   As noun, **barbarī**, -ōrum,
m., pl., *strangers, foreigners ; natives, barbarians*.   [barbarous.

Basilus, -ī, m., *Lucius Minucius Basilus*, (mị-nū' sh[y]ụs bas' ị-lụs), an
officer of Caesar, afterwards one of
the conspirators against him ; murdered in 43 B.C. on account of cruelty
to his slaves.

Batāvī, -ōrum, m., pl., *the Batavians,
Batavi*, (bạ-tā' vī), a people dwelling
near the mouth of the Rhine.   iv.
10.

Belgae, -ārum, m., pl., *the Belgians,
Belgae*, (bel' jē), inhabitants of one
of the three main divisions of Gaul,
divided into many small states.

Belgium, -ī, n., (bel′j[y]ụm), *the land of the Belgians, Belgic Gaul, Belgium.* v. 12, 25. [Belgium.

bellicōsus, -a, -um, comp. -ior, sup. -issimus, [bellicus], adj., *warlike, fond of war.* i. 10. [bellicose.

bellicus, -a, -um, [bellum], adj., *of war, martial, military.* vi. 24.

bellō, -āre, -āvī, -ātus, [bellum], 1, *wage war, carry on war, fight.*

Bellovacī, -ōrum, m., pl., (be̥-lov′-ḁ-sī), a powerful Belgic people.

bellum, -ī, n., *war, warfare.* **bellum gerere**, *to wage war.* **bellum īnferre**, *to make war.* **bellum parāre**, *to prepare for war.*

bene, comp. **melius**, sup. **optimē**, [bonus], adv., *well, ably, successfully.*

beneficiārius, -ī, [beneficiārius, -a, -um, from beneficium], m., *privileged soldier,* who, by order of the commander, was exempt from ordinary tasks and detailed for special duties (C. III. 88). [beneficiary.

beneficium, -ī, [bene + faciō], n., *kindness, favor, service.* [benefice.

benevolentia, -ae, [benevolus], f., *good will, friendly disposition, kindly feeling, friendship.* [benevolence.

Bibracte, -is, n., [bi̥-brak′tē], capital of the Aeduans, situated on a mountain now called *Mont Beuvray* (height, 2,690 ft.).

Bibrax, -actis, f., (bī′brḁks), a town of the Remi, north of the Axona (*Aisne*). ii. 6.

Bibrocī, -ōrum, m., pl., (bib′rọ-sī), a people in the southern part of Britain. v. 21.

bīduum, -ī, [bi-, = bis, cf. diēs], n., *space of two days, two days.*

biennium, -ī, [bi-, = bis, cf. annus], n., *period of two years, two years' time.* i. 3. [biennial.

Bigerriōnēs, -ōnum, m., pl., (bī″jer-

ri̥-ō′nēz), a people in Aquitania iii. 27.

bīnī, -ae, -a, [bis], distributive adj., *two by two, two each, by twos, two.*

bipedālis, -e, [bi-, = bis, + pedālis, from pēs], adj., *two feet* in width, length, or height; *two feet thick* (iv. 17).

bipertītō, [bipartītus, bi-, = bis, + partītus], adv., *in two divisions.* i. 25; v. 32. [cf. bipertite.

bis, [for duis, cf. duo], num. adv., *twice.*

Biturīgēs, -um, m., pl., (bit-ụ-rī′jēz), a people in Central Gaul (Fig. 195).

Figure 195. — A coin of the Bituriges.

Electrum, gold alloyed with silver.
Obverse, head of crude but bold design.
Reverse, above the horse, a bird; underneath, a three-leaf ornament. This coin may possibly belong to the Pictones.

Boduognātus, -ī, m., (bod″ ụ-ọg-nā′tụs), a leader of the Nervians. ii. 23.

Boiī, -ōrum, m., pl., *Boians, Boii* (bō′i̥-ī), a Celtic people once widely dif-

Figure 196. — Coin of the Boians.

Silver, struck in Cisalpine Gaul.
Obverse, a laurel wreath encircles the head.
Reverse, the horseman wears a crown.

fused over Central Europe (Fig.
196).

bonitās, -tātis, [bonus], f., *goodness,
excellence;* of land, *fertility* (i. 28).

bonus, -a, -um, comp. melior, sup.
optimus, adj., *good, advantageous;
pleasant, well-disposed, friendly.* As
noun, bonum, n., *profit, advantage;*
pl., bona, -ōrum, *goods, property,
possessions.* [bonus; optimist.

bōs, bovis, gen. pl. boum, m. and f.,
ox, bull, cow. [bovine.

bracchium, -ī, [= βραχίων], n., *arm,
forearm.*

Brannovīcēs, -um, (bran-ọ-vī′ sēz),
m., pl., see Aulercī.

Brātuspantium, -ī, n., (brat-ụs-pan′
sh[y]ụm), a stronghold of the Bellovaci. ii. 13.

brevis, -e, comp. -ior, sup. -issimus,
adj., *short, brief.* [brief.

brevitās, -tātis, [brevis], f., *shortness* (ii. 20); *smallness, small stature*
(ii. 30). [brevity.

breviter, comp. -ius, sup. -īssimē,
[brevis], adv., *briefly, with few
words, concisely.* vii. 54.

Britannī, -ōrum, m., pl., *natives of
Britain, Britons.*

Britannia, -ae, f., (brị-tan′ ị-ạ), *Britain.*

Britannicus, -a, -um, adj., *of Britain, British.* v. 4.

brūma, -ae, [for *brevuma, sup.
of brevis, sc. diēs], f., *winter solstice, shortest day; winter* (v. 13).

Brundisium, -ī, [βρεντάσιον], n.,
(brụn-dizh′ ị-ụm), a city of Italy on
the Adriatic, the principal port of
embarcation for Greece ; now *Brin-
disi.* C. iii. 87.

Brūtus, -ī, m., *Decimus Junius Brutus
Albinus*, (jūn′ yụs brū′tụs al-bī′ nus),
an officer of Caesar, both in the Gallic
and in the Civil War ; afterwards a
conspirator against him.

būcinātor, -ōris, [būcina, *trumpet*],
m., *trumpeter.* C. ii. 35.

C

C, in expressions of number, = 100.

C., see Gāius.

Cabūrus, -ī, m., *Gaius Valerius
Caburus*, (vạ-lē′ rị-ụs kạ-bū′ rụs), a
Gaul who received the Roman citi-
zenship.

cacūmen, -inis, n., *end, point* (vii.
73); *peak, summit.* [cacuminous.

cadāver, -eris, [cf. cadō], n., *corpse,
dead body.* [cadaver.

cadō, cadere, cecidī, cāsūrus, 3,
fall; be slain, die. [chance.

Cadūrcī, -ōrum, m., pl., (kạ-dėr′
sī), a people in Aquitania. Sing.
Cadūrcus, -ī, m., *a cadurcan* (vii.
5).

caedēs, -is, [caedō], f., *killing;
slaughter, murder, massacre.*

caedō, caedere, cecīdī, caesus, 3,
cut, cut down; cut to pieces, slay.

caelestis, -e, [caelum], adj., *heavenly.* As noun, caelestēs, -ium,
m., pl., *the gods* (vi. 17). [celestial.

caelum, -ī, n., *heaven, the heavens, the
sky.* C. ii. 5.

caerimōnia, -ae, f., *religious cere-
mony, sacred rite.* vii. 2. [cere-
mony.

Caerōsī, -ōrum, m., pl., (sẹ-rō′ sī),
a people in Belgic Gaul. ii. 4.

caeruleus, -a, -um, adj., *deep blue,
dark blue.* v. 14. [cerulean.

Caesar, -aris, m. :

  (1) *Gaius Julius Caesar* (gā′yụs
jūl′ yụs sē′ zạr).

  (2) *Lucius Julius Caesar*, consul
in 64 b.c., a distant relative of the
great Caesar, under whom he served
as lieutenant, in 52 b.c. vii. 65.

caespes, -itis, m., *sod, turf.*

calamitās, -tātis, f., *loss, damage;
disaster, defeat.* [calamity.

Caletī, -ōrum, also **Caletēs**, -um, m., pl., (kal′ ẹ-tì, kal′ ẹ-tēz), a people near the mouth of the Sequana (*Seine*).

callidus, -a, -um, comp. -ior, sup. -issimus, [**calleō**, *be skillful*], adj., *skillful ; tactful, crafty* (iii. 18).

cālō, -ōnis, m., *soldier's servant, camp servant.*

campester, -tris, -tre, [**campus**], adj., *of level ground, flat, level.*

campus, -ī, m., *plain.* [campus.

Camulogenus, -ī, m., (kam-ū-loj′ ẹ-nụs), an Aulercan, commander of the Parisii against Labienus.

Canīnius, -ī, m., *Gaius Caninius Rebilus*, (kạ-nin′ ị-ụs reb′ ị-lụs), a lieutenant of Caesar's in the latter part of the Gallic War, and in the Civil War ; made consul by Caesar for a few hours to fill a vacancy on the last day of December, B.C. 45. vii. 83, 90 ; C. II. 34.

canō, **canere**, **cecinī**, 3, *sing ;* of a musical instrument, *sound, play.*

Cantabrī, -ōrum, m., pl., *Cantabrians, Cantabri* (kan′ tạ-brī), a warlike people in northern Spain.

Cantium, -ī, n., *Kent, Cantium,* (kan-sh[y] ụm), a district in the southeast part of England.

capillus, -ī, [cf. **caput**], m., *hair of the head, hair.* [capillary.

capiō, **capere**, **cēpī**, **captus**, 3, *take, get ; seize, capture ; occupy, take possession of ; select, win over, charm, captivate ; receive ;* of vessels, *reach, make ; deceive* (i, 40). **initium capere**, *to begin.* **cōnsilium capere**, *to form a plan.* **dolōrem capere**, *to be grieved.* [capture.

Capitōlium, -ī, n., *the Capitol,* the temple of Jupiter, Juno, and Minerva on the Capitoline hill in Rome ; sometimes referring to the hill as a whole, *the Capitoline hill.* C. I. 6. [Capitol.

capra, -ae, [**caper**], f., *she-goat.*

captīvus, -a, -um, [cf. **capiō**], adj., *taken prisoner, captured* (C. II. 5). As noun, **captīvus**, -ī, m., *captive, prisoner* (vi. 43). [captive.

captus, -a, -um, see **capiō**.

captus, -ūs, [**capiō**], m., *capacity ; understanding, notion* (iv. 3).

Capua, -ae, f., (kap′ ū-ạ), a city in Italy, in Campania. C. III. 71.

caput, -itis, n., *head ;* by metonymy, *person, man, life, safety ;* of a river, *mouth* (IV. 10). **capitis poena**, *capital punishment* (vii. 71). **duo milia capitum**, *two thousand souls.* [capital.

Carcasō, -ōnis, f., (kär′ kạ-sō), a town in southern Gaul, now *Carcassonne* (III. 20).

careō, -ēre, -uī, -itūrus, 2, *be without, lack, want.* vi. 38 ; vii. 17.

carīna, -ae, f., *keel of a ship.*

Carnutēs, -um, m., pl., (kär′ nụ-tēz), a people in Central Gaul, north of the Liger (*Loire*) ; chief city, Cenabum (Fig. 197).

Figure 197. — Coin of the Carnutes.

Bronze. Obverse, head of Hercules ; inscription [A]CUSSROS.

Reverse, boar.

Copied from a Roman coin, except the name.

carō, **carnis**, f., *flesh, meat.* [carnage.

carpō, -ere, -sī, -tus, 3, *pluck ; censure, criticise* (iii. 17). [carp.

carrus, -ī, m., *cart, wagon.* [car.

cārus, -a, -um, comp. -ior, sup. **carissimus**, adj., *dear, precious.*

Carvilius, -ī, m., (kạr-vil′ ị-ụs), one of four British rulers in Kent. v. 22.

casa, -ae, f., *hut, cottage, barrack.*

cāseus, -ī, m., *cheese.* vi. 22.

Cassī, -ōrum, m., pl., (kas′ ī) a tribe in Britain. v. 21.

Cassiānus, -a, -um, [Cassius], adj., *of Cassius.* i. 13.

cassis, -idis, f., *helmet* of metal.

Cassius, -ī, m., *Lucius Cassius Longinus*, (kash′ [y]ụs lọn-jī′ nụs), praetor 111 B.C.; when consul, 107 B.C., he engaged in battle with the Tigurians in the territory of the Allobroges, and was defeated and slain. i. 7, 12.

Cassivellaunus, -ī, m., *Cassivellaunus* (kas″ ị-vẹ-lä′ nụs), *Caswallon*, leader of the British army against Caesar in 54 B.C.

castellum, -ī, [dim. of castrum], n., *redoubt, fortress, stronghold.* [castle.

Casticus, -ī, m., (kas′ tị-kụs), a prominent Sequanian. i. 3.

castīgō, -āre, -āvī, -ātus, I, *reprove.* C. III. 60. [castigate.

castra, -ōrum, n., [pl. of castrum, *fortress*], *camp, encampment; military service* (I. 39); *day's march* (VII. 36). **castra movēre**, *to break camp.* **castra pōnere**, *to encamp, camp.* [-chester *in* Ro-chester, etc.

cāsus, -ūs, [cadō], m., *fall; chance, occurrence, happening, fortune; opportunity, event; accident, mishap, evil plight, death.* **cāsū**, *by chance.* [case.

Catamantāloedis, -is, m., (kat-ạ-man-tạ-lē′ dịs), a leader among the Sequanians before Caesar's time. i. 3.

catēnae, -ārum, f., pl., *chains; fetters.*

Caturīgēs, -um, m., pl., (kat-ū-rī′ jēz), a Gallic people in the eastern part of the Province. i. 10.

Catuvolcus, -ī, m., (kat-ū-vol′ kụs), a ruler of the Eburones; despairing of success in the war against Caesar, he took poison. v. 24, 26 ; vi. 31.

causa, -ae, f., *cause, ground, reason; pretext, excuse; condition, state, case, suit.* **causā**, with gen., *for the sake of, on account of.* [cause.

cautē, comp. -ius, sup. -issimē, [cautus, from caveō], adv., *cautiously, carefully.* v. 49.

cautēs, -is, f., *jagged rock, cliff.* iii. 13.

Cavarillus, -ī, m., (kav-ạ-ril′ ụs), an Aeduan of high rank. vii. 67.

Cavarīnus, -ī, m., (kav-ạ-rī′ nụs), a ruler among the Senones. v. 54; vi. 5.

caveō, **cavēre**, **cāvī**, **cautūrus**, 2, *be on one's guard, beware of, take precaution; give security.* [cautious.

Cavillōnum, -ī, n., (kav-ị-lō′ nụm), an Aeduan city on the Arar, now *Châlon-sur-Saône.* VII. 42, 90.

Cebenna, -ae, f., *Cebenna* (sẹ-ben′ ạ), *the Cévennes*, a mountain range in southern Gaul, about 250 miles long.

cēdō, **cēdere**, **cessī**, **cessūrus**, 3, *go away, depart, withdraw, retreat; yield, give up to; abandon.* [cede.

celer, -eris, -ere, comp. -ior, sup. celerrimus, adj., *quick, speedy.*

celeritās, -tātis, [celer], f., *speed, quickness, swiftness, rapidity, despatch.* [celerity.

celeriter, comp. celerius, sup. celerrimē, [celer], adv., *quickly, speedily, at once, immediately.*

cēlō, -āre, -āvī, -ātus, I, *conceal, hide, keep secret.* ii. 32; vii. 80.

Celtae, -ārum, m., pl., *Celts, Celtae* (sel′ tē), inhabitants of central Gaul, divided into many states.

Celtillus, -ī, m., (sẹl-til′ ụs), an Arvernian ruler, father of Vercingetorix. vii. 4.

Cēnabēnsēs, -ium, [Cēnabum], m., pl., *the inhabitants of Cenabum.*

Cēnabum, -ī, n., (sen′ a̤-bṳm), chief city of the Carnutes, later called *Aurelianensis Urbs*, whence comes *Orléans*, name of the city on the site of Cenabum.

Cēnimagnī, -ōrum, m., pl., (sen-i̤-mag′ nī), a British people. v. 21.

Cēnomanī,-ōrum, (se̤-nom′ a̤-nī), see **Aulercī**.

cēnseō, -ēre, -uī, -us, 2, *estimate; think, hold, judge; decree, resolve upon, determine; vote for, favor.*

cēnsus, -ūs, [cēnseō], m., *count, enumeration.* i. 29. [census.

centum, or C, indeclinable num. adj., *hundred.* [cent. *in* per cent.

centuriō, -ōnis, [centuria], m., *centurion.* [centurion.

cernō, **cernere**, **crēvī**, 3, *separate; distinguish, discern, see, perceive.*

certāmen, -inis, [certō], n., *contest, rivalry* (v. 44); *struggle, battle, engagement* (iii. 14).

certē, comp. **certius**, [certus], adv., affirmative, *certainly, surely* (vi. 31); restrictive, *at least, at any rate* (IV. 25, V. 29, VII. 50).

certus, -a, -um, comp. -ior, sup. -issimus, [part. of **cernō**], adj., *certain, fixed, definite; positive, undoubted, trustworthy, true.* **certiōrem facere**, *to inform.* **certior fierī**, *to be informed.* Neut. as noun, **certī quid esset**, *what was really going on* (vii. 45); **prō certō**, *as a certainty, as certain* (vii. 5). [certain.

cervus, -ī, m., *stag* (vi. 26); in military language, *stag's horns*, a device for hindering the approach of an enemy (vii. 72). [cervine.

cēterus, -a, -um, nom. sing. m. not in use, adj., *other, the other, the rest, remainder;* pl., *the rest, all the others, the other.* As noun, **cēterī**,

-ōrum, m., pl., *the others, all the rest, every one else;* **cētera**, -ōrum, n., pl., *the rest, all else, everything else.*

Ceutronēs, -um, m., pl. (sū′ tro̤-nēz):
   (1) A Belgic people, subject to the Nervians. v. 39.
   (2) A people in the eastern part of the Province. v. 10.

chara, -ae, f., *chara*, a plant the tuberous roots of which were used by Caesar's soldiers for food. C. III. 48.

Cheruscī, -ōrum, m., pl., (ke̤-rus′ ī), a German people north of the Suebi. vi. 10.

cibāria, -ōrum, [cibārius, from **cibus**], n., pl., *provisions, rations.*

cibus, -ī, m., *food, nourishment.*

Cicerō, -ōnis, m., *Quintus Tullius Cicero* (tul′ i̤-ṳs sis′ e̤-rō), brother of Marcus Tullius Cicero, the orator, born about 102 B.C. He became a lieutenant of Caesar in Gaul in 55, and made a heroic defence of his camp in 54; he held aloof from Caesar in the Civil War, but was reconciled with him in 47; he was put to death by order of the triumvirs in 43 B.C.

Ciliciēnsis, -e, [Cilicia], adj., *Cilician, of Cilicia,* a province in the southern part of Asia Minor.

Cimberius, -ī, m., (si̤m-bē′ ri̤-ṳs), a leader of the Suebi. i. 37.

Cimbrī, -ōrum, m., pl., *Cimbrians, Cimbri* (sim′ brī), a Germanic people that joined with the Teutones in the invasion of Gaul.

Cingetorīx, -īgis, m., (si̤n-jet′ o̤-ri̤ks):
   (1) Rival of Indutiomarus for the headship of the Treverans, and loyal to Caesar. v. 3, 4, 56, 57; vi. 8.
   (2) A British ruler. v. 22.

cingō, **cingere**, **cīnxī**, **cīnctus**, 3, *surround, encircle; invest.* [cincture.

cippus, -ī, m., *stake, post.* vii. 73.

circinus, -ī, [= κίρκινος], m., *pair of compasses.* i. 38.

circiter, [**circus**, *circle*], adv. and prep.:
  (1) As adv., *about, not far from, near.*
  (2) As prep., with acc. only, *about* (i. 50).

circuitus, -ūs, [**circumeō**], m., *a going around; detour, circuit, winding path, way around.* [circuit.

circum, [acc. of **circus**, *circle*], adv. and prep.:
  (1) As adv., *about, around.*
  (2) As prep. with acc., *around, about; in the neighborhood of, near, near by.*

circumcīdō, -cīdere, -cīdī, -cīsus, [**circum** + **caedō**], 3, *cut around, cut.* v. 42.

circumcīsus, -a, -um, [part. of **circumcīdō**], adj., *cut off; steep, precipitous.* vii. 36.

circumclūdō, -dere, -sī, -sus, [**circum** + **claudō**], 3, *encircle.* vi. 28.

circumdō, -dare, -dedī, -datus, [**circum** + **dō**, *place*], 1, *place around, encompass, surround, encircle.*

circumdūcō, -dūcere, -dūxī, -ductus, [**circum** + **dūcō**], 3, *lead around; trace* (i. 38). [circumduct.

circumeō, -īre, -iī, -itus, [**circum** + **eō**], irr., *go around, pass around; surround, encircle; go about, visit for inspection* (v. 2).

circumfundō, -fundere, -fūdī, -fūsus, [**circum** + **fundō**], 3, *pour around; surround, hem in;* pass. often used reflexively, *spread (themselves) around, crowd around.*

circumiciō, -icere, -iēcī, -iectus, [**circum** + **iaciō**], 3, *throw around, place around.* ii. 6.

circummittō, -mittere, -mīsī, -mis-sus, [**circum** + **mittō**], 3, *send around.* v. 51 ; vii. 63.

circummūniō, -īre, -īvī, -ītus, [**circum** + **mūniō**], 4, *surround with walls, fortify; hem in* (ii. 30).

circumplector, -plectī, 3, dep., *embrace, encompass, surround.* vii. 83.

circumsistō, -sistere, -stetī or -stitī, [**circum** + **sistō**], 3, *stand around, surround, take a position around.*

circumspiciō, -icere, -exī, -ectus, [**circum** + **speciō**, *look*], 3, *look about, survey; ponder, consider; look about for, look over* (v. 31). [circumspect.

circumvāllō, -āre, -āvī, -ātus, [**circum** + **vāllō**], 1, *surround with a rampart, blockade, inves'.*

circumvehor, -vehī, -vectus, [**circum** + **vehō**], 3, pass. as dep., *ride around* (vii. 45); *sail around.*

circumveniō, -venīre, -vēnī, -ventus, [**circum** + **veniō**], 4, *come around, go around; surround, encompass; ensnare, overreach, deceive.* [circumvent.

cis, prep. with acc., *on this side of.*

Cisalpīnus, -a, -um, [**cis** + **Alpīnus**], adj., *Cisalpine, on this* (the Italian) *side of the Alps.* [Cisalpine.

Cisrhēnānus, -a, -um, [**cis** + **Rhēnānus**], adj., *on this side* (the west side) *of the Rhine.* vi. 2.

Cita, (sī' ta), see **Fūflus.**

citātus, -a, -um, comp. -ior, sup. -issimus, [**citō**], adj., *rapid.* iv. 10.

citerior, -us, [**citer**, from **cis**], comp. adj., *on this side, hither, nearer.*

citō, -āre, -āvī, -ātus, [freq. of **ciëō**, *set in motion*], 1, *urge on.* C. III. 96. [cite.

cito, comp. **citius**, sup. **citissimē**, [**citus**], adv., *speedily.* **citissimē**, *with the utmost rapidity* (iv. 33).

citrā, [citer, from cis], prep. with acc. only, *on this side of.*

citrō, [citer, from cis], adv., *hither.* ultrō citrōque, *to and fro, back and forth* (i. 42).

cīvis, -is, m. and f., *citizen, fellow-citizen.* [civil.

cīvitās, -tātis, [cīvis], f., *body of citizens, state, nation; citizenship* (i. 47). [city.

clam, [cf. cēlō], adv., *secretly.*

clāmitō, -āre, -āvī, -ātus, [freq. of clāmō], I, *cry out loudly, shout.*

clāmor, -ōris, [cf. clāmō, *cry out*], m., *outcry, shout, din.* [clamor.

clandestīnus, -a, -um, [clam], adj., *secret, hidden.* vii. I, 64. [clandestine.

clārē, [clārus], adv., *loudly, distinctly.* C. iii. 94.

clārus, -a, -um, comp. -ior, sup. -issimus, adj., *clear, distinct;* of the voice, *loud* (v. 30); *famous.* [clear.

classicum, -ī, [classicus, -a, -um, from classis], n., *trumpet signal.* C. iii. 82.

classis, -is, f., *a class; a fleet.* [class.

Claudius, -ī, m., *Appius Claudius Pulcher,* (klâ' dĭ-ŭs pul' kẹr), brother of Clodius (see below); praetor in 57 B.C., and consul in 54. v. I.

claudō, claudere, clausī, clausus, 3, *shut, close.* [close.

clāvus, -ī, m., *nail, spike.* iii. 13.

clēmentia, -ae, [clēmēns], f., *forbearance, mercifulness.* [clemency.

Cleopātra, -ae, f., (klē-ọ-pā' trạ), sister of the young Egyptian king, Ptolemy, and afterwards queen of Egypt. C. iii. 103.

cliēns, -entis, m., *retainer, dependent, client, adherent.* [client.

clientēla, -ae, [cliēns], f., *relation of client to patron, clientship, vassalage;* pl., *following of clients* (vii. 32), *dependencies* (vi. 12). [clientele.

clīvus, -ī, m., *slope.* VII. 46.

Clōdius, -ī, m., (klō' dĭ-ŭs) :

(1) *Publius Clodius Pulcher,* the enemy of Cicero, who as tribune in 58 B.C. drove the orator into exile; he was killed in 52 B.C. VII. I.

(2) *Aulus Clodius,* a mutual friend of Caesar and of Scipio. C. iii. 90.

Cn., = Gnaeus (nē' ŭs), a Roman first name.

co-, see com-.

coacervō, -āre, -āvī, -ātus, [co- + acervō], I, *heap up, pile up.* ii. 27.

coāctus, pf. pass. part. of cōgō.

coāctus, -ūs, [cōgō], m., only abl. sing. in use, *compulsion.* v. 27.

coagmentō, -āre, -āvī, -ātus, [coagmentum, cf. cōgō], I, *fasten together.* vii. 23. [coagment.

coartō, -āre, -āvī, -ātus, [co- + artō, *make close*], I, *press together, crowd together.* vii. 70.

Cocosātēs, -um, m., pl., (kok-ọ-sā' tēz), a people in Aquitania. iii. 27.

coëmō, -emere, -ēmī, -ēmptus, [co- + emō], 3, *buy up, purchase.*

coëō, -īre, -īvī or -iī, -itum est, [co- + eō], irr., *come together, join together.* vi. 22.

coepī, -isse, coeptus, def., (present supplied by incipiō), *have begun, began.*

coërceō, -ercēre, -ercuī, -ercitus, [co- + arceō, *shut up*], 2, *confine; restrain, check* (i. 17; v. 7). [coerce.

cōgitō, -āre, -āvī, -ātus, [co- +, agitō], I, *think about, think; intend, purpose, plan.* [cogitate.

cognātiō, -ōnis, [cognātus], f., *blood-relationship; blood-relations, kindred.* [cognation.

cognōscō, -gnōscere, -gnōvī, cognitus, [co- + (g)nōscō], 3, *become acquainted with, learn, learn of, ascertain; be familiar with, know, recognize; spy out, examine; take cognizance of.* [cognizance.

cōgō, cōgere, coēgī, coāctus, [co-+agō], 3, *drive together, bring together, collect, gather, assemble; compel, force, oblige.* [cogent.

cohors, -hortis, f., *cohort, battalion,* the tenth part of a legion. [cohort.

cohortātiō, -ōnis, [cohortor], f., *encouraging, exhortation.* ii. 25.

cohortor, -ārī, -ātus, [co-+hortor], 1, dep., *encourage; urge, exhort; address* with encouraging words. [cohortative.

collabefīō, -fierī, -factus, [com-+labefīō, *be shaken loose*], pass., *be shattered.* C. II. 6.

collātus, see **cōnferō.**

collaudō, -āre, -āvī, -ātus, [com-+laudō], 1, *praise warmly, commend.*

colligō, -āre, -āvī, -ātus, [com-+ligō, *bind*], 1, *bind together, fasten together.* i. 25.

colligō, -ligere, -lēgī, -lēctus, [com-+legō, *gather*], 3, *gather together, collect, assemble; obtain, get.* **sē colligere,** *to gather themselves together; to form* in battle order (III. 19); *to recover themselves, rally.* [collect.

collis, -is, m., *hill, height, elevation.*

collocō, -āre, -āvī, -ātus, [com-+locō, *place*], 1, *place, set, post, station; set in order, arrange;* with or without **nūptum,** *give in marriage* (i. 18). [collocate.

colloquium, -i, [colloquor], n., *conference, interview.* [colloquy.

colloquor, -loquī, -locūtus, [com-+loquor], 3, dep., *talk with, hold a conference, hold a parley.*

colō, colere, coluī, cultus, 3, *cultivate, till* (iv. 1; v. 12); *honor, worship* (vi. 17).

colōnia, -ae, [colōnus], f., *colony, settlement.* vi. 24. [colony.

color, -ōris, m., *color.* [color.

com-, co-, prep., old form of **cum,** *with,* found only in composition; see **cum.**

combūrō, -ūrere, -ussī, -ustus, [com-+*būrō,=ūrō, *burn*], 3, *burn up, consume* by fire. i. 5. [combustion.

comes, -itis, [co-+eō], m. and f., *companion, comrade.* [count (title).

comitātus, -ūs, [comes], m., *retinue, company.* C. III. 61, 96. [county.

comitia, -ōrum, [sing. **comitium,** *meeting-place* for elections], n., pl., *elections* (vii. 67; C. III. 82).

comitor, -ārī, -ātus, [comes], 1, dep., *accompany, attend.* vi. 8.

commeātus, -ūs, [commeō], m., *passing to and fro, trip, voyage* (v. 23); *supplies, provisions,* often including grain, **frūmentum.**

commemorō, -āre, -āvī, -ātus, [com-+memorō], 1, *call to mind, recount, relate.* [commemorate.

commendō, -āre, -āvī, -ātus, [com-+mandō], 1, *commit* to one *for protection, entrust; ask favor for, commend.* [commend.

commentārius, -ī, [commentor], m., *note-book, source-book.* [commentary.

commeō, -āre, -āvī, -ātus, [com-+meō, *go*], 1, *go to and fro, visit, resort to.* i. 1; vii. 36.

commīlitō, -ōnis, [com-+mīlitō, from **mīles**], m., *fellow-soldier, comrade.*

comminus, [com-+manus], adv., *hand to hand, at close quarters.*

commissūra, -ae, [committō], f., *joint, seam, juncture.* vii. 72.

committō, -mittere, -mīsī, -missus, [com-+mittō], 3, *join, bring together, connect; entrust, commit; cause, do, perpetrate.* **committere proelium,** *to join battle, begin the engagement.* [commit.

Commius, -i, m., *Comm, Commius,*
(kom′ i-ṳs), an Atrebatian, loyal and
useful to Caesar (especially in the
British campaigns) till the uprising
in 52, when he became a commander
in the Gallic army raised for the
relief of Alesia.

commodē, comp. -ius, sup. -issimē,
[commodus], adv., *conveniently,
opportunely, to advantage; readily,
easily; fitly, suitably, properly.*

commodus, -a, -um, comp. -ior,
sup. -issimus, [com- + modus, i.e.
having full measure], adj., *convenient, advantageous, easy; good, favorable; suitable, fit.* As noun,
commodum, -ī, n., *convenience,
advantage, profit.* [commodious.

commonefaciō, -facere, -fēcī, -fac-
tus, [commoneō + faciō], 3, *remind; impress upon* one (i. 19).

commoror, -ārī, -ātus, [com- +
moror], 1, dep., *delay, linger.*

commoveō, -movēre, -mōvī, commōtus, [com- + moveō], 2, *disturb, disquiet, alarm; move, stir.*
[commotion.

commūnicō, -āre, -āvī, -ātus, [com-
mūnis], 1, *share together, share with,
divide with; communicate, impart;
consult with* (v. 36). [communicate.

commūniō, -īre, -īvī or -iī, -ītus,
[com- + mūniō], 4, *fortify on all
sides, strongly fortify, intrench.*

commūnis, -e, [com- + mūnus],
adj., *common, in common, general,
public; indiscriminate* (VI. 9).
commūnī cōnciliō, *in accordance
with the general plan, by common
consent.* **in commūnī conciliō,**
at a general council (ii. 4; vii. 15).
[common.

commūtātiō, -ōnis, [commūtō], f.,
complete change, alteration.

commūtō, -āre, -āvī, -ātus, [com-
+ mūtō], 1, *change, wholly change,*

alter; exchange (vi. 22). [com-
mute.

comparō, -āre, -āvī, -ātus, [com-
+ parō], 1, *prepare, make ready, get
together; acquire, secure; amass,*
(I. 18).

comparō, -āre, -āvī, -ātus, [com-
par, *like*], 1, *match, compare.*
[compare.

compellō, -pellere, -pulī, -pulsus,
[com- + pellō], 3, *drive together,
collect; drive, force.* [compel.

compendium, -ī, [com- + pendō],
n., *profit, gain.* vii. 43. [compend.

comperiō, -perīre, -perī, -pertus,
[com- + PER in *experior*], 4,
ascertain, learn, discover, find out.

complector, -plectī, -plexus, [com-
+ plectō, *braid*], 3, dep., *embrace,*
(i. 20); *surround, include, encompass* (vii. 72, 74). [complex.

compleō, -plēre, -plēvī, -plētus,
[com- + pleō, *fill*], 2, *fill up, fill;
complete, cover;* of troops, *fully
occupy, fill full.* [complete.

complexus, see **complector.**

complūrēs, -a, [com- + plūrēs,
from plūs], adj., pl., *several, a number of; many.* As noun, **complūrēs,** -ium, m., pl., *a great many,
quite a number, many.*

comportō, -āre, -āvī, -ātus, [com-
+ portō], 1, *bring in, carry, convey, bring over.* [comport.

comprehendō, -hendere, -hendī,
-hēnsus, [com- + prehendō], 3,
grasp; seize; arrest, capture; of
fire, *catch* (v. 43). [comprehend.

comprobō, -āre, -āvī, -ātus, [com-
+ probō], 1, *approve fully, justify.*

cōnātum, -ī, [n. of cōnātus, part. of
cōnor], n., *attempt, undertaking.*

cōnātus, -ūs, [cōnor], m., *attempt.*

cōnātus, pf. part. of **cōnor.**

concēdō, -cēdere, -cessī, -cessūrus,
[com- + cēdō], 3, *withdraw, de-*

part; give up, yield, cede; submit;
allow, grant; grant permission,
permit. [concede.

concelebrō, -āre, -āvī, -ātus,
[com- + celebrō], I, *frequent;*
publish abroad, make known. C. III.
72.

concessus, -ūs, [concēdō], m., *used*
only in abl. sing., permission, leave.

concidō, -cidere, -cidī, [com- +
cadō], 3, *fall down, fall; perish, be*
slain.

concīdō, -cīdere, -cīdī, -cīsus,
[com- + caedō], 3, *cut up, cut off;*
cut to pieces, kill, slay, destroy.

conciliō, -āre, -āvī, -ātus, [conci-
lium], I, *win over, reconcile; win,*
gain, procure. [conciliate.

concilium, -ī, n., *meeting, assembly.*
[council.

concinō, -ere, -uī, [com- + canō],
3, *sound together.* C. III. 92.

concitō, -āre, -āvī, -ātus, [com- +
citō], I, *rouse, stir up.*

conclāmō, -āre, -āvī, -ātus, [com-
+ clāmō, *shout*], I, *cry aloud to-*
gether, shout, cry out.

conclūsus, -a, -um, [conclūdō],
adj., *confined, shut in.* II!. 9.

Conconnetodumnus, -ī, m., (kọn-
kọn*ǁ* ẹ -tọ-dum*ʹ* nụs), *a chief of the*
Carnutes. vii. 3.

concrepō, -āre, -uī, -itus, [com- +
crepō, *rattle*], I, *rattle, clash.* vii.
21.

concurrō, -currere, -cucurrī or
-currī, -cursum est, [com- +
currō], 3, *run together, run up,*
rush; charge; gather; resort (VI.
13). [concur.

concursō, -āre, [freq. of concurrō],
I, *rush to and fro, run about.*

concursus, -ūs, [concurrō], m.,
running together; dashing together,
collision (v. 10; C. II. 6); *onset,*
charge (vi. 8; vii. 62). [concourse.

condemnō, -āre, -āvī, -ātus, [com-
+ damnō], I, *condemn, find guilty*
(of). vii. 19. [condemn.

condiciō, -ōnis, [com- + DIC, *de-*
clare], f., *condition, situation, state;*
terms, stipulation. [condition.

condōnō, -āre, -āvī, -ātus, [com-
+ dōnō], I, *give up, overlook,*
disregard, pardon. i. 20. [con-
done.

Condrūsī, -ōrum, m., pl. (kọn-drū*ʹ*
sī), *a Belgic people on the right bank*
of the Mosa (Meuse).

condūcō, -dūcere, -dūxī, -ductus,
[com- + dūcō], 3, *bring together,*
collect; hire. [conduce.

cōnfectus, see cōnficiō.

cōnferō, -ferre, -tulī, collātus,
[com- + ferō], irr., *bring together,*
gather, collect, convey; compare (i.
31); *ascribe, refer* (i. 40); *put off,*
postpone (i. 40). sē cōnferre, *to*
betake one's self, turn, proceed. [con-
fer.

cōnfertus, -a, -um, comp. -ior, sup.
-issimus, [part of cōnferciō], adj.,
crowded together, close, dense.

cōnfestim, adv., *immediately, at once,*
speedily.

cōnficiō, -ficere, -fēcī, -fectus,
[com- + faciō], 3, *do thoroughly,*
complete, finish, accomplish, do;
bring to an end, wear out, exhaust,
enfeeble; of troops, bring together,
furnish (ii. 4). [confectionery.

cōnfīdō, -fīdere, -fīsus sum, [com-
+ fīdō, *trust*], 3, semi-dep., *trust*
firmly, rely upon, have confidence
in; believe, be confident. [confide.

cōnfīgō, -fīgere, -fīxī, -fīxus, [com-
+ fīgō, *fasten*], 3, *fasten together,*
join. iii. 13.

cōnfīnis, -e, [com- + fīnis], adj.,
bordering on, adjoining. vi. 3.

cōnfīnium, -ī, [cōnfīnis], n., *boun-*
dary, frontier. v. 24. [confine.

cōnfīō, -fierī, [com- + fīō], irr., sometimes used instead of cōnficior, pass. of cōnficiō, *be accomplished, be done.* vii. 58.

cōnfīrmātiō, -ōnis, [cōnfīrmō], f., *assurance.* iii. 18. [confirmation.

cōnfīrmātus, -a, -um, [cōnfīrmō], adj., comp. cōnfīrmātior, *encouraged, confident.* C. iii. 84.

cōnfīrmō, -āre, -āvī, -ātus, [com-, cf. fīrmus], 1, *strengthen, confirm; arrange for, establish; reassure, encourage; assert, declare; assure.* [confirm.

cōnfīsus, -a, -um, see cōnfīdō.

cōnfiteor, -fitērī, -fessus, [com- + fateor, *confess*], 2, dep., *confess, acknowledge.* v. 27. [confess.

cōnfīxus, -a, -um, see cōnfīgō.

cōnflagrō, -āre, -āvī, -ātus, [com- + flagrō, *blaze*), 1, *be in flames, be on fire.* v. 43. [conflagration.

cōnflīctō, -āre, -āvī, -ātus, [freq. of cōnflīgō], 1, dep., *harass, assail.* v. 35. [conflict.

cōnflīgō, -flīgere, -flīxī, -flīctus, [com- + flīgō, *strike*], 3, *dash together; contend, fight.*

cōnfluēns, -entis, [cōnfluō], m., *flowing together* of two streams, *confluence.* iv. 15.

cōnfluō, -fluere, -flūxī, [com- + fluō], 3, *flow together; flock* (vii. 44). [confluent.

cōnfugiō, -fugere, -fūgī, [com- + fugiō], 3, *flee for refuge.* vi. 5.

cōnfundō, -fundere, -fūdī, -fūsus, [com- + fundō], 3, *pour together; mass together* (vii. 75). [confound.

congerō, -gerere, -gessī, -gestus, [com- + gerō], 3, *bring together, collect.* C. ii. 37.

congredior, -gredī, -gressus, [com- + gradior, *step*], 3, dep., *come together, meet, unite with; join battle, engage, contend.*

congressus, -a, -um, see congredior.

congressus, -ūs, [congredior], m., *meeting; encounter, engagement* (iii. 13). [congress.

conicio, -icere, -iēcī, -iectus, [com- + iaciō], 3, *throw together, hurl, cast; throw up, throw; place, put.* in fugam conicere, *to put to flight.*

coniectūra, -ae, [coniciō], f., *inference.* [conjecture.

coniūnctim, [coniungō], adv., *jointly, in common.*

coniūnctus, -a, -um, comp. -ior, sup. -issimus, [part of coniungō], adj., *connected; closely allied* (vii. 33). [conjunct.

coniungō, -iungere, -iūnxī, -iūnctus, [com- + iungō], 3, *join together, unite, join.* [conjoin.

coniūnx, coniugis, [coniungō], m. and f., *husband; wife, spouse* (vii. 14). [conjugal.

coniūrātiō, -ōnis, [coniūrō], f., *union bound by oath, league; conspiracy, plot.*

coniūrō, -āre, -āvī, -ātus, [com- + iūrō], 1, *take oath together* (vii. 1); *form a league, conspire, plot.* [conjure.

cōnor, -ārī, -ātus, 1, dep., *endeavor, attempt, undertake, try.* [conative.

conquiēscō, -ere, -quiēvī, -quiētūrus, [com- + quiēscō, *rest*], 3, *take complete rest, repose.* vii. 46.

conquīrō, -quīrere, -quīsīvī, -quīsītus, [com- + quaerō], 3, *seek out, hunt up; bring together, collect.*

conquīsītus, see conquīrō.

cōnsanguineus, -a, -um, [com- + sanguineus, from sanguis], adj., *of the same blood.* As noun, m., and f., *relative, kinsman;* pl., *kinsfolk, blood-relations.* [consanguineous.

cōnscendō, -scendere, -scendī, -scēnsus, [com- + scandō, *climb*],

3, *mount, ascend.* nāvēs cōnscendere, *to embark.*

cōnscientia, -ae, [cōnsciō], f.,
knowledge (v. 56); with animī,
moral sense, conscience (C. III. 60).
[conscience.

cōnscīscō,-scīscere,-scīvī,-scītus,
[com-+scīscō, *approve*], 3, *decree,
appoint; inflict, bring upon.* sibi
mortem cōnscīscere, *to commit
suicide* (i. 4; iii. 22).

cōnscius, -a, -um, [com-, cf. sciō],
adj., *conscious, aware* (*of*). [con-
scious.

cōnscrībō, -scrībere, -scrīpsī,
-scrīptus, [com-+ scrībō], 3,
write (v. 48); *enrol, levy, enlist.*
[conscript.

cōnscrīptus, see cōnscrībō.

cōnsecrātus, -a, -um, [part. of cōn-
secrō], adj., *holy, sacred.* [conse-
crate.

cōnsector,-ārī,-ātus,[cōnsequor],
I, dep., *follow up, pursue.*

cōnsecūtus, see cōnsequor.

cōnsēnsiō, -ōnis, [cōnsentiō], f.,
common feeling, agreement. vii.
76.

cōnsēnsus, -ūs, [cōnsentiō], m.,
*common feeling, agreement, under-
standing.* [consensus.

cōnsentiō,-sentīre,-sēnsī,-sēnsus,
[com-+ sentiō], 4; *agree; plot together, conspire.* [consent.

cōnsequor,-sequī,-secūtus,[com-
+ sequor], 3, dep., *follow after,
follow; pursue, overtake; obtain, secure, gain.* [consequence.

cōnservō, -āre, -āvī, -ātus, [com-
+ servō], I, *save, spare;* of laws
or rights, *observe, maintain.* [con-
serve.

cōnsīderātē, [cōnsīderātus, from
cōnsīderō], adv., *circumspectly.*
Comp. cōnsīderātius, *with unusual
caution* (C. III. 82).

Cōnsidius, -ī, m., *Publius Considius,*
(kon-sid'i-us), an officer in Caesar's
army.

cōnsīdō, -sīdere, -sēdī, -sessum,
[com- + sīdō, *sit*], 3,*sit down, seat
one's self; halt, encamp; take up an
abode, establish one's self, settle.*

cōnsilium, -ī, [cf. cōnsulō], n., *consultation, deliberation, counsel; gathering for deliberation, council; advice; decision, plan, design, scheme;
project, proposal; good judgment, pru-
dence, discretion.* cōnsilium inīre
or habēre, *to form a plan.* [coun-
sel.

cōnsimilis, -e, [com-+ similis],
adj., *very like, quite like.*

cōnsistō, -sistere, -stitī, [com-+
sistō, *set, place*], 3,*stand, stop, halt;
take a position, be posted, make a
stand; stay, remain; sojourn, settle;
consist* (*in*), *depend* (*on*). in orbem
cōnsistere, *to form a circle* (v. 33).
[consist.

cōnsobrīnus, -ī, [com-, cf. soror],
m., *cousin.* vii. 76. [cousin.

cōnsōlor,-ārī,-ātus,[com-+sōlor,
comfort], I, dep., *comfort, cheer, encourage.* [console.

cōnspectus, -ūs, [cōnspiciō], m.,
sight, view, presence. [conspectus.

cōnspiciō, -spicere, -spexī, -spec-
tus, [com-+ speciō, *look*], 3, *observe, behold, see, perceive.*

cōnspicor, -ārī, -ātus, I, dep., *catch
sight of, see, observe.*

cōnspīrō, -āre, -āvī, -ātus, [com-
+ spīrō, *breathe*], I, *agree; com-
bine, form a league, conspire* (iii.
10). [conspire.

cōnstanter, comp. -ius, sup. -issimē,
[cōnstāns],adv., *resolutely* (iii. 25);
uniformly, unanimously (ii. 2).

cōnstantia, -ae,[cōnstāns], f.,*firmness, resolution.* [constancy.

cōnsternō, -āre, -āvī, -ātus, I,

alarm, terrify. vii. 30. [conster-
nation.

cōnsternō, -sternere, -strāvī, -strā-
tus, [com- + sternō], 3, *strew over,
cover* (IV. 17); *strew, carpet* (C. III.
96).

cōnstīpō, -āre, -āvī, -ātus, [com-
+ stīpō, *press*], I, *crowd together,
crowd closely.* v. 43.

cōnstituō, -stituere, -stituī, -stitū-
tus, [com- + statuō], 3, *station,
place, draw up; bring to a halt, stop*
(vii. 47); *of ships, moor; appoint,
establish; resolve upon, determine,
decide, fix, settle.* [constitute.

cōnstō, -stāre, -stitī, -stātūrus,
[com- + stō], I, *stand firm; remain the same* (vii. 35); *remain, lie*
(vii. 21); *depend on* (vii. 84); *cost*
(vii. 19); *be made up of* (C. II. 36).
cōnstat, impers., *it is certain, well-
known, evident, it is clear.*

cōnsuēscō, -suēscere, -suēvī, -suē-
tus, [com- + suēscō, *become used*],
3, *form a habit, become accustomed,
be accustomed, be wont.*

cōnsuētūdō, -inis, [cōnsuēscō], f.,
*habit, practice, custom, usage; mode
of life* (v. 14, vi. 21); *practice in*
speaking a language (i. 47). **cōnsuētūdō vīctūs,** *standard of living*
(I. 31). [custom.

cōnsuētus, see cōnsuēscō.

cōnsul, -ulis, m., *consul,* one of the
two chief magistrates at Rome, chosen
annually. [consul.

cōnsulāris, -e, [cōnsul], adj., *consular.* C. I. 6. [consular.

cōnsulātus, -ūs, [cōnsul], m., *consulship.* i. 35. [consulate.

cōnsulō, -sulere, -suluī, -sultus, 3,
consult, deliberate, take counsel of;
with dat., *have regard for, look out
for.*

cōnsultō, [cōnsulō], adv., *on purpose, designedly, purposely.*

cōnsultō, -āre, -āvī, -ātus, [freq. of
cōnsulō], I, *deliberate, take counsel.*
v. 53; vii. 77. [consult.

cōnsultum, -ī, [cōnsultus, from
cōnsulō], n., *deliberation; resolution, decree, decision.*

cōnsūmō, -sūmere, -sūmpsī,
-sūmptus, [com- + sūmō], 3, *use
up, devour, eat up; waste, exhaust,
destroy;* of time, *spend, pass.* [con-
sume.

cōnsūmptus, see cōnsūmō.

cōnsurgō, -surgere, -surrēxī, con-
surrēctum est, [com- + surgō,
rise], 3, *rise together, arise, stand up.*

contabulō, -āre, -āvī, -ātus, [com-,
cf. tabula, *board*], I, *construct of
boards; build up in stories.* vii. 22.

contāgiō, -ōnis, [cf. contingō], f.,
contact. vi. 13. [contagion.

contāminō, -āre, -āvī, -ātus, [con-
tāmen, = contāgiō], I, *taint, pol-
lute.* vii. 43. [contaminate.

contegō, -tegere, -tēxī, -tēctus,
[com- + tegō], 3, *cover, cover up*
(vii. 85).

contemnō, -temnere, -tempsī,
-temptus, [com- + temnō, *despise*], I, *despise, hold in contempt.*
[contemn.

contemptiō, -ōnis, [cf. contemnō],
f., *a despising, contempt, scorn.*

contemptus, -ūs, [contemnō], m.,
scorn. [contempt.

contendō, -tendere, -tendī, -ten-
tus, [com- + tendō], 3, *put forth
effort, strive for, make effort, strive;
demand* (vii. 63, C. III. 97); *hasten,
make haste, push forward; struggle,
contend, vie; maintain, insist, protest* (vi. 37, 41, 43). [contend.

contentiō, -ōnis, [contendō], f.,
*effort; struggle, fight, contest; dis-
pute, controversy.* [contention.

contentus, -a, -um, [part. of con-
tineō], adj., *satisfied.* [content.

contexō, -texere, -texuī, -textus, [com- + texō, *weave*], 3, *weave together, weave; bind together, join, construct.* [context.

continēns, -entis, [part. of contineō], adj., *adjoining; continuous, unbroken, consecutive.* continentī impetū, *without pausing* (vii. 28). As noun, (originally sc. terra), f., *mainland.* [continent.

continenter, [continēns], adv., *constantly, incessantly, without interruption, continually.*

continentia, -ae, [continēns], f., *self-restraint, moderation.* vii. 52.

contineō, -tinēre, -tinuī, -tentus, [com- + teneō], 2, *hold together; hold; hold back, keep in hand; keep, retain, detain, shut in;* of places and regions, *hem in, bound, border;* of space, *fill* (i. 38); of a rite, pass., *consist of* (vii. 2). [contain.

contingō, -tingere, -tigī, -tāctus, [com- + tangō], 3, *touch, extend to, border on, reach; happen, fall to the lot of* (i. 43). [contact.

continuātiō, -ōnis, [verb continuō], f., *succession.* iii. 29. [continuation.

continuō, [continuus], adv., *forthwith, immediately, at once.*

continuus, -a, -um, [com-, cf. teneō], adj., *successive, uninterrupted.* [continuous.

cōntiō, -ōnis, [for *coventiō, co-, cf. veniō], f., *assembly, meeting* (v. 52, vii. 52); *address, harangue.* hāc habitā cōntiōne, *having delivered this address* (vii. 53).

cōntiōnor, -ārī, -ātus, [cōntiō], 1, dep., *address* an assembly, *make an address.* C. I. 7.

contrā, [related to com-], adv. and prep.:
(1) As adv., *opposite, in opposition, on the other side; on the other hand, on the contrary* (v. 31). contrā atque, *otherwise than, contrary to what* (iv. 13).
(2) As prep., with acc. only, *opposite to, facing, over against, contrary to; against, in hostility to, to the disadvantage of, in spite of; in reply to* (v. 29).

contrahō, -trahere, -trāxī, -trāctus, [com- + trahō], 3, *bring together, collect; draw in, contract, make smaller* (v. 49; vii. 40). [contract.

contrārius, -a, -um, [contrā], adj., *opposite, contrary.* ex contrāriō, *on the contrary* (vii. 30). [contrary.

contrōversia, -ae, [contrōversus], f., *dispute, debate, controversy, quarrel.* minuere contrōversiās, *to settle the questions at issue* (v. 26; vi. 23). [controversy.

contumēlia, -ae, f., *insult, indignity;* of waves, *buffeting* (iii. 13). [contumely.

convalēscō, -valēscere, -valuī, [com- + valēscō, inch. from valeō], 3, *grow strong, get well, recover.* vi. 36. [convalesce.

convallis, -is, [com- + vallis], f., *valley, ravine, defile.*

convehō, -vehere, -vexī, -vectus, [com- + vehō], 3, *bring together, collect, store.* vii. 74.

conveniō, -venīre, -vēnī, -ventum est, [com- + veniō], 4, *come together, gather, assemble, meet, come in a body; come* to an assembly (v. 56); *be agreed upon* (i. 36, ii. 19); impers., *be fitting* (vii. 85); *fall in with, meet* (i. 27). [convene.

conventus, -ūs, [cf. conveniō], m., *assembly, meeting; court.* [convent.

conversus, see convertō.

convertō, -vertere, -vertī, -versus, [com- + vertō], 3, *turn, direct, turn about, wheel around; change* (i. 41). conversa signa īnferre, *to face* *about and advance* (i. 25; ii. 26). [convert.

Convictolitāvis, -is, acc. -im, (vii. 55), m., (kon″vĭk-tọ-lĭ-tā′ vĭs), an Aeduan whose claims to the office of Vergobret were sustained by Caesar.

convictus, see **convincō**.

convincō, -vincere, -vīcī, -victus, [com- + vincō], 3, *prove clearly, establish, prove* (i. 40). [convict.

convocō, -āre, -āvī, -ātus, [com-+ vocō], 1, *call together, summon, assemble.* [convoke.

coörior, -orīrī, -ortus, [co-+orior], 4, dep., *arise;* of storm and wind, *arise, rise, spring up;* of war, *break out* (iii. 7).

coörtus, see **coörior**.

cōpia, -ae, [= co-opia, from co- + ops], f., *quantity, abundance, supply, plenty.* Pl., **cōpiae**, -ārum, *means, resources, wealth; forces, troops.*

cōpiōsus, -a, -um, comp. -ior, sup. -issimus, [cōpia], adj., *well-supplied, wealthy, rich.* i. 23. [copious.

cōpula, -ae, [co- + AP in aptus], f., *band;* pl., *grappling-hooks* (iii. 13). [copula.

cor, cordis, n., *heart.* **cordī esse**, *to be dear* (vi. 19). [cordial.

cōram, [co-, cf. ōs, *face*], adv., *face to face, in person.* **cōram perspicit** (v. 11) or **cernit** (vi. 8), *he sees with his own eyes.* As prep., with the ablative, *in the presence of.*

Coriosolitēs, -um, m., pl., (kō″rĭ-ọ-sol′ ĭ-tēz), a people along the northwestern coast of Gaul.

corium, -ī, n., *hide.* vii. 22.

Cornēlius, -a, -um, adj., *of Cornelius, Cornelian.* **castra Cornēlia**, *Cornelian camp,* near Utica (C. ii. 37).

cornū, -ūs, n., *horn;* of a deer, *antler* (vi. 26); of an army, *wing.*

corōna, -ae, [= κορώνη], f., *crown,*

wreath (iii. 16); of soldiers, *continuous cordon, cordon* (vii. 72). [crown.

corpus, -oris, n., *body.* [corporal.

corripiō, -ripere, -ripuī, -reptus, [com- + rapiō], 3, *snatch up; seize, carry away* (C. iii. 64).

corrumpō, -rumpere, -rūpī, -ruptus, [com- + rumpō, *break*], 3, *spoil, destroy.* vii. 55, 64. [corrupt.

cortex, corticis, m. and f., *bark* of a tree. ii. 33, C. iii. 49.

Cōrus, -ī, m., *northwest wind.* v. 7.

coss., = cōnsulibus, from cōnsul.

cotīdiānus, -a, -um, [cotīdiē], adj., *daily; ordinary, usual.*

cotīdiē, [quot + diēs], adv., *daily, every day.*

Cotta, -ae, m.:

(1) *L. Aurunculeius Cotta,* see **Aurunculeius.**

(2) *L. Aurelius Cotta* (â-rē′ lĭ-ụs kot′ ạ), consul in 65 B.C. C. i. 6.

Cotuātus, -ī, m., (kot-ū-ā′ tụs), a leader of the Carnutes. vii. 3.

Cotus, -ī, m., (kō′ tụs), an Aeduan, rival of Convictolitavis for the office of Vergobret. vii. 32, 33, 39, 67.

crassitūdō, -inis, [crassus, *thick*], f., *thickness.* iii. 13; vii. 73.

Crassus, -ī, m., (kras′ ụs):

(1) *Marcus Licinius Crassus,* member of the triumvirate with Caesar and Pompey, consul in 55 B.C.; perished in the disastrous Parthian expedition, 53 B.C. i. 21; iv. 1.

(2) *Publius Licinius Crassus,* younger son of the triumvir, lieutenant of Caesar in Gaul, B.C. 58–56; returning to Rome in 55, he followed his father to the East and fell in the same battle, 53 B.C. i. 52; ii. 34; iii. 7, 8, 9, 11, 20–27.

(3) *Marcus Licinius Crassus,* elder son of the triumvir, quaestor in Caesar's army after his brother

Publius left Gaul. v. 24, 46, 47;
vi. 6.

Crāstinus, -ī, [**crās**], m., (kras' ṭi-
nụs), a brave soldier in Caesar's
army. C. III. 91, 99.

crātēs, -is, f., *wicker-work, wattle;
hurdle, fascine.* [crate, grate.

crēber, -bra, -brum, comp. **crēbrior,**
sup. **crēberrimus,** adj., *thick, numerous, frequent, a great many.*

crēbrō, comp. **crēbrius,** sup. **crē-
berrimē,** [**crēber**], adv., *frequently,
in quick succession.* vii. 41.

crēdō, crēdere, crēdidī, crēditus,
3, *trust, believe, think, suppose; intrust, consign* (vi. 31). [creed,
credit.

cremō, -āre, -āvī, -ātus, 1, *burn;
burn to death* (i. 4.) [cremate.

creō, -āre, -āvī, -ātus, 1, *create,
make; choose, elect, appoint.* [create.

crēscō, crēscere, crēvī, crētus, 3,
inch., *grow; become great, become
powerful* (i. 20); of a river, *become
swollen* (vii. 55). [crescent.

Crētēs, -um, accusative **Crētas,**
[Κρῆτες], m., pl., *Cretans,* inhabitants of Crete.

Critognātus, -ī, m., (krit-ọg-nā' tụs),
a prominent Arvernian. vii. 77, 78.

cruciātus, -ūs, [**cruciō,** *torture*], m.,
torture, cruelty, torment, suffering.

crūdēlitās, -tātis, [**crūdēlis**], f.,
cruelty, barbarity. [cruelty.

crūdēliter, comp. **crūdēlius,** sup.
crūdēlissimē, [**crūdēlis**], adv.,
cruelly, with cruelty. i. 31; vii. 38.

crūs, crūris, n., *leg.* vi. 27.

cubīle, -is, [cf. **cubō,** *lie down*], n.,
bed, resting-place. vi. 27.

culmen, -inis, n., *height, summit, top.*
iii. 2. [culminate.

culpa, -ae, f., *blame, fault, error.* iv.
27; v. 52. [culpable.

cultūra, -ae, [cf. **colō**], f., *tilling,
cultivation.* [culture.

cultus, -ūs, [**colō**], m., *cultivation,
care; mode of life, civilization.*
[cult.

cum, prep. with ablative only, *with,
along with, together with.*

In composition the earlier form
com- is used, which remains unchanged before **b, p, m,** but is
changed to **col-** or **con-** before **l, cor-**
or **con-** before **r, con-** before other
consonants, and **co-** before vowels
and **h;** implies doing anything *in
concert with* others, or *thoroughly*
and *completely.*

cum, conj., temporal, *when, while, as
often as, as;* causal, *since;* adversative, *although.* **cum . . . tum,**
both . . . and, not only . . . but also.
cum prīmum, *as soon as.*

cunctātiō, -ōnis, [**cunctor**], f., *delay, hesitation.* iii. 18, 24.

cunctor, -ārī, -ātus, 1, dep., *delay,
hesitate.* iii. 23; iv. 25.

cūnctus, -a, -um, adj., *all together,
all.* As noun, **cūnctī, -ōrum,** m.,
pl., *all in a body* (vii. 11).

cuneātim, [**cuneātus, cuneus**],
adv., *in the form of a wedge; in
wedge-shaped masses* (vii. 28).

cuneus, -ī, m., *wedge;* of troops,
wedge-shaped mass (vi. 40).

cunīculus, -ī, m., *rabbit;* in military
language, *underground passage, mine.*
iii. 21; vii. 22, 24.

cupidē, comp. **-ius,** sup. **-issimē,**
[**cupidus**], adv., *eagerly, ardently.*

cupiditās, -tātis, [**cupidus**], f., *ar-
dent desire, eagerness.* [cupidity.

cupidus, -a, -um, comp. **-ior,** sup.
-issimus, [cf. **cupiō**], adj., *desirous,
eager for, fond of.*

cupiō, cupere, cupīvī, cupītus, 3,
desire; wish well to (i. 18).

cūr, adv., *why? wherefore?*

cūra, -ae, f., *care, attention, anxiety,
trouble.* [cure (noun).

Cūriō, -ōnis, m., *Gaius Scribonius
Curio*, (scrĭ-bō' nĭ-ŭs kū' rĭ-ō), a
lieutenant of Caesar's army. C. II. 3,
34 et seq.

cūrō, -āre, -āvī, -ātus, [cūra], I,
*take care, provide for, superintend,
arrange.* **nāvēs aedificandās
cūrāre**, *to have ships built* (v. I).
[cure (verb).

currus, -ūs, [cf. currō], m., *chariot.*

cursus, -ūs, [cf. currō], m., *running; speed; course.* [course.

cūstōdia, -ae, [cūstōs], f., *a watching; guard, watch;* pl., *watch stations* (C. II. 5). [custody.

cūstōdiō, -īre, -īvī, -ītus, [cūstōs],
4, *guard, keep.* vi. 4.

cūstōs, -tōdis, m. and f., *guard,
keeper, watch.*

D

D., with proper names, = Decimus.

D = quīngentī, 500.

d., see a. d.

Dācī, -ōrum, m., pl., *the Dacians,
Daci* (dā' sī), a people living north of
the lower course of the Danube
River, in the countries now called
Hungary and *Rumania.* vi. 25.

Damasippus, -ī, see Licinius.

damnō, -āre, -āvī, -ātus, [dam-
num], I, *condemn, sentence.* **capitis damnāre**, *to condemn to death*
(C. III. 83). Part. as noun, **dam-
nātī**, -ōrum, m., pl., *those condemned, criminals* (v. 55).

damnum, -ī, n., *loss.* vi. 44.

Dānuvius, -ī, m., *the Danube.* vi. 25.

dē, prep. with abl., denoting separation, *from, down from, away from;
out of, of; from among; on account of,
for, through, by; concerning, about,
in respect to; after, during, in the
course of, in.*

dēbeō, dēbēre, dēbuī, dēbitus, [dē
+ habeō], 2, *owe;* pass., *be due;*
followed by infin., *ought, must,
should.* [debit.

dēcēdō, -cēdere, -cessī, -cessūrus,
[dē + cēdō], 3, *go away, retire,
withdraw; avoid, shun; die* (vi. 19).

decem, or **x**, indeclinable num., *ten.*

dēceptus, see dēcipiō.

dēcernō, -cernere, -crēvī, -crētus,
[dē + cernō], 3, *pass judgment, decide; resolve upon, resolve, determine;
assign* by vote (C. I. 6).

dēcertō, -āre, -āvī, ātus, [dē +
certō, *contend*], I, *fight to a finish,
fight a decisive battle.*

dēcessus, -ūs, [dēcēdō], m., *departure, withdrawal.* [decease.

Decetia, -ae, f., (dĕ-sē' sh[y]ạ), a
town of the Aeduans, on the Liger
(*Loire*). vii. 33.

dēcidō, -cidere, -cidī, [dē + cadō],
3, *fall down, fall off.* [deciduous.

decimus, -a, -um, or **x**, [decem],
num. adj., *tenth.* [decimal.

Decimus, -ī, m., (des' ĭ-mŭs), a Roman
first name.

dēcipiō, -cipere, -cēpī, -ceptus,
[dē + capiō], 3, *catch; deceive* (i.
14). [deceive.

dēclārō, -āre, -āvī, -ātus, [dē +
clārō, from clārus], I, *make clear,
announce.* i. 50. [declare.

dēclīvis, -e, [dē + clīvus], adj., *sloping, descending.* As noun, **dēclīvia**,
n., pl., *slopes, declivities* (vii. 88).

dēclīvitās, -tātis, [dēclīvis], f., *descent.* [declivity.

dēcrētum, -ī, [dēcernō], n., *decree,
decision.* [decree.

decumānus, -a, -um, [decimus],
adj., *of a tenth part, decuman.*
decumāna porta, *rear gate* of the
Roman camp, opposite the **porta
praetōria.**

decuriō, -ōnis, [decuria], m., *decurion,* a cavalry officer in charge of a
decuria, consisting of 10 horsemen.

dēcurrō, -currere, -cucurrī or -currī, -cursūrus, [dē + currō], 3, *run down, rush down, hasten.*

dēdecus, -oris, [dē + decus, *honor*], n., *disgrace, dishonor.* iv. 25.

dēditīcius, -ī, [dēditus, from dēdō], adj., *that has surrendered, subject.* As noun, dēditīciī, -ōrum, m., p¹., *prisoners of war, captives.*

dēditiō, -ōnis, [dēdō], f., *surrender.* accipere or recipere in dēditiōnem, *to receive by capitulation.* in dēditiōnem venīre, *to surrender* (vi. 3, 9).

dēditus, -a, -um, [part. of dēdō], adj., *devoted* (VI. 16).

dēdō, -dere, -didī, -ditus, [dē + dō], 3, *give up, surrender; devote* (iii. 22).

dēdūcō, -dūcere, -dūxī, -ductus, [dē + dūcō], 3, *lead down; lead away, lead off, withdraw; lead, induce; conduct, bring;* of ships, *draw down, launch* (v. 2, 23) ; *bring home* as a bride, *marry* (v. 14). [deduce.

dēfatīgātiō, -ōnis, [dēfatīgō], f., *weariness, exhaustion.* iii. 19.

dēfatīgō, -āre, -āvī, -ātus, [dē + fatīgō, *weary*], 1, *tire out, exhaust.*

dēfectiō, -ōnis, [dēficiō], f., *a failing; desertion, revolt.* [defection.

dēfendō, -fendere, -fendī, -fēnsus, 3, *ward off, repel; defend, guard, protect.* [defend.

dēfēnsiō, -ōnis, [dēfendō], f., *defence.* i'. 7; vii. 23.

dēfēnsor, -ōris, [dēfendō], m., *defender, protector;* of piles protecting a bridge, *guards* (iv. 17).

dēfēnsus, see dēfendō.

dēferō, -ferre, -tulī, -lātus, [dē + ferō], irr., *bring down; carry away, bear away; bring* (*to*), *carry* (*to*); *refer* (*to*), *confer upon, lay before; report, announce.* [defer.

dēfessus, -a, -um, [part. of dēfetīscor], adj., *worn out, exhausted.* As noun, dēfessus, -ī, m., *one exhausted* (iii. 4), pl., *the exhausted* (vii. 25, 41, C. III. 94).

dēfetīscor, -ī, dēfessus, [dē + fatīscor], 3, dep., *become exhausted* (vii. 88).

dēficiō, -ficere, -fēcī, -fectus, [dē + faciō], 3, *fail, be lacking; fall away, revolt, rebel.* dēficere animō, *to lose heart* (vii. 30). [deficit.

dēfīgō, -fīgere, -fīxī, fīxus, [dē + fīgō, *fasten*], 3, *make fast, fix, fasten; stick fast* (v. 44).

dēfīniō, -īre, -īvī, -ītus, [dē + fīniō], 4, *set bounds to; define, fix, set* (vii. 83); *apportion* (C. III. 82). [define.

dēfore, see dēsum.

dēfōrmis, -e, comp. -ior, [dē + fōrma], adj., *ill-shaped* (iv. 2); *unsightly* (vii. 23). [deform.

dēfugiō, -fugere, -fūgī, [dē + fugiō], 3, *flee from, shun, avoid.*

dēiciō, -icere, -iēcī, -iectus, [dē + iaciō], 3, *throw down, cast down, throw; dislodge, drive from, rout;* of a ship, pass., *be carried* (iv. 28); of lots, *cast* (C. III. 6) ; *kill, destroy; disappoint.* [dejection.

dēiectus, see dēiciō.

dēiectus, -ūs, [dēiciō], m., *descent, slope, declivity.* ii. 8, 22, 29.

deinceps, [dein, = deinde, + CAP in capiō], adv., *one after the other, in succession, in turn; without interruption* (III. 29).

deinde, [dē + inde], adv., *thereafter, afterwards, then, next.*

dēlātus, see dēferō.

dēlectō, -āre, -āvī, -ātus, [freq. of dēliciō], 1, *please;* in pass., *have pleasure in* (iv. 2). [delectation.

dēlēctus, see dēligō.

dēlĕo, -ēre, -ēvī, -ētus, 2, *destroy, annihilate;* of disgrace, *wipe out* (ii. 27). [delete.

dēlīberō, -āre, -āvī, -ātus, [dē, cf. lībra, *balance*], 1, *deliberate, ponder.* Impersonal, dēlīberātur, *the question is discussed* (vii. 15). [deliberate.

dēlībrō, -āre, ——, -ātus, [dē + liber, *bark*], 1, *strip off the bark, peel.* vii. 73.

dēlīctum, -ī, [dēlinquō, *do wrong*], n., *offence, crime.* vii. 4. [delict.

dēligō, -āre, -āvī, -ātus, [dē + ligō, *bind*], 1, *bind fast, make fast, tie, fasten.*

dēligō, -ligere, -lēgī, -lēctus, [dē + legō], 3, *choose, select, pick out.*

dēlĭtēscō, -lĭtēscere, -lĭtuī, [dē + latēscō, from lateō], 3, *conceal one's self.* iv. 32.

dēmentia, -ae, [dēmēns], f., *madness, folly.* iv. 13. [dementia.

dēmessus, see dēmetō.

dēmetō, -metere, -messuī, -messus, [dē + metō], 3, *reap.* iv. 32.

dēmigrō, -āre, -āvī, -ātus, [dē + migrō, *depart*], 1, *move from, withdraw; depart, migrate.*

dēminuō, -minuere, -minuī, -minūtus, [dē + minuō], 3, *lessen, make smaller; impair.* [diminish.

dēmissus, -a, -um, comp. -ior [part. of dēmittō], adj., *low.* vii. 72.

dēmittō, -mittere, -mīsī, -missus, [dē + mittō], 3, *send down, let down;* of the head, *bow* (i. 32). dēmissae, *letting themselves down* (vii. 47). sē dēmittere, *to go down, come down, descend* (v. 32; vi 40; vii. 28). sē animō dēmittere, *to be discouraged* (vii. 29). [demit.

dēmō, dēmere, dēmpsī, dēmptus, [dē + emō], 3, *take down.* v. 48.

dēmōnstrō, -āre, -āvī, -ātus, [dē + mōnstrō, *show*], 1, *point out, state, mention; show, explain.* [demonstrate.

dēmoror, -ārī, -ātus, [dē + moror], 1, dep., *delay, retard, hinder.*

dēmptus, see dēmō.

dēmum, adv., *at length, finally.*

dēnegō, -āre, -āvī, -ātus, [dē + negō], 1, *refuse, deny.* i. 42. [deny.

dēnī, -ae, -a, [decem], distributive num. adj., *ten each, ten apiece.*

dēnique, adv., *at last, finally; in a word, in short; at any rate* (ii. 33).

dēnsus, -a, -um, comp. -ior, sup. -issimus, adj., *thick, closely packed, dense, crowded.* [dense.

dēnūntiō, -āre, -āvī, -ātus, [dē + nūntiō], 1, *announce, declare; threaten* (i. 36); *order* (vi. 10); *admonish* (C. iii. 86). [denounce.

dēpellō, -pellere, -pulī, -pulsus, [dē + pellō], 3, *drive away, dislodge;* of disease, *ward off* (vi. 17).

dēperdō, -dere, -didī, -ditus, [dē + perdō, *destroy*], 3, *lose.*

dēpereō, -īre, -iī, -itūrus, [dē + pereō], irr., *be destroyed* (v. 23); *be lost, perish* (vii. 31, C. iii. 87).

dēpōnō, -pōnere, -posuī, -positus, [dē + pōnō], 3, *lay aside, lay down, place; give up, resign* (vii. 33). [deposit.

dēpopulor, -ārī, -ātus, [dē + populor], 1, dep., *lay waste, plunder;* part. dēpopulātus, pass., *laid waste, devastated* (i. 11; vii. 77). [depopulate.

dēportō, -āre, -āvī, -ātus, [dē + portō], 1, *remove.* iii. 12. [deport.

dēposcō, -poscere, -poposcī, [dē + poscō], 3, *demand, earnestly desire.*

dēpositus, see dēpōnō.

dēprāvō, -āre, -āvī, -ātus, [dē, prāvus], 1, *distort, corrupt.* [deprave.

dēprĕcātor, -ōris, [dēprecor], m., *intercessor, mediator.* [deprecator.

dēprecor, -ārī, -ātus, [dē + precor, *pray*], 1, dep., *pray to be delivered from, beg to escape; ask for quarter, beg for mercy* (iv. 7, vi. 4). [deprecate.

dēprehendō, -hendere, -hendī, -hēnsus, [dē + prehendō], 3, *catch, seize; surprise.*

dēprehēnsus, see dēprehendō.

dēprimō, -primere, -pressī, -pressus, [dē + premō], 3, *press down; sink* (C. II. 6, 7, 43). [depress.

dēpugnō, -āre, -āvī, -ātus, [dē + pugnō], 1, *fight decisively, fight it out* (vii. 28).

dēpulsus, see dēpellō.

dērēctē, comp. -ius, [dērēctus], adv., *directly, straight up and down* (iv. 17).

dērēctus, -a, -um, [part. of dērigō], adj., *laid straight, straight; straight up and down, perpendicular.* [direct.

dērigō, -rigere, -rēxī, -rēctus, [dē + regō], 3, *lay straight;* of a line of battle, *draw up, form* (vi. 8). [dress.

dērivō, -āre, -āvī, -ātus, [dē + rīvus, *brook*], 1, *draw off, turn aside.* vii. [derive.

dērogō, -āre, -āvī, -ātus, [dē + rogō], 1, *withdraw.* vi. 23. [derogate.

dēscendō, -scendere, -scendi, dēscēnsum est, [dē + scandō, *climb*], 3, *come down, descend;* with **ad** and the acc., *resort to, stoop to.* [descend.

dēsecō, -cāre, -cuī, -ctus, [dē + secō], 1, *cut off.* vii. 4.

dēserō, -serere, -seruī, -sertus, [dē + serō, *join*], 3, *leave, abandon, desert.* [desert.

dēsertor, -ōris, [dēserō], m., *deserter, runaway.* vi. 23.

dēsertus, see dēserō.

dēsertus, -a, -um, comp. -ior, sup.

-issimus, [part. of dēserō), adj., *deserted, solitary.* v. 53.

dēsīderō, -āre, -āvī, -ātus, 1, *wish for, want, long for, miss; lack, lose;* pass. often, especially of soldiers, *be missing, be lost.* [desideratum.

dēsidia, -ae, [dēses, *idle,* cf. dēsideō], f., *indolence, idleness.* vi. 23.

dēsignō, -āre, -āvī, -ātus, [dē + signō, *mark*], 1, *point out; indicate, evidence* (C. III. 96); *designate* (1. 18). [designate.

dēsiliō, -silīre, -siluī, -sultus, [dē + saliō, *leap*], 4, *leap down, jump down;* from horses, *dismount.*

dēsistō, -sistere, -stitī, -stitūrus, [dē + sistō], 3, *leave off, cease; desist from, stop, give up.* dēsistere sententiā, *to give up the notion* (vi. 4). [desist.

dēspectus, see dēspiciō.

dēspectus, -ūs, [dēspiciō], m., *a looking down* from an elevation, *view.*

dēspērātiō, -ōnis, [dēspērō], f., *despair, hopelessness.* [desperation.

dēspērātus, -a, -um, comp. -ior, sup. -issimus, [part. of dēspērō], adj., *without hope, beyond hope, desperate.* vii. 3. [desperate.

dēspērō, -āre, -āvī, -ātus, [dē + spērō], 1, *give up hope of, despair of, have no hope of.* [despair.

dēspiciō, -spicere, -spexī, -spectus, [dē + speciō, *look*], 3, *look down upon; despise, disdain.* [despise.

dēspoliō, -āre, -āvī, -ātus, [dē + spoliō], 1, *despoil, rob.* ii. 31. [despoil.

dēstinō, -āre, -āvī, -ātus, 1, *make fast, bind, stay.* operī dēstinātī, *detailed for the work* (vii. 72). [destine.

dēstituō, -stituere, -stituī, -stitūtus, [dē + statuō], 3, *desert, abandon, leave.* i. 16. [destitute.

dēstrictus, see dēstringō.

dēstringō, -stringere, -strīnxī, -strictus, [dē + stringō, *pluck off*], 3, *unsheathe, draw.* i. 25; vii. 12.

dēsum, deesse, dēfuī, [dē + sum], irr., *be wanting, fail, be lacking.*

dēsuper, [dē + super], adv., *from above.* i. 52.

dētendō, -ere, ——, dētēnsus, [dē + tendō], 3, *relax;* of tents, *strike* (C. iii. 85).

dēterior, -us, comp., sup. dēterrimus, [dē], adj., *worse, poorer; of less value* (i. 36). [deteriorate.

dēterreō, -terrēre, -terruī, -territus, [dē + terreō], 2, *frighten off, prevent, deter; repress* (v. 7). dēterrēre nē, quō minus, or quīn, *to prevent from.* [deter.

dētestor, -ārī, -ātus, [dē + testor], 1, dep., *curse, execrate.* [detest.

dētineō, -tinēre, -tinuī, -tentus, [dē + teneō], 2, *hold back.* iii. 12. [detain.

dētrāctus, see dētrahō.

dētrahō, -trahere, -trāxī, trāctus, [dē + trahō], 3, *draw off, take off; take away, remove.* [detract.

dētrectō, -āre, -āvī, -ātus, [dē + tractō], 1, *avoid.* vii. 14.

dētrīmentōsus, -a, -um, [dētrīmentum], adj., *hurtful, detrimental.* vii. 33.

dētrīmentum, -ī, [dē, cf. terō, *wear away*], n., *loss, damage, injury; loss in war, repulse, reverse, defeat.* quid dētrīmentī, *any harm* (C. I. 7). [detriment.

dēturbō, -āre, -āvī, -ātus, [dē + turbō, *disturb*], 1, *force back in disorder, dislodge.* v. 43; vii. 86.

deūrō, -ūrere, -ussī, -ūstus, [dē + ūrō], 3, *burn up.* vii. 25.

deus, -ī, m., *god.* [deity.

dēvehō, -vehere, -vexī, -vectus, [dē + vehō], 3, *carry away, remove, convey.*

dēveniō, -venīre, -vēnī, -ventūrus, [dē + veniō], 4, *come.* ii. 21.

dēvexus, -a, -um, [dēvehō], adj., *sloping.* As noun, dēvexa, n., pl., *sloping places, slopes* (vii. 88).

dēvincō, -vincere, -vīcī, -victus, [dē + vincō], 3, *conquer completely, subdue.* vii. 34, C. iii. 87.

dēvocō, -āre, -āvī, -ātus, [dē + vocō], 1, *call away.* in dubium dēvocāre, *to risk, endanger* (vi. 7).

dēvōtus, [part. of dēvoveō], adj., *bound by a vow.* As noun, dēvōtī, -ōrum, m., pl., *faithful followers* (iii. 22).

dēvoveō, -vovēre, -vōvī, -vōtus, [dē + voveō], 2, *vow, devote* (iii. 22); *offer* to the gods, *consecrate* (vi. 17). [devote.

dexter, -tra, -trum, adj., *right.* [dexterous.

dextra, -ae, [dexter, sc. manus], f., *right hand.* i. 20.

Diablintēs, -um, m., pl., (dī-ạblin′ tēz), a small people in north-western Gaul, probably a division of the Aulercī. iii. 9.

diciō, -ōnis, pl. and nom. sing. not in use, f., *sway, sovereignty, authority, lordship.* i. 31, 33; ii. 34.

dicō, -āre, -āvī, -ātus, 1, *dedicate; devote, offer* (VI. 12, 13).

dīcō, dīcere, dīxī, dictus, 3, *say, converse, speak; mention, tell, utter; appoint;* of a case, *plead;* of a day, *set.*

dictiō, -ōnis, [dīcō], f., *speaking; pleading* (i. 4). [diction.

dictum, -ī, [dīcō], n., *saying, word; command, order.* dictō audiēns, audientēs, *obedient to (his) order.* [dictum.

dīdūcō, -dūcere, -dūxī, -ductus, [dis- + dūcō], 3, *lead in different*

directions (VI. 34); *divide, separate*
(III. 23); *distribute*. [diduce.

dīes, dīēī, m. and f., *day; time* (i.
7). in dīes, *day by day, every
day*. diem dīcere, *to set a day*.

differō, differre, distulī, dīlātus,
[dis- + ferō], irr., *spread, scatter*
(v. 43); *put off, delay* (vii. 11, C. III.
85); *differ, be different*. [differ.

difficilis, -e, comp. difficilior, sup.
difficillimus, [dis- + facilis], adj.,
difficult, hard. [difficile.

difficultās, -tātis, [difficilis], f., *difficulty, trouble*. [difficulty.

difficulter, comp. difficilius, sup.
difficilimē, [difficilis], adv., *with
difficulty ;* comp., *with too great difficulty* (vii. 58).

diffīdō, -fīdere, -fīsus sum, [dis- +
fīdō], 3, semi-dep., *distrust, lose confidence in, despair of*. [diffident.

diffīsus, -a, -um, part. of diffīdō.

diffluō, -ere, diffluxī, [dis- + fluō],
3, *flow* in different directions, *divide*.
IV. 10. [diffluent.

diffundō, -fundere, -fūdī, -fūsus,
[dis- + fundō], 3, *pour forth;
spread out, extend* (vi. 26). [diffuse.

digitus, -ī, m., *finger ;* as a measure,
finger's breadth (vii. 73), the 16th
part of a Roman foot, .728 of an
inch. digitus pollex, *thumb* as a
measure (iii. 13). [digit.

dignitās, -tātis, [dignus], f., *worth,
merit; self-respect* (vi. 8); *greatness, rank, reputation*. [dignity.

dignus, -a, -um, comp. -ior, sup.
-issimus, adj., *worthy, worth, de-
serving*. vii. 25.

dīiūdicō, -āre, -āvī, -ātus, [dis- +
iūdicō], 1, *decide*. v. 44. [dijudi-
cate.

dīlēctus, see dīligō.

dīlēctus, -ūs, [dīligō], m., *levy,
draft, enlistment*.

dīligenter, comp. dīligentius, sup.

dīligentissimē, [dīligēns], adv.,
*carefully, punctually, with painstak-
ing*.

dīligentia, -ae, [dīligēns], f., *care,
painstaking, activity*. [diligence.

dīligō, -ligere, -lēxī, -lēctus, [dis-
+ legō, *choose*], 3, *love, prize*. vi.
19.

dīmēnsus, see dīmētior.

dīmētior, -mētīrī, -mēnsus [dis- +
mētior], 4, dep., passive in Caesar,
measure, measure off (IV. 17); of
work, *lay out* (ii. 19). [dimension.

dīmicātiō, -ōnis, [dīmicō], f., *combat, engagement, encounter*. vii. 86.

dīmicō, -āre, -āvī, -ātum est, [dis- +
micō], 1, *fight, contend, struggle*.

dīmidius, -a, -um, [dis- + medius],
adj., *half* (vi. 31). As noun, dīmi-
dium, -ī, n., *half*.

dīmittō, -mittere, -mīsī, -missus,
[dis- + mittō], 3, *send in different
directions, send about; dismiss, send
off; let go, let slip, lose; abandon,
leave; give up* (vii. 17); *disband*
(II. 14). [dismiss.

dirimō, -imere, -ēmī, -ēmptus, [dis-
+ emō, *take*], 3, *take apart; break
off, put an end to* (i. 46).

dīripiō, -ripere, -ripuī, -reptus, [dis-
+ rapiō, *seize*], 3, *tear asunder;
ravage, plunder, pillage*.

dis- (dī-), inseparable prep., used only
as a prefix with other words, adding
the force of *apart, asunder, in different directions, utterly, entirely;
not, un-*.

In Composition **dis-** becomes **dif-**
before f, **dir-** before vowels, **dī-**
before d, g, l, m, n, r, and v.

Dīs, Dītis, m., with pater, *Dis pater*
(dis pā′ter), *Father Dis*, god of the
Underworld. vi. 18.

discēdō, -cēdere, -cessī, -cessūrus,
pf. pass. impers., discessum est,
[dis- + cēdō], 3, *go apart, disperse*,

scatter; depart, withdraw, leave, go away, go off. ab armīs discēdere, *to lay down one's arms.*

disceptātor, -ōris, [disceptō, *decide*], m., *arbitrator, umpire, judge.* vii. 37.

discernō, -cernere, -crēvī, -crētus, [dis- + cernō], 3, *distinguish between, know apart, keep separate* (vii. 75). [discern.

discessus, -ūs, [discēdō], m., *departure, going away.*

disciplīna, -ae, [discipulus], f., *instruction, training; system.* [discipline.

disclūdō, -clūdere, -clūsī, -clūsus, [dis- + claudō], 3, *keep apart, hold apart* (iv. 17); *separate* (vii. 8).

discō, discere, didicī, 3, *learn.*

discrīmen, -inis, [cf. discernō], n., *interval; crisis, peril* (vi. 38).

discutiō, -cutere, -cussī, -cussus, [dis- + quatiō, *shake*], 3, *shatter; remove, clear away* (vii. 8). [discuss.

disiciō, -icere, -iēcī, -iectus, [dis- + iaciō], 3, *drive asunder; disperse, scatter, rout* (i. 25; iii. 20).

disiectus, see disiciō.

dispār, -paris, [dis- + pār], adj., *unequal, unlike.* v. 16; vii. 39.

disparō, -āre, -āvī, -ātus, [dis- + parō], 1, *divide, separate.* [disparate.

dispergō, -spergere, -spersī, -spersus, [dis- + spargō, *scatter*], 3, *scatter, scatter about, disperse.* [disperse.

dispersus, see dispergō.

dispōnō, -pōnere, -posuī, -positus, [dis- + ponō], 3, *set in various places, distribute; station, post.* [dispose.

disputātiō, -ōnis, [disputō], f., *discussion, debate, dispute.* [disputation.

disputō, -āre, -āvī, -ātus, [dis- + putō], 1, *treat, investigate, discuss.* vi. 14. [dispute.

dissēnsiō, -ōnis, [dissentiō], f., *disagreement, dissension.* [dissension.

dissentiō, -sentīre, -sēnsī, -sēnsus, [dis- + sentiō], 4, *differ in opinion, disagree.* v. 29; vii. 29. [dissent.

disserō, -serere, [dis- + serō, *sow*], 3, *plant here and there, place at intervals.* vii. 73.

dissimulō, -āre, -āvī, -ātus, [dis- + simulō], 1, *make unlike; conceal, keep secret* (iv. 6). [dissimulate.

dissipō, -āre, -āvī, -ātus, 1, *scatter, disperse.* [dissipate.

dissuādeō, -suādēre, -suāsī, -suāsūrus, [dis- + suādeō], 2, *advise against, object, oppose.* vii. 15. [dissuade.

distendō, -tendere, -tendī, -tentus, [dis- + tendō], 3, *stretch out.* C. iii. 92. [distend.

distineō, -tinēre, -tinuī, -tentus, [dis- + teneō], 2, *keep apart, hold apart, separate; hinder, delay* (vii. 37).

distō, -āre, [dis- + stō], 1, *stand apart, be separated, be distant.* distantēs inter sē bīnōs pedēs, *two feet apart* (vii. 23). [distant.

distrahō, -trahere, -trāxī, -trāctus, [dis- + trahō, *draw*], 3, *wrench asunder* (vii. 23); *draw apart* (C. iii. 92). [distract.

distribuō, -tribuere, -tribuī, -tribūtus, [dis- + tribuō], 3, *distribute, divide, assign, apportion.* [distribute.

dītissimus, see dīves.

diū, comp. diūtius, sup. diūtissimē, adv., *long, for a long time.* quam diū, *as long as* (i. 17).

diurnus, -a, -um, [cf. diēs], adj., *of the day, by day.* [diurnal.

diūtinus, -a, -um, [diū], adj., *long-continued, lasting.* v. 52.

diūtissimē, see diū.

diūtius, see diū.

diūturnitās, -tātis, [diūturnus], f., *long continuance, length (of time)*, *long duration.* i. 40; iii. 4.

diūturnus, -a, -um, comp. -ior, [diū], adj., *long, prolonged.* i. 14.

dīversus, -a, -um, [part. of dīvertō], adj., *opposite; separate, apart; different; remote* (vi. 25). [diverse.

dīvertō, -ere, -tī, -sus, [dis- + vertō], 3, *separate.* ii. 24. [divert.

dīves, -itis, comp. dītior, sup. dītissimus, adj., *rich, wealthy.* i. 2.

Dīviciācus, -ī, m., (div″ i̯-shi̯-ā′ kŭs) : (1) An Aeduan of influence, loyal to Caesar, who at his intercession pardoned Dumnorix (i. 18–20), and the Bellovaci (ii. 14, 15). (2) A ruler of the Suessiones. ii. 4.

Dīvicō, -ōnis, m., (div′ i̯-kō), leader of the Helvetians in their war with Cassius, 107 B.C., and head of an embassy to Caesar, 58 B.C. i. 13, 14.

dīvidō, -videre, -vīsī, -vīsus, 3, *separate, divide.* [divide.

dīvīnus, -a, -um, comp. -ior, sup. -issimus, [dīvus], adj., *divine, sacred.* [divine.

dīvīsus, see dīvidō.

dō, dare, dedī, datus, irr., *give, give up, give over, grant; offer, furnish, allow.* in 'fugam dare, *to put to flight.* operam dare, *to take pains* (v. 7). [date.

doceō, docēre, docuī, doctus, 2, *teach; inform; point out, state; show* (vi. 1). [doctor.

documentum, -ī, [doceō], n., *proof, warning.* vii. 4. [document.

doleō, dolēre, doluī, dolitūrus, 2, *suffer; be grieved, be annoyed.*

dolor, -ōris, [doleō], m., *pain, suffering; grief, distress.* [dolors.

dolus, -ī, m., *cunning, fraud, deceit* (i. 13; iv. 13). [dole.

domesticus, -a, -um, [domus], adj., *home, native, internal; their own* (ii. 10); *of their own household* (C. iii.60). domesticum bellum, *civil war* (v. 9). [domestic.

domicilium, -ī, [domus], n., *dwelling, abode, habitation.* [domicile.

dominor, -ārī, -ātus, [dominus], 1, dep., *be master, have dominion.* ii. 31. [dominate.

dominus, -ī, [domō, *subdue*], m., *master, lord.* vi. 13. [dominie.

Domitius, -ī, m., (dọ-mish′ [y]ụs) : (1) *Lucius Domitius Ahenobarbus,* consul with Appius Claudius Pulcher, 54 B.C. (v. 1), in the Civil War a general on the side of Pompey. (2) *Gnaeus Domitius,* a cavalry officer in Curio's army in Africa. C. ii. 42. (3) *Gnaeus Domitius Calvīnus,* a general in Caesar's army. C. iii. 89.

domus, -ūs, f., *house, home.* [dome.

Donnotaurus, -ī, m., *Gaius Valerius Donnotaurus* (don-ọ-tâ′ rụs), a leader among the Helvii. vii. 65.

dōnō, -āre, -āvī, -ātus, [dōnum], 1, *give, grant, confer.* i. 47; vii. 11. [donate.

dōnum, -ī, [dō], n., *gift, present.*

dorsum, -ī, n., *back;* of a mountain, *long summit,* like the back of an animal (vii. 44). [dorsal.

dōs, dōtis, [cf. dō], f., *dowry, marriage portion.* vi. 19. [dot (dowry).

Druidēs, -um, m., pl., *Druids.*

Dubis, -is, m., (dū′ bis), a river in Gaul, tributary of the Arar (*Saône*); now the *Doubs.* i. 38.

dubitātiō, -ōnis, [dubitō], f., *doubt, hesitation.* [dubitation.

dubitō, -āre, -āvī, -ātus, [dubius], 1, *be uncertain, doubt; hesitate, delay.*

dubius, -a, -um, adj., *doubtful, uncertain.* [dubious.

ducentī, -ae, -a, or CC, [duo + centum], adj., *two hundred*.

dūcō, dūcere, dūxī, ductus, 3, *lead, guide, conduct, bring, take;* of a trench, *make; protract, prolong, put off; think, consider, reckon.* in mātrimōnium dūcere, *to marry* (i. 9, 53). [ductile.

ductus, -ūs, [dūcō], m., *generalship, command.* vii. 62, C. I. 7. [duct.

dum, conj., *while; until.*

Dumnorīx, -īgis, m., (dum' nọ-rĭks), an Aeduan, brother of Diviciacus, and son-in-law of Orgetorix; a bitter enemy of Caesar, and leader of an Aeduan anti-Roman party; slain by Caesar's orders while trying to escape from him, 54 B.C. (Fig. 42.)

dumtaxat, [dum + taxat], adv., *merely, only.* C. II. 41.

duo, -ae, -o, or II, adj., *two.* [duet.

duodecim, or XII, [duo + decem], indecl. num. adjective, *twelve.* [duo-decimal.

duodecimus, -a, -um, [duodecim], num. adj., *twelfth.*

duodēnī, -ae, -a, gen. pl. duodēnum (vii. 36), [duodecim], distributive num. adj., *twelve at a time, by twelves.*

duodēseptuāgintā, or LXVIII, [duo + dē + septuāgintā], indeclinable num. adj., *sixty-eight.* i. 29.

duodētrīgintā, or XXVIII, [duo + dē + trīgintā], indeclinable num. adj., *twenty-eight.* v. 2.

duodēvīgintī, -ae, -a, or XVIII, [duo + dē + vīgintī], num. adj., *eighteen.*

duplex, -icis, [duo, cf. plicō, *fold*], adj., *twofold, double.* [duplex.

duplicō, -āre, -āvī, -ātus, [duplex], 1, *make double, double.* [duplicate.

dūritia, -ae, [dūrus], f., *hardness; severe mode of life* (vi. 21). [duress.

dūrō, -āre, -āvī, -ātus, [dūrus], 1, *harden, make hardy.* vi. 28.

Dūrocortorum, -ī, n., (dū-rọ-cor' tọ-rụm), capital of the Remi, now *Reims.* vi. 44.

dūrus, -a, -um, comp. -ior, sup. -issi-mus, adj., *hard, severe, difficult;* of a season, *inclement* (vii. 8).

Dūrus, -ī, m., *Quintus Laberius Du-rus*, (lạ-bē' rĭ-ụs dū' rụs), a military tribune. v. 15.

dux, ducis, [dūcō, *lead*], m., *leader, guide; general, commander.* [duke.

Dyrrachīnus, -a, -um, [Dyrra-chium], adj., *at Dyrrachium, of Dyrrachium.* C. III. 84, 87, 89.

Dyrrachium, -ī, [Δυρράχιον], n., (dir-rā' kĭ-ụm), a city on the east coast of the Adriatic, formerly called *Epidamnus;* now *Durazzo*, in Albania. C. III. 53.

E.

ē, see **ex**.

eā, [properly abl. of is, sc. parte], adv., *there, on that side.* v. 51.

Eburōnēs, -um, m., pl., (eb-ū-rō' nēz), a Belgic people north of the Treve-rans. In 54 B.C. they destroyed a detachment of Caesar's army under Sabinus and Cotta, and were afterwards almost exterminated by him.

Eburovīcēs, -um, m., pl., (eb'' ū-rọ-vī' sēz), a division of the Aulercī.

ēdiscō, -discere, -didicī, [ex + discō], 3, *learn by heart.* vi. 14.

ēditus, -a, -um, comp. -ior, [part. of ēdō], adj., *elevated; rising* (II. 8).

ēdō, -dere, -didī, -ditus, [ex + dō], 3, *put forth; inflict* (i. 31). [edit.

ēdoceō, -docēre, -docuī, -doctus, [ex + doceō], 2, *teach carefully, instruct, inform, tell.*

ēdūcō, -dūcere, -dūxī, -ductus, [ex + dūcō], 3, *lead out, lead forth;* of a sword, *draw* (v. 44). [educe.

effēminō, -āre, -āvī, -ātus, [ex + fēmina], 1, *make womanish, weaken, enervate*. i. 1; iv. 2. [effeminate.

effarciō, -īre, effertus, [ex+farciō, *stuff*], 4, *fill in*. vii. 23.

efferō, -ferre, extulī, ēlātus, [ex + ferō], irr., *bring out, carry forth, carry away* (i. 5; v. 45); *spread abroad, publish* (i. 46; vi. 14; vii. 1, 2); *lift up, pull up; extol* (C. III. 87); *elate* (v. 47, VII. 47). [elate.

efficiō, -ficere, -fēcī, -fectus, [ex+ faciō], 3, *make out, bring about; accomplish, effect, produce; make, render; build, construct*. [effect.

effodiō, -fodere, -fōdī, -fossus, [ex + fodiō], 3, *dig out; of the eyes, gouge out* (VII. 4).

effossus, see effodiō.

effugiō, -fugere, -fūgī, [ex+fugiō], 3, *escape*.

effundō, -fundere, -fūdī, -fūsus, [ex + fundō], 3, *pour out*. **sē effundere**, of a crowd, *pour out, rush forth* (C. II. 7); of cavalry, *dash forth* (V. 19). [effusive.

egēns, egentis, comp. egentior, sup. -issimus, [part. of egeō], adj., *needy*. As noun, egentēs, -ium, m., pl., *the needy, destitute men* (vii. 4, C. III. 59).

egeō, egēre, eguī, 2, *lack, be in want (of)*. vi. 11.

egestās, -tātis, [egēns], f., *privation, destitution, want*. vi. 24.

ego, meī, personal pron., *I;* pl. nōs, nostrum, *we*. [egotism.

egomet pl. nōsmet [ego+-met, enclitic suffix = 'self'], personal pronoun, *I myself, ourselves*. vii. 38.

ēgredior, -gredī, -gressus, [ex + gradior, *step*], 3, dep., *go out, go forth, come forth, leave;* from a ship, *land, disembark*.

ēgregiē, [ēgregius], adv., *remarkably well, admirably, splendidly*.

ēgregius, -a, -um, [ex + grex, *herd, crowd*], adj., *eminent, marked, distinguished, excellent*. [egregious.

ēgressus, see ēgredior.

ēgressus, -ūs, [ēgredior], m., *departure; disembarking, landing* (v. 8). [egress.

Egus, -ī, m., (ē' gus), an Allobrogian, son of Roucillus. C. III. 59.

ēiciō, -icere, -iēcī, -iectus, [ex + iaciō], 3, *throw out, cast out, thrust out, expel; cast up* (v. 10). **sē ēicere**, *to rush, sally forth*. [eject.

eius modī, see modus.

ēlābor, -lābī, -lāpsus, [ex + lābor], 3, dep., *slip away; escape* (v. 37). [elapse.

ēlātus, see efferō.

Elaver, Elaveris, n., (el' a-ver), a tributary of the Liger (*Loire*), into which it flows from the south after a course of about 200 miles; now *Allier*.

ēlēctus, -a, -um, comp. -ior, sup. -issimus, [part. of ēligō], adj., *chosen, picked*. ii. 4, C. III. 91. [elect.

elephantus, -ī, [ἐλέφας], m., *elephant*. vi. 28. [elephant.

Eleutetī, -ōrum, m., pl., (e-lū' te-tī), a people of Central Gaul. vii. 75.

ēliciō, -licere, -licuī, [ex+laciō, *entice*], 3, *entice forth, lure forth; bring out, draw out*. [elicit.

ēloquor, -ī, ēlocūtus, [ex + loquor], 3, dep., *speak out, utter, declare*. C. II. 34. [eloquent.

Elusātēs, -ium, m., pl., (el-ū-sā' tēz), a people in Central Aquitania. iii. 27.

ēmigrō, -āre, -āvī, [ex + migrō, *depart*], 1, *go forth* to remain, *move, emigrate*. i. 31. [emigrate.

ēmineō, -minēre, -minuī, 2, *project, stand out*. vii. 72, 73. [eminent.

ēminus [ex + manus, *hand*], adv., *at a distance, from afar*. vii. 24.

ēmissus, see ēmittō.

ēmittō, -mittere, -mīsī, -missus, [ex + mittō], 3, *send out; hurl, cast, shoot, discharge* (ii. 23); *throw away, let go* (i. 25). [emit.

emō, emere, ēmī, ēmptus, 3, *buy, purchase.* i. 16; ii. 33.

ēnāscor, -nāscī, -nātus, [ex + nāscor], 3, dep., *grow out;* of branches, *shoot out* (ii. 17).

enim [nam], conj., postpositive, *for, for in fact.* neque enim, *and (with good reason) for . . . not, for in fact . . . not.*

ēnītor, -ī, ēnīsus, [ex + nītor], 3, dep., *make effort* (C. ii. 6); *force one's way out* (C. ii. 34).

ēnūntiō, -āre, -āvī, -ātus [ex + nūntiō], 1, *report, reveal, disclose.* [enounce.

eō, abl. of is (*44*).

eō, [cf. is], adv., *thither, to that place, there.*

eō, īre, iī, itūrus, ītum est, irr., *go, pass, march, advance.*

eōdem [īdem], adv., *to the same place; to the same thing* (i. 14), *to the same end* (iv. 11).

ephippiātus, -a, -um, adj., *riding with saddle-cloths.* iv. 2.

ephippium, -ī, [ἐφίππιον, from ἐπί + ἵππος], n., *saddle-cloth.* iv. 2.

Epīrus, -ī, ["Ηπειρος], f., (e-pī'rus), a province in the northern part of Greece, east of the Adriatic. C. iii. 47, 61.

epistula, -ae, [ἐπιστολή], f., *letter, despatch.* v. 48. [epistle.

Eporēdorīx, -īgis, m., (ep-o-red'o-rĭks):

(1) A leader of the Aeduans, captured by Caesar. vii. 67.

(2) A young Aeduan of rank, for a time friendly to Caesar, afterwards one of the commanders of the Gallic army raised for the relief of

Alesia. vii. 38, 39, 40, 54, 55, 63, 64, 76.

epulae, -ārum, f., pl., *feast.* vi. 28.

eques, -itis, [equus], m., *horseman, cavalryman, trooper;* as a member of a social order, *knight.*

equester, -tris, -tre, [eques], adj., *of cavalry, cavalry-.* [equestrian.

equitātus, -ūs, [equitō, *ride*], m., *cavalry; knighthood,* collectively *knights* (i. 31).

equus, -ī, m., *horse.* [equine.

Eratosthenēs, -is, ['Ερατοσθένης], m., (er-a-tos'thě-nēz), a Greek, born at Cyrene, in Africa, B.C. 276; died about B.C. 196; librarian of the great library at Alexandria in Egypt, and famous as a geographer, mathematician, historian, and grammarian. vi. 24.

ērēctus, -a, -um, comp. -ior, [part. of ērigō], adj., *high, elevated.* iii. 13. [erect (adj.).

ēreptus, see ēripiō.

ergā, prep. with acc., *towards.* v. 54.

ergō, adv., *therefore, then.* vii. 77.

ērigō, -rigere, -rēxī, -rēctus, [ex + regō], 3, *raise to a standing position,* (vi. 27); *erect.* [erect (verb).

ēripiō, -ripere, -ripuī, -reptus, [ex + rapiō, *seize*], 3, *take away, snatch away; rescue, save* (i. 53). sē ēripere, *to rescue one's self, make one's escape.*

errō, -āre, -āvī, -ātus, 1, *wander; be mistaken, delude one's self.* [err.

error, -ōris, [errō], m., *wandering; mistake.* (C. iii. 73). [error.

ērumpō, -rumpere, -rūpī, -ruptus, [ex + rumpō, *break*], 3, *burst forth, sally forth.* iii. 5. [erupt.

ēruptiō, -ōnis, [ērumpō], f., *a bursting forth; sally, sortie.* [eruption.

essedārius, -ī, [essedum], m., *fighter from a chariot, chariot-fighter.*

essedum, -ī, n., two-wheeled *war-chariot.* iv. 32, 33; v. 9, 16, 17.

Esuviī, -ōrum, m., pl., (ę-sū′ vi̧-ī), a people in northwestern Gaul.

et, conj., *and.* et . . . et, *both . . . and.*

etiam [et + iam], conj., *also; even.* nōn sōlum . . . sed etiam, *not only . . . but also.*

etsī [et + sī], conj., *although, though, even if.*

ēvādō, -vādere, -vāsī, -vāsūrus, [ex + vādō], 3, *escape.* iii. 19. [evade.

ēvellō, -vellere, -vellī, -vulsus, [ex + vellō, *pluck*], 3, *pull out.* i. 25.

ēveniō, -venīre, -vēnī, -ventūrus, [ex + veniō], 4, *turn out, happen.* iv. 25.

eventus, -ūs, [cf. ēveniō], m., *outcome, result; chance, fortune* (vi. 42); *fate, accident* (iv. 31). [event.

ēvocātus, -ī, [part. of ēvocō], m., *veteran volunteer,* a soldier serving voluntarily after the completion of his time of service. vii. 65.

ēvocō, -āre, -āvī, -ātus, [ex + vocō], 1, *call out, call forth, call, summon; invite* (v. 58). [evoke.

ēvolō, -āre, -āvī, [ex + volō, *fly*], 1, *fly forth, rush out, dash out.*

ex, often before consonants ē, prep. with abl., *from, out of, down from; since, after; of; by reason of, by, because of, in consequence of; according to, with, in, on.* ex ūnā parte, *on one side.*

In composition ex becomes ef before f, ē before b, d, g, i consonant, l, m, n, and v.

exāctus, see exigō.

exagitō, -āre, -āvī, -ātus, [ex + agitō, freq. of agō], 1, *disturb, harass.* ii. 29; iv. 1.

exāminō, -āre, -āvī, -ātus, [ex-

āmen, *tongue of a balance*], 1, *weigh,* v. 12. [examine.

exanimō, -āre, -āvī, -ātus, [exanimus], 1, *deprive of life, kill;* pass., *be out of breath, weakened, exhausted* (ii. 23, iii. 19; C. iii. 92).

exārdēscō, -ārdēscere, -ārsī, -ārsūrus, [ex + ārdēscō], 3, *take fire; be incensed* (v. 4).

exaudiō, -dīre, -dīvī, -dītus, [ex + audiō], 4, *hear distinctly, hear plainly.*

excēdō, -cēdere, -cessī, -cessūrus, [ex + cēdō], 3, *go out, leave, withdraw, depart.* [exceed.

excellēns, -entis, comp. -ior, sup. -issimus, [excellō], adj., *surpassing, excellent.* C. iii. 99. [excellent.

excellō, -cellere, participial adj. excelsus, 3, *be eminent, surpass.* vi. 13. [excel.

excelsus, -a, -um, comp. -ior, sup. -issimus, [part. of excellō], adj., *high* (vi. 26). [excelsior.

exceptō, -āre, -āvī, -ātus, [freq. of excipiō], 1, *catch up* with the hands, *take hold of* (vii. 47).

exceptus, see excipiō.

excīdō, -cīdere, -cīdī, -cīsus, [ex + caedō], 3, *cut out; cut down* (vii. 50). [excise.

excipiō, -cipere, -cēpī, -ceptus, [ex + capiō], 3, *take out; take up* (vii. 3); *take in* (vii. 28); *cut off, catch* (vi. 28, 35 ; vii. 20); *receive, withstand* (i. 52, iii. 5, iv. 17, C. iii. 92); *cope with, encounter* (iii. 13); *take the place of, relieve, succeed, follow* (v. 16; vii. 51, 88, C. ii, 7, iii. 87). [except.

excitō, -āre, -āvī, -ātus, [ex + citō, *move*], 1, *erect, raise rapidly* (iii. 14; v. 40); *stir up, rouse, spur on; kindle* (vii. 24). [excite.

exclūdō, -clūdere, -clūsī, -clūsus, [ex + claudō], 3, *shut out, shut off, cut off; hinder, prevent.* [exclude.

excōgitō, -āre, -āvī, -ātus, [ex + cōgitō], 1, *think out, think of.* v. 31. [excogitate.

excruciō, -āre, -āvī, -ātus, [ex + cruciō, from crux, *cross*], 1, *torment, torture.* [excruciate.

excubitor, -ōris, [excubō], m., *soldier in bivouac; watchman, sentinel.* vii. 69.

excubō, -cubāre, -cubuī, [ex + cubō, *lie down*], 1, *lie out* of doors, *bivouac; keep watch, keep guard.*

exculcō, -āre, [ex + calcō, from calx, *heel*], 1, *tread down, pack down* by stamping. vii. 73.

excursiō, -ōnis, [ex, cf. currō], f., *a running out; sally, sortie* (ii. 30). [excursion.

excursus, -ūs, [excurrō], m., *a running forth; onset, attack* (C. iii. 92). [excursus.

excūsātiō, -ōnis, [excūsō], f., *excuse, apology, defence.* vi. 4.

excūsō, -āre, -āvī, -ātus, [ex, cf. causa], 1, *excuse, make excuse for.* iv. 22. [excuse.

exemplum, -ī, [cf. eximō], n., *example, precedent;* as an example to warn others, *kind of punishment* (i. 31). [example.

exeō, -īre, -iī, -itum est, [ex + eō], irr., *go forth, go out; withdraw, leave.*

exerceō, -ercēre, -ercuī, -ercitus, [ex + arceō], 2, *exercise, practice; train, discipline.* [exercise.

exercitātiō, -ōnis, [exercitō, freq. of exerceō], f., *practice, exercise, training.*

exercitātus, -a, -um, comp. -ior, sup. -issimus, [exercitō, freq. of exerceō], adj., *practiced, experienced, trained.*

exercitus, -ūs, [exerceō], m., *army,* as a trained and disciplined body.

exhauriō, -haurīre, -hausī, -haustus, [ex + hauriō, *draw up*], 4, *take out.* v. 42. [exhaust.

exigō, -igere, -ēgī, -āctus, [ex + agō], 3, *drive out;* of time, *spend, complete, end* (iii. 28; vi. 1); of money, *demand, require* (C. i. 6). [exact.

exiguē [exiguus], adv., *barely, hardly.* vii. 71.

exiguitās, -ātis, [exiguus], f., *smallness* (iv. 30); *scantness* (iv. 1); *small number, fewness* (iii. 23); *shortness* (ii. 21, 33).

exiguus, -a, -um, sup. -issimus, [exigō], adj., *small, scanty, little.*

eximius, -a, -um, [cf. eximō], adj., *distinguished, excellent.* ii. 8.

exīstimātiō, -ōnis, [exīstimō], f., *opinion, judgment* (i. 20; v. 44); *good name, reputation* (C. i. 7).

exīstimō, -āre, -āvī, -ātus, [ex + aestimō, *compute*], 1, *reckon; think, consider, judge, suppose, believe.*

exitus, -ūs, [exeō], m., *a going out, egress* (vii. 44); *passage* (vii. 28); *conclusion, end; issue, event, outcome.* [exit.

expediō, -pedīre, -pedīvī, -pedītus, [ex, cf. pēs], 4, *disengage, set free; get ready, make ready.* [expedite.

expedītiō, -ōnis, [expediō], f., *rapid march.* v. 10. [expedition.

expedītus, -a, -um, comp. -ior, sup. -issimus, [part. of expediō], adj., *with light equipment, unencumbered, light-armed; convenient, easy.* **legiōnēs expedītae,** *legions in light marching order,* without baggage. As noun, **expedītus,** -ī, m., *soldier with light equipment, light-armed soldier.*

expellō, -pellere, -pulī, -pulsus, [ex + pellō], 3, *drive out, drive away, remove.* [expel.

experior, -perīrī, -pertus, 4, dep., put to the test, try. [expert.

expiō, -āre, -āvī, -ātus, [ex + piō, appease], 1, atone for, make amends for. v. 52. [expiate.

expleō, -plēre, -plēvī, -plētus, [ex + pleō, fill], 2, fill up, fill full; fill out, complete.

explicō, -āre, -āvī and -uī, explicitus, explicātūrus, [ex + plicō, fold], 1, unfold; of troops, with sē, deploy (C. III. 93). [explicate.

explōrātor, -ōris, [explōrō], m., scout, patrol.

explorātus, -a, -um, comp. -ior, sup. -issimus, [part. of explōrō], adj., established, certain, settled, sure. Neut. as noun in prō explōrātō, lit. for a certainty, as certain (vi. 5).

explōrō, -āre, -āvī -ātus, 1, search out, investigate, explore; spy out, reconnoitre; gain, secure. [explore.

expōnō, -pōnere, -posuī, -positus, [ex + pōnō], 3, set out, put out; place in full view, array (iv. 23); from ships, set on shore, land; set forth, state, explain. [expose.

exportō, -āre, -āvī -ātus, [ex + portō], 1, carry away. iv. 18. [export.

exposcō, -poscere, -poposcī, [ex + poscō], 3, earnestly request, clamor for. vii. 19; C. III. 90.

exprimō, -primere, -pressī, -pressus, [ex + premō], 3, press out; force out (i. 32); raise, increase (vii. 22). [express.

expugnātiō, -ōnis, [expugnō], f., storming, assault. vi. 41.

expugnō, -āre, -āvī, -ātus, [ex + pugnō], 1, take by storm, take by assault, capture.

expulsus, see expellō.

exquīrō, -quīrere, -quīsīvī, -quīsītus, [ex + quaerō], 3, seek out, search out (i. 41); ask for, inquire into (iii. 3). [exquisite.

exquīsītus, see exquīrō.

exsequor, -sequī, -secūtus, [ex + sequor], 3, dep., follow up; maintain, enforce (i. 4). [execute.

exserō, -serere, -seruī, -sertus, [ex + serō], 3, thrust out; thrust out from one's garments, bare (vii. 50).

exsertus, see exserō.

exsistō, -sistere, -stitī, [ex + sistō], 3, appear; spring up, arise, ensue; of a horn, project (vi. 26). [exist.

exspectō, -āre, -āvī, -ātus, [ex + spectō], 1, look out for, wait for, await; look to see, expect. [expect.

exspoliō, -āre, -āvī, -ātus, [ex + spoliō], 1, deprive, rob. vii. 77.

exstinguō, -stinguere, -stīnxī, -stīnctus, [ex + stinguō], 3, quench completely. v. 29. [extinguish.

exstō, -stāre, [ex + stō], 1, stand out, project. v. 18. [extant.

exstruō, -struere, -strūxī, -strūctus, [ex + struō, pile], 3, pile up, heap up; rear, build, construct, make (vii. 72).

exsul, -ulis, m. and f., outlaw, exile. v. 55.

exter or exterus, -a, -um, comp. exterior, sup. extrēmus, [ex], adj., outward, outer. Sup. extrēmus, last, extreme, at the end. As noun, extrēmī, -ōrum, m., pl., the rear (v. 10); neut. sing. in ad extrēmum, at the end, finally (iv. 4). [extreme.

externus, -a, -um, [exter], adj., outward; foreign (C. II. 5). [external.

exterreō, -ēre, -uī, -itus, [ex + terreō, scare], 2, greatly frighten, terrify.

extimēscō, -timēscere, -timuī, [ex + timēscō, fear], 3, fear greatly, dread. iii. 13.

extorqueō, -torquēre, -torsī, -tortus, [ex + torqueō, *twist*], 2, *force from ; wrest from* (vii. 54). [extort.

extrā [exter], prep. with acc., *outside of, beyond, without.* [extra.

extrahō, -trahere, -trāxī, -trāctus, [ex + trahō, *draw*], 3, *draw out; draw out* to no purpose, *waste* (v. 22). [extract.

extrūdō, -trūdere, -trūsī, -trūsus, [ex + trūdō], 3, *thrust out; shut out* (iii. 12). [extrude.

exuō, -uere, -uī, -ūtus, 3, *strip, strip off, despoil, deprive.*

exūrō, -ūrere, -ussī, -ūstus, [ex + ūrō, *burn*], 3, *burn up.* i. 5.

F.

faber, fabrī, m., *skilled workman, mechanic, artisan.* v. 11. [fabric.

Fabius, -ī, m., (fā′ bi-us) :

(1) *Quintus Fabius Maximus* (mak′ si-mus), called *Allobrogicus* (al-o-broj′ i-kus), in honor of his victory over the Allobroges, Arvernians, and Ruteni in the year of his consulship, B.C. 121. i. 45.

(2) *Gaius Fabius,* a lieutenant of Caesar in the Gallic War, and in the first year of the Civil War.

(3) *Lucius Fabius,* a centurion, killed at Gergovia. vii. 47, 50.

(4) *Fabius, the Paelignian,* a soldier in Curio's army. C. II. 35.

facile, comp. facilius, sup. facillimē, [facilis], adv., *easily, readily.*

facilis, -e, comp. facilior, sup. facillimus, [cf. faciō], adj., *easy, not difficult, not hard.* [facile.

facinus, -oris, [faciō], n., *action; wicked action, misdeed, crime.*

faciō, facere, fēcī, factus, 3, *do, make; act, perform, accomplish, form; bring about, cause; furnish, give.* For pass., fīō, fierī, factus sum, see fīō. certiōrem facere,

to inform. imperāta facere, *to obey commands.* iter facere, *to march.* vim facere, *to use violence* (i. 8, v. 7). [factor.

factiō, -ōnis, [faciō], f., *party, political party ; league.* [faction.

factū, pass. supine of faciō.

factum, -ī, [faciō], n., *deed, action, achievement.* [fact.

facultās, -ātis, [facilis], f., *ability, capability; opportunity, chance; abundance; supply* (iii. 9). Pl., *resources, wealth.* [faculty.

fāgus, -ī, f., *beech-tree.* v. 12.

fallō, fallere, fefellī, falsus, 3, *deceive, cheat ; disappoint.*

falsus, -a, -um, [part. of fallō], adj., *false, ungrounded.* [false.

falx, falcis, f., *sickle ;* sickle-shaped *hook.*

fāma, -ae, [cf. fārī, *to speak*], f., *report, rumor, common talk; reputation, fame* (vii. 77). [fame.

famēs, -is, f., *hunger, starvation.* [famine.

familia, -ae, [famulus, *servant*], f., *body of slaves* in one household, *household; family* (vii. 33); including the whole body of serfs and retainers under the authority of a nobleman, *retinue* (i. 4). pater familiae, *head of a family, householder* (vi. 19); patrēs familiae, *heads of families* (C. II. 44). mātrēs familiae, *matrons* (i. 50; vii. 26, 47, 48). antīquissimā familiā, *of a very old family* (vii. 32). amplissimā familiā, *of a very distinguished family* (vii. 37). [family.

familiāris, -e, comp. -ior, sup. -issimus, [familia], adj., *belonging to a family, private.* rēs familiāris, *private property, estate, private fortune* (i. 18; vii. 14, 64). As noun, familiāris, -is, m., *intimate friend, companion.* [familiar.

familiāritās, -ātis, [familiāris], f.,
intimacy, close friendship. [famili-
arity.

fānum, -ī, n., *shrine*. C. I. 6. [fane.

fās, only nom. and acc. sing. in use,
[cf. **fārī**, *to speak*], indecl., n., *right
according to the laws of God and
nature*. **fās est**, *it is right, allow-
able, lawful;* of an event, *it is predestined* (I. 50).

fascis, -is, m., *bundle* of reeds or
twigs; especially pl., **fascēs**, -ium,
the fasces, a bundle of rods with an
axe, carried before the highest magistrates as an emblem of authority
(C. III. 71).

fastīgātē [fastīgātus], adv., *sloping;
slanting* (iv. 17).

fastīgātus, -a, -um, [cf. **fastīgium**],
adj., *sloping, sloping down*. ii. 8.

fastīgium, -ī, n., of a roof, *top;* of a
hill, *summit, peak* (vii. 69); *sloping
side, slope, descent, declivity*.

fatīgō, -āre, -āvī, -ātus, I, *weary*.
C. III. 95. [fatigue.

fātum, -ī, [cf. **fārī**, *to speak*], n., *fate,
destiny*. i. 39. [fate.

Faustus, -ī, see Sulla.

faveō, favēre, fāvī, fautūrus, 2, *be
favorable, be inclined toward, favor,
countenance*. [favor.

fax, facis, f., *torch, firebrand*. vii.
24.

fēlīcitās, -ātis, [fēlīx, *happy*], f.,
good fortune (i. 40, C. III. 73); *success* (vi. 43). [felicity.

fēlīciter, comp. fēlīcius, sup. fēlīcis-
simē, [fēlīx], adv., *with good fortune, luckily, happily* (iv. 25; C. I. 7).

fēmina, -ae, f., *woman; female*. vi.
21, 26. [feminine.

femur, -oris and -inis, n., *thigh*. v.
35; vii. 73. [femoral.

fera, -ae, [ferus, *wild*], f., *wild beast,
wild animal*. vi. 25, 28.

ferāx, -ācis, comp. ferācior, sup.

ferācissimus, [ferō], adj., *fertile,
productive*. ii. 4. [feracious.

ferē, adv., *almost, nearly;* with words
denoting time, *about; for the most
part, as a rule, usually, generally*.

ferō, ferre, tulī, lātus, irr., *bear,
carry, bring; endure, support, suffer, hold out against; bear away;
obtain, receive; assert, report, say*
(vi. 17). **signa ferre**, *to advance*.

ferrāmentum, -ī, [ferrum], n., *iron
tool*. v. 42.

ferrāria, -ae, [ferrum], f., *iron mine*.
vii. 22.

ferreus, -a, -um, [ferrum], adj., *of
iron, iron*. **ferreae manūs**, *grappling-hooks* (C. II. 6). [ferreous.

ferrum, -ī, n., *iron* (v. 12); figura-
tively, *the iron*, with a barbed point,
at the end of a pike (i. 25), *sword*
(v. 30).

fertilis, -e, comp. -ior, sup. -issimus,
[ferō], adj., *fertile, fruitful, productive*. vi. 24; vii. 13. [fertile.

fertilitās, -ātis, [fertilis], f., *produc-
tiveness*. ii. 4. [fertility.

ferus, -a, -um, adj., *wild; rude, savage, fierce*. [fierce.

fervefaciō, -facere, -fēcī, -factus,
[ferveō + faciō], 3, *make hot, heat,
heat red-hot*. v. 43; vii. 22.

ferveō, -ēre, 2, *be boiling hot, be heated,
glow*. Present Participle as Adj.,
fervēns, -tis, *red-hot* (v. 43).
[fervent.

fībula, -ae, [cf. **fīgō**, *fasten*], f.,
clasp; brace, bolt (iv. 17).

fidēlis, -e, comp. -ior, sup. -issimus,
[fidēs], adj., *faithful, trustworthy*
(vii. 76); *true, loyal* (iv. 21).

fidēs, -eī, f., *good faith, fidelity, loyalty; pledge of good faith, promise;
confidence, trust; protection, alliance*. [faith.

fīdūcia, -ae, [fīdus], f., *reliance, confidence, assurance*. [fiduciary.

figūra, -ae, [cf. fingō], f., *form, shape.* [figure.

fīlia, -ae, f., *daughter*.

fīlius, -ī, m., *son.* [filial.

fingō, fingere, fīnxī, fīctus, 3, *form, shape; conceive, imagine, think of* (vi. 37); *invent, devise* (iv. 5); *of the features, change, control* (i. 39). [feign.

fīniō, fīnīre, fīnīvī, fīnītus, [fīnis], 4, *bound, define* (iv. 16); *measure, limit* (vi. 18, 25). [finite.

fīnis, -is, m., *limit, border, boundary, end.* Pl., *borders,* hence *territory, country, land.* [finis.

fīnitimus, -a, -um, [fīnis], adj., *bordering on, neighboring, adjoining.* As noun, fīnitimī, -ōrum, m., pl., *neighbors, neighboring peoples.*

fīō, fierī, factus, irr., used as pass. of faciō, *be made, be done; be performed,* (II. 5); *become, take place, happen; come about, come to pass.* certior fierī, *to be informed.*

fīrmiter, [fīrmus], adv., *steadily, firmly.* iv. 26.

fīrmitūdō, -inis,[fīrmus],f.,*strength, solidity; rigidity.* iii. 13; iv. 17.

fīrmō, -āre, -āvī, -ātus, [fīrmus], I, *make firm, strengthen, fortify.* vi. 29.

fīrmus, -a, -um, comp. -ior, sup. -issimus, adj., *strong, firm; steadfast, powerful.* [firm.

fistūca, -ae, f., *rammer, pile-driver.* iv. 17.

Flaccus, -ī, (flak'us), see Valerius (2) and (7).

flāgitō, -āre, -āvī, -ātus, I, *ask earnestly, importune, demand.* i. 16.

flamma, -ae, f., *blazing fire, flame, fire.* v. 43; vi. 16. [flame.

flectō, flectere, flexī, flexus, 3, *bend, turn, curve.* iv. 33; vi. 25. [flex.

Flegīnās, -ātis, m., *Gaius Fleginas* (fle-jī'nas), a Roman knight killed in action near Dyrrachium. C. III. 71.

fleō, flēre, flēvī, flētus, 2, *weep, shed tears, cry.*

flētus, -ūs, [fleō], m., *weeping.*

flō, -āre, -āvī, -ātus, I, *blow.* v. 7.

flōrēns, -entis, comp. -entior, sup. -entissimus, [flōreō, *bloom*], adj., *flourishing, prosperous* (I. 30, IV. 3); *influential* (vii. 32).

flōs, flōris, m., *flower.* vii. 73. [flower.

fluctus, -ūs, [cf. fluō], m., *wave.*

flūmen, -inis, [cf. fluō], n., *flowing water, current; stream, river.* adversō flūmine, *up the stream.*

fluō, fluere, flūxī, sup. flūxum, 3, *flow.* [flux.

fodiō, fodere, fōdī, fossus, 3, *dig, dig out.* vii. 73.

foedus, foederis, n., *treaty, compact, league.* vi. 2.

forāmen, -inis, [forō, *bore*], n., *hole.* C. III. 53.

fore = futūrum esse; see sum.

forem = essem; see sum.

forīs, [foris, *door*], adv., *out of doors; outside of a city, without* (vii. 76).

fōrma, -ae, f., *shape, form.* [form.

fors, fortis, [cf. ferō], f., *chance, luck, accident.* ii. 21; vii. 87.

fortasse, [forte], adv., *perhaps, possibly.* C. III. 60.

forte [abl. of fors], adv., *by chance, by accident; perchance, perhaps.*

fortis, -e, comp. -ior, sup. -issimus, adj., *strong; brave, courageous.* [fort.

fortiter, comp. fortius, sup. fortissimē, [fortis], adv., *bravely, boldly, courageously.*

fortitūdō, -inis, [fortis], f., *courage, bravery.* i. 2. [fortitude.

fortuītō, [abl. of fortuītus, from forte], adv., *by chance.* [fortuitous.

fortūna, -ae, [fors], f., *luck, lot, fate, chance, fortune; good fortune; the goddess Fortune* (Fig. 198); Pl., *fortunes* (III. 12; v. 3; VI. 7; VII. 77); *pos-*

sessions, property (i. 11; v. 43; vi. 35; vii. 8). [fortune.

Figure 198. — The Goddess Fortune as conceived by the Romans.

Marble Statue, in Rome. The goddess wears a broad diadem. Her left hand holds a cornucopia, filled with good things for those whom she favors. Her right hand grasps a steering-paddle, with which, noiselessly but remorselessly, she guides the affairs of mankind; the steering-paddle rests upon a globe symbolizing the world.

Some such picture as this presented itself to Caesar's mind when he vividly personified *fortuna*, which in certain passages of his text (as v. 44) is sometimes written with a capital letter. But his vision was too broad and his mind too philosophical to believe in Fortuna as those did who worshipped at her shrine.

fortūnātus, -a, -um, comp. -ior, sup. -issimus, [part. of fortūnō, from fortūna], adj., *prosperous, fortunate.* vi. 35. [fortunate.

forum, -ī, n., *market-place.* vii. 28. [forum.

fossa, -ae, [cf. fodiō], f., *trench, intrenchment.* [fosse.

fovea, -ae, f., *pit, pitfall.* vi. 28.

frangō, frangere, frēgī, frāctus, 3, *break; dash to pieces, wreck* (iv. 29); *crush, dishearten* (i. 31). [fracture.

frāter, -tris, m., *brother;* pl. as a name of honor applied to allies, *brethren* (i. 33, 44; ii. 3).

frāternus, -a, -um, [frāter], adj., *of a brother, brotherly.* [fraternal.

fraudō, -āre, -āvī, -ātus, [fraus], 1, *cheat; embezzle* (C. III. 59, 60).

fraus, fraudis, f., *deception, imposition.* vii. 40. [fraud.

fremitus, -ūs, [cf. fremō, *roar*], m., *uproar, noise, din.*

frequēns, -entis, comp. frequentior, sup. -issimus, adj., *in large numbers, crowded.* [frequent.

fretum, -ī, n., *strait.* fretum Siciliae, *Sicilian strait, strait of Messina* (C. II. 3).

frētus, -a, -um, adj., *relying on, depending on;* followed by abl.

frīgidus, -a, -um, comp. -ior, sup. -issimus, [frīgeō, *be cold*], adj., *cold.* iv. 1. [frigid.

frīgus, frīgoris, n., *cold, cold weather.* Pl., *cold seasons, cold climate.*

frōns, frontis, f., *forehead; front.* ā mediā fronte, *in the middle of the forehead* (vi. 26). [front.

frūctuōsus, -a, -um, sup. -issimus, [frūctus], adj., *fruitful, fertile.* i. 30.

frūctus, -ūs, m., *fruit, product; profit, interest, income* (vi. 19); *advantage, gain, reward* (vii. 27, 86). [fruit.

frūgēs, -um, f., pl., *produce, crops, fruits.* i. 28. [frugal.

frūmentārius, -a, -um, [frūmentum], adj., *relating to grain* or *supplies* of grain; *productive* of grain (i. 10). rēs frūmentāria, *supply of grain, supplies.*

frūmentātiō, -ōnis, [frūmentor), f., *obtaining of grain, expedition in quest of grain.*

frūmentor, -ārī, -ātus, [frūmentum], 1, dep., *get grain, forage.*

frūmentum, -ī, n., *grain;* pl. often *crops of grain, grain-crops.*

fruor, fruī, frūctus, 3, dep., *enjoy;* followed by abl. iii. 22.

frūstrā, adv., *in vain, without effect; for nothing, without reason.* [frustrate.

Fūfius, -ī, m., *Gaius Fufius Cita* (fū′fi̯-u̯s sī′ta̯), a Roman knight. vii. 3.

fuga, -ae, f., *flight.* **in fugam dare,** *to put to flight, rout.*

fugiō, fugere, fūgī, 3, *flee, run away, make off; avoid, shun* (vii. 30); *escape* (vii. 38).

fugitīvus, -a, -um, [fugiō], adj., *fleeing, runaway.* As noun, **fugitīvus, -ī,** m., *runaway slave* (i. 23). [fugitive.

fugō, -āre, -āvī, -ātus, [fuga], 1, *put to flight, rout.* vii. 68.

fūmō, -āre, [fūmus], 1, *smoke.* vii. 24. [fume.

fūmus, -ī, m., *smoke.* ii. 7; v. 48.

funda, -ae, f., *sling.*

funditor, -ōris, [funda], m., *slinger.*

fundō, fundere, fūdī, fūsus, 3, *pour* (vii. 24); *scatter, rout* (iii. 6). [foundry.

fūnebris, -e [fūnus], adj., *funeral.* As noun, **fūnebria, -ium,** neuter plural, *funeral rites* (vi. 19).

fungor, fungī, fūnctus, 3, dep., *discharge, perform.* vii. 25. [function.

fūnis, -is, m., *rope;* rope *cable* (III. 13, IV. 29, V. 10); *halyards* (III. 14).

fūnus, -eris, n., *funeral.* vi. 19. [funeral.

furor, -ōris, [furō, *rage*], m., *rage, madness, fury.* [furor.

fūrtum, -ī, [fūr, *thief*], n., *theft.*

fūsilis, -e, [cf. fundō], adj., *molten;* of clay, *kneaded, molded.* v. 43. [fusile.

futūrus, -a, -um, see **sum.**

G.

Gabalī, -ōrum, m., pl., (gab′a̯-lī), a people in Southern Gaul, subject to the Arvernians. VII. 7, 64, 75.

Gabīnius, -ī, m., *Aulus Gabinius* (ga̯-bin′i̯-u̯s), consul with Lucius Calpurnius Piso, 58 B.C. i. 6; C. III. 103.

gaesum, -ī, n., *heavy javelin* used by the Gauls. iii. 4.

Gaius, -ī, abbreviation **C.,** m., *Gaius* (gā′yu̯s), sometimes in English written *Caius,* a Roman first name.

Galba, -ae, m., (gal′ba̯) :

(1) *Servius Sulpicius Galba,* a lieutenant of Caesar in the earlier part of the Gallic War, Praetor at Rome in 54 B.C.; afterwards named among the conspirators who took Caesar's life. iii. 1–6.

(2) *Galba,* a ruler of the Suessiones. ii. 4, 13.

galea, -ae, f., *helmet.* ii. 21.

Figure 199. — Coin struck at Lugdunum, now Lyons.

Silver, issued by order of Galba, latter half of first century A.D. Inscription, TRES GALLIA[E], 'Three Gauls.' The identification of the heads is uncertain; an ear of wheat projects in front of each.

Gallia, -ae, [Gallus], f., *Gallia* (gal′i̯-a̯), *Gaul,* used of Transalpine Gaul, and of the middle one of its three parts, Celtic Gaul (i. 1);

also of Cisalpine Gaul, and of the
Province ; once in the plural, Galliae, as referring to the several divisions (IV. 20). After Caesar's
conquest the plural was used of three
provinces in Transalpine Gaul (Fig.
199). [Gaul.

Gallicus, -a, -um, [Gallus], adj., *of
Gaul, Gallic.*

gallīna, -ae, [gallus, *cock*], f., *hen.*

Gallus, -a, -um, adj., *Gallic.* As
noun, m., *a Gaul;* pl., Gallī,
-ōrum, *Celts,* Galli (gal' ī), used by
Caesar as referring to the inhabitants
of *Gallia Celtica,* the middle of the
three main divisions of Gaul.

Gallus, -ī, m., see Trebius.

Garumna, -ae, f., (ga-rum' na), the
great river of southwestern France,
which rises in the Pyrenees Mountains and flows in a northwesterly
direction to the Atlantic Ocean, after
a course of about 350 miles; now
Garonne. i. 1.

Garumnī, -ōrum, m., pl.,(ga-rum' nī),
a people in Aquitania, probably near
the sources of the Garonne. iii. 27.

Gatēs, -ium, m., pl., (gā' tēz), a people in Aquitania. iii. 27.

gaudeō, gaudēre, gāvīsus sum, 2,
semi-dep., *rejoice, be glad.* iv. 13.

gāvīsus, see gaudeō.

Geidumnī, -ōrum, m., pl., (je-
dum' nī), a people of Belgic Gaul,
clients of the Nervians. v. 39.

Genava, -ae, f., (jen' a-va), a city of
the Allobroges, on the lacus Lemannus; now *Geneva.* i. 7.

gener, generī, m., *son-in-law.* v. 56.

generātim [genus], adv., *by kind;
by peoples, by tribes, nation by nation* (i. 51; vii. 19).

gēns, gentis, f., *clan, family* (vi. 22);
nation, people. [gentile.

genus, generis, n., *birth, descent,
family; race* (iv. 3; vii. 22, 42);

*kind, species; class, rank; method,
nature.* [genus.

Gergovia, -ae, f., (jer-gō' vi-a), chief
city of the Arvernians, situated on a
narrow plateau (elevation, 2,440 ft.)
about six miles south of Clermont-
Ferrand.

Germānia, -ae, [Germānus], f.,
Germany. [Germany.

Germānicus, -a, -um, [Germānī],
adj., *German.*

Germānus, -a, -um, adj., *of* or *from
Germany, German.* As noun, Germānī, -ōrum, m., pl., *Germans,
the Germans.* [German.

gerō, gerere, gessī, gestus, 3, *bear,
carry; manage, transact, do, carry
on; carry out, perform, accomplish;*
of an office, *fill;* of war, *wage.* rem
gestam perscrībit, *he wrote a full
account of what had been done* (v.
47). [jest.

gestus, see gerō.

gladius, -ī, m., *sword.* [gladiolus.

glāns, glandis, f., *acorn; slingshot,
bullet* hurled by a sling (v. 43); vii.
81). [gland.

glēba, -ae, f., *lump of earth, clod;
lump, mass* (vii. 25). [glebe.

glōria, -ae, f., *fame, renown.* [glory.

glōrior, -ārī, -ātus, [glōria], 1, dep.,
boast, brag (i. 14).

Gnaeus, -ī, abbreviation Cn., m.,
(nē' us), a Roman first name.

Gobannitiō, -ōnis, m., (gob-a-nish'
[y]ō), an uncle of Vercingetorix,
hostile to him. vii. 4.

Gorgobina, -ae, f., (gor-gob' i-na),
a city in the country of the Aeduans,
inhabited by Boians (vii. 9).

Gracchī, -ōrum, m., pl., *the Grac-
chi,* (grak' ī), Tiberius and Gaius
Sempronius Gracchus, leaders in re-
forms which led to violence; Tiberius Gracchus was killed in 133 B.C.,
Gaius in 121 B.C. C. I. 7.

Graecus, -a, -um, [Γραικός], adj., *Greek, Grecian*. As noun, **Grae-cus**, -ī, m., *a Greek* (vi. 24).

Graiocelī, -ōrum, m., pl., (grạ-yō'-sẹ-lī), a Gallic people in the Alps. i. 10.

grandis, -e, comp. -ior, sup. -issimus, adj., *large, great*. [grand.

Grānius, -ī, m., *Aulus Granius*, (grā'-nị-ụs), a Roman knight killed in action near Dyrrachium. C. iii. 71.

grātia, -ae, [grātus], f., *favor, gratitude; esteem, regard; recompense, requital* (i. 35, v. 27); *popularity; influence* (i. 9, 18, 20, 43, etc.). Pl., **grātiae**, -ārum, *thanks*. **grātiās agere**, *to thank*. **grātiā**, *for the sake of* (vii. 43). [grace.

grātulātiō, -ōnis, [grātulor], f., *rejoicing, congratulation*. [gratulation.

grātulor, -ārī, -ātus, [grātus], 1, dep., *offer congratulations, congratulate*. i. 30. [gratulate.

grātus, -a, -um, comp. -ior, sup. -issimus, adj., *acceptable, pleasing* (vi. 16). Neut. as noun, **grātum**, -ī, *a kindness, a favor* (i. 44). [grateful.

gravis, -e, comp. -ior, sup. -issimus, adj., *heavy* (iv. 24); *heavily laden* (v. 8); *severe, hard, serious, troublesome; of age, advanced* (iii. 16). [grave (adjective).

gravitās, -ātis, [gravis], f., *weight* (v. 16); *importance* (iv. 3). [gravity.

graviter, comp. **gravius**, sup. **gravissimē**, [gravis], adv., *heavily* (iii. 14); *severely, warmly, bitterly; seriously, with great displeasure*. **graviter ferre**, *to be annoyed, be disturbed*.

gravō, -āre, -āvī, -ātus, [gravis], 1, *weigh down*. Pass. as dep., *hesitate, be unwilling* (i. 35).

Grudiī, -ōrum, m., pl., (grū' dị-ī), a Belgic people near the Nervians. v. 39.

gubernātor, -ōris, [gubernō, *steer*], m., *helmsman, pilot*. [governor.

gustō, -āre, -āvī, -ātus, [gustus, *tasting*], 1, *taste, taste of*. [gustatory.

H.

habeō, **habēre**, **habuī**, **habitus**, 2, *have, hold, possess, keep; regard, think, consider; account, repute, reckon; of a count, make* (i. 29). **ōrātiōnem habēre**, *to make a speech, deliver an address*. [habit.

haesitō, -āre, -āvī, -ātus, [freq. of **haereō**], 1, *stick fast, remain fixed*. vii. 19. [hesitate.

hāmus, -ī, m., *hook; barbed hook* (vii. 73). [hamate.

harpagō, -ōnis, [= ἁρπάγη], m., *grappling-iron, grappling-hook*, a pole with an iron hook at the end. vii. 81.

Harūdēs, -um, m., pl., (hạ-rū' dēz), a German tribe between the Danube and the upper part of the Rhine.

haud, adv., *not at all, not*. v. 54.

hedera, -ae, f., *ivy*. C. iii. 96.

Helvēticus, -a, -um, adj., *Helvetian*. **Helvēticum proelium**, *the battle with the Helvetians* (vii. 9).

Helvētius, -a, -um, adj., *of the Helvetians, Helvetian*. **cīvitās Helvētia**, *the State of the Helvetians, Helvetian State*, divided into four cantons, the names of two of which, **pāgus Tigurīnus**, **pāgus Verbigenus**, are known (i. 12). As noun, **Helvētiī**, -ōrum, m., pl., *the Helvetians, Helvetii* (hẹl-vē' sh[y]ī).

Helviī, -ōrum, m., pl., (hẹl' vị-ī), a Gallic people in the Province.

Hercynius, -a, -um, adj., *Hercynian*. **Silva Hercynia** [in Greek Ἀρκύνια ὄρη, Ἑρκύνιοι δρυμοί], a forest in southern Germany and Austria, which followed the course of the Danube from its source eastward beyond modern Vienna to the Carpathian Mountains. [hercynite.

hērēditās, -ātis, [hērēs, *heir*], f., *inheritance*. vi. 13. [heredity.

Hibernia, -ae, f., *Hibernia* (hī-bér'-nĭ-a), *Ireland*. v. 13. [Hibernian.

hībernus, -a, -um, [hiems], adj., *of winter*. As noun, **hīberna**, -ōrum (sc. **castra**), n., pl., *winter-quarters*. [hibernal.

hīc, haec, hōc, gen. **huius**, dem. pron., *this, the following, he, she, it*.

hīc, [pron. **hīc**], adv., *here, at this place;* of time, *at this point*.

hiemō, -āre, -āvī, -ātūrus, [hiems], 1, *pass the winter, winter*.

hiems, hiemis, f., *winter; wintry storm, stormy weather* (iv. 36).

hinc [hīc], adv., *hence, from this place, from this point*.

Hirrus, -ī, m., see **Lūcīlius**.

Hispānia, -ae, f., *Spain*. Pl., **Hispāniae**, -ārum, *Spanish provinces*, referring to the division into the two parts, **Hispānia** **citerior**, *Hither Spain*, and **ulterior**, *Further Spain* (C. iii. 73). [Spain.

Hispānus, -a, -um, adj., *Spanish*. v. 26. [spaniel, *i.e.* 'Spanish dog.'

homō, hominis, m. and f., *human being, man*.

honestus, -a, -um, comp. -ior, sup. -issimus [honōs], adj., *honorable, noble; of good family*, (vii. 3; C. ii. 5). **locō nātus honestō**, *of excellent family* (v. 45, C. iii. 61). [honest.

honōrificus, -a, -um, comp. **honōrificentior**, sup. -centissimus, [honōs, cf. **faciō**], adj., *conferring honor, complimentary*. i. 43. [honorific.

honōs, or **honor**, -ōris, m., *honor, esteem, respect, dignity; public office, office, post*. [honor.

hōra, -ae, [= ὥρα], f., *hour*, a twelfth part of the day, from sunrise to sunset, the Roman hours varying in length with the season of the year.

hordeum, -ī, n., *barley*. C. iii. 47.

horreō, horrēre, horruī, 2, *tremble at, shudder at, dread*. i. 32.

horribilis, -e, comp. -ior, [horreō], adj., *dread-inspiring*. [horrible.

horridus, -a, -um, comp. -ior, [horreō], adj., *wild, frightful* (v. 14). [horrid.

hortātus, -ūs, [hortor], m., *encouragement, urging*. C. iii. 86.

hortor, -ārī, -ātus, 1, dep., *urge, encourage; exhort, incite, press*.

hospes, hospitis, m., *host; guest* (vi. 23); *friend* bound by hospitality, *guest-friend* (i. 53, v. 6). [host.

hospitium, -ī, [hospes], n., *relation of guest and host, tie of hospitality, hospitality*. [hospice.

hostis, -is, m., public *enemy, foe;* in this book both the sing. and the pl., **hostēs**, -ium, in most cases = *the enemy*. Cf. **inimīcus**. [host (army).

hūc, [hīc], adv., *hither, here, to this place*.

huius modī, see **modus**.

hūmānitās, -ātis, [hūmānus], f., *humanity; refinement, culture* (i. 1. 47). [humanity.

hūmānus, -a, -um, comp. -ior, sup. -issimus, [homō], adj., *of man, human* (C. i. 6); *refined, civilized* (iv. 3; v. 14). [human.

humilis, -e, comp. -ior, sup. **humillimus**, [humus, *ground*], adj., *low; shallow* (v. 1); *mean, humble, insignificant, weak*. [humble.

humilitās, -ātis, [humilis], f., *lowness* (v. 1); *humble position, insignificance* (v. 27). [humility.

I.

iaceō, iacēre, iacuī, iacitūrus, 2, *lie, lie prostrate; lie dead* (vii. 25). Pres. part. as noun, **iacentēs, -ium,** m., pl., *the fallen* (ii. 27).

iaciō, iacere, iēcī, iactus, 3, *throw, cast, hurl; throw up, construct* (ii. 12); of an anchor, *drop* (iv. 28).

iactō, -āre, -āvī, -ātus, [freq. of **iaciō**], 1, *throw, cast* (vii. 47); *throw about, jerk back and forth* (i. 25); *discuss, agitate* (i. 18); *boast of, vaunt* (C. III. 83).

iactūra, -ae, [**iaciō**], f., *a throwing; loss, sacrifice, cost.*

iactus, see **iaciō.**

iaculum, -ī, [cf. **iaciō**], n., *javelin.* v. 43, 45.

iam, adv., *already, now; at once, immediately* (vi. 35, vii. 38); *at length* (i. 42); *actually* (iii. 17); *in fact, indeed* (iii. 9).

ibi or **ibī,** adv., *in that place, there.*

Iccius, -ī, m., (ik′sh[y]us), a leader of the Remi.

ictus, -ūs, [**īcō,** *strike*], m., *blow, stroke.* i. 25; vii. 25.

Īd., abbreviation for **Īdūs.**

idcircō, [**id** + abl. of **circus**], adv., *on that account, therefore.* v. 3.

īdem, eadem, idem, eiusdem, dem. pron., *the same.* [identity.

identidem, [**idem et idem**], adv., *repeatedly, again and again.* ii. 19.

idōneus, -a, -um, adj., *suitable, convenient, fit, capable.*

Īdūs, -uum, f., pl., abbreviation **Īd.,** *the Ides,* the fifteenth day of March, May, July, and October; the thirteenth day of other months. i. 7.

īgnis, -is, m., *fire.* Pl., **īgnēs,** *fire-signals, watch-fires* (ii. 33). [igneous.

ignōbilis, -e, [**in-** + (**g**)**nōbilis**], adj., *unknown; obscure* (v. 28). [ignoble.

ignōminia, -ae, [**in-** + (**g**)**nōmen**], f., *disgrace, dishonor.* [ignominy.

ignōrō, -āre, -āvī, -ātus, [cf. **ignōscō**], 1, *be ignorant of, not to know, be unaware; overlook* (i. 27). **nōn ignōrāns,** *being not unfamiliar with* (vi. 42), *not unaware* (vii. 33). [ignore.

ignōscō, -gnōscere, -gnōvī, -gnōtus, [**in-** + (**g**)**nōscō,** *know*], 3, *pardon, overlook; forgive, excuse.*

ignōtus, -a, -um, comp. **-ior,** sup. **-issimus,** [**in-** + (**g**)**nōtus**], adj., *unknown; unfamiliar* (iv. 24).

illātus, see **īnferō.**

ille, illa, illud, illīus, dem. pron., used with or without a noun, *that; he, she, it.*

illīc [loc. of **ille**], adv., *there, in that place, in that region.* i. 18; vii. 20.

illigō, -āre, -āvī, -ātus, [**in** + **ligō,** *bind*], 1, *tie on; bind* (iv. 17); *fasten* (v. 45).

illō [**ille**], adv., *thither, to that place; to that end* (iv. 11).

illūstris, -e, comp. **-ior,** sup. **-issimus,** [**in,** cf. **lūx**], adj., *prominent, distinguished; remarkable, noteworthy* (vii. 3). [illustrious.

Illyricum, -ī, n., (i-lir′i-kum), a region along the east coast of the Adriatic Sea, now *Istria* and *Dalmatia.* ii. 35; iii. 7; v. 1.

imbēcillitās, -ātis, [**imbēcillus,** *weak*], f., *weakness.* [imbecility.

imber, imbris, m., *rain, rainstorm.* **magnus imber,** *a violent rainstorm* (vii. 27).

imitor, -ārī, -ātus, 1, dep., *copy, imitate.* vi. 40; vii. 22. [imitate.

immānis, -e, comp. **-ior,** sup. **-issimus,** adj., *huge, enormous, immense.*

immineō, -minēre, [**in** + **mineō,** *overhang*], 2, *overhang; be near at hand, threaten* (vi. 38). [imminent.

immittō, -mittere, -mīsī, -missus, [in + mittō], 3, *send into; send against* (vii. 40); of pikes, *hurl, cast* against (v. 44, vi. 8, C. III. 92); of timbers, *let down* into (iv. 17), *let in between* (iv. 17).

immolō, -āre, -āvī, -ātus, [in, cf. mola, *meal*], 1, lit. *sprinkle meal on* a victim for sacrifice; *sacrifice, offer up* (vi. 16, 17). [immolate.

immortālis, -e, [in- + mortālis, from mors], adj., *immortal*. [immortal.

immūnis, -e, [in- + mūnus], adj., *free from taxes*. vii. 76. [immune.

immūnitās, -ātis, [immūnis], f., *freedom* from public burdens, *exemption* (vi. 14). [immunity.

imparātus, -a, -um, sup. -issimus, [in- + parātus], adj., *not ready, unprepared*. vi. 30.

impedīmentum, -ī, [impedīō], n., *hindrance, interference* (i. 25; ii. 25). Pl. **impedīmenta**, -ōrum, *heavy baggage, baggage; pack-animals* (vii. 45). [impediment.

impediō, -pedīre, -pedīvī, -pedītus, [in, cf. pēs], 4, *hinder, obstruct, interfere with; prevent, disorder;* of the mind, *occupy, engage* (v. 7); *make unpassable* (vii. 57). [impede.

impedītus, -a, -um, comp. -ior, sup. -issimus, [part. of impediō], adj., *encumbered* with baggage, *hindered, hampered, obstructed, embarrassed; difficult, hard* (ii. 28, iii. 9); of places, *hard, inaccessible*.

impellō, -pellere, -puli, -pulsus, [in + pellō], 3, *strike against; urge, urge on, drive on, impel*. [impel.

impendeō, -pendēre, [in + pendeō, *hang*], 2, *hang over, overhang*. i. 6; iii. 2. [impend.

impēnsus, -a, -um, comp. -ior, [part. of impendō, *expend*], adj., *ample, great;* of price, *dear, high* (iv. 2).

imperātor, -ōris, [imperō], m., *com-mander-in-chief, commander, general*. [emperor.

imperātōrius, -a, -um, [imperātor], adj., *of a commander, general's*. C. III. 96.

imperātum, -ī, [imperō], n., *command, order*. **ad imperātum**, *in accordance with his command* (vi. 2).

imperītus, -a, -um, comp. -ior, sup. -issimus, [in- + perītus], adj., *inexperienced, unskilled, unacquainted with*.

imperium, -ī, [cf. imperō], n., *command, order; control, government, dominion; military authority*. **nova imperia**, *a revolution* (ii. 1). [empire.

imperō, -āre, -āvī, -ātus, 1, *command, order; exercise authority over, rule* (i. 31, 36); *requisition, order to furnish, levy, draft, demand*. After **imperō, ut** is ordinarily to be translated by *to*, and **nē** by *not to*, with the infin. [imperative.

impetrō, -āre, -āvī, -ātus, [in + patrō, *execute*], 1, *obtain* by request, *procure, get; accomplish, bring to pass; gain one's request*. **rē impetrātā**, *the request having been granted, after the request had been granted*.

impetus, -ūs, [in, cf. petō], m., *attack, assault, charge; raid* (I. 44); *fury, impetuosity, force*. [impetus.

impius, -a, -um, [in- + pius], adj., *wicked, impious*. As noun, **impiī**, -ōrum, m., pl., *the wicked* (vi. 13). [impious.

implicō, -āre, -āvī or -uī, -ātus or -itus, [in + plicō, *fold*], 1, *infold; interweave* (vii. 73). [implicate.

implōrō, -āre, -āvī, -ātus, [in + plōrō, *cry out*], 1, *beseech, implore* (i. 51); *invoke, appeal to* (v. 7, C. III. 82). **auxilium implōrāre**, *to solicit aid* (i. 31, 32). [implore.

impōnō, -pōnere, -posuī, -positus, [in + pōnō], 3, *put on, place on, put; impose (upon); levy upon* (i. 44); of horses, *mount* (i. 42). [impose.

importō, -āre, -āvī, -ātus, [in + portō], 1, *bring in, import.* i. 1; iv. 2; v. 12. [import.

improbus, -a, -um, comp. -ior, sup. -issimus, [in- + probus, *good*], adj., *bad, shameless.* i. 17.

imprōvīsō [imprōvīsus], adv., *unexpectedly, suddenly.* i. 13.

imprōvīsus, -a, -um, comp. -ior, [in + part. of prōvideō], adj., *unforeseen, unexpected.* Neut. as noun in dē imprōvīsō, *unexpectedly, suddenly.*

imprūdēns, -entis, [contr. from imprōvidēns, in- + part. of prōvideō], adj., *unawares, off one's guard.* iii. 29; v. 15. [imprudent.

imprūdentia, -ae, [imprūdēns], f., *lack of foresight, indiscretion, ignorance.* [imprudence.

impūbēs, -eris, [in- + pūbēs], adj., *under age; unmarried* (vi. 21).

impugnō, -āre, -āvī, -ātus, [in + pugnō], 1, *attack, make an attack on* (i. 44); *fight* (iii. 26). [impugn.

impulsus, -ūs, [impellō], m., *push; instigation* (v. 25). [impulse.

impulsus, see impellō.

impūne [impūnis, from in- + poena], adv., *without punishment, with impunity.* i. 14.

impūnitās, -ātis, [impūnis, from in- + poena], f., *exemption from punishment, impunity.* i. 14. [impunity.

īmus, see īnferus.

in, prep. with acc. and abl.:

(1) With the acc.: *into, to, up to, towards, against; until, till; for, with a view to; in, respecting, concerning, according to; after, over.*

(2) With the abl.: *in, within, on, upon, among, over; in the course of, within, during, while; involved in, in case of, in relation to, respecting.*

In composition in retains its form before the vowels and most of the consonants; is often changed to il- before l, ir- before r; usually becomes im- before m, b, p.

in-, inseparable prefix, = *un-, not,* as in incertus, *uncertain.*

inānis, -e, comp. -ior, sup. -issimus, adj., *empty* (v. 23); *vain, useless* (vii. 19). [inane.

incautē, comp. incautius, [incautus], adv., *carelessly.* vii. 27.

incautus, -a, -um, comp. -ior, [in- + cautus, cf. caveō], adj., *off one's guard.* vi. 30. [incautious.

incēdō, -cēdere, -cessī, [in + cēdō, *go*], 3, *go forward, move (forward); come upon, enter* (C. iii. 74).

incendium, -ī, [cf. incendō], n., *fire, conflagration.* [incendiary.

incendō, -cendere, -cendī, -cēnsus, [in, cf. candeō, *shine*], 3, *set on fire; burn; rouse, excite* (vii. 4). [incense.

incēnsus, see incendō.

inceptus, see incipiō.

incertus, -a, -um, comp. -ior, sup. -issimus, [in- + certus], adj., *uncertain, doubtful; undecided* (vii. 62); *indefinite* (vii. 16); of reports, *unreliable, unauthenticated* (iv. 5); of a military formation, *in disorder* (iv. 32).

incidō, -cidere, -cidī, [in + cadō], 3, with in and the acc., *fall in with, come upon, fall in the way of* (i. 53; vi. 30); *occur, happen* (vii. 3); of war, *break out* (ii. 14, vi. 15). [incident.

incīdō, -cīdere, -cīdī, -cīsus, [in + caedō], 3, *cut into.* ii. 17. [incise.

incipiō, -cipere, -cēpī, -ceptus, [in

+ **capiō**], 3, *begin, commence, undertake.* [incipient.

incīsus, see incīdō.

incitātiō, -ōnis, [incitō], f., *a rousing, spurring on.* C. III. 92.

incitō, -āre, -āvī, -ātus, [in + citō, *move rapidly*], 1, *urge, urge on, hurry;* of vessels, *drive forward* with oars, *drive* (iii. 14; iv. 25; vii. 60; C. II. 6); of horses, *urge on, spur;* of water, with sē, *rush against* (iv. 17), *run in* (iii. 12); of men, *rouse, stir up, excite; spur on* (iii. 10); *exasperate* (vii. 28). [incite.

incognitus, -a, -um, [in- + part. of cognōscō], adj., *unknown, not known.* iv. 20, 29. [incognito.

incolō, -colere, -coluī, [in + colō], 3, intrans., *live, dwell;* trans., *inhabit, dwell in, live in.*

incolumis, -e, adj., *safe, unharmed, uninjured, unhurt.*

incommodē, comp. -ius, sup. -issimē, [incommodus], adv., *inconveniently; unfortunately* (v. 33).

incommodum, -ī, [incommodus], n., *inconvenience, disadvantage; misfortune, disaster, injury, defeat.* **quid incommodī,** *any harm* (vi. 13), *what disadvantage* (vii. 45).

incrēdibilis, -e, [in- + crēdibilis], adj., *beyond belief, extraordinary, incredible.* [incredible.

increpitō, -āre, [freq. of increpō, *chide*], 1, *reproach, rebuke* (ii. 15); *taunt* (ii. 30).

incumbō, -ere, incubuī, incubitus, [in + cumbō for cubō, *lie*], 3, *press upon; devote one's self to* (vii. 76). [incumbent.

incursiō, -ōnis, [incurrō], f., *invasion, raid, inroad.* [incursion.

incursus, -ūs, [incurrō], m., *onrush* (ii. 20); *assault, attack* (vii. 36).

incūsō, -āre, -āvī, -ātus, [in + causa], 1, *find fault with, accuse; chide, rebuke* (i. 40; ii. 15).

inde, adv., of place, *from that place, thence;* of time, *after that, then* (vii. 48).

indicium, -ī, [cf. indicō, *reveal*], n., *information, disclosure.*

indīcō, -dīcere, -dīxī, -dictus, [in + dīcō], 3, *proclaim, declare;* of a council, *call, appoint.* [indict.

indictus, see indīcō.

indictus, -a, -um, [in- + dictus], adj., *unsaid;* of a case, *untried* (VII. 38).

indigeō, -ēre, indiguī, [indu, for in, + egeō], 2, *be in want of, lack.* C. II. 35. [indigent.

indignē, comp. -ius, sup. indignissimē, [indignus], adv., *unworthily, shamefully.* vii. 38.

indignitās, -ātis, [indignus], f., *shamefulness* (vii. 56); *indignity, ill-treatment* (ii. 14). [indignity.

indignor, -ārī, -ātus, [indignus], 1, dep., *consider unworthy; be indignant* (vii. 19). [indignant.

indignus, -a, -um, comp. -ior, sup. -issimus, [in- + dignus], adj., *unworthy.* v. 35; vii. 17.

indīligēns, -entis, comp. -ior, [in- + dīligēns], adj., *negligent, remiss.* vii. 71.

indīligenter, comp. -ius, [indīligēns], adv., *negligently, carelessly.* ii. 33.

indīligentia, -ae, [indīligēns], f., *negligence, carelessness.* vii. 17.

indūcō, -dūcere, -dūxī, -ductus, [in + dūcō], 3, *lead in; lead on, induce, influence* (i. 2, 27); *cover* (ii. 33). [induce.

inductus, see indūcō.

indulgentia, -ae, [indulgēns], f., *favor, kindness.* vii. 63. [indulgence.

indulgeō, -dulgēre, -dulsī, 2, *be kina
to, favor*. [indulge.

induō, -duere, -duī, -dūtus, 3, *put
on* (ii. 21); with sē, *pierce, stab
themselves* (vii. 73, 82).

industria, -ae, [industrius], f., *activity, energy*. C. II. 4, III. 73. [in-
dustry.

industriē [industrius], adv., *actively, energetically*. vii. 60, C. III.
95.

indūtiae, -ārum, f., pl., *truce, armis-
tice*. iv. 12, 13.

Indutiomārus, -ī, m., (ĭn-dū″ sh(y)ǫ-
mā′ rǔs), a Treveran, rival of Cingetorix and hostile to Caesar.

ineō, -īre, -iī, -itus, [in + eō], irr.,
enter, enter upon, begin; of favor,
win (vi. 43); of a plan, *form;* of
an account or enumeration, *cast up,
make.*

inermis, -e, and (i. 40) inermus, -a,
-um, [in- + arma], adj., *unarmed,
without arms.*

iners, -ertis, comp. inertior, sup. in-
ertissimus, [in- + ars], adj., *indo-
lent; unmanly* (iv. 2). [inert.

infāmia, -ae, [infāmis, from in- +
fāma], f., *disgrace, dishonor*. [in-
famy.

infāns, -antis, comp. infantior, sup.
-issimus, [in- + part. of for, *speak*],
adj., *without speech*. As noun, m.
and f., (lit. *one not speaking*), *child,
infant* (vii. 28, 47). [infant.

infectus, -a, -um, [in- + factus],
adj., *not done, unaccomplished*. in-
fectā rē, *without accomplishing his
(their) purpose* (vi. 12, vii. 17, 82).

inferō, -ferre, intulī, illātus, [in +
ferō], irr., *bring in, import* (ii. 15);
throw upon (vii. 22), *throw into* (vi.
19); of injuries, *inflict;* of hope
and fear, *inspire, infuse;* of an excuse, *offer, allege* (i. 39); of wounds,
make, give. bellum inferre, *to*

make war. signa inferre, *to advance*. in equum inferre, *to put
on a horse* (vi. 30). [infer.

inferus, -a, -um, comp. inferior, sup.
infimus or īmus, adj., *below, underneath;* comp., *lower, inferior;* sup.,
lowest, at the bottom. sub infimō
colle, *at the foot of the hill* (vii. 49).
Neut. as noun, ab infimō, *from the
foot* (vii. 19), *at the bottom* (vii. 73);
ad infimum, *toward the bottom*
(vii. 73); ab īmō, *from the bottom*
(iii. 19), *at the lower end* (iv. 17).
[inferior.

infestus, -a, -um, comp. -ior, sup.
-issimus, adj., *hostile, threatening.*

inficiō, -ficere, -fēcī, -fectus, [in +
faciō], 3, *stain*. v. 14. [infect.

infidēlis, -e, sup. -issimus, [in- +
fidēlis], adj., *unfaithful, untrust-
worthy*. vii. 59. [infidel.

infīgō, -fīgere, -fīxī, -fīxus, [in +
fīgō], 3, *fasten in*. vii. 73. [in-
fix.

infimus, see inferus.

infīnitus, -a, -um, comp. -ior, [in- +
fīnitus, from fīniō], adj., *unlimited, boundless; vast, immense; num-
berless* (v. 12). [infinite.

infirmitās, -ātis, [infirmus], f., *weakness, feebleness* (vii. 26); *fickleness*
(iv. 5, 13). [infirmity.

infirmus, -a, -um, comp. -ior, sup.
-issimus, [in- + firmus], adj., *not
strong, weak; depressed, timid* (iii.
24); comp., *less strong* (iv. 3). [in-
firm.

inflātē, comp. inflātius, [inflātus],
adv., *boastfully*. C. II. 39.

inflectō, -flectere, -flexī, -flexus,
[in + flectō], 3, *bend*. i. 25; ii.
17. [inflect.

inflexus, see inflectō.

influō, -fluere, -flūxī. [in + fluō], 3,
flow into, flow; drain into (vii. 57).
[influx.

īnfodiō, -fodere, -fōdī, -fossus, [in
+ fodiō], 3, *bury.* vii. 73.

īnfrā, [for īnferā, sc. **parte**], adv.
and prep.:

   (1) As adv., *below.* iv. 36; vii.
61.

   (2) As prep., with acc., *below.*
vi. 28, 35.

īnfringō, -fringere, -frēgī, -frāctus,
[in + frangō], 3, *break off; break,
lessen* (C. III. 92). [infraction.

ingēns, -entis, comp. **ingentior**, adj.,
large, vast, great; of size of body,
huge (I. 39).

ingrātus, -a, -um, comp. -ior, sup.
-issimus, [in- + grātus], adj., *un-
acceptable, unwelcome.* [ingrate.

ingredior, -gredī, -gressus, [in +
gradior, *step*], 3, dep., *advance;
enter, go into* (ii. 4; v. 9). [ingress.

iniciō, -icere, -iēcī, -iectus, [in +
iaciō], 3, *throw in; lay on* (iv. 17);
place on, put on (vii. 58); *inspire,
infuse* (i. 46); of fear, *strike into*
(iv. 19; vii. 55). [inject.

iniectus, see iniciō.

inimīcitia, -ae, [inimīcus], f., *en-
mity.* vi. 12.

inimīcus, -a, -um, comp. -ior, sup.
-issimus, [in- + amīcus], adj., *unfriendly, hostile.* As noun, inimīcus, -ī, m., *enemy, personal enemy*, as distinguished from **hostis**,
a public enemy; adversary. [inimi-
cal.

inīquitās, -ātis, [inīquus], f., *un-
evenness; unfairness, unreasonable-
ness; disadvantage.* inīquitās
locī, *unfavorableness of (the) position, disadvantageous position.* [in-
iquity.

inīquus, -a, -um, comp. -ior, sup.
-issimus, [in- + aequus], adj., *uneven, sloping; unfavorable, disadvantageous; unfair, unjust* (i.
44).

initium, -ī, [cf. ineō], n., *beginning;
commencement;* pl., *elements, first
principles* (vi. 17). [initial.

initūrus, see ineō.

initus, -a, -um, see ineō.

iniungō, -iungere, -iūnxī, -iūnctus,
[in + iungō], 3, *fasten upon, impose.* vii. 77. [enjoin.

iniūria, -ae, [iniūrius, in- + iūs],
f., *wrong, outrage, injustice, injury.*
[injury.

iniussus, -ūs, [in- + iussus], m.,
only abl. in use, *without command,
without orders.* i. 19; v. 28.

innāscor, -nāscī, -nātus, [in + nās-
cor], 3, dep., *be born in, be latent
in* (vii. 42, C. III. 92); *spring up in,
arise in* (i. 41). [innate.

innātus, -a, -um, see innāscor.

innītor, -nītī, -nīxus or -nīsus, [in +
nītor], 3, dep., *support one's self
with, lean upon.* ii. 27.

innīxus, see innītor.

innocēns, -entis, comp. **innocen-
tior**, sup. -issimus, [in- + nocēns,
from noceō], adj., *blameless, innocent.* As noun, innocentēs, -ium,
m., pl., *the innocent* (vi. 9), *innocent
men* (vi. 16). [innocent.

innocentia, -ae, [innocēns], f.,
blamelessness, integrity. i. 40. [in-
nocence.

inopia, -ae, [inops, *needy*], f., *want,
lack, need, shortage, scarcity.*

inopīnāns, -antis, [in- + opīnāns,
from opīnor], adj., *not expecting,
unawares, off one's guard.*

inquam, inquis, inquit, present indicative, def., *say, says.*

īnsciēns, -entis, [in- + sciēns, from
sciō], adj., *not knowing, unaware.*

īnscientia, -ae, [īnsciēns], f., *ignorance, lack of knowledge.*

īnscius, -a, -um, [in-, cf. sciō], adj.,
not knowing, unaware, ignorant.

īnsecūtus, see īnsequor.

īnsequor, -sequī, -secūtus, [in +
sequor], 3, dep., *follow up, pursue,
follow in pursuit.*

īnserō, -serere, -seruī, -sertus, [in
+ serō], 3, *fasten in.* iii. 14. [in-
sert.

īnsidiae, -ārum, [cf. īnsideō], f.,
pl., *ambush, ambuscade; artifice,
device, trap, pitfall.* **per īnsidiās,**
by stratagem (i. 42; iv. 13). [in-
sidious.

īnsidior, -ārī, -ātus, [īnsidiae], 1,
dep., *lurk in ambush, lie in wait.*

īnsigne, -is, [īnsignis], n., *sign,
mark, signal; decoration.* [ensign.

īnsignis, -e, comp. -ior, [in + sig-
num], adj., *noteworthy.* i. 12.

īnsiliō, -silīre, -siluī, [in + saliō,
leap], 4, *leap upon.* i. 52.

īnsimulō, -āre, -āvī, -ātus, [in +
simulō], 1, *charge* with, *accuse* of;
with gen. vii. 20, 38.

īnsinuō, -āre, -āvī, -ātus, [in +
sinuō, *curve*], 1, *push in;* with sē,
make one's way (iv. 33). [insinu-
ate.

īnsistō, -sistere, -stitī, [in + sistō],
3, *stand, stand upon, keep one's footing; press on; follow, pursue* (iii.
14). **tōtus īnsistit in,** *he devotes
himself wholly to* (vi. 5). [insist.

īnsolēns, -entis, [īn-, soleō], adj.,
unusual. **īnsolēns bellī,** *unaccustomed to war* (C. II. 36). [inso-
lent.

īnsolenter [īnsolēns], adv., *arrogantly, haughtily.* i. 14.

īnsolitus, -a, -um, [in- + solitus],
adj., *unaccustomed.* C. III. 85.

īnspectō, -āre, only pres. part. in
use, [freq. of īnspiciō], 1, *look at,
look.* **īnspectantibus nōbīs,**
under our own eyes (vii. 25). [in-
spect.

īnstabilis, -e, [in- + stabilis, from
stō], adj., *unsteady.* iv. 23.

īnstāns, -antis, comp. **īnstantior,**
[part. of īnstō], adj., *impending,
pressing.* vi. 4. [instant.

īnstar, n., indecl., *likeness;* followed
by gen., *like* (ii. 17).

īnstīgō, -āre, -āvī, -ātus, 1, *urge on,
incite.* v. 56. [instigate.

īnstituō, -stituere, -stituī, -stitū-
tus, [in + statuō], 3, *of troops,
draw up, arrange; devise, build,
construct; make; make ready, furnish; obtain* (III. 9); *establish, insti-
tute* (vi. 16); *undertake, commence,
begin; resolve upon, determine;
train, teach.* [institute (verb).

īnstitūtum, -ī, [īnstituō], n., *plan,
practice* (i. 50; vii. 24); *custom,
usage* (iv. 20; vi. 18); *institution*
(i. 1); *arrangement, disposition*
(C. III. 84). [institute (noun).

īnstitūtus, see īnstituō.

īnstō, -stāre, -stitī, -stātūrus, [in +
stō], 1, *be near at hand, approach;
press on, press forward.*

īnstrūmentum, -ī, [īnstruō], n.,
tool; singular with collective force,
stock, outfit. **mīlitāre īnstrūmentum,** *stock of weapons* (vi. 30).
[instrument.

īnstruō, -struere, -strūxī, -strūc-
tus, [in + struō, *build*], 3, *build,
construct;* of troops, *draw up, form;
fit out, equip, supply* (v. 5; vii. 59;
C. III. 61). [instruct.

īnsuēfactus, -a, -um, [īnsuēscō +
faciō], adj., *accustomed, trained.*
iv. 24.

īnsuētus, -a, -um, [part. of īnsuēs-
cō], adj., *unaccustomed.*

īnsula, -ae, f., *island.* [insular.

īnsuper [in + super], adv., *above,
on top.* iv. 17; vii. 23.

integer, -gra, -grum, comp. **inte-
grior,** sup. **integerrimus,** [in- +
TAG in tangō], adj., *untouched,
whole, unhurt, undamaged; fresh,*

vigorous. rē integrā, *at the outset* (vii. 30). As noun, integrī,
-ōrum, m., pl., *fresh troops.* [integer.

integō, -tegere, -tēxī, -tēctus, [in
+ tegō], 3, *cover, cover over.*

intellegō, -legere, -lēxī, -lēctus,
[inter + legō], 3, *understand, see
clearly, realize.* [intelligent.

intentus, -a, -um, comp. -ior, sup.
-issimus, [part. of intendō], adj.,
attentive, eager, intent. [intent.

inter, prep. with acc., *between, among;*
of time, *during, for* (i. 36). inter sē, *with each other, among themselves, with one another.*

intercēdō, -cēdere, -cessī, -cessū-
rus, [inter + cēdō], 3, *go between,
be placed between* (ii. 17); *lie between* (i. 39; v. 52; vii. 26, 46, 47);
of time, *intervene, pass* (i. 7; v. 53);
take place, occur (v. 11). [intercede.

intercessiō, -ōnis, [intercēdō], f.,
interposition, protest. C. I. 7. [in-
tercession.

intercipiō, -cipere, -cēpī, -ceptus,
[inter + capiō], 3, *cut off, intercept.* [intercept.

interclūdō, -clūdere, -clūsī, -clū-
sus, [inter + claudō], 3, *shut off,
cut off; block up, blockade, hinder.*

interdīcō, -dīcere, -dīxī, -dictus,
[inter + dīcō], 3, *forbid, prohibit,
exclude, interdict;* followed by a
prohibition, *enjoin* (v. 58; vii. 40).
[interdict.

interdiū, [inter, cf. diēs], adv., *in
the daytime, by day.*

interdum, [inter + dum], adv., *for
a time, for a season* (i. 14); *sometimes* (i. 39).

intereā, [inter + eā], adv., *in the
mean time, meanwhile.*

intereō, -īre, -iī, -itūrus, [inter +
eō], 4, *perish, be destroyed, die.*

interficiō, -ficere, -fēcī, -fectus, [in-
ter + faciō], 3, *slay, kill.*

intericiō, -icere, -iēcī, -iectus, [in-
ter + iaciō], 3, *throw between,
place between, put between;* pass.
part., interiectus, *lying between,
intervening.* [interject.

interiectus, see intericiō.

interim, [inter + -im], adv., *in the
mean time, meanwhile.*

interior,-ius,gen.-ōris, sup.intimus,
[inter], adj. in comp. degree, *inner,
interior.* As noun, interiōrēs,
-um, m., pl., *those living in the interior* (v. 14), *those within* the city
(vii. 82, 86). [interior.

interitus, -ūs, [intereō], m., *destruction, death.* v. 47.

intermittō,-mittere, -mīsī,-missus,
[inter + mittō], 3, *leave an interval, leave vacant; leave off, leave;
stop, break, cease, discontinue; inter-
rupt, suspend;* pass., of fire, *abate*
(v. 43), of wind, *fail* (v. 8). [inter-
mittent.

interneciō, -ōnis, [cf. internecō, *destroy*], f., *slaughter* (I. 13); *utter
destruction* (ii. 28). [internecine.

interpellō, -āre, -āvī, -ātus, I, *inter-
rupt; disturb, hinder* (i. 44). [in-
terpellate.

interpōnō, -pōnere, -posuī, -posi-
tus, [inter + pōnō], 3, *place between, put between, interpose; put
forward* (i. 42); *present, manifest*
(iv. 32); of time, *suffer to elapse.*
fidem interpōnere, *to pledge one's
honor* (v. 6, 36). [interpose.

interpres, -pretis, m., *interpreter,*
i. 19; v. 36. [interpreter.

interpretor,-ārī, -ātus,[interpres],
I, dep., *explain, expound.* vi. 13.
[interpret.

interrogō, -āre, -āvī, -ātus, [inter
+ rogō], I, *ask, question.* vii. 20.
[interrogate.

interrumpō, -rumpere, -rūpī, -rup-
tus, [inter + rumpō], 3, *break*

down, *destroy.* vii. 19, 34. [inter-
rupt.

interscindō, -scindere, -scidī, -scis-
sus, [inter + scindō], 3, *cut down*
(ii. 9); *cut through* (vii. 24).

intersum, -esse, -fuī, irr., *be between,*
lie between; be present at, take part
in. Impers., **interest,** *it concerns,*
is important. **magnī interest,** *it*
is of great importance (v. 4, vi. 1).
neque interest, *and it makes no*
difference (vii. 14). [interest.

intervāllum, -ī, [inter + vāllum],
n., *room between two palisades, interval, space, distance.* [interval.

interveniō, -venīre, -vēnī, -ventum
est, [inter + veniō], 4, *arrive* (VI.
37); *appear, present one's self* (vii.
20). [intervene.

interventus, -ūs, [interveniō], m.,
intervention. iii. 15.

intexō, -texere, -texuī, -textus, [in
+ texō, *weave*], 3, *weave in, interweave.* ii. 33.

intoleranter, comp. -ius, sup. -issimē,
[intolerāns], adv., *unendurably;*
violently (VII. 51).

intrā, [for interā, sc. parte], prep.
with acc., *inside of, within.*

intrītus, [in- + part. of terō, *rub*],
adj., *unworn; unwearied, fresh* (iii.
26).

intrō, adv., *within, inside.*

intrō, -āre, -āvī, -ātus, [in + *trō,
cf. trāns], 1, *enter, go in.* [enter.

intrōdūcō, -dūcere, -dūxī, -ductus,
[intrō + dūcō], 3, *lead into, bring*
into. [introduce.

introeō, -īre, -īvī, [intrō + eō], irr.,
go in; come in, enter (v. 43).

introitus, -ūs, [introeō], m., *an*
entering; entrance (v. 9). [introit.

intrōmissus, see intrōmittō.

intrōmittō, -mittere, -mīsī, -mis-
sus, [intrō + mittō], 3, *send into,*
send in; let in; bring in (v. 58).

intrōrsus, [intrō + versus], adv.,
within, inside.

intrōrumpō, -rumpere, -rūpī, -rup-
tus, [intrō + rumpō, *break*], 3,
burst into; break in (v. 51).

intueor, -tuērī, -tuitus, [in + tu-
eor], 2, dep., *look upon.* i. 32.
[intuition.

intuleram, see īnferō.

intulī, see īnferō.

intus, adv., *within, on the inside.*

inūsitātus, -a, -um, comp. -ior, [in-
+ part. of ūsitor, freq. of ūtor],
adj., *unfamiliar, unwonted, unprecedented.*

inūtilis, -e, comp. -ior, [in- + ūtilis],
adj., *useless, unserviceable, of no use;*
disadvantageous (vii. 27). [inutile.

inveniō, -venīre, -vēnī, -ventus, [in
+ veniō], 4, *come upon, find, discover; find out, learn* (ii. 16). [in-
vent.

inventor, -ōris, [inveniō], m., *originator, inventor.* vi. 17. [inventor.

inveterāscō, -ere, inveterāvī, [in
+ veterāscō, from vetus], 3, *grow*
old; become established, become fixed
(v. 41); *establish one's self* (ii. 1).
[cf. inveterate.

invictus, -a, -um, [in- + part. of
vincō], adj., *unconquerable, invincible.* i. 36.

invideō, -vidēre, -vīdī, -vīsus, [in
+ videō], 2, *look askance at; envy*
(ii. 31).

invidia, -ae, [invidus], f., *envy,*
jealousy. [envy.

inviolātus, -a, -um, [in- + part. of
violō], adj., *inviolable.* iii. 9. [in-
violate.

invīsitātus, -a, -um, [in- + vīsitā-
tus], adj., *unseen.* C. II. 4.

invītō, -āre, -āvī, -ātus, 1, *invite,*
request (i. 35; iv. 6); *entice, attract*
(v. 51; vi. 35). [invite.

invītus, -a, -um, sup. -issimus, adj.,

unwilling, reluctant. **sē invītō** . (I. 8; IV. 16), **eō invītō** (i. 14), *against his will.*

ipse, -a, -um, gen. **ipsīus,** dem. pron., *self; himself, herself, itself, themselves; he, they* (emphatic); *very.* **hōc ipsō tempore,** *just at this moment* (vi. 37).

īrācundia, -ae, [**īrācundus**], f., *anger, passion.* vi. 5; vii. 42.

īrācundus, -a, -um, comp. **-ior,** [**īra**], adj., *passionate, quick-tempered.* i. 31. [iracund.

irrīdeō, -rīdēre, -rīsī, -rīsus, [**in +** **rīdeō,** *laugh*], 2, *laugh at, make fun of, ridicule.* ii. 30.

irrīdiculē, [**in-** + **rīdiculē**], adv., *without wit.* i. 42.

irrumpō, -rumpere, -rūpī, -ruptus, [**in +** **rumpō,** *break*], 3, *break into, burst into, rush in.*

irruptiō, -ōnis, [**irrumpō**], f., *raid* (vii. 7); *attack* (vii. 70). [irruption.

is, ea, id, gen. **eius,** dem. pron., *he, she, it; that, this, the, the one;* before **ut, is =** **tālis,** *such;* after **et,** *and that too;* after **neque,** *and that not* (iii. 2); with comparatives, abl. **eō =** *the, all the,* as **eō magis,** *all the more.*

iste, -a, -ud, gen. **istīus,** dem. pron., *that, that of yours.* vii. 77.

ita, [cf. **is**], adv., *in this way, so, thus; in the following manner, in such a way, accordingly.* **nōn ita,** *not so very, not very* (iv. 37; v. 47).

Italia, -ae, f., *Italy.* [Italy.

itaque, = et **ita,** *and so* (i. 52).

itaque, [**ita** + **-que**], adv., *and thus, accordingly, therefore, consequently.*

item, adv., *also, further; just so, in like manner.* [item.

iter, itineris, [cf. **eō, īre**], n., *journey, line of march, march; road, route.* **magnum iter,** *forced march,* from 20 to 25 miles a day.

ex itinere, *directly after marching, from the line of march;* used of a force which turns from marching at once, without encamping, to attack an enemy in the field (i. 25), to storm a town (ii. 6, 12; iii. 21), or to retreat (ii. 29). [itinerary.

iterum, adv., *again, a second time.*

Itius, -ī, m., *portus Itius* (ish′ [y]us), harbor from which Caesar sailed to Britain, probably *Boulogne.*

itūrus, see **eō.**

iuba, -ae, f., *mane.* i. 48.

Iuba, -ae, m., *Juba* (jū′ ba̧), a king of Numidia, who joined the side of Pompey in the Civil War.

iubeō, iubēre, iussī, iussus, 2, *order, give orders, bid, command.* [jussive.

iūdicium, -ī, [**iūdex,** *judge*], n., *legal judgment, decision, decree; place of judgment, trial* (i. 4); *opinion, judgment.* [judicial.

iūdicō, -āre, -āvī, -ātus, [**iūdex**], 1, *judge, decide; think, be of the opinion; pronounce, declare* (v. 56). [judge (verb).

iugum, -ī, [**IUG,** cf. **iungō**], n., *yoke* (i. 7, 12); iv. 33); *of hills and mountains, ridge, summit, height.*

iūmentum, -ī, [for *iugumentum,* root IUG in **iungō**], n., *yoke-animal, beast of burden, draught-animal,* used of horses, mules, and asses.

iūnctūra, -ae, [**iungō**], f., *juncture, joint.* iv. 17. [juncture.

iūnctus, see **iungō.**

iungō, -ere, iūnxī, iūnctus, 3, *join together, join, connect, unite.* [join.

iūnior, see **iuvenis.**

Iūnius, -ī, m., *Quintus Junius* (jūn′- yus), a Roman of Spanish birth in Caesar's army. v. 27, 28.

Iuppiter, Iovis, m., *Jupiter* (jū′ pi̧- tȩr). vi. 17. Fig. 200. [jovial.

Iūra, -ae, m., *Jura* (jū′ ra̧), a range of mountains extending from the

Rhine to the Rhone (about 170 miles), and forming the boundary between the Helvetians and the Sequanians. i. 2, 6, 8.

Figure 200. — Bust of Jupiter, discovered at Pompeii.

Of marble. "The god is following with closest attention the course of events in some far distant place, affairs that in the next moment may require his intervention; excitement and expectancy are seen in the raised upper lip. The ideal of this sculptor was the wise and powerful king, whose watchful and all-protective eye sees to the furthest limits of his kingdom "

iūrō, -āre, -āvī, -ātus, [iūs], 1, *take an oath, swear.* [jury.

iūs, iūris, n., *right, justice, authority.* **iūre bellī**, *by the laws of war* (i. 44; vii. 41). **in suō iūre**, *in the exercise of his own rights* (1. 36, 44).

iūs reddere, *to render justice* (vi. 13). **iūs dīcere**, *to administer justice* (vi. 23). **iūra in hōs**, *rights over these* (vi. 13).

iūs iūrandum, iūris iūrandī, [iūs + gerundive of iūrō], n., *oath.*

iussus, -ūs, [iubeō], m., used only in abl. sing., *order, bidding, command.* vii. 3.

iūstitia, -ae, [iūstus], f., *justice, fair-dealing.* [justice.

iūstus, -a, -um, comp. -ior, sup. -issimus, [iūs], adj., *just, rightful, fair; proper, suitable, due.* [just.

iuvenis, -e, comp. iūnior, adj., *young.* As noun, iūniōrēs, -um, m., pl., *younger men,* of military age, under forty-six years (vii. 1). [junior.

iuventūs, -ūtis, [iuvenis], f., *youth; young men.*

iuvō, -āre, iūvī, iūtus, 1, *help, aid, assist.*

iūxtā, adv., *near by, near.* [jostle.

K.

Kal. = **Kalendae.**

Kalendae, -ārum, f., pl., *Calends,* the first day of the month. [Calendar.

L.

L., with proper names = **Lūcius.**

Laberius, -ī, m., see **Dūrus.**

Labiēnus, -ī, m., *Titus Labienus* (lā-bĭ-ē′ nŭs), the most prominent of

Caesar's lieutenants in the Gallic War; in the Civil War he went over to the side of Pompey, but displayed small abilities as a commander, and fell at the battle of Munda, 45 B.C.

lābor, lābī, lāpsus, 3, dep., *slip; go astray* (v. 3); *fail, be deceived, be disappointed* (v. 55). [lapse.

labor, -ōris, m., *toil, work, exertion, labor; endurance* (iv. 2). [labor.

labōrō, -āre, -āvī, -ātus, [labor], 1, *make effort, labor, strive* (i. 31; vii. 31); *be hard pressed, be in distress, be in danger*. [labor (verb).

labrum, -ī, [LAB, cf. lambō, *lick*], n., *lip* (v. 14); *edge* (vii. 72); *rim, brim* (vi. 28).

lac, lactis, n., *milk*. [lacteal.

lacessō, -ere, -īvī, -ītus, [obsolete laciō, *entice*], 3, *arouse, provoke; harass, assail, attack*.

lacrima, -ae, f., *tear*. [lachrymal.

lacrimō, -āre, -āvī, -ātus, [lacrima], 1, *shed tears, weep*. vii. 38.

lacus, -ūs, m., *lake*. [lake.

laedō, laedere, laesī, laesus, 3, *injure; break, violate* (vi. 9).

laetitia, -ae, [laetus], f., *rejoicing, joy, delight*. v. 48, 52; vii. 79.

laetus, -a, -um, comp. -ior, sup. -issimus, adj., *joyful, glad*. iii. 18.

languidē, comp. languidius, [languidus], adv., *feebly, lazily*. vii. 27.

languidus, -a, -um, comp. -ior, [cf. languor], adj., *weak, faint, exhausted*. iii. 5. [languid.

languor, -ōris, [langueō, *be faint*], m., *faintness; exhaustion, weariness* (v. 31). [languor.

lapis, -idis, m., *stone*. [lapidary.

lāpsus, see lābor.

laqueus, -ī, m., *noose*. vii. 22.

largior, largīrī, largītus, [largus, *abundant*], 4, dep., *give freely, supply, bestow* (vi. 24); *bribe* (i. 18).

largiter, [largus, *abundant*], adv., *abundantly, much*.

largītiō, -ōnis, [largior], f., *lavish giving, bribery*. i. 9. [largition.

Lārīsa, -ae, [Λάρισσα], f. (la̱-ris′ a̱), a city in Thessaly, now *Larissa*. C. III. 96, 97, 98.

lassitūdō, -inis, [lassus, *weak*], f., *faintness, weariness*. [lassitude.

lātē, comp. lātius, sup. lātissimē, [lātus], adv., *widely, broadly, extensively*. quam lātissimē, *as far as possible*.

latebra, -ae, [cf. lateō], f., *hiding-place*. vi. 43. [latebricole.

lateō, latēre, latuī, 2, *lie hid* (ii. 19); *be unnoticed* (iii. 14). [latent.

lātissimē, see lātē.

lātitūdō, -inis, [lātus], f., *width, breadth, extent*. [latitude.

lātius, see lātē.

Latobrīgī, -ōrum, m., pl., (lat-o̱-brī′ jī), a people near the Helvetians.

latrō, -ōnis, m., *freebooter, robber*.

latrōcinium, -ī, [latrōcinor, *plunder*], n., *freebooting, brigandage, robbery*. vi. 16, 23, 35.

lātūrus, see ferō.

lātus, -a, -um, comp. -ior, sup. -issimus, adj., *broad, wide; of territory, extensive* (ii. 4; vi. 22).

latus, -eris, n., *side; of an army, flank*. latus apertum, *exposed flank*. ab latere, *on the flank*. [lateral.

laudō, -āre, -āvī, -ātus, [laus], 1, *praise, commend, compliment*. [laud (verb).

laurea, -ae, [laurus, *laurel*], f., *laurel tree; laurel* (C. III. 71). [laureate.

laus, laudis, f., *praise, glory, commendation, distinction*. [laud.

lavō, -āre, lāvī, lautus and lōtus, 1, *wash;* pass. lavārī, used reflexively, *bathe* (iv. 1). [lave.

laxō, -āre, -āvī, -ātus, 1, *make wide,
spread out, extend.* [laxative.

lēgātiō, -ōnis, [lēgō, *despatch*]; f.,
envoyship, mission (i. 3); referring
to persons (= lēgātī), *deputation,
embassy, envoys.* [legation.

lēgātus, -ī, [lēgō, *despatch*], m., *envoy;* of the army, *lieutenant, lieutenant-general.* [legate.

legiō, -ōnis, [cf. legō, *collect*], f.,
legion. [legion.

legiōnārius, -a, -um, [legiō], adj.,
of a legion, legionary. [legionary.

legō, -ere, lēgī, lēctus, 3, *bring together; single out, select* (C. III. 59);
read. [legible.

legūmen, -inis, [legō, *gather*], n.,
pulse. C. III. 47. [legume.

Lemannus, -ī, m., with lacus, *Lake
Geneva.*

Lemovīcēs, -um, m., pl., (lem-ọ-
vī′sēz), a Gallic people west of the
Arvernians.

lēnis, -e, comp. -ior, sup. -issimus,
adj., *smooth, gentle.* [lenient.

lēnitās, -ātis, [lēnis], f., *smoothness*
(I. 12); *gentleness* (C. III. 98).
[lenity.

lēniter, comp. lēnius, sup. -issimē,
[lēnis], adv., *mildly, gently, slightly.*

lentē, [lentus], adv., comp. lentius,
slowly. C. II. 40.

Lentulus, -ī, m., (len′ chū lụs):
　(1) *Lucius Lentulus,* consul in 49
B.C., a partisan of Pompey, who was
with him at the time of the battle of
Pharsalus (C. III. 96).
　(2) See Spinther.

lēnunculus, -ī, m., *boat, skiff.* C. II.
43.

Lepontiī, -ōrum, m., pl., (lẹ-pon′-
sh[y]ī), a people in the Alps.

Leptitānī, -ōrum, [Leptis], m.,
pl., (lep-tị-tā′nī), the inhabitants
of Leptis Minor, a city on the coast
of Africa southeast of Thapsus.

lepus, -oris, m., *hare.* v. 12.

Leucī, -ōrum, m., pl., (lū′sī), a Gallic state south of the Mediomatrici.
i. 40.

Levācī, -ōrum, m., pl., (lẹ-vā′sī), a
Belgic people, dependents of the
Nervians. v. 39.

levis, -e, comp. -ior, sup. -issimus,
adj., *light, slight;* of a report, *baseless, unfounded* (vii. 42); of an engagement, *unimportant* (vii. 36, 53).
Comp., *more capricious* (v. 28); *less
serious* (vii. 4).

levitās, -ātis, [levis], f., *lightness*
(v. 34); *fickleness, instability* (ii. 1;
vii. 43). [levity.

leviter, [levis], adv., comp. levius,
sup. levissimē, *lightly.* C. III. 92.

levō, -āre, -āvī, -ātus, [levis], 1,
lighten; relieve, free from (v. 27).

lēx, lēgis, f., *law, enactment.* [legal.

Lexoviī, -ōrum, m., pl., (lẹks-ō′vị-ī),
a Gallic state on the coast west of
the Sequana (*Seine*). Fig. 201.

Figure 201. — Coin of the Lexovii.

Bronze. Obverse, portrait; inscription,
CISIAMBOS, probably the name of the man
whose portrait appears.

Reverse, eagle; inscription, PUBLICOS
CIMISSOS LIXOVIO.

libenter, comp. libentius, sup. liben-
tissimē, [libēns, *glad*], adv., *willingly, gladly, cheerfully.*

līber, -era, -erum, comp. -ior, sup.
līberrimus, adj., *free, independent;
unimpeded, unrestricted.* [liberal.

līberālitās, -ātis, [līberālis], f., *gen-
erosity* (i. 18); *generous help* (I. 43).
[liberality.

līberāliter, comp. **līberālius**, sup.
-**issimē**, [**līberālis**], adv., *gra-
ciously, courteously, kindly*.

līberē, comp. -**ius**, [**līber**], adv.,
freely, without hindrance (vii. 49);
boldly (v. 19); *openly* (i. 18; vii. 1).

līberī, -**ōrum**, m., pl., *children*.

līberō, -**āre**, -**āvī**, -**ātus**, [**līber**], 1,
set free, free; release, relieve. [liberate.

lībertās, -**ātis**, [**līber**], f., *freedom,
liberty, independence*. [liberty.

Libō, -**ōnis**, m., *Lucius Scribonius
Libo* (skrĭ-bō′ nĭ-ŭs lī′ bō), a partisan
of Pompey in the Civil War. C. iii.
90.

lībrīlis, -**e**, [**lībra**, *pound*], adj.,
weighing a pound. vii. 81.

licentia, -**ae**, [**licēns**, **licet**], f., *law-
lessness; presumption* (vii. 52).
[license.

liceor, **licērī**, **licitus**, 2, dep., *bid,
make a bid*, at an auction. i. 18.

licet, **licēre**, **licuit** and **licitum est**,
2, impers., *it is allowed, lawful, permitted*. **licet mihi**, *I am allowed,
I may*. **petere ut liceat**, *to ask
permission*. [licit.

Licinius, -**ī**, m., *Licinius* (lĭ-sĭn′ ĭ-ŭs),
a Roman name:
(1) *Licinius Crassus*, see **Crassus**.
(2) *Licinius Damasippus* (dam-
ạ-sĭp′ ŭs), a Roman senator on the
side of Pompey in the Civil War.
C. ii. 44.

līctor, -**ōris**, m., *lictor*, an attendant
upon a Roman magistrate. C. i. 6.

Liger, -**eris**, m., (lī′ jẹr), *Loire*, which
rises in the Cévennes (*Cebenna*)
mountains, flows northwest, receives
as a tributary the Allier (*Elaver*),
flows west, and empties into the
Atlantic, after a course of more than
500 miles. iii. 9; vii. 5, 11, 55, 59.

lignātiō, -**ōnis**, [**lignor**, from **lignum**], f., *getting wood*. v. 39.

lignātor, -**ōris**, [**lignor**, from **lignum**], m., *wood-cutter*. Pl., *men
sent to get wood, wood foragers* (v. 26).

līlium, -**ī**, n., *lily*. vii. 73. [lily.

līnea, -**ae**, [**līneus**, from **līnum**], f.,
line. vii. 23. [line.

Lingonēs, -**um**, m., pl., (ling′ gǫ-
nēz), a Gallic people west of the Sequanians.

lingua, -**ae**, f., *tongue; language* (i. 1,
47). [language.

lingula, -**ae**, [dim. of **lingua**], f.,
tongue of land. iii. 12.

linter, -**tris**, f., *boat, skiff*.

līnum, -**ī**, n., *flax*. iii. 13.

līs, **lītis**, f., *strife; lawsuit; damages*,
adjudged by legal process (v. 1).

Liscus, -**ī**, m., (lis′ kŭs), chief magistrate (vergobret) of the Aeduans in
58 B.C.

Litaviccus, -**ī**, m., (lit-ạ-vik′ us), a
prominent Aeduan.

littera, -**ae**, f., *letter, character*, of the
alphabet.   Pl. **litterae**, -**ārum**,
writing (vi. 14); *letter, despatch*.
litterae pūblicae, *public records*
(v. 47). [letter.

lītus, -**oris**, n., *shore* of the sea, *strand,
beach*. [littoral.

locuplēs, -**ētis**, [**locus**, cf. **plēnus**],
adj., *wealthy, opulent*. C. iii. 59.

locus, -**ī**, m., pl. **loca**, -**ōrum**, n.,
*place, ground; position, situation;
room; social position, rank, standing; opportunity;* pl. **loca** often
region, country. [local.

locūtus, see **loquor**.

longē, comp. **longius**, sup. **longissimē**, [**longus**], adv., *at a distance,
far, by far*. Comp., of space,
further; of time, *further, longer*.
quam longissimē, *as far as possible*.

longinquus, -**a**, -**um**, comp. -**ior**,
[**longus**], adj., *far removed, remote,
distant; long-continued, prolonged,
lasting*. [longinquity.

longitūdō, -inis, [longus], f., *length.*
[longitude.

longurius, -ī, [longus], m., *long pole.*

longus, -a, -um, comp. -ior, sup.
-issimus, adj., *long, extended, distant;* used of either space or time.
nāvis longa, *battleship, galley.*

loquor, loquī, locūtus, 3, dep., *speak,
say.* [loquacious.

lōrīca, -ae, [cf. lōrum, *leather strap*],
f., *cuirass* of leather; *breastwork*
(v. 40; vii. 72, 86). [loricate.

Lūcānius, -ī, m., *Quintus Lucanius*
(lū-kā′ nĭ-ŭs), a brave centurion.
v. 35.

Lūcīlius, -ī, m., a Roman name. Lūcīlius Hirrus (lū-sil′ ĭ-ŭs hir′ ŭs),
a leader on the side of Pompey in
the Civil War. C. III. 82.

Lūcius, -ī, m., (lū′ sh[y]ŭs), a Roman
first name; abbreviation, L.

Lucterius, -ī, m., (lŭk-tē′ rĭ-ŭs), a
Cadurcan, a helper of Vercingetorix
in the great uprising of 52 B.C.

lūctus, -ūs, [lūgeō], m., *mourning,
lamentation.* C. II. 7.

Lugotorīx, -īgis, m., (lū-got′ ǫ-rĭks),
a British chief. v. 22.

lūna, -ae, f., *moon.* [lunar.

Lūna, -ae, f., *moon* as a divinity,
moon-goddess. vi. 21.

Lutecia, -ae, f., (lū-tē′ sh[y]ạ), a
city of the Parisii on an island in the
Seine, *Paris.* vi. 3; vii. 57, 58.

lūx, lūcis, f., *light, daylight.* prīmā
lūce, *at daybreak.*

lūxuria, -ae, [lūxus, *excess*], f., *high
living, luxury.* ii. 15. [luxury.

M.

M., with proper names = Mārcus.

M as a designation of number = 1000.

māceria, -ae, [cf. mācerō, *soften*], f.,
originally *wall of soft clay; wall of
loose stone* (vii. 69, 70.)

māchinātiō, -ōnis, [māchinor, *con-
trive*], f., *mechanical appliance,
machine.* [machination.

maestus, -a, -um, sup. -issimus, [cf.
maereō, *be sad*], adj., *sad, dejected.*

magis, sup. maximē, [cf. magnus],
adv. in comp. degree, *more, rather.*
eō magis, *all the more.* Sup. maximē, *very greatly, exceedingly,
chiefly, especially.* quam maximē,
as much as possible.

magister, -trī, m., *master* of a ship,
captain (C. III. 43). [master.

magistrātus, -ūs, [magister], m.,
*magistracy, civil office; one holding a
magistracy, magistrate.* [magistrate.

magnificus, -a, -um, comp. magnifi-
centior, sup. -issimus, [magnus,
cf. faciō], adj., *splendid, magnifi-
cent.* vi. 19. [magnificent.

magnitūdō, -inis, [magnus], f.,
greatness, extent; size, bulk; of winds
and waves, *violence.* [magnitude.

magnopere, [for magnō opere, abl.
of magnum + opus], adv., *very
much, greatly, specially, deeply; earnestly, urgently.*

magnus, -a, -um, comp. maior, sup.
maximus, adj., *great, large, powerful;* of wind, *violent;* of voices,
loud (iv. 25). Sup., *greatest, very
great, largest, very large.* As noun,
maiōrēs, -um, m., pl., *forefathers,
ancestors.* maiōrēs nātū, lit. *those
older by birth, the old men, elders*
(ii. 13, 28; iv. 13). [maximum.

maiestās, -ātis, [maior], f., *greatness, dignity.* vii. 17. [majesty.

maiōrēs, -um, see magnus.

malacia, -ae, [μαλακία], f., *calm, dead
calm.* iii. 15.

male, comp. peius, sup. pessimē,
[malus, *bad*], adv., *badly, ill, unsuccessfully.*

maleficium, -ī, [maleficus], n., *mischief, wrong-doing, outrage, harm.*

mālō, **mālle**, **māluī**, [magis + volō], irr., *prefer*, *choose rather*, *had rather*.

mālus, -ī, m., *upright pole*, *upright;* of a ship, *mast.* iii. 14; vii. 22.

mandātum, -ī, [part. of mandō], n., *commission*, *order; command; injunction, instruction.* [mandate.

mandō, -āre, -āvī, -ātus, [manus + dō], 1, *commit*, *entrust*, *commission; order, direct.* [mandatory.

Mandubiī, -ōrum, m., pl., *Mandubians, Mandubii* (man-dū′ bī-ī), a Gallic people north of the Aeduans; chief city Alesia, now *Alise-Ste-Reine.*

Mandubracius, -ī, m., (man-du-brā′-sh[y]us), a British chieftain, loyal to Caesar. v. 20, 22.

māne, adv., *in the morning.*

maneō, **manēre**, **mānsī**, **mānsūrus**, 2, *stay, remain; continue.* [manse.

manipulāris, -ē, [manipulus], adj., *of a maniple.* As noun, **manipulāris**, -is, m., *soldier of a maniple, fellow-manipular.* vii. 47, 50.

manipulus, -ī, [manus + PLE in pleō, the first standard of a maniple being a *handful* of hay raised on a pole], m., *company* of soldiers, *maniple*, one-third of a cohort. [maniple.

Mānlius, -ī, m., *Lucius Manlius* (man′ lī-us), a proconsul in Gaul. iii. 20.

mānsuēfaciō, -facere, -fēcī, -factus, pass. **mānsuēfīō**, -fierī, [mānsuētus, *tame*, + faciō], 3, *make tame, tame.* vi. 28.

mānsuētūdō, -inis, [mānsuētus, *tame*], f., *gentleness, compassion.*

manus, -ūs, f., *hand;* of troops, *band, force.* [manicure.

Mārcellīnus, -ī, m., *P. Cornelius Lentulus Marcellinus* (len′ chū-lus mar-se-lī′ nus), a quaestor in Caesar's army in the Civil War. C. iii. 64.

Mārcellus, -ī, m., *Gaius Claudius Marcellus* (klâ′ dī-us mar-sel′ us), one of the consuls in 49 B.C. C. i. 6.

Mārcius, -ī, m., *Marcius Rufus* (mär′ sī-us rū′ fus), a quaestor in Curio's army (C. ii. 43).

Marcomanī, -ōrum, m., pl., (mar-kom′ a-nī), a Germanic people.

Mārcus, -ī, m., (mär′ kus), a Roman first name, our *Mark.*

mare, -is, n., *the sea.* [marine.

maritimus, -a, -um, [mare], adj., *of the sea, by the sea, near the sea; maritime, sea-.* **maritimae rēs**, *naval operations* (iv. 23). [maritime.

Marius, -ī, m., *Gaius Marius* (mā′-rī-us), a great Roman general; born 157 B.C., near Arpinum, died 86 B.C.; famous for his victories over Jugurtha, and the Cimbrians and Teutons; seven times consul, remaining to the end the bitter foe of the aristocratic party. i. 40.

Marrūcīnī, -ōrum, m., pl., (mär-ū-sī′ nī), a people of Central Italy, on the Adriatic coast. C. ii. 34.

Mārs, **Mārtis**, m., *Mars* (märz), god of war (vi. 17). [March.

mās, **maris**, m., *male.* vi. 26. [male.

Massilia, -ae, [Μασσαλία], f., (ma-sil′ i-a), a city in southern Gaul, founded by Greeks from Phocaea; now *Marseilles.* C. ii. 3, 7.

Massiliēnsēs, -ium, [Massilia], m., pl., *inhabitants of Massilia, Massilians.*

matara, -ae, f., *javelin, spear.* i. 26.

māter, -tris, f., *mother.* **mātrēs familiae**, *matrons.* [maternal.

māteria, -ae, and **māteriēs**, acc. (vii. 24) **māteriem**, [māter], f., *material, stuff; timber, wood; woodwork* (vii. 23). [material.

māterior, -ārī, [māteria], 1, dep., *procure timber, get wood.* vii. 73.

Matiscō, -ōnis, f., (mạ-tis′kō), an Aeduan city on the Arar (*Saône*), now *Mâçon*. vii. 90.

mātrimōnium, -ī, [māter], n., *marriage*. [matrimony.

Matrona, -ae, f., *Matrona* (mat′rọnạ), *Marne*, a tributary of the Sequana (*Seine*), into which it flows four miles above Paris, after a course of more than two hundred miles. i. 1.

mātūrē, comp. **mātūrius**, sup. **mātūrrimē**, [mātūrus], adv., *early*. **quam mātūrrimē**, *as early as possible* (i. 33).

mātūrēscō, [mātūrus], -ere, **mātūruī**, 3, *become ripe, ripen*. vi. 29.

mātūrō, -āre, -āvī, -ātus, [mātūrus], 1, *make haste, hasten*. [maturate.

mātūrrimē, see **mātūrē**.

mātūrus, -a, -um, comp. -ior, sup. **mātūrrimus**, adj., *ripe; early* (iv. 20). [mature.

Maurētānia, -ae, (mâ-rẹ-tā′nị-ạ), a country of northern Africa reaching from Numidia west to the Atlantic Ocean. C. i. 6.

maximē, [maximus], see **magis**.

maximus, see **magnus**.

Maximus, see **Fabius** (1).

medeor, -ērī, 2, dep., *heal; remedy, provide for* (v. 24). [medicine.

mediocris, -cre, [medius], adj., *common, ordinary;* of distance, *moderate, short*. [mediocre.

mediocriter, comp. **mediocrius** [mediocris], adv., *moderately, in a slight degree*.

Mediomatricī, -ōrum, m., pl., (mē′′dị-ọ-mat′rị-sī), a Gallic people near the Rhine.

mediterrāneus, -a, -um, [medius + terra], adj., *inland*. v. 12. [Mediterranean.

medius, -a, -um, adj., *middle, in the midst, mid-*. **media nox**, *midnight*.

dē mediā nocte, *just after midnight*. [medium.

Meldī, -ōrum, m., pl., (mel′dī), a Gallic people on the Matrona (*Marne*), east of the Parisii. v. 5.

melior, adj., see **bonus**.

melius, adv., see **bene**.

membrum, -ī, n., *limb*. [member.

meminī, -isse, def., *remember, bear in mind*. iii. 6; vii. 37.

memor, -oris, adj., *mindful, remembering*. C. ii. 6.

memoria, -ae, [memor], f., *memory, recollection, remembrance*. **memoriā tenēre**, *to recollect*. **memoriā prōditum**, *reported, handed down, by tradition* (v. 12). [memory.

Menapiī, -ōrum, m., pl., (mẹ-nā′-pị-ī), a people in the northeast part of Belgic Gaul.

mendācium, -ī, [mendāx, *false*], n., *lie, falsehood*. [mendacious.

mēns, mentis, f., *mind; temper* (iii. 19); *attitude of mind, feeling* (i. 41; vii. 64). **et mente et animō**, *heart and soul* (vi. 5). [mental.

mēnsis, -is, m., *month*.

mēnsūra, -ae, [mētior], f., *measuring* (vi. 25); *measure*. **ex aquā mēnsūra**, *water-clock* (v. 13). [measure.

mentiō, -ōnis, [MEN in memini], f., *mention*. vi. 38. [mention.

mercātor, -ōris, [mercor, *trade*], m., *trader, merchant*.

mercātūra, -ae, [mercor, *trade*], f., *traffic, trade;* pl., *commercial transactions* (vi. 17).

mercēs, -ēdis, f., *pay, hire*. i. 31.

Mercurius, -ī, [cf. merx, *merchandise*], m., *Mercury*, messenger of the gods, patron of traders and thieves, promoter of eloquence, and conductor of souls to the lower world; also, patron divinity of athletes and athletics. vi. 17.

mereō, -ēre, -uī, -itus, and **mereor**,
-ērī, -itus, 2, dep., *deserve, merit;*
serve (vii. 17). [merit.

merīdiānus, -a, -um, [merīdiēs],
adj., *of mid-day.* **merīdiānō ferē**
tempore, *about noon* (v. 8). [me-
ridian.

merīdiēs, -ēī, [medī-diē, loc.], m.,
mid-day; south (v. 13).

meritum, -ī, [part. of mereō], n.,
desert, merit, service. [merit.

meritus, see **mereor.**

Messāla, -ae, m., *Marcus Valerius*
Messala (va̤-lē′ ri̤-ṳs me̤-sā′ la̤), consul, 61 B.C. i. 2, 35.

Messāna, -ae, [Μεσσήνη], f., (me̤-
sā′ na̤), a city of northeastern Sicily,
now *Messina.* C. II. 3.

-met, enclitic, *self;* see **egō.**

mētior, mētīrī, mēnsus, 4, dep.,
measure, measure out, distribute.

Metius, -ī, m., *Marcus Metius* (mē′-
sh[y]ṳs), an envoy of Caesar to
Ariovistus.

Metlosēdum, -ī, n., (met-lo̤-sē′ dum),
a town of the Senones, on an island
in the Sequana (*Seine*), 28 miles
above Paris; later called Melodūnum,
now *Melun.*

metō, metere, messuī, messus, 3,
reap. iv. 32.

metus, -ūs, m., *fear, apprehension.*

meus, -a, -um, [mē], adj., *my, mine.*

mīles, -itis, m., *soldier, foot soldier.*

mīlitāris, -e, [mīles], adj., *of a sol-*
dier, military. **rēs mīlitāris,** *art*
of war. [military.

mīlitia, -ae, [mīles], f., *military ser-*
vice. vi. 14, 18; vii. 14. [militia.

mīlle or **M,** indecl. adj., *a thousand.*
As noun, **mīlia,** -um, n., pl., *thou-*
sand, thousands. [mile.

Minerva, -ae, f., (mi̤-nėr′ va̤), goddess of wisdom and the arts; identified with a Gallic divinity (vi. 17).

minimē, see **parum.**

minimus, -a, -um, see **parvus.**

minor, -us, see **parvus.**

Minucius, see **Basilus.**

minuō, -uere, -uī, -ūtus, 3, *lessen,*
diminish, reduce; of the tide, *ebb*
(iii. 12); of controversies, *settle, put*
an end to (v. 26; vi. 23). [minute.

minus, see **parum.**

mīror, -ārī, -ātus, [mīrus], 1, dep.,
wonder, wonder at. i. 32; v. 54.

mīrus, -a, -um, [mīror], adj., *won-*
derful, remarkable, marvellous.

miser, -era, -erum, comp. -ior, sup.
miserrimus, adj., *wretched, unfor-*
tunate, pitiable; poor (vi. 35). As
noun, **miserī,** -ōrum, m., pl., *the*
wretched (ii. 28). [miser.

misericordia, -ae, [misericors], f.,
pity, compassion, mercy.

miseror, -ārī, -ātus, [miser], 1, dep.,
lament, deplore. i. 39; vii. 1.

missus, -ūs, [mittō], m., used only
in abl. sing., *a sending, despatching.*
missū Caesaris, *being sent by*
Caesar (v. 27; vi. 7).

missus, -a -um, see **mittō.**

mītissimē, [mītis, *mild*], adv., sup.,
very gently, very kindly. **quam**
mītissimē potest, *in as kind a*
manner as possible (vii. 43).

mittō, mittere, mīsī, missus, 3,
send, despatch; release, let go; of
weapons, *throw, hurl, shoot.* [mis-
sile.

mōbilis, -e, comp. -ior, sup. -issimus,
[cf. **moveō**], adj., *fickle, changeable.*
iv. 5. [mobile.

mōbilitās, -tātis, [mōbilis], f., *quick-*
ness of movement, speed (iv. 33, C.
II. 6); *instability, changeableness*
(ii. 1). [mobility.

mōbiliter, [mōbilis], adv., *easily*
(iii. 10).

moderor, -ārī, -ātus, [modus], 1,
dep., *keep under control* (iv. 33);
manage, control (vii. 75). [moderate.

modestia, -ae, [modestus], f., *self-control; subordination* (vii. 52). [modesty.

modo, [modus], adv., *only, merely, even;* of time, *lately, just now* (vi. 39, 43). **nōn modo . . . sed etiam,** *not only . . . but also.*

modus, -ī, m., *measure, amount* (vi. 22); *plan* (v. 1); *manner, fashion, style.* **ad hunc modum,** *after this manner, in this way.* **eius modī,** *of such a character,* or *of that kind.* **quem ad modum,** *in what way, how; in whatever way, just as* (i. 36). **modō,** abl., with a dependent genitive, *after the manner of, as* (iv. 17, 27). **nūllō modō,** *by no means* (vi. 12). **omnibus modīs,** *by all means, in every way* (vii. 14). [mode.

moenia, -ium, n., pl., *walls* of a city, *fortifications* as a whole.

mōlēs, -is, f., *mass, massive structure; dam, dike* (iii. 12). [mole.

molestē, comp. -ius, sup. -issimē, [molestus, *troublesome*], adv., *with annoyance.*

mōlīmentum, -ī, [cf. mōlior, from mōlēs], n., *great effort.* i. 34.

molitus, see molō.

molliō, -īre, -īvī, -ītus, [mollis], 4, *soften; make easy* (vii. 46).

mollis, -e, comp. -ior, sup. -issimus, adj., *pliant, gentle; smooth* (v. 9); *weak, yielding* (iii. 19); *effeminate.*

mollitia, -ae (vii. 77), and (vii. 20) **mollitiēs,** -ēī, [mollis], f., *weakness, irresolution.*

molō, -ere, -uī, -itus, 3, *grind.*

mōmentum, -ī, [for *movimen-tum, cf. moveō], n., *movement; thrust, forward movement* (C. II. 6); *influence* (vii. 85); *importance, account* (vii. 39). [moment.

Mona, -ae, f., (mō' na̤), the *Isle of Man,* in the Irish Sea. v. 13.

moneō, -ēre, -uī, -itus, 2, *advise, warn, remind, admonish.*

mōns, montis, m., *mountain, mountain-range, elevation, height.* **summus mōns,** *top of the height* (i. 22). **rādīcēs montis,** *foot of the mountain* or *height* (i. 38; vii. 36). [mount.

mora, -ae, f., *delay.*

morātus, -a, -um, see moror.

morbus, -ī, [cf. morior, mors], m., *disease, sickness.* vi. 16, 17. [morbid.

Morinī, -ōrum, m., pl., (mor' i̤-nī), a Belgic people, on the seacoast opposite Kent.

morior, morī, mortuus, 3, dep., *die.* i. 4; vi. 13. [mortuary.

Moritasgus, -ī, m., (mor-i̤-tas' gṳs), a chief of the Senones. v. 54.

moror, -ārī, -ātus, [mora], 1, dep., *delay, wait, stay; hinder, delay, check, impede.* [moratorium.

mors, mortis, f., *death.* [mortal.

mortuus, -a, -um, see morior.

mōs, mōris, m., *usage, custom, way, wont, practice.* Pl., *customs, manners.* [moral.

Mosa, -ae, f., *Mosa* (mō' sa̤), *Meuse,* or *Maas,* which rises in the western spurs of the Vosges, pursues a northerly course till joined by the Waal, then flows westward into the North Sea.

mōtus, -ūs, [moveō], m., *movement, motion; disturbance, revolt, uprising.*

moveō, movēre, mōvī, mōtus, 2, *move, set in motion, remove;* of feelings, *disturb; stir, touch* (vii. 76). **castra movēre,** *to break camp.* [move.

mulier, -eris, f., *woman.*

mūliō, -ōnis, [mūlus], m., *muleteer, mule-driver.* vii. 45.

multitūdō, -inis, [multus], f., *great*

number, *host*, *large body; crowd.*
[multitude.

multō, -āre, -āvī, -ātus, [multa, *a fine*], 1, *punish; deprive of*, by way of punishment (vii. 54, C. III. 83).
[mulct.

multō, multum, comp. **plūs**, sup. **plūrimum**, [multus], adv., *much, by far, greatly.* **multum posse** or **valēre**, *to have great power, influence.*

multum, adv., see **multō**.

multus, -a, -um, adj., comp. **plūs**, sup. **plūrimus**, *much;* pl., *many.* As noun, m., pl., **multī**, -ōrum, *many* (people); **plūrēs**, -ium, *more, quite a number, several;* neut., sing., **multum**, *much;* **plūs**, *more;* **plūrimum**, *very much:* neut., pl., **multa**, *many things, many considerations.* [plural.

mūlus, -ī, m., *mule.* vii. 45. [mule.

Mūnātius, see **Plancus**.

mundus, -ī, m., *world, universe.* vi. 14. [mundane.

mūnicipium, -ī, [mūniceps], n., *free town, municipality.* [municipal.

mūnīmentum, -ī, [mūniō], n., *fortification, defence, barrier.* ii. 17. [muniment.

mūniō, -īre, -īvī, -ītus, [moenia], 4, *fortify; protect, make secure.* **mūnīre iter**, *to construct a road* (vii. 58).

mūnītiō, -ōnis, [mūniō], f., *a fortifying, building of fortifications; works of fortification, fortification, intrenchment, defences.* **mūnītiōnī castrōrum**, *for the fortifying of the camp* (v. 9). [munition.

mūnītus, -a, -um, comp. -ior, sup., -issimus, [part. of mūniō], adj., *fortified, protected, secure.* **mūnītissima castra**, *a camp very strongly fortified* (v. 57).

mūnus, -eris, n., *duty, service, func-*

tion; present, gift (i. 43). **mūnus mīlitiae**, *military service* (vi. 18).

mūrālis, -e, [mūrus], adj., *of a wall, wall-.* **mūrālis falx**, *wall-hook* (iii. 14). **mūrāle pīlum**, *wall-pike* (v. 40; vii. 82). [mural.

mūrus, -ī, m., *wall; rampart, line of works* (i. 8). [mure, immure.

mūsculus, -ī, [dimin. of mūs], m., *little mouse;* in military language, *long shed, mousie.* vii. 84. [muscle.

mutilus, -a, -um, adj., *maimed, broken.*

mūtuor, -ārī, -ātus, [mūtuus], 1, dep., *obtain a loan of, borrow.* C. III. 60.

N.

nactus, -a, -um, see **nancīscor**.

nam, conj., introducing an explanation or reason, *for.*

-nam; enclitic, *possible;* see **quisnam**.

Nammeius, -ī, m., (na̡-mē′ yu̡s), a Helvetian sent as envoy to Caesar. i. 7.

Namnetēs, -um, m., pl., (nam′ ne̡-tēz), a Gallic state north of the mouth of the Liger (*Loire*); the name survives in *Nantes.* iii. 9.

namque [nam + -que], conj., *for indeed, for truly, and* (with good reason) *for.*

nancīscor, -cīscī, **nactus**, and **nanctus**, 3, dep., *come upon, find, obtain; get, secure, get hold of.*

Nantuātēs, -um, m., pl., (nan-tu̡-ā′-tēz), a Gallic people southeast of Lake Geneva.

Narbō, -ōnis, m., (när′ bō), capital of the Province, which was later named from it, *Gallia Narbonensis;* originally a city of the Volcae Arecomici, but made a Roman colony in 118 B.C.; now *Narbonne.* iii. 20; vii. 7.

nāscor, nāscī, nātus, 3, dep., *be born, produced; is found* (v. 12); *rise* (ii. 18); *arise* (vi. 22; vii. 43). [nascent.

Nāsidiānus, -a, -um, adj., *of Nasidius.* C. II. 7.

Nāsīdius, -ī, m., *Lucius Nasidius* (na̯-sid′ i̯-u̯s), a naval commander on the side of Pompey in the Civil War. C. II. 3, 4.

Nasua, -ae, m., (nash′ ū̯-a̯), a chieftain of the Suebi. i. 37.

nātālis, -e, [nātus], adj., *of birth.* diēs nātālis, *birth-day* (vi. 18). [natal.

nātiō, -ōnis, [nāscor], f., *birth; people, tribe.* [nation.

nātīvus, -a, -um, [cf. nātus], adj., *natural, native.* vi. 10. [native.

nātūrāliter, [nātūrālis], adv., *by nature, naturally.* C. III. 92.

nātūra, -ae, [nātus, from nāscor], f., *nature, character; natural features, situation; nature of things, Nature.* nātūrā et opere, *naturally and artificially.* v. 9, 21. [nature.

nātus, -ūs, [cf. nāscor], m., used only in abl. sing., *birth.* maiōrēs nātū, see magnus.

nauta, -ae, [for * nā vi t a from nāvis], m., *sailor, seaman.* iii. 9; v. 10.

nauticus, -a, -um, [= ναυτικός], adj., *naval, nautical.* [nautical.

nāvālis, -e, [nāvis], adj., *naval.* As noun, nāvālia, -ium, n., pl., *shipyards.* C. II. 3. [naval.

nāvicula, -ae, [dim. of nāvis], f., *boat, skiff* (i. 53); *small ship* (C. II. 3).

nāvigātiō, -ōnis, [nāvigō], f., *navigation, sailing; voyage.* [navigation.

nāvigium, -ī, [nāvigō], n., *vessel, boat.* See speculātōrius.

nāvigo, -āre, -āvī, -ātus, [nāvis, cf.

agō], 1, *sail, go by water.* [navigate.

nāvis, -is, f., *ship, vessel;* for river navigation, *barge.* nāvis longa, *battleship, galley.* nāvis onerāria, *a transport* (Fig. 202). [nave.

Figure 202. — Ancient transport.

The transport is just entering the harbor, gliding into still water. The helmsman sits at the stern, and one of the two steering-paddles is plainly seen; the sailors are furling the large sail. From a relief on a tomb at Pompeii, symbolizing entrance into a haven of rest, after the stormy voyage of life.

nāvō, -āre, -āvī, -ātus, [(g)nāvus, *busy*], 1, *do with zeal.*

nē, adv., *not.* nē . . . quidem, *not . . . even.*

nē, conj., *that . . . not, lest, not to,* after words of fearing, *that;* after words of beseeching, ordering, commanding, *not to.* nē quis, *that no one.* nē qua spēs . . . *that no hope.* dēterrēre nē . . . *to frighten from.*

-ne, enclitic interrog. particle, *whether.* -ne . . . an, or -ne . . . -ne (vii. 14), *whether . . . or.*

nec, conj., see neque.

necessāriō, [necessārius], adv., *of necessity, unavoidably.*

necessārius, -a, -um, [necesse], adj., *needful, necessary; urgent, pressing.* As noun, necessārius, -ī, m., *relative, kinsman* (i. 11, C. III. 82). [necessary.

necesse, indecl. adj., *necessary, unavoidable, inevitable.*

necessitās, -tātis, [necesse], f., *necessity, need, urgency.* [necessity.

necessitūdō, -inis, [necesse], f., *close relationship, friendship.* i. 43.

necne, [nec + -ne], conj., *or not.* utrum ... necne, *whether or not* (i. 50).

necō, -āre, -āvī, -ātus, 1, *put to death, kill, destroy.* [noyade.

necubi, [nē + *cubi for ubi], conj., *that nowhere, lest anywhere.* vii. 35.

nefārius, -a, -um, [nefās], adj., *execrable, atrocious.* [nefarious.

nefās [ne, = nē, + fās], n., indecl., *a crime* against divine law, *impious deed.* nefās est, *it is wrong, it is not permitted* (vii. 40).

neglegō, -legere, -lēxī, -lēctus, [nec + legō], 3, *disregard, leave out of consideration, be indifferent to; neglect* (iii. 27; iv. 38); *overlook, leave unnoticed* (i. 35, 36; iii. 10). [neglect.

negō, -āre, -āvī, -ātus, 1, *deny, say not, say no,* often = dīcit nōn; *refuse* (v. 6, 27). [negative.

negōtiātor, -ōris, [negōtior], m., *wholesale dealer, wholesaler.* C. III. 103. [negotiator.

negōtior, -ārī, -ātus, [negōtium], 1, dep., *transact business.* negōtiandī causā, *in order to carry on business* (VII. 3, 42, 55). [negotiate.

negōtium, -ī, [neg-, = nē, + ōtium], n., *business, enterprise, task; effort, trouble, difficulty.* nihil negōtiī, *no trouble,* (v. 38).

Nemetēs, -um, m., pl., (nem' e-tēz), a Germanic people, settled west of the Rhine.

nēmō, dat. nēminī, [nē + *hemō = homō], m., *no one, nobody.*

nēquāquam [nē + quāquam, *anywhere*], adv., *not at all, by no means.*

neque or **nec** [ne, = nē, + -que], adv., *nor, and ... not.* neque ... neque or nec, *neither ... nor.*

nē ... quidem, see nē.

nēquīquam [nē + quīquam], adv., *in vain, to no purpose.* ii. 27.

Nervicus, -a, -um, adj., *of the Nervians.* Nervicum proelium, *battle with the Nervians* (iii. 5).

Nervius, -ī, m., *a Nervian* (v. 45). Pl., Nerviī, -ōrum, *the Nervians, Nervii* (nèr' vi̯-ī), a warlike people of Belgic Gaul.

nervus, -ī, m., *sinew, muscle* (vi. 21); pl., *power, force* (i. 20). [nerve.

neu, see nēve.

neuter, -tra, -trum, gen. neutrīus, [nē + uter], pron. adj., *neither.* As noun, neutrī, -ōrum, m., pl., *neither side* (vii. 63), *neither force* (ii. 9). [neuter.

nēve or **neu,** [nē + -ve, *or*], conj., *or not, and not, and that not, nor.* neu ... -que, *and not ... but* (ii. 21). neu ... et, *and not ... but* (v. 34).

nex, necis, f., *death* by violence.

nihil [ne, = nē, + hīlum, *trifle*], n., indecl., *nothing;* as adverbial acc., = emphatic nōn, *not at all.* [nihilism.

nihilō sētius, see sētius.

nihilum, -ī, [ne, = nē, + hīlum], n., *nothing.* nihilō, abl. of degree of difference, lit. *by nothing;* nihilō minus, *none the less.*

nimius, -a, -um, [nimis], adj., *excessive, too great.* vii. 29, C. III. 96.

nisi [ne, = nē, + sī], conj., *if not, unless, except.*

Nitiobrogēs, -um, m., pl., (nish-i̯-ob' ro-jēz), a people in Northern Aquitania.

nītor, nītī, nīxus and nīsus, 3, dep., *strive, endeavor; rely upon, depend on* (i. 13).

nix, nivis, f., *snow.* vii. 8, 55.

nōbilis, -e, comp. -ior, sup. -issimus, [cf. nōscō], adj., *noted, renowned* (vii. 77); *of high rank, noble* (i. 2, 18; v. 22; vii. 67). As noun, nō-bilēs, -ium, m., pl., *nobles, men of rank* (i. 44; vi. 13); nōbilissimus, -ī, m., *man of highest rank;* pl., *men of highest rank* (i. 7, 31). [noble.

nōbilitās, -tātis, [nōbilis], f., *nobility, rank* (ii. 6); collective (for nōbilēs), *nobility, nobles, men of rank.* [nobility.

nocēns, -entis, comp. nocentior, sup. -issimus, [part. of noceō], adj., *guilty.* As noun, nocentēs, -um, m., pl., *the guilty* (vi. 9).

noceō, -ēre, -uī, -itūrus, 2, *hurt, do harm, injure.*

noctū, [cf. nox], adv., *by night, at night, in the night.*

nocturnus, -a, -um, [cf. nox], adj., *by night, of night.* nocturnus labor, *the toil of the night* (vii. 83). nocturnum tempus, *night-time* (v. 11, 40). [nocturnal.

nōdus, -ī, m , *knot; node,* on the joint of an animal (vi. 27). [node.

nōlō, nōlle, nōluī, [nē + volō], irr., *be unwilling, not wish, not want.* nōlī, nōlīte, with infin., *do not.*

nōmen, -inis, n., *name, appellation, title; reputation, renown; account.* suō nōmine, *on his own account* (i. 18), *on their own account* (vii. 75). [noun.

nōminātim [nōminō], adv., *by name.*

nōminō, -āre, -āvī, -ātus, [nōmen], 1, *name, call* by a name (vii. 73); *mention* (ii. 18). [nominate.

nōn, adv., *not; no.* nōn nihil, *to some extent, somewhat* (iii. 17). nōn nūllus, *some, several.* nōn num-quam, *sometimes.*

nōnāgintā, or **xc**, indeclinable num. adj., *ninety.*

nōndum [nōn + dum], adv., *not yet.*

nōn nihil, see nōn.

nōn nūllus, -a, -um, see nōn.

nōn numquam, see nōn.

nōnus, -a, -um, [novem], numeral ord. adj., *ninth.* [noon.

Nōreia, -ae, f., (no̱-rē′ya), chief city of the Norici (nor′i̱-sī), now *Neu-markt.* i. 5.

Nōricus, -a, -um, adj., *of the Norici, Norican* (i. 5). As noun, Nōrica, -ae, f., *Norican woman* (i. 53).

nōs, see ego.

nōscō, nōscere, nōvī, nōtus, 3, *ob-tain a knowledge of, learn;* in tenses from the pf. stem, *know, be familiar with, be acquainted with.*

nōsmet, see egomet.

noster, -tra, -trum, [nōs], pron. adj., *our, our own.* As noun, nostrī, -ōrum, m., pl., *our men, our side.* [nostrum.

nōtitia, -ae, [nōtus], f., *knowledge, acquaintance.* [notice.

notō, -āre, -āvī, -ātus, [nota, *mark*], 1, *brand* (C. iii. 74); *reprimand, check* (C. i. 7). [note.

nōtus, -a, -um, comp. -ior, sup. -issi-mus, [part. of nōscō], adj., *known, well-known, familiar.*

novem, or **viiii**, indeclinable num. adj., *nine.*

Noviodūnum, -ī, [Celtic word, = 'Newtown'], n., (no̱′′ vi̱-o̱-dū′num), name of three towns :

(1) Of the Aeduans, on the right bank of the Liger (*Loire*); now *Nevers.* vii. 55.

(2) Of the Bituriges, south of Cenabum. vii. 12, 14.

(3) Of the Suessiones, on the Axona (*Aisne*). ii. 12.

novitās, -tātis, [novus], f., *novelty, newness, strangeness.*

novus, -a, -um, adj., *new, fresh, strange.* Sup. novissimus, *last, at* *the rear.* As noun, novissimī, -ōrum, m., pl., *those at the rear, the rear.* novissimum agmen, *rear of the line of march, the rear.* [novice.

nox, noctis, f., *night.* multā nocte, *late at night, when the night was far spent.* [nocti- in noctivagant, etc.

noxia, -ae, [noxius, -a, -um, *hurtful*], f., *hurt, offence, crime* (vi. 16).

nūbō, nūbere, nūpsī, supine nūptum, 3, *veil one's self* for marriage, *marry, wed.* i. 18. [nuptial.

nūdō, -āre, -āvī, -ātus [nūdus], 1, *strip, make bare; clear* (II. 6); *expose, leave unprotected.*

nūdus, -a, -um, adj., *naked, bare; unprotected* (i. 25). [nude.

nūllus, -a, -um, gen. nūllīus, dat. nūllī, [ne, = nē, + ūllus], adj., *none, no.* As noun, especially in the dat., m., *no one.*

num, interrogative particle, expecting the answer No.

nūmen, -inis, [cf. nuō, *nod*], n., *divine will; divine majesty* (vi. 16).

numerō, -āre, -āvī, -ātus, [numerus], 1, *count, reckon.* C. III. 53. [numerate.

numerus, -ī, m., *number, amount; estimation, account* (vi. 13). obsidum numerō, *as hostages* (v. 27). [number.

Numidae, -ārum, [νομάς, *wanderer*, pl. νομάδες], m., pl., *Numidians*, a people in Northern Africa, in the country now called Algeria, famous as archers, and employed by Caesar as light-armed troops (ii. 7, 10, 24). Numidians under Juba destroyed the army of Curio in 49 B.C. (C. II. 39, 41).

nummus, -ī, m., *piece of money, money, coin.* v. 12.

numquam [ne, = nē, + umquam], adv., *never, not at any time.*

nunc, adv., *now, at present.*

nūncupō, -āre, -āvī, -ātus, [nōmen, cf. capiō], 1, *name publicly;* of vows, *offer publicly* (C. I. 6).

nūntiō, -āre, -āvī, -ātus, [nūntius], 1, *announce, report; give orders* (iv. 11). Impers. nūntiātur, *word is brought, it is reported.*

nūntius, -ī, m., *messenger, agent* (i. 44); *message, tidings.* [nuncio.

nūper, sup. nūperrimē, adv., *lately, recently.*

nūtus, -ūs, [nuō, *nod*], m., *nod, nodding* (v. 43); *bidding, command* (i. 31; iv. 23).

O.

ob, prep. with acc., *on account of, for.* ob eam causam, *for that reason.* ob eam rem, *on that account, therefore.* quam ob rem, *wherefore* (I. 34); *for what reason* (i. 50).

obaerātus, -a, -um, comp. -ior, [ob, cf. aes], adj., *in debt.* As noun, obaerātus, -ī, m., *debtor, serf* (i. 4).

obdūcō, -dūcere, -dūxī, -ductus, [ob + dūcō], 3, *lead forward;* of a trench, *prolong, extend* (ii. 8).

obeō, -īre, -iī, -itus, [ob + eō], irr., *go to meet; attend to.* omnia per sē obīre, *to see to everything in person* (v. 33).

obiciō, -icere, -iēcī, -iectus, [ob+ iaciō], 3, *throw before; place in front, place; put in the way, expose;* of taunts, *cast up at; twit of* (C. III. 96); of difficulties, *present* (vii. 59). [object.

obiectātiō, -ōnis, [obiectō], f., *reproach.* C. III. 60.

obiectō, -āre, -āvī, -ātus, [freq. of obiciō], 1, *accuse of; twit of* (C. III. 48).

obiectus, -a, -um, see obiciō.

obitus, -ūs, [cf. obeō], m., *destruction.* ii. 29. [obituary.

oblātus, see offerō.

oblīquē, [obliquus], adv., *obliquely,
with a slant.* iv. 17.

oblīquus, -a, -um, adj., *slanting,
crosswise.* vii. 73. [oblique.

oblīvīscor, -līvīscī, -lītus, 3, dep.,
forget. [oblivion.

obses, -idis, [cf. obsideō], m. and
f., *hostage.*

obsessiō, -ōnis, [cf. obsideō], f.,
siege (vii. 36); *blockade* (vi. 36).
[obsession.

obsessus, see obsideō.

obsideō, -sidēre, -sēdī, -sessus, [ob

Figure 203. — A Roman document, tied and sealed.

The writing is on the two inside faces of the two tablets, which were securely tied together.
The seals of the 8 witnesses were stamped in wax over the ends of the cord, a groove of
suitable width being cut in the wood of the tablets for the purpose.

The names of those who stamped their seals were written with ink on the wood at the
right, in the genitive case. The number of witnesses was often 7 (cf. p. 467), sometimes 8,
as here, sometimes 9 or more.

The illustration is from a charred tablet found at Pompeii, restored ; it was sealed about
100 years after Caesar's death.

The names of the first three and last three witnesses are: L. LAELIUS FUSCUS, SEXTUS
NONIUS SCAMANDER, P. AEFULANUS CRYSANTUS ; L. MELISSAEUS COERASUS, L. COR-
NELIUS DEXTER, and L. NAEVOLEIUS NYMPHUS. The fourth and fifth names are uncertain.

obsecrō, -āre, -āvī, -ātus, [ob +
sacrō, from sacer], 1, *beseech* in
the name of that which is sacred,
implore, beg. [obsecrate.

obsequentia, -ae, [obsequēns], f.,
compliance, complaisance. vii. 29.

observō, -āre, -āvī, -ātus, [ob +
servō], 1, *watch, observe* (vii. 16);
keep track of (vi. 18); *heed, comply
with* (i. 45; v. 35). [observe.

+ sedeō], 2, *besiege, blockade;* of
roads, *seize upon, block* (iii. 23, 24;
v. 40). [obsess.

obsidiō, -ōnis, [cf. obsideō], f., *siege,
blockade; oppression* (iv. 19).

obsignō, -āre, -āvī, -ātus, [ob +
signō], 1, *seal up, seal* (Fig. 203).

obsistō, -sistere, -stitī, [ob +
sistō], 3, *withstand.* vii. 29.

obstinātē [obstinātus, part. of ob-

stinō, *persist*], adv., *firmly, stead-
fastly, persistently.* v. 6.

obstrictus, -a, -um, see **obstringō**.

obstringō, -stringere, -strīnxī,
-strictus, [ob + stringō, *tie*], 3,
bind, place under obligation. i. 9,
31.

obstruō, -struere, -strūxī, -strūc-
tus, [ob + struō, *pile*], 3, *block up,
stop up.* v. 50, 51; vii. 41. [ob-
struct.

obtemperō, -āre, -āvī, -ātus, [ob +
temperō], 1, *submit to, obey.*

obtentūrus, fut. act. part. of **obtineō**.

obtestor, -ārī, -ātus, [ob + testor],
1, dep., *call as witness, appeal to;
implore, adjure.*

obtineō, -tinēre, -tinuī, -tentus,
[ob + teneō], 2, *hold fast, maintain, keep, retain, hold* (i. 3); *get
possession of, obtain* (i. 18; vi. 12);
possess, occupy, inhabit (i. 1). [ob-
tain.

obtrectātiō, -ōnis, [obtrectō], f.,
disparagement. C. 1. 7.

obveniō, -venīre, -vēnī, -ventūrus,
[ob + veniō], 4, *fall in with, encounter* (ii. 23); *fall to the lot of,
fall to* (vii. 28, 81, C. 1. 6).

obviam, [ob + acc. of **via**], adv., *in
the way, against.* **obviam Caesarī
proficīscitur**, *goes to meet Caesar*
(vii. 12).

occāsiō, -ōnis, [cf. occidō], f., *opportunity, favorable moment; surprise* (vii. 45). [occasion.

occāsus, -ūs, [cf. occidō], m., *going
down, setting.* **sōlis occāsus**, *sunset, the west* (i. 1; iv. 28).

occidēns, -entis, [part. of occidō],
adj., *of the sun, setting.* **occidēns
sōl**, *the west* (v. 13). [occident.

occidō, -cidere, -cidī, [ob + cadō],
3, *fall* (vi. 37).

occīdō, -cīdere, -cīdī, -cīsus, [ob +
caedō], 3, *kill, slay.*

occīsus, -a, -um, see **occīdō**.

occultātiō, -ōnis, [occultō], f., *concealment.* vi. 21.

occultē, comp. -ius, sup. -issimē,
[occultus], adv., *secretly, in secret.*

occultō, -āre, -āvī, -ātus, [freq. of
occulō, *cover*], 1, *hide, conceal;
keep secret.*

occultus, -a, -um, comp. -ior, sup.
-issimus, [part. of occulō, *cover*],
adj., *hidden, secret, concealed.* As
noun, **ex occultō**, *from ambush, in
ambush* (vi. 34); **sē in occultum
abdere**, *to go into hiding* (vii. 30);
in occultō, *in hiding, in concealment* (ii. 18; vi. 35; vii. 27, 35), *in
a secret place* (i. 31, 32). [occult.

occupātiō, -ōnis, [occupō], f., *employment, engagement.* [occupation.

occupō, -āre, -āvī, -ātus, [ob, cf.
capiō], 1, *seize upon, seize, take possession of; fill, occupy* (ii. 8); *of the
attention, engage, occupy.* **occu-
pātus**, -a, -um, as adj., *engaged;
busied* (ii. 19). [occupy.

occurrō, -currere, -currī, rarely -cu-
currī, -cursūrus, [ob + currō],
3, *run to meet, come to meet, meet;
meet with, fall in with, encounter;
match, offset* (vii. 22); *come into
mind, occur* (vii. 85). [occur.

Ōceanus, -ī, ['Ωκεανός], m., *Ocean,*
considered by Caesar as one body
of water, including the Atlantic
Ocean, the English Channel, and
the North Sea; *the sea.* [ocean.

Ocelum, -ī, n., (ōs′ ę-lụm), a town of
the Graioceli in the Alps, west of
modern Turin. i. 10.

octāvus, -a, -um, [octō], numeral
ord. adj., *eighth.* [octave.

octingentī, -ae, -a, or DCCC, [octō
+ centum], num. adj., *eight hundred.*

octō, or VIII, indeclinable num. adj.,
eight. [October.

octōdecim, or **XVIII,** [octō + decem], indeclinable num. adj., *eighteen*.

Octodūrus, -ī, m., (ok-tọ-dū'rụs), chief town of the Veragri, in the Rhone valley southeast of Geneva. iii. 1.

octōgēnī, -ae, -a, or **LXXX,** [octō], distrib. num. adj., *eighty* in each case.

octōgintā, or **LXXX,** [octō], indeclinable num. adj., *eighty*.

octōnī, -ae, -a, [octō], distrib. num. adj., *eight each, eight at a time*.

oculus, -ī, m., *eye*. [oculist.

ōdī, ōdisse, ōsūrus, def., *hate*.

odium, -ī, [ōdī], n., *hatred*. [odium.

offendō, -fendere, -fendī, -fēnsus, 3, *hit against; hurt, wound* (i. 19). Impersonal, **offendī posset,** *injury could be inflicted, a disaster might occur* (vi. 36); **esset offēnsum,** *a reverse had been experienced* (C. III. 72). [offend.

offēnsiō, -ōnis, [offendō], f., *hurting, wounding; reverse*.

offerō, -ferre, obtulī, oblātus, [ob + ferō], irr., *bring before; offer, present; put in one's way, afford*. **sē offerre,** *to offer one's self* (vii. 89), *expose one's self* (vii. 77), *rush against* (iv. 12). [offer.

officium, -ī, [for *opificium, ops + FAC in faciō], n., *service, duty; allegiance; sense of duty* (i. 40). [office.

Ollovicō, -ōnis, m., (ọ-lov'ị-kō), a king of the Nitiobroges. vii. 31.

omittō, -mittere, -mīsī, -missus, [ob + mittō], 3, *lay aside, throw away* (vii. 88); *neglect, disregard* (ii. 17). **omnibus omissīs rēbus,** *laying aside everything else* (vii. 34). [omit.

omnīnō, [omnis], adv., *altogether; after negatives, at all; with numer-als, in all, altogether, only*. **nihil omnīnō,** *nothing at all*.

omnis, -e, adj., *every, all; as a whole*. As noun, pl., **omnēs,** -ium, m., *all men, all;* **omnia,** -ium, n., *all things, everything*. [omnibus.

onerārius, -a, -um, [onus], adj., *of burden;* see **nāvis.** [onerary.

onerō, -āre, -āvī, -ātus, [onus], 1, *load*. v. 1. [onerate.

onus, -eris, n., *load, burden, weight; cargo* (v. 1). [onus.

opera, -ae, [opus], f., *effort, work, pains; service, aid, assistance*. **dare operam,** *to take pains*. [opera.

opīniō, -ōnis, [opīnor, *think*], f., *idea, notion; good opinion, reputation; expectation*. **opīniō timōris,** *impression of fear*. **iūstitiae opīniō,** *reputation for fair dealing* (vi. 24). [opinion.

oportet, oportēre, oportuit, 2, impers., *it is necessary, it is needful; it behooves; ought; is proper* (vii. 33).

oppidānus, -a, -um, [oppidum], adj., *of the town*. As noun, **oppidānī,** -ōrum, m., pl., *townspeople, inhabitants of the town*.

oppidum, -ī, n., *fortified town, city; fortified enclosure, stronghold* (v. 21).

oppleō, -ēre, -ēvī, -ētus, [ob + pleō], 2, *fill completely*. C. III. 73.

oppōnō, -pōnere, -posuī, -positus, [ob + pōnō], 3, *place over against, set against, oppose*. [oppose.

opportūnē, sup. -issimē, [opportūnus], adv., *conveniently, seasonably, opportunely*.

opportūnitās, -ātis, [opportūnus], f., *fitness, favorableness, seasonableness; favorable situation, advantage*. [opportunity.

opportūnus, -a, -um, comp. -ior, sup. -issimus, adj., *fit, suitable, favorable, advantageous*. [opportune.

oppositus, -a, -um, [part. of oppōnō], adj., *placed opposite; lying in the way* (vii. 56). [opposite.

opprimō, -primere, -pressī, -pressus, [ob + premō], 3, *weigh down; overwhelm, crush; take by surprise, surprise, fall upon.* [oppress.

oppugnātiō, -ōnis, [oppugnō], f., *storming* of a city or camp, *assault, attack, besieging.*

oppugnō, -āre, -āvī, -ātus, [ob + pugnō], 1, *attack, assault; storm, besiege; take* by storming.

ops, opis, nom. and dat. sing. not in use, f., *help, power, might.* Pl., **opēs,** -um, *help* (vi. 21); *resources, means, wealth; influence; strength* (vii. 76). [opulent.

optātus, -a, -um, comp. -ior, sup. -issimus, [part. of optō], adj., *desired; welcome* (vi. 42).

optimē, see **bene.**

optimus, see **bonus.**

opus, n., used only in nom. and acc., *necessity, need.* **opus est,** *there is need, it is necessary.*

opus, operis, n., *work, labor;* that produced by labor, *structure, works; line of works, fortification.* Cf. **quantus.** [opus.

ōra, -ae, f., *coast, shore.* **ōra maritima,** *sea-coast* (iv. 20); place put for people, *inhabitants of the coast, people along the sea* (iii. 8, 16).

ōrātiō, -ōnis, [ōrō], f., *speech, words, remarks, plea.* [oration.

ōrātor, -ōris, [ōrō], m., *speaker; envoy* (iv. 27). [orator.

orbis, -is, m., *circle.* **in orbem cōnsistere,** *to form a circle* (v. 33). **orbis terrārum,** *the world* (vii. 29). [orb.

Orcynia, -ae, f., (or-sin′ ĭ-ạ), with **silva,** *the Hercynian forest.* vi. 24.

ōrdō, -inis, m., *row, series; layer* (vii. 23); *rank, order; century* (half a maniple), *company* (i. 40,

v. 35); *officer commanding a century, centurion.* [order.

Orgetorīx, -īgis, m., (or-jet′ ọ-rĭks), a Helvetian nobleman who formed a plot to seize the supreme power.

Ōricum, -ī, ['Ωρικόν], n., (or′ ĭ-cụm), a seaport on the east coast of the Adriatic, now *Palaeocastro,* on the bay of Valona. C.′ III. 90.

oriēns, -entis, [part. of orior], adj., *rising.* **oriēns sōl,** *rising sun; the east* (i. 1; v. 13; vii. 69). [orient.

orior, orīrī, ortus, 4, dep., *rise, arise; begin, spring from; start from* (i. 39). **oriente sōle,** *at sunrise* (vii. 3). **ortā lūce,** *at daybreak* (v. 8).

ōrnāmentum, -ī, [ōrnō], n., *decoration; distinction, honor* (i. 44; vii. 15). [ornament.

ōrnātus, -a, -um, comp. -ior, sup. -issimus, [part. of ōrnō], adj., *equipped.* [ornate.

ōrnō, -āre, -āvī, -ātus, 1, *furnish, equip; provide* (vii. 33).

ōrō, -āre, -āvī, -ātus, [ōs, *mouth*], 1, *plead, beg, entreat.* [orate.

ortus, -ūs, [orior], m., *rising.* **ortus sōlis,** *sunrise* (vii. 41).

ortus, see **orior.**

ōs, ōris, n., *mouth; face* (v. 35; vi. 39; C. III. 99). [oral.

Osismī, -ōrum, m., pl., (ọ-sis′ mī), a small state in the northwest corner of Gaul.

ostendō, -tendere, -tendī, -tentus, [obs, for ob, + tendō], 3, *show, display; point out, set forth, declare.*

ostentātiō, -ōnis, [ostentō], f., *display, show; ostentation* (vii. 53). **ostentātiōnis causā,** *in order to attract attention* (vii. 45). [ostentation.

ostentō, -āre, -āvī, -ātus, [freq. of ostendō], 1, *display, show;* with **sē,** *show off* (vii. 19).

ōtium, -ī, n., *rest, quiet, peace.*

ōvum, -ī, n., *egg.* iv. 10. [oval.

P.

P. with proper names = **Pūblius.**

pābulātiō, -ōnis, [pābulor], f., *foraging, getting fodder.* [pabulation.

pābulātor, -ōris, [pābulor], m., *forager.* v. 17.

pābulor, -ārī, -ātus, [pābulum], 1, dep., *forage, obtain fodder.*

pābulum, -ī, n., *fodder, forage.* [pabulum.

pācātus, -a, -um, comp. -ior, sup. -issimus, [part. of **pācō**], adj., *peaceful, quiet.* [pacate.

pācō, -āre, -āvī, -ātus, [pāx], 1, *pacify, tranquillize.* [pacable.

pactum, -ī, [pacīscor], n., *agreement; manner, way* (vii. 83). [pact.

Padus, -ī, m., (pā′ dụs), *Po,* the great river of Northern Italy. v. 24.

Paelignus, -a, -um, *Paelignian, of the Paeligni* (pẹ-lig′ nī), a people of Central Italy, whose chief city was Corfinium. C. ii. 35.

Paemānī, -ōrum, m., pl., (pē-mā′ nī), a people in Belgic Gaul. ii. 4.

paene, adv., *almost, nearly.*

paenitet, -ēre, -uit, 2, impers., *it makes sorry, it causes regret.* [penitent.

pāgus, -ī, m., *district, canton,* generally referring to the inhabitants rather than to the country; *clan.* [pagan.

palam, adv., *openly, publicly.*

palma, -ae, f., *palm* of the hand; *hand* (vi. 26, C. iii. 98). [palm.

palūdātus, -a, -um, *wearing a general's cloak* (palūdāmentum); as we say, *in uniform.* C. i. 6.

palūs, -ūdis, f., *marsh, swamp, bog.*

palūster, -tris, -tre, [palūs], adj., *marshy, swampy* (vii. 20).

pandō, pandere, pandī, passus, 3, *spread out;* of hair, *dishevel* (vii. 48). passīs manibus, *with hands outstretched.*

pānis, -is, m., *bread;* pl., *loaves of bread* (C. iii. 48). [pantry.

pār, paris, adj., *like, similar, same; equal; corresponding* (vii. 74). pār atque, *same as.* [par.

parātus, -a, -um, comp. -ior, sup. -issimus, [part. of **parō**], adj., *ready, prepared; provided.*

parcē, comp. -ius, [parcus], adv., *sparingly.* vii. 71.

parcō, parcere, pepercī and parsī, parsūrus, 3, *use sparingly* (vii. 71); with dat., *spare, give quarter to.*

parēns, -entis, [pariō], m. and f., *parent.* [parent.

parentō, -āre, -ātus, [parēns], 1, *offer a sacrifice in honor of* deceased *parents* or relatives; *take vengeance for the death of any one, avenge* (vii. 17).

pāreō, pārēre, pāruī, 2, *obey; submit to, be subject to.*

pariō, parere, peperī, partus, 3, *bring forth; obtain, get, acquire.*

Parīsiī, -ōrum, m., pl., (pạ-rish′[y]ī), a Gallic people on the Sequana (*Seine*); the name survives in *Paris.*

Figure 204. — A coin of the Parisii.

Gold. Obverse, head with decorative treatment of the hair.

Reverse, chariot design conventionalized, the outline of the horse alone being distinctive.

parō, -āre, -āvī, -ātus, 1, *prepare, make ready, make ready for; obtain, secure.* [pare.

pars, partis, f., *part, portion, share, number; region, district, division; side, direction; party, faction* (vi. 11, l. 15). pars maior, *the majority.* ūnā ex parte, *on one side.* in omnēs partēs, *in every direction.* [part.

Parthī, -ōrum, m., pl., *the Parthians,* a Scythian people in the region of the Caspian Sea. C. III. 82.

particeps, -cipis, [pars, cf. capiō], adj., *sharing in.* C. III. 60. [participle.

partim, [acc. of pars], adv., *partly, in part.*

partior, partīrī, partītus, [pars], 4, dep., *divide, divide up, share.* Part. partītus in a passive sense, *divided, shared.* [partite.

partus, see pariō.

parum, comp. minus, sup. minimē, adv., *too little, not enough.* Comp., *less.* Sup., *least, very little; not at all, by no means.* [minus.

parvulus, -a, -um, [dim. of parvus], adj., *very small; very young; slight, trifling.*

parvus, -a, -um, comp. minor, sup. minimus, adj., *small, trifling, insignificant.* Comp., *smaller, less.* As noun, minus, n., *less;* minimum, n., *the least.* [minimum.

passim, [passus, from pandō], adv., *in all directions* (iv. 14); *here and there* (C. II. 38).

passus, -ūs, m., *step, pace;* as a measure of length, *pace* (reckoned as a double step, from the place where either foot is raised to the place where the same foot rests on ground again), = 5 Roman feet, or 4 feet, 10¼ inches by English measurement. mīlle passūs, *mile;* pl., mīlia passuum, *miles.* [pace.

passus, see pandō.

passus, see patior.

patefaciō, -facere, -fēcī, -factus, pass., patefīō, -fierī, -factus, [pateō + faciō], 3, *lay open, open.*

patēns, -entis, comp. patentior, [part. of pateō], adj., *open.* [patent.

pateō, patēre, patuī, 2, *be open, lie open, stand open; extend.*

pater, -tris, m., *father.* Pl., patrēs, -um, *fathers, forefathers.* [paternal.

patiēns, -entis, [patior], adj., comp. patientior, sup. patientissimus, *long-suffering, patient.* C. III. 96. [patient.

patienter, comp. patientius, [patiēns], adv., *patiently.* vii. 77.

patientia, -ae, [patiēns], f., *endurance* (vi. 24); *forbearance* (vi. 36). [patience.

patior, patī, passus, 3, dep., *suffer, bear, endure; permit, allow.* [passive.

patrius, -a, -um, [pater], adj., *of a father; ancestral, of (their) forefathers* (ii. 15).

patrōnus, -ī, [pater], m., *protector, patron.* vii. 40. [patron.

patria, -ae, [patrius, sc. terra], f., *native land, fatherland* (C. II. 7).

patruus, -ī, [pater], m., *father's brother, uncle* on the father's side.

paucitās, -ātis, [paucus], f., *fewness, small number.* [paucity.

paucus, -a, -um, comp. -ior, sup. -issimus, adj., *little;* pl., *few.* As noun, paucī, -ōrum, m., pl., *few, only a few;* n., pl., pauca, -ōrum, *a few words* (i. 44).

paulātim, [paulum], adv., *little by little, by degrees; gradually; one by one* (iv. 30).

paulisper, [paulum, per], adv., *for a short time, a little while.*

paulō, [abl. of paulus], adv., *by a little, just a little.*

paululum [paulus], adv., *a very little, only a little.* ii. 8.

paulum, [neut. acc. of **paulus**], adv., *a little, somewhat.*

pāx, pācis, f., *peace.* [peace.

peccō, -āre, -āvī, -ātus, 1, *do wrong.*

pectus, -oris, n., *breast.* [pectoral.

pecūnia, -ae, [cf. **pecus,** *cattle*], f., *property; money.* Pl., **pecūniae,** *contributions of money* (C. I. 6).

pecūniārius, -a, -um, [**pecūnia**], adj., *of money, pecuniary.* [pecuniary.

pecus, -oris, n., *cattle,* general term for domestic animals; *flesh* of cattle, *meat* (IV. 1).

pedālis, -e, [**pēs**], adj., *measuring a foot, a foot thick.* iii. 13. [pedal.

pedes, -itis, [**pēs**], m., *foot-soldier.* Pl., **peditēs, -um,** *infantry.*

pedester, -tris, -tre, [**pēs**], adj., *on foot.* **pedestrēs cōpiae,** *infantry.* [pedestrian.

peditātus, -ūs, [**pedes**], m., *infantry.*

Pedius, -ī, m., *Quintus Pedius* (pē'-dị-ụs), nephew of Julius Caesar, under whom he served as lieutenant in the Gallic and Civil Wars. He was consul in 43 B.C. ii. 2, 11.

peior, see **malus.**

pellis, -is, f., *skin, hide.* [pelisse.

pellō, pellere, pepulī, pulsus, 3, *drive out, drive off; rout, defeat.*

Pēlūsium, -ī, [Πηλούσιον], n., (pẹ-lū'-shị-ụm), a city and fortress in Egypt, at the easternmost mouth of the Nile. C. III. 103.

pendō, pendere, pependī, pēnsus, 3, *weigh out; pay.* [pendent.

penes, prep. with acc., *in the power of, in the possession of.*

penitus, adv., *far within.* vi. 10.

per, prep. with acc., *through; across, along, over, among; during, in the course of; by, by the hands of, by means of, under pretence of; by reason of.* In oaths, *in the name of, by.*

per agrōs, *over the country* (vi. 31; vii. 3).

In composition, **per** adds the force of *through, thoroughly, very much, very.*

peragō, -agere, -ēgī, -āctus, [**per + agō**], 3, *finish, complete, bring to an end.*

perangustus, -a, -um, [**per + angustus**], adj., *very narrow.* vii. 15.

percellō, -ere, perculī, perculsus, 3, *beat down; cast down, demoralize* (C. III. 47).

perceptus, see **percipiō.**

percipiō, -cipere, -cēpī, -ceptus [**per + capiō**], 3, *get, secure, gain; hear* (v. 1); *learn* (vi. 8). [perceive.

percontātiō, -ōnis, [**percontor,** *inquire*], f., *questioning, inquiry.*

percurrō, -currere, -cucurrī or **-currī, -cursūrus,** [**per + currō**], 3, *run through; run along* (iv. 33).

percussus, see **percutiō.**

percutiō, -cutere, -cussī, -cussus, [**per + quatiō,** *shake*], 3, *thrust through.* v. 44. [percuss.

perdiscō, -discere, -didicī, [**per + discō**], 3, *learn thoroughly, learn by heart.* vi. 14.

perditus, -a, -um, comp. **-ior,** sup. **-issimus,** [part. of **perdō,** *ruin*], adj., *abandoned, desperate* (iii. 17). As noun, **perditī, -ōrum,** m., pl., *desperate men, the desperate* (vii. 4).

perdūcō, -dūcere, -dūxī, -ductus, [**per + dūcō**], 3, *lead through, bring, conduct, convey; bring over, win over* (vi. 12); *draw out, prolong* (v. 31, C. III. 95); *extend, construct, make.*

perendinus, -a, -um, [**perendiē,** *day after to-morrow*], adj., *after to-morrow.* **perendinō diē,** *day after to-morrow* (v. 30).

pereō, -īre, -iī, -itūrus, [per + eō],
irr., *perish, be lost.* [perish.

perequitō, -āre, -āvī, [per +
equitō, *ride*], 1, *ride through* (vii.
66); *ride about* (iv. 33).

perexiguus, -a, -um, [per + exi-
guus], adj., *very small.*

perfacilis, -e, [per + facilis], adj.,
very easy.

perfectus, see perficiō.

perferō, -ferre, -tulī, -lātus, [per +
ferō], irr., lit. *carry through; carry,
convey, bring, report; endure, suffer;
bear, submit to.*

perficiō, -ficere, -fēcī, -fectus, [per
+ faciō], 3, *finish, complete; perform, accomplish, carry out; cause,
effect; bring about, arrange.* [per-
fect.

perfidia, -ae, [perfidus], f., *faith-
lessness, bad faith, treachery.* [per-
fidy.

perfringō, -fringere, -frēgī, -frāc-
tus, [per + frangō], 3, *break
through.*

perfuga, -ae, [perfugiō], m., *deserter.*

perfugiō, -fugere, -fūgī, [per + fu-
giō], 3, *flee for refuge, flee.*

perfugium, -ī, [cf. perfugiō], n.,
place of refuge, refuge. iv. 38.

pergō, pergere, perrēxī, perrēc-
tus, [per + regō], 3, *proceed, advance.*

perīclitor, -ārī, -ātus, [perīculum],
1, dep., *try, prove, make trial of,
test; be in danger, incur danger*
(vi. 34; vii. 56).

perīculōsus, -a, -um, comp. -ior,
sup. -issimus, [perīculum], adj.,
full of danger, dangerous. I. 33,
vii. 8. [perilous.

perīculum, -ī, n., *trial, test* (i. 40);
attempt (iv. 21); *risk, danger, haz-
ard.* [peril.

perītus, -a, -um, comp. -ior, sup.

-issimus, adj., *skilled, practised; familiar with.*

perlātus, see perferō.

perlēctus, see perlegō.

perlegō, -legere, -lēgī, -lēctus,
[per + legō], 3, *read through, pe-
ruse.* v. 48. [perlection.

perluō, -luere, -luī, -lūtus, [per +
luō, *wash*], 3, *wash.* Pass. used
reflexively, *bathe* (vi. 21).

permagnus, -a, -um, [per + mag-
nus], adj., *very large, very great.*

permaneō, -manēre, -mānsī, mānsūrus, [per + maneō], 2, *continue,
stay, remain.* [permanent.

permisceō, -miscēre, -miscuī, -mix-
tus, [per + misceō, *mix*], 2, *mix,
mingle.* vii. 62.

permittō, -mittere, -mīsī, -missus,
[per + mittō], 3, *give over, entrust,
commit; grant, allow.* [permit.

permixtus, see permisceō.

permōtus, see permoveō.

permoveō, -movēre, -mōvī, -mō-
tus, [per + moveō], 2, *deeply move,
disturb, alarm; arouse, stir; influence, induce.*

permulceō, -ēre, -sī, -sus, [per +
mulceō, *soothe*], 2, *calm, soothe.*
iv. 6.

permulsus, see permulceō.

perniciēs, -ēī, [per, cf. nex], f., *ruin,
destruction.* i. 20, 36.

perniciōsus, -a, -um, [perniciēs],
adj., *ruinous.* C. I. 7. [pernicious.

pernīcitās, -tātis, [pernīx, *nimble*],
f., *quickness of movement, nimbleness.*
C. III. 84.

perpaucī, -ae, -a, [per + paucus],
adj., *very few.* As noun, **perpaucī,**
-ōrum, m., pl., *a very few.*

perpendiculum, -ī, [cf. perpendō],
n., *plumb-line.* [perpendicular.

perpetior, -petī, -pessus, [per +
patior], 3, dep., *bear patiently, endure.* vii. 10; C. III. 47.

perpetuō [perpetuus], adv., *contin-ually, constantly* (vii. 41); *always, forever* (i. 31).

perpetuus, -a, -um, [per, cf. petō], adj., *continuous, unbroken, unceasing, entire, perpetual.* As noun, in perpetuum, *for ever, ever after.* [perpetual.

perquīrō, -quīrere, -quīsīvī, -quīsī-tus, [per + quaerō], 3, *make careful inquiry about, inquire about.* vi. 9.

perrumpō, -rumpere, -rūpī, -rup-tus, [per + rumpō, *break*], 3, *break through, burst through, force a passage.*

perruptus, see perrumpō.

perscrībō, -scrībere, -scrīpsī, -scrīp-tus, [per + scrībō], 3, *write fully, report* in writing.

persequor, -sequī, -secūtus, [per + sequor], 3, dep., *follow up, pursue; assail, attack* (i. 13; v. 1); *avenge* (vii. 38). [persecute.

persevērō, -āre, -āvī, -ātus, [perse-vērus, *very strict*], 1, *continue* stead-fastly, *persist.* [persevere.

persolvō, -solvere, -solvī, -solūtus, [per + solvō], 3, *pay in full, pay.*

perspectus, see perspiciō.

perspiciō, -spicere, -spexī, -spec-tus, [per + speciō, *look*], 3, *see, look; inspect, survey; perceive, observe, ascertain.* [perspective.

perstō, -stāre, -stitī, -stātūrus, [per + stō], 1, *stand firmly, persist.*

persuādeō, -suādēre, -suāsī, -suā-sum est, [per + suādeō, *per-suade*], 2, *convince, persuade, prevail upon, induce.* mihi persuādētur, *I am convinced.* [persuade.

perterreō, -terrēre, -terruī, -terri-tus, [per + terreō], 2, *greatly alarm, frighten, terrify, dismay.* Part., perterritus, -a, -um, often *panic-stricken.*

pertinācia, -ae, [pertināx, per + tenāx, from teneō], f., *obstinacy, stubbornness.* [pertinacity.

pertineō, -tinēre, -tinuī, [per + teneō], 2, *reach out, extend; pertain to, concern, belong to.* [pertain.

perturbātiō, -ōnis, [perturbō], f., *disturbance, confusion.* [perturba-tion.

perturbō, -āre, -āvī, -ātus, [per + turbō, *disturb*], 1, *disturb greatly, disorder, confuse.* [perturb.

pervagor, -ārī, -ātus, [per + va-gor], 1, dep., *roam about.*

pervehō, -ere, pervexī, [per + vehō], 3, *carry through;* pass. with middle sense, *sail along* (C. II. 3).

perveniō, -venīre, -vēnī, -ventum est, [per + veniō], 4, *come (to), arrive (at), reach;* of an inheritance, *fall to* (vi. 19).

pēs, pedis, m., *foot;* as a measure of length, = .9708 of the English foot, or 296 millimetres. pedem re-ferre, *to retreat.* [pedestrian.

pestilentia, -ae, [pestilēns], f., *plague, pestilence.* C. III. 87. [pes-tilence.

petītus, see petō.

petō, petere, petīvī and petiī, petī-tus, 3, *make for, try to reach, seek; get, secure; beg, ask, request.* pe-tere ut liceat, *to ask permission.*

Petrocoriī, -ōrum, m., pl., (pet-ro̧-ko' ri̧-ī), a Gallic people north of the Garumna (*Garonne*) river. vii. 75.

Petrōnius, -ī, m., *Marcus Petronius* (pȩ-trō' ni̧-u̧s), a centurion of the eighth legion (vii. 50).

Petrosidius, -ī, m., *Lucius Petrosi-dius* (pet-ro̧-sid' i̧-u̧s), a brave stand-ard-bearer. v. 37.

phalanx, -angis, Greek acc. sing., (i. 52) phalanga, [φάλαγξ], f., *com-pact host, mass, phalanx.* [phalanx.

Philippus, -ī, m., *Lucius Marcus Philippus* (fĭ-lip′ ŭs), consul in 56 B.C. C. I. 6.

Pictonēs, -um, m., pl., (pĭk′ tọ-nēz), a Gallic people bordering on the Atlantic south of the Liger (*Loire*). Fig. 205.

Figure 205. — A coin of the Pictones.

Silver. Reverse, cavalryman with a shield. The object underneath has not been explained.

The hair of the head on the obverse is shown in thick masses.

pietās, -ātis, [pius, *dutiful*], f., *dutiful conduct, devotion,* to the gods, one's country, or one's kindred; *loyalty* (v. 27), [piety.

pīlum, -ī, n., *javelin, pike.* [pile.

pīlus, -ī, [pīlum], m., with prīmus, *maniple of the triarii,* a division in the army containing the most experienced soldiers.   **prīmī pīlī cen- turiō**, *first centurion of the first maniple of the triarii, first centurion* of the legion in rank (iii. 5).   **prī- mum pīlum dūcere**, *to lead the first maniple of the triarii, to hold the rank of first centurion* (v. 35; vi. 38 ; C. III. 91).

pinna, -ae, f., *feather;* in military language, *battlement.* [pen.

Pīrustae, -ārum, m., pl., (pī-rus′tē), a people in Illyricum. v. i.

piscātōrius, -a, -um, [piscātor, *fisherman*], adj., *of a fisherman.* **nāvēs piscātōriae**, *fishing-smacks* (C. II. 4). [piscatory.

piscis, -is, m., *fish.* iv. 10. [Pisces.

Pīsō, -ōnis, m., (pī′ sō) :

(1) *Lucius Calpurnius Piso Cae- soninus,* consul 112 B.C. i. 12.

(2) *Lucius Calpurnius Piso Cae- soninus,* consul with *Aulus Gabi- nius,* 58 B.C.; father-in-law of Cae- sar. i. 6, 12.

(3) *Marcus Pupius Piso Calpur- nianus,* consul with *M. Valerius Messala,* 61 B.C. i. 2, 35.

(4) *Piso,* a brave Aquitanian. iv. 12.

pix, picis, f., *pitch.* [pitch.

Placentia, -ae, f., (plạ-sen′ sh[y]ạ), a city in northern Italy, on the Po River; now *Piacenza.* C. III. 71.

placeō, placēre, placuī, placitum est, 2, *please, be agreeable, be wel- come to.* Used impersonally, **placet**, *it pleases, it seems good; it is agreed, it is settled; it is resolved, it is de- cided.*   **eī placuit**, *he resolved* (i. 34). [please.

placidē, comp. -ius, [placidus], adv., *quietly, calmly.* vi. 8.

plācō, -āre, -āvī, -ātus, 1, *appease, conciliate.* vi. 16. [placate.

Plancus, -ī, m., *Lucius Munatius Plancus* (mụ-nā′ sh[y]ŭs plang′- kŭs), a lieutenant in Caesar's army. v. 24, 25.

plānē, comp. -ius, sup. -issimē, [plā- nus], adv., *clearly, distinctly* (iii. 26); *entirely, quite* (vi. 43).

plānitiēs, -ēī, [plānus], f., *level ground, plain.*

plānus, -a, -um, comp. -ior, sup. -issimus, adj., *level, even* (iv. 23); *flat* (iii. 13). [plain.

plēbs, plēbis, or plēbēs, -eī, f., *the common folk, the common people, the masses.* **apud plēbem**, *among the masses.* [plebeian.

plēnē, comp. -ius, [plēnus], adv., *fully, completely.* iii. 3.

plēnus, -a, -um, comp. -ior, sup. -issimus, adj., *full.*

plērumque, [n. acc. of plērusque], adv., *commonly, generally, usually, for the most part.*

plērusque, -aque, -umque, [plērus, *very many*], adj., *very many, most.* As noun, plērīque, -ōrumque, m., pl., *the most, the greater part, the majority, most.*

Pleumoxiī, -ōrum, m., pl., (plū-mok'-sị-ī), a Belgic people, subject to the Nervians. v. 39.

plumbum, -ī, n., *lead.* plumbum album, *tin* (v. 12.) [plumber.

plūrēs, plūrimum, see multus.

plūs, plūrimum, see multum.

pluteus, -ī, m., *breastwork* of planks or wickerwork, placed on ramparts (vii. 41), or on the stories of a tower (vii. 25); *wood construction* (vii. 72); *movable mantelet,* to protect besiegers.

pōculum, -ī, n., *cup, beaker.* vi. 28.

poena, -ae, f., *compensation, fine* (v. 1); *punishment, penalty.* poenās pendere (vi. 9) or persolvere, (i. 12), *to pay the penalty.* [penal.

pollex, pollicis, m., *thumb, great toe.*

polliceor, -licērī, -licitus, [por- + liceor], 2, dep., *promise, offer.*

pollicitātiō, -ōnis, [pollicitor, freq. of polliceor], f., *promise, offer.*

pollicitus, see polliceor.

Pompeiānus, -a, -um, [Pompeius], adj., *of Pompey.* As noun, Pompeiānī, -ōrum, m., pl., *soldiers of Pompey, Pompey's men.* (C. III. 48. 72).

Pompeius, -ī, m., (pọm-pē' yụs):

(1) *Gnaeus Pompeius Magnus, Pompey,* Caesar's son-in-law and rival, born B.C. 106; conquered by Caesar at the battle of Pharsalus, and afterwards murdered in Egypt.

(2) *Gnaeus Pompeius,* an interpreter serving under Titurius Sabinus. v. 36.

pondus, ponderis, [cf. pendō], n., *heaviness, weight* (ii. 29; vi. 27; v. 22); *a weight* as a standard of value (v. 12); *quantity* (C. III. 96). [ponderous.

pōnō, pōnere, posuī, positus, 3, *place, put; lay down* (iv. 37); *set aside* (vi. 17); *station; pitch.* Pass. often *be situated, be dependent, depend on.* castra pōnere, *to pitch camp, encamp.* [positive.

pōns, pontis, m., *bridge.* [pontoon.

populātiō, -ōnis, [populor], f., *a laying waste, ravaging.* i. 15.

populor, -ārī, -ātus, 1, dep., *lay waste, devastate.* i. 11.

populus, -ī, m., *people* as a political whole, *nation.* [people.

por-, in composition, *forth, forward.*

porrigō, -rigere, -rēxī, -rēctus, [por- + regō], 3, *reach out, extend.*

porrō, adv., *moreover, furthermore.* v. 27.

porta, -ae, f., *gate* of a city, *gateway;* of a camp, *gate, entrance, passage.* [porter (door-keeper).

portō, -āre, -āvī, -ātus, 1, *carry, bring, convey, take.* [portage.

portōrium, -ī, n., *toll, tax, customs duties.* i. 18; iii. 1.

portus, -ūs, m., *harbor, haven.* [port.

poscō, poscere, poposcī, 3, *demand, ask for urgently;* of things, *require, make necessary* (vii. 1).

positus, -a, -um, see pōnō.

possessiō, -ōnis, [cf. possīdō], f., *possession.* [possession.

possideō, -sidēre, -sēdī, [por- + sedeō], 2, *hold, occupy, possess.* i. 34; ii. 4; vi. 12. [possess.

possīdō, -sīdere, -sēdī, -sessus, [por- + sīdō], 3, *gain possession of, possess one's self of.* iv. 7.

possum, posse, potuī, [potis, *able,* + sum], irr., *be able, can; have power, have influence.* multum

posse, *to have great influence;* **plūrimum posse,** *to have very great power, influence.* [posse.

post, adv., *afterwards, later, after;* with abl. of degree of difference, **annō post,** *a year later, the following year.* **paucīs post diēbus,** *a few days later.*

post, prep. with acc. only:

(1) Of place, *behind.* **post tergum,** *in the rear.*

(2) Of time, *after.* **post mediam noctem,** *after midnight.*

posteā [post eā], adv., *afterwards.* **posteā quam,** with the force of a conjunction, *after that, after.*

posterus, -a, -um, nom. sing. m. not in use, comp. **posterior,** sup. **postrēmus,** [post], adj., *the following, next.* As noun, **posterī,** -ōrum, m., pl., *posterity* (vii. 77). [postern.

postpōnō, -pōnere, -posuī, -positus, [post + pōnō], 3, *put after, lay aside.* **omnia postpōnere,** *to disregard everything else* (vi. 3). **omnibus rēbus postpositīs,** *laying everything else aside* (v. 7). [postpone.

postpositus, see postpōnō.

postquam [post + quam], conj., *after that, after, when;* post and quam are often separated by intervening words.

postrēmō [abl. of postrēmus, sc. tempore], adv., *at last, finally.*

postrīdiē, [locative from posterus diēs], adv., *the next day.* **postrīdiē eius diēī,** *the next day, the following day.*

postulātum, -ī, [part. of postulō], n., *demand, claim, request.*

postulō, -āre, -āvī, -ātus, 1, *claim, demand, ask, request;* of things, *require, make necessary, demand; accuse of* (C. III. 83). [postulate.

potēns, -entis, comp. **potentior,** sup.

-issimus, [part. of possum], adj., *powerful.* As noun, **potentior,** -ōris, m., *one more powerful* (vi. 11); pl., *the more powerful* (ii. 13, 22). **potentissimī,** -ōrum, m., pl., *the most powerful* (vi. 22). [potent.

potentātus, -ūs, [potēns], m., *power, headship, supremacy.* I. 31. [potentate.

potentia, -ae, [potēns], f., *might, power, influence.* [potency.

potestās, -ātis, [potis], f., *might, power, authority, lordship; possibility, opportunity.* **potestātem facere,** *to give opportunity; to grant permission* (iv. 15; v. 41).

potior, potīrī, potītus, [potis, *able*], 4, dep., *obtain possession of, become master of, acquire, obtain.*

potius, adv. in comp. degree, sup. **potissimum,** [potis], adv., *rather, more, preferably.* **potius quam,** *rather than.*

prae, prep. with abl., *in comparison with* (ii. 30), *on account of* (vii. 44).

praeacuō, -cuere, -cuī, -cūtus, 3, *sharpen at the end.*

praeacūtus, -a, -um, [part. of praeacuō], adj., *sharpened at the end, sharpened, pointed; very sharp.*

praebeō, -ēre, praebuī, praebitus, [prae + habeō], 2, *hold forth; exhibit, manifest; furnish, provide* (ii. 17); *produce* (iii. 17). [prebendary.

praecaveō, -cavēre, -cāvī, -cautus, [prae + caveō], 2, *take precautions.* i. 38. [precaution.

praecēdō, -cēdere, -cessī, -cessūrus, [prae + cēdō], 3, *go before; surpass, excel* (i. 1). [precede.

praeceps, -cipitis, [prae + CAP in caput], adj., *headlong, with great speed, head over heels* (ii. 24; v. 17); *steep, precipitous* (iv. 33). [precipitous.

praeceptum, -ī, [part. of praecipiō], n., *order, command, instruction, injunction; precept.* v. 35; vi. 36. [precept.

praecipiō, -cipere, -cēpī, -ceptus, [prae + capiō], 3, *anticipate* (VII. 9; C. III. 87); *order, direct, instruct.*

praecipitō, -āre, -āvī, -ātus, [praeceps], I, *hurl headlong, fling down.* [precipitate.

praecipuē, [praecipuus], adv., *especially, specially, particularly.*

praecipuus, -a, -um, [prae + CAP in capiō], adj., *especial, particular.*

praeclūdō, -clūdere, -clūsī, -clūsus, [prae + claudō], 3, *close up, block.* v. 9. [preclude.

praecō, -ōnis, m., *herald, crier.*

Praecōnīnus (prę-cǫ-nī′ nụs), see Valerius (I).

praecurrō, -currere, -cucurrī or -currī, [prae + currō], 3, *run forward, hasten forward* (vi. 39, C. II. 34); *hasten in advance* (vii. 37); *anticipate* (vii. 9). [precursor.

praeda, -ae, [cf. praehendō], f., *booty, spoil, plunder.* [prey.

praedicō, -āre, -āvī, -ātus, [prae + dicō], I, *make known, declare, announce; boast* (i. 44, C. II. 39). [preach.

praedīcō, -dīcere, -dīxī, -dictus, [prae + dīcō], 3, *say beforehand; order, give orders,* in advance (C. III. 92). [predict.

praedō, -ōnis, [praeda], m., *robber, pirate.* C. III. 104.

praedor, -ārī, -ātus, [praeda], I, dep., *obtain booty, pillage, plunder.*

praedūcō, -dūcere, -dūxī, -ductus, [prae + dūcō], 3, *extend, make in front.* vii. 46, 69.

praefectus, see praeficiō.

praefectus, -ī, [praeficiō], m., *commander, prefect; subsidiary official* (I. 39). [prefect.

praeferō, -ferre, -tulī, -lātus, [prae + ferō], irr., *carry before; put before, prefer to* (v. 54). **sē praeferre**, *to show one's self superior to* (ii. 27). [prefer.

praeficiō, -ficere, -fēcī, -fectus, [prae + faciō], 3, *place in command of, appoint to command.*

praefīgō, -fīgere, -fīxī, -fīxus, [prae + fīgō, *fasten*], 3, *fix in front.* **sudibus praefīxīs**, *by driving stakes in front* (v. 18). [prefix.

praefringō, -fringere, -frēgī, -frāctus, [prae + frangō], 3, *break off, shatter.* C. II. 6.

praemetuō, -ere, [prae + metuō, *fear*], 3, *be anxious.* vii. 49.

praemittō, -mittere, -mīsī, -missus, [prae + mittō], 3, *send forward, send ahead, send in advance.* [premise.

praemium, -ī, [prae, cf. emō], n., *reward, distinction.* [premium.

praeoccupō, -āre, -āvī, -ātus, [prae + occupō], I, *take possession of beforehand, seize first* (vii. 26). [preoccupy.

praeoptō, -āre, -āvī, -ātus, [prae + optō], I, *choose rather, prefer.* I. 25.

praeparō, -āre, -āvī, -ātus, [prae + parō], I, *make ready beforehand, make ready, prepare.* [prepare.

praepōnō, -pōnere, -posuī, -positus, [prae + pōnō], 3, *set over, place in command of.*

praerumpō, -rumpere, -rūpī, -ruptus, [prae + rumpō, *break*], 3, *break off in front, break off.* iii. 14.

praeruptus, -a, -um, [part. of praerumpō], adj., *steep, precipitous.*

praesaepiō, -saepīre, -saepsī, -saeptus, [prae + saepiō], 4, *fence in; block, bar* (vii. 77).

praesaeptus, see praesaepiō.

praescrībō, -scrībere, -scrīpsī,

-scrīptus, [prae + scrībō], 3, *give
directions, direct* (i. 36, 40); *determine* (ii. 20). [prescribe.

praescrīptum, -ī, [part. of prae-
scrībō], n., *direction, order, instructions.* i. 36. [prescript.

praesēns, -entis, comp. -ior, [part.
of praesum], adj., *at hand, present.*
[present.

praesentia, -ae, [praesēns], f., *presence* (v. 43); *present time.* in
praesentiā, *for the present.* [pres-
ence.

praesentiō, -sentīre, -sēnsī, -sēn-
sus, [prae + sentiō], 4, *perceive
beforehand.* v. 54; vii. 30.

praesertim [prae, cf. serō, *join*],
adv., *especially, particularly.*

praesidium, -ī, [praeses, *guard*], n.,
*guard, detachment, garrison, protec-
tion; post, redoubt; safety* (ii. 11).

praestō, -stāre, -stitī, -stitus, [prae
+ stō], 1, *surpass, excel; exhibit,
display, manifest; discharge, perform, do.* Impers. praestat, *it is
preferable, it is better.*

praestō, adv., *at hand.* praestō
esse, *to meet* (v. 26).

praesum, -esse, -fuī, [prae + sum],
irr., *preside over; be at the head of,
have command of, have charge of.*

praeter, prep. with acc. only, *beyond*
(i. 48); *except, besides; contrary to.*

praetereā [praeter + eā], adv., *besides, further.*

praetereō, -īre, -īvī or -iī, -itus,
[praeter + eō], irr., *pass over*
(vii. 25, 77); *pass, go by* (vii. 77).
[preterit.

praeteritus, see praetereō.

praetermittō, -mittere, -mīsī, missus, [praeter + mittō], 3, *pass
over, let pass, allow to go by.*

praeterquam [praeter + quam],
adv. with comparative force, *other
than, besides.* vii 77.

praetor, -ōris, [*praeitor, from
praeeō], m., *general, commander*
(i. 21); *praetor,* a Roman magistrate, next in rank to the consul.

praetōrium, -ī, [praetōrius], n.,
general's tent. C. III. 82.

praetōrius, -a, -um, [praetor], adj.,
of the commander, general's (i. 40,
42); *pretorian.* As noun, praetōrius, -ī, m., *ex-praetor, man of prae-
torian rank* (C. III. 82). [preto-
rian.

praetūra, -ae, [praetor], f., *the office
of praetor, praetorship* (C. III. 82).

praeūstus, -a, -um, [part. of prae-
ūrō], adj., *burnt at the end, hardened at the end by burning.*

praevertō, -vertere, -vertī, [prae
+ vertō], 3, *outstrip; attend to first*
(vii. 33).

prāvus, -a, -um, comp. -ior, sup.
-issimus, adj., *bad, wicked.* vii. 39.

precēs, see prex.

premō, -ere, pressī, pressus, 3,
press, harass, oppress; pass., *be hard
pressed, be beset, be burdened, be in
need.* [press.

prēndō (for prehendō), prēndere,
prēndī, prēnsus, 3, *take, grasp.*
i. 20.

pretium, -ī, n., *price, value.* [price.

prex, precis, f., generally pl., nom.
and gen. sing. not in use, *prayer,
entreaty, supplication; curse, impre-
cation* (vi. 31).

prīdiē, adv., *the day before, the previous day.* prīdiē eius diēī, *the
day before that day, on the previous
day* (i. 47).

prīmipīlus, -ī, [prīmus + pīlus], m.,
= prīmus pīlus, *first centurion;*
see pīlus. ii. 25, C. III. 53.

prīmō [abl. of prīmus], adv., *at first,
in the first place.*

prīmum [acc. of prīmus], adv., *first,
before everything else, in the first*

place. quam prīmum, *as soon as possible.* cum prīmum, *as soon as.*

prīmus, see prior.

prīnceps, -ipis, [prīmus + CAP in capiō], adj., *first, chief, at the front.* As noun, m., *leading man, leader,* pl. often *leading men.* [prince.

prīncipātus, -ūs, [prīnceps], m., *chief authority, headship.* [principate.

prior, -us, gen. priōris, adj. in comp. degree, sup. prīmus, [cf. prō], *former, previous, first.* As noun, priōrēs, -um, m., pl., *those in advance* (ii. 11). Sup. prīmus, *first, the first.* As noun, prīmī, -ōrum, m., pl., *the foremost men, the first.* prīma, -ōrum, n., pl., in the phrase in prīmīs, *especially.* [prior, prime.

prīstinus, -a, -um, [*prīs, = prius, + -tinus], adj., *former, previous, earlier, old-time.* [pristine.

prius [prior], adv., *before, sooner, earlier.*

priusquam, prius quam, conj., *before, sooner than;* prius and quam are often separated by intervening words.

prīvātim [prīvātus], adv., *privately, as individuals,* opposed in meaning to pūblicē. i. 17; v. 55.

prīvātus, -a, -um, [part. of prīvō], adj., *private, personal.* As noun, prīvātus, -ī, m., *private individual* (vi. 13). [private.

prīvō, -āre, -āvī, -ātus, 1, *rob, deprive.* C. III. 90.

prō, prep. with abl. only, *in front of, before; for, in behalf of; instead of, as; on account of, in return for; in accordance with* (ii. 31); *in proportion to, considering* (i. 2, 51; vi. 19; vii. 56, 74).

probō, -āre, -āvī, -ātus, [probus], 1, *approve; show to be worthy, display* (v. 44); *prove* (v. 27); *show, demonstrate* (i. 3). [probe.

prōcēdō, -cēdere, -cessī, [prō + cēdō], 3, *advance, go forward.* [proceed.

Procillus, (pro-sil′ us), see Valerius (4).

prōclīnō, -āre, -āvī, -ātus, [prō + clīnō, *bend*], 1, *bend forward, lean forward;* pass., *become desperate* (vii. 42).

prōcōnsul, -ulis, [prō + cōnsul], m., *proconsul,* an ex-consul appointed as governor of a province.

procul, adv., *at a distance, from afar, far off.*

prōcumbō, -cumbere, -cubuī, [prō + cumbō, for cubō, *lie down*], 3, *fall prostrate* (vii. 15); *sink down* (ii. 27); *be beaten down* (vi. 43); *lie down* (vi. 27); *lean forward* (iv. 17).

prōcūrātiō, -ōnis, [prōcūrō], f., *charge, management.* C. III. 104.

prōcūrō, -āre, -āvī, -ātus, [prō + cūrō], 1, *look after, have charge of, regulate.* vi. 13. [procure.

prōcurrō, -currere, -cucurrī or -currī, [prō + currō], 3, *run forward, hasten forward, rush forward.*

prōdeō, -īre, -iī, -itum est, [prōd-, for prō, + eō], irr., *come out, come forth, advance.*

prōdesse, see prōsum.

prōditiō, -ōnis, [prōdō], f., *treachery.*

prōditor, -ōris, [prōdō], m., *traitor.*

prōditus, see prōdō.

prōdō, -dere, -didī, -ditus, [prō + dō], 3, *give forth, make known; transmit, hand down; surrender, betray; give up, abandon* (iv. 25).

prōdūcō, -dūcere, -dūxī, -ductus, [prō + dūcō], 3, *bring out, lead forth; prolong* (iv. 30). [product.

prōductus, see prōdūcō.

proelior, -ārī, -ātus, [proelium], 1, dep., *fight.*

proelium, -ī, n., *battle, combat, engagement.*

profectiō, -ōnis, [proficīscor], f., *departure, setting out.*

prōfectus, see prōficiō.

profectus, see proficīscor.

prōferō, -ferre, -tulī, -lātus, [prō + ferō], irr., *bring out, bring forth.*

prōficiō, -ficere, -fēcī, -fectus, [prō + faciō], 3, *effect, gain, accomplish.* [profit.

proficīscor, -ficīscī, -fectus, [prōficiō], 3, dep., *set out, depart; set out (for), proceed.*

profiteor, -fitērī, -fessus, [pro, = prō, + fateor, *confess*], 2, dep., *declare openly, avow* (VII. 2, 37); *offer, promise.* [profess.

prōflīgō, -āre, -āvī, -ātus, [prō + flīgō, *strike*], 1, *put to flight, rout.* ii. 23; vii. 13. [profligate.

prōfluō, -fluere, -flūxī, [prō + fluō], 3, *flow forth.* IV. 10.

profugiō, -fugere, -fūgī, [pro, = prō, + fugiō], 3, *flee, escape.*

prōfuī, see prōsum.

prōfundō, -fundere, -fūdī, -fūsus, [prō + fundō], 3, *pour forth.* sē prōfūdit, *rushed forward* (C. III. 93).

prōgnātus, -a, -um, [prō + (g)nātus, from (g)nāscor], adj., *sprung, descended.* ii. 29; vi. 18.

prōgredior, -gredī, -gressus, [prō + gradior, *step*], 3, dep., *advance, go forward, proceed.* [progress.

prōgressus, see prōgredior.

prohibeō, -hibēre, -hibuī, -hibitus, [prō + habeō], 2, *hold, restrain; keep off, prevent, hinder; cut off, shut off; protect, defend.* [prohibit.

prōiciō, -icere, -iēcī, -iectus, [prō + iaciō], 3, *throw forward, throw, fling, cast;* of arms, *throw down; abandon, lose* (ii. 1/5). sē prōicere, *to leap down* (iv. 25), *to prostrate one's self* (i. 27, 31). proiectae,

pass. as middle, *casting themselves* (vii. 26). [project.

proinde [prō + inde], adv., *hence, therefore, and so.* proinde ac sī, *just as if* (C. III. 60).

prōmineō, -minēre, -minuī, 2, *bend forward, lean forward.* [prominent.

prōmiscuē [prōmiscuus], adv., *in common, promiscuously.* vi. 21.

prōmissus, -a, -um, [part. of prōmittō], adj., of hair, *hanging down, flowing.* v. 14.

prōmōtus, see prōmoveō.

prōmoveō, -movēre, -mōvī, -mōtus, [prō + moveō], 2, *move forward, push forward.* [promote.

prōmptus, -a, -um, comp. -ior, sup. -issimus, [part. of prōmō, *bring forward*], adj., *ready, quick.* [prompt.

prōmunturium, -ī, [cf. prōmineō], n., *headland.* iii. 12. [promontory.

prōnē [prōnus], adv., *bending forward, leaning forward.* iv. 17.

prōnūntiō, -āre, -āvī, -ātus, [prō + nūntiō], 1, *tell openly, declare; announce, give notice.* Impers., prōnūntiātur, *notice is given.* [pronounce.

prope, comp. propius, sup. proximē, adv., *near, nearly, almost;* followed by the acc., *near.* proximē, *nearest, next, very near; last, most recently.*

prōpellō, -pellere, -pulī, -pulsus, [prō + pellō], 3, *drive away, put to flight, rout; force back* (v. 44). [propel.

properō, -āre, -āvī, -ātus, [properus, *quick*], 1, *hurry, make haste, hasten.*

propinquitās, -ātis, [propinquus], f., *nearness, vicinity; relationship* (ii. 4). [propinquity.

propinquus, -a, -um, comp. -ior, [prope], adj., *near, neighboring.* As noun, propinquus, -ī, m., *rela-*

tive; pl., propinquī, -ōrum, m., *relatives, kinsfolk;* propinquae, -ārum, f., *female relatives* (i. 18).

propior, -us, gen. propiōrīs, adj. in comp. degree, sup. **proximus,** [cf. **prope**], positive wanting, *nearer.* **proximus,** -a, -um, *nearest, next, last,* of space or time. **proximā nocte,** *on the following night.* [proximate.

propius. see **prope.**

prōpōnō, -pōnere, -posuī, -positus, [prō + pōnō], 3, *set forth, put forward, present; declare, explain; propose, intend; raise, display* (ii. 20). [propose.

prōpositum, -ī, [prōpositus], n., *intention, purpose.* C. III. 84.

prōpositus, see **prōpōnō.**

proprius, -a, -um, adj., *one's own, particular, peculiar, characteristic.* vi. 22, 23. [proper.

propter, prep. with acc. only, *on account of, in consequence of.*

proptereā [propter + eā], adv., *for this reason, therefore.* **proptereā quod,** *because.*

prōpugnātor, -ōris, [prōpugnō], m., *defender.* vii. 25.

prōpugnō, -āre, -āvī, -ātus, [prō + pugnō], 1, *come forth to fight* (v. 9); *fight* on the defensive (ii. 7; vii. 86).

prōpulsō, -āre, -āvī, -ātus, [freq. of prōpellō], 1, *drive off, drive back* (i. 49); *ward off, repel* (vi. 15).

prōra, -ae, [πρῷρα], f., *prow.* [prow.

prōruō, -ere, -uī, -utus, 3, *throw down; tear down* (iii. 26).

prōsequor, -sequī, -secūtus, [prō + sequor], 3, dep., *follow after; follow up, pursue; address* (ii. 5). [prosecute.

prōspectus, -ūs, [cf. prōspiciō], m., *view, sight.* **in prōspectū,** *in sight, visible* (v. 10). [prospect.

prōspiciō, -spicere, -spexī, -spectus, [prō + speciō, *look*], 3, *look out, see to it* (v. 7); *provide for, look out for* (i. 23; vii. 50).

prōsternō, -sternere, -strāvī, -strātus, [prō + sternō, *scatter*], 3, *overthrow, utterly cast down, destroy.* vii. 77. [prostrate.

prōsum, prōdesse, prōfuī, [prō, prōd-, + sum], irr., *be of advantage to.* VI. 40.

prōtegō, -tegere, -tēxī, -tēctus, [prō + tegō], 3, *cover, protect.* [protect.

prōterō, -terere, -trīvī, -trītus, [prō + terō], 3, *wear away, destroy.* C. II. 41.

prōterreō, -ēre, -uī, -itus, [prō + terreō], 2, *frighten away, drive off* by means of fright. v. 58; vii. 81.

prōtinus [prō + tenus], adv., *forthwith, at once, immediately.*

prōturbō, -āre, -āvī, -ātus, [prō + turbō, *disturb*], 1, *drive away, repulse.* ii. 19; vii. 81.

prōvectus, see **prōvehō.**

prōvehō, -vehere, -vexī, -vectus, [prō + vehō], 3, *carry forward* (v. 8); pass. in a middle sense, *put out* to sea.

prōveniō, -venīre, -vēnī, -ventum est, [prō + veniō], 4, *come forth; grow* (v. 24).

prōventus, -ūs, [cf. prōveniō], m., *issue, result, outcome.* vii. 29, 80.

prōvideō, -vidēre, -vīdī, -vīsus, [prō + videō], 2, *foresee, perceive in advance; provide for, look out for.* [provide.

prōvincia, -ae, f., *province;* often *the Province,* the part of Transalpine Gaul subdued by the Romans before 58 B.C. [province.

prōvinciālis, -e, [prōvincia], adj., *of the province.* vii. 7. [provincial.

prōvīsus, see **prōvideō.**

prōvolō, -āre, -āvī, [prō + volō,
fly], 1, *fly forward, dash forth.* ii. 19.

proximē, see prope.

proximus, -a, -um, see propior.

prūdentia, -ae, [prūdēns, for prō-
videns, *far-seeing*], f., *foresight,
good judgment.* ii. 4. [prudence.

Ptiāniī, -ōrum, m., pl., (tī-ā′ nį-ī), a
small state in Aquitania. iii. 27.

Ptolomaeus, -ī, [Πτολεμαῖος], m.,
Ptolemy, king of Egypt in 49 B.C.,
brother of Cleopatra. C. iii. 103.

pūberēs, -um, [adj. pūbēs used as a
noun], m., pl., *adults.* v. 56.

pūblicē [pūblicus], adv., *in the name
of the state, as a state, publicly.*

pūblicō, -āre, -āvī, -ātus, [pūbli-
cus], 1, *make public; confiscate* (v.
56; vii. 43). [publish.

pūblicus, -a, -um, adj., *of the state,
public, common.* litterae pūblicae, *state documents* (v. 47). rēs
pūblica, *the state, public business,
public interest.* As noun, pūblicum, -ī, n., *a public place* (vi. 28;
vii. 26). in pūblicō, *in a public
place* (vi. 18). [public.

Pūblius, -ī, m., (pub′ lị-ụs), a Roman
first name.

pudet, pudēre, puduit or puditum
est, 2, impers. form of pudeō, *it
shames; it makes ashamed* (vii. 42).

pudor, -ōris, [cf. pudeō], m., *shame,
sense of shame.*

puer, puerī, m., *child, boy.*

puerīlis, -e, comp. -ior, [puer], adj.,
of a child. [puerile.

pugna, -ae, f., *fight, combat, battle.*

pugnō, -āre, -āvī, -ātus, [pugna], 1,
fight, engage in battle. pugnātum
est, *the battle raged.*

pulcher, -chra, -chrum, comp. -ior,
sup. pulcherrimus, adj., *beautiful*
(vii. 15); *noble* (vii. 77).

Pullō, -ōnis, m., (pul′ ō), a brave centurion. v. 44.

pulsus, see pellō.

pulsus, -ūs, [pellō], m., *stroke;* of
oars, *movement* (iii. 13). [pulse.

pulvis, pulveris, m., *dust.* [pul-
verize.

puppis, -is, f., *stern* of a ship. [poop.

pūrgō, -āre, -āvī, -ātus, [for *pū-
rigō; pūrus + agō], 1, *make clean;
free from blame, excuse, clear.* suī
pūrgandī causā, *in order to excuse
themselves.* [purge.

Puteolī, -ōrum, m., pl., (pū-tē′ ǫ-lī),
a city on the coast of Campania, now
Pozzuoli. C. iii. 71.

putō, -āre, -āvī, -ātus, 1, *think, consider, believe, judge.* [putative.

Pȳrēnaeus, -a, -um, [Πυρηναῖος], adj.,
of Pyrene. Pȳrēnaeī montēs, *the
Pyrenees Mountains.* i. 1.

Q.

Q. = Quīntus.

quā [abl. fem. of quī, originally sc.
viā or parte], adv., *where.*

qua, nom. sing. fem., and neut. pl.,
of the indefinite pron. quis, or quī.

quadrāgēnī, -ae, -a,[quadrāgintā],
num. distributive adj., *forty each,
forty in each case.* iv. 17; vii. 23.

quadrāgintā, or XL, [quattuor],
indeclinable num. adj., *forty.*

quadringentī, -ae, -a, or CCCC,
[quattuor + centum], numeral
adj., *four hundred.*

quaerō, -ere, quaesīvī, quaesītus,
3, *look for, seek* (ii. 21; vii. 37);
ask, inquire, make inquiry. [query.

quaestiō, -ōnis, [cf. quaerō], f., *inquiry; examination, investigation.*
[question.

quaestor, -ōris, [cf. quaerō], m.:

　(1) *quaestor, state treasurer,* the
lowest in rank of the great officers
of state.

　(2) *quarter-master, quaestor,* an
officer accompanying the army on

campaigns, having charge of money and supplies, sometimes detailed for military service in charge of troops.

quaestus, -ūs, [cf. **quaerō**], m., *getting* of money, *gain.* vi. 17, C. III. 60.

quālis, -e, [cf. **quis**], inter. adj., *of what sort ? what sort of ?* i. 21.

quam [**quī**], adv. and conj., *how much, how;* with superlatives (with or without **possum**), *as possible;* after comparatives and comparative expressions, *than, as;* with expressions of time, *after.* **quam vetus,** *how old.* **quam diū,** *as long as.* **nāvēs quam plūrimās,** *as many ships as possible.* **quam celerrimē,** *as quickly as possible.* **post diem quārtum quam,** *the fourth day after.*

quamvīs [**quam** + **vīs**, from **volō**], adv., *however much; however* (IV. 2).

quandō, adv., *ever, at any time.*

quantō opere, see **quantus.**

quantus, -a, -um, adj., *how great, how much, how large;* after **tantus,** *as;* **tantum ... quantum,** *so much, so far ... as.* As noun, with gen. of the whole, **quantum bonī,** *how much advantage, how great advantage* (i. 40); **quantum agrī,** *as much land as* (vi. 22). **quantō opere,** *how much, how deeply* (ii. 5). **quantō opere ... tantō opere,** *as much as ... so much* (vii. 52).

quantusvīs, quantavīs, quantumvīs, [**quantus** + **vīs**, from **volō**], adj., *however great, no matter how great.*

quārē [**quā** + **rē**], adv., *wherefore, and for this reason.*

quārtus, -a, -um, [**quattuor**], adj., *fourth.* **quartus decimus,** or XIIII, *fourteenth.* [quart.

quasi [**quam** + **sī**], conj., *as if.*

quattuor, or IIII, indeclinable num. adj., *four.*

quattuordecim, or XIIII, [**quattuor** + **decem**], indeclinable num. adj., *fourteen.*

-que, enclitic conj., *and,* appended to a word which in construction belongs after it.

quem ad modum, see **modus.**

queror, querī, questus, 3, dep., *complain, lament; complain of, make complaint of.* [querulous.

questus, see **queror.**

quī, quae, quod, gen. **cuius,** rel. and inter. pron. :

(1) As rel. pron., *who, which;* at the beginning of a clause often best rendered by a personal or demonstrative pron., with or without *and.* **īdem quī,** *the same as.*

(2) As inter. adj. pron., *what? what kind of ?*

quī, quae or **qua, quod,** indef. pron., *any, any one,* or *anything,* used both as subst. and as adj. **sī quī,** if *any one.*

quicquam, see **quisquam.**

quīcumque, quaecumque, quodcumque, indef. pron., *whoever, whatever, whichever.*

quid, see **quis.**

quīdam, quaedam, quiddam, indef. pron., *a certain one, a certain thing.* As adj., **quīdam, quaedam, quoddam,** *a certain, some, certain.*

quidem, adv., *indeed, at least.* **nē ... quidem,** *not even.*

quidnam, see **quisnam.**

quiēs, -ētis, f., *rest, repose.* [quiet (noun).

quiētus, -a, -um, [part. of **quiēscō,** from **quiēs**], adj., *at rest, calm, quiet; peaceful, at peace.* [quiet (adj.).

quīn, [old abl **quī** + **ne**], conj., *that not, but that, without;* after words expressing doubt or suspicion, *that;* after **dēterreō, retineō**, etc., trans. by *from* with a participle. **quīn** *etiam, moreover.*

quincunx, -ūncis, [quīnque + ūncia], f., *quīncūnx,* an arrangement of trees or other objects like the five spots on the dice (*quīncūnx*), thus:

. . . . .

. . . . . vii. 73.

quīndecim, or **XV,** [quīnque + decem], indeclinable num. adj., *fifteen.*

quīngentī, -ae, -a, or **D,** [quīnque + centum], num. adj., *five hundred.*

quīnī, -ae, -a, [quīnque], distrib. num. adj., *five each, five at a time.*

quīnquāgintā, or **L,** [quīnque], indeclinable num. adj., *fifty.*

quīnque, or **V,** indeclinable num. adj., *five.*

quīntus, -a, -um, [quīnque], adj., *fifth.* [quint.

Quīntus, -ī, m., (kwin' tŭs), a Roman first name.

quis, ——, quid, inter. pron., *who? what?* Neut. **quid,** with gen. of the whole, **quid cōnsiliī,** *what plan?* neut. **quid,** as adverbial acc., *why?* **quid vōs sectāminī,** *why do ye pursue?* (vi. 35).

quis, ——, quid, indef. pron., *any one, anything.* As adj., **quī, quae** or **qua, quod,** *any.* **sī quis,** *if any one.* **nē quis,** *that not any one, that no one.* Neut. **quid,** with partitive gen., *any;* as, **sī quid cōnsiliī,** *if any plan.*

quisnam, ——, quidnam, inter. pron., *who, pray? what, pray?* As adj., **quīnam, quaenam, quodnam,** *of what kind, pray* (ii. 30).

quispiam, ——, quidpiam, indef. pron., *any one, anything* (vi. 17). As adj., **quispiam, quaepiam, quodpiam,** *any* (v. 35).

quisquam, ——, quicquam, indef. pron., *any one, anything.* As adj., *any* (acc. **quemquam,** vi. 36).

quisque, ——, quidque, indef. pron., *each one, each thing.* As adj., **quisque, quaeque, quodque,** *each.*

quisquis, ——, quicquid, indef. rel. pron., *whoever, whatever.*

quīvīs, quaevīs, quidvīs, [quī + vīs, from **volō**], indef. pron., *any one, anything you please.* As adj., **quīvīs, quaevīs, quodvīs,** *any whatever.*

quō, see **quī.**

quō, adv. and conj.:

(1) **quō** [dat. or abl. of **quī**], adv., relative and interrogative, *whither, where;* indefinite, after **sī** and **nē,** *to any place, at any point, anywhere.*

(2) **quō** [abl. of **quī**], conj., used especially with comparatives, followed by subj., *in order that, that, that thereby.* **quō minus,** *that not,* often best translated by *from* with a participle.

quoad [quō + ad], conj., *as long as* (iv. 12); *until, till* (iv. 11; v. 17, 24).

quod [acc. of **quī**], conj., *because, inasmuch as, since; as to the fact that, so far as.*

quō minus, see **quō** (2).

quoniam [quom, old form of **cum,** + iam], conj., *since, seeing that, because, inasmuch as.*

quoque, conj., following the emphatic word of a clause, *also, too.*

quōque, abl. of **quisque,** which see.

quōque = et **quō.**

quōque versus, see **versus.**

quot, indeclinable adj., *how many, as many as.* iv. 22, vii. 19.

quotannīs [quot + abl. pl. of annus], adv., *yearly, every year.*

quotiēns [quot], adv., *as often as*

(v. 34); *how often* (i. 43, C. III. 72).
[quotient.

quotiēnscumque, [quotiēns +
-cumque], adv., *just as often as.*
C. I. 7.

R.

rādīx, -īcis, f., *root* (vi. 27); of an
elevation, *foot, base.* **rādīcēs collis**, *the foot of the hill* (vii. 51, 69).
rādīcēs montis, *the base of the
height, the foot of the mountain.*
[radish.

rādō, -ere, rāsī, rāsus, 3, *shave.*
[razor.

raeda, -ae, f., *wagon* with four wheels.
i. 51; vi. 30.

rāmus, -ī, m., *branch, bough, limb.*

rapiditās, -ātis, [rapidus, *swift*],
f., *swiftness.* iv. 17. [rapidity.

rapīna, -ae, [cf. rapiō, *seize*], f., *pillaging, plundering.* i. 15. [rapine.

rārus, -a, -um, comp. -ior, sup. rā-
rissimus, adj., *not thick ;* pl., *few,
scattered, in small parties.* [rare.

rāsus, see rādō.

ratiō, -ōnis, [reor, *reckon*], f., *reckoning, enumeration ; account ; method,
means, way ; plan, theory, system,
science ; reason, ground ; condition,
situation.* **ratiōnem habēre**, *to
keep an account* (vi. 19), *take account
of* (v. 27, VII. 71; C. III. 82). **ratiōne initā**, *having made calculation*
(vii. 71). **abs tē ratiōnem reposcent**, *they will call you to account, will hold you responsible* (v.
30). [ratio, ration, reason.

ratis, -is, f., *raft.*

Raurācī, -ōrum, m., pl., (râ′ ra̜-sī), a
people along the upper Rhine, north
of the Helvetians.

re-, red-, used only in composition,
again, back.

rebelliō, -ōnis, [rebellis, from re- +
bellum], f., *renewal of fighting, up-*

rising. **rebelliōnem facere**, *to
enter into rebellion, rebel, revolt.*
[rebellion.

Rebilus, (reb′ i̜-lu̜s), see Canīnius.

recēdō, -cēdere, -cessī, -cessūrus,
[re- + cēdō], 3, *withdraw.* [re-
cede.

recēns, -entis, adj., *fresh ; recent,
late.* As noun, **recentēs**, -ium,
m., pl., *those who were fresh, the unwearied* (v. 16; vii. 48; C. III. 94).
[recent.

recēnseō, -ēre, recēnsuī, [re- +
cēnseō], 2, *review, mobilize.* vii. 76.

receptāculum, -ī, [receptō], n.,
place of shelter, retreat. [receptacle.

receptus, see recipiō.

receptus, -ūs, [recipiō], m., *retreat ;
avenue of retreat* (vi. 9); *recall,* a
signal given with a musical instrument to call soldiers back (vii. 47).

recessus, -ūs, [recēdō], m., *a reced-
ing ; opportunity to draw back* (v.
43). [recess.

recidō, -cidere, -cidī, -cāsūrus, [re-
+ cadō], 3, *fall back ; come upon,
fall to the lot of* (vii. 1).

recipiō, -cipere, -cēpī, -ceptus,
[re- + capiō], 3, *take back, get back,
recover, win ; receive, admit ; take
upon one's self* (C. III. 82). **sē
recipere**, *to retreat, withdraw ; to
recover one's self* (ii. 12; iv. 27, 34).
recipere in dēditiōnem, *receive
into submission.* [receive.

recitō, -āre, -āvī, -ātus, [re- + citō,
quote], 1, *read aloud, recite.* v. 48.
[recite.

reclīnō, -āre, -āvī, -ātus, [re- +
clīnō, *bend*], 1, *bend back.* **sē
reclīnāre**, *to lean back* (vi. 27);
part. **reclīnātus**, *leaning back* (vi.
27). [recline.

recordor, -ārī, -ātus, [re-, cor], 1,
dep., *remember, call to mind.* C. III.
47, 72, 73. [record.

recreō, -āre, -āvī, -ātus, [re- + creō], 1, *restore, renew.* C. III. 74. [recreate.

rēctē, comp. -ius, sup. -issimē, [rēctus], adv., *rightly, properly; nobly* (vii. 80); *safely* (vii. 6).

rēctus, -a, -um, comp. -ior, sup. rēctissimus, [part. of regō], adj., *straight, direct.*

recuperō, -āre, -āvī, -ātus, [re-, cf. capiō], 3, *get back, recover.* [recuperate.

recūsātiō, -ōnis, [recūsō], f., *refusal, objection, protest.* C. III. 98.

recūsō, -āre, -āvī, -ātus, [re-, cf. causa], 1, *refuse, make refusal, decline; raise objections* (v. 6).

redāctus, see redigō.

redditus, see reddō.

reddō, -dere, -didī, -ditus, [red- + dō], 3, *give back, restore, return; render, make* (ii. 5). iūs reddere, *to dispense justice* (vi. 13). supplicātiōnem reddere, *to proclaim a thanksgiving* (vii. 90). vītam prō vītā reddere, *to give life for life* (vi. 16). [rendition.

redēmptus, see redimō.

redeō, -īre, -iī, -itum est, [red- + eō], irr., *go back, come back, return; slope down* (ii. 8); *be reduced* (v. 48); *be referred* (vi. 11). ad gladiōs redīre, *to resort to swords, draw swords* (C. III. 93).

redigō, -igere, -ēgī, -āctus, [red- + agō], 3, *force back; reduce; render, make* (ii. 27; iv. 3). [redact.

redimō, -imere, -ēmī, -ēmptus, [red- + emō], 3, *buy back, purchase;* of revenues, *buy up, farm* (i. 18). [redeem.

redintegrō, -āre, -āvī, -ātus, [red- + integrō, *make whole*], 1, *commence again, renew; revive.* [redintegrate.

reditiō, -ōnis, [cf. redeō], f., *a going back, returning.* i. 5.

reditus, -ūs, [cf. redeō], m., *returning, return.* iv. 30; vi. 29, 36.

Redonēs, -um, m., pl., (red′o̯-nēz), a people in northwestern Gaul (Fig. 206).

Figure 206. — Coin of the Redones.

Gold. Obverse, head with chaplet of laurel.

Reverse, horseman brandishing a spear and shield; in front of the horse, a head of wheat.

redūcō, -dūcere, -dūxī, -ductus, [re- + dūcō], 3, *lead back, bring* or *conduct back; draw back* (vii. 22, 24); *carry back, put back,* (vii. 72). [reduce.

refectus, see reficiō.

referō, -ferre, rettulī, -lātus, [re- + ferō], 3, *bring back, carry back* (iv. 28); *bring, carry, convey* to a place or person; *report, announce.* pedem referre, *to retreat.* grātiam referre, *to make return, requite.* [refer.

reficiō, -ficere, -fēcī, -fectus, [re- + faciō], 3, *repair, refit, restore;* of troops, *refresh* (iii. 5; vii. 32, 83); *recruit* (C. III. 87). [refectory.

refrāctus, see refringō.

refringō, -fringere, -frēgī, -frāctus, [re- + frangō], 3, *break* (vii. 56); *burst in, break down* (ii. 33). [refract.

refugiō, -fugere, -fūgī, [re- + fugiō], 3, *flee back* (v. 35); *flee away, escape.* [refuge.

Rēgīnus, (re̯-jī′nus), see Antistius.

regiō, -ōnis, [cf. regō, *keep straight*], f., *direction, line ; boundary ; region, tract, territory.* rēctā regiōne, *in a direct line* (vii. 46); *along the line* (vi. 25). ē regiōne, *directly opposite.* [region.

rēgius, -a, -um, [rēx], adj., *kingly, royal.* vii. 32, C. iii. 104.

rēgnō, -āre, -āvī, -ātus, [rēgnum], 1, *be king, reign.* v. 25. [reign.

rēgnum, -ī, [cf. regō], n., *kingship, sovereignty, royal power ; absolute authority ; territory* subject to a king or ruler, *kingdom.* [reign (noun.)

regō, -ere, rēxī, rēctus, 3, *keep straight ; regulate ; control, manage* (iii. 13); *conduct, carry on* (vi. 17).

reiciō, -icere, -iēcī, -iectus, [re- + iaciō], 3, *throw back, hurl back* (i. 46); of ships, *cast back, carry back* (v. 5, 23); *drive back, repulse* (i. 24; ii. 33); *cast away* (v. 30); *throw away* (i. 52). [reject.

reiectus, see reiciō.

relanguēscō, -ere, -uī, [re- + languēscō], 3, *become enfeebled, become enervated.* ii. 15.

relātus, see referō.

relēgō, -āre, -āvī, -ātus, [re- + lēgō, *depute*], 1, *banish, remove, treat as an outlaw.* [relegate.

relīctus, see relinquō.

religiō, -ōnis, f., *religious scruple, religious obligation, religious observance, superstition.* [religion.

religō, -āre, -āvī, -ātus, [re- + ligō, *bind*], 1, *bind back ; bind fast* (C. ii. 6).

relinquō, -linquere, -līquī, -lictus, [re- + linquō, *quit*], 3, *leave, leave behind ; desert, abandon ;* of a siege or attack, *leave off, give up.* [relinquish.

reliquus, -a, -um, [cf. relinquō], adj., *remaining, left, the rest.* As noun, reliquī, -ōrum, m., pl., *the*

rest ; reliquī, gen. sing. neut., in nihil reliquī, *nothing left* (i. 11).

remaneō, -manēre, -mānsī, [re- + maneō], 2, *remain, stay behind.* [remain.

rēmex, -igis, [rēmus, cf. agō], m., *rower.* iii. 9.

Rēmī, -ōrum, m., pl., (rē′ mī), a Belgic people, about the headwaters of the Axona (*Aisne*); chief city, Durocortorum, now *Reims.*

rēmigō, -āre, [rēmex], 1, *row.* v. 8.

remigrō, -āre, -āvī, [re- + migrō, *remove*], 1, *move back, return.* iv. 4, 27. [remigrate.

reminīscor, -minīscī, [re- + MEN in mēns], 3, dep., *remember, recollect.* i. 13. [reminiscent.

remissus, -a, -um, comp. -ior, [part. of remittō], adj., *relaxed ; mild.* remissior, *less severe* (v. 12). [remiss.

remittō, -mittere, -mīsī, -missus, [re- + mittō], 3, *send back ; give back, restore* (vii. 20); *relax, diminish* (ii. 15; v. 49); *impair, lose* (vi. 14); of a tax, *remit* (i. 44). [remit.

remollēscō, -lēscere, [re- + mollēscō, *grow soft*], 3, *become weak.* iv. 2.

remōtus, -a, -um, comp. -ior, sup. -issimus, [removeō], adj., *far off, remote.* i. 31; vii. 1. [remote.

removeō, -movēre, -mōvī, -mōtus, [re- + moveō], 2, *move back, remove ; dismiss* (i. 19). [remove.

remūneror, -ārī, -ātus, [re-, cf. mūnus], 1, dep., *recompense, repay.* i. 44. [remunerate.

rēmus, -ī, m., *oar.*

Rēmus, -ī, m., *one of the Remi, a Reman.*

rēnō, -ōnis, m., *reindeer skin, deerskin.* vi. 21.

renovō, -āre, -āvī, -ātus, [re- + novō, from novus], 1, *renew, again commence.* [renovate.

renūntiō, -āre, -āvī, -ātus, [re- + nūntiō], 1, *bring back word, announce; declare elected* (vii. 33). [renounce.

repellō,-pellere, reppulī, repulsus, [re- + pellō], 3, *drive back, force back, repulse.* [repel.

repente, [abl. of repēns, *sudden*], adv., *suddenly.*

repentīnus, -a, -um, [repēns, *sudden*], adj., *sudden, unexpected.*

reperiō, -perīre, repperī, repertus, 4, *find, find out; discover, ascertain, learn.*

repetō, -petere, -petīvī or -petiī, -petītus, [re- + petō], 3, *seek again, again try to obtain* (v. 49); *demand* (i. 31); *exact* (i. 30). [repeat.

repleō, -plēre, -plēvī, -plētus, [re- + pleō, *fill*], 2, *fill up; supply amply* (vii. 56). [replete.

repōnō, -pōnere, -posuī, -positus, [re- + pōnō], 3, *replace; place, rest* (C. ii. 41). [repository.

reportō, -āre, -āvī, -ātus, [re- + portō], 1, *carry back, convey back.* [report.

reposcō, -poscere, [re- + poscō], 3, *demand, require.* v. 30.

repraesentō, -āre, -āvī, -ātus, [re- + praesentō, from praesēns], 1, *do at once, do forthwith.* i. 40. [represent.

reprehendō, -hendere, -hendī, -hēnsus, [re- + prehendō], 3, *hold back; criticise, blame.* [reprehend.

repressus, see reprimō.

reprimō, -primere, -pressī, -pressus. [re- + premō], 3, *restrain, check; repress.* [repress.

repudiō, -āre, -āvī, -ātus, 1, *reject, scorn.* i. 40. [repudiate.

repugnō, -āre, -āvī, -ātus, [re- + pugnō], 1, *fight back, resist.* [repugnant.

repulsus, see repellō. [repulse.

requiēscō, -ere, requiēvī, requiētus, [re- + quiēscō], 3, *take rest, rest.* C. iii. 98.

requīrō, -quīrere, -quīsīvī, -quīsītus, [re- + quaerō], 3, *require, demand* (vi. 34); *wish back again, miss* (vii. 63); *seek* (C. ii. 35). [require.

rēs, reī, f., *matter, affair; circumstance, fact, transaction; object, project, business.* rēs mīlitāris, *warfare, military science.* rēs novae, *a revolution.* praemia reī pecūniāriae, *rewards in money* (C. iii. 59). [real.

rescindō, -scindere, -scidī,-scissus, [re- + scindō], 3, *cut down, break up, destroy.* [rescind.

rescīscō, -scīscere, -scīvī, or -sciī, -scītus, [re- + scīscō, *inquire*], 3, *discover, find out.* i. 28.

rescrībō, -scrībere, -scrīpsī, -scrīptus, [re- + scrībō], 3, *write again; enroll anew, transfer* from one branch of the service to another (i. 42). [rescribe.

reservō, -āre, -āvī, -ātus, [re- + servō], 1, *keep back, keep.* [reserve.

resideō,-sidēre, -sēdī, [re-+ sedeō, *sit*], *linger, remain.* [reside.

resīdō, -sīdere, -sēdī, [re- + sīdō, *sit down*], 3, *settle down, subside.* vii. 64.

resistō, -sistere, -stitī, [re- + sistō, *set*], 3, *remain, stay; stand still* (C. ii. 35); *oppose, withstand, offer resistance.* [resist.

respiciō, -spicere, -spexī, -spectus, [re- + speciō, *look*], 3, *look back* (ii. 24; v. 43, C. ii. 35); *look at; consider* (vii. 77). [respect.

respondeō, -spondēre, -spondī,

-spōnsus, [re- + spondeō, *promise*], 2, *answer, reply.* [respond.

respōnsum, -ī, [part. of respondeō], n., *answer, reply.* [response.

res pūblica, see pūblicus.

respuō, -spuere, -spuī, [re- + spuō], 3, *spit out ; reject* (i. 42).

restinguō, -stinguere, -stīnxī, -stīnctus, [re- + stinguō, *quench*], 3, *put out, extinguish.* vii. 24, 25.

restituō, -uere, -uī, -ūtus, [re- + statuō], 3, *replace, restore ; renew, revive ; rebuild* (i. 28). [restitution.

retentus, see retineō.

retineō, -tinēre, -tinuī, -tentus, [re- + teneō], 2, *restrain, detain, keep back ; hold* (vii. 21). [retain.

retrahō, -trahere, -trāxī, -trāctus, [re- + trahō], 3, *bring back* by force. v.· 7. [retract.

revellō, -vellere, -vellī, -vulsus, [re- + vellō, *pull*], 3, *pull back* (i. 52); *tear away* (vii. 73).

reversus, see revertor.

revertō, revertī, [re- + vertō], 3, only in tenses from pf. stem, and revertor, -vertī, -versūrus, 3, dep., *return, go back.* [revert.

revinciō, -vincīre, -vinxī, -vinctus, [re- + vinciō], 4, *bind back, bind securely, fasten.*

revocō, -āre, -āvī, -ātus, [re- + vocō], 1, *call back, recall.* [revoke.

rēx, rēgis, [cf. regō, *rule*], m., *king, ruler, chieftain.*

Rhēnus, -ī, m., *the Rhine.*

Rhodanus, -ī, m., *the Rhone,* which rises in the Alps near the sources of the Rhine, and passing through Lake Geneva, follows at first a south-westerly direction, then flows south, reaching the Mediterranean after a course of about 500 miles.

rīpa, -ae, f., *bank* of a stream. [river.

rīvus, -ī, m., *stream, brook.* [rival.

rōbur, -oris, n., *oak* (ii. 13); *strength* (C. iii. 87). [robust.

rogō, -āre, -āvī, -ātus, 1, *ask, request.* [rogation.

Rōma, -ae, f., *Rome.*

Rōmānus, -a, -um, [Rōma], adj., *Roman.* As noun, Rōmānus, -ī, m., ·*a Roman ;* usually pl., *the Romans, Romans.* [Roman.

Rōscius, -ī, m., *Lucius Roscius* (rosh'-[y]ŭs), a lieutenant in Caesar's army.

rōstrum, -ī, [cf. rōdō, *gnaw*], n., *beak ;* of a ship, *beak.* [rostrum.

rota, -ae, f., *wheel.* [rotary.

Roucillus, -ī, m., (rṳ-sil'ŭs), *an Allobrogian,* brother of Egus. C. iii. 59.

rubus, -ī, m., *brier, bramble.* ii. 17.

Rūfus, -ī, [rūfus, *reddish*], m., (rṳ'-fŭs), a Roman cognomen.

rūmor, -ōris, m., *rumor, report, gossip.* [rumor.

rūpēs, -is, [cf. rumpō], f., *cliff.* ii. 29.

rūrsus, [for revorsus, from re- vertō], adv., *again, anew ; in turn, on the contrary.*

Rutēnī, -ōrum, m., pl., (rṳ-tē'nī), a Gallic people, west of the Cebenna (*Cévennes*) Mountains; part of them were in the Province, and were called Rutēnī prōvinciālēs.

Rutilus (rṳ'tĭ-lŭs), see Semprōnius.

S.

Sabīnus, see Titūrius.

Sabis, -is, m., *Sabis* (sā'bĭs), *the Sambre,* a river in the central part of Belgic Gaul flowing northeast into the Mosa (*Meuse*). ii. 16, 18.

Saburra, -ae, m., (sạ-bū'rạ), a general in Juba's army. C. ii. 38–42.

sacerdōs, -dōtis, [sacer, cf. dō], m. and f., *priest.* vii. 33. [sacerdotal.

sacerdōtium, -ī, [sacerdōs], n., *priesthood.* C. iii. 82, 83.

sacrāmentum, -ī, [sacrō, *set apart as sacred*], n., *oath*. [sacrament.

Sacrātivir, -ī, m., *Marcus Sacrativir*, (sa̤-krat′ i̤-vir), a Roman knight. C. iii. 71.

sacrificium, -ī, [sacrificus, from sacrum + FAC in faciō], n., *sacrifice*. vi. 13, 16, 21. [sacrifice.

saepe, comp. -ius, sup. -issimē, adv., *often, frequently*. Comp., *too often* (iii. 6). saepe numerō, *oftentimes, repeatedly*.

saepēs, -is, f., *hedge*. ii. 17, 22.

saeviō, -īre, -iī, -ītus, [saevus, *fierce*], 4, *rage; be violent* (iii. 13).

sagitta, -ae, f., *arrow*.

sagittārius, -ī, [sagitta], m., *archer, bowman*. [Sagittarius.

sagulum, -ī, [dim. of sagum, *mantle*], n., *small cloak, cloak*. v. 42.

sāl, salis, m., *salt*. C. ii. 37. [salad.

salīnae, -ārum, f., pl., [sāl], *saltworks*. C. ii. 37.

saltem, adv., *at any rate*. C. i. 6.

saltus, -ūs, m., *wooded valley, defile, glen, thicket*. vi. 43; vii. 19.

salūs, -ūtis, [cf. salvus, *well*], f., *health, welfare; safety*. [salutary.

salūtō, -āre, -āvī, -ātus, [salūs], 1, *greet, address*. C. iii. 71. [salute.

Samarobrīva, -ae, f., (sam″ a̤-ro̤-brī′ va̤), a city of the Ambiani on the Samara (*Somme*); now *Amiens*.

sanciō, sancīre, sānxī, sānctus, 4, *make sacred; make binding, ratify*. [sanction.

sānctus, -a, -um, comp. -ior, sup. -issimus, [sanciō], adj., *hallowed, sacred*. [saint.

sanguis, -inis, m., *blood*. [sanguine.

sānitās, -tātis, [sānus], f., *soundness* of mind, *good sense*. [sanity.

sānō, -āre, -āvī, -ātus, [cf. sānus], 1, *make sound; make good, remedy* (vii. 29).

Santonēs, -um, or **Santonī**, -ōrum, m., pl., (san′ to̤-nēz, san′ to̤-nī), a Gallic people on the seacoast north of the Garumna (*Garonne*). Fig. 207.

Figure 207. — Coin of the Santones.

Silver. Obverse, helmeted head; inscription, SANTONOS.
Reverse, a galloping horse.

sānus, -a, -um, comp. -ior, sup. sānissimus, adj., *sound, healthy, rational*. As noun, prō sānō, *as a prudent man* (v. 7). [sane.

sapiō, -ere, -īvī, 3, *taste; be sensible, understand* (v. 30). [sapient.

sarcinae, -ārum, [sarciō], f., pl., *packs*, carried by the soldiers on their backs.

sarciō, -īre, sarsī, sartus, 4, *mend; make good* (vi. 1; C. iii. 73); *wipe out* (C. iii. 74). [sartorial.

sarmentum, -ī, [sarpō, *prune*], n., *a branch;* pl., *brushwood* (iii. 18).

satis, adv., *enough, sufficiently, tolerably, rather;* often used as a noun, especially with a gen. of the whole, as satis causae, *sufficient reason*.

satisfaciō [satis + faciō], -facere, -fēcī, -factus, irr., *satisfy, give satisfaction; make restitution* (i. 14, v. 1); *appease, placate* (vii. 89); *make apology, apologize* (i. 41, v. 54). [satisfy.

satisfactiō, -ōnis, [satisfaciō], f., *apology, excuse*. [satisfaction.

Sāturnīnus, -ī, m., *L. Appuleius Saturninus* (sat-ṳr-nī′ nṳs), a tribune in 100 B.C. C. i. 7.

satus, see serō.

saucius, -a, -um, adj., *wounded* (v. 36). As noun, saucius, -ī, m., *a wounded man* (iii. 4).

saxum, -ī, n., *stone, rock.*

Scaeva, -ae, m., *Cassius Scaeva* (sē′va), a brave centurion in Caesar's army. C. III. 53.

scālae, -ārum, [cf. scandō, *climb*], f., pl., *ladder, scaling-ladder.* [scale.

Scaldis, -is, m., *the Schelde*, which rises in France near the headwaters of the *Somme* (Samara), and flows northeast to the sea. vi. 33.

scapha, -ae, [σκάφη], f., *skiff, small boat.*

scelerātus, -a, -um, comp. -ior, sup. -issimus, [part. of scelerō, from scelus], adj., *wicked, infamous* (vi. 34). As noun, scelerātus, -ī, m., *a crime-polluted man* (vi. 13).

scelus, sceleris, n., *crime, wickedness.* i. 14.

scienter, comp. scientius, sup. scientissimē, [sciēns], adv., *cleverly, skilfully.* vii. 22.

scientia, -ae, [sciēns], f., *knowledge, skill.* [science.

scindō, -ere, scidī, scissus, 3, *tear, cut, split; tear down, break down* (iii. 5; v. 51).

sciō, scīre, scīvī, scītus, 4, *know, understand.*

Scīpiō, -ōnis, m., *Q. Caecilius Metellus Scipio* (sip′i-ō), a prominent partisan of Pompey, who married his daughter Cornelia as fifth wife. C. III. 82, 83, 88, 90.

scorpiō, -ōnis, [σκορπίων], m., *a scorpion; scorpion*, a military engine (vii. 25). [scorpion.

scrībō, scrībere, scrīpsī, scrīptus, 3, *write, write down.* [scribe.

scrobis, -is, m. and f., *hole, pit; wolfhole, wolf-pit.* [scrobicule.

scūtum, -ī, n., *oblong shield.*

sē, sēsē, see suī.

sē-, sēd-, in composition, *apart from, without.*

sēbum, -ī, n., *fat, tallow.* [sebaceous.

sēcessiō, -ōnis, [sēcēdō], f., *withdrawal.* C. I. 7. [secession.

sēclūdō, -ere, -sī, -sus, [sē- + claudō], 3, *shut off.* C. III. 97. [seclude.

secō, -āre, -uī, -tus, 1, *cut.* [sector.

sēcrētō [sēcrētus], adv., *secretly, privately.* i. 18, 31.

sectiō, -ōnis, [secō], f., *booty.* [section.

sector, -ārī, -ātus, [freq. of sequor], 1, dep., *pursue, chase.* vi. 35.

sectūra, -ae, [secō], f., *a cutting through earth, digging, excavation.* iii. 21.

secundum, [sequor], prep. with acc. only, *along, next to, by the side of* (ii. 18; vii. 34); *according to* (iv. 17); *besides* (i. 33).

secundus, -a, -um, comp. -ior, sup. -issimus, [sequor], adj., *second, next; propitious, fortunate, favorable.* [second.

secūris, -is, [cf. secō], f., *axe;* pl. referring to the axes of the lictors, *the lictor's axe* (vii. 77).

sed, conj., *but; yet, but yet.*

sēd-, see sē-.

sēdecim, or XVI, [sex + decem], indeclinable num. adj., *sixteen.*

sēdēs, -is, [cf. sedeō, *sit*], f., *seat, habitation, abode, settlement, home.*

sēditiō, -ōnis, [sēd- + itiō, from īre], f., *mutiny, revolt.* vii. 28. [sedition.

sēditiōsus, -a, -um, sup. -issimus, [sēditiō], adj., *mutinous.* [seditious.

Sedulius, -ī, m., (se̞-dū′li̞-u̞s), a leader of the Lemovices. vii. 88.

Sedūnī, -ōrum, m., pl., (se̞-dū′nī), a people in the Alps southeast of Lacus Lemannus (*Lake Geneva*).

Sedusii, -ōrum, m., pl., (se̦-dū'-sh[y]-ī), a German tribe. i. 51.

seges, -etis, f., *grain-field.* vi. 36.

Segnī, -ōrum, m., pl., (seg'nī), a German tribe settled in Belgic Gaul. vi. 32.

Segontiācī, -ōrum, m., pl., (seg''-o̦n-shi̦-ā'sī), a people in the southern part of Britain. v. 21.

Segovax, -actis, m., (seg'o̦-vaks), a British chieftain. v. 22.

Segusiāvī, -ōrum, m., pl., (seg''ū-shi̦-ā'vī), a Gallic people, subject to the Aeduans. Fig. 208.

Figure 208.— A Coin of the Segusiavi.

Silver. Obverse, helmeted head; inscription, SEGVSIAVS, perhaps a man's name. Reverse, Hercules with his club and lion's skin.

semel, adv., *once.*

sēmentis, -is, [sēmen, *seed*], f., *sowing, seeding* (i. 3).

sēmita, -ae, f., *path, by-way.*

semper, adv., *always, ever, constantly.*

Semprōnius, -ī, m., *Marcus Sempronius Rutilus* (sem-prō'ni̦-u̦s rū'ti̦-lu̦s), a Roman cavalry officer. vii. 90.

senātor, -ōris, [cf. **senex**], m., member of the Roman Senate, *senator;* member of a Gallic state-council, *councillor, senator* (ii. 28). [senator.

senātōrius, -a, -um, [senator], adj., *senatorial.* ōrdō senātōrius, *senatorial rank* (C. iii. 83, 97). [senatorial.

senātus, -ūs, [cf. **senex**], m., *council of elders, senate.* [senate.

senex, -is, comp. **senior,** adj., *old, aged.* As noun, m., *old man* (i.

29); seniōrēs, -um, m., pl., *older men* (C. ii. 4). [senile.

sēnī, -ae, -a, [sex], distrib. num. adj., *six each, six.* i. 15.

Senonēs, -um, m., pl., (sen'o̦-nēz), a Gallic people south of the Matrona (*Marne*); chief city Agedincum, now *Sens.*

sententia, -ae, [cf. **sentiō**], f., *opinion, view, notion, conviction; decision, judgment.* sententiam dīcere, *to express an opinion.* sententiās ferre, *to vote* (C. iii. 83). [sentence.

sentiō, sentīre, sēnsī, sēnsus, 4, *perceive* through the senses, *become aware, learn; feel, think; know.* [sense.

sentis, -is, m, *thorn-bush.* ii. 17.

sēparātim [sēparātus], adv., *separately, apart.*

sēparātus, -a, -um, [part. of sēparō], adj., *separate, marked off.* [separate.

sēparō, -āre, -āvī, -ātus, [sē- + parō], 1, *part, separate.* vii. 63. [separate (verb).

septem, or VII, indeclinable num. adj., *seven.* [September.

septentriō, -ōnis, [septem + triō, *plough-ox*], m., generally pl., septentriōnēs, -um, *the seven plough-oxen,* the seven stars forming the constellation of the Great Bear; *the North.* [septentrional.

Septimius, -ī, m., *Lucius Septimius* (sep-tim'i̦-u̦s), a military tribune. C. iii. 104.

septimus, -a, -um, [septem], num. adj., *the seventh.* [septimal.

septingentī, -ae, -a, or DCC, [septem + centum], num. adj., *seven hundred.* v. 13; vii. 51.

septuāgintā, or LXX, indeclinable num. adj., *seventy.* [Septuagint.

sepultūra, -ae, [cf. sepeliō, *bury*], f., *burial.* i. 26. [sepulture.

Sēquana, -ae, f., *Sequana* (sek′-
wạ-nạ), *the Seine,* the principal river
of Northern France.

Sēquanī, -ōrum, m., pl., *the Sequanians, Sequani* (sek′ wạ-nī), a Gallic
people west of the Jura; chief city
Vesontio, now *Besançon.*

Sēquanus, -a, -um, adj., *Sequanian,
of the Sequanians* (i. 31). As noun,
Sēquanus, -ī, m., *a Sequanian*
(i. 3).

sequor, -quī, -cūtus, 3, dep., *follow,
follow after; pursue; take advantage
of* (v. 8); *hold to, maintain* (vii. 63).
Caesaris fidem sequī, *to attach
one's self to Caesar* (v. 20, 56).
[*sequence.*

Ser., = Servius.

sermō, -ōnis, m., *talk, conversation.*
[*sermon.*

sērō, comp. sērius, sup. -issimē, [sē-
rus, *late*], adv., *late; too late* (v. 29).

serō, serere, sēvī, satus, 3, *sow,
plant.*

Sertōrius, -ī, m., *Quintus Sertorius*
(sẹr-tō′ rị-ụs), a Roman general.
III. 23.

servīlis, -e, [servus], adj., *servile, of
slaves.* i. 40; vi. 19. [*servile.*

serviō, -īre, -iī, -ītus, [servus], 4,
be the slave of, follow (iv. 5); *devote
one's self to* (vii. 34). [*serve.*

servitūs, -tūtis, [servus], f., *slavery,
bondage, subjection.* [*servitude.*

Servius, -ī, m., (sẹr′ vị-ụs), a Roman
first name.

servō, -āre, -āvī, -ātus, 1, *save; keep,
maintain, retain; save up* (vi. 19);
keep watch of, watch (v. 19); *keep
up the watch* (ii. 33).

servus, -ī, m., *slave.* [*serf.*

sescentī, -ae, -a, or DC, [sex +
centum], num. adj., *six hundred.*

sēsē, see suī.

sēsquipedālis, -e, [sēsqui-, *one half
more,* + pedālis ; sēsqui- = sē-

mis, *one half,* + -que], adj., *a foot
and a half* in thickness. iv. 17.

sēstertius, -a, -um, [for sēmis tertius, *three less one half*], num. adj.,
two and a half. As subst., **sēstertius,** -ī, (originally sc. nummus),
gen. pl. sēstertium, m., *sesterce,* a
small silver coin, originally 2½ *asses,*
= about 4$\frac{1}{10}$ cents.

sētius, adv., comp., *less.* **nihilō
sētius,** *none the less, nevertheless.*

seu, see sīve.

sevēritās, -tātis, [sevērus, *severe*],
f., *sternness, rigor, strictness.* vii. 4.
[*severity.*

sēvocō, -āre, -āvī, -ātus, [sē- +
vocō], 1, *call apart, call aside.*

sex, or VI, indeclinable num. adj.,
six. [*sextet.*

sexāgintā, or LX, indeclinable num.
adj., *sixty.*

Sextius, -ī, m., (seks′ tị-ụs) :
(1) *Publius Sextius Baculus,* see
Baculus.
(2) *Titus Sextius,* a lieutenant.

sī, conj., *if, whether.* **quod sī,** *but if,
now if.* **sī quidem,** *if indeed, in
so far as* (vi. 36).

Sibusātēs, -um, m., pl., (sib-ụ-sā′-
tēz), a people in Aquitania. iii. 27.

sīc, adv., *so, in this way, thus; as
follows* (II. 4). **ut . . . sīc,** *as
. . . so.* **sīc . . . ut,** *so . . . that.*

siccitās, -tātis, [siccus, *dry*], f.,
dryness, drouth.

Sicilia, -ae, f., the island of *Sicily.*

sīcut or **sīcutī,** [sīc + utī], adv.,
just as, as.

sīdus, -eris, n., *constellation;* pl.,
sīdera, *heavenly bodies,* sun, moon
and stars (vi. 14). [*sidereal.*

signifer, -ferī, [signum, cf. ferō],
m., *standard-bearer, ensign.* ii. 25.

significātiō, -ōnis, [significō], f.,
sign, signal, intimation; demeanor
(vii. 12). **significātiōnem facere,**

to give notice, convey information
(II. 33, V. 53, VI. 29). [significa-
tion.

significō, -āre, -āvī, -ātus, [signum,
+ FAC in faciō], 1, *show by signs,
show, intimate, indicate; transmit
the news* (vii. 3). [significant.

signum, -ī, n., *signal; standard, ensign.* signum dare, *to give the
signal.* [sign.

Sīlānus, -ī, m., *Marcus Silanus* (sị-
lā′nụs), a lieutenant of Caesar.
vi. 1.

silentium, -ī, [silēns, *silent*], n., *silence, stillness.* [silence.

Sīlius, -ī, m., *Titus Silius* (sil′ị-ụs),
a military tribune. iii. 7, 8.

silva, -ae, f., *wood, forest.* [sylvan.

silvestris, -e, [silva], adj., *covered
with woods, wooded.* [sylvestral.

similis, -e, comp. similior, sup. si-
millimus, adj., *like, similar.* [sim-
ilar.

similitūdō, -inis, [similis], f., *likeness, similarity.* [similitude.

simul, adv., *at the same time, at once;
as soon as* (iv. 26). simul . . .
simul, *both . . . and, partly . . .
partly.* simul atque, *as soon as.*

simulācrum, -ī, [cf. simulō], n.,
image. vi. 16, 17.

simulātiō, -ōnis, [cf. simulō], f.,
pretence, deceit. [simulation.

simul atque, see simul.

simulō, -āre, -āvī, -ātus, [similis],
1, *make like; pretend, feign* (i. 44;
iv. 4). [simulate.

simultās, -tātis, [simul], f., *rivalry,
jealousy, bitterness* toward a rival
(v. 44).

sīn [sī + ne], conj., *if however, but if.*

sincērē [sincērus, *pure*], adv.,
frankly, sincerely. vii. 20.

sine, prep. with abl. only, *without.*

singillātim [singulī], adv., *one by
one, singly.* iii. 2; v. 4, 52.

singulāris, -e, [singulī], adj., *one by
one, one at a time* (iv. 26; vii. 8);
singular, extraordinary. [singular.

singulī, -ae, -a, distrib. num. adj., *one
to each, one by one, one apiece; separate, single.* [single.

sinister, -tra, -trum, adj., *left.* [sin-
ister.

sinistra, -ae, [sc. manus], f., *left
hand* (i. 25). sub sinistrā, *on the
left* (v. 8).

sinistrōrsus [sinister + vorsus, cf.
vertō], adv., *to the left.* vi. 25.

sī quidem, see sī.

situs, -ūs, [cf. sinō], m., *situation,
location, site.* [site.

sīve or **seu** [sī + ve], conj., *or if.*
sīve (seu) . . . sīve (seu), *if
. . . or if, whether . . . or, either
. . . or, it might be . . . or.*

socer, -erī, m., *father-in-law.* i. 12.

societās, -tātis, [socius], f., *fellow-
ship; alliance, confederacy* (vi. 2);
corporation, association for business
purposes (C. III. 103). [society.

socius, -ī, m., *comrade, ally;* in Caesar generally pl., sociī, *allies.*
[social.

sōl, **sōlis**, m., *the sun.* oriente
sōle, *at sunrise* (VII. 3). [solar.

Sōl, -is, m., *god of the sun, sun-god.*
vi. 21.

sōlācium, -ī, [cf. sōlor, *console*], n.,
consolation, comfort. vii. 15. [solace.

soldurius, -ī, m., *retainer, follower,
vow-beholden.* iii. 22.

soleō, -ēre, -itus sum, semi-dep., 2,
be wont, be accustomed.

sōlitūdō, -inis, [sōlus], f., *wilderness, waste* (iv. 18; vi. 23). [soli-
tude.

sollertia, -ae, [sollers, *skilful*], f.,
skill, cleverness, ingenuity.

sollicitō, -āre, -āvī, -ātus, [sollici-
tus, *agitated*], 1, *instigate, urge, incite; tamper with, tempt.* [solicit.

sollicitūdō, -inis, [sollicitus], f., *anxiety, apprehension.* [solicitude.

solum, -ī, n., *lowest part, ground;* of a trench, *bottom* (VII. 72). **agrī solum**, *the bare ground* (i. 11).

sōlum [acc. of sōlus], adv., *only.* **nōn sōlum . . . sed etiam**, *not only . . . but also.*

sōlus, -a, -um, gen. sōlīus, adj., *only, alone.* [sole.

solvō, -ere, solvī, solūtus, [se-, = sē-, + luō, *loose*], 3, *loose; set sail* (iv. 23, 28; v. 23). [solve.

somnus, -ī, m., *sleep.* C. II. 38.

sonitus, -ūs, [cf. sonō, *sound*], m., *noise, sound.* vii. 60, 61.

sonus, -ī, m., *sound.* vii. 47. [sound.

soror, -ōris, f., *sister.* [sorority.

sors, sortis, f., *lot, chance.* [sort.

Sōtiātēs, -ium, m., pl., (sō-shị-ā′-tēz), a people in northern Aquitania. iii. 20, 21.

spatium, -ī, n., *space, distance; interval, time, period, duration.* **nactus spatium**, *having gained time* (v. 58). [space.

speciēs, -iēī, [cf. speciō, *look*], f., *sight, show, appearance; pretence.* **ad speciem**, *for show* (i. 51). [species.

spectō, -āre, -āvī, -ātus, [freq. of speciō, *look*], 1, *look at, regard* (i. 45; v. 29); *have in view* (C. III. 85); *face, lie* (i. 1; v. 13; vii. 69). [spectacle.

speculātor, -tōris, [speculor], m., *spy, scout.* [speculator.

speculātōrius, -a, -um, [speculātor], adj., *scouting, spying.* **speculātōrium nāvigium**, *spy-boat* (iv. 26). [speculatory.

speculor, -ārī, -ātus, [cf. specula, *watch-tower*], 1, dep., *spy out, spy.* i. 47. [speculate.

spērō, -āre, -āvī, -ātus, [cf. spēs], 1, *hope, expect.*

spēs, speī, f., *hope, expectation.*

Spinther, -ēris, m., (spin′ thẹr), *P. Cornelius Lentulus Spinther,* a prominent adherent of Pompey in the Civil War. C. III. 83.

spīritus, -ūs, [cf. spīrō, *breathe*], m., *breath, air;* pl., *haughtiness, pride* (i. 33; ii. 4). [spirit.

spoliō, -āre, -āvī, -ātus, [spolium, *booty*], 1, *strip, despoil.* [spoil (verb).

spolium, -ī, n., usually in pl., *booty, spoils.* C. II. 39. [spoil (noun).

sponte, abl., and **spontis**, gen., only forms in use of an obsolete nom. **spōns**, f., *of one's own accord, willingly.* **suā sponte**, *of their own accord, of their own initiative* (I. 44, vi. 14, C. III. 93); *on their own account, unaided* (v. 28; vii. 65); *by their own influence* (i. 9). [spontaneous.

stabiliō, -īre, -īvī, -ītus, [stabilis], 4, *make steady; make fast* (vii. 73).

stabilitās, -tātis, [stabilis], f., *steadiness.* iv. 33. [stability.

statim [stō], adv., *on the spot; immediately, at once, straightway.*

statiō, -ōnis, [cf. stō], f., *outpost, picket, guard; reserves* (v. 16). **in statiōne**, *on guard.* [station.

statuō, -uere, -uī, -ūtus, [status], 3, *set, place; determine, resolve; judge, think.* [statute.

statūra, -ae, [cf. stō], f., *height, stature.* ii. 30; vi. 21. [stature.

status, -ūs, [stō], m., *condition, position, situation.* [status.

stimulus, -ī, m., *goad; pricker* like a goad (vii. 73, 82). [stimulus.

stīpendiārius, -a, -um, [stīpendium], adj., *tributary, subject to payment of tribute* (i. 30, 36). As noun, **stīpendiāriī**, -ōrum, m., pl., *tributaries, dependents* (vii. 10). [stipendiary.

stīpendium, -ī, [stips, *coin,* cf.

pendō, *weigh*], n., *tribute ;* of soldiers, *pay.* [stipend.

stīpes, -itis, m., *stock* of a tree, *log.*
vii. 73.

stirps, -is, f., *stem ; stock, race* (vi. 34).

stō, stāre, stetī, statūrus, 1, *stand,
stand upright* (vi. 27) ; *be posted, be
placed* (v. 35, 43) ; *abide by* (vi.
13).

strāmentum, -ī, [cf. sternō, *strew*],
n., *thatch* of houses (v. 43) ; *pack-
saddle* (vii. 45).

strepitus, -ūs, [strepō], m., *noise,
uproar.*

stringō, -ere, strīnxī, strictus, 3,
bind tight ; of a sword, *draw* (C. iii.
93). [stringent.

struō, -ere, strūxī, strūctus, 3,
build, construct. C. iii. 96.

studeō, -ēre, -uī, 2, *be eager for,
strive for ; be devoted to, pay heed to ;
eagerly desire, strive.* [student.

studiōsē, comp. -ius, sup. -issimē,
[studiōsus, *eager*], adv., *eagerly,
diligently.*

studium, -ī, [cf. studeō], n., *eagerness, energy, enthusiasm ; goodwill*
(i. 19) ; *pursuit.* studia reī mīlitāris, *pursuits of war, military pursuits* (vi. 21). [study.

stultitia, -ae, [stultus], f., *folly, lack
of foresight.* vii. 77.

stultus, -a, -um, adj., *foolish.* C. iii.
59. [stultify.

sub, prep. :
(1) With acc., after verbs of motion, *under, towards, near to, just
before.*
(2) With abl., *under, at the foot
of, close by ;* of time, *on, in, during.*

subāctus, see subigō.

subdolus, -a, -um, [sub + dolus],
adj., *crafty, cunning.* vii. 31.

subdūcō, -dūcere, -dūxī, -ductus,
[sub + dūcō], 3, *lead up* from a
lower to a higher position (i. 22,

24) ; of ships, *draw up, haul on
shore, beach* (iv. 29 ; v. 11, 24).

subductiō, -ōnis, [subdūcō], f.,
hauling on shore, beaching. v. 1.

subeō, -īre, -iī, -itūrus, [sub + eō],
irr., *go under* (i. 36) ; *come up,
approach, go up* (*to*), from a lower
position (ii. 25, 27 ; vii. 85) ; *un-
dergo, suffer.*

subfodiō, -fodere, -fōdī, -fossus,
[sub + fodiō], 3, *stab underneath.*
iv. 12.

subfossus, see subfodiō.

subiciō, -icere, -iēcī, -iectus, [sub
+ iaciō], 3, *throw under, place near ;
throw from beneath* (i. 26) ; *expose*
(iv. 36, C. iii. 85) ; *make subject*
(vii. 1, 77).

subiectus, -a, -um, comp. -ior,
[subiciō], adj., *lying near, adjacent.* v. 13. [subject.

subigō, -igere, -ēgī, -āctus, [sub +
agō], 3, *subdue ; constrain, reduce
to straits* (vii. 77).

subitō, [abl. of subitus], adv., *suddenly, on a sudden.*

subitus, -a, -um, [subeō], adj., *sudden, unexpected.*

sublātus, see tollō.

sublevō, -āre, -āvī, -ātus, [sub +
levō], 1, *lift up, support, hold up*
(i. 48 ; vi. 27 ; vii. 47) ; *relieve, assist, aid, support* (i. 16, 40 ; vii. 14,
65) ; of labor, *lighten* (vi. 32) ; *re-
trieve* (C. iii. 73).

sublica, -ae, f., *stake, pile.*

subluō, -luere, ——, -lūtus, [sub +
luō], 3, *wash* (vii. 69) ; *flow at the
foot of* (C. iii. 97).

subruō, -ruere, -ruī, -rutus, [sub
+ ruō, *fall*], 3, *undermine.*

subsequor, -sequī, -secūtus, [sub
+ sequor], 3, dep., *follow close
upon, follow after, follow up.* [sub-
sequent.

subsidium, -ī, [cf. subsīdō], n., *reserve, reserve force, auxiliaries; support, relief, help, aid; relieving force; resource, remedy. **mittere subsidiō**, to send help. [subsidy.

subsīdō, -sīdere, -sēdī, [sub + sīdō, sit], 3, stay behind, remain behind. vi. 36. [subside.

subsistō, -sistere, -stitī, [sub + sistō, set], 3, halt, make a stand (i. 15); hold out (v. 10). [subsist.

subsum, -esse, [sub + sum], irr., be near (i. 25; v. 29); of time, be close at hand, not far off (iii. 27; v. 23, C. III. 97).

subtrahō, -trahere, -trāxī, -trāctus, [sub + trahō], 3, carry off, draw off underneath (vii. 22); withdraw, take away (i. 44). [subtract.

subvectiō, -ōnis, [subvehō], f., transportation. vii. 10.

subvehō, -vehere, -vexī, -vectus, [sub + vehō], 3, bring up. i. 16.

subveniō, -venīre, -vēnī, subventum est, [sub + veniō], 4, come to the help of, come to the rescue of; assist, succor, render assistance. [subvention.

succēdō, -cēdere, -cessī, -cessūrus, [sub + cēdō], 3, come up, approach, advance; succeed to another's place, take the place of, relieve, follow; become the successor (vi. 13); prosper, succeed (vii. 26). [succeed.

succendō, -cendere, -cendī, -cēnsus, [sub, cf. candeō], 3, set on fire, set fire to.

succīdō, -cīdere, -cīdī, -cīsus, [sub + caedō], 3, cut down.

succumbō, -cumbere, -cubuī, [sub + cumbō, for cubō], 3, yield, succumb. vii. 86. [succumb.

succurrō, -currere, -currī, -cursum est, [sub + currō], 3, run to help, succor. v. 44; vii. 80. [succor.

sudis, -is, f., stake, pile.

sūdor, -ōris, [cf. sūdō, sweat], m., sweat; toil, effort (vii. 8). [sudary.

Suēba, -ae, [Suēbus, cf. Suēbī], f., a Swabian woman. i. 53.

Suēbī, -ōrum, m., pl., the Swabians, Suebi (swē′bī), a powerful German people.

Suessiōnēs, -um, m., pl., (swes-i̯-ō′-nēz), a Belgic people north of the Matrona (Marne); the name survives in Soissons.

sufficiō, -ficere, -fēcī, -fectus, [sub + faciō], 3, hold out. vii. 20. [suffice.

suffrāgium, -ī, n., vote. [suffrage.

Sugambrī, -ōrum, m., pl., (sū-gam′-brī), a German people.

suggestus, -ūs, [suggerō, raise up], m., platform (vi. 3).

suī, sibi, sē or sēsē, nom. wanting, reflex. pron., himself, herself, itself, themselves, him, her, it.

Sulla, -ae, m., (sul′a̯) :
   (1) Lucius Cornelius Sulla, born 138 B.C.; consul 88, dictator 81–79 B.C.; leader of the aristocratic party in the first Civil War, enemy of Marius; died 78 B.C. i. 21; C. I. 7.
   (2) Faustus Cornelius Sulla, son of the dictator. C. I. 6.
   (3) Publius Cornelius Sulla, nephew of the dictator, who fought under Caesar. C. III. 89, 99.

Sulpicius, -ī, m., (sul-pish′[y]u̯s) :
   (1) Publius Sulpicius Rufus, a lieutenant of Caesar in Gaul and afterwards in the Civil War. iv. 22, vii. 90.
   (2) Servius Sulpicius, a Roman senator. C. II. 44.

sum, esse, fuī, futūrus, irr., be, exist. [future.

summa, -ae, [summus; sc. rēs], f., sum total, aggregate, whole (i. 29; vi. 11, 34; C. III. 89); general management, control, administra-

tion ; determination, deciding (vi.
11). **summa imperiī,** *the supreme command.* [sum.

sumministrō, -āre, -āvī, -ātus, [sub
+ ministrō, *serve*], 1, *supply, provide, furnish.*

summittō, -mittere, -mīsī, -missus,
[sub + mittō], 3, *send secretly ;
send as reinforcement, send as help.*
[submit.

summoveō, -movēre, -mōvī, -mō-
tus, [sub + moveō], 2, *force back.*

summus, see superus.

sūmō, sūmere, sūmpsī, sūmptus,
3, *take* (i. 7, 16; vii. 65); *take to
one's self, take on, assume* (i. 33; ii.
4); *put forth, expend, spend* (iii. 14).
dē aliquō supplicium sūmere,
to inflict punishment on any one
(i. 31; vi. 44).

sūmptuōsus, -a, -um, comp. -ior,
[sūmptus], adj., *costly.* vi. 19.
[sumptuous.

sūmptus, -tūs, [sūmō], m., *expense.*
i. 18. [sumptuary.

superbē, comp. -ius, sup. -issimē,
[superbus, *proud*], adv., *haughtily.*

superior, see superus.

superō, -āre, -āvī, -ātus, [superus],
1, *conquer, overcome, vanquish, defeat ; surpass* (vi. 24); *surmount*
(vii. 24); *rise above* (iii. 14); *prove
superior* (iii. 14); *carry the day* (v.
31); *survive* (vi. 19). [superable.

supersedeō, -sedēre, -sēdī, [super
+ sedeō, *sit*], 2, *refrain from.* ii.
8. [supersede.

supersum, -esse, -fuī, [super +
sum], irr., *remain, be left* (i. 23;
iii. 28; v. 22; C. III. 91); *survive*
(i. 26; ii. 27, 28).

superus, -a, -um, comp. **superior,**
sup. **summus** or **suprēmus,** [su-
per], adj., *above, on high.* Comp.
superior, -ius, *higher, upper, superior ;* of time, *former, earlier,* as

superiōre nocte, *the previous night*
(v. 10). Sup., **summus,** -a, -um,
*highest ; greatest, very great ; most
important, chief ; all together, all* (v.
17; vii. 41); often denoting a part,
as **summus mōns,** *the top of the
height* (i. 22). As noun, **summum,**
-ī, n., *top, end.* **ab summō,** *from
the top* (ii. 18); *at the end* (vii. 73);
from the end (vi. 26). [superior,
supreme.

suppetō, -petere, -petīvī or -iī, -pe-
tītus, [sub + petō], 3, *be at hand,
be available ; hold out* (vii. 77, 85).

supplēmentum, -ī, [suppleō, *fill
up*], n., *raw contingent,* a body of
recruits under training, not yet
assigned to the legions in which
they will serve. [supplement.

supplex, -icis, m. and f., *suppliant.*
ii. 28.

supplicātiō, -ōnis, [supplicō], f.,
solemn thanksgiving, thanksgiving.
[supplication.

suppliciter [supplex], adv., *after
the manner of a suppliant, humbly.*

supplicium, -ī, [cf. supplex], n.,
*punishment ; death-penalty, execu-
tion.*

supportō, -āre, -āvī, [sub + portō],
1, *bring up, transport, convey.* [sup-
port.

suprā, adv. and prep. :
(1) As adv., *above ; before, previously.*
(2) As prep., with acc., *above ;*
of time, *beyond, before* (vi. 19).

suscipiō, -cipere, -cēpī, -ceptus,
[subs, for sub, + capiō], 3, *undertake, take up ; take upon one's self,
assume* (i. 3). **bellum suscipere,**
to commence war. [susceptible.

suspectus, -a, -um, comp. -ior, adj.,
under suspicion. [suspect.

suspīciō, -ōnis, f., *suspicion ; reason
to suspect* (i. 4). [suspicion.

suspicor, -ārī, -ātus, [cf. suspiciō], 1, dep., *suspect, mistrust, surmise.*

sustentō, -āre, -āvī, -ātus, [freq. of sustineō], 1, *sustain, endure, bear, hold out.*

sustineō, -tinēre, -tinuī, -tentus, [subs, for sub, + teneō], 2, *hold up* (vii. 56); *check, pull up* (iv. 33); *hold out, bear, endure; hold out against, withstand.* [sustain.

sustulī, see tollō.

suus, -a, -um, [cf. suī], possessive pronominal adj., *his, her, its, their; his own, her own, their own,* etc.; with locō, locīs, *favorable to himself, to themselves.* As noun, suī, m., pl., *his, their friends, people, party, side;* suum, -ī, n., *their own* (i. 43); sua, n., pl., *his, her, their property, possessions.* sē suaque, *themselves and their possessions* (i. 11, ii. 31).

Syria, -ae, [Συρία], f., (sir′ i-a), a country lying east of the Mediterranean Sea, between Cilicia and Palestine; organized into a Roman province in 64 B.C. C. I. 6, III. 103.

Syriacus, -a, -um, [Syria], adj., *Syrian.* C. III. 88.

T.

T. = Titus (tī′tụs), a Roman first name.

tabella, -ae, [dim. of tabula], f., *tablet; voting-tablet, ballot* (C. III. 83).

tabernāculum, -ī, [taberna, *hut*], n., *tent, hut.* [tabernacle.

tabula, -ae, f., *board; writing-tablet; list* written on a tablet (i. 29). [table.

tabulātum, -ī, [cf. tabula], n., *floor, story.* vi. 29. [tabulate.

taceō, -ēre, -uī, -itus, 2, *be silent, remain silent* (i. 17); *say nothing of, pass over in silence* (i. 17).

tacitus, -a, -um, [part. of taceō], adj., *silent.* i. 32. [tacit.

tālea, -ae, f., *stick, block* (vii. 73); *bar* (v. 12). [tally.

tālis, -e, adj., *such.*

tam, adv., *so, so very.*

tamen, adv., *yet, still, for all that, nevertheless, however.*

Tamesis, -is, m., *the Thames.*

tametsī [tam, = tamen, + etsī], conj., *although, though.*

tandem [tam], adv., *at length, finally;* in questions, *pray* (i. 40).

tangō, tangere, tetigī, tāctus, 3, *touch, border on.* v. 3. [tact.

tantopere [tantō opere], adv., *so earnestly, with so great effort.* i. 31.

tantulus, -a, -um, [dim. of tantus], adj., *so small, so slight, so trifling.*

tantum [acc. of tantus], adv., *only so much, so far, merely.* tantum modo, *only* (iii. 5).

tantundem [acc. neut. of tantusdem], adv., *just so much.* vii. 72.

tantus, -a, -um, adj., *so great, so large, so much, so extensive, so important.* tantus . . . quantus, *so great, so much, only so much . . . as.*

Tarbellī, -ōrum, m., pl., (ṭar-bel′ ī), a people in Aquitania, near the Ocean. iii. 27.

tardē, comp. -ius, sup. -issimē, [tardus], adv., *slowly;* comp., *rather slowly* (iv. 23, C. III. 82).

tardō, -āre, -āvī, -ātus, [tardus], 1, *check, delay, impede, hinder.*

tardus, -a, -um, comp. -ior, sup. -issimus, adj., *slow.* Comp., *less active* (ii. 25). [tardy.

Tarusātēs, -ium, m., pl., (tär-ụ-sā′-tēz), a people in Aquitania. iii. 23, 27.

Tasgetius, -ī, m., (ṭas-jē′ sh[y]ụs), a ruler of the Carnutes. v. 25, 29.

Taurois, -entis, acc. Tauroenta, [Ταυρόεις], (tâ′ rọ-ịs), a fortified place

on the seacoast near Massilia. C.
II. 4.

taurus, -ī, m., *bull.* vi. 28. [Taurus.

Taximagulus, -ī, m., (tak-sĭ-mag' ū̆-lŭs), a British chieftain. v. 22.

taxus, -ī, f., *yew.* vi. 31.

Tectosagēs, -um, m., pl., (tĕk-tos'-ā-jēz), a division of the Volcae, in the Province; represented also by a branch settled near the Hercynian forest (vi. 24).

temere, adv., *blindly, recklessly, rashly* (I. 40, v. 28; vii. 37, C. III. 87); *without good reason* (iv. 20).

temeritās, -tātis, [cf. temere], f., *rashness, recklessness.* [temerity.

tēmō, -ōnis, m., *pole, tongue,* of a wagon or chariot. iv. 33.

Tempē [Τέμπη], n., indeclinable pl., *Tempe,* a narrow valley, famed for its beauty, in the northern part of Thessaly, through which the river

Figure 209. — A view in the Vale of Tempe.

Through this beautiful valley Pompey rode in mad haste after the battle of Pharsalus.

tēctum, -ī, [tegō], n., *roof* (i. 36); *house* (vii. 66).

tegimentum, -ī, [tegō], n., *covering.* ii. 21; vi. 21. [tegument.

tegō, tegere, tēxī, tēctus, 3, *cover* (v. 43); *hide, conceal, protect.*

tēlum, -ī, n., general word for *missile; dart, spear.*

temerārius, -a, -um, [temere], adj., *rash, headstrong.* I. 31; VI. 20.

Xerias (ancient *Peneius*) flows eastward to the sea; it lies between Mt. Olympus and Mt. Ossa (Map 19, and Fig. 209).

temperantia, -ae, [temperāns, *temperate*], f., *moderation, sound judgment.* i. 19. [temperance.

temperātus, -a, -um, comp. -ior, [temperō], adj., *moderate, temperate, mild* (v. 12). [temperate.

temperō, -āre, -āvī, -ātus, [cf. tempus], 1, *control one's self, refrain* (i. 7, 33). [temper.

tempestās, -tātis, [tempus], f., *weather; stormy weather, bad weather, storm.* [tempest.

templum, -ī, n., *temple.* C. I. 7, II. 5. [temple.

temptō, -āre, -āvī, -ātus, [freq. of tendō], 1, *try, attempt; make an attack on, attack, assail* (vii. 73, 86); *try to win over* (vi. 2). [tempt.

tempus, -oris, n., *period of time; time, period; season; occasion, circumstances.* **prō tempore**, *according to the emergency* (v. 8). **in reliquum tempus**, *for the future, for all time to come.* [temporal.

Tencterī, -ōrum, m., pl., (tengk'-te̜-rī), a German people, driven from their territories by the Suebi.

tendō, tendere, tetendī, tentus, 3, *stretch, extend; put up* (C. III. 82); *have one's tent* (vi. 37). [tend.

tenebrae, -ārum, f., pl., *darkness.*

teneō, tenēre, tenuī, 2, *hold, keep, occupy; hold in, keep in, hold back, restrain, hem in; bind* (i. 31). **sē tenēre**, *to keep one's self, to remain.* [tenet.

tener, -era, -erum, comp. -ior, sup. tenerrimus, adj., *tender, young.* ii. 17. [tender (adj.).

tenuis, -e, comp. tenuior, sup. tenuissimus, adj., *thin; poor, trifling* (vi. 35); *feeble, delicate* (v. 40).

tenuitās, -ātis, [tenuis], f., *thinness; weakness; poverty, destitution* (vii. 17). [tenuity.

tenuiter, comp. tenuius, sup. -issimē, [tenuis], adv., *thinly.* iii. 13.

ter, num. adv., *three times, thrice.*

teres, -etis, [cf. terō, *rub*], adj., *smooth* (vii. 73).

tergum, -ī, n., *back.* **ā tergō**, *post*

tergum, *in the rear, on the rear.* **terga vertere**, *to flee.* [tergant.

ternī, -ae, -a, [ter], distrib. num. adj., *by threes, three each.* [ternary.

terra, -ae, f., *earth; land, ground; territory, country, region.* [terrace.

Terrasidius, -ī, m., (ter-a̜-sid' i̜-u̜s), an officer under Publius Crassus. iii. 7, 8.

terrēnus, -a, -um, [terra], adj., *of earth, earthy.* i. 43. [terrain.

terreō, -ēre, -uī, -itus, 2, *frighten, terrify, alarm;* followed by quō minus, *deter, frighten* from an action (vii. 49).

territō, -āre, [freq. of terreō], 1, *frighten greatly, terrify.* **metū territāre**, *to fill with apprehension* (v. 6).

terror, -ōris, [cf. terreō], m., *fear, fright, alarm.* **īnferre terrōrem**, *to strike terror* (vii. 8). [terror.

tertius, -a, -um, [ter], num. ord. adj., *third.* **tertius decimus**, or **XIII**, *thirteenth.* [tertiary.

testāmentum, -ī, [cf. testor], n., *will.* i. 39. [testament.

testimōnium, -ī, [cf. testis], n., *proof, evidence.* [testimony.

testis, -is, m. and f., *witness.*

testūdō, -inis, [cf. testa, *potsherd*], f., *turtle; turtle-shell roof, testudo*, a covering formed by the soldiers' shields held above their heads and overlapping (ii. 6; v. 9; vii. 85); *turtle-shell shed*, a movable shed to protect soldiers near the enemy's wall (v. 42, 43, 52). [testudinate.

Teutomatus, -ī, m., (tū-tom' a̜-tu̜s), a king of the Nitiobroges. vii. 31, 46.

Teutonī, gen. -um, m., pl., *Teutons, Teutoni* (tū' to̜-nī); see **Cimbrī**.

Thessalia, -ae, [Θεσσαλία], f., *Thessaly*, the northeastern part of Greece. C. III. 82.

Thrācēs, -um, m., pl., *Thracians,* natives of Thrace, east of Macedonia. C. III. 95.

tignum, -ī, n., *log, pile.* iv. 17.

Tigurīnus, -a, -um, adj., *Tigurian.* As noun, **Tigurīnī,** -ōrum, m., pl., *the Tigurians,* one of the four divisions of the Helvetians. i. 12.

timeō, -ēre, -uī, 2, *fear, be afraid of; be afraid, be apprehensive* (i. 14, 41). Pres. part. as noun, **timentēs,** m., pl., *the fearful* (vii. 7).

timidē, comp. -ius, [timidus], adv., *timidly.* iii. 25; v. 33.

timidus, -a, -um, comp. -ior, sup. -issimus, [cf. timeō], adj., *timid, cowardly.* i. 39; vi. 40. [timid.

timor, -ōris, [cf. timeō], m., *fear, apprehension, alarm.* [timorous.

Titūrius, -ī, m., *Quintus Titurius Sabinus* (tǐ-tū' rǐ-ǔs sạ-bī' nǔs), a lieutenant of Caesar.

Titus, -ī. m., (tī' tǔs), a Roman first name; abbreviation, T.

tolerō, -āre, -āvī, -ātus, 1, *bear, support, endure; sustain* (VII. 77); *hold out* (vii. 71). [tolerate.

tollō, tollere, sustulī, sublātus, 3, *lift, raise;* of an anchor, *weigh* (iv. 23); *take on board* (iv. 28); *puff up, elate* (i. 15; v. 38, C. II. 37); *take away, remove* (vi. 17; vii. 14); *do away with* (I. 42).

Tolōsa, -ae, f., (tǫ-lō' sạ), a city in the Province, now *Toulouse.* iii. 20.

Tolōsātēs, -ium, [Tolōsa], m., pl., (tol-ǫ-sā' tēz) a people in the territory of the Volcae Tectosages, in the Province, about Tolosa.

tormentum, -ī, [cf. torqueō, *twist*], n., *windlass* (vii. 22); as a military term, pl., *torsioners, engines, artillery* (vii. 41, 81); *missile,* thrown by the torsioners (iv. 25); *means of torture, rack, torture* (vi. 19; vii. 4). [torment.

torreō, torrēre, torruī, tostus, 2. *roast; burn, scorch* (v. 43). [torrid.

tot, indeclinable num. adj., *so many.*

totidem [tot], indeclinable num. adj., *just as many, just so many.*

tōtus, -a, -um, gen. tōtīus, adj., *the whole, all, all the, entire.* [total.

trabs, trabis, f., *beam, timber.*

trāctus, see trahō.

trādō, -dere, -didī, -ditus, [trāns + dō], 3, *hand over, give up, deliver, surrender; intrust, commit, confide; commend, recommend* (vii. 39); *hand down* (iv. 7); *teach, impart* (vi. 14, 17; vii. 22).

trādūcō, -dūcere, -dūxī, -ductus, [trāns + dūcō], 3, *lead across, bring over; lead, transport, transfer; win over* (VI. 12, VII. 37). [traduce.

trāgula, -ae, f., *dart, javelin,* perhaps having a barbed point, and hurled by means of a leather thong.

trahō, trahere, trāxī, trāctus, 3, *drag along* (i. 53); *draw along, drag* (VI. 38). [tract.

trāiciō, -icere, -iēcī, -iectus, [trāns + iaciō], 3, *throw across; strike through, pierce, transfix* (v. 35, 44; vii. 25, 82). [trajectory.

trāiectus, see trāiciō.

trāiectus, -ūs, [cf. trāiciō], m., *passage.* iv. 21; v. 2.

trānō, -āre, -āvī, [trāns + nō, *swim*], 1, *swim across.* i. 53.

tranquillitās, -ātis, [tranquillus, *still*], f., *stillness, calm* (iii. 15). **summa tranquillitās,** *a profound calm* (v. 23). [tranquillity.

trāns, prep. with acc. only, *across, over; on the further side of, beyond.*

Trānsalpīnus, -a, -um, [trāns + Alpīnus, from Alpēs], adj., *beyond the Alps, Transalpine.* vii. 1, 6.

trānscendō, -scendere, -scendī, [trāns + scandō, *climb*], 3, *climb* *over* (vii. 70); of ships, *board* (III. 15). [transcend.

trănseō, -īre, -iī or -īvī, -itum est, [trāns + eō], irr.,*go over, go across, pass over, cross over ; pass by, march through ;* of time, *pass* (iii. 2). [transit (verb).

trănsferō, -ferre, -tulī, -lātus, [trāns + ferō], irr., *carry across; transfer.* [transfer.

trănsfīgō, -fīgere, -fīxī, -fīxus, [trāns + fīgō, *fix*], 3, *pierce through, transfix.* [transfix.

trănsfīxus, see **trănsfīgō**.

trănsfodiō, -fodere, -fōdī, -fossus, [trāns + fodiō], 3, *pierce through, impale* (vii. 82).

trănsgredior, -gredī, gressus, [trāns + gradiŏr, *walk, go*], 3, dep., *pass over, go across, cross.* ii. 19; vii. 25, 46. [transgress.

trănsitus, -ūs, [cf. **trănseō**], m., *going over, crossing* (v. 55; vi. 7; vii. 57). [transit (noun).

trănslātus, see **trănsferō**.

trănsmarīnus, -a, -um, [trāns + mare], adj., *beyond the sea.* vi. 24. [transmarine.

trănsmissus, -ūs, [cf. **trănsmittō**], m., *passage.* v. 13.

trănsmittō, ·mittere, -mīsī, -missus, [trāns + mittō], 3, *send across, convey across.* vii. 61. [transmit.

Trānspadānus, -a, -um, [trāns + Padus], adj., *beyond the Po.* C. III. 87. [Transpadane.

trănsportō, -āre, -āvī, -ātus, [trāns + portō], 1, *carry over, convey across, transport.* [transport.

Trānsrhēnānus, -a, -um, [trāns + Rhēnus], adj., *beyond the Rhine, on the other side of the Rhine* (v. 2). As noun, **Trānsrhēnānī**, -ōrum, m., pl., *the people beyond the Rhine* (iv. 16; vi. 5). [Transrhenane.

trānstrum, -ī, [trāns], n., *thwart, cross-beam.* iii. 13.

trănsversus [part. of **trănsvertō**], adj., *crosswise.* ii. 8. [transverse.

Trebius, -ī, m., *Marcus Trebius Gallus* (trē′ bi̯-u̯s gal′ u̯s), an officer under Publius Crassus. iii. 7, 8.

Trebōnius, -ī, m., (tre̦-bō′ ni̯-u̯s) :

(1) *Gaius Trebonius*, quaestor 60 B.C., tribune of the people 55 B.C., a lieutenant of Caesar in the Gallic and Civil wars; afterwards one of the conspirators against Caesar's life.

(2) *Gaius Trebonius*, a Roman knight. vi. 40.

trecentī, -ae, -a, or CCC, [trēs + centum], num. adj., *three hundred.*

trepidō, -āre, -āvī, -ātus, [cf. trepidus], 1, *hurry about anxiously.* v. 33; vi. 37. [trepidation.

trēs, tria, gen. trium, or III, num. adj., *three.*

Trēverī, -ōrum, m., pl., *Treverans, Treveri* (trev′ e̦-rī) a Belgic people near the Rhine.

Trēverus, -a, -um, adj., *Treveran, of the Treveri* (ii. 24).

Triārius, -ī, m., *Gaius Triarius* (tri̦-ā′ ri̯-u̯s), a commander under Pompey. C. III. 92.

Tribocēs, -um, or **Tribocī**, -ōrum, m., pl., (trib′ o̦-sēz, trib′ o̦-sī), a German people near the Rhine.

tribūnīcius, -a, -um, [tribūnus], adj., *of a tribune, tribunicial.* C. I. 7.

tribūnus, -ī, [tribus, *tribe*], m., *tribune.* tribūnus mīlitum, *military tribune.* tribūnus plēbis, *tribune of the people.* [tribune.

tribuō, -ere, -uī, -ūtus, [cf. tribus], 3, *assign, ascribe; allot, give, concede; grant, pay, render.*

tribūtum, -ī, [part. of **tribuō**], n., *tax, tribute.* vi. 13, 14. [tribute.

trichila, -ae, f., *arbor, bower.* C. III. 96.

trīduum, -ī, [tri, = trēs, cf. **diēs**], n., *space of three days, three days.*

triennium, -ī, [tri-, = trēs,+annus], n., *period of three years, three years.* iv. 4. [triennial.

trīgintā, or **XXX**, indeclinable num. adj., *thirty.*

trīnī, -ae, -a, [trēs], distrib. num. adj., *three each; three; threefold, triple* (i. 53). [trinal.

Trinovantēs, -um, m., pl., (trin-ọ-van′tēz), a tribe in Britain.

tripertītō, [tripertītus, tri- + par-tītus], adv., *in three divisions, in three columns.* [tripertite.

triplex, -icis, [tri, = trēs, cf. **plicō**, *fold*], adj., *threefold, triple.* [triple.

triquetrus, -a, -um, adj., *three-cornered, triangular.* v. 13.

trirēmis, -e, [trī, = trēs, + rēmus], adj., *having three banks of oars.* C. ii. 6. [trireme.

trīstis, -e, comp. -ior, sup. -issimus, adj., *sad, dejected, disconsolate.* i. 32.

trīstitia, -ae, [trīstis], f., *sadness, dejection.* i. 32.

Troucillus, -ī, m., *Gaius Valerius Troucillus* (tru̧-sil′ u̧s), a Gaul who acted as interpreter for Caesar. i. 19.

truncus, -ī, m., *trunk* of a tree. [trunk.

tū, **tuī**, pl. **vōs**, **vestrum**, personal pron., *thou, you.*

tuba, -ae, f., *trumpet.* [tuba.

tueor, **tuērī**, 2, dep., *gaze at, behold, watch; guard, protect, defend.*

tulī, see **ferō**.

Tulingī, -ōrum, m., pl., (tū-lin′ jī), a people near the Helvetians.

Tullius, see **Cicero**.

Tullus, see **Volcacius**.

tum, adv., *then, at that time; thereupon; besides, moreover.* **cum** . . . **tum**, *both . . . and, not only . . . but also.*

tumultuor, -ārī, -ātus, [tumultus],

1, dep., *make a disturbance; be in confusion* (vii. 61).

tumultuōsē, comp. -ius, sup. -issimē, [tumultuōsus], adv., *with confusion.* Comp., *with more confusion* than usual (vii. 45).

tumultus, -ūs, m., *disturbance, confusion, disorder, uproar; uprising, rebellion* (i. 40; v. 26). [tumult.

tumulus, -ī, [tumeō, *swell*], m., *mound, hillock.* [tumulus.

tunc, adv., *then, at that time, at this juncture.* v. 41.

turba, -ae, f., *disorder, confusion.* C. ii. 35.

turma, -ae, f., *troop, squadron* of cavalry.

turmātim, [turma], adv., *by squadrons.* C. iii. 93.

Turonī, -ōrum, m., pl., (tū′ rọ-nī), a Gallic people, on the Liger (*Loire*).

turpis, -e, comp. -ior, sup. -issimus, adj., *ugly; disgraceful, shameful.*

turpiter, comp. -ius, sup. -issimē, [turpis], adv., *basely, disgracefully.*

turpitūdō, -inis, [turpis], f., *baseness, disgra͟ce.* ii. 27. [turpitude.

turris, -is, f., *tower;* movable *tower*, built on wheels so that it could be moved up to the wall of a besieged city. [tower.

Tūticānus, -ī, m., (tū-ti̧-kā′ nu̧s), a Gaul in Caesar's army. C. iii. 71.

tūtō, comp. **tūtius**, [abl. of tūtus], adv., *in safety, safely, securely.*

tūtus, comp. -ior, sup. -issimus, [part. of tueor], adj., *safe, secure.*

tuus, -a, -um, [tū], possessive pronominal adj., *thy, your.* v. 44.

U.

ubi or **ubī**, adv., of place, *where;* of time, *when.* **ubi prīmum**, *as soon as.*

Ubiī, -ōrum, m., pl., *Ubians, Ubii* (ū′ bi̧-ī), a German people.

ubíque [ubí + -que], adv., *anywhere,
everywhere*. iii. 16. [ubiquity.

Ubius, -a, -um, adj., *Ubian, of the
Ubians* (vi. 29).

ulcíscor, ulcíscí, ultus, 3, dep.,
take vengeance on (i. 14; iv. 19; v.
38); *avenge* (i. 12); *to take vengeance* (vi. 34).

úllus, -a, -um, gen. úllíus, adj., *any*.
As noun, *anyone, anybody* (i. 8).

ulterior, -ius, [ultrá], adj. in comp.
degree, *farther, beyond, more remote,
more distant*. Sup. **ultimus**,
*farthest, most distant, most remote;
last*. As noun, ulteriórés, -um,
m., pl., *those who were further off*
(vi. 2); ultimí, -órum, m., pl., *the
last* (v. 43). [ulterior, ultimate.

ultrá, prep. with acc. only, *on the
farther side of; beyond* (i. 48, 49).

ultró, adv., *to the farther side; besides,
moreover, also* (v. 28, vi. 35); *actually* (v. 40); *of one's own accord,
voluntarily*.

ultus, see ulcíscor.

ululátus, -ús, [ululó, *yell*], m., only
in acc. and abl., *shouting, yell*.

umerus, -í, m., *shoulder*. vii. 50,
56.

umquam, adv., *at any time, ever*.

úná [únus], adv., *into one place* (vii.
87); *in the same place* (ii. 29; vii.
38); *at the same time; together, in
company*. **úná cum**, *along with, together with*.

unde, adv., *whence, from which*.

úndecim, or **XI**, [únus + decem],
indeclinable num. adj., *eleven*.

úndecimus, -a, -um, [undecim],
num. ord. adj., *eleventh*.

úndéquadrágintá, or **XXXIX**, [únus
+ dé + quadrágintá], indeclinable
num. adj., *thirty-nine*.

úndévígintí, or **XVIIII**, [únus +
dé + vígintí], indeclinable num.
adj., *nineteen*. i. 8.

undique [unde + -que], adv., *from
all sides, on all sides, everywhere*.

úniversus, -a, -um, [únus + versus,
from vertó], adj., *all together, all,
in a body; the whole of, entire*. As
noun, úniversí, -órum, m., pl., *all
the men together, the whole body, all
together*. [universe.

únus, -a, -um, gen. uníus, num. adj.,
*one; one alone, only one, only, sole;
one and the same*. Pl., úní, *alone,
only*. **únó tempore**, *at one and
the same time*. **ad únum omnés**,
all to a man (v. 37). [unite.

urbánus, -a, -um, [urbs], adj., *of
the city*, referring to Rome. [urban.

urbs, urbis, f., *city;* often *the city*,
referring to Rome.

urgeó, urgére, ursí, 2, *press;* pass.,
be hard pressed (ii. 25, 26).
[urge.

úrus, -í, m., *wild ox*. vi. 28.

Usipetés, -um, m., pl., (ū-sip'ę-tēz),
a German people.

úsitátus, -a, -um, comp. -ior, sup.
-issimus, [part. of úsitor], adj.,
usual; common, familiar (vii. 22).

úsque, adv., *as far as, even*. **úsque
ad**, *as far as;* of time, *up to, until*
(i. 50; iii. 15). **úsque eó**, *even
so far as this, even to this degree* (vi.
37; vii. 17).

úsus, see útor.

úsus, -ús, [cf. útor], m., *use, practice, exercise, employment; experience, familiarity* (with), *skill;
control; advantage, benefit; need,
necessity*. **ex úsú**, *of advantage*.
[use (noun).

ut, utí, adv. and conj. :
(1) As adv., interrogative, *how* (i.
43, 46); relative, *as, just as*.
(2) As conj., with indic., *as* (i. 4);
when, as soon as (i. 31); with subj.,
*that, so that; in order that; though,
although* (iii. 9).

uter, utra, utrum, gen. utrīus, pronominal adj., often used as subst., *which* of two, *whichever, which.*

uterque, -traque, -trumque, gen. utrīusque, [uter + -que], adj., *each, both.* As subst., uterque, utrīusque, m., *both, each.* Pl., utrīque, *both sides, both forces* (iv. 26; v. 50; vii. 70, 80, 85); *both peoples* (ii. 16; vii. 7).

utī, see ut.

Utica, -ae, f., (ū′ tĭ-cạ), a city in northern Africa, on the sea-coast.

Uticēnsēs, -ium, m., pl., *Uticans, the inhabitants of Utica.* C. ii. 36.

ūtilis, -e, comp. -ior, sup. -issimus, [ūtor], adj., *useful, serviceable* (iv. 7; vii. 20); *helpful* (vii. 76).

ūtilitās, -ātis, [ūtilis], f., *usefulness, advantage, benefit.* [utility.

ūtor, ūtī, ūsus, 3, dep., *use, employ, adopt; avail one's self of, have, enjoy, find; observe, maintain; exercise, display, show.* [use (verb).

utrimque [uterque], adv., *on both sides.*

utrum, [uter], conj., *whether.*

uxor, -ōris, f., *wife.* [uxorious.

V.

Vacalus, -ī, m., *Waal, Vacalus* (vak′ ạ-lụs), an arm of the Rhine, which flows west into the Meuse. iv. 10.

vacātiō, -ōnis, [cf. vacō], f., *exemption.* vi. 14. [vacation.

vacō, -āre, -āvī, -ātus, 1, *be unoccupied, lie waste.* [vacate.

vạcuus, -a, -um, sup. vacuissimus, [vacō], adj., *empty, clear, vacant, unoccupied; destitute* (ii. 12). [vacuum.

vadum, -ī, n., *shoal, shallow* (iii. 9, 12, 13; iv. 26); *ford, shallow place.*

vāgīna, -ae, f., *scabbard, sheath.* v. 44.

vagor, -ārī, -ātus, 1, dep., *wander, wander about, roam about.*

valeō, -ēre, -uī, -itūrus, 2, *be powerful, be strong; have power, have influence; prevail.* [value.

Valerius, -ī, m., (vạ-lē′ rĭ-ụs):

(1) *Lucius Valerius Praeconinus,* a lieutenant defeated and killed in Aquitania a few years before 56 B.C. iii. 20.

(2) *Gaius Valerius Flaccus,* a Roman governor in Gaul. i. 47.

(3) *Gaius Valerius Caburus,* a Gaul who received the Roman franchise, B.C. 83. i. 47; vii. 65.

(4) *Gaius Valerius Procillus,* son of (3); sent by Caesar as envoy to Ariovistus. i. 47, 53.

(5) *Gaius Valerius Donnotaurus,* a Gaul, son of (3). vii. 65.

(6) *Gaius Valerius Troucillus,* see Troucillus. i. 19.

(7) *Valerius Flaccus,* an officer in Pompey's army. C. iii. 53.

Valetiācus, -ī, m., (val′ ẹ-shĭ-ā′ kụs), vergobret of the Aeduans in 53 B.C. vii. 32.

valētūdō, -inis, [cf. valeō], f., *health.* v. 40; vii. 78. [valetudinarian.

vallēs or **vallis, -is,** f., *valley.* [valley.

vāllum, -ī, [vāllus], n., *rampart* set with palisades, *wall, intrenchment.* [wall.

vāllus, -ī, m., *stake, pole; rampart stake, palisade;* rampart stakes in position, *stockade, palisade;* sharpened *point* (vii. 73).

Vangionēs, -um, m., pl., (vạn-jī′ ọ-nēz), a German tribe. i. 51.

varietās, -ātis, [varius], f., *variety, diversity* (vii. 23); *mottled appearance* (vi. 27). [variety.

varius, -a, -um, adj., *different, diverse.* [various.

Vārus, -ī, a Roman name: see **Attius**

vāstō, -āre, -āvī, -ātus, [vāstus], 1, *lay waste, devastate.*

vastus, -a, -um, comp. -ior, sup. -issimus, adj., *vast, immense.* [vast.

vāticinātiō, -ōnis, [vāticinor, *predict*], f., *prophecy.* i. 50. [vaticination.

Vatīnius, -ī, m., *Publius Vatinius* (vạtin′ ị-ụs), a partizan of Caesar. C. III. 90.

-ve, enclitic conj., *or.*

vectīgal, -ālis, [cf. vehō], n., *tax, tribute* (v. 22); *revenue* (i. 18, 36).

vectīgālis, -e, [vectīgal], adj., *paying tribute, tributary.* iii. 8; iv. 3.

vectōrius, -a, -um, [vector, cf. vehō], adj., *for carrying.* vectōrium nāvigium, *transport ship* (v. 8). [vectorial.

vehementer, comp. vehementius, sup. -issimē, [vehemēns, *eager, violent*], adv., *vigorously, violently; exceedingly, greatly.*

vehō, -ere, vexī, vectus, 3, *carry.* equō vectus, *riding on horseback* (C. II. 44). [vehicle.

vel, [volō], conj., *or.* vel . . . vel, *either . . . or.* As adv., *even* (vii. 37).

Velānius, -ī, m., *Quintus Velanius* (vẹ-lā′ nị-us), an officer under Crassus. iii. 7, 8.

Veliocassēs, -ium, and **Veliocassī,** -ōrum, m., pl., (vel″ ị-ọ-kas′ ēz, vel″ ị-ọ-kas′ ī), a small state north of the Sequana (*Seine*).

Vellaunodūnum, -ī, n., (vel″ â-nọdū′ nụm), a town of the Senones. vii. 11, 14.

Vellaviī, -ōrum, m., pl., (vẹ-lā′ vị-ī), a small state in the Cebenna (*Cévennes*) Mountains. vii. 75.

vēlōcitās, -ātis, [vēlōx], f., *swiftness, speed.* vi. 28. [velocity.

vēlōciter, comp. vēlōcius, sup. vēlōcissimē, [vēlōx], adv., *swiftly, quickly.* v. 35.

vēlōx, -ōcis, comp. -ior, sup. -issimus, adj., *swift, fast.* i. 48. [velox.

vēlum, -ī, n., *sail.* iii. 13, 14.

velut [vel + ut], adv., *just as.* velut sī, *just as if* (i. 32).

vēnātiō, -ōnis, [cf. vēnor, *hunt*], f., *hunting, hunting expedition.*

vēnātor, -ōris, [vēnor, *hunt*], m., *hunter.* vi. 27.

vēndō, -dere, -didī, -ditus, [vēnum, *sale,* + dō], 3, *sell.* [vend.

Venellī, -ōrum, m., pl., (vẹ-nel′ ī), a Gallic people, on the northwest coast (Fig. 210).

Figure 210. — A Venellan coin.

Gold. Reverse, two-horse chariot; the charioteer holds aloft the model of a ship. In front of the horses is a head of wheat, on a sinuous stalk.

The head on the obverse wears a laurel wreath.

Venetī, -ōrum, m., pl., *Venetans, Veneti* (ven′ ẹ-tī), a sea-faring Gallic people, on the west coast.

Venetia, -ae, f., (vẹ-nē′ sh[y]ạ), *the country of the Venetans.* iii. 9.

Veneticus, -a, -um, [Venetia], adj., *of the Venetans, Venetan.* Veneticum bellum, *the war with the Venetans* (iii. 18; iv. 21).

venia, -ae, f., *pardon, forgiveness* (vi. 4); *permission* (vii. 15). [venial.

veniō, venīre, vēnī, ventum est, 4, *come.*

ventitō, -āre, -āvī, [freq. of veniō], 1, *come often, go often, keep coming.*

ventus, -ī, m., *wind.* [ventilate.

vĕr, vēris, n., *spring.* prīmō vēre,

at the commencement of spring (vi. 3). [vernal.

Veragrī, -ōrum, m., pl., (ver′ ạ-grī), an Alpine tribe.

Verbigenus, -ī, m., *Verbigen, Verbigenus* (vẹr-bij′ ẹ-nụs), a canton of the Helvetians. i. 27.

verbum, -ī, n., *word.* verba facere, *to speak* (ii. 14). [verb.

Vercassivellaunus, -ī, m., (vẹr-kas′′-ị-vẹ-lâ′ nụs), one of the four generals in command of the Gallic army raised for the relief of Alesia.

Vercingetorīx, -ĭgis, m., (vẹr-sịn-jet′ ọ-riks), an Arvernian, commander-in-chief of the Gallic forces in 52 B.C.

vereor, -ērī, -ĭtus, 2, dep., *fear, be afraid ; be afraid of, dread.*

vergō, -ere, 3, *lie, slope ; be situated.* [verge.

vergobretus, -ī, m., [Celtic word, ' He that renders judgment '; as a title, ' Dispenser of Justice '], *vergobret,* title of the chief magistrate of the Aeduans. i. 16.

veritus, see vereor.

vērō [abl. neuter of vērus], adv., *in truth, in fact, truly, certainly ; but, but in fact, however.*

versō, -āre, -āvī, -ātus, [freq. of vertō], 1, *turn often ; shift, change the position of* (v. 44). Pass. **versor**, -ārī, -ātus, as dep., lit., *turn one's self about, move about* in any place; *dwell, live, be ; be occupied, be engaged, be busy.* in bellō versārī, *to engage in war* (vi. 15). [versatile.

versus, -ūs, [vertō], m., *line, verse* (vi. 14). [verse.

versus, [part. of vertō], prep. and adv. :

(1) As prep., with acc. only, sometimes following a word governed by ad or in, *towards, in the direction*

of. ad . . . versus, in . . . versus, *towards.*

(2) As adv., *turned, facing.* quōque versus, *in all directions* (iii. 23; vii. 4, 14).

Verticō, -ōnis, m., (vẹr′ tị-kō), a Nervian of rank. v. 45, 49.

vertō, vertere, vertī, versus, 3, *turn, turn about ; change.* terga vertere, *to turn and flee, to flee.*

Verucloetius, -ī, m., (ver-ụ-klē′-sh[y]ụs), a Helvetian who went as envoy to Caesar. i. 7.

vērus, -a, -um, comp. -ior, sup. vērissimus, adj., *true* (i. 18, 20); *right, proper, fitting* (iv. 8). As noun, vērum, -ī, n., *the truth.* vērī similis, *probable* (iii. 13).

verūtum, -ī, [verū, *spit* for roasting meat], n., *dart.* v. 44.

Vesontiō, -ōnis, m., (vẹ-son′ sh[y]ō), chief city of the Sequanians, on the Dubis (*Doubs*) river; now *Besançon.* i. 38, 39.

vesper, -erī, m., *evening.* [vespers.

vester, -tra, -trum, [vōs], possessive pronominal adj., *your, yours.*

vēstīgium, -ī, n., *footprint, track* (vi. 27); *spot, place* (iv. 2); of time, *moment, instant.* [vestige.

vestiō, -īre, -īvī, -ītus, [vestis], 4, *clothe* (v. 14); vii. 31); *cover* (vii. 23). [vestment.

vestis, -is, f, *clothing.* vii. 47. [vest.

vestītus, -ūs, [cf. vestiō], m., *clothing, garb.* iv. 1; vii. 88.

veterānus, -a, -um, [vetus], adj., *old, veteran.* i. 24. [veteran.

vetō, -āre, -uī, -ĭtus, 1, *forbid* (ii. 20); *not allow* (vii. 33). [veto.

vetus, -eris, sup. veterrimus, adj., *old, former ; ancient, long-standing.*

vetustās, -ātis, [vetustus, vetus], f., *antiquity, ancient times.* C. 1. 6.

vēxillum, -ī, [cf. vēlum], n., *banner, flag.*

vexō, -āre, -āvī, -ātus, [freq. of vehō], 1, *harass, assail* (i. 14; vi. 43); *lay waste, overrun* (ii. 4; iv. 15). [vex.

via, -ae, f., *way, road; journey, march.* bīduī via, *a two days' march* (vi. 7). [via.

viātor, -ōris, [cf. via], m., *traveller, wayfarer.* iv. 5.

vīcēnī, -ae, -a, [vīgintī], distrib. num. adj., *twenty each, twenty.*

vīcēsimus, -a, -um, [vīgintī], num. adj., *twentieth.* vi. 21.

vīciēs [vīgintī], num. adv., *twenty times.* vīciēs centum mīlia passuum, *two thousand miles* (v. 13).

vīcīnitās, -ātis, [vīcīnus, *near*], f., *neighborhood; neighbors* (vi. 34). [vicinity.

vicis, -is, f., nom., dat. and voc. sing. and gen. and voc. pl. not in use, *change, succession.* in vicem, *in turn* (iv. 1, C. III. 98). [vicar.

victima, -ae, f., *victim.* vi. 16. [victim.

victor, -ōris, [vincō], m., *conqueror, victor.* As adj., *victorious* (i. 31; vii. 20, 62). [victor.

victōria, -ae, [victor], f., *victory.* [victory.

victus, see vincō.

vīctus, -ūs, [vīvō], m., *living* (i. 31); *mode of life* (vi. 24); *food, provisions* (vi. 22, 23). [victuals.

vīcus, -ī, m., *village, hamlet.*

videō, vidēre, vīdī, vīsus, 2, *see, perceive, observe; understand.* Pass., generally as dep., videor, vidērī, vīsus sum, *be seen, seem, appear; seem proper, seem good, seem best.* [vision.

Vienna, -ae, f., (vi̯-en′a̯), a city of the Allobroges; now *Vienne.* vii. 9.

vigilia, -ae, [vigil, *watchman*], f., *watching, sleeplessness* (v. 31, 32); *watch*, a division of the night; *sentry duty* (C. III. 49). [vigil.

vīgintī, or XX, indeclinable num. adj., *twenty.*

vīmen, -inis, n., *pliant shoot, twig, withe.* ii. 33; vii. 73. [Viminal.

vinciō, vincīre, vinxī, vinctus, 4, *bind.* i. 53.

vincō, vincere, vīcī, victus, 3, *conquer, overcome, defeat, subdue; exceed, surpass* (vi. 43); *carry one's point, have one's own way* (v. 30). victī, -ōrum, part., used as noun, m., pl., *the conquered.* [vincible.

vinculum, -ī, [vinciō], n., *chain, bond, fetters.* [vinculum.

vindicō, -āre, -āvī, -ātus, [cf. vindex], 1, *claim, demand* (vii. 76); *restore* to liberty (vii. 1); *inflict punishment* (iii. 16). [vindicate.

vīnea, -ae, f., *arbor-shed, sappers' hut.*

vīnum, -ī, n., *wine.* [wine.

violō, -āre, -āvī, -ātus, ['v̄s], 1, *do violence to, maltreat* (vi. 23); *invade, lay waste* (vi. 32). [violate.

vir, virī, m., *man; husband* (vi. 19). [virile.

vīrēs, see vīs.

virgō, -inis, f., *maiden.* [virgin.

virgultum, -ī, [virga, *a shoot*], n., *small brush; fascine.* iii. 18; vii. 73.

Viridomārus, -ī, m., (vir′′i̯-do̯-mā′-rу̯s), a prominent Aeduan.

Viridovīx, -icis, m, (vi̯-rid′-o̯-viks), a leader of the Venelli. iii. 17-18.

virītim, [vir], adv., *man by man, to each individually.* vii. 71.

Viromanduī, -ōrum, m., pl., (vir-o̯-man′du̯-ī), a Belgic people about the headwaters of the Samara (*Somme*) and the Scaldis (*Schelde*). Fig. 211.

virtūs, -ūtis, [vir], f., *manliness; courage, bravery, prowess; vigor, energy, initiative* (vii. 6, 59); *efficiency, effort* (v. 8; vii. 22); *worth* (i. 47). Pl., *remarkable qualities, virtues* (i. 44). [virtue.

vīs, acc. **vim**, abl. **vī**, pl. **vīrēs**, **-ium**, f., *strength* (vi. 28); *force, violence; influence, control* (vi. 14, 17); *number* (vi. 36). Pl., *physical powers, strength.* [vim.

Figure 211.—A Viromanduan coin.
Bronze; crude fanciful designs.

vīsus, see **videō**.

vīta, **-ae**, [cf. **vīvō**], f., *life.* [vital.

vitium, **-ī**, n., *defect, failing, fault.* C. II. 4, III. 72. [vice.

vītō, **-āre**, **-āvī**, **-ātus**, 1, *shun, avoid, try to escape.*

vitrum, **-ī**, n., *woad,* a plant used for dyeing blue. v. 14.

vīvō, **vīvere**, **vīxī**, **vīctūrus**, 3, *live;* with abl., *sustain life, live on* (iv. 1, 10; v. 14). [vivacious.

vīvus, **-a**, **-um**, [cf. **vīvō**], adj., *living, alive.* As noun, **vīvī**, **-ōrum**, m., pl., *the living* (vi. 19). [vivi-section.

vix, adv., *scarcely, barely; with difficulty, hardly* (i. 6; vi. 37; vii. 46).

Vocātēs, **-ium**, m., pl., (vǫ-kā′ tēz), a people in Aquitania. iii. 23, 27.

Vocciō, **-ōnis**, m., (vok′ sh[y]ō), a king of the Norici. i. 53.

vocō, **-āre**, **-āvī**, **-ātus**, [cf. **vōx**], 1, *call, summon; call for, demand; name, call* (v. 21). [vocative.

Vocontiī, **-ōrum**, m., pl., (vǫ-kon′-sh[y]ī), a Gallic people in the Province. i. 10.

Volcācius, **-ī**, m., *Gaius Volcacius Tullus* (vol-kā′ sh[y]ụs tul′ ụs), an officer in Caesar's army.

Volcae, **-ārum**, m., pl., (vol′ sē), a Gallic people in the Province having two branches, **Arecomicī** and **Tectosagēs**.

volō, **velle**, **voluī**, irr., *be willing, wish, desire; mean, intend, purpose.*

voluntārius, **-a**, **-um**, [**volō**], adj., *willing; serving as a volunteer* (C. III. 91). As noun, **voluntārius**, **-ī**, m., *volunteer* (v. 56). [voluntary.

voluntās, **-ātis**, [**volō**], f., *will, wish, inclination, desire; good-will, loyalty* (i. 19; v. 4; vii. 10); *consent, approval* (i. 7, 20, 30, 39).

voluptās, **-ātis**, [**volō**], f., *pleasure, indulgence, enjoyment; amusement* (v. 12). [voluptuous.

Volusēnus, **-ī**, m., *Gaius Volusenus Quadratus* (vol-ụ̄-sē′ nụs kwạ-drā′-tus), a military tribune.

Vorēnus, **-ī**, m., *Lucius Vorenus* (vǫ-rē′ nụs), a centurion. v. 44.

Vosegus, **-ī**, m., (vos′ ẹ-gụs), a range of mountains in eastern Gaul, now *Vosges* (vōzh).

vōtum, **-ī**, [**voveō**], n., *vow.* C. I. 6. [vote.

voveō, **vovēre**, **vōvī**, **vōtus**, 2, *vow.* vi. 16. [vow.

vōx, **vōcis**, f., *voice* (ii. 13; v. 30; IV. 25); *utterance* (VII. 17); *word, reply* (I. 32). Pl. **vōcēs**, *words, sayings, language, speeches, statements.* [voice.

Vulcānus, **-ī**, m., *Vulcan,* son of Jupiter and Juno, god of fire and of work in metals. vi. 21. [volcano.

vulgō [**vulgus**], adv., *generally, commonly, everywhere.* i. 39; ii. 1; v. 33.

vulgus, **-ī**, n., *common people; multitude, crowd;* of soldiers, *rank and file* (I. 46). [vulgar.

vulnerō, **-āre**, **-āvī**, **-ātus**, [**vulnus**], 1, *wound, hurt.* [vulnerable.

vulnus, **-eris**, n., *wound.*

vultus, **-ūs**, m., *countenance, features, expression of face.* i. 39.

ENGLISH–LATIN VOCABULARY [1]

Regular verbs of the first conjugation are indicated by the figure 1.

abandon, relinquō, -ere, -līquī, -līctus.
ability, virtūs, -tūtis, *f.*
  natural ability, ingenium, -iī, *n.*
  have ability, possum, posse, potuī.
able, be able, possum, posse, potuī.
about, concerning, dē, *prep. with abl.*
  about, around, circum, *prep. with acc.*
  about (*with numerals*), circiter.
accept, accipiō, -ere, -cēpī, -ceptus.
accident, cāsus, -ūs, *m.*
accomplish, perficiō, -ere, -fēcī, -fectus; cōnsequor, -ī, -secūtus.
account, on account of, propter, *prep. with acc.*
accuse, accūsō, 1.
accustomed, be accustomed, soleō, -ēre, solitus.
across, trāns, *prep. with acc.*
act (*noun*), factum, -ī, *n.*
act (*verb*), faciō, -ere, fēcī, factus.
actively, ācriter.
admit, cōnfiteor, -ērī, -fessus.
adopt, *of a plan,* ūtor.
advance, prōgredior, -gredī, -gressus.
advantage, bonum, -ī, *n.;* commodum, -ī, *n.*
advise, moneō, -ēre, -uī, -itus.
affair, rēs, reī, *f.*
  public affairs, rēs pūblica.
afraid, be afraid, timeō, -ēre, -uī.
after, post, *prep. with acc.;* postquam, *conj.*
afterward, post, posteā.
again, iterum.
against, in, ad, contrā, *prepositions with acc.*
ago, ante.

agriculture, agrī cultūra, -ae, *f.*
aid (*noun*), auxilium, -iī, *n.*
aid (*verb*), adiuvō, -āre, -iūvī, -iūtus, *with acc.*
alarm, permoveō, -ēre, -mōvī, -mōtus.
all, omnis, -e; tōtus, -a, -um.
allow, patior, patī, passus.
ally, socius, -iī, *m.*
almost, ferē, paene.
alone, sōlus, -a, -um.
already, iam.
also, quoque (*postpositive*).
  not only . . . but also, nōn modo . . . sed etiam.
although, cum, quamquam.
always, semper.
ambassador, lēgātus, -ī, *m.*
ambuscade, īnsidiae, -ārum, *f., pl.*
among, apud, *prep. with acc.*
ancestors, maiōrēs, -um, *m.*
anchor, ancora, -ae, *f.*
  at anchor, ad ancoram.
and, et, atque, -que.
and . . . not, neque.
  and so, itaque.
announce, nūntiō, 1.
another, alius, -a, -ud.
answer, respondeō, -ēre, -dī, respōnsus.
any, any one, anything, aliquis, aliqua, aliquid (quod); *after* sī, nisi *or* nē, quis, qua, quid (quod); *with negatives,* quisquam quidquam (*pron.*); ūllus, -a, -um (*adj.*).
appeal to, implōrō, 1.
approach, appropinquō, 1.
approve, probō, 1.

[1] Reproduced, with the consent of the authors, from *Latin Composition,* by Bernard M. Allen and John L. Phillips.

arise, coörior, -īrī, -ortus.
arm, armō, 1.
arms, arma, -ōrum, n.
army, exercitus, -ūs, m.
arouse, incitō, 1.
arrival, adventus, -ūs, m.
arrive, perveniō, -īre, -vēnī, -ventum est.
as, just as, ut, sīcut, with indic.
  as if, quasi, velut sī.
  as soon as, simul atque.
ask, request, rogō, 1.
  ask, seek, petō, -ere, -īvī or -ĭī, -ītus.
  ask, inquire, quaerō, -ere, -sīvī or -sĭī, -sītus.
assistance, auxilium, -ĭī, n.
at, in with abl.; ad with acc.; sign of locative case.
Atrebatian, Atrebās, -ātis, m.
attack (noun), impetus, -ūs, m.
attack (verb), oppugnō, 1; adgredior, -ī, -gressus; lacessō, -ere, -īvī or -ĭī, -ītus.
  make an attack on, impetum faciō in with acc.
attempt (noun), cōnātus, -ūs, m.
attempt (verb), cōnor, 1.
authority, auctōritās, -tātis, f.
avenge, ulcīscor, -ī, ultus.
avoid, vītō, 1.
await, exspectō, 1.
away, be away, absum, abesse, āfuī, āfutūrus.

baggage, impedīmenta, -ōrum, n., pl.
band (of men), manus, -ūs, f.
barbarian, barbarus, -ī, m.
battle, pugna, -ae, f.; proelium, -ĭī, n.
be, sum, esse, fuī, futūrus.
  be at hand, adsum, adesse, affuī.
bear, ferō, ferre, tulī, lātus.
because, quod.
  because of, propter, prep. with acc.
befall, accidit, -ere, accidit.
before (adv.), ante, anteā.
before (conj.), prius quam, ante quam.
before (prep.), ante, with acc.
before (adj.), prior, superior.
  on the day before, prīdiē.
beg, ōrō, 1; petō, -ere, -īvī or -ĭī, -ītus.
began, coepī, coepisse, coeptus. Use the pass. when the inf. is pass.

begin, incipiō, -e.e (see began).
behalf, in behalf of, prō, prep. with abl.
behind, post, prep. with acc.
  behind him, them, etc., post tergum.
Belgians, Belgae, -ārum, m., pl.
believe, crēdō, -ere, crēdidī, crēditus; putō, 1.
belittle, minuō, -ere, -uī, -ūtus.
betray, prōdō, -ere, -didī, -ditus.
between, inter, prep. with acc.
bitterly, ācriter.
board, go on board, nāvem (nāvēs) ascendō, -ere, -scendī, -scēnsus.
body, corpus, -oris, n.
both, each, uterque, utraque, utrumque.
  both . . . and, et . . . et.
boundaries, fīnēs, -ium, m.
brave, fortis, -e.
bravely, fortiter.
break down, perfringō, -ere, -frēgī, -frāctus.
bridge, pōns, pontis, m.
bring, ferō, ferre, tulī, lātus; dūcō, -ere, dūxī, -ductus.
  bring about, cōnficiō, -ere, -fēcī, -fectus.
bring on, upon, īnferō.
bring to, afferō, afferre, attulī, allātus; addūcō, -ere, -dūxī, -ductus.
  bring together, comportō, 1.
Britain, Britannia, -ae, f.
Britons, Britannī, -ōrum, m., pl.
brother, frāter, -tris, m.
build,
  (of a bridge), faciō, -ere, fēcī, -factus.
  (of a road), mūniō, -īre, -īvī, or -ĭī, -ītus.
  (of a rampart), perdūcō, -dūcere, -dūxī, -ductus.
building, aedificium, -ĭī, n.
burn, set fire to, incendō, -ere, -cendī, -cēnsus.
burning, incendium, -ĭī, n.
but, sed.
buy, emō, -ere, ēmī, ēmptus.
by, abl. case; ab, with abl. of agent.

call (by name), appellō, 1.
camp, castra, -ōrum, n., pl.
can, possum, posse, potuī.

capture, capiō, -ere, cēpī, captus.
(*by storming*), expugnō, 1.
care, cūra, -ae, *f.*
carefully, dīligenter.
carriage with four wheels, wagon, raeda, *f.*
carry, ferō, ferre, tulī, lātus.
  carry back, referō, referre, rettulī, relātus.
  carry on, gerō, -ere, gessī, gestus.
  carry out, accomplish, perficiō, -ere, -fēcī, -fectus.
case, causa, -ae, *f.*
  in the case of, in, *prep. with abl.*
cast off, cast out, abiciō, -ere, -iēcī, -iectus; ēiciō.
cause (*noun*), causa, -ae, *f.*
cause (*verb*), efficiō, -ere, -fēcī, -fectus; faciō, -ere, fēcī, factus.
cavalry (*adj.*), equester, -tris, -tre.
cavalry (*noun*), equitātus, -ūs, *m.*; equitēs, -um, *m., pl.*
Celts, Celtae, -ārum, *m., pl.*
centurion, centuriō, -ōnis, *m.*
certain (*indef. pron.*), quīdam, quaedam, quiddam.
certainly, certē.
chain, vinculum, -ī, *n.*
chance, occāsiō, -ōnis, *f.*
  by chance, forte.
charge,
  be in charge, praesum, -esse, -fuī.
  put in charge, praeficiō, -ere, -fēcī, -fectus.
chariot, currus, -ūs, *m.*
chief, chief man, prīnceps, -cipis, *m.*
children, puerī, -ōrum, *m., pl.*
  (*free born*), līberī, -ōrum, *m., pl.*
choose, legō, -ere, lēgī, lēctus; deligō, -ere, -lēgī, -lēctus.
citizen, cīvis, -is, *m.*
city, urbs, urbis, *f.*
clear, make clear, dēclārō, 1.
  it is clear, cōnstat.
client, cliēns, -entis, *m.*
close, be close at hand, subsum, -esse.
cohort, cohors, cohortis, *f.*
come, veniō, -īre, vēnī, ventum est.
  come back, redeō, -īre, -iī, -itum est.
  come together, conveniō, -īre, -vēnī, -ventum est.

come to pass, fīō, fierī, factum est.
come up, arise, coörior, -īrī, -ortus.
comfort, cōnsōlor, 1.
command, iubeō, -ēre, iussī, iussus; imperō, 1.
  be in command, praesum, -esse, -fuī, *with dat.*
commander, imperātor, -ōris, *m.*
commence battle, proelium committō, -ere, -mīsī, -missus.
commit, do, faciō, -ere, fēcī, factus.
common, commūnis, -e.
  common people, plēbs, plēbis, *f.*
companion, socius, -iī, *m.*
compare, comparō, 1.
compel, cōgō, -ere, coēgī, coāctus.
complain, queror, -ī, questus.
concern, it concerns, interest, -esse, -fuit.
concerning, dē, *prep. with abl.*
confer, colloquor, -ī, -locūtus.
conference, colloquium, -iī, *n.*
confess, cōnfiteor, -ērī, -fessus.
confidence, fidēs, -eī, *f.*
  have confidence in, cōnfīdō, -ere, -fīsus.
conquer, vincō, -ere, vīcī, victus; superō, 1.
consider, believe, putō, 1; exīstimō, 1.
  consider, regard, habeō, -ēre, habuī, habitus.
conspiracy, coniūrātiō, -ōnis, *f.*
conspire, coniūrō, 1.
consul, cōnsul, -is, *m.*
consulship, cōnsulātus, -ūs, *m.*
  in the consulship of, *abl. absol. with* cōnsul.
consult, cōnsulō, -ere, -uī, -sultus.
contention, contentiō, -ōnis, *f.*
continent, continēns, -entis, *f.*
contrary to, contrā, *prep. with acc.*
convict, damnō, 1.
council, concilium, -iī, *n.*
council of war, cōncilium, -iī, *n.*
counsel, advice, cōnsilium, -iī, *n.*
  take counsel, cōnsulō, -ere, -uī, -sultus.
courage, virtūs, -ūtis, *f.*
  have courage, audeō, -ēre, ausus.
courageously, fortiter.
course, cursus, -ūs, *m.*

court of law, jūdicium, -iī, *n.*

covet, adamō, 1.

crime, facinus, -oris, *n.*; scelus, -eris, *n.*

cross, trānseō, -īre, -iī, -itum est.

crowd, multitūdō, -inis, *f.*

crush, frangō, -ere, frēgī, frāctus.

custom, mōs, mōris, *m.*; cōnsuētūdō, -dinis, *f.*

cut down (*of grain*), succīdō, -ere, -cīdī, -cisus; (*of a bridge*), rescindō, -ere, -scidī, -scissus.

cut off, interclūdō, -ere, -clūsī, -clūsus.

daily, cotīdiānus, -a, -um.

damage, afflīgō, -ere, -flīxī, -flīctus.

danger, perīculum, -ī, *n.*

dangerous, perīculōsus, -a, -um.

dare, audeō, -ēre, ausus.

daughter, fīlia, -ae, *f.*

day (*noun*), diēs, -ēī, *m.*

on the next day, postrīdiē.

on the day before, prīdiē.

day (*adj.*), diurnus, -a, -um.

death, mors, mortis, *f.*

decide, cōnstituō, -ere, -uī, -ūtus.

decision, iūdicium, -iī, *n.*

declare, dēclārō, 1; cōnfirmō, 1.

decree, dēcernō, -ere, -crēvī, -crētus.

deed, factum, -ī, *n.*

deep, altus, -a, -um.

defeat, superō, 1.

defend, dēfendō, -ere, -fendī, -fēnsus.

delay, wait, moror, 1.

deliver (*of a speech*), habeō, -ēre, -uī, -itus.

demand (*noun*), postulātum, -ī, *n.*

demand (*verb*), imperō, 1, *with dat. of person from whom;* postulō, 1, *with* ab *and abl.*

deny, negō, 1.

depart, discēdō, -ere, -cessī, -cessum est.

descendants, posterī, -ōrum, *m.*

deserve, mereor, -ērī, meritus.

design (*noun*), cōnsilium, -iī, *n.*

desire, cupiō, -ere, -īvī *or* -iī, -ītus.

desirous, cupidus, -a, -um.

despoil, spoliō, 1.

destroy, dēleō, -ēre, -ēvī, -ētus.

detain, teneō, -ēre, -uī; dētineō, -ēre, -uī, -tentus.

determine, cōnstituō, -ere, -uī, -ūtus.

devise, cōgitō, 1.

devote, dō, dare, dedī, datus; dēdō, -ere, dēdidī, dēditus.

devoted, dēditus, -a, -um.

devotion, studium, -iī, *n.*

die, morior, morī, mortuus.

die, be put to death, *pass. of* interficiō, -ere, -fēcī, -fectus.

die, perish, pereō, -īre, -iī, -itūrus.

differ, differō, -ferre, distulī, dīlātus.

difference, there is a difference, interest, -esse, -fuit.

difficult, difficilis, -e.

difficulty, difficultās, -tātis, *f.*

diminish, dēminuō, -ere, -uī, -ūtus.

direction, pars, partis, *f.*

in that direction, in eam partem.

disaster, calamitās, -tātis, *f.*

discover, reperiō, -īre, repperī, repertus.

disembark (*trans.*), ex nāvī (nāvibus) expōnō, -ere, -posuī, -positus; (*intrans.*), ex nāvī (nāvibus) ēgredior, -ī, -gressus.

disgraceful, turpis, -e.

dislodge, summoveō, -ēre, -mōvī, -mōtus.

dismiss, dīmittō, -ere, -mīsī, -missus.

dismount, ex equō (equīs) dēsiliō, -īre, -uī, -sultus.

disorder, tumultus, -ūs, *m.*

disregard, neglegō, -ere, -lēxī, -lēctus.

distance, at a distance, procul, in locīs longinquīs.

disturb, commoveō, -ēre, -mōvī, -mōtus; perturbō, 1.

divide, dīvidō, -ere, -vīsī, -vīsus.

do, faciō, -ere, fēcī, factus.

be done, happen, fīō, fierī, factum est.

be done, go on, *pass. of* gerō, -ere, gessī, gestus.

do not (*in prohibitions*), nōlī, nōlīte, *with inf.*

doubt, dubitō, 1.

there is no doubt, nōn est dubium.

doubtful, dubius, -a, -um.

draw up (*of soldiers*), īnstruō, -ere, -strūxī, -strūctus; (*of ships*), subdūcō, -ere, -dūxī, -ductus.

drive, pellō, -ere, pepulī, pulsus.

drive back, repellō, -ere, repulī, repulsus.

dry, āridus, -a, -um.
  dry land, āridum, -ī, *n.*
Dumnorix, Dumnorīx, -rīgis, *m.*
dust, pulvis, -veris, *m.*
duty, officium, -iī, *n.*
  do one's duty, officium praestō, -āre, -stitī, -stitus.

each (*of any number*), quisque, quaeque, quidque *and* quodque.
eager, cupidus, -a, -um.
eagle, aquila, -ae, *f.*
  eagle-bearer, aquilifer, -erī, *m.*
easily, facile.
easy, facilis, -e.
effort, labor, -ōris, *m.*
eight, octō.
either . . . or, aut . . . aut.
elect, faciō, -ere, fēcī, factus ; creō, 1.
else (*adj.*), reliquus, -a, -um.
  nothing else, nihil aliud.
eminent, clārus, -a, -um.
empty (*of a river*), īnfluō, īnfluere, -flūxī.
encounter, occurrō, -ere, -currī, -cursūrus, *with dat.;* subeō, -īre, -iī, -itus, *with acc.*
encourage, hortor, 1.
end, fīnis, -is, *m.*
  each end, utraque pars, utrīusque partis, *f.*
endure, ferō, ferre, tulī, lātus.
enemy (*in war*), hostis, -is, *m.*, hostēs, -ium, *pl.;* (*personal*), inimīcus, -ī, *m.*
enjoy, fruor, -ī, frūctus.
enlist, enroll, cōnscrībō, -ere, -scrīpsī, -scrīptus.
enough (*adv. and indecl. noun*), satis.
entreat, ōrō, 1.
envoy, lēgātus, -ī, *m.*
equal, pār, paris ; īdem, eadem, idem.
equinox, aequinoctiī diēs.
escape, effugiō, -ere, -fūgī.
establish, cōnstituō, -ere, -uī, -ūtus.
  become established, inveterāscō, -ere, -rāvī.
even, etiam.
  not even, nē . . . quidem.
  even if, etsī, etiam sī.
ever, umquam.

every, all, omnis, -e.
  every, each, quisque, quaeque, quidque *and* quodque.
  everybody, omnēs, -ium, *m., pl.*
  everything, omnia, omnēs rēs.
  every part of, tōtus, -a, -um ; omnis, -e.
  every sort of, omnis, -e.
  in every way, omnī modō.
evidence, indicium, -iī, *n.*
evident, it is evident, cōnstat.
except, praeter, *prep. with acc.;* nisi (*conj.*).
exchange, inter sē dō, dare, dedī, datus.
excuse, pūrgō, 1.
exercise, exercitātiō, -ōnis, *f.*
exist, sum, esse, fuī, futūrus.
  exposed, apertus, -a, -um.
extend, pertineō, -ēre, -uī.

face to face, adversus, -a, -um.
fact, rēs, reī, *f.*
fall, cadō, -ere, cecidī, cāsūrus.
  fall on, fall in with, incidō, -ere, -cidī, -cāsūrus.
  fall upon, overwhelm, opprimō, -ere, -pressī, -pressus.
far, longē.
  far and near, longē latēque.
farther, ulterior, -ius.
father, pater, -tris, *m.*
favorable, secundus, -a, -um.
fear (*noun*), timor, -ōris, *m.;* metus, -ūs, *m.*
fear (*verb*), timeō, -ēre, timuī.
feel, sentiō, -īre, sēnsī, sēnsus.
feeling, sēnsus, -ūs, *m.*
  feelings, animus, -ī, *m.*
fellow soldier, commīlitō, -ōnis, *m.*
few, paucī, -ae, -a.
  not a few, complūrēs, -ia *or* -a.
fickleness, levitās, -ātis, *f.*
field, ager, agrī, *m.*
fiercely, ācriter.
fifteen, quīndecim, XV.
fight (*noun*), pugna, -ae, *f.;* proelium, -iī, *n.*
fight (*verb*), pugnō, 1 ; contendō, -ere, -tendī, -tentus ; congredior, -ī, -gressus.
fill, compleō, -ēre, -ēvī, -ētus.

finally, dēnique, postrēmō.

find, inveniō, -īre, -vēnī, -ventus; nancīscor, -ī, nactus *or* nanctus.

find out, reperiō, -īre, repperī, repertus.

finish, end, cōnficiō, -ere, -fēcī, -fectus.

finish, make perfect, perficiō, -ere, -fēcī, -fectus.

fire, set fire to, incendō, -ere, -cendī, -cēnsus.

first, prīmus, -a, -um.

at first, prīmō.

in the first place, prīmum.

fit, idōneus, -a, -um.

five, quīnque, V.

flank, latus, -eris, *n.*

flee, fugiō, -ere, fūgī.

flight, fuga, -ae, *f.*

put to flight, in fugam dō, dare, dedī, datus.

foe, *see* **enemy.**

follow, sequor, -ī, secūtus; īnsequor.

foot, pēs, pedis, *m.*

on foot, pedibus.

for (*conj.*), nam, enim (*postpositive*).

for, in behalf of, prō, *prep. with abl.*

for, toward, in, *prep. with acc.; often expressed by dat. case.*

force, vīs, *f.*

forces, cōpiae, -ārum, *f., pl.*

forest, silva, -ae, *f.*

forget, oblīvīscor, -ī, oblītus.

form, make, faciō, -ere, fēcī, factus; (*of plans*), capiō, -ere, cēpī, captus.

former, early, prīstinus, -a, -um.

fortify, mūniō, -īre, -īvī *or* -iī, -ītus.

fortune, good fortune, fortūna, -ae, *f.*

four, quattuor, IIII.

free, līber, -era, -erum.

free, unencumbered, expedītus, -a, -um.

free, set free, līberō, I.

freedom, lībertās, -ātis, *f.*

friend, amīcus, -ī, *m.*

friendship, amīcitia, -ae, *f.*

frighten, terreō, -ēre, -uī, -itus.

from, *sign of abl. case;* ā *or* ab, ē *or* ex, dē, *prepositions with abl.*

front, frōns, frontis, *f.*

in front of, prō, *prep. with abl.;* ante, *prep. with acc.*

full, plēnus, -a, -um.

gain, cōnsequor, -ī, -secūtus.

gain possession of, potior, -īrī, -ītus, *with abl.*

gather, bring together, cōgō, -ere, coēgī, coāctus.

Gaul, Gallia, -ae, *f.*

Gauls, Gallī, -ōrum, *m., pl.*

general, dux, ducis, *m.*; imperātor, -ōris, *m.*

Germans, Germānī, -ōrum, *m., pl.*

get to, arrive, perveniō, -īre, -vēnī, -ventum est.

get possession of, potior, -īrī, -ītus, *with abl.*

give, dō, dare, dedī, datus.

give up, *see* **surrender.**

give opportunity, potestātem faciō, -ere, fēcī, factus.

glad, be glad, gaudeō, -ēre, gavīsus.

glory, glōria, -ae, *f.*

go, eō, īre, īvī, *or* iī, itum est.

go back, redeō, -īre, -iī, -itum est.

go out, exeō, -īre, -iī, -itum est.

go on, be done, *pass. of* gerō, -ere, gessī, gestus.

god, deus, deī, *m.*

good, bonus, -a, -um.

grain (*threshed*), frūmentum, -ī, *n.*; (*growing or unthreshed*), frūmenta, -ōrum, *n., pl.*

grain supply, rēs frūmentāria, reī frūmentāriae, *f.*

gratitude, grātia, -ae, *f.*

great, magnus, -a, -um.

greatly, magnopere.

grief, dolor, -ōris, *m.*

guard (*noun*), praesidium, -iī, *n.*

off one's guard, inopīnāns, -antis.

on guard, in statiōne (statiōnibus).

habit, cōnsuētūdō, -inis, *f.*

hand, manus, -ūs, *f.*

on the other hand, contrā.

be at hand, adsum, -esse, affuī.

happen, accidit, -ere, accidit; fit, fierī, factum est.

harbor, portus, -ūs, *m.*

harm, dētrīmentum, -ī, *n.*

hasten, contendō, -ere, -tendī, -tentus.

hastily, repente.

hate, ōdī, ōdisse, ōsūrus.

have, habeō, -ēre, -uī, -itus.

have in mind, propōnō, -ere, -posuī, -positus, *with reflex.*

he, is, hīc, ille. *Usually not expressed.*

hear, hear of, audiō, -īre, -īvī *or* -iī, -ītus.

height, altitūdō, -inis, *f.*

held, cf. hold.

help (*noun*), auxilium, -iī, *n.*

help (*verb*), adiuvō, -āre, -iūvī, -iūtus.

helpful, ūsuī, *dat. of* ūsus.

Helvetians, Helvētiī, -ōrum, *m., pl.*

here, hīc (*adv.*).

hesitate, dubitō, 1, *with inf.*

hide, abdō, -ere, -didī, -ditus.

high (*of position*), superus, -a, -um.
 (*of extent*), altus, -a, -um.
 (*of wind or tide*), magnus, -a, -um.

himself, ipse (*intensive*); suī (*reflexive*).

hinder, impediō, -īre, -īvī *or* -iī, -ītus.

hire, condūcō, -ere, -dūxī, -ductus.

his, eius; suus, -a, -um (*reflex.*).

hold, teneō, -ēre, -uī.
 (*of an office*), gerō, -ere, gessī, gestus.
 (*of a council*), habeō, -ēre, -uī, -itus.

home, house, domus, -ūs, *f.*
 at home, domī.
 from home, domō.
 (*to one's*) **home**, domum.

honor, honor, -ōris, *m.*

honorable, honestus, -a, -um.

hope (*noun*), spēs, -eī, *f.*

hope (*verb*), spērō, 1.

horse, equus, -ī, *m.*

horseman, eques, -itis, *m.*

hostage, obses, -idis, *m.*

hostile, īnfēstus, -a, -um.

hour, hōra, -ae, *f.*

house, domus, -ūs, *f.*

how, in what degree, quam; **in what way**, quō modō, quem ad modum.
 how many, quot, quam multī, -ae, -a.
 how much, quantus, -a, -um; *as subst.*, quantum, -ī, *n.*
 how often, quotiēns.

however (*adv.*), quamvīs.

however (*conj.*), autem (*postpositive*).

human, hūmānus, -a, -um.

hundred, centum, C.

hurl, coniciō, -ere, -iēcī, -iectus.

hurry (*intrans.*), contendō, -ere, -tendī, -tentus.

hurry off (*trans.*), rapiō, -ere, -uī, raptus.

I, ego, meī. *Usually not expressed.*

if, sī.
 if not, nisi.
 if only, dum modo.
 if (*in indirect questions*), num, -ne.
 but if, quod sī; *after another condition*, sīn.

immortal, immortālis, -e.

import, importō, 1.

importance, it is of importance, rēfert.

impunity, impūnitās, -ātis, *f.*
 with impunity, impūne.

in, in, *prep. with abl.*

increase (*trans.*), augeō, -ēre, auxī, auctus.
 (*intrans.*), crēscō, -ere, crēvī, crētus.

incredible, incrēdibilis, -e.

incur, subeō, -īre, -iī.

induce, addūcō, -ere, -dūxī, -ductus.

infantry, peditēs, -um, *m., pl.*; peditātus, -ūs, *m.*

inflict, īnferō, -ferre, intulī, illātus.

influence, auctōritās, -ātis, *f.*

influence (*verb*), addūcō, -ere, -dūxī, -ductus.

inform, certiōrem (certiōrēs) faciō, -ere, fēcī, factus.

inhabit, incolō, -ere, -uī.

injury, iniūria, -ae, *f.*

inquire, quaerō, -ere, -sīvī *or* -iī, -sītus.

inspire, iniciō, -ere, -iēcī, -iectus, *with dat. of person and acc. of thing.*

intention, concilium, -iī, *n.*

interests of state, rēs pūblica, reī pūblicae, *f.*
 highest interests of state, summa rēs pūblica.
 it is to the interest, interest, interesse, interfuit.

intimate friend, familiāris, -is, *m.*

into, in, *prep. with acc.*

investigate, search into, quaerō, -ere, -sīvī *or* -siī, -sītus.

investigate, inspect, perspiciō, -ere, -spexī, -spectus.

invincible, invictus, -a, -um.

island, īnsula, -ae, *f.*
it, hīc, haec, hoc; is, ea, id.
Italy, Italia, -ae, *f.*
its, eius; suus, -a, -um (*reflex.*).
itself, ipse, ipsa, ipsum.

javelin, pīlum, -ī, *n.*
journey, iter, itineris, *n.*
judge, pass judgment, iūdicō, 1.
jump down, dēsiliō, -īre, -uī, -sultus.
Jupiter, Juppiter, Jovis, *m.*
just as, sīcut.
justly, iūre.

keep, teneō, -ēre, -uī.
  keep, hold, contineō, -ēre, -uī, -tentus.
  keep, prevent, prohibeō, -ēre, -uī, -itus.
kill, interficiō, -ere, -fēcī, -fectus; occīdō, -ere, -cīdī, -cīsus.
knight, eques, -itis, *m.*
know, sciō, scīre, scīvī, scītus.
  know, have learned, cognōvī.
  not know, ignōrō, 1; nesciō, -īre, -īvī.
known, nōtus, -a, -um.

lack, be lacking, be wanting, dēsum, -esse, -fuī.
lake, lacus. Lake Geneva, lacus Lemannus.
land, ager, agrī, *m.*
large, magnus, -a, -um.
  large number, multitūdō, -inis, *f.*
last (*adv.*), proximē.
  at last, tandem.
later (*adv.*), posteā.
latter, the latter, hīc, haec, hoc.
law, lēx, lēgis, *f.*
lay aside, dēpōnō, -ere, -posuī, -positus.
lay down (*of arms*), pōnō, -ere, posuī, positus.
lead, dūcō, -ere, dūxī, ductus.
  lead across, trādūcō, -ere, -dūxī, -ductus.
  lead back, redūcō, -ere, -dūxī, -ductus.
  lead out, ēdūcō, -ere, -dūxī, -ductus.
leader, dux, ducis, *m.*
  leading man, prīnceps, -cipis, *m.*

leadership, prīncipātus, -ūs, *m.*
learn, cognōscō, -ere, -ōvī, -itus; reperiō, -īre, repperī, repertus.
leave, relinquō, -ere, -līquī, -līctus; discēdō, -ere, -cessī, -cessūrus, *followed by* ab *with abl,*
legion, legiō, -ōnis, *f.*
less, minor, minus, *gen.* minōris.
liberty, lībertās, -ātis, *f.*
lieutenant, lēgātus, -ī, *m.*
life, vīta, -ae, *f.*
line of battle, aciēs, -ēī, *f.*
listen to, audiō, -īre, -īvī *or* -iī, -ītus.
little, parvus, -a, -um.
  a little while, breve tempus, -oris, *n.*
live, vīvō, -ere, vīxī, vīctus.
  live in, inhabit, incolō, -ere, -uī (with accusative).
long, longus, -a, -um.
  for a long time, diū.
look at, spectō, 1.
lose, āmittō, -ere, -mīsī, -missus.
loud, magnus, -a, -um.
low, īnferus, -a, -um.

madness, furor, -ōris, *m.*; āmentia, -ae, *f.*
make, faciō, -ere, fēcī, factus.
  make (*of a plan*), capiō, -ere, cēpī, captus; ineō, inīre, iniī, initus.
  make war, bellum faciō, *or* bellum īnferō, īnferre, intulī, illātus, *both with dat.*
  make use of, ūtor, -ī, ūsus.
man, homō, hominis, *m.*; vir, virī, *m.*
  men, soldiers, mīlitēs, -um, *m.*
  a man who, is quī.
many, multī, -ae, -a; complūrēs, -a *or* -ia.
march, iter, itineris, *n.*
  march, make a march, iter faciō, -ere, fēcī, factus.
Mark, Mārcus, -ī, *m.*
marriage, mātrimōnium, -iī, *n.*
material, māteria, -ae, *f.*
matter, rēs, reī, *f.*
meet (*trans.*), conveniō, -īre, -vēnī, -ventum est, *with acc.*; occurrō, -ere, -currī, -cursūrus, *with dat.*
mercy, misericordia, -ae, *f.*
mere, ipse, -a, -um.
message, nūntius, -iī, *m.*

messenger, nūntius, -iī, *m.*

miles, mīlia passuum.

military matters, rēs mīlitāris, reī
    mīlitāris, *f.*

mind, mēns, mentis, *f.*; animus,
    -ī, *m.*

misdeed, facinus, -oris, *n.*

misfortune, calamitās, -ātis, *f.*

month, mēnsis, -is, *f.*

moon, lūna, -ae, *f.*

more (*adj.*), plūs, plūris; (*adv.*), magis.

moreover, autem (*postpositive*).

motive, causa, -ae, *f.*

move, moveō, -ēre, mōvī, mōtus.

moved, disturbed, commōtus, -a, -um.

much (*adj.*), multus, -a, -um; (*adv.*),
    multum; *in comparisons*, multō.

multitude, multitūdō, -inis, *f.*

name, nōmen, -inis, *n.*

narrow, angustus, -a, -um.

nation, nātiō, -ōnis, *f.*

nature, nātūra, -ae, *f.*

near at hand, be near at hand, adsum,
    -esse, affuī.

nearer (*adj.*), propior, -ius; (*adv.*), pro-
    pius.

nearly, ferē.

necessary, necessārius, -a, -um.

  it is necessary, opus est; necesse est.

neglect, neglegō, -ere, -lēxī, -lēctus.

neighbor, fīnitimus, -ī, *m.*

neither . . . nor, neque . . . neque;
    nec . . . nec.

never, numquam.

nevertheless, tamen.

new, novus, -a, -um.

news, nūntius, -iī, *m.*

next, proximus, -a, -um.

  on the next day, posterō diē.

night, nox, noctis, *f.*

  by night, noctū.

no, nūllus, -a, -um.

  no one, nobody, nēmō, *m. and f.*,
    gen. nūllīus, *dat.* nēminī, *acc.*
    nēminem, *abl.* nūllō.

noise, strepitus, -ūs, *m.*

not, nōn; *in negative purpose, wish,
    or command*, nē.

  and not, neque.

not only . . . but also, nōn sōlum
    . . . sed etiam.

not yet, nōndum.

notable, īnsignis, -e.

nothing, nihil (*indecl.*).

notice, animadvertō, -ere, -vertī,
    -versus.

now, at the present time, nunc; by
    this time, iam.

number, numerus, -ī, *m.*

obtain a request, impetrō, 1.

occur, occurrō, -ere, -currī, -cursūrus.

of, concerning, dē, *prep. with abl.*

offer, offerō, -ferre, obtulī, oblātus;
    of terms, ferō.

office, magistrātus, -ūs, *m.*; honor,
    -ōris, *m.*

often, saepe.

on, in, *prep. with abl.*

once, at once, statim.

one, ūnus, -a, -um.

  one . . . another, alius . . . alius.

  one who, is quī.

  only (*adv.*), modo.

  only one, sōlus, -a, -um.

opinion, opīniō, -ōnis, *f.*

opportunity, facultās, -ātis, *f.*

oppose, resistō, -ere, -stitī.

oppress, premō, -ere, pressī, pressus.

or, aut; *in questions*, an.

order, iubeō, -ēre, iussī, iussus,
    with acc. and inf.; imperō,
    1, *with dat.*, ut *and subj.*

  in order that, ut, *with subj.*

other, another, alius, -a, -ud.

  on the other hand, autem (*post-
    positive*).

others, the remaining, cēterī, -ae, -a.

ought, dēbeō, -ēre, -uī, -itus; oportet,
    -ēre, oportuit.

our, noster, -tra, -trum.

  our men, nostrī, -ōrum, *m., pl.*

outcry, clāmor, -ōris, *m.*

overwhelm, opprimō, -ere, -pressī,
    -pressus.

own, *reflex. poss. adj., or gen. of* ipse.

pack-animal, iūmentum, -ī, *n.*

pain, dolor, -ōris, *m.*

pardon, ignōscō, -ere, -nōvī, -nctus.

part, pars, partis, *f.*

party, pars, partis, *f.*

pass judgment, iūdicō, 1.

peace, pāx, pācis, *f.*
people, populus, -ī, *m.*
  their people (*reflex.*), suī, suōrum, *m.*, *pl.*
perceive, perspiciō, -ere, -spexī, -spectus.
peril, perīculum, -ī, *n.*
perish, pereō, -īre, -iī, -itūrus.
permission, it is permitted, licet, licēre, licuit, *with dat. and inf.*
permit, patior, patī, passus, *with acc. and inf.;* permittō, -ere, -mīsī, -missus, *with dat.,* ut, *and subj.*
personal enemy, inimīcus, -ī, *m.*
persuade, persuādeō, -ēre, -suāsī, -suāsum est, *with dat.,* ut, *and subj.*
picked, dēlēctus, -a, -um.
pick out, dēligō, -ere, -lēgī, -lēctus.
pitch camp, castra pōnō, -ere, posuī, positus.
place (*noun*), locus, -ī, *m.*; *pl.* loca, -ōrum, *n.*
place (*verb*), collocō, 1; pōnō, -ere, posuī, positus.
  place (*in different positions*), dīspōnō.
plan (*noun*), cōnsilium, -iī, *n.*
plan, arrange, cōnstituō, -ere, -uī, -ūtus.
plan, think (**of**), cōgitō, 1.
pleasure, voluptās, -ātis, *f.*
plot, ambuscade, īnsidiae, -ārum, *f.*, *pl.*
plot against, īnsidior, 1, *with dat.*
point, at this point, hīc.
possession, gain possession of, potior, -īrī, -ītus.
power, ability, facultas, -ātis, *f.*; **power, might,** potentia, -ae, *f.*; **military power,** imperium, -iī, *n.*
powerful, to be very, plūrimum posse.
practice, exercitātiō, -ōnis, *f.*
praetor, praetor, -ōris, *m.*
praise, laus, laudis, *f.*
pray (*verb*), vōtum faciō, -ere, fēcī, factum.
pray (*in commands and questions*), tandem.
prefer, mālō, mālle, māluī.
prepare, comparō, 1; parō, 1.
prepared, parātus, -a, -um.

preserve, cōnservō, 1.
press hard, premō, -ere, pressī, pressus.
pretend, simulō, 1.
prevail, valeō, -ēre, -uī, -itūrus.
prevent, prohibeō, -ēre, -uī, -itus, *with inf.*
  not prevent, nōn dēterreō, -ēre, -uī, -itus, *with* quīn *and subj.*
previous, superior, -ius; prior, -us.
private, prīvātus, -a, -um.
privilege, give the privilege, potestātem faciō.
prolong, prōdūcō, -ere, -dūxī, -ductus.
proof, indicium, -iī, *n.*
property, rēs, reī, *f.*
proportion, in proportion to, prō.
prosperous, flōrēns, -entis.
protect, dēfendō, -ere, -dī, -fēnsus.
protection, praesidium, -iī, *n.*
prove, probō, 1.
provided, provided that, dum.
province, prōvincia, -ae, *f.*
provision, make provision, prōvideō, -ēre, -vīdī, -vīsus.
public, pūblicus, -a, -um.
public welfare, rēs pūblica, reī pūblicae, *f.*
punish, ulcīscor, -ī, ultus.
punishment, supplicium, -iī, *n.*; poena, -ae, *f.*
purpose, mēns, mentis, *f.*
put down, conquer, superō, 1.
put in charge, praeficiō, -ere, -fēcī, -fectus.
put to death, interficiō, -ere, -fēcī, -fectus.
put to flight, fugō, 1.
put under the power, permittō, -ere, -mīsī, -missus.

quickly, celeriter.

rampart, vāllum, -ī, *n.*
rank, ōrdō, -inis, *f.*
rather, potius.
reach, perveniō, -īre, -vēnī, -ventum est, *with* ad *and acc.*
reach (*of land*), attingō, -ere, -tigī, -tāctus.
ready, parātus, -a, -um.
  get ready, comparō, 1.

realize, intellegō, -ere, -lēxi, -lēctus.
reason, causa, -ae, *f.*
  for this reason, quā dē causā.
reasonable, iūstus, -a, -um.
reasonableness, ratiō, -ōnis, *f.*
recall, revocō, 1.
receive, accipiō, -ere, -cēpī, -ceptus.
  receive under protection, in fidem
  recipiō.
recently, nūper.
recklessness, audācia, -ae, *f.*
regard, in regard to, dē *with abl.*
region, regiō, -ōnis, *f.*
reject, repudiō, 1.
rejoice, gaudeō, -ēre, gāvīsus sum.
relief, subsidium, -iī, *n.*
remain, maneō, -ēre, mānsī, mānsūrus.
remove, tollō, -ere, sustulī, sublātus;
  removeō, -ēre, -mōvī, -mōtus.
renown, glōria, -ae, *f.*
repair, reficiō, -ere, -fēcī, -fectus.
repeatedly, saepe.
repent, paenitet, -ēre, -uit.
reply, respondeō, -ēre, -spondī,
  -spōnsus.
report, nūntiō, 1.
report back, renūntiō, 1.
republic, rēs pūblica, reī pūblicae, *f.*
reputation, opīniō, -ōnis, *f.*
request, obtain a request, impetrō, 1,
reserve, reservō, 1.
resist, resistō, -ere, -stitī, *with dat.*
rest of, remaining, reliquus, -a,
  -um.
restore, restituō, -ere, -uī, -ūtus;
  reddō, -ere, -didī, -ditus.
restrain, retineō, -ēre, -uī, -tentus;
  prohibeō, -ēre, -uī, -itus; reprimō, -ere, -pressī, -pressus.
retreat (*noun*), receptus, -ūs, *m.*
retreat (*verb*), recipiō, -ere, -cēpī,
  -ceptus, *with reflexive.*
return (*noun*), reditus, -ūs, *m.*
return, give back, reddō, -ere, -didī,
  -ditus.
return, go back, redeō, -īre, -iī,
  -tum est; revertor, -ī.
  in return for, prō *with abl.*
revolt, tumultus, -ūs, *m.*
reward, praemium, -iī, *n.*
Rhine, Rhēnus, -ī, *m.*
Rhone, Rhodanus, -ī, *m.*

right, fair (*adj.*), aequus, -a, -um.
  right (*in the sight of the gods*),
  fās, *n., indecl. noun.*
rightly, iūre.
risk, perīculum, -ī, *n.*
river, flūmen, -inis, *n.*
road, via, -ae, *f.*; iter, itineris, *n.*
Roman, Rōmānus, -a, -um.
Rome, Rōma, -ae, *f.*
royal power, regnum.
rule, regō, -ere, rēxī, rēctus.
rumor, rūmor, -ōris, *m.*

safe, incolumis, -e; tūtus, -a, -um.
safely, tūtō; *translate when possible
  by adj.*, safe.
safety, salūs, -ūtis, *f.*
sail (*verb*), nāvigō, 1.
sake, for the sake of, causā, *following
  its gen.*
same, īdem, eadem, idem.
savage, ferus, -a, -um.
save, cōnservō, 1.
say, dīcō, -ere, dīxī, dictus.
sea, mare, -is, *n.*
secure, (*adj.*), tūtus, -a, -um.
secure (*verb*), cōnsequor, -ī, -secūtus;
  conciliō, 1; nancīscor, -ī, nactus.
see, see to it, videō, -ēre, vīdī, vīsus.
seek, petō, -ere, -īvī *or* -iī, -ītus.
seem, videor, -ērī, vīsus.
seize, occupō, 1; comprehendō, -ere,
  -hendī, -hēnsus.
self, myself, etc. *If emphatic*, ipse,
  -a, -um; *if reflexive*, meī, tuī, suī,
  etc.
senate, senātus, -ūs, *m.*
senator, senātor, -ōris, *m.*
send, mittō, -ere, mīsī, missus.
  send ahead, praemittō, -ere, -mīsī,
  -missus.
  send back, remittō, -ere, -mīsī,
  -missus.
  send out or **away** (*in different
  directions*), dīmittō, -ere, -mīsī,
  -missus.
separate, dīvidō, -ere, -vīsī, -vīsus.
serious, gravis, -e.
servant, servus, -ī, *m.*
service, officium, -iī, *n.*; meritum, -ī, *n.*
service, be of service, prōsum,
  prōdesse, prōfuī.

set fire to, incendō, -ere, -cendī, -cēn-
sus.

set out, proficīscor, -ī, -fectus.

set sail, solvō, -ere, solvī, solūtus,
with or without navem *or* nāvēs.

settle (*down*), cōnsīdō, -ere, -sēdī,
-sessūrus.

seventh, septimus, -a, -um.

several, complūrēs, -a *or* -ia.

shield, scūtum, -ī, *n.*

ship, nāvis, -is, *f.*
war ship, nāvis longa.

short, brevis, -e.

shout, shouting, clāmor, -ōris, *m.*

show, ostendō, -ere, -dī, -tus; indicō,
ı ; doceō, -ēre, -uī, doctus.

shrewdness, cōnsilium, -iī, *n.*

sight, cōnspectus, -ūs, *m.*

since, cum, *with subj.;* quoniam,
with indic.

sister, soror, -ōris, *f.*

situation, locus, -ī, *m.;* *pl.* loca,
-ōrum, *n.*

skilful, skilled, perītus, -a, -um, *with
gen.*

slave, servus, -ī, *m.*

slay, occīdō, -ere, -cīdī, -cīsus.

slight, parvus, -a, -um.

so (*with adjectives and adverbs*), tam;
(*with verbs*), ita, sīc.
and so, itaque.
so great, tantus, -a, -um.
so long, tam diū.
so long as, dum, *with indic.*
so much (*as noun*), tantum, -ī, *n.*
so often, totiēns.

soldier, mīles, -litis, *m.*

some (*adj.*), aliquī, -qua, -quod;
nōn nūllus, -a, -um; *pl. as subst.*
some one, something (*subst.*), aliquis, aliquid.
some . . . others, aliī . . . aliī.
some in one direction, others in
another, aliī aliam in partem.
there are some who, sunt quī.

sometimes, nōn numquam.

soon, brevī tempore.
as soon as, simul atque.

sort, genus, -eris, *n.*
of this sort, ēius modī.

spare, parcō, -ere, pepercī *or* parsī,
parsūrus.

speak, dīcō, -ere, dīxī, dictus.

speech, ōrātiō, -ōnis, *f.*

speed, celeritās, -ātis, *f.*
at full speed (*of horses*), incitātus,
-a, -um.

spot, locus, -ī, *m.;* *pl.* loca, -ōrum, *n.*

spy, spy out, speculor, ı.

stab, percutiō, -ere, -cussī, -cussus.

stand, stō, stāre, stetī, stātus.
stand, get a footing, consistō,
-ere, -stitī.
stand in the way of, obsistō, -ere,
-stitī, *with dat.*

standard, signum, -ī, *n.*

start, proficīscor, -ī, profectus.

state, cīvitās, -ātis, *f.*

stay, maneō, -ēre, mānsī, mānsūrus.

still, now, nunc; still, nevertheless,
tamen.

stir up, concitō, ı.

storm, tempestās,-ātis,*f.*

strange, novus, -a, -um.

strangeness, novitās,-tātis,*f.*

strong, fīrmus, -a, -um.

such, of such a sort, tālis, -e; so
great, tantus, -a, -um.

suddenly, subitō.

sufficient, satis (*indecl.*), *n.*

sufficientiy, satis.

suitable, idōneus, -a, -um, *with dat.*
or ad *with acc.*

summon, vocō, ı.

sun, sōl, sōlis, *m.*

supplies, commeātus, -ūs, *m.*

support, alō, -ere, -uī, altus *or* alitus.

suppose, crēdō, -ere, -didī, -ditus;
exīstimō, ı.

sure, certus, -a, -um.

surpass, superō, ı, *with acc.;* praestō,
-stāre, -stitī, -stitus, *with dat.*

surrender (oneself), dēdō, -ere,
dēdidī, dēditus, *with reflex.*

surround, get around, circumveniō,
-īre, -vēnī, -ventus.

suspect, suspicor, ı.

suspicion, suspīciō, -ōnis, *f.*

Swabians, Suēbī, -ōrum, *m., pl.*

sword, gladius, -iī, *m.*

take, bear, ferō, ferre, tulī, lātus.
take, lead, dūcō, -ere, dūxī,
ductus.

take, take up, capture, capiō, -ere, cēpī, captus.

take away, ēripiō, -ere, -uī, -reptus.

take by storm, expugnō, 1.

take place, fīō, fierī, factum est.

take possession of, potior, -īrī, -ītus.

tear, lacrima, -ae, f.

tear up, ēripiō, -ere, -uī, -reptus.

tell, dīcō, -ere, dīxī, dictus; prō-nūntiō, 1.

tell, show, doceō, -ēre, -uī, doctus.

tempest, tempestās, -ātis, f.

ten, decem.

tenth, decimus, -a, -um.

terms, condiciō, -ōnis, f., sing. or pl.

terrify, perterreō, -ēre, -uī, -itus.

territory, territories, ager, agrī, m.; fīnēs, -ium, m.

than, quam, or abl. after a comparative.

that (dem. pron.), ille, illa, illud; is, ea, id.

that, so that, in order that, ut; after verbs of fearing, nē; after negative expressions of doubt, quīn.

that . . . not, introducing a negative clause of purpose, nē.

would that, utinam.

their, suus, -a, -um (reflex.); eōrum.

them, cf. he.

then, at that time, tum.

then, therefore, igitur (usually postpositive).

there, in that place, ibi.

therefore, itaque.

these, cf. this.

thing, rēs, reī, f.

think, putō, 1; exīstimō, 1; arbitror, 1.

think, feel, sentiō, -īre, sēnsī, sēnsus.

this, hīc, haec, hoc.

though, cum.

thousand, mīlle (indecl. adj.).

thousands, mīlia, -ium, n., pl. (followed by partitive gen.).

threaten, impendeō, -ēre.

three, trēs, tria.

a period of three days, trīduum, -ī, n.

three hundred, trecentī, -ae, -a.

through, per, prep. with acc.

throw, iaciō, -ere, iēcī, iactus; coniciō, -ere, -iēcī, -iectus.

throw back, rēiciō, -ere, -iēcī, -iectus.

throw down, away, abiciō, -ere, -iēcī, -iectus.

tide, aestus, -ūs, m. .

tilling the land, agrī cultūra, -ae, f.

time, tempus, -oris, n.

on time, ad tempus.

time and again, semel atque iterum.

timid, timidus, -a, -um.

to, ad, prep. with acc.; often translated by dat.

to-day, hodiē.

together with, ūnā cum, with abl.

toward (in space), ad with acc.

town, oppidum, -ī, n.

trader, mercātor, -ōris, m.

transport, adj., onerārius, -a, -um.

travel, eō, īre, iī or ivī, itum est.

treachery, īnsidiae, -ārum, f., pl.

trial, iūdicium, -iī, n.

tribe, gēns, gentis, f.

tribune, tribūnus, -ī, m.

tribune of the people, tribūnus plēbis.

tributary, vectīgālis, -e.

troops, cōpiae, -ārum, f., pl.

true, vērus, -a, -um.

truth, vērum, -ī, n.

try, cōnor, 1.

turn and flee, tergum vertō, -ere, vertī, versum.

twelve, duodecim; XII.

two, duo, -ae, -o.

unacquainted, imperītus, -a, -um, with gen.

unbelievable, incrēdibilis, -e.

uncertain, incertus, -a, -um.

uncovered, nūdus, -a, -um.

understand, intellegō, -ere, -lēxī, -lēctus.

undertake, suscipiō, -ere, -cēpī, -ceptus.

ungrateful, ingrātus, -a, -um.

unharmed, incolumis, -e.

unjust, inīquus, -a, -um.

unjustly, iniūriā.

unless, nisi.

unprepared, imparātus, -a, -um.

unskilful, imperītus, -a, -um.
until, ad, *prep. with acc.*
until, dum; quoad, *conj.; when
    equivalent to* before, prius quam.
urge, hortor, 1; cohortor, 1.
use (*noun*), ūsus, -ūs, *m.*
    of use, ūsuī (*dative*).
use, make use of, ūtor, -ī, ūsus.

vacant, lie vacant, vacō, 1.
valor, virtūs, -ūtis, *f.*
vengeance, take vengeance on, ulcīs-
    cor, -ī, ultus.
verdict, iūdicium, -iī, *n.*
very (*adj.*), ipse, -a, -um.
victory, victōria, -ae, *f.*
village, vīcus, -ī, *m.*
violence, vīs, *f.*
virtue, virtūs, -ūtis, *f.*
voice, vōx, vōcis, *f.*

wait, delay, moror, 1.
    wait for, exspectō, 1.
wander about, vagor, 1.
war, bellum, -ī, *n.*
warn, admoneō, -ēre, -uī, -itus.
way, manner, modus, -ī, *m.*
    way, road, via, -ae, *f.*
we, nōs, *gen.*, nostrum *or* nostrī.
weapon, tēlum, -ī, *n.*
weather, tempestās, -ātis, *f.*
weigh (*of anchor*), tollō, -ere, sustulī,
    sublātus.
welfare, salūs, -ūtis, *f.*
    public welfare, rēs pūblica, reī
    pūblicae.
what (*inter. pron.*), quid; (*inter.
    adj.*), quī, quae, quod.
what (*rel. pron.*), (id) quod, (ea) quae.
what great, how great, quantus,
    -a, -um.
whatever, quidquid.
what sort of, quālis, -e.
when, cum; ubi.
where (*place in which*), ubi; (*place
    to which*), quō.
wherever, whithersoever, quōcumque.
whether, num, -ne, sī, utrum.

which, *see* who.
which (*of two*), uter, utra, utrum.
while, dum.
who, what (*inter. pron.*), quis, quid.
who, which, what (*rel. pron.*), quī,
    quae, quod.
whoever, whatever, quīcumque,
    quaecumque, quodcumque.
whole, tōtus, -a, -um.
wholly, omnīnō.
why, cūr.
wicked, improbus, -a, -um.
wide, lātus, -a, -um.
width, lātitūdō, -inis, *f.*
wife, uxor, -ōris, *f.*
willing, be willing, volō, velle, voluī.
winter, hiems, hiemis, *f.*
    pass the winter, hiemō, 1.
    winter quarters, hīberna, -ōrum,
    n., pl.
wisdom, cōnsilium, -iī, *n.*
wish, volō, velle, voluī.
    not wish, nōlō, nōlle, nōluī.
with, cum, *prep. with abl.*
with, near, apud, *prep. with acc.*
withdraw, go away, discēdō, -ere,
    -cessī, -cessūrus.
without, sine, *prep. with abl.*
withstand, sustineō, -ēre, -uī, -tentus.
woman, mulier, -eris, *f.*
word, verbum, -ī, *n.*
work (*noun*), opus, operis, *n.*
work (*verb*), labōrō, 1.
worth, virtūs, -ūtis, *f.*
would that, utinam.
wound, volnus, -eris, *n.*
wrong, do wrong, peccō, 1.

year, annus, -ī, *m.*
    every year, quotannīs.
yet, tamen.
yield, cēdō, -ere, cessī, cessūrus.
you, tū, tuī.
young man, adulēscēns, adulēscentis,
    m.
your (*sing.*), tuus, -a, -um; (*plu.*)
    vester, -tra, -trum.

zeal, studium, -iī, *n.*

INDEX

The references are to sections and paragraphs of the *Essentials of Latin Grammar*, pp. 479–586

debeo - ui - ought, owe
acies - line of battle
terga vertere = to retreat

cocus - i - m. - cook
cocina - ae - f. - kitchen
culter - tri - m. - butcher-knife
porcellus - i - m. - pig
testamentum - last will and testament
modius - month
vico - live
mei domine - Good Sirs

Margaret Brookes
Phylis LaPine
Marian Cootie
Pearl Case

stipendium - tribute

conficio - conficere - to defeat &

undique - on all sides

perfacile - very easily

constituo - ere - to determine

coegit - collect

cogo - ere - coegi - coactus

arbitror - ari - atus - think

conor - ari - atus - try or attempt

negat - deny

nova res - revolution

plurimum posse - very powerful

fio - fieri - make or do

passive form of facere

se suaque themselves and their
possessions

futurum - would be

colloquium = conference

licet = be allowed